HIPPOCRENE STANDARD DICTIONARY

ARABIC-ENGLISH
ENGLISH-ARABIC

HIPPOCRENE STANDARD DICTIONARY

ARABIC-ENGLISH
ENGLISH-ARABIC

John Wortabet and Harvey Porter

HIPPOCRENE BOOKS
New York, NY

Hippocrene paperback edition, 1995.
Third printing, 1998.

For information, address:
HIPPOCRENE BOOKS, INC.
171 Madison Avenue
New York, NY 10016

ISBN 0-7818-0383-7

Printed in the United States of America.

ARABIC-ENGLISH

قاموس عربي وانكليزي

ARABIC-ENGLISH DICTIONARY.

ا

أ	As a numerical sign = 1.
أ	Particle of interrogation.
أَبٌ مث أَبَوَانِ ج آبَاءٌ	Father.
آبٌ	Month of August.
أَبَوِيٌّ	Fatherly, paternal.
أُبُوَّةٌ	Fatherhood.
أَبَدٌ	Time, eternity (future).
أَبَدَ ٱلآبِدِينَ	For ever.
أَبَداً	Ever ; always.
أَبَدِيٌّ وَمُؤَبَّدٌ	Eternal.
أَبَدِيَّةٌ	Eternity, perpetuity.
إِبْرَةٌ ج إِبَرٌ	Needle.
مِئْبَرٌ ج مَآبِرُ	Needle-case.
إِبْرِيزٌ	Pure gold.
أَبْرَشِيَّةٌ	Diocese.
إِبْرِيقٌ ج أَبَارِيقُ	Water-jug.
إِبْزِيمٌ ج أَبَازِيمُ	Buckle, clasp.
إِبْطٌ ج آبَاطٌ	Arm-pit.
أَبِقَ يَأْبِقُ	To run away.
آبِقٌ	Runaway (slave).
إِبْلٌ	Camels (coll noun).
إِبْلِيسٌ ج أَبَالِسَةٌ	Satan.
أَبَّنَ	To praise the dead.
إِبَانَ	Time or season of a thing.
إِبْنٌ ج أَبْنَاءٌ وَبَنُونَ	Son.
إِبْنَةٌ أَوْ بِنْتٌ ج بَنَاتٌ	Daughter.
أَبَنُوسٌ	Ebony.
أُبَّهَةٌ	Beauty. Greatness,
أَبَى يَأْبَى	To refuse, refrain.
أَبِيٌّ	Refusing, disdaining.

إِبَاءٌ	Refusal, rejection.
أَتَانٌ ج أُتُنٌ وَأُتْنٌ	She-ass.
أَتُونٌ ج أُتُنٌ	Oven, furnace.
أَتَى يَأْتِي	To come, arrive.
آتَى إِيتَاءً	To give ; requite.
تَأَتَّى	To happen.
إِتْيَانٌ	Arrival, coming.
آتٍ	Comer, one who arrives.
أَلْآتِي	The future ; coming next.
أَثَّ يَئِثُّ	To abound.
أَثَاثٌ	Household furniture.
أَثَرَ يَأْثُرُ	To choose.
أَثَّرَ فِي	To impress.
آثَرَ	To choose, prefer.
تَأَثَّرَ	To follow one's tracks
أَثَرٌ ج آثَارٌ	Trace, impression.
تَأَثُّرٌ	Influence ; impression.
مَأْثُرَةٌ ج مَآثِرُ	Memorable deed.
مُؤَثِّرٌ	Impressive.
أَثْلٌ	A kind of tamarisk.
أَثِمَ يَأْثَمُ	To sin.
أَثَّمَ	To accuse of sin.
إِثْمٌ ج آثَامٌ	Sin, crime.
أَثِيمٌ ج أُثَمَاءُ	Guilty.
مَأْثَمَةٌ وَمَأْثَمٌ ج مَآثِمُ	Sin, crime.
أَجَّ يَؤُجُّ أَجِيجاً	To burn, blaze.
أَجَرَ يَأْجُرُ	To pay ; let on hire.
آجَرَ	To pay, let for money.
إِسْتَأْجَرَ	To hire, take on hire.
أَجْرٌ ج أُجُورٌ	Recompense.
أُجْرٌ وَأُجْرَةٌ	Wages, salary.
آجُرٌّ	Baked bricks.
إِيجَارٌ	Lease, hire, rent.
أَجِيرٌ ج أُجَرَاءُ	Hired labourer.
مُؤْجِرٌ وَمُؤَاجِرٌ	Landlord.
مُسْتَأْجِرٌ	Tenant.
إِجَّاصٌ وَإِنْجَاصٌ	Pear (fruit).
أَجِلَ يَأْجَلُ	To delay, tarry.

To grant a delay. أَجَّلَ

Appointed time. الأَجَلُ

Cause, reason, sake. أَجْلٌ

Postponed, future. آجِلٌ

Thicket, jungle. أَجَمٌ ج آجَامٌ

To unify. آحَدَ وَوَحَّدَ

To unite with ; join. إِتَّحَدَ بِ

One. احَدٌ م إِحْدَى ج آحَادٌ

Sunday. الأَحَدُ

Units. آحَادٌ

Union ; agreement. إِتِّحَادٌ

To take. اخَذَ يَاخُذُ

To begin, to say. أَخَذَ يَقُولُ

To seize, take hold of. أَخَذَ بِ

To aid, assist. أَخَذَ بِيَدِهِ

To blame. آخَذَ مُؤَاخَذَةً بِ أَوْ عَلَى

To take to himself. إِتَّخَذَ

Source. Way. مَأْخَذٌ ج . مآخذٌ

To postpone. أَخَّرَ تَأْخِيراً

To tarry, delay. تَأَخَّرَ

Other, another. آخَرُ م اخْرَى

End, last. آخِرٌ ج أَوَاخِرُ

The future life. الآخِرَةُ

Last, extreme. أَخِيرٌ ج أَخِيرُونَ

At the end, finally, lastly. أخيراً

Posterior part. مُؤَخَّرٌ

Brotherhood. إِخَاءٌ وَاخُوَّةٌ

Brother. أَخٌ ج إِخْوَةٌ وَإِخْوَانٌ

Sister. أُخْتٌ ج أَخَوَاتٌ

Fraternal, brotherly. أَخَوِيٌّ

Stable. أَخُورٌ

To be educated. أَدُبَ يَأْدُبُ

To invite to a meal. أَدَبَ يَأْدِبُ

To discipline, chastise. أَدَّبَ

Become well-educated. تَأَدَّبَ

Liberal education. أَدَبٌ ج آدَابٌ

Polite literature. عِلْمُ الأَدَبِ

Chastisement. تَأْدِيبٌ

Moral. Polite. أَدَبِيٌّ

Literary, learned. أَدِيبٌ ج أُدَبَاءُ

Condiment, seasoning. إِدَامٌ

Human skin. أَدَمَةٌ

Dark or tawny colour. أُدْمَةٌ

Human being. آدَمِيٌّ

To give up, deliver. أَدَّى

To bring to أَدَّى إِلَى

Payment, discharge. أَدَاءٌ

Tool, utensil. أَدَاةٌ ج أَدَوَاتٌ

When. Lo. إِذْ

Behold! When. إِذَا

Therefore. إِذاً وإِذَنْ

March (month). آذَارُ

To give leave to. أَذِنَ لِ يَأذَن

To call to prayer. أَذَّنَ

To ask permission. إِسْتَأْذَنَ

Permission, leave. إِذْنٌ

Ear. Handle. أُذْنٌ وأُذُنٌ ج آذانٌ

The Moslem call to prayer. أَذَانٌ

Minaret. مِئْذَنَةٌ ومَأْذَنَةٌ ج مَآذِنُ

One who calls to prayer. مُؤَذِّنٌ

To injure, annoy. آذَى إِيذَاءً

Injury, damage. أَذًى وأَذِيَّةٌ

Hurtful, harmful. مُؤْذٍ

Need, want. أَرَبٌ ج آرَابٌ

In pieces, limb by limb. إِرْباً إِرْباً

Groin. اُرْبِيَّةٌ

Purpose. مَأْرَبَةٌ ومَأْرَبٌ ج مَآرِبُ

Europe. اورُبَّا

European. أورُبِّيٌّ

Inheritance. (*See* وَرِث) إِرْثٌ

Purple (*n*). أُرْجُوَانٌ

Purple (*adj*). ارْجُوَانِيٌّ

To date ; write a history. أَرَّخَ

Epoch, history. تَأْرِيخٌ ج تَوَارِيخُ

Historian. مُؤَرِّخٌ

Dated مُؤَرَّخٌ

Ardeb, (corn measure).	إِرْدَبٌّ
Cedar or pine (tree).	أَرْزٌ
Rice.	أَرْزٌ وَأُرُزٌّ وَرُزٌ
Earth, soil, land.	أَرْضٌ
Terrestrial.	أَرْضِيٌّ
To be sleepless.	أَرِقَ يَأْرَقُ
Wakefulness; insomnia.	أَرَقٌ
Hare, rabbit	ارنبٌ ج أَرَانِبُ
To flow.	ازَبَ يَازِبُ ازْبًا
Drain.	مِيزابٌ ج مَيَازِيبُ
To assist, strengthen.	ازَرَ
A long wrapper, veil.	إِزَارٌ
Succour, assistance.	مُؤَازَرَةٌ
An apron.	مِئْزَرٌ ج مَآزِرُ
Eternity.	أَزَلٌ وَأَزَلِيَّةٌ
Eternal (of past time).	ازَلِيٌّ
Distress ; draught.	أَزْمَةٌ
In front, opposite to.	إِزَاءَ
To found.	أَسَّسَ
To be founded, built.	تَأَسَّسَ
Foundation.	اسَاسٌ ج أُسُسٌ
Fundamental.	اسَاسِيٌّ
Founder.	مُؤَسِّسٌ
Founded, established.	مُؤَسَّسٌ
Spinach, spinage.	أَسْبَانَخ
Master, professor.	اسْتَاذ ج أَسَاتِذَةٌ وَأَسَاتِيذُ
Lion.	اَسَدٌ ج اسُودٌ
To take captive.	اسَرَ يَأْسِرُ
To submit as a captive.	إِسْتَأْسَرَ
All, the whole of.	بِأَسْرِهِ
Captivity, retention.	أَسْرٌ
Near relations.	اسرَةٌ
Captive.	أَسِيرٌ ج اسَرَاءُ وَأَسْرَى
Stable.	إِسْطَبْلٌ ج إِسْطَبْلاتٌ
Fleet.	أُسْطُولٌ ج اسَاطِيلُ
To regret.	أَسِفَ وَتَأَسَّفَ
Sorrow, grief, regret.	أَسَفٌ
Oh ! Alas !	اَسَفِيٌّ وَيَا أَسَفَا

إِسْفِنْجٌ	Sponge.
إِسْكِلَةٌ ج أَسَاكِلُ	Harbour.
إِسْمٌ ج أَسْمَاءٌ	Name ; noun.
أَسِيَ يَأْسَى	To be grieved.
أَسًى وَأَسًا	Grief, sorrow.
أَصُلَ يَأْصُلُ	To be firmly rooted.
تَأَصَّلَ	To be firmly rooted.
إِسْتَأْصَلَ	To extirpate.
أَصْلٌ ج أُصُولٌ	Root ; principle.
أَصْلِيٌّ	Radical, original.
أَصِيلٌ	Noble ; judicious.
اَلْأَصِيل	Evening.
إِفْرَنْجٌ وَإِفْرَنْجَةٌ	Franks.
إِفْرَنْجِيٌّ	A European.
أُفُقٌ ج آفَاقٌ	Horizon ; region.
أَفَكَ يَأْفِكُ	To tell a lie.
إِفْكٌ وَإِفْكَةٌ	A lie.
أَفَلَ يَأْفُلُ	To disappear, set.
أَفْيُونٌ	Opium.
أُقْحُوَانٌ	Camomile.
اقةٌ ج اقَقٌ وَاقَاتٌ	Oke.
أَكَّدَ	To assure.
تَأَكَّدَ	To be assured.
أَكِيدٌ	Firm ; certain.
تَأْكِيدٌ	Assurance, certitude,
أَكَلَ يَأْكُلُ	To eat.
أُكْلَةٌ	A morsel, mouthful.
آكِلَةٌ وَأَكَلَةٌ	Corroding ulcer.
أَكِيلٌ وَأَكُولٌ	Glutton.
مَأْكَلٌ ج مَآكِلُ	Food.
أَكَمَةٌ ج آكَامٌ	Hill. Mound.
أَلْ	The (definite article).
أَلَا	Is it not so ? Surely.
أَلَّا أَنْ لَا	That-not.
إِلَّا	Unless, except.
أَلَّذِي مث أَللَّذَانِ ج أَلَّذِينَ	Who, which (*Masc*).
التِي ج اللَّوَاتِي	Who, Which (*Fem*).

أَلِفَ يَأْلَفُ	To be accustomed
آلَفَ	To be friendly.
أَلَّفَ	To compile a book.
تَأَلَّفَ	To be united.
إِلْفٌ وَأَلِيفٌ	Friend, companion.
أَلْفٌ ج أُلُوفٌ وآلافٌ	Thousand.
أُلْفَةٌ	Friendship, alliance.
إِئْتِلافٌ	Accord, harmony.
تَأْلِيفٌ ج تَآلِيفُ	Compilation.
مَأْلُوفٌ	Customary, usual.
مُؤَالَفَةٌ	Friendship, familiarity.
مُؤَلِّفٌ	Author (of a book).
مُؤَلَّفٌ	Book. Composed.
أَلِمَ يَأْلَمُ	To suffer, feel pain.
أَلَّمَ وَآلَمَ	To pain, cause pain.
تَأَلَّمَ	To feel pain, ache.
أَلَمٌ ج آلامٌ	Pain, grief, ache.
أَلِيمٌ وَمُؤْلِمٌ	Painful.
أَلْمَاسٌ	Diamond.
إِلٰهٌ ج آلِهَةٌ	A god, divinity.
الله	God ; the One True God.
أَلَّهَ	To deify.
اللّٰهُمَّ	O God !
أُلُوهَةٌ وَأُلُوهِيَّةٌ	Divinit y.
أَلْيَةٌ ج الأَلَايَا وَأَلَيَاتٌ	Rump.
الأَلْيُ ج الأَلَايَاتٌ	Regiment.
إِلَى	To, unto, until.
إِلَى أَنْ	Until, till.
إِلَى مَتَى	Until when ? How long ?
أَمَّ يَؤُمُّ	To seek ; lead.
أُمٌّ ج أُمَّاتٌ وَأُمَّهَاتٌ	Mother.
أَمَامَ	Before, in-front.
إِمَامٌ ج أَئِمَّةٌ	Imam, leader.
أُمَّةٌ ج أُمَمٌ	Nation, people.
أُمِّيٌّ	Maternal, Illiterate.
أَمَّا	But, but as to.
إِمَّا ـ وَإِمَّا	Either, or.
أَمَدٌ ج آمَادٌ	Limit, end, term

To order, command.	أَمَرَ يَأْمُرُ
To consult.	آمَرَ مُؤَامَرَةً فِي
Command, order.	أَمْرٌ ج أَوَامِرُ
Matter, affair.	أَمْرٌ ج أُمُورٌ
Prefecture, power.	إِمَارَةٌ
Chief, prince.	أَمِيرٌ ج أُمَرَاءُ
Colonel.	أَمِيرُ أَلَايِ
Admiral.	أَمِيرُ ٱلْبَحْرِ
Caliph.	أَمِيرُ ٱلْمُؤْمِنِينَ
Princely.	أَمِيرِيٌّ
Taxes.	أَلْمَالُ ٱلأَمِيرِيُّ
Sub-governor.	مَأْمُورٌ
Yesterday.	أَمْسِ
To hope, hope for.	أَمَلَ يَأْمُلُ
To meditate, reflect upon.	تَأَمَّلَ
Hope, desire.	أَمَلٌ ج آمَالٌ
Hoped, expected.	مَأْمُولٌ
To be faithful.	أَمُنَ يَأْمُنُ
To be or feel safe.	أَمِنَ يَأْمَنُ

To entrust.	أَمَّنَ وَآمَنَهُ عَلَى
To believe in.	آمَنَ إِيمَانًا بِ
To protect	أَمَّنَهُ
To trust, rely upon.	إِئْتَمَنَ
Safety, protection.	أَمْنٌ وَأَمَانٌ
Safe, secure.	آمِنٌ
Faithfulness, fidelity.	أَمَانَةٌ
Faithful.	أَمِينٌ ج أُمَنَاءُ
Treasurer.	أَمِينُ ٱلصُّنْدُوقِ
Amen ; so be it.	آمِينَ وَأَمِينَ
Creed, belief.	إِيمَانٌ
Trustworthy.	مَأْمُونٌ
Believer, faithful.	مُؤْمِنٌ
Female slave.	أَمَةٌ ج إِمَاءٌ
That (*particle*).	أَنْ وَأَنَّ
If. Not.	إِنْ
Certainly, truly.	أَنَّ وَإِنَّ
Only , but. Verily.	إِنَّمَا
To groan ; moan.	أَنَّ يَئِنُّ أَنِينًا

أنا ج نحن — I, we.

أنتَ ج أنتم م أنتِ ج أنتنَّ — Thou.

انتما — You two, both of you.

أنثى ج إناث وأناثى — Female.

مؤنَّث — Feminine, effeminate.

ألإنجيل — The Gospel.

أنِسَ يأنَسُ — To be polite, affable.

آنسَ مؤانسة — To be sociable.

آنَسَ إيناساً — To cheer.

انس — Social life. Cheerfulness.

إنس — Mankind.

إنسان ج أناس — Man.

إنسانيّ — Human ; polite.

إنسانيّة — Humanity ; politeness.

انيس ومؤانس — Friendly, gentle.

أنِفَ يأنَفُ — To hate, disdain.

إستأنف — To recommence; appeal.

أنف ج آناف وانوف — Nose.

آنفاً — Little while age.

أنفة — Dislike. Scorn.

انوف — Disdainful.

مجلس الاستئناف — Court of appeal

أنِقَ بِ يأنَق — To be pleased.

تأنَّق — To be dainty.

أنام وآنام — Men, mankind.

تأنَّى — To act deliberately.

أناة — Patience, deliberateness.

إناء ج آنية وأوان — Vessel.

تأنّ — Deliberateness.

متأنّ — Deliberate, careful.

أنيسون — Anise.

أنَّى = من أين — Whence ?

آه وآها — Ah ! Alas !

أهَّبَ — To equip, get one ready.

تأهَّب لِ — To get ready.

أُهبة ج اُهَب — Apparatus, tools.

اهَّل لِ — To render fit for.

أهَّل به — To bid welcome.

تَأَهَّلَ	To marry.
إِسْتَأْهَلَ	To deserve, merit.
أَهْلاً وَسَهْلاً	Welcome !
أَهْلٌ ج أَهَالٍ	Family ; relations.
أَهْلٌ لِ	Worthy of, fit for.
أَهْلِيٌّ	Domestic.
اهْلِيَةٌ	Aptitude, fitness.
مُسْتَأْهِلٌ	Deserving, meriting.
أَو	Or, unless.
آبَ يَؤُوبُ إِيَاباً	To return.
إِوَز	Geese.
آسٌ	Myrtle.
آفَةٌ ج آفَاتٌ	Injury, damage.
آلَ يَؤُول	To result in.
أَوَّلَ	To explain, make clear.
آلٌ	Family ; kinsfolk.
آلَةٌ ج آلاَتٌ	Instrument.
آلِيٌّ	Organic.
أَوَّلُ ج أَوَائل	First, beginning.
أَوَّلاً	Firstly, in the first place.
أَوَّلاً فَاوَّلاً	Successively.
اولَئِكَ	Those, these.
إِيَالَة ج إِيَالاَتٌ	Province.
تَاوِيلٌ	Interpretation.
مَآلٌ	End, result, issue.
آنٌ وَاوَانٌ	Time.
أَلآنَ	Now at present.
إِيوَانٌ إِيوَانَاتٌ	Porch, hall.
أَوى يَأْوِي	To resort for shelter.
مَأْوًى ج مَآوٍ	Abode shelter.
إِبْنُ آوى	Jackal.
أَيْ	That is to say; namely.
أَيٌّ	Whoever, whichever.
آيَةٌ ج آيَاتٌ	Sign ; miracle.
إِيَّاهُ	Him.
إِيَّاي	Me.
ايَّدَ	To strengthen, aid.
ايَّار	May (month).

أيِسَ يأْيسُ	To despair.
إِيَاسٌ	Despair.
أَيِسٌ وَآئِسٌ	Despairing.
أَيِّلٌ وَإِيَّلٌ	Deer, stag.
أَيْلُولُ	September.
آنَ يَئِينُ	Its time comes.
أَيْنَ	Where ? whither ?
أَيْنَمَا	Whither ; everywhere.
إِلَى أَيْنَ	Whither ? where ?
مِنْ أَيْنَ	From whence ?

ب

ب	As a numerical sign 2.
بِ	With, during, by, at, in.
بِاللّٰهِ	By God !
بِمَا أَنْ	By reason of, inasmuch.
بَابَا ج بَابَاوَات	Pope ; father.
بَابَوِيٌّ وَبَابَاوِيٌّ	Papal.
بُؤْبُؤُ الْعَيْنِ	Pupil of the eye.
بَابُوجٌ ج بَوَابِيجُ	Slipper.
بَابُونَجٌ	Camomile.
بَاذِنْجَانٌ	Egg-plant.
بِئْرٌ ج آبَارٌ	Well, cistern.
بَارَةٌ ج بَارَاتٌ	Para (coin).
بَارُودٌ	Gunpowder.
بَارُودَةٌ ج بَوَارِيدُ	Gun.
بَازٌ	Falcon, hawk.
بَازَارٌ	Market.
بَازِرْكَانٌ	Cloth-merchant.
بِئْسَ	Evil ! Bad, very bad. !
بَأْسٌ	Courage , boldness.
بَأْسٌ وَبُؤْسٌ	Misfortune.

Misfortune, distress.	اَلْبأْسَاءُ
Unfortunate, poor.	بائِسٌ
Pasha.	بَاشَا ج بَاشاوَاتٌ
Sparrow-hawk.	بَاشَقٌ ج بَوَاشِق
Bunch of flowers, bouquet.	بَاقَةٌ
Bale (of merchandise).	بَالَةٌ
Okra.	بَامِيَا وَبَامِيَةٌ
Parrot.	بَبْغَاءُ ج بَبْغَاوَاتٌ
To cut off ; decide.	بَتَّ يَبتُّ
Irrevocably; not at all.	اَلْبَتَّةَ وَبَتَّةً
To cut off; amputate.	بَتَرَ يبتُرُ
Virgin.	بَتُولٌ
Virginity.	بتُولِيَةٌ
To disperse, publish.	بَثَّ يَبثُّ
To be divulged, spread.	إِنْبَثَّ
Pustule.	بَثْرٌ ج بُثُورٌ
To break out.	بَثَقَ يبثق
To proceed from.	إِنْبَثَقَ من
To dawn.	إِنْبَثَقَ اَلْفجر
Stork.	بَجَعٌ
To be great.	بَجُلَ يَبْجُلُ بَجَالَةً
To honour, praise.	بَجَّل
To be hoarse.	بَحَّ يبَحُّ بَحًّا
Hoarseness ; rough voice.	بُحَّةٌ
Hoarse.	أَبَحُّ وَمَبْحُوحٌ
To investigate.	بَحَثَ عَنْ
To discuss.	بَاحَثَ وتَبَاحَث
Examination, enquiry.	بَحْثٌ
Research.	مَبْحَثٌ ج مَبَاحِثُ
Discussion, controversy.	مُبَاحَثَةٌ
To scatter.	بَخْثَرَ
Sea.	بَحْرٌ ج أَبْحُر وَبُحُورٌ
The Atlantic Ocean.	بَحْرُ اَلظُّلُمَاتِ
The Red Sea.	اَلْبَحْرُ اَلأَحْمَرُ
The Black Sea.	اَلْبَحْرُ الاسْوَدُ
The Caspian Sea.	بَحْرُ اَلْخَزَرِ
The Pacific Ocean.	اَلْبَحْرُ اَلْمحيط
The Mediterranean.	اَلْبَحْرُ اَلْمُتَوَسِّطُ اوْ بَحْرُ اَلرُّومِ

بُحْرَةٌ ج بُحَارٌ	Basin, pool.
بُحَيْرَةٌ ج بُحَيْرَاتٌ	Lake.
بَحْرِيٌّ	Nautical.
بَحْرِيٌّ ج بَحْرِيَّةٌ	Sailor.
بَخْتٌ	Fortune, good luck.
بَخْتَرَ وَتَبَخْتَرَ	To swagger.
بَخَرَ يَبْخَرُ بَخْراً	To steam.
بَخَّرَ	To fumigate, steam.
بَاخِرَةٌ ج بَوَاخِر	Steamship.
بُخَارٌ ج أَبْخِرَةٌ	Vapour steam.
بَخُورٌ	Incense.
بَخُورُ مَرْيَم	Cyclamen (plant).
أَبْخَرُ	Having a foul breath.
مِبْخَرَةٌ ج مَبَاخِر	Censer.
بَخَسَ يَبْخَسُ	To diminish.
بَخْسٌ	Defective, low price.
بَخُلَ يَبْخُلُ	To be miserly.
بُخْلٌ	Avarice, stinginess.
بَخِيلٌ ج بُخَلاءُ	Miser ; miserly.
بَدَّدَ	To disperse ; squander.
تَبَدَّدَ	To be dispersed.
إِسْتَبَدَّ	To be arbitrary.
لاَ بُدَّ	By all means, necessarily.
بَدَأَ يَبْدَأُ	To begin ; create.
بَدَّأَ	To give precedence.
أَبْدَأَ	To create ; produce.
إِبْتَدَأَ ب	To begin, commence.
بَدْءٌ وَبَدَاءَةٌ	Beginning.
إِبْتِدَائِيٌّ	Initial, primary.
مَبْدَأٌ ج مَبَادِئُ	Principle.
بَدْخٌ	Dissipation ; pride.
بَدَرَ إِلَى	To hasten towards.
بَادَرَ وَابْتَدَرَ	To hasten.
بَدْرٌ ج بُدُورٌ	Full moon.
بَيْدَرٌ ج بَيَادِر	Thrashing-floor.
بَدَعَ يَبْدَعُ	To originate.
أَبْدَعَ وَابْتَدَعَ	To originate.
بِدْعَةٌ ج بِدَعٌ	Innovation.

بَدِيعٌ	Astonishing.
عِلْمُ ٱلْبَدِيعِ	Rhetoric.
إِبْدَاعٌ وَٱبْتِدَاعٌ	Invention.
مُبْدِعٌ	Inventor. Creator.
بَدَلَ يَبْدُلُ	To change, exchange.
تَبَدَّلَ	To be changed or altered.
إِسْتَبْدَلَ	To take in exchange.
بَدَلٌ وَبَدِيلٌ	Substitute.
بَدَلَ أَنْ	Instead of.
بَدَلاً مِنْ	In exchange for.
تَبَادُلٌ	Reciprocity.
مُتَبَادَلٌ	Reciprocal
بَدَنٌ ج أَبْدَانٌ	Body, trunk.
بَدَهَ ج يَبْدَهُ	To come suddenly.
بَدَاهَةٌ	Intuitive knowledge.
بَدِيهًا. عَلَى ٱلْبَدِيهَةِ	Intuitively.
بَدِيهِيَّةٌ	Axiom.
بَدَا يَبْدُو	To appear.
أَبْدَى	To make plain, reveal.
أَلْبَدْوُ	Nomads, bedouins.
بَادِيَةٌ ج بَوَادٍ	Desert.
بَدَاوَةٌ	Desert life ; desert.
بَدَوِيٌّ	Beduin ; nomad.
بَذِخَ يَبْذَخُ	To be proud.
بَذَخٌ	Pride, haughtiness.
بَذَرَ يَبْذُرُ	To sow ; disperse.
بَذْرٌ ج بِذَارٌ	Seed, grain.
تَبْذِيرٌ	Dissipation, prodigality.
مُبَذِّرٌ	Prodigal.
بَذَلَ يَبْذُلُ	To give.
بَذْلٌ	Generous gift, present.
بَرَّرَ	To justify.
تَبَرَّرَ	To be justified.
بِرٌّ	Goodness, piety.
بُرٌّ	Wheat.
بَرٌّ	Land as opposed to sea.
بَرًّا وَبَحْرًا	By land and by sea.
بَارٌّ ج أَبْرَارٌ	Just, pious.

بَرّانِيٌّ ج بَرّانِيُّون	External.
بَرِّيٌّ	Wild (tree or animal).
بَرِّيَّةٌ ج بَرارِيٌّ	Desert, waste.
تَبرِيرٌ	Justification.
بَرَأَ يَبرَأ	To create.
بَرَأَ وبَرِئَ يَبْرَأ	To be innocent of. Recover from an illness.
بَرَّأ مِن	To acquit.
بُرْءٌ وبُرْءٌ	Recovery, cure.
بَرِيٌّ ج أبرِياء	Innocent.
بَراءةٌ	Immunity. Document.
أَلْبارِئُ	Creator (God).
بَرِيَّةٌ ج بَرايَا	Creature, creation.
بَربَرِيٌّ	Native of Barbary.
بُرتُقانٌ وبُردُقانٌ	Oranges.
بُرجٌ ج بُروجٌ	Tower, castle.
بُروجُ الأفْلاكِ	Signs of zodiac.
بارِجَةٌ ج بَوارِجُ	Man-of-war.
بَرِحَ يَبْرَحُ	To part from.
ما بَرِحَ	To continue, persevere.
بَرَّحَ	To cause pain.
اَلْبارِحُ وأَلْبارِحةُ	Yesterday.
اَلْبارِحَةَ الأولى / اوَّلَ البارِحَةِ	Day before yesterday.
بَرَدَ يَبرُدُ	To become cold.
بَرَدَ	To file (iron).
بَرَّدَ	To make cool or cold.
بَرْدٌ	Cold.
بَرَدٌ	Hail ; hail stones.
بُرَداء وبَرديَّة	Fever and ague.
بَرْدِيٌّ	Reed, papyrus reed.
بارِدٌ	Cold.
برودة	Freshness, coolness.
بَرِيدٌ ج بُرُدٌ	Courier, post.
مِبْرَدٌ ج مَبارِدُ	File.
بَرْدَعَة	Donkey-saddle.
بَرَزَ يَبرز	To appear, issue.
بارَزَ	To go to battle.

To publish, bring out. أَبْرَزَ

Combat, duel. بِرَاز وَمُبَارَزَة

Appearance. بُرُوز

Champion ; fighter. مُبَارِز

Isthmus. بَرْزَخ ج بَرَازِخ

Alexandrian clover. بِرْسِيم

Stramonium. بِرْش

Piebald, spotted. أَبْرَش م بَرْشَاء

Soft-boiled egg. بِرِشْت

Wafer. بِرْشَان

Leprosy. بَرَص

Leper. أَبْرَص م بَرْصَاء ج بُرْص

To bribe. بَرْطَلَ بَرْطَلَة

Bribe. بِرْطِيل ج بَرَاطِيل

To excel. بَرَعَ يَبْرَع

To bestow of free will. تَبَرَّعَ ب

Distinguished ; perfect. بَارِع

Distinction ; elegance. بَرَاعَة

Bud. بُرْعُم ج بَرَاعِم

Flea. بُرْغُوث ج بَرَاغِيث

Small flies ; gnats. بَرْغَش

A small fly ; gnat. بَرْغَشَة

Wheat coarsely ground. بُرْغُل

Screw. بُرْغِيّ ج بَرَاغِيّ

To flash, lighten. بَرَقَ يَبْرُقُ

To flash, gleam. أَبْرَقَ

Lightning. بَرْق ج بُرُوق

Borax. بُورَق

To veil the face. بَرْقَعَ

A lady's veil. بُرْقُع ج بَرَاقِع

Yellow plum ; apricot. بَرْقُوق

Ewer. إِبْرِيق ج أَبَارِيق

To kneel. بَرَكَ يَبْرُك

To bless. بَارَكَ فِي أَوْ عَلَى

To seek blessing. تَبَرَّكَ بِ

To be blessed. تَبَارَكَ

Blessing. بَرَكَة ج بَرَكَات

Pool, pond ; tank. بِرْكَة ج بِرَك

Blessed.	مُبَارَك
Compasses.	بِرْكَارٌ وَبِيكَارٌ
Volcano.	بُرْكَانٌ ج براكين
To twist.	بَرَمَ يَبْرُمُ
To make firm.	أَبْرَمَ
Gimlet; augur.	بَيْرَمٌ وَبَرِّيمَةٌ
Affirmed, assured.	مُبْرَمٌ
Twisted cord.	مَبْرُومٌ
Barrel ; cask.	بِرْمِيلٌ ج بَرَامِيلُ
A kind of cloak.	بُرْنُسٌ
Hat.	بُرْنَيْطَةٌ
Space of time.	بُرْهَةٌ
To prove	بَرْهَنَ عَلَى أَو عَنْ
To be demonstrated.	تَبَرْهَنَ
Proof, evidence.	بُرْهَانٌ ج بَرَاهِينُ
Demonstrated, proved.	مُبَرْهَنٌ
Frame.	بِرْوَازٌ ج بَرَاوِيز
To pare ; emaciate.	بَرَى يَبْرِي
To vie with.	بَارَى وَٱنْبَرَى
Creation, universe.	بَرِيَّةٌ ج بَرَايَا
Mended or cut (pen).	مَبْرِيٌّ
Linen or cotton clothes.	بَزٌّ
Udder, nipple.	بِزٌّ ج أَبْزَازٌ
Seed, grain.	بِزْرٌ ج بُزُورٌ
A grain or seed.	بِزْرَةٌ
To peep forth (sun).	بَزَغَ يَبْزَغُ
Rising of sun or moon.	بُزُوغٌ
To spit.	بَزَقَ يَبْزُقُ بَزْقاً
Spittle, saliva.	بُزَاقٌ
Snail. (*coll.* بَزَاقٌ)	بَزَّاقَةٌ
Spittoon.	مِبْزَقَةٌ
To split. Tap a cask.	بَزَلَ يَبْزُلُ
Perforator.	بِزَالٌ وَمِبْزَلٌ
Buckle.	إِبْزِيمٌ
Bath-tub.	الإِبْزَنُ ج اَبَازِنُ
Cat. (بُسَيْنٌ م بُسَيْنَةٌ)	بَسٌّ م بَسَّةٌ
Garden ; orchard.	بُسْتَانٌ ج بَسَاتِين
Gardener.	بُسْتَانِيٌّ

بَاسُورٌ	Piles.
بَسَطَ يبسُطُ	To spread out ; cheer.
إِنْبَسَطَ	To be cheerful, merry.
بِسَاط ج بُسُطٌ	Carpet.
بَسِيط ج بُسطاء	Simple.
أَلْبَسِيطَة	The Earth.
إِنْبِسَاط وبسطٌ	Cheerfulness.
مبْسوطٌ	Extended ; happy.
بَسَقَ يبْسق بَسقاً	To spit.
بَسُلَ يبْسل	To be brave.
بَاسِل ج بسلاء	Bold, brave.
بسَالَةٌ	Bravery ; heroism.
بَسَمَ يَبْسِم وتَبَسَّم وا بْتَسَم	To smile.
تبسُّمٌ وآبْتِسامٌ	Smile.
بَشَّ	To be cheerful.
بَشَاشَة	Cheerfulness of face, gentleness.
بَشَر يبْشِرُ	To rejoice at.
بَشَّر	To announce good news.
بَاشَر	To manage an affair.
بَشَرَةٌ	Epidermis ; cuticle.
بَشَرٌ	Man ; mankind ; humanity.
أَلْبَشَر	Mankind, men.
بِشْرى	Good news.
بَشَرِيٌّ	Human.
بِشَارة ج بشائر	Good news ; gospel.
بَشِيرٌ	Bearer of good news.
مُبَشِّرٌ	Announcer of news ; preacher.
بَشِعَ يَبْشع	To be ugly, deformed.
بشَاعَةٌ	Bad taste (food); ugliness.
بَشِعٌ وبَشِيعٌ	Ugly ; repulsive.
بَشَمٌ	Indigestion.
بَشْنينٌ	Lotus (plant).
بَصَّ يبِصُّ	To shine, glitter.
بَصَّةٌ	A live coal.
بَصَّاصٌ ج بَصَّاصون	Spy.
بصر يبْصر بصر يبْصر	To see.
تبَصَّر	To consider, observe.
بَصَرٌ ج أَبصَارٌ	Sight.

Intelligent. بَصِيرٌ ج بُصَرَاء

Consideration ; reflection. تَبَصُّرٌ

To spit. بصق يَبْصُقُ بصقًا

Spittle, saliva. بُصَاق

Onion ; bulb. بَصَلٌ

To cut, incise. بَضَعَ يبضَع

A small number. بِضْعٌ وبِضْعَةٌ

A few days. بِضْعَةُ أَيامٍ

Merchandise. بِضَاعة ج بَضَائِع

Knife ; lancet. مِبْضَعٌ ج مبَاضِع

To lance a tumour. بط يَبُطُّ

Duck. بطةٌ ج بَطٌّ

Bottle. بَطةٌ ج بُطَطٌ

To linger. بَطُؤَ يَبْطُؤُ

To be slow, dally. تَبَاطَأَ في

Slowness. بِطَاءٌ وبطْءٌ وبُطُوءٌ

Slow, tardy, dilatory. بَطِيءٌ

Water-course. بِطحَاءُ وبَطِيحَة

Water-melon. بِطِّيخٌ أحمر

Musk-melon. بِطِّيخٌ أَصْفَر

To exult. بطِرَ يبطَر بَطَرًا

Exultation. Wantonness. بَطَرٌ

Toshoe animals بَيْطَرَ

Farrier. بِيْطَارٌ ج بَيَاطِرة

Veterinary art . بَيطَرَةٌ

Battery (of cannons). بطَّاريَّة

Patriarch. بطْرِكٌ ج بطَارِكَةٌ

Patriarchate. بَطْرِيرَكِيَّةٌ وبَطْرِكيَّةٌ

To assault. بَطَشَ يبطِش ب

Power ; violence. بَطْشٌ

A marked ticket. بطَاقَةٌ

To cease. بطَل يَبطُل

To repeal, abolish. بطل وأَبْطَل

Vanity ; lie. بطْلٌ وبطْلان

Hero. بطَلٌ ج أَبْطَالٌ

False, vain, useless. بَاطِلٌ

Lazy, idle ; useless. بَطَّالٌ

Idleness ; holidays. بِطَالَة

Abolition, repeal.	إِبْطَالٌ
Marine muscle.	بَطلَينوسٌ
Terebinth.	بُطْمٌ
To line (clothes).	بطَن وأَبْطَنَ
Belly, abdomen.	بَطْنٌ ج بُطونٌ
Inner lining.	بطانَةٌ
Inner, hidden.	بَاطِن ج بواطِن
Internally, secretly.	باطناً
To send.	بعَث يبْعَث إلى
To raise the dead.	بعَثَ
Cause, motive.	باعِثٌ
Sent. Envoy.	مَبعوثٌ
To scatter, uncover.	بعْثَرَ
To be far distant.	بعد يبعد
To make distant.	بَعَّدوأَبعَد
To be far from.	تَبَاعَدعَن
To go far from.	إبتعدعَن
To regard improbable.	إستَبعَدَ
Distance ; interval.	بُعْدٌ
Then ; afterwards ; after.	بَعْدُ
Distant ; far.	بعيدٌ
Camel.	بعيرٌ ج بعْوانٌ
To scatter, dissipate.	بعزق
Portion, part ; some.	بَعضٌ
Gnats, mosquitoes.	بعوضٌ
A gnat or mosquito.	بعوضةٌ
Husband, wife.	بعلٌ ج بعولٌ
Unwatered land.	بَعْلٌ
To take by surprise.	بَغَتَ يَبغَتُ وبَاغتَ
Surprise.	بَغْتة ج بغْتات
Suddenly, unexpectedly.	بغتَةً
Strait.	بوغاز ج بوَاغيزُ
To hate, detest.	أَبْغضَ
Hatred ; enmity.	بُغْضٌ
Violent hatred.	بغضةٌ وبَغْضَاء
One who hates.	مُبْغِضٌ
Mule.	بغلٌ ج بِغال وأَبغَال
Muleteer.	بَغالٌ

بُغْمَةٌ	Necklace.
بَغَى يَبْغِي	To seek ; desire.
بَغَى عَلَى	To be unjust ; oppress.
يَنْبَغِي أَنْ	It is desirable.
بَغْيٌ	Injustice ; aggression.
بَغَاءٌ وَٱبْتِغَاءٌ	Wish, desire.
بُغْيَةٌ وَبَغِيَّةٌ	Anything wished for or sought.
بَاغٍ ج بُغَاةٌ	Unjust aggressor.
بُقْجَةٌ ج بُقَجٌ	Bundle of clothes.
بَقْدُونَسٌ	Parsley.
بَقَرٌ ج أَبْقَارٌ	Oxen.
بَقَرَةٌ ج بَقَرَاتٌ	Cow.
بَقْسٌ	Box-tree.
بَقِعَ يَبْقَعُ بَقَعاً	To be spotted.
بُقَعٌ	Spots, stains.
بُقْعَةٌ ج بُقَعٌ وَبِقَاعٌ	Piece of land.
بَقْلٌ ج بُقُولٌ	Vegetables, herbs.
بَقَّالٌ	Green-grocer.
بَقَّمٌ	Logwood.

بَقِيَ يَبْقَى	To remain ; continue.
أَبْقَى وَٱسْتَبْقَى	To preserve.
تَبَقَّى	To be left.
بَقَاءٌ	Continuance, uration.
بَقِيَّةٌ ج بَقَايَا	Remainder.
بَاقٍ ج بَاقُونَ	Remaining.
اَلْبَاقِي	The Everlasting (God).
بَاقِيَةٌ	Vetch.
أَبْقَى	More enduring.
بَكَّتَ	To reprove, scold.
بَكَّرَ وَبَاكَرَ	To come early.
بِكْرٌ ج أَبْكَارٌ	First-born ; virgin.
بُكْرَةٌ	Dawn ; to-morrow.
بَكْرَةٌ ج بَكَرٌ	Pulley.
بَكَارَةٌ	Virginity.
بَاكِراً	Early.
بَاكُورَةٌ	First fruits.
بَكِمَ يَبْكَمُ	To be dumb.
أَبْكَمَ	To cause to be silent.

Dumbness.	بَكَمٌ
Dumb ; mute.	أَبْكَم ج بُكْمٌ
To weep.	بَكَى يَبْكِي
To cause to weep.	بَكَّى وأَبْكَى
Weeping.	بُكَاءٌ وبُكًى
But ; nay but.	بَلْ
To wet, moisten.	بَلَّ يَبُلُّ
To become wet	تَبَلَّلَ وابْتَلَّ
Wet, moistened.	مَبْلُولٌ ومُبَلَّلٌ
To mix, confound.	بَلْبَلَ
Nightingale.	بُلْبُلٌ ج بَلَابِلُ
Intense anxiety.	بَلْبَالٌ
Dates (*Coll.*)	بَلَحٌ
To be stupid.	بَلُدَ يَبْلُدُ
Town ; land.	بَلَدٌ ج بِلَادٌ وبُلْدَانٌ
Native ; urban.	بَلَدِيٌّ
Stupidity ; dullness.	بَلَادَة
Imbecile, stupid.	بَلِيدٌ وأَبْلَد
Crystal.	بَلُّورٌ وبِلَّوْرٌ
Devil, Satan.	ابْلِيسٌ ج أَبَالِسَةٌ
Balsam, balm.	بَلْسَمٌ
Elder-tree.	بَلَسَانٌ
To tax illegally.	بَلَصَ يَبْلُصُ
Oppressive taxation.	بَلْصٌ
To pave with flage-stones.	بَلَّطَ
Axe, battle-axe.	بَلْطَة
Flag-stones ; pavement.	بَلَاط
Oak-tree, acron.	بَلُّوطٌ
Sapper, executioner.	بَلْطَجِيٌّ
Act of paving.	تَبْلِيطٌ
Paver.	مُبَلِّطٌ
Paved.	مُبَلَّطٌ
To swallow.	بَلَعَ يَبْلَعُ
Swallowing.	بَلْعٌ وابْتِلَاعٌ
Sink, sewer, gutter.	بَالُوعَةٌ
Gullet.	بُلْعُومٌ
To reach, attain.	بَلَغَ يَبْلُغُ بُلُوغًا
To inform.	بَلَّغَ

بالغ في	To exaggerate.
بالغ	Mature ; of full age.
بلاغ	Message.
بلاغة	Elegance of style.
علم البلاغة	Rhetoric.
بلوغ	Arrival, maturity.
بليغ	Eloquent efficacious.
مبلغ ج مبالغ	Sum, amount.
مبالغة	Exaggeration.
بلغم ج بلاغم	Phlegm.
بلغمي	Phlegmatic.
أبلق م بلقاء ج بلق	Spotted.
بلان	A thorny plant.
بله وبلاهة	Stupidity, idiocy.
أبله م بلهاء ج بله	Stupid ; simpleton, idiot.
بلا يبلو	To test, try ; afflict.
بلي يبلى	To decay.
بالى بـ	To be attentive to.
بلى	Decay ; rottenness.
بلى	Yes, certainly.
بلاء	Trial. Grief ; calamity.
بلوى ج بلايا	Affliction.
بال	Used up ; rotten.
بم	Wherewith ?
بما ان	Because, inasmuch as
بن	Coffee-berries ; coffee.
بنان	Fingers.
بنج	To drug, stupefy.
بنج	Henbane, Hyoscyamus.
بند ج بنود	Section. Banner.
بندورة	Tomatoes.
بنديرة	Flag, banner.
بندقة وبندق	Hazel-nut.
بندقية	Musket, gun.
بندوق ج بنادیق	Bastard.
بنفسج	Violet (*plant*).
بنفسجي	Violet (*colour*).
بنصر ج بناصر	Ring-finger.

بَنْكٌ ج بُنُوكَةٌ	Seat. Bank.
بَنَى يَبْنِي	To construct, build.
تَبَنَّى	To adopt a son.
بِنَاءٌ وَبِنَايَةٌ	Building, edifice.
بِنَاءً عَلَى	In consequence of.
بَنَّاءٌ ج بَنَّاؤُونَ	Mason.
بُنْيَةٌ	Form ; constitution.
إِبْنٌ ج بَنُونَ وَأَبْنَاءٌ	Son, boy.
إِبْنَةٌ وَبِنْتٌ ج بَنَاتٌ	Daughter.
إِبْنُ ٱلسَّبِيلِ	Traveller, wayfarer.
مَبْنِيٌّ	Built. Indeclinable.
بُهِتَ يُبْهَتُ	To be astonished ; faded.
بَهَتَ يَبْهَتُ	To astonish, perplex.
بُهْتَانٌ	Lie ; slander.
بَهَجَ وَأَبْهَجَ	To rejoice, cheer.
بَهِجَ وَٱبْتَهَجَ	To rejoice at.
بَهْجَةٌ	Joy, gladness ; beauty
مُبْهِجٌ	Cheering ; causing joy.
بَهَرَ يَبْهَرُ	To shine.
بَهِرَ	To be dazzled.
بَاهِرٌ	Beautiful, admirable.
بَاهِظٌ	Heavy, distressing.
إِبْتَهَلَ إِلَى	To supplicate.
إِبْتِهَالٌ	Supplication.
بَهْلَوَانٌ	Rope-dancer.
أَبْهَمَ وَٱسْتَبْهَمَ	To be doubtful.
بَهِيمَةٌ ج بَهَائِمُ	Brute, beast.
إِبْهَامٌ	Doubt ; ambiguity.
إِبْهَامٌ ج أَبَاهِمُ	Thumb.
مُبْهَمٌ	Ambiguous ; doubtful.
بَهَا يَبْهُو	To be beautiful.
بَاهَى	To rival in beauty.
بَهَاءٌ	Beauty, brilliancy.
بَهِيٌّ	Beautiful splendid.
بَابٌ ج أَبْوَابٌ	Door. Chapter.
أَلْبَاب ٱلْعَالِي	The Sublime Porte.
بَوَّابٌ	Door-keeper.
بَوَّابَةٌ	Large door, gate.

Storehouse.	بائِكَةٌ ج بَوَائِك
To micturate. Melt ; flow.	بالَ يَبُولُ
Condition ; mind ; thought.	بالٌ
To occur to mind	خَطَر بِبَال
Bale.	بَالَةٌ
Urine.	بَوْلٌ
Steel.	بُولاَدٌ (فولاَذٌ)
An owl.	بُومَةٌ
Bill ; order ; receipt.	بُولِيصَةٌ ج بَوَالِص
The Egyptian willow.	بَانٌ
Distance ; difference.	بَوْنٌ
To pass the night.	بَاتَ يَبِيت
House, room. Verse of poetry.	بَيت ج بيوتٌ وأَبْيَاتٌ
Water-closet ; latrine ; privy.	بَيْت ٱلْمَاء بيْتُ ٱلْخَلاَء بَيْتُ ٱلْفَضَاء
Public treasury.	بيتُ ٱلْمَال
Cobweb.	بَيت ٱلعَنْكَبوتِ
Jerusalem.	بيتُ ٱلْمقدِس

To be known.	باحَ يبُوح
To divulge.	باحَ ب
To allow.	أَبَاحَ
To consider lawful.	إِستَبَاح
Revealing, licence.	إِبَاحَةٌ
Permissable; lawful.	مُبَاحٌ
To abate ; fade.	باخَ يَبُوخ
To perish.	بارَ يَبور
Uncultivated land.	بورٌ
Destruction, ruin.	بَوَارٌ
Borax ; natron.	بُورَق
Falcon, hawk.	بَاز ج بِيزَانٌ
To kiss.	باسَ يَبُوس بَوْساً
Post ; mail.	بُوسطَةٌ
Postman.	بُوسْطَجِيٌّ
A fathom.	باعٌ ج ابْوَاعٌ
Generous. Able.	طَوِيل ٱلْبَاعِ
To blow a trumpet.	بَوَّق
Trumpet; shell.	بُوقٌ ج أَبْوَاقٌ

The Kaaba in Mecca.	أَلْبَيْت آلْحَرام
House, night's lodging.	مَبِيت
To perish, vanish.	بَاد يَبِيد
To destroy, annihilate.	أَبَاد
Desert.	بيداء ج بِيدٌ
Foot-soldier.	بَيَّادِيٌّ بَيَّادة
But, although.	بَيْدَ أَنْ
Thrashing-floor.	بَيْدَرٌ
Well of water.	بِئْرٌ
Banner.	بَيْرَقٌ بَيَارِق
To lay eggs.	بَاض يَبِيض
To whiten, bleach.	بَيَّض
To become white.	إِبْيَضّ
Eggs.	بَيْضٌ ج بُيُوضٌ
An egg. Testicle.	بَيْضَة
Oval, ovate ; elliptical.	بَيْضِيٌّ
Whiteness.	بَيَاضٌ
White.	أَبْيَض م بيضاء ج بِيضٌ
Tinner; white-washer.	مُبَيِّضٌ
To shoe a horse.	بَيْطَر
To sell.	بَاع يَبِيع
To swear fealty.	بَايَع مبايعة
To buy from.	إِبْتَاع مِن
Selling, sale.	بَيْعٌ
Church, synagogue.	بَيْعَةٌ ج بِيَعٌ
Seller.	بَائِعٌ ج بَاعَة
Seller.	بَيَّاع
Sale ; place of sale.	مَبِيع
Bey.	بَيْكٌ و بَك
Pair of compasses.	بِيكَارٌ
Elder (tree).	بَيْلَسَانٌ
Hospital.	بِيمَارِسْتان
To be distinct, separate.	بَان يَبِين
To render clear ; explain.	بَيَّن
To quit, abandon.	بَايَن
To be clear, lucid.	تَبَيَّن
Between, among.	بَيْنَ
Middling.	بَيْنَ بَيْنَ

بَيْنَا وبَيْنَمَا — Whilst, while.

بَيان — Explanation.

عِلْم ٱلْبَيَان — A branch of Rhetoric.

بائِن وبيّن — Distinct, evident.

بيّنة ج بَيّنات — Evidence.

تبَاين — Difference ; contrast.

مبيْن و بيّن — Clear, evident.

ت

ت — As a numeral sign=400

تَاللّه — I swear by God.

تَابوت ج توَابِيت — Chest. Coffin.

تارةً — Once ; sometimes.

توأمة ج توائِم — Twin.

توأم — Twins ; double.

ألتوأمان — The sign of Gemini.

تَب يَتب — To suffer loss.

إستَتَب — To be established.

تَبّاً لَهُ — Evil be to him !

تبْر — Native gold.

تَبع يتْبَع واتّبَع — To follow.

أتْبَع — To cause to follow.

تَابع متابعة عَلَى — To follow.

تتبع — To follow up.

تَتَابع — To follow consecutively.

تبع ج اتباع — Follower.

متتابِع — Successive.

تبغ — Tobacco.

تبَّل وتَابَل — To season (a dish).

تَوَابِلُ	Condiments.
مُتَبَّلٌ	Seasoned (dish.)
تِبْنٌ	Straw.
تَتَرٌ	Tartars (*coll.*)
تَتَرِيٌّ	A Tartar.
تَتْرَى	One after another.
تُتُنٌ	Tobacco
تَجَرَ يَتْجُرُ وتَاجَرَ	To trade.
تِجَارَةٌ	Commerce, trade.
تَاجِرٌ ج تُجَّارٌ	Merchant.
مَتْجَرٌ ج مَتَاجِرُ	Commerce.
تُجَاهَ	In front of, opposite to.
تَحْتَ	Under, below, beneath.
تَحْتَانِيٌّ	Inferior, placed below.
أَتْحَفَ ب	To present with.
تُحْفَةٌ	Precious object, gift.
تَخْتٌ ج تُخُوتٌ	Bench ; bedstead.
تَخْتَرْوَان	Palanquin.
تَخْتُ ٱلْمُلْكِ	Capital of a kingdom.
تَخَمَ يَتْخُمُ تَخْمًا	To confine, limit.
تَاخَمَ	Adjoin, border upon.
أَتْخَمَ	To cause indigestion.
تَخْمٌ ج تُخُومٌ	Boundary.
مُتَاخِمٌ	Adjoining.
تُخَمَةٌ	Indigestion.
تَرَّبَ	To cover with earth.
تُرَابٌ ج أَتْرِبَةٌ	Earth, dust.
تُرْبَةٌ ج تُرَبٌ	Cemetery. Soil.
أُتْرُجٌّ وأُتْرُنْجٌ	Citron.
تَرْجَمَ	To translate.
تَرْجَمَةٌ	Translation.
تَرْجُمَانٌ	Dragoman, interpreter.
مُتَرْجِمٌ	Translator, interpreter.
مُتَرْجَمٌ	Translated, interpreted.
تَرَحٌ ج أَتْرَاحٌ	Sorrow, grief.
تُرْسٌ ج أَتْرَاسٌ	Shield.
مِتْرَاسٌ ج مَتَارِيسُ	Bulwark.
تَرْسَانَةٌ وتَرْسَخَانَة	Arsenal.

Channel, canal.	تُرْعَةٌ ج تُرَع
Luxury ; ease.	تَرَفٌ وتُرْفَةٌ
Collar-bone, clavicle.	تَرْقُوَةٌ
To abandon, allow.	تَرَكَ يَتْرُكُ
To leave to, bequeath.	ترك لِ
Abandoning leaving.	تَرْكٌ
Turk.	تُرْكٌ ج أَتْرَاكٌ
A turk ; Turkish.	تُرْكِيٌّ
Estate of one dead.	تِرْكَةٌ وتَرِكَةٌ
Abandoned, omitted.	مَتْرُوكٌ
Lupine.	تُرْمُسٌ
Theriac ; antidote.	تِرْيَاقٌ
Nine.	تِسْعَةٌ م تِسْعٌ
A ninth (part).	تُسْعٌ
Ninth (*ord. num.*)	تَاسِعٌ
Ninety, ninetieth.	تِسْعُونَ
October.	تِشْرِينُ ٱلْأَوَّلُ
November.	تِشْرِينُ ٱلثَّانِي
Come !	تَعَالَ
To become tired.	تَعِبَ يَتْعَبُ
To give trouble ; tire.	أَتْعَبَ
Fatigue, toil.	تَعَبٌ ج أَتْعَابٌ
Tired, fatigued.	تَعِبٌ
Toilsome, fatiguing.	مُتْعِبٌ
Fatigued.	مُتْعَبٌ
To stumble	تَعِسَ يَتْعَسُ
Misfortune.	تَعْسٌ وتَعَاسَةٌ
Unhappy, unlucky.	تَعِسٌ
Apple.	تُفَّاحٌ
An apple, apple-tree.	تُفَّاحَةٌ
To spit.	تَفَلَ يَتْفُلُ
Spittle, saliva.	تُفْلٌ
Spittoon.	مَتْفَلَةٌ
To be mean, foolish.	تَفِهَ يَتْفَهُ
Insipidity.	تَفَاهَةٌ
To arrange skilfully.	أَتْقَنَ
Perfection (of a work).	تَقَانَةٌ
Skilful elaboration.	إِتْقَانٌ

مُتْقَن Skilfully made.

تَقِيّ Pious.

تَقْوى Piety.

تَلّ ج تِلال Small hill.

تَلِف يَتْلَف تَلَفًا To perish.

أَتْلَف To ruin.

تَلَف Destruction.

مُتْلِف Destroyer, waster.

مِتْلاف Squanderer.

تِلْك That (*fem.*)

تَلَم ج اتْلام Furrow, rut.

تَلْمَذ To be a pupil.

تِلْمِيذ ج تَلامِيذ Disciple, pupil.

تَلا يَتْلُو تُلُوًّا To follow ; succeed.

تَلا يَتْلُو تِلاوة To read ; recite.

تِلاوة Reading, recitation.

تال Following, next.

تَمّ يَتِمّ To be complete.

تَمَّم وأَتَمّ To complete, finish.

تَمام Completion, end.

تَمامًا وبالتَّمام Completely.

تَمِيمة ج تَمائِم Talisman, amulet

تامّ م تامّة Perfect, complete.

تَتِمّة Complement.

تَمْتام Stammerer.

تَمْر ج تُمور Ripe dates.

تَمْرهِنْدِيّ Tamarind (*fruit*).

تَموز وتمُّوز July.

تِمْساح ج تماسِيح Crocodile.

تِنّين ج تَنانِين Dragon.

تَنْباك Persian tobacco.

تَنْبَل ج تَنابِل Idler, lazy.

تَنُّور ج تَنانِير Oven-pit.

تَنَك Tin.

أَتْهَم واتَّهَم To suspect, accuse.

تُهْمَة Suspicion. Accusation.

تاب يتوب To repent.

تَوْبَة Repentence ; penitence.

تائبٌ	Repentant, penitent.
تُوتٌ	White mulberry.
تُوتٌ شَامِيٌّ	Black mulberry.
تُوتُ ٱلْعُلَّيْقِ	Blackberry.
تُوتِيَاءُ	Zinc.
تَوَّجَ	To crown.
تَتَوَّجَ	To be crowned.
تَاجٌ ج تِيجَانٌ	Crown, diadem.
تَوْرَاةٌ	Pentateuch. Bible.
تَارَةً	One time.
تَاقَ يَتُوقُ إِلَى	To long for, desire.
تَوْقٌ وَتَوَقَانٌ	Passion, desire.
تَائِقٌ	Yearning, desiring.
تَاهَ يَتُوهُ	To lose one's way.
تَيَّارٌ	A strong, deep current.
تَاحَ وَأَتَاحَ لِ	To be appointed, decreed to.
تَيْسٌ ج تُيُوسٌ	He-goat.
تِينٌ	Figs ; fig-trees.
تِينَةٌ	A fig, a fig tree.
تَاهَ يَتِيهُ	To be proud. Wander.
تِيهٌ	Desert. Pride.
تَائِهٌ	Lost, wandering. Proud.

ث

ث	As a numeral sign = 500
تَثَاءَبَ تَثَاؤُباً	To yawn.
ثَأْرٌ وَثَارٌ ج اثَارٌ	Revenge.
ثُؤْلُولٌ ج ثَآلِيلُ	Wart.
ثَبَتَ يَثْبُتُ	To stand firm.
ثَبَتَ عِنْدَ	To be certain, assured.

ثَبَّتَ وَأَثْبَتَ	To prove.
ثَبَاتٌ وَثُبُوتٌ	Firmness. Reality.
ثَابِتٌ	Firm ; certain sure.
ثَابِتَةٌ ج ثَوَابِتُ	Fixed star.
مُثْبَتٌ وَثَابِتٌ	Firm ; proved.
ثَابَرَ عَلَى مُثَابَرَةً	To persevere in.
مُثَابِرٌ	Assiduous, persevering.
ثَخُنَ يَثْخُنُ	To be thick.
أَثْخَنَ	To make slaughter.
ثُخْنٌ وَثُخُونَةٌ	Thickness; hardness.
ثَخِينٌ ج ثِخَانٌ	Thick, firm.
ثَدْيٌ ج ثُدِيٌّ	Breast (mamma).
ثَرْبٌ ج ثُرُوبٌ	Omentum, caul.
ثَرِيدٌ	Bread with broth.
ثَرِيَ وَأَثْرَى	To abound in wealth.
ثَرَاءٌ وَثَرْوَةٌ	Wealth, riches.
ثُرَيَّا	The Pleiades.
ثَرًى ج أَثْرَاءٌ	Moisture ; earth.
ثُعْبَانٌ ج ثَعَابِينُ	Large serpent.
ثَعْلَبٌ ج ثَعَالِبُ	Fox.
دَاءُ ٱلثَّعْلَبِ	Alopecia, falling of hair.
ثَغَرَ يَثْغَرُ	To make a breach.
ثَغْرٌ ج ثُغُورٌ	Frontier. Mouth.
ثُغْرَةٌ ج ثُغُورٌ	Opening ; breach.
ثُقْلٌ	Sediment, dregs.
ثَقَبَ يَثْقُبُ ثَقْبًا	To pierce.
تَثَقَّبَ وَٱنْثَقَبَ	To be pierced.
ثَقْبٌ ج ثُقُوبٌ	Hole.
ثَاقِبٌ	Penetrating.
مِثْقَبٌ ج مَثَاقِبُ	Gimlet, drill.
مَثْقُوبٌ	Pierced, perforated.
ثَقِفَ يَثْقَفُ	To be skilful.
ثَقَافَةٌ	Sagacity, intelligence.
مُثَقَّفٌ	Well-made; educated.
ثَقُلَ يَثْقُلُ	To be heavy.
ثَقَّلَ	To make heavy.
ثَقُلَ عَلَى	To burden, annoy.
إِسْتَثْقَلَ	To deem heavy

ثِقْلٌ ج أَثْقَالٌ	Weight, burden.
أَلثَّقَلَانِ	Mankind and geni.
ثَقِيلٌ ج ثُقَلَاءُ وَثِقَالٌ	Heavy.
مُثَقَّلٌ	Overburdened.
مِثْقَالٌ ج مَثَاقِيلُ	$1\frac{3}{7}$ dirhems.
ثَاكِلٌ وَثَكْلَى	Mother bereft of children.
ثَلَبَ يَثْلِبُ	To blame, censure.
ثَلْبٌ	Censure, reproach.
مَثْلَبَةٌ ج مَثَالِبُ	Fault, vice.
ثَلَّثَ	To make three.
أَثْلَثَ	To become three.
ثُلْثٌ وَثُلُثٌ	Third part, third.
ثَالِثٌ	Third.
ثَالِثًا	Thirdly.
ثَلَاثًا	Thrice, three times.
أَلثُّلَاثَاءُ وَأَلثَّلَثَاءُ	Tuesday.
ثَلَاثَةٌ أَوْ ثَلٰثَةٌ م ثَلَاثٌ	Three.
ثُلَاثِيٌّ	Triliteral.
ثَلَاثُونَ وَثَلٰثُونَ	Thirty.

مُثَلَّثٌ	Triangular ; triangle.
ثَالُوثٌ	Trinity.
عِلْمُ ٱلْمُثَلَّثَاتِ	Trigonometry.
ثَلَجَ يَثْلُجُ وَأَثْلَجَ	To snow.
ثَلْجٌ ج ثُلُوجٌ	Snow.
ثَلِجٌ	Icy cold.
ثَلَمَ يَثْلِمُ ثَلْمًا وَثَلَّمَ	To blunt.
ثَلِمَ وَتَثَلَّمَ وَٱنْثَلَمَ	To be blunted.
ثَلْمٌ	Furrow ; breach.
ثَمَّ	Yonder ; there.
ثُمَّ وَثُمَّتْ	Then ; moreover.
إِثْمِدٌ	Antimony.
ثَمَرَ يَثْمُرُ وَأَثْمَرَ	To bear fruit.
ثَمَرٌ ج أَثْمَارٌ وَثِمَارٌ	Fruit.
ثَمَرَةٌ ج ثَمَرٌ وَثَمَرَاتٌ	A fruit.
مُثْمِرٌ	Productive, fruitful.
ثَمَلٌ	Intoxication.
ثَمَّنَ	To value, estimate.
ثَمَنٌ ج أَثْمَانٌ	Price, value.

ثُمْنٌ ج أَثْمَانٌ	Eighth part.
ثَامِنٌ	Eighth.
ثَمَانِيَةٌ م ثَمَانٍ	Eight.
ثَمَانُونَ	Eighty.
ثَمِينٌ وَمُثْمِنٌ	Costly, precious.
تَثْمِينٌ	Valuation, estimation.
مُثَمِّنٌ	Estimator appraiser.
مُثَمَّنٌ	Octagon. Estimated.
ثَنَى يَثْنِي ثَنْياً	To fold, double.
ثَنَى عَنْ	To dissuade.
ثَنَّى	To make two.
أَثْنَى عَلَى	To praise a person.
إِنْثَنَى	To be bent, folded.
إِنْثَنَى عَنْ	To desist from.
إِسْتَثْنَى مِن	To exclude.
ثَنَاءٌ ج أَثْنِيَةٌ	Praise, eulogy.
ثَانٍ م ثَانِيَةٌ	Second.
ثَانِياً وَثَانِيَةً	Secondly.
ثَانِيَةٌ ج ثَوَانٍ	Second, (time).
في إِثْنَاءِ ذَلِكَ	Meanwhile.
إِثْنَانِ م ثِنْتَانِ وَاثْنَتَانِ	Two.
يَوْمُ الإِثْنَيْنِ	Monday.
إِسْتِثْنَاءٌ	Exception, exclusion.
إِسْتِثْنَائِيٌّ	Exceptional.
مُثَنًّى	Put in the dual, (noun).
أَلْمُثَنَّى	The dual.
مُسْتَثْنًى	Excpeted, excluded.
ثَوَّبَ	To reward, recompense.
أَثَابَ إِثَابَةً	To reward.
ثَوْبٌ ج ثِيَابٌ وَأَثْوَابٌ	Garment.
ثَوَابٌ	Reward, recompense.
ثَارَ يَثُورُ	To rise up ; break out.
ثَوَّرَ وَأَثَارَ	To stir up ; rouse.
ثَوْرٌ ج أَثْوَارٌ وَثِيرَانٌ	Bull, ox.
ثَوْرَةٌ	Excitement. Mutiny.
ثُومٌ	Garlic.
ثَوَى يَثْوِي	To abide. To die.
مَثْوًى ج مَثَاوٍ	Abode.
ثَيِّبٌ ج ثَيِّبَاتٌ	Woman freed from her husband

ج

ج — As a numeral sign = 3.

جَاثَلِيقٌ — Primate of Christians.

جَاشٌ — Agitation, commotion.

جَبَّ يَجُبُّ — To lop ; cut off.

جُبٌّ ج أَجْبَابٌ — A deep well.

جُبَّةٌ ج جُبَبٌ — A long coat.

جَبَرَ يَجْبِرُ — To set a broken bone. To repair.

جَبَرَ عَلَى — To force, compel.

جَبَّرَ — To set a broken bone.

أَجْبَرَ عَلَى — To constrain, force.

تَجَبَّرَ عَلَى — To be haughty.

جَبْرٌ — Compulsion.

أَلْجَبْرُ — Algebra.

جَبِرَةٌ ج جَبَائِرُ — Bandage ; splint.

جَبَّارٌ ج جَبَابِرَةٌ — Strong, Proud.

أَلْجَبَّارُ — God. Orion.

مُجَبِّرٌ — Bone-setter.

مَجْبُورٌ — Set (bone) ; constrained.

جَبْرِيلُ — The Angel Gabriel.

جِبْسٌ — Gypsum.

جَبَلَ يَجْبُلُ — To form, knead.

جَبَلٌ ج أَجْبَالٌ وَجِبَالٌ — Mountain.

جِبْلَةٌ وَجِبِلَّةٌ — Natural temper.

جَبَلِيٌّ — Mountainous.

جِبِلِّيٌّ — Natural, inborn.

مَجْبُولٌ — Kneaded ; formed.

جَبُنَ يَجْبُنُ — To be timid, cowardly.

تَجَبَّنَ — To become curdled.

جُبْنٌ وَجَبَانَةٌ — Cowardice.

جُبْنٌ وَجُبُنٌ — Cheese.

جَبِينٌ — Brow forehead.

جَبَانٌ ج جُبَنَاءُ — Coward.

جَبَّانَةٌ — Burying-ground.

جَبْهَةٌ — Brow, forehead.

جَبَا يَجْبُو وَيَجْبِي — To gather taxes.

إِجْتَبَى — To choose.

Tribute, tax.	جِبَايَةٌ ج جِبَايَاتٌ
Tax-gatherer.	جَابٍ
Corpse ; body.	جُثَّةٌ ج جُثَثٌ
To kneel.	جَثَا يَجْثُو جُثُوًّا
To deny ; disbelieve.	جَحَدَ يَجْحَدُ
Denying. An apostate.	جَاحِدٌ
Unbelief ; denial.	جُحُودٌ
Den, hole.	جُحْرٌ ج أَجْحَارٌ وَأَجْحِرَةٌ
Foal of an ass.	جَحْشٌ ج جِحَاشٌ
To protrude (eye).	جَحَظَ ـَ جُحُوظًا
To look sharply at.	جَحَظَ إِلَى
To injure ; oppress.	أَجْحَفَ بِ
Damage ; injury.	إِجْحَافٌ
Large fire ; hell.	جَحِيمٌ
To exert oneself.	جَدَّ يَجِدُّ
To be new.	جَدَّ جِدَّةً
To renew ; restore.	جَدَّدَ
To be renewed, restored.	تَجَدَّدَ
To become new.	إِسْتَجَدَّ
Fortune, success.	جَدٌّ
Exertion, seriousness.	جِدٌّ
Much ; very ; seriously.	جِدًّا
Grandfather.	جَدٌّ ج جُدُودٌ
Grandmother.	جَدَّةٌ ج جَدَّاتٌ
New, recent.	جَدِيدٌ ج جُدُدٌ
Drought ; dearth.	جَدْبٌ
Sterile, bare.	أَجْدَبُ م جَدْبَاءُ
Imbecile, idiot.	مَجْذُوبٌ
Grave.	جَدَثٌ ج أَجْدَاثٌ
Wall, enclosure.	جِدَارٌ ج جُدُرٌ
Small-box.	جُدْرِيٌّ
Fit, worthy of.	جَدِيرٌ بِ
More worthy, fitted.	أَجْدَرُ
To cut off, main.	جَدَعَ يَجْدَعُ
Mutilation.	جَدْعٌ
Maimed, mutilated.	أَجْدَعُ
To row.	جَدَفَ
To blaspheme.	جَدَفَ عَلَى

تَجْدِيفٌ ج تَجَادِيفُ	Blasphemy.
مِجْدَافٌ ج مَجَادِيفُ	Oar, paddle.
جَدَلَ يَجْدُلُ جَدْلاً	To twist.
جَدَّلَ	To braid the hair.
جَادَلَ	To contend, dispute.
جِدَالٌ وَمُجَادَلَةٌ	Contention, dispute.
جَدْوَلٌ ج جَدَاوِلُ	Brook. List.
مَجْدُولٌ	Plaited, twisted.
اجْدَى	To be useful, profitable.
جَدْوَى	Gift. Benefit.
جَدْيٌ ج جِدَاءٌ	Kid. Capricorn.
جَذَبَ يَجْذِبُ	To draw ; attract.
إِنْجَذَبَ	To be drawn, attracted.
قُوَّةٌ جَاذِبَةٌ	Power of attraction.
جَذَرَ يَجْذِرُ	To lop, cut off.
جَذْرٌ ج جُذُورٌ	Root, origin. Root of number.
جَذَعٌ وَجُذْعَانٌ	Lad, youth.
جِذْعٌ	Trunk of tree.
جَذَفَ يَجْذِفُ	To row (a boat).
مِجْذَافٌ مَجَاذِيفُ	Oar.
جَذَمَ يَجْذِمُ وَجَذَمَ	To cut off.
جُذَامٌ	Leprosy.
أَجْذَمُ ج جَذْمَى	Leper.
جَرَّ يَجُرُّ جَرًّا	To draw, drag.
إِنْجَرَّ	To be pulled, drawn.
إِجْتَرَّ	To chew the cud.
هَلُمَّ جَرًّا	And so on, et cetera.
حُرُوفُ ٱلْجَرِّ	Prepositions.
جَرُّ ٱلأَثْقَالِ	Mechanics.
جَرَّةٌ ج جِرَارٌ	Earthen jar.
جَارٌّ وَمَجْرُورٌ	Preposition and case governed by it.
جَيْشٌ جَرَّارٌ	Large army.
جَرِيرَةٌ ج جَرَائِرُ	Sin, crime.
أَلْمَجَرَّةُ	Milky-way.
جَرُؤَ يَجْرُؤُ جَرَاءَةً	To be bold.
جَرَّأَ	To embolden, encourage.
إِجْتَرَأَ	To bare, venture.
جُرْأَةٌ وَجَرَاءَةٌ	Boldness, courage.

جَرِبَ يَجْرَبُ To have the itch.
جَرَّبَ To put to the test, try.
جَرَبٌ Itch, scabies.
جِرَابٌ ج أَجْرِبَةٌ Leathern sack.
أَجْرَبُ Suffering from itch.
جَرِيبٌ ج أَجْرِبَةٌ A corn-measure.
تَجْرِبَةٌ ج تَجَارِبُ Trial, experiment; temptation.
مُجَرَّبٌ Tried, tested.
جُرْثُومَةٌ ج جَرَاثِيمُ Root; germ.
جَرْجِيرٌ Cress, water-cress.
جَرَحَ يَجْرَحُ To wound, hurt.
جُرْحٌ ج جُرُوحٌ Wound, cut.
جِرَاحَةٌ ج جِرَاحٌ Wound.
عِلْمُ ٱلْجِرَاحَةِ Surgery.
جَرَّاحٌ وَجِرَاحِيٌّ Surgeon.
جَرِيحٌ ج جَرْحَى Wounded.
جَارِحَةٌ ج جَوَارِحُ Beast of prey.
مَجْرُوحٌ ج مَجَارِيحُ Wounded.
مُجَرَّحٌ Covered with wounds.

جَرَّدَ To strip, abstract.
تَجَرَّدَ To be stripped, bared.
جَرَادٌ Locusts.
جَرِيدٌ Branch of palm-tree.
أَجْرَدُ م جَرْدَاءُ Naked, hairless.
مُجَرَّدٌ Separated; bare, naked.
مُجَرَّدًا لِ Solely for.
مُجَرَّدَاتٌ Abstractions.
جُرَذٌ ج جِرْذَانٌ Field-rat.
جُرْزَةٌ Bundle of sticks.
جَرَسٌ ج أَجْرَاسٌ Bell.
جَرَشَ يَجْرُشُ To bruise; bray.
جَارُوشٌ ج جَوَارِيشُ Hand-mill.
جَرَعَ يَجْرَعُ وَٱجْتَرَعَ To swallow.
جُرْعَةٌ Draught of water.
جَرَفَ يَجْرُفُ To sweep away.
مِجْرَفَةٌ Shovel; hoe.
جَرَمَ وَأَجْرَمَ To commit a crime.
تَجَرَّمَ To impute a crime falsely.

جُرْمٌ ج جُرُومٌ وَأَجْرَامٌ Sin, crime.

جُرْمٌ ج أَجْرَامٌ Body, bulk.

الأَجْرَامُ الفَلَكِيَّةُ The celestial bodies.

جَرْمٌ ج جُرُومٌ Boat, lighter.

لَا جَرَمَ Verily, truly.

جَرِيمَةٌ ج جَرَائِمُ Sin, guilt, crime.

مُجْرِمٌ Criminal, guilty.

جُرْنٌ ج أَجْرَانٌ Mortar, basin.

جَرْوٌ ج أَجْرِيَةٌ Cub, whelp.

جَرَى يَجْرِي جَرْيًا وَجَرَيَانًا To flow.

جَرَّى وَأَجْرَى To cause to flow.

أَجْرَى To carry out, execute.

جَارَى فِي To agree with.

جِرَايَةٌ Rations of a soldier.

جَارٍ Running ; current.

جَارِيَةٌ Slave-girl, girl.

إِجْرَاءٌ Execution of an order.

مَجْرًى ج مَجَارٍ Course ; duct.

جَزَّ يَجُزُّ To shear, cut, mow.

جِزَّةٌ Fleece, shorn wool.

جَزَّازٌ Shearer.

مِجَزٌّ Shears, scissors.

مَجْزُوزٌ Shorn, cut.

جَزَّأَ To divide into portions.

تَجَزَّأَ To be divided into parts.

جُزْءٌ ج أَجْزَاءٌ Part, portion.

جُزْئِيٌّ Partial, particular.

جُزْئِيَّةٌ Particular proposition.

جُزْئِيَّاتٌ Details, parts ; trifles.

أَجْزَائِيٌّ Apothecary, druggist.

أَجْزَائِيَّةٌ Pharmacy.

مُتَجَزِّئٌ Divided into parts.

جَزَرَ يَجْزُرُ To slaughter, kill.

جَزَرَ يَجْزُرُ جَزْرًا To ebb (sea).

جَزْرٌ Slaughter. Ebb.

جَزَرٌ Carrots.

جَزَّارٌ Butcher ; slaughterer.

جَزِيرَةٌ ج جَزَائِرُ وَجُزُرٌ Island.

Peninsula.	شِبْهُ جَزِيرَةٍ
Algiers.	أَلْجَزَائِر
Slaughter-house.	مَجْزَرٌ ج مَجَازِر
To grow impatient.	جَزِعَ يَجْزَعُ
Impatience, grief.	جَزَعٌ وجُزُوعٌ
Impatient.	جَزْعٌ وجَزُوعٌ
At random, by conjecture.	جَزْفٌ وَمجَازَفَةٌ وَجِزَافًا
To abound.	جَزَلَ يَجْزُلُ جَزَالَةً
To give largely.	أَجْزَلَ
Abundant ; much.	جَزِيلٌ
Very venerable.	جَزِيلُ ٱلْاحْتِرَامِ
To decide ; make binding.	جَزَمَ يَجْزِمُ جَزْمًا
Boot.	جَزْمَةٌ ج جَزْمَات
Decisive.	جَازِمٌ ج جَوَازِمُ
To recompense.	جَزَى يَجْزِي
To reward.	جَازَى
To be rewarded or punished.	تَجَازَى
Requital, reward.	جَزَاءٌ وَمُجَازَاةٌ
Tax on a tributary ; land tax.	جِزْيَةٌ
To touch.	جَسَّ يَجُسُّ وَٱجْتَسَّ
To spy out.	جَسَّ وَتَجَسَّسَ
Spy.	جَاسُوسٌ ج جَوَاسِيسُ
To assume a body.	تَجَسَّدَ
Body, flesh.	جَسَدٌ ج أَجْسَادٌ
Corporeal.	جَسَدِيٌّ وَجُسْدَانِيٌّ
Incarnation.	تَجَسُّدٌ
To dare venture.	جَسَرَ يَجْسُرُ
To venture boldly.	تَجَاسَرَ
Bridge. Dike.	جِسْرٌ ج أَجْسُرٌ
Courage, audacity.	جَسَارَةٌ
Bold, courageous.	جَسُورٌ
Courage, audacity.	تَجَاسُرٌ
To be large.	جَسُمَ جَسَامَةً
To assume a form.	تَجَسَّمَ
Body.	جِسْمٌ ج أَجْسَامٌ
Bodily ; material.	جُسْمَانِيٌّ
Importance.	جَسَامَةٌ

جَسِيمٌ	Large. Important.
مُجَسَّمٌ	Solid, corporeal, bulky.
جَشَّأَ وَتَجَشَّأَ	To belch, eruct.
جُشَاءٌ	Eructation.
جَشِمَ وَتَجَشَّمَ	To undertake a difficult task.
جَصٌّ	Gypsum ; mortar.
جَعْبَةٌ ج جِعَابٌ	Quiver.
جَعُدَ يَجْعُدُ	To be curly (hair).
تَجَعَّدَ	To be curly, wrinkled.
جُعَيْدِيٌّ	Buffoon ; low fellow.
جَعَلَ يَجْعَلُ	To put, place, make.
جَعَلَ يَبْكِي	He began to weep.
جِعَالَةٌ وَجُعْلٌ	Pay, wages; bribe.
جَفَّ يَجِفُّ جَفَافاً	To become dry.
جَفَّفَ	To dry cause to dry.
تَجَفَّفَ	To become dry.
جَافٌّ وَجَفِيفٌ	Dry, withered,
جَفَلَ وَأَجْفَلَ	To be frightened, shy.
جَفَّلَ	To put to flight ; frighten.
جَفْنٌ ج جُفُونٌ وَأَجْفَانٌ	Eyelid.
جَفَا يَجْفُو جَفَاءً	To treat rudely.
جَافَى	To shun, turn away from.
جِفْوَةٌ وَجَفَاءٌ	Harshness.
جَافٍ	Thick, coarse, rude.
جَلَّ يَجِلُّ جَلَالاً	To be great.
جَلَّ وَتَجَالَّ عَنْ	To disdain.
اجَلَّ	To honour, magnify.
جُلٌّ ج أَجْلَالٌ	Pack-saddle.
جُلُّ الأَمْرِ	The gist of a matter.
جَلَالٌ	Splendour, majesty.
جَلَالَاتِيٌّ	Maker of pack-saddles.
جَلَالَةٌ	Human greatness ; majesty.
جَلِيلٌ ج أَجِلَّاءُ	Great.
مَجَلَّةٌ	Book ; review.
جَلَبَ يَجْلِبُ	To gather ; bring.
إِنْجَلَبَ	To be led, imported.
جَلْبٌ	Importation, import.
جَلَبٌ	Camlour, noise, tumult.

Imported slaves, cattle.	جَلَبٌ
Scab. Hunger, distress.	جُلْبَةٌ
Clamour, tumult.	جَلَبَةٌ
Cattle or slave-dealer.	جَلاَبٌ
Julep, raisin-water.	جُلاَبٌ
Drawn ; imported.	مَجْلُوبٌ
Little bell.	جُلْجُلٌ ج جَلاَجِلُ
Baldness on the temples.	جَلْحَةٌ
Bald on the temples.	أَجْلَحُ
To whet (a razor).	جَلَخَ وَجَلَّخَ
Grindstone.	جَلْخٌ
To scourge.	جَلَدَ يَجْلِدُ جَلْداً
To be frozen.	جَلَدَ يَجْلَدُ جَلْداً
To bind a book.	جَلَّدَ
To bear patiently.	تَجَلَّدَ
Endurance. Firmament.	جَلَدٌ
Skin, hide, leather.	جِلْدٌ ج جُلُودٌ
Endurance.	جَلاَدَةٌ وَجُلُودَةٌ
Executioner.	جَلاَّدٌ
Hoar-frost, ice.	جَلِيدٌ
Book-binder.	مُجَلِّدٌ
Bound in leather, book.	مُجَلَّدٌ
To sit, sit up.	جَلَسَ يَجْلِسُ
To sit in company with.	جَالَسَ
To cause to sit.	أَجْلَسَ
A single sitting ; session.	جَلْسَةٌ
Sitting. Straight.	جَالِسٌ
Act of sitting.	جُلُوسٌ
Companion.	جَلِيسٌ ج جُلَسَاءُ
Council.	مَجْلِسٌ ج مَجَالِسُ
Council of ministers.	مَجْلِسُ ٱلْوُزَرَاءِ
Court of the First Instance.	أَلْمَجْلِسُ ٱلاِبْتِدَائِيُّ
Court of Appeal.	مَجْلِسُ ٱلاِسْتِئْنَافِ
Mixed Tribunal.	أَلْمَجْلِسُ ٱلْمُخْتَلَطُ
Council of war.	مَجْلِسٌ حَرْبِيٌّ
To tear, scrape.	جَلَفَ يَجْلِفُ جَلْفاً
Large sack.	جُوَالِقُ ج جَوَالِيقُ
Catapult.	مَنْجَلِيقٌ وَمَنْجَنِيقٌ

To polish ; remove.	جَلَا يَجْلُو
To become evident.	جَلَا لِـ
To depart.	جَلَا عَن
To emigrate.	أَجْلَى
To appear.	تَجَلَّى لِ
To be disclosed.	إِنْجَلَى
Clearness. Emigration.	جَلَاءٌ
Clear, evident, manifest.	جَلِيٌّ
Clearly, evidently.	جليا
Transfiguration.	أَلتَّجَلِّي (عيد)
Polished, planed.	مَجْلُوٌّ وَمَجْلِيٌّ
To polish.	جَلَى يَجْلِي جَلْيًا
Great number, crowd.	جَمٌّ غَفِيرٌ
Skull.	جُمْجُمَةٌ ج جَمَاجِم
To be restive, run-away (horse).	جَمَحَ يَجْمَحُ
Refractory.	جَامِحٌ وَجَمُوحٌ
To congeal, harden.	جَمَدَ يَجْمُدُ
Underived word.	جَامِدٌ ج جَوَامِد
The mineral kingdom	اَلْجَوَامِد
Mineral, solid.	جَمَادٌ
The fifth and sixth months of the Mohammedan year.	جُمَادَى ٱلْاولَى / » ٱلْآخِرَة
Live coal. Tribe.	جَمْرَةٌ ج جَمْرٌ
Carbuncle (*disease*).	جَمْرَةٌ
Censer ; fire-pan.	مِجْمَرَةٌ ج مَجَامِر
Sycamore.	جُمَّيْزٌ وَجُمَّيْزَى
Buffalo.	جَامُوسٌ ج جَوَامِيس
To gather, add.	جَمَعَ يَجْمَعُ
To bring together.	جَمَعَ بَيْنَ
To agree upon.	أَجْمَعُوا عَلَى
To assemble, be gathered.	تَجَمَّعَ وَاجْتَمَعَ
Assembly ; plural.	جَمْعٌ ج جُمُوع
Whole plural.	أَلْجَمْعُ ٱلسَّالِم
Broken plural.	جَمْعُ ٱلتَّكْسِير
Week.	جُمْعَةٌ ج جُمَع
Friday.	اَلْجُمْعَةُ
Party ; community.	جَمَاعَةٌ
Collector ; comprehensive.	جَامِعٌ

Mosque. جَامِعٌ ج جَوَامِعُ

All, the whole of. جَمِيع

All; altogether. جَمِيعاً

Company; committee. جَمْعِيَّةٌ

All, whole. أَجْمَعُ ج أَجْمَعُونَ

Unanimity. إِجْمَاعٌ

Assembly, gathering. إِجْتِمَاعٌ

Confluence. Society of learned men. مَجْمَعٌ ج مَجَامِعُ

United, total. مَجْمُوعٌ ج مَجَامِيعُ

Pay, salary. جَامَكِيَّةٌ

To embellish, adorn. جَمَّلَ

To treat with affability. جَامَلَ

Camel. جَمَلٌ ج جِمَال

Sum, total. Sentence, phrase, paragraph. جُمْلَةٌ ج جُمَلٌ

In the aggregate. بِالْجُمْلَةِ

Beauty, grace. جَمَالٌ

Camel-driver. جَمَّالٌ

Handsome, good deed. جَمِيلٌ

Generally speaking. بالإِجمال

Sum, total; summary. مُجْمَلٌ

Multitude. جُمْهُورٌ ج جَمَاهِيرُ

Republican. جُمْهُورِيٌّ

Republic. جُمْهُورِيَّةٌ

To be dark (night). جَنَّ يَجُنُّ

To become mad. جُنَّ

To madden. جَنَنَ وَأَجَنَّ

Demons, genii. جِنٌّ وَجَانٌ وَجِنَّةٌ

Garden, paradise. جَنَّةٌ ج جَنَّات

Heart, mind. جَنَانٌ ج أَجْنَانٌ

Madness, insanity. جُنُونٌ

Embryo, fœtus. جَنِين ج أَجِنَّةٌ

Small garden. جُنَيْنَةٌ

Shield. مِجَنٌّ ج مَجَانّ

Mad, insane. مَجْنُونٌ ج مَجَانِينُ

To shun, avoid. تَجَنَّبَ وَاجْتَنَبَ

Side, flank. جَنْبٌ ج جُنُوبٌ

Pleurisy. ذَاتُ الْجَنْبِ

Flank, part. جَانِبٌ ج جَوَانِبُ

Mild, gentle. لَيِّنُ ٱلْجَانِبِ

Title of respect. جَنَابٌ

South ; south wind. جَنُوبٌ

Southern. جَنُوبِيٌّ

Foreign. أَجْنَبِيٌّ ج أَجَانِبُ

Act of avoiding. إِجْتِنَابٌ وَتَجَنُّبٌ

To incline towards. جَنَحَ يَجْنَحُ

Wing. جَنَاحٌ ج أَجْنِحَة

Sin, crime, guilt. جُنَاحٌ

To levy troops. جَنَّدَ

To be enlisted, enrolled. تَجَنَّدَ

Army. جُنْدٌ ج جُنُودٌ

A soldier. جُنْدِيٌّ

Grasshopper. جُنْدَبٌ ج جَنَادِبُ

To throw a man down. جَنْدَلَ

A kind of plum. جنريك

Funeral, corps. جَنَازَةٌ ج جَنَائِزُ

Funeral rites. جُنَازٌ ج جَنَانِيز

Verdigris. جِنْزَارٌ

To make similar. جَنَّسَ

To appear similar. جَانَسَ

Genus, kind, race, sex ; nationality. جِنْسٌ ج أَجْنَاسٌ

Generic noun. إِسْمُ جِنْسٍ

Nationality. جِنْسِيَّةٌ

Of the same kind. مُجَانِس

To act unjustly. جَنَفَ وَأَجْنَفَ

Wrong, injustice. جَنَفٌ

Coarse linen. جِنْفَاصٌ وَجَنْفِيصٌ

Catapult. مَنْجَنِيقٌ ج مَجَانِقُ وَمَجَانِيقُ

To gather (fruit). جَنَى ـِ وَٱجْتَنَى

To commit a crime. جَنَى جِنَايَةً

To accuse falsely. تَجَنَّي عَلَى

A gatherer. Criminal. جَانٍ

Crime ; sin. جِنَايَةٌ

To toil. جَهُدَ

To weary, fatigue. جَهَّدَ

To struggle. جَاهَدَ مُجَاهَدَةً وَجِهَاداً

To strive after. إِجْتَهَدَ فِي

جُهْدٌ	Exertion, effort.
أَفْرَغَ جَهْدَهُ	He did his best.
جِهَادٌ	Combat, struggle.
جِهَادِيٌّ	Military.
إِجْتِهَادٌ	Diligence, effort.
مُجَاهِدٌ	Champion.
جَهَرَ بِ	To publish.
جَهِرَ يَجْهَرُ	To be dazzled.
جَاهَرَ بِ	To declare publicly.
تَجَاهَرَ	To appear in public.
جَهْرًا وَجِهَارًا	Publicly, openly.
أَجْهَرُ م جَهْرَاءُ	Day-blind.
مِجْهَرٌ	Microscope.
جَهَّزَ	To equip, fit out.
تَجَهَّزَ	To get ready.
جَهَازٌ ج أَجْهِزَة	Trousseau. Requisites, apparatus.
تَجْهِيزٌ	Equipment, expedition.
جَهِلَ يَجْهَلُ	To be ignorant.
جَهَّلَ	To impute ignorance.
تَجَاهَلَ	To affect ignorance.
إِسْتَجْهَلَ	To deem one ignorant.
جَهْلٌ وَجَهَالَةٌ	Ignorance. Folly.
جَاهِلٌ	Ignorant, fool.
أَلْجَاهِلِيَّةُ	Pre-islamic age.
مَجْهُولٌ	Unknown. Passive verb.
جَهَنَّمُ	Hell.
جَهَنَّمِيٌّ	Hellish, infernal.
جَوٌّ	Sky, atmosphere.
جَابَ يَجُوبُ	To travel.
جَاوَبَ	To answer, reply.
أَجَابَ	To answer, respond.
إِسْتَجَابَ	To answer ; listen to.
جَوَابٌ ج أَجْوِبَة	Answer reply.
إِجَابَةٌ وَآسْتِجَابَةٌ	Compliance.
مُجِيبٌ وَمُسْتَجِيبٌ	Answerer.
مُسْتَجَابٌ	Answered (prayer).
جُوخٌ ج أَجْوَاخٌ	Broadcloth.
جَوَّاخٌ	Cloth-maker or dealer.

جادَ يَجُودُ جُودَةً	To excel.
جَادَ جُوداً	To give abundantly.
جَوَّدَ	To make good.
جُودٌ	Liberality, generosity.
جُودَةٌ	Goodness, excellence.
جَوَادٌ ج أَجْوادٌ	Generous.
جَوَادٌ ج جِيَاد	Fleet (horse).
جَيِّدٌ ج جِيَاد	Good, excellent.
جَيِّداً	Very well.
جارَ يَجُورُ عَلَى	To oppress.
جَاوَرَ	To be contiguous.
أَجَارَ إِجَارَةً	To save ; protect.
تَجَاوَرَ	To be neighbours.
إِسْتَجَارَ	To seek protection.
جَارٌ ج جِيرَانٌ	Neighbour.
جَوْرٌ	Oppression, tyranny.
جُوَارٌ	Neighbourhood, vicinity.
مُجَاوِرٌ	Neighbour ; contiguous.
مُجِيرٌ	Protector, defender.
جَوْرَبٌ ج جَوَارِبُ	Stocking.
جَازَ يَجُوزُ	To pass, travel.
جَازَ جَوَازاً	To be allowable.
جَوَّزَ	To allow ; permit.
جَاوَزَ مُجَاوَزَةً	To exceed.
أَجَازَ إِجَازَةً	To allow ; permit.
تَجَاوَزَ	To exceed the bounds.
تَجَاوَزَ عَنْ	To overlook.
إِجْتَازَ بِ	To pass by.
جَوْزٌ	Nut, nut-tree. Walnut.
جَوْزٌ هِنْدِيٌّ	Cocoa-nut.
جَوْزُ ٱلطِّيبِ	Nutmeg.
ٱلْجَوْزَاءُ	Twins. Orion.
جَائِزٌ	Passing ; lawful.
جَوَازٌ	Lawfulness ; passage.
جَائِزَةٌ ج جَوَائِزُ	Present, prize.
إِجَازَةٌ	Permission ; licence.
مَجَازٌ	Passage. Figurative.
مَجَازِيٌّ	Metaphoric.

جَوْشَنٌ ج جَوَاشِنُ — Coat of mail.

جَاعَ يَجُوعُ — To be hungry.

جَوَّعَ وَأَجَاعَ — To starve.

جُوعٌ — Hunger.

جَائِعٌ ج جِيَاعٌ — Hungry.

مَجَاعَةٌ — Famine ; hunger.

جَوَّفَ — To hollow.

جَوْفٌ ج أَجْوَافٌ — Cavity. Belly.

اجْوَف — Empty, hollow.

تَجْوِيفٌ ج تَجَاوِيف — Cavity.

مُجَوَّفٌ — Hollow, empty.

جَوْقَةٌ ج جَوْقَاتٌ — Crowd.

جَالَ يَجُولُ — To travel.

جَائِلٌ — Travelling roaming.

جَوَلَانٌ — Act of travelling about.

مَجَالٌ — Range ; sphere of action.

جَامٌ ج جَامَاتٌ — Vessel, tray.

جَاهٌ — Honour, rank, dignity

جَوْهَرٌ ج جَوَاهِر — Jewels, pearls, Essence, nature element.

أَلْجَوْهَر ٱلْفَرْدُ — Atom ; monad.

جَوْهَرَةٌ — A jewel, pearl.

جَوْهَرِيٌّ — Jeweller. Essential.

جَوَّانِيٌّ — Interior, inward.

جَاءَ يَجِيءُ — To come, arrive.

جَاءَ ب — To bring.

مَجِيءٌ — Act of coming, arrival.

جَيْبٌ ج جُيُوبٌ — Pocket, Sinus.

جِيدٌ ج أَجْيَادٌ وَجُيُودٌ — Neck.

جِيرٌ — Gypsum ; quicklime.

جَيَّشَ — To collect an army.

جَأْشٌ وَجَاشٌ — The soul.

جَيْشٌ ج جُيُوشٌ — Army.

جِيفَةٌ ج جِيَفٌ — Corpse, carcass.

جِيلٌ ج أَجْيَالٌ — Race ; generation.

ح

ح	As a numeral sign = 8.
حَبَّ يحِبُّ حِبًّا وَحُبًّا	To love.
حَبَّبَ إِلَى	To make lovable.
أَحَبَّ	To love ; like.
تَحَبَّبَ	To show love.
إِسْتَحَبَّ عَلَى	To prefer.
حَبٌّ ج حُبُوبٌ	Grain ; seed ; berry; pill ; pustule.
حُبٌّ وَمحبةٌ	Love, friendship.
حَبَّةٌ ج حَبَّاتٌ	A grain.
حَبِيبٌ ج احبَّاء	Lover ; beloved.
حبًّا وَ كَرَامةً	With all my heart.
أحَبُّ	Dearer ; preferable.
محِبٌّ	Lover ; friend.
محْبوبٌ	Beloved ; liked.
حَبَّذَا . يا حَبذَا	Well done.
حبِرَ يحْبَرُ حُبُوراً	To be glad.
حَبْرٌ ج أَحْبَارٌ	Learned, good man.
الْحَبْرُ الأَعْظَمُ	High priest, the Pope.
حِبْرٌ	Ink.
حُبُورٌ	Joy, gladness, happiness.
مَحْبَرَةٌ ج محابِرُ	Inkstand.
حَبَسَ يَحْبِسُ	To imprison.
حَبَسَ عَنْ	To restrain.
حَبْسٌ ج حُبُوسٌ	Prison.
حَبْسٌ وَآحْتِبَاسٌ	Imprisonment.
إِحْتِبَاسٌ	Retention.
مَحْبُوسٌ	Imprisoned ; arrested.
حَبَشٌ وَحَبَشَةٌ	The Abyssinians.
حَبَشِيٌّ	An Abyssinian.
بلَادُ ٱلْحَبشِ وٱلْحَبَشَةِ	Abyssinia.
حَبَطَ يَحْبِطُ	To fail ; perish.
حُبُوطٌ	Failure.
حَبَقٌ	Basil, penny-royal.
حبكَ يَحْبكُ	To weave ; unite.

Well woven ; strong.	مَحْبُوكٌ
To conceive (woman).	حَبِلَتْ تَحْبَلُ
To be entangled.	تَحَبَّلَ
Rope, cable.	حَبْلٌ ج حِبَالٌ
Jugular vein.	حَبْلُ ٱلْوَرِيدِ
Pregnancy, conception.	حَبَل
Net, snare.	أُحْبُولَةٌ ج حَبَائِل
Pregnant (woman).	حَبْلَى ج حَبَالى
Rope-maker.	حَبَّالٌ
To creep, crawl.	حَبَا يَحْبُو
To be partial to.	حَابَى
Partiality, favour.	مُحَابَاةٌ
Partial.	مُحَاب
To rub off.	حَتَّ يَحُتُّ حَتًّا
Bit of anything.	حَتَّةٌ ج حَتَتٌ
Until, to, as far as, even.	حَتَّى
So that.	حَتَّى أَنْ
Death.	حَتْفٌ ج حتوفٌ
Natural death.	حَتْفَ أَنْفِهِ
To decide, decree.	حَتَمَ يَحْتِمُ
To decide ; order.	حَتَمَ ب
To compel.	حَتَمَ عَلَى
Final decision.	حَتْمٌ ج حُتُومٌ
Decided, fixed.	مَحْتُومٌ
To exhort, instigate.	حَثَّ يَحُثُّ
Instigation.	حَثٌّ وَإِحْثَاثٌ
To go as a pilgrim to Mecca.	حَجَّ يَحِجُّ
To overcome in argument.	حَجَّهُ
To dispute, contend with.	حَاجَّ
To offer as a proof.	إِحْتَجَّ ب
To argue against.	إِحْتَجَّ عَلَى
Pilgrimage to Mecca.	حَجٌّ وَحِجَّةٌ
Proof ; title, deed. Pretext, excuse.	حُجَّةٌ ج حُجَجٌ
The last month of the Mohammedan year.	ذو ٱلْحِجَّةِ
Pilgrim to Mecca.	حَاجٌّ ج حُجَّاجٌ
To hide, cover.	حَجَبَ يَحْجُبُ
To prevent.	حَجَبَ عَنْ
To conceal one's self.	إِحْتَجَبَ

To hop, leap. حَجَلَ يَحْجِلُ
Partridge. حَجَلٌ ج حِجْلَانٌ
Having white foot, or feet, (horse). مُحَجَّلٌ
To cup, scarify. حَجَمَ يَحْجُمُ
To be cupped. إِحْتَجَمَ
Bulk ; size. حَجْمٌ ج حُجُومٌ
Art of cupping, cupping. حِجَامَةٌ
Cupper. حَجَّامٌ
Cupping instrument. مِحْجَمٌ
To propose riddles. تَحَاجَى
Intelligence. حِجًى ج أَحْجَاءٌ
Enigma ; riddle. اُحْجِيَّةٌ ج أَحَاجِيُّ
To confine, define. حَدَّ يَحُدُّ
To go into mourning. حَدَّ حِدَادًا
To confine ; define ; sharpen. حَدَّدَ
To look sharply. أَحَدَّ ٱلنَّظَرَ
To be limited ; defined. تَحَدَّدَ
To be excited. إِحْتَدَّ
Limit, boundary. حَدٌّ ج حُدُودٌ

Partition; veil. حِجَابٌ ج حُجُبٌ
Diaphragm. أَلْحِجَابُ ٱلْحَاجِزُ
Chamberlain. Door-keeper. حَاجِبٌ ج حُجَّابٌ
Eye-brow. حَاجِبٌ ج حَوَاجِبُ
To prevent, restrain. حَجَرَ يَحْجُرُ
To be turned into stone. تَحَجَّرَ
Prevention, prohibition. حَجْرٌ
Stone. حَجَرٌ ج أَحْجَارٌ وَحِجَارَةٌ
Nitrate of silver. حَجَرُ جَهَنَّمَ
Chamber ; sepulchre. حُجْرَةٌ
Stone-cutter. حَجَّارٌ ج حَجَّارُونَ
Larynx. حَنْجَرَةٌ ج حَنَاجِرُ
To prevent, hinder. حَجَزَ يَحْجُزُ
To separate. حَجَزَ بَيْنَ
To sequester goods. حَجَزَ عَلَى
Prevention, restraint. حَجْزٌ
Arabia Petrœa, Hijas. أَلْحِجَازُ
A barrier. حَاجِزٌ ج حَوَاجِزُ
Hindered, prevented. مَحْجُوزٌ

Impetuosity ; acerbity. حِدَّةٌ

Sharp, pointed ; pungent. حَادٌّ

Acute angle. زَاوِيَةٌ حَادَّةٌ

Mourning. حِدَادٌ

Blacksmith. حَدَّادٌ

Iron. حَدِيدٌ

A piece of iron. حَدِيدَةٌ

Demarcation. تَحْدِيدٌ

Limited ; bounded. مَحْدُودٌ

Kite (hawk). حِدَأَةٌ ج حِدَاءٌ

To become convex. تَحَدَّبَ

To be hump-backed. إِحْدَوْدَبَ

Hump-backed. أَحْدَبُ م حَدْبَاءُ

Convex ; bulging. مُحَدَّبٌ

To happen, occur. حَدَثَ يَحْدُثُ

To tell ; relate. حَدَّثَ

To converse. حَادَثَ مُحَادَثَةً

To cause to exist. أَحْدَثَ

To converse together. تَحَادَثَ

Event. حَادِثَةٌ ج حَوَادِثُ

Newness, youth. حَدَاثَةٌ

New, recent. حَدِيثٌ

Story, tale. Mohammedan tradition. حَدِيثٌ ج أَحَادِيثُ

Tale. أُحْدُوثَةٌ ج أَحَادِيثُ

Conversation. مُحَادَثَةٌ

To descend. إِنْحَدَرَ

Descent. حُدُورٌ وَٱنْحِدَارٌ

To surmise. حَدَسَ يَحْدِسُ فِي

Conjecture; guess. حَدْسٌ

Hypotheses. حَدَسِيَّاتٌ

To surround, enclose. أَحْدَقَ بِ

To look sharply at. حَدَّقَ إِلَى

The pupil of the eye. حَدَقَةٌ

Garden. حَدِيقَةٌ ج حَدَائِقُ

Glow (of a fire). حَدْمٌ وَحَدَمٌ

Growing with heat. مُحْتَدِمٌ

Camel-driver. حَادٍ ج حُدَاةٌ

The eleventh.	حَادِي عَشَرَ
To be cautious.	حَذِرَ يَحْذَرُ
To warn.	حَذَّرَ
To be cautious.	تَحَذَّرَ وَٱحْتَذَرَ
Caution ; distrust.	حِذْرٌ وَحَذَرٌ
Cautious.	حَذِرٌ ج حَذِرُون
Take care !	حَذَارِ
A thing to be avoided.	مَحْذُورٌ
To cut off ; drop.	حَذَفَ يَحْذِفُ
To throw at.	حَذَفَ بِ
Elision ; suppression.	حَذْفٌ
Cut off ; suppressed.	مَحْذُوفٌ
To be skilful.	حَذَقَ يَحْذِقُ
Sharpness, skill.	حِذْقٌ
Sharp ; clever.	حَاذِقٌ ج حُذَّاقٌ
To imitate, emulate.	حَذَا يَحْذُو حَذْواً
To be opposite to.	حَاذَى
Opposite to ; vis-à-vis.	حِذَاءَ
Shoe, sandal.	حِذَاءٌ ج أَحْذِيَةٌ
Placed opposite ; vis-a-vis.	مُحَاذٍ
To be hot.	حَرَّ يَحِرُّ
To set free, free (a slave).	حَرَّرَ
To be set free, freed.	تَحَرَّرَ
Heat.	حَرٌّ
Freeman ; noble.	حُرٌّ ج أَحْرَارٌ
Heat warmth.	حَرَارَةٌ
Liberty, freedom.	حُرِّيَّةٌ
Silk ; silk-stuff.	حَرِيرٌ
Letter, note.	تَحْرِيرٌ ج تَحَارِيرُ
Hot, burning ; fervent.	حَارٌّ
Liberated ; set free.	مُحَرَّرٌ
Heated (with anger, etc.)	مَحْرُورٌ
To fight.	حَارَبَ مُحَارَبَةً
To fight one another.	تَحَارَبَ
War, battle.	حَرْبٌ ج حُرُوبٌ
Enemy's territory.	دَارُ ٱلْحَرْبِ
Chameleon.	حِرْبَاءٌ ج حَرَابِيُّ
Lance ; bayonet.	حَرْبَةٌ ج حِرَابٌ

مِحْرَابٌ	Place of prayer.
حَرَثَ يَحْرُثُ حَرْثًا	To till.
حِرَاثَةٌ	Agriculture.
حَارِثٌ وَحَرَّاثٌ	Ploughman.
مِحْرَثٌ وَمِحْرَاثٌ	A plough.
حَرِجَ يَحْرَجُ	To be in difficulty.
حَرِجَ عَلَى	To be forbidden.
حَرِجٌ	Narrow. Forbidden.
لَا حَرَجَ	No blame or sin.
حَرَاجٌ	Auction.
حَرِدَ يَحْرَدُ	To be angry.
حَرَدٌ	Anger, grudge, hatred.
حِرْذَوْنٌ ج حَرَاذِينَ	Lizard.
حَرَزَ يَحْرُزُ	To guard carefully.
أَحْرَزَ	To guard. Obtain.
تَحَرَّزَ وَاحْتَرَزَ	To guard against.
حِرْزٌ	Caution ; amulet.
حَرِيز	Fortified ; valued.
حَرَسَ يَحْرُسُ	To guard, watch.
تَحَرَّسَ وَاحْتَرَسَ	To be cautioned.
حِرَاسَةٌ	Watch, guard.
حَارِسٌ ج حُرَّاسٌ	Watchman, guard.
حَرَّشَ بَيْنَ	To excite discord.
تَحَرَّشَ بِ	To meddle with.
حُرْشٌ ج أَحْرَاشٌ	Wood, thicket.
حَرَصَ يَحْرِصُ	To covet eagerly.
حِرْصٌ	Greed, cupidity.
حَرِيصٌ ج حُرَصَاءُ	Covetous.
حَرَّضَ عَلَى	To incite, instigate.
حَرَفَ يَحْرِفُ عَنْ	To turn from.
حَرَّفَ	To falsify, garble.
إِنْحَرَفَ عَنْ	To deviate from.
إِحْتَرَفَ	To earn sustenance.
حَرْفٌ ج حِرَفٌ	Edge, border.
حَرْفٌ ج حُرُوفٌ وَأَحْرُفٌ	Letter, particle (in grammer).
حَرْفِيٌّ	Literal.
حِرْفَةٌ ج حِرَفٌ	Trade, craft.

Pungency.	حرافة
Sharp, pungent.	حِرِّيفٌ
Falsified.	مُحَرَّفٌ
Oblique ; trapezium	مُنْحَرِفٌ
To burn.	حرق يَحْرِقُ وَأَحْرَقَ
To be burned.	اِحْتَرَقَ وَتَحَرَّقَ
Heat, burning pain.	حُرْقَةٌ
Heat, conflagration.	حَرِيقٌ
Blister ; tinder.	حَرَّاقَةٌ ج حَرَّاقَات
Hip-bone.	حَرْقَفَةٌ ج حَرَاقِف
To be in motion.	حَرَكَ يَحْرُكُ
To move a thing	حَرَّكَ
To be moved.	تَحَرَّكَ
Brisk, nimble.	حَرِكٌ
Motion ; gesture.	حَرَكَةٌ ج حَرَكَاتٌ
Vowel-point.	(َ ُ ِ)
Motion.	حِرَاكٌ
Withers of a horse.	حَارِكٌ
Act of moving.	تَحْرِيكٌ
To refuse, forbid.	حَرَمَ يَحْرِمُ
To be unlawful.	حَرُمَ يَحْرُمُ
To forbid.	حَرَّمَ
To be forbidden.	تَحَرَّمَ
To honour, venerate.	إِحْتَرَمَ
To hold as unlawful.	إِسْتَحْرَمَ
Excommunication.	حِرْمٌ
Sacred (territory).	حَرَمٌ
Sacred territory at Mecca.	اَلْحَرَمُ
Mecca and Medina.	اَلْحَرَمَانِ
Sacredness. Wife.	حُرْمَةٌ ج حُرَمٌ
Unlawful, sacred.	حَرَامٌ
El Kaaba.	اَلْمَسْجِدُ ٱلْحَرَامُ
The month.	اَلشَّهْرُ ٱلْحَرَامُ . مُحَرَّمٌ
Robber, thief.	حَرَامِيٌّ ج حَرَامِيَةٌ
Women of a household.	حَرِيمٌ
Unlawful ; first month of the Moslem year.	مُحَرَّمٌ
Denied, refused. Excommunicated.	مَحْرُومٌ
Venerable, respected.	مُحْتَرَمٌ

حَرَنَ يَحْرُنُ — To rear and kick.
حَرُونٌ — Restive, refractory.
حَرِيَ بِ — To be adapted to.
تَحَرَّى — To seek, aim at.
حَرِيٌّ بِ — Suitable, proper for.
أَحْرَى — More suited, better.
كَمْ بِالْحَرِيِّ — How much more.
بِالأَحْرَى — Rather.
حَزَّ يَحُزُّ — To cut, incise, notch.
حَزَازٌ وَحَزَازَةٌ — Dandruff, scurff.
حَزَبَ — To collect parties.
حِزْبٌ ج أَحْزَابٌ — Troop; party.
مُتَحَزِّبٌ — Leagued; partisan.
حَزَرَ يَحْزُرُ — To guess, compute.
حَزِيرَانُ — June (month).
حَزَمَ يَحْزِمُ — To tie together.
حَزُمَ يَحْزُمُ — To be firm, prudent.
حُزْمَةٌ ج حُزَمٌ — Bundle, parcel.
حَزْمٌ — Firmness, resolution, discretion.

حِزَامٌ ج أَحْزِمَةٌ — Belt, girth.
حَازِمٌ — Prudent, resolute.
مِحْزَمٌ ج مَحَازِمُ — Belt, girth.
حَزِنَ يَحْزَنُ — To grieve.
حَزِنَ يَحْزَنُ — To be grieved.
أَحْزَنَ — To grieve another.
حُزْنٌ ج أَحْزَانٌ — Sadness.
حَزِينٌ — Sad, sorrowful.
مُحْزِنٌ — Sad thing, sorrowful.
مَحْزُونٌ — Saddened, grieved.
حَسَّ يَحِسُّ — To feel; perceive.
أَحَسَّ بِ — To feel; perceive.
حِسٌّ — Perception, sense.
حِسِّيٌّ وَمَحْسُوسٌ — Perceptible.
حَاسَّةٌ ج حَوَاسُّ — Faculty of each of the five senses; feeling.
اَلْحَوَاسُّ اَلْخَمْسُ — The five senses.
مِحَسَّةٌ — Curry-comb.
حَسَبَ يَحْسُبُ — To count.

To suppose, consider.	حَسِبَ يَحْسِبُ
To account with.	حَاسَبَ
To settle an account.	تَحَاسَبَ
Sufficient ; sufficiency.	حَسْبُ
According to.	بِحَسَبِ
Honour ; pedigree.	حَسَبٌ
Account, calculation.	حِسَابٌ
Arithmetic.	عِلْمُ ٱلْحِسَابِ
Noble	حَسِيبٌ ج حُسَبَاءُ
Counted, calculated.	مَحْسُوبٌ
To envy.	حَسَدَ يَحْسُدُ
Envy, grudge.	حَسَدٌ
Envious.	حَاسِدٌ وَحَسُودٌ ج حُسَّادٌ
Envied ; object of envy.	مَحْسُودٌ
To grieve for.	حَسِرَ يَحْسَرُ عَلَى
To feel regret.	تَحَسَّرَ عَلَى
Grief.	حَسْرَةٌ ج حَسَرَاتٌ
Alas !	يا حَسْرَتِي . وَاحَسْرَتَاه
Hatred. Thistle.	حَسَكٌ

To cut off ; stop.	حَسَمَ يَحْسِمُ
Sharp sword.	حُسَامٌ
To be handsome.	حَسُنَ يَحْسُنُ
To embellish, adorn.	حَسَّنَ
To treat well.	حَاسَنَ
To do a thing well.	احْسَنَ
To confer a benefit.	أَحْسَنَ إِلَى
To approve.	إِسْتَحْسَنَ
Beauty ; good.	حُسْنٌ ج مَحَاسِن
Beautiful ; good.	حَسَنٌ ج حِسَانٌ
Good deed.	حَسَنَةٌ ج حَسَنَاتٌ
Goldfinch.	حَسُّونٌ
More beautiful, better.	احْسَنُ
How beautiful.	مَا أَحْسَنَ
Benefit, beneficence.	إِحْسَانٌ
Good deeds or qualities.	مَحَاسِن
To cut hay.	حَشَّ يَحُشُّ حَشًّا
Smoker of hashish.	حَشَّاشٌ
Grass; hay. Hashish.	حَشِيشٌ

حَشَدَ يَحْشُدُ	To assemble, *v. t.*
إِحْتَشَدَ	To be assembled.
حَشْدٌ	Troop, assembly.
مَحَاشِدُ	Places of assembling.
حَشَرَ يَحْشُرُ حَشْرًا	To assemble.
يَوْمُ ٱلْحَشْرِ	Day of Judgment.
مَحْشَرٌ ج مَحَاشِرُ	Place of gathering.
حَشَرَةٌ ج حَشَرَاتٌ	Insect.
إِحْتَشَمَ	To stand in awe. or shame.
حَشَمٌ	Attendants, retinue.
حِشْمَةٌ	Reverence ; modesty.
احْتِشَامٌ	Reverence ; modesty.
حَشَا يَحْشُو	To stuff, cram.
إِحْتَشَى وَانْحَشَى	To be filled.
حَشًا ج أَحْشَاءٌ	Viscera, bowels.
حَشْوٌ	Stuffing, wadding.
تَحَاشَى عَنْ	To abstain, disdain.
حَاشَا	Except. God forbid!
حَاشِيَةٌ ج حَوَاشٍ	Annotation. Followers.
حِصَّةٌ ج حِصَصٌ	Part, share.
حَصْبٌ	Stones, firewood.
حَصْبَةٌ	Measles.
حَصَدَ يَحْصُدُ	To mow, reap.
حَاصِدٌ وَحَصَّادٌ	Mower, reaper.
حَصَادٌ	Harvest, harvest-time.
حَصِيدٌ وَمَحْصُودٌ	Mown, reaped.
حَصَرَ يَحْصُرُ	To confine, restrict.
حَاصَرَ مُحَاصَرَةً	To besiege.
حَصْرٌ	Restriction ; confinement.
بِالْحَصْرِ	Strictly speaking.
حِصَارٌ وَمُحَاصَرَةٌ	Siege, blockade.
حُصُرِيٌّ	Maker or seller of mats.
حَصِيرٌ وَحَصِيرَةٌ ج حَصَائِرُ	Mat.
مُحَاصِرٌ	Besieger ; blockader.
مَحْصُورٌ	Besieged ; restricted.
حِصْرِمٌ	Green grapes.
حَصَافَةٌ	Sound judgment.
حَصَلَ – لِ	To happen to one.

حَصَلَ عَلَى	To obtain, acquire.
تَحَصَّلَ	To be obtained.
حَاصِلٌ ج حَوَاصِلُ	Result.
الحَاصِلُ	The result ; in short.
تَحْصِيلٌ	Acquisition.
مَحْصُولٌ ج مَحَاصِيل	Result, produce.
حَصُنَ يَحْصُنُ	To be fortified.
حَصَّنَ	To fortify.
تَحَصَّنَ	To be entrenched.
حِصْنٌ ج حُصُونٌ	Fortress.
حِصَانٌ ج حُصُنٌ وَأَحْصِنَةٌ	Horse.
حَصِينٌ	Strongly fortified.
أَبُو ٱلحُصَيْنِ	Fox.
احْصَى	To count, number.
حَصًى	Small pebbles.
حَصَاةٌ	Small pebble.
غَيْرُ مُحْصًى	Innumerable.
حَضَّ يَحُضُّ	To instigate, incite.
حَضِيضٌ	Foot of a mountain.
حَضَرَ يَحْضُرُ	To be present.
حَضَرَ إِلَى	To come.
حَضَّرَ وَأَحْضَرَ	To bring.
تَحَضَّرَ	To be ready.
إِسْتَحْضَرَ	To cause to come.
حَضَرٌ	Towns, cultivated land.
حَضْرَةٌ	Presence. Highness.
حَاضِرٌ	Present, ready.
أَلحَاضِرُ	Present tense.
مُحْتَضَرٌ	Approach of death.
حَضَنَ يَحْضُنُ	To embrace.
حِضْنٌ ج حُضُون	Bosom.
حِضَانَةٌ	Nursing ; incubation.
حَطَّ يَحُطُّ	To fall, go down.
حط	To put down.
انْحَطَ	To descend, fall.
إِنْحِطَاطٌ	Falling.
مَحَطٌّ وَمَحطة	Railway station.
مُنْحَط	Fallen, depressed.

مَحْطُوطٌ	Placed, laid, deposited.
إِحْتَطَبَ	To collect fire-wood.
حَطَبٌ	Fuel, wood.
حَطَّابٌ	Wood-cutter.
حَطَمَ يَحْطِمُ وَحَطَّمَ	To break.
تَحَطَّمَ وَٱنْحَطَمَ	To crumble.
حِطْمَةٌ وَحُطَامٌ	Piece, fragment.
حُطَامُ ٱلدُّنْيَا	Goods or vanities of this world.
حَظَّ يَحِظُّ	To be fortunate.
حَظٌّ ج حُظُوظٌ	Happiness.
مَحْظُوظٌ	Happy.
حَظَرَ يَحْظُرُ عَلَى	To forbid.
حَظِيرَةٌ ج حَظَائِرُ	Enclosure.
مَحْظُورَاتٌ	Prohibited things.
حَظِيَ يَحْظَى بِ	To obtain.
حَفَّ بِ	To encompass.
خُبْزٌ حَافٌّ	Dry bread.
حَافَّةٌ	Edge, rim, border.
مِحَفَّةٌ	Kind of litter.
مَحْفُوفٌ	Surrounded.
حَفِيدٌ ج حَفَدَةٌ	Grandson.
حَفَرَ يَحْفِرُ وَٱحْتَفَرَ	To dig.
حُفْرَةٌ ج حُفَرٌ	Ditch, pit.
حَافِرٌ ج حَوَافِرُ	Hoof.
حَفَّارٌ	Grave-digger.
مَحْفُورٌ	Dug, dug out.
حَفِظَ يَحْفَظُ	To guard, keep.
حَافَظَ عَلَى	To be careful of.
تَحَفَّظَ	To be watchful.
حِفْظٌ	Guard ; careful watch.
حِفَاظٌ	Truss.
(أَلْقُوَّةُ) ٱلْحَافِظَةُ	Memory.
مُحَافِظٌ	Guardian, keeper.
مُحَافَظَةٌ	Guardianship.
مَحْفُوظٌ	Guarded, preserved.
حَفَلَ يَحْفُلُ	To gather, assemble.
إِحْتَفَلَ لَهُ	To receive with houour.
إِحْتَفَلَ بِ	To give attention to.

حَفْلٌ	Large assembly ; care.
حَافِلٌ	Entirely full (hall &c.)
إِحْتِفَالٌ	Celebration ; pomp.
مَحْفِلٌ ج مَحَافِلُ	Assembly.
مُحْتَفَلٌ	Place of assembly.
حَفْنَةٌ ج حَفَنَاتٌ	Handful.
حَفِيَ يَحْفَى	To go bare-foot.
حَفِيَ وَاحْتَفَى بِ	To show joy and honour.
حَفَاءٌ وَحُفْوَةٌ	Bare-footedness.
حَافٍ	Bare-foot ; unshod.
حَقَّ يَحُقُّ	To be true, right.
حَقَّقَ	To verify, confirm.
تَحَقَّقَ	To assure one's self.
إِسْتَحَقَّ	To deserve ; fall due.
حَقٌّ ج حُقُوقٌ	Right ; truth ; obligation, worth ; true ; truthful.
حَقٌّ عَلَى	Duty.
حَقٌّ بِ	Worthy of.
حَقًّا وَبِالْحَقِّ	Truly, indeed.
حُقٌّ ج حِقَاقٌ	Socket.
حُقَّةٌ ج حُقَقٌ	Case, casket.
حَقِيقَةٌ ج حَقَائِق	Reality, truth. ssence.
حَقِيقَةً وَفِي ٱلْحَقِيقَةِ	Truly.
حَقِيقِيٌّ	Real ; proper (sense).
أَحَقُّ بِ	More worthy of.
إِسْتِحْقَاقٌ ج إِسْتِحْقَاقَاتٌ	Merit.
تَحْقِيقٌ	Verification.
مُحَقَّقٌ	Verified, confirmed.
مُسْتَحِقٌّ	Worthy of, deserving.
حُقْبٌ ج أَحْقَابٌ	A long time.
حَقِيبَةٌ	Saddle-bag.
حَقَدَ يَحْقِدُ	To bear spite.
حِقْدٌ	Hatred, grudge, spite.
حَاقِدٌ وَحَقُودٌ	Spiteful.
حَقَرَ يَحْقِرُ وَاحْتَقَرَ	To despise.
حَقُرَ يَحْقُرُ	To be contemptible.
حَقَارَةٌ	Contempt ; vileness.
حَقِيرٌ	Despised ; mean ; paltry.

Field. حَقْلٌ ج حُقُولٌ

To retain. Inject. حَقَنَ يَحْقُنُ

To be congested. إِحْتَقَنَ

Clyster ; syringe. حُقْنَةٌ ج حُقَنٌ

Waist ; loins. حَقْوٌ ج حِقَاءٌ

To rub, scrape. حَكَّ يَحُكُّ

To rub against. إِحْتَكَّ بِ

Rubbing ; scratching. حَكٌّ

Magnetic compass. حكٌّ

An itching. حِكَّةٌ وَحُكَاكٌ

Touchstone. مِحَكٌّ

To withhold grain for sale at high prices. تَحَكَّرَ وَٱحْتَكَرَ

Usurious grain-trade. حُكْرَةٌ

To give judgment. حَكَمَ يَحْكُمُ

To judge in favour of. حَكَمَ لِ

To judge against. حَكَمَ عَلَى

To appoint one to judge. حَكَّمَ

To contest in law. حَاكَمَ

To do a thing well. أَحْكَمَ

To go together to law. تَحَاكَمَ

Judgment ; government ; authority, rule. حُكْمٌ ج أَحْكَامٌ

Wisdom. حِكْمَةٌ ج حِكَمٌ

Judge ; governor. حَاكِمٌ

Judgment ; government. حُكُومَةٌ

Wise. حَكِيمٌ ج حُكَمَاءُ

Well made. مُحْكَمٌ

Tribunal. مَحْكَمَةٌ ج مَحَاكِمُ

To tell, relate. حَكَى يَحْكِي

To resemble. حَكَى وَحَاكَى

Story, tale, narrative. حِكَايَةٌ

To alight, abide. حَلَّ يَحُلُّ

To solve (a problem) حَلَّ يَحُلُّ حَلًّا dissolve (a solid) ; loosen.

To come upon one. حَلَّ عَلَى

To be lawful. حلَّ يَحِلُّ

To permit. Analyze. حلَّلَ

To allow, permit. أَحلَّ

To deem lawful. إِسْتَحَلَّ

A solving, dissolving. حَلٌّ

Lawful. حِلٌّ

Garment. حُلَّةٌ ج حُلَلٌ

Lawful ; right. حَلَالٌ

An alighting, abiding. حُلُولٌ

Husband ; wife. حَلِيلٌ م حَلِيلَةٌ

Deeming lawful. إِسْتِحْلَالٌ

Dissolving ; analysis. تَحْلِيلٌ

Place ; quarter. مَحَلٌّ ج مَحَال

Inn ; stopping-place. مَحَلَّةٌ

To milk. حَلَبَ يَحْلُبُ

To flow ; exude. تَحَلَّبَ وَانْحَلَبَ

Aleppo. حَلَبُ

Fenugreek. حُلْبَةٌ

Milkman. حَالِبٌ وَحَلَّابٌ

Fresh milk. حَلِيبٌ

Emulsion. مُسْتَحْلَبٌ

Assafoetida. حِلْتِيتٌ

To card cotton. حَلَجَ يَحْلِجُ

Carding of cotton. حِلَاجَةٌ

Cotton-carder. حَلَّاجٌ

Instrument for carding. مِحْلَجٌ

Snail. حَلَزُونٌ

Spiral. حَلَزُونِيٌّ

To swear. حَلَفَ يَحْلِفُ

To make swear. حَلَّفَ وَاسْتَحْلَفَ

To be in league with. حَالَفَ

To confederate. تَحَالَفَ

Oath ; league. حِلْفٌ

Confederate. حَلِيفٌ ج حُلَفَاءُ

Alliance. تَحَالُفٌ وَمُحَالَفَةٌ

To shave. حَلَقَ يَحْلِقُ

Throat, palate. حَلْقٌ ج حُلُوقٌ

Guttural letters. حُرُوفُ الْحَلْقِ

Circle ; link, ear-ring. حَلَقَةٌ

Barber. حَلَّاقٌ

Barber's trade. حِلَاقَةٌ

حَلِيقٌ ج حَلْقَى	Shaved, shorn.
مَحْلُوقٌ	Shaved.
حُلْقُومٌ ج حَلَاقِيمُ	Throat.
حَلَكٌ	Intense blackness.
حَالِكٌ	Very black.
حَلَمَ يَحْلُمُ	To dream.
حَلُمَ يَحْلُمُ	To be gentle, mild.
حِلْمٌ	Gentleness, clemency.
حُلْمٌ ج أَحْلَامٌ	Dream, vision.
حَلَمَةٌ	Teat, nipple.
حَلِيمٌ ج حُلَمَاءُ	Gentle, mild.
حَلَا يَحْلُو	To be sweet.
حَلَّى تَحْلِيَةً	To sweeten.
إِسْتَحْلَى	To find sweet.
حُلْوٌ	Sweet, agreable.
حُلْوَانٌ	Present ; gratuity.
حَلَوَانِيٌّ	Confectioner.
حَلْوَى	Sweetmeats.
حَلَاوَةٌ	Sweetness.
مُحَلًّى	Sweetened, sugared.
حَلِيَ يَحْلَى	To be adorned.
حَلَّى	To adorn (with jewels).
حَلَّى بِذَهَبٍ	To gild.
تَحَلَّى	To be adorned.
حَلْيٌ ج حُلِيٌّ	Jewels ; ornaments.
حِلْيَةٌ ج حِلًى	Adornment.
حُمَّ	To have fever.
إِسْتَحَمَّ	To take a bath.
حُمَّى ج حُمَّيَاتٌ	Fever.
حَمَّةٌ	Thermal spring.
حِمَامٌ	Fate ; death.
حَمَامَةٌ ج حَمَامٌ	Dove ; pigeon.
حَمَّامٌ ج حَمَّامَاتٌ	Bath.
مَحْمُومٌ	Suffering from fever.
حَمَدَ يَحْمَدُ	To praise ; thank.
حَمْدٌ	Praise ; thanks.
أَلْحَمْدُ لِلّٰهِ	Praise be to God.
حَمِيدٌ	Praised.

Praised, praiseworthy.	مَحْمُودٌ
To dye red ; redden.	حَمَّرَ
To become red; blush.	إِحْمَرَّ
Bitumen.	حُمَّرٌ
Redness. Erysipelas.	حُمْرَةٌ
Ass, donkey.	حِمَارٌ ج حَمِيرٌ
Wild ass.	حِمَارُ ٱلْوَحِشِ
Ass-driver.	حَمَّارٌ ج حمارَةٌ
Red.	أَحْمَرُ م حَمْرَاءُ ج حُمْرٌ
Rubefacient.	مُحَمِّرٌ
To be hard in religion, etc.	حَمِسَ يَحْمَسُ
To irritate.	حَمَّسَ وَأَحْمَسَ
Bravery energy.	حَمَاسَةٌ
To roast, toast.	حَمَّصَ
To be roasted.	تَحَمَّصَ
Hems (city).	حِمْصُ
Chick-peas.	حِمِّصٌ
To be sour, acid.	حَمَضَ يَحْمَضُ
Acid ; sour.	حَامِضٌ
Acidity ; sourness.	حُمُوضَةٌ
Sorrel (plant).	حُمَاضٌ وَخُمَّيْضٌ
Acidulated, acid, sour.	مُحَمَّضٌ
To be foolish.	حَمِقَ يَحْمَقُ
Stupidity, folly.	حُمْقٌ وَحَمَاقَةٌ
Chicken-pox.	حماقٌ
Stupid, foolish.	أَحْمَقُ
To carry, lift.	حَمَلَ يَحْمِلُ
To conceive (woman).	حَمَلَتْ
To attack, charge.	حَمَلَ على
To bear fruit.	حَمَلَ يَحْمِلُ
To overflow (river).	حَمَلَ ٱلنَّهْرُ
To burden, load.	حَمَّلَ
To suffer patiently.	تَحَمَّلَ
To bear, suffer.	إِحْتَمَلَ
To be possible.	إِحْتَمَلَ أَنْ
Carrying. Pregnancy.	حَمْلٌ
Burden, load.	حِمْلٌ ج أَحْمالٌ
Lamb.	حَمَلٌ ج حُمْلَانٌ

أَلحَمَلُ	Sign of the Ram (Aries).
حَمْلَةٌ	Attack ; charge in battle.
حَمَّالٌ	Porter.
إِحتِمَالٌ	Patience ; endurance.
مَحْمِلٌ ج مَحَامِلِ	Litter.
مَحْمُولٌ	Borne ; suffered.
مُحتَمَلٌ	Bearable. Possible.
حَمْوٌ ج أَحمَاءٌ	Father-in-law.
حَمَاةٌ ج حَمَوَاتٌ	Mother-in-law.
حَمَى يَحْمِي	To protect, defend.
حَمِيَ يَحْمَى	To be very hot.
أَحمَى إِحْمَاءً	To make hot.
حَامَى عَنْ	To defend.
إِحتَمَى	To protect one's self.
حِمًى ج أَحْمَاءٌ	Interdicted place.
حِمْيَةٌ	Care of diet.
حَمِيَّةٌ	Anger, rage. Disdain.
حُمَةٌ	Venom, sting.
حَامٍ	Protector. Hot.
حَامِيَةٌ	Guard, garrison.
حِمَايَةٌ	Protection. Protégé,
مُحْمًى	Heated.
مُحَامٍ	Protector ; advocate.
حَنَّ يَحِنُّ إِلَى	To yearn.
تَحَنَّنَ عَلَى	To have compassion.
حَنَانٌ وَحُنُونٌ	Compassionate, tender.
حَنَّأَ	To dye with *Henna*.
حِنَاءٌ	The plant *henna*.
حَانُوتٌ ج حَوَانِيتُ	Shop.
حَنِثَ يَحْنَثُ	To break an oath.
حِنثٌ	Perjury. Sin, crime.
حَانِثٌ	A perjurer.
حَنَشٌ ج أَحنَاشٌ	Snake.
حَنَّط وَأَحْنَطَ	To embalm.
حِنْطَةٌ	Wheat.
حَنْظَلٌ	Colocynth.
حَنَفِيَّةٌ	Tap.
حَنِقَ يَحْنَقُ	To be enraged.

حَنَق — Violent anger ; spite.

حنكَ وَأَحْنَكَ — To make wise.

حَنَكٌ ج احْنَاكٌ — Palate.

مُحَنَّكٌ — Experienced.

حَنَى يَحْنِي — To bend, incline.

تَحَنَّى وَانْحَنَى — To be bent.

حَنُوٌّ — Tenderness, compassion.

حَانِيَةٌ — Wine-house, tavern.

مُنْحَنٍ — Bent, crooked ; inclined.

حُوتٌ ج حِيتَانٌ — Large fish. Whale.

أَحْوَجَ — To compel.

إِحْتَاجَ — To want, need, require.

حَاجَةٌ ج حَاجَات وَحَوَائِجُ — Want ; need ; necessity ; object ; desire.

إِحْتِيَاجٌ — Want ; having need.

مُحْتَاجٌ إِلى — In want or need of.

اسْتَحْوَذَ على — To overcome.

حوذِيٌّ — Coachman, cabman.

حَارَ يَحَارُ — To be bewildered.

حَاوَرَ — To converse, debate.

حَوْرٌ — Leather. Poplar tree.

حَوَارِيٌّ — Disciple of a prophet.

حَارَةٌ — A quarter of a town.

مَحَارَةٌ — Panier. Oyster.

مِحْوَرٌ ج مَحَاوِر — Pivot.

مُحَاوَرَة — Conversation ; debate.

حَازَ يَحُوز — To get ; possess.

إِنْحَازَ عَنْ — To drow aside from.

إِنْحَازَ إِلَى — To turn to and join.

حَيِّزٌ — Space occupied by a body.

حَوَّش — To gather, collect.

إِنْحَاشَ — To be taken in.

حَوْشٌ ج احْوَاشٌ — Fold ; court.

حَوَشٌ — Mixed people ; rabble.

حِيَاصَةٌ — Saddle-girth, girdle.

حَوْصَلَة — Stomach of a bird.

حَوْضٌ ج أَحْوَاضٌ — Reservoir, tank.

حَوَّطَ — To surround ; enclose.

احَاطَ ب — To invest, surround.

حَائِطٌ ج حِيطَانٌ	Wall.
إِحتِيَاطٌ	Investment. Caution.
مُحِيطٌ	Circumference.
أَلْبَحْرُ ٱلْمُحِيطُ	The ocean.
حَافَةٌ ج حَافَاتٌ	Edge, border.
حَاقَ يَحُوقُ بِ	To surround.
حَوَّقَ	To strike out, erase.
حَاكَ يَحُوكُ	To weave.
حَائِكٌ ج حَاكَةٌ	Weaver.
حِيَاكَةٌ	The art of weaving.
حَالَ وَتَحَوَّلَ	To be changed.
حَالَ بَيْنَ	To come between.
حَوَّلَ إِلَى	To change, alter.
حَاوَلَ	To attempt.
اِحْتَالَ	To use stratagem.
إِسْتَحَالَ	To be changed. Absurd.
حَالٌ ج أَحْوَالٌ	State, condition.
حَالاً وَفِي ٱلْحَالِ	Immediately.
حَالَمَا	As soon as.
حَالَةٌ ج حَالَاتٌ	State, condition.
حَوْلٌ ج احْوَالٌ	Power. Year.
حَوْلَ	All around, around.
حَوَلٌ	Squint.
حَوَالَةٌ	Transfer of a debt.
حِيلَةٌ ج حِيَلٌ	Stratagem ; means.
عِلْمُ ٱلْحِيَلِ	Mechanics.
حِيَالَ	In front of, opposite to.
أَحْوَلُ م حَوْلَاءُ	Squint-eyed.
أَحْيَلُ	More cunning, crafty.
تَحْوِيلٌ	Transferring.
مُحَالٌ	Absurd, unreasonable.
لَا مَحَالَةَ	Undoubtedly.
مُحْتَالٌ	Cunning, sly, wily.
مُسْتَحِيلٌ	Impossible ; absurd.
حَامَ يَحُومُ	To run around ; hover.
حَانَةٌ وَحَانُوتٌ	Wine-shop.
حَوَّاءُ	Eve (mother of mankind).
حَوَى يَحْوِي	To possess ; contain.

To comprise.	إحْتَوَى عَلَى
Snake-charmer. Containing.	حَاوٍ
Where, where there.	حَيْثُ
Wherever.	حَيْثُمَا
In respect of, since.	مِنْ حَيْث
So that.	بِحَيْثُ انْ
To deviate ; turn aside.	حَادَ يَحِيدُ
To avoid, shun.	حَايَدَ مُحَايَدَةً
To be bewildered.	حَارَ يَحَارُ
To bewilder, perplex.	حيرَ
To be perplexed.	تَحَيرَ فِي
Perplexity.	حيرَةٌ وَتَحَيُّرٌ
Street ; quarter.	حَارَةٌ ج حَارَاتٌ
Confused, perplexed.	حائِرٌ
Planet.	مُتَحَيِّرَةٌ ج مُتَحَيِّرَاتٌ
Space occupied by a body.	حيِّزٌ
To menstruate.	حاضَتْ تَحِيض
Menstruation ; menses.	حَيْضٌ
To be unjust.	حَافَ يَحِيفُ
Injustice, oppression.	حيفٌ
To surround, befall.	حَاقَ يَحِيق ب
Strength, power, might.	حَيْلٌ
To draw near (time).	حَانَ يَحِينُ
Wine-house, tavern.	حَانٌ وَحَانَةٌ
Time, season.	حِينٌ ج أَحْيَانٌ
Instantaneously ; at once.	لِلْحِين
From time to time.	أَحْيَانًا
Then ; at that time.	حِينَئِذ
To live.	حَيِيَ يَحْيَا حَيَاةً
To be ashamed of.	حَيِيَ حَيَاءً مِنْ
To salute, greet.	حَيَّا تَحِيَةً
To bring to life.	أَحْيَا
To spare one's life.	إِسْتَحْيَا
To be ashamed.	إِسْتَحْيَا وَٱسْتَحَى
Come ! come quickly !	حَيَّ
Shame ; modesty.	حَيَاءٌ
Life ; life-time.	حَيَاةٌ أَوْ حَيَوةٌ
Alive. Tribe. Quarter of a town.	حَيٌّ ج أَحْيَاءٌ

حَيَّةٌ ج حَيَّاتٌ	Snake.
حَيَوَانٌ ج حَيَوَانَاتٌ	Animal.
عِلْمُ ٱلْحَيَوَانِ	Zoology.
حَيَوَانِيٌّ	Animal (*Adj.*)
حَيَوِيٌّ	Vital.
تَحِيَّةٌ ج تَحِيَّاتٌ	Greeting.
مُحَيًّا	Face.
مُحْيٍ	Vivifying, giving life.

خ

خ	As a numeral sign =600.
خَبَّ يَخُبُّ	To trot, amble.
خَبَبٌ	Ambling pace, trot.
خَبَا يَخْبَأُ وَخَبَّأَ	To conceal, hide.
إِخْتَبَأَ وَتَخَبَّأَ	To be concealed.
خِبَاءٌ ج أَخْبِئَةٌ	Small tent.
خَابِيَةٌ ج خَوَاب	Large jug.
مَخْبَأٌ ج مَخَابِئُ	A hiding place.
خَبُثَ يَخْبُثُ	To be corrupt.
خُبْثٌ وَخَبَاثَةٌ	Wickedness.
خَبِيثٌ ج خُبَثَاءُ	Vile, malicious.
خَبَائِثُ	Infamous actions.
مَخْبَثَةٌ	A cause of evil.
خَبَرَ يَخْبُرُ	To test, try, prove.
خَابَرَ	To negotiate.
خَبَّرَ وَأَخْبَرَ بِ	To inform.
إِخْتَبَرَ	To learn by experience.
إِسْتَخْبَرَ	To ask for information
خَبَرٌ ج اخْبَارٌ	New report.
خُبْرَةٌ	Knowledge ; experience.
خَبَرِيَّةٌ	Report ; story.
خَبِيرٌ ج خُبَرَاءُ	Well informed.
أَخْبَرُ	Better informed.
خَبَزَ يَخْبِزُ	To bake bread.
خُبْزٌ	Bread.
خُبْزَةٌ	Loaf of bread.

خِبَازَةٌ Baker's trade.

خَبَّازٌ م خَبَّازَةٌ Baker.

خُبَّازَى وَخُبَّيْزَةٌ Mallow (plant).

مَخْبُوزٌ وَخَبِيزٌ Any thing baked.

خَبَصَ يَخْبِصُ To mix ; bungle.

خَبَّاصٌ Rash bungler.

خَبَطَ يَخْبِطُ To strike.

خَبْطُ عَشْوَاءَ At random.

خَبَلَ يَخْبُلُ To be or make insane.

خَبِلٌ وَأَخْبَلُ وَمُخَبَّلٌ Mad, insane.

مَخْبُولٌ Fatigued ; weakened.

خِبَاءٌ ج أَخْبِيَةٌ Tent of wool.

خَابِيَةٌ ج خَوَابٍ Large jug, jar.

خَتَلَ يَخْتِلُ وَخَاتَلَ To cheat.

مُخَاتَلَةٌ Fraud, deceit.

خَتَمَ يَخْتِمُ To seal, stamp.

خَتَمَ To conclude, terminate.

خَاتِمٌ ج خَوَاتِمُ Seal-ring, signet.

خَاتِمَةٌ End, conclusion.

خِتَامٌ ج خُتُمٌ End, conclusion.

مَخْتُومٌ Sealed ; closed.

خَتَنَ يَخْتِنُ To circumcise.

إِخْتَتَنَ To be circumcised.

خَتَنٌ Any relation on side of wife.

خَاتُونٌ ج خَوَاتِينُ Noble lady.

خِتَانٌ وَخِتَانَةٌ Circumcision.

خَثَرَ يَخْثُرُ وَتَخَثَّرَ To coagulate.

خَثَّرَ وَأَخْثَرَ To thicken.

خُثَارَةٌ Sediment, dregs.

خَاثِرٌ Coagulated ; thickened.

خَجِلَ يَخْجَلُ To be ashamed, blush.

خَجَّلَ وَأَخْجَلَ To put to shame.

خَجَلٌ Shame, confusion.

خَجْلَانُ وَمَخْجُولٌ Modest, bashful.

خَدٌّ ج خُدُودٌ Cheek.

خَدٌّ وَأُخْدُودٌ Furrow, pit.

خُدَّةٌ ج خُدَدٌ Furrow, track.

خُدَيْدِيَةٌ Small cushion.

مِخَدَّةٌ Cushion, pillow.
خَدِرَ يَخْدَرُ To be benumbed.
خَدَّرَ To benumb.
خِدْرٌ ج خُدُورٌ Curtain, veil.
خَدَرٌ Numbness ; stupefaction.
مُخَدِّرٌ Sedative, anæsthetic.
مُخَدَّرَةٌ Girl kept in seclusion.
خَدَشَ يَخْدِشُ خَدْشًا To scratch.
خَدَعَ يَخْدَعُ وَخَادَعَ To deceive.
خُدعَةٌ Deceit, guile.
إِنْخَدَعَ To be deceived.
خَدِيعَةٌ ج خَدَائِعُ Deceit.
خَادِعٌ Impostor ; deceitful.
خَدَّاعٌ Impostor, great cheat.
مُخْدَعٌ ج مَخَادِعُ Chamber.
مَخْدُوعٌ Deceived, deluded.
خَدَمَ يَخْدُمُ خِدْمَةً To serve.
إِسْتَخْدَمَ To employ.
خِدْمَةٌ Service ; official duty.
خَادِمٌ ج خَدَمٌ وَخُدَّامٌ Servant.
خِدْنٌ ج أَخْدَانٌ Friend.
خُدَيْوِيٌّ Prince, viceroy.
خَذَلَ يَخْذُلُ خَذْلاً To forsake.
إِنْخَذَلَ To be forsaken.
مَخْذُولٌ Forsaken, unaided.
خَرَّ يَخِرُّ To gurgle, rumble.
خَرَّ لِ To prostrate one's self.
خَرِيرٌ Gurgling, murmur.
خَرِئَ يَخْرَأُ To ease the bowels.
خُرْءٌ وَخِرَاءٌ Excrement.
خَرِبَ يَخْرَبُ To be ruined.
خَرَبَ يَخْرِبُ To demolish, ruin.
تَخَرَّبَ To be destroyed.
خِرْبَةٌ ج خِرَبٌ A ruin, waste.
خَرَابٌ Devastation ; ruin.
خَرُّوبٌ وَخُرْنُوبٌ Carob-tree.
تَخْرِيبٌ Devastation, destruction.
خَرْبَشَ To scratch a writing.

خَرْبَقٌ	Hellebore.
خَرَجَ يَخْرُجُ	To get out ; emerge.
أَخْرَجَ	To take out ; expel.
تَخَرَّجَ	To be well trained.
إِسْتَخْرَجَ	To draw out, extract.
خَرْجٌ	Expenditure.
خُرْجٌ ج أَخْرَاجٌ	Saddle-bags.
خَارِجٌ	Exterior, quotient.
اَلْأُمُورُ ٱلْخَارِجِيَّةُ	Fareign affairs.
خَرَاجٌ	Land-tax ; tribute, tax.
خُرَاجٌ ج خُرَاجَاتٌ	Abscess.
مَخْرَجٌ	Outlet ; issue.
مُخَرَّجٌ	Skilful, well-trained.
خَرْخَرَ	To rattle, snore.
خُرْدُقٌ	Small shot.
خَرْدَلٌ	Mustard.
خَرَزَ يَخْرِزُ	To pierce ; bore.
خَرَزٌ	Small shells, beads.
خَرَزَاتُ ٱلظَّهْرِ	Vertebræ of the back.
مِخْرَزٌ ج مَخَارِزُ	Awl.
خَرِسَ يَخْرَسُ	To be dumb.
خَرَسٌ	Dumbness.
أَخْرَسُ	Dumb.
خُرْصٌ ج خِرْصَانٌ	Ear-ring.
خَرَطَ يَخْرِطُ	To turn on a lathe.
إِخْتَرَطَ	To unsheathe a sword.
خِرَاطَةٌ	Trade of a turner.
خُرَاطَةٌ	Shavings of a lathe.
خَرَّاطٌ	Turner. Liar.
مِخْرَطَةٌ ج مَخَارِطُ	Lathe.
مَخْرُوطٌ	Cone.
مَخْرُوطِيٌّ	Conical.
خُرْطُومٌ ج خَرَاطِيمُ	Snout.
إِخْتَرَعَ	To invent, devise.
خِرْوَعٌ	Castor-oil-plant.
إِخْتِرَاعٌ ج إِخْتِرَاعَاتٌ	Invention.
خَرِفَ يَخْرَفُ	To dote from old age.
خَرَفٌ وَخَرَافَةٌ	Dotage.

Doting, idiotic.	خَرِفٌ وَخَرْفَانٌ
Fictitious tale, fable.	خَرَافَةٌ
Lamb, sheep.	خَرُوفٌ ج خِرَافٌ
Autumn.	خَرِيفٌ
To pierce.	خَرَقَ يَخْرُقُ خَرْقًا
To be pierced.	إِنْخَرَقَ
To traverse.	إِخْتَرَقَ
Rent, hole.	خَرْقٌ ج خُرُوقٌ
Stupid, awkward.	خَرِقٌ وَاخْرَقُ
Rag, tatter.	خِرْقَةٌ ج خِرَقٌ
Unusual.	خَارِقٌ ج خَوَارِقُ
To slit. Fail.	خَرَمَ يَخْرِمُ
To embroider.	خَرَّمَ
To be torn, slit, pierced.	إِنْخَرَمَ
Bore.	خُرْمٌ ج خُرُومٌ
Acromion (anatomy).	أَلاَخْرَمُ
Embroidery.	تَخْرِيمٌ
Embroidered, chased.	مُخَرَّمٌ
To scratch.	خَرْمَشَ
See. خَرُّوبٌ	خُرْنُوبٌ
Silk-stuff.	خَزٌّ ج خُزُوزٌ
Caspian Sea.	بَحْرُ ٱلْخَزَرِ
Ratan, Bamboo.	خَيْزُرَانٌ
A fable.	خُزَعْبَلَةٌ ج خُزَعْبَلاَتٌ
Earthenware, pottery.	خَزَفٌ
Potter.	خَزَفِيٌّ وَخَزَافٌ
To penetrate; tear.	خَزَقَ يَخْزِقُ
To impale.	خَوْزَقَ
To cut off.	خَزَلَ يَخْزِلُ خَزْلاً
To pierce the nose.	خَزَمَ يَخْزِمُ
Nose-ring.	خِزَامٌ
Lavender. Hyacinth.	خُزَامَى
To store, hoard.	خَزَنَ يَخْزُنُ
Treasury.	خَزْنَةٌ وَخِزَانَةٌ
Treasure.	خَزْنَةٌ وَخَزِينَةٌ ج خَزَائِنُ
Library.	خِزَانَةُ ٱلْكُتُبِ
Armoury.	خِزَانَةُ ٱلسِّلاَحِ
Treasurer.	خَازِنٌ ج خَزَنَةٌ

مَخْزَنٌ ج مَخَازِنُ	Magazine.
خَزَا يَخْزُو خَزْواً	To subdue.
خَزِيَ يَخْزَى	To be despised.
خَزِيَ مِنْ	To be ashamed of.
خِزْيٌ	Shame, disgrace.
خِزْيَةٌ	Shameful thing.
خَسَّ يَخِسُّ خَسَاسَةً	To be mean.
خَسٌّ	Lettuce.
خَسِيسٌ	Vile, mean (miserly).
خَسِرَ يَخْسَرُ	To lose.
خَسَّرَ	To cause loss, damage.
خُسْرٌ وخَسَارَةٌ وخُسْرَانٌ	Loss.
خَاسِرٌ	Losing, loser.
خَسَفَ يَخْسِفُ	To sink into the earth and vanish. Be eclipsed.
إِنْخَسَفَ	To be eclipsed.
خُسُوفٌ	Eclipse.
مَخْسُوفٌ	Eclipsed.
خَشَّ يَخُشُّ	To enter, penetrate.
خَشَبٌ	Timber-wood.
خَشَبَةٌ	A piece of wood.
خَشِبٌ	Coarse ; hard.
خَشابٌ	Wood-seller.
خَشْخَشَ	To rustle ; clink.
خَشْخَاشٌ	Poppy.
خَشْخَاشَةٌ	Charnel-house.
خُشَارٌ وخُشَارَةٌ	Refuse.
خَشَعَ يَخْشَعُ	Te be submissive.
تَخَشَّعَ	To humble one's self.
خُشُوعٌ	Lowliness ; humility.
خَاشِعٌ ج خَاشِعُونَ	Humble.
خِشْفٌ وخِشْفَةٌ	Young gazelle.
خُشَّافٌ	Bat (animal).
خَشْمٌ . خَيْشُومٌ ج خَيَاشِيمُ	Nose.
خَشُنَ يَخْشُنُ	To be rough.
خَاشَنَ	To treat one harshly.
خُشْنَةٌ وخُشُونَةٌ	Roughness.
خَشِنٌ ج خِشَانٌ	Rough.

To fear, dread.	خَشِيَ يَخْشَى
Fear.	خَشْيَةٌ وَخِشْيَانٌ
For fear that.	خَشْيَةَ أَنْ
Fearful.	خَاشٍ وَخَشْيَانُ
To distinguish by	خَصَّ يَخُصُّ بِ
To be special to.	خَصَّ خُصُوصًا
To assign.	خَصَّصَ بِ
To be one's property.	إِخْتَصَّ بِ
Hut, booth.	خُصٌّ ج خِصَاصٌ
Special to.	خَاصٌّ لِ وبِ
Quality, property.	خَاصَّةٌ ج خَوَاصٌّ
Particularly.	خَاصَّةً
The notables.	اَلْخَاصَّةُ وَالْخَوَاصُّ
Particular property.	خَاصِيَّةٌ
Especially.	عَلَى ٱلْخُصُوصِ وَخُصُوصًا
Special, particular.	خُصُوصِيٌّ
To be fertile.	خَصِبَ يَخْصَبُ
Fertility.	خِصْبٌ
Fertile.	خَصِبٌ وَمُخْصِبٌ
To abridge	إِخْتَصَرَ
Waist.	خَصْرٌ ج خُصُورٌ
Side ; flank.	خَاصِرَةٌ ج خَوَاصِرُ
Abridgment.	إِخْتِصَارٌ
In short ; briefly.	بِٱلْإِخْتِصَارِ
Whip, staff.	مِخْصَرَةٌ ج مَخَاصِرُ
Abridged ; compend.	مُخْتَصَرٌ
Habit, quality.	خَصْلَةٌ ج خِصَالٌ
Lock of hair. Bunch.	خُصْلَةٌ ج خُصَلٌ
To dispute, contend with.	خَاصَمَ
Adversary.	خَصْمٌ ج خُصُومٌ
Adversary.	خَصِيمٌ ج خُصَمَاءُ
Dispute, quarrel.	خِصَامٌ
To geld, castrate.	خَصَى يَخْصِي
Eunuch.	خَصِيٌّ ج خِصْيَانٌ
Testicle.	خُصْيَةٌ ج خُصًى
To stir (water).	خَضَّ وَخَضْخَضَ
To dye.	خَضَبَ يَخْضِبُ
To be dyed.	تَخَضَّبَ وَاخْتَضَبَ

To err, sin.	خَطِئَ يَخْطَأُ
To charge with mistake.	خَطَّأَ
To err, transgress ; miss one's aim.	أَخْطَأَ
Error ; sin, mistake.	خَطَأٌ وَخَطَاءٌ
Sin.	خَطِيئَةٌ ج خَطَايَا
Sinner.	خَاطِئٌ ج خَطَأَةٌ وَخُطَاةٌ
Erring, missing.	مُخْطِئٌ
To make a speech.	خَطَبَ يَخْطُبُ
To betroth, ask in marrigae.	خَطَبَ يَخْطُبُ
To talk or converse with.	خَاطَبَ
Calamity.	خَطْبٌ ج خُطُوبٌ
Address, speech.	خُطْبَةٌ وَخِطَابٌ
Betrothal.	خِطْبَةٌ
Preacher.	خَطِيبٌ ج خُطَبَاءُ
Second person, (*Gram.*)	مُخَاطَبٌ
To occur to his mind.	خَطَرَ لَهُ
To expose to danger.	خَاطَرَ بِ
Danger, risk.	خَطَرٌ ج أَخْطَارٌ
Thought, idea.	خَاطِرٌ ج خَوَاطِرُ

Dye, colour.	خِضَابٌ
To be green.	خَضِرَ يَخْضَرُ
To become green.	خَضَّرَ
Greenness. Vegetables.	خُضْرَةٌ ج خُضَرٌ
Green.	أَخْضَرُ م خَضْرَاءُ ج خُضْرٌ
Fruits ; herbs.	خِضْرَاوَاتٌ
To submit ; obey.	خَضَعَ يَخْضَعُ
To subdue.	خَضَّعَ وَأَخْضَعَ
To humble one's self.	تَخَضَّعَ
Submissive.	خَاضِعٌ وَخَضُوعٌ
Submission.	خُضُوعٌ
To trace ; write.	خَطَّ يَخُطُّ
To mark with lines.	خَطَّطَ
Line, streak.	خَطٌّ ج خُطُوطٌ
Equator.	خَطُّ ٱلْاسْتِوَاءِ
Equinoctial line.	خَطُّ ٱلْاعْتِدَالِ
Meridian.	خَطُّ نِصْفِ ٱلنَّهَارِ
Imperial edict.	خَطٌّ شَرِيفٌ
Affair. Line of action.	خُطَّةٌ

Admonition, warning.	إِخْطَارٌ
Great ; important.	خَطِيرٌ
Dangerous.	مُخْطِرٌ وَخطِرٌ
Risks, dangers, perils.	مَخَاطِرُ
To seize, abduct.	خطفَ يَخْطفُ
To snatch away, rob.	إِخْتَطَفَ
Robbery ; abduction.	خَطْفٌ
Seizing with violence.	خَاطِفٌ
Swallow (bird).	خطّافٌ ج خطاطِيفُ
To muzzle.	خطَمَ يَخْطِمُ
Marsh-mallow.	خطمِيٌّ
To step, walk.	خَطَا يَخطُو
To pass beyond.	تَخَطى
Step, pace.	خُطْوَةٌ ج خُطْوَاتٌ
Sin, transgression.	خَطِيَةٌ
To be light (in weight).	خَفَّ يَخِفُّ
To make light, ease.	خَفَّفَ
To make light of.	إِستَخَفَّ
Boot, shoe.	خُفٌّ ج اخْفَافُ
Lightness ; agility.	خِفَّةٌ
Light (in weight) ; quick.	خَفِيفٌ
Slighting, despising.	إِستِخْفَافٌ
Alleviating, lightening.	تَخْفِيفٌ
To protect, guard.	خفَرَ يَخْفرُ
Sentry, guard.	خَفَرٌ
Sentry, escort.	خَفِيرٌ ج خفَرَاءُ
Bat (animal).	خُفَّاشٌ ج خَفَافِيشُ
To depress, lower.	خفضَ يَخْفِضُ
To let down, lower.	خَفَّضَ
To become low.	إِنْخَفَضَ
Abasement.	خفْضٌ
To beat. Flutter.	خَفَقَ يَخْفقُ
To fail, miss.	أَخْفَقَ
Palpitation.	خَفَقَانٌ
To be hidden.	خفِيَ يَخْفَى خَفَاءً
To go out of sight.	خَفِيَ خفْيَةً
To conceal.	أَخْفَى إِخْفَاءً
To be concealed.	تَخفَّى

To disappear. إِخْتَفَى مِنْ

Secret ; unperceived. خَفَاً وَخَفَاء

Cocealed, secret. خَفاً ج خَفَايا

Secretly ; in secret. خُفْيَةً

King. خاقَانٌ ج خَوَاقِينُ

To become vinegar. خَلَلَ

To be remiss in, neglect. اخَلَّ بِ

To penetrate, enter. تَخَلَّلَ فِي

To be shaky, faulty. اخْتَلَّ

Vinegar. Slit, rent. خَلٌّ

Intimate friend. خِلٌّ ج أَخْلاَلٌ

Defect ; injury. خَلَلٌ

Quality, habit. خلةٌ ج خِلاَلٌ

Friend. خَلِيل ج أَخِلاء وَخِلانٌ

Mental disorder ; fault. إِخْتِلاَلٌ

Leading to disorder. مُخِلٌّ

Claw, talon. مِخْلَبٌ ج مَخَالِبُ

To quiver. خَلَجَ يَخْلُجُ خَلْجاً

To contend with. خالَجَ

To tremble, quiver. إِخْتَلَجَ

Bay, gulf; canal. خَلِيجٌ ج خُلْجَانٌ

To be displaced. تَخَلْخَلَ

Ankle-ring. خَلْخَالٌ ج خَلاخِيلُ

To be eternal. خَلَدَ يَخْلُدُ

Eternity ; immortality. خُلُودٌ

Mole (animal). خُلْدٌ ج مَنَاجِذ

Everlasting. خَالِدٌ وَمُخَلَّدٌ

To steal. خَلَسَ يَخْلِسُ وَٱخْتَلَسَ

Theft, robbery. إِخْتِلاَسٌ

Thief, robber. مُخْتَلِسٌ وخَالسٌ

To be pure. Escape. خلَصَ يَخْلص

To deliver, rescue, save. خَلَّصَ

To be sincere. أَخْلَصَ

To be saved ; escape. تَخَلَّص

Rescue ; salvation. خَلاَصٌ

Essence ; extract. خُلاَصَةٌ

Pure, unmixed ; free. خَالِصٌ

Sincerity. إِخْلاَصٌ وَخلوصٌ

مُخْلِصٌ	Sincere.
اَلْمُخَلِّصُ	The Saviour.
خَلَطَ يَخْلِطُ	To mix, mingle.
خَلَّطَ	To confuse, disorder.
خَالَطَ وَتَخَالَطَ	To associate with.
إِخْتَلَطَ	To be mixed, mingled.
خَلْطٌ ج أَخْلَاطٌ	Mixture.
خُلْطَةٌ	Social intercourse.
خَلَعَ يَخْلَعُ	To cast off, strip. Depose ; unhinge ; dislocate.
خَلَّعَ	To disjoint, pull to pieces.
إِنْخَلَعَ	To be removed ; dislocated.
خَلْعٌ	Dislocation. Deposition.
خِلْعَةٌ ج خِلَع	Robe of honour.
خَلَاعَةٌ	Disorderly life. Vice.
مُخَلَّعٌ	Unhinged ; feeble, weak.
خَلَفَ يَخْلُفُ	To succeed ; replace.
خَلَّفَ	To leave behind.
خَالَفَ مُخَالَفَةً وَخِلَافًا	To oppose.
أَخْلَفَ الْوَعْدَ	To break one's promise.
تَخَلَّفَ عَنْ	To remain behind.
تَخَالَفَ وَاخْتَلَفَ	To disagree.
خَلْفَ	Behind, after.
خَلَفٌ	Successor, descendant.
خُلْفَةٌ وَاخْتِلَافٌ	Difference.
خِلَافٌ	Disagreement.
خِلَافًا لِذَلِكَ	Contrary to that.
خِلَافَةٌ	Caliphate. Succession.
خَلِيفَةٌ ج خُلَفَاء	Successor. Caliph.
مُخَالَفَةٌ	Opposition.
مُخْتَلِفٌ	Varied, different.
خَلَقَ يَخْلُقُ خَلْقًا	To create.
خَلُقَ يَخْلُقُ	To be worn out.
خَلُقَ بِ وَلِ	To be adapted to.
إِخْتَلَقَ	To invent, forge lies.
تَخَلَّقَ بِ	To affect, feign.
خَلْقٌ	Creation ; creatures. Mankind.
خِلْقَةٌ ج خِلَقٌ	Natural shape.
خُلُقٌ ج أَخْلَاقٌ	Inbron quality.

خَلْقِيٌّ	Congenital.
خَالِقٌ وَخَلَّاقٌ	Creator (God).
خَلِيقٌ ج خُلَقَاءُ بِ	Fit, suitable.
خَلِيقَةٌ ج خَلَائِقُ	Creature.
اَلْمَخْلُوقَاتُ	Created things.
خَلَا يَخْلُو	To be vacant ; alone.
خَلَا مِنْ وَعَنْ	To be free from.
خَلَا بِ	To meet privately.
خَلَّى	To leave, let alone.
اخْلَاهُ	To vacate a place.
تَخَلَّى عَنْ	To withdraw from.
تَخَلَّى لِ	To confine himself to.
خَلَاءٌ	Empty space ; solitude.
بَيْتُ ٱلْخَلَاءِ	Water-closet.
خَلَا وَمَا خَلَا	Except.
خُلُوٌّ	Emptiness.
خَلْوَةٌ	Privacy, solitude.
عَلَى خَلْوَةٍ	Aside, apart.
خَلِيَّةٌ ج خَلَايَا	Bee-hive ; cell.

خَالٍ	Empty, vacant. Free.
اَلْقُرُونُ ٱلْخَالِيَةُ	Past ages.
مِخْلَاةٌ	Feed-bag (for animals).
خَمَّ يَخُمُّ	To be putrid.
خَمَّ يَخُمُّ خَمًّا	To examine a country.
خُمٌّ	Hen-coop.
خَمَدَ يَخْمُدُ	To subside ; abate.
خَامِدٌ	Silent ; dead.
خُمُودٌ	Abatement, subsidence.
خَمَرَ يَخْمُرُ	To veil, conceal.
خَمَّرَ	To conceal. Leaven.
خَامَرَ	To be mixed with.
تَخَمَّرَ	To veil the head, face.
إِخْتَمَرَ	To ferment ; rise (dough).
خَمْرٌ وَخَمْرَةٌ	Wine.
خِمَارٌ ج خُمُرٌ	Covering ; veil.
خَمِيرٌ وَخَمِيرَةٌ	Leaven.
خَمَّارٌ	Wine-merchant.
خَمَّارَةٌ	Wine-shop.

Fermented.	مُخَمَّرٌ
To be the fifth.	خَمَسَ يَخْمُسُ
To make pentagonal.	خَمَّسَ
The fifth part.	خُمْسٌ ج أَخْمَاسٌ
Five.	خَمْسَةٌ م خَمْسٌ
Fifth.	خَامِسٌ
Fifty, fiftieth.	خَمْسُونَ
Thursday.	يَوْمُ ٱلْخَمِيسِ
Pentagon. Pentagonal.	مُخَمَّسٌ
To scratch.	خَمَشَ يَخْمِشُ
Hollow of the foot.	أَلأَخْمَصُ
To limp.	خَمَعَ يَخْمَعُ
Nap of cloth.	خَمْلٌ
To be obscure (man).	خَمَلَ يَخْمُلُ
Villi of stomach.	خَمَلُ ٱلْمِعْدَةِ
Velvet.	مُخْمَلٌ
To surmise.	خَمَنَ يَخْمُنُ وخَمَّنَ
By supposition.	عَلَى ٱلتَّخْمِينِ
To snuffle.	خَنَّ يَخِنُّ خَنِينًا

Nasal twang.	خُنَّةٌ
Sunffles (disease).	خُنَانٌ
To be effeminate.	خَنِثَ يَخْنَثُ
Hermaphrodite.	خُنْثَى
Poniard.	خَنْجَرٌ ج خَنَاجِرُ
Trench, moat.	خَنْدَقٌ ج خَنَادِقُ
Canals of the Nile.	خَنَادِلُ
Hog, pig.	خِنْزِيرٌ ج خَنَازِيرُ
Wild boar.	خِنْزِيرٌ بَرِّيٌّ
Scrofula.	دَاءُ ٱلْخَنَازِيرِ
The stars.	أَلْخُنَّسُ
Satan.	أَلْخَنَّاسُ
Fern (plant).	خِنْشَارٌ
Sucking, pig.	خِنَّوْصٌ ج خَنَانِيصُ
The little finger.	خِنْصِرٌ ج خَنَاصِرُ
Black beetle	خُنْفُسَاءُ ج خَنَافِسُ
To strangle.	خَنَقَ يَخْنُقُ
To be strangled.	إِخْتَنَقَ وٱنْخَنَقَ
Quinsy (disease).	خُنَّاقٌ

Strangled.	خنقٌ وَمَخْنوقٌ
Foul words.	الْخَنَى
Suffocation ; asphyxia.	إِخْتِنَاقٌ
(Mister, Mr.	(خَوَاجَه خَوَاجَاتٌ
(Teacher.	(خوجَه ج خوجَات
Plum ; peach.	خَوْخٌ
Helmet.	خُوذَةٌ ج خُوَذٌ
To bellow.	خارَ يَخُورُ
To fail (strength).	خارَ خَؤُوراً
Bellowing of cattle.	خُوَارٌ
Curate, person.	خُورِيٌّ ج خَوَارِنَةٌ
To be unsaleable.	خاسَ يخُوسُ
Leaves of the plam-tree.	خوصٌ
Having a deformed eye.	أَخْوَصُ
To wade ; ford.	خَاضَ يَخوضُ
Ford.	مَخَاضَةٌ ج مَخَاوِضُ
To fear, be afraid of.	خافَ يَخَافُ
To frighten.	خوَّفَ وَأَخَافَ
Fear, fright.	خوفٌ وَمَخَافة وَخِيفَةٌ
Timid, fearing.	خَائِفٌ
Intimidation.	تَخْوِيفٌ
Fearful, perilous.	مُخَوِّفٌ
Terrible, inspiring fear.	مُخِيفٌ
Cause of fear.	مَخَافَةٌ ج مَخَاوِفُ
To bestow upon.	خَوَّلَ
Maternal uncle.	خَالٌ ج أَخْوَالٌ
Mole on the face.	خَالٌ ج خِيلانٌ
Maternal aunt.	خَالَةٌ ج خَالاَتٌ
Steward.	خَوْلِيٌّ ج خَوَلٌ
Calico.	خَامٌ
To be unfaithful.	خانَ يَخُونُ
To accuse of treachery.	خوَّنَ
Inn (Prince).	خانٌ ج خَانَاتٌ
Deceit, treachery.	خَوْنٌ وَخِيَانَةٌ
Table for food.	خِوَانٌ ج أَخْوِنَةٌ
Unfaithful, traitor.	خَائِنٌ
Treacherous.	خَؤُونٌ وَخَوَّانٌ
To be waste, empty.	خَوَى يَخْوِي

خاوٍ	Empty, hollow ; void.
خَابَ يَخِيب	To be disappointed.
خَيَّبَ وَا خاب	To disappoint.
خَيْبَةٌ	Failure, disappointment.
خَائِبٌ	Frustrated.
خَيَّرَ عَلَى	To deem better ; prefer.
خَيَّرَ	To give one a choice.
إِخْتار	To choose, select, prefer.
خَيْرٌ ج خِيَارٌ	A good thing.
خَيْرٌ مِنْ	Better than.
خَيْرُ ٱلنَّاسِ	The best of men.
خَيْرِيٌّ	Good, benevolent.
خِيَارٌ	Choice. Cucumber.
خَيْرٌ	Good, liberal.
خَيْرٌ (اخْيَرُ)	Better ; preferable.
اخْتِيَارٌ	Choice, election.
اخْتِيَارِيٌّ	Voluntary.
مُخَيَّرٌ	Free to choose.
مُخْتَارٌ	Preferred.
خَارَصِينِي	Zinc.
خَيْشٌ	Coarse canvas.
خَيْشَةٌ ج خَيْشَاتٌ	Large sack.
خَاطَ يَخِيط وَخَيَّطَ	To sew.
خَيْطٌ ج خُيُوطٌ وَخِيطَانٌ	Thread.
خِيَاطَةٌ	Needle-work, sewing.
خَيَّاط	Tailor.
مَخِيطٌ وَمَخْيُوطٌ	Sewn, stitched.
خَالَ يَخَال	To conceive; imagine.
خُيِّلَ لِ وَإِلَى	To seem to.
تَخَيَّلَ	To imagine, fancy.
خَيْلٌ ج خُيُول	Horse ; cavalry.
خَيَالٌ ج اخْيِلَةٌ	Spectre, phantom.
خَيَالِيٌّ	Imaginary ideal.
أَلْمُخَيِّلَةَ	Faculty of imagination.
خَيَّالٌ ج خَيَّالَةٌ	Horseman.
خَيَّمَ	To pitch a tent ; abide.
خَامٌ	Unbleached cloth.
خَيْمَةٌ ج خِيَامٌ	Tent ; booth.

د

د As a numerical sign=4.

دَابٌ State, condition ; habit.

دَبَّ يَدِبُّ To crawl, creep.

دُبٌّ ج أَدْبَابٌ Bear (animal).

دَابَّةٌ ج دَوَابُّ Animal ; beast.

دُوَيْبَّةٌ Little animal ; reptile.

دِيبَاجٌ Silk brocade.

دِيبَاجَةٌ Introduction, preface.

دَبْدَبَ To tread, crawl.

دَبَّرَ To plan ; manage well.

أَدْبَرَ To go back, retreat.

تَدَبَّرَ To regard attentively.

دُبْرٌ ج أَدْبَارٌ Back, hind part.

تَدْبِيرٌ ج تَدَابِيرُ Management.

مُدْبِرٌ One who turns back.

مُدَبِّرٌ Administrator ; director.

دِبْسٌ Thick juice of grapes.

دَبُّوسٌ ج دَبَابِيس Mace. Pin.

دَبَغَ يَدْبُغُ To tan (leather).

دِبَاغَةٌ Trade of a tanner.

دَبَّاغٌ Tanner.

مَدْبَغَةٌ ج مَدَابِغ Tannery.

مَدْبُوغٌ Tanned.

دَبِقَ يَدْبَقُ ب To adhere to.

دِبْقٌ Glue, bird-lime.

دَثَرَ يَدْثُرُ To be effaced.

دَثَّرَ To cover with a blanket.

إِنْدَثَرَ To be destroyed.

دَاثِرٌ That which perishes.

دُجَاجٌ Poultry.

دُجَاجَةٌ A hen.

دُجَاجُ ٱلْهِنْدِ Turkey.

دُجَاجُ ٱلأَرْضِ	Woodcock.
دُجَاجُ ٱلْبَرِّ	Partridge.
مُدَجَّجٌ	Completely armed.
دجَلَ يَدْجُلُ	To lie ; cheat.
دَجَّالٌ	Liar ; imposter ; quack.
دِجْلة	Tigris (river).
دَجَنَ يَدْجُنُ	To be cloudy, dark. To become tame.
دَجَنَ دُجونَا بِ	To abide.
دُجْنَةٌ ج دُجَنٌ	Darkness.
دَاجِنٌ ج دَوَاجِنُ	Tame animal.
دجىً	Darkness.
دَحَرَ يَدْحَرُ	To drive away.
دَحْرَجَ	To roll down (*tran*).
تَدَحْرَجَ	To be rolled.
دُحَيْرِجَةٌ	Lucern.
دَاحِسٌ	Whitlow.
دَحَشَ يَدْحَشُ	To force into.
أَدْحَضَ	To rebut, refute.
إِنْدَحَضَ	To be refuted, rebutted.
دَخَلَ يَدْخل	To enter.
دخلَ تَحتَ وَفي	To be included.
أَدْخَلَ	To cause to enter.
تَدَاخَلَ فِي	To intermeddle.
دَخْلٌ	Income, revenue.
دَخْلَكَ وَدَخِيلَكَ	I beseech you.
دَاخِلٌ	Interior, inside.
وَزِيرُ ٱلدَّاخِلِيَّةِ	Home Secretary.
دَخِيلٌ ج دُخَلاءُ	Stranger. Guest.
مَدْخَلٌ ج مدَاخِلُ	Door ; access.
مَدْخُولٌ ج مَدَاخِيل	Revenue.
دَخَنَ وَدَخَّنَ وَأَدْخَنَ	To smoke.
دُخْنٌ	Millet.
دُخَّانٌ	Smoke. Tobacco.
مَدْخَنَةٌ ج مَدَاخِنُ	Chimney.
دَرَّ يَدُرُّ	To flow copiously.
دَرٌّ	Copious flow of milk.
لِلّٰهِ دَرُّهُ	How exquisite !
دُرَّةٌ ج دُرَّاتٌ	Pearl. Parrot.

To sew, stitch.	دَرَزَ يَدْرُزُ
Seam.	دَرْزٌ ج دُرُوزٌ
Druze.	دُرْزِيٌّ ج دُرُوزٌ
To efface.	دَرَسَ يَدْرُسُ
To read, study.	دَرَسَ يَدْرِسُ
To tread out corn, thresh.	دَرَسَ
To study or read under a teacher.	دَرَسَ عَلَى
To teach, lecture.	دَرَّسَ
To be effaced.	إِنْدَرَسَ
Lesson. study.	دَرْسٌ ج دُرُوسٌ
Threshing.	دِرَاسٌ وَدِرَاسَةٌ
School.	مَدْرَسَةٌ ج مَدَارِسُ
Teacher, professor.	مُدَرِّسٌ
To put on a coat of mail.	إِدَّرَعَ وَتَدَرَّعَ
Coat of mail.	دِرْعٌ ج دُرُوعٌ
Armoured.	مُدَرَّعٌ
Water jug.	دَوْرَقٌ ج دَوَارِقُ
Peach.	دُرَاقِنٌ وَدُرَّاقٌ
To make responsible for.	دَرَّكَ

Copious flow.	مِدْرَارٌ
To guide, direct.	دَرَّبَ
To be practised in.	تَدَرَّبَ
Path ; way.	دَرْبٌ ج دُرُوبٌ
Training ; drill.	تَدْرِيبٌ
Trained ; excercised.	مُدَرَّبٌ
Balustrade.	دَرَبْزِينٌ وَدَرَابزُون
To proceed gradually.	درَجَ يَدْرُجُ
To introduce.	أَدْرَجَ وَدَرَّجَ في
To proceed by degrees.	تَدَرَّجَ
Roll of Paper.	دَرْجٌ ج أَدْرَاجٌ
Box, case.	دُرْجٌ ج أَدْرَاجٌ
Road, path.	دَرَجٌ ج ادرَاجٌ وَدِرَاجٌ
Step; degree.	درَجةٌ ج دَرَجَاتٌ
Gradually.	تَدْرِيجاً وَبِٱلتَّدْرِيجِ
Common, current.	دَارِجٌ
Francolin.	دُرَّاجٌ
To lie unconscious.	انْدَرَجَ
Elm.	دَرْدَارٌ

To overtake.	دَارَكَ
To reach ; comprehend.	أَدْرَكَ
To overtake ; rectify.	تَدَارَكَ
To seek to obviate.	إِسْتَدْرَكَ
Comprehension.	إِدْرَاكٌ
To be filthy.	درِنَ يدْرَن
Dirt. Tubercle.	دَرَنٌ ج أَدْرَانٌ
Polluted, dirty,	دِرْنٌ
Drachm ; money.	دِرْهَمٌ ج دَرَاهِم
Dervish.	دَرْوِيشٌ ج دَرَاوِيشُ
To know.	دَرَى يَدْرِي
To treat kindly, cajole.	دَارَى
To acquaint, inform.	ادْرَى بِ
Knowledge.	دِرَايَةٌ
To hide, insert.	دَسَّ يَدُسُّ
To plot against,	دَسَّ عَلَى
To be hidden, concealed.	إِنْدَسَّ
Spy.	داسُوسٌ ج دَوَاسِيسُ
Intrigue.	دَسِيسَةٌ ج دَسَائِسُ
A game. Copper pot,	دَسْتٌ ج دُسُوتٌ
Rule, regulation.	دُسْتُورٌ
Town, village.	دَسْكَرَةٌ ج دَسَاكِرُ
To be fatty.	دَسِمَ يَدْسَمُ
Fat, grease.	دَسَمٌ وَدُسُومَةٌ
To dismiss ; leave.	دَشَرَ
Let ! (*imp. from* وَدَعَ)	دَعْ
To sport, jest with.	دَعَبَ وَدَاعَبَ
Wickedness.	دَعَرٌ وَدِعَارَةٌ
To tread under foot.	دَعَسَ يدْعَسُ
A track, foot-print.	دَعْسَةٌ
To rup.	دَعَكَ يَدْعَكُ
To contend with.	دَاعَكَ مُدَاعَكَةً
To prop.	دَعَمَ يَدْعُمُ دَعْماً
Support, prop.	دِعَامَةٌ ج دَعَائِمُ
To call ; pray,	دَعَا يَدْعُو
To invite.	دَعَا دَعْوَةً
To pray for.	دَعَا لِ
To invoke a curse upon.	دَعَا عَلَى

إدّعى بِ	To claim ; pretend.
إدّعى على	To claim against.
إستدعى	To call, invite.
دُعاءٌ ج ادعيةٌ	Call ; prayer.
دَعوةٌ	Invocation ; invitation. Imprecation.
دعوى ج دَعاوٍ	Claim ; law-suit.
دَاعٍ ج دُعاةٌ	Calling. Preacher.
دَاعيةٌ ج دَوَاعٍ	Cause ; motive.
إدّعاءٌ	Claim, pretention.
مُدَّعٍ	Pretender ; plaintiff.
مُدَّعًى عَلَيْهِ	Defendant.
دَغْدَغَ دَغْدَغَةً	To tickle.
دَغَشٌ	Darkness ; nightfall.
دَغَلٌ ج أَدْغَالٌ	Corruption. Thicket.
دَفٌّ ج دفوفٌ	Tambourine.
دَفَّةٌ	Side. Rudder.
دَفِئَ يَدْفَأُ	To be warm.
دَفَّأَ وَأَدْفَأَ	To warm.
تَدَفَّأَ	To warm one's self.
دِفْءٌ	Heat, warmth.
دَفْتَرٌ ج دفاتِرُ	Register. Account-book.
دَفْتَرْدَارٌ	Minister of Finances.
دَفَرَ يَدْفَرُ	To push back.
دِفْرَان	Juniper tree.
دَفَشَ يَدْفُش	To push.
دَفَعَ يَدْفَعُ	To push back, repel.
دَفَعَ إِلَى وَلِ	To hand over to.
دَافَعَ	To contend with. Defer.
دَافَعَ عَنْ	To protect, defend.
إِنْدَفَعَ	To be thrust back.
دَفْعٌ	Pushing back. Payment.
قُوَّةٌ دَافِعَةٌ	Expulsive force.
مِدْفَعٌ ج مَدَافِعُ	Cannon.
دَفَقَ يَدْفُقُ	To pour forth (water).
تَدَفَّقَ وَانْدَفَقَ	To be poured out.
مُتَدَفِّقٌ	Overflowing.
دِفْلٌ وَدِفْلَى	Oleander.
دَفَنَ يَدْفِنُ	To bury ; conceal.

To be buried.	إِندَفَنَ
Burying, burial.	دَفْنٌ
Buried treasure.	دَفِينَةٌ ج دَفَائِنُ
Tomb.	مَدْفَنٌ ج مَدَافِنُ
To be fine, thin.	دقَّ يَدِقُّ
To crush ; knock.	دَقَّ يَدُقُّ
To ring the bell.	دق ٱلْجرَس
To be precise.	دَقَقَ
To examine minutely.	دَقَقَ ٱلنظَرَ
Exactness, accuracy.	دِقَّةٌ
Pestle.	مِدَقٌّ وَمِدَقَّةٌ
Fine : thin. Fine flour.	دَقِيقٌ ج أَدِقَّةٌ وَدِقَاقٌ
Minute (time).	دَقِيقَةٌ ج دَقَائِقُ
Exactness, precision.	تَدْقِيقٌ
Exact, precise.	مُدَقَّقٌ
To demolish. To charge a gun.	دَكَّ يَدُكُّ
Wide bench, seat.	دَكَّةٌ
Ramrod.	مِدَكٌّ
Loaded (gun).	مَدْكُوكٌ

To be blackish.	دَكِنَ يَدْكَنُ
Blackish colour.	دُكْنَةٌ
Shop.	دُكَّانٌ ج دَكَاكِينُ
Shop-keeper.	دُكَّنْجِيٌّ
Blackish.	أَدْكَنُ م دَكْنَاءُ
To point out, show.	دَلَّ يَدُلُّ على
To spoil (a child).	دَلَّلَ
To sell at auction.	دلَّلَ على
To be coquettish.	تَدَلَّلَ
To seek, or to find a proof.	إِستَدَلَّ على
Coquetry.	دَلالٌ
Broker, auctioneer.	دَلَّالٌ
Sign, proof.	دَلِيلٌ ج أَدِلَّةٌ
Guide.	دَلِيلٌ ج أَدِلَّاءُ
Plane-tree.	دُلْبٌ
Water-wheel.	دُولَابٌ ج دَوَالِيبُ
Deceit.	دَلَسٌ وَدُلْسَةٌ
To loll the tongue.	دَلَعَ لِسَانَهُ
To leak.	دَلَفَ يَدْلِفُ دَلْفًا

Dolphin.	دُلْفِينٌ ج دَلَافِينُ
To pour out (a liquid).	دَلَقَ يَدْلُقُ
To rub.	دَلَكَ يَدْلُكُ دَلْكاً ب
Rubbing stone.	مِدْلَاكٌ وَمِدْلَكَةٌ
To be very dark.	ادْلَهَمَّ
Very black.	مُدْلَهِمٌّ
To draw a bucket.	دَلَا يَدْلُو
To let down.	دَلَّى وَادْلَى
To be let down.	تَدَلَّى
Bucket.	دَلْوٌ ج دِلَاءٌ
Aquarius.	الدَّلْوُ
Grape-vine.	دَالِيَةٌ ج دَوَالٍ
Blood.	دَمٌ
Bloody.	دَمَوِيٌّ
To be gentle.	دَمُثَ يَدْمُثُ
Mild, soft.	دَمْثٌ وَدَمِيثٌ
Gentleness, delicacy.	دَمَاثَةٌ
To be joined.	دَمَجَ يَدْمُجُ وَانْدَمَجَ
Compact.	مُدْمَجٌ وَمُنْدَمِجٌ
To murmur against.	دَمْدَمَ عَلَى
To perish utterly.	دَمَرَ يَدْمُرُ
To annihilate, destroy.	دَمَرَ وَدَمَّرَ
Destruction, annihilation.	دَمَارٌ
Palmyra.	تَدْمُرُ
To be dense, (darkness).	دَمَسَ يَدْمُسُ
To conceal, bury.	دَمَسَ يَدْمُسُ
Dark, (night).	دَامِسٌ
Damascus.	دِمَشْقُ
To shed tears, (eyes).	دَمَعَ يَدْمَعُ
Tears.	دَمْعٌ ج دُمُوعٌ وَأَدْمُعٌ
A tear, a drop.	دَمْعَةٌ
To mark by branding.	دَمَغَ يَدْمَغُ
Mark, brand.	دَمْغَةٌ
Brain.	دِمَاغٌ ج أَدْمِغَةٌ
To manure land.	دَمَلَ يَدْمِلُ
To be healed.	دَمَلَ يَدْمُلُ وَانْدَمَلَ
Pustule, boil.	دُمَّلٌ ج دَمَامِلُ
Manure.	دَمَالٌ

Bracelet. دُمْلُجٌ ج دَمالِجُ

To manure land. دَمَنَ وَدَمَّنَ

To be permanent. دَمِنَ يَدْمَنُ

To persevere in, cleave to. ادْمَنَ

Constant practice. إِدْمَانٌ

Addicted to. مُدْمِنٌ

To bleed, flow (blood). دَمِيَ يَدْمَى

To cause to bleed. دَمَّى وَادْمَى

Blood. دَمٌ ج دِمَاءٌ

Bloody. دَمِيٌّ وَدَمَوِيٌّ

Large wine-jar. دَنٌّ ج دِنَانٌ

To be low, vile. دَنَا يَدْنَا

Meanness; weakness. دَنَاءَةٌ

Low; worthless. دَنِيءٌ ج أَدْنِيَاءُ

A gold coin. دِينَارٌ ج دَنَانِيرُ

To be defiled. دَنِسَ يَدْنَسُ

To stain, pollute. دَنَّسَ

To be defiled. تَدَنَّسَ

Filth, pollution. دَنَسٌ ج أَدْنَاسٌ

Soiled, foul. دَنِسٌ ج ادْنَاسٌ

To be near death. أَدْنَفَ

To perish with cold. دَنِقَ يَدْنَقُ

Small coin. دَانِقٌ ج دَوَانِقُ

To approach. دَنَا يَدْنُو

Nearness; proximity. دَنَاوَةٌ

Meanness, baseness. دَنَايَةٌ

Vile. Near. دَنِيءٌ ج أَدْنِيَاءُ

Anything base. دَنِيَّةٌ ج دَنَايَا

The (present) world. دُنْيَا

Worldly. دُنْيَوِيٌّ

Nearer. Viler, worse. ادْنَى

Time; age. دَهْرٌ ج دُهُورٌ

For ever and ever. دَهْرُ الدَّاهِرِينَ

To be bewildered. دَهِشَ يَدْهَشُ

To perplex. دَهَّشَ وَأَدْهَشَ

Astounded. دَهِشٌ وَمَدْهُوشٌ

Confusion; perplexity. دَهْشَةٌ

Vestibule. دِهْلِيزٌ ج دَهَالِيزُ

To scatter.	دَهَكَ يَدْهَكُ دَهْكًا
To come unexpectedly.	دَهِمَ يَدْهَمُ
Blackness.	دُهْمَةٌ
Black (horse).	أَدْهَمُ
To anoint, paint.	دَهَنَ يَدْهِنُ
To beguile ; coax.	دَاهَنَ
To be anointed.	تَدَهَّنَ
Oil, grease.	دُهْنٌ ج أَدْهَانٌ
Paint. Ointment.	دِهَانٌ وَدَهُونٌ
Painter.	دَهَّانٌ
Dissimulation ; flattery.	مُدَاهَنَةٌ
Painted.	مُدَهَّنٌ وَمَدْهُونٌ
To be sly, subtle.	دَهِيَ يَدْهَى
Cunning, craft.	دَهَاءٌ
Calamity.	دَاهِيَةٌ ج دَوَاهٍ
Sagacious, cunning.	دَاهٍ وَدَاهِيَةٌ
To throw down.	دَهْوَرَ
To tumble down.	تَدَهْوَرَ
Illness, disease.	دَاءٌ ج أَدْوَاءٌ
Gout.	دَاءُ ٱلْمُلُوكِ
Hydrophobia.	دَاءُ ٱلْكَلْبِ
Elephantiasis.	دَاءُ ٱلْفِيلِ
To be giddy, sea sick.	دَاخَ يَدُوخُ
To subdue, conquer.	دَوَّخَ
Giddiness.	دَوْخَةٌ
A worm.	دُودَةٌ ج دِيدَانٌ وَدُودٌ
Silk-worm.	دُودَةُ ٱلْقَزِّ
David.	دَاوُدُ
To revolve, circulate.	دَارَ يَدُورُ
To set going ; administer.	أَدَارَ
To be round.	تَدَوَّرَ وَٱسْتَدَارَ
House.	دَارٌ ج دُورٌ وَدِيَارٌ
The world to come.	دَارُ ٱلْبَقَاءِ
The world that is.	دَارُ ٱلْفَنَاءِ
The two worlds (of time and eternity).	أَلدَّارَانِ
Turn ; age, period.	دَوْرٌ ج أَدْوَارٌ
Rotation, circulation.	دَوَرَانٌ
Sparrow.	دُورِيٌّ

Revolving ; roaming. دَائِرٌ

Circle; or bit of a planet. Calamity. Department. دَائِرَةٌ ج دَوَائِرُ

Encyclopedia. دَائِرَةُ ٱلْعُلُومِ

Giddiness. دُوَارٌ

Convent. دَيْرٌ ج أَدْيِرَةٌ

Administration. إِدَارَةٌ

Circular form. إِسْتِدَارَةٌ

Pivot, axis. مَدَارٌ

Round, circular. مُدَوَّرٌ وَمُسْتَدِيرٌ

Inspector ; director. مُدِيرٌ

Territory of a Mudir. مُدِيرِيَّةٌ

To tread, trample. دَاسَ يَدُوسُ

To be trodden upon. إِنْدَاسَ

Shoe, sandal. مَدَاسٌ

To alternate. دَاوَلَ مُدَاوَلَةً

To do by turns. تَدَاوَلَ

Dynasty ; empire. دَوْلَةٌ ج دُوَلٌ

Vine, grapes. دَوَالِيٌّ

By turns, alternately. مُدَاوَلَةٌ

Used, employed commonly. مُتَدَاوَلٌ

To continue ; endure. دَامَ يَدُومُ

As long as it stands. مَادَامَ قَائِمًا

To persist in. دَاوَمَ عَلَى

To prolong. أَدَامَ

To continue. إِسْتَدَامَ

Continuance. دَوَامٌ وَدَيْمُومَةٌ

The ban palm. دَوْمٌ

Continually ; for ever. عَلَى ٱلدَّوَامِ

Spinning-top. دُوَّامَةٌ

Continuing, lasting. دَائِمٌ

Always. دَائِمًا

Wine. مُدَامٌ وَمُدَامَةٌ

Perseverance. مُدَاوَمَةٌ

To write out. دَوَن

Beneath. Before, behind. دُونَ

Except. دُونَ أَنْ

بِدُونِ وَمِنْ دُونِ Without.

دُونٌ Low, mean, vile, bad.

دُونَكَ Take it !

دِيوَانٌ ج دَوَاوِينُ Court of justice ; tribunal Poems.

مُدَوَّنٌ Inserted, registered.

دَاوَى To treat medically.

دَوَاءٌ ج أَدْوِيَةٌ Medicine, remedy.

دَوَاةٌ وَدَوَايَةٌ Inkstand.

دَوِيٌّ Hum, buzz; rustling.

مُدَاوَةٌ Treatment, cure.

مُدَاوٍ Physician.

دِيكٌ ج دُيُوكٌ Cock.

دَانَ يَدِينُ To borrow ; lend.

دَانَ دِيناً To judge, requite. Follow a religion.

دانَ لِ To submit, yield to.

دَيَّنَ وَأَدَانَ To lend money.

تَدَيَّنَ وَٱسْتَدَانَ مِنْ To borrow.

تدَيَّنَ بِ To follow a religion.

دَيْنٌ ج دُيُونٌ Debt, loan.

دِينٌ ج اَدْيَانٌ . دِيَانَةٌ ج دِيَانَاتٌ Religion ; belief.

يوْمُ ٱلدِّينِ The Judgment Day.

دَيْنُونَةٌ Judgment.

دَائِنٌ Debtor ; creditor.

دَيَّانٌ Judge.

مَدِينَةٌ City. (*see* مدن)

مَدْيُونٌ ج مَدْيُونون Debtor.

ذ

ذ As a numeral sign=700.

ذا ج اولاءِ This, this one.

ذَاكَ ج اولئِكَ That, that one.

ذلِك ج اوْلائِكَ That, that one.

لمَاذا What ? مَاذاَ Why ?

كذا Thus, like this.

هذَا مث هذَانِ ج هؤُلاَءِ This.

هـكَذا Thus, like this.

ذِئْبٌ ج ذِئَابٌ Wolf.

ذبَّ يَذُبُّ عَنْ To repel ; defend.

ذُبَابٌ ج ذِبَّانٌ Fly.

ذُبَابَةٌ A fly.

ذبَحَ يَذْبَحُ To slaughter, slay.

تَذابَحَ To kill one another.

ذَبْحٌ Act of slaughtering.

ذُبْحَة Angina, croup.

ذَبِيحٌ Slaughtered.

ذَبِيحَةٌ ج ذَبائِحُ Sacrifice.

مَذْبَحٌ ج مَذابِحُ Alter.

مذبُوحٌ Slaughtered, immolated.

ذَبْذَبَ To swing to and fro.

مُذَبْذَبٌ وَمُتَذَبْذِبٌ Wavering.

ذَبَلَ يَذْبُلُ ذُبُولاً To wither.

أَذْبَلَ To cause to wither, dry up.

ذابِلٌ Withered, withering.

ذَخَرَ يَذْخَرُ وَآذخَرَ To treasure up.

ذُخْرٌ ج أَذْخَارٌ وَذَخِيرَةٌ ج ذَخائِر
Treasure ; stores.

ذرَّ يَذُرُّ ذَرًّا To scatter, sprinkle.

ذرٌّ Young or small ants.

ذَرَّةٌ An atom.

ذُرّيَةٌ ج ذَراريُّ Descendants.

Spanish fly. ذَرَّاحٌ ج ذَرَارِيح

To scatter, strew. ذَرْذَرَ

Power, capacity. ذَرْعٌ

To be unable. ضَاقَ ذَرْعًا

Arm ; cubit. ذِرَاعٌ ج أَذْرُعٌ

Sudden, rapid. ذَرِيعٌ

To flow; shed (tears). ذَرَفَ يَذْرِفُ

To winnow ; scatter. ذَرَى يَذْرِي

To winnow. ذَرَّى وَأَذْرَى

To seek shelter. ذَرَّى وَاسْتَذْرَى

A kind of millet. ذُرَةٌ

Maize. ذُرَةٌ صَفْرَاءُ

Dispersed dust. Shelter. ذَرًى

Summit. ذَرْوَةٌ ج ذُرًى

Winnowing fork. مِذْرًى

To frighten. ذَعَرَ يَذْعَرُ وَأَذْعَرَ

To be terrified. ذَعِرَ وَانْذَعَرَ

Fright, terror. ذُعْرٌ

Bewilderment. ذَعَرٌ

Bewildered ; frightened. مَذْعُورٌ

To obey. ذَعِنَ يَذْعَنُ وَأَذْعَنَ لِ

To confess, submit. اَذْعَنَ بِ

Submission. إِذْعَانٌ

Obedient, submissive. مُذْعِنٌ

Strong odour. ذَفَرٌ

Chin ; beard. ذَقْنٌ ج ذُقُونٌ

To remember. ذَكَرَ يَذْكُرُ

To mention, relate. ذَكَرَ

To remind of ذَكَّرَ وَأَذْكَرَ

To confer with. ذَاكَرَ فِي

To remember, think of. تَذَكَّرَ

To confer together. تَذَاكَرَ فِي

Memory ; praise. Mention. ذِكْرٌ

Male. Male organ. ذَكَرٌ ج ذُكُورٌ

Remembrance. ذِكْرَى

Faculty of memory. ذَاكِرَةٌ

Permit, passport. تَذْكِرَةٌ ج تَذَاكِرُ

Remembrance. تَذْكَارٌ

Frequent remembrance. تَذَكُّرٌ
Conference. مُذَاكَرَةٌ
Masculine, (word). مُذَكَّرٌ
Mentioned. Praised. مَذْكُورٌ
To be quick, (in intellect). ذَكِيَ يَذْكَى
Quick understanding. ذَكَاءٌ
Intelligent. ذَكِيٌّ ج أَذْكِيَاءُ
Quicker in perception. أَذْكَى
To be low ; submissive. ذَلَّ يَذِلُّ
To humble, humiliate. ذَلَّلَ وَأَذَلَّ
To render tractable. ذَلَّلَ
To humble one's self. تَذَلَّلَ
Submissiveness. ذُلٌّ
Humiliation. ذُلٌّ وَمَذَلَّةٌ
Low, abject. ذَلِيلٌ ج أَذِلَّاءُ
This ; that. (*see* ذَا) ذَلِكَ
To blame, censure. ذَمَّ يَذُمُّ
Blame, rebuke. ذَمٌّ وَمَذَمَّةٌ
Covenant ; security. ذِمَّةٌ ج ذِمَمٌ

Protected tributaries. أَهْلُ الذِّمَّةِ
Conscience ; moral sense. ذِمَّةٌ
Blamed ; censured. ذَمِيمٌ
Blameworthy action. مَذَمَّةٌ
Blamed ; censured. مَذْمُومٌ
To murmur against. تَذَمَّرَ عَلَى
To be guilty. أَذْنَبَ
Crime guilt. ذَنْبٌ ج ذُنُوبٌ
Tail, extremity. ذَنَبٌ ج أَذْنَابٌ
Comet. نَجْمٌ ذُو ذَنَبٍ
Guilty ; criminal. مُذْنِبٌ
To go, depart. ذَهَبَ يَذْهَبُ
To think, believe. ذَهَبَ إِلَى
To gild. ذَهَّبَ وَأَذْهَبَ
To cause to disappear. أَذْهَبَ
Gold. ذَهَبٌ
Golden, of gold. ذَهَبِيٌّ
Nile-boat. ذَهَبِيَّةٌ
Going ; passing. ذَاهِبٌ

Departure. ذَهَابٌ

Gilt. مُذَهَّبٌ

Way. Creed. مَذْهَبٌ ج مَذَاهِبُ

To embrace a creed. تَمَذْهَبَ

Gold powder. ماءُ ٱلذهَبِ

To forget, neglect. ذَهَلَ يَذْهَلُ عَنْ

To be astonished. ذَهَلَ وَٱنْذَهَلَ

To cause to forget. أَذْهلَ عَنْ

Astonishment. إِنْذِهَالٌ

Astonished, bewildered. مُنْذَهِلٌ

Mind, intellect. ذِهْنٌ ج أَذْهَانٌ

Intellectual, subjective. ذِهْنِيٌّ

Master, possessor. ذُو ج ذَوُو

Essence; person, self. ذَاتٌ

To the right. ذاتَ ٱلْيمينِ

On a certain day. ذَاتَ يَوْمٍ

In person. بذاتهِ

In itself. في ذَاتِهِ

Essential, personal. ذَاتِيٌّ

Selfishness. مَحَبَّة ٱلذاتِ

To dissolve, melt. ذَابَ يذُوبُ

To cause to melt. ذوَّب وَاذابَ

Melting, in a fluid state. ذَائِبٌ

Manager. مِذْوَدٌ ج مَذَاوِد

To taste; try. ذَاقَ يذُوقُ

To give to taste. أَذاقَ

Taste, sense of taste. ذَوْقٌ

Sound taste. ذَوْقٌ سَلِيمٌ

Flavour. مَذَاقٌ

That, yonder. (*See* اذا) ذَاكَ

To wither, (plant). ذَوَى يَذْوِي

This, (*fem. of* ذا) ذِي وَهذي

To be public, (news). ذَاعَ يذِيعُ

To make public. اَذَاعَ وَبِ

Publication. إِذَاعَة

To add an appendix. ذَيَّلَ

Tail, skirt. Fringes. Appendix. ذَيْلٌ ج ذُيُولٌ

Appendix, supplement. تَذْييل

ر

ر As a numeral sign=200.

رَاتِينَجٌ Resin.

رَأَسَ يَرْأَسُ To be a chief.

رَأَّسَ To make one a leader.

تَرَأَّسَ To become a chief.

رَأْسٌ ج رُؤُوسٌ Head; peak; cape; chief, leader; principal part.

رَأْساً Directly; completely.

عَلَى ٱلرَّأْسِ وَٱلْعَيْنِ Most willingly.

رَأْسُ ٱلْمَالِ Capital; stock.

رِآسَةٌ وَرِيَاسَةٌ Headship, authority.

رَئِيسٌ ج رُؤَسَاءُ President, chief.

أَلْأَعْضَاءُ ٱلرَّئِيسَةُ The vital organs.

مَرْؤُوسٌ Under authority.

رَأَفَ يَرْأَفُ To show pity.

رَأْفَةٌ Compassion, pity, mercy.

رَؤُوفٌ وَرَئِفٌ Compassionate.

رِئْمٌ ج آرَامٌ White antelope.

رَأَى يَرَى To see, perceive; judge.

رَأَى رُؤْيَا To have a vision.

رَاءَى مُرَاءَاةً To dissemble.

يَا تُرَى Do you suppose?

أَرَى إِرَاءَةً To show.

تَرَأَّى وَتَرَاءَى لِ To appear to.

إِرْتَأَى To consider.

رَأْيٌ ج آرَاءٌ Opinion; view.

رَايَةٌ Military banner.

رِيَاءٌ Hypocrisy.

رِئَةٌ ج رِئَاتٌ Lung.

ذَاتُ ٱلرِّئَةِ Inflammation of lung.

رُؤْيَا ج رُؤًى Dream, vision.

رُؤْيَةٌ ج رُؤًى Act of seeing.

مِرْآةٌ ج مَرَايَا	Mirror.
مُرَاءٍ	Hypocrite.
مُرَاءَاة	Hypocrisy.
رَبٌّ ج أَرْبَابٌ	Lord, master.
أَلرَّبُّ	The Lord.
رُبٌّ ج رِبَابٌ	Syrup.
رُبَّ وَرُبَّمَا	Often. Seldom.
رَبَّانِيٌّ	Divine. Rabbi.
رَبَابٌ	A kind of violoncello.
رُبَّانٌ	Captain of ship; chief.
رَبِحَ يَرْبَحُ رِبْحًا	To gain.
رَبَّحَ	To cause one to gain.
رِبْحٌ ج أَرْبَاحٌ	Profit, gain.
رِيبَاسٌ	A kind of sorrel (plant).
تَرَبَّصَ	To wait, expect.
رُوبَاصٌ	Pure, refined, (silver).
رَبَضَ يَرْبِضُ	To lie in wait.
رَبَضٌ ج أَرْبَاضٌ	Suburb.
مَرْبِضٌ ج مَرَابِضُ	Enclosure.
رَبَطَ يَرْبُطُ	To tie, bind, fasten.
تَرَابَطَ	To agree upon.
إِرْتَبَطَ	To be tied.
رَبْطَةٌ ج رَبْطَاتٌ	Bundle, parcel.
رَابِطُ ٱلدَّرْبِ	Highway-robber.
رِبَاطٌ ج رُبُطٌ	Bond, rope.
رَابِطَةٌ	Connective, copula.
مَرْبَطٌ ج مَرَابِطُ	Stable.
مِرْبَطٌ	Cord, rope; halter.
رَبَعَ بِ	Pasture freely in.
رَبَّعَ	To square.
تَرَبَّعَ	To sit cross-legged.
رُبْعٌ ج ارْبَاعٌ	Fourth part.
رَبْعَةٌ	Medium in stature.
رَابِعٌ رَابِعَةٌ	Fourth.
رُبَاعِيٌّ	Quadrilateral.
رَبِيعٌ	Spring-time.
رَبِيعُ ٱلأَوَّلُ	The third month of the Mohammedan year.

The fourth month.	رَبِيعُ ٱلآخِرُ
Four.	أَرْبَعَةٌ م أَرْبَعُ
Quadrupeds.	ذَوَاتُ ٱلأَرْبَعِ
Wednesday.	ٱلأَرْبَعَاءُ
Forty.	أَرْبَعُونَ
Square form or number.	مُرَبَّعٌ
Of medium stature.	مَرْبُوعٌ
Jerboa.	يَرْبُوعٌ ج يَرَابِيعُ
To entangle, bind.	رَبَقَ يَرْبُقُ رَبْقًا
Loop, noose.	رِبْقٌ وَرِبْقَةٌ
To mix, confuse.	رَبَكَ يَرْبُكُ
To be entangled.	رَبِكَ وَٱرْتَبَكَ
Confused, entangled.	مُرْتَبِكٌ
Captain of a ship.	رُبَّانٌ
To increase ; grow.	رَبَا يَرْبُو
To nourish ; train up.	رَبَّى
To take usury.	رَابَى مُرَابَاةً
To increase *v. t.*	أَرْبَى
To be brought up.	تَرَبَّى
Usury, interest.	رِبًا وَرِبَاءٌ
Asthma, panting.	رَبْوٌ
Hill, height.	رَبْوَةٌ ج رُبًى
Ten thousand.	رَبْوَةٌ ج رَبَوَاتٌ
Hill, height.	رَابِيَةٌ ج رَوَابٍ
Education, training.	تَرْبِيَةٌ
Groin.	ارْبِيَةٌ
Usurer.	مُرَابٍ
Educator, trainer.	مُرَبٍّ
Educated, trained up.	مُرَبًّى
To set in order.	رَتَّبَ
To be arranged.	تَرَتَّبَ
To result from.	تَرَتَّبَ عَلَى
Rank, position.	رُتْبَةٌ ج رُتَبٌ
Salary, pension.	رَاتِبٌ
Arrangement, order.	تَرْتِيبٌ
Grade, rank.	مَرْتَبَةٌ ج مَرَاتِبُ
To live in abundance.	رَتَعَ يَرْتَعُ
To repair.	رَتَقَ يَرْتُقُ رَتْقًا

To sing.	رَتَلَ
Large spider.	رُتَيْلاَءُ ج رُتَيْلاَوَاتٌ
Singing, chanting.	تَرْتِيلٌ ج تَرَاتِيلُ
To be ragged.	رَثَّ يَرِثُّ
Worn out. Rags.	رَثٌّ
Squalor, raggedness.	رَثَاثَةٌ
To bewail (the dead).	رَثَى يَرْثِي
To sympathize with, pity.	رَثَى لِ
Elegy.	رِثَاءٌ
Elegy.	مَرْثِيَةٌ ومَرْثَاةٌ ج مَرَاثٍ
To move, shake.	رَجَّ يَرُجُّ
Agitation, trembling.	إرْتِجَاجٌ
To put off, defer.	أَرْجَأَ
The seventh month of the Moslem year.	رَجَبٌ
To over-weigh.	رَجَحَ يَرْجَحُ
To prefer.	رَجَّحَ عَلَى
To be more probable.	تَرَجَّحَ
Outweighing, preferable.	رَاجِحٌ
Preferable, more probable.	أَرْجَحُ
Swing.	أُرْجُوحَةٌ
Preference, probability.	تَرْجِيحٌ
A poetical metre.	رَجَزٌ
Poem of رَجَزَ metre.	ارْجُوزَةٌ
To defile one's self.	رَجَسَ يَرْجُسُ
Pollution.	رِجْسٌ ورَجَسٌ ورَجَاسَةٌ
Dirty, foul.	رَجِسٌ
To return.	رَجَعَ يَرْجِعُ
To have recourse to.	رجعَ إلى
To renounce.	رَجَعَ عن
To restore.	رَجَّعَ
To review.	رَاجَعَ
To restore.	أَرْجَعَ
To reclaim.	إستَرْجَعَ
Return.	رُجُوعٌ
Review, repetition.	مُرَاجَعَةٌ
To quake, tremble.	رَجَفَ يَرْجُفُ
To shake, agitate.	أَرْجَفَ
To tremble.	إرْتَجَفَ

To hope, expect.	رَجَا يَرْجُو
To hope for.	تَرَجَّى وَٱرْتَجَى
To beg, entreat.	تَرَجَّى
To put off, defer.	أَرْجَى
Hope.	رَجَاءٌ
To be spacious (place).	رَحِبَ يَرْحَبُ
To make wide.	رَحَّبَ وَأَرْحَبَ
To welcome.	رَحَّبَ وَتَرَحَّبَ بِ
Ample, spacious.	رَحْبٌ وَرَحِيبٌ
Welcome.	تَرْحَابٌ
Welcome !	مَرْحَبًا بِكَ
wash.	رَحَضَ يَرْحَضُ
Wash-tub, water, closet.	مِرْحَاضٌ ج مَرَاحِيضُ
Choice wine.	رُحَاقٌ وَرَحِيقٌ
To depart, migrate.	رَحَلَ يَرْحَلُ وَٱرْتَحَلَ
Pack-saddle.	رَحْلٌ ج رِحَالٌ
Journey.	رِحْلَةٌ وَٱرْتِحَالٌ
Migration.	رَحِيلٌ وَٱرْتِحَالٌ
Traveller.	رَاحِلٌ ج رُحَّلٌ
Trembling, shaking.	رَجْفَةٌ
Seditious rumours.	أَرَاجِيفُ
To go on foot.	رَجَلَ يَرْجُلُ
To dismount.	تَرَجَّلَ
To speak extempore.	إِرْتَجَلَ
Foot, leg.	رِجْلٌ ج أَرْجُلٌ
A man.	رَجُلٌ ج رِجَالٌ
Pedestrain.	رَجِلٌ وَرَاجِلٌ
Manliness ; virility.	رُجُولِيَّةٌ
Extemporizing.	إِرْتِجَالٌ
Caldron.	مِرْجَلٌ ج مَرَاجِلُ
Improvised (speech).	مُرْتَجَلٌ
To stone ; kill.	رَجَمَ يَرْجُمُ
To guess.	رَجَمَ بِٱلْغَيْبِ
To be heaped up.	إِرْتَجَمَ
Heap of stones.	رَجَمٌ ج رِجَامٌ
Tomb-stone.	رُجْمَةٌ ج رُجَمٌ
Stoned, killed. Cursed.	رَجِيمٌ
Coral.	مَرْجَانٌ

رَحَّالٌ وَرَحَّالَةٌ	Great traveller.
مَرْحَلَةٌ ج مَرَاحِلُ	Day's journey.
رَحِمَ يَرْحَمُ	To pity, to be merciful.
تَرَحَّمَ عَلَى	To have, or pray for, pity for one.
إِسْتَرْحَمَ	To implore pity.
رَحِمٌ ج أَرْحَامٌ	Uterus, womb.
رَحْمَةٌ	Pity, compassion.
رَحِيمٌ ج رُحَمَاءُ	Compassion.
الرَّحْمَانُ ٱلرَّحِيمُ	The Merciful.
مَرْحَمَةٌ ج مَرَاحِمُ	Act of mercy.
مَرْحُومٌ	Deceased (person).
رَحًى ج أَرْحَاءٌ	Mill-stone.
رخ	A fabulons bird.
رَخْتٌ ج رُخُوتٌ	Saddle.
رَخُصَ يَرْخُصُ	To be cheap.
رَخُصَ رَخَاصَةً	To be soft, supple.
رَخَّصَ	To lower the price.
رَخَّصَ لِ	To allow, permit.
إِسْتَرْخَصَ	To consider a thing cheap. To ask leave.
رَخْصٌ م رَخْصَةٌ	Soft, tender.
رُخْصٌ	Cheapness of price.
رَخِيصٌ	Cheap. Soft, tender.
رَخَّمَ يَرْخُمُ	To be soft (voice).
رُخَامٌ	Marble.
رَخِيمٌ وَرَخَمٌ	Soft (voice).
تَرْخِيمٌ	Elision of last letter of a word.
رَخِيَ يَرْخَى	To be soft, flaccid.
أَرْخَى	To loosen, let down.
تَرَاخَى	To flag, be slow.
إِرْتَخَى وَاسْتَرْخَى	To become lax.
رَخَاءٌ	Relaxation ; abundance.
رَخْوٌ	Lax, soft, loose.
رَخَاوَةٌ	Softness, slackness.
رَخِيُّ ٱلْبَالِ	Free from care.
إِرْتِخَاءٌ وَٱسْتِرْخَاءٌ	Relaxation.
رَدَّ يَرُدُّ	To return, send back, turn away. Refer.
رَدَّدَ	To ponder ; repeat.
تَرَدَّدَ إِلَى	To frequent (a place).

To waver ; hesitate.	تَرَدَّدَ فِي
To go back, retreat, revert.	إِرْتَدَّ
To be converted to.	ارْتَدَّ إِلَى
To depart from.	إِرْتَدَّ عَنْ
To reclaim ; revoke.	اسْتَرَدَّ
Repulse. Return. Reply.	رَدٌّ
Conversion to.	إِرْتِدَادٌ إِلَى
Apostasy.	إِرْتِدَادٌ عَنْ
Reclamation, recovery.	اسْتِرْدَادٌ
Frequenting. Wavering.	تَرَدُّدٌ
Setting aside, repelling.	مَرَدٌّ
Convert ; apostate.	مُرْتَدٌّ
Vacillating, hesitating.	مُتَرَدِّدٌ
Rejected ; refuted.	مَرْدُودٌ
Divorced woman.	مَرْدُودَةٌ
Evil, malice.	رَدَاءَةٌ وَرَدَاوَةٌ
Bad, wicked.	رَدِيءٌ ج أَرْدِيَاء
Worse, more wicked.	أَرْدَأ
Corn measure.	أَرْدَبٌّ

Restrain, prevent.	رَدَعَ يرْدَعُ عَنْ
To be restrained.	إِرْتَدَعَ عَنْ
To follow.	رَدَفَ يرْدُفُ
To be synonymous, (words).	تَرَادَفَ
The reserves, (soldiers).	رَدِيفٌ
Synonymous (words).	مُتَرَادِفٌ
To stop, fill up.	رَدَمَ يَرْدِمُ
To be stopped up.	إِرْتَدَمَ
Ruins of a wall, debris.	رَدْمٌ
To spin. Purr (cat).	رَدَنَ يرْدِنُ
Sleeve.	رِدْنٌ ج أَرْدَانٌ
The Jordan.	الأرْدُنّ
Spindle.	مِرْدَنٌ ج مَرَادِنُ
A large hall.	رَدْهَةٌ ج رِدَاه
To perish.	رَدِيَ يرْدَى رَدًى
To put on a mantle.	تَرَدَّى
Mantle, cloak.	رِدَاءٌ ج أَرْدِيَةٌ
Enveloped in a mantle.	مُتَرَدٍّ
To be mean, base.	رَذَلَ يَرْذُلُ

To reject.	رَذَلَ يَرْذُلُ رَذْلاً
Ignoble, base.	رَذِيلٌ ج رُذَلَاءُ
Vileness.	رَذَالَةٌ ج رَذَالَاتٌ
Vice.	رَذِيلَةٌ ج رذَائِلُ
Rice.	رُزٌّ (*for* أُرُزٌّ)
Iron peg.	رَزَّةٌ ج رَزَّاتٌ
To diminish. Afflict.	رَزَأَ يَرْزَأُ
Misfortune.	رَزِيئَةٌ ج رَزَايَا
Iron rod.	إِرْزَبَّةٌ وَمِرْزَبَةٌ
Satrap.	مَرْزُبَانٌ ج مَرَازِبَةٌ
To fall from fatigue.	رَزَحَ يَرْزَحُ
Extreme fatigue.	رُزُوحٌ
Fatigued, exhausted.	رَازِحٌ
District.	رُزْدَاقٌ ج رُزْدَاقَاتٌ
To grant, bestow.	رَزَقَ يَرْزُقُ
To receive means of life.	إِرْتَزَقَ
To seek means of life.	إِسْتَرْزَقَ
Means of living.	رِزْقٌ ج أَرْزَاقٌ
God.	اَلرَّازِقُ وَٱلرَّزَّاقُ
Blessed with worldly goods.	مَرْزُوقٌ
To wrap up a package.	رَزَمَ يَرْزُمُ
Package, bale.	رِزْمَةٌ ج رِزَمٌ
To be grave, dignified.	رَزَنَ يَرْزُنُ
Gravity, dignity.	رَزَانَةٌ
Weighty, grave, calm.	رَزِينٌ
Almanac.	رُزْنَامَةٌ
To settle down. (liquid).	رَسَبَ يَرْسُبُ
Sediment.	رُسُوبٌ وَرُسَابَةٌ
Theatre.	مَرْسَحٌ ج مَرَاسِحُ
To be firm, stable.	رَسَخَ يَرْسَخُ
Firm, stable.	رَاسِخٌ ج رَاسِخُونَ
Well instructed.	رَاسِخٌ فِي ٱلْعِلْمِ
The ankle, wrist.	رُسْغٌ ج أَرْسَاغٌ
To correspond about.	رَاسَلَ
To dismiss, send.	أَرْسَلَ
To hang loose, (hair).	إِسْتَرْسَلَ
Message, letter, epistle. Mission.	رِسَالَةٌ ج رَسَائِلُ
Messenger, apostle.	رَسُولٌ ج رُسُلٌ

One sent, missionary.	مُرْسَلٌ
Correspondent.	مُرَاسِلٌ
Correspondence.	مُرَاسَلَةٌ
To trace ; design.	رَسَمَ يَرْسُمُ عَلَى
To prescribe, enjoin.	رَسَمَ لِ
To ordain to a sacred office.	رَسَمَ رِسَامَةً
Trace ; sign. Tax.	رَسْمٌ ج رُسُومٌ
Official, authoritative.	رَسْمِيٌّ
Marked. Ordained.	مَرْسُومٌ
Halter.	رَسَنٌ ج أَرْسُنٌ وَأَرْسَانٌ
To be firm.	رَسَا يَرْسُو
To cast anchor.	أَرْسَى إِرْسَاءً
At anchor, (ship).	رَاسٍ
Port. Anchorage.	مَرْسًى ج مَرَاسٍ
Anchor.	مِرْسَاةٌ ج مَرَاسٍ
To sprinkle.	رَشَّ يَرُشُّ
Watering-pot.	مِرَشَّةٌ ج مِرَشَّاتٌ
To exude, ooze.	رَشَحَ يَرْشَحُ رَشْحاً
To train, bring up.	رَشَّحَ لِ
To be trained for.	تَرَاشَحَ لِ
Cold in the heat.	رَشْحٌ
Trained. Candidate.	مُرَشَّحٌ
To direct, guide.	أَرْشَدَ
To ask for guidance.	إِسْتَرْشَدَ
Rectitude. Maturity.	رُشْدٌ
Cress, pepperwort.	رَشَادٌ
Follower of right way.	رَاشِدٌ وَرَشِيدٌ
To sip. suck.	رَشَفَ يَرْشُفُ
To hurl (a weapon).	رَشَقَ يَرْشُقُ
Fine, elegant form.	رَشِيقٌ
Elegance of from.	رَشَاقَةٌ
Window.	رَوْشَنٌ ج رَوَاشِنُ
To bribe.	رَشَا يَرْشُو رَشْواً
To receive a bribe.	إِرْتَشَى
To ask for a bribe.	إِسْتَرْشَى
Bribe.	رَشْوَةٌ ج رُشًى
To press, squeeze.	رَصَّ يَرُصُّ
To overlay with lead.	رَصَّصَ

رَصَاصٌ Lead.

رَصَاصَةٌ Piece of lead ; bullet.

رَصَاصِيٌّ Lead-colour.

مَرْصُوصٌ Firm, compact.

رَصَدَ يَرْصُدُ To watch for.

رَصَدَ لِ To lie in wait for.

تَرَصَّدَ To observe, watch.

رَصْدٌ Watching, observation.

رَصِيدٌ Balance of account.

مَرْصَدٌ ج مَرَاصِدُ Observatory.

مِرْصَادٌ Highway, lurking-place.

رَصَّعَ To set with jewels

مُرَصَّعٌ Inlaid with gold-work.

رَصَفَ يَرْصُفُ رَصْفًا To pave.

رَصَافَةٌ Firmness, solidity.

رَصِيفٌ Firm. Paved road.

رَصُنَ يَرْصُنُ To be solid, grave.

رَصَانَةٌ Gravity, sedateness.

رَصِينٌ Firm, dignified, grave.

رَضَّ يَرُضُّ To pound, bruise.

تَرَضَّضَ وَٱرْتَضَّ To be bruised.

رَضٌّ وَرَضَّةٌ Bruise, contusion.

رُضَابٌ Saliva.

رَضَخَ يَرْضَخُ رَضْخًا لِ To submit.

رَضِعَ يَرْضَعُ To nurse (infant).

أَرْضَعَ To nurse, (mother).

رَضِيعٌ Infant at the breast.

إِرْضَاعٌ Act of nursing a child.

مُرْضِعَةٌ ج مُرْضِعَاتٌ Wet-nurse.

رَضِيَ يَرْضَى To be pleased.

رَضِيَ بِ To consent to.

رَاضَى To satisfy, conciliate.

أَرْضَى إِرْضَاءٌ To satisfy, please.

إِرْتَضَى To be content with.

رِضًى وَرِضْوَانٌ Satisfaction.

رَاضٍ ج رَاضُونَ Satisfied, content.

عِيشَةٌ رَاضِيَةٌ Comfortable life.

تَرَاضٍ Mutual agreement.

Satisfying, pleasing. مُرْضٍ

To be moist, damp. رَطِبَ يَرْطَبُ

To moisten; cool. رَطَّبَ

To be moistened. تَرَطَّبَ

Fresh, ripe dates. رُطَبٌ

Moisture; humidity. رُطُوبَةٌ

449.28 grammes. رَطْلٌ ج أَرطَالٌ

To stick in mire. إِرْتَطَمَ

The rabble, dregs of men. رَعَاعٌ

To frighten. رَعَبَ يَرْعَبُ

To terrify. رَعَبَ وَأَرْعَبَ

To be frightened. إِرْتَعَبَ

Fright, fear. رُعْبٌ وَرُعُبٌ

Causing fear. رَاعِبٌ وَمُرْعِبٌ

To thunder. رَعَدَ يَرْعُدُ

To tremble, be afraid. إِرْتَعَدَ

Thunder. رَعْدٌ ج رُعُودٌ

To tremble. رَعَشَ يَرْعَشُ وَآرْتَعَشَ

To cause to tremble. أَرْعَشَ

A trembling, shaking. رَعَشٌ

To bleed, (nose). رَعِفَ يَرْعَفُ

Bleeding from the nose. رُعَافٌ

Sun-stroke. رَعْنٌ

Stupidity رَعَنٌ وَرُعُونَةٌ

To graze; tend (cattle). Rule (subjects). Have regard to. رَعَى يَرْعَى

To have regard for. رَاعَى

To pasture, graze. إِرْتَعَى وَتَرَعَّى

Guarding; pasturing. رِعَايَةٌ

Subjects (of a ruler). رَعِيَّةٌ ج رَعَايَا

Shepherd. Pastor. رَاعٍ ج رُعَاةٌ

Pasturage, pasture. مَرْعًى ج مَرَاعٍ

Observed, regarded. مَرْعِيٌّ

Out of regard for. مُرَاعَاةً لِ

To desire, long for. رَغِبَ يَرْغَبُ فِي

To have no desire for, refrain from. رَغِبَ عَنْ

To implore, entreat. رَغِبَ إِلَى

To inspire with desire. رَغَّبَ

رَغْبَةٌ Strong desire, eagerness.
رَغِيبَةٌ ج رَغَائِبُ A desired object.
رَغْدٌ ورَغِيدٌ Comfortable, easy.
رَغِيفٌ ج أَرْغِفَةٌ Loaf (of bread).
أَرْغَمَ To humiliate, vex ; force.
رَغْماً عَنْهُ In spite of him.
رَغَا يَرْغُو To effervesce, froth.
رَغْوَةٌ Foam, froth, cream.
رَفَّ يَرِفُّ To shine ; flutter.
رَفٌّ ج رُفُوفٌ Flock. Shelf.
رَفَأَ يَرْفَأ To mend (a garment).
رَفَأَ بَيْن To make peace between.
رَفَاءٌ Peace, concord, accord.
مَرْفَأ Harbour for ships.
رَفَتَ يَرْفُتُ To refuse, reject.
رَفْتِيَّةٌ Permit (for goods).
رَفَخَ To rise, swell (dough).
رَفَدَ يَرْفِدُ To aid. Dress (a wound).
إِسْتَرْفَدَ To ask help.

رِفْدٌ ج أَرْفَادٌ Assistance.
رِفَادَةٌ Cushion ; bandage.
رَفْرَفَ To flap the wings.
رَفَسَ يَرْفِسُ To kick.
رَفْسَةٌ A kick.
رَفَشَ يَرْفُشُ رَفْشاً To shovel.
رَفْشٌ Winnowing-shovel.
رَفَضَ يَرْفُضُ To leave, reject.
إِرْفَضَّ To be separated, disperse.
رَافِضٌ ج رَفَضَةٌ One who rejects.
مُتَرَفِّضٌ A fanatic.
مَرْفُوضٌ Rejected.
رَفَعَ يَرْفَعُ To raise ; take away.
رَفُعَ يَرْفُعُ To be exalted.
رَفَعَ إِلَى To present to ; inform.
رَافَعَ إِلَى To cite before a judge.
تَرَافَعَ To bring a cause together before a judge.
إِرْتَفَعَ To rise high ; carried off.
رَفْعٌ Act of raising, elevating.

رِفْعَةٌ	High rank, dignity.
رَفِيعٌ	High, elevated.
إِرْتِفَاعٌ	Elevation, height.
مَرْفَعٌ ج مَرَافِعُ	Carnival.
مَرْفُوعٌ	Raised up. Carried off.
رَفِقَ يَرْفُقُ ب	To be gentle towards.
رَافَقَ	To accompany one.
تَرَفَّقَ ب	To treat with kindness.
تَرَافَقَ	To be companions.
رِفْقٌ	Kindness, compassion.
رِفْقَةٌ ج رُفَقٌ	Company.
رَفِيقٌ ج رُفَقَاءُ	Companion.
مِرْفَقٌ وَمَرْفِقٌ ج مَرَافِقُ	Elbow.
مُرْتَفَقٌ	Water-closet
رَفُهَ يَرْفُهُ	To live in luxury.
رَفَهَ يَرْفُهُ	To be comfortable, (life).
رَفَاهَةٌ وَرَفَاهِيَةٌ	Good living.
رَقَّ يَرِقُّ	To be thin, fine.
رَقَّ لَهُ	To pity one.
رَقَّ رِقًّا	To become a slave.
رَقَّقَ وَأَرَقَّ	To make thin, fine.
إِسْتَرَقَّ	To enslave.
رِقٌّ	Slavery.
رِقٌّ ج رُقُوقٌ	Parchment ; paper.
رِقَّةٌ	Fineness. Compassion.
رِقَّةُ ٱلْقَلْبِ	Tender-heartedness.
رُقَاقٌ ج رِقَاقٌ	Thin bread.
رَقِيقٌ ج رِقَاقٌ	Thin. Slave.
رَقِيقُ ٱلْحَالِ	Not rich.
رَقَبَ يَرْقُبُ	To watch, observe.
رَاقَبَ	To guard, keep. Observe.
تَرَقَّبَ	To expect, look for.
رَقَبَةٌ ج رِقَابٌ	Neck. Slave.
رَقِيبٌ ج رُقَبَاءُ	Guardian.
مَرْقَبٌ ج مَرَاقِبُ	Watch-tower.
مِرْقَبٌ	Telescope.
رَقَدَ يَرْقُدُ	To sleep.
أَرْقَدَ	To put to sleep.

رُقَاد Sleep.

مَرْقَدٌ ج مَرَاقِدُ Bed ; dormitory.

رَقَشَ يَرْقُشُ وَرَقَّشَ To variegate.

تَرَقَّشَ To be embellished.

أَرْقَشُ رَقْشَاءُ ج رُقْشٌ Variegated.

رَقَصَ يَرْقُصُ رَقْصاً To dance.

رَقَّصَ وَأَرْقَصَ To cause to dance.

رَقْصٌ Dancing, leaping.

رَقَّاصٌ Dancer. Pendulum.

تَرَقَّطَ To be spotted.

أَرْقَطُ م رَقْطَاءُ ج رُقْطٌ Spotted.

رَقَعَ يَرْقَعُ وَرَقَّعَ To patch.

رَقُعَ يَرْقُعُ رَقَاعَةً To be foolish.

رُقْعَةٌ ج رِقَاعٌ Patch scrap.

رَقَاعَةٌ Folly, stupidity.

رَقِيعٌ Firmament.

مُرَقَّعٌ Patched, mended.

رَقَمَ يَرْقُمُ رَقْماً To write.

رَقَّمَ وَرَقَمَ To mark with stripes.

رَقْمٌ ج أَرْقَامٌ Numerical sign.

الرَّقْمُ الْهِنْدِيُّ Indian numerals.

مَرْقُومٌ Written. Embroidered.

تَرْقُوَةٌ Clavicle. collar-bone.

رَقِيَ يَرْقَى To ascend, rise.

رَقَى يَرْقِي رُقْيَةً To use magic.

رَقَّى To raise high, elevate.

تَرَقَّى وَارْتَقَى فِي وَإِلى To rise high.

رُقْيَةٌ Magic, incantation.

رَاقٍ ج رُقَاةٌ Charmer, magician.

تَرَقٍّ وَارْتِقَاءٌ Rising, progress.

مَرْقًى وَمِرْقَاةٌ ج مَرَاقٍ Ladder, stairs.

رَكَّ يَرِكُّ رَكَاكَةً To be weak.

رَكَّ يَرُكُّ To make a foundation.

رَكَّةٌ Rubble used in masonry.

رَكِيكٌ ج رِكَاكٌ Weak.

مَرْكُوكٌ Pressed.

رَكِبَ يَرْكَبُ To ride ; embark.

رَكِبَ هَوَاهُ To follow one's fancy.

To brave danger. رَكِبَ ٱللَّيْلَ

To compose, mix. رَكَّبَ

To be constructed, mixed. تَرَكَّبَ

To commit a crime. إِرْتَكَبَ

Band of horsemen. رَكْبٌ

Knee. رُكْبَةٌ ج رُكَبٌ

Stirrup. رِكَابٌ ج رُكُبٌ

Rider. Passenger. رَاكِبٌ ج رُكَّابٌ

Composition, structure. تَرْكِيبٌ

Ship, vessel. مَرْكَبٌ ج مَرَاكِبُ

Carriage. مَرْكَبَةٌ

Shoes. مَرْكُوبٌ ج مَرَاكِيبُ

Compound. Joined. مُرَكَّبٌ

To be still, motionless. رَكَدَ يَرْكُدُ

Still, stagnant. رَاكِدٌ

To fix in (the ground). رَكَزَ يَرْكُزُ

Prop, buttress. رَكِيزَةٌ ج رَكَائِزُ

Centre. مَرْكَزٌ ج مَرَاكِزُ

To run. رَكَضَ يَرْكُضُ رَكْضًا

To vie with in running. رَاكَضَ

Good runner. رَكُوضٌ

To bow (in prayer); kneel. رَكَعَ يَرْكَعُ

To cause one to bow. رَكَّعَ وَأَرْكَعَ

Bowing in (prayer). رَكْعَةٌ ج رَكَعَاتٌ

To heap up. رَكَمَ يَرْكُمُ رَكْمًا

To be heaped up. تَرَاكَمَ وَٱرْتَكَمَ

Heap, pile. رَكْمٌ وَرُكَامٌ

To rely upon. رَكَنَ يَرْكُنُ إِلَى

To trust in. أَرْكَنَ إِلَى

To take to fight. أَرْكَنَ إِلَى ٱلْفِرَارِ

Support, prop. رُكْنٌ ج أَرْكَانٌ

The elements (of things). الأَرْكَانُ

Firmness; gravity. رُكُونَةٌ وَرَكَانَةٌ

To rely upon. تَرَكَّى وَٱرْتَكَى عَلَى

Small vessel. رَكْوَةٌ ج رَكَوَةٌ

Well. رَكِيَّةٌ ج رَكَايَا

To mend, restore. رَمَّ يَرُمُّ وَرَمَّمَ

To become decayed. رَمَّ وَأَرَمَّ

To be repaired by degrees.	تَرَمَّمَ
Altogether.	بِرُمَّتِهِ
Decayed bones.	رِمَّةٌ ج رِمَمٌ
Decayed (bone).	رَمِيمٌ
Lance, spear.	رُمْحٌ ج رِمَاحٌ
Lancer, spearman.	رَامِحٌ
To have sore eyes.	رَمِدَ يَرْمَدُ
Ophthalmia.	رَمَدٌ
Ashes.	رَمادٌ
Having ophthalmia.	رَمْدَانُ
Grey, ash-coloured.	رَمادِيٌّ
To indicate by a sign.	رَمَزَ يَرْمُزُ
To be intelligent.	رَمُزَ يَرْمُزُ رَمَازَةً
Sign. Allegory.	رَمْزٌ ج رُمُوزٌ
Model, specimen.	رَامُوزٌ ج رَوَامِيزُ
Alluded to.	مَرْمُوزٌ إِلَيْهِ
To conceal; bury.	رَمَسَ يَرْمُسُ
Tomb, grave.	رَمْسٌ ج رُمُوسٌ
Lupine (herb).	تُرْمُسٌ
To be very hot.	رَمِضَ يَرْمَضُ
Intense heat.	رَمْضَاءُ
The ninth month of the Moslem year.	رَمَضَانُ
To glance furtively.	رَمَقَ يَرْمُقُ
The last breath of life.	رَمَقٌ
To put sand into.	رَمَلَ
To become sandy.	أَرْمَلَ
To become a widow or widower.	أَرْمَلَ وَتَرَمَّلَ
Sand.	رَمْلٌ ج رِمَالٌ وَأَرْمَالٌ
Hour-glass.	سَاعَةٌ رَمْلِيَّةٌ
Widower; widow.	أَرْمَلٌ ج أَرْمَلَةٌ
Pomegranate.	رُمَّانٌ
The Armenians.	أَلأَرْمَنُ
Armenian.	أَرْمَنِيٌّ
To throw; hit; accuse.	رَمَى يَرْمِي
To be thrown.	إِرْتَمَى آرْتِمَاءً
Throw, hit.	رَمْيَةٌ ج رَمِيَاتٌ
Archer, slinger.	رَامٍ ج رُمَاةٌ
Sagittarius (of the Zodiac).	الرَّامِي

مِرْمىً ج مرَامٍ	Instrument for throwing (projectile, arrow).
مِرْماةٌ ج مرَام	Arrow, missile.
رَنَّ يرِن رَنِيناً	To twang, ring.
رنينٌ وَرَنَّةٌ	Sound, tone, echo.
أَرْنَبٌ ج أَرَانِبُ	Hare.
رنحَ	To make giddy, (wine).
ترنَّحَ	To stagger.
روْنقٌ	Lustre, brilliancy.
رنِمَ يرْنَمُ ورنّمَ وَترَنمَ	To sing.
ترْنيمةٌ	Poem. Hymn.
ترَنُّمٌ	Singing, psalmody.
رهبَ يرْهَبُ رُهْبَةً	To fear, dread.
رهَّبَ وَارْهبَ	To frighten.
ترَهَّبَ	To become a monk.
رُهْبَةٌ	Fear.
رَهْبَنَةٌ ورهبَانيةٌ	Monachism.
راهِبٌ ج رُهبَانٌ	Monk.
راهبَةٌ ج راهِبَاتٌ	Nun.
رَهِيبٌ	Fearful, awful.
رهجٌ	Dust. Excitement.
إِرْتهَطَ	To assemble, congregate.
رهْطٌ ج أَرْهُطٌ	Company of men.
رَهُفَ يرْهُفُ	To be thin, sharp.
رَهِيفٌ وَمرْهَفٌ	Thin, slender.
راهَقَ	To approach puberty.
مرَاهِقٌ	Boy at puberty.
مَرْهمٌ ج مَرَاهِمُ	Ointment.
رَهَنَ يَرْهنُ رهْناً	To be firm.
رَهْنَ عِنْدَ	To pledge with.
رَاهَنَ	To bet, lay a wager.
ترَاهَنَ	To bet together.
إِرْتَهَنَ	To receive a pledge.
إِسْترْهَنَ	To require a pledge.
رَهْنٌ ج رِهَانٌ	Pledge, mortgage.
رَاهِنٌ	Fixed, stable, durable.
رهينٌ وَمُرْتهَنٌ ومرْهُونٌ	Pledged.
رَهينَةٌ ج رَهَائِنُ	Pledge, security.

رهْوَانُ	Ambling-horse.
رَابَ يَرُوبُ	To curdle, (milk.)
رَائِبُ وَمَرَوَّبٌ	Curdled ; churned.
رَوْبَةٌ	Ferment of; milk.
رَاثَ يَرُوثُ رَوْثًا	To void excrement, (horse).
رَاجَ يَرُوجُ	To be current.
رَوَّجَ	To put in circulation.
رَوَاجٌ	Currency. Good market.
رَائِجٌ	Selling well. Current.
رَاحَ يَرُوحُ	To go, depart.
أَرَاحَ إِرَاحَةً	To give rest.
إِرْتَاحَ	To be pleased.
إِسْتَرَاحَ	To rest.
رَاحٌ	Wine. Mirth.
رَاحَةٌ	Rest ease, quietude.
رَاحَةٌ رَاحَاتٌ	Palm of the hand.
بَيْتُ ٱلرَّاحَةِ	Water-closet.
رُوحٌ ج أرْوَاحٌ	Breath, spirit.
رُوحُ ٱلْقُدُسِ	The Holy Spirit.
طَوِيلُ ٱلرُّوحِ	Long-suffering.
رُوحَانِيٌّ	Spiritual, incorporeal.
رِيحٌ ج رِيَاحٌ	Wind. Odour.
رِيحُ ٱلشَّوكَةِ	Whitlow.
رِيحَةٌ	Odour. Puff of wind.
رَيْحَانٌ ج رَيَاحِينُ	Myrtle.
رَائِحَة ج رَوَائِحُ	Odour.
أَرِيحِيٌّ	Generous, liberal.
مُرَاحٌ	Cattle-fold.
مِرْوَحٌ وَمِرْوَحَةٌ ج مَرَاوِحُ	Fan.
مُسْتَرَاحٌ	Water-closet.
رَادَ يَرُودُ	To ask for. Seek (food).
رَاوَدَ	To beguile, seduce ; entice.
أَرَادَ	To wish, desire.
أَرَادَ بِ	To mean, intend.
رُوَيْداً	Slowly, gently.
إِرَادَةٌ	Will ; volition.
إِرَادِي	Voluntary.
مُرَادٌ	Desired. Purpose · meaning.

رَوَّضَ	To train, discipline.
رَوْضٌ	Garden, flower-bed.
رَوْضَةٌ ج رِيَاضٌ	Meadow.
رِيَاضَةٌ	Exercise, training.
عِلْمُ ٱلرِّيَاضَاتِ	Mathematics.
رَاعَ يَرُوعُ وَٱرْتَاعَ	To fear.
رَاعَ وَرَوَّعَ وَأَرَاعَ	To frighten.
رَوْعٌ وَرَوْعَةٌ	Fear, fright.
رَاغَ يَرُوغُ رَوْغًا	To act slyly.
رَاوَغَ	To employ a ruse.
مُرَاوَغَةٌ	Ruse, trick.
رَاقَ يَرُوقُ	To be clear, limpid.
رَوَّقَ	To render clear, clarify.
أَرَاقَ	To pour out or forth.
ٱتْرَوَّقَ	To breakfast.
رِوَاقٌ ج أَرْوِقَةٌ	Tent, portico.
رَائِقٌ	Clear, limpid, pure.
رَامَ يَرُومُ	To desire strongly.
رُومٌ ج أَرْوَامٌ	Roman. Greek.

بَحْرُ ٱلرُّومِ	Mediterranean Sea.
رُومِيَّةٌ ج رَوَامِيُّ	Rafter.
مَرَامٌ	Desire, purpose.
رِوَنْدٌ وَرَاوَنْدٌ	Rhubarb.
رَوَى يَرْوِي رِوَايَةً	To report, quote.
رَوِيَ يَرْوَى	To quench one's thirst.
تَرَوَّى	To consider attentively.
أَرْوَى إِرْوَاءً	To quench thirst.
رِوَايَةٌ	Narration, tale.
رَاوٍ ج رُوَاةٌ وَرَاوُونَ	Narrator.
رِيٌّ	Rain ; irrigation.
رَيَّانٌ	Well watered.
مَرْوِيٌّ	Well watered. Cited.
رَابَ يَرِيبُ	To make doubtful.
أَرَابَ	To trouble, disquiet.
إِرْتَابَ	To have doubts.
رَيْبٌ وَرَيْبَةٌ ج رِيَبٌ	Doubt.
ٱرْتِيَابٌ	Doubt, hesitation.
مُرِيبٌ	Causing, doubt.

رَيْثَمَا	As long as ; while.
رِيشٌ ج رِيَاش	Feathers.
رِيشَةٌ	A feather.
رِيَاشٌ	Furniture, goods.
رَيْعَانٌ	The best part.
رِيفٌ ج أَرْيَافٌ	A fertile land along the banks of a river.
رِيفُ الْبَحْرِ	Sea-coast.
رَاقَ يَرِيقُ	To pour out.
أَرَاقَ	To pour out a liquid.
رِيقٌ	Saliva.
على الرِّيقِ	Before breakfast.
رَالَ يَرِيلُ رَيلاً	To droll (child).
رِيَالٌ	Saliva. Dollar.
رِيمٌ	White gazelle or antelope.
رَايَة ج رَايَاتٌ	Flag ; standard.

ز

ز	As a numeral sign=7.
زِئْبِرٌ وَزُئْبُرٌ	Nap of cloth.
زِئْبَقٌ	Mercury, quicksilver.
زَأَرَ يَزْأَرُ وَزَئِرَ	To roar (lion).
زَائِرٌ	Roaring ; angry ; enemy.
زُوَانٌ	Tares, (seed and plant).
زَبَبٌ	Hairiness, Down.
زَبِيبٌ	Raisins, dried figs.
أَزَبُّ م زَبَّاء	Hairy.
عامٌ أَزَبُّ	Fertile year.
زَبَدَ يَزْبُدُ	To churn (butter).
زَبَدَ وَأَزْبَدَ	To foam, froth.
زَبَدٌ	Foam, froth.
زُبْدٌ وَزُبْدَةٌ	Butter.

Cream.	زُبْدَةٌ
A kind of perfume; civet.	زَبَادٌ
Foaming. Enraged.	مُزْبِدٌ
Psalms of David.	زَبُورٌ ج زُبُرٌ
Powerful man.	زِبِّيرٌ
Chrysolite.	زَبَرْجَدٌ
A whirlwind.	زَوْبَعَةٌ ج زَوَابِعُ
To manure.	زَبَلَ يَزْبِلُ وَزَبَّلَ
Manure.	زِبْلٌ وَزِبْلَةٌ
Dirt; sweepings.	زُبَالَةٌ
Manure-gatherer.	زَبَّالٌ
Basket, pannier.	زِنْبِيلٌ ج زَنَابِيلُ
Dung-hill.	مَزْبَلَةٌ ج مَزَابِلُ
Customer.	زَبُونٌ ج زَبَائِنُ
To thrust with a lance.	زَجَّ يَزُجُّ زَجًّا
Point of a spear.	زُجٌّ ج زِجَاجٌ
Glass; glass vessels.	زُجَاجٌ
Piece, or cup, of glass.	زُجَاجَةٌ
Glass-manufacturer	زَجَّاجٌ
Glass-merchant.	زُجَاجِيٌّ
Having long eyebrows.	أَزَجُّ م زَجَّاءُ
To forbid. Rebuke.	زَجَرَ يَزْجُرُ
To be forbidden.	إِنْزَجَرَ
Play. Uproar.	زَجَلٌ
Carrier-pigeons.	حَمَامُ ٱلزَّاجِلِ
To remove a thing.	زَحَّ يَزُحُّ
To strain in breathing.	زَحَرَ يَزْحِرُ
Straining. Dysentery.	زَحِيرٌ
To remove a thing.	زَحْزَحَ عَنْ
To march. Creep.	زَحَفَ يَزْحَفُ
Marching. An army.	زَحْفٌ
Reptiles.	ٱلزَّحَافَةُ وَٱلزَّحَّافَاتُ
To depart; retire.	زَحَلَ يَزْحَلُ عَنْ
To move a thing.	زَحَّلَ وَأَزْحَلَ
The planet Saturn.	زُحَلُ
To crowd; press.	زَحَمَ يَزْحَمُ وَزَاحَمَ
To be crowded.	تَزَاحَمَ وَٱزْدَحَمَ
Pressure; throng.	زَحْمَةٌ وَزِحَامٌ

زَاخِرٌ — Full ; copious.

زَخِيرَةٌ ج زَخَائِرُ — Munitions of war.

زَخْرَفَ زَخْرَفَةً — To adorn.

زُخْرُفٌ ج زَخَارِفُ — Vain show.

مُزَخْرَفٌ — Adorned with tinsel.

زَخْمَةٌ — Whip of thong. Strap.

زَرَّ يَزُرُّ زَرًّا وَزَرَّرَ — To button.

زِرٌّ ج أَزْرَارٌ — Button. Knob.

زَرَبَ يَزْرُبُ — To make a sheep-fold.

زَرِبَ يَزْرَبُ زَرَبًا — To flow ; leak.

زِرَابَةٌ — Payment for stabling.

زَرِيبَةٌ ج زَرَائِبُ — Flod for cattle ; lurking place.

زَارُوبٌ ج زَوَارِيبُ — Narrow street.

مِزْرَابٌ ج مَزَارِيبُ — Water-course.

زَرِدَ يَزْرَدُ وَازْدَرَدَ — To swallow.

زَرَدٌ ج زُرُودٌ — Coat of mail.

زَرَدَةٌ — Ring, or link of a chain.

زُرْدِى — A kind of pudding.

زُرْزُورٌ ج زَرَازِيرُ — Starling.

زَرَعَ يَزْرَعُ — To sow ; plant.

زَارَعَ مُزَارَعة — To sow in shares.

زَرْعٌ ج زُرُوعٌ — Seed. Off-spring.

زَارِعٌ ج زُرَّاعٌ — Husbandman.

زِرَاعَةٌ — Seed. Agriculture.

مَزْرَعَة ج مَزَارِعُ — Plantation.

زَرَافَةٌ ج زَرَافى — Giraffe.

زَرَقَ يَزْرُقُ — To thrust ; dung, (bird).

إِزْرَقَّ آزْرِقَاقًا — To become blue.

زُرْقَةٌ — Blue (colour).

أَلزَرْقَاء — Sky ; heavens.

زُرَيْقٌ — A black singing bird.

زُرَيْقَاءُ — A kind of bread-salad.

أَزْرَقُ م زَرْقَاءُ ج زُرْق — Blue.

عَدُوٌّ ازْرَقُ — Bitter enemy.

مِزْرَاقٌ ج مَزَارِيقُ — Short spear.

زَرَكَ يَزْرُكُ — To press, vex.

زَرْكَةٌ — Crowd, throng.

زَرْكَشَ — To embroider.

Brocade of silk.	زَرْكَشٌ
Arsenic.	زِرْنِيخٌ
To reproach.	زَرَى يَزْرِي عَلَى
To despise.	ازْدَرَى إِزْدِرَاءً ب
Contemptible.	زَرِيٌّ
Despiser.	مزْدَرٍ
To cheat by tricks.	زَعْبَرَ زَعْبَرَةً
Juggler.	مزَعْبِرٌ
Thyme. (see صَعْتَرٌ)	زَعْتَرٌ
To disturb.	زَعَجَ يَزْعَجُ وَأَزْعَجَ
To be troubled.	إِنْزَعَجَ
Agitation ; trouble.	زَعَجٌ وَانْزِعَاجٌ
Medlar (tree and fruit).	زُعْرُورٌ
Thin haired. Thief.	ازْعَرُ ج زُعْرَانٌ
To shake ; move.	زَعْزَعَ
To be shaken ; moved.	تَزَعْزَعَ
Violent wind.	زَعْزَعٌ ج زَعَازِعُ
Inconstant ; unstable.	مُتَزَعْزِعٌ
Quick in killing.	زُعَافٌ
Saffron.	زَعْفَرَانٌ
To cry out, shout.	زَعَقَ يَزْعَقُ
To frighten.	زَعَقَ ب وَأَزْعَقَ
Thunderbolt. (see صَاعِقَةٌ)	زَاعِقَةٌ
To be angry ; bored.	زَعِلَ يَزْعَلُ
Angry, bored.	زَعْلَانُ
To assert.	زَعَمَ يَزْعَمُ زَعْماً
Assertion.	زُعْمٌ وَزَعْمَةٌ
Honour. Authority.	زَعَامَةٌ
Chief. Spokesman.	زَعِيمٌ
Fin.	زِعْنِفَةٌ ج زَعَانِفُ
Down ; fine hair, feathers.	زَغَبٌ
Nap of cloth.	زِغْبِرٌ وَزَغْبَرٌ
To adulterate.	زَغَلَ يَزْغَلُ زَغْلاً
Young pigeon.	زُغْلُولٌ ج زَغَالِيلُ
To lead a bride home.	زَفَّ يَزِفُّ
Procession of joy.	زِفَّةٌ
To cover with pitch.	زَفَتَ
Pitch.	زِفْتٌ

مزفّتٌ	Covered with pitch.
زفر يزفِر	To expire breath.
زفرةٌ ج زفرَاتٌ	Deep sigh.
زفيرٌ	Expiration. Deep sigh.
زيزَفونٌ	Oleaster.
زِقٌّ ج زقاقٌ	Water-skin.
زُقاقٌ ج ازِقةٌ	Street, lane.
زكيبةٌ	A sack made of hair.
زُكرةٌ ج زُكَرٌ	A wine-skin.
زكزكَ	To tickle.
زكِمَ	To have a cold in the head.
زُكامٌ وزكمةٌ	A cold in the head ; catarrh.
زكَنَ يزكَنُ	To consider.
زكا يزكو	To be pure.
زكّى	To give alms. Justify.
تَزَكّى	To be justified.
زكوة (زكاةٌ) ج زكا	Alms.
زكِيٌّ ج أزكياء	Pure ; just.
زلَّ يزِلُّ زلاًّ	To stumble ; slip.
زَلَلٌ	A slip ; fault.
زلّةٌ ج زَلات	A fault, fall.
زُلالٌ	Clear, pure, cool (water). (White of an egg).
(زلحفةٌ زلاحفُ)	Tortoise.
زَلْزَلَ زلزلةً وزُلْزالاً	To shake.
زَلْزَلَةٌ ج زلازلُ	Earth-quake.
(تَزلطَ)	To strip one's self.
زَلْعومٌ ج زَلاعِيمُ	Throat.
زلّفَ	To exaggerate.
أَزْلفَ	To bring near.
زُلْفةٌ وزُلْفى	Nearness.
زلَقَ يزْلقُ زَلقاً	To slip, glide.
زَلَقٌ ومَزْلَقَةٌ	Slippery (place).
زَلقُ الامْعاء	Diarrhœa.
زليْقٌ	A kind of fish.
زلَمٌ ج أَزْلامٌ	Arrow for devining.
(زَلَمةٌ ج زلْمٌ)	Man. Footman.
زمَّ يزُمُّ زما	To tighten. Strap.
زمَامٌ ج ازمةٌ	Halter. Shoe-strap.

زمجر زمجرة	To shout ; roar.
زمَّر يزمّر	To play on a reed.
زمرٌ ج زمورٌ	Musical reed.
زمرةٌ ج زمرٌ	Group ; party.
زمّارٌ	A piper.
زمارةٌ ومزمارٌ ج مزاميرُ	A pipe.
لسانُ المزمار	Epiglottis.
مزمورٌ ج مزاميرُ	Psalm.
زمرّدٌ	Emerald.
أزمع	To be about to happen.
مزمعٌ	About to happen.
زاملةٌ ج زواملُ	Beast of burden.
زميلٌ ج زملاء	Comrade ; companion.
إزميلٌ ج أزاميل	Chisel.
أزمن	To continue a long time.
زمنٌ وزمانٌ ج أزمنة	Time.
زمنيٌّ	Temporal ; transient.
مزمنٌ (مرضٌ)	Chronic disease.
زمهر وازمهرّ	To be inflamed.
زمهريرٌ	Intense cold.
تزنبر على	To scorn ; frown.
زنبورٌ ج زنابيرُ	Wasp ; hornet.
زنبركٌ	Spring of a watch.
زنبقٌ	Lily. Iris, (flower and plant).
زنجٌ ج زنوجٌ	The black races.
زنجيٌّ	A black ; negro.
زنجبيلٌ	Ginger.
زنجر	To bind with a chain.
زنجارٌ	Verdigris.
زنجيرٌ (جنزيرٌ) ج زناجير	Chain.
حسابُ الزنجير	Book-keeping.
زنجفرٌ وزنجفر	Cinnabar.
زنخ يزنخ	To become rancid.
زندٌ ج زنادٌ	Ulna (bone).
زنادٌ	Steel for atriking fire.
تزندق	To disbelive religion.
زنديقٌ ج زنادقة	Unbeliever.
تزنّر	To gird one's self.

Girdle. زُنَّارٌ ج زَنَانِيرُ

Melia (tree). زَنْزَلَخْتٌ (أَزْدَرَخْتٌ)

Necklace. Shackle. زِنَاقٌ

To commit adultery. زَنَى يَزْنِي

Adulterer. زَانٍ ج زُنَاةٌ

Munition. (زَهْبٌ وزُهْبَةٌ)

To renounce. (فِي وعَنْ) زَهَدَ يَزْهَدُ

To become an ascetic. تَزَهَّدَ

Indifference. زُهْدٌ

Ascetic ; indifferent. زَاهِدٌ ج زُهَّادٌ

Little. Insignificant. زَهِيدٌ

To shine. زَهَرَ يَزْهَرُ زُهُوراً

To blossom ; flourish. أَزْهَرَ

Flower. زَهْرَةٌ ج أَزْهَارٌ

Dice. زَهْرُ ٱلنَّرْدِ

The planet Venus. أَلزُّهَرَةُ

A Mosque in Cairo. أَلْجَامِعُ ٱلازْهَرُ

A graduate of الأَزْهَر أَزْهَرِيٌّ

In blossom ; flourishing. مُزْهِرٌ

Lute. Timbrel. مِزْهَرٌ ج مَزَاهِرُ

To vanish. زَهَقَ يَزْهَقُ زُهُوقاً

To blossom. زَهَا يَزْهُو زَهْواً وازْهَى

Pomp of this world. زَهَا ٱلدُّنْيَا

Quantity ; number. زُهَاءٌ

About a hundred. زُهَاءَ مِئَةٍ

Beautiful ; bright. زَاهٍ

To give in marriage. زَوَّجَ

To marry a woman. تَزَوَّجَ

Copperas ; vitriol. زَاجٌ

Husband. Pair. زَوْجٌ ج أَزْوَاجٌ

Pair, couple. زَوْجَانِ

Wife. زَوْجَةٌ ج زَوجَاتٌ

Marriage. زَوَاجٌ وَزِيجَةٌ

Married. مُزَوَّجٌ ومُتَزَوِّجٌ

Double ; doubled. مُزْدَوِجٌ

To leave its place. زَاحَ يَزُوحُ

To move from its place. أَزَاحَ

To provide food for journey. زَوَّدَ

To take provisions. تَزَوَّدَ

Food for the journey. زَادٌ

Sack for food. مِزْوَدٌ ج مَزَاوِدُ

Water-skin. مَزَادٌ ج مَزَاوِدُ

To visit. زَارَ يَزُورُ زِيَارَةً وَمَزَاراً

To falsify ; forge. زَوَّرَ

Falsehood. زُورٌ

Visitor. Pilgrim. زَائِرٌ ج زُوَّارٌ

Baghdad. اَلزَّوْرَاءُ

Visit. Pilgrimage. زِيَارَة

Crooked. ازْوَرَ

Falsification ; forgery. تَزْوِيرٌ

Shrine. مَزَارٌ ج مَزَارَاتٌ

Falsifier ; counterfeiter. مُزَوِّرٌ

Falsified ; conterfeited. مُزَوَّرٌ

Small boat. زَوْرَقٌ ج زَوَارِق

To deviate. زَاغَ يَزُوغُ زَوْغاً

Hyssop (plant). زُوفَاءُ وَزُوفى

To embellish. زَوَّقَ تَزْوِيقاً

Embellished, decorated. مُزَوَّقٌ

To pass away ; cease. زَالَ يَزُولُ

To continue. مَا زَالَ وَلَا يَزَالُ

To remove. زَوَّلَ وَأَزَالَ

To strive, prevail. زَاوَلَ مُزَاوَلَةً

Disappearance. Cessation. زَوَالٌ

Vanishing ; transient. زَائِلٌ

Juice. زُومٌ

To be apart ; removed. إِنْزَوَى

Tares. زُوَانٌ

Angle, corner. زَاوِيَةٌ ج زَوَايَا

Acute angle. زَاوِيَةٌ حَادَّةٌ

Obtuse angle. زَاوِيَةٌ مُنْفَرِجَة

Right anlge. زَاوِيَةٌ قَائِمَةٌ

Quicksilver. زِيبَق وزِئْبَق

To oil. زَيَّتَ

Oil. زَيْتٌ ج زُيُوت

Olive (tree and fruit). زَيْتُونٌ

Olive-coloured. زَيْتُونِيٌّ

Astronomical tables. Plumb-line.	زِيجٌ
To depart ; deviate.	زَاحَ يَزِيحُ
To move away ; remove.	أَزَاحَ
Line.	زِيحٌ ج أَزْيَاحٌ
To increase, (*v. t. & i.*)	زَادَ يَزِيد
To exceed.	زَادَ عَنْ وعَلَى
To bid higher.	زَايَدَ
To increase gradually.	تَزَايدَ
To be increased.	إِزْدَادَ
An increase.	زِيَادَةٌ ج زِيَادَاتٌ
In excess ; superfluous.	زَائِدٌ
More ; more abundant.	أَزْيَدُ
Auction.	مَزَادٌ ج مَزَادَاتٌ
Increased.	مَزِيدٌ ج مَزِيدَاتٌ
Large water-jar.	زِيرٌ ج أَزْيَارٌ
A kind of cricket.	زِيرٌ
To deviate.	زَاغَ يَزِيغُ زَيغَانًا وزِيغًا
To cause to deviate.	أَزَاغَ
A kind of crow.	زَاغٌ ج زِيغَانٌ
To be counterfeit.	زَافَ يَزِيفُ
To counterfeit money.	زَيَّفَ
Counterfeit.	زَائِفٌ ج زُيُوفٌ
To adorn.	زَانَ يَزِينُ وَزَيَّنَ
To be adorned.	تَزَيَّنَ تَزَيُّنًا وَازْدَانَ
Ornament ; finery.	زِينَةٌ ج زِيَنٌ
Barber ; hair-dresser.	مُزَيِّنٌ
To assume the costume, or habits of others.	تزيا
Form. Costume.	زِيٌّ ج أَزْيَاء

س

As a numeral sign=60.	س
Remaining ; the rest ; all.	سَائِرٌ
To ask; request.	سَأَلَ يَسْأَلُ
To beg (alms).	تَسَآلَ وَتَسَوَّلَ
Question, request.	سُؤَالٌ
Questioner. Beggar.	سَائِلٌ
Question; request.	مَسْأَلَةٌ ج مَسَائِلُ
Questioned. Responsible.	مَسْؤُولٌ
Responsibility.	مَسْؤُولِيَّةٌ
To loathe.	سَئِمَ يَسْأَمُ مِن
To revile, defame.	سَبَّ يَسِبُّ
To cause, occasion.	سَبَّبَ
To be caused.	تَسَبَّبَ
To live by.	تَسَبَّبَ بِ
Abuse, invective.	سَبٌّ
Cause, reason ; means ; means of living.	سَبَبٌ ج أَسْبَابٌ
Causality.	سببية
Forefinger, index.	سَبَّابَةٌ
Caused.	مُسَبَّبٌ وَمُتَسَبَّبٌ عَنْ
Trader.	مُتَسَبِّبٌ
Sabbath. Saturday.	سَبْتٌ ج سُبُوتٌ
Heavy sleep, lethargy.	سُبَاتٌ
To swim, float.	سَبَحَ يَسْبَحُ سِبَاحَةً
To praise, magnify God.	سَبَّحَ
Praise be to God !	سُبْحَانَ ٱللهِ
Rosary.	سُبْحَةٌ ج سُبَحٌ وَسُبُحَاتٌ
Swimming floating.	سِبَاحَةٌ
Ships. Stars.	سَابِحَاتٌ
Fleet horses	سَوَابِحُ

تَسْبِحَةٌ ج تَسَابِيحُ	Hymn.
تَسْبِيح	Act of praising God.
مِسْبَحَةٌ ج مَسَابِحُ	Rosary.
سَبِخٌ	Salty, marshy (sod).
سَبْخَةٌ ج سِبَاخٌ	Salty, marsh.
سَبَرَ يسْبُرُ	To probe. Try, test.
سَبْرٌ	Probing, sounding.
مِسْبَرٌ ج مَسَابِرُ	Surgeon's probe.
سبطٌ ج أَسْبَاطٌ	Tribe Jewish).
شُبَاطُ	February (month).
سَبَّعَ	To make (in) seven.
أَسْبَعَ	To become seven.
سَبْعةٌ م سَبْعٌ	Seven.
سُبْعٌ ج اسْبَاعٌ	Seventh part.
سَبُعٌ ج سِبَاعٌ	Beast of prey.
سَابِعٌ	Seventh.
سُبَاعِيٌّ	Composed of seven.
سَبْعُونَ	Seventy ; seventieth.
أُسْبُوعٌ ج أَسَابِيع	Week.
مُسَبَّعٌ	Heptagon.
أَسْبَغَ عَلى	To give abundantly.
سَبَقَ يسبُقُ	To go before, precede.
سَبَقَ إِلى	To go hastily to one.
سَابَقَ سِبَاقاً	To try to precede.
تَسَابَقَ	To contend for precedence.
سَابِقٌ	Previous, former.
سَابِقاً	Formerly, before, of old.
سَابِقَةٌ ج سَوَابِق	Antecedent.
سِبَاقٌ وَمُسَابَقَةٌ	Racing ; a race.
سَبَكَ يَسْبِكُ سَبْكاً	To melt metals ; cast into a mould.
سَبِيكٌ وَمَسْبُوكٌ	Melted; moulded.
سَبِيكَةٌ ج سَبَائِكُ	Ingot.
مَسْبَكٌ ج مسابِكُ	Foundery.
اسْبَلَ	To lower the veil ; let fall.
أَسْبَلَ الزَّرْعُ	To put forth ears, (grains).
سُبُلٌ	Ears of grain.
سَبِيلٌ ج سبلٌ	Road, way ; manner; means. Public fountain.

إِبْنُ ٱلسَّبِيلِ	Traveller, wayfarer.
سَبَانِخُ وَاسْبَانَاخٌ	Spinage.
سَبَى يَسْبِي	To take prisoner, captivate.
سَبْيٌ وَسَبِيٌّ ج سَبَايَا	Captives. Booty.
سِتَّةٌ م سِتٌّ	Six.
(سِتٌّ ج سِتَّاتٌ)	Lady.
سِتُّون	Sixty ; sixtieth.
سَتَرَ يَسْتُرُ	To cover, veil.
تَسَتَّرَ وَاسْتَتَرَ	To be covered.
سِتْرٌ ج سُتُورٌ	Veil, curtain, cover.
سِتَارٌ ج سُتُرٌ	Veil, cover.
أَلسَّتَّارُ	God who covers sins.
مُسْتَتِرٌ	Concealed. Understood, (pronoun).
أَلإِسْتَانَةُ	Constantinople.
إِسْتٌ ج أَسْتَاهٌ	Anus, podex.
سَجَدَ يَسْجُدُ	To worship, adore.
سَاجِدٌ ج سُجَّدٌ	Worshipper.
سَجَّادَةٌ	Prayer-carpet.
سُجُودٌ	Prostration, adoration.
مَسْجِدٌ ج مَسَاجِدُ	Mosque.
سَجَسٌ	Turbidness ; agitation.
سَجَعَ يَسْجَعُ	To coo ; rhyme.
سَجْعٌ وَتَسْجِيعٌ	Rhymed prose.
مُسَجَّعٌ وَمَسْجُوعٌ	Rhymed (prose).
سَجْفٌ ج سُجُوفٌ	Curtain, veil.
سَجَّلَ	To register, record.
سِجِلٌّ سِجِلَّاتٌ	Record ; scroll.
سَجَمَ يَسْجُمُ وَٱنْسَجَمَ	To flow, stream.
سَجَمَ يَسْجُمُ وَأَسْجَمَ	To shed.
إِنْسِجَامٌ	Flowing effusion.
سَجَنَ يَسْجُنُ سَجْنًا	To imprison.
سِجْنٌ ج سُجُونٌ	Prison.
سَجَّانٌ	Jailor.
سَجِينٌ ج سُجَنَاءُ	Imprisoned.
سَجِيَّةٌ ج سَجَايَا	Natural disposition.
سَحَّ يَسُحُّ سَحًّا	To flow.
سَحَبَ يَسْحَبُ سَحْبًا	To drag, trail.
إِنْسَحَبَ	To be dragged, drawn.

Cloud. سَحَابٌ وَسَحَابَةٌ ج سُحُبٌ

To scratch, rub off. سَحَجَ يَسْحَجُ

To be rubbed off. تَسَحَّجَ وَٱنْسَحَجَ

Dysentery. سَحْجٌ

To bewitch, fascinate. سحرَ يسْحَرُ

To take a morning meal. تَسَحَّرَ

Magic, enchantment. سِحْرٌ

Early daybreak. سَحَرٌ ج أَسْحَارٌ

Sorcerer, magician. ساحِرٌ ج سَحَرَةٌ

Wooden box. سَحَّارَةٌ

Meal before daybreak. سُحُورٌ

To pound, crush. سَحَقَ يَسْحَقُ

To be crushed. تَسَحَّقَ وَٱنْسَحَق

Bruised, powdered. مَسْحُوق

Contrition. إِنْسِحَاقُ ٱلْقَلْبِ

Shore ; coast. ساحِلٌ ج سَوَاحِلُ

To break, crush. سَحَنَ يسحَنَ

Aspect ; complexion. سَحْنَةٌ

Tanned leather. سِخْتِيَان

To compel to labour without wages. سَخَرَ يَسْخَرُ وَسَخَّر

To laugh at, mock. سَخِرَ يَسْخَرُ مِنْ

Compulsory labour. سُخْرَةٌ

To be angry. سَخِطَ يَسْخَطُ و تَسَخَّطَ

To provoke to anger. اسْخَطَ

Anger, displeasure. سُخْطٌ وَسَخَطٌ

To be weak. سَخُفَ يَسْخُفُ سَخَافَةً

Shallowness, weakness. سَخَافَةٌ

To blacken with soot. سَخَّمَ

Soot, crock. سُخَامٌ

To be hot ; have fever. سَخُنَ يَسْخُنُ

To warm, heat. سَخَّنَ وَأَسْخَن

Heat. Fever ; illness. سُخُونَة

Warm, hot. سُخْن

Hot ; sick, ill. ساخِنٌ ج سُخَّان

So be liberal. سَخَا يَسْخُو وَسَخِيَ يَسْخَى

Generosity. سَخَاءٌ وَسَخَاوةٌ

Generous, liberal. سَخِيٌّ ج اسخِيَاء

To close, stop up. سَدَّ يَسُدُّ سَدًّا

To take the place of. سَدَّ مَسَدًّا

Balance, pay an account. سَدَّدَ

To be stopped. إِنْسَدَّ وَٱسْتَدَّ

To collect a debt. إِسْتَدَّ

Barrier ; dam. سَدّ ج أَسْدَادٌ

Vestibule, porch. سُدَّة

A stopper, a cork. سِدَادَةٌ

Right, true. سَدّ وَسَدِيدٌ

Stopped, corked. مَسْدُودٌ

Simplicity of mind. سَذَاجَة

A species of lotus. سِدْرٌ ج سُدُورٌ

To be the sixth. سَدَسَ يَسْدِسُ

To make six. سَدَّسَ

Sixth part. سُدْسٌ ج أَسْدَاسٌ

Sixth. سَادِسٌ

Consisting of six. سُدَاسِيٌّ

Hexagon. مُسَدَّسٌ

To let down. سَدَلَ يَسْدِلُ وَأَسْدَلَ

To be let down. تَسَدَّلَ وَٱنْسَدَلَ

Mist. Nebula. سَدِيمٌ

In vain, to no purpose. سُدًى

Warp (of cloth). سَدَاةٌ ج أَسْدِيَةٌ

Rue-plant. سَذَابٌ

To gladden, cheer. سَرَّ يَسُرُّ

To rejoice at. سُرَّ سُرُوراً بِ

To cheer, gladden. أَسَرَّ

To impart a secret. سَارَّ مُسَارَّةً

To keep secret, conceal. أَسَرَّ

To confide a secret to. أَسَرَّ إِلَى

Secret, mystery. سِرٌّ ج أَسْرَارٌ

Secretary. كَاتِمُ ٱلْأَسْرَارِ

Navel. سُرَّةٌ ج سُرَّاتٌ وَسُرُورٌ

Happy state of life. سَرَّاءُ

Mysterious, secret. سِرِّيٌّ

Joy, pleasure. سُرُورٌ وَمَسَرَّةٌ

Bed, cradle ; throne. سَرِيرٌ ج أَسِرَّةٌ

Hidden thought. سَرِيرَةٌ ج سَرَائِرُ

Concubine. سُرِّيَّةٌ ج سَرَارِيُّ

Joy, pleasure. مَسَرَّةٌ ج مَسَرَّاتٌ

Happy, pleased. مَسْرُورٌ

To drive to pasture. سَرَّبَ

Troop, flock. سِرْبٌ ج أَسْرَابٌ

Aqueduct, canal. سَرَبٌ ج أَسْرَابٌ

Mirage. سَرَابٌ

Shirt; dress. سِرْبَالٌ ج سَرَابِيلُ

To saddle (a horse). سَرَجَ يَسْرِجُ

Saddle. سَرْجٌ ج سُرُوجٌ

Dung, manure. سرجين

Lamp, torch. سِرَاجٌ ج سُرُجٌ

Glow-worm. سِرَاجُ ٱللَّيْلِ

Glanders. Saddlery. سِرَاجَةٌ

Saddler. سَرَّاجٌ وَسُرُوجِيٌّ

Sesame oil. سِيرَجٌ وَشَيْرَجٌ

Lamp-stand. مِسْرَجَةٌ ج مَسَارِجُ

To pasture at will. سَرَحَ يَسْرَحُ

To send away; set free. سَرَّحَ

Pasture. مَسْرَحٌ ج مَسَارِحُ

Comb. مِسْرَحٌ ج مَسَارِحُ

Cellar, vault. سِرْدَابٌ ج سَرَادِيبُ

Strip of leather. سَرِيدَةٌ ج سَرَائِدُ

Awning. سُرَادِقٌ ج سُرَادِقَاتٌ

Sticking-paste. سِرَاسٌ (*for* شِرَاسٌ)

Way, street, road. سِرَاطٌ وَصِرَاطٌ

Crab. Cancer. سَرَطَان

Cancer (of the Zodiac). ٱلسَّرَطَانُ

To hasten, hurry. سَرُعَ يَسْرُعُ

To hasten to do. أَسْرَعَ فِي

Quickness, haste, speed. سُرْعَةٌ

Quick, rapid, swift. سَرِيعٌ

To be extravagant, act immoderately. أَسْرَفَ

Extravagance. سَرَفٌ وَإِسْرَافٌ

A spendthrift. مُسْرِفٌ

To steal, rob. سَرَقَ يَسْرِقُ

To steal away. إِنْسَرَقَ

Theft, robbery. سِرْقَةٌ وَسَرِقَةٌ

Thing stolen. سَرِقَةٌ وسَرَاقَةٌ

Thief. سَارِقٌ ج سُرَّاقٌ وسَرَقَةٌ

Great thief. سَرَّاقٌ

Dung. سَرْقِينٌ

Continuing endlessly. سَرْمَدٌ

Eternal. سَرْمَدِيٌّ

Cypress (tree). سَرْوٌ

Liberal, noble. سَرِيٌّ ج سَرَاةٌ

Trowsers. سِرْوَالٌ ج سَرَاوِيلُ

To travel. سَرَى يَسْرِي

To cause to travel. أَسْرَى بِ

Night-journey. سُرًى

Night-traveller. سَارٍ ج سُرَاةٌ

Column ; mast. سَارِيَةٌ ج سَوَارٍ

Palace. سَرَايَا ج سَرَايَاتٌ

The Syriac language. السُّرْيَانِيَّةُ

To spread out. سَطَحَ يَسْطَحُ وسَطَّحَ

To be spread out. تَسَطَّحَ

Surface ; terrace. سَطْحٌ ج سُطُوحٌ

Flat, plane, even. مُسَطَّحٌ

To write. سَطَرَ يَسْطُرُ

Line ; row. سَطْرٌ ج أَسْطُرٌ وسُطُورٌ

Large knife. سَاطُورٌ ج سَوَاطِيرُ

Fable, legend. أُسْطُورَةٌ ج أَسَاطِيرُ

Ruler (for lines).
Sample. مَسْطَرَةٌ

New wine. مُسْطَارٌ

Authority, guardianship. سَيْطَرَةٌ

To rise ; gleam. سَطَعَ يَسْطَعُ

Pail, bucket. سَطْلٌ

Ship of war. Fleet. أُسْطُولٌ

To stop up, bar. سَطَمَ يَسْطُمُ

Cork, stopper ; bolt. سِطَامٌ

Cylinder. أُسْطُوَانَةٌ ج أَسَاطِينُ

Cylindrical. أُسْطُوَانِيٌّ

To attack ; assail. سَطَا يَسْطُو عَلَى

Attack ; power. سَطْوَةٌ ج سَطَوَاتٌ

Thyme (plant). سَعْتَرٌ (أَوْ صَعْتَرٌ)

To be fortunate. سَعَدَ يَسْعَدُ

سَاعَدَ	To help, assist.
أَسْعَدَ	To make happy.
سَعْدٌ ج سُعُودٌ	Luck, success.
سَعْدَانٌ ج سَعَادِينُ	Monkey.
سَاعِدٌ ج سَوَاعِد	Fore-arm.
سَعَادَةٌ	Happiness, felicity.
سعادَتُكَ	Your Excellency.
سعيدٌ ج سُعَدَاءُ	Fortunate.
سعر يَسعُرُ	To light a fire.
سعَّرَ	To fix, estimate a price.
تَسَعَّرَ	To be fixed, (price).
إِسْتَعَرَ	To blaze, spread.
سِعْرٌ ج أَسْعَارٌ	Price.
سعِيرٌ	Flame, blaze. Fire.
سَعُوطٌ	Snuff.
سَعَفَ يَسْعَفُ وأَسْعَفَ بِ	To assist.
سَاعَفَ	To assist, help.
سَعَفٌ	Branches of palm-tree.
سعَلَ يَسْعُلُ سُعَالاً	To cough.
سُعَالٌ	Cough.
سَعَى يَسْعَى سَعْياً	To run. Seek.
سَعَى بِ	To calumniate.
سَعْيٌ	Effort, exertion.
سَاعٍ ج سُعَاةٌ	Messenger.
مَسْعًى ج مَسَاعٍ	Effort ; enterprise.
سَفُوفٌ	Medicine (in powder).
سُفْتَجَةٌ ج سَفَاتِجُ	Bill of exchange.
سَفَحَ يَسْفَحُ سُفُوحاً وَسَفْحاً	To shed.
سَافَحَ	To fornicate.
سَفْحٌ	Foot of a mountain.
سِفَاحٌ	Fornication.
سَفُّودٌ ج سَفَافِيدُ	Roasting-fork.
سَفَرَ يَسْفُرُ سَفَراً	To travel.
سَفَّرَ	To send on a journey.
سَافَرَ	To depart, travel.
أَسْفَرَ	To shine, (dawn).
سِفْرٌ ج اسْفَارٌ	Written book.
سَفَرٌ ج اسْفَارٌ	Journey.

سَفْرَةٌ ج سَفَرَاتٌ	A journey.
سُفْرَةٌ	Table-cloth ; table.
مُسَافِرٌ	Traveller.
سِفَارَةٌ	Embassy.
سَفِيرٌ ج سُفَرَاءُ	Ambassador.
سَفَرْجَلٌ ج سَفَارِجُ	Quince.
سَفْسَطَةٌ وَسِفْسِطَةٌ	Sophism.
سَفْسَطِيٌّ	Sophistical ; sophist.
سَفَقَ يَسْفِقُ	To shut, slap.
سَفِيقٌ	Thick, compact.
سَفِيقُ ٱلْوَجْهِ	Impudent, insolent.
سَفَكَ يَسْفُكُ سَفْكًا	To shed.
إِنْسَفَكَ	To be shed.
سَفَّاكٌ لِلدِّمَاءِ	Blood-shedder.
مَسْفُوكٌ	Shed, (blood, &c.)
سَفَلَ يَسْفُلُ	To be low, sink.
سَفُلَ سَفَالَةً	To be mean.
سِفْلٌ	The lowest part, bottom.
سُفْلِيٌّ	The lower part.
سَفَالَةٌ	Baseness, vileness.
سَافِلٌ ج سَفَلَةٌ	Low, vile.
اسْفَلُ	The lowest part.
سَفِينٌ وَإِسْفِينٌ	Wedge.
سَفِينَةٌ ج سُفُنٌ	Ship, boat.
سَفْنَجٌ وَسِفِنْجٌ	Sponge.
سَفِهَ يَسْفَهُ سَفَهًا	To be foolish.
تَسَفَّهَ عَلَى	To revile.
سَفَهٌ وَسَفَاهَةٌ	Stupidity.
سَفِيهٌ ج سُفَهَاءُ	Stupid, foolish.
سَقَطَ يَسْقُطُ	To fall, fall down.
أَسْقَطَ	To cause to fall, let fall. Discount. Subtract.
تَسَاقَطَ	To fall by degrees.
سَقَطٌ ج أَسْقَاطٌ	Refuse. Defect.
سَقْطَةٌ	Fall, slip, fault, error.
سَاقِطٌ ج سُقَّاطٌ	Low, worthless.
سُقَاطَةٌ	Refuse, what is rejected.
سَقَاطَةٌ	Door-latch.
سُقُوط	Falling, downfall.

Discount. Subtraction. إِسْقَاطٌ

Native place. مَسْقَطُ ٱلرَّأْسِ

To roof. سَقَفَ يَسْقُفُ سَقْفاً وَسَقَّفَ

Roof ; ceiling. سَقْفٌ ج سُقُوفٌ

Porch, roof. سَقِيفَةٌ ج سَقَائِفُ

Bishop. أُسْقُفٌ ج أَسَاقِفَةٌ

Bishopric. اسْقُفِيَّةٌ

A Slavonian. سَقْلَبِيٌّ ج سَقَالِبَةٌ

To be weak, diseased. سَقِمَ يَسْقَمُ

To make ill. أَسْقَمَ

Disease, illness. سُقْمٌ ج اسْقَامٌ

Diseased, weak. سَقِيمٌ ج سُقَمَاءُ

Scammony, (plant). سَقَمُونِيَا

To give to drink, irrigate. سَقَى يَسْقِي

To draw water ; ask for water. إِسْتَقَى

To be dropsical. إِسْتَسْقَى

Giving to drink, watering. سَقْيٌ

Water-skin. سِقَاءٌ ج أَسْقِيَةٌ

Water-carrier. سَقَّاءٌ ج سَقَّاؤُونَ

Cup-bearer. سَاقٍ

Water-wheel. Irrigation-canal. سَاقِيَةٌ ج سَوَاقٍ

Dropsy. إِسْتِسْقَاءٌ

Dropsical. مُسْتَسْقٍ

To coin money. سَكَّ ٱلنُّقُودَ

Ploughshare. Road, high road. Coined money. سِكَّةٌ ج سِكَكٌ

Railway. سِكَّةُ حَدِيدٍ

To pour out ; melt. سَكَبَ يَسْكُبُ

To flow. سَكَبَ سُكُوباً وَٱنْسَكَبَ

Melting, flowing. سَكْبٌ

To be silent, still. سَكَتَ يَسْكُتُ

To silence, still. سَكَّتَ وَأَسْكَتَ

Silence ; pause. سَكْتٌ وَسُكُوتٌ

Apoplexy. A pause. سَكْتَةٌ

Silent, reserved. سَكُوتٌ

To become intoxicated. سَكِرَ يَسْكَرُ

To intoxicate. سَكَّرَ وَأَسْكَرَ

Drunkenness. سُكْرٌ

Agony of death.	سَكْرَةُ ٱلْمَوْتِ
Wooden lock to a door.	سَكْرَةٌ
Sugar.	سُكَّرٌ
Intoxicated.	سَكْرَانُ ج سُكَارَى
Habitual drunkard.	سِكِّيرٌ
Trade of a shoemaker.	سِكَافَة
Shoemaker.	إِسْكَافٌ ج أَسَاكِفَةٌ
Threshold.	أُسْكُفَّةٌ
To subside.	سَكَنَ يَسْكُنُ سُكُونًا
To dwell in.	سَكَنَ سَكَنًا وفِي
To rely upon, trust in.	سَكَنَ إِلَى
To calm, pacify, quiet.	سَكَّنَ
To make to dwell.	أَسْكَنَ
Habitation.	سَكَنٌ
An inhabitant.	ساكِنٌ ج سُكَّانٌ
Rest, quiescence.	سُكُونٌ
Knife.	سِكِّينٌ ج سَكَاكِينُ
Quiet.	سَكِينَةٌ
House. abode.	مَسْكَنٌ ج مَسَاكِنُ
Poverty ; lowliness.	مَسْكَنَةٌ
Inhabited; possessed.	مَسْكُونٌ
The world.	أَلْمَسْكُونَةُ
Poor ; lowly.	مِسْكِينٌ ج مَسَاكِينُ
To draw a sword.	سَلَّ يسلُّ وَٱسْتَلَّ
To slip away.	تسلل وَٱنسَلَّ
Basket.	سَلٌّ وَسَلَّةٌ ج سِلَالٌ
Consumption, (disease).	داء ٱلسُّلِّ
Offspring, progeny.	سُلَالَةٌ
Child ; male offspring.	سَلِيلٌ
Large needle. Obelisk.	مِسَلَّةٌ
Unsheathed. Phthisical.	مسلُول
To melt, clarify (butter).	سَلَأَ يَسْلا
To rob. Seize.	سَلَبَ يسْلُبُ وٱسْتَلَبَ
Robbery. Negation.	سَلْبٌ
Robbed, plundered.	مسْلُوبٌ
Method, way.	أُسْلوبٌ ج أَسَاليبُ
To arm equip.	سَلَّح بِ
To arm one's self.	تسلَّحَ

سِلَاحٌ ج أَسْلِحَةٌ	Arms, weapons.
سلحفَاةٌ ج سَلَاحِفُ	Tortoise.
سَلَخَ يَسْلُخُ سَلْخًا	To skin, flay.
انْسَلَخَ	To be stripped off.
سَلْخٌ وَمُنْسَلَخٌ	End of (the month).
مَسْلَخٌ مَسَالِخُ	Slaughter-house.
سَلِسَ يَسْلَسُ	To be loose, docile.
سَلَس وَسَلَاسَة	Docility.
سَلِس	Docile ; compliant.
سَلْسَلَ ب	To chain.
سَلْسَلَ إِلَى	To trace a pedigree.
سِلْسِلَةٌ ج سَلَاسِل	Chain.
سَلْسَبِيلٌ	Artificial fountain.
تَسَلْسُلٌ	A continued series.
سلطهُ	To make one a ruler.
تَسَلطَ عَلى	To overcome ; rule.
سلطَةٌ وَتَسَلط	Rule, dominion.
سلطنَةٌ	Power, dominion.
سلطَانٌ	Absolute power.

سُلْطَانٌ ج سَلَاطِينُ	Sultan.
سُلْطَانِيٌّ	Imperial.
طَرِيقٌ سُلْطَانِيٌّ	High road.
سِلْعَةٌ ج سِلَعٌ	Article for sale.
سَلَفَ يَسْلُفُ	To pass away ; precede.
سَلَّفَ وَأَسْلَفَ	To give in advance.
تَسَلَّفَ وَاسْتَلَفَ	To borrow ; receive payment in advance.
سَلَفٌ	Payment in advance.
سَلَفٌ ج أَسْلَافٌ	Predecessor.
سُلَافُ ٱلْعَسكَرِ	Vanguard of army.
سَالِفٌ	Preceding ; former.
سَلَقَ يسلقُ سَلْقًا	To boil.
تَسَلَّقَ	To scale or climb a wall.
سُلَاقٌ	Ulceration of eye-lids.
سَلُوقِيٌّ	Greyhound.
سلِيقَةٌ ج سَلَائِقُ	Natural trait.
بِٱلسَّلِيقَة	Naturally, instinctively.
مَسْلُوقٌ	Boiled.

سلك يسلُكُ	To travel, enter. Behave.
أسْلَكَ	To make to enter.
سِلكٌ ج أَسْلاكٌ	String ; wire.
سُلوكٌ	Conduct, behaviour.
علمُ ٱلسُّلُوك	Good manners.
سالِك	Ordinary, usual, current.
مَسْلَك ج مَسَالِكُ	Path road.
سَلِمَ يسلَمُ	To be sound, safe.
سلمَ مِنْ	To be free from.
سَلَّمَ مِنْ	Tsave ; preser ove.
سلمَ بِ	To admit.
سلمَ لِ	To surrender, yield.
سلَّمَ إِلى	To give over, hand to.
سلم عَلَى	To salute, greet.
سَالَم	To keep peace with.
اسْلَمَ	To deliver up.
أَسْلَمَ	To profess Islâm.
تَسلم	To take possession of.
إِستَسلمَ	To yield, surrender.
سِلْمٌ	Peace, reconciliation.
سُلمٌ ج سَلاَلِمُ	Ladder, stairs.
سَلاَمٌ وَسلاَمَةٌ	Peace, well-being.
سَلاَمٌ	Greeting ; salutation.
سَالِمٌ	Sound and safe.
أَلْجَمْعُ ٱلسالِمُ	Sound plural.
سلِيمٌ ج سُلَمَاء	Sound, safe.
سُلَيْمَانِيٌّ	Corrosive sublimate.
أَسلَمُ	More secure, safer.
الإِسْلاَمُ	Religion of Islâm.
تَسْلِيمٌ	Delivery ; surrender.
مسْلِمٌ ج مُسْلِمُونَ	Moslem.
مُسَلمٌ	Delivered ; conceded.
سُلاَ يَسلو	To forget.
سَلَّى	To divert, cheer, amuse.
تَسَلى	To be diverted.
سُلْوَةٌ وَتسْلِيَة وَتسَلٍّ	Diversion.
سلْوَى	Quail. Consolation.
سُلْوَانٌ	Consolation.

To poison. سَمَّ يَسُمُّ سَمًّا

Hole. Poison. سَمٌّ ج سُمُومٌ

Arsenic ; ratsbane. سَمُّ ٱلْفَارِ

Poisonous. سَامٌّ

Hot wind. سَمُومٌ

Holes ; pores. مَسَامٌّ

Poisoned. مَسْمُومٌ

Way ; manner. سَمْتٌ

Azimuth. أَلسَّمْتُ ج سُمُوتٌ

Zenith. سَمْتُ ٱلرَّاسِ

To be ugly. سَمُجَ يَسْمُجُ سَمَاجَةً

Ugly, horrid ; foul. سَمْجٌ وَسَمِيجٌ

To grant, permit ; pardon. سَمَحَ يَسْمَحُ

To pardon, excuse. سَامَحَ

Kindness ; grace. سَمَاحٌ وَسَمَاحَةٌ

Allowed ; permitted. مَسْمُوحٌ بِهِ

Periosteum. سِمْحَاق

To manure the soil. سَمَّدَ

Manure. سَمَادٌ

Semolino. سَمِيذٌ وَسَمِيدٌ

To be brownish. سَمُرَ يَسْمُرُ وَاسْمَرَّ

To nail. سَمَرَ وَسَمَّرَ

To converse with. سَامَرَ وَتَسَامَرَ

Brownish colour. سُمْرَةٌ

Samaria (in Palestine). ٱلسَّامِرَةُ

Samaritan. سَامِرِيٌّ

Sable (animal). سَمُّورٌ

Brownish. أَسْمَرُ م سَمْرَاءُ ج سُمْرٌ

Nail. Foot-corn. مِسْمَارٌ ج مَسَامِيرُ

To act as a broker. سَمْسَرَ

Brokerage ; fee of a broker. سَمْسَرَةٌ

Broker. سِمْسَارٌ ج سَمَاسِرَةٌ

Sesame. سِمْسِمٌ

Sesamoid bone. سِمْسِمَانِيٌّ

To strap with thongs. سَمَّطَ

Thong. سِمْطٌ ج سُمُوط

Table-cloth. سِمَاطٌ ج أَسْمِطَةٌ

To hear, listen. سَمِعَ يَسْمَعُ وَاسْتَمَعَ

To hear of.	سَمِعَ ب
To accept, obey.	سَمِعَ لِ ومن
Sense of hearing.	سَمْعٌ
You shall be obeyed.	سَمْعاً وَطَاعَةً
Report, fame.	سُمْعَةٌ
Irregular, traditional.	سَمَاعِيٌّ
The hearer of all (God).	السَّمِيعُ
Sumach, (tree and fruit).	سُمَّاقٌ
To become thick.	سَمُكَ سَمَاكَةً
To thicken, make thick.	سَمَّكَ
Depth, thickness.	سَمْكٌ وسَمَاكَةٌ
Fish.	سَمَكٌ ج اسْمَاكٌ
A fish.	سَمَكَةٌ
Deep, thick.	سَمِيكٌ
To grow fat.	سَمِنَ يَسْمَنُ سِمَناً
To butter; fatten.	سَمَّنَ
Clarified butter.	سَمْنٌ
Seller of butter. Grocer.	سَمَّان
Quail.	(سُمَنَةٌ ج سُمَّنٌ وَسَمَامِنُ)
Fat, corpulent.	سَمِينٌ ج سِمَانٌ
To be high ; rise high.	سَمَا يَسْمُو
Give a name ; name.	سَمَّى
To be named ; mentioned.	تَسَمَّى
Name ; noun.	إِسْمٌ ج أَسْمَاءٌ
The name of God.	إِسْمُ ٱلْجَلَالَةِ
Height ; greatness.	سُمُوٌّ
Heaven.	سَمَاءٌ ج سَمَوَاتٌ
Heavenly.	سَمَاوِيٌّ وَسَمَائِيٌّ
High ; sublime.	سَامٍ ج سُمَاةٌ
Grand vizierial order.	أَمْرٌ سَامٍ
Named, determined.	مُسَمًّى
To sharpen, whet.	سَنَّ يَسُنُّ
To introduce a law.	سَنَّ سُنَّةً
To become aged.	اسَنَّ
Tooth. Age in life.	سِنٌّ ج اسْنَانٌ
To become old.	طَعَنَ فِي ٱلسِّنِّ
Law ; usage.	سُنَّةٌ ج سُنَنٌ
Head of a spear.	سِنَانٌ ج أَسِنَّة

سُنِّيٌّ ج سُنِّيَّةٌ A Sunnite.

مِسَنٌّ Whet-stone.

مُسِنٌّ Advanced in age.

سُنْبُوقٌ Skiff, small boat.

سُنْبُلَةٌ ج سَنَابِل An ear of corn.

اَلسُّنْبُلَةُ Virgo (of the Zodiac).

سِنْجَابٌ Squirrel.

سِنْجَقٌ ج سَنَاجِقُ Standard, flag.

سَنَحَ يَسْنَحُ To occur to the mind.

سَنَحَ عَن To dissuade.

سِنْخٌ ج اسْنَاخٌ Socket of a tooth.

سَنَدَ يَسْنُدُ وَاسْتَنَدَ إِلى To lean upon.

سَنَّدَ To support firmly.

أَسْنَدَ إِلَى To ascribe, trace up.

سَنَدٌ ج أَسْنَادٌ Support; refuge.

سَنْدَانٌ ج سَنَادِينُ Anvil.

سِنْدِيَانٌ Evergreen oak; ilex.

مِسْنَدٌ ج مَسَانِدُ Cushion, pillow.

مُسْتَنَدٌ Supported, propped.

المُسْنَد Predicate.

اَلْمُسْنَدُ إِلَيْهِ Subject.

سِنْدَرُوسٌ Sandarach.

سُنْدُسٌ Silk brocade; fine silk.

سِنَّوْرٌ ج سَنَانِيرُ Cat.

سَنْط Acacia (*Nilotica*).

سِنْطِيرٌ وَسَنْطُورٌ A kind of harp.

سَنْكَرِيٌّ ج سَنَاكِرَةٌ Tinker.

سَنَامٌ ج أَسْنِمَةٌ Hump of camel.

مُسَنَّمٌ Raised; convex.

تَسَنَّى To ascend. Be easy.

سَنًى Brightness, gleaming.

سَنَاءٌ Sublimity; high rank.

سَنَا مَكَّةَ Senna, (plant).

سَنَةٌ سِنُونٌ وَسَنَوَاتٌ Year.

سَنِيٌّ High, sublime, noble.

سَنَوِيٌّ Annual, yearly.

سُنُونُو Swallow.

أَسْهَبَ To be lengthy, prolix.

To give largely. اسْهَبَ فِي ٱلْعَطَاء

Prolixity ; amplification. اسْهَابٌ

Loquacious ; diffuse. مُسْهِبٌ

To be sleepless. سَهِدَ يَسْهَدُ

To deprive of sleep. سَهَّدَ

Sleeplessness. سُهْدٌ وَسُهَادٌ

To keep awake. سَهِرَ يَسْهَرُ

Awake. سَاهِرٌ وَسَهْرَان

To be level ; easy. سَهُلَ يَسْهُلُ

To smooth ; facilitate. سَهَّلَ

To be level ; become easy. تَسَهَّلَ

To be accommodating. تَسَاهَلَ

To regard as easy. إِسْتَسْهَلَ

Plain ; level. سَهْلٌ ج سُهُولٌ

Gentle. سَهْلُ ٱلْخُلُقِ

Easy ; smooth, soft. سهلٌ

Ease, facility. Evenness. سُهُولَةٌ

Canopus, (star). سُهَيْلٌ

Diarrhœa. إِسْهَال

Purgative, laxative. مُسْهِلٌ

Arrow. سَهْمٌ ج سِهَامٌ

Lot, share. سَهْمٌ ج اسْهُمٌ

Sagittarius. سَهْمُ ٱلرَّامِي

To overlook, neglect. سَهَا يَسْهُو عَنْ

Oversight, forgetfulness. سَهْوٌ

Thoughtlessly. سَهْواً

Forgetful, negligent. سَاهٍ

To be evil, bad. سَاءَ يَسُوءُ

To treat badly ; offend. سَاءَ سُوءًا

To be evil to ; offend. أَسَاءَ إِلَى

To suspect evil. أَسَاءَ ٱلظَّنَّ

Evil. سُوءٌ ج أَسْوَاءٌ وَمَسَاوِئُ

Evil, bad. سَيِّئٌ م سَيِّئَةٌ

Sin ; calamity. سَيِّئَةٌ ج سَيِّئَاتٌ

Teak-tree. سَاجٌ

See under. سيح سَاحَ يَسُوحُ

Court ; yard. سَاحَةٌ ج سَاحَاتٌ

Traveller. سَائِحٌ ج سُيَّاحٌ

To rule a people. To groom a horse. ساسَ يَسُوس

To be moth-eaten. سَوَّسَ

Moth, worm. Liquorice. سُوس

Political administration. سِيَاسَة

Groom. سَائِس ج سَاسَة وَسُوَّاس

Lily. سُوسَن وَسُوسَان

To whip. سَاطَ يَسُوط سَوْطاً

Whip, lash. سَوْط ج سِيَاط

Hour. Watch. سَاعَة ج سَاعَات

Sun-dial. سَاعَة شَمْسِيَّة

Hour-glass. سَاعَة رَمْلِيَّة

Watch-maker. سَاعَاتِيّ

To be permitted, lawful. سَاغَ لَ

To allow, permit. سَوَّغَ لِ

Lawful, allowable. سَائِغ

To put off, defer. سَوَّفَ

Row, course. سَاف ج سَافَات

A particle which changes the *present* tense into a future; سَوْفَ

e.g. Thou shalt see. سَوْفَ تَرَى

To rule. سَادَ يَسُود سِيَادَةً

To become black. إِسْوَدَّ

To blacken; write a rough draft. سَوَّدَ

To be blackened. تَسَوَّدَ

Dominion; honour. سُؤْدَد وَسِيَادَة

Black bile. Melancholy. سَوْدَاء

Sudan (country). بِلَادُ ٱلسُّودَانِ

Blackness. Large number. سَوَاد

Power, authority. سِيَادَة

Master, lord. سَيِّد ج سَادَة

Black. أَسْوَدُ م سَوْدَاء ج سُود

First copy, rough draft. مُسْوَدَّة

Glass bottle. مُسَوَّدَة ج مُسَوَّدَات

To wall in a town. سَوَّرَ

Wall, ramparts. سُور ج أَسْوَار

Chapter of Koran. سُورَة ج سُوَر

Syria. سُورِيَّة

Bracelet. سِوَار وَأَسْوَار ج أَسْوِرَة

Surrounded with walls. مُسَوَّر

Distance.	مَسَافَةٌ
To drive, urge on.	سَاقَ يَسُوقُ
To lead to.	سَاقَ إِلَى
To be driven, urged on.	إِنْسَاقَ
Leg. Stem (of a plant). Side of a triangle.	سَاقٌ ج سُوقٌ وسِيقَانٌ
Market.	سُوقٌ ج أَسْوَاق
Fine flour.	سَوِيقٌ
Logical connection.	سِيَاقٌ
Driver, driving.	سَائِقٌ
To clean one's teeth.	تَسَوَّكَ
Toothpick.	سِوَاكٌ وَمِسْوَاك
To deceive, incite to evil.	سَوَّلَ لِ
To compel.	سَامَ يَسُومُ
To bargain.	سَاوَمَ مُسَاوَمَةً
Sign, mark.	سِيمَةٌ وَسِيمَاء
To be worth.	سَوِيَ يَسْوَى وَسَاوَى
To adjust, rectify.	سَوَّى تَسْوِيَةً
To be equal.	سَاوَى وَٱسْتَوَى
To be ripe, well cooked.	إِسْتَوَى
To sit upon.	إِسْتَوَى عَلَى
Just, right. Same, alike.	سَوَاء
Alike, equally.	عَلَى حَدٍّ سَوَاء
Equally ; together.	سَوِيَّةً وَسَوَاءً
Chiefly, principally.	لَا سِيَّمَا
Equally, alike, (both).	هُمَا سِيَّان
Equator.	خَطُّ الإِسْتِوَاء
Equaliy. Moderation.	مُسَاوَاةٌ
Equal.	مُسَاوٍ وَمُتَسَاوٍ
Common gender.	مُسْتَوٍ
To set free.	سَيَّبَ
Left free, at liberty.	سَائِبٌ
Unguarded ; free.	مُسَيَّبٌ
To hedge in, enclose.	سَيَّجَ
Hedge.	سِيَاجٌ ج سِيَاجَاتٌ
Surrounded by a hedge.	مُسَيَّجٌ
To travel. Flow.	سَاحَ يَسِيحُ
Long journery.	سِيَاحَة

سَائِحٌ ج سيَّاحٌ — Traveller.

سيَّاحٌ — Great traveller.

مَسَاحَةٌ — Area.

عِلْمُ ٱلْمَسَاحَةِ — Land surveying.

سِيخٌ ج أَسْيَاخٌ — Large knife.

سَارَ يَسِير — To go ; travel.

سَارَ بِ — To carry away.

سيْرٌ ج سيورٌ — Journey. Thong.

سيرَةٌ ج سِيَرٌ — Conduct. Biography.

سائرٌ — Current, customary.

سَيَّارَةٌ ج سَيَّارَاتٌ — Planet.

مَسِيرٌ — Journey, road.

سَيْفٌ ج سُيُوفٌ — Sword.

سَالَ يَسِيلُ — To flow ; become liquid.

سَيَّلَ وَأَسَالَ — To liquify.

سَيْلٌ ج سُيُولٌ — Stream ; torrent.

سيَلَانٌ — Flow ; flux.

سيْلَانُ — Ceylon.

سيْلَانٌ — Ruby ; carbuncle.

سَائِلٌ ج سَوَائِلُ — Liquid, fluid.

مسِيلٌ — Water-course.

ش

ش As a numeral sign=300.

شَؤُمَ وَشُئِمَ To be inauspicious.

تَشَاءَمَ To take as a bad omen.

شُؤْمٌ Evil omen, ill luck.

الشَّامُ Syria. Damascus.

شَامِيٌّ Syrian. Damascene.

شِئْمَةٌ Nature, disposition.

مَشُومٌ Inauspicious, unlucky.

شَأْنٌ Thing ; state ; honour.

عَظِيمُ ٱلشَّأْنِ Of great importance.

شَاهِينٌ ج شَوَاهِينُ White falcon.

شَبَّ يَشِبُّ To grow up, (youth).

شَبَّ يَشُبُّ To blaze (fire, war).

شَبٌّ Vitriol. Alum.

شَابٌّ ج شُبَّانٌ Young man.

شَابَّةٌ ج شَابَّاتٌ Young woman.

شَبَابٌ وَشَبِيبَةٌ Youth.

شَبَّابَةٌ A reed or musical pipe.

تَشَبَّثَ ب To take firm hold.

شِبِتٌّ Dill (plant).

شَبَحٌ ج أَشْبَاحٌ Object of vision.

شُبْحَةٌ A horse's shackle.

شِبْرٌ ج أَشْبَارٌ Span.

شَبَّطَ To scarify.

شُبَاطُ وَسُبَاطُ February.

شَبِعَ يَشْبَعُ To be satiated.

أَشْبَعَ To satiate, satisfy.

شِبَعٌ Satiety, satiation.

شَبْعَانُ Satiated, satisfied.

شَبَكَ يَشْبِكُ To entwine, entangle.

To be entangled. تَشَبَّكَ وَٱشْتَبَكَ	Resemblance. مُشَابَهَةٌ
Fishing-net. شَبَكَةٌ ج شَبَكٌ	To be scattered. شَتَّ يَشِتُّ
Window. شُبَّاكٌ ج شَبَابِيكُ	To scatter. شَتَّ وَشَتَّتَ وَأَشَتَّ
Cub of a lion. شِبْلٌ ج أَشْبَالٌ	To be dispersed. تَشَتَّتَ
Groomsman. شَبِينٌ م شَبِينَةٌ	Disunion. شَتٌّ وَشَتَاتٌ
To liken, compare. شَبَّهَ ب	Great is the difference ! شَتَّانَ
To resemble. شَابَهَ وَأَشْبَهَ	Various things. أَشْيَاءُ شَتَّى
To imitate. تَشَبَّهَ ب	Nursery-plant. شَتْلَةٌ
To resemble one another. تَشَابَهَ	Plant-nursery. مَشْتَلٌ
To be obscure. إِشْتَبَهَ	To revile. شَتَمَ يَشْتُمُ شَتْمًا
To be in doubt. إِشْتَبَهَ فِي	Defamation. شَتِيمَةٌ ج شَتَائِمُ
A similar person or thing. شِبْهٌ	Reviled. شَتِيمٌ وَمَشْتُومٌ
Similarity ; likeness. شَبَهٌ	To pass the winter. شَتَا يَشْتُو وَشَتَّى
Point of resemblance. وَجْهُ ٱلشَّبَهِ	Winter ; rain. شِتَاءٌ
Doubt, suspicion. شُبْهَةٌ ج شُبُهَاتٌ	Pertaining to winter. شَتَوِيٌّ
Resembling, like. شَبِيهٌ	Wintry ; rainy. شَاتٍ
Ambiguity ; doubt. اشْتِبَاهٌ	Winter abode. مَشْتًى
Comparison ; metaphor. تَشْبِيهٌ	To wound the head. شَجَّ يَشُجُّ
Doubtful, obscure. مُشْتَبِهٌ	Wound in the head. شَجَّةٌ

To become woody. شَجَّرَ

To quarrel with. شَاجَرَ مُشَاجَرَةً

To abound in trees. شَجَرَ

To dispute, quarrel. تَشَاجَرَ

Tree; shrub, bush. شَجَرٌ ج أَشْجَارٌ

A tree. شَجَرَةٌ

Abounding in trees. شَجِرٌ وَمُشْجِرٌ

Dispute, contest. مُشَاجَرَةٌ

To be brave. شَجُعَ يَشْجُعُ شَجَاعَةً

To encourage, embolden. شَجَّعَ

To take courage. تَشْجِيعٌ

Courage, bravery. شَجَاعَةٌ

Brave, bold. شُجَاعٌ ج شُجْعَانٌ

To grieve. Coo. شَجَنَ يَشْجُنُ شَجَنًا

Grief. شَجَنٌ ج شُجُون

To cause anguish. شَجَا يَشْجُو

To be grieved. شَجِيَ يَشْجَى شَجًا

Anxiety, grief. شَجًا وَشَجْوٌ

Grieved, anxious, sad. شَجٍ وَشَجِيٌّ

To be niggardly. شَحَّ يَشُحُّ شُحًّا

To contend together. تَشَاحَّ

Avarice, covetousness. شِحٌّ

Avaricious. شَحِيحٌ ج شِحَاحٌ

Incontestable. لَا مُشَاحَّةَ فِي

To ask for alms, beg. شَحَذَ يَشْحَذُ

Mendicity. شِحَاذَةٌ

Importunate beggar. شَحَّاذٌ

Stye on the eyelid. شَحَّاذُ ٱلْعَيْنِ

To drag along. شَحَطَ يَشْحَطُ

Grease, lard, fat. شَحْمٌ ج شُحُومٌ

Lobe of the ear. شَحْمَةُ ٱلْأُذُنِ

To fill, load. شَحَنَ يَشْحَنُ وَأَشْحَنَ بِ

To treat with enmity. شَاحَنَ

Freight, cargo. شَحْنٌ وَشَحْنَةٌ

Hatred, enmity. شَحْنَاءُ وَشِحْنَةٌ

Garrison. شِحْنَةٌ

Hatred, enmity. مُشَاحَنَةٌ

To micturate. شَخَّ يَشِخّ شَخًّا

شِخَاخٌ	Urine.
شَخَرَ يَشْخِرُ شَخِيراً	To snore ; snort.
شَخَصَ بِبَصَرِهِ إِلَى	To gaze at.
شَخَصَ مِنْ وَإِلَى	To go from . . to . .
شَخَصَ	To distinguish.
تَشَخَّصَ	To be distinct.
شَخْصٌ ج أَشْخَاصٌ	Person, individual.
تَشْخِيصٌ	Diagnosis of (disease).
شَدَّ يَشُدُّ شَدًّا	To strap, bind.
شَدَّدَ	To bind fast, strengthen.
شَدَّدَ عَلَى	To treat with severity.
تَشَدَّدَ وَاشْتَدَّ	To be strengthened.
إِشْتَدَّ	To be strong, intense.
شِدَّةٌ	Violence, intensity.
شِدَّةٌ ج شَدَائِدُ	Hardship, distress.
شَدَّةٌ	Name of the sign (ّ).
شَدِيدٌ ج اشِدَّاءُ	Violent, strong.
شَدِيدُ الْبَاسِ	Courageous, brave.
أَشَدُّ	More intense, stronger.
أَشَدُّ سَوَاداً	Blacker.
أَشَدُّ غَضَباً	More or most angry.
إِشْتِدَادٌ	Violence. Strength.
شِدْقٌ	Cheek.
شَدْيَاقٌ ج شَدَايِقَة	Deacon
مُتَشَدِّقٌ	Diffuse in speech.
شَادِنٌ	A young gazelle.
شَدَا يَشْدُو وَأَشْدَى	To sing.
شَذَّ يَشِذُّ	To be exceptional.
شَاذٌّ ج شَوَاذ	Irregular, rare.
شُذُوذٌ	Irregularity ; rarity.
شَرٌّ ج شُرُورٌ	Anything bad, evil.
شَرٌّ ج أَشْرَارٌ	Wicked. Worse.'
شَرَارَةٌ	A spark.
شَرِيرٌ ج أَشْرَارٌ	Bad, wicked.
شِرِّيرٌ ج شِرِّيرُونَ	Very wicked.
أَلشِّرِّيرُ	The Evil One, Satan.
شَرِبَ يَشْرَبُ	To drink, swallow.
شَرِبَ الدُّخَّانَ	To smoke tobacco.

To saturate. شَرَّبَ

To absorb, imbibe. تَشَرَّبَ

Act of drinking. شُرْبٌ

Draught. Water-jug. شَرْبَةٌ

Drink, beverage. شَرَابٌ ج أَشْرِبَةٌ

Syrup. شَرَابٌ

Tassel. شَرَّابَةٌ ج شَرَارِيب

Moustache. شَارِبٌ ج شَوَارِبُ

Addicted to drink. شِرِّيبٌ

Inclination. مَشْرَبٌ ج مَشَارِبُ

To entangle, confuse. شَرْبَكَ

A species of fir. شَرْبِينٌ

To baste. شَرَّجَ

Sesame-oil. شَيْرَجٌ وَسِيرَجٌ

To explain. شَرَحَ يَشْرَحُ

To dissect. شَرَّحَ

To be enlarged. Happy. إِنْشَرَحَ

Commentary. شَرْحٌ ج شُرُوحٌ

Commentator. شَارِحٌ ج شُرَّاحٌ

Long slice of meat. شَرِيحٌ وَشَرِيحَةٌ

Dissection. تَشْرِيح

Anatomy. عِلْمُ ٱلتَّشْرِيحِ

Anatomist. مُشَرِّحٌ ج مُشَرِّحُونَ

Prime of youth. شَرْخٌ

To flee, take fright. شَرَدَ يَشْرُدُ

To depart from. شَرَدَ عَنْ

Roaming, fugitive. شَارِدٌ

Strange, unusual. شَوَارِدُ

Small number of men. شِرْذِمَةٌ

To be ill-natured. شَرِسَ يَشْرَسُ

Ill-natured. شَرِسٌ

Sticking-paste. شِرَاسٌ وَسِرَاسٌ

Extremity of a rib. شُرْسُوفٌ

Epigastric region. أَلْقِسْمُ ٱلشَّرَاسِيفِيُّ

Root. شِرْسٌ ج شُرُوسٌ

A fringe. شَرْشَرَةٌ ج شَرَاشِرُ

Bed-sheet. شَرْشَفٌ ج شَرَاشِفُ

To stipulate. شَرَطَ يَشْرُطُ وَٱشْتَرَطَ

شَرَطَ وَشَرَّطَ — To make incisions.
شَارَطَ وَتَشَارَطَ — To stipulate with.
شَرْطٌ ج شُرُوطٌ — Condition, stipulation, contract.
شَرْطِيٌّ ج شُرْطَةٌ — Guard's-man.
شَرِيطٌ ج شُرُط — Wire ; tape.
مِشْرَط ج مَشَارِط — Bistoury.
مُشَارَطَةٌ — Stipulation. Betting.
شَرَعَ يَشْرَعُ وَاشْتَرَعَ — To make a law.
شَرَعَ شُرُوعاً — To begin.
شَرَعَ يَقُولُ — He began to say.
شَرَعَ فِي — To engage in an affair.
شَرْع — Divine or religious law.
شَرْعِيٌّ — Legitimate, legal.
شَارِعٌ ج شَوَارِعُ — Main street. Legislator.
شِرَاعٌ ج أَشْرِعَةٌ — A sail.
شَرِيعَةٌ ج شَرَائِع — Law, statute.
أَلشَّرِيعَةُ — Jordan (river).
تَثْنِيَةُ الاشْتِرَاعِ — Deuteronomy.
مُشْتَرِعٌ — Legislator.

ثَرُفَ يَشْرُف — To be noble.
شَرَفَ يَشْرُفُ شَرَفاً — To be high.
شَرَّفَ — To exalt, honour.
أَشْرَفَ عَلَى — To be near to ; overtop.
تَشَرَّفَ — To be honoured.
شَرَفٌ ج أَشْرَافٌ — Elevated place. Eminence.
شَرَفٌ — Honour, nobility ; height.
شُرْفَةٌ ج شُرُفَاتٌ — Battlement.
شَرِيفٌ ج أَشْرَافٌ — Noble.
أَلْخَطُّ الشَّرِيف — An edict by the Sultan's own hand.
مُشْرِفٌ — Projecting, overlooking.
شَرَقَ يَشْرُقُ — To rise (sun).
شَرَّقَ — To go eastward.
أَشْرَقَ — To rise, shine, beam.
شَرْق — East ; Orient.
شَرْقِيٌّ — Eastern ; Oriental.
مَشْرِقٌ ج مشَارِق — East ; Orient. Levant.
شَارَكَ مُشَارَكَةً — To share with.
أَشْرَكَ فِي — To take a partner.

To be a polytheist. أَشْرَكَ بِاللهِ

To share. اشَارَكَ وَٱشْتَرَكَ

Polytheism. شِرْكٌ

Snare. شَرَكٌ ج أَشْرَاكٌ

Company ; partnership. شُرْكَةٌ

Shoe-string. شِرَاكٌ ج شُرُكٌ

Partner. شَرِيكٌ ج شُرَكَاء

Polytheist, idolater. مُشْرِكٌ

Associate. Subscriber. مُشْتَرِكٌ

Common to several. مُشْتَرَكٌ

To split, slit. شَرَمَ يَشْرُمُ شَرْماً

To be split. شَرِمَ وَتَشَرَّمَ وَٱنْشَرَمَ

Split, rent. شَرْمٌ ج شُرُومٌ

Cocoon. شَرْنَقَةٌ ج شَرَانِقُ

To be greedy for. شَرِهَ يَشْرَهُ إِلَى

Inordinate desire. شَرَهٌ وَشَرَاهَة

Greedy. Glutton. شَرِهٌ وَشَرْهَانُ

Trowsers. شِرْوَالٌ وَسِرْوَالٌ

To buy. شَرَى يَشْرِي شِرَاءً وَشِرًى

To buy. إِشْتَرَى

Purchase. شِرَاءٌ وشِرًى

Nettle-rash ; urticaria. شَرَى

Artery. شَرْيَانٌ ج شَرَايِين

Buyer. شَارٍ وَمُشْتَرٍ ج شُرَاةٌ

Jupiter (planet). اَلْمُشْتَرِي

To look askance at. شَزَرَ يَشْزُرُ إِلَى

To be distant. شَسَعَ يَشْسَعُ شُسُوعاً

Very remote, distant. شَاسِعٌ

Water-closet. (شَشْمَةٌ)

Sample. (شَشْنَةٌ)

Fish-hook. شِصٌّ ج شُصُوصٌ

To go beyond bounds. شَطَّ فِي

Shore, bank. شَطٌّ ج شُطُوطٌ

Excess. Injustice. شَطَطٌ

Shore. Coast. شَاطِئٌ ج شَوَاطِئ

To cut into strips. Deviate. شَطَبَ يَشْطُبُ

To divide, halve. شَطَرَ يَشْطُرُ

To balve with another. شَاطَرَ

شَطْرٌ ج شُطُورٌ	Half ; part.
شَاطِرٌ ج شُطَّارٌ	Wicked ; sharper.
مَشْطُورٌ	Divided into halves.
مُشَاطِرٌ	Adjacent, neighbouring.
شَطْرَنْجٌ	Chess.
شَطَفَ يَشْطُفُ شَطْفًا	To wash ; rinse.
شَيْطَنَ وَتَشَيْطَنَ	To be rebellious.
شَيْطَنَةٌ	Devilishness.
شَيْطَانٌ ج شَيَاطِين	Satan, devil.
شَظِيَّةٌ ج شَظَايَا	Splinter. Fibula.
شَعَّ يَشِعُّ شَعَاعًا	To disperse.
شَعَّ يَشِعُّ	To be dispersed.
أَشَعَّ	To emit rays.
شُعَاعٌ ج أَشِعَّةٌ وَشَعَاعٌ	Sun-beam.
تَشَعَّبَ وَٱنْشَعَبَ	To ramify.
شِعْبٌ ج شِعَابٌ	Mountain-pass.
شَعْبٌ ج شُعُوب	People, nation.
شُعْبَةٌ ج شُعَبٌ	Branch. Portion.
شَعْبَانُ	The eighth lunar month.
مُتَشَعِّبٌ	Ramified.
شَعْبَذَ	To juggle.
مُشَعْبِذٌ	Juggler.
شَعِثَ وَتَشَعَّثَ	To be dishevelled.
شَعَرَ يَشْعُرُ بِ	To know ; feel.
أَشْعَرَهُ بِ	To inform.
شِعْرٌ ج أَشْعَارٌ	Poetry, verse.
شَعْرٌ ج شُعُورٌ	Hair.
شَعْرَةٌ ج شَعَرَات	A hair.
شِعْرِيٌّ	Poetical.
أَلشِّعْرَى	Sirius, Dog-Star.
لَيْتَ شِعْرِي	Would that I knew !
أَشْعَرُ ج شُعْرٌ	Hairy, shaggy.
شِعَارٌ وَشَعَائِرُ	Rites.
شَعْرِيَّةٌ ج شَعْرِيَّات	Trellis-work.
شَاعِرٌ ج شُعَرَاءُ	Poet.
شُعُورٌ	Knowing, perceiving.
شَعِيرٌ	Barley.
مَشْعَرٌ ج مَشَاعِر	Sense (sight, &c.)

To kindle. شَعَلَ يَشْعُلُ وَشَعَّلَ وَاشْعَلَ

To be kindled. شَعِلَ وَاشْتَعَلَ

To be enraged. إِشْتَعَلَ غَضَبًا

Firebrand, flame. شُعْلَةٌ ج شُعَلٌ

Burning wick. شَعِيلَةٌ ج شُعُلٌ

Conflagration. إِشْتِعَالٌ

Lamp ; torch. مِشْعَلٌ ج مَشَاعِلُ

Palm-Sunday. عِيدُ ٱلشَّعَانِينِ

To juggle. شَعْوَذَ

Jugglery. شَعْوَذَةٌ

Juggler. مُشَعْوِذٌ

To stir up discord, evil. شَغَبَ يَشْغَبُ

Discord, tumult ; revolt. شَغْبٌ

To inflame with love. شَغَفَ حُبًّا

To be smitten. شُغِفَ بِ

Passionate love. شَغَفٌ

Passionately taken up. مَشْغُوفٌ

To occupy. شَغَلَ يَشْغُلُ

To divert from. شَغَلَ عَنْ

To busy, occupy much. شَغَّلَ

To be occupied. To act. إِشْتَغَلَ

Occupation, work. شُغْلٌ ج أَشْغَالٌ

Busying affair. شَاغِلٌ ج شَوَاغِلُ

Occupation. إِشْتِغَال

Occupied ; busy. مَشْغُولٌ

To be very fine, transparent. شَفَّ يَشِفُّ

Thin, fine dress. شَفٌّ ج شُفُوفٌ

Transparent. شَفَّافٌ

Transparency. شُفُوفٌ

Edge, border. شُفْرٌ ج أَشْفَارٌ

Blade. شَفْرَةٌ ج شِفَارٌ

Border of a valley. شَفِيرُ ٱلْوَادِي

To plead, intercede. Couple, double. شَفَعَ يَشْفَعُ

To make double. شَفَّعَ

Right of pre-emption. شُفْعَةٌ

Intercession, mediation. شَفَاعَةٌ

Intercessor. شَافِعٌ وَشَفِيعٌ ج شُفَعَاء

To pity. شَفِقَ يَشْفَقُ وَأَشْفَقَ عَلَى

شَفَقٌ Evening twilight.

شَفَقَةٌ Compassion ; tenderness.

شَفُوقٌ وَشَفِيقٌ Compasionate.

شَافَهَ To speak mouth to mouth.

شَفَةٌ ج شِفَاهٌ وَشَفَهَاتٌ وَشَفَوَاتٌ Lip.

شَفَهِيٌّ وَشَفَوِيٌّ Labiat.

مُشَافَهَةً وَشِفَاهاً By word of mouth.

شَفَى يَشْفِي شِفَاءً مِنْ To cure, heal.

أَشْفَى على To be very near.

إِشْتَفَى To recover (one's health).

إِسْتَشْفَى To seek a cure.

شِفَاءٌ Cure, recovery.

شَفاً Brink, edge, extremity.

شَافٍ Curing, healing.

جَوَابٌ شَافٍ A clear answer.

مُسْتَشْفًى وَدَارُ ٱلشِّفَاءِ Hospital.

شَقَّ يَشُقُّ شَقًّا To split, cleave.

شَقَّ مَشَقَّةً على To trouble, distress.

شَقَّ ٱلْعَصَا To rebel.

شَقَّقَ To split into pieces

إِنْشَقَّ To be split or separated.

شَقٌّ ج شُقُوقٌ Split, rent ; crack.

شِقٌّ وَمَشَقَّةٌ Great hardship.

شِقٌّ Half, one side of a thing.

شِقَّةٌ ج شِقَقٌ Piece of cloth.

شَاقٌّ Troublesome, hard.

شِقَاقٌ Separation, discord.

شَقِيقٌ ج أَشِقَّاءُ Full brother.

شَقَائِقُ ٱلنُّعْمَانِ Red anemone.

إِشْتِقَاقٌ Derivation of a word.

إِنْشِقَاقٌ Separation, division.

مَشَقَّةٌ ج مَشَاقٌّ Great hardship.

مُشْتَقٌّ Derived (word).

شُقْرَةٌ Light red, sorrel colour.

أَشْقَرُ Of fair complexion, sorrel.

شِقِرَّاقٌ The green wood pecker.

شَقْشَقَةُ ٱللِّسَانِ Verbosity.

To pile up. شَقَعَ يَشْقَعُ شَقْعًا

To split, cut into pieces. شَقَّفَ

Earthen pot ; piece. شَقَفَةٌ ج شَقَفٌ

To lift up. شَقَلَ يَشْقُلُ شَقْلاً

To be miserable. شَقِيَ يَشْقَى

To labour, toil. شَقِيَ فِي

To struggle with. شَاقَى

To make miserable. أَشْقَى

Misery. شَقًا وَشَقَاءٌ وَشَقَاوَةٌ

Miserable. شَقِيٌّ ج أَشْقِيَاءُ

To doubt. شَكَّ يَشُكُّ وَتَشَكَّكَ فِي

To pierce through. شَكَّ

To throw into doubt. شَكَّكَ فِي

Uncertainty, doubt. شَكٌّ ج شُكُوكٌ

Thrust (of a lance, &c.) شَكَّةٌ

Armed. شَاكُّ السِّلَاحِ

Doubtful, uncertain. مَشْكُوكٌ فِيهِ

To thank. شَكَرَ يَشْكُرُ وَتَشَكَّرَ لِ

Thanks. شُكْرٌ وَشُكْرَانٌ ج شُكُورٌ

Thankful. شَاكِرٌ وَشَكُورٌ

Hemlock. شَوْكَرَانٌ وَشَيْكَرَانٌ

To be stubborn. شَكُسَ يَشْكُسُ

Refractory. شَكِسٌ وَشَكُسٌ

To be obscure. شَكَلَ يَشْكُلُ وَاشْكَلَ عَلَى

To tether, tie up. شَكَلَ وَشَكَّلَ

To resemble. شَاكَلَ

To be fashioned, shaped. تَشَكَّلَ

To resemble one another. تَشَاكَلَ

To be ambiguous. إِشْتَكَلَ

To deem dubious. إِسْتَشْكَلَ

Likeness ; form. Fashion. Kind, sort. Vowel point. شَكْلٌ ج أَشْكَالٌ

Tether. شِكَالٌ ج شُكُلٌ

Side. Way. شَاكِلَةٌ ج شَوَاكِلُ

Resemblance. مُشَاكَلَةٌ وَتَشَاكُلٌ

Difficulty. مُشْكِلٌ ج مَشَاكِلُ

Mouth-bit. شَكِيمَةٌ

To complain to. شَكَا يَشْكُو إِلَى

To complain of pain. شَكَا أَلَمًا

To complain. تَشَكَّى وَٱشْتَكَى إِلَى

Complaint ; accusation. شَكَايَةٌ

Plaintiff. شَاكٍ وَمُشْتَكٍ

Accused. مَشْكُوٌّ وَمُشْتَكَى عَلَيْهِ

To be paralyzed. شَلَّ يَشَلُّ وَشَلَّ

To paralyze, disable. أَشَلَّ

Paralysis. شَلَلٌ

Cataract. شَلَّالٌ ج شَلَّالَاتٌ

To strip, undress. شَلَحَ يَشْلَحُ

To strip, plunder. شَلَّحَ

Mantle. مَشْلَحٌ

Body after decay. شِلْوٌ ج أَشْلَاءٌ

Darnel-grass. شَيْلَمٌ

To smell. شَمَّ يَشَمُّ شَمًّا

To make one smell. شَمَّمَ وَأَشَمَّ

Sense of smell. شَمٌّ

A fragrant, striped melon. شَمَّامٌ

To rejoice شَمِتَ يَشْمَتُ شَمَاتَةً بِ at the affliction of an enemy.

To disappoint. شَمَّتَ

To be high, lofty. شَمَخَ يَشْمَخُ

To be high ; be proud. تَشَامَخَ

High ; proud. شَامِخٌ ج شُمَّخٌ

Pride, haughtiness. تَشَامُخٌ

Proud, haughty. مُتَشَامِخٌ

To tuck up a garment. شَمَرَ يَشْمُرُ

To be ready for. تَشَمَّرَ وَٱنْشَمَرَ لِ

Fennel. شَمْرَةٌ وَشَمَارٌ

To abhor. شَمَزَ يَشْمُزُ مِنْ

To shrink from. اشْمَأَزَّ ٱشْمِئْزَازًا

To be sunny. شَمِسَ يَشْمُسُ وَأَشْمَسَ

To be restive. شَمَسَ يَشْمُسُ

To expose in the sun. شَمَّسَ

Sun. شَمْسٌ ج شُمُوسٌ

Solar. شَمْسِيٌّ

Umbrella ; sun-shade. شَمْسِيَّةٌ

Deacon. شَمَّاسٌ ج شَمَامِسَةٌ

Restive, refractory. شَمُوسٌ

Exposed to the sun. مُشَمَّسٌ

Whiteness, hoariness. شَمَطٌ

Gray-haired, graizzled. أَشْمَطُ

To wax ; cover with wax. شَمَّعَ

Wax. شَمْعٌ ج شُمُوعٌ

Wax-candle. شَمَعَةٌ ج شَمَعَاتٌ

Waxed. Oil-cloth. مُشَمَّعٌ

Candlestick. شَمْعَدَانٌ

To shift to north. شَمَلَ يَشْمُلُ

To take the left side. شَمَلَ يَشْمُلُ

To include, contain. شَمَلَ يَشْمِلُ

To comprise, contain. إِشْتَمَلَ عَلَى

Union. شَمْلٌ

Comprehensive ; general. شَامِلٌ

Left side ; north. شِمَالٌ

Northern, northerly. شِمَالِيٌّ

Endowed. Included. مشْمُولٌ

Beet (root). شَمَنْدَرٌ وَشَمَنْدُرٌ

To attack. شَنَّ وَأَشَنَّ ٱلغَارَةَ عَلَى

To hate, detest. شَنَأَ وَشَنِئَ يَشْنَأَ

Hatred, detestation. شَنْءٌ

Hater, enemy. شَانِئٌ ج شُنَاءٌ

Hated ; hateful. مشْنُوءٌ

Moustache. شَنَبٌ ج اشْنَابٌ

A grain-measure. شُنْبُلٌ ج شَنَابِلُ

Spasmodic contraction. تَشَنُّجٌ

Nature, disposition. شِنْشِنَةٌ ج شَنَاشِنُ

To be bad. شَنُعَ يَشْنُعُ شَنَاعَةً

To disgrace, revile. شَنَعَ شَنْعاً

To accuse him of evil. شَنَّعَ عَلَيْهِ

To regard as foul. إِسْتَشْنَعَ

Infamy, ugliness. شُنْعَةٌ وَشَنَاعَةٌ

Foul, ugly. شَنِعٌ شَنِيعٌ وَأَشْنَعُ

To embellish. شَنَّفَ

Ear-ring. شَنْفٌ ج شُنُوفٌ

To hang. شَنَقَ يَشْنِقُ شَنْقاً

Hanging. شَنْقٌ

Longing, yearning. شَنِقٌ وَشَانِقٌ

Cord, rope. شِنَاقٌ ج أَشْنِقَة

Gibbet, gallows. مِشْنَقَةٌ ج مَشَانِقُ

Hanged. مَشْنُوقٌ

Gray colour. شُبْهَةٌ وشَهَبٌ

Meteor. شِهَابٌ ج شُهُبٌ

Gray. أَشْهَبُ م شَهْبَاءُ ج شُهْبٌ

Aleppo. أَلشَّهْبَاءُ

To witness, be present. شَهِدَ يَشْهَدُ

To witness against. شَهِدَ يَشْهَدُ على

To bear witness to. شَهِدَ بِ

To be an eye-witness ; see. شَاهَدَ

Call to witness. أَشْهَدَ وَٱسْتَشْهَدَ

To die as a martyr. أُسْتُشْهِدَ

Honeycomb. شُهْدٌ ج شِهَادٌ

Eye-witness. شَاهِدٌ ج شُهُودٌ

Testimony. Diploma. شَهَادَةٌ

Martyrdom. شَهَادَةٌ وَٱسْتِشْهَادٌ

Witness. Martyr. شَهِيدٌ ج شُهَدَاءُ

Assembly. Aspect. مَشْهَدٌ

Vision, sight, scene. مُشَاهَدَة

To make public. شَهَرَ يَشْهَرُ

To make known, publish. أَشْهَرَ

To become known ; be celebrated ; notorius. إِشْتَهَرَ

Month. شَهْرٌ ج شُهُورٌ وأَشْهُرٌ

Celebrity, fame, repute. شُهْرَةٌ

Celebrated, notorious. شَهِيرٌ

Well-known. مَشْهُورٌ ج مَشَاهِيرُ

According to usage. عَلَى ٱلْمَشْهُورِ

To draw the breath. شَهَقَ يَشْهَقُ

A single cry. شَهْقَةٌ

High, lofty. شَاهِقٌ ج شَوَاهِقُ

Inspiration and expiration in breathing. أَلشَّهِيقُ وٱلزَّفِيرُ

A mixture of two colours. شَهَلٌ

To be sagacious. شَهُمَ يَشْهُمُ

Honourable. شَهْمٌ ج شِهَامٌ

Sagacity. Honour. شَهَامَةٌ

Falcon. شَاهِينٌ ج شَوَاهِين

شَهَا يَشْهُو	To crave for.
شَهَّى	To excite a desire.
إِشْتَهَى	To desire eagerly.
شَهْوَةٌ ج شَهَوَاتٌ	Strong desire, appetite, passion, lust.
شَهِيٌّ وَمُشْتَهًى	Desired, pleasant.
شَهَوَانِيٌّ	Sensual.
أَشْهَى	More desirable, delicious.
إِشْتِهَاءٌ	Desire, craving.
مُشْتَهًى ج مُشْتَهَيَاتٌ	Craved.
شَابَ يَشُوبُ شَوْبًا	To mix.
شَائِبَةٌ ج شَوَائِب	Blemish.
شُوحَةٌ	A species of kite.
أَشَارَ إِلَى	To point out or at.
أَشَارَ عَلَى ب	To counsel, advise.
شَاوَرَ وَاسْتَشَارَ	To consult.
تَشَاوَرَ عَلَى	To consult together.
مَشْوَرَةٌ وَمَشُورَةٌ	Consultation.
أَهْلُ ٱلشُّورَى	Councillors.
مَجْلِسُ ٱلشُّورَى	Council.
إِشَارَةٌ	Sign ; signal ; allusion.
إِسْمُ ٱلإِشَارَةِ	Demonstrative pronoun.
مُشَارٌ إِلَيْهِ	Indicated, referred to.
مُشِيرٌ	Councillor ; minister.
مُسْتَشَارٌ	Councillor.
شَوْرَبَةٌ	Soup.
شَوَّشَ	To trouble, confuse.
تَشَوَّشَ	To be confused ; sick.
شَاشٌ	Thin muslin.
شَاوِيشٌ (جَاوِيشٌ)	Sergeant.
شُوشَةٌ	Hair of head.
تَشْوِيشٌ	Confusion. Sickness.
مُشَوَّشٌ	Confused. Ill.
أَشْوَصُ م شَوْصَاءُ	Squint-eyed.
شَافَ يَشُوفُ شَوْفًا	To see.
شَوَّفَ	To show.
شَاقَ وَشَوَّقَ إِلَى	To fill with longing.
تَشَوَّقَ وَاشْتَاقَ إِلَى	To long for.

Strong desire. شَوْقٌ ج أَشْوَاق

Desirable, charming. شَائِقٌ

Ardently longing. مُشْتَاقٌ

To pierce with a thorn. شَاكَ وَشَوَّكَ

Thorns, prickles. شَوْكٌ ج أَشْوَاكٌ

A thorn, sting. شَوْكَةٌ

Shawl. شَالٌ ج شَالاَتٌ

Desert. شَوْلٌ ج أَشْوَالٌ

Large sack. شُوَالٌ ج شُوَالاَتٌ

The tenth lunar month. شَوَّالٌ

Watch-tower. Barn. شُونَةٌ ج شُوَن

To disfigure. شَوَّهَ

To be ugly, disfigured. تَشَوَّهَ

Deformity, ugliness. شَوَهٌ

Deformed ugly. أَشْوَهُ م شَوْهَاءُ

King ; Shah, (*Persian*). شَاهٌ

Royal, imperial. شَاهَانِيٌّ

Sheep, lamb. شَاةٌ ج شَاءٌ وشِيَاهٌ

Ugly, deformed. Stupid. شَوٌّ

To roast, broil (meat). شَوَى يَشْوِي

To be roasted, grilled. إِنْشَوَى

Roasted, grilled. شَوِي وَمَشْوِيٌّ

Gridiron. مِشْوًى ومِشْوَاةٌ

To will, wish, desire. شَاءَ يَشَاءُ

Thing, something. شَيْءٌ ج أَشْيَاءُ

Gradually. شَيْئًا فشَيْئًا

A small thing ; a little. (شُوَيَّةٌ)

Will, wish, desire. مَشِيئَةٌ

To become gray. شَابَ يَشِيبُ

To make gray. أَشَابَ وَشَيَّبَ

Old age. شَيْبٌ وَمَشِيبٌ

White or hoary beard. شَيْبَةٌ

Hoary ; old. شَائِبٌ وَأَشْيَبُ

Cotton-prints. شِيتٌ

Artemesia ; wormwood. شِيْحٌ

To grow old. شَاخَ يَشِيخُ وَشَيَّخَ

Old man, Sheikh. شَيْخٌ ج شُيُوخ

Religious Chief of the Moslems. شَيْخُ ٱلإِسْلاَمْ

شَيْخُوخَةٌ Old age.

مَشْيَخَةٌ Republic. Senate.

شادَ يَشيدُ وَشَيَّدَ To build up.

مَشيدٌ وَمُشَيَّدٌ High, elevated.

شَاطَ يَشيطُ To be slightly burnt.

إِسْتَشاطَ عَلَى To get angry.

شَيْطانٌ Satan, devil.

مُسْتَشيطٌ Inflamed by anger.

شَاعَ يَشِيعُ To be spread abroad.

شاعَ ب وَأَشَاعَ To publish.

شَيَّعَ To see a guest off.

شَايَعَ To escort, follow.

أَشاعَ ٱلْخَبَرَ To publish the news.

شِيعَةٌ Party, sect ; the Shites.

شِيعِيٌّ A Shite.

شَائِعٌ وَمُشاعٌ Public ; common.

مُشَايِعٌ لِ Partisan of.

شَالَ يَشِيلُ شَيْلاً To lift up, carry.

شِيَالَةٌ To trade of a porter.

شَيَّالٌ A porter.

شَامَةٌ ج شَامَاتٌ Black spot ; mole.

أَلشَّامُ Syria.

شِيمَةٌ ج شِيَمٌ Character, nature.

كَرِيمُ ٱلشِّيَمِ Of noble qualities.

شانَ يَشِينُ شَيْناً To disgrace.

شَيْنٌ A disgraceful thing.

شَايٌ Tea.

ص

ص As a numeral sign=90.

صَبَّ يَصُبُّ صبًّا To pour out.

صَبَّ عَلَى To dart or rush upon.

صَبَّ يَصَبُّ صبابَةً To be in love.

أَصبَّ To descend.

إِنْصبّ To be poured out. Incline.

صَبٌّ Longing lover.

صُبَّةٌ Catarrh of the nose.

صَبَابَةٌ Excessive love or desire.

صَبِيبٌ Poured forth.

مَصَبّ Mouth of a river.

صَابِئٌ ج صَابِئُونَ Sabian.

صَبُحَ يَصْبُحُ To be handsome.

صَبَّحَ To bid good morning.

أَصْبَحَ To rise in the morning.

أَصْبَحَ عَالِماً He became learned.

أَصْبَحَ يَفْعَلُ To take to doing.

صُبْحٌ ج أَصْبَاحٌ Dawn. Morning.

صُبْحَةٌ Early part of forenoon.

صَبَاحٌ Morning.

صَبَاحَةٌ Beauty, comeliness.

صَبِيحَةٌ Morning.

مِصْبَاحٌ ج مَصَابِيحُ Lamp.

صَبَرَ يَصْبِرُ To be patient. Confine.

صَبَّرَ To ask one to be patient. Embalm Ballast.

تَصَبَّرَ وَاصْطَبَرَ To be patient.

صَبْرٌ Patience, endurance.

صَبِرٌ وَصَبْرٌ Aloe. Aloe-plant.

صَابِرٌ ج صَابِرُونَ Patient.

صَبَّارٌ وَصَبُورٌ Very patient.

صُبَّيرٌ Cactus.

صَابُورَةٌ Ballast (of a ship).

صَابُورِيَّةٌ A kind of basket.

أَصْبَعٌ ج أَصَابِعُ Finger, toe.

مُصَبَّعٌ Gridiron.

صَبَغَ يَصْبُغُ To dye, colour.

إِصْطَبَغَ To be baptized ; dyed.

صِبْغٌ وَصِبَاغٌ Dye ; paint.

صِبْغَةٌ Dye. Religion. Baptism.

صَبَّاغٌ Dyer.

صِبَاغَةٌ Art of dyeing.

مَصْبَغَةٌ A dye-house.

صَبَّنَ وَصَوْبَنَ To wash with soap.

صَبَّانٌ Soap-maker.

صَابُونٌ Soap.

مَصْبَنَةٌ Soap factory.

صَبَا ـُ إِلَى To incline to, long for.

أَلصَّبَا Light east-wind.

الصِّبَا Youth, boyhood. Love.

صَبْوَةٌ Youth.

صَبِيٌّ ج صِبْيَانٌ Boy, youth.

صَبِيَّةٌ ج صَبَايَا Young woman.

صَحَّ يَصِحُّ To recover from disease. To be sound ; true.

صَحَّحَ تَصْحِيحاً To cure a sick person. Correct ; render sound.

صِحَّةٌ Health. Soundness. Truth.

صَحِيحٌ ج أَصِحَّاءُ Healthy, sound. True.

إِصْحَاحٌ ج إِصْحَاحَاتٌ Chapter.

تَصْحِيحٌ Correction.

صَحِبَ يَصْحَبُ وَصَاحَبَ To accompany.

تَصَحَّبَ لِ To take the part of.

تَصَاحَبَ مَعْ To associate with.

إِصْطَحَبَ To associate together.

صُحْبَةٌ Companionship.

صَاحِبٌ ج أَصْحَابٌ Friend. Owner.

صَاحِبُ مَالٍ Wealthy.

مَصْحُوبٌ Accompanied.

صَحْرَاءُ ج صَحْرَاوَاتٌ Desert.

To alter a word. صحَّفَ تَصْحِيفاً
Large plate. صَحْفَةٌ ج صِحَافٌ
A written page. صَحِيفَةٌ ج صَحَائِفُ
The Koran. مُصْحَفٌ ج مَصَاحِفُ
Plate (for food). صحْنٌ ج صحونٌ
Court (of a house). صحْنُ الدَّارِ
To become clear (sky). صَحَا يَصْحُو وَصَحِيَ يَصْحَى
To recover consciousness after intoxication or sleep.
To rouse. أَصحى
Fair weather; clear sky. صَحْوٌ
Mental clearness. صَحْوَةٌ
Clear (sky); conscious. صَاحٍ
To shout, clamour. صخبَ
Clamourous. صخِبٌ وَصَخوبٌ
Rock. صخرٌ وَصَخرَةٌ ج صُخورٌ
Rocky; stony. صخِرٌ وَمُصخِرٌ
To turn away from. صَدَّ يَصُدُّ عَنْ
To oppose; prevent. صَدَّ صَدًّا
Aversion; opposition. صَدٌّ

Subject in hand. صَدَدٌ
Pus; matter. صَدِيدٌ
To become rusty. صَدِئَ يَصْدَأُ
To confront; face. تصَدَّى لِ
Rust. صَدَأٌ
To sing. صَدَحَ يَصْدُحُ
Singer. صَادِحٌ
To take place; occur. صَدَرَ ـُ
To proceed from. صَدَرَ مِنْ
To arise, result from. صَدَرَ عَنْ
To go to. صدَرَ إِلَى
To begin (a book) with. صَدَّرَ بِ
To show forth; issue. أَصْدَرَ
Chest; bosom. صَدْرٌ ج صُدُورٌ
The first part. Chief.
Prime Minister. اَلصَّدْرُ الأَعْظَم
Vest. صدْرِيَّةٌ صَدَارَةٌ
The office of Prime Minister. صَدَارَةٌ
Going out. صَادِرٌ
(*opp. to* وارد coming in).

مَصْدَرٌ ج مَصَادِرُ	Origin; source. Noun of action.
صَدِعَ وَصُدِّعَ	To have a sprain.
صَدَّعَ	To trouble; annoy.
إِنْصَدَعَ	To be sprained.
صَدْعٌ ج صُدُوعٌ	Fissure. Sprain.
صُدَاعٌ	Headache.
صَدَغَ يَصْدَغُ إِلَى	To incline to.
صُدْغٌ ج أَصْدَاغٌ	Temple; temporal region.
صَدَفَ يَصْدُفُ	To meet by chance.
صَادَفَ مُصَادَفَةً	To encounter.
تَصَدَفَ	To happen by chance.
تَصَادَفَ	To meet together.
صَدَفٌ	Sea-shells.
صَدَفَةٌ ج صَدَفَاتٌ	A see-shell.
صُدْفَةٌ ج صِدَفٌ	Chance.
صَدَقَ يَصْدُقُ	To say the truth.
يَصْدُقُ عَلَى	It applies correctly to.
صَدَقَ	To believe. Verify.
صَادَقَ	To treat as a friend.
صَادَقَ عَلَى	To ratify, confirm.
تَصَدَّقَ	To give alms, charity.
صِدْقٌ	Truth; veracity; sincerity.
صَدَقَةٌ ج صَدَقَاتٌ	Alms; charity.
صَدَاقٌ	Dower given to a wife.
صَدَاقَةٌ	True friendship.
صَادِقٌ	True, sincere.
صَدِيقٌ ج أَصْدِقَاءُ	True friend.
صِدِّيقٌ ج صِدِّيقُونَ	Righteous.
أَصْدَقُ	More, most, true.
تَصْدِيقٌ	Belief; faith. Verification.
مُصَدِّقٌ	Believer. Verifying. Confirming.
مُتَصَدِّقٌ	One who gives alms.
صَيْدَلَةٌ	An apothecary's trade.
صَيْدَلَانِيٌّ ج صَيَادِلَةٌ	Druggist.
صَيْدَلِيَّةٌ	A pharmacy.
صَدَمَ يَصْدِمُ	To strike; repel.
صَادَمَ	To dash against; thrust.

To collide. تَصَادَمَ وَٱصْطَدَمَ

Shock, collision. صَدْمَةٌ

To return an echo. أَصْدَى إِصْدَاءً

Echo ; sound. صَدًى ج أَصْدَاءٌ

To tie up. صَرَّ يَصُرُّ صَرًّا

Creak ; chirp ; tingle. صَرَّ يَصِرُّ

To persist in. أَصَرَّ عَلَى

Parcel ; packet. صُرَّةٌ ج صُرَرٌ

Persistence. إِصْرَارٌ

Grating noise. صَرِيرٌ

To be pure, clear. صَرُحَ يَصْرُحُ

To make clear proclaim. صَرَّحَ

Pure, clear. Explicit. صَرِيحٌ

Clearness. Purity. صَرَاحَةٌ

Clear expression. تَصْرِيحٌ

To cry out. صَرَخَ يَصْرُخُ

A loud cry. صَرْخَةٌ

Cries, screams. صُرَاخٌ وَصَرِيخٌ

Crying out. صَارِخٌ

Intense cold. صَرْصَرٌ

A cockroach. صُرْصُرٌ وَصُرْصُورٌ

Violent, cold wind. رِيحٌ صَرْصَرٌ

Way ; path. صِرَاطٌ

To strike down. صَرَعَ يَصْرَعُ

To have a fit. صُرِعَ

To wrestle. صَارَعَ وَتَصَارَعَ

To be thrown down. إِنْصَرَعَ

Epilepsy. صَرْعٌ

Epileptic. صَرِيعٌ وَمَصْرُوعٌ

Hemistich. مِصْرَاعٌ ج مَصَارِيعُ
Half of a folding door.

Wrestler, combatant. مُصَارِعٌ

To send away ; صَرَفَ يَصْرِفُ
change or spend (money).

To avert from. صَرَفَ عَنْ

To turn him to. صَرَفَهُ إِلَى

To conjugate, decline. صَرَّفَ

To commit to. صَرَّفَ فِي

To be inflected. تَصَرَّفَ

To carry out.	تَصَرَّفَ فِي
To depart; be inflected.	إِنْصَرَفَ
Etymology.	صَرْفٌ
Pure, unmixed.	صِرْفٌ
Evils of fortune.	صُرُوفُ ٱلدَّهْرِ
Broker's trade ; brokerage.	صَرَافَةٌ
Money-changer.	صَرَّافٌ ج صَيَارِفَةٌ
Departing, going off.	إِنْصِرَافٌ
Freedom of action.	تَصَرُّفٌ
Inflection of words.	تَصْرِيفٌ
Vicissitudes of time.	تَصَارِيفُ الدَّهْرِ
Expense.	مَصْرُوفٌ مَصَارِيفُ
Having free action. Inflected word. Governor.	مُتَصَرِّفٌ
A governor's district.	مُتَصَرِّفِيَّةٌ
A word capable of inflection.	مُتَصَرَّفٌ
To cut off, sever.	صَرَمَ يَصْرِمُ
To cease.	تَصَرَّمَ وَٱنْصَرَمَ
Sharp severe.	صَارِمٌ ج صَوَارِمُ

Severity.	صَرَامَةٌ
Shoe.	(صِرْمَايَةٌ ج صَرَامِيُّ)
The past year.	اَلْعَامُ ٱلْمُنْصَرِمُ
Mast.	صَارٍ وَصَارِيَةٌ ج صَوَارٍ
Platform.	مِصْطَبَةٌ ج مَصَاطِبُ
To be difficult.	صَعُبَ يَصْعُبُ
To make difficult.	صَعَّبَ وَتَصَعَّبَ
To find difficult.	إِسْتَصْعَبَ
To be difficult.	تَصَعَّبَ وَاسْتَصْعَبَ
Difficult, hard.	صَعْبٌ ج صِعَابٌ
Difficulty.	صُعُوبَةٌ
Difficulties, troubles.	مَصَاعِبُ
Thyme.	صَعْتَرٌ (أَوْ سَعْتَرٌ)
To ascend.	صَعِدَ يَصْعَدُ صُعُوداً
To take or carry up.	صَعِدَ بِ
To cause to ascend.	أَصْعَدَ
Distress, calamity.	صَعْدَاءُ
Sighing, deep sigh.	صُعَدَاءُ
Henceforth.	مِنَ ٱلآنَ فَصَاعِداً

Earth. Elevated land. صَعِيدٌ

Upper Egypt. صَعِيدُ مِصْرَ

Place of ascent. مَصْعَدٌ ج مَصَاعِدُ

Vehement sound, cry. صَعَقٌ

Thunderbolt. صَاعِقَةٌ ج صَوَاعِقُ

Poor, pauper. صُعْلُوكٌ ج صَعَالِيك

To be small. صَغُرَ يَصْغُرُ

To be base. صَغِرَ يَصْغَرُ

To make small. صَغَّرَ وَأَصْغَرَ

To change a noun into the diminutive form. صَغَّرَ ٱلْإِسْمَ

To become small, or base. تَصَاغَرَ

To esteem as little. إِسْتَصْغَرَ

Smallness. صِغَرٌ وصَغَارَةٌ

Adject. صَاغِرٌ ج صاغِرُونَ

Little, small. صَغِيرٌ ج صِغَارٌ

A small sin. صَغِيرَةٌ ج صَغَائِرُ

Smaller, younger; least. أَصْغَرُ

The minor proposition of a syllogism. أَلصُّغْرَى

Act of diminishing. تَصْغِيرٌ

Noun in the diminutive form. مُصَغَّرٌ

To incline to. صَغَا يَصْغُو إِلَى

To listen to. صَغَا وَأَصْغَى إِلى

Attention, listening. إِصْغَاءٌ

To set in a line. صَفَّ يَصُفُّ

To take position in line. إِصْطَفَّ

Row, line, class. صَفٌّ ج صُفُوفٌ

Line of battle. مَصَفٌّ ج مَصَافٌّ

To consider, examine. صَفَحَ ـَ

To turn away from, leave. Pardon, forgive. صَفَحَ ـَ عَنْ

To cover with plates (metal). صَفَّحَ

To clap the hands. صَفَّحَ بِالْيَدِ

To take by the hands (in saluting). صَافَحَ مُصَافَحَةً وصِفَاحًا

To examine attentively. تَصَفَّحَ

Forgiveness. صَفْحٌ

To disregard. ضَرَبَ عَنْهُ صَفْحًا

Page of a book. صَفْحَةٌ ج صَفَحَاتٌ

Generous, forgiving. صَفُوحٌ

Plate of metal. صَفِيحَة ج صَفَائِحُ
Grasp of the hand. مُصَافَحَةٌ
Broad, flat. Plated. مُصَفَّحٌ
To shackle, fetter. صَفَدَ يَصْفِدُ
Bond, fetter. صَفَدٌ ج أَصْفَادٌ
To whistle. صَفَرَ يَصْفِرُ صَفِيراً
To be empty. صَفِرَ يَصْفَرُ صَفَراً
To make, or dye, yellow. صَفَّرَ
To make vacant. صَفَّرَ وَأَصْفَرَ
To become poor. أَصْفَرَ
To become yellow, pale. إِصْفَرَّ
Empty. صِفْرٌ ج أَصْفَارٌ
Having nothing. صِفْرُ ٱلْيَدَيْنِ
Zero. صِفْرٌ ج وَسِفْرٌ ج أَصْفَارٌ
Second month of lunar year. صَفَرٌ
Yellowness, paleness. صُفْرَةٌ
Whistle. صَافُورَةٌ وَصُفَّيْرَةٌ
Yolk of an egg. صَفَارُ ٱلْبَيْضِ
Golden oriole. صُفَارِيَّةٌ

Yellow. أَصْفَرُ م صَفْرَاءُ ج صُفْرٌ
(Yellow) bile. صَفْرَاءُ
A poor man, destitute. مُصْفِرٌ
Desert, plain. صَفْصَفٌ
Willow, osier. صَفْصَافٌ
To slap. صَفَعَ يَصْفَعُ صَفْعاً
A slap. صَفْعَةٌ
To strike; flap. صَفَقَ يَصْفُقُ صَفْقاً
To be strong. صَفُقَ يَصْفُقُ صَفَاقَةً
To clap the hands. صَفَّقَ
To agree upon. اصْفَقَ عَلَى
They ratified a compact. تَصَافَقُوا
Side, flank, face. صَفْقٌ ج صُفُوقٌ
Contract, bargain. صَفْقَةٌ
Fascia; aponeurosis. صِفَاقٌ
Thick, firm (texture). صَفِيقٌ
Scrotum. صَفَنٌ ج أَصْفَانٌ
Saphena vein. صَافِنٌ ج صَوَافِنُ
To be clear. صَفَا يَصْفُو

To purify, filter. صَفَّى وَأَصْفَى

To be sincere. صَافَى وَاصْفَى ٱلْوُدَّ

To choose, select. إِصْطَفَى

Smooth stone. صَفَا ج أَصْفَاء

Serenity of life, pleasure. صَفَاء

Clearness. صَفْوٌ وَصَفَاء وَصَفْوَةٌ

Pure ; chosen. صَفِيٌّ ج أَصْفِيَاء

Pure, lear, climpid. صَافٍ

Strainer. مِصْفَاةٌ ج مَصَافٍ

Purified, filtered. مُصَفًّى

Chosen. مُصْطَفًى

To strike. صَقَرَ يَصْقُرُ

Hawk. صَقْرٌ ج أَصْقُرٌ

Hell. صَقَرُ

A pickaxe. صَاقُورٌ

To be covered with frost. صُقِعَ

To be cold, icy. صَقَعَ

Region, district. صُقْعٌ ج اصْقَاعٌ

Intenseness of cold. صَقْعَةٌ

Hoar-frost. صَقِيعٌ

To polish, give lustre. صَقَلَ يَصْقُلُ

Staging. صَقَالَةٌ ج صَقَائِلُ

Polisher. صَقَّالٌ ج صَيَاقِلَةٌ

Polished. Sword. صَقِيلٌ

Sclav. صَقْلَبِيٌّ ج صَقَالِبَةٌ

To strike coin (money). صَكَّ يَصُكُّ

To trip, stumble. صَكَّ يَصُكُّ

To strike each other. إِصْطَكَّ

A legal deed. صَكٌّ ج صُكُوكٌ

Deadly serpent. صِلٌّ ج أَصْلَالٌ

To crucify. صَلَبَ يَصْلُبُ صَلْبًا

To become hard, tough. صَلُبَ يَصْلُبُ

To render hard. To make the sign of the cross. صَلَّبَ

To become hard, firm. تَصَلَّبَ

Crucifixion. صَلْبٌ وَتَصْلِيبٌ

The loins. صُلْبٌ ج أَصْلَابٌ

Hardness, firmness. صَلَابَةٌ

Cross. صَلِيبٌ ج صُلْبَانٌ

صَلِيبِيٌّ ج صَلِيبِيَّةٌ — Crusader.

مُصَالَبَةً — Crosswise.

مُصَلَّبٌ — Crossing at right angles.

مَصْلُوبٌ ج مَصَالِيبُ — Crucified.

صَلْتٌ — Fair ; wide.

صَوْلَجَانٌ وَصَوْلَجَانَةٌ — Sceptre.

صَلَحَ يَصْلُحُ — To be good, right.

صَلَحَ لِ — To be suitable, good for.

صَالَحَ مُصَالَحَةً — To make peace.

صَالَحَ عَلَى — To agree upon.

أَصْلَحَ — To repair, improve.

أَصْلَحَ بَيْنَ — To make peace between (two parties).

تَصَالَحَ وَاصْطَلَحَ — To be reconciled.

إِصْطَلَحَ — To become better.

إِصْطَلَحَ عَلَى — To agree upon. ...

صُلْحٌ — Peace, reconciliation.

صَالِحٌ — Good ; fit ; just. (one's good, self-interest).

صَالِحَةٌ ج صَالِحَاتٌ — A good deed.

صَلاَحٌ — Goodness, virtue.

إِصْلاَحٌ — Reformation ; improvement.

إِصْطِلاَحٌ — Technical use.

إِصْطِلاَحِيٌّ — Conventional.

مُصْلِحٌ — Peacemaker, reformer.

مَصْلَحَةٌ ج مَصَالِحُ — Advantage. Department.

مُصَالَحَةٌ — Reconciliation.

صَلَدَ يَصْلُدُ صَلْداً — To be hard.

صَلْصَلَ وَتَصَلْصَلَ — To sound.

صِلْصَالٌ — Clay.

صَلَحٌ — Baldness of the head.

صَلَعَةٌ وَصُلْعَةٌ — Bald spot.

أَصْلَعُ م صَلْعَاءُ ج صُلْعٌ — Bald.

صَلْعَمَ — *Abbreviation of the formula:* صَلَّى ٱللّٰهُ عَلَيْهِ وَسَلَّمَ

صَلَفَ يَصْلَفُ وَتَصَلَّفَ — To boast.

صَلَفٌ — Boasting.

صَلَّى صَلاَةً أَوْ صَلْوَةً — To pray.

صَلَّى عَلَى — To pray for ; bless.

صَلاَةٌ ج صَلَوَاتٌ — Prayer. Mercy.

Place of prayer. مُصَلًّى
One who prays. مصَلٍّ
To roast, broil. صَلَى يَصْلِي
To put into the fire. أَصْلَى
To warm one's self by the fire. تصلَّى وَاصْطَلَى بِالنَّارِ
Fuel ; fire. صلاَءٌ
To stop (a flask). صَمَّ يصمُّ صَمًّا
To become deaf. صَمَّ وَأَصَمَّ
To determine upon. صَمَّم على
Deafness. صَمَمٌ
Stopper, cork. Valve. صِمامٌ
Most sincerely. مِنْ صَمِيمِ ٱلْقَلْبِ
Deaf. أصمُّ م صَمَّاءُ ج صُمٌّ
Hard stone. حَجَرٌ أَصَمُّ
A surd root. جِذْرٌ أَصَمُّ
To be silent. صَمَتَ يَصْمُتُ صَمْتًا
To silence. صمَّتَ وأَصْمَتَ
Silence. صَمْتٌ وصمات وَصُمُوتٌ
Solid (not hollow). مصْمَتٌ

Canal of the ear. صِمَاخٌ ج أَصْمِخَةٌ
To arrange ; adorn. صَمَدَ يَصْمُدُ صَمْدًا
To lay up, save. صَمَّدَ
Solid ; not hollow. صَمَدٌ
The Eternal (God). أَلصَّمَدُ
Cell of a recluse. صَوْمَعَةٌ ج صَوَامِع
To gum, put gum into. صَمَّغَ
Gum. صَمْغٌ ج صُمُوغٌ
Gum Arabic. أَلصَّمْغُ ٱلْعَرَبِيُّ
To have a fetid odour. أَصَنَّ
Stench. صَنَّةٌ وَصُنَانٌ
Tube, pipe. صُنْبُورٌ
Pine tree. صَنَوْبَرٌ
Cone-shaped. صَنَوْبَرِيٌّ
Cymbal. صَنْجٌ ج صنوجٌ
Valiant. صِنْدِيدٌ ج صَنَادِيد
Chest, trunk. صُنْدُوقٌ ج صَنَادِيقُ
Sandal-wood. صَنْدَلٌ
Fish-hook. صِنَّارَةٌ ج صَنَانِير

To make; construct. صَنَعَ يَصْنَعُ

To arrange skilfully. صَنَّعَ

To coax, flatter. صَانَعَ مُصَانَعَةً

To effect good manners. تَصَنَّعَ

To make; have made. إِصْطَنَعَ

Act of making; deed. صُنْعٌ

Good deed; benefit. صُنْعٌ

Work. Carft, trade. صَنْعَةٌ

Craft, صِنَاعَةٌ ج صِنَاعَاتٌ
trade, industry. Art.

Artisans. أَصْحَابُ ٱلْحِرَفِ

Maker, artisan. صَانِعٌ ج صُنَّاعٌ

Artificial. صِنَاعِيٌّ

Deed. Good deed. صَنِيعَةٌ ج صَنَائِعُ

Affectation. تَصَنُّعٌ

Factory. مَصْنَعٌ وَمَصْنَعَةٌ ج مَصَانِعُ

Affected; artificial. مُصَنَّعٌ

Made. Fabricated. مَصْنُوعٌ

To assort; compose. صَنَّفَ

Sort, kind. صِنْفٌ ج صُنُوفٌ

Literary work. مُصَنَّفٌ ج مُصَنَّفَاتٌ

Author. مُصَنِّفٌ

Idol. Camel's hump. صَنَمٌ ج أَصْنَامٌ

Hush! Be silent! صَهْ

A reddish colour. صَهَبٌ وَصُهْبَةٌ

Reddish. أَصْهَبُ م صَهْبَاءُ ج صُهْبٌ

A very cold day. يَوْمٌ أَصْهَبُ

(Red) wine. اَلصَّهْبَاءُ

To melt. Smite. صَهَرَ يَصْهَرُ

To become related to by marriage. صَاهَرَ

Son-in-law, brother-in-law. صِهْرٌ ج أَصْهَارٌ

Water-tank. صِهْرِيجٌ ج صَهَارِيجُ

To neigh (horse). صَهَلَ يَصْهِلُ

Neighing. صَهِيلٌ وَصُهَالٌ

To hit the mark. صَابَ ـُ وأَصَابَ

To approve. Point, aim. صَوَّبَ

To attain one's pnrpose. أَصَابَ

To be right. أَصَابَ فِي قَوْلِهِ

To do right. أَصَابَ فِي عَمَلِهِ

To assail, smite. أَصَابَ

To descend, (rain). أَنْصَاب

To hold to be right. إِسْتَصْوَبَ

Side, course, direction. صَوْبٌ

Right, correct. صَائِبٌ وَمُصِيبٌ

What is right, correct. صَوَابٌ

Struck, stricken. مُصَابٌ

Affliction. مُصِيبَةٌ ج مَصَائِبُ

To make a noise. صَاتَ يَصُوتُ وَصَوَّتَ

Sound, voice. صَوْتٌ ج أَصْوَاتٌ

Reputation, fame. صِيتٌ

To fashion, shape, picture. صَوَّرَ

To imagine. صَوَّرَ لَهُ

To be formed. To imagine. تَصَوَّرَ

Tyre (city). Horn, trumpet. صُورٌ

Picture, form. صُورَةٌ ج صُوَرٌ

Imagination, idea. تَصَوُّرٌ

Sculptor. Painter. مُصَوِّرٌ

Young chick. صُوصٌ ج صِيصَانٌ

To measure grain. صَاعَ يَصُوعُ

A measure for grain. صَاعٌ

To form, fashion. صَاغَ يَصُوغُ صَوْغًا

Pure, unmixed. صَاغٌ

Money at its legal value. صَاغٌ

Grammatical form. صِيغَةٌ ج صِيَغٌ

Goldsmith. صَائِغٌ ج صَاغَةٌ وَصُيَّاغٌ

Goldsmith's art. صِيَاغَةٌ

Jewelry. مَصَاغٌ

To become a *Sûfi*. تَصَوَّفَ

Wool. صُوفٌ ج أَصْوَافٌ

A tuft of wool. صُوفَةٌ

Tinder, agaric. صُوفَانٌ

Religious mystic ; *Sûfi*. صُوفِيٌّ

To overpower, subdue. صَالَ يَصُولُ عَلَى

To clean wheat. صَوَّلَ ٱلْحِنْطَةَ

To soak, slake. صَوَّلَ

صَولَةٌ	Power ; rule ; force.
صُوَالةٌ	Rubbish, refuse matter.
مِصْوَلٌ ج مَصَاوِلُ	Implement for cleaning wheat ; trough.
صَوْلَجَانٌ	Sceptre.
صَامَ يَصُومُ صَوْماً وَصِيَاماً	To fast.
صَامَ عَنْ	To abstain from.
صَوَّمَ	To cause to fast.
صَوْمٌ وَصِيَامٌ	Fast ; abstinence.
صَائِمٌ ج صُوَّامٌ وَصِيَّمٌ	Fasting.
صَوْمَعَةٌ ج صَوَامِعُ	Hermit's cell.
صَانَ يَصُونُ	To keep, preserve, guard.
صَوَّنَ	To enclose with a wall.
صَوْنٌ وَصِيَانَةٌ	Act of preserving.
صَوَّانَةٌ ج صَوَّانٌ	Flint, flint-stone.
مَصُونٌ	Guarded, preserved.
صَاحَ يَصِيحُ	To cry out ; crow, (cock).
صَاحَ بِ	To call out to.
صَاحَ عَلَى	To cry out against.
صِيَاحٌ	Cry ; crowing of a cock.
صَيْحَةٌ	Cry, shout.
صَيَّاحٌ	Clamorous (man).
صَادَ يَصِيدُ وَتَصَيَّدَ وَاصْطَادَ	To hunt; trap, snare ; catch fish
صَيْدٌ	Hunting, fishing ; game.
صَيَّادٌ	Hunter, fisherman.
صَيْدَاءُ	Sidon (city).
مِصْيَدَةٌ ج مَصَايِدُ	Trap, snare.
مَصِيدٌ	Prey taken in hunting.
صَيْدَلَةٌ	Pharmacy.
صَيْدَلَانِيٌّ	Druggist.
صَارَ يَصِيرُ	To become ; change into.
صَارَ لَهُ	To happen to, befall.
صَارَ يَفْعَلُ	To begin to do.
صَارَ مَصِيراً إِلَى	To arrive at.
صَيَّرَ	To cause to become.
صِيرَةٌ ج صِيَرٌ	Fold (for sheep).
صَيْرُورَةٌ	Act of becoming.

Destination, end, result.	مصيرٌ
To pass the summer.	صافَ يَصِيفُ
Summer.	صَيْفٌ
Belonging to summer.	صيْفِيٌّ
A hot day.	يومٌ صائِفٌ
Summer residence.	مَصِيفٌ
China.	أَلصِّينُ
Chinese, Chinese porcelain.	صِينِيٌّ
Tray.	صينِيَّةٌ
Large tent. Pavilion.	صيوَانٌ
External ear.	صِيوَان ٱلأُذُن

ض

As a numeral sign=800.	ض
To shout in battle.	ضَاضَأَ
Shouts of war.	ضَوْضَى وَضوْضَاءُ
Thin ; small.	ضَئِيلٌ ج ضُؤَلاَءُ
Sheep, (*coll noun*).	ضأْنٌ
To grasp, keep.	ضبَّ وَاضَبَّ على
Lizard.	ضبٌّ ج ضِبَابٌ
Mist ; thin cloud.	ضَبَابَةٌ ج ضَبَابٌ
To guard. Do a thing well ; perfect.	ضَبَطَ يضبطُ ضَبْطاً
To withhold, restrain.	ضَبَطَ عَلَى
Exactness, correctness.	ضَبْطٌ
Rule ; canon.	ضَابطٌ ج ضَوَابطُ
Military officer.	ضَابطٌ ج ضُبَّاطٌ
Almighty (God).	ضَابِطُ ٱلْـكُلِّ
Policeman.	ضَابِطِيٌّ ج ضَابِطِيَّة

Written sentence, decision. (*law*). مَضْبَطَةٌ ج مَضَابِطُ

Well-regulated ; exact. مَضْبُوطٌ

Hyena. ضَبْعٌ وَضَبُعٌ ج ضِبَاعٌ

To cry, shout. ضَجَّ يَضِجُّ وَأَضَجَّ

To contend with. ضَاجَّ

Tumult, cry. ضَجَّةٌ وضَجِيجٌ

To be irritated, impatient, bored. ضَجِرَ يَضْجَرُ وَتَضَجَّرَ مِنْ

To bore, vex, distress. أَضْجَرَ

Uneasiness. ضَجَرٌ وَضُجْرَةٌ

Uneasy ; irritable. ضَجِرٌ وَمُتَضَجِّرٌ

Vexing, distressing. مُضْجِرٌ

To lie down. ضَجَعَ يَضْجَعُ وَاضَّجَعَ

To lie with (a woman). ضَاجَعَ

To make one to lie down. أَضْجَعَ

Bed-fellow. ضَجِيعٌ

Bed, bed-chamber. مَضْجَعٌ ج مَضَاجِعُ

To laugh. ضَحِكَ يَضْحَكُ ضُحْكاً

To laugh at. ضَحِكَ مِنْ وَعَلَى

To make one laugh. أَضْحَكَ

Pleasantry. ضُحْكَةٌ وَاضْحُوكَةٌ

Comic, causing laughter. مُضْحِكٌ

To appear. ضَحَا يَضْحُو ضَحْواً

To come in the morning. ضَحَّى

To sacrifice an animal. ضَحَّى بِ

To show, reveal. أَضْحَى وَضَحَّى عَنْ

He took to laughing. أَضْحَى يَضْحَكُ

ضَحَاءٌ وَضَحْوَةٌ وَضُحًى وَضَحِيَّةٌ
Early morning after sunrise.

Sacrifice. ضَحِيَّةٌ ج ضَحَايَا

Suburb, region. ضَاحِيَةٌ ج ضَوَاحٍ

Bright ; cloudless. أَضْحَى م ضَحْيَاءُ

Day of sacrifice. يَوْمُ ٱلأَضْحَى

(tenth of the month. ذُو ٱلْحِجَّةِ)

To be large. ضَخُمَ يَضْخُمُ

Large bulk ; corpulence. ضَخَامَةٌ

Large ; heavy. ضَخْمٌ ج ضِخَامٌ

To overcome. ضَدَّ يَضُدُّ

To oppose.	ضَادَّ مُضَادَّةً
To disagree.	تَضَادَّ تَضَادًّا
Contrary; enemy.	ضِدٌّ ج أَضْدَادٌ
Two opposites.	ضِدَّانِ
Contrast; opposition.	تَضَادٌّ
To injure.	ضَرَّ يَضُرُّ وَأَضَرَّ بِ
To receive an injury.	تَضَرَّرَ
To force, compel.	إِضْطَرَّ إِلَى
To be forced.	اضْطُرَّ إِلَى
Harm; evil.	ضُرٌّ وَضَرَرٌ
Adversity.	ضَرَّاءُ
A fellow-wife to a woman's husband.	ضَرَّةُ ٱلْمَرْأَةِ ج ضَرَائِرُ
Necessity.	ضَرُورَةٌ ج ضَرُورَاتٌ
Necessarily.	بِالضَّرُورَةِ وَضَرُورَةً
Indispensable.	ضَرُورِيٌّ
Necessary things.	ضَرُورِيَّاتٌ
Blind.	ضَرِيرٌ ج أَضِرَّاءُ
Necessity.	إِضْطِرَارٌ
Injurious, harmful.	مُضِرٌّ
Injury; means of harm.	مَضَرَّةٌ
To strike.	ضَرَبَ يَضْرِبُ ضَرْبًا
Multiply, (*Arith*). Pitch (tent). Strike (money).	
To impose a tax.	ضَرَبَ عَلَى
To overlook.	ضَرَبَ عَنْهُ صَفْحًا
To incline to blackness.	ضَرَبَ إِلَى ٱلسَّوَادِ
To blow a trumpet.	ضَرَبَ فِي ٱلْبُوقِ
To travel.	ضَرَبَ فِي ٱلْأَرْضِ
To give a parable.	ضَرَبَ مَثَلًا
To be silent.	أَضْرَبَ
To quit, cease.	أَضْرَبَ عَنْ
To speculate.	ضَارَبَ مُضَارَبَةً
To fight together.	تَضَارَبَ
To be agitated.	إِضْطَرَبَ
To be confused.	إِضْطَرَبَ ٱلْأَمْرُ
Multiplication. (*Arith*).	ضَرْبٌ
Kind, form.	ضَرْبٌ ج ضُرُوبٌ

ضَرْبَةٌ ج ضَرَبات A blow, stroke.
صَارِبٌ Striking. Multiplier.
ضَرِيبَةٌ ج ضَرَائِبُ Impost, tax.
إِضْطِرَابٌ Agitation.
مَضْرَبٌ ج مَضَارِبُ Large tent.
مَضْرُوبٌ Struck. Multiplicand.
مُضَارِب Sharer in traffic.
مُضْطَرِبٌ Agitated, confused.
ضَرَجَ يَضْرِجُ ضَرْجاً To smear.
ضَرَّجَ To dye red. Adorn.
ضَرِيحٌ ج ضَرَائِحُ Grave.
ضَرِسَ يَضْرَسُ To be set on edge (teeth).
ضَارَسَ To contend with.
ضِرْسٌ ج أَضْرَاسٌ Molar tooth.
أَضْرَاسُ ٱلْعَقْلِ Wisdom teeth.
مُضَرَّسٌ Experienced man.
ضَرَعَ يَضْرَعُ إِلى To beseech.
ضَارَعَ مُضَارَعة To resemble.
تَضَرَّعَ إِلى To beseech.

ضَرْعٌ ج ضُرُوعٌ Udder.
تَضَرُّعٌ Prayer with humility.
مضارِعٌ Present-future tense. of verbs; (*e.g.* يَضْرِبُ)
ضِرْغَامٌ Lion. Brave man.
ضَرِمَ يَضْرَمُ وَٱضْطَرَمَ To burn, blaze.
أَضْرَمَ To kindle a fire.
إِضْطَرَمَ To be kindled.
ضِرَامٌ Firewood. Blazing.
مُضْطَرِمٌ Blazing.
ضَارٍ ج ضَوَارٍ Rapacious animal.
ضِعَةٌ Humiliation, (*from* وَضَعَ).
ضَعْضَعَ ضَعْضَعَةً To pull down, rase.
ضَعُفَ يَضْعُفُ To be weak, feeble.
ضَعَّفَ يُضَعِّفُ وَضَاعَفَ To double.
أَضْعَفَ To weaken, enfeeble.
تَضَاعَفَ To be doubled.
ضُعْفٌ Weakness, feebleness.
ضِعْفٌ ج أَضْعَافٌ Double.

ضَعِيفٌ ج ضُعَفَاء Weak, feeble.

ضَغَثَ يَضْغَثُ To mix, confuse.

ضَغَطَ يَضْغَطُ ضَغْطًا To press, squeeze.

إِنْضَغَطَ To be pressed.

ضَغْطَةٌ Pressure. Compulsion.

ضَاغُوطٌ Night-mare.

ضَغِنَ يَضْغَنُ عَلَى To bear malice.

تَضَاغَنَ To bear malice or hatred against each other.

ضَغِنٌ Spiteful, malevolent.

ضِغْنٌ ج أَضْغَانٌ Hatred, malice.

ضَغِينَةٌ ج ضَغَائِنُ Malice, spite.

ضِفَّةٌ Side of a river.

ضِفْدَعٌ ج ضَفَادِعُ Frog.

ضَفَرَ يَضْفِرُ وَضَفَّرَ To braid, plait.

إِنْضَفَرَ To be braided, twisted.

ضَفِيرَةٌ ج ضَفَائِرُ Braid; tress.

ضَفَا يَضْفُو To be ample.

ضَلَّ يَضِلُّ To err; wander from.

أَضَلَّ إِضْلَالًا To lead into error.

ضَلٌّ وَضَلَالٌ وَضَلَالَةٌ Error.

ضَالٌّ ج ضَالُّونَ Strayed; erring.

ضَالَّةٌ A stray animal.

أُضْلُولَةٌ ج أَضَالِيلُ Error.

مُضِلٌّ Leading astray.

مَضَلَّةٌ Cause of error.

ضَلُعَ يَضْلُعُ ضَلَاعَةً To be strong.

تَضَلَّعَ To be full, strong.

ضِلْعٌ ج ضُلُوعٌ وَأَضْلَاعٌ وَأَضْلُعٌ (م) Rib. Side of a triangle, &c.

ضَلِيعٌ Strong, powerful; large.

مُضَلَّعٌ Ribbed; striped.

ضَمَّ يَضُمُّ ضَمًّا To join, add. To vocalize a letter with. (ُ).

ضَمَّ عَلَى To grasp, seize.

إِنْضَمَّ To be joined, annexed.

ضَمٌّ وَضَمَّةٌ . The vowel-point. (ُ)

مَضْمُومٌ Collected, joined. Having the vowel-point.

إِضْمَحَلَّ To vanish.

ضَمَدَ يَضْمِدُ وَضَمَّدَ. To dress a wound.

ضِمَادٌ Dressing for a wound.

ضِمَادَةٌ Bandage.

ضَمُرَ يَضْمُرُ To be thin, emaciated.

أَضْمَرَ To conceal, hide.

أَضْمَرَ فِي نَفْسِهِ To resolve.

تَضَمَّرَ وَٱنْضَمَرَ To be shrivelled.

ضُمُورٌ Emaciation, atrophy.

ضَمِيرٌ ج ضَمَائِرُ Secret thought. Heart, Conscience. Pronoun.

مُضْمَرٌ Secret; understood. (*Gram*).

ضَمِنَ يَضْمَنُ To stand surety. To farm or rent.

ضَمَّنَ To make one responsible for. To put in; inclose.

تَضَمَّنَ To include, comprise.

ضِمْنَ Within. Inclosed.

ضَمَانٌ Suretyship. Responsibility.

ضَامِنٌ وَضَمِينٌ Responsible for.

مَضْمُونٌ ج مَضَامِينُ Sense; meaning. Ensured; assured.

ضَنَّ يَضِنُّ ضَنًّا To be avaricious.

ضِنٌّ ج ضَنَائِنُ A prized thing.

ضَنِينٌ Avaricious, stingy.

ضَنُكَ يَضْنُكُ To be larrow; feebne.

ضَنْكٌ Distress. Narrowness.

ضَنِيَ يَضْنَى ضَنًى To be sickly.

ضَانَى مُضَانَاةً To suffer, endure.

أَضْنَى To consume (disease).

إِنْضَنَى To be consumed slowly.

ضَنًى Disease; weakness.

مُضْنًى Sickly, emaciated.

ضَهَدَ يَضْهَدُ To overcome.

إِضْطَهَدَ To maltreat; persecute

إِضْطِهَادٌ Presecution.

مُضْطَهِدٌ Persecutor.

ضَاهَى مُضَاهَاةً To resemble.

ضَاءَ يَضُوءُ To shine; glitter.

ضَوَّأَ تَضْوِئَةً To illuminate.

أَضَاءَ إِضَاءَةً To shine.

To seek light. إِسْتَضَاءَ

Light. ضِيَاءٌ وَضَوْءٌ ج أَضْوَاءٌ

Light-giving ; brilliant. مُضِيءٌ

Tumult of war. ضَوْضَى وَضَوْضَاءُ

To injure. ضَارَ يَضِيرُ ضَيْراً

To suffer pain. تَضَوَّرَ

To be lost ; perish. ضَاعَ يَضِيعُ

To lose. Destroy. ضَيَّعَ وَأَضَاعَ

Lost. Neglected. ضَائِعٌ

Unmissed. ضَيَاعاً

Village. ضَيْعَةٌ ج ضِيَعٌ وَضِيَاعٌ

To be a guest. ضَافَ يَضِيفُ

To treat with hospitality. أَضَافَ

To join, add. To put a noun in the construct state. أَضَافَ إِلَى

To be joined. إِنْضَافَ إِلَى

To seek hospitality. إِسْتَضَافَ

Guest. ضَيْفٌ ج أَضْيَافٌ وَضُيُوفٌ

Entertainment. ضِيَافَةٌ

Annexation. إِضَافَةٌ

Two nouns in the construct state (*e.g.* كِتَابُ زَيْدٍ) اَلْمُضَافُ وَٱلْمُضَافُ إِلَيْهِ

Host. مُضِيفٌ

Hospitable. مِضْيَافٌ

To be narrow. ضَاقَ يَضِيقُ ضِيقاً

To be inabequate. ضَاقَ عَنْ

To make narrow. ضَيَّقَ

To annoy ; oppress. ضَايَقَ

To feel oppressed. تَضَايَقَ

Narrowness. Distress. ضِيقٌ

Poverty. Misery. ضِيقَةٌ

Narrow ; contracted. ضَيِّقٌ

Narrower. أَضْيَقُ

Narrowplace. مَضِيقٌ ج مَضَايِقُ

To oppress. ضَامَ يَضِيمُ ضَيْماً

Wrong ; injury. ضَيْمٌ

ط

ط	As a numeral sign=9.
طَاطَا	To bend down.
تَطَاطَأَ	To be depressed, abased.
طَبَّبَ تَطْبِيباً	To treat the sich.
طِبٌّ	Medical treatment.
عِلْمُ ٱلطِّبِّ	The science of medicine.
طِبِّيٌّ	Medical.
طَبِيبٌ ج أَطِبَّاءُ	Physician.
طَبَخَ يَطْبُخُ طَبْخاً	To cook.
انْطَبَخَ	To be cooked.
طَبْخٌ	Cooking. Food cooked.
طَبَّاخٌ	Cook.
طِبَاخَةٌ	Art of cookery.
طَبِيخٌ	Cooked food.
مَطْبَخٌ ج مَطَابِخُ	Kitchen.
مَطْبُوخٌ	Cooked.
طَبَرِيَّة	Tiberias.
طَابُورٌ	Battalion.
طَبَاشِيرُ	Chalk.
طَبَعَ يَطْبَعُ	To stamp. Print.
طَبَّعَ	To break in (a horse).
تَطَبَّعَ	To assume a character.
إِنْطَبَعَ	To be imprinted.
طَبْعٌ ج طِبَاعٌ	Natural disposition.
طِبَاعَة	Art of printing.
طَبِيعَةٌ ج طَبَائِعُ	Nature.
طَبِيعِيٌّ	Natural. Naturalist.
عِلْمُ ٱلطَّبِيعِيَّات	Physics.
مَطْبَعَةٌ ج مَطَابِعُ	Printing-press.
مَطْبُوعٌ	Impressed, printed.

To fit, suit. طَابَقَ مُطَابَقَةً

To make to agree. طَبَّقَ وطَابَقَ بَيْنَ

To cover, close, shut. أَطْبَقَ

To agree upon. أَطْبَقَ عَلَى

To agree. تَطَابَقَ

To apply to something. إِنْطَبَقَ عَلَى

Suitable, conformable to. طِبْقٌ

Cover. Tray. طَبَقٌ ج أَطْبَاقٌ

Layer ; stratum. طَبَقَةٌ ج طَبَقَاتٌ
Class ; Grade. Stage.

A hard year سَنَةٌ مُطْبِقَةٌ

Conformable to. مُطَابِقٌ

Agreement, accord. مُطَابَقَةٌ

To beat the drum. طَبَّلَ

Drum. طَبْلٌ ج طُبُولٌ

Drummer. طَبَّالٌ

Pistol. طَبَنْجَةٌ ج طَبَنْجَاتٌ

To fry. طَجَنَ يَطْجُنُ طَجْناً

Frying-pan. طَاجِنٌ ج طَوَاجِنُ

To strain in breathing. طَحَرَ يَطْحِرُ

Straining. طُحَارٌ وَطَحِيرٌ

Spleen. طِحَالٌ ج طُحُلٌ

Water-moss. طُحْلُبٌ وَطِحْلِبٌ

To rush upon. طَحَمَ يَطْحَمُ عَلَى

Impetuous ; violent. طَحُومٌ

To grind (flour). طَحَنَ يَطْحَنُ طَحْناً

Miller. طَحَّانٌ

Mill. طَاحُونٌ وَطَاحُونَةٌ ج طَوَاحِينُ

Grinders, (teeth). طَوَاحِنُ

Flour. طَحِينٌ

Dregs of sesame-oil. طَحِينَةٌ

Mill-machine. مِطْحَنَةٌ

Mill. مِطْحَنَةٌ ج مَطَاحِنُ

All ; every one. طُرًّا

To happen to. طَرَأَ يَطْرَأُ عَلَى

To overwhelm with praise. أَطْرَأَ

Fresh, juicy, moist. طَرِيٌّ

Unexpected calamity. طَارِئَةٌ

Exaggerated praise. إِطْرَاءٌ

To be joyful. طَرِبَ يَطْرَبُ طَرَباً

To sing, chant, trill. طَرَّبَ

To gladden. طَرَّبَ وَأَطْرَبَ

Mirth, glee. طَرَبٌ

One who feels merry. طَرِبٌ

Exciting mirth or delight. مُطْرِبٌ

Red cap, fez. طَرْبُوشٌ ج طَرَابِيشُ

To throw. Subtract. طَرَحَ يطْرَحُ

Casting. Subtraction. طَرْحٌ

Abortion, miscarriage. طِرْحٌ

Veil worn by a female. طَرْحَةٌ

Sheet of paper. طَرْحِيَّةُ وَرق

Cushion to sit on. طَرَّاحَةٌ

Cast down. طَرِيحَةٌ ج طَرْحَى

Place. مَطْرَحٌ ج مَطَارِح

Tarragon. طَرْخُونٌ (نَبَاتٌ)

To drive awry ; chase. طَرَدَ يَطْرُدُ

To attack, charge, assault. طَارَدَ

To be sent away. انْطَرَدَ

To follow regularly. إِطَّرَدَ

To digress. إِسْتَطْرَدَ اَسْتِطْرَاداً

Bale of goods. طَرْدٌ ج طُرُودٌ

Attack ; charge ; pursuit. طِرَادٌ

Expelled, outcast. طَرِيدٌ

Chased game. طَرِيدَةٌ ج طَرَائِدُ

Having no exception. مُطَّرِدٌ

To embroider. طَرَّزَ

Form, shape, manner. طَرْزٌ

Mode, manner. طِرَازٌ

Embroiderer. طَرَّازٌ وَمُطَرِّزٌ

Embroidered. مُطَرَّزٌ

To be deaf. طَرِشَ يَطْرَشُ

To whitewash. (طَرَّشَ يطَرِّشُ)

Deafness. طَرَشٌ

Lime for whitewashing. (طَرْشٌ)

Whitewasher. (طَرَّاشٌ)

Deaf. اطْرَشُ م طَرْشَاءُ ج طُرْشٌ

A high pointed cap. طَرْطُورٌ

طَرَفَ يَطْرِفُ To hurt the eye.

تَطَرَّفَ To go to an extreme.

طَرْفٌ The eye.

طَرْفُ ٱلْعَيْنِ The eyelid.

طَرَفٌ ج أَطْرَافٌ Side. End part.

أَلأَطْرَافُ Limbs, extremities.

أَطْرَافُ ٱلْحَدِيثِ Choice subjects of conversation.

أَطْرَافُ ٱلنَّاسِ The lower classes.

طَرْفَةٌ Twinkling of an eye.

طَرْفَاءُ Tamarisk (tree).

طَرَقَ يَطْرُقُ طَرْقًا To strike, knock.

أَطْرَقَ To be silent.

تَطَرَّقَ إِلى To find or seek a way.

إِسْتَطْرَقَ To take a way.

طَارِقَةٌ ج طَوَارِقُ Calamity; evil.

طَرِيقٌ ج طُرُقٌ Way; road, path.

طَرِيقَةٌ ج طَرَائِقُ Way; manner.

مِطْرَقَةٌ ج مَطَارِقُ Hammer.

مَطْرُوقٌ وَمُسْتَطْرَقٌ Beaten (road).

طَارِمَةٌ Cabin of a ship.

طَرَّى To soften, moisten.

أَطْرَى إِطْرَاءً To praise highly.

طَرِي Tender; fresh; juicy.

طَسْتٌ وطَشْتٌ ج طُسُوتٌ وَطُشُوتٌ
Basin for washing.

طَعَّمَ To graft. Vaccinate.

أَطْعَمَ To give food.

تَطَعَّمَ To be grafted, inoculated.

إِسْتَطْعَمَ To taste.

طَعْمٌ ج طُعُومٌ Taste; flavour.

طُعْمٌ Bait thrown to fish.

طَعَامٌ ج أَطْعِمَةٌ Food.

مَطْعَمٌ ج مَطَاعِمُ Food. Place of food.

طَعَنَ يَطْعُنُ بِ Thrust, pierce.

طَعَنَ فِي وَعَلَى To defame.

طَعَنَ فِي ٱلسِّنِّ To become old.

طَعْنَةٌ A thrust.

طَاعُونٌ ج طَوَاعِينُ Plague.

طُغْرَاءُ ج طُغْرَاءَاتٌ The Turkish Imperial cypher.

طُغْمَةٌ A company ; order.

طغَا يَطْغو To overflow.

طَاغٍ ج طُغَاةٌ Highly wicked.

الطَّاغُوتُ Idol. Tempter.

أطَفَّ عَلَى To look down upon.

طَفِيفٌ Small quantity.

أطْفَأَ To put out (fire) ; allay.

انْطَفَأَ انْطِفَاءً To be extinguished.

طَفَحَ يَطْفَحُ To be full ; overflow.

طَفَّحَ واطْفَحَ To fill to overflowing.

طَفْحانُ وَطَافِحٌ Ove flowing.

طَفَرَ يطْفِرُ طَفْراً To jump, leap.

طَفْرَةٌ A leap. Eruption.

طَفِقَ يَفْعَلُ To commence to do.

أطْفَلَ To have a child, (woman).

أَطْفَلَتِ ٱلشَّمْسُ To approach setting.

تَطَفَّلَ To intrude.

طَفَلٌ Time before sunset.

طِفْلٌ ج اطْفَالٌ Infant.

طُفُولِيَّةٌ Infancy. Childhood.

طُفَيْلِيٌّ Intruder.

طَفَا يَطْفو To rise high, (water).

طَفَا فَوْقَ ٱلْمَاءِ To float.

طُفَاوَةٌ Scum.

طَقَّ يطُقُّ To make a sound.

طَقْسٌ ج طُقُوسٌ Weather. Religious rite.

طَقْطَقَ طَقْطَقَةً To make a noise.

طَقْمٌ ج طُقُومَةٌ Suit of clothes. Set.

أطَلَّ عَلَى To look down upon.

طَلٌّ Finest rain ; dew.

مطَلٌّ Overlooking place.

طَلَبَ يطْلُبُ To seek ; ask ; desire.

طَلَبَ إلى To beseech ; pray.

طَالَبَ To demand ; claim.

تَطَلَّبَ To demand repeatedly.

طَلَبٌ وطِلْبَةٌ Desire. Request.

طَالِبٌ ج طُلاَّبٌ وَطَلَبَة . Seeker.

طَالِبُ عِلْمٍ A student.

مَطْلَبٌ ج مَطَالِبُ Demand ; desire.

مَطْلوبٌ ج مَطَالِيبُ Claim. Object sought or desired.

طَلَحَ يَطْلَحُ طَلاَحًا To be wicked.

طَلْحٌ A kind of thorny acacia.

طَالِحٌ ج طُلَّحٌ وَطَالِحُونَ Wicked.

طَلاَحٌ Wickedness.

طَلْحِيَّةٌ ج طَلاَحِيٌّ Sheet of paper.

طَلَسَ يَطْلِس To blot. Obliterate.

أَطْلَس Satin. Atlas.

طَيْلَسَانٌ ج طَيَالِسَةٌ A particular robe worn by learned men.

طَلْسَمَ To write a talisman.

طَلْسَمٌ ج طَلاَسِمُ Talisman.

طَلَعَ يَطْلُعُ To rise, (sun). Sprout.

طَلَعَ وطَلِعَ يَطْلَعُ To ascend.

طَالَعَ مُطَالَعَةً To study ; read.

أَطْلَعَ To appear. Sprout.

أَطْلَعَ عَلى To inform.

تَطَلَّعَ إِلى To look at, or for.

إِطَّلَعَ عَلَى To know, see.

إِسْتَطْلَعَ To examine.

طَلْعٌ Spadix, spathe.

طَلْعَةٌ Face. Aspect.

طَالِعٌ ج طَوَالِع Star (of fortune).

طُلُوعٌ Rising ; appearance.

طَلِيعَةٌ ج طَلاَئِعُ Vanguard.

مَطْلَعٌ First line of a poem.

طَلُقَ يطْلُقُ To be freed.

طَلُقَ يَطْلُقُ To have a cheerful face.

طَلَّقَ To divorce (his wife).

أَطْلَقَ To free, liberate.

أَطْلَقَ اَلْقَوْل To generalize.

أَطْلَقَ لَهُ To permit him.

أُطْلِقَ To be applied ; apply.

إِنْطَلَقَ To go, depart.

طَلْقٌ Pains of childbirth.

Liberal.	طَلْقُ ٱلْيَدَيْنِ
Cheerful.	طَلْقُ ٱلْوَجْهِ
Eloquent.	طَلْقُ ٱللِّسَانِ
Divorce.	طَلَاقٌ
Divorced (woman).	طَالِقٌ وَطَالِقَةٌ
Absolutely.	عَلَى ٱلإِطْلَاقِ وَمُطْلَقًا
Free. Absolute.	مُطْلَقٌ
Loaf of bread.	طُلْمَةٌ ج طُلَمٌ
Beauty ; grace.	طلاوَةٌ
To anoint ; cover with.	طلى يَطْلِي
Ointment ; tar ; plaster.	طِلَاءٌ
Smeared, covered.	مَطْلِيٌّ
Calamity.	طامَّةٌ
To cover up.	طَمَّ يَطُمُّ طَمًّا
To be filled, covered up.	إِنْطَمَّ
Menstruation ; menses.	طَمْثٌ
To gaze at.	طَمَحَ يَطْمَحُ إِلى
Aspring. Proud.	طامِحٌ وطَمُوحٌ
To bury, conceal.	طمر يَطْمِرُ
Accumulated.	مُطْمَرٌّ
To efface.	طَمَسَ يَطْمُسُ وَطَمَّسَ
To be effaced.	تَطَمَّسَ وَٱنْطَمَسَ
Obliterated.	طَمِيسٌ وَمَطْمُوسٌ
To covet, hope.	طَمِعَ يَطْمَعُ فِي وَب
Covetousness ; avidity.	طَمَعٌ
A coveted object.	طَمَعٌ ج أَطْمَاعٌ
Covetous.	طَامِعٌ وَطَمِعٌ وَطَمَّاعٌ
Thing coveted.	مَطْمَعٌ ج مَطَامِعُ
To tranquillize ; reassure.	طَمْأَنَ
To be low, (land). To be free from disquietude.	إِطْمَأَنَّ
To abide, dwell.	إِطْمَأَنَّ بِٱلْمَوْضِعِ
To trust implicitly.	إِطْمَأَنَّ إِلى
Tranquility.	طُمَأْنِينَةٌ وَٱطْمِئْنَانٌ
Tranquil ; composed.	مُطْمَئِنٌّ
To rise high, (water).	طَمَا يَطْمُو
High (water, sea).	طَامٍ
To buzz ; ring.	طَنَّ يَطِنُّ طَنِينًا
Humming ; ringing.	طَنِينٌ

طَنَّانٌ Sonorous. Wide-spread.

أَطْنَبَ فِي To be eloquent ; exert one's self in.

طُنُبٌ ج أَطْنَابٌ Tent-rope.

إِطْنَابٌ Superfluity, prolixity.

مُطْنِبٌ An immoderate praiser.

مُطَنَّبٌ Made fast with ropes.

طُنْبُورٌ ج طَنَابِيرُ Tambour.

طَنْجَرَةٌ ج طَنَاجِرُ A cooking pan.

طَنَّ طَنْطَنَةً To hum, ring.

طُنُفٌ ج أَطْنَافٌ Peak.

طِنْفِسَةٌ ج طَنَافِسُ A carpet.

طَهُرَ يَطْهُرُ To be clean, pure.

طَهَّرَ To cleanse. Circumcise.

تَطَهَّرَ To be cleansed, purified.

طَهَارَة Purity. Holiness.

طَاهِرٌ ج أَطْهَارٌ Pure. Holy.

مَطْهَرَة Purgatory.

مُطَهَّرٌ Purified.

طَاهٍ ج طُهَاة A cook.

طُوبٌ Brick, canon.

طُوبْجِيٌّ Gunner ; artillery-man.

طُوبَى Blessedness.

طَاحَ يَطُوحُ To perish.

طَوَّحَ وَأَطَاحَ To mislead.

تَطَوَّحَ To wander ; perish.

طَوَائِحُ وَمَطَاوِحُ Adversities.

طَوْدٌ ج أَطْوَادٌ High mountain.

مُنْطَادٌ Lofty ; rising high.

طَوْراً بَعْدَ طَوْرٍ Time after time.

طَوْرٌ ج أَطْوَارٌ State, manner.

طُورٌ Mountain.

أَلطُّورُ Mount Sinai.

طَاسٌ ج طَاسَاتٌ Drinking-cup.

طَاوُوسٌ ج طَوَاوِيسُ Peacock.

طَوْشٌ Frivolity.

طَوَاشِي ج طَوَاشِيَةٌ Eunuch; gelding.

طَاعَ يَطُوعُ وَأَطَاعَ To obey.

طَاوَعَ مُطَاوَعَةً To consent; follow.

تَطَوَّعَ — To volunteer.

إِسْتَطَاعَ — To be able.

طَوْعٌ وطَائِعٌ — Obedient.

طَوْعاً — Voluntarily ; willingly.

طَاعةٌ — Obedience ; submission.

أَطْوَعُ — More submissive.

إِسْتِطَاعَةٌ — Ability ; power.

تَطَوُّعٌ — Voluntary action.

مُطَاعٌ — Obeyed. Accepted.

طَافَ يَطُوفُ حَوْلَ وفي — To go around.
To travel. Circumambulate.

طَوَّفَ — To lead around.

أَطَافَ ب — To surround.

طَوْفٌ — Night-police. Raft.

طُوفَانٌ — Flood ; deluge.

طَائِفَةٌ ج طَوَائِفُ — Party, sect.

طَوَافٌ — Circumambulation.

مُطَوِّفٌ — A Mecca guide.

طَاقَ يَطُوقُ وأَطَاقَ — To be able.

طَوَّقَ — To put a collar on.

طَاقٌ ج طَاقَاتٌ — Window.

طَوْقٌ ج أَطْوَاقٌ — Collar.

طَاقَةٌ — Ability. Window.

إِطَاقَةٌ — Ability ; power.

طَالَ يَطُولُ طُولاً — To be long.

طَوَّلَ وأَطَالَ — To lengthen.

طَاوَلَ في — Defer, put off.

تطَاول عَلَى — To wrong.

إِسْتَطَالَ — To be long, extend.

طَالَمَا — During a long time.

طُولٌ — Length. Duration.

خطوطُ الطُّول — Longitude.

طَائِلٌ — Advantage ; benefit.

طَاوِلَةٌ — Table.

طَوِيلٌ ج طِوَالٌ — Long. Tall.

طَوِيلُ البَاعِ — Competent.

أَطْوَلُ — Longer.

تَطْوِيلٌ — Lengthening.

Parallelogram.	مُسْتَطِيلٌ
To fold, fold up.	طَوَى يَطْوِي طَيًّا
To suffer hunger.	طَوِيَ يَطْوَى
To be folded up.	إِنْطَوَى
Folding. Traversing.	طَيٌّ
Within it.	فِي طَيِّهِ
Hunger.	طَوًى
Folded up.	مَطْوِيٌّ
To be good.	طَابَ يَطِيبُ طِيبًا
To be cheerful.	طَابَتْ نَفْسُهُ
To perfume.	طَيَّبَ
To be perfumed.	تَطَيَّبَ
To find good.	إِسْتَطَابَ وَٱسْتَطْيَبَ
Perfume.	طِيبٌ ج أَطْيَابٌ
Ball used in play.	(طَابَةٌ)
Good. In good health	طَيِّبٌ
Cheerful, happy.	طَيِّبُ ٱلنَّفْسِ
A good thing.	طَيِّبَةٌ ج طَيِّبَاتٌ
A tax on houses, &c.	(طَابُو)
How good it is !	مَا أَطْيَبَهُ
Blessedness.	طُوبَى
To fly, (bird).	طَارَ يَطِيرُ طَيَرَانًا
To hasten to...	طَارَ إِلَى
To make to fly.	طَيَّرَ أَوْ أَطَارَ
To draw a bad omen.	تَطَيَّرَ
To be dispersed.	تَطَايَرَ تَطَايُرًا
Evil augury or omen.	طَيَرَ
Flight (of birds, &c.)	طَيَرَانٌ
Bird.	طَائِرٌ ج طَيْرٌ وَطُيُورٌ
Paper-kite.	طَيَّارَاتٌ
Spreading.	مُسْتَطِيرٌ
To be light-headed.	طَاشَ يَطِيشُ
To miss, (an arrow).	طَاشَ عَنْ
Frivolity.	طَيْشٌ وَطَيْشَانٌ
Light, fickle, frivolous.	طَائِشٌ
Apparition ; spectre.	طَيْفٌ
To plaster with clay.	طَيَّنَ
Clay ; mortar.	طِينٌ ج أَطْيَانٌ
A lump of clay.	طِينَةٌ
Plasterer.	طَيَّانٌ

ظ

As a numeral sign=900.	ط
Gazelle.	ظَبْيٌ م ظَبْيَةٌ ج ظِبَاءٌ
To adorn, embellish.	ظَرَّفَ
To deem beautiful.	إِسْتَظْرَفَ
Vessel, receptacle.	ظَرْفٌ ج ظُرُوفٌ
Adverbial noun of time or place.	
Beautiful. Witty.	ظَرِيفٌ ج ظُرَفَاءُ
To travel.	ظَعَنَ يَظْعَنُ ظَعْنًا
Camel.	ظَعُونٌ ج ظُعُنٌ
Litter for woman.	ظَعِينَةٌ ج أَظْعَانٌ
To scratch with the nail.	ظَفَرَ يَظْفِرُ
To obtain. Overcome.	ظَفِرَ بِ وعَلَى
To give victory.	ظَفَّرَ وَأَظْفَرَ
Nail ; claw ; hoof.	ظِفْرٌ ج اظفار
Pterygium.	ظَفْرٌ وظَفَرَة
Success ; victory.	ظَفَرٌ
Victorious ; conqueror.	مُظَفَّرٌ
To continue.	ظَلَّ يظل
To continue to act.	ظَلَّ يَفْعَلُ
To cover ; shade.	ظَلَّلَ وَأَظَلَّ
To be in the shade of.	تَظَلَّلَ بِ
To seek the shade.	إِسْتَظَلَّ بِ
Shade ; protection.	ظِلٌّ ج أَظْلَالٌ
Cover. Cloud.	ظُلَّةٌ ج ظِلَالٌ
Cloud.	ظَلَالٌ وَظِلَالٌ وظِلَالَةٌ
Giving shade,	ظَلِيلٌ ومُظِلٌّ
Shady. Cloudy.	مُظِلٌّ ومُظَلَّلٌ
Tent. Umbrella.	مِظَلَّةٌ ج مَظَالٌّ
Hoof.	ظِلْفٌ ج ظُلُوفٌ وأَظْلَافٌ
To wrong ; oppress.	ظَلَمَ يَظْلِمُ

ظَلِمَ يَظْلَمُ وَأَظْلَمَ — To be dark.

ظَلَّمَ — To accuse of injustice.

تَظَلَّمَ مِنْ — To accuse of injustice.

انْظَلَمَ — To suffer injustice.

ظُلْمٌ — Injustice ; oppression.

ظُلْمَةٌ ج ظُلُمَاتٌ — Darkness.

بَحْرُ ٱلظُّلُمَاتِ — Atlantic Ocean.

ظَالِمٌ ج ظَالِمُونَ وَظَلَمَةٌ — Tyrant.

ظَلَامٌ وَظَلْمَاءُ — Darkness.

ظَلَّامٌ وَظَلُومٌ — Great tyrant.

مَظْلَمَةٌ ج مَظَالِمُ — Wrong ; injustice.

مَظْلُومٌ وَظَلِيمٌ — Wronged.

ظَلِمٌ — Dark ; obscure.

ظَمِئَ يَظْمَأُ — To be thirsty.

ظَمْءٌ ج أَظْمَاءٌ — Thirst. Longing.

ظَمِئٌ وَظَمْآنُ — Thirsty ; desirous.

ظَنَّ يَظُنُّ ظَنًّا — To suppose.

ظَنَّ وَاظَّنَّ وَأَظَنَّ بِ — To suspect.

ظَنٌّ ج ظُنُونٌ — Supposition

ظِنَّةٌ ج ظِنَنٌ — Suspicion.

مَظَنَّةٌ — Presumption.

مَظْنُونٌ — Supposed.

مَظْنُونَاتٌ — Probable propositions.

ظَهَرَ يَظْهَرُ ظُهُوراً — To appear.

ظَهَرَ عَلَى — To overcome, subdue.

ظَاهَرَ مُظَاهَرَةً — To aid, assist.

أَظْهَرَ — To show, manifest.

تَظَاهَرَ بِ — To show forth.

إِسْتَظْهَرَ بِ — To seek help or aid.

إِسْتَظْهَرَ عَلَى — To overcome.

ظَهْرٌ ج ظُهُورٌ — Back.

عَنْ ظَهْرِ ٱلْقَلْبِ — From memory.

ظُهْرٌ ج أَظْهَارٌ — Mid-day ; noon.

ظَاهِرٌ — Clear ; evident. External.

فِي ٱلظَّاهِرِ — Apparently.

ظَاهِرَةٌ ج ظَوَاهِرُ — Phenomenon.

ظُهُورٌ — Appearance.

ظَهِيرَةٌ — Mid-day ; hour of noon.

إِظْهَارٌ — Disclosure, manifestation.

ع

As a numeral sign=70. ع

Covering of bosom. عُبٌّ ج عِبَابٌ

Torrent, billows. عُبَابٌ

To care for. عبَأَ يَعْبا عبْأً

Woollen cloak. عَبَاءٌ وَعَبَاءَةٌ ج أَعْبِئَةٌ

To play. عَبِث يَعْبَث عَبَثًا

Play, sport. Useless. عَبَثٌ

To no purpose, in vain. عَبَثًا

To worship, adore. عَبَد يَعْبُدُ

To take one as a slave. تَعَبَّد

To devote one's self to ... تَعَبَّدَ لِ

To enslave. إِسْتَعْبَدَ

Servant, slave. عَبْدٌ ج عَبِيدٌ

Mankind. أَلعِبَادُ

Worshipper. عابِدٌ ج عَبَدَةٌ وَعُبَّادٌ

Religious worship. عِبادَة

Slavery, servitude. عُبُودِيَّةٌ

Self-consecration to God. تَعَبُّدٌ

Place of worship. مَعْبَدٌ ج معَابِدُ

Object of worship. معْبُودٌ

To pass; pass away. عبَر يَعبُر

To cause to pass over. عَبَّرَ

To explain. عَبَّرَ عَنْ

To consider. إِعْتَبَرَ

To take warning from. اعْتَبَرَ بِ

On the other side. عبْرٌ

Tear; sobbing. عَبْرَةٌ ج عَبَرَاتٌ

Admonition. عِبْرَةٌ ج عِبَرٌ

Hebrew. عِبْرِيٌّ وَعِبْرَانِيٌّ

A wayfarer. عابر سَبيل

Expression. Style, diction. عِبَارَةٌ

This means. هٰذَا عِبَارَةٌ عَنْ

Act of passing over. عُبُورٌ

Perfume. عَبِيرٌ

Consideration, regard. إِعْتِبَارٌ

Explanation. تَعْبِيرٌ

Ferry, passage. مَعْبَرٌ ج مَعَابِرُ

Esteemed ; important. مُعْتَبَرٌ

To frown. عَبَسَ يَعْبِسُ

Austere, stern. عَابِسٌ وَعَبُوسٌ

Very stern. Lion. عَبَّاسٌ

Frowning, sternness. عُبُوسٌ

To injure. عَبَطَ يَعْبِطُ عَبْطًا

To carry off in the flower of one's age, (death). أَعْبَطَ وَاعْتَبَطَ

A pure lie. عَبْطٌ

An act without reason. إِعْتِبَاطٌ

To be diffused, (perfume). عَبِقَ ـَ

Sense of suffocation. عَبَقَةٌ

Fine, excellent. عَبْقَرِيٌّ

To pack (goods). عَبَا يَعْبُو وَعَبَّى

To be filled ; arranged. تَعَبَّى

To importune ; rebuke. عَتَّ يَعُتُّ

To blame, censure. عَتَبَ يَعْتُبُ عَلَى

To blame, censure. عَاتَبَ مُعَاتَبَةً

Threshold. عَتَبَةٌ ج عَتَبَاتٌ

Blame. عِتَابٌ وَمَعْتَبَةٌ ج مَعَاتِبُ

To be ready. عَتُدَ يَعْتُدُ عَتَادًا

About to happen ; ready. عَتِيدٌ

To become old. عَتُقَ يَعْتُقُ عِتْقًا

To set free. عَتَقَ يَعْتِقُ

To make old, let grow old. عَتَّقَ

To set free, emancipate. أَعْتَقَ

Antiquity, oldness. عِتْقٌ

Emancipation. عَتْقٌ وَعَتَاقٌ

Shoulder. عَاتِقٌ ج عَوَاتِقُ

Old. Emancipated. عَتِيقٌ ج عِتَاقٌ

Kept long, made old. مُعَتَّقٌ

Acting corruptly. عاث ج عثاةٌ

To cry out. عجَّ يَعُجُّ عَجًّا وَعَجِيجًا

To raise the dust, (wind). عجَّ

Outcry, clamour. عَجٌّ وَعَجِيجٌ

Omelet. (عُجَّة)

Dust, smoke. عَجَاجٌ وَعَجَاجَة

عجب يَعْجَب عَجَبًا مِنْ وَلِ وَتعَجَّب

To wonder at. وَٱسْتَعْجَبَ مِنْ

To cause to wonder. عجَّبَ وَأَعْجَبَ

To please. أَعْجَبَ

To be vain, conceited. اعْجِبَ بِنَفْسِهِ

Pride, vanity, self-conceit. عُجْبٌ

Astonishment. عَجَبٌ

Very wonderful. عَجَبٌ وعجَابٌ

O wonderful يا لِلْعَجَبِ

Wonderful, extraordinary. عجيبٌ

عجِيبَة ج عَجَائِبُ وَأُعْجُوبَةٌ ج أَعَاجِيب

Wonderful thing, marvel.

More wonderful. أَعْجَب

Freed, emancipated. مَعْتُوقٌ

Shoulder-pole. عَتَلَةٌ

Porter. عَتَّالٌ ج عَتَّالَةٌ

Porterage. عِتَالَةٌ

To become dark. عَتم يَعْتِمُ وَعَتَمَ

Darkness of night. عَتْمٌ وَعَتْمَةٌ

Obscure, dark. مُعْتِمٌ وَمُعْتَمٌ

To be idiotic. عتهَ عَتَاهَةً

Idiocy, stupidity. أَعْتَهٌ وَعَتَاهَة

Idiot ; mad. مَعْتُوهٌ

To be proud, rebel. عتا يَعْتُوعُتُوًّا

Proud rebellious. عاتٍ ج عُتَاةٌ

Moth-worm. عُثَّةٌ ج عُثٌّ

To stumble, trip. عثرَ يَعْثُرُ عَثْرًا

To stumble upon. عثَرَ يَعْثُرُ عَلَى

To cause to stumble. عثّرَ وَأَعْثَرَ

A false step. عَثْرَةٌ ج عثرَاتٌ

Young bastard. Serpent. عُثْمَانٌ

To do evil, mischief. عثا يعْثُو عُثُوًّا

تَعَجُّبٌ Wonder, astonishment.

مُعْجَبٌ بِنَفْسِهِ Vain, self-conceited.

عُجْرَةٌ ج عُجَرٌ Knot, knob.

عَجُورٌ A kind of melon.

تَعَجْرَفَ عَلَى To act haughtily.

عَجْرَفَةٌ Coarseness, rudeness.

عَجَزَ يَعْجِزُ عَجْزاً To lack strength.

عَجَّزَ وَأَعْجَزَ To render unable.

عَجْزٌ Weakness, impotence. Second hemistich of a verse.

عَجُزٌ ج أَعْجَازٌ The posterior part.

عَاجِزٌ ج عَوَاجِزُ Feeble.

عَجُوزٌ ج عَجَائِزُ Old woman.

مُعْجِزَةٌ ج مُعْجِزَاتٌ Miracle.

عَجِفَ يَعْجَفُ عَجَفاً To be lean.

عَجِفٌ م عَجْفَاءُ ج عِجَافٌ Very lean.

عَجِلَ يَعْجَلُ وَاسْتَعْجَلَ To hasten.

عَجَّلَ وَاسْتَعْجَلَ To press one on.

عَجَلٌ وَعَجَلَةٌ وَاسْتِعْجَالٌ Haste.

عِجْلٌ ج عُجُولٌ Calf.

عَجَلَةٌ ج عَجَلٌ Cart ; wheel.

عَجُولٌ Hasty, quick.

أَعْجَلُ More hasty, expeditious.

مُعَجَّلٌ Hastened, accelerated.

عَجَمٌ Foreigners. *sp.* Persians.

أَعْجَمُ وَبِلَادُ ٱلْعَجَمِ Persia.

عُجْمَةٌ Foreign origin of a word.

أَعْجَمِيٌّ ج أَعْجَامٌ Foreigner.

مُعْجَمٌ Marked with vowel-points (letters). Obscure.

عَجَنَ يَعْجِنُ عَجْناً To knead (dough).

عِجَانٌ The perinæum.

عَجِينٌ Kneaded ; dough.

مِعْجَنٌ ج مَعَاجِنُ Kneading-trough.

مُعَجَّنَاتٌ Pastry.

مَعْجُونٌ ج مَعَاجِنُ Electuary.

عَجْوَةٌ Pressed dates.

عَدَّ يَعُدُّ To number ; regard.

أَعَدَّ To prepare, make ready.

تَعَدَّدَ To be multiplied.

لا يُعْتَدُّ بِهِ — Of no account.

اِسْتَعَدَّ — To be ready, prepare.

عَدَدٌ ج أَعْدَادٌ — Number.

عُدَّةٌ ج عُدَدٌ — Implements.

عَدِيدٌ — Numerous.

إِسْتِعْدَادٌ — Preparation.

تَعْدَادٌ — Enumeration.

مُعَدٌّ — Reday, prepared.

مُعْتَدٌّ بِهِ — Important.

مَعْدُودٌ — Numbered, counted.

مُسْتَعِدٌّ — Reday, prepared.

عَدَسٌ — Lentils.

عَدَسَةٌ — Lens. A small pustule.

عَدَسِيٌّ — Lenticular.

عَدَلَ يَعْدِلُ عَدْلاً — To act justly.

عَدَلَ عُدُولاً عَنْ — To deviate.

عَدَلَ بَيْنَ — To act with equity.

عَدَّلَ — To make just, equal.

عَادَلَ مُعَادَلَةً — To be equal to.

تَعَدَّلَ — To be valued at.

تَعَادَلَ — To be equal, (two things).

إِنْعَدَلَ عَنْ — To turn aside from.

إِعْتَدَلَ — To become right.

عَدْلٌ — Equity, justice.

عَادِلٌ ج عُدُولٌ — Just, equable.

عَدَالَةٌ — Justice, equity.

عَدِيلٌ وَعِدْلٌ — Like, equal.

عَدِيلَةٌ — Bag, sack.

إِعْتِدَالٌ — Equality, equity. Moderation. Equinox.

إِعْتِدَالِيٌّ — Equinoctial.

مُعَادِلٌ — Equal, like.

مُعَادَلَةٌ — Equation. Equilibrium.

مُعَدَّلٌ — Average.

مُعْتَدِلٌ — Temperate, moderate.

عَدِمَ يَعْدَمُ عَدَماً — To lack, want.

أَعْدَمَ — To deprive of ; annihilate.

إِنْعَدَمَ — To cease to exist.

عَدَمٌ — Non-existence.

عَدِيمٌ ج عُدَمَاءُ — Lacking.

مَعْدُومٌ — Non-existent.

عَدَنَ وَعَدَّنَ — To manure land.

عَدْنٌ — Eden. Abode.

جَنَاتُ عَدْنٍ — Paradise.

مَعْدِنٌ ج مَعَادِنُ — Mine. Metal, mineral. Origin, source.

مَعْدِنِيٌّ — Mineral, metallic.

عَدَا يَعْدُو عَدْواً — To run.

عَدَاهُ — To pass beyond it.

عَدَّى — To cause to go beyond.

عَادَي — To treat with enmity.

أَعْدَى — To infect (disease).

تَعَدَّى — To pass the limit ; transgress. Be transitive (verb).

إِعْتَدَى عَلَى — To be hostile toward.

عَدَا وَمَا عَدَا — Except.

عِدًّى (قَوْمٌ) — Hostile party.

عَدْوَى — Infection or contagion.

عُدْوَانٌ — Gross injustice.

عَدَاوَةٌ — Hostility, enmity.

عَدُوٌّ ج أَعْدَاءٌ وَأَعَادٍ وعُدِى — Enemy.

إِعْتِدَاءٌ وَتَعَدٍّ — Injustice.

مُعْدٍ — Infectious, contagious.

مُتَعَدٍّ وَمُعْتَدٍ عَلَى — Unjust.

مُتَعَدٍّ — Transitive (verb).

عَذُبَ يَعْذُبُ عُذُوبَةً — To be sweet.

عَذَّبَ — To punish, torment.

تَعَذَّبَ — To be punished ; suffer.

عَذْبٌ — Sweet, (water).

عَذَابٌ — Punishment ; torment.

عُذُوبَةٌ — Sweetness, agreeableness.

عَذَرَ يَعْذِرُ — To excuse.

تَعَذَّرَ وَاعْتَذَرَ — To apologize.

تَعَذَّرَ عَلَى — To be impossible.

إِسْتَعْذَرَ — To ask to be excused.

عُذْرٌ ج أَعْذَارٌ — Excuse, apology.

عَذْرَاءُ ج عَذَارَى — Virgin.

الْعَذْرَاءُ — The sign Virgo.

عِذَارٌ ج عُذُرٌ Halter. Cheek.

خَلَعَ ٱلْعِذَارَ To throw off restraint.

إِعْتِذَارٌ Excuse pretext.

تَعَذُّرٌ Difficulty, impossibility.

مَعْذِرَةٌ ج مَعَاذِرُ Excuse.

مَعْذُورٌ Excused, excuseable.

عَذَلَ يَعْذِلُ عَذْلاً To blame.

إِعْتَذَلَ وَتَعَذَّلَ To blame one's self.

عَذْلٌ وَعَذَلٌ Censure, blame.

عَاذِلٌ ج عُذَّالٌ One who blames.

عَذِيَةٌ (أَرْضٌ) Salubrious, (land).

عَرَّبَ To arabicize a foreign word.

أَعْرَبَ To speak clearly.

تَعَرَّبَ وَٱسْتَعْرَبَ To become an Arab.

أَلْعَرَبُ وَعُرْبَانٌ The Arabs.

أَلْعَرَبُ أَلْعَرْبَاءُ The pure Arabs.

عَرَبَةٌ وَعَرَبَانَةٌ Carriage, coach.

عَرَبِيٌّ Arabic; An Arabian.

أَلْعَرَبِيَّةُ The Arabic language.

عَرَبَجِيٌّ Coachman.

إِعْرَابٌ Syntax; parsing.

أَعْرَابِيٌّ ج أَعْرَابٌ Bedouin.

مُعْرَبٌ Declinable, capable of receiving all the vowel-points.

مُعَرَّبٌ Arabicized.

عَرْبَسَ To embroil, trouble.

عَرْبَنَ To give a pledge.

عُرْبُونٌ ج عَرَابِينُ Pledge.

عَرَجَ يَعْرُجُ فِي To ascend, mount.

عُرِجَ بِهِ To be taken up.

عَرَجَ عَرْجاً To limp, be lame.

عَرَّجَ وَتَعَرَّجَ عَلى To halt, stop at.

إِنْعَرَجَ To incline, decline.

عَرَجٌ وَعَرَجَانٌ Lameness.

أَعْرَجُ م عَرْجَاءُ ج عُرْجٌ Lame.

مُنْعَرَجٌ Sloping. Bend.

عِرْزَالٌ ج عَرَازِيلُ Booth.

عِرْسٌ ج أَعْرَاسٌ Husband, wife.

Wedding.	عُرْسٌ ج أَعْرَاسٌ
Weasel.	إِبْنُ عِرْسٍ
Bridegroom.	عَرِيسٌ ج عُرْسٌ
Bride.	عَرُوسٌ ج عَرَائِسُ
Throne. Booth.	عَرْشٌ ج عُرُوشٌ
Grape-vine.	عَرِيشٌ ج عَرَائِشُ
Court of a house.	عَرْصَةٌ ج أَعْرَاصٌ
To happen.	عَرَضَ يَعْرِضُ
To offer.	عَرَضَ عَلَى
To be wide, broad.	عَرُضَ يَعْرُضُ
To make broad.	عَرَّضَ
To expose to.	عَرَّضَ لِ
To oppose ; contradict.	عَارَضَ
To turn away from.	أَعْرَضَ عَنْ
To be exposed.	تَعَرَّضَ وَٱعْتَرَضَ
To interfere in.	تَعَرَّضَ لِ
To review an army.	إِعْتَرَضَ ٱلْجُنْدَ
To be in the way of.	إِعْتَرَضَ دُونَ
To oppose, object to.	اعْتَرَضَ عَلَى
Breadth, width.	عَرْضٌ ج عُرُوضٌ
Latitude.	خُطُوطُ ٱلْعَرْضِ
Day of Judgment.	يَوْمُ ٱلْعَرْضِ
Petition.	عَرْضُحَالٍ ج عَرْضُحَالَاتٍ
Honour.	عِرْضٌ ج أَعْرَاضٌ
Accident.	عَرَضٌ ج اعْرَاضٌ
By chance, accidentally.	عَرَضًا
Accidental.	عَرَضِيٌّ
Cross-beam.	عَارِضَةٌ ج عَوَارِضُ
Science of prosody.	عِلْمُ ٱلْعَرُوضِ
Broad.	عَرِيضٌ ج عِرَاضٌ
Opposition, objection.	إِعْتِرَاضٌ
Exposition.	مَعْرِضٌ
Opposition, contradiction.	مُعَارَضَةٌ
Offered, presented.	مَعْرُوضٌ
Transverse; obstructing.	مُعْتَرِضٌ
Parenthetic clause.	جُمْلَةٌ مُعْتَرِضَةٌ
Juniper-tree.	عَرْعَرٌ
To know.	عَرَفَ يَعْرِفُ

To make known. Define. عَرَّفَ

To be known. تَعَرَّفَ

To acknowledge. إِعْتَرَفَ ب

Odour, (*sp.* fragrant). عَرْفٌ

Comb of a cock. عرفٌ

Cock's-comb, (plant). عرفُ ٱلدِّيكِ

Common usage. عُرْفِيٌّ

Mount Arafât. عَرَفَاتٌ

Knowing. Skilled. عَارِفٌ

The diviner's art. عِرَافَةٌ

Diviner, astrologer. عَرَّافٌ

Overseer. عَرِيفٌ ج عُرَفَاء

Confession. إِعْتِرَافٌ

Tariff. Defining. تَعْرِيفٌ ج تَعْرِيفَاتٌ

The definite article. حرفُ ٱلتَّعْرِيفِ

Knowledge. مَعْرِفَةٌ ج مَعَارِفُ

Determinate, noun.

Determinate, definite. مُعَرَّفٌ

Known. Kindness. مَعْرُوفٌ

To sweat. عَرِقَ يَعْرَقُ عَرَقًا

To cause to sweat. عَرَّقَ

Extend its roots, (tree). أَعْرَقَ

Sweat. Distilled spirits. عَرَقٌ

Root. Vein. عِرْقٌ ج عُرُوقٌ

Sweating, perspiring. عَرْقَانُ

Irak. بِلَادُ ٱلْعِرَاقِ

Rooted. Noble. عَرِيقٌ

Diaphoretic. مُعَرِّقٌ

To hamstring (a beast). عَرْقَبَ

Hamstring. عُرْقُوبٌ ج عَرَاقِيبُ

To confuse, complicate. عَرْقَلَ

To be dangled, confused. تَعَرْقَلَ

Difficulties. عَرَاقِيل

To rub. عَرَكَ يَعْرُكُ عَرْكًا

To fight. عَارَكَ مُعَارَكَةً وَعِرَاكًا

Nature. عَرِيكَةٌ ج عَرَائِكُ

Gentle, tractable. لَيِّنُ ٱلعَرِيكَةِ

Battle. مَعْرَكَةٌ ج مَعَارِك

A heap.	عُرْمَةٌ ج عُرَمٌ
Numerous, (army).	عَرَمْرَمٌ
Covert, lair.	عَرِين وَعَرِينَةٌ
To be fall.	عَرَا ـ وَاعْتَرَى
Loop, button-loop.	عُرْوَةٌ ج عُرًى
The firmest support.	اَلْعُرْوَةُ ٱلْوُثْقَى
Overtaken (by).	مُعْتَرًى
To be naked ; free from.	عَرِيَ يَعْرَى
To strip, denude.	عَرَّى وَأَعْرَى
To be stripped.	تَعَرَّى
Nakedness.	عُرْيٌ وَعَرْيَةٌ
Naked ; free from.	عارٍ ج عُرَاةٌ
Naked.	عُرْيَانٌ ج عُرْيَانُونَ
Naked, denuded.	مُعَرًّى
To be mighty, noble.	عَزَّ يَعِزُّ
To be distressing to.	عَزَّ عَلَيْهِ
God, exalted and magnified (be His name!).	أَللّٰهُ عَزَّ وَجَلَّ
To render powerful.	عَزَّزَ
To love.	اَعَزَّ
To become powerful.	تَعَزَّزَ
To overcome.	إِعْتَزَّ وَاسْتَعَزَّ عَلَى
Might. Honour.	عِزٌّ وَعِزَّةٌ
Self-respect.	عِزَّةُ ٱلنَّفْسِ
Mighty ; noble ; dear.	عَزِيزٌ ج أَعِزَّاءُ
The mighty God.	اَلْعَزِيزُ
Governor of Egypt.	عَزِيزُ مِصْرَ
Dear, or dearer.	أَعَزُّ
Celibacy.	عُزْبَةٌ وَعُزُوبَةٌ
To be celibate.	عَزَبَ يَعْزُبُ
Unmarried.	أَعْزَبُ م عَزْبَاءُ ج عُزْبٌ
To punish ; reprove.	عَزَّرَ
Punishment.	تَعْزِيرٌ
The angel of death.	عِزْرَائِيل
To play upon a musical instrument.	عَزَفَ يَعْزِفُ
To furrow (the earth).	عَزَقَ يَعْزِقُ عَزْقًا
A hoe.	مِعْزَقٌ وَمِعْزَقَةٌ ج مَعَازِقُ
To set aside ; depose.	عَزَلَ يَعْزِلُ

To clean out.	عَزَّلَ
To separate one's self.	إِعْتَزَلَ
Removal (of an officer).	عَزْلٌ
Retirement. seclusion.	عُزْلَةٌ
Retirement.	إِعْتِزَالٌ وَآنْعِزَالٌ
Place of seclusion.	معزل
Away, aloof from.	بِمَعْزِلٍ عَنْ
Seceder.	مُعْتَزِلٌ
Removed, separated.	مَعْزُولٌ
To resolve to do.	عَزَمَ يَعْزِمُ عَلَى
To invite. Recite charms.	عَزَّمَ
Resolution, firm purpose.	عَزْمٌ
Firm, resolute.	عَازِمٌ ج عَزَمَةٌ
Magician, charmer.	عَزَّامٌ وَمُعَزِّمٌ
Determined, resolute.	عَزُومٌ
To comfort.	عَزَّى تَعْزِيَةً
To be comforted.	تَعَزَّى
Patience. Mourning.	عَزَاءٌ
Comforter, consoler.	مُعَزٍّ
Consoled, comforted.	مُعَزًّى
To ascribe, attribute.	عَزَى يَعْزُو
To patrol.	عَسَّ يَعُسُّ وَآعْتَسَّ
Night-patrol.	عَسٌّ وَعَسَسٌ
Male-bee. Chief.	يَعْسُوبٌ
Bax-thorn.	عَوْسَجٌ
Gold. Gem.	عَسْجَدٌ
To be difficult for.	عَسُرَ يَعْسُرُ عُسْراً عَلَى
To make difficult.	عَسَّرَ
To treat harshly.	عَاسَرَ
To become poor.	أَعْسَرَ
To become difficult.	تَعَسَّرَ
To find difficult.	إِسْتَعْسَرَ
Difficulty.	عُسْرٌ وَعُسْرَى وَمَعْسُرَةٌ
Difficult, hard.	عَسِرٌ وَعَسِيرٌ
Left-handed.	أَعْسَرُ م عَسْرَاءُ
Poor, indigent.	مُعْسِرٌ
To treat unjustly.	عَسَفَ يَعْسِفُ
Injustice, oppression.	عَسْفٌ

To form a camp. عَسْكَرَ

Army, troops. عَسْكَرٌ ج عَسَاكِرُ

Soldier. عَسْكَرِيٌّ ج عَسَاكِرُ

Military service. عَسْكَرِيَّةٌ

Military camp. مُعَسْكَرٌ

Honey. عَسَلٌ

To make honey, (bees). عَسَّلَ

Tender shoot. عُسْلُجٌ ج عَسَالِجُ

Stiffness of the wrist. عَسَمٌ

Having stiff wrist or ankle. أَعْسَمُ

To become hard. عَسَا يَعْسُو

Thick, coarse, rough. عَاسٍ

It may be that, perhaps. عَسَى أَنْ

To make a nest. عَشَّشَ وَاعْشَشَّ

Bird's nest. عِشٌّ ج أَعْشَاشٌ

To produce herbage. أَعْشَبَ

Green herb. عُشْبٌ ج اعشَابٌ

To take tithes. عَشَرَ وَعَشَرَ

To consort with. عَاشَرَ

To associate together. تَعَاشَرَ

Tithe ; a tenth. عُشْرٌ ج أَعْشَارٌ

Social intercourse. عِشْرَةٌ وَمُعَاشَرَةٌ

Ten. عَشَرَةٌ م عَشْرٌ ج عَشَرَاتٌ

Twenty. عِشْرُونَ

Tenth. عَاشِرٌ

Tithe-gatherer. عَشَّارٌ ج عَشَّارُونَ

Associate, friend. عَشِيرٌ ج عُشَرَاءُ

Kinsfolk. عَشِيرَةٌ ج عَشَائِرُ

Decimal. (*arith.*) أَعْشَارِيٌّ

Community. مَعْشَرٌ ج مَعَاشِرُ

Familiar friend. مُعَاشِرٌ

Companionship. مُعَاشَرَةٌ

To love passionately. عَشِقَ يَعْشَقُ

Passionate love. عِشْقٌ وَمَعْشَقٌ

Beloved one. عَشِيقٌ وَمَعْشُوقٌ

Passionate lover. عَاشِقٌ ج عُشَّاقٌ

To sup. عَشَا يَعْشُو وَتَعَشَّى

Weakness of sight. عَشًا وَعَشَاوَةٌ

Supper. عَشَاءٌ

The Eucharist. اَلْعَشَاءُ ٱلسِّرِّيُّ

Evening. عَشِيَّةٌ ج عَشَايَا

Yesterday evening. عَشِيَّةُ أَمْسِ

Darkness of night. عَشْوَةٌ وَعَشْوَاءُ

Cook. عَشِّيٌّ

To bind up. عَصَبَ وَعَصَّبَ

To defend a cause. تَعَصَّبَ فِي

To take the part of. تَعَصَّبَ لِ

To league against. تَعَصَّبَ عَلَى

To be leagued. إِعْتَصَبَ

Sinew. Nerve. عَصَبٌ ج أَعْصَابٌ

Male relations. عَصَبَةٌ ج عَصَبَاتٌ

Troop, band. عُصْبَةٌ ج عُصَبٌ

Nervous. عَصَبِيٌّ

Partisanship. Male relations. عَصَبِيَّةٌ

Bandage. Troop. عِصَابَةٌ ج عَصَائِبُ

Obstinacy, fanaticism. تَعَصُّبٌ

A zealous partisan. مُتَعَصِّبٌ

Bound, tied. مَعْصُوبٌ

To press, squeeze. عَصَرَ يَعْصِرُ

To be contemporary with. عَاصَرَ

To be pressed. تَعَصَّرَ وَٱنْعَصَرَ

A time, period. عَصْرٌ ج أَعْصُرٌ

Latter part of the day. عَصْرٌ

The afternoon prayer. صَلَاةُ ٱلْعَصْرِ

Juice, extract. عَصِيرٌ وَعُصَارَةٌ

A press. مِعْصَرَةٌ ج مَعَاصِرُ

Contemporary. مُعَاصِرٌ

Tail-bone. عُصْعُصٌ ج عَصَاعِصُ

To blow violently. عَصَفَ يَعْصِفُ

Hurricane. عَاصِفَةٌ ج عَوَاصِفُ

Chaff, straw. عُصَافَةٌ

Safflower. عُصْفُرٌ

Small bird. عُصْفُورٌ ج عَصَافِيرُ

To prevent ; defend. عَصَمَ يَعْصِمُ

To take refuge. اعْتَصَمَ وَٱسْتَعْصَمَ

Prevention, defence. عِصْمَةٌ

عَاصِمَةٌ	Capital of a country.
مَعْصَمٌ ج مَعَاصِم	Wrist.
مَعْصُومٌ	Preserved, protected.
عَصاً ج عِصِيٌّ	Staff, rod, cane.
عَصَا ٱلرَّاعِي	Knot-grass.
عَصَى يَعْصِي	To disobey, rebel.
عَاصٍ ج عُصَاةٌ	Rebellious.
نَهْرُ ٱلعَاصِي	The river Orontes.
عِصْيَانٌ وَمَعْصِيةٌ	Disobedience.
عَضَّ يَعَضُّ عَضًّا	To bite.
عَضَّ بِلِسَانِهِ	To defame.
عَضَدَ يَعْضُدُ وَعَاضَدَ	To aid, assist.
تَعَاضَدَ	To aid one another.
إِعْتَضَدَ ب	To seek assistance of.
عَضْدٌ ج أَعْضَادٌ	Aid Assistance.
عِضْدٌ ج أَعْضَادٌ	The upper arm.
عِضَادَةٌ	Side, side-post.
عَضَلَ وَأَعْضَلَ	To be difficult.
عَضِلٌ	Muscular.
عَضَلَةٌ ج عَضَلٌ وَعَضَلَاتٌ	Muscle.
عُضَالٌ وَمُعْضِلٌ	Severe; difficult.
مُعْضِلَةٌ ج مُعْضِلَاتٌ	Difficult case.
عِضْوٌ ج أَعْضَاءٌ	Member, limb.
عَطِبَ يَعْطَبُ عَطَباً	To perish.
اعْطَبَ	To destroy. Damage.
عَطَّرَ	To perfume.
تَعَطَّرَ	To perfume one's self.
عِطْرٌ ج أَعْطَارٌ	Perfume.
عِطْرُ ٱلوَرْدِ	Ottar of roses.
عَطِرٌ م عَطِرَةٌ	Aromatic.
عَطَّارٌ ج عَطَّارُونَ	Grocer.
عِطَارَةٌ	Grocery.
عُطَارِدُ	The planet Mercury,
عَطَسَ يَعْطُسُ	To sneeze.
عَطَّسَ	To make one sneeze.
عَطْسَةٌ وَعُطَاسٌ	A sneezing.
عَطُوسٌ	Snaff.
عَطِشَ يَعْطَشُ عَطَشاً	To thirst.

عَطَّشَ وَأَعْطَشَ To cause to thirst.

عَطَشٌ Thirst.

عَطْشَانُ ج عَطَاشَى Thirsty.

عَطَفَ يَعْطِفُ إِلى To incline towards.

عَطَفَ وَتَعَطَّفَ عَلَى To be kind to.

عَطَفَ كَلِمَةً To join one word to another by a conjunction.

عَطَفَ عَنْ To turn away from.

إِنْعَطَفَ To be bent, inclined.

إِسْتَعْطَفَ To seek favour.

حَرْفُ عَطْفٍ A conjunction.

عِطْفٌ ج أَعْطَافٌ Side, flank.

عَاطِفٌ Conjunctive particle.

عَاطِفَة ج عَوَاطِفُ Kindness, pity.

مَعْطُوفٌ Joined ; inclined.

مَعْطُوفٌ عَلَيْهِ A word to which another is joined by a conjunction.

مُنْعَطَفٌ A bend.

عَطِلَ وَتَعَطَّلَ To be without work. Be spoiled.

عَطَّلَ To leave unemployed. Ruin.

عُطْلٌ وَضَرَرٌ Damage and loss.

عُطْلُ ٱلْمَالِ Interest on money.

عُطْلَةٌ وَعَطَالَةٌ Vacant time.

عَاطِلٌ Spoiled, useless.

مُعَطَّلٌ Without work ; useless.

عَطَنٌ وَعَطْنَةٌ Mouldiness.

عَطِنٌ وَمُعَطَّنٌ Mouldy.

أَعْطَى To give present, offer.

تَعَطَّى وَٱسْتَعْطَى To beg.

تَعَاطَى To engage in.

عَطًا وَعَطَاءٌ وَعَطِيَّةٌ Gift.

مُعْطٍ Giver.

عَظُمَ يَعْظُمُ To be great, large.

عَظُمَ عَلَى To be hard upon.

عَظَّمَ To make large ; magnify.

تَعَظَّمَ To be great ; proud.

تَعَاظَمَ To magnify one's self.

إِسْتَعْظَمَ To regard as great.

عَظْمٌ ج عِظَامٌ Bone.

عِظَمٌ وَعَظَمَةٌ Pride ; majesty.

عَظِيمٌ ج عُظَمَاء وَعِظَامٌ Great.

أَلْعَظِيمُ The Great (God).

عَظِيمَةٌ ج عَظَائِمُ A great thing.

أَعْظَمُ م عُظْمَى Greater.

مُعْظَمٌ Greater, or chief part.

مُعَظَّمٌ Exalted, made great.

عَفَّ يَعِفُّ عَنْ To abstain from wrong.

عَفِيفٌ ج أَعِفَّاء Virtuous.

عِفَّة Continence, chastity.

عَفَرَ يَعْفِرُ To cover with dust.

عَفَرٌ وَعَفْرٌ Dust.

عِفْرِيتٌ ج عَفَارِيت Demon.

عَفَشَ يَعْفِشُ To heap up.

عَفْشٌ Trash. Baggage.

عَفْصٌ Galls.

عَفِنَ يَعْفَنُ وَعَفَّنَ وتَعَفَّنَ To become decayed, rotten, mouldy.

وعُفُونَة Mildew.

عَفِنٌ وَمَعْفُونٌ وَمُعَفَّنٌ Decayed.

مُتَعَفِّنٌ Putrid, mouldy.

عَفَا يَعْفُو عَنْ To pardon, forgive.

عَافَى To restore to health.

عَافَاكَ Bravo ! Well done.

أَعْفَى مِن To exempt, excuse.

تَعَافَى To be restored to health.

إِسْتَعْفَى To ask to be released.

عَفْوٌ Pardon, amnesty. Young ass.

عَفْواً Spontaneously ; easily.

عَافِيَةٌ ج عَوَافٍ وَعَافِيَاتٌ Health.

إِسْتِعْفَاء Resignation.

مُعَافَاةٌ Restoration to health.

مُتَعَافٍ Convalescent.

عَقِيقٌ Cornelian.

عَقَبَ ـُ عَقْباً To succeed.

عَقَبَ وَأَعْقَبَ وَاعْتَقَبَ To follow.

عَاقَبَ To punish.

تَعَقَّبَ To follow out.

To follow (one another).	تَعَاقَبَ
Heel of foot.	عِقبٌ ج أَعْقَابٌ
Mountain road.	عَقَبَةٌ ج عِقَابٌ
End, issue.	عقبى
End, result.	عَاقِبَةٌ ج عَوَاقِبُ
Punishment.	عِقَابٌ وَمُعَاقَبَةٌ
Eagle.	عقَابٌ ج أَعْقُبٌ وَعِقْبَانٌ
That which follows.	عقيبٌ
To tie, knot. Conclude. Ratify.	عَقَدَ يعقِدُ
To determine upon.	عقَدَ عَلَى
To make a contract with.	عَاقَدَ
To be complicated.	تَعَقَّدَ
To unite in a contract.	تَعَاقَدَ
To believe firmly.	إِعْتَقَدَ
Contract. Vault.	عقْدٌ ج عقُودٌ
Necklace.	عِقْدٌ ج عقود
Knot. Joint.	عُقْدَةٌ ج عُقَدٌ
Maker of silk-cord.	عقَّادٌ
Ally, confederate.	عقيدَةٌ
Article of faith.	عَقِيدَةٌ ج عَقَائِدُ
Belief, creed.	إِعْتِقَادٌ
Bond, contract, union.	إِنْعِقَادٌ
Obscurity, complexity.	تَعْقِيدٌ
Very knotty ; tangled.	مُعَقَّدٌ
Doctrine, belief.	مُعْتَقَدٌ
To cut, wound.	عَقَرَ يعقِرُ عَقْراً
To persevere in.	عاقَرَ
To be wounded.	إِنعَقَرَ
Wounding, wound.	عَقْرٌ
Barrenness.	عقْرٌ وعُقْرَةٌ وَعَقَارَةٌ
Barren.	عَاقِرٌ ج عَوَاقِرُ
Real estate.	عَقَارٌ ج عَقَارَاتٌ
A drug.	عقَّارٌ ج عَقَاقِيرُ
Scorpion.	عقرَبٌ ج عَقَارِبُ
Scorpion (of the zodiac).	أَلعَقْرَبُ
To plait (the hair).	عقَصَ يعقِصُ
To sting.	(عَقَصَ يَعقُصُ وَعَقَّصَ)
Plait (of hair).	عَقِيصَةٌ ج عَقَائِصُ

عِقَاصٌ	Hair-filet.
عَقَفَ يَعْقِفُ	To crook, bend.
تَعَقَّفَ وَٱنْعَقَفَ	To become bent.
أَعْقَفُ وَمَعْقُوفٌ	Bent, hooked.
عَقَلَ يَعْقِلُ وَٱعْتَقَلَ	To bind.
عَقَلَ مَعْقُولاً	To understand.
تَعَقَّلَ	To conceive, know.
إِعْتَقَلَ	To withhold, restrain.
عَقْلٌ ج عُقُولٌ	Mind, intellect.
عَقْلِيٌّ	Rational ; mental.
عَاقِلٌ ج عُقَّالٌ وَعُقَلَاءُ	Intelligent.
عِقَالٌ ج عُقُلٌ	Rope cord.
عَقِيلَةٌ ج عَقَائِلُ	A noble woman.
مَعْقِلٌ ج مَعَاقِلُ	Fortress, refuge.
مَعْقُولٌ	Intelligible, reasonable.
عِلْمُ ٱلْمَعْقُولَاتِ	Mental science.
عَقِمَ يَعْقَمُ	To be barren.
عَقَّمَ وَأَعْقَمَ	To render barren.
عُقْمٌ	Barrenness.

عَقِيمٌ ج عُقُمٌ	Barren, sterile.
عَكَّةُ وَعَكَّاءُ	Acre, (town).
عَكِرَ يَعْكَرُ وَتَعَكَّرَ	To become turbid.
عَكَّرَ وَأَعْكَرَ	To render turbid.
عَكَرٌ	Dregs, lees, sediment.
عَكِرٌ وَمُعَكَّرٌ	Troubled, turbid.
عَكَزَ وَتَعَكَّزَ عَلَى	To lean upon (a staff.)
عُكَّازٌ ج عَكَاكِيزُ	Staff ; crosier.
عَكَسَ يَعْكِسُ	To reverse, invert.
عَاكَسَ	To invert, oppose.
إِنْعَكَسَ	To be inverted, reflected.
إِنْعِكَاسٌ	Inversion, reflection.
بِٱلْعَكْسِ	On the contrary.
عَكِشٌ	Thick, dense.
عَكَفَ يَعْكُفُ عَكْفاً	To detain.
عَكَفَ عَلَى	To persevere in.
عَكَفَ وَٱعْتَكَفَ فِي	To abide in.
عَاكِفٌ	Keeping to.
إِعْتِكَافٌ	Religious seclusion.

عَكَمَ يَعْكِمُ	To tie up. Muzzle.
عُلَّ علة	To become ill.
علَّلَ بِ	To Divert. Account for.
تَعَلَّلَ	To offer excuses.
تَعَلَّلَ بِ	To divert one's self.
إعْتَلَّ	To become diseased, sick.
علَّ وَلَعَلَّ	May-be, perhaps.
علةٌ ج عِلَلٌ	Cause. Malady.
حُرُوفُ ٱلعِلَة	The weak letters.
عِلِّيَّةٌ ج عَلَالِيُّ	Upper chamber.
عَلِيلٌ وَمَعْلُولٌ	Sick, diseased.
تَعْلِيلٌ	Assignment of a cause.
مُعْتَلٌّ	Ill, diseased. Containing one of the weak letters.
عُلْبَةٌ ج عُلَبٌ	Small box.
عَالَجَ	To work at. Treat (a disease).
تَعَالَجَ	To take medical treatment.
تَعَالَجَ	To strive with one another.
عِلَاجٌ وَمُعَالَجَةٌ	Treatment of disease. Remedy, cure.

مُعَالَجَةٌ	Dispute, contention.
عَلَفَ يَعْلِفُ	To feed (a beast).
عَلَفٌ	Fodder (for beasts).
عَلَّافٌ	Seller of provender.
مَعْلَفٌ ج مَعَالِفُ	Manger.
مُعَلَّفٌ	Fattened (animal),
عَلِقَ يَعلَقُ وَٱعْتَلَقَ بِ	To hang to.
عَلِقَ عُلُوقًا	To conceive, (woman).
عُلِقَ عُلُوقًا بِهِ	To love.
عَلِقَ يَعْلَقُ	To begin to do.
عَلَّقَ	To attach.
عَلَّقَ فِي	To note down.
تَعَلَّقَ بِ	To be attached to.
عَلَقَةٌ ج عَلَقَاتٌ وَعَلَقٌ	Leech.
علاقةٌ ج عَلَائِقُ	Connection.
عَلِيقٌ	Forage, for animals.
عُلَّيْقٌ	Climbing plant ; brier.
تَعَلُّقٌ	Connection.
مُعَلَّقٌ	Attached, suspended.

Attached to. مُتَعَلِّقٌ بِ

Very bitter plant. عَلْقَمٌ

To chew. عَلَكَ يَعْلُكُ عَلْكًا

To know, perceive. عَلِمَ يَعْلَمُ

To teach. To mark. عَلَّمَ

To inform. أَعْلَمَ

To learn. تَعَلَّمَ

To desire to know ; ask. إِسْتَعْلَمَ

Sign. Banner. عَلَمٌ ج أَعْلَامٌ

Proper name. إِسْمُ عَلَمٍ

Science, knowledge. عِلْمٌ ج عُلُومٌ

Scientific. عِلْمِيٌّ

Knowing ; learned. عَالِمٌ ج عُلَمَاءُ

World. عَالَمٌ ج عَوَالِمُ وعَالَمُونَ

The animal kingdom. عَالَمُ ٱلْحَيَوَانِ

The vegetable kingdom. عَالَمُ ٱلنَّبَاتِ

The mineral kingdom. عَالَمُ ٱلْمَعَادِنِ

Very learned. عَلَّامٌ وَعَلَّامَةٌ

Sign, mark. عَلَامَةٌ

Learned, savant. عَلِيمٌ ج عُلَمَاءُ

Announcement, notice. إِعْلَامٌ

Instruction. Doctrine. تَعْلِيمٌ

Instructions ; orders. تَعْلِيمَاتٌ

Taught. Marked. مُعَلَّمٌ

Teacher, master. مُعَلِّمٌ

Known. Active voice, (verb). Certainly, of course. مَعْلُومٌ

To be open, manifest. عَلَنَ يَعْلُنُ

To publish, reveal. أَعْلَنَ

To be manifest. إِعْتَلَنَ وَاسْتَعْلَنَ

Manifest, open. عَلَنٌ وَعَالِنٌ

Openly, publicly. عَلَانِيَةً

Manifestation, announcement. Advertisement. إِعْلَانٌ

To be high ; ascend. عَلَا يَعْلُو

To overcome. عَلَا عَلَى

To elevate. عَلَّى وَأَعْلَى

To be elevated. تَعَلَّى وَتَعَالَى

God, the exalted one. أَللّٰهُ تَعَالَى

Come ! come here !	تَعالَ
To rise high.	اِعْتَلَى وَاسْتَعْلَى
Nobility ; eminence.	عَلاَءٌ وَعُلى
Height. Grandeur.	عُلُوٌّ
In addition to.	علاوَةٌ
High ; elevated ; noble.	عَلِيٌّ ج عَلِيُّونَ
God, the most High.	اَلْعَلِيُّ
Upper chamber.	عِلِّيَّةٌ ج عَلاَلِيٌّ
High, sublime.	عالٍ
The Sublime Porte.	اَلْبَاب العَالِي
Higher, nobler.	أَعْلَى ج أَعالٍ
The exalted, (God).	اَلْمُتَعَالِي
To address a letter.	عَلْوَنَ
Address ; title.	عُلْوَانٌ
To ascend.	عَلِيَ يَعْلِي عَلْيًا وَعُلِيًّا
Upon, with, for, at.	عَلَى
You ought to do ...	عَلَيْكَ ان تَفْعَلَ...
He is in debt.	عَلَيْهِ دَيْنٌ
In his time.	عَلَى عَهْدِهِ
By means of.	عَلَى يَدِ فُلاَنٍ
To be general ; include.	عَمَّ يَعُمُّ
To generalize.	عَمَّمَ
Paternal uncle.	عَمٌّ ج أَعْمَامٌ
Paternal aunt.	عَمَّةٌ ج عَمَّاتٌ
Cousin on the father's side. Husband.	إِبْنُ ٱلْعَمِّ
Cousin on the father's side. Wife.	بِنْتُ ٱلْعَمِّ
For what ?	عَمَّ (عَنْ ما)
For whom ?	عَمَّنْ (عَنْ مَنْ)
General, universal.	عَامٌّ
The common people.	اَلْعَامَّةُ
They all came.	جَاءَ الْقَوْمُ عَامَّةً
To common people.	اَلْعَوَامُّ
Vulgar, common.	عَامِّيٌّ
Turban.	عِمَامَةٌ ج عَمَائِمُ
Universality, totality.	عُمُومٌ
Ingeneral, universally.	عُمُوماً

General, universal.	عُموميّ
More common or general.	أَعَمّ
Turbaned.	مُعَمَّم ومُتَعَمِّم
To prop up, support.	عَمَدَ يَعْمِدُ
To intend, purpose.	عَمَدَ وتَعَمَّدَ
To aim at, seek, repair to.	عَمَدَ إِلَى
To baptize.	عَمَدَ وعَمَّدَ
To be baptized.	تَعَمَّدَ واعْتَمَدَ
To depend upon.	اعْتَمَدَ عَلَى
Intentionally.	عَمْداً وتَعَمُّداً
Prop. Committee.	عُمْدَة
Column, pillar.	عَمُود ج أَعْمِدَة
Perpendicular line.	خَطّ عَمُودِيّ
Representative.	مُعْتَمَد
Baptism.	مَعْمُودِيَّة
To live a long time.	عَمَرَ يَعْمُرُ
To be inhabited.	عَمَرَ يَعْمُرُ
To inhabit.	عَمَرَ عِمَارَة
To build.	عَمَرَ عِمَارَة
To make inhabited.	أَعْمَرَ
To be flourishing.	عَمَرَ يَعْمُرُ
To build, construct.	عَمَّرَ
To colonize.	أَعْمَرَ واسْتَعْمَرَ
Life-time ; age.	عُمْر ج أَعْمَار
By my life!	لَعَمْرِي
Prosperity of a land. Civilization.	عُمْرَان
Edifice. Cultivation.	عِمَارَة ج عَمَائِر
Inhabited.	عَامِر وعَمِير ومَعْمُور
Mason.	مِعْمَار ومِعْمَارِيّ ج مِعْمَارِيَة
Colony.	مُسْتَعْمَرَة
Weakness of sight.	عَمَش
Weak in sight.	أَعْمَش
To be deep.	عَمُقَ يَعْمُقُ
To make deep.	عَمَّقَ وأَعْمَقَ
To go deeply into.	تَعَمَّقَ فِي
Depth.	عَمْق وعُمْق ج أَعْمَاق
Deep, profound.	عَمِيق
To work, do, make.	عَمِلَ يَعْمَلُ

To act upon. عَمِلَ فِي

To deal with. Treat. عَامَلَ

To employ, use, exert. اعْمَلَ

To deal with one another. تَعَامَلَ

To labour, work. إِعْتَمَلَ

To use ; employ. إِسْتَعْمَلَ

Work, service, deed, action ; occupation. عَمَلٌ ج اعمالٌ

An evil deed. عَمْلَةٌ

Money. عُمْلَة

Practical. Artificial. عَمَلِي

Operation. عَمَلِيَّةٌ

Workman, doer. عامِلٌ ج عُمَّالٌ

A word that governs another (*in gram.*) عامِلٌ ج عَوَامِلُ

Commercial agent. عَمِيلٌ

Use, employment. إِسْتِعْمَالٌ

Mill, factory. مَعْمَلٌ ج مَعَامِلُ

Transaction. Manner of treatment. مُعَامَلَةٌ ج مُعَامَلاتٌ

Made. Governed (word). مَعْمُولٌ

To become blind. عَمِيَ يَعْمَى

To be blind to. عَمِيَ عَنْ

To be obscure to. عَمِيَ ٱلْأَمْرُ عَلَى

To render blind. اعْمَى

To feign blindness. تَعَامَى

Blindness. عَمًى

Blind. أَعْمَى م عَمْيَاءُ ج عُمْيٌ

For, from, at. عَنْ

He left us. ذَهَبَ عَنَّا

After a little while. عَنْ قَلِيلٍ

To the last man. عَنْ آخِرِهِمْ

At his right hand. عَنْ يَمِينِهِ

Life for life. نَفْسٌ عَنْ نَفْسٍ

Because of a promise. عَنْ وَعْدٍ

To appear. عَنَّ يَعِنُّ عَنًّا

Clouds. عَنَانٌ

Reins. عِنَانٌ ج اعِنَّة

Grapes. عِنَبٌ

عُتَّابٌ	Jujube tree and fruit.
عَنْبَرٌ	Ambergris. Ship-hold. A kind of Mimosa.
عَنَّتَ	To treat with rigour.
عِنْدَ	At, near, with, on.
جِئْتُ مِنْ عِنْدِهِ	I came from him.
عِنْدَ طُلُوعِ ٱلشَّمْسِ	At sunrise.
جَلَسَ عِنْدَهُ	He sat with him.
عِنْدِي مَالٌ	I have property.
عِنْدِي كَذَا	Such is my opinion.
عِنْدَ مَا صَارَ	When it happened.
عِنْدَ ذٰلِكَ	Then ; thereupon.
عَنَدَ يَعْنُدُ	To be obstinate.
عَانَدَ عِنَاداً وَمُعَانَدَةً	To resist.
تَعَانَدَ	To oppose one another.
عَنِيدٌ ج عُنُدٌ وَمُعَانِدٌ	Obstinate.
عَنْزٌ ج عُنُوزٌ وَعِنَازٌ	She-goat.
عُنْصُرٌ ج عَنَاصِرُ	Element. Origin.
أَلْعَنْصَرَةُ	Feast of Pentecost.
عُنْصُرِيٌّ	Simple, elemental.
عَنْصَلٌ	Wild onion ; squill.
عَنُفَ يَعْنُفُ	To be harsh ; rude.
عَنَّفَ وَأَعْنَفَ	To upbraid.
عُنْفٌ	Roughness, harshness.
عُنْفاً	Violently.
عُنْفُوَانٌ	The first of a thing.
عُنْفُوَانُ ٱلشَّبَابِ	Prime of youth.
عَنِيفٌ	Harsh, violent.
عَانَقَ وَٱعْتَنَقَ	To embrace.
عُنُقٌ ج أَعْنَاقٌ	Neck.
عِنَاقٌ وَمُعَانَقَةٌ	Embrace.
أَلْعَنْقَاءُ	Fabulous bird ; griffin.
عُنْقُودٌ ج عَنَاقِيدُ	Bunch.
عَنْكَبُوتٌ ج عَنَاكِبُ	Spider.
عَنَا يَعْنُو	To trouble, distress.
عَنَا (ل)	To submit to.
عَنَّى وَأَعْنَى	To subdue.
عَنْوَةٌ	Force, violence.

Captive ; submissive.	عَانٍ ج عُنَاةٌ
To address a letter.	عَنْوَنَ
Title ; address.	عُنْوَانٌ
To mean, intend.	عَنَى يَعْنِي
To concern.	عُنِيَ عِنَايَةً
To distress, afflict.	عَنَّى وأَعْنَى
To suffer, endure.	عَانَى
To care for, manage.	إِعْتَنَى بِ
Difficulty, trouble.	عَنَاءٌ
Care, solicitude.	عِنَايَةٌ وَآعْتِنَاءٌ
Divine Providence.	أَلْعِنَايَةُ ٱلإِلٰهِيَّةُ
Meaning, sense.	مَعْنًى ج مَعَانٍ
Rhetoric.	عِلْمُ ٱلْمَعَانِي
Ideal, mental.	مَعْنَوِيٌّ
To know.	عَهِدَ يَعْهَدُ عَهْداً
To enjoin, charge.	عَهِدَ إِلَى
To make an agreement.	عَاهَدَ
To swear to one.	عَاهَدَهُ
To be careful of.	تَعَهَّدَ وَتَعَاهَدَ
To make an engagement.	تَعَاهَدَ
Covenant, agreement. Time, epoch.	عَهْدٌ ج عُهُودٌ
The Old Testament.	أَلْعَهْدُ ٱلْقَدِيمُ
The New Testament.	اَلْعَهْدُ ٱلْجَدِيدُ
Presumptive heir.	وَلِيُّ ٱلْعَهْدِ
Compact. Responsibility.	عُهْدَةٌ
Treaty, alliance.	مُعَاهَدَةٌ
Stipulated. Known.	مَعْهُودٌ
Debauchery.	عَهْرٌ وَعَهَارَةٌ
To stop ; pass by.	عَاجَ يَعُوجُ
To crook, bend, contort.	عَوَّجَ
To become bent.	تَعَوَّجَ وَٱعْوَجَّ
Ivory.	عَاجٌ
Crookedness.	عِوَجٌ وَٱعْوِجَاجٌ
Crooked.	أَعْوَجُ م عَوْجَاءُ ج عُوْجٌ
Crooked, tortuous.	مُعَوَّجٌ
To return to.	عَادَ يَعُودُ إِلَى
To repeat.	عَادَ وَأَعَادَ
To visit (the sick).	عَادَ عِيَادَةً

عَوَّدَ	To accustom.
أَعَادَ إِلَى	To restore.
تَعَوَّدَ وَٱعْتَادَ	To be accustomed.
عَادَةٌ ج عَادَاتٌ	Custom.
عَادِيٌّ	Old. Customary.
أَلْعَادِيَّاتُ	Ancient monuments.
عَوْدٌ	Return ; repetition.
عُودٌ ج عِيدَانٌ	Stick. Lute.
أَلْعُودُ	Aloes-wood.
عِيدٌ ج أَعْيَادٌ	Festival, feast-day.
عَائِدٌ	A visitor, (*sp.* of the sick).
عَائِدَةٌ ج عَوَائِدُ	Benefit ; utility.
إِعَادَةٌ	Repetition.
إِعْتِيَادِيٌّ	Habitual, customary.
أَلْمَعَادُ	The future life.
مُعَوَّدٌ وَمُعْتَادٌ	Habituated.
عَاذَ يَعُوذُ بِ	To seek protection.
عَوْذٌ وَعِيَاذٌ	Taking refuge.
مَعَاذٌ وَمَعَاذَةٌ	Refuge, asylum.
مَعَاذَ ٱللهِ	God forbid !
عَوِرَ وَٱعْوَرَّ	To lose one eye.
أَعَارَ	To lend.
إِسْتَعَارَ	To borrow.
عَوْرَةٌ ج عَوْرَاتٌ	Private parts.
إِعَارَةٌ	Loan ; act of lending.
إِسْتِعَارَةٌ	Borrowing. Metaphor.
إِسْتِعَارِيٌّ	Metaphorical.
أَعْوَرُ م عَوْرَآءُ ج عُورٌ	One-eyed.
مُسْتَعَارٌ	Borrowed. Metaphorical.
عَازَ يَعُوزُ وَأَعْوَزَ	To want, lack.
أَعْوَزَهُ ٱلشَّيْءُ	He needed it.
أَعْوَزَهُ ٱلدَّهْرُ	Fortune has reduced him to poverty.
عَوَزٌ	Poverty, need.
عَوِزٌ وَعَائِزٌ وَأَعْوَزُ وَمُعْوِزٌ	Needy.
مَعَاوِزُ	Wants.
عَوِصَ يَعْوَصُ	To be difficult.

Difficulty, obscurity.	عَوَصٌ
Difficult.	عَوِيصٌ م عَوْصَاءُ
To give something in exchange.	عَاضَ يَعُوضُ وَعَوَّض
To receive in compensation for.	تَعَوَّضَ وَٱعْتَاضَ عَنْ أَوْ مِنْ
Thing in exchange.	عِوَضٌ
Compensation.	عِوَضٌ وَتَعْوِيضٌ
Instead of.	عِوَضًا عَنْ أَوْ مِنْ
To hinder.	عَاقَ يَعُوقُ وَعَوَّقَ وَأَعَاقَ
To be hindered.	تَعَوَّقَ
Delay.	عَاقَةٌ
Obstacle.	عَائِقٌ وَعَائِقَةٌ ج عَوَائِقُ
Capella (star).	أَلْعَيُّوقُ
Act of retarding.	إِعَاقَةٌ وَتَعْوِيقٌ
To support ; nourish.	عَالَ يَعُولُ
To be unfaithful in.	عَالَ فِي
His patience was exhausted.	عَالَ وَعِيلَ صَبْرُهُ
To wail.	عَوَّلَ وَأَعْوَلَ وَٱعْتَوَلَ
To rely upon.	عَوَّلَ عَلَى وَبِ
To sustain a family.	أَعَالَ
Wailing.	عَوْلٌ وَعَوْلَةٌ وَعَوِيلٌ
Family.	عَائِلَةٌ ج عَائِلَاتٌ
A family, household.	عِيَالٌ
Pickaxe.	مِعْوَلٌ ج مَعَاوِلُ
To swim, float.	عَامَ يَعُومُ عَوْمًا
A year.	عَامٌ ج أَعْوَامٌ
Swimming.	عَائِمٌ
To aid, assist.	عَاوَنَ وَأَعَانَ عَلَى
To give mutual aid.	تَعَاوَنَ
To seek the aid of.	إِسْتَعَانَ بِ
Aid, assistance.	عَوْنٌ وَمَعُونَةٌ
Aider, assistant.	عَوْنٌ ج أَعْوَانٌ
Aid, assistance.	إِعَانَةٌ وَمُعَاوَنَةٌ
Assistant, coadjutor.	مُعَاوِنٌ
Bane, pest, blight.	عَاهَةٌ
To howl, bark.	عَوَى يَعْوِي عُوَاءً

عُوَاءٌ Howling, crying, barking.
عَابَ يَعِيبُ To be faulty.
عَابَ وَعَيَّبَ To find fault with.
عَيْبٌ ج عُيُوبٌ Blemish ; shame.
عَائِبٌ Defective, faulty.
مَعِيبٌ وَمَعْيُوبٌ Shameful.
عَاثَ يَعِيثُ To act corruptly.
عَيَّدَ To celebrate a feast.
عِيدٌ ج أَعْيَادٌ Feast, festival.
عِيدُ ٱلْمِيلَادِ Christmas.
عَارَ يَعِيرُ To go about ; journey.
عَيَّرَ To upbraid, reproach. To verify by weighing.
عَارٌ Disgrace, shame.
عِيَارٌ Standard of weight.
عِيسَى Jesus (Christ).
عِيسَوِيٌّ Christian.
عَاشَ يَعِيشُ عَيْشًا To live.
عَيَّشَ وَأَعَاشَ To nourish.

تَعَيَّشَ To seek means of living.
عَيْشٌ وَعِيشَةٌ Life.
عَيْشٌ Wheat, bread, food.
عَائِشٌ Living, living well.
مَعَاشٌ وَمَعِيشَةٌ Means of living.
عَيَّطَ To cry out, shout.
عِيَاطٌ Shouting.
عَافَ يَعَافُ وَيَعِيفُ To dislike.
عَالَ يَعِيلُ To become poor.
أَعْيَلَ To have a large family.
عَائِلَةٌ ج عِيَالٌ Family.
مُعْيِلٌ Having a large family.
عَيَّنَ To appoint ; specify.
عَايَنَ مُعَايَنَةً وعِيَانًا To see.
تَعَيَّنَ To be specified ; appointed.
عَيْنٌ ج أَعْيُنٌ وَعُيُونٌ Eye. Self.
ٱلْأَعْيَانُ The chief men, notables.
عينٌ ج عيُون Fountain.

هُوَ هُوَ عَيْنُهُ	It is he himself.
عَيْنُ ٱلْيَقِين	Certain knowledge.
عِيَانٌ ومُعَايَنَةٌ	Act of seeing.
عِيَانًا	Clearly, evidently.
عِيَانِيٌّ	Occular (witness).
عُوَيْنَاتٌ	Spectacles, eye-glasses.
تَعْيِينٌ	Specification, designation.
مُعَيَّنٌ	Designated, appointed.
مُعَيَّنٌ	A rhombus, (*geom.*).
الشَّبِيهُ بالمُعَيَّنِ	A rhomboid.
مُتَعَيِّنٌ	Designated, appointed.
عَاهَةٌ	Bane, scourge, blight.
عَيِيَ يَعْيَى عِيًّا	To be unable.
أَعْيَا	To be disabled ; disable.
عَيَاءٌ	Weakness, disease.
عَيٌّ ج أَعْيَاءٌ	Weak.
عَيَّانٌ	Weak, incapable, sick.

غ

غ	As a numeral sign=1000.
غَبَّ ـُ	To visit at intervals.
غِبًّا	At intervals.
غِبَّ	After.
غَبَّرَ وَأَغْبَرَ	To raise the dust.
تَغَبَّرَ	To become dusty.
إِغْبَرَّ	To become dust-coloured.
غُبْرَة و غَبَرَةٌ وَغُبَارٌ	Dust.
غَابِرٌ	Remaining. Passing away.
أَغْبَرُ م غَبْرَاءُ ج غُبْرٌ	Dust-coloured.
غَبَسٌ وغُبْسَةٌ	Duskiness.
اغْبَسُ م غَبْسَاءُ	Ash-coloured.

إِغْتَبَطَ To be in a happy state.
غَبْطٌ وَغِبْطَةٌ Happy state.
غَبِيطٌ ج غُبُطٌ Channel of water.
مَغْبُوطٌ Fortunate ; blessed.
غَبَنَ يَغْبِنُ غَبْناً To cheat.
غَبَنَ وَٱغْتَبَنَ To conceal.
إِنْغَبَنَ To be deceived, or cheated.
غَبْنٌ وَغَبِينَةٌ Fraud, deceit.
غَبِيَ عَلَى To be hidden from.
غَبَاوَةٌ Ignorance, heedlessness.
غَبِيٌّ ج أَغْبِيَاءُ Ignorant, stupid.
غَثٌّ وَغَثِيثٌ Lean, meagre.
غُثْمَةٌ Ash-colour.
غَثَا يَغْثِي غَثَيَانًا To be nauseated.
غُدَّةٌ ج غُدَدٌ Wen ; gland.
غَدَرَ يَغْدِرُ غَدْراً بِ To deceive.
غَادَرَ To leave, abandon.
غَدْرٌ Perfidy, treachery.
غَادِرٌ وَغَدَّارٌ Treacherous.

غَدَّارَةٌ ج غَدَّارَاتٌ Small pistol.
غَدِيرٌ ج غُدْرَانٌ Pool of water.
غَدَا يَغْدُو To go forth early.
تَغَدَّى To breakfast.
غَدَّى To give breakfast.
غَداً وَفِي ٱلْغَدِ To-morrow.
بَعْدَ ٱلْغَدِ Day after to-morrow.
غَدَاءٌ Morning meal ; lunch.
غُدُوٌّ وَغَدَاةٌ Early morning.
غَذَا ـُ وَغَذَّى To nourish (food).
تَغَذَّى وَٱغْتَذَى To be fed.
غِذَاءٌ ج أَغْذِيَةٌ Food nutriment.
مُغَذٍّ Nourishing (food).
غَرَّ يَغُرُّ غُرُوراً To beguile.
إِغْتَرَّ To be deceived.
غُرَّةٌ ج غُرَرٌ White mark on the forehead of a horse. The new moon. The best of anything.
غَرَّارٌ وَغَرُورٌ Very deceitful.
غِرٌّ ج أَغْرَارٌ Unexperienced, ignorant.

False things, vanities. غُرُورٌ

Beautiful. Noble. أَغَرُّ م غَرَّاءُ

Deceived, deluded. مَغْرُورٌ

To depart ; set (sun). غَرَبَ يَغْرُبُ

To go west. غَرَّبَ وَأَغْرَبَ

To go to a strange land. تَغَرَّبَ

To regard as strange. إِسْتَغْرَبَ

The west. غَرْب

Travelling in a foreign land. غُرْبَةٌ وَتَغَرُّبٌ وَٱغْتِرَابٌ

A crow. غُرَابٌ ج غِرْبَانٌ

Strangeness, obscurity. غَرَابَةٌ

Setting, sun-set. غُرُوبٌ

A stranger. غَرِيبٌ ج غُرَبَاءُ

Strange event. غَرِيبَةٌ ج غَرَائِب

The west. مَغْرِبٌ ج مَغَارِبُ

Hour of sun-set. مَغْرِبُ ٱلشَّمْسِ

Moor, Arab of N. W. Africa. مَغْرِبِيٌّ ج مَغَارِبَةٌ

To sift ; disperse. غَرْبَلَ

Sieve. غِرْبَالٌ ج غَرَابِيلُ

To warble. غَرِدَ يَغْرَدُ وَغَرَّدَ

To prick. غَرَزَ يَغْرِزُ غَرْزاً ب

To insert. غَرَزَ وَغَرَّزَ وَأَغْرَزَ

Nature ; natural, innate quality. غَرِيزَةٌ ج غَرَائِزُ

Natural, innate. غَرِيزِيٌّ

To plant. غَرَسَ يَغْرِسُ غَرْساً

To be planted. إِنْغَرَسَ

Planted tree. غَرْسٌ ج أَغْرَاسٌ

Plantation. مَغْرِسٌ ج مَغَارِسُ

Planted (tree). مَغْرُوسٌ

Piastre. غُرْشٌ ج غُرُوشٌ

Aim, object. غَرَضٌ ج أَغْرَاضٌ

To gargle. غَرْغَرَ

A gargle. غَرْغَرَةٌ

To dip out with a ladle. غَرَفَ يَغْرُفُ وَٱغْتَرَفَ

Upper chamber. غُرْفَةٌ ج غُرَفٌ

Handful. غُرْفَةٌ ج غِرَافٌ

مِغْرَفَةٌ ج مَغَارِفُ	Ladle.
غَرِقَ يَغْرَقُ	To sink, be drowned.
غَرَّقَ وَأَغْرَقَ	To drown.
إِسْتَغْرَقَ	To take in, comprise.
غَرَقٌ	Drowning, sinking.
غَرِيقٌ ج غَرْقَى	Drowned.
غَرِمَ يَغْرَمُ	To pay a tax, fine.
غَرَّمَ وَأَغْرَمَ	To impose a fine.
اغْرِمَ ب	To be very fond of.
تَغَرَّمَ	To pay a tax ; fine.
غَرَامَةٌ	Fine, tax ; loss.
غَرَامٌ	Fond attachment.
غَرِيمٌ ج غُرَمَاءُ	Debtor ; litigant.
مُغْرَمٌ	Eagerly desirous.
غُرْنُوقٌ ج غَرَانِقُ	Crane ; stork.
غَرَا يَغْرُو وَغَرَّى	To glue.
أَغْرَى	To incite, urge.
تَغَرَّى	To be glued.
غِرَاءٌ	Glue.
لاَ غَرْوَ	No wonder !
إِغْرَاءٌ	Incitement, instigation.
مِغْرَاةٌ	Glue pot.
غَزَّ يَغُزُّ ب	To prick.
غَزَّةُ	Gaza, (town).
غَزُرَ يَغْزُرُ	To be copious.
غَزَارَةٌ	Abundance.
غَزِيرٌ ج غِزَارٌ	Abundant.
غَزَلَ يَغْزِلُ غَزْلاً	To spin.
تَغَزَّلَ	To say amatory words.
غَزْلٌ	Spun thread or yarn.
غَزَلٌ وَتَغَزُّلٌ	Amatory words.
غَزَالٌ ج غِزْلاَنٌ	Gazelle.
غَزَالَةٌ	Female gazelle. The sun.
مِغْزَلٌ ج مَغَازِلُ	Spindle.
مَغْزُولٌ	Spun.
غَزَا يَغْزُو	To wage war, invade the enemy's country.
غَزْوٌ	Military expedition.

An incursion. غَزْوَةٌ ج غَزَوَاتٌ

Warrior ; invader. غَازٍ ج غُزَاةٌ

Sense, meaning. مَغْزَى ٱلْكَلَامِ

To become very dark. غَسَقَ يَغْسِقُ

Early darkness of night. غَسَقٌ

To wash. غَسَلَ يَغْسِلُ وَغَسَّلَ

To be washed. إِنْغَسَلَ

To wash one's self. إِغْتَسَلَ

Washing, ablution. غُسْلٌ

Washerwoman. غَسَّالَةٌ

Clothes that are washed. غَسِيلٌ

To deceive, falsify. غَشَّ يَغُشُّ

To be deceived. إِنْغَشَّ

Deceit, dishonesty, fraud. غِشٌّ

Deceitful. غَاشٌّ وَغَشَّاشٌ

Deceived ; falsified. مَغْشُوشٌ

Inexperience. غُشْمٌ

Inexperienced. غَشِيمٌ ج غُشَمَاءُ

Film (on the eyes) غَشَاوَةٌ

To cover, conceal. غَشِيَ يَغْشَى

To be dark, (night). غَشِيَ وَأَغْشَى

He swooned. غُشِيَ عَلَيْهِ غَشَيَانًا

To put a covering upon. غَشَّى

Cover ; membrane. غِشَاءٌ ج أَغْشِيَةٌ

Swoon. غَشْيَةٌ وَغَشَيَانٌ

Covered, enveloped. مُغْشًى وَمُغَشًّى

Swooning, senseless. مَغْشِيٌّ عَلَيْهِ

To be choked. غَصَّ يَغَصُّ

To choke. Grieve. أَغَصَّ

Choking. Grief. غُصَّةٌ ج غُصَصٌ

To force. غَصَبَ يَغْصِبُ غَصْبًا عَلَى
To take by violence.

To violate. غَصَبَ وَٱغْتَصَبَ مِنْ

Violence. غَصْبٌ

In spite of him. غَصْبًا عَنْهُ

Oppressor. غَاصِبٌ وَمُغْتَصِبٌ

Violence, tyranny. إِغْتِصَابٌ

Forced. مَغْصُوبٌ وَمُغْتَصَبٌ

غُصْنٌ ج أَغْصَانٌ Branch, twig.

غَضَّ يَغِضُّ To be fresh (plant).

غَضَّ ٱلطَّرْفَ To take no notice.

غَضٌّ Fresh, juicy, luxuriant.

غَضِبَ يَغْضَبُ To be angry.

غَاضَبَ وَأَغْضَبَ To make angry.

تَغَضَّبَ To be angry.

غَضَبٌ Anger, rage, passion.

غَضْبَانٌ ج غَضْبَى Angry, enraged.

غَضُوبٌ Stern, austere, angry.

مَغْضُوبٌ عَلَيْهِ Object of anger.

غَضَارَةٌ Ease of life, affluence.

غَضْرُوفٌ ج غَضَارِيفُ Cartilage.

غَضْنٌ Wrinkle, fold.

فِي غُضُونِ كَذَا During.

غَضَا يَغْضُو To become dark.

أَغْضَى عَنْهُ To close the eyes to.

تَغَاضَى عَنْ To neglect, disregard.

غَطَّ يَغِطُّ غَطًّا To immerse, dip.

غَطَّ يَغِطُّ غَطِيطًا To snore.

إِنْغَطَّ To be plunged, immersed.

غَطْرَسَ غَطْرَسَةً To be proud.

غَطَسَ يَغْطِسُ غَطْسًا فِي To immerse. To plunge.

غَطَّسَ To immerse.

عِيدُ ٱلْغِطَاسِ Feast of Epiphany.

غَطَّاسٌ Diver.

مِغْطَسٌ ج مَغَاطِسُ Bath-tub.

مَغْنَطِيسٌ وَمَغْنَاطِيسٌ Magnet.

غَطَّى To cover up, conceal.

تَغَطَّى To be covered, concealed.

غِطَاءٌ ج أَغْطِيَةٌ Cover, covering.

غَفَرَ ـ وَغَفَّرَ To cover, veil.

غَفَرَ ـِ لِ To forgive, pardon.

إِسْتَغْفَرَ To ask for pardon.

غَفَرٌ Guard, escort.

غُفْرَانٌ Pardon, forgiveness.

غَفَّارٌ وَغَفُورٌ Forgiving, (God).

غَفِيرٌ وَخَفِيرٌ	Guard, sentinel.
مَغْفِرَةٌ	Pardon, forgiveness.
غَفَلَ يَغْفُلُ عَنْ	To be heedless of.
أَغْفَلَ	To make one unmindful.
أَغْفَلَ	Forget, disregard.
تَغَافَلَ عَنْ	To be unmindful of.
إِسْتَغْفَلَ	To watch for one's unmindfulness.
غَفَلٌ وَغَفْلَةٌ وَغُفُولٌ	Heedlessness.
غَفْلَةً وَعَلَى غَفْلَةٍ	Unawares.
غَافِلٌ	Unmindful, heedless.
مُغَفَّلٌ	Simpleton.
غَفَا يَغْفُو وَغَفِيَ يَغْفَى	To sleep.
غَافٍ	Sleepy ; sleeping.
غَلَّ يَغُلُّ	To fetter, shackle.
أَغَلَّ وَغَلَّ	To yield income.
إِسْتَغَلَّ	To take the proceeds.
غِلٌّ وَغَلِيلٌ	Rancour, malice.
غُلٌّ ج أَغْلَالٌ	Manacle, shackle.
غَلِيلٌ	Burning of love &c.
غَلَّةٌ ج غَلَّاتٌ وَغِلَالٌ	Proceeds, revenue from land, crops.
غَلِيلٌ	Burning of love or grief.
مُغِلٌّ	Fruitful, productive.
مَغْلُولٌ	Manacled, shackled.
غَلَبَ يَغْلِبُ	To conquer, subdue.
غَالَبَ	To contend for victory.
تَغَلَّبَ عَلَى	To prevail, overcome.
إِنْغَلَبَ	To be overcome, defeated.
غَلَبَةٌ	Victory, conquest.
غَالِبٌ ج غَلَبَةٌ	Victor, conqueror.
غَالِبًا وَفِي ٱلْغَالِبِ	Usually.
مَغْلُوبٌ	Conquered, overcome.
غَلَسٌ	The last darkness of night.
غَلَسًا	At early dawn.
غَلِطَ يَغْلَطُ	To make a mistake.
غَلَّطَ	To accuse one of mistake.
غَلَطٌ ج أَغْلَاطٌ	Mistake, error.

غَلْطَةٌ	Single mistake, fault.
مغلَّط وَمَغلوطٌ	Erroneous.
مغالَطَةٌ	Sophism.
غَلُظَ يَغْلُظُ	To be thick, bulky.
غَلَّظَ على	To be hard, severe.
أغْلَظَ لهُ	To be rough, uncivil.
غلاظَةٌ	Thickness, incivility.
غَليظٌ ج غِلاظٌ	Thick ; rough.
غَلَّفَ	To put into an envelope.
تَغَلَّفَ وَاغْتَلَفَ	To have a cover.
غِلافٌ ج غُلُفٌ	Covering, sheath.
(مُغَلَّفٌ ج مُغَلَّفَاتٌ	Envelope.
أغْلَفُ ج غُلفٌ	Uncircumcised.
أغلَقَ	To close, shut.
إنغَلَقَ	To be closed, shut.
غَلَقٌ ج أغْلاَقٌ	Lock.
مُغلَقٌ	Closed, locked.
غِلاقَةُ حِسَاب	Balance of account.
غُلاَمٌ ج غِلمَانٌ	Boy, youth.
غَيْلَمٌ	Tortoise.
غَلَّنَ	To become calm, (sea).
(غَلِّينَة)	Quiet, calmness of the sea.
غَلاَ يَغْلُو غُلُوًّا	To be excessive.
غَلاَ غَلاَءً	To be high in price.
غَلَّى	To make the price high.
غَالَى مُغَالاَةً في	To go too far.
إستَغْلَى	To find it high-priced.
غَلاَءٌ	High price ; dearness.
غُلُوٌّ	Excess, exaggeration.
غَلْوَةٌ ج غَلَوَاتٌ	Furlong.
غَالٍ	High-priced, dear.
أغْلَى	Of higher price, dearer.
غَلَى يَغْلي	To boil (pot).
غَلَّى وَأغْلَى	To cause to boil.
غَلْيٌ وَغَلَيَانٌ	Boiling, ebullition.
غَلْيُونٌ ج غلاَيِينُ	Tobacco-pipe.
غَلاَّيَةٌ	Vessel for heating water.

غَمَّ يَغُمُّ	To cover, to grieve.
إِنغَمَّ وَاغْتَمَّ	To be grieved.
غَمٌّ ج غُمُومٌ	Grief, sorrow.
غَمَامٌ ج غَمَائِمُ	Clouds, (*coll*).
غَمَامَةٌ	A cloud.
مغمٌّ	Sorrowful, mournful.
مَغْمُومٌ	Afflicted, grieved.
غَمَدَ يَغْمُدُ وَأَغْمَدَ	To sheathe; cover.
غَمَّدَ وَتَغَمَّدَ	To cover, veil.
غِمْدٌ ج أَغْمَادٌ	Scabbard, sheath.
غَمَرَ يَغْمُرُ	To submerge (water).
غَمُرَ يَغْمُرُ	To be abundant.
إِنغَمَرَ وَاغْتَمَرَ	To be submerged.
غَمْرٌ	Abundant (water).
غَمْرَةٌ	Deep water. Difficulty.
غَمَرَاتُ ٱلْمَوْتِ	Pangs of death.
غَمَزَ يَغْمُزُ غَمْزاً	To wink. Press.
غَمْزٌ	Sign made with the eye.
غَمَسَ يَغْمُسُ	To immerse, dip.
إِنغَمَسَ وَٱغْتَمَسَ	To be plunged.
غَمُضَ يَغْمُضُ	To be obscure.
غَمَّضَ وَاغْمَضَ	To shut (the eyes).
إِنغَمَضَ	To be closed, (eye).
غَامِضٌ ج غَوَامِضُ	Obscure.
مُغَمَّضٌ	Closed (eye). Obscure.
(غُمْقٌ)	Depth.
(غَمِيقٌ)	Deep.
غُمِيَ عَلَيْهِ وَاغْمِيَ عَلَيْهِ	To swoon.
غَمْيٌ وَإِغْمَاءٌ	Swooning, swoon.
مُغْمًى عَلَيْهِ	In a swoon.
غَنِجَ -	To be coquettish.
غُنْجٌ وَغِنَاجٌ	Coquetry.
غَنِجَةٌ وَغَنُوجَةٌ	Coquette.
غَنِمَ يَغْنَمُ	To plunder ; obtain.
غَنَّمَ	To give a free gift.
إِغْتَنَمَ	To seize as spoil.

إِغْتَنَمَ وَٱسْتَغْنَمَ ٱلْفُرْصَةَ — To seize the opportunity.

غُنْمٌ وَغَنِيمَةٌ ج غَنَائِمُ — Booty.

غَنَمٌ ج أَغْنَامٌ — Sheep (*coll.*).

غَنَّامٌ — Shepherd.

غَانِمٌ — Spoiler ; successful.

غَنِيَ يَغْنَى — To be rich.

غَنِيَ بِ — To be content with.

غَنِيَ عَنْ — To be in no need of.

غَنَّى — To sing, chant.

أَغْنَى — To free from want.

إِغْتَنَى وَٱسْتَغْنَى — To become rich.

إِسْتَغْنَى عَنْ — To be in no need of.

غِنًى وَغَنَاء — Wealth, opulence.

مَا لَهُ عَنْهُ غِنًى — He cannot do without it.

غِنَاء وأُغْنِيَّةٌ ج أَغَانٍ وَأَغَانِيُّ — Song.

غَنِيٌّ ج أَغْنِيَاء — Rich, opulent.

غَانِيَةٌ ج غَوَانٍ — Beautiful woman.

مُغَنٍّ ج مُغَنِّيَةٌ — Singer.

غَيْهَبٌ ج غَيَاهِبُ — Very dark, black.

غَاثَ يَغُوثُ وَأَغَاثَ — To aid, succour.

إِسْتَغَاثَ وَب — To seek aid.

غَوْثٌ وَإِغَاثَةٌ — Aid, succour.

إِسْتِغَاثَةٌ — Request of aid.

غَارَ يَغُورُ — To sink deep.

أَغَارَ عَلَى — To attack, invade.

غَارٌ — Laurel (plant).

غَارَةٌ ج غَارَاتٌ — Raid, incursion.

شَنَّ ٱلْغَارَةَ — He made a raid.

غَوْرٌ — Bottom, depth. Low land.

مَغَارَةٌ ج مَغَائِرُ — Cave, cavern.

غَاصَ يَغُوصُ فِي — To plunge into.

غَوَّصَ — To plunge dip (*v.t.*).

غَائِصٌ — One who plunges.

غَوَّاصٌ — Diver, (*sp.* pearl-fisher).

(غَوِيصٌ) — Deep.

غَاطَ يَغُوطُ — To dig, excavate. Sink.

To void excrement. تَغَوَّطَ

Low ground. غَوْطٌ وَغَوْطَةٌ

Excrement, fæces. غَائِطٌ

To destroy. غَالَ يَغُولُ وَٱغْتَالَ

To slay covertly. إِغْتَالَ

Goblin, demon. غُولٌ ج غِيلَانٌ

Evil, mischief. غَائِلَةٌ ج غَوَائِلُ

To err. غَوِيَ يَغْوَى غَوًى

To seduce. غَوَى وَأَغْوَى

To be led into error. إِنْغَوَى

Error, leading astray. غَيٌّ وَغَوَايَةٌ

Error. غَيَّةٌ ج غَيَّاتٌ

Erring ; deceiver. غَاوٍ ج غُوَاةٌ

To be absent, distant. غَابَ يَغِيبُ

To set ; disappear. غَابَ غِيَابًا

To lose one's reason. غَابَ عَنِ ٱلصَّوَابِ

To slander. غَابَ وَٱغْتَابَ

To go away, travel. غَابَ وَتَغَيَّبَ

To conceal from. غَيَّبَ عَنْ

Absence. غَيْبٌ وَغَيْبَةٌ وَغِيَابٌ

Hidden thing. غَيْبٌ ج غُيُوبٌ

From memory. غَيْبًا وَعَلَى ٱلْغَائِبِ

The unseen world. عَالَمُ ٱلْغَيْبِ

Forest. غَابَةٌ ج غَابَاتٌ

Calumny, backbiting. غِيبَةٌ

Absent, hidden. غَائِبٌ

Time or place of the setting of the sun. مَغِيبُ ٱلشَّمْسِ

To water with rain. غَاثَ يَغِيثُ

Rain. غَيْثٌ ج غُيُوثٌ

Fresh, tender (woman) غَادَةٌ

Tender. أَغْيَدُ م غَيْدَاءُ ج غِيدٌ

To be jealous. غَارَ يَغَارُ

To alter, change. غَيَّرَ

To make jealous. أَغَارَ

To be changed. تَغَيَّرَ

To differ. غَايَرَ وَتَغَايَرَ

غَيْرُ	Other ; another. Except.
وَغَيْرُ ذَلِكَ	Et cætera.
غَيْرُ خَالِصٍ	Not pure, impure.
مِنْ غَيْرِ ذَلِكَ	Without that.
غَيْرَ أَنْ	Although.
لاَ غَيْرُ	Nothing else.
غَيْرَةٌ	Jealously ; zeal.
غَيُورٌ	Very jealous.
(مِغْيَارٌ)	Unhealthy (climate).
غَيْضَةٌ ج غِيَاضٌ	Thicket, wood.
غَاظَ يَغِيظُ وَأَغَاظَ	To anger, enrage.
إِغْتَاظَ وَتَغَيَّظَ	To become angry.
غَيْظٌ	Anger, rage, wrath.
مُغْتَاظٌ	Angry, enraged.
غَاقٌ	Crow, raven.
(غَالٌ ج غَالاَتٌ)	Lock.
غِيلٌ ج أَغْيَالٌ	Thicket, jungle.
غِيلَةٌ	Subterfuge, deception.
غَائِلَةٌ	Rancour, malice ; evil.
غَامَ وَأَغْيَمَ وَتَغَيَّمَ	To be cloudy.
غَيْمٌ ج غُيُومٌ	Clouds (*coll.*)
غَايَةٌ ج غَايَاتٌ	Extremity, term. Ultimate object.
إِلَى ٱلْغَايَةِ	Extremely.

ف

ف And ; then. As a numeral sign=80.

فُؤَادٌ ج أَفْئِدَةٌ Heart ; soul ; mind.

فَأْرٌ ج فِئْرَانٌ Rat ; mouse.

فَأْرَةٌ ج فَأْرَاتٌ A mouse.

فَأْسٌ ج فُؤُسٌ Axe ; hatchet.

تَفَأَّلَ وَتَفَاءَلَ بِ To draw a favourable augury.

فَأْلٌ وَتَفَاؤُلٌ Good or evil omen.

فِئَةٌ ج فِئَاتٌ Company, band.

فَتَّ يَفُتُّ To break in pieces.

تَفَتَّتَ وَٱنْفَتَّ To be crumbled.

فُتَاتٌ Small pieces ; crumbs.

فَتِيتٌ وَمَفْتُوتٌ Crumbled.

فَتِيءَ يَفْتَأُ عَنْ To cease from.

مَا فَتِيءَ يَفْعَلُ He continued to do.

فَتَحَ يَفْتَحُ To open. Conquer (a country).

فَتَحَ عَلَى To succour. Reveal.

فَاتَحَ To address one first.

تَفَتَّحَ وَٱنْفَتَحَ To be opened.

إِفْتَتَحَ To open, commence. Attack and conquer (a land).

إِسْتَفْتَحَ To begin. Seek succour.

فَتْحٌ ج فُتُوحٌ Victory, conquest.

فُتُوحَاتٌ Conquered countries.

فَتْحَةٌ The short vowel *fatha*.(َ)

فَتْحَةٌ An opening.

فَاتِحٌ Conqueror. Light-coloured.

فَاتِحَةٌ Introduction, preface.

أَلْفَاتِحَةُ First chapter of the Koran.

فَتَّاحٌ He who opens, conquers.

افْتِتَاحٌ Introduction. Conquest.

افْتِتَاحِيٌّ Introductory.

مِفْتَاحٌ ج مَفَاتِيحُ Key.

مَفْتُوحٌ Opened. Vocalized by the vowel *fatha*.

فَتَرَ يَفْتُرُ To subside; be tepid.

فَتَرَ عَنْ To desist; abate.

فَتَّرَ To allay. Make tepid.

فِتْرٌ Measure between extended thumb and index finger.

فَتْرَةٌ ج فَتَرَاتٌ Intermission.

فَاتِرٌ Languid; lukewarm.

فُتُورٌ Lukewarmness, languor.

فَتَّشَ To examine, investigate.

تَفْتِيشٌ Examination, inquest.

مُفَتِّشٌ Examiner, inspector.

(فَتْفَتَ) To crumble (*v.t.*).

فَتَقَ يَفْتُقُ وفَتَّقَ To cleave, slit, rip.

تَفَتَّقَ وَٱنْفَتَقَ To be split; ripped.

فَتْقٌ وَفِتَاقٌ Rupture, hernia. Rent.

مَفْتُوقٌ Ruptured, ripped.

فَتَكَ بِ To assault; kill.

فَاتِكٌ ج فُتَّاكٌ Bold, daring.

فَتَلَ يَفْتِلُ فَتْلاً وَفَتَّلَ To twist.

تَفَتَّلَ وَٱنْفَتَلَ To be twisted.

فَتَّالٌ Twister (of rope, &c.)

فَتِيلٌ وَمَفْتُولٌ Twisted (rope, &c.)

فَتِيلَةٌ ج فَتَائِلُ Wick of a lamp.

فَتَنَ يَفْتِنُ To please; infatuate.

أَفْتَنَ To please; seduce.

افْتَتَنَ To lead, or to be led, into error.

فِتْنَةٌ Seduction. Trial, affliction. Sedition.

فَاتِنٌ ج فُتَّانٌ Seducer; charmer.

مَفْتُونٌ Infatuated; seduced.

فَتِيَ يَفْتَى فَتًى وَفَتَاءً To be young.

أَفْتَى (ٱلْعَالِمُ) فِي مَسْأَلَةٍ To answer a learned question.

To affect youth. تَفَتَّى
To ask the solution of a learned question, sp. judicial. إِسْتَفْتَى
A young man. فَتًى ج فِتْيَانٌ
A young woman. فَتَاةٌ ج فَتَيَاتٌ
Manliness, generosity. فُتُوَّةٌ
Judicial sentence. فَتْوَى ج فَتَاوٍ
A lawyer. Mufti. مُفْتٍ (اَلْمُفْتِي)
Way, path. فَجٌّ ج فِجَاجٌ
Unripe (fruit). فِجٌّ وَفَجٌّ
To attack or befall suddenly. فَجَأَ يَفْجَأُ وَفَاجَأَ
Suddenly ; unawares. فَجْأَةً
To give exit to water. فَجَرَ يَفْجُرُ
To live in open sin. فَجَرَ يَفْجُرُ
To flaw. Dawn. تَفَجَّرَ وَآنْفَجَرَ
Dawn, day-break. فَجْرٌ
Wicked (man). فَاجِرٌ ج فُجَّارٌ
Great wickedness. فُجُورٌ
To give pain. فَجَعَ يَفْجَعُ فَجْعًا

To suffer pain from loss. فُجِعَ بِ
To grieve, complain. تَفَجَّعَ
Calamitous. فَاجِعٌ وَفَجُوعٌ
Great calamity. فَاجِعَةٌ ج فَوَاجِعُ
Radish (plant). فُجْلٌ
To notch, blunt. فَجَمَ يَفْجُمُ فَجْمًا
To be excessive ; foul. فَحُشَ يَفْحُشُ
To use foul words. فَحَشَ وَأَفْحَشَ
Shameless evil. Excess. فُحْشٌ
Evil. Excessive. فَاحِشٌ
Atrocious sin. فَاحِشَةٌ ج فَوَاحِشُ
To examine. فَحَصَ ـَ وَتَفَحَّصَ
Examination. (فَحْصٌ ج فُحُوصٌ)
To become formidable. اِسْتَفْحَلَ
Male. Strong man. فَحْلٌ ج فُحُولٌ
Elites in science. فُحُولُ الْعُلَمَاءِ
To be silence. فَحَمَ يَفْحَمُ
To blacken. فَحَّمَ

To silence by argument. أَفْحَمَ
Charcoal. فَحْمٌ
Coal. فَحْمُ ٱلْحَجَرِ أَوْ فَحْمٌ حَجَرِيٌّ
Seller of charcoal. فَحَّامٌ ج فَحَّامَة
Blackness ; darkness. فُحْمَةٌ
(Answer) that silences. مُفْحِمٌ
Meaning ; sense. فَحْوى وَفَحْوَاء
Trap, snare. فَخٌّ ج فِخَاخٌ وفخوخٌ
To break through. فَخَتَ يَفْخَتُ
To be perforated. إِنفَخَتَ
Hole, break, perforation. فَخْت
Thigh. Sub-tribe. فَخْذٌ ج أَفْخَاذٌ
To glory, boast. فَخَرَ يَفْخُرُ وَٱفْتَخَرَ
To prefer. فَخَرَ وفَخَّرَ وَأَفْخَرَ عَلَى
To compete or vie with. فَاخَرَ
Glory, excellence. فَخْرٌ
Glorious ; excellent. فَاخِرٌ
Pottery ; earthen-ware. فَخَّارٌ
Potter. فَخَّارِيٌّ وَفَاخُورِيٌّ
Glorious trait. مَفْخَرَةٌ ج مَفَاخِرُ
To be great. فَخُمَ يَفْخُمُ فَخَامَةً
To show great honour. فَخَّمَ
Highly honoured. مُفَخَّمٌ
Club-footed. أَفْدَعُ ج فُدْعٌ
To wound the head. فَدَغَ يَفْدَغُ
Yoke of oxen. Field-measure, acre. فَدَّان وفَدَان ج فَدَادِين
Plum-line. فَادِنٌ ج فَوَادِن
To redeem, ransom. فَدَى يَفْدِي
To ransom. إِفْتَدَى
Ransom. Redemption. فِدَاء
May it be a ransom to you ! فِدَاكَ
The Redeemer. الْفَادِي
To become apart. فَذَّ يَفِذُّ
One alone, single. فَذٌّ
One by one. فَذَاذَى وَفُذَاذاً
Resumé, gist. فَذْلَكَةٌ
To flee ; escape. فَرَّ يَفِرُّ فَرًّا

فَارٌّ وفَرَّارٌ	Fleeing, fugitive.
فُرِّيٌّ	Snipe, quail.
فرارٌ	Flight ; escape.
مَفَرٌّ	Escape. Place of escape.
فرأٌ وفراءٌ	Wildass ; onager.
أَلْفُرَاتُ	The Euphrates (river).
(فُرْتيكَةٌ)	Fork.
فُرْتُونَةٌ)	Storm at sea.
فَرْثٌ	Excrement, fæces.
فَرَجَ يَفْرِجُ فَرْجًا	To relieve.
أَفرَجَ بَينَ	To separate.
فَرَجَ لِ	To make place for.
فَرَّجَ	To open ; widen. Relieve.
فَرَّجَ عَلَى	To show,
تَفَرَّجَ	To see a new thing.
انفرج	To be opened, separate ; to diverge. Be relieved.
فَرَجٌ	Relief.
فُرْجَة ج فُرَجٌ	Opening Show.
فَرَجِيَّةٌ	Over-garment.
فَرُّوجٌ ج فَرَارِيجُ	Chicken.
مَفْروجٌ	Open. Relieved.
مُنْفَرِجٌ	Diverging.
أَلزَّاوِيَةُ ٱلْمُنْفَرِجَةُ	Obtuse angle.
فَرِحَ يَفْرَحُ فَرَحًا بِ	To rejoice.
فَرَّحَ وأَفْرَحَ	To make glad.
فَرَحٌ	Joy, gladness, happiness.
فَرِحٌ ج فرحونَ	Happy, glad.
فَرْحَانٌ م فَرْحَانَةٌ	Glad, rejoicing.
فَرَّخَ وَأَفْرَخَ	To sprout ; hatch.
فَرْخٌ ج فُروخ	Sprout. Chick
فَرْخَةٌ	Chicken.
فرد عَنْ	To separate one's self.
أَفْرَدَ	To make single ; set apart.
تَفَرَّدَ وَٱنفرد	To be alone.
إِستَفْرَدَ	To seek privacy.
فَرْدٌ ج أَفْرَادٌ	One ; one of a pair. Individual.

Atom ; monad. اَلْجَوْهَرُ ٱلْفَرْدُ

Pistol. فَرْدٌ ج فُرُودَةٌ

Bale of goods. فَرْدَةٌ

One by one. فُرَادًا وَفُرَادَى

Unique, matchless. فَرِيدٌ

Precious gem. فَرِيدَةٌ ج فَرَائِدُ

Singular number (*gram.*). مُفْرَدٌ

Alone; insolated. مُنْفَرِدٌ

Paradise. فِرْدَوْسٌ ج فَرَادِيس

To set aside. فَرَزَ يَفْرِزُ وَأَفْرَزَ

To go aside, or away. إِنْفَرَزَ

Cornice, frieze. إِفْرِيزٌ ج أَفَارِيز

To perceive ; gaze ' تَفَرَّسَ

To capture (prey). اِفْتَرَسَ

Horse. فَرَسٌ ج أَفْرَاسٌ

Hippopotamus. فَرَسُ ٱلْبَحْرِ

Horseman. فَارِسٌ ج فُرْسَان

Persia. بِلَادُ فَارِسَ وبِلَادُ ٱلْفُرْسِ

Persian. فَارِسِيٌّ وَفُرْسِيٌّ ج فُرْسٌ

The Persian language. أَلْفَارِسِيَّةُ

Horsemanship. فَرَاسَةٌ وفُرُوسَةٌ

Skilful discernment. فِرَاسة

Physiognomy. عِلْمُ الفِرَاسَةِ

Prey (of a lion). فَرِيسَة

Pharisee. فَرِّيسِيٌّ ج فَرِّيسِيُّونَ

Parasang; league. فَرْسَخ ج فَرَاسِخ

To spread out. فَرَشَ يَفْرُشُ

To be spread out. إِفْتَرَشَ وَٱنْفَرَشَ

House-furniture. فَرْشٌ وَمَفْرُوشٌ

Brush. فُرْشَةٌ

Bed. فِرَاشٌ وفَرْشَةٌ ج فُرُشٌ

Moth ; butterfly. فَرَاشَةٌ ج فَرَاشٌ

Furnished (house). مَفْرُوشٌ

To separate the feet. فَرْشَخَ

Occasion; chance. فُرْصَة ج فُرَصٌ

To avail one's self of an opportunity. إِنْتَهَزَ ٱلْفُرْصَةَ

To appoint ; ordain. Estimate ; suppose. Allot. فَرَضَ يَفْرِضُ

To notch, cut. فرَض وفرّض

To impose. فرَضَ وآفترَض عَلى

To enact (a law). إفترَضَ

Decree. Supposition. فرْضٌ ج فُرُوضٌ

On the supposition. على فَرْض

Harbour. فُرْضَةٌ ج فُرَضٌ

Ordinance; duty. Alloted portion. فرِيضَةٌ ج فَرَائِض

The science of the laws of inheritance. عِلْم الفرَائض

Enactment. Supposition. إفتِرَاضٌ

Supposed. Enacted. مفرُوضٌ

To lose an opportunity. فرَطَ يفرُط

To do a thing hastily. فرَطَ مِنْ

To miss ; neglect. فرّط (في)

To go to excess. أفْرَطَ افرَاطًا

Excess. فرْطٌ ج أفراط

Cheap. فرط

Excessive, immoderate. مفرَطٌ

To flatten ; make broad. فرْطَح

Broad ; flattened. مفرْطَحٌ

To derive, deduce. فرّعَ مِنْ

To ramify ; branch forth. تفرّعَ

Branch. Derivative. فرْعٌ ج فروعٌ

Hatchet. فرّاعةٌ

To be very proud. تَفَرْعَن

Pharaoh. فرْعَوْنٌ ج فرَاعنَةٌ

To be empty, vacant. فرَغَ يفرُغ

To finish a thing. فرَغَ مِنْ

To pour out. Empty. فرّغ وأفْرَغ

To be free from, be at leisure. تفرّغ منْ

To devote one's self to. تفرّغ ل

To exhaust ; vomit. إستفرَغ

Empty, vacant. فرِغٌ وفارِغ

Emptiness ; cessation. فَرَاغ

To flap the wings. فرْفَرَ فرْفرَة

Light-headed, noisy. فرْفارٌ

To divide. Distinguish. فَرَقَ يَفْرُقُ بَيْنَ

To scatter ; disperse. فَرَّقَ

To distribute among. فَرَّقَ على

To stir up dissention. فَرَّقَ بَيْنَ

To abandon. Die. فَارَقَ

To be separated. تَفَرَّقَ وَٱفْتَرَقَ

To leave one another. تَفَارَقَ

To be separated from. إِنْفَرَقَ عَنْ

Difference, distinction. فَرْقٌ

The Koran. الْفُرْقَانُ

Party of men. فِرْقَةٌ ج فِرَقٌ

Separation. فُرْقَةٌ وَٱفْتِرَاقٌ

Separation. Death. فِرَاقٌ

General of a division. فَرِيقٌ

Africa. أَفْرِيقِيَةُ

Separation, dispersion. تَفْرِيقٌ

In parts, in detail. بِٱلتَّفْرِيقِ

A point from which a road branches. مَفْرَقٌ ج مَفَارِقُ

To rub. فَرَكَ يَفْرُكُ فَرْكاً

To be mature, (grain). أَفْرَكَ

To be rubbed and pressed. إِنْفَرَكَ

To become full (grain). إِسْتَفْرَكَ

Act of rubbing ; friction. فَرْكٌ

Rubbed soft grain. فَرِيكٌ

To mince. فَرَمَ يَفْرِمُ فَرْماً

To change the teeth, (child). فَرَّمَ

A small piece. (فَرْمَةٌ)

Firman. فَرَمَانٌ

Oven. فُرْنٌ ج أَفْرَانٌ

Baker. فَرَّانٌ

Europeans. Franks. إِفْرَنْجٌ وَفِرِنْجٌ

France. فَرَنْسَا

French. فَرَنْسِيٌّ فَرَنْسَاوِيٌّ

To line with fur. فَرَّى تَفْرِيَةً

Garment of fur. فَرْوٌ ج فِرَاءٌ

Scalp. Fur-cloak. فَرْوَةٌ

Furrier. فَرَّاءٌ

إِفْتَرَى ٱلْكَذِب — To fabricate a lie.

فِرْيَةٌ ج فِرًى — Wilful lie.

فَرِيٌّ — Unusual thing.

فَزَّ ـِ — To be excited.

فَزَّ وَأَفَزَ — To frighten, disturb.

إِسْتَفَزَّ — To excite, incite.

فَزَرَ يَفْزُرُ فَزْراً — To cut ; break.

فَزِعَ يَفْزَعُ فَزَعاً — To be afraid.

فَزِعَ إِلَى — To flee for help to.

فَزَّعَ وَأَفْزَعَ — To frighten.

فَزَعٌ — Fear ; fright.

فَزِعٌ — Frightened, afraid.

مَفْزَعٌ — Refuge. Succour.

فُسْتُقٌ — Pistachio (tree and fruit).

فُسْقِيَّةٌ — Basin ; reservoir.

فُسْتَانٌ ج فَسَاتِينُ — Female gown.

فَسَحَ يَفْسَحُ وأَفْسَحَ لَهُ فِي — To make place for ; permit.

فَسُحَ يَفْسُحُ — To be spacious, (place).

فَسَّحَ — To make roomy, wide.

إِنْفَسَحَ صَدْرُهُ — His bosom was dilated (with joy).

فُسْحَةٌ ج فُسَحٌ — Space ; court-yard.

فَسَاحَةٌ — Spaciousness, width.

فَسِيحٌ — Spacious, roomy, ample.

فَسَخَ يَفْسَخُ — To annul, abrogate.

فَسَّخَ — To split.

إِنْفَسَخَ — To be annulled, split.

فَسْخٌ — Abrogation. Separation.

فُسْخَةٌ — A part, a piece.

فَسِيخٌ — Salted fish.

فَسَدَ يَفْسُدُ — To become corrupt.

فَسَّدَ وَأَفْسَدَ — To corrupt.

أَفْسَدَ بَيْنَ — To stir up strife.

إِنْفَسَدَ — To be corrupted, bad.

فَسَادٌ — Corruption, mischief. Invalidity. Decomposition.

فَاسِدٌ — Bad. Invalid. Spoilt.

مُفْسِدٌ — Causing mischief or strife.

مَفْسَدَةٌ ج مَفَاسد Cause of evil.

فَسَّر To make plain ; explain.

إِستَفْسَر To seek an explanation.

تَفسِيرٌ ج تَفَاسِير Explanation.

فُسْطَاطٌ Pavilion ; tent.

فُسْفُورٌ وَفُصْفُورٌ Phosphorus.

فَسَافِس Bugs ; bed-bugs.

فُسَيْفِسَاء Mosaic-pavement.

فَسَقَ يَفسُق To be impious.

فِسقٌ وَفُسُوق Impiety.

فَاسِقٌ Impious, dissolute.

فَاسِقَة Adulteress.

فشَّ يَفُشُّ فَشًّا To pick a lock.

فشَّ خُلْقُه To vent one's anger.

فَشَخَ يَفْشَخ Do take a wide step.

فَشْخَةٌ A step.

فَشَرَ وَفَشَّر To talk incoherently.

فُشَارٌ Incoherent talk ; babbling.

فَشَكَةٌ ج فَشَكٌ) Cartridge.

فَشِلَ يَفْشَل To be faint-hearted.

تَفَشَّل To fail, be disappointed.

فَشَلٌ Disappointment.

فَشَا يَفْشُو فُشُوًّا To be spread.

أَفْشَى To spread. Divulge.

تَفَشَّى To become wide ; extend.

فَصٌّ ج فُصُوصٌ Stone or gem of a signet-ring. Lobe.

فَصَهٌ A species of clover.

فصَحَ يَفْصَح To break forth, (light).

افْصَح To appear clearly.

تَفَاصَح To affect eloquence.

فِصْحٌ Passover ; Easter.

فَصَاحَةٌ Lucidity ; eloquence.

فَصِيحٌ ج فُصَحَاء Elegant speaker.

فَصَدَ يَفْصِدُ فَصْدًا To open a vein.

إِنفَصَد To be bled.

فَصَّادٌ Bleeder, phlebotomist.

A person who is bled. مَفْصُودٌ

Lancet. مِفْصَدٌ

To cut off ; separate. فَصَلَ يَفْصِلُ
Decide a disputed point.

To divide into parts. فَصَّلَ

To bargain for a price. فَاصَلَ

To expire ; die. أَفْصَلَ

To be separated ; detatched. إِنْفَصَلَ

To go away from. إِنْفَصَلَ عَنْ

Separation. Chapter. فَصْلٌ ج فُصُولٌ
A season of the year.

That which separates. فَاصِلٌ

Decisive judgment. حُكْمٌ فَاصِلٌ

Family ; species. فَصِيلَةٌ ج فَصَائِلُ

Judge, arbiter. فَيْصَلٌ ج فَيَاصِلُ

Detailed statement. تَفْصِيلٌ ج تَفَاصِيلُ

In detail. بِالتَّفْصِيلِ

Joint. مَفْصِلٌ ج مَفَاصِلُ

Rheumatism. دَاءُ الْمَفَاصِلِ

Cut out. Detailed. مُفَصَّلٌ

In detail. مُفَصَّلاً

Hinge. مُفَصَّلَةٌ ج مُفَصَّلَاتٌ

Detached. مَفْصُولٌ وَمُنْفَصِلٌ

To break, crack. فَصَمَ يَفْصِمُ

To be broken, cracked. إِنْفَصَمَ

To break open. فَضَّ يَفُضُّ فَضًّا

To cover with silver. فَضَّضَ

To be dispersed. إِنْفَضَّ

Silver. Para. فِضَّةٌ

To divulge, disgrace. فَضَحَ يَفْضَحُ

Disgrace. فَضِيحَةٌ ج فَضَائِحُ

To remain over. فَضَلَ يَفْضُلُ

To excel, surpass. فَضَلَ وَعَلَى

To prefer. فَضَّلَ عَلَى

To show favour. أَفْضَلَ وَتَفَضَّلَ

Do me the favour. تَفَضَّلْ

To leave a part. إِسْتَفْضَلَ مِنْ

فَضْلٌ ج فُضُولٌ	Excess Favour. Superiority, excellence.
فَضْلاً عَن	Besides.
فَضْلَةٌ	Portion remaining.
فَاضِلٌ وَفَضِيلٌ	Superior; excellent.
فُضُولٌ	Officiousness.
فُضُولِيٌّ	Meddlesome.
فَضِيلَةٌ ج فَضَائِل	Virtue. Excellence.
أَفْضَل ج أَفَاضِل	Better.
اَلأَفْضَلُ	The best.
حِسَابُ ٱلتَّمَامِ وَٱلتَّفَاضُلِ	Calculus (integral and differential).
تَفْضِيلٌ	Preference.
إِسْمُ ٱلتَّفْضِيلِ	Adjective in the comparative degree, *as* : أَكْبَرُ
مُفَضَّلٌ	Preferable.
مِفْضَالٌ	Distinguished for excellence.
فَضَا يَفْضُو فَضَاءً	To be empty.
فَضَّى	To empty, turn out.
أَفْضَى إِلى	To reach. Lead to.
تَفَضَّى لِ	To have leisure for.
فَضَاءٌ	Open space.
فاضٍ	Empty ; unoccupied.
فَطْراً	To create, (God).
فَطَر وأَفْطَر	To bre ak one's fast.
تَفَطَّرَ وَٱنفَطَرَ	To be broken.
فُطْرٌ	Fungus.
عيد ٱلفِطْرِ	Feast of Ramadan.
فِطْرَةٌ ج فِطَرٌ	Innate quality.
فَاطِرٌ	Creator.
فُطُورٌ	Midday, meal.
فَطِيرٌ	Unleavened.
عِيدُ الفِطْرِ	Jewish feast of unleavened bread.
فَطِيرَةٌ ج فَطَائِرُ	Pastry-cake.
فَطَسَ يَفْطِسُ فُطُوساً	To die.
فَطَسَ يَفْطَس	To be suffocated.
فَطَّس	To kill. Suffocate.
أَفْطَسُ م فطساء ج فُطْسٌ	Flat-nosed.

فَطَمَ يَفْطِمِ To wean (an infant).

إِنْفَطَم To be weaned.

إِنْفَطَم عَنْ To cease from.

فِطَامٌ Weaning.

فَطِيمٌ وَمَفْطُومٌ Weaned (child).

فَطَنَ يَفْطِنُ بِ To remember ; consider. Understand.

فَطَّنَ بِ To remind.

تَفَطَّنَ لِ To understand. Remember.

فِطْنَةٌ Understanding ; sagacity.

فَطِنٌ وَفَطِينٌ Intelligent.

فَظَ يَفَظ فَظَاظَةً To be rough, rude.

فَظ ج فِظَاظ Rough, rude.

فَظَعَ يَفْظَع فَظَاعَةً To be horrid.

فَظِعٌ وَفَظِيعٌ Atrocious ; horrid.

فَعَلَ يَفْعَل To do ; perform ; act.

إِنْفَعَل To be affected. Be done.

افْتَعَلَ To forge ; invent.

فِعْلٌ ج افْعَالٌ Act, deed. Verb.

فَاعِلٌ ج فَعَلَةٌ Doer. Agent or subject of the verb.

إِسْم ٱلْفَاعِلِ Noun of agent.

نَائِب ٱلْفَاعِلِ Agentor subject of the passive verb.

فَعَّالٌ Effective, efficient.

إِنْفِعَالٌ ج إِنْفِعَالاتٌ Influence, impression.

إِنْفِعَالٌ نَفْسَانِيٌّ Emotion.

تَفْعِيلٌ ج تَفَاعِيل Foot (*in prosody*).

مَفْعُولٌ ج مَفَاعِيل Something done. Impression ; influence.

مَفْعُولٌ بِهِ Object of transitive verb.

إِسْم ٱلْمَفْعُولِ Noun of patient.

مُفْتَعَلٌ Invented. Done purposely.

فَعَمَ يَفْعَم To fill (a vessel).

فَعِمَ يَفْعَم فُعُومَة To be full.

مُفْعَمٌ Filled, full.

أَفْعَى وَافْعُوانٌ ج افَاعٍ Viper.

فَغَرَ يَفْغَر To open (the mouth).

فَغَرَ وَٱنْفَغَر To open.

فَقَأَ يَفْقَأ To open (an abscess). Put out an eye.

To burst; break.	تَفَقَّأَ وَٱنْفَقَأَ
To lose.	فَقَدَ يَفْقِدُ فَقْداً وَفُقْدَاناً
To deprive of, cause to lose.	أَفْقَدَ
To seek a lost object.	تَفَقَّدَ
To miss, fail to find. Visit a sick person.	إِفْتَقَدَ
Lost object. Dead.	فَقِيدٌ وَمَفْقُودٌ
To slit, perforate.	فَقَرَ يَفْقُرُ
To impoverish.	أَفْقَرَ
To become poor.	إِفْتَقَرَ
To need.	إِفْتَقَرَ إِلى
Poverty; need.	فَقْرٌ
Vertebra.	فَقْرَةٌ ج فِقَرٌ
Poor; needy.	فَقِيرٌ ج فُقَرَاءُ
To hatch eggs (bird).	فَقَسَ يَفْقِسُ فَقْساً
To be hatched.	تَفَقَّسَ وَٱنْفَقَسَ
Small melon.	فَقُّوسٌ
To break open.	فَقَشَ يَفْقُشُ فَقْشاً
Only.	فَقَطْ
To die from heat or grief.	فَقَعَ
To be cleft or rent.	إِنْفَقَعَ
Very bright-coloured.	فَاقِعٌ
Bubble of air.	فَقَّاعَةٌ ج فَقَاقِيعُ
Unripe figs.	(فُقَّيْعٌ)
Excessive poverty.	فَقْرٌ مُفْقِعٌ
To be full, (vessel).	فَقِمَ يَفْقَمُ
To become very serious.	تَفَاقَمَ
Seal. (sea-animal).	فُقْمَةٌ وَفُقَّمَةٌ
To understand.	فَقِهَ يَفْقَهُ فِقْهاً
To be skilled in the Law.	فَقُهَ يَفْقُهُ
To teach.	فَقَّهَ وَأَفْقَهَ
To understand; learn.	تَفَقَّهَ
Knowledge; intelligence.	فِقْهٌ
Science of Law.	عِلْمُ ٱلْفِقْهِ
Understanding; learning.	فَقَاهَةٌ
Skilled in Law.	فَقِيهٌ ج فُقَهَاءُ

فلكَ يفلُكُ فكًّا To separate; untie.
فكّكَ To separate ; disentangle.
إنفكّ To be separated ; untied.
مَا انفكَّ Not to cease.
إستفكّ To seek redemption.
فك ج فكوك Jaw-bone.
فكّرَ يفكِّر وفكَّر وتفكَّر وافتكرَ في To think of ; consider.
(فكّر) To remind.
فكرٌ ج أفكارٌ Thought ; reflection.
فكِّيرٌ Very thoughtful.
(فاكورةٌ ج فواكير) Latch.
فكِهَ يفكَهُ فكاهةً To be gay.
فكّهَ To cheer by wit.
تفكّه بِ To enjoy.
تفاكه To jest with another.
فَكِهٌ ج فكِهون Merry ; cheerful.
فاكِهَة ج فواكِهُ Fruit.
فكاهة Jesting ; merriment.

فلّ يفلُّ فلًّا To blunt or notch.
فُلٌّ Arabian Jasmine.
فلَتَ يفلِتُ To free, liberate.
أفلتَ وتفلّتَ وانفلتَ To escape
تفلّتَ على To spring on.
فلتٌ Escape.
فلْتةٌ Sudden event.
فلتةً Suddenly. Undesignedly.
(فلتيٌّ) Vagabond.
فالتٌ Loose, free.
(كلامٌ فالتٌ) Improper language.
فلِجَ وانفلجَ To be paralyzed.
انفلجَ To shine, (day break).
فالِجٌ Paralysis ; palsy.
مفلوجٌ Paralysed ; paralytic.
فلَحَ يفلَحُ To plough ; till.
أفلحَ To prosper; be successful.
فلْحٌ ج فلوحٌ Furrow.
فلاحٌ Prosperity ; success.

فَلاَحَةٌ Agriculture.

فَلاَّحٌ ج فَلاَّحُونَ Farmer, peasant.

فِلذة ج أَفْلاَذ A piece.

فَالُوذ وَفَالُوذَجٌ A sweet pastry.

فُولاَذٌ (بُولاَدٌ) Steel.

فِلِزٌّ Bronze. Metal.

فَلَّسَ To proclaim bankrupt.

أَفْلَسَ To become bankrupt.

فَلْسٌ ج فُلُوسٌ A small coin. *Pl.* scales of fish. Money.

إِفْلاَسٌ Insolvency, bankruptcy.

مُفْلِسٌ Bankrupt ; penniless.

فِلِسْطِين Palestine.

تَفَلْسَفَ To philosophize.

فَلْسَفَةٌ Philosophy.

أَلْفَلْسَفَةُ الطَّبِيعِيَّةُ Physics.

أَلْفَلْسَفَةُ العَقْلِيَّةُ Psychology.

فَلْسَفِيٌّ Philosophical.

فَيْلَسُوفٌ ج فَلاَسِفَة Philosopher.

(فَلَشَ) To spread out.

(إِنفَلَشَ) To be spread out.

(فَلَصَ يفْلُص مِنْ) To escape from.

افْلَصَ وتَفَلَّصَ وانْفَلَصَ To escape.

فَلطَحَ To flatten, make broad.

مُفَلْطَحٌ Flattened ; broad.

فَلْفَلَ To pepper.

فُلْفُلٌ وفِلْفِلٌ Pepper (tree or fruit).

فُلَيفِلَةٌ Pepper plant.

مُفَلْفَلٌ Peppered.

فَلَقَ يَفلِقُ To cleave ; split.

أَفْلَقَ وَافْتَلَقَ To be skilled in.

تَفَلَّقَ وانْفَلَقَ To be split, cleft.

انْفَلَقَ الصُّبْحُ The dawn broke.

فَلَقٌ ج أَفْلاَق Dawn. Stocks.

فِلْقَةٌ ج فِلَقٌ Lobe. Cotyledon.

مُفْلِق Distinguished (poet).

فَلَّكَ وتَفَلَّكَ To augur or predict.

فُلْكٌ Ship. Noah's ark.

فَلَكٌ ج أَفْلَاكٌ — Celestial sphere.

عِلْمُ ٱلفَلَك — Astronomy.

فَلَكِيٌّ — Astronomer.

(فُلُوكَةٌ) — Small ship ; boat.

فُلَانٌ — A certain person.

فُلَانِيٌّ — Such and such.

(فَلَا) — Open space ; the open air.

فِلْوٌ ج فَلَاوَى وَأَفْلَاءٌ — Foal.

فَلَاةٌ ج فَلَوَاتٌ — Open country.

فَلَّى — To clean from lice.

فِلِّينٌ — Cork. Bottle-cork.

فَلْيُونٌ — God-son.

فَمٌ وَفَمٌّ — Mouth. (*see* فوه)

فَنٌّ ج فُنُونٌ — Form ; kind. Art.

تَفَنَّنَ — To be accomplished.

مُتَفَنِّنٌ — Accomplished ; skilful.

فِنْجَانٌ ج فَنَاجِينُ — Small cup.

فَنَّدَ — To state in detail. Accuse of untruth or error.

فَنْدٌ فُنُودٌ — Branch. Taper.

فُنْدُقٌ ج فَنَادِق — Inn ; hotel.

فَنَارٌ ج فَنَارَاتٌ — Lantern. Light-house.

فَانُوسٌ ج فَوَانِيسُ — Lantern. Lamp.

أَفْنِيَ يَفْنَى — To perish.

أَفْنَى — To annihilate ; destroy.

فَنَاءٌ — Destruction. Vanishing.

فَانٍ — Transient ; perishing.

فَهْدٌ ج فُهُود — Panther ; lynx.

فَهْرَسَ — To make index.

فِهْرِسٌ وَفِهْرِسْتٌ ج فَهَارِس — Catalogue. Index, table of contents.

فَهِمَ يَفْهَمُ — To understand.

فَهَّمَ وَأَفْهَمَ — To make understand.

إِنْفَهَمَ — To be understood.

إِسْتَفْهَمَ — To seek to know.

فَهْمٌ — Understanding.

فَهِيمٌ وَفَهَّامَة — Very intelligent.

إِسْتِفْهَامٌ — Interrogation.

إِسْمُ اسْتِفْهَامٍ — Interrogative pronoun.

مَفْهومٌ	Understood. Meaning.
فَاتَ يفوتُ	To pass. Miss.
فَوَّتَ	To make pass ; omit.
تَفَاوتَ	To differ ; be dissimilar.
فَوتٌ وفواتٌ	Passing ; missing.
تَفاوتٌ	Dissimilarity ; difference.
فوجٌ ج أَفْواجٌ	Troop ; company.
افواجًا أَفواجًا	In troops, crowds.
فاح يَفوح	To be diffused, (odour).
فار يَفور فَوراً وفوراَنًا	To boil.
أَفَار وفَوَّر	To make boil.
فارٌ ج فيرانٌ	Mice.
فارةٌ	Mouse. Carpenter's plane.
علَى ٱلْفَوْر	Immediately ; at once.
فَوَّارةٌ	Jet d'eau ; fountain.
فازَ يَفوز	To win, succeed.
فاز بِ	To obtain ; attain.
فَوْزٌ	Success. Escape.
مفازَةٌ ج مفازاتٌ ومَفاوزُ	Desert.
(فاش يَفوش فَوْشًا)	To float.
فَوَّض إلى	To commit to.
فاوض	To converse with.
تَفاوض	To converse together.
فَوْضَى	Anarchy.
مُفاوضَةٌ	Conversation.
فُوطَةٌ ج فوطٌ	Napkin ; towel.
فاق يَفوق	To surpass; excel.
فَاقَ فَوَاقًا	To hiccough.
أَفاق واَسْتفاق مِن	To awake.
فَوقُ	Above ; upon ; beyond.
إلى فوقُ	Upwards.
فَما فوقُ	And upwards.
فاقةٌ	Poverty ; want ; need.
فَوقانيٌّ	What is above.
فُواقٌ	Hiccough.
فائقٌ	Surpassing, excelling.
فائِقُ ٱلْوصْف	Beyond description.
فولٌ	Horse-beans. (*sing.* فولَة)

Cook or seller of beans. فوّالٌ

Garlic. فومٌ

To speak ; utter. فَاهَ يفوهُ وتفوَّه

Mouth, فوهٌ وفمٌ ج أفواهٌ وأفمَامٌ

Madder-root. فوّةٌ وفوَّةٌ

Opening. فوَّهةٌ ج فوَّهاتٌ وأفواهٌ

In, among, with, at. في

To shade. فَاءَ وفَيّاً

To shade one's self. تفيّأ

Shadow. فيءٌ ج أفياءٌ

Party ; company. فئةٌ ج فئاتٌ

To flow. فاحَ يفيح فيْحاً وفيحَاناً

To spill, shed. أفَاحَ

Wide ; extensive. أفيَح م فيْحاءُ

To benefit ; serve ; mean. أفَاد

To be benefited ; acquire. إستفاد

Benefit ; use ; profit. Interest (on money). فَائدةٌ ج فوائد

Bestowal of benefit. إفَادةٌ

Beneficial ; useful. مفيدٌ

Turquoise (stone). فيروزٌ

See under. فَصْلٌ فيصلٌ

To abound ; overflow, (river.) Be full, (vessel). فَاض يفَيض فيضَاناً

To pour (water) ; fill. أفَاض

Abundance. فَيْضٌ ج فيوضٌ

Periodic overflow or inundation of the Nile. فيضَان النّيل

Waterless desert. فيفَاءُ ج فيَافٍ

Elephant. فيلٌ ج أفْيالٌ وفيلَة

An army-corps. فيْلقٌ ج فيالقُ

Why? Wherefore ? فيم (في ما)

To be niggardly. فَان يفَين فيناً

ق

ق	As a numeral sign=100.
قَبَّب	To make convex.
(قَبَّة)	Collar (to a shirt, &c.).
قُبَّةٌ ج قُبَبٌ	Cupola, dome.
قَبَّانٌ ج قَبَابين	Large steelyard.
مقبب	Surmounted with a dome.
قَبح يقْبَحُ	To be ugly, vile.
قَبَّح	To render, or deem ugly.
قَابَح	To revile, insult.
اقبَح	To act meanly, shamefully.
إستقبح	To detest, abhor.
قُبْحٌ وقَبَاحةٌ	Ugliness, foulness.
قبحاً لهُ	Fie on him !
قبيحٌ ج قباحٌ	Ugly, infamous.
قَبيحةٌ ج قبائح	Vile action.
قَبَر يقـبر قبْراً	To bury, inter.
قبْرٌ ج قُبورٌ	Grave, sepulchre.
قنبرةٌ ج قَنَابر	Sky-lark, lark.
قُبَّارٌ	Capers.
مقبرةٌ ج مقَابر	Cemetery.
مقبورٌ	Interred, buried.
قُبرس	Cyprus (island).
قُبْرسيٌّ	Of Cyprus ; Cypriote.
قَبَس يقبس واقتَبَس من	To seek fire, or knowledge, from.
إقتَبَس من	To quote an author.
قَبْسةٌ	A coal, a fire-brand.
قبض يقبض	To seize, grasp ; arrest. To contract.
قَبَض	To receive (money).

قَبَّضَهُ	God caused him to die.
قُبِض	To die.
قَبَّض	To make a payment to.
تَقَبَّض وانقَبَض	To shrink.
قَبْضٌ	Grasping, taking possession. Constipation.
قَبْضَةٌ	A grasp ; handful.
قَبْضَةٌ	Handle, haft, hilt.
قَابِضٌ	Astringent.
إِنقِبَاضٌ	Contraction, constipation.
مَقْبَضٌ ج مَقَابِض	Handle, hilt.
مَقبوضٌ	Seized ; received. Dead.
قُبْطٌ وأَقبَاط	Copts.
قِبْطِيٌّ	A Copt ; Coptic.
قُبْعٌ وقُبَّعَة	Hood, cowl.
قَبقَابٌ ج قَبَاقِيب	Clogs.
قَبِلَ يَقبَلُ قبولاً	To receive, accept, admit ; consent, agree to.
أَقبَلَ عَلَى	To take up.
أَقبَلَ	To approach, be near.
قَبَّلَ	To kiss.
قَابَلَ	To correspond to ; meet.
قَابَلَ بِ	To compare, collate.
تَقَبَّلَ	To receive, accept.
تَقَابَلَ	To meet ; be compared.
إِستَقبَل	To go to meet, receive.
قبلُ وَقَبْلاً ومِن قَبْلُ	Previously.
قِبلٌ	Side, direction.
مِنْ قبَله	With respect to ; from.
قِبلَةٌ	Direction of Mecca. South.
قُبلَةٌ ج قُبَلٌ . وتَقْبِيلٌ	Kiss.
قِبلِيٌّ	Southern.
قَابِلٌ ل	Capable of, subject to.
قَابِلَةٌ ج قوابِلُ	Midwife. Receiver.
قَابِلِيَّةٌ	Capacity ; appetite.
قُبَالَةٌ	Over against.
قِبَالة	Midwifery.
قبولٌ	Consent ; reception.
مِنْ هذَا القبيل	As regards this.

قَبِيلَةٌ ج قَبَائِل — Tribe.

إِقْبَالٌ — Approach. Prosperity.

إِسْتِقْبَالٌ — The future. Reception.

مُقَابَلَةٌ — Meeting. Collation (of two texts). Antithesis.

مُقْبِلٌ — Coming, approaching.

مُقَابِلٌ — Opposite to, in front of.

مَقْبُولٌ — Accepted ; received.

مُسْتَقْبَلٌ — The future ; Facing.

قَبَنَ — To weigh with steelyard.

قَبَّانٌ — Steelyard.

قِبَانَةٌ — Trade of a weigher.

قَبَّانِيٌّ — One who weighs.

قَبُونَةٌ — Weighing.

قَبَا يَقْبُو قَبْواً — To bend, curve.

قَبَاءٌ ج أَقْبِيَةٌ — Outer garment.

قَبْوٌ ج أَقْبِيَةٌ — Vault.

قَتَبٌ ج أَقْتَابٌ — Small pack-saddle.

قَتَرَ وأَقْتَرَ عَلَى — To be niggardly.

قَتْرٌ وَتَقْتِيرٌ — Avarice, economy.

قَاتِرٌ وَمُقَتِّرٌ — Parsimonious, economical.

قَتَلَ يَقْتُلُ — To kill, murder.

قَاتَلَ مُقَاتَلَةً — To fight against.

تَقَاتَلَ واقْتَتَلَ — To combat with one another, fight.

إِسْتَقْتَلَ — To seek death, stake one's life.

قَتْلٌ — Murder ; execution.

قَاتِلٌ ج قَتَلَةٌ — Murderer, assassin.

قِتَالٌ وَمُقَاتَلَةٌ — Battle, combat.

قَتَّالٌ — Deadly, causing death.

قَتِيلٌ ج قَتْلَى . وَمَقْتُول — Killed.

مَقْتَلٌ — Vital part (of the body).

مُقَاتِلٌ — Warrior, combatant.

قِتَامٌ — Darkness.

قَاتِمٌ وأَقْتَمُ — Dark-coloured.

قِثَّاءٌ — Cucumber.

قِثَّاءُ الحِمَار — *Elaterium.*

(قَحَّ يَقُحُّ) — To cough.

قُحٌّ ج اقْحَاحٌ — Pure, unmixed.

A cough. (قَحَّة)

Cough. Prostitute. قَحْبَةٌ ج قِحَابٌ

To be rainless. قَحِطَ يَقْحَطُ وأَقْحَطَ

Drought, famine. قَحْطٌ

Year of drought. عَامٌ مقحط

To sweep away. قَحَفَ يَقْحَفُ

Skull. قِحْفٌ ج أَقْحَافٌ

What is swept away. قُحَافَةٌ

Winnowing-fan; dust-pan. مِقْحَفَةٌ

To dry up, wither. قَحِلَ يَقْحَلُ قَحْلاً

To dry, cause to wither. أَقْحَلَ

Dryness, aridity. قُحُولَةٌ

To rush. قَحَمَ يَقْحُمُ قُحُوماً في

To draw near to. قَحَمَ إلى

To rush upon. إِقْتَحَمَ

Anthemis, camomile. أُقْحُوان

Particle, e. g. Zeid has *just* ~~isen. قد. قَدْ قَامَ زَيْدٌ

The liar *sometimes* peaks the truth. قَدْ يَصْدُقُ الْكَذُوبُ

Verily he prospers. قَدْ أَفْلَحَ

To cut, cleave. قَدَّ يَقُدُّ قَدًّا

To cut and dry (meat). قَدَّدَ

To be cut and dried. تَقَدَّدَ

To be cut, slit, divided. إِنْقَدَّ

Stature, size. قَدٌّ ج قُدُودٌ

Equal to in measure. عَلَى قَدِّهِ

Goodly in form. حَسَنُ الْقَدِّ

Cured meat. قَدِيدٌ ومُقَدَّدٌ

To bore, pierce. قَدَحَ يَقْدَحُ

To strike fire. قَدَحَ واقْتَدَحَ

To revile, censure. قَدَحَ في

Drinking-cup. قَدَحٌ ج أَقْدَاحٌ

Slanderer, calumniator. قَادِحٌ

Gimlet. مِقْدَحٌ ومِقْدَاحٌ

To be able. قَدَرَ يَقْدِرُ عَلَى

To measure; compute. قَدَرَ وقَدَّرَ

To decree for. قَدَرَ وقَدَّرَ عَلَى

To prepare, assign. قدر لِ

To put a value upon. قدَّر

To enable. قَدر على

To be preordained. تقدَّر

To be powerful, or rich. اقتدر

Quantity, measure. قَدْرٌ

Fate ; divine decree. Powder, position. قَدْرٌ ج أَقْدارٌ

Cooking-pot. قدرٌ ج قُدورٌ

Might, power, authority. قدرةٌ

Powerful ; able. قَادرٌ وقديرٌ

The Omnipotent. أ لقدير

Predestination. تقديرٌ ج تقادير

Suppositon. Implied meaning. Evaluation.

Hypothetically. تقديراً

Quantity, fixed measure. مقدارٌ

As much as. بِمِقْدار مَا

Power, ability. مقدرةٌ

Valuer, estimator. مقدّرٌ

Predestinated. مقدَّرٌ ومقدورٌ

To hallow ; sanctify. قَدَّس

To be purified, sanctified. تَقَدَّس

Holiness. قُدْسٌ وقداسةٌ

Jerusalem. القُدْس

The Holy Ghost. (ألروح ٱلقدس)

Mass, liturgy. قداسٌ ج قداديس

The All-Holy (God). القدوس

Saint. قدّيسٌ ج قدّيسونَ

Sanctification. تقديسٌ

Jerusalem. بيت ٱلمَقَدس

Sanctified. مقدسٌ ومُتقدّسٌ

The Holy Bible. أَلْكِتَاب ٱلمقدَّس

To arrive from. قدِم يقدُم من

To be old. قدم يقْدم . وتقادم

To prefer (a thing). قدَّمهُ علَى

To present, offer to. قَدم ل

To undertake boldly. اقْدم على

To advance, lead. تقدَّم

To advance towards. تقدَّم إِلى

To surpass. تقدَّم على

Antiquity. قدْمٌ وقِدْمَةٌ

Precedence. قِدَمٌ

Foot. قدمٌ ج أَقْدَامٌ

Priority, precedence. قُدْمَةٌ

Comer ; coming. قَادِمٌ

In front of, before. قُدَّام

Courageous, bold. قَدُومٌ ج قُدُمٌ

Hatchet, adze. قَدُومٌ وقَدُّومٌ

Ancient, old. قَدِيمٌ ج قُدَمَاءُ

The Eternal (God). أَلْقَدِيم

Formerly. قَدِيمًا وفِي ٱلْقَدِيم

In olden times. مِن ٱلْقَدِيم

More ancient. أَقْدَم ج أَقْدَمُون

The ancients. أَلأَقْدَمُون

Boldness ; diligence. إِقْدَامٌ

Present ; offering. تَقْدِمَةٌ ج تَقَادِم

Presenting, offering. تَقْدِيمٌ

Pre-eminence ; progress. تَقَدُّم

Antiquity, oldness, &c. تَقَادُمٌ

Front part, fore part. مُقَدَّمٌ

Advance guard of (an army). Preface ; premise. مُقَدَّمَةٌ

One who is in advance. مُتَقَدِّمٌ

Afore-mentioned. مُتَقَدِّمٌ ذِكْرُه

Courageous, energetic. مِقْدَامٌ

To imitate, emulate. اقتدى ب

Model for imitation. قُدْوَةٌ

Way, manner. قِدْيَةٌ

Imitation. اقتِداءٌ

To be unclean. قَذُرَ يَقْذُرُ وقذِر يَقذر

To foul, render unclean. قَذَّرَ

Filth. قذرٌ ج أَقْذَارٌ وقاذورةٌ

Dirty, filthy ; unclean. قذرٌ

To throw. Row. قذف يقذف

To accuse of. قذف بِ

Throwing ; abusing. قَذْف

Rower. قذّافٌ

Oar.	مقذافٌ ومقذفٌ ج مقاذيف
Mote, or small particle.	قَذًى
To stay, dwell.	قَرَّ يَقِرُّ
To persist, persevere in.	قَرَّ على
He was content.	قَرَّ عيناً
To settle, fix, establish.	قَرَّر
To cause one to stay.	قَرَّر وأقرَّ
To cause one to confess. To settle, fix.	قَرَّر
To decide upon.	قَرَّر في نَفْسِهِ أن
To confess, avow.	أقَرَّ ب
To refresh, console.	أقَرَّ عينَهِ
To be stated, determined.	تَقَرَّر
To dwell, inhabit.	إستَقَرَّ في
Water-cress. Darling.	قُرَّةُ العَيْن
Dwelling ; stability.	قَرارٌ
Refrain, (music).	قَرارٌ
Continent, firm-land.	قَارَةٌ
Glass bottle.	قَارورةٌ ج قَوارِيرُ
Consoled, content.	قَرِيرُ العَين
Affirmation ; confession.	إقْرارٌ
Report.	تَقريرٌ
Residence.	مقَرٌّ ومستَقَرٌّ
To read.	قَرَأَ يَقرَأُ قِراءَةً
To study with (a teacher).	قَرَأَ على
To send, or deliver, a greeting.	أقرأهُ السَّلام
To investigate.	إستَقْرَأَ
Act of reading.	قِراءَةٌ ج قراءاتٌ
The Coran.	ألْقرآن
Reader, reciter.	قارئٌ ج قرّاء
Read, recited.	مَقْروءٌ ومقْريٌّ ومقْروٌّ
To approach.	قَرُب يَقْرُب الى ومن
To bring near ; offer.	قَرَّبَ
To be near to.	قاربَ
To be on the point of.	قَاربَ أن
To approach.	تقرَّب تقرباً إلى
To be near one another.	تَقارب
To approach.	إقترب

Nearness. قُرْبٌ

Near ; soon. عن قُرْب

In the vicinity of. بِٱلْقُرْبِ مِن

Skin-bag. قُرْبَةٌ ج قُرْبَاتٌ وَقِرَبٌ

Offering to God. قُرْبَانٌ ج قَرَابِين

Sheath, scabbard. قِرَابٌ ج اقرِبَةٌ

Kinship ; relations. قرابةٌ وَقُرْبَى

Boat, skiff. قَارِبٌ ج قَوَارِب

Near ; related ; قريبٌ ج أَقْرِبَاء
neighbour, followman ; relation.

Shortly, soon. عن قَرِيب

Nearer ; more probable. أَقْرَبُ

Approximation. تَقْرِيبٌ

Approximately. تَقْرِيباً و بٱلتَّقْرِيب

Pommel. قَرَبُوسٌ ج قَرَابِيس

To wound. قَرَحَ يَقْرَحُ قَرْحاً

To finish teething (horse). قَرَحَ يَقْرَحُ

To invent ; improvise. Demand. إِقْتَرَحَ

A wound ; an ulcer. قُرْحَةٌ

Pure (water). قَرَاحٌ

Talent, genius. قَرِيحَةٌ ج قرائح

Ape, monkey. قِرْدٌ ج قُرُودٌ

Tick, (insect). قُرَادٌ ج أَقْرِدَةٌ

To burn, blaze (coal). قَرْدَحَ

Armourer. قَرْدَاحِيٌّ وَقَرْدَحْجِيٌّ

To freeze. قَرِسَ يَقْرَسُ قَرَساً

Intense cold. قَارِسٌ وقَرِيسٌ

A kind of plum. (قَرَاسِيَا)

To curdle (milk). قَرَشَ ٱلْحَلِيب

Piastre. قِرْشٌ ج قُرُوشٌ

Tribe of Koreish. قُرَيْشٌ

Sweet curd. قَرِيشَةٌ

Rich. (مُقَرِّشٌ)

To pinch. قَرَصَ يَقْرُصُ قَرْصاً

To cut out (dough). قَرَّصَ

Disc ; cake. قُرْصٌ ج أَقْرَاصٌ

Nettle (plant). قُرَّاصٌ وَ(قُرَّيْصٌ)

Corsairs, pirates. قُرْصَانٌ

قَرَضَ يَقْرِض	To cut ; nibble.
أَقْرَض	To lend one money.
إِنقَرَض	To die out, perish.
إِقتَرَض وآستَقْرَض	To borrow.
قَرْضٌ ج قروضٌ	Loan, debt.
قُرَاضَةٌ	Cuttings, clippings.
قَرِيضٌ	Poetry.
مِقْراضٌ ج مَقَارِيض	Scissors.
قَرَط يَقرِط	To cut.
قَرَّطَ عَلَى	To give little to.
قُرْطٌ ج أَقْرَاطٌ	Ear-ring. Cluster.
قِيراطٌ ج قَرَارِيط	Carat, inch.
قُرْطُبَة	Cordova (in Spain).
قُرْطَاسٌ ج قراطِيس	Paper.
قَرْطَلٌ ج قراطل	Reed-basket.
قَرَّظَ	To laud, eulogize.
تَقْرِيظٌ	Eulogy. Panegyric.
قَرَعَ يَقْرَع قَرْعاً	To knock, rap.
قَرَّعَ	To scold, rebuke.
قَارَعَ مقارعةً وقِرَاعاً	To fight.
تَقَارَع	To cast lots, or play dice.
إِقترع فِي وعَلَى	To cast lots for.
قَرْعٌ	Knocking. Gourd.
قَرَعَةٌ	Baldness ; scald-head.
قُرْعَةٌ	A gourd, Chemical retort.
قُرْعَةٌ ج قُرَعٌ	Lot. Ballot.
أَلْقُرْعَةُ لَهُ	He wins.
القُرْعَةُ عَلَيْهِ	He loses.
قَارِعَةٌ	Middle part of the way.
القَارِعَةُ	Day of judgement.
أَقْرَعُ	Bald, scald-headed. Bare.
مِقْرَعَةٌ ج مَقَارِع	Whip, knocker.
قَرَف وقَرَّف ب	To suspect, blame.
قَرِف يَقْرَف قَرَفاً	To loathe.
أَقْرَف	To cause disgust.
إِقتَرَف	To commit (a crime).
قَرَفٌ	Disgust, loathing.
قِرفةٌ	Suspicion. Cinnamon.

Disgusting. مُقْرِفٌ

To cluck, (hen). قَرَقَ يقرق قرقاً

Hernia in the scrotum. (قُرقٌ)

Sitting-hen. (قُرقَةٌ)

To dry, become hard. (قرقَدَ)

Squirrel. قَرقذانٌ وقَرْقَذونٌ

To rumble, (stomach). قَرْقَرَ

Rumbling. قرقَرَةٌ ج قَرَاقر

Lamb. (قَرقورٌ)

To gnaw at. (قَرقَشَ)

To cut into small pieces. (قَرْقَطَ)

To rumble, clatter. (قَرقَعَ)

A rattling, rumbling. (قرقَعَةٌ)

To gnaw off. قَرَمَ يقرُم قرماً

The Crimea. أَلقَرْم

Stump of a tree. قرمةٌ ج قرمٌ

Tile, brick. قرميدٌ

Cochineal; crimson. قِرْمِزٌ

Of a crimson colour. قرمزيٌّ

A Karmathian. قرمطيٌّ

Sect of Karmathians. قَرَامِطَةٌ

To join. قرنَ يقرن قرناً بِ

To join together. أقرنَ

To be joined; married. إِقتَرَنَ ب

Horn. Century, age. قَرْنٌ ج قرونٌ

Alexander the Great. ذو ٱلقَرْنَين

Rhinoceros. وحيد القَرن

One's equal. قِرْنٌ ج أقرانٌ

Projecting angle or corner. قرنَةٌ

Close union. قِرَانٌ وَمقارنَةٌ

Comrade; husband. قَرينٌ ج قُرَنَاءُ

Wife. Context. قَرينَةٌ ج قَرَائِنُ

Horned; angled. مُقَرَّنٌ

Joined, yoked. مَقْرونٌ ومقترَنٌ

Cauliflower. قَرْنَبيطٌ (قُنَّبيطٌ)

Cloves. Carnation (plant). قَرَنفلٌ

Cloves. كَبش ٱلقرنفل

A pink, carnation.	قَرَنْفُلَةٌ
To follow out.	قَرَاَ ُ . واستَقْرَى
Analogy. (*See* إستَقْرأَ)	إستِقْراءٌ
To receive hospitably.	قَرا يَقرِي
Entertainment ; feasting.	قِرى
Village.	قَريةٌ ج قُرًى
To feel aversion to.	قَزَّ يَقَزُّ عَنْ
Raw-silk, floss silk.	قَزٌّ
Silk-worm.	دود القَزّ
Glass, glass-ware. (زُجاجٌ)	قَزازٌ
Silk, or glass merchant.	قَزَّازٌ
Iris (of the eye).	قُزَحيَّةٌ
Tin. (عوض : قَصدِيرٌ)	قَزْدِيرٌ
To limp.	قَزَل يقزل قَزَلاً
Limping.	قَزَلٌ
Lame.	أقْزَل قَزْلاءُ ج قُزْلٌ
To be small, mean.	قَزُم يَقزُم
Mean, dwarfish.	قَزَمٌ وقَزْمٌ

Clergyman, minister.	قَسٌّ ج قسوسٌ. وقسّيسٌ ج قسّيسون
Sebesten plum. *Cordia Myxa L.*	مِقْساسٌ
To force, compel.	قَسَر يقسر
Violence, compulsion.	قَسْرٌ
By force.	قَسْراً
To act unjustly, swerve from what is right, to separate, distribute.	قسط يَقْسِط قَسْطًا وقسوطًا
To do justice.	قَسَط يقسطواَقسَط
To pay by instalments.	قَسَّط
To divide equally.	تَقَسَّط بَيْن
Justice ; just, equitable.	قِسطٌ
Part, portion.	قِسْطٌ ج اقْسَاطٌ
Pipe, conduit.	قَسْطَلٌ ج قَسَاطِل
To divide.	قَسَم يقسم قَسْماً وقَسَّم
To share mutually.	قَاسَم
To swear by God.	أقْسَم بِالله
To be divided, separated.	تَقَسَّم
To share.	تَقَاسَم وانْقَسَم

تَقَاسم To take mutual oaths.

إنقسم To be divided.

قَسَمٌ ج أقْسَامٌ Oath.

قِسمٌ ج أقْسَامٌ Part; share.

قِسْمَةٌ ج قِسَمٌ Division, share, lot.

خَارج آلقسمَةَ Quotient, (arith.).

قَسِيمٌ ج أقسِمَاء Sharer ; lot.

مُقَسَّمٌ Divided, distributed.

مقسومٌ Dividend (arith.).

مقسومٌ عَلَيه Divisor, (arith.).

قسا يَقْسُو To be hard, unyielding.

قَسَّى وأَقسى To harden.

قاسى To endure, suffer.

قَسَاوة Hard-heartedness.

قَاس ج قُسَاة Hard, severe.

قَش يَقُشّ To gather, collect. Sweep. Skim.

قَشٌّ Straw.

قشة A single straw.

قَشَّاشٌ Cleaner (sweeper).

مِقَشَّةٌ Broom.

مُقَشَّشَةٌ Demijohn.

قَشَبٌ Chapped skin.

قِشْدَةٌ Cream.

قَشَرَ يَقشرُ قَشْراً To peel, skin.

تَقَشَّرَ وآنْقَشَرَ To be peeled.

قِشْرٌ ج قشورٌ Rind, bark, shell.

قشرةٌ وقشَارةٌ A rind, bark, shell.

مُقَشَّرٌ Peeled.

قَشَطَ يَقشط قَشْطاً عن To strip off.

قَشَّط To strip; rob.

تَقَشَّطَ وآنقشط To be stripped.

(قَشْطَةٌ) Sugar-candy. Cream.

(قشَاطٌ) Leather strap.

(قَشَع يقشَعُ) To see.

أقْشَعَ To be dispersed, (clouds).

أقْشَعَ عن To be dispelled.

To be seen. Dispelled.	انقشع
To shudder, shiver.	إقشعرّ
Shudder ; shivering.	قُشَعْرِيرَة
To be wretched.	قَشِفَ يَقْشَفُ قَشَافَة
To lead an ascetic life.	تَقَشَّفَ
Life in misery.	قَشَفٌ
Ascetic.	مُتَقَشِّفٌ
Barrack.	(قُشْلَة)
To out off, clip.	قَصَّ يَقُصُّ قَصًّا
To tell ; narrate.	قَصَّ يَقُصُّ على
To punish.	قَاصَّ مُقَاصَّةً وقِصَاصًا
To be clipped, cut off.	انْقَصَّ
To take vengeance. Tell.	اقْتَصَّ
Sternum.	قَصٌّ
Tale, story.	قِصَّةٌ ج قِصَصٌ
Punishment.	قِصَاصٌ
Cuttings ; parings.	قُصَاصَةٌ
Scissors.	مِقَصٌّ ج مَقَاصُّ
Reeds. Thread of gold.	قَصَبٌ
Sugar-cane.	قَصَبُ ٱلسُّكَّرِ
A reed or cane. City ; capital.	قَصَبَةٌ ج قَصَبٌ
Œsophagus.	قَصَبَةُ ٱلْمَرِيءِ
Windpipe.	قصبةُ ٱلرِّئَةِ
Bone of the nose.	قَصَبَةُ ٱلْأَنْفِ
Butcher's trade.	قِصَابَةٌ
Butcher.	قَصَّابٌ
Slaughter-house.	مَقْصَبَةٌ
To purpose; repair to.	قصد يَقْصِدُ
To economise.	قصد وٱقْتَصَدَ في
Intention, purpose, aim.	قصدٌ
Visitor. Legate.	قاصدٌ ج قُصَّادٌ
Intended, desired.	مقصودٌ
A poem.	قَصِيدَةٌ ج قَصَائِد
Moderation ; economy.	إِقْتِصَادٌ
Intention, aim.	مَقْصَد ج مقاصد
Tin.	قصديرٌ
To be short.	قَصُرَ يَقْصُر
To lack power.	قَصَرَ أو قصّر عنْ

To shorten. قَصَّرَ وَأَقْصَرَ

To bleach. قَصَرَ قَصْراً وقِصارة

To shut up, confine. قَصَرَهُ في

To limit, restrict. قَصَرَ على

To lag, fall short of. قَصَّرَ في

To desist from. اقصَرَ عن

To shrink, contract. تَقَصَّرَ

To limit one's self to. إقتَصَرَ عَلَى

Shortness. قَصْرٌ وقِصَر

Remissness. قصورٌ

End (of an affair). قُصارى

Castle, palace. قَصرٌ ج قصورٌ

Minor, under age. قاصرٌ

Powerless. قاصر اليَدِ

Fuller, bleecher. قَصَّارٌ

Art of bleaching. قِصارَةٌ

Cæsar, emperor. قَيصَرٌ ج قَياصِرةٌ

Short; small. قَصيرٌ ج قِصارٌ

Shorter. أَقْصَرُ م قُصرى ج أَقاصِرُ

Abbreviation ; neglect. تقصيرٌ

Limited. Bleached. مَقصورٌ

A large room. مقصورةٌ ج مقاصير

Large dish. قَصْعَةٌ ج قَصَعَاتٌ

To break. قَصَفَ يَقصِف قَصْفاً

To roar, (thunder). قَصَفَ يقصف

To be broken. تَقَصَّفَ وانقصف

Brittle, easily broken. قَصِفٌ

Breaking, roaring. قَاصِفٌ

Pleasure-house. مَقصَفٌ

To cut off, mow. قَصَلَ يَقصِلُ قَصْلاً

Stubble, chaff. قَصَلٌ وقَصَالَةٌ

Green food for animals. قَصيل

To break in pieces. قَصَمَ يقصم قَصْماً

To be broken. تَقَصَّمَ وانقصم

Brittle, fragile. قَصِمٌ

Broken shattered. قَصيمٌ ومقصومٌ

To be very distant. قَصَا يَقصو

To penetrate deeply ; follow out to the end. تَقَصَّى واستَقصَى في

Distance. قَصًا وَقَصَاءٌ

Very distant. قَاصٍ ج أَقْصَاءٌ

Investigation. إِسْتِقْصَاءٌ

More distant. أَقْصَى م قُصْوَى ج أَقَاصٍ

The extreme end ; highest purpose. الغَايَةُ القُصْوَى

The uttermost parts of the earth. أَقَاصِي الأَرْضِ

To break, crush. قَضَّ يَقُضُّ قَضًّا

To swoop down (bird). To fall. إِنْقَضَّ

To cut off, prune. قَضَبَ وَاقْتَضَبَ

To be pruned. تَقَضَّبَ وَانْقَضَبَ

Prunings. قُضَابَةٌ

Rod, stick. قَضِيبٌ ج قُضْبَانٌ

Improvised (speech). مُقْتَضَبٌ

To nibble at, gnaw. قَضِمَ يَقْضَمُ

Roasted peas. (قَضَامَةٌ أَوْ قَضَامِيٌّ)

To decide, fulfil (a duty) ; satisfy (a want) ; execute (an order). قَضَى يَقْضِي

To judge. قَضَى بَيْنَ يَقْضِي

To require. قَضَى عَلَى

To die. قَضَى أَوْ قَضَى أَجَلَهُ أَوْ نَحْبَهُ

To spend the time. قَضَى الزَّمَانَ

To pay a debt. قَضَى الدَّيْنَ

To judge in favour of. قَضَى لِ

To fulfil a purpose. قَضَى الوَطَرَ

To execute, carry out. قَضَّى

To summon before a judge. قَاضَى

To be carried out ; cease. إِنْقَضَى

They had a law-suit. تَقَاضَيَا

To be required ; necessary. إِقْتَضَى

Judgment. قَضًى وَقَضَاءٌ ج أَقْضِيَةٌ

Event ; fact, matter ; question, proposition. قَضِيَّةٌ ج قَضَايَا

A judge. قَاضٍ ج قُضَاةٌ

Supreme Judge. قَاضِي القُضَاةِ

Death. القَاضِيَةُ

End ; completion. إِنْقِضَاءٌ

Exigency ; requisite. إِقْتِضَاءٌ

مَقْضِيٌّ Accomplished.

مُقْتَضًى Required, necessary.

بِمُقْتَضَى In conformity with.

قَطَّ يَقُطُّ To cut (a reed-pen).

قَطُّ وقَطْ Never, not at all.

مَا رَأَيْتُهُ قَطُّ I never saw him.

قِطٌّ ج قِطَاطٌ Tom-cat, cat.

قِطَّةٌ Female cat.

قَطَبَ يَقْطِبُ قُطُوبًا. وقَطَّبَ To frown.

قُطْبٌ ج قُطُوبٌ Axis, pivot.

قُطْبٌ Pole, pole-star. Leader.

نَجْمَةُ ٱلْقُطْبِ Pole-star.

قُطْبَةٌ One of the earth's poles.

قُطْبِيٌّ Polar.

قَاطِبٌ وقَطُوبٌ One who frowns.

قَاطِبَةً All together.

قَطَرَ يَقْطُرُ قَطْرًا To trickle.

قَطَرَ يَقْطُرُ To place in line or file.

تَقَطَّرَ To fall in drops.

تَقَاطَرَ To come from all sides.

إِسْتَقْطَرَ To distil.

قَطْرٌ وقَطَرَانٌ Dropping.

قَطْرٌ Rain ; drops.

قُطْرٌ ج أَقْطَارٌ Side, region. Diameter.

قُطْرُ ٱلدَّائِرَةِ Diameter of a circle.

قُطْرُ ٱلْمُرَبَّعِ اوْ ٱلْمُسْتَطِيل Diagonal of a square or parallelogram.

قَطْرَةٌ A drop. Collyrium.

قَطْرَانٌ Liquid pitch ; tar.

قِطَارٌ File or string ; train.

تَقْطِيرٌ Distillation.

مِقْطَرَةٌ Hand-cuffs ; stocks.

قَطَعَ يَقْطَعُ قَطْعًا To cut off, cross.

قَطَعَ ٱلطَّرِيقَ To carry on highway robbery.

قَطَعَ عَنْ To sever ; prevent.

قَطَعَ لَهُ To assign a portion.

قَطَعَ فِي ٱلْقَوْلِ To speak decisively.

قَطَّعَ To cut off entirely.

قَطَّعَ ٱلشِّعْرَ	To scan poetry.
قَطَّعَ ٱلزَّمَانَ	To while away time.
قَاطَعَ	To separate from.
أَقْطَعَ	To take across (a river). Give land as a fief.
تَقَطَّعَ وَٱنْقَطَعَ	To be cut off.
إِنْقَطَعَ	To be interrupted ; cease.
إِنْقَطَعَ إِلى	To be devoted to.
إِقْتَطَعَ مِنْ	To cut off a part.
قَطْعٌ	Amputation. Section. Size.
قَطْعٌ زَائِدٌ	Hyperbola.
قَطْعٌ نَاقِصٌ	Ellipse.
قَطْعٌ مُكَافِئٌ	Parabola.
قَطْعُ ٱلْمَخْرُوطِ	Conic section.
قَطْعًا	Certainly ; not at all.
قُطْعَةٌ ج قِطَعٌ	A part, piece.
قَاطِعٌ	Sharp ; decisive.
(قَاطِعُ ٱلنَّهْرِ)	Opposite side of a river.
قَاطِعُ ٱلطَّرِيقِ	Highway-man.
قَطَاعَةٌ ج قَطَائِعُ	Lent.
قَطِيعٌ ج قُطْعَانٌ	Herd, flock.
قَطِيعَةٌ ج قَطَائِعُ	Fief-land. Tax.
إِنْقِطَاعٌ	Separation ; interruption.
تَقْطِيعٌ تَقَاطِيعُ	Scanning.
مَقْطَعٌ ج مَقَاطِعُ	Syllable.
مَقْطَعُ ٱلنَّهْرِ	Ford of a river.
مُقَاطَعَةٌ ج مُقَاطَعَاتٌ	Province.
(بِالْمُقَاطَعَةِ)	Work by the job.
مُقَطَّعٌ	Cut into pieces.
مُنْقَطِعٌ	Separated, detached.
مَقْطُوعٌ	Cut off ; amputated.
قَطَفَ يَقْطِفُ وَٱقْتَطَفَ	To cull, pluck, gather.
قَطْفٌ	Act of gathering fruit.
قِطَافٌ	Time of gathering.
قَطَائِفُ	A kind of sweet cake
مِقْطَفٌ	Basket, panier.
قَطَمَ يَقْطِمُ قَطْمًا	To cut off.

Piece, fragment. قُطَيْمَةٌ

To inhabit (a place). قَطَنَ يَقْطُنُ فِي

Loins ; lumbar region. قَطْنٌ

Cotton. قُطْنٌ ج أَقْطَانٌ

Settled inhabitant. قَاطِنٌ ج قُطَّانٌ

Pumpkin, squash. يَقْطِينٌ

A kind of snipe. قَطَاةٌ ج قَطًا

To sit down ; dwell. قَعَدَ يَقْعُدُ

To lie in wait for. قَعَدَ لِ

To desist from. قَعَدَ عَنْ

To cause to sit, seat. اقْعَدَ

To be unable to walk. اقْعِدَ

To neglect. تَقَعَّدَ وَتَقَاعَدَ عَنْ

Eleventh month of the Arabian year. ذُو ٱلْقَعْدَةِ

Foundation, base; rule, canon ; model. قَاعِدَةٌ ج قَوَاعِدُ

Capital of a country. قَاعِدَةُ ٱلْبِلَادِ

Sitting ; inactivity. قُعُودٌ

A place of sitting. مَقْعَدٌ ج مَقَاعِدُ

Infirm ; cripple. مُقْعَدٌ

Pensioner. Neglectful. مُتَقَاعِدٌ

To be deep. قَعُرَ يَقْعُرُ قَعَارَةً

To make concave. قَعَّرَ

To dig deep. قَعَّرَ وَأَقْعَرَ

Bottom ; depth. قَعْرٌ ج قُعُورٌ

Dug ; hollow ; concave. مُقَعَّرٌ

To clatter, rattle. قَعْقَعَ ج قَعْقَعَةً

Magpie. قَعْقَعٌ وَقُعْقُعٌ ج قُعْقُعَانٌ

Large basket, panier. قُفَّةٌ ج قُفَفٌ

To track. قَفَرَ يَقْفُرُ قَفْرًا وَتَقَفَّرَ وَٱقْتَفَرَ

To be waste, deserted. اقْفَرَ

Desert, waste (land). قَفْرٌ ج قِفَارٌ

Bee-hive ; basket. قَفِيرٌ ج قُفْرَانٌ

To jump, leap. قَفَزَ يَقْفِزُ قَفْزًا

Jump, leap. قَفْزَةٌ ج قَفَزَاتٌ

A certain measure. قَفِيزٌ ج أَقْفِزَةٌ

Bird-cage ; coop. قَفَصٌ ج أَقْفَاصٌ

قفقف To shiver from cold.

قفل يقفل قفولاً To return.

قفل يقفل قفلاً To guard, lock up.

قفّل وأقفل To lock, shut.

أقفل عن To cause to return.

إنقفل To be locked, bolted.

قفل ج أقفال Lock, bolt. Caravan.

قافلة ج قوافل Caravan.

قيفال Vein in the arm.

قفا يقفو To walk behind, follow.

قفّى ب To send after.

تقفّى واقتفى To follow, imitate.

اقتفى To prefer, select, chose.

قفا وقفاء Back side, reverse.

قافية ج قوافٍ Rhyme, (final word).

إقتفاء Imitation ; preference.

ألكلام المقفّى Rhymed prose.

قاقلّة Cardamon.

قلّ يقلّ To be little in quantity, be scarce, happen rarely.

قلّما (قلّ ما) Rarely.

قلّ قلاً وأقلّ To bear, carry.

قلّل وأقلّ To diminish, lessen.

أقلّ To have little property.

إستقلّ To find small, paltry.

إستقلّ ب To be independent.

قلّة ج قلل Earthen water-jug.

قِلّة Littleness, small quantity.

جمع القلّة Plural which signifies from 3 to 10 objects.

قلّية وقلاّية A (monk's) cell.

قليل ج قليلون Few, little, scarce.

قليلاً Rarely, seldom, slightly.

أقلّ Less, rarer.

ألأقلّ Least, rarest.

أقلّ ومقلّ Poor, having but little.

تقليل Diminishing, lessening.

إستقلال Independence.

Independent. مُستَقِلٌّ

To change, alter. To overturn ; overthrow. قَلَبَ يَقلِبُ

To manipulate ; prove. قلَّب

To be turned ; be fickle. تقَلَّبَ

To be turned upside down. انقَلَبَ

To return to. إِنقَلَبَ إِلى

Change of letters (*in gram*). قَلْبٌ

Heart, mind, thought ; centre, core. قَلْبٌ ج قُلُوبٌ

Sincere, earnest, hearty. قَلْبِيٌّ

Mould, cast, last. قَالَبٌ ج قَوَالِب

Loaf of sugar. قَالِبُ سُكَّرٍ

Revolution ; overthrow. إِنقِلابٌ

Solstice. إِنقِلاَبُ ٱلشَّمْسِ

Change ; inconstancy. تقَلُّبٌ

Vicissitudes. تقَلُّبَاتٌ

Turned, turned over. مقلُوبٌ

Final resting place. مُنقَلَبٌ

To wind round ; adorn. Imitate. قَلَّدَ

To undertake an affair. تقَلَّدَ الأَمرَ

To put on the sword. تقَلَّدَ ٱلسَّيفَ

Necklace ; collar. قِلاَدَةٌ ج قَلاَئِدُ

Imitation. Church tradition. تقلِيدٌ ج تَقَالِيدُ

Imitator, counterfeiter. مُقَلِّدٌ

Imitated, counterfeited. مُقَلَّدٌ

Management of affairs. مقَالِيدُ الامُورِ

Red Sea. بَحْرُ ٱلقُلْزُمِ

Hood, cap. قَلَنسُوَةٌ

Eel. أَنقَلِيسٌ وَإِنقِلِيس

To contract, shrink. قلَصَ يَقْلِصُ

To be wrinkled, shrunk. تقَلَّصَ

To tear from its place, pull out, uproot. قَلَعَ يَقلَعُ

To set sail. أَقلَعَ

To withdraw from. أَقْلَعَ عَنْ

To be taken away. إِنقَلَعَ

To pull out, uproot. إِقْتَلَعَ

قِلْعٌ ج قُلُوعٌ — Sail.

قَلْعَةٌ ج قِلاعٌ — Castle, fortress.

قُلاعٌ — Sores in the mouth, (aphthæ).

مَقْلَعٌ ج مَقَالِعُ — Stone-quarry.

مِقْلاعٌ ج مَقَالِيعُ — Sling.

مَقْلُوعٌ — Uprooted, pulled out.

قَلَفَ يَقْلُفُ — To circumcise.

قَلَفَ وَقَلَّفَ — To calk a ship.

قَلَفَةٌ وَقُلْفَةٌ ج قُلَفٌ — Prepuce.

قِلافَةٌ — Trade of calking ships.

أَقْلَفُ — Uncircumcised.

قَلِقَ يَقْلَقُ قَلَقًا — To be agitated.

أَقْلَقَ — To agitate, disturb.

قَلَقٌ — Disquietude, trouble.

قَلِقٌ — Disturbed; restless.

قُلْقَاسٌ — Colocassia (plant).

قَلْقَلَ قِلْقَالاً — To move, shake.

تَقَلْقَلَ — To be moved, shaken.

قَلْقَلَةٌ — Agitation.

قَلَمَ ـ وَقَلَّمَ — To pare (the nails).

قَلَمٌ ج أَقْلامٌ — Pen; handwriting. Style.

قَلَمُ رُصَاص — Pencil.

قَلَمُ حَجَرٍ — Slate-pencil.

قُلامَةٌ — Parings (of nails &c.).

إِقْلِيمٌ ج أَقَالِيمُ — Region, tract, province; climate.

مُقَلَّمٌ — Cut, pared.

مِقْلَمَةٌ — Pen-case.

قَلَنْسُوَةٌ ج قَلانِسُ — Cowl, cap.

قَلا يَقْلُو قَلْوًا وَقَلَى يَقْلِي قَلْيًا — To fry.

قِلًى وَقِلْيٌ — Ash of alkaline plants.

قِلاَّيَةٌ — Cell of a monk.

قَلِيَّةٌ — Fried food.

مِقْلًى وَمِقْلاةٌ — A frying-pan.

مَقْلِيٌّ وَمُقْلًى — Fried, roasted.

قِمَّةٌ ج قِمَمٌ — Summit, top.

قَمْحٌ — Wheat.

قَمْحَةٌ — Grain of wheat; grain (weight).

To play a game of chance. قَمَرَ يَقْمُرُ

To gamble. قَامَرَ مُقَامَرَةً وَقِمَاراً

To be moonlight. أَقْمَرَ

To play at dice. تَقَامَرَ

Moon. قَمَرٌ ج أَقْمَارٌ

Moonlit (night). قَمِرَةٌ

Lunar ; moonlike. قَمَرِيٌّ

Small window. قَمَرِيَّةٌ

Gambling. قِمَارٌ

Moonlit (night). مُقْمِرَةٌ

Gambler. مُقَامِرٌ

To jump. قَمَزَ يَقْمُزُ قَمْزاً

To dive. قَمَسَ يَقْمُسُ قَمْساً

Dictionary. قَامُوسٌ ج قَوَامِيسُ

Whip. قَمْشَةٌ

Woven stuff. قُمَاشٌ ج أَقْمِشَةٌ

Household things. قُمَاشُ ٱلْبَيْتِ

To jump, leap. قَمَصَ يَقْمِصُ

To transmigrate (soul). تَقَمَّصَ

Shirt. قَمِيصٌ ج أَقْمِصَةٌ وَقُمْصَانٌ

Transmigration (soul). تَقَمُّصٌ

To bind ; swaddle. قَمَطَ وَقَمَّطَ

Swaddling-cloth. قِمَاطٌ ج قُمُطٌ

Bound up, swaddled. مُقَمَّطٌ

To tame, subdue. قَمَعَ يَقْمَعُ وَأَقْمَعَ

To prevent. قَمَعَ وَأَقْمَعَ عَنْ

To be subdued, tamed. إِنْقَمَعَ

Subjugating. قَمْعٌ وَإِقْمَاعٌ

Funnel. قِمْعٌ ج أَقْمَاعٌ

To murmur, find fault. تَقَمْقَمَ

Jar, cup; flask. قُمْقُمٌ ج قَمَاقِمُ

Lice, vermin. قَمْلٌ

Infested with lice. قَمِلٌ وَمُقَمَّلٌ

A louse. قَمْلَةٌ

Very small insects. قُمَّلٌ

Oven to heat baths. قَمِينٌ

Poultry-house, hen-coop. قُنٌّ

Small mountain. Peak. قُنَّةٌ ج قُنَنٌ

Rule, canon, law. Kind of harp. قَانُونٌ ج قَوَانِينُ

Canonical, legal. قَانُونِيٌّ

Glass bottle, phial. قِنِّينَةٌ ج قَنَانِيُّ

To be very red. قَنَأَ يَقْنَأُ قُنُوءً

Very dark red. أَحْمَرُ قَانِئٌ

Hemp ; coarse rope. قُنَّبٌ

Lark. قُنْبَرَاءُ وَقُنْبُرَةٌ ج قَنَابِرُ

Crest of a cock. قُنْبُرَةٌ ج قَنَابِرُ

Cauliflower. قُنَّبِيطٌ وَقَرْنَبِيطٌ

Bomb-shell. قُنْبُلَةٌ ج قَنَابِلُ

To obey God. قَنَتَ يَقْنُتُ وَأَقْنَتَ

To eat sparingly. قَنَتَ يَقْنُتُ قَنَاتَةً

Pious. قَانِتٌ م قَانِتَةٌ

Piety, submission to God. قُنُوتٌ

Lamp. قِنْدِيلٌ ج قَنَادِيلُ

To hunt. قَنَصَ يَقْنِصُ وَاقْتَنَصَ

Hunting. قَنْصٌ وَاقْتِنَاصٌ

Prey ; game. قَنَصٌ وَقَنِيصٌ

Hunter. قَانِصٌ وَقَنَّاصٌ

Crop, gizzard. قَانِصَةٌ ج قَوَانِصُ

Consul. قُنْصُلٌ ج قَنَاصِلُ

Consulate. قُنْصُلِيَّةٌ وَقُنْصُلَاتُو

To despair. قَنَطَ يَقْنِطُ وَقَنُطَ يَقْنُطُ

To throw into despair. قَنَّطَ

Despair. قَنَطٌ وَقُنُوطٌ

Discouraged ; despairing. قَنِط

To fall from a horse. قَنْطَرَ وَتَقَنْطَرَ

Arch. قَنْطَرَةٌ ج قَنَاطِر

100 rottles. قِنْطَارٌ ج قَنَاطِيرُ

Centaury. قِنْطَارِيُونٌ

Collected together. مُقَنْطَرٌ

To be contented. قَنِعَ يَقْنَعُ

To convince, persuade. قَنَّعَ وَأَقْنَعَ

To veil one's self. تَقَنَّعَ

To be content. To be persuaded, convinced. إِقْتَنَعَ بِ

Content, temperate. قَنِعٌ وَقُنُوعٌ

قَانِعٌ	Contented.
قِنَاعٌ ج قُنُعٌ	Veil for the head.
قَنَاعَةٌ وقُنُوعٌ	Contentedness.
مقَنَّعٌ	Wearing an iron helmet.
قِنفَذٌ ج قَنَافِذُ	Porcupine.
قَنَا يَقْنُو واَقْتَنَى	To acquire.
قَنَّى	To dig a canal.
أَقْنَى	To give one possession.
قُنْوَةٌ	Acquisition ; possession.
قَنَاةٌ ج قَنَوَاتٌ	Canal. Lance.
قِنْيَةٌ ج قِنًى	That which is acquired.
قَانٍ	Possessor, proprietor, owner.
أَقْنَى	Having an aquiline nose.
قَهَرَ يَقْهَرُ	To subdue, oppress.
قَاهَرَ	To treat with violence.
قَهْرٌ	Violence ; oppression.
قَهْراً	By force, inspite of.
قَاهِرٌ	Victor, conqueror.
أَلقَاهِرَةُ	Cairo, *i.e. Victirx.*
أَلقَهَّارُ	God, the Almighty.
مقْهُورٌ	Forced, conquered.
قَهْرَمَانٌ ج قَهَارِمَةٌ	Steward.
قَهقَرَ وَتَقَهقَرَ	To go backwards.
قَهقَرَى	Retrograde movement.
قُهقُورٌ (وَقَعقُورٌ)	Pile of stones.
قَهقَهَ	To laugh immoderately.
قَهقَهَة	Immoderate laughter.
قَهْوَةٌ	Coffee. Wine.
قَهْوَةٌ ج قَهَوَاتٌ	Coffee-house ; café.
(قَهْوَجِيٌّ)	Coffee-house keeper.
قَابُ قَوْسٍ	A bow's length.
قُوْبَاءُ	Ring-worm, tetter.
قَاتَ يَقُوتُ	To nourish, feed.
تَقَوَّتَ وَاَقْتَاتَ	To be nourished.
قُوتٌ ج أَقْوَاتٌ	Food, victuals.
مُقِيتٌ	Sustainer, guardian.

To lead, guide.	قَادَ يَقُودُ وَٱقْتَادَ
To be guided, led.	إِنْقَادَ وَٱقْتَادَ
To obey.	إِنقَادَ لِ
Leading, guiding.	قَوْدٌ وَقِيَادَةٌ
Guide ; leader.	قَائِدٌ ج قُوَّادٌ
Halter.	مِقْوَدٌ ج مَقَاوِدُ
Led, guided.	مَقُودٌ وَمَقْوُودٌ
Small, isolated mountain.	قَارَةٌ ج قَارَاتٌ
A thing with a hole in its middle.	مُقَوَّرٌ
To measure.	قَاسَ يَقُوسُ وَٱقْتَاسَ
To be bent.	قَوِسَ يَقْوَسُ وَتَقَوَّسَ
To shoot with a gun.	(قَوَّسَ)
To be shot, fired.	(تَقَوَّسَ)
Bow, arc.	قَوْسٌ ج قُسِيٌّ وَأَقْوَاسٌ
Rainbow.	قَوْسُ قُزَحَ
Cavass ; archer.	قَوَّاسٌ ج قَوَّاسَةٌ
Sage (plant).	قُوَيْسَةٌ
Crupper.	(قُوشٌ ج أَقْوَاشٌ)
To demolish.	قَاضَ وَقَوَّضَ
Exchange.	قَوْضٌ
Plain ; bottom-land.	قَاعٌ ج قِيعٌ
Courtyard. Hall.	قَاعَةٌ ج قَاعَاتٌ
To cackle (hen).	قَاقَ يَقُوقُ قَوْقًا
Cylindrical hat.	قَاوُوقٌ ج قَوَاوِيقُ
To speak, say, propose.	قَالَ يَقُولُ
To give as an opinion.	قَالَ بِ
To speak against.	قَالَ عَلَى
It is said, has been said.	قِيلَ
To argue, bargain with.	قَاوَلَ
To make a false report.	تَقَوَّلَ
To converse together.	تَقَاوَلَ
Talk.	قَالٌ وَقِيلٌ
Saying, word, speech ; promise.	قَوْلٌ ج أَقْوَالٌ وَأَقَاوِيلُ
Author of a saying.	قَائِلٌ
Treatise ; chapter ; article.	مَقَالَةٌ
Said ; word, sentence.	مَقُولٌ

Conference. Contract.	مُقاوَلَةٌ
Colic.	قُولَنْجٌ
Colon (intestine).	أَلْقُولُونُ
To rise ; stand.	قَامَ يَقُومُ
To rise against, revolt.	قَامَ عَلَى
To rise to honour one.	قَامَ لِ
To take one's place.	قَامَ مَقَامَهُ
To carry on (a matter).	قَامَ بِ
To keep a promise.	قَامَ بِوَعْدِهِ
She began to cry.	قَامَتْ تَنُوحُ
To erect ; straighten.	قَوَّمَ
To oppose, dispute with.	قَاوَمَ
To set up ; establish.	أَقَامَ
To stay (in a place).	أَقَامَ بِ
To persevere in.	اقَامَ عَلَى
To appoint to.	أَقَامَهُ على
He brought a charge against him.	أَقَامَ عَلَيْهِ ٱلدَّعْوَى
To be straightened.	تَقَوَّمَ
To be upright, straight.	إِسْتَقَامَ
People ; company.	قَوْمٌ ج أَقْوَامٌ
The enemy.	أَلْقَوْمُ
Consistence.	قَوَامٌ
Support ; sustenance.	قِوَامٌ
Stature ; fathom.	قَامَةٌ ج قَامَاتٌ
Price, value, worth.	قِيمَةٌ ج قِيَمٌ
Upright, vertical ; firm.	قَائِمٌ
Governor. Lt.-Colonel.	قَائِمَقَام
Right-angled.	قَائِمُ ٱلزَّاوِيَةِ
Right angle.	زَاوِيَةٌ قَائِمَةٌ
Foot of a quadruped.	قَائِمَةٌ ج قَوَائِمُ
List, catalogue.	قَائِمَةٌ ج قَوَائِمُ
Resurrection.	قِيَامَةٌ
Manager ; agent.	قَيِّمٌ
Straight ; true.	قَوِيمٌ ج قِيَامٌ
The Self-Existent (God)	أَلْقَيُّومُ
Abiding ; preforming.	إِقَامَةٌ

إِسْتِقَامَةٌ Uprightness ; rectitude.

تَقْوِيمُ ٱلسَّنَةِ Calendar.

تَقْوِيمُ ٱلْبِلَادِ Valuation of a country for purposes of taxation.

مُقَامٌ Place, rank, office.

مُقَاوِمٌ Resisting ; adversary.

مُقَاوَمَةٌ Resistance, opposition.

مُسْتَقِيمٌ Straight. Upright.

قَوِيَ يَقْوَى To be, or grow, strong.

قَوِيَ عَلَى ٱلْأَمْرِ To be able to do it.

قَوَّى To strengthen.

تَقَوَّى وَٱسْتَقْوَى To grow strong.

قُوَّةٌ ج قُوَّات وَقُوًى Strength, faculty, ability ; potentiality.

أَلْقُوَى ٱلْعَقْلِيَّةُ The mental faculties.

أَلْقُوَّةُ ٱلنَّظَرِيَّةُ Perception.

أَلْقُوَّةُ ٱلْعَمَلِيَّةُ Reasoning.

أَلْقُوَّةُ ٱلْحَافِظَةُ Memory.

قَوِيٌّ ج أَقْوِيَاءُ Strong, powerful.

تَقْوِيَةٌ Act of strengthening.

مُقَوٍّ Strengthening, fortifying.

قَاءَ يَقِيءُ قَيْئًا To vomit.

قَيَّأَ تَقْيِئَةً وَأَقَاءَ To make vomit.

قَيْءٌ Act of vomiting.

مُقَيِّئٌ Emetic.

قِيثَارٌ ج قَيَاثِيرُ Guitar.

قَاحَ يَقِيحُ وَقَيَّحَ وَتَقَيَّحَ To suppurate.

قَيْحٌ Pus, suppuration.

قَيَّدَ To bind. Register. To restrict. (the sense of a word).

تَقَيَّدَ To be bound, registered.

تَقَيَّدَ بِ To be bound to.

قَيْدٌ ج قُيُودٌ Fetter, chain, limit.

تَقْيِيدٌ Limitation, restriction. Registration.

مُقَيَّدٌ Bound ; Registered.

قِيرٌ وَقَارٌ Pitch, tar.

أَلْقَيْرَوَانُ Cyrene.

قَاسَ يَقِيسُ To measure, compare.

قَايَسَ مُقَايَسَةً	To measure.
قَايَسَ بَيْنَ	To compare a thing with another.
إِنْقَاسَ	To be measured.
قِيَاسٌ ج أَقْيِسَةٌ	Measure ; rule, analogy. Syllogism.
قِيَاسِيٌّ	According to rule.
مُقَايَسَةٌ	Estimate by analogy.
مِقْيَاس ج مقَايِيسُ	A measure.
مقْيَاس ٱلنِّيلِ	Nilometer.
قَاضَ بِ مِنْ	To exchange for.
قَايَضَ مُقَايَضَةً	To exchange with.
تَقَيَّضَ	To be broken down.
قِيَاضٌ وَمُقَايَضَةٌ	Exchange.
(قِيطَانٌ)	Silk-cord.
قَاظَ يَقِيظ قَيْظًا	To be very hot.
قَيْظٌ	Heat of summer. Drought.
قَيْقَبٌ	Maple (tree).
قَالَ يَقِيلُ	To take a siesta.
أَقَالَ	To abrogate a sale.
إِسْتَقَالَ	To seek abrogation.
قِيلَةٌ	Hydrocele.
قَيْلُولَةٌ	Mid-day nap, siesta.
إِقَالَةٌ	Annulment of a bargain.
مَقِيلٌ	Place of a mid-day nap.
قَيْنَةٌ	Maid-servant. Female singer.

ك

ك — As a numeral sign=20.

كَ وَكِ — Pronominal suffix.

ضَرَبَكَ — He struck thee.

كِتَابُكِ — Thy book.

كَ — As, like.

كَالاسَدِ — Like a lion.

كَئِبَ يَكْأَبُ وَاكْتَأَبَ — To be sad.

كَأْبٌ وَكَآبَةٌ — Grief, sorrow.

كَئِبٌ وَكَئِيبٌ وَمُكْتَئِبٌ — Grieved.

كَأْسٌ ج كَاسَاتٌ وَكُؤُوس — Cup.

كَأْسُ ٱلْمَنِيَّةِ — Death.

كَأَنَّ وَكَأَنْ — As if, as though.

كَأَنَّ زَيْدًا أَسَدٌ — As if Zeid were a lion.

كَبَّ يَكُبُّ كَبًّا — To invert; overthrow.

أَكَبَّ عَلَى — To be intent upon.

إِنْكَبَّ — To fall prostrate.

كُبَّةٌ ج كُبَبٌ — Ball of thread.

كَبَاب — Broiled bits of meat.

كَبَابَةٌ (نبات) — Cubeb.

كَبَابَةُ ٱلشَّوْكِ — Hedge-hog.

مِكَبٌّ ج مِكَبَّاتٌ — Thread-reel.

كَبُّوتٌ ج كَبَابِيتُ — Over-coat.

كَبَحَ يَكْبَحُ — To pull in a horse.

كَبَحَ عَنْ — To restrain, prevent.

كَبَّدَ وَتَكَبَّدَ — To be in the zenith.

كَابَدَ — To suffer, endure.

كَبْدٌ	The middle of the sky.
كَبْدٌ وَكَبِدٌ ج أَكْبَادٌ وَكُبُودٌ	Liver.
كَبَدٌ	Interior ; middle.
كَبَّادٌ	Citron.
كَبِرَ يَكْبَرُ	To be advanced in age.
كَبُرَ يَكْبُرُ	To be large ; grow.
كَبُرَ عَلَيْهِ ٱلْأَمْرُ	It became formidable to him.
كَبَّرَ	To enlarge ; magnify.
تَكَبَّرَ وَٱسْتَكْبَرَ	To grow proud.
إِسْتَكْبَرَ	To deem great.
كُبْرٌ	Greatness, glory, pride.
كِبَرٌ	Greatness, advanced age.
كَبَرٌ وَ(كَبَّارٌ وَقَبَّارٌ)	Caper-bush.
كُبْرَى	Major proposition, (*logic*).
كِبْرِيَاءُ	Greatness ; pride.
كَبِيرٌ ج كِبَارٌ وَكُبَرَاءُ	Great, large.
كَبِيرَةٌ ج كَبَائِرُ	Great crime.
أَكْبَرُ	Greater ; older.
أَللّٰهُ أَكْبَرُ	God is great !
اَلْأَكَابِرُ	The grandees.
تَكَبُّرٌ	Pride, haughtiness.
تَكْبِيرٌ	Magnifying God.
مُتَكَبِّرٌ	Proud, haughty.
كِبْرِيت	Sulphur ; matches.
مُكَبْرَتٌ	Sulphuretted.
كَبَسَ يَكْبِسُ	To press. Surprise.
كَبَّسَ	To train an animal.
تَكَبَّسَ	To be pressed, squeezed.
كَبْسٌ	Assault. Pressure.
كَبْسَةٌ	A sudden attack.
كَابُوس ج كَوَابِيسُ	Nightmare.
كَبِيس	Pickles.
سَنَةٌ كَبِيسَة	Leap year.
مِكْبَسٌ ج مَكَابِسُ	Hand-press.
مَكْبُوس	Assailed, pressed. Pickled.
كَبَشَ يَكْبُشُ كَبْشًا	To grasp.

Ram, male sheep. كَبْشٌ ج كِبَاشٌ
Mulberry-fruit. كَبْشُ ٱلتُّوتِ
Cloves. كَبْشُ ٱلقُرُنْفُلِ
A handful. (كَبْشَةٌ)
To bind, fetter. كَبَلَ يَكْبِلُ وَكَبَّلَ
To be fettered. تَكَبَّلَ
Heavy fetter. كَبْلٌ ج كُبُولٌ
Fettered. مُكَبَّلٌ وَمَكْبُولٌ
Horse-blanket. (كُوبَانٌ)
To fall , trip. كَبَا يَكْبُو كَبْواً
Trip, stumble. كَبْوَةٌ
Charpie, lint. كَتِيتٌ
To write. كَتَبَ يَكْتُبُ كِتَابةً
To prescribe, appoint. كَتَبَ عَلَى
To arrange troops in order. كَتَّبَ
To correspond with. كَاتَبَ
To assemble in squadrons. تَكَتَّبَ
To write to one another. تَكَاتَبَ

To enrol one's self. اِكْتَتَبَ
To ask to write. إِسْتَكْتَبَ
Book-seller. كُتُبِيٌّ
Writer, clerk. كَاتِبٌ ج كُتَّابٌ
Writing, book. كِتَابٌ ج كُتُبٌ
Christians. Jews. أَهْلُ ٱلْكِتَابِ
School. كُتَّابٌ ج كَتَاتِيبُ
Writing ; calligraphy. كِتَابَةٌ
Squadron. كَتِيبَةٌ ج كَتَائِبُ
School. Office. مَكْتَبٌ ج مَكَاتِبُ
Library ; study. مَكْتَبَةٌ ج مَكَاتِبُ
Correspondent. مُكَاتِبٌ
Correspondence by letter. مُكَاتَبَةٌ
Inscribed, registered. مُكْتَتِبٌ
Written ; letter. مَكْتُوبٌ ج مَكَاتِيبُ
Crippled. Whole. أَكْتَعُ م كَتْعَاءُ ج كُتْعٌ
To tie the hands back. كَتَّفَ
To cross the arms. تَكَتَّفَ

Shoulder. كَتِفٌ ج أَكْتَافٌ

Heap, lump. كُتْلَةٌ ج كُتَلٌ

Catholic. كَاثُولِيكِيٌّ ج كَاثُولِيكٌ

To conceal, hide. كَتَمَ يَكْتُمُ

To be concealed, hidden. إِنْكَتَمَ

To confide a secret. إِسْتَكْتَمَ

Concealing. كَتْمٌ وَكِتْمَانٌ

Private secretary. كَاتِمُ ٱلْأَسْرَار

Constipation, costiveness. كُتَامٌ

Kept secret. مَكْتُومٌ وَمُكْتَتَمٌ

Flax, linen. كَتَّانٌ

Linseed. بِزْرُ كَتَّان

Thick, dense. كَثٌّ وَكَثِيثٌ

To be much, many ; increase, multiply. كَثُرَ يَكْثُرُ

To increase ; do too much. كَثَّرَ

To be rich ; increase, grow. أَكْثَرَ

To speak much. أَكْثَرَ فِي ٱلْكَلَامِ

To increase multiply. تَكَاثَرَ

To regard as much. إِسْتَكْثَرَ

To thank. إِسْتَكْثَرَ بِخَيْرِهِ

Great number, plenty, abundance كُثْرٌ وَكَثْرَةٌ

Much, many ; abundant. كَثِيرٌ

Abundantly, often, very. كَثِيراً

Tragacanth, goat's thorn. كَثِيرَاءُ

More, more frequent. أَكْثَرُ

Most people. أَكْثَرُ ٱلنَّاسِ

Growth, increase. تَكَاثُرٌ

Rich. مُكْثِرٌ

To be thick, dense. كَثُفَ يَكْثُفُ

Thickness, denseness. كَثَافَةٌ

Thick, dense, compact. كَثِيفٌ

To apply collyrium, or paint, to one's eyes. تَكَحَّلَ وَٱكْتَحَلَ

An eye-salve or paint. كُحْلٌ

Black antimony-powder. كُحَالٌ

Horse of best breed. كَحِيلٌ ج كَحَائِلُ

أَكْحَلُ م كَحْلَاءُ ج كُحلٌ Having the eye-lashes black.

مِكْحَلٌ وَمِكْحَالٌ Pencil with which the *kohl* is applied.

مُكْحُلَةٌ ج مَكَاحِلُ Vessel containing the *kohl*.

كَاخِيَةٌ ج كَوَاخٍ Secretary.

كَدَّ يَكُدُّ To toil hard. To weary.

كَدٌّ Toil ; effort, exertion.

كدودٌ Laborious.

كَدِرَ يَكْدَرُ To be muddy, turbid.

كَدَّرَ To trouble ; make turbid.

تَكَدَّرَ To be troubled ; muddy.

كَدَرٌ Turbidness ; vexation.

كَدِرٌ وَمُكَدَّرٌ Troubled ; turbid.

كَدَسَ يَكْدِسُ To heap reaped grain.

كُدْسٌ ج أَكْدَاسٌ Heap of grain.

كَدَشَ يَكْدِشُ To bite (horse).

كَدِيشٌ ج كُدْشٌ Pack-horse.

كَدَمَ يَكْدُمُ كَدْماً To bite.

كَدْمٌ ج كُدُومٌ Scar.

كَدَنَ يَكْدُنُ To yoke oxen.

كَذَا وَكَذَلِكَ Thus, like this.

كَذَا وَكَذَا So and so.

كَذَبَ يَكْذِبُ To lie, speak falsely.

كَذَّبَ To accuse of lying.

كَذَّبَ To discredit a thing.

كَذَّبَ وَأَكْذَبَ نَفْسَهُ To contradict one's self ; belie one's self.

كِذْبٌ وأُكْذُوبَةٌ ج أَكَاذِيبُ Lie, fraud.

كَذُوبٌ وَكَاذِبٌ وَكَذَّابٌ Liar.

أَكْذَبُ More false.

مَكْذُوبٌ عَلَيْهِ Falsely accused.

مَكْذَبَةٌ ج مَكَاذِبُ Falsehood.

كَرَّ يَكُرُّ كُرُوراً To return.

كَرَّ كَرّاً To return against.

كَرَّرَ To repeat. Purify, refine.

تَكَرَّرَ To be repeated.

Return, return to attack. كَرٌّ

Turn, time. كَرَّةٌ ج كَرَّاتٌ

Globe, ball. كُرَةٌ ج كُرَاتٌ

Succession of ages. كُرُورُ ٱلدُّهُورِ

Repetition. تِكْرَارٌ وَتَكْرِيرٌ

Repeatedly. تَكْرَاراً

Repeated. Refined. مُكَرَّر

To grieve. كَرَبَ يَكْرُبُ كَرْباً

To offect with sorrow. أَكْرَبَ

To be in distress, grief. إِكْتَرَبَ

Grief, sorrow. كَرْبٌ ج كُرُوبٌ

Cherub. كَرُوبٌ

Grieved. كَرِيبٌ وَمَكْرُوبٌ

Horse-whip. كُرْبَاجٌ ج كَرَابِيجُ

To impose a quarantine. كَرْتَنَ

To be kept in quarantine. تَكَرْتَنَ

Quarantine. كَرَنْتِينَةٌ

Paste-board. كَرْتُونٌ

To look after. إِكْتَرَثَ لِ وَبِ

Leek. كُرَّاثٌ

Georgia. بِلَادُ ٱلْكُرْجِ

Georgian. كُرْجِيٌّ

Kurd. كُرْدٌ وَأَكْرَادٌ

A Kurd. كُرْدِيٌّ

Neck chain. (كُرْدَانٌ)

To divide into squadrons. كَرْدَسَ

The Kurds country. كُرْدِسْتَانُ

Squardon. كُرْدُوسَةٌ ج كَرَادِيسُ

To preach. كَرَزَ يَكْرِزُ كَرْزاً

Preaching. كَرْزٌ وَكِرَازَةٌ

Cherry, cherry tree. كَرَزٌ

The leading ram. كَرَّازٌ

Earthen flask. كَرَازٌ وَكَرَّارٌ

To consecrate. (كَرَّسَ)

To be devoted to God. تَكَرَّسَ

Pamphlet. كُرَّاسَةٌ ج كَرَارِيسُ

Chair. كُرْسِيٌّ ج كَرَاسِيُّ وَكَرَاسٍ

Carriage. (كَرُّوسةٌ ج كَرُّوسَاتٌ)

Consecration, dedication. (تَكْرِيسٌ)

Vetch. كِرْسِنَّةٌ

To be wrinkled. كَرِشَ يَكْرَشُ وَتَكَرَّشَ

Stomach. كِرْشٌ ج كُرُوشٌ

To sip water. كَرَعَ يَكْرَعُ

Celery. كَرَفْسٌ

Distilling-retort. كَرَكَةٌ

Crane (bird). كَرْكِيٌّ ج كَرَاكِيُّ

To disarrange, confuse. كَرْكَبَ

Rhinoceros. كَرْكَدَّنٌ

To laugh loud. كَرْكَرَ

Saffron. كُرْكُمٌ

To be generous, noble. كَرُمَ يَكْرُمُ

To exalt, honour. كَرَّمَ وأَكْرَمَ

How generous he is ! مَا أَكْرَمَهُ

To act generously. تَكَرَّمَ

Grace, liberality. كَرَمٌ

Vine (grape). كَرْمٌ ج كُرُومٌ

A vine-tree. كَرْمَةٌ

Vine-dresser. كَرَّامٌ

Generosity ; honour. كَرَامةٌ

Most gladly ! حبًّا وَكَرَامَةً

Noble, liberal. كَرِيمٌ ج كِرَامٌ

Precious object. كَرِيمَةٌ

More noble, or generous. أَكْرَمُ

Respect, reverence. إِكْرَامٌ

For the sake of. إِكْرَامًا لِ

Honouring, honour. تَكْرِيمٌ

Honoured. مُكْرَمٌ وَمُكَرَّمٌ

Noble action. مَكْرَمَةٌ ج مَكَارِمُ

Cabbage. كُرُنْبٌ وَكَرَنْبٌ

To loathe, abhor. كَرِهَ يَكْرَهُ

To be loathsome. كَرُهَ يَكْرُهُ

To render hateful. كَرَّهَ

أَكْرَهَ على — To force one to . .
تَكَرَّهَ وتَكَارَهَ — To loathe.
إِسْتَكْرَهَ — To find loathsome.
كُرْهٌ وكَرَاهَةٌ — Aversion, disgust.
كَرِهٌ وكَرِيهٌ — Detestable.
كَرِيهَةٌ ج كَرَائِهُ — Adversity.
إِكْرَاهٌ — Compulsion.
مَكْرُوهٌ — Abhorred, detested.
كَرَوْيَا وكَرَاوِيَا — Caraway.
كَرِيَ يَكْرَى كَرًى — To slumber.
كَارَى وأَكْرَى — To let, rent.
إِكْتَرَى وإِسْتَكْرَى — To hire, rent.
كِرَاءٌ وكِرْوَةٌ — Hire, wages; rent.
كُرَةٌ ج كُرَاتٌ وكُرًى — Globe, ball.
كُرَةُ الأَرْضِ — Terrestrial globe.
كُرَوِيٌّ — Globular, spherical.
إِكْرَاءٌ — Act of renting, letting.
إِكْتِرَاءٌ — Act of hiring.

مُكَارٍ ج مُكَارُون — Muleteer.
مُكْرٍ — Hirer out, letter.
مُكْرًى — Hired, rented, let.
كَزَّ يَكَزُّ — To dry up; become rigid.
كُزَازٌ وكُزَّازٌ — Tetanus.
كُزْبَرَةٌ وكُزْبُرَةٌ — Coriander.
كَسَبَ يَكْسِبُ — To earn; acquire.
كَسَّبَ وأَكْسَبَ — To bestow; give.
إِكْتَسَبَ — To seek gain; acquire.
كِسْبٌ — Earnings, gain.
إِكْتِسَابٌ — Acquiring, earning.
إِكْتِسَابِيٌّ — Acquired.
مَكْسَبٌ ج مَكَاسِبُ — Gain, profit.
مَكْسُوبٌ ومُكْتَسَبٌ — Acquired.
(كَسْتَنَا) — Chestnut.
كَسَحَ يَكْسَحُ كَسْحًا — To cut off.
كَسِحَ يَكْسَحُ كَسَحًا — To be crippled.
كُسَاحَةٌ — Rickets. Sweepings.

Lame, crippled. كَسِيحٌ ج كُسْحَانٌ

A cripple. أَكْسَحُ م كَسْحَاءُ ج كُسْحٌ

To sell badly. كَسَدَ يَكْسُدُ

Worthless ; selling badly. كَاسِدٌ

To break ; rout, defeat. كَسَرَ يَكْسِرُ

To break into pieces. كَسَّرَ

To seek an abatement. كَاسَرَ

To be broken into pieces. تَكَسَّرَ

To be broken ; routed ; become a bankrupt, fail. إِنْكَسَرَ

Breach, fracture. كَسْرٌ

Fraction (*arith*). كَسْرٌ ج كُسُورٌ

Fragment. كِسْرَةٌ ج كِسَرٌ

The vowel. (ِ) كَسْرَةٌ ج كَسَرَاتٌ
A fracture ; defeat.

Chosroes. كِسْرَى ج أَكَاسِرَةٌ

Bird of prey. كَاسِرَةٌ ج كَوَاسِرُ

A fragment. كُسَارَةٌ

Elixir. إِكْسِيرٌ

Defeat ; bankruptcy. إِنْكِسَارٌ

Broken plural. جَمْعُ ٱلتَّكْسِيرِ

Broken into pieces. مُكَسَّرٌ

Routed ; bankrupt. مَكْسُورٌ

To be eclipsed. كَسَفَ وَٱنْكَسَفَ

Eclipse. كُسُوفٌ وَٱنْكِسَافٌ

Heavy-hearted. كَاسِفُ ٱلْبَالِ

Eclipsed. مَكْسُوفٌ وَمُنْكَسِفٌ

To be lazy. كَسِلَ يَكْسَلُ وَتَكَاسَلَ

Laziness, idleness. كَسَلٌ وَتَكَاسُلٌ

Lazy, idle. كَسْلَانُ ج كَسَالَى

Mode, fashion. كَسْمٌ

To clothe. كَسَا يَكْسُو وَأَكْسَى

To be dressed, clothed. إِكْتَسَى

Garment, dress. كِسَاءٌ ج أَكْسِيَةٌ

Clothing, dress. كُسْوَةٌ ج كُسًى

To frown. Chase away. (كَشَّ)

Lock of hair. كُشَّةٌ

A thimble. (كِشْتْبَانٌ)

كَشَحَ ـُ	To disperse.
إِنكَشَحَ عَنْ	To retire from.
كَشْحٌ ج كُشُوحٌ	Flank ; waist.
كَشَرَ عَنْ نَابِهِ	To snarl (beast).
كَشَطَ يَكْشِطُ	To strip ; scrape.
تَكَشَّطَ	To be dispersed (clouds).
إِنْكَشَطَ	To be taken off.
كَشَفَ يَكْشِفُ وَكَشَّفَ	To uncover.
كَاشَفَ بِ	To reveal, disclose.
إِنْكَشَفَ	To be uncovered.
إِكْتَشَفَ	To discover ; find out.
إِسْتَكْشَفَ	To try to discover.
كَشْفٌ	Unveiling, revealing.
كَاشِفٌ ج كَشَفَةٌ)	Overseer. Test.(
مَكْشُوفٌ	Uncovered, disclosed.
إِكْتِشَافٌ ج إِكْتِشَافَاتٌ	Discovery.
مُكْتَشِفٌ	Discoverer.
كَشْكَشٌ	Ruffle of a garment.
كَشْكُولٌ	A beggar's bag.
كِشْمِشٌ	Currants.
كَظَّ يَكُظُّ	To surfeit (food).
كَظَّةٌ	Indigestion ; surfeit.
كَظَمَ يَكْظِمُ	To shut ; restrain.
كَاظِمٌ	Silent, speechless.
كَظِيمٌ	Suppressing anger.
كَعَّبَ	To cube (a number).
كَعْبٌ	Ankle. Cube, (*arith*).
أَلْكَعْبَةُ	*The kaba* in Mecca.
مُكَعَّبٌ	Cubic ; cube.
كُعْبُرَةٌ	The radius (bone).
كَعْكٌ	Biscuit, cake, bun.
كَعَمَ يَكْعَمُ	To muzzle.
كِعَامٌ	Muzzle of the camel.
كَعِيمٌ وَمَكْعُومٌ	Muzzled.
كَعَا يَكْعُو	To be timid.
(كَعَّى)	To defy.

كَاغِدٌ Paper.

كَفَّ يَكُفُّ كَفًّا To hem, seam.

كَفَّ عَنْ To prevent. To cease.

كُفَّ بَصَرُهُ To become blind.

إِنْكَفَّ عَنْ To abstain from.

كَفٌّ ج كُفُوفٌ Palm of hand.

كَفَّةٌ Scale (of a balance).

كَفِيَّةٌ Silk handkerchief.

كَافَّةً All.

كَفَافٌ Equal ; daily bread.

كَفِيفٌ وَمَكْفُوفٌ ج مَكَافِيفُ Blind.

كَافَأَ مُكَافَأَةً وَكِفَاءً To reward.

إِنْكَفَأَ To retreat ; turn back.

كَفَأٌ وَكَفَاءَةٌ Equality, likeness.

كِفَاءٌ وَكُفْوءٌ Equal, like.

كَفَحَ يَكْفَحُ وَكَافَحَ To face.

كَافَحَ عَنْ To fight for, defend.

أَكْفَحَ عَنْ To drive back.

تَكَافَحَ To encounter one another.

كِفَاحٌ وَمُكَافَحَةٌ Battle, combat.

كَفَرَ يَكْفُرُ وَكَفَّرَ To cover.

كَفَرَ يَكْفُرُ To be an infidel.

كَفَرَ بِ To renounce, deny.

كَفَّرَ To expiate.

كَفْرٌ ج كُفُورٌ Village, hamlet.

كُفْرٌ Unbelief ; infidelity.

كَافِرٌ ج كُفَّارٌ وَكَفَرَةٌ Infidel.

كَافُورٌ Camphor.

كَفَّارَةٌ Atonement ; expiation.

تَكْفِيرٌ Atonement ; expiation.

كَفَلَ يَكْفُلُ To take charge of.

كَفَلَ يَكْفِلُ To stand security.

كَفَّلَ To make one give bail.

تَكَفَّلَ لَهُ بِ To guarantee.

كَفَلٌ ج أَكْفَالٌ Buttocks.

كَافِلٌ One who stands bail.

أَلْكَافِلُ God.
كَفَالَةٌ Bail, security, pledge.
كَفِيلٌ كُفَلاءُ A surety.
مَكْفُولٌ Guaranteed.
إِكْفَهَرَّ To be very dark (night).
كَفَّنَ To shroud the dead.
كَفَنٌ ج أَكْفَانٌ Shroud.
كَفَى يَكْفِي To suffice ; satisfy.
كَفَاهُ ٱلشَّرَّ To prevent evil.
كَافَى بِـ To recompense.
إِكْتَفَى To be contented.
كَفِيٌّ وَكَافٍ Sufficient.
كِفَايَةٌ Sufficient quantity.
مُكَافَأَةٌ Recompense, requital.
كَلَّ يَكِلُّ To be tired, weary.
كَلَّ وَكَلَّلَ To be dim, dull.
كَلَّلَ To crown. To join in wedlock, marry.
أَكَلَّ To fatigue ; to dim.

تَكَلَّلَ To be crowned.
كَلٌّ وَكَلَالٌ Weariness ; dulness.
كَلٌّ وَكَلِيلٌ Blunt ; dim.
كُلٌّ All ; each, every.
كِلَا Both of. (كِلْتَا *dual fem*)
كَلَّا No ! by no means.
كُلَّةٌ ج كُلَلٌ Cannon ball.
كُلَّمَا As often as, whenever.
كُلِّيٌّ م كُلِّيَّةٌ Universal, general.
أَلْكُلِّيَّةُ General term, (*logic*).
بِالْكُلِّيَّةِ Altogether, entirely.
كَالٌّ Fatigued ; dim ; blunt.
إِكْلِيلٌ ج أَكَالِيلُ Crown ; umbel.
مُكَلَّلٌ Crowned.
كَلَأٌ Forage ; herbage.
كَلِبَ ـَ To have hydrophobia.
كَلْبٌ ج كِلَابٌ Dog.
كَلْبُ ٱلْبَحْرِ Shark.

To be freckled. كَلِفَ يَكْلَفُ كَلَفًا

To be devoted to. كَلِفَ بِ

To impose a difficult matter upon one. كَلَّفَ وَإِلى

To cost. كَلَّفَ

To take the trouble (to do anything). كَلَّفَ خَاطِرَهُ

Please do this! كَلِّفْ خَاطِرَكَ

To take pains. تَكَلَّفَ

Ardent love. Freckles. كَلَفٌ

Trouble, labour, hardship. Cost, expense. كُلْفَةٌ ج كُلَفٌ

Freckled; maculated. أَكْلَفُ

Trouble. تَكْلِيفٌ ج تَكَالِيفُ

Without ceremony. بِلاَ تَكْلِيف

Expensive. مُكْلِفٌ وَمُكَلِّفٌ

Responsible agent. مُكَلَّفٌ

Intruder. مُتَكَلِّفٌ

Raft. كَلَكٌ

To wound. كَلَمَ يَكْلُمُ وَكَلَّمَ

Beaver. كَلْبُ ٱلْمَاءِ

Canis major. أَلْكَلْبُ ٱلْأَكْبَرُ

Canis minor. أَلْكَلْبُ ٱلْأَصْغَرُ

Hydrophobia. كَلِبٌ

Seized with hydrophobia. كَلِبٌ

Female dog, bitch. كَلْبَةٌ

Tongs, forceps. كَلْبَتان

Hook; grapnel. كُلَّابٌ ج كَلَالِيبُ

See: كِلَا Both, (*fem*). كِلْتَا

To frown. كَلَحَ يَكْلَحُ وَأَكْلَحَ وتكلّحَ

Austere, severe. كَالِحٌ

To plaster with lime. كَلَّسَ

Lime mortar. كِلْسٌ

Sock, stocking. (كَلْسَةٌ)

Lime-kiln. كَلَّاسَةٌ

Lime-burner; plasterer. مُكَلِّسٌ

Plastered with lime. مُكَلَّسٌ

Eel. أَنْكَلِيسٌ

To speak ; speak to. كَلَّمَ

To converse with. كَالَمَ

To talk, converse. تَكَلَّمَ

Wound. كَلْمٌ ج كُلُومٌ وَكِلَامٌ

Incomplete sentence. كَلِمٌ

Word, sentence. كَلِمَةٌ ج كَلِمَاتٌ

Speech, saying. كَلَامٌ

Talking, speech. تَكَلُّمٌ

Speaker, 1st person, (*gram*). مُتَكَلِّمٌ

Wounded. مَكْلُومٌ وَكَلِيمٌ

Both. (*dual*). كِلَا م كِلْتَا

Kidney. كُلْيَةٌ ج كُلًى

How much ? How many ? كَمْ

How many men ? كَمْ رَجُلاً

Pronominal suffix. كُمْ

Your book (*pl. m.*). كِتَابُكُمْ

Your book (*dual*). كِتَابُكُمَا

As, even as, just as. كَمَا

To muzzle (an animal). كَمَّ

Quantity. كَمٌّ وَكَمِّيَّةٌ ج كَمِّيَّاتٌ

Calyx, spathe. كِمٌّ ج أَكْمَامٌ

Sleeve. كُمٌّ ج أَكْمَامٌ

Muzzle. كِمَامَةٌ وَكِمَامٌ

Muzzled. مَكْمُومٌ

Truffle. كَمْءٌ وَكَمْأَةٌ

Bill ; cheque. كَمْبِيَالَةٌ

Rate, or bill of exchange. كَمْبِيُو

Dark brown, bay. كُمَيْتٌ

Pear. كُمَّثْرَى

A pear. كُمَّثْرَاةٌ ج كُمَّثْرَيَاتٌ

Scum ; film. كَمْخَةٌ

To be sad. كَمِدَ يَكْمَدُ كَمَداً

To make sad. أَكْمَدَ

Change of colour. كَمَدٌ وَكُمْدَةٌ

Concealed grief.

A kind of belt. كَمَرٌ ج أَكْمَارٌ

Duty ; custom-house. كُمْرُكٌ

Receiver of customs. كُمْرُكْجِيّ

Chyme. كَيْمُوسُ

To grasp. (كَمَشَ)

To be wrinkled. إِنْكَمَشَ وَتَكَمَّشَ

A handful. (كَمْشَةٌ)

Carpenter's pincers. (كَمَّاشَةٌ)

كَمَلَ يَكْمُلُ وَتَكَمَّلَ وَتَكَامَلَ وَاكْتَمَلَ

To be complete, finished.

To finish, complete. كَمَّلَ وَأَكْمَلَ

Entire, complete. كَامِلٌ

Perfection. كَمَالٌ

Finishing; perfecting. تَكْمِيلُ

Completed, finished. مُكَمَّلٌ

To hide; hide one's self. كَمَنَ ـُ وَاكْتَمَنَ

To lie in ambush. كَمَنَ ل

Ambush. كَمْنَةٌ ج كِمَانٌ

State of being hidden. كُمُونٌ

Cumin. كَمُّونٌ

Hidden; ambush. كَمِينٌ ج كُمَنَاءُ

Place of ambush. مَكْمَنٌ ج مَكَامِنُ

Hidden, concealed. مُكْتَمِنٌ

Violin. كَمَنْجَةٌ

Blindness. كَمَهٌ

Blind. أَكْمَهُ م كَمْهَاءُ ج كُمْهٌ

Pronominal suffix. كُنَّ

Your book, (*fem*). كِتَابُكُنَّ

To conceal, secrete. كَنَّ يَكُنُّ

To be concealed. إِكْتَنَّ

To retire; be quiet. إِسْتَكَنَّ

Cover, shelter. كِنٌّ ج أَكْنَانٌ

Son's wife. كَنَّةٌ ج كَنَائِنُ

Roof for shelter. كُنَّةٌ ج كِنَانٌ

Hearth, stove. كَانُونٌ ج كَوَانِينُ

December. كَانُونُ الأَوَّل

January. كَانُونُ آلثَّانِي

Concealed. كَنِينٌ وَمَكْنُونٌ

Callousness (of hand). كَنَبٌ

كُنُودٌ Ingratitude.

كُنْدُرٌ Frankincense.

(كُنْدُرَةٌ ج كَنَادِرُ) Shoe.

كَنَارٌ Hem, border.

كَنَارِيٌّ Canary bird.

كَنَّارَةٌ ج كَنَّارَاتٌ Lute, harp.

كَنَزَ يَكْنِزُ To treasure, store.

إِكْتَنَزَ To be firm, hard.

كَنْزٌ ج كُنُوزٌ Treasure.

مُكْتَنِزٌ Firm and compact.

مَكْنُوزٌ Hidden, buried (treasure).

كَنَسَ يَكْنِسُ كَنْسًا وكَنَّسَ To sweep.

كَنَّاسٌ Sweeper.

كُنَاسَةُ Sweepings.

كَنِيسٌ Synagogue.

كَنِيسَةٌ ج كَنَائِسُ Church.

كَنَائِسِيٌّ و كَنَسِيٌّ Ecclesiastical.

مِكْنَسَةٌ ج مَكَانِسُ Broom.

كَنْعَانُ Canaan.

اَلْكَنْعَانِيُّونَ The Canaanites.

كَنَفَ يَكْنُفُ كَنْفًا To shelter.

تَكَنَّفَ وَاكْتَنَفَ To surround.

كَنَفٌ ج أَكْنَافٌ Refuge.

كَنَافَةٌ A kind of sweet pastry.

كَنِيفٌ ج كُنُفٌ Privy, sewer.

كُنْهٌ Substance, essence.

كَنَى يَكْنِي كِنَايَةً عَنْ To hint at.

كَنَّى بِ To give a surname.

تَكَنَّى بِ To take a surname.

كُنْيَةٌ Surname. Epithet.

كِنَايَةٌ Metaphor, metonomy.

كِنَايَةً عَنْ Instead or in place of.

كَهْرَبَ To electrify.

كَهْرَبَاءُ Yellow amber.

كَهْرَبَائِيٌّ Electric.

كَهْرَبَائِيَّةٌ Electricity.

مُكَهْرَبٌ Electrified.

كَهْفٌ ج كُهُوفٌ Cavern, cave.

كَهَلَ يَكْهَلُ To be middle-aged.

كَهْلٌ ج كُهُولٌ Middle-aged.

كُهُولَةٌ وَكُهُولِيَّةٌ Mature age.

كَهَنَ يَكْهَنُ To divine, foretell.

كَاهِنٌ ج كَهَنَةٌ Soothsayer ; priest.

كَهَانَةٌ Soothsaying ; divination.

كَهَنُوتٌ Priesthood.

كُوبٌ ج أَكْوَابٌ A large cup.

(كُوبَانٌ) A horse cloth.

كَوْثَلٌ Stern of ship ; helm.

كُوخٌ ج أَكْوَاخٌ Hut.

كَادَ يَكُودُ كَوْدًا To restrain, hinder.

كَادَ يَفْعَلُ He almost did.

مَا كَادَ يَفْعَلُ He hardly did.

كَارٌ ج كَارَاتٌ Art, profession.

كُورٌ ج أَكْوَارٌ Furnace, forge.

كُورَةٌ ج كُوَرٌ Small district.

كُوَارَةُ نَحْلٍ Bee-hive

كُورَنْتِينَا Quarantine.

كَازٌ Petroleum. Gas.

كُوزٌ ج أَكْوَازٌ Drinking-mug.

كَاسٌ ج كُؤُوسٌ Drinking-cup.

كُوسَا Vegetable marrow.

كُوعٌ ج أَكْوَاعٌ Elbow.

اَلْكُوفَةُ Kufa (city).

كُوفِيٌّ Kufic (writing) ; of Kufa.

كُوفِيَّةٌ Head-wrapper.

كَوْكَبٌ ج كَوَاكِبُ Planet, star.

كَوْكَبَةٌ A party ; assembly.

كَوَّمَ To make a heap.

كُومَةٌ ج كُوَمٌ وَأَكْوَامٌ A heap.

كَانَ يَكُونُ To be, exist.

كَانَ لَهُ مَالٌ He had wealth.

كَانَ قَائِمًا He was standing.

He was doing. كَانَ يَفْعَلُ

He had said. كَانَ قَدْ قَالَ

To create, form. كَوَّنَ

To be created, formed. تَكَوَّنَ

Existence, nature. كِيَانٌ

Nature ; universe. كَوْنٌ ج أَكْوَان

Being ; creature. كَائِنٌ

Incident, event. كَائِنَةٌ ج كَائِنَاتٌ

All created things. أَلْكَائِنَاتُ

Formation, creation. تَكْوِينٌ

Book of Genesis. سِفْرُ ٱلتَّكْوِينِ

Place. مَكَانٌ ج أَمْكِنَةٌ وَأَمَاكِنُ

Adverb of place. ظَرْفُ ٱلْمَكَانِ

Place ; rank. مَكَانَةٌ ج مَكَانَاتٌ

Creator. مُكَوِّنٌ

Window. كُوَّةٌ ج كُوَّات وَكُوًى

To burn, cauterise. كَوَى يَكْوِي

(To iron clothes). كَوَى

To be cauterised. إِكْتَوَى

Cauterisation, ironing. كَيٌّ

Smoothing-iron. مِكْوَاةٌ ج مَكَاوٍ

Cauterised ; ironed. مَكْوِيٌّ

In order that. كَيْ وَلِكَيْ

In order not... كَيْ لاَ وَلِكَيْ لاَ

So and so. كَيْتَ وَكَيْتَ

To deceive... كَادَ يَكِيدُ كَيْداً وَكَايَدَ

Stratagem, guile. كَيْدٌ

Same as كَيْدٌ. مَكِيدَةٌ ج مَكَائِدُ.

To be shrewd. كَاسَ يَكِيسُ

To put into a bag. كَيَّسَ

Intelligence. كَيْس وَكِيَاسَةٌ

Bag, purse. كِيسٌ ج أَكْيَاسٌ

Clever ; handsome. كَيِّسٌ

Handsome, pretty. (كُوَيِّسٌ)

More handsome. اكْوَسُ

To take a special form. تَكَيَّفَ

كَيْفَ How ; in what way?

(كَيْف) Enjoyment. Quality.

كَيفما كَانَ Howsoever.

كَيفِيَّةٌ ج كَيفِيَّاتٌ Quality ; form.

كَالَ يَكِيلُ وَكَيْلَ To measure.

إِكْتَالَ To measure out.

كَيْلٌ ج أَكْيَال Measure of grains
(٦ أَمْدَادٍ) = 6 *mudds.*

كَيلَة ج كَيْلاَت A small measure.

كِيَالَة Measuring, weighing.

كَيَّالٌ One who measures.

مِكْيَلٌ Measure of capacity.

مَكِيلٌ وَمَكْيُولٌ Measured.

كَيْلُوسٌ Chyle.

كَيْمَا (كَيْ مَا) In order that.

كِيميا وَكِيمِيَاء Chemistry.

كِيمِيّ Chemist ; chemical.

كِينَا Quinine.

خَشَبُ ٱلْكِينَا Cinchona bark.

ل

ل As a numeral sign=30.

لِ To, for.

لِيَكْتُبْ Let him write.

لَعَمْرُكَ By thy life!

لاَ No ; not.

لاَ وَلاَ Neither, nor.

No, there is not or no...	لَاتَ
An Arabian godess.	أَللاَّتُ
Lapis lazuli.	لَازَوَرْدٌ
Azure-blue.	لَازَوَرْدِيٌّ
Angel.	مَلَاكٌ وَمَلَكٌ ج مَلَائِكَةٌ
To shine, glitter.	لأْلأَ وَتَلألأَ
Pearls.	لُؤْلُوءٌ
A pearl.	لُؤْلُؤَةٌ ج لَآلِئُ
Pearl-coloured.	لُؤْلُؤِيٌّ
To bind up a wound.	لَأَمَ يَلْأَمُ
To be of a low character.	لَؤُمَ
To agree with.	لَاءَمَ
To reconcile.	لَاءَمَ بَيْنَ
To assemble. Unite. *v. i.*	إِلْتَأَمَ
Avarice, meanness.	لُؤْمٌ
Base, sordid.	لَئِيمٌ ج لِئَامٌ
Convenient ; suitable.	مُلَائِمٌ
Suitableness.	مُلَاءَمَةٌ
Assembled, gathered.	مُلْتَئِمٌ
To stay in.	أَلَبَّ بِ
Marrow, pith.	لُبٌّ ج لُبُوبٌ
Heart ; mind.	لُبٌّ ج أَلْبَابٌ
Intelligent.	لَبِيبٌ ج أَلِبَّاءُ
First milk.	لِبَأٌ
Lioness.	لَبُوَةٌ ج لَبُوَاتٌ
To tarry, abide in.	لَبِثَ يَلْبَثُ بِ
He did not delay to do.	مَالَبِثَ أَنْ فَعَلَ
A tarrying.	لَبْثٌ وَلُبْثٌ وَلَبَاثٌ
A short stay, delay.	لُبْثَةٌ
To beat. To abuse.	لَبَخَ يَلْبُخُ
Persea (tree).	لَبَخَ (وَلَبْخٌ)
Poultice, cataplasm.	لَبْخَةٌ ج لَبَخَاتٌ
To abide, dwell in.	لَبَدَ وَأَلْبَدَ بِ
To cram, compress.	لَبَّدَ
To be compact together.	تَلَبَّدَ
To stick to, cleave to.	تَلَبَّدَ بِ

إِلْتَبَدَ	To be pressed closely.
لبَّادَةٌ	Cap of cloth or felt.
لَبَسَ يَلْبِسُ عَلَى	To make obscure.
لَبِسَ يَلْبَسُ	To put on a dress.
لَبَّسَ	To render obscure. To clothe.
أَلْبَسَ	To cover, clothe.
إِلْتَبَسَ	To be dark, obscure.
إِلْتَبَسَ بِ	To be confused with.
لَبْسٌ وَٱلْتِبَاسٌ	Ambiguity.
لُبْسٌ ج لُبُوسٌ	Clothing, dress.
لِبَاسٌ ج أَلْبِسَةٌ	Garment.
مَلْبَسٌ ج مَلاَبِسُ	Clothing.
مُلْتَبِسٌ	Obscure; doubtful.
(مُلَبَّسٌ)	Sugar-plums.
مَلْبُوسٌ ج مَلاَبِيسُ	Garment.
(لَبَّشَ)	To collect pell-mell.
لَبَشٌ	Baggage, chattels.
لَبَطَ يَلْبُطُ لَبْطًا	To kick.
لَبْطَةٌ	A kick.
لَبِقَ بِ	To fit, become one.
لَبَقٌ ولَبَاقَةٌ	Wit and cleverness.
لَبِقٌ وَلَبِيقٌ	Skilful, clever.
لَبَكَ يَلْبُكُ ولَبَّكَ	To mix; confuse.
تَلَبَّكَ وٱلْتَبَكَ	To be confused, embarrassed.
لَبْكٌ وَلَبْكَةٌ	Confused affair.
مُلْتَبِكٌ وَمَلْبُوكٌ	Embarrassed.
لَبْلاَبٌ	Egyptian bean.
لَبَنٌ ج أَلْبَانٌ	Milk; sour milk. Sap.
لَبِنٌ وَلِبْنٌ	Brick, tile.
لَبِنَةٌ	A brick.
لُبْنَان	Mount Lebanon.
لُبْنَانِيٌّ	Of Mount Lebanon.
لُبَانٌ	Frankincense. Pine.
لَبَّانٌ	Brick-maker. Milk-man.
لَبْوَةٌ ج لَبَوَاتٌ	Lioness.
لَبَّى	To obey, respond.

لَبَّيْكَ Here I am!

لَتَّ يَلُتُّ لَتًّا To speak nonsense.

اَللّاتُ والعُزَّى Two idols.

اَلَّتِي مث اَللَّتَانِ ج اَللَّوَاتِي Who, which (*fem*).

لَثِغَ يَلْثَغُ To stammer, lisp.

لَثَغٌ ولُثْغَةٌ Stammering, lisping.

أَلْثَغُ م لَثْغَاءُ ج لُثْغٌ Lisper.

لَثَمَ يَلْثُمُ ولَثِمَ يَلْثَمُ لَثْمًا To kiss.

لَثَمَ ولَثَّمَ To muffle the mouth.

لَثْمَةٌ A kiss.

لِثَامٌ Veil.

لِثَةٌ ج لِثَاتٌ Gums (of the teeth).

لَجَّ يَلِجُّ To persist, persevere.

لَجَّ عَلَى To importune.

لاجَّ To wrangle with.

لُجَّةٌ ج لُجَجٌ High sea; the deep.

لاجٌّ ولَجُوجٌ Pertinacious.

لَجَاجٌ ولَجَاجَةٌ Pertinacity.

لَجَأَ يَلْجَأُ ولَجِئَ يَلْجَأُ والْتَجَأَ إِلَى To take refuge in, repair to.

لَجَّأَ وأَلْجَأَ إِلَى To force, compel.

أَلْجَأَ To defend, protect.

لَجَأٌ ومَلْجَأٌ ج مَلاجِئُ Refuge.

لاجِئٌ ومُلْتَجِئٌ Seeking shelter.

لَجْلَجَ وتَلَجْلَجَ To stammer.

لَجْلاجٌ One who stutters.

لَجَمَ وأَلْجَمَ To bridle (a horse).

إِلْتَجَمَ To be bridled.

لِجَامٌ ج أَلْجِمَةٌ ولُجُمٌ Bridle, curb.

مُلْجَمٌ Bridled.

لَجْنَةٌ Committee.

لَحَّ يَلُحُّ لَحًّا To be close, near.

أَلَحَّ في السُّؤَالِ To persist in one's demands.

أَلَحَّ عَلَيْهِ To importune, press.

إِلْحَاحٌ Importunity; persistence.

مُلِحٌّ ومِلْحَاحٌ One who insists.

To bury. لَحَدَ يَلْحَدُ لَحْداً وَأَلْحَدَ

To swerve from. أَلْحَدَ عنْ

To apostatize. أَلْحَدَ وَٱلْتَحَدَ

A grave. لَحْدٌ ج أَلْحَادٌ وَلُحُودٌ

Apostasy ; heresy. إِلْحَادٌ

An apostate. مُلْحِدٌ ج مُلْحِدُون

To lick. لَحِسَ ـَ لَحْساً

To regard, observe. لَحَظَ يَلْحَظُ لَحْظاً

To look at attentively. لَاحَظَ

Glance, moment. لَحْظَةٌ

Observation. مُلَاحَظَةٌ

Regarded. مَلْحُوظٌ ج مَلْحُوظَاتٌ

To wrap up لَحَفَ يَلْحَفُ

To wrap one's self up. إِلْتَحَفَ

Foot of a mountain. لَحْفُ

Cover, blanket. لِحَافٌ ج لُحُفٌ

An outer dress. مِلْحَفَةٌ ج مَلَاحِفُ

To reach, overtake. لَحِقَ يَلْحَقُ

To pursue, follow. لَاحَقَ

To annex, join to. أَلْحَقَ ب

To reach ; be annexed. إِلْتَحَقَ بِ

Overtaking, reaching. لَاحِقٌ

Adding ; annexing. إِلْحَاقٌ

Appendix ; supplement. مُلْحَقٌ

To be fleshy. لَحِمَ يَلْحَمُ لَحْماً

To be killed, massacred. لَحِمَ لَحْماً

To solder. لَحَمَ يَلْحُمُ لَحْماً

To join, unite. لَاحَمَ وَأَلْحَمَ ب

To kill one another. تَلَاحَمَ

To be soldered, united. إِلْتَحَمَ

To grow bloody, (combat). اِلتحم

Flesh, meat. لَحْمٌ ج لُحُومٌ

Woof (of a stuff). لُحْمَةٌ ج لُحَمٌ

Solder. لِحَامٌ

Butcher ; flesh-monger. لَحَّامٌ

Union ; alliance. إِلْتِحَامٌ

مَلْحَمَةٌ ج مَلاَحِمُ Combat, battle.

لَحَنَ يَلْحَنُ To make grammatical mistakes in speaking.

لَحَّنَ فِي ٱلْقِرَاءَةِ To chant.

لَحْنٌ ج أَلْحَانٌ Tone; chant, air.
Error of pronunciation.

صِنَاعَةُ ٱلأَلْحَانِ Musical art.

تَلْحِينٌ Chanting.

إِلْتَحَى To let one's beard grow.

لَحْيٌ مث لَحْيَانِ ج لُحِيٌّ Jaw-bone.

لِحَاءٌ Bark, (*sp.* inner bark).

لِحْيَةٌ ج لِحًى Beard.

لِحْيَةُ ٱلتَّيْسِ Wild salsify.

لَخَّةٌ Obscurity in speech.

لَخَّصَ To extract; sum up.

تَلْخِيصٌ Abstract. Explanation.

مُلَخَّصٌ Summary, abstract

لَدَّ يَلُدُّ لَدًّا To quarrel; oppose.

أَلَدُّ Violent in opposition.

لَدَغَ يَلْدَغُ لَدْغًا To sting, bite.

لَدْغَةٌ Sting, poisonous bite.

لَدُنَ يَلْدُنُ To be pliable, flexible.

لَدْنٌ ج لُدْنٌ Soft; supple.

لَدُنْ At, by, to, with, near to.

لَدَانَةٌ وَلُدُونَةٌ Softness, flexibility.

لَدَى At, by, to, with.

لَدَيْكَ Near or by thee; to thee.

لَذَّ يَلَذُّ To be sweet, agreeable.

لَذَّ وَٱلْتَذَّ وَٱسْتَلَذَّ بِ To enjoy.

تَلَذَّذَ To delight.

لَذَّةٌ ج لَذَّاتٌ Pleasure, delight.

لَذِيذٌ Sweet, pleasant.

مَلَذَّةٌ ج مَلاَذُّ Delight, pleasure.

لَذَعَ يَلْذَعُ لَذْعًا To burn, brand.

إِلْتَذَعَ To feel a burning pain.

لَذْعَةٌ A burn.

لَذَّاعٌ Stinging pungent.

لَوْذَعٌ وَلَوْذَعِيٌّ Ingenious; witty.

أَللاَّذِقِيَّةُ Latakia (*city*).

أَلَّذِي مث أَللَّذَانِ ج أَلَّذِينَ Who, which.

لَزَّ يَلُزُّ لَزًّا To press.

اِلْتَزَّ بِهِ To adhere to it.

لَازِبٌ Necessary; constant.

لَزِجَ يَلْزَجُ To stick, adhere.

لَزِجٌ Viscid, sticky, cohesive.

لُزُوجَةٌ Viscidity, stickiness.

لَزِقَ يَلْزَقُ وَاِلْتَزَقَ بِ To stick to.

لَازَقَ To adhere to another.

أَلْزَقَ وَلَزَّقَ To glue together.

لِزْقٌ That which adjoins.

لَزْقَةٌ وَلَزُوقٌ Poultice, plaster.

لَزِمَ يَلْزَمُ To adhere to; persist in; be necessary, follow of necessity.

لَازَمَ To cling to, persevere in.

أَلْزَمَ إِلْزَامًا To impose as a duty, compel.

إِلْتَزَمَ To be responsible; be forced. To farm taxes.

اِسْتَلْزَمَ To find necessary.

لَازِمٌ Necessary, unavoidable. Intransitive verb (*Gram.*).

لُزُومٌ Necessity.

اِلْزَامٌ Compulsion.

إِلْتِزَامٌ ج إِلْتِزَامَاتٌ Necessity; obligation. Renting; farming

(مِلْزَمَةٌ ج. مَلَازِمُ) Hand-vice; press.

مُلَازِمٌ Lieutenant (*mil.*).

مُلَازَمَةٌ Assiduity, application.

مَلْزُومٌ Obliged, compelled.

مُلْتَزِمٌ Farmer of revenues.

لَسَعَ يَلْسَعُ لَسْعًا To sting.

لَسِنَ يَلْسَنُ لَسَنًا To be eloquent.

لَسِنٌ ج لُسْنٌ Eloquent.

لِسَانٌ ج أَلْسُنٌ Tongue; language. Cape of land.

لِسَانُ ٱلْمِزْمَارِ Epiglottis.

لِسَانُ ٱلْحَالِ Speaking for itself.

لِسَانًا By word of mouth.

ذُو لِسَانَيْنِ Double dealer, false.

لِسَانِيٌّ Lingual.

لَاشَى	To destroy, annihilate.
تَلَاشَى	To vanish, perish.
مُلَاشَاةٌ وَتَلَاشٍ	Annihilation.
لِصٌّ ج لُصُوصٌ	Thief, robber.
لُصُوصِيَّةٌ	Robbery, thieving.
لَصِقَ يَلْصَقُ وَٱلْتَصَقَ بِ	To stick to.
لَاصَقَ	To cling to, be devoted to
أَلْصَقَ بِ	To fasten, join.
لَصُوقٌ	A dressing (for wounds).
مُلَاصِقٌ	Contiguous.
مُلَاصَقَةٌ	Contiguity, adherence.
لَطَخَ يَلْطَخُ وَلَطَّخَ بِ	To soil with.
تَلَطَّخَ بِ	To be soiled with.
لُطْخَةٌ	A soil, stain.
لَطُفَ يَلْطُفُ بِ	To be kind.
لَطَّفَ	To soften, mitigate.
لَاطَفَ	To treat with kindness.
تَلَطَّفَ لِ	To be polite, courteous to.
إِسْتَلْطَفَ	To find pretty or nice.
لُطْفٌ	Friendliness. Favour.
حَرَكَةُ لُطْفٍ	Light illness.
لَطَافَةٌ	Delicacy. Tenuity.
لَطِيفٌ ج لُطَفَاءُ	Graceful; kind. Rare (not dense).
أَللَّطِيفُ	God.
لَطِيفَةٌ ج لَطَائِفُ	Witty saying.
تَلَطُّفٌ	Friendliness; courtesy.
مُلَاطَفَةٌ	Friendly treatment.
لَطَمَ يَلْطِمُ لَطْمًا	To slap.
تَلَاطَمَ وَٱلْتَطَمَ	To clash, collide.
لَطْمَةٌ ج لَطَمَاتٌ	Slap on the face.
لَطَا يَلْطُو	To take shelter.
لَظَّ يَلُظُّ	To cleave to.
لَظِيَ يَلْظَى لَظًى	To blaze (fire).
تَلَظَّى وَٱلْتَظَى	To be enflamed.
لَظًى	Fire; flame
لَعِبَ ـِ لَعْبًا	To play, sport, jest.

لَاعَبَ — To play, sport with.
لَعْبٌ ولَعِبٌ — Play, sport.
لَعْبُ ٱلْقِمَارِ — Gambling.
لُعْبَةٌ ج لُعَبٌ — A game, sport.
لُعَابٌ — Saliva, spittle. Mucilage.
لُعَابِيٌّ — Mucilaginous, slimy.
لَعَّابٌ وَلَعِّيبٌ — Professional player.
أُلْعُوبَةٌ — Play, pleasantry.
تَلَاعُبٌ — Sporting, jesting.
مَلْعَبٌ ج مَلَاعِبُ — Place to play in.
مَلْعَبَةٌ — Toy, plaything.
(مَلْعُوبٌ ج مَلَاعِيبُ) — A trick in play.
لَعَجَ يَلْعَجُ لَعْجًا — To pain, burn.
لَاعِجٌ ج لَوَاعِجُ — Burning pain.
لَعِقَ يَلْعَقُ لَعْقًا — To lick.
لَعُوقٌ — Electuary.
مِلْعَقَةٌ ج مَلَاعِقُ — Spoon.
لَعَلَّ وَعَلَّ — Perhaps, may be.
لَعَلَّ زَيْدًا قَائِمٌ — It may be that Zeid is standing.
لَعْلَعَ وتَلَعْلَعَ — To shine, gleam.
لَعَنَ يَلْعَنُ لَعْنًا — To curse.
تَلَاعَنَ — To curse one another.
لَعْنٌ وَلَعْنَةٌ ج لَعَنَاتٌ — Imprecation.
أَللَّعِينُ — Satan.
مَلْعُونٌ ج مَلَاعِينُ — Cursed.
لَغُبَ ـُ — To be very tired.
تَلَغَّبَ — To chase long.
لُغْزٌ ج أَلْغَازٌ — Riddle; enigma.
مُلْغَزٌ — Enigmatic, ambiguous.
لَغَطَ يَلْغَطُ — To speak indistinctly.
لَغْطٌ ج أَلْغَاطٌ — Noise; sound.
لُغْمٌ ج لُغُومٌ — Mine, blast.
لُغْمَجِيٌّ — Miner; blaster.
لَغَا يَلْغُو — To speak.
أَلْغَى — To exclude, abolish.
لُغَةٌ ج لُغَاتٌ — Language, dialect; idiom, expression.

عِلْمُ ٱللُّغَةِ Lexicography.

أَهْلُ ٱللُّغَةِ Lexicographers.

لَغْوٌ Faulty language, nonsense.

لُغَوِيّ Etymological ; linguistic.

إِلْغَاءٌ Abolishing, annulling.

مُلْغًى Suppressed, abolished.

لَفَّ يَلُفُّ لَفًّا To wrap up, roll.

ٱلْتَفَّ To wrap one's self up.

إِلْتَفَّ To be entwined.

(لَفَّةٌ ج لَفَّاتٌ) A turban.

لِفَافَةٌ ج لَفَائِف Bandage.

لَفِيفٌ Mixed crowd.

مَلْفُوفٌ Wrapped up. Cabbage.

لَفَتَ يَلْفِتُ لَفْتًا To twist, turn.

إِلْتَفَتَ إِلَى To consider, regard.

لِفْتٌ Turnip, rape.

لَفْتَةٌ ج لَفَتَات Side-glance.

إِلْتِفَاتٌ Attention ; favour.

لَفَحَ يَلْفَحُ لَفْحًا To burn, scorch.

لَفُوحٌ وَلَافِحٌ ج لَوَافِحُ Scorching.

لُفَّاحٌ Mandrake (plant).

لَفَظَ يَلْفِظُ To pronounce. Dei.

لَفَظَ وَتَلَفَّظَ بِ To utter.

لَفْظٌ ج أَلْفَاظٌ Utterance ; word.

لَفْظًا وَمَعْنًى As regards the wording and the meaning.

لَفْظَةٌ ج لَفَظَاتٌ A word ; an utterance.

لَفْظِيٌّ Verbal.

لَفَقَ يَلْفِقُ لَفْقًا To seam.

لَفَّقَ To interpolate, falsify, lie.

مُلَفَّقٌ Embellished by falsehood.

لَفْلَفَ To wrap up, envelop.

تَلَافِيفُ ٱلدِّمَاغِ Convolutions of the brain.

أَلْفَى إِلْفَاءً To find.

تَلَافَى To mend ; take up.

لَقَّبَ بِ To give a title

لَقَبٌ ج أَلْقَابٌ Surname ; title.

Surnamed; having a title. مُلَقَّبٌ

To fecundate. لَقَحَ يَلْقَحُ لَقْحاً

To be fecundated. لَقِحَ يَلْقَحُ لَقَحاً

To fecundate. لَقَّحَ وَأَلْقَحَ

Fecundation. لَقْحٌ

Pollen. لِقَاحٌ

To delay, be late. (تَلَقَّسَ)

To pick up; glean. لَقَطَ يَلْقُطُ

To glean. Catch. تَلَقَّطَ وَٱلْتَقَطَ

Freed slave. لَاقِطٌ م لَاقِطَةٌ

Picking up; gleaning. لِقَاطٌ

What is picked up. لُقَاطَةٌ

Foundling. لَقِيطٌ ج لُقَطَاءُ

Pincers; tongs. مِلْقَطٌ ج مَلَاقِطُ

To snatch away. لَقِفَ وَٱلْتَقَفَ

Stork. لَقْلَقٌ وَلَقْلَاقٌ ج لَقَالِقُ

To swallow. لَقِمَ يَلْقَمُ لَقْماً

To feed. لَقَّمَ وَأَلْقَمَ

To swallow. تَلَقَّمَ وَٱلْتَقَمَ

Morsel, mouthful. لُقْمَةٌ ج لُقَمٌ

To understand readily. لَقِنَ يَلْقَنُ

To instruct, teach. لَقَّنَ

To learn. تَلَقَّنَ

Of quick understanding. لَقِنٌ

Facial paralysis. لَقْوَةٌ

To meet; see, find. لَقِيَ يَلْقَى

To go to meet, meet. لَاقَى لِقَاءً

To throw away, fling. أَلْقَى بِ

To cast away from. أَلْقَى عَنْ

To propound, propose. أَلْقَى عَلَى

To receive. To encounter. تَلَقَّى

To meet one another. تَلَاقَى وَٱلْتَقَى

To lie on one's back. إِسْتَلْقَى عَلَى

Towards. تِلْقَاءَ

Spontaneously. مِنْ تِلْقَاءِ نَفْسِهِ

Mutual encounter. تَلَاقٍ

يَوْمُ ٱلتَّلاقي	The day of resurrection.
ملتقًى عَلَى	Leaning or resting upon.
مُلْتقًى وملْتقًى	Meeting-place.
ملاقاةٌ	Meeting.
لَكٌّ	Lac (resin) ; sealing wax.
لكٌّ ج ألكاكٌ	Ten millions. Lac.
لكز يلكز لكزاً	To push, thrust.
لكِع يلْكعُ لكْعاً ولكاعة	To be vile.
لكَعٌ م لكاع	Dirty, vile, abject.
لكم يلْكمُ لكماً	To strike with the fist.
ملاكمة	Boxing, fighting.
لكِنْ ولكِنَّ	But, yet, however.
(لكَنٌ ج ألْكانٌ)	Large copper basin.
ألْكنُ م لكْناء ج لُكْنٌ	Stammerer.
لكَي ولِكيْما	In order that.
لمْ	Not, not yet.
لَمْ يأكل	He has not eaten.
لمْ	Why ? (for لِمَا)
أَلَمْ وأَفلَمْ وأَوَلمْ	Was it not ?
لَمَّ يلُمُّ لمّاً	To gather, amass.
أَلَمَّ ب	To come upon, befall.
لمَّا	When. Not yet.
لمَّا كانَ	Inasmuch as...
لِمَاذا (لِمَا ـ ذا)	Why ?
لمَّةٌ	Calamity ; misfortune.
لِمَّة ج لِممٌ ولِمامٌ	Lock of hair.
لَممٌ	Slight madness.
إِلْمام	Knowledge, experience.
مُلِمَّةٌ ج مُلِمَّاتٌ	Calamity ; chance.
ملْمومٌ	Collected. Slightly mad.
لمْحةٌ	Light meal before lunch.
لمَح يلْمحُ إلى	To glance at.
لمح بالْبصر	To direct the sight.
لمَح يلْمح	To shine, gleam.
لمَّح إِلَى	To hint at, suggest.
لمْحةُ	A glance resemblance.

لَامِحٌ ولُمُوحٌ	Gleaming, shining.
تَلْمِيحٌ	Allusion, hint.
مَلَامِحُ	Points of resemblance.
لَمَسَ يَلْمِسُ لَمْسًا وَلَامَسَ	To touch.
تَلَمَّسَ	To seek for repeatedly.
إِلْتَمَسَ مِنْ	To entreat, ask for.
لَمْسٌ ومَلْمَسٌ	Touch, feeling.
إِلْتِمَاسٌ	Entreaty supplication.
مَلْمُوسٌ	Touched.
لَمَعَ يَلْمَعُ وَٱلْتَمَعَ	To shine, flash.
أَلْمَعَ بِ	To beckon with.
لَمْعٌ ولَمَعَانٌ	Flash, brightness.
لُمْعَةٌ ج لُمَعٌ	A small quantity.
لَامِعٌ ج لُمَّعٌ	That which shines.
أَلْمَعِيٌّ	Having a sharp genius.
أَلْمَعِيَةُ	Genius, wit.
مُلَمَّعٌ	Mottled, spotted.
لَمْلَمَ	To gather, get together.
تَلَمْلَمَ	To be gathered.
لَمْلَمٌ	A numerous army.
لَنْ	Not. By no means.
لَهِبَ يَلْهَبُ	To flame, blaze(fire).
لَهَّبَ وَأَلْهَبَ	To make to blaze.
تَلَهَّبَ وَٱلْتَهَبَ	To flame, blaze.
لَهَبٌ ولَهِيبٌ	Flame.
إِلْتِهَابُ ج إِلْتِهَابَاتٌ	Inflammation.
أَللَّاهُوتُ	The divine nature.
عِلْمُ ٱللَّاهُوتِ	Theology.
لَاهُوتِيٌّ	Theologian.
لَهَثَ يَلْهَثُ	To pant. Thirst.
لَهْثَانُ	Thirsty ; out of breath.
لَهِجَ يَلْهَجُ بِ	To be addicted to.
أَلْهَجَ بِ	To be taken up with.
لَهْجَةٌ	Voice, tone.
لَهِفَ يَلْهَفُ وتَلَهَّفَ عَلَى	To regret.
لَهْفٌ	Regret, grief, sadness.

Oh ! Alas ! يا لَهفاهُ وَيا لهفي على

Grieved. لَهفانُ م لهفى

To swallow at one gulp. لَهِم يَلْهمُ والْتَهم

To inspire. الْهمَ

Greedy, voracious. لَهِمٌ

Divine guidance. إِلْهامُ ج إِلْهاماتٌ

To play. لَها يَلْهو لهْواً

To be infatuated with. لَهَا بِ

To forget ; neglect. (لها عنْ)

To preoccupy. لَهَّى وأَلْهى (عنْ)

To be diverted. تلاهى وَالْتهى

Amusement ; diversion. لَهْوٌ

Soft palate. لُهاةٌ ج لَهواتٌ

Palatial. لَهَوِيٌّ

Diverted, thoughtless. لاهٍ

Amusement. ملْهًى ج مَلاهٍ

If. O that. لوْ

Although, though. و لَوْ

Unless ; if not. لوْ لَمْ

Were it not for... لوْلاَ ولَوْ ما

To thirst. Be restless. لاَبَ يَلُوبُ

Beans. لُوباء ولُوبِيَا

Pl. of. ٱلّتِي أَللوَاتي

To stain ; soil. Mix. لوَّثَ

To be soiled. تَلوَّثَ تَلَوُّثاً

To glimmer ; appear. لاَحَ يلُوحُ

Plate ; tablet. Shoulder-blade. لوْحٌ ج أَلْوَاحٌ

Schedule. لاَئِحَةٌ ج لوَائِح

Appearances. لَوائحُ

To take refuge in (ب) لاَذَ يلُوذُ

Refuge ; fortress. ملاَذٌ

Almond (tree and fruit). لوْزٌ

The tonsils. (أَللَّوزَتَان)

To taste. لاَس يَلُوسُ لوْساً

To be impatient. لاَعَ يَلُوعُ

To torture. لوَّعَ تَلْوِيعاً

لَوْعَةٌ — Pain ; anguish ; torture.

لُوفٌ — A plant, the Arum.

لَاكَ يَلُوكُ لَوْكًا — To masticate.

(لُوكَنْدَةٌ) — Hotel (*Ital*).

لَوْلَا — Were it not for....

لَوْلَبٌ ج لَوَالِبُ — Screw.

لَوْلَبِيٌّ — Spiral.

لَامَ يَلُومُ لَوْمًا — To blame censure.

تَلَاوَمَ — To blame ; one another.

لَوْمٌ — Blame ; censure.

لَائِمٌ — Blamer ; censurer.

مَلَامٌ وَمَلَامَةٌ — Blame ; censure.

مَلُومٌ — Blamable ; reprehensible.

أَلْعَظْمُ ٱللَّامِيُّ — Hyoid bone.

(لُومَانٌ) — State-prison.

لَوَّنَ تَلْوِينًا — To colour.

تَلَوَّنَ — To be coloured.

لَوْنٌ ج أَلْوَانٌ — Colour. Kind.

مُتَلَوِّنٌ — Changeful.

(لَوَنْدَا) — Lavander.

لَوَى يَلْوِي لَيًّا — To twist.

لَوَّى وَأَلْوَى — To bend.

إِلْتَوَى — To be bent, deflected.

لِوَاءٌ ج أَلْوِيَةٌ — Flag, standard. District.

أَمِيرُ ٱللِّوَاءِ — A general of the army.

إِلْتِوَاءٌ — Curvature.

لَيْتَ — O that ! Would that !

لَيْتَ زَيْدٌ ذَاهِبٌ — Would that Zeid were going !

لَيْتَنِي فَعَلْتُهُ — Would that I had done it !

لَيْثٌ ج لُيُوثٌ — Lion.

لَيْسَ — Not.

لَيْسَ ٱللّٰهُ بِظَالِمٍ — God is not unjust.

لِيفٌ — Fiber of palm, &c.

لَاقَ يَلِيقُ — To be fit, suitable.

لَائِقٌ — Suitable, proper.

لَيْلٌ ج لَيَالٍ . وَلَيْلَةٌ ج لَيْلَاتٌ — Night.

Lest. (From لِأَنْ لَا) لئَلَّا

Lest he should say. لِئَلَّا يَقُولَ

Lemon. ايمُونٌ

To be soft, tender. لانَ يَلِين

To soften. لَيَّن تَلْيِيناً وأَلانَ إِلاَنَةً

To conciliate. لاين مُلاَينَة

To become soft, tender. تَلَيَّنَ

To coax, conciliate. تَلَيَّنَ لَهُ

Tender, flexible. لِينٌ ج لَيِّنُونَ

Softness. Diarrhœa. لِيِّنٌ

Softness, pliability. لُيُونَةٌ

Laxative, aperient. مُلَيِّنٌ

Portico. (لِيوَانٌ) إِيوَانٌ

م

As a numeral sign=40. م

What? مَا

What has he done? ما فعلَ

What he has done. ما صَنَعَ

A certain affair. أَمْرٌ مَا

As long as I live. ما دُمْتُ حيًّا

How beautiful! ما أَجْمَلَهُ

I do not know. مَا أَدْرِي

What? ما ذا

What art thou doing? مَاذَا تَفْعَلُ

Why hast thou come? لِمَا ذا جِئْتَ

Nature, essence. مَاهِيَّةٌ

Wages, pay. ماهيّةٌ ج مَاهيات

Water (*see* موه) مَاءٌ ج مِياهٌ

Inner angle of the eye. مُوق

To provide. مأن يمأن مأنا

Provisions. مؤونةٌ ومؤنةٌ ج مؤن

One hundred. مِئةٌ ومائةٌ ج مِئات

Centenary. مِئويّ

Metre (measure). مترٌ ج امتارٌ

To grant. متّع وأمتع ب

To enjoy. تمتّع بِ ومِن

Enjoyment, privilege. متعةٌ ج مِتعٌ

Furniture, effects. متاعٌ ج امتعةٌ

Enjoyment, privilege. تمتّعٌ واستمتاعٌ

To be firm. مَتن يمتن متانةً

Text of a book. مَتْنٌ

Solidity, firmness. مَتانةٌ

Strong, solid, robust. مَتينٌ

When? When. مَتى

When, at the time when. مَتى مَا

To resemble. مثَل يمثُل ومَاثل

To compare to. مثّل ومَاثل بِ

To stand before someone. مَثل يمثُل بَيْن يديه

He imagined (a thing). تمثّل لهُ

To imitate. تمثّل بِ

To resemble each other. تماثل

To be nearly convalescent. تماثل مِن علّتهِ

To obey order. إمتثل الأمرَ

Similar, like. مِثْلٌ ج أمثالٌ

As well as. مِثلما

Proverb; a saying. مَثَلٌ ج أمثالٌ

To give an example. ضرب مَثلاً

Model. Example. مِثالٌ ج امثِلةٌ

Lesson. (مَثالةٌ ج مثالاتٌ ومَثائل)

Resembling. مثيلٌ ج مثُلٌ

The best. أمثل م مثلى ج اماثِل

Example. Lesson. أُمثولةٌ

Image, figure. تِمْثالٌ ج تَماثِيلُ

Assimilation. Analogy. تَمْثِيلُ

Bladder. مَثانَةٌ ج مَثانَاتٌ

To spit; reject. مجَّ يَمُجُّ مَجًّا

To be great, glorious. مجدَ يَمْجدُ

To glorify; exalt, honour. مجدَ

To be glorified, praised. تمجدَ

Glory, praise. مجدٌ ج أَمجادٌ

Glorification, praising. تمجيدٌ

Noble, glorious. مَجِيدٌ وماجدٌ

The Glorious (God). أَلْمجيدُ

More glorious. أَمجدُ ج أَماجدُ

Hungarian. مجرٌ

Hungary. بِلادُ آلْمجرِ

Magians. مجوسٌ

Creed of the Magians. أَلْمجُوسيَّةُ

Code, book, (*see* جلل) مَجَلَّةُ

To jest. مجن يمجن مُجُوناً

Buffoon, jester. مجّانٌ

Gratuitously; freely. مَجَّاناً

Yolk of an egg. مُحٌّ

Litter, panier. محَّارةٌ

To purify. مَحَص يَمْحص مَحْصاً بِ

To purify. To try, prove. مَحَّصَ

To be sincere. مَحَضَ يَمْحَضُ مَحْضاً لهُ

Pure, unmixed. مَحْضٌ

To blot out, efface. محقَ يَمْحقُ مَحْقاً

To be effaced. إِمْتَحَقَ وآمَّحقَ

Perdition, annihilation. مَحْقٌ

Waning of the moon. مَحاقٌ

To brawl, dispute. مَحَكَ يَمْحَكُ مَحْكاً

To quarrel with one. مَاحَكَهُ

A quarrel, brawl. مُماحكَةٌ

Quarrelsome. مَحِكٌ ومَاحِكٌ

To be sterile. مَحَلَ يَمْحَلُ وَأَمْحلَ

Sterility, barrenness. مَحْلٌ

مَحَّالٌ Cunning, deceitful.

ماحِلٌ وَمُمْحِلٌ Barren, unfruitful.

مَحَنَ يَمْحَنُ محنًا To try, test.

إِمْتَحن To try, examine.

مِحْنَةٌ ج مِحَنٌ Trial, affliction.

إِمْتِحانٌ Experience; examination.

مَحا يَمْحُو مَحْوًا To efface, blot out.

امَّحى (إِنْمحى) To be blotted out.

ممحوٌّ Effected; blotted out.

مِمحَاةٌ A wiper.

مُخٌّ ج مِخاخٌ Marrow; brain.

مَخر يَمْخَرُ To plough the water.

ماخِرةٌ ج مَواخِرُ A ship.

ماخورٌ Wine shop. House of ill-fame.

مَخض يَمخَضُ مَخْضًا To churn.

مَخَضَتْ تَمْخَضُ وَتمخَّضت To suffer the pains of childbirth.

تمخَّض وَامْتخض To be churned.

مَخاضٌ Labour of childbirth.

مخيضٌ Butter-milk.

مِمخضٌ A churning-vessel.

مَخط يَمْخط To blow the nose.

مُخاطٌ Mucus.

مُخاطُ ٱلشَّيْطانِ أَوِ ٱلشَّمْسِ Gossamar.

مُخاطيٌّ Mucous.

مُخْلٌ ج أَمخَالٌ ومُخُولٌ Lever.

(مَخْمَضَ فاهُ وتَمَخْمَضَ) To rinse the mouth.

مدَّ يمدُّ مدًّا To spread, extend.

مدَّ ٱلْقَلمَ To dip the pen in ink.

مَدَّ وَأَمَدَّ To help, aid, assist.

إِمْتَدَّ إِلى To reach; extend to.

تمدَّدَ To be extended, lie down.

إِستَمدَّ To seek help.

مَدٌّ ج مُدُودٌ Tide; flux.

مَدٌّ ومدَّةٌ The sign. (آ)

مُدٌّ ج أَمدادٌ A dry measure.

مدَّةٌ ج مُددٌ Period; while.

Assistance. مَدَدٌ وَإِمْدَادٌ

Ink. Oil (f a lamp). مِدَادٌ

Matter. مَادَّةٌ ج مَوَادُّ

Material. مَادِّيٌّ

Long. مَدِيدٌ

Extensin ; dilatati n. تَمَدُّدٌ

Prolonged ; extended. مُمْتَدٌّ

A letter with. مَدّة (آ) مَمْدُودٌ

To braise, extol. مَدَحَ يَمْدَحُ

To praise, Be extended. إِمْتَدَحَ

Eulogy. مَدْحٌ .وَمَدِيحٌ ج مَدَائِحُ

Panegyrist. مَادِحٌ وَمَدَّاحٌ

Village, town, city. مَدَرٌ

Inhabitants of towns. أَهْلُ ٱلْمَدَرِ

To build cities ; civilize. مَدَّنَ

To become civilized. تَمَدَّنَ

Refinement, civilizati n. تَمَدُّنٌ

City, town. مَدِينَةٌ ج مُدُنٌ وَمَدَائِنُ

Medina (in Arabia). أَلْمَدِينَةُ

Bagdad. مَدِينَةُ ٱلسَّلَام

Citizen, townsman. مَدَنِيٌّ

To grant one a delay. مَادَى

To take a long time. تَمَادَى

Distance, extent ; end. مَدًى

Large knife. مُدْيَةٌ ج مُدًى

Since. مُذْ

To become rotten. مَذِرَ يَمْذَرُ

To disperse, scatter. مَذَّرَ

Hither and thither. شَذَرَ مَذَرَ

Spoilt, rotten (egg) ; foul. مَذِرٌ

Insincere, dissembler. مُمَاذِقٌ

To pass, pass by. مَرَّ يَمُرُّ

To embitter, make bitter. مَرَّرَ

He caused him to pass. أَمَرَّهُ

To continue ; last. إِسْتَمَرَّ

Course, succession. مَرٌّ وَمُرُورٌ

مُرٌّ	Bitter. Myrrh (plant).
مَرَّةٌ ج مِرَارٌ وَمَرَّاتٌ	Once.
مِرَارًا	Several times, often.
مِرَّةٌ ج مِرَرٌ	Gall; bile.
أَلْمَارُّ ذِكْرُهُ	Aforesaid.
مَرَارَةٌ	Bitterness. Gall-bladder.
أَمَرُّ	More bitter.
مَمَرٌّ	Passage; pathway.
مُسْتَمِرٌّ	Continued, continual.
مَرِئَ يَمْرَأُ	To be healthy (food).
مَرْءٌ وَامْرُؤٌ	Man.
مَرْأَةٌ وَامْرَأَةٌ	Woman.
مُرُوءَةٌ وَمُرُوَّةٌ	Courage, bravery.
مَرِيءٌ	Gullet, œsophagus.
مَرَثَ يَمْرُثُ	To moisten, soak.
مَرْجٌ ج مُرُوجٌ	Meadow, pasture.
هَرْجٌ وَمَرْجٌ	Confusion, disorder.
مَرْجَانٌ	Coral.
مَرِحَ يَمْرَحُ	To be very gay.
مَرِحٌ ج مَرْحَى وَمَرَاحَى	Very gay.
مَرْحَبًا	(*See* رحب)
مَرَخَ يَمْرَخُ مَرْخًا	To anoint.
مَرُوخٌ	Liniment.
أَلْمِرِّيخُ	Mars (planet).
مَرَدَ يَمْرُدُ وَتَمَرَّدَ	To rebel, revolt.
تَمَرَّدَ عَلَى	To be proud, insolent.
مَارِدٌ ج مَرَدَةٌ	Rebellious.
أَمْرَدُ ج مُرْدٌ	Beardless (youth).
مَرْدَقُوشٌ وَمَرْزَنْجُوشٌ	Marjoram.
مَرَسَ يَمْرُسُ	To steep, soak.
مَارَسَ	To exercise, practice.
مَرَسَةٌ ج مَرَسٌ وَأَمْرَاسٌ	Rope, cord.
مُمَارَسَةٌ	Exercise, practice.
مَرْسِينٌ	Myrtle-tree.
مَارِسْتَانٌ	Hospital.
مَرِضَ يَمْرَضُ	To fall ill, be sick.

To nurse the sick.	مَرَّضَ
To make ill, or sick.	أَمْرَضَ
To feign illness.	تَمارَضَ
Disease, illness.	مَرَضٌ ج امْراضٌ
Sick, ill.	مَرِيضٌ ج مَرْضَى
To pull out (hair).	مَرَطَ يَمْرُطُ مَرْطاً
Scanty-haired.	أَمْرَطُ م مَرْطاء
To graze (cattle).	مَرَعَ يَمْرَعُ مَرْعاً
To roll one in the dust.	مَرَّغَ
To roll in the dust.	تَمَرَّغَ
To penetrate, pass.	مَرَقَ يَمْرُقُ مِنْ
Broth ; gravy, sauce.	مَرَقٌ ومَرَقَةٌ
A heretic.	مارِقٌ
Marble.	مَرْمَرٌ
To become elastic.	مَرَنَ يَمْرُنُ
To be accustomed to.	مَرَنَ عَلَى
To train, habituate.	مَرَّنَ عَلَى
To be habituated to.	تَمَرَّنَ عَلَى
Elastic, flexible.	مَرِنٌ
Elasticity, flexibility.	مُرُونَةٌ
Maronite.	مَارُونِيٌّ ج مَوارِنَةٌ
Practice; exercise.	تَمْرِينٌ وتَمَرُّنٌ
Trained ; inured.	مُمَرَّنٌ
Ointment.	مَرْهَمٌ ج مَراهِمُ
Saint *(Syriac)*.	مار ومَاري
Dispute, quarrel.	مِرْيَةٌ
To suck.	مَزَّ يَمُزُّ مَزًّا
Sourish. Insipid.	مُزٌّ ومَزَّةٌ
To mix.	مَزَجَ يَمْزُجُ مَزْجاً
To associate with.	مازَجَ
To get mixed with...	إِمْتَزَجَ ب
Mixture, amalgamation.	إِمْتِزاجٌ
Mixture, alloy.	مَزِيجٌ
Temperament.	مِزاجٌ ج امْزِجَة
To joke, jest.	مَزَحَ يَمْزَحُ مَزْحاً
To jest together.	تَمازَحَ

Jesting, bantering.	مُزاحٌ
A kind of beer.	مِزْرٌ
To tear to pieces.	مَزَق يَمْزِق وَمَزَّق
To disperse (a crowd).	مَزَّق
To be torn into pieces.	تَمَزَّق
Merit; trait.	مَزِيَّةٌ ج مزايا
To touch.	مَسَّ يَمَسُّ مَسًّا
To touch one another.	تَمَاسَّ
Touch; contact. Insanity.	مَسٌّ
Urgent business.	حاجةٌ مَاسةٌ
Tangent *(geom.)*.	مُمَاسٌّ
Touched. Insane.	مَمْسُوسٌ
A kind of shoe.	مِسْتٌ ج مُسُوتٌ
To wipe; anoint.	مَسَح يَمْسَحُ مَسْحًا
To measure land.	مَسَح الأَرْض
Wiping. Anointing.	مَسْحٌ
Sack-cloth.	مِسْحٌ ج مُسُوحٌ
Land-survey.	مِسَاحَةٌ
Mensuration.	عِلْمُ المِسَاحَةِ
Anointed.	مسيحٌ ج مُسَحاء وَمَسْحى
Christ, the Messiah.	أَلْمسيحُ
Antichrist.	أَلْمسيحُ الدَّجَّالُ
Christian.	مَسِيحيٌّ ج مَسيحيُّون
Christianity.	أَلْمسيحيةُ
Land-surveyor.	مسَّاحٌ ج مَسَّاحون
Flat barren land.	مسحاء
Crocodile.	تِمْساحٌ ج تماسيحُ
To change; distort.	مَسَخ يَمْسَخُ مَسْخًا
Distorted, corrupted.	مِسْخ
To plait or twist.	مَسَد يَمْسُدُ
To rub with the hand.	(مَسَّدَ)
Cord of fibres.	مَسَدٌ ج مِسَادٌ
Massage.	(تمسيدٌ)
To hold, seize.	مَسَكَ يَمْسُكُ وأَمْسَكَ
To retain, hold back.	أَمْسَكَ
To refrain from.	أَمْسَكَ عن

مِسْكٌ Musk.
إِمْسَاكٌ Avarice. Abstinence.
مُمَسَّكٌ Scented with musk.
مَسَّى To wish one good evening.
أَمْسَى To enter into the evening.
مَسَاءٌ Eve, evening.
مَسَاءَ ٱلْخَيْرِ Good evening.
مَشَطَ يَمْشُطُ وَمَشَّطَ To comb (the hair).
مُشْطٌ ج أَمْشَاطٌ Comb; rake.
مُشْطُ ٱلرِّجْلِ Instep of the foot.
مَاشِطٌ م مَاشِطَةٌ Hair-dresser.
مَشْقٌ Slenderness.
مُشَاقَةٌ The refuse of silk.
مَمْشُوقٌ Slim, Slender.
مِشْمِشٌ Apricots.
مِشْمِشَةٌ An apricot.
مَشَى يَمْشِي وَتَمَشَّى To walk; go.
مَشَّى وَأَمْشَى To cause to walk.
مَاشَى To walk with one.
مَشْيٌ Walking, marching.
مَاشٍ ج مُشَاةٌ Walker on foot; foot-soldier.
مَاشِيَةٌ ج مَوَاشٍ Flocks, cattle.
مَمْشًى ج مَمَاشٍ Corridor.
مَصَّ يَمُصُّ وَٱمْتَصَّ To suck; sip.
إِمْتَصَّ To absorb.
مُصَّةٌ وَمُصَاصٌ What is sucked.
(قَصَبُ ٱلْمَصِّ) Sugar-cane.
خَيْطٌ مَصِيصٌ Twine, pack-thread.
مِمَصٌّ Siphon; sucking tube.
إِمْتِصَاصٌ Absorption.
مَصَّرَ To build cities.
مِصْرُ Egypt. Cairo.
مِصْرٌ ج أَمْصَارٌ Great city. Limits.
مِصْرِيٌّ ج مِصْرِيُّونَ Egyptian.
مُصْرَانٌ ج مَصَارِينُ Intestines.
مُصْطَكَى Mastic (kind of gum).

To drop, trickle. مَصَل يَمْصُلُ

Whey. Serum. مَصْلٌ

To cause pain. مَضَّ يَمُضُّ وَأَمَضَّ

Pain, grief. مَضٌّ وَمَضَّةٌ وَمَضَضٌ

To masticate, chew. مَضغ يَمْضَغُ

Mastication, chewing. مَضْغٌ

Morsel. مَضْغَةٌ ج مُضَغٌ

To rinse, wash. مَضْمَضَ

To pass; go, depart. مضى يَمْضي

To sign (a letter). مَضَى على

To take, carry off. مضى بِ

To execute, accomplish. أَمْضَى

To pass off, carried out. تَمَضَّى

Execution, Signature. إِمْضَاءٌ

The past; past tense. الْمَاضي

Signer; subscriber. مُمْضٍ

To draw; stretch. مطّ يَمُطُّ

To rain. مَطَر يَمْطُرُ وَامطر

To pray for rain. إِسْتَمْطَرَ

Rain; heavy rain. مَطَرٌ ج امْطَارٌ

Rainy (weather). مَاطِرٌ وَمُمْطِرٌ

A water-skin. مَطَرَةٌ

Bishop. مُطْرَانٌ ج مطارِنَةٌ

To defer, put off. مَطَلَ وَمَاطَل

Delay, putting off. مَطْلٌ وَمُمَاطَلَةٌ

One who puts off. مُمَاطِلٌ

Deferred. مَمْطُولٌ

To mount, ride. أَمْطَى وَامْتَطَى

Beast of burden. مَطِيَّةٌ ج مَطَايَا

With, together with. مع وَمَعْ

Nevertheless, yet. مع ذَلِك

Although. مع أَنْ

Together, simultaneously. مَعاً

Company, attendance. معيةٌ

Stomach. معدةٌ وَمِعدةٌ ج مِعدٌ

Goats *(coll noun)*. معزٌ ومعزَى

A goat.	ماعِزٌ ج مَواعِز
Goat-herd.	معازٌ
To crush.	(مَعَسَ يَمْعَسُ مَعْساً)
To pull out (hair).	معَطَ يَمْعَطُ
Hairless.	أَمْعَطُ م معْطاءُ ج مُعْطٌ
To rub.	معَكَ يَمْعَكُ مَعْكاً
To delay paying.	ماعَكَ بدَيْنِهِ
Tumult of battle.	مَعْمَعَةٌ ج مَعامِعُ
To consider.	أَمْعَنَ ٱلنَّظَرَ. وَتَمَعَّنَ
Consideration.	إِمْعانٌ وَتَمَعُّنٌ
Utensil ; boat.	ماعُونٌ ج مَواعِينُ
Running water.	مَعِينٌ ج مُعُنٌ
Intestine.	معيٌ ومِعًى ج أَمْعاءٌ
Red earth for dyeing.	مَغَرَةٌ
To suffer from colic.	مُغِصَ
Colic gripes.	مَغْصٌ
To stretch.	مَغَطَ يَمْغَطُ. وَمَغَّطَ
To be stretched.	تَمَغَّطَ وَٱمْتَغَطَ

To draw (a sword).	إِمْتَغَطَ
To speak indistinctly.	مَغْمَغَ ٱلْكَلامَ
To magnetize.	(مَغْطَسَ)
The magnet.	مَغْنَطِيسٌ
To hate, detest.	مَقَتَ يَمْقُتُ مَقْتاً
Hatred ; aversion.	مَقْتٌ
Hated, detested.	مقيتٌ وَمَمْقُوتٌ
Sebesten (*Cordia myxa*).	مِقْساسٌ
To look at.	مَقَلَ يَمْقُلُ مَقْلاً
The eye ; eye-ball.	مُقْلَةٌ ج مُقَلٌ
Mecca (city in Arabia).	مَكَّةُ
Meccan.	مَكِّيٌّ وَمَكَّاوِيٌّ
Weaving-shuttle.	مَكُّوكُ
To abide, dwell.	مَكَثَ يَمْكُثُ
Sojourn, stay.	مَكْثٌ
To deceive.	مَكَرَ يَمْكُرُ وَمَاكَرَ
Trick, deceit, fraud.	مَكْرٌ
Cunning, deceitful.	ماكِرٌ ج مَكَرَةٌ

مَكَّارٌ Deceiver ; trickster.

مَكَسَ وَمَكَّسَ To collect taxes.

مَكْسٌ ج مُكُوسٌ Custom duties.

ماكِسٌ وَمَكَّاسٌ Tax-gatherer.

مَكُنَ يَمْكُنُ To be strong.

مَكَّنَ To strengthen.

مَكَّنَ وَأَمْكَنَ مِن To enable.

أَمْكَنَهُ To be possible for (him).

يُمْكِنُ أَنْ It is possible that...

تَمَكَّنَ To be stable, firm, solid.

تَمَكَّن مِنْ To be able, overcome.

مَكْنَةٌ Possibility. Power.

مَكان ج أَماكِن Place ; station.

مَكانَةٌ Influence ; power.

إِمْكانٌ Possibility ; power.

مُمْكِنٌ Possible.

مُتَمَكِّنٌ Declinable noun.

مَلَّ يَمُلُّ مَلاًّ To tack, baste.

مَلَّ يَمَلُّ مِنْ To tire of.

أَمَلَّ To cause weariness.

تَمَلَّلَ To be restless, tired.

مِلَّةٌ ج مِلَلٌ A religion, creed.

مَلَلٌ ومَلالٌ وَمَلالَةٌ Weariness.

مُلاَّ Mollah, a Turkish judge.

مَلُّولٌ Acorn-tree ; kind of oak.

مَلأَ يَمْلأُ مَلأً To fill up.

مَلِئَ يَمْلأُ وَامْتَلأَ مِن To be filled.

مَلَّأَ تَمْلِئَةً To fill, fill up.

مِلْءٌ Quantity which fills up.

مَلأٌ ج أَمْلاءٌ An assembly.

مُلاءَةٌ وَمِلايَةٌ A kind of garment.

مَلآنُ م مَلأَى وَمَلآنَةٌ Full.

إِمْتِلاءٌ Fullness Plethora.

مَمْلُوءٌ وَمَمْلُوٌّ وَمُمْتَلِئٌ Full.

مَلَحَ يَمْلَحُ وَمَلَّحَ To salt (food.)

مَلُحَ يَمْلُحُ مُلُوحَةٌ To be salty. Be beautiful.

ما أَمْلَحَهُ	How handsome he is!
مِلْحٌ ج أَمْلاحٌ	Salt.
مُلْحَةٌ ج مُلَحٌ	Pleasant anecdote.
مَلاحَةٌ	Beauty, goodliness.
مِلاحَةٌ	The art of navigation.
مَلَّاحٌ	Sailor. Salt merchant.
مَلَّاحَةٌ	Salt-works, salt mine.
مُلوحَةٌ	Saltness.
مَلِيحٌ ج مِلاحٌ	Goodly, pretty.
مُمَلَّحٌ	Salted.
مَمْلَحَةٌ ج مَمالِحُ	Salt-cellar.
مُلوخِيَّةٌ ومُلُوخِيا	Jew's mallow.
مَلُسَ يَمْلُسُ	To be smooth.
مَلَّسَ	To make smooth.
مَلَسُ الظَّلامِ	Twilight, dawn.
مَلاسَةٌ	Smoothness.
أَمْلَسُ م مَلْساءُ ج مُلْسٌ	Smooth.
مَلَصَ وتَمَلَّصَ مِنْ	To escape.
مَلَطَ يَمْلِطُ ومَلَّطَ	To plaster.
مِلاطٌ	Plaster.
مالِطَةٌ	Malta (Island).
مالِطيٌّ	Maltese.
أَمْلَطُ م مَلْطاءُ	Scanty-haired.
مَلِقَ يَمْلَقُ . وماَلَقَ	To flatter.
تَمَلَّقَ تَمَلُّقاً	To flatter, cajole.
مَلَقٌ وتَمْلِيقٌ وتَمَلُّقٌ	Flattery.
مَلِقٌ ومَلَّاقٌ	Adulator, flatterer.
مَلَكَ يَمْلِكُ وتَمَلَّكَ	To possess.
مَلَكَ على	To reign or rule over.
مَلَّكَ	To give in possession.
تَمَلَّكَ	To rule, possess.
تَمالَكَ عَنْ	To abstain from.
مِلْكٌ ج أَمْلاكٌ	Property; goods.
مُلْكٌ	Power, authority, reign.
مَلَكٌ ومَلاكٌ ج مَلائِكَةٌ	Angle.
مَلِكٌ ج مُلوكٌ	King.

Queen. مَلِكَةٌ

Custom, habit. مَلَكَةٌ ج مَلَكات

Royalty. Kingdom. مَلَكُوتٌ

Royal, Kingly. مَلَكِيٌّ وَمُلُوكِيٌّ

Possessor, proprietor. مالِكٌ

Heron (bird). مالِكُ ٱلْحزين

Possessor. King. مليكٌ ج ملكاء

Kingdom. مَمْلَكةٌ ج ممالِكُ

Mamluk. مَمْلُوكٌ ج مَماليكُ

To be restless. تَمَلْمَلَ

Melancholy; black bile. مَلَنْخوليا

To dictate a writing. أَملى عَلى

A long time. مليًّا مِنَ الدهر

Dictation. إِملاء ج أمال

Million. مليونٌ ج مَلايين

For what? From what? مِمَّا (مِنْ ما)

Who? Whoever. مَنْ

From; of; for; than. مِنْ

Some *of* them say. مِنْهُمْ مَنْ يَقُولُ

He drew nigh *to* him. قَرُبَ مِنهُ

Better *than*. أَفْضَلُ مِنْ

He came at once. جاءَ مِنْ ساعَتِهِ

To be gracious. مَنَّ يَمُنُّ وَٱمْتَنَّ

To reproach for benefits. مَنَّ وَمَنَّنَ

Gift, benefit. Manna. مَنٌّ

By the grace of God. بِمَنِّهِ تَعالى

Grace, bounty. مِنَّةٌ ج مِنَنٌ

Generous. مَنَّانٌ

God, the Giver of good. أَلْمَنَّانُ

Death. Ill-fortune. اَلْمَنُونُ

Reproach for benefit. إِمْتِنانٌ

Under obligation. (مَمْنُونٌ)

Obligation. (مَمْنُونِيَّة)

Battering-ram. مَنْجَنِيقٌ وَمَنْجَلِيقٌ

To give, grant. مَنَحَ يَمْنَحُ مَنْحًا

Gift, favour. مِنْحَةٌ ج مِنَحٌ

مُنذُ ومُذْ	Since.
منع يَمْنَعُ عَنْ ومِنْ	To refuse; prohibit.
منُعَ يَمْنُعُ	To be inaccessible.
مانَعَ	To refuse; oppose.
تَمَنَّعَ عَنْ	To abstain from.
تَمَنَّعَ بِ	To intrench one's self.
إِمْتَنَعَ	To be impossible.
إِمْتَنَعَ وتَمَنَّعَ	To refrain from.
مَنْعٌ	Prevention.
مَنيعٌ	Impregnable, inaccessible.
مانِعٌ	Something which prevents.
مُمْتَنِعٌ	Impossible.
مَمْنُوعٌ	Interdicted, prohibited.
مَنَّى تَمْنِيَةً	To grant one's desire.
تَمَنَّى	To wish, desire.
مَنا ج أَمْناء	A measure.
مَنِيَّةٌ ج مَنايا	Death. Destiny.
مُنْيَة ج مُنًى	Wish, desire.
أُمْنِيَّةٌ ج أَمانِيُّ	Wish, vain wish.
مُهْجَةٌ ج مُهَجٌ	Soul, life.
مَهَدَ يَمْهَدُ ومَهَّدَ	To level; prepare.
تَمَهَّدَ	To be made easy.
مَهْدٌ ج مُهُودٌ	Bed; child's cradle.
مَهَرَ يَمْهَرُ	To be skilful.
تَمَهَّرَ	To become skilful.
مَهْرٌ ج مُهُورٌ	Dowry.
مُهْرٌ ج مِهارٌ	Foal. Signet.
مُهْرْدارٌ	Seal-bearer, secretary.
مُهْرَةٌ ج مُهُرات	Filly.
مَهارَةٌ	Skilfulness, dexterity.
ماهِرٌ ج مَهَرَة	Skilful.
مَهَلَ يَمْهَلُ . وتَمَهَّلَ	To act slowly.
مَهَّلَ وأَمْهَلَ	To grant a delay.
إِسْتَمْهَلَ	To ask for a delay.
مَهْلٌ	Deliberate action.
مَهْلاً	Go slowly; softly!

إِمْهالٌ	Concession of a delay.
تَمَهُّلٌ	Slowness, delay.
مَهْما	Whatever.
مَهَنَ يَمْهَنُ	To serve. Overwork.
إِمْتَهَنَ	To employ. Despise.
مِهْنَةٌ ج مِهَنٌ	Art, trade.
مَهاةٌ ج مَهاً	Antelope.
مَاتَ يَمُوتُ مَوْتاً	To die, expire.
مَوَّتَ وَأَماتَ	To kill.
تَماوَتَ	To feign death.
اسْتَماتَ	To act desperately.
مَوْتٌ ومَوْتَة	Death, decease.
مَوْتانٌ ومُوتانٌ	Cattle-plague.
مائتٌ ج مَائِتُونَ	Dying.
مَيْتٌ ومَيِّتٌ ج أَمْواتٌ	Dead.
مِيتَة	Kind of death.
مَماتٌ	Death, decease.
مُمِيتٌ	Deadly, mortal, fatal.
مُسْتَمِيتٌ	Bold, desperate.
ماجَ يَمُوجُ وتَمَوَّجَ	To be agitated.
مَوْجٌ ج أَمْواجٌ	Wave, billow.
تَمَوُّجٌ	Commotion ; fluctuation.
مارِسْتانٌ	A hospital; asylum.
مَوْزٌ	Banana (tree or fruit).
ماسٌ	Diamond.
مُوسَى أَوْ مُوسَى و (مُوسٌ) ج مَواسٍ	A razor.
مُوسَى	Moses.
مُوسِيقَى	Music.
مُوسِيقِي	Musician. Musical.
مَاشٌ	Indian peas.
مُوقٌ	Inner angle of the eye.
مَالَ يَمُولُ	To be wealthy, rich.
تَمَوَّلَ	To become rich.
مالٌ ج أَمْوالٌ	Goods, riches.
بَيْتُ ٱلْمال	Public Treasury.

Financial ; pecuniary.	مالِيٌّ
Finance; ministry of...	ألْمالِيَةُ
Minister of Finance.	وزيرُ ٱلْمالِيَة
A wealthy man.	مُتَموِّلٌ
A kind of bitumen.	مومِياً
Mummy.	مومِيَةٌ ج مُومِيَاتٌ
To furnish.	مَانَ يَمُونُ . ومَوَّنَ
To lay in a store.	تَموَّنَ
Provisions.	مُونَةٌ (مُؤُنَةٌ)
Store-room.	بَيْتُ ٱلْمُونَةِ
To gild, or silver.	مَوَّهَ
To falsify (news).	مَوَّهَ
Water.	ماءٌ ج أمْواهٌ ومِيَاهٌ
Watery; fluid. Aquatic.	مائِيٌّ
Nature, essence. Salary.	ماهِيَةٌ
Falsified (narrative).	مُمَوَّهٌ
Equivocation.	تَمْوِيهٌ
To give a gift.	مَاحَ يَمِيحُ
To seek a gift.	إِسْتِماحَ
A table.	مَائِدَةٌ ج مَائِداتٌ وموائِدُ
Race-field; arena.	ميدانٌ ج مَيادِينُ
Taxes.	مِيرِيٌّ أَوْ مِيرَةٌ (أَميرِيٌّ)
To detect, distinguish.	مَيَّزَ
To be distinguished.	تَمَيَّزَ وٱمْتازَ
Separation ; distinction.	تَمْيِيزٌ
The age of reason.	سِنُّ ٱلتَّمْيِيزِ
Distinction; privilege ; preference.	إِمْتِيازٌ
Distinguishing.	مُتَمَيِّزٌ
Distinguished.	مُتَمَيِّزٌ ومُمْتَازٌ
Hackberry tree.	مَيْسٌ
To flow (liquid).	ماعَ يَميعُ
Incense, perfume. Balm.	مَيْعَةٌ
Fluid, liquid.	مَائِعٌ
To be inclined to.	مالَ يَمِيلُ إلى
To deviate from.	مال عَنْ
To be adverse to...	مال عَلَى

مال يميلُ	To decline, (sun).
تَمايَلَ	To reel in walking.
إِستمالَ	To conciliate.
ميَّلَ وأَمالَ	To incline, bend.
مَيْلٌ ج مُيُولٌ	Inclination.
مِيلٌ ج أَميالٌ	A probe. A mile.
مَائِلٌ	Bent, inclined.
مَيَّالٌ	Very much inclined.
مَانَ يَمِينُ	To lie, tell a falsehood.
مَيْنٌ ج مُيُونٌ	A lie, falsehood.
مينَا	A harbour, port. Enamel.

ن

ن	As a numeral sign=50.
نَارَجِيلٌ وَنَارِجِيلٌ	Cocoa-nut.
نَأَى يَنْأَى عَنْ	To be far from.
انتَأَى عَنْ	To go far from.
نَاءٍ	One who is far away, remote.
أُنبُوبٌ ج أَنَابِيب	A tube, pipe.
نبا عَلَى	To assault.
نَبَأَ بِ	To lead to.
نَبَّأَ وَأَنْبَأَ	To announce, inform.
تَنَبَّأَ	To prophesy; foretell.
إِستَنْبَأَ	To seek information.
نَبَأٌ ج أنباء	News; information.
نُبُوءَةٌ وَنُبُوَّةٌ	A prophecy.
نَبَوِيٌّ	Prophetic.

نَبِيٌّ ج أَنْبِيَاء وَنَبِيُّونَ	A prophet.
نَبَتَ يَنْبُتُ	To sprout (plant).
أَنْبَتَ	To cause to sprout.
نَبْتٌ	A plant; herb; sprout.
نَبَاتٌ ج نَبَاتَات	Plant, vegetation.
عِلْمُ ٱلنَّبَاتِ	Botany.
عَالَمُ ٱلنَّبَاتِ	The vegetable world.
نَبَاتِيٌّ	Botanist. Vegetable.
نَابِتٌ	Sprouting, germinating.
نَبُّوتٌ ج نَبَابِيتُ	A club.
مَنْبَتٌ ج مَنَابِت	Herbarium. Origin.
نَبَحَ يَنْبَحُ نَبْحاً	To bark (dog).
نُبَاحٌ	Barking.
نَبَذَ يَنْبِذُ	To throw ; give up.
أَنْبَاذُ ٱلنَّاسِ	The rabble, mob.
نُبْذَةٌ ج نُبَذٌ	Section, article.
نَبِيذٌ ج أَنْبِذَة	Wine.
نَبَرَ يَنْبِرُ نَبْرًا	To speak loud.
نِبْرٌ ج أَنَابِر	A store; granary.
نَبْرَةٌ	Emphasis (in speaking).
مِنْبَرٌ ج مَنَابِرُ	Stage, pulpit.
نِبْرَاسٌ ج نَبَارِيس	A lamp.
نَبَشَ يَنْبُشُ	To unearth, dig up.
نَبِيشَةٌ	Earth or pit dug out.
نَبَّاشٌ	A digger.
نَبَضَ يَنْبِضُ	To pulsate, throb.
نَبْضٌ	Pulsation; pulse.
نَبْضَةٌ	A throb, pulsation.
إِسْتَنْبَطَ	To invent (something).
نَبَطٌ ج أَنْبَاطٌ	The Nabathæns.
• كَلِمَةٌ نَبَطِيَّةٌ	A vulgar word.
إِسْتِنْبَاطٌ	Discovery, invention.
نَبَعَ يَنْبَعُ	To spring, gush (water).
نَبْعٌ	Spring of water.
مَنْبَعٌ ج مَنَابِعُ	Source, origin.
يَنْبُوعٌ ج يَنَابِيع	A fountain.

نَبَغَ يَنْبُغُ — To arise ; appear.

نَابِغةٌ ج نَوابِغُ — Distinguished.

انْبِيقٌ ج أَنابِيقُ — Chemical retrot.

نَبَلَ يَنْبُلُ نَبْلاً — To shoot arrows.

نَبُلَ يَنْبُلُ — To have genius, skill.

تَنَبَّلَ — To become skilful.

نَبْلٌ ج نِبَالٌ — Arrows, darts.

نَبِيلٌ ج نِبالٌ — Highly intelligent.

نَبْلةٌ — An arrow, dart.

نَبالةٌ — Ability; ; superiority.

نَبِهَ يَنْبَهُ نَبْهاً لِ — To perceive.

نَبِهَ نُبْهاً مِنَ ٱلنَّوْمِ — To awake.

نَبَّهَهُ مِنَ النَّوْمِ — To wake ; one up.

نَبَّهَ عَلَى أَوْ إِلَى — To warn inform.

تَنَبَّهَ وَٱنْتَبَهَ — To awake.

تَنَبَّهَ لِ — To be awake to.

إِنْتَبَهَ لِ — To perceive.

نَبَاهةٌ — Celebrity. Intelligence.

إِنْتِباهٌ — Attention; wakefulness.

تَنْبِيهٌ — Warning. Notice.

مُتَنَبِّهٌ وَمُنْتَبِهٌ — Awake, Attentive.

نَتَأَ يَنْتَأُ نُتُوءًا — To project.

نَاتِئٌ — Projecting; jutting out.

نَتَجَ يَنْتِجُ — To bring forth.

نَتَجَ عَنْ — To arise, result from...

إِسْتَنْتَجَ — To deduce, infer.

نَتِيجةٌ ج نَتائِجُ — Conclusion. Result; consequence.

نَتَرَ يَنْتُرُ — To pull, snatch.

نَتَشَ يَنْتِشُ نَتْشاً — To snatch, pluck.

نَتَفَ يَنْتِفُ — To pluck, pull out.

تَنَتَّفَ — To be plucked off.

نُتْفةٌ ج نُتَفٌ — A small quantity.

نَتُنَ يَنْتُنُ نَتْناً وَٱنْتَنَ — To stink.

نَتْنٌ وَنَتَانَةٌ — Stench.

نَتِنٌ وَمُنْتِنٌ — Stinking, putrid.

نتوءٌ ج نتوّآتٌ — Tuberosity.

Swollen. Projecting.	ناتٍ
To disperse, scatter.	نَثَرَ يَنْثُرُ
To be scattered.	تَنَاثَرَ وَٱنْتَثَرَ
Prose, (*opp. to* نَظْم).	نَثْرٌ
Gilly-flower.	مَنْثُورٌ
To be noble.	نَجُبَ يَنْجُب
To choose, select.	إِنْتَجَبَ
Nobility.	نَجَابَة
Noble.	نَجِيبٌ ج نُجَبَاء
The choicest parts.	نَجَائِب
To succeed, prosper.	نَجَحَ يَنْجَح
To give success.	نَجَّحَ وَأَنْجَحَ
Success, prosperity.	نُجْحٌ وَنَجَاحٌ
Successful, thriving.	نَاجِحٌ
To help, aid.	نَجَدَ يَنْجُد. وَأَنْجَدَ
To upholster.	نَجَّدَ
To bring help to.	نَاجَدَ مُنَاجَدَةً
To invoke assistance.	إِسْتَنْجَد
High land.	نَجْدٌ ج أَنْجُد
Help, succour.	نَجْدَةٌ ج نَجَدَاتٌ
An upholsterer.	نَجَّادٌ وَمُنَجِّدٌ
To plane (wood).	نَجَرَ يَنْجُرُ
Carpentry.	نِجَارَةٌ
Shavings chips of wood.	نُجَارَة
Carpenter.	نَجَّارٌ ج نَجَّارُونَ
To finish a thing.	نَجَزَ يَنْجُزُ وَنَجَّزَ
To come to an end.	نَجِزَ يَنْجَزُ
To achieve; accomplish.	أَنْجَزَ
Achievement.	نَجْز وَنَجَاز
Ready, present.	نَاجِزٌ وَنَجِيزٌ
To be impure.	نَجِسَ يَنْجَسُ نَجَساً
To defile, pollute.	نَجَّسَ وَأَنْجَسَ
To become polluted.	تَنَجَّسَ
Filth. Legal impurity.	نَجَاسَةٌ
Impure, filthy.	نَجْسٌ ج أَنْجَاسٌ
Title of the Abyssinian kings.	النَّجَاشِيُّ

To benefit, profit. نَجَعَ يَنْجَعُ

Profitable, useful. Dark red blood. نَجِيعٌ

Child, son. نَجْلٌ ج أَنْجَالٌ

Gospel. إِنْجِيلٌ ج أَنَاجِيلُ

Evangelical; evangelist. إِنْجِيلِيٌّ

A sickle. مِنْجَلٌ ج مَنَاجِلُ

To appear. نَجَمَ يَنْجُمُ وَأَنْجَمَ

To arise, or result from. نَجَمَ عَنْ

A star. Shrub. نَجْمٌ ج أَنْجُمٌ وَنُجُومٌ

Astronomy. عِلْمُ ٱلنُّجُومِ

Astrology. عِلْمُ ٱلتَّنْجِيمِ

Astronomer. Astrologer. مُنَجِّمٌ

Mine. Source. مَنْجَمٌ ج مَنَاجِمُ

To escape. نَجَا يَنْجُو نَجَاةً

To confide a secret to. نَاجَى

To save deliver. نَجَّى وَأَنْجَى مِنْ

To commune secretly. تَنَاجَى

Deliverance. نَجَاةٌ وَنَجَاءٌ

An asylum. مَنْجًى ج مَنَاجٍ

Secret communication. مُنَاجَاةٌ

To weep, cry, wail. نَحَبَ يَنْحَبُ

Bitter weeping. Death. نَحْبٌ

To die. قَضَى نَحْبَهُ

Wailing. Lamenation. نَحِيبٌ

To cut, hew, carve. نَحَتَ يَنْحِتُ

Fragments, chips. نُحَاتَةٌ

Stone-cutter. Sculptor. نَحَّاتٌ

Cut, hewed. نَحِيتٌ وَمَنْحُوتٌ

Sculptor's chisel. مِنْحَتٌ ج مَنَاحِتُ

To kill (an animal). نَحَرَ يَنْحَرُ

To contend together. تَنَاحَرَ

To commit suicide. إِنْتَحَرَ

Skilled. نِحْرِيرٌ ج نَحَارِيرُ

Lower part of neck. نَحْرٌ ج نُحُورٌ

Throat. مَنْحَرٌ

To cover with copper. نَحَسَ

Ill-luck. نَحْسٌ ج نُحُوسٌ

Unlucky. نَحْسٌ وَمَنْحُوسٌ

Brass. نُحَاسٌ

Copper. نُحَاسٌ أَحْمَرُ

A piece of copper. نُحَاسَةٌ

A copper merchant. نَحَّاسٌ

To be slim. نَحِفَ يَنْحَفُ نَحَافَةً

To make thin. أَنْحَفَ

Leanness ; slenderness. نَحَافَةٌ

Thin, meagre. نَحِيفٌ ج نِحَافٌ

To become thin. نَحَلَ يَنْحَلُ

To make thin. أَنْحَلَ

To plagiarize. تَنَحَّلَ وَانْتَحَلَ

To embrace a religion. انْتَحَلَ

Bees. نَحْلٌ

A bee. نَحْلَةٌ

A religious sect. نِحْلَةٌ ج نِحَلٌ

Thinness, leanness. نُحُولٌ

Thin, emaciated. نَحِيلٌ

We. نَحْنُ

To move towards. نَحَا يَنْحُو

To send away. نَحَّى عَنْ

To go aside. تَنَحَّى عَنْ

Towards. Nearly, about. For example. نَحْوَ

Region. Method. نَحْوٌ ج أَنْحَاءٌ

Grammar, *sp.* syntax. عِلْمُ النَّحْوِ

Grammarian. نَاحٍ ج نُحَاةٌ

Grammatical. نَحْوِيٌّ

Side, direction. نَاحِيَةٌ ج نَوَاحٍ

To select. نَخَبَ يَنْخُبُ وَانْتَخَبَ

Choice, election. نَخْبٌ وَانْتِخَابٌ

Chosen. Choice. نُخْبَةٌ ج نُخَبٌ

Elector. مُنْتَخِبٌ

Chosen ; elected. مُنْتَخَبٌ

To snore ; snort. نَخَرَ يَنْخُرُ

To be rotten. نَخِرَ يَنْخَرُ نَخَراً

Rotten, decayed. نَخِرٌ وَناخِرٌ

Nostril ; nose. مِنْخَرٌ ج مَناخِيرُ

To prick with. نَخَرَ يَنْخُرُ بِ

To prick. نَخَسَ يَنْخُسُ نَخْساً

Cattle-trade ; slave-trade. نِخاسَةٌ

Cattle, or slave trader. نَخَّاسٌ

A goad, spur. مَنْخَسٌ ج مَناخِسُ

To hawk, clear the throat. تَنَخَّعَ

Marrow. Brain. نُخاعٌ ج نُخُعٌ

Phlegm, mucus. نُخاعَةٌ

To sift, bolt flour. نَخَلَ يَنْخُلُ

The palm-tree. نَخْلٌ وَنَخِيلٌ

A palm-tree. نَخْلَةٌ

Bran. نُخالَةٌ

A sieve. مُنْخُلٌ ج مَناخِلُ

To blow the nose. تَنَخَّمَ

Mucus ; phlegm. نُخامَةٌ

To incite, instigate. نَخى وأَنْخى

Pride. Sense of honour. نَخْوَةٌ

To expose one's faults. نَدَّدَ بِ

A kind of perfume. نَدٌّ

Similar to, an equal. نِدٌّ ج أَندادٌ

To weep, lament. نَدَبَ يَندُبُ

To call, appoint. نَدَبَ وَٱنْتَدَبَ

To be cicatrized. نَدِبَ يَندَبُ

To respond to a call. إِنْتَدَبَ لِ

Scar. نَدْبَةٌ ج نُدُوبٌ وَأَندابٌ

An elegy, a lamentation. نُدبَةٌ

A weeper, lamenter. نادِبٌ

Mourned. Commissioner. مَندوبٌ

Liberty of action. مَندوحَةٌ

To be rare. نَدَرَ يَندُرُ

Rarity ; infrequency. نَدْرَةٌ

A rare thing. نادِرٌ ج نَوادِرُ

Rarely, seldom. نادِراً وفي ٱلنَّادِرِ

To card (cotton). نَدَفَ يَندِفُ

نِدافةٌ Trade of carding.
نَدّافٌ Wool or cotton carder.
مَندوفٌ Carded.
مَنديلٌ ج مَنادِيلُ A towel. Veil.
ألأندلُسُ Andalusia. Spain.
اندلُسِيٌّ Andalusian.
نَدِمَ يَندَمُ . وتَنَدَّمَ على To regret.
نادَمَ مُنادَمةً To associate with.
نَدَمٌ ونَدامةٌ Regret, repentance.
نادِمٌ Repentant contrite.
نَديمٌ ج نُدَماءُ Associate, friend.
نَدِيَ يَندَى To be wet.
ندَّى تندِيةً To dampen, wet.
نادَى مُناداةً ونِداءً To call.
نادَى ب To proclaim ; publish.
أندَى إِنداءً To be liberal.
تَندَّى Ta become wet.
انتَدَى To assemble *v.i*

نَدًى ج أنداءٌ Moisture. Dew.
نداءٌ Call. Proclamation.
حرفُ النِّداء Vocative particle.
نَدوةٌ An assembly, a meeting.
نادٍ ج أندِيةٌ Place of assembly.
مُنادٍ A public crier.
مُنتدًى Assembly-hall.
نَذَرَ ـُ To make a vow; dedicate
أنذرَ إِنذاراً ب To warn.
نَذْرٌ ج نُذُورٌ A vow.
إِنذارٌ A warning. Prognosis.
نَذِيرٌ ج نُذُرٌ Vowed. Preacher.
مَنذُورٌ Vowed, consecrated.
نَذُلَ يَنذُلُ نَذالةً To be abject.
نَذْلٌ ج أنذالٌ Vile, mean.
نرجِسٌ Narcissus (plant).
نارِجيلٌ ونارَجيلٌ Cocoa-nut.
نارَجيلةٌ Nargileh.

نَرْدٌ	Backgammon.
نَارِدِينٌ وَنَرْدِينٌ	Spikenard.
نَارَنْجٌ	Orange.
نَوْرَجٌ	Thrashing-harrow.
نَزَّ يَنِزُّ نَزًّا	To exude.
نَزٌّ ج نُزُوزٌ	Leakage.
نَزَحَ يَنْزَحُ	To exhaust a well.
نَزِحَ بِهِ وَانْتَزَحَ	To emigrate.
نَازِحٌ وَنَزِيحٌ	Distant, Emigrant.
نَزْرٌ	Little ; mean.
نَزَعَ يَنْزَعُ وَٱنْتَزَعَ	To remove.
نَازَعَ	To fight, dispute with.
تَنَازَعَ	To contend among themselves.
إِنْتَزَعَ	To be taken away.
نَزْعٌ وَنِزَاعٌ	Agony of death.
نِزَاعٌ وَمُنَازَعَةٌ	Contention.
مَنْزُوعٌ	Taken away, removed.
نَزِفَ	To be exhausted (well).
نَزَفَ	To have a flow of blood.
نَزْفُ ٱلدَّمِ	Hemorrhage
نَزِقٌ	Quick, hot-tempered.
نَيْزَكٌ ج نَيَازِكُ	A falling star.
نَزَلَ يَنْزِلُ نُزُولاً	To descend.
نَزَلَ فِي وَعَلَى	To stop at a place.
نَزَّلَ وَأَنْزَلَ	To bring down.
نَزَّلَ وَأَنْزَلَ عَلَى	To reveal.
نَازَلَ	To fight with.
تَنَزَّلَ عَنْ	To renounce.
تَنَازَلَ	To condescend.
اسْتَنْزَلَ	To seek or offer hospitaliy.
نَزْلٌ	Place where men gather.
نُزُولٌ ج أَنْزَالٌ	Guests.
نَزْلَةٌ	A cold in the head.
نَازِلَةٌ ج نَوَازِلُ	Calamity.
نَزِيلٌ ج نُزَلَاءُ	A guest.
إِنْزَالٌ وَتَنْزِيلٌ	A revelation.

Condescension, affability. تَنَازُلٌ

Hostlery ; house. مَنْزِلٌ ج مَنَازِلُ

Domestic economy. تَدْبِيرُ ٱلْمَنْزِلِ

Degree, rank. مَنْزِلَةٌ

To abstain from evil. نَزِهَ يَنْزَهُ

To walk, divert one's self. تَنَزَّهَ

To be free from. تَنَزَّهَ عَنْ

Purity of the soul. نُزْهٌ وَنَزَاهَةٌ

Pure, upright. نَزِيهٌ ج نُزَهَاءُ

Amusement. نُزْهَةٌ ج نُزَهٌ

Place of recreation. مُنْتَزَهٌ

To attribute, ascribe. نَسَبَ إِلَى

To resemble. Be suitable. نَاسَبَ

To correspond with. تَنَاسَبَ

To trace one's genealogy. إِنْتَسَبَ

To approve. إِسْتَنْسَبَ

Lineage. نَسَبٌ ج أَنْسَابٌ

Arithmetical proportion. نُسْبَةٌ

Relation, affinity. نِسْبَةٌ ج نِسَبٌ

Kinsman. نَسِيبٌ ج أَنْسِبَاءُ

Proportion. مُنَاسَبَةٌ وَتَنَاسُبٌ

Suited to, convenient. مُنَاسِبٌ

Proportioned. مُتَنَاسِبٌ

Ascribed, imputed. مَنْسُوبٌ إِلَى

Human nature. نَاسُوتٌ

To weave. نَسَجَ يَنْسُجُ نَسْجًا

To be woven. إِنْتَسَجَ

The art of weaving. نِسَاجَةٌ

Weaver. نَسَّاجٌ

Woven tissue. نَسِيجٌ ج نُسُجٌ

Loom. مِنْسَجٌ

Woven ; tissue. مَنْسُوجٌ

To abrogate. نَسَخَ يَنْسَخُ نَسْخًا
abolish To copy, transcribe.

To follow successively. تَنَاسَخَ

To copy a (book). إِنْتَسَخَ وَٱسْتَنْسَخَ

To annul, abrogate. إِنْتَسَخَ

Abrogation. Transcribing. نَسْخٌ

Copy ; manuscript, نُسْخَةٌ ج نُسَخٌ

Transmigration of souls. تَنَاسُخٌ

Abolished. Copied. مَنْسُوخٌ

An eagle ; vulture. نَسْرٌ ج نُسُورٌ

A fistula, sinus. نَاسُورٌ ج نَوَاسِيرُ

Beak of a bird. مِنْسَرٌ ج مَنَاسِرُ

A scented white rose. نِسْرِينٌ

Nestorian. نُسْطُورِيٌّ ج نَسَاطِرَةٌ

To demolish winnow. نَسَفَ يَنْسِفُ

Chaff. Froth. نُسَافَةٌ

Winnowing-fan. مِنْسَفٌ ج مَنَاسِفُ

A razing machine. مِنْسَفَةٌ

To compose. نَسَقَ يَنْسُقُ نَسْقًا

To place in order; arrange. نَسَّقَ

To be arranged. تَنَسَّقَ وتَنَاسَقَ

Order ; system, method. نَسَقٌ

To lead an ascetic's life. نَسَكَ وَتَنَسَّكَ

A hermit's life. نَسْكٌ وَنُسُكٌ

A hermit. نَاسِكٌ ج نُسَّاكٌ

To beget. نَسَلَ يَنْسِلُ نَسْلًا

To multiply (men). تَنَاسَلَ

Posterity, progeny. نَسْلٌ

Descent by generation. تَنَاسُلٌ

To blow gently. نَسَمَ يَنْسِمُ

To breathe. تَنَسَّمَ

Breath of life. Man. نَسَمَةٌ ج نَسَمَاتٌ

A soft breeze. نَسِيمٌ

An ape. نَسْنَاسٌ

Women. نُسْوَةٌ وَنِسَاءٌ وَنِسْوَانٌ

Sciatica. عِرْقُ ٱلنَّسَا

To forget. نَسِيَ يَنْسَى نَسْيًا وَنِسْيَانًا

To cause to forget. نَسَّى وَأَنْسَى

To feign forgetfulness. تَنَاسَى

Forgetfulness. نَسْوَةٌ وَنِسْيَانٌ

Forgotten. مَنْسِيٌّ

To dry up ; ooze. نَشَّ يَنِشُّ

Blotting-paper. وَرَقٌ نَشَّاشٌ

To grow up. (child). To live, orginate. Rise. نَشَأَ يَنْشَأُ وَنَشُوَ يَنْشُؤُ

To follow, proceed from. نَشَأَ مِنْ

To create ; originate. Train up. أَنْشَأَ

He began to say. أَنْشَأَ يَقُولُ

Growing, developing. نُشُوءٌ

Growing. Resulting. نَاشِئٌ

Composition ; style. Origination. إِنْشَاءٌ

Native country. Source. مَنْشَأٌ

A creator. Author. مُنْشِئٌ

To break out (war). نَشِبَ ـُ بَيْنَ

An arrow (of wood). نُشَّابٌ

An archer. نَشَّابٌ

To seek a lost object. نَشَدَ يَنْشُدُ

To abjure by God. نَشَدَهُ ٱللهَ

To cause to swear. نَاشَدَ

To recite (verses). أَنْشَدَ

Chanting. Song. نَشِيدٌ

The Song of Songs. نَشِيدُ ٱلأَنْشَادِ

A poem. Song. أُنْشُودَةٌ ج أَنَاشِيدُ

Ammonia. نُشَادِرٌ وَنُوشَادِرٌ

To spread out. To saw. نَشَرَ يَنْشُرُ

To publish. نَشَرَ يَنْشُرُ

To resuscitate, raise to life. نَشَرَ يَنْشُرُ

To be extended. تَنَشَّرَ وَٱنْتَشَرَ

To be published. إِنْتَشَرَ

Resurrection. Publication. نَشْرٌ

Day of Resurrection. يَوْمُ ٱلنُّشُورِ

A written open paper. نَشْرَةٌ

Shavings, saw-dust. نُشَارَةٌ

Art of sawing. نِشَارَةٌ

Dissemination. إِنْتِشَارٌ

Dispersed. مَنْشُورٌ وَمُنْتَشِرٌ

A saw. مِنْشَارٌ ج مَنَاشِيرُ

Prism. Circular. مَنْشُورٌ

مَنْشُورِيّ — Prismatic form.

نَشِطَ يَنْشَطُ. وَتَنشّطَ — To be active.

نَشَطَ يَنشُطُ — To knot (a cord).

نَشَّطَ إِلى وَفِي — To encourage in.

نَشَاطٌ — Ardour, energy.

نَشِيطٌ ج نِشَاطٌ — Active, energetic.

أُنشُوطَةٌ ج أَنَاشِيط — A knot, noose.

نَشِفَ يَنشَفُ — To become dry.

تَنَشَّفَ — To dry, wipe (the body).

نَاشِفٌ — Dry.

تَنشِيفٌ — Wiping, drying up.

مِنشَفَةٌ ج مَنَاشِفُ — A towel.

نَشِقَ يَنشَقُ. وَٱستَنشَقَ — To inhale.

أَنشَقَ — To cause one to inhale.

نَشُوقٌ — Snuff.

نَشَلَ يَنشُلُ وَٱنتَشَلَ — To snatch; steal.

نَشَّالٌ — A pickpocket.

مَنْشَلٌ وَمِنْشَالٌ ج مَنَاشِلُ — A ladle.

نَشِيَ ـ نَشْوًا وَنَشْوَةً — To be drunk.

نَشِيَ وَاستَنْشَى — To smell. Be drunk.

نَشَّى — To starch (linen).

نَشًا وَنَشَاءٌ — Starch.

نَشْوَةٌ — Odour. Exhiliration of wine..

نَشْوَانُ م نَشْوَى ج نَشَاوَى — Drunk.

نَصَّ ـُ ل — To dictate a writing.

نَصٌّ ج نُصُوصٌ — Text (of a book).

مَنْصُوصٌ عَلَيْهِ — Clearly stated.

نَصَبَ يَنْصُبُ — To fix, plant; raise.

نَصِبَ ـَ نَصَبًا — To strive, toil.

نَصَّبَ — To appoint to an office.

نَاصَبَ — To resist, oppose.

إِنْتَصَبَ — To rise; stand erect.

نُصْبٌ ج أَنْصَابٌ — Idol, statue.

نُصْبَ عَيْنِي — Before my eye.

نِصَابٌ ج نُصُبٌ — Origin Handle.

نَصَّابٌ — Swindler.

Portion ; lot. نَصِيبٌ ج أَنْصِبَةٌ

Fatiguing, toilsome. نَاصِبٌ

Rank ; place. مَنْصِبٌ ج مَنَاصِبُ

Elevated, erected. مَنْصُوبٌ

To listen to نَصَتَ يَنْصِتُ وَأَنْصَتَ لِ

To silence. أَنْصَتَ

To listen. تَنَصَّتَ

To advise, counsel. نَصَحَ يَنْصَحُ

To act sincerely. نَصَحَ نُصْحاً

To receive advice. إِنْتَصَحَ

A sincere adviser. نَاصِحٌ

Sincere. نَصُوحٌ وَنَصِيحٌ

Advice, counsel. نَصِيحَةٌ ج نَصَائِحُ

To assist aid. نَصَرَ يَنْصُرُ

To become a Christian. تَنَصَّرَ

To strive to assist. تَنَصَّرَ لِ

To help one another. تَنَاصَرَ

To conquer, vanquish. اِنْتَصَرَ عَلَى

To seek aid from. إِسْتَنْصَرَ بِ

Help. Victory. نَصْرٌ وَنُصْرَةٌ

A Christian. نَصْرَانِيٌّ ج نَصَارَى

Christianity. أَلنَّصْرَانِيَّةُ

Victory, triumph. إِنْتِصَارٌ

Helper. نَاصِرٌ ج نُصَّارٌ وَأَنْصَارٌ

Helper. نَصِيرٌ ج نُصَرَاءُ

Victorious, conquering. مُنْتَصِرٌ

Aided Conqueror. مَنْصُورٌ

To be pure, unmixed. نَصَعَ يَنْصَعُ

Pure, unmixed (color) نَاصِعٌ

To divide into two halves. نَصَّفَ

To be just, equitable. أَنْصَفَ

To get one's due. إِنْتَصَفَ

To be mid-day. إِنْتَصَفَ آلنَّهَارُ

Half. Middle. نِصْفٌ ج أَنْصَافٌ

Justice, equity. إِنْصَافٌ

Middle (of anything). مُنْتَصَفٌ

To come out. (نَصَلَ يَنْصُلُ نَصْلاً)
Blade ; arrow-head. نَصْلٌ ج نِصَالٌ
Forelock. نَاصِيَةٌ ج نَوَاصٍ
To ooze, flow out. نَضَّ يَنِضُّ نَضًّا
Remainder, rest. نُضَاضَةٌ
To be well cooked ; ripe. نَضِجَ يَنْضَجُ
Cooked well, ripe. نَاضِجٌ
Of mature judgment. نَضِيجُ ٱلرَّأْيِ
To ooze ; exude. نَضَحَ يَنْضَحُ نَضْحًا
To sprinkle with. نَضَحَ بِ
To pile up. نَضَدَ يَنْضُدُ . وَنَضَّدَ
Laid in layers. نَضِيدٌ وَمَنْضُودٌ
To be soft. Blooming. نَضَرَ يَنْضُرُ
Bloom, freshness. نَضْرَةٌ وَنَضَارَةٌ
Blooming, verdant. نَضِرٌ وَنَضِيرٌ
To defend. نَاضَلَ عَنْ
Combat. نِضَالٌ وَمُنَاضَلَةٌ
A horse-shoe. نَضْوَةٌ

To jump, skip. (نَطَّ يَنِطُّ نَطًّا)
To butt. نَطَحَ يَنْطَحُ نَطْحًا
To butt one another. تَنَاطَحَ
Butted ; gored. نَطِيحٌ وَمَنْطُوحٌ
To guard. To wait. نَطَرَ يَنْطُرُ
Keeper (of gardens). نَاطُورٌ ج .نَوَاطِيرُ
A watch-tower. مَنْطَرَةٌ ج مَنَاطِرُ
Very learned. نَطِسٌ وَنِطَاسِيٌّ
To speak utter. نَطَقَ يَنْطِقُ
To gird. نَطَّقَ
To gird one's self. تَنَطَّقَ وَٱنْتَطَقَ
To question, examine. إِسْتَنْطَقَ
Speech ; articulation. نُطْقٌ
Belt, girdle. نِطَاقٌ ج نُطُقٌ
Endowed with speech. نَاطِقٌ
The human soul. أَلنَّفْسُ ٱلنَّاطِقَةُ
Speech, language. Logic. مَنْطِقٌ
Logical. Logician. مَنْطِقِيٌّ

مِنْطَقةٌ ج مَناطِقُ A girdle, belt.

مِنْطَقَةُ ٱلبُرُوجِ The Zodiac.

مَنْطُوقٌ Proper signification.

مُستَنْطِقٌ Examiner (*law*).

نَطَلَ يَنْطُلُ ۰ وَنَطَّلَ To foment.

نَطُولٌ ج نُطُولَاتٌ A fomentation.

نَظَرَ يَنْظُرُ وَإِلَى To see, look at.

نَظَرَ يَنْظُرُ فِي To consider.

نَاظَرَ To resemble ; rival. Debate. Superintend, inspect.

تناظَرَ To debate with one another.

إِنْتَظَرَ وَٱسْتَنْظَرَ To expect.

نَظَرٌ ج أَنْظَارٌ Vision. Favour.

نَظَرًا وَبِالنَّظَرِ إِلَى As regards.

نَظْرَةٌ A look, a glance.

نَظَرِيٌّ Theoretical. Subjective.

نَظَرِيةٌ ج نَظَرِياتٌ A problem.

نَاظِرٌ ج نُظَّارٌ Inspector. Director.

نَاظِرُ ٱلنظارِ Prime Minister.

نَاظِرُ الاشغالِ Minister of Works.

نَاظِرُ ٱلْمعارفِ العُمُومِيةِ Minister of Public Instruction.

نَاظِرُ ٱلماليةِ Minister of Finance.

نَاظِرُ ٱلخارجيةِ Minister of Foreign Affairs.

نَاظِرُ الدَّاخِلِيةِ Minister of the Interior.

نَاظِرُ ٱلحربيةِ Minister of War.

نَاظِرُ ٱلحَقَّانِيةِ Minister of Justice.

نِظَّارَةٌ Administration. Ministry.

نَظَّارَةٌ وَنَاظُورٌ A telescope.

نَظَّارَاتٌ Spectacles.

نَظِيرٌ ج نُظَرَاءُ Similar, equal to.

إِنْتِظَارٌ وَٱسْتِنْظَارٌ Expectation.

مَنْظَرٌ ج مَنَاظِرُ View. Aspect.

مِنْظَارٌ Speculum.

مُنَاظِرٌ Similar to. Inspector.

مُنَاظَرَةٌ Rivalry. Inspection.

نَظُفَ يَنْظُفُ To be clean ; comely.

نَظَّفَ To cleanse, purify.

تَنَظَّفَ To become clean.

نَظَافَةٌ Cleanliness. Beauty.

نَظِيفٌ ج نظفاء Clean; comely.

نَظَمَ ـِ To arrange ; compose (verses).

تَنَظَّمَ وَٱنْتَظَمَ To be arranged.

نَظْمٌ Arrangement. Poetry.

نِظَامٌ ج أَنْظِمَةٌ System , method.

مُنَظَّمٌ Well-arranged.

مَنْظُومٌ Arranged, composed.

نَعَتَ يَنْعَتُ نَعْتًا To describe.

نَعْتٌ Qualification; attribute.

نَعْتٌ ج نُعُوت Adjective.

مَنْعُوتٌ A qualified noun.

نَعْجَةٌ ج نِعَاجٌ A sheep, an ewe.

نُعَّارٌ A kind of finch (bird).

(نَعَّارَةٌ ج نَعَائِرُ) Earthen cooler.

نَاعُورَةٌ ج نَوَاعِير Irrigating wheel.

نَعَسَ يَنْعَسُ To grow sleepy.

أَنْعَسَ To make sleepy.

تَنَاعَسَ To feign sleep.

نُعَاسٌ Sleepiness; drowsiness

نَاعِسٌ وَنَعْسَان ج نُعَّسٌ Sleepy.

نَعَشَ يَنْعَشُ . وَأَنْعَشَ To cheer, refresh.

إِنْتَعَشَ To be revived, animated.

نَعْشٌ Bier.

بنات نَعْشٍ الكبرى Ursa Major.

نَعَقَ يَنْعَقُ To croak, (crow).

نَعَلَ يَنْعَلُ نَعْلًا To shoe (an animal).

نَعْلٌ ج نِعَالٌ Shoe. Horse-shoe.

نَعِمَ يَنْعَمُ To live in ease.

نَعُمَ يَنْعُمُ To be soft to the touch.

نِعْمَ الرَّجُلُ Excellent man !

نِعِمَّا Excellent! Good !

نَعَّمَ To make one easy in life.

أَنْعَمَ عَلَيْهِ To bestow, confer on.

تَنَعَّمَ To enjoy life ; enjoy.

Yes, certainly, assuredly. نَعَمْ

Cattle, camles. نَعَمٌ ج أَنْعَامٌ

Blessing, favour. نِعْمَةٌ ج نِعَمٌ

Opulent, rich. وَاسِعُ ٱلنِّعْمَةِ

An ostrich. نَعَامَةٌ ج نَعَائِمُ وَنَعَامَاتٌ

Softness, smoothness. نُعُومَةٌ

Anemone. شَقَائِقُ ٱلنُّعْمَانِ

Soft, tender. نَاعِمٌ م نَاعِمَةٌ

Contented, tranquil. نَعِيمُ ٱلْبَالِ

Goodness, favour. إِنْعَامٌ ج إِنْعَامَاتٌ

Luxury; enjoyment. تَنَعُّمٌ

Benefactor ; beneficent. مُنْعِمٌ

Mint (plant). نَعْنَعٌ وَنَعْنَاعٌ

To announce death. نَعَى يَنْعَى

News of death. نَعِيَّةٌ

Announcer of death. نَاعٍ ج نُعَاةٌ

To be troubled. نَغِصَ يَنْغَصُ نَغْصاً

To trouble, vex. نَغَّصَ وَأَنْغَصَ عَلَى

To be annoyed (in life). تَنَغَّصَ

To be inflamed, (wound). نَغِلَ يَنْغَلُ

Bastard. Hinny. نَغْلٌ

To sing softly. نَغَمَ يَنْغُمُ . وَنَغَّمَ

Melody, tune. نَغْمَةٌ ج نَغَمَاتٌ

To spit out. نَفَثَ يَنْفُثُ

Expectoration. Puff. نَفْثٌ

To blow (wind). نَفَحَ يَنْفَحُ نَفْحاً

A breath. A gift. نَفْحَةٌ ج نَفَحَاتٌ

To blow with the mouth. نَفَخَ يَنْفُخُ

To be puffed up proud. إِنْتَفَخَ

Breath, puff; blowing. نَفْخٌ

A water-bubble. Vesicle. نُفَّاخَةٌ

Bellows. مِنْفَاخٌ وَمِنْفَخٌ ج مَنَافِخُ

Inflated, swollen, مَنْفُوخٌ

To be spent, consumed. نَفِدَ يَنْفَدُ

To consume. أَنْفَدَ وَٱسْتَنْفَدَ

To pierce through. نَفَذَ يَنْفُذُ مِنْ

To be executed (an order). نَفَذَ

To reach, arrive at. نَفَذَ إِلى

To send, execute. نَفَّذَ وَأَنفَذ

Execution; efficiency. نَفاذٌ وَنفوذٌ

Efficacious, effective. نافِذٌ

Window. نافِذَةٌ ج نَوافِذُ

Outlet, passage. مَنفَذٌ ج مَنافِذُ

To turn away from. نَفَرَ يَنفُرُ مِنْ

To cause aversion. نَفَّرَ

To have mutual aversion. تَنافَرَ

A number of men. نَفَرٌ ج أَنْفار

Contest, repulsion. تَنافُرٌ

A trumpet, bugle. نَفيرٌ

To be precious. نَفُسَ يَنفُسُ

To give birth. نَفِسَتْ تَنْفَسُ

To breathe. تَنَفَّسَ

To sigh deeply. تَنَفَّسَ الصُّعَداء

To contend together. تَنافَسَ

Soul, self. نَفسٌ ج نُفوسٌ وَأَنفُسٌ

He himself came. جاءَ نَفسُهُ

A woman at child-birth. نُفَساء

The thing itself. نَفسُ الشَّيء

Breath. Style. نَفَسٌ ج أَنفاسٌ

Confinement, child-birth. نِفاسٌ

Respiration, breathing. تَنَفُّس

A valuable thing. نَفيسٌ ج نَفائِسُ

More precious. أَنفَسُ

To teaze (cotton). نَفَشَ ـ وَنَفَّشَ

To bristle (hair), ruffle (feathers). تَنَفَّشَ

To shake, shake off. نَفَضَ ـُ وَنَفَّضَ

A plate for ashes. مِنفَضة ج مَنافِض

Matches. نَفطٌ

Naptha, bitumen. نِفطٌ

Pustule, vesicle. نَفطة

A vesicating medicine. مُنفِطٌ

To be useful. نَفَعَ يَنفَعُ نَفعاً

إنتفعَ بِ وَمِنْ To profit by.

إِسْتَنفَعَ To seek benefit.

نَفعٌ وَمنفَعةٌ Advantage, benefit.

نَافِعٌ Useful, profitable.

نفق ينفُقُ نفاقاً To have a brisk sale
To be exhausted.

نفّقَ وَأنفَقَ To sell well.

نَافقَ To be hypocritical.

انفقَ To exhaust one's means.

نَفقةٌ ج نَفقاتٌ Cost, expenses.

نَافِقٌ Selling briskly.

نفاقٌ وَمنَافقَةٌ Hypocrisy.

منَافِقٌ A hypocrite ; deceiver.

نفلٌ A supererogatory deed.

نفلٌ ج أَنفالٌ Booty. Present.

نفلةٌ Clover.

نفى ينفي To expel ; deny, exclude.

نفى مِنْ To banish, exile.

؛ في To oppose, be incompatible.

إِنتفى To be excluded, rejected.

نَفْيٌ Banishment. Negation.

حرْفُ ٱلنَّفْيِ Particle of negation.

نُفاوَةٌ وَنُفايَة Rejected as useless.

مَنفِيٌّ Excluded. Exiled.

تناف ومنافاةٌ Incompatibility.

مَنفًى ج مُناف Exile.

نَقبَ يَنقُبُ نَقباً To dig through.

نَقَبَ في To travel over.

نَقَبَ عَنْ To examine.

تَنقبَ وَانتَقَبَ To put on a veil.

نَقبٌ ج انقابُ A hole in a wall.

نِقاب ج نقبٌ Veil of a woman.

نقيب ج نقباء Chief. Magistrate.

مَنقَبةٌ ج مَناقبُ Worthy deed.

نقّحَ وَأنقحَ To revise, correct.

تَنقيحٌ Revision, correction. –

نَقدَ يَنقُدُ نَقداً To peck (bird).

To pay in cash.	نَقَدَ لِ
To sort, pick out.	نَقَدَ وَتَنَقَّدَ
Ready money, cash.	نَقْدٌ
Money, cash.	نُقُودٌ وَنَقْدِيَّةٌ
Testing ; criticism.	إِنْتِقَادٌ
Beak (of a bird).	مِنْقَادٌ ج مَنَاقِيدُ
To deliver, save.	نَقَذَ يَنْقُذُ وَأَنْقَذَ
Rescue, déliverance.	نَقْذٌ
Deliverer.	مُنْقِذٌ
To cut into (stone, wood) ; peck (bird).	نَقَرَ يَنْقُرُ
To examine.	نَقَرَ وَنَقَّرَ عَنْ
To dispute with.	نَاقَرَ مُنَاقَرَةً
Cavity. Carving.	نَقْرٌ
Hollow, cavity.	نُقْرَةٌ ج نُقَرٌ
Sculptor, carver.	نَقَّارٌ
A small tambourine.	(نَقَّارَةٌ وَنُقَيْرَةٌ)
Hunting-horn.	نَاقُورٌ ج نَوَاقِيرُ
Beak of a bird.	مِنْقَارٌ ج مَنَاقِيرُ
Gout.	نِقْرِسٌ
To skip.	نَقَزَ يَنْقِزُ
A church-bell.	نَاقُوسٌ ج نَوَاقِيسُ
To paint; sculpture.	نَقَشَ يَنْقُشُ
To reckon with.	نَاقَشَ مُنَاقَشَةً
Painting. Tracing.	نَقْشٌ ج نُقُوشٌ
Painting. Sculpture.	نِقَاشَةٌ
Painter. Engraver.	نَقَّاشٌ
Brush. Chisel.	مِنْقَشٌ وَمِنْقَاشٌ
To reduce, decrease.	نَقَصَ يَنْقُصُ
To decrease gradually.	تَنَاقَصَ
To defame.	إِنْتَقَصَ
Diminution ; loss.	نَقْصٌ وَنُقْصَانٌ
Diminished, defective.	نَاقِصٌ
Fault ; vice.	نَقِيصَةٌ ج نَقَائِصُ
To demolish; annul.	نَقَضَ يَنْقُضُ
To contradict.	نَاقَضَ
To be annulled.	إِنْتَقَضَ

Destruction, dissolution. نَقْضٌ

Beam, joist. نَقْضَةٌ

The contrary, opposite. نقيضٌ

Contrariety. تَناقضٌ ومناقَضَةٌ

To mark with dots. نقَطَ ينقُطُ و نقَّط

Dot of a letter. نقْطَةٌ ج نقطٌ

Geometrical point. A drop.

Centre of a circle. نقطَةُ الدَّائرة

Epilepsy. داءُ النقْطَةِ

To soak, macerate. نقَعَ ينقَعُ

To become stagnant. إستنقع

Penetrating, pervading. ناقعٌ

Infusion. نقيعٌ ومنقوعٌ

Dried apricots. (نُقوعٌ)

A marsh, swamp. مُستنقعٌ ونقعٌ

To take out. إنتقف

To remove, transport. نقَلَ ينقل

To copy from ; quote. نقَلَ عنْ

To emigrate. انتقَلَ منْ إلى

To die. إنتقَلَ إلى رحمَةِ ٱللهِ

Transpsrt. Quotation. نقْلُ

Narrator. Bearer. Copyist. ناقِلٌ

Movable (estate). مُنتقِلٌ

Transferred ; quoted. مَنقولٌ

To punish, chastise. إنتقَمَ منْ

Vengeance. نقمَةٌ وٱنتقامٌ

An avenger. ناقِمٌ ومنتقِمٌ

To recover (from illness). نقه ينقَهُ نقْهاً

Convalescent. ناقِهٌ و نقِهٌ ج نُقَّهٌ

To be pure. نقِيَ ينقى

To clean, purify. نقّى وأنقى

To choose, select. تنَقى وٱنتقى

To cleanse one's body. إستنقى

Purity. Innocence. نقاءٌ و نقاوةٌ

Pure. clean. Innocent. نقيٌّ

Purer, cleaner. أنقى

To afflict. نَكَبَ يَنكُبُ نَكْباً

Unfortunate.	مَنْكُودُ ٱلْحَظّ
To be ignorant of.	نَكِرَ يَنْكَرُ
To deny.	أَنْكَرَ
To disapprove of.	أَنْكَرَ عَلَى
To be disguised.	تَنَكَّرَ
To deny. To censure.	إِسْتَنْكَرَ
Cunning.	نُكْرٌ وَنَكَارَةٌ
Indefinite noun.	نَكِرَةٌ ج نَكِرَاتٌ
Denial. Repudiation.	إِنْكَارٌ
Disguise.	تَنَكُّرٌ
Illicit deed.	مُنْكَرٌ ج مُنْكَرَاتٌ
Indeterminate noun.	مُنَكَّرٌ
To push; prick.	نَكَزَ يَنْكُزُ نَكْزاً
To upset.	نَكَسَ يَنْكُسُ وَنَكَّسَ
To be upset, inverted.	تَنَكَّسَ
To have a relapse.	نُكِسَ وَٱنْتَكَسَ
A relapse.	نُكْسٌ وَٱنْتِكَاسٌ
Reversed.	مَنْكُوسٌ وَمُنْتَكِسٌ

To swerve from.	نَكَبَ عَنْ
Adversity.	نَكْبَةٌ ج نَكَبَاتٌ
Shoulder; side.	مَنْكِبٌ ج مَنَاكِبُ
Afflicted, smitten.	مَنْكُوبٌ
To find fault with.	نَكَّتَ عَلَى
Speck. Witty saying.	نُكْتَةٌ ج نُكَتٌ
Criticism.	تَنْكِيتٌ
To break a compact.	نَكَثَ يَنْكُثُ
To be broken (promise).	إِنْتَكَثَ
Broken, violated.	مَنْكُوثٌ
To marry.	نَكَحَ يَنْكِحُ نِكَاحاً
To give in marriage.	أَنْكَحَ
Marriage contract.	نِكَاحٌ
To be hard.	نَكِدَ ـَ نَكَداً
To molest, annoy.	نَكَّدَ وَنَاكَدَ
To molest each other.	تَنَاكَدَ
Irritable, peevish.	نَكِدٌ م نَكْدَاءُ
Annoyance, molestation.	تَنْكِيدٌ

To exhaust. To dig. نَكَشَ يَنْكُشُ

Pickaxe. مِنْكَاشٌ ج مَنَاكِيشُ

To withdraw from. نَكَصَ يَنْكُصُ عَنْ

To turn back. نَكَصَ عَلَى عَقِبَيْهِ

To abstain from, reject. نَكَفَ يَنْكُفُ عَنْ

To discuss, contend. تَنَاكَفَ

To disdain, scorn. إِسْتَنْكَفَ

To punish severely. نَكَلَ وَنَكَّلَ بِ

A strong fetter. نِكْلٌ ج أَنْكَالٌ

Chastisement; warning. نَكَالٌ

Smell of breath. نَكْهَةٌ

To overcome; vex. نَكَى يَنْكِي نِكَايَةً

To make mischief. نَمَّ ـ بَيْنَ

A calumniator. نَمَّامٌ وَنَمُومٌ

Calumny, slander. نَمِيمَةٌ ج نَمَائِمُ

To mark with numbers. (نَمَرَ)

Leopard; panther. Tiger. نِمْرٌ ج نُمُورَةٌ

Number (For). (نمرة ج نُمَرٌ)

Ichneumon; weasel. نِمْسٌ ج نُمُوسٌ

Law. Mosquito. نَامُوسٌ ج نَوَامِيسُ

Mosquito-net. نَامُوسِيَّةٌ

Freckles. نَمَشٌ

A straight sword. انمشةٌ

Freckled. نَمِشٌ م نَمْشَاءُ ج نُمْشٌ

Cropped grass. نَمِيصٌ

Manner; fashion. نَمَطٌ ج نِمَاطٌ

To write well, embellish. نَمَّقَ

To be numb. نَمِلَ ـ نَمَلاً

An ant. A pustule. نَمْلَةٌ ج نَمْلٌ

Tip of the finger. أَنْمِلَةٌ ج أَنَامِلُ

To embellish, adorn. نَمْنَمَ

To grow, develop. نَمَا يَنْمُو

To attribute, ascribe, to. نَمَا إِلَى

Growth, increase. نُمُوٌّ

Example. نَمُوذَجٌ ج نَمُوذَجَاتٌ

To grow, increase. نَمَى يَنْمِي

To ascribe to one. نمى إلى

To cause to grow. أنمى

To trace one's origin to. إِنْتَمى إِلى

Growing, increasing. نَام

To plunder. نَهَبَ يَنْهَبُ وَانْتَهَبَ

Pillage, rapine. نَهْبٌ

Booty, plunder, spoil. نُهْبَةٌ

Pillager, depredator, نَهَّابٌ

Pillaged, plundered. مَنْهُوبٌ

To follow (the way). نَهَجَ يَنْهَجُ

To be out of breath: نَهِجَ يَنْهَجُ

Rapid breathing, panting. نَهَجٌ

A plain road. Way. مَنْهَجٌ ومِنْهَاجٌ ج مَنَاهِج

To contend with in battle. نَاهَدَ

To sigh, groan. تَنَهَّدَ

To flow. نَهَرَ يَنْهَرُ نَهْراً

To chide, check. نَهَرَ وَانْتَهَرَ

River. نَهْرٌ ج أَنْهُرٌ وَأَنْهَارٌ

Day. نَهَارٌ ج نُهُرٌ

To be near. نَهَزَ يَنْهَزُ نَهْزاً

To approach, be close to. نَاهَزَ

To seize an opportunity. إِنْتَهَزَ

Opportunity. نُهْزَةٌ ج نُهَزٌ

To bite. نَهَشَ يَنْهَشُ نَهْشاً

To rise, get up. نَهَضَ يَنْهَضُ. عَنْ.

To revolt, rise against. نَهَضَ عَلى

To rush towards. نَهَضَ إِلَى

To urge ; cause to rise, أَنْهَضَ

To rise up. إِنْتَهَضَ

To urge, incite. إِسْتَنْهَضَ لِ

Lifting ; rising. نُهُوضٌ

To bray. نَهَقَ يَنْهَقُ نُهَاقاً وَنَهِيقاً

To overcome, wear out. نَهَكَ يَنْهَكُ

To defame. نَهَكَ عِرْضَهُ وَانْتَهَكَ

To weaken. نَهَكَ وَانْتَهَكَ

Enfeebled, weakened. مَنْهُوكٌ

To drink. نَهَلَ يَنْهَلُ نَهلاً

A watering place. مَنْهَلٌ ج مَناهِلُ

To be ravenous. نَهِمَ يَنْهَمُ

An insatiable avidity. نَهْمٌ

Greedy ; glutton. نَهِمٌ وَنَهِيمٌ

To prohibit. نَهَى يَنْهَى عَنْ

To accomplish, achieve. أَنْهَى

To inform. أَنْهَى إِلَى

To lead to. إِنتَهَى إِلَى

To be completed. تَناهَى وَآنْتَهَى

To abstain from. تَناهَى وَآنْتَهَى عَنْ

Prohibition, interdiction. نَهْيٌ

Intelligence. نُهًى

End, utmost. نِهايَةٌ ج نِهايَاتٌ

One who forbids. نَاهٍ

What a man ! نَاهِيكَ مِنْ رَجُلٍ

End, termination ; limit. إِنْتِهاءٌ

Prohibited. مَنْهِيٌّ عَنْهُ

Prohibited things. أَلْمَناهِي

Infinite ; endless. غَيْرُ مُتَناهٍ

End, extremity ; limit. مُنْتَهَى

The final plural. مُنْتَهَى آلجُمُوعِ

Storm ; tempest. نَوْءٌ ج أَنْوَاءٌ

To take one's place. نَابَ يَنُوبُ عَنْ

To repent. نَابَ وَأَنَابَ إِلَى اللهِ

To overtake, befall. نَابَ وَآنْتَابَ

To appoint a substitute. أَنَابَ

To do a thing in turn. تَناوَبَ عَلَى

The Nubians. نُوبٌ وَنُوبَةٌ

A Nubian. نُوبِيٌّ

A turn ; time. نَوْبَةٌ ج نُوَبٌ

Musical concert. نَوْبَةٌ ج نَوْبَاتٌ

Lieutenancy, vicarship. نِيَابَةٌ

In place of, instead of. نِيَابَةٌ عَن

Substitute, deputy. نَائِبٌ ج نُوَّابٌ

The subject of a passive verb. نَائِبُ آلفَاعِلِ

مَجْلِسُ ٱلنوَّابِ	Parliament.
نائِبَةٌ ج نَوائِبُ	Misfortune.
نُوتِيٌّ ج نَوتِيَّةٌ	Mariner, sailor.
نَاحَ يَنوحُ	To wail ; coo (pigeon).
نَاحَ عَلى	To bewail the dead.
نَوْحٌ وَنُواحٌ وَنِياحٌ	Lamentation.
نَائِحٌ	A mourner, weeper.
نَائِحَةٌ ج نَوائِحُ وَنائِحاتٌ	Wailing women.
أَنَاخَ	To cause a camel to kneel.
أَناخَ بِالْمَكانِ	To abide in a place.
مَناخٌ ج مَناخاتٌ	Climate.
نارَ يَنورُ وَأَنارَ	To shine, sparkle.
نَوَّرَ وَأَنارَ	To flower, blossom (plant).
نَوَّرَ وَأَنارَ	To light up.
إِستَنارَ بِ	To be enlightened by.
نَارٌ ج نِيرانٌ	Fire.
جَبَلُ ٱلنَّارِ	A volcano.
مَرْكَبُ ٱلنَّارِ	A steam-ship.
نورٌ ج أَنْوارٌ	Light.
نُورِيٌّ ج نَوَرٌ	Gipsy.
إِنارَةٌ وَتَنْوِيرٌ	Illumination.
نَيِّرٌ م نَيِّرَةٌ	Shining, bright.
مُنِيرٌ	Giving light ; shining.
مَنارَةٌ	A light-house. Minaret.
نَوْرَجٌ	A threshing-harrow.
نَاسٌ	Men; people. (*for* أُناسٌ)
نَاوُوسٌ ج نَواوِيسُ	Sarcophagus.
نَاوَشَ	To engage in a combat.
تَناوَشَ	To attack one another.
إِنتَاشَ	To take out.
نَاصَ يَنوصُ عَنْ	To flee away.
مَناصٌ	A refuge, an asylum.
نَاطَ يَنوطُ وَأَناطَ بِ	To suspend to.
مَنوطٌ بِ	Dependent on.
نَوَّعَ	To divide, classify, specify.
تَنَوَّعَ	To be of different kinds.

Kind, sort species. نَوْعٌ ج أنْواعٌ

Diversified ; diverse. مُتَنَوِّعٌ

To overlook, surmount. نَافَ — عَلَى

More, upwards of. نَيْفٌ وَنَيْفٌ

Upwards of ten. عَشَرَةٌ وَنَيِّفٌ

Water-lily. نَوْفَرٌ

Jet d'eau. نَوْفَرَةٌ

She-camel. نَاقَةٌ ج نُوقٌ وَنِيَاقٌ

Dainty, fastidious. نَيِّقٌ

To give to, hand over. نَاوَلَ

To procure for one. أَنَالَ

To obtain, receive. تَنَاوَلَ

A loom. نَوْلٌ ج أَنْوَالٌ

Freight money. نَاوُلُونٌ

Mode, manner, fashion. مِنْوَالٌ

To sleep. نَامَ يَنَامُ نَوْماً وَنِيَاماً

To put to sleep. نَوَّمَ وَأَنَامَ

To feign sleep تَنَاوَمَ

Sleep, slumber. نَوْمٌ

Sleeping ; sleeper. نَائِمٌ ج نِيَامٌ

Sleep. A dream. مَنَامٌ

A dormitory. مَنَامٌ وَمَنَامَةٌ

Hypnotic, soporific. مُنَوِّمٌ

To mark with the double vowels (ٌ) (ً) و (ٍ) . نَوَّنَ تَنْوِيناً

A dimple on chin. نُونَةٌ

To purpose, resolve. نَوَى يَنْوِي

Distance, absence. نَوًى

A fruit stone. Nucleus. نَوَاةٌ ج نَوًى

Intention. نِيَّةٌ ج نِيَّاتٌ

Intended, purposed. مَنْوِيٌّ

Raw, underdone. نِيءٌ وَنِيٌّ

Canine tooth ; tusk. نَابٌ ج أَنْيَابٌ

To give rest. (نَيَّحَ)

To die. تَنَيَّحَ

Yoke. نِيرٌ ج أَنْيَارٌ وَنِيرَانٌ

نِيرٌ ج أنيارٌ	Woof.
نِيرَةٌ	Tooth-gum.
نيسانُ	April.
نيشانٌ ج نَياشِينُ	A decoralion.
ناف يَنيفُ على	To surpass, exceed.
نيافة	Eminence, (*title of honour*).
نيّفٌ و نيْفٌ . نوف	*See under*
نالَ يَنالُ	To obtain, acquire.
نالَ وأَنالَ	To cause to obtain.
نِيْلٌ	Indigo-plant ; indigo.
ألنّيلُ	The Nile.
نيلُوفَرٌ ونِينوفَرٌ	Nenuphar, lotus.
نينَوَى	Nineveh.
نايٌ ج نايَاتٌ	A kind of flute.

ه

ه	As a numeral sign = 5.
ه	His, him, it.
هَا	Her, it.
هَا	Lo ! Behold !
هاكَ	Take thou ! Here you are !
هَبْ	Grant ! (*Imp, of* وَهَبَ
هَبْنِي قلت	Suppose I said.
هَبَّ يَهُبُّ	To blow (wind).
هَبَّ وأَهَبَّ	To shake (a sword).
هَبَّ يَفْعَلُ	To begin to do.
هَبَّ مِنَ ٱلنَّوْمِ	To awake from sleep.
هَبَابٌ	Fine dust in the air.

Blowing (of wind). هُبُوب
Place of blowing of wind. مَهَبّ
Flesh, a piece of meat. هَبْرٌ
A wind raising dust. رِيح هُبارِيَّةٌ
Flakes. Scurf. هِبْرِيَّةٌ
To descend ; fall. هَبَطَ يَهْبُطُ
To cause to come down. أَهْبَطَ
Fall ; abatement. هَبْطٌ وهُبُوطٌ
A fall; a descent. هَبْطَةٌ
To take a vapour bath. (تَهَبَّلَ)
Vapour; steam. (هَبْلَةٌ)
Fumigation. (تَهبيلٌ)
Dust flying in the a ir. هَباءٌ
To defame. هَتَرَ يَهْتِرُ هَتْراً
To be reckless; neglect. إِسْتَهْتَرَ
To call, shout. هَتَفَ يَهْتِفُ هُتافاً
Call, cry, shauting. هُتافٌ
To tear off ; divulge. هَتَكَ يَهْتِكُ

To defame, disgrace. هَتَكَ سِتْرَه
To be disclosed, divulged. تَهَتَّكَ
Solution of continuity. هَتْكٌ
Disgrace, dishonour. (هَتِيكَةٌ)
Rapid, quick (march). هَجاجٌ
To subside. هَجَأَ يَهْجَأُ هَجْأً
To spell (a ward). تَهَجَّأَ
To forsake, renounce. هَجَرَ يَهْجُرُ
To emigrate. هاجَرَ مِنْ
Forsaking. هَجْرٌ وهِجْرانٌ
Separation; flight. هِجْرَةٌ
The Hegira, Moslem Era. أَلْهِجْرَةُ
Hot mid-day. هاجِرَةٌ وهَجِيرَةٌ
Emigrant. مُهاجِرٌ
Emigration. مُهاجَرَةٌ
Deserted, forsaken. مَهْجُورٌ
To occur to the mind. هَجَسَ يَهْجِسُ
A troubled thought. هاجِسٌ

To sleep; subside. هجع يَهجَعُ هجُوعاً

Part of the night. هَجيعٌ مِنَ ٱللَّيلِ

To assail, surprise. هجم يَهجِمَ عَلَى

To attack suddenly. هَاجَم

A surprise, sudden attack. هَجْمَةٌ

Sudden attack or surprise. هُجوم

To be low, vile. هجن يَهجُن هجنةٌ

To consider mean. إِسْتَهجن

Fault, meanness. هجنةٌ

Fast dromedary. هجِينٌ

To mock, ridicule. هجا يَهجُو هجْواً

To spell. هجا وَهجى وتَهجى

A satire, lampoon. هجاء

Spelling. هجاء وتَهجيةٌ وتَهجٍّ

The alphabet. حرُوفُ ٱلهجاء

Satire. هجُوَّةٌ واهجيةٌ ج أهاجي

To pull down, demolish. هدَّ يَهدُّ

To threaten, menace. هَدَّدَ وتَهدَّدَ

To be pulled down. إِنْهَدَّ

Destruction, demolition. هَدٌّ

Threatening. تَهدِيدٌ وتَهدُّدٌ

Sledge-hammer. مِهَدَّةٌ

To subside, calm down. هَدَأَ يَهدَأُ

To calm, appease. هَدَّأَ تَهدِئَة

Rest, tranquillity, quiet. هُدوء

Eye-lashes; fringe. هدْبٌ ج أهدابٌ

To be spent uselessly. Squander. هَدرَ يَهدِر

Roaring (of waves, &c.) هَدِيرٌ

To approach. هَدَفَ يَهدِفُ إِلَى

Target, aim. هَدَفٌ ج أهدافٌ

To let down. هدل ـ هدْلاً

To hang down. هدِل وتَهدَّل

A bovine epidemic. Rinderpest. أبُو هَدلانَ

To pull down. هَدَمَ يَهدِمُ هدماً

To be destroyed. تَهدَّمَ وٱنْهدمَ

Destruction, demolition. هَدْمٌ

(هدومٌ)	Clothes, garments.
هادِمُ آللَّذاتِ	Death.
مهدومٌ	Destroyed, demolished.
هادَنَ	To come to an agreement.
تهادنَ	To make a truce.
هدنَةٌ ومُهادَنَةٌ	Armistice, truce.
هدْهدٌ ج هداهدُ	Hoopoo (bird).
هدى يهدِي	To lead aright, guide.
أهدى	To give a present.
تَهادى	To make mutual presents.
اهْتدى	To be rightly guided.
إستهدى	To ask for guidance.
هدايةٌ وهُدًى	The right path.
هَديَّةٌ ج هدايا	A present, gift.
هادٍ ج هُداةٌ	Guide, leader.
مهديٌّ	Rightly guided, offered.
هذَّ ـ هذيذاً في	To ponder over.
هَذا م هَذهِ وَهَذي	This.
هذان	Dual of هَذا
هذَّب	To trim; improve.
تَهذَّبَ	To be educated; improved.
تهذيبٌ	Education. Correction.
مُهذَّبٌ ومُتهذبٌ	Refined. polished.
هَذرَ يهذُرُ هَذْراً	To babble,
هَذهِ	*Fem of.* هذا
هَذى يهذي	To talk irrationally.
هذاءٌ وَهَذيان	Delirium.
هرٌّ ج هِررةٌ	A cat.
هرَّةٌ ج هررٌ	A she-cat.
هَريرٌ	Whining, yelping.
هرئ يهرا	To become tattered,
هَربَ يهرُبُ	To run away, flee.
هرب	To put to flight; smuggle.
هَربٌ	Escape, flight.
هَاربٌ	A fugitive.
مَهربٌ ج مَهارب	Place of refuge.

هرَّجَ	To joke, jest.
هرْجٌ	Agitation, tumult.
هارِجٌ وَمُهرِّجٌ	Jester ; buffoon.
هرس يهرس	To pound, crush.
هرَّشَ بَيْنَ	To excite discord.
تَهارَشَ وَاهترش	To sport.
هرَاشٌ	Tumult, row.
هرْطوقيٌّ ج هَراطقَةٌ	Heretic.
هرَعَ يهرَعُ هَرعاً	To walk fast.
هرَقَ يهرق. وهرَّق	To pour out.
إهراقٌ	Effusion, shedding.
هرَقْلٌ	Heraclius *(Emperor)*.
هرِمَ يهرَمُ	To be decrepit.
هَرمَ يهرِمُ.وهرَّمَ	To cut, hash.
هرَّمَ وَأهرمَ	To render one old.
هرم	Decrepitude.
هرَمٌ ج أهرامٌ	A pyramid.
هرِمٌ ج هَرِمونَ	Very old.
هَرْوَلَ	To walk fast.
هِراوةٌ ج هَراوَى	A cudgel.
(هَرَى يهري هَرْياً)	To wear out.
(إهترَى)	To get worn out.
هرْيٌ ج أهراء	Granary.
هزَّ يهز هزّاً	To shake, brandish.
إهتزَّ وَانهزَّ	Ta be shaken.
هزَّةٌ	Earthquake.
هَزِيزٌ	Sound. Rustling.
هزَأَ وَهزِئَ يهزَأُ بِ	To mock at.
تهزَّأَ وَاستهزَأَ بِ	To ridicule.
هَزْءٌ وهُزُوءٌ وَاستهزاء	Mockery.
هزِيجٌ منَ اللَّيْلِ	Part of the night.
اهزوجَـةٌ ج أهازيج	A song.
هزيعٌ منَ اللَّيْل	Part of the night.
هَيْزَعةٌ	Fear. Tumult.
هَزَلَ يهزِلُ هَزْلاً	To joke, jest.
هَزَلَ هُزْلاً . وَهزَّلَ	To emaciate.

To be emaciated. هَزَلَ يَهزُلُ

Sport, jest, joke. هزْلٌ وهزَالةٌ

Thinness, emaciation. هزالٌ

Thin, meagre. هزيل وَمَهْزول

To put to flight. هَزَم يهزِم

To be put to flight. إِنهزام

Rout, defeat. هَزْم وَهَزيمة

Thunder. Rain. هزيم

To shake, agitate. هزْهَز

To be cheerful. هشَّ يهِشُّ

Joyous cheerful. هشٌّ

Tender, soft. هَشٌّ وَهشاشٌ

To roam about. (هشل يَهشل هَشْلاً)

To drive away, expel. (هَشلَ)

To crush, break. هشم يَهْشم وَهشَّم

To be crushed. تَهشَّم وانهشَمَ

A hill. هَضْبةٌ ج هِضابٌ

To break. To digest. هضم يهضِم

To oppress. هَضَمَ وتهضَّم واهتضَم

To wrong. هَضم حقَّهُ

To be digested (food). إِنهضَمَ

Digestion. هَضْم وَانهِضام

Indigestion. سُوءُ الهَضْمِ

Injury, wrong. هَضيمة ج هَضائِم

To rain. هَطل يَهْطِل هَطلاً

Fine but continuous rain. هَطلٌ

To rustle; walk quickly. هَفَّ يَهِفُّ

To long for. هَفَّ إِلى

To fly up and down. هَفت يَهفِت

To rush to, or into. تَهافت عَلى

A slip, fault. هفْوة ج هَفَوات

Famished. هَافٍ

Thus, so. هَكذا

To mock at, deride. تهكَّم على

Mockery. Irony. Sarcasm. تَهكُّم

Particle of Interrogation. هَل

هَلْ كَتَبْتَ — Did you write ?
هَلَّا — Is not ? Why not ?
حيَّ هلْ — Come! Hasten!
هَلَّ يَهِلُّ — To appear, (new moon).
هلَّل — To praise God.
تهلَّل — To exult, be joyous.
إنهلَّ — To pour down (rain).
هِلٌّ و هَلَّةٌ — The new moon.
هلالٌ — New moon. Crescent.
هِلاليٌّ — Semi-lunar, crescentic.
تهليلٌ — Act of parising God.
أهلِيلجيٌّ — Elliptical. Oval.
هلك يَهْلِكُ — To perish, die.
هلك وأهْلَكَ — To ruin. destroy.
إستهلك — To squander, exhaust.
هلاكٌ — Ruin, loss. Death.
هالِكٌ — Perishing, lost, dead.
تهلُكةٌ — Perdition, ruin.

مهلكةٌ — Dangerous place.
هَلُمَّ — Here ! Come here !
هَلُمَّ جرًّا — And so on, *et cœtera*.
هُلامٌ — Jelly.
هُلاميٌّ — Jelly-like, gelatinous.
هُمْ — They ; their ; them.
كِتابُهُمْ — Their book.
ضَرَبَهُمْ — He struck them.
هَمَّ يَهُمُّ. وأهَمَّ — To cause anxiety.
هَمَّ يَهُمُّ هَمًّا ب — To desire, seek.
إهتمَّ — To be grieved.
إهتمَّ بِ — To take pains in...
إهتمَّ لِ — To be solicitous about
هَمٌّ ج هُمُومٌ — Care, anxiety.
هِمَّةٌ ج هِمَم — Concern ; energy.
هَامَّةٌ ج هَوامٌّ — Reptile, insect.
هُمامٌ — Energetic.
أهَمُّ — More important.

Care, effort.	إِهتِمامٌ
Important matter.	مُهِمٌّ ج مَهامٌّ
Provisions, necessaries.	مُهِمَّاتٌ
Preoccupied, anxious.	مَهْمومٌ
Stupid, savage people.	هَمَجٌ
To subside.	هَمَدَ يَهْمُدُ هُموداً
To extinguish ; clam.	هَمَّدَ وأَهْمَدَ
To pour out.	هَمَرَ يَهْمُرُ
To be poured out, flow.	إِنهَمَرَ
To beat ; push.	هَمَزَ يَهمِزُ هَمزاً
A hemza = (ء)	هَمزَةٌ ج هَمَزاتٌ
A spur, goad.	مِهْمازٌ ج مَهامِيزُ
Marked with a hemza.	مَهْموزٌ
To mumble.	هَمَسَ يَهْمِسُ هَمْساً
Margin of a book.	هامِشٌ
To shed tears.	هَمَعَ يَهْمَعُ
To press, urge.	هَمَكَ يَهْمِكُ
To be engrossed in.	إِنهَمَكَ في
To rain quietly.	هَمَلَ يَهْمُلُ
To neglect, forget.	أَهْمَلَ
To be negligent.	(تَهامَلَ في)
Negligence, carelessness.	(تَهامُلٌ)
Unused, obsolete (word).	مُهْمَلٌ
Neglected.	مُهْمَلٌ
To mumble, mutter.	هَمْهَمَ
To fall, flow, run.	هَمَا يَهْمُو
Belt.	هِمْيانٌ ج هَمايِينُ
Royal.	هَمايُونٌ وَهَمايُونِيٌّ
They ; their · them, *fem.*	هُنَّ
To congratulate.	هَنَّأَ ب
To enjoy, relish.	هَنِئَ يَهْنَأُ ب
To enjoy, relish.	تَهَنَّأَ تَهَنُّؤًا ب
Wholesome. Pleasant.	هَنِيءٌ
Congratulation.	تَهْنِئَةٌ
India, the Indies.	أَلْهِندُ
Cocoa-nut.	جَوْزُ ٱلْهِند

An Indian. هنديّ ج هُنُود

Endive, wild chicory. هندباء

To make a plan. هندسَ

Engineering. Architecture. هندَسةٌ

Geometry. علمُ الهندَسةِ

Geometrical. هندسيّ

Geometrician. Architect. Engineer. مُهندِس

To arrange, adorn. هندمَ

Here (*adv*). هنا وَهَهنا

There, yonder. هنا وهُنالِكَ

A little while, trifle. هنيةٌ وهُنيهةٌ

He, it. هُوَ

An abyss. هُوّةٌ ج هُوَت

To become a Jew. هادَ وتهوَّدَ

To abate price. هاوَدَ

Jews. يهودُ

Jew. يهوديّ

Jewess. Judea. يهوديّة

Camel-litter. هوْدَجٌ ج هوادِج

Lo! Behold! هوذا

To roll down, fall down. تهوَّرَ

To rush imprudently. تهوَّرَ

Rashness. Collapse. تهوُّرٌ

Folly. Passionate desire. هَوَس

Scorched green wheat. (هَوِيسٌ)

To be agitated; (bark). هاشَ يهوشُ

Tumult. هَوْشةٌ ج هَوْشاتٌ

To vomit. هاعَ يهاعُ ويهوعُ هَوْعاً

To frighten. هَالَ يَهُولُ

To threaten with. هوَّلَ عليهِ بِ

To be terrified. إهتالَ

Terror, fright. هَولٌ ج أهوالٌ

The sphinx. أبو الهَوْلِ

Frightful, terrible. هَائلٌ ومَهولٌ

Halo (of moon). هَالةٌ ج هَالاتٌ

Head. Chief. هامَةٌ ج هَاماتٌ

هانَ يَهُونُ هَوْنًا عَلى To be easy.
هَانَ يَهُونُ هُونًا To be despised.
هَوَّنَ على To facilitate.
أهانَ To despise.
تهاوَنَ ب To neglect.
هَوانٌ Contemptibleness.
إهانَةٌ ج إهانات Disdain ; insult.
تهاوُن Negligence ; idleness.
هَاوُنٌ Mortar (for pounding).
هيّنٌ وَهيْنٌ Light, easy to do.
أهْون Lighter, easier.
مُهانٌ Disdained ; injured.
مَهانَةُ Contempt, shame.
هوى يهوي هَويًّا To fall.
هوي يَهْوى To love ; desire.
هوَّى تهْوِيَة To ventilate.
أهْوى To fall down ; descend.
هوى ج أهْواء Passionate desire.

هَوِيٌّ Ringing in the ears.
هَواءٌ ج أهْوِيَةٌ Air, atmosphere.
هَوائِيٌّ Atmospherical.
ألْهاوِيَةُ The lower world ; hades.
هِيَ ج هُنَّ She, it ; they.
هَيَّأ تهيئة To prepare.
تَهَيَّأ لِ To be prepared for.
هَيئَةٌ ج هَيئات Form, aspect.
عِلْمُ ٱلْهيئَةِ Astronomy.
هَابَ يَهابُ وآهْتابَ To fear ; revere.
هَبْ *Imp. of* هَاب *and* وَهَب
هَيبَةٌ Respect, awe, veneration.
أَهيب More respected.
مَهيبٌ Venerable ; respected.
مَهابَة Fear ; veneration, respect.
هاتِ ج هاتُوا Give !
هَاجَ يَهيج To be agitated, excited.
هَاجَ وَهَيَّجَ To excite, agitate.

تهيّج واهتاجَ — To be agitated.

هيجانٌ — Agitation, excitement.

هيجاء — Battle, combat ; strife.

هائجٌ — Agitated, excited.

هيضةٌ — Diarrhœa.

أهيفُ م هَيفاء ج هِيفٌ — Slim.

هيكلٌ ج هَياكل — Temple ; alter.

الهيكلُ العظميُّ — The skeleton.

هيولى — Matter.

هيوليٌّ وهيولانيٌّ — Material *(adj)*.

هام يَهيم — To love passionately.

هيامٌ — Passionate love.

هائمٌ ج هيَّمٌ وهيّامٌ — Love stricken.

ليلٌ أهيمُ — Starless night.

قلبٌ مستهامٌ — Heart lost in love.

ألمهيمن — God (the Protector).

هَيْنٌ وهيِّنٌ — Easy.

هَيهاتَ — Far ! Far away !

هيّا وهيِّ — Come ! Quick !

و

و — As a numeral sign=6.

و — And.

والله — By God !

وا — Oh ! Ah ! Alas !

إبةٌ — Shame. Dishonour.

وباءٌ ووباءٌ ج أوبئةٌ وأوباءٌ — Pestilence.

وبائيٌّ — Epidemic ; pestiiential.

وبيءٌ وموبوءٌ — Pestilential.

To rebuke, reprimand. وبَّخ

Scolding, rebuking. تَوْبيخٌ

Cony. وَبْرٌ ج وُبُورٌ وَوِبَارٌ

Soft hair (of animals). وَبْرٌ

Nomad people. أهلُ ٱلوبَر

Low people. وَبَشٌ ج أوْبَاشٌ

To rain. وَبَلَ يَبِلُ وَبْلاً

To be unhealthy, (land). وَبُلَ يَوْبُلُ

A heavy shower. وَبْلٌ وَوَابِلٌ

Unhealthiness. Hardship. وَبَالٌ

Unhealthy. Hard. وَبِيلٌ

To make firm. وَتَدَ يَتِدُ وَوَتَّدَ

Wooden peg. A kind of foot *(Prosody)*. وَتَدٌ ج أوْتَادٌ

Mountains. أوْتَادُ ٱلأرْضِ

To string a bow. وَتَرَ وَوَتَرَ وَأَوْتَرَ

To be strained hard. توتر

To follow one another. تواتر

Single; odd number. وِتْرٌ

Cord of a circle. وَتَرٌ وَوَتَرٌ

String of a bow, or musical instrument. Tendon وَتَرٌ ج أوْتَارٌ

Succession. تَوَاتُرٌ

Repeated at intervals. مُتَوَاتِرٌ

Often, repeatedly. مُتَوَاتِراً

A bruise or wound. وَثْءٌ وَوَثَاءَةٌ

To leap. وَثَبَ يَثِبُ وَثْباً وَوُثُوباً

A leap, jump. An assault. وَثْبَةٌ

To rely upon. وَثِقَ يَثِقُ بِ

To be firm. وَثُقَ يَوْثُقُ وَثَاقَةً

To make firm. وَثَّقَ

To make a covenant with. وَاثَقَ

To fetter, tie fast. أوْثَقَ بالوِثَاقِ

To trust, rely upon. إِسْتَوْثَقَ مِنْ

Confidence. ثِقَةٌ

A tie, fetter, rope, strap. وِثَاقٌ

Firm or solid. Reliable. وَثِيقٌ

Compact, alliance. وَثِيقَةٌ ج وَثَائِقُ

أوثق م وُثقى	Firmer, firmest.
ألعُرْوَةُ ٱلوُثقى	The strongest hold.
مِيثاقٌ ج مَواثيقَ	Covenant.
وَثنٌ ج أوْثانَ	An idol.
وَثنِيٌّ ج وَثَنِيُّون	Idolater ; heathen.
وَثْيٌ	A sprain.
وَجَبَ يجِبُ	To be necessary, due.
أوْجَبَ	To make binding.
إستَوْجَبَ	To be worthy of.
وَجْبَةٌ	A set of the same kind.
وُجُوبٌ	Necessity, duty.
ايجابٌ	Affirmation.
إيجابيٌّ	Affirmative, positive.
وجبٌ	Necessary, obligatory.
وَاجِبٌ ج وَاجِبَاتٌ	Duty.
مُوْجِبٌ	Cause, motive, reason.
بِمُوْجِبِ	According to.
وَجَدَ يَجِدُ	To find.
وجد	To be ; to exist.
أوْجَدَ إيجاداً	To create, produce.
تَوَجَّدَ لِ	To be grieved for.
جِدَةٌ	Wealth, competence.
وَجْدٌ	Love ; joy ; grief.
وُجْدانٌ	Inner consciousness.
وُجُودٌ	Existence.
مَوْجُودٌ	Found ; existing.
ألمَوْجُوداتُ	Existing things.
وَجْرٌ ج أوْجارٌ	Grotto, cave.
وِجَارٌ ج أوْجِرَةٌ	Den, lair.
وَجَزَ يَجِزُ	To be brief in speech.
أوْجَزَ	To abbreviate, abridge.
وَجِيزٌ ومُوجَزٌ	Abridged, concise.
إيجازٌ	Conciseness, brevity.
وَجِعَ يَوْجَعُ وَيَيْجَعُ	To feel pain.
أوْجَعَ	To cause or inflicl pain.

Face. Chief. وجهٌ ج أوْجهٌ وَوجوه
Manner. Aim. Surface.

To do for God. عملهُ لوجهِ ٱللّٰه

In some manner. بوجهٍ

Side. Dimension. (*Geom*). جِهةٌ ج جِهاتٌ

Concerning. منْ جِهتهِ

Consideration, position. وَجاهةٌ

Opposite to, in front of. تجاهَ

Chief, prince. وَجيهٌ ج وَجهاء

Going, turning to. متوجّهٌ

To be alone. وَحدَ يحدُ

To reduce to one ; unify. وَحَّد

To be one, single, alone. توحَّد

To be united. إتّحد

Separately. على حِدَةٍ

Alone. وَحْدَهُ

Unity, being unique. وَحْدانيةٌ

Solitude, isolation. وَحْدةٌ

To feel pain. توجَّع

To feel pain for. توجَّع ل

Beer, ale. جِعَةٌ

Pain. Disease. وجعٌ ج أوْجاعٌ

Painful ; sore. وجيعٌ ومُوْجعٌ

Fire-place, hearth. وُجاقٌ وأوْجاقٌ

To fear. وَجِلَ يَوْجَلُ

Fear, terror. وَجلٌ ج أوْجالٌ

Timorous. وجلٌ ج وَجِلُون

Cheek (face). وجنةٌ ج وَجَناتٌ

Mallet. ميجنةٌ ج مَوَاجنُ

To be respected. وجُهَ يوْجهُ

To turn a thing towards. وَجَّه

To send. وَجَّه

To meet one. واجَهَ مُواجهةً

To repair to. توجَّه نحوَ وإلى

To have an interview. (تَوَاجَهَ)

To turn towards.

وَاحِدٌ One; single; unique.

الوَاحِد The only one.

أَحَدٌ م إِحْدى ج آحادٌ One.

الأَحَدُ Sunday.

وحيدٌ م وحيدَةٌ Unique.

إِتِّحادٌ Union ; harmony ; accord.

تَوْحيدُ Unification. Belief in the unity of God.

تَوَحُّد Isolation, solitude.

تَوَحُّدٌ A unitarian.

مُتَوَحِّدٌ Isolated, alone. One.

وَحَشَ وَتَوَحَّشَ To be unpeopled.

تَوَحَّش To grow savage.

إِسْتَوْحَشَ To feel lonely.

وَحْشٌ ج وُحوشٌ Wild beast.

حِمارُ وَحْشٍ Onager, wild ass.

وَحْشَةٌ Grief ; solitude.

وحْشيٌّ Wild, ferocious cruel.

تَوَحُّشٌ Savage state. Barbarity.

مُتَوَحِّشٌ Savage, brute-like.

وحْلٌ ج وُحُولٌ Thin mud, mire.

وحِلٌ Muddy, miry.

وَحنَ يحِنُ To be spiteful.

أَوْحى إِلى To inspire. Send.

وَحيٌ Divine inspiration.

وَحى Haste, hurry.

وَآخذ مواخذةً) To find fault with.

(لا تُواخِذْني) Excuse me.

وَخزَ يخِزُ وخْزاً To prick.

وَخَطهُ الشَّيْبُ To be grizzled.

وَخُمَ يَوْخمُ To be unhealthy.

أَتخمَ To surfeit (food).

إِتَّخم To be ill (from food).

وَخِمٌ وَوَخيمٌ Dirty unclean.

تخمةٌ Indigestion.

وخّى وَتوخّى To seek diligently.

(وَآخى مُوآخاةً) To fraternize with.

To love; wish for. وَدَّ يَوَدّ

To show love to. تَوَدَّدَ إِلى

To have mutual love. تَوادَّ تَوادًّا

Love; friendship. وُدّ وَوِدادٌ

It is my wish. بودّي (بدّي)

Lover, affectionate. وُدّ وَوَدُود

Affection, friendship. مَوَدَّة

Mutual, love. موادَّة وَتَوادٌّ

Jugular vein. وَداج مث وَداجان

To forsake, leave. وَدَع يَدَع

Let me, allow me! دَعْني

To take leave of. وَدَّعَ يُوَدّع

To conciliate. ودع وداعًا

To deposit with. أَوْدع عِنْد

To bid farewell. Deposit. إِسْتَوْدَعَ

White shell. وَدْعَة ج وَدَعاتٌ

Bidding adieu, farewell. وَداعٌ

Mildness, gentleness. وَداعَة

Rest, quiet; gentleness. دَعَة

Quiet, gentle. وديع ج ودعاء

Deposit; trust, charge. وَدِيعَةٌ

Depositor. مستَوْدِعٌ

Depository. مستَوْدَعٌ

Race-field. ميدان ج مَيادين

To send. وَدَّى

To perish. أَوْدى إِيداءً

Blood-money. دِيَة ج دِياتٌ

Valley. وادٍ ج أَوْدِيَة

Let him alone. وذَر — ذَرْهُ

Behind. Beyond. وَرَاءَ

To equivocate. وَارَب مُوارَبَة

Obliquity. Diagonal. (وَرْبٌ)

To inherit. وَرِثَ يرِثُ إِرْثًا وَوِراثَةً

To bequeath. وَرَّثَ وَاوْرَثَ

To bring on (an evil). أَوْرَثَ

تواَرَثَ	To inherit.
إِرْثٌ وورِاثةٌ	Inheritance.
وارثٌ ج وَرَثَةٌ وورَّاثٌ	Heir.
موْرُوثٌ	Inherited ; hereditary.
مِيراثٌ ج موَاريثُ	Inheritance.
وَرَدَ يرِدُ ورُودًا	To come, arrive.
وَرْدٌ ج ورودٌ	Flower. Rose.
وَرْدَةٌ	A rose.
بنْتُ وَرْدانَ	Cockroach.
وَرْدِيٌّ	Red, rose-coloured.
واردٌ	Coming, arriving.
إِيرادات	Revenue.
وريدُ ج اوْرِدَةٌ	Vein.
حبْلُ الوَرِيدِ	Jugular vein.
موْرِدٌ ج موَارد	Access, entrance.
مورَّدٌ	Of a rose colour, rosy.
ورِشٌ	Brick, restless.
(ورْشةٌ)	Work-shop.
وَرَّط	To throw into difficulty.
تورَّط	To fall into difficulty.
وَرْطةٌ ج وَرَطاتٌ	Difficulty.
وَرِعَ يرِعُ	To be pious.
وَرَعٌ	Fear of God. Piety.
وَرِعٌ ج أَوْرَاعٌ	A pious man.
وَرَقٌ ج أَوْرَاقٌ	Foliage, paper.
أَوْرَقَ	To put forth leaves.
وَرَقةٌ	A leaf (of a tree) ; a piece of paper ; ticket.
مُورِّقٌ	Stationer. Plasterer.
وَرِكٌ ووِرْكٌ	Hip bone ; hip.
وَرَلٌ ج ورْلانٌ	A large lizard.
وَرِمَ يرِمُ وَرَماً . وتورَّمَ	To swell.
ورَّمَ	To cause to swell.
وَرَمٌ ج أَوْرَام	Swelling. Tumour.
وَرْوَارُ ج وَرَاوِير	Bee-eater (bird).
ورَّى وَوَارَى	To conceal.
توَارَى عَن	To hide one's self.

Creatures ; mankind. وَرًى

Behind. وَرَاءَ

The Pentateuch. Bible. تَوْرَاةٌ

Using a word in a double sense. تَوْرِيَةٌ

Geese. وَزّ (اوز)

A goose. وَزَّةٌ

To flow. وَزَبَ يزبُ وُزُوبا

Water-drain. مِيزَابٌ ج مَيَازِيبُ

To commit a sin. وَزَرَ يَزِرُ

To aid, help. وَازَرَ عَلَى

To become a vizier. تَوَزَّرَ

To put on a وَزْرَة . إِتَّزَرَ

Burden. Crime. وِزْرٌ ج أَوْزَارٌ

Loin-cloth. وَزْرَةٌ ج وَزْرَاتٌ

Office of a vizier. وِزَارَةٌ

Vizier. وَزِيرٌ ج وُزَرَاءُ

Assistant. مُوَازِرٌ

To distribute. وَزَّعَ وَأَوْزَعَ بَيْنَ

To be divided, distributed. تَوَزَّعَ

Scotch broom. (وَزَّالٌ)

To weigh. وَزَنَ يَزِنُ وَزْنًا وَزِنَةً

To compose (a verse) according to measure scan. وَزَنَ ٱلشِّعْرَ

To be heavy. وَزُنَ يَوْزُنُ وَزَانَةً

To be equal in weight. وَازَنَ

To compare. وَازَنَ بَيْنَ

To be equal in weight. تَوَازَنَ

Weighing ; weigh. وَزْنٌ وَزِنَةٌ

Weight; measure; metre of a verse. وَزْنٌ ج أَوْزَانٌ

A weight. Talent. وَزْنَةٌ ج وَزْنَاتٌ

A weigher. Of full weight. وَازِنٌ

Prudent, reflecting. وَزِينُ ٱلرَّأْيِ

Equal, equivalent to. مُوَازِنٌ

Equilibrium. مُوَازَنَةٌ

Weighed ; measured. مَوْزُونٌ

Scales, balance. Standard. Measure. مِيزَانٌ ج مَوَازِينُ

Libra (zodiac). أَلْمِيزَانُ

To correspond to, be parallel with.	وازَى
To correspond to,	تَوازَى
Correspondence.	مُوازَاةٌ
Parallel (line).	مُتَوازٍ
To be foul, soiled,	وَسِخَ يَوْسَخُ
To soil.	وَسَّخَ وَأَوْسَخَ
Dirt, uncleanness.	وَسَخٌ ج أَوْسَاخٌ
Dirty, unclean, soiled.	وَسِخٌ
To prop with a pillow.	وسد
A pillow, cushion.	وِسَادٌ ج وُسُدٌ
A pillow.	وِسَادَةٌ ج وِسَادَاتٌ
To put in the middle.	وَسَّطَ
To take a middle position.	تَوَسَّطَ
To mediate between.	تَوَسَّطَ بَيْنَ
Middle, centre.	وَسَطٌ وَوَسْطٌ
Means.	وَاسِطَةٌ ج وَسَائِط
By means of, through.	بِوَاسِطَةِ
Intermediation.	وَسَاطَة وَتَوَسُّط

Mediator.	وَسِيط ج وُسَطاء
The middle finger.	الوُسْطَى
Intermediate. Mediator.	مُتَوَسِّط
Mediterranean.	أَلبَحْرُ المُتَوَسِّطُ
To be spacious, wide.	وَسُعَ يَوْسُعُ
To contain, hold.	وَسِعَ يَسَعُ سَعَةً
Thou canst not.	لا يَسَعُكَ انْ
To widen, enlarge.	وَسَّعَ وَأَوْسَعَ
To enrich (God).	وَسَّعَ وَأَوْسَعَ على
To be at ease.	تَوَسَّعَ في
To be enlarged.	إِتَّسَعَ وَاسْتَوْسَعَ
Power, ability.	وُسْعٌ وَسِعَةٌ
Width ; capacity.	سَعَة واتِّساع
Extent, dilatation.	إِتِّساعُ
Spacious.	واسع وَوَسيع وَمُتَّسع
Wider, more vast.	اوْسَع
Rich, wealthy, opulent.	مُوسِعٌ
To load; to freight.	وَسَقَ يَسِقُ وَسْقًا

وَسْق ج أَوْسَاق A load ; cargo.

مَوْسُوق Freighted, loaded.

تَوَسَّل إلى To implore, seek.

وسيلة ج وَسَائِل Means.

تَوَسُّل Supplication.

وَسَمَ يَسِم وَسْمًا وَسِمَة To brand.

وَسْم ج وُسُوم. سِمَة ج سِمَات Sign, mark.

وِسَام Badge of honour.

مَوْسِم ج مَوَاسِم Season.

مَوْسُوم Marked. Branded.

وَسِنَ يَوْسَن To slumber.

سِنَة Slumber; unconsciousness.

وَسْوَسَ لِ To suggest wicked things.

وَسْوَاس ج وَسَاوِس Hallucination.

الوَسْوَاس Satan.

مُوسَى و (موس) A razor.

مُوسَى Moses.

مُوسَوِيّ Mosaic; a Jew.

وَشَّح To adorn.

تَوَشَّح وَاتَّشَح To put on.

وُشَاح A sash set with jewels.

مُوَشَّحة Double-rhymed poetry.

وَشَرَ يَشِر To saw (wood).

مَوْشُور ج مَوَاشِير A prism.

مِيشَار A saw.

وَشُكَ يَوْشُك وَشْكًا To be quick.

أَوْشَك أَنْ To be on the point of.

وَشْك Celerity ; haste, hurry.

وَشِيك Swift ; on the point of.

وَشَمَ يَشِم وَشْمًا وَوَشَّم To tattoo.

وَشْوَش وَتَوَشْوَش To whisper.

وَشَى يَشِي . وَوَشَّى To embellish.

وَشَى بفلانٍ إلى To slander.

وَاشٍ ج وُشَاة وَوَاشُون Slanderer.

مُوَشَّى Coloured ; embroiderd.

وَصَبٌ ج أَوْصَاب Illnes, pain.

أُوْصَدَ To shut, close (a door).
مُوصَدٌ Shut, closed.
وصَفَ يَصِفُ To describe, qualify.
وَصَفَ لِ To prescribe medicine to a sick person, (physician).
إِتَّصَفَ To be qualified.
وَصْفٌ ج أوْصَافٌ Description.
وَصفةٌ Prescription of physician.
وَصفيّ Descriptive.
صِفةٌ ج صِفاتٌ Quality ; adjective.
وصيف ج وصَفاء Young servant.
موْصُوف Qualified noun.
وَصَلَ يَصِلُ ب To unite, join.
وَصَلَ إلى To reach, arrive at.
وَصَلَ To give, bestow.
وَصَّلَ وَأوْصَلَ إلى To bring to.
واصَلَ To persevere in.
توصَّلَ إلى To arrive at.
تواصَلَ To be joined.
إِتَّصَلَ To be continuous.
إِتَّصَلَ إلى To arrive at, reach.
إِتَّصَلَ بِ To be united to.
وصلٌ Connection. Receipt.
وُصلةٌ وَاتّصالٌ Junction, union.
وِصالٌ Union of the friends.
صِلةٌ ج صِلاتٌ Union. Gift.
وُصُول ج وُصُولاتٌ Arrival. Receipt.
إِتّصَالٌ Continuity ; connexion.
مُواصَلةٌ Continuity. Union.
مُوصِلٌ Connective.
مُتَّصِلٌ Joined. Continual.
الضَّمِيرُ المتَّصِلُ Suffixed pronoun.
مَوْصُولٌ United, joined.
ألاسْمُ المَوْصُول Relative Pronoun.
وَصْمٌ وَوَصْمةٌ Fault; shame.
وَصْوَصَ To peep through a hole.
وَصّي وأوْصَى To bequeath.

To recommend.	وَصَّى إِلَى بِ
To charge, commend.	وَصَّى وَأَوْصَى
A testator, Executor of a will. Guardian.	وَصِيٌّ ج أَوْصِيَاء
An order, charge. Will, testament.	وَصِيَّةٌ ج وَصَايَا
Testator.	مُوصٍ
What is bequeathed.	مُوصًى بِهِ
A legatee, legatory.	مُوصًى لَهُ
To be clean.	وَضُؤَ يَوْضُؤُ وَضُوءًا
To perform ablutions.	تَوَضَّأَ
Water for ablutions.	وَضُوء
Cleanliness ; beauty.	وَضَاءَةٌ
Ablutions before prayers.	تَوَضُّؤ
To be clear, evident.	وَضَحَ يَضِحُ
To explain clearly.	وَضَّحَ وَأَوْضَحَ
To become clear.	تَوَضَّحَ وَٱتَّضَحَ
To ask for explanation.	إِسْتَوْضَحَ
Distinctness.	وُضُوحٌ وَٱتِّضَاحٌ
Clear, manifest, evident.	وَاضِحٌ
Clear exposition.	إِيضَاحٌ وَتَوْضِيحٌ
Evident, manifest, clear.	مُتَّضِحٌ
To lay put down.	وَضَعَ يَضَعُ
To give birth.	وَضَعَتْ تَضَعُ
To humiliate, abase.	وَضَعَ فُلَانًا
To be humble.	تَوَاضَعَ وَٱتَّضَعَ
To be humbled.	إِتَّضَعَ
Position, site.	وَضْعٌ ج أَوْضَاعٌ
Humiliation.	ضِعَةٌ
Laying down. Founder.	وَاضِعٌ
Humble, low.	وَضِيعٌ ج وُضَعَاء
Humility.	تَوَاضُعٌ وَٱتِّضَاعٌ
Place, site, spot.	مَوْضِعٌ ج مَوَاضِعُ
Humble, meek.	مُتَّضِعٌ وَمُتَوَاضِعٌ
Object; subject.	مَوْضُوعٌ ج مَوَاضِيعُ
To tread upon.	وَطِئَ يَطَأُ
To mount.	وَطِئَ (ٱلفَرَسَ)
To prepare, render easy.	وَطَّأَ

واطأ وتواطأ على To agree upon.

وَطاءٌ وَوطْءٌ Low ground.

وِطأةٌ Pressure, violence.

واطئٌ Low.

مَوْطِئٌ ج مَوَاطِئ Foot-stool.

وطد يَطد وَوَطّد To fix, make firm.

توَطّد To be made firm, fixed.

أَوْطادُ Mountains.

وَطيدٌ Firm, solid, immovable.

وَطرٌ ج أَوْطار Object purpose.

وَطَنَ يطِنُ. وَأَوْطَنَ ب To reside in.

وطّن وَٱستوْطَنَ To inhabit.

وطّن نفسهُ To resolve.

وَطنٌ ج أَوْطانٌ Native place.

موْطِنٌ ج مَوَاطِن Abode, home.

وَطواطٌ ج وَطاويطُ A bat.

وَطّى To lower, let down.

وَظبَ يَظبُ وظوبًا وَوَاظبَ على To persevere in.

مُواظبَةٌ Perseverance, assiduity.

وظّفَ To give an office to one.

تَوَظّفَ To be employed.

وَظيفةٌ ج وظائِفُ Pay, Office, function, employment.

عِلمُ وَظائِفِ ٱلأَعْضاء Physiology.

مُتَوَظّفٌ Functionary ; official.

وَعبَ يَعبُ To take up wholly.

أوْعبَ إِيعَابا To fill up; complete.

إِستوعَب To contain, hold.

وَعَد يعدُ To promise.

وَاعَدَ To make an appointment.

توَعّدَ To threaten.

توَاعَدَ To promise one another.

عِدةٌ وَوَعدٌ ج وُعُود A promise.

وَعيدٌ Menaces, threats.

مَوْعدٌ ج مَوَاعد Appointed time

ميعادٌ Appointed time or place.

وَعرٌ ج وعور Rugged place.

Rugged, difficult.	وعِر
To intimate.	وَعزـِ وَأوْعزَ إليهِ في
To exhort, warn.	وَعظ يَعِظ
To listen to warning.	إتعظَ
Sermon ; exhortation.	وعظٌ وَعظةٌ وَموعِظةٌ
A preacher.	واعِظُ ج وعَّاظُ
To be ill, indisposed.	توَعَّكَ
An illness.	وَعْكةٌ
Antelope.	وَعلٌ ج أوْعالُ
Good morning.	وَعِمَ — عِمْ صَباحاً
To gather ; contain.	وَعَى يَعي
To put into a vessel.	أوْعى إيعاء
To be careful.	توَعَّى وَٱستَوْعى
Attention, care.	وَعيٌ
Vessel, receptacle.	وِعاء ج أوْعيةٌ
Remembering. Cautious.	واعٍ
To be very hot.	وغر يَغر وَغراً
Intense heat. Anger.	وغرٌ
Tumult ; battle.	وَغى وَوَغيٌ
To come, arrive.	وَفد يَفدُ على
To send (an envoy).	وَفد وأوْفد
A deputation.	وفدٌ ج وفُودٌ
Epidemic.	وَافدٌ ج وفُودٌ
To increase, multiply.	وَفرَ يَفرُ
To economise ; save.	وَفَّرَ
Wealth, affluence.	وَفرٌ ج وفُورٌ
Economy ; saving.	وَفرٌ وَتوْفِيرٌ
Abundant, plentiful.	وَافرٌ
More abundant.	أوْفرُ
To make fit. To assist.	وَفَّقَ
To reconcile.	وَفَّقَ وَوَافقَ بَيْنَ
To agree or accord with.	وَافقَ
To succeed.	توَفَّقَ
To agree together.	توَافقَ في
To agree upon.	إتَّفقَ على أوْ في
To happen, occur.	إتفقَ لِ

وِفْقٌ وَوِفاقٌ Accord, agreement.

وفقًا لِ In accordance with.

مُوافقة Agreement, fitness.

إِتّفاقُ Coincidence. Accord.

اتّفاقي Accidental, by chance.

تَوفيقٌ Success. Prosperity.

مُوافِقٌ Convenient, suitable.

مُتَوَفّقٌ Prosperous, successful.

وفى يفي وأَوْفى To keep one's promise. To pay a debt.

وفى وَفيًّا To be perfect, complete.

وَافى To come to, meet.

وَفى حَقّه To pay the whole.

تُوُفّيَ وَتَوَفّاهُ اللّهُ To die.

وَفاء وإِيفاء Payment of a dept.

وَفاةٌ ج وَفَيَاتٌ Death, decease.

وَافٍ Complete.

وَقبٌ ج أَوْقابٌ Cavity, hole.

وقت وَوَقّتَ To appoint a time.

وَقتٌ ج أَوْقاتٌ Time, season.

وقتئذٍ Then, at that time.

لِلوقتِ ولِوقتِهِ Immediately.

وَقتيّ Temporal, provisional.

وَقَحَ يَقحُ وتَوَقّحَ To be impudent.

وقِحٌ Impudent, brazen-faced.

وَقاحةٌ وَقِحةٌ Impudence.

وَقَدَ يَقِدُ. وتَوَقَدَ وَٱتّقد To burn, blaze (a fire).

أَوْقدَ To kindle (a fire); light.

وَقُودٌ وَوَقِيدٌ Fuel.

مَوْقدٌ وَمَوْقدةٌ Fire-grate.

مَوْقُودٌ ومُتَقدٌ Lit, kindled.

وَقّرَ To honour, respect.

أَوْقرَ إِيقارًا To load (an animal).

وِقرٌ ج أَوْقارٌ Load, burden.

وَقارٌ Dignified bearing.

وَقُورٌ Venerable.

وَقَعَ يَقعُ To fall, fall down.

To happen, occur to one.	وقعَ لِ
To slander, insult one.	وقعَ في
To attack, assail.	وقَعَ وَأَوْقعَ ب
To let fall. Seal, sign.	توقَّعَ
To charge, rush upon.	واقِعَ
To tune, put in tune.	أَوقَعَ
To expect.	توقَّعَ وَآستوْقعَ
To fight together.	تواقَعَ
To beseech humbly.	تَواقعَ على
Event. Battle.	وَقعة ج وَقَعاتٌ
Imploring help.	وقيعٌ
Actually, in fact.	في الْوَاقع
Event, catastrophe.	وَاقعةٌ
Harmony of sounds.	إِيقاع
Expectation ; hope.	توقُّع
Signature.	توقيع ج تواقيع
Place.	مَوقع ج مواقع
To stop ; stand.	وَقفَ يَقِفُ
To endow.	وَقفَ لِ وَعلى
To inform. Know.	وَقفَ وُقوفاً على
To seize. To arrest.	وَقَّفَ وَأَوْقف
To contend with.	وَاقفَ في
To hesitate.	توَقَّفَ في
To abstain from.	توَقَّفَ عَنْ
To depend on.	توَقَّفَ على
Endowment.	وَقفٌ ج أَوْقافٌ
Standing. Pause.	وَاقِفٌ ج وُقوفٌ
Standing ; stopping.	وُقوف
Hesitation ; arrest.	توَقف
Suspension ; arrest.	توْقيف
A stand, station.	مَوْقِفٌ ج مَوَاقِف
Dependent on, stopped. Endowed.	مَوْقوف
To guard, protect.	وقى يَقي
To be on one's guard.	توَقى وَآتقى
To fear God.	إِتقى يَتقي
Protection.	وقايَةٌ وَوِقاء

Fear of God, piety. تقًى و تقْوى

Pious, God-fearing. تقيٌّ ج أتقياء

Sixty drams. A pharmaceutical ounce. اوْقيةٌ ج أواقٍ

A man who fears God. مُتّقٍ

To lean upon. تَوَكَّأَ وَٱتَّكَأَ على

To sit leaning on the side. إِتَّكَأَ

A staff; a couch. مُتَّكأٌ ج مُتَّكآت

To advance slowly. وكب يَكب

A procession. موْكبٌ ج مَوَاكبُ

To affirm, confirm. وكّد وَأكّد

To be confirmed. توَكَّد وَتأكَّد

Certain, affirmed. أكيدٌ وَمؤَكَّدٌ

Affirmation, confirmation. Emphasis. توْكيدٌ وَتأكيدٌ

Certatinly. بالتّأكيدِ

Nest of a bird. وكْرٌ ج أوْكارٌ

To push, thrust. وَكز ـــِ

To be defective. وَكَس ـــِ

Diminution of value; loss. وكْسٌ

To sell at a loss. بَاعَ بِٱلوَكس

To drop, trickle. وَكفَ يَكِفُ

Trickling, leaking. وَكْفٌ

To confide to. وكلَ يَكلُ إِلى

To appoint as an agent. وَكّلَ

To trust in. توَكَّل وَٱتَّكل على

Agency. وَكالةٌ ج وكالات

Substitute, agent. وَكيلٌ ج وُكلاء

Trust, confidence. إِتّكالٌ

Committed to. موْكُول إِلى

To enter. وِلَجَ يَلِجُ وُلُوجا وَفي

To commit to. وَلّج وَإِلى

To beget bring, forth. ولد يَلد

To act as a midwife. وَلّد

To originate from. توَلّد منْ

Child, son. وَلدٌ ج أوْلادٌ

Birth, parturition. وِلادةٌ

Midwifery. عِلمُ ٱلوِلادَةِ

Father; sire. وَالِدٌ ج وَالِدُونَ

Mother; dam. وَالِدَةٌ ج وَالِدَاتٌ

Father and mother. أَلْوَالِدَانِ

Generation. مَوْلِدٌ ج مَوَالِدُ

Birthday. مِيلَادٌ ج مَوَالِيدُ

Christmas. عِيدُ ٱلْمِيلَادِ

Unclassical (word) مُوَلَّدَةٌ

Midwife. مُوَلِّدَةٌ

Born. Child. مَوْلُودٌ ج مَوَالِيدُ

To be attached to. وَلِعَ يَوْلَعُ بِ

To light or kindle. وَلَّعَ

Material for lighting with. (وَلْعَةٌ)

Violent love, passion. وَلَعٌ

Passionately addicted. مُوْلَعٌ بِ

To associate with. وَالَفَ مُؤَالَفَةً

To entertain. أَوْلَمَ

Entertainment. وَلِيمَةٌ ج وَلَائِمُ

To grieve much. وَلِهَ يَلِهُ

Grief, passion, love. وَلَهٌ

Overcome with grief. وَلْهَانُ م وَلْهَى

To wail, lament. وَلْوَلَ وَلْوَلَةً

To follow. وَلِيَ وَوَلِيَ يَلِي

To rule. وَلِيَ وِلَايَةً وَعَلَى

To make one a ruler. وَلَّى

To turn away from. وَلَّى عَنْ

He turned and fled. وَلَّى هَارِبًا

He turned his face. وَلَّى وَجْهَهُ

To help, protect. وَالَى مُوَالَاةً

To do a good deed. أَوْلَى مَعْرُوفًا

To take charge of. تَوَلَّى

To follow one another. تَوَالَى

To take possession. إِسْتَوْلَى

Master, lord. وَلِيٌّ ج أَوْلِيَاءُ

Friend of God. وَلِيُّ ٱللهِ

Province. Rule. وِلَايَةٌ ج وِلَايَاتٌ

Heir apparent. وَلِيُّ ٱلْعَهْدِ

وَلِيُّ آلنعمِ Benefactor.

وَال ج وُلاةٌ Ruler, governor.

أَوْلى بِ More deserving, fit.

مَوْلى ج مَوالٍ Master, lord.

مُتَوَلٍّ Invested with power.

مُتَوالٍ Successive.

مُتَوالٍ ج مَتاوِلَةٌ A Sheïte.

وَمَا يَمَأُ . وَأَوْمَأَ إِلى To beckon to.

وَمأٌ وَإِيماءٌ Indication by sign.

أَلمُومَا إِلَيْهِ Indicated.

مُومِسَةٌ وَمُومِسٌ A prostitute.

وَمَض يَمِض . وَأَوْمَض To flash.

وَمِيضٌ Lightning; flash; gleam.

وَنَبَ To reprove, reprimand.

وَنى يَني . وَوَنِيَ To be faint, weak.

تَوانى في To relax one's efforts.

وَنًى وَوَناءٌ Fatigue, faintness.

تَوانٍ Slowness, slackness.

مُتَوانٍ Lazy, languid ; slow.

مِينا Enamel.

مِينا وَمِيناءٌ ج مَوانٍ Port, harbour.

وَهَبَ يَهَبُ To grant, give.

هَبْ Grant ! (*Imp. of* وَهَبَ)

إِستَوْهَبَ To ask for a present.

هِبَةٌ ج هِباتٌ Gift, present.

مَوْهِبَةٌ ج مَواهِبُ Donation, gift.

وَهَّابِيٌّ Mohammedan Wahhabite.

وَهَجَ يَهِجُ To blaze, burn.

أَوْهَجَ إِيهاجاً To kindle (a fire).

تَوَهَّجَ To glow burn.

وَهَجٌ Glow, heat (of fire, sun).

وَهَّاجٌ Intensely glowing.

وَهدَةٌ ج وَهَدٌ Deep pit ; abyss.

وَهَّطَ وَأَوْهَطَ To lead into evil.

تَوَهَّطَ في To rush rashly into.

وَهْطَةٌ ج وِهْطٌ Precipice, abyss.

Terror, fear, fright.	وَهلٌ وَوهلةٌ
At first sight.	أوَّل وهلةٍ
To imagine, fancy.	وَهم يَهم
To lead into error.	وهَّم وأوهم
To suspect, accuse.	إتَّهم بِ
To suppose, imagine.	توهَّم
To be suspected.	أُتهم ب
Opinion, idea.	وَهمٌ ج أوهامٌ
The imagination.	ألقوَّة ألوهمية
Imaginary, hypothetical.	وهميٌّ
Ambiguity. Misleading.	إيهامٌ
Suspicion, charge.	تُهمةٌ ج تُهمٌ
Suspected person.	مُتهمٌ
Fanciful imagination.	توهُّمٌ
To be weak.	وَهن يهنُ . وَوهن ـ
To weaken.	وهَّن وأوْهن
Weak, frail.	واهنٌ ج وهْنٌ
To be weak.	وَهى ووَهي يهي
To weaken, break.	أوْهى .
Feeble, frail.	واهٍ م واهيهٌ ج واهون
Wonderful! Alas!	واهاً ل
Woe to you!	ويْك
Oasis.	واحةٌ ج واحات
Woe to!	ويْحٌ ويلٌ
Disaster, calamity.	وَيلٌ
Woe to me!	وَيْلي
Disgrace.	ويلةٌ ج ويلات

ي

ي As a numeral sign=10.

ي My, me, e. g.

كِتَابي My book.

معي With me.

ضَرَبَني He struck me.

يّ *A particle of relation, e.g.*

مِصْرِيٌّ Egyptian.

يا *Interjection,* O e.g.

يا زَيدُ O Zeid !

يَئِسَ يَيأَسُ ويَيئِسُ من To despair of,

يَأْسٌ Despair, loss of hope.

يَؤُسٌ ويَؤُوس Despairing.

يَبِسَ يَيبَسُ To dry up, wither.

يَبَّسَ وأَيْبَسَ To cause to dry.

أليَبْسُ والْيابسة To dry land.

يابس Dry.

يُبوسة Dryness.

يَتَّمَ To make one an orphan.

تَيَتَّمَ To become an orphan.

يُتْمٌ State of orphanage.

يتيمٌ ج يتامى وأَيْتامٌ Orphan.

درة يتيمة A rare pearl.

(يَخْنَةٌ) A kind of stew.

يَدٌ ج أيدٍ وأيادٍ Hand; arm. Power. Handle.

عنْ يَدٍ By force.

بَيْنَ يَدَيهِ In his presence.

لهُ يد بيضاء He is well versed.

أليد الطولى Power, influence.

Manual. يَدِيٌّ ويَدَوِيٌّ

Scattered. ايدِي سَبا

Jerboa (animal). يرْبوعٌ

Glow-worm. Reed-pen. يرّاعٌ

Jaundice. Blight. يرْقانٌ

To be easy. يسر ييسر يُسْرًا

To facilitate, make easy. يَسَّرَ

To become easy. تَيسرَ واستَيسرَ

To be feasible to one. تيسَّرَ لهُ

Facility, ease; affluence. يُسْرٌ

Left side. Ease. يسارٌ ج يُسْر

Easy. Small quantity. يسيرٌ

More easy. أيْسر

The left side. ألأيْسر واليُسرى

Rich, affluent. موْسرٌ ج مَياسِير

Gambling. مَيْسِرٌ

Ease, affluence, wealth. مَيْسُرةٌ

Left side. مَيْسرةٌ ج مياسر

Feasible, easy. مَيْسورٌ ج مياسير

Arrest, interdicted. (يَسَقْ)

A cavass (*Turk*). (يسقجيٌّ)

Jasmine (jessamine). ياسَمينٌ

Male bee. Chief. يَعسوبٌ

Fontanelle. يَافوخٌ

A young man. Lad. يافِعٌ ج يفَعَةٌ

Ruby. ياقُوتٌ

To be awake. يقِظَ ييقَظُ

To awaken. يقَّظَ وأيقظَ

To wake up. تيقَّظ واستَيقظ

Wakefulness. Attention. يَقظةٌ

Awake, watchful. يَقظٌ ويقظانُ

To be certain, sure. يَقِنَ ييقَنُ

To believe firmly. أيقنَ واستَيقنَ

To know, be sure of. تيقَّنَ

Certain belief, conviction. يَقينٌ

He is sure of it. هو على يقينٍ منهُ

Certainly, undoubtedly. يَقيناً

Certain knowledge. علمُ اليقينِ

حقُّ اليقين Indubitable truth.
يقينيّات Certain truths; axioms.
موقنٌ Confident, sure.
يمّ ج يموم Sea, ocean.
يمام ويمامة Wood-pigeon.
يمَّن ويامَن To go to the right.
تيمَّن ب To seek a blessing.
إستيمن To exact an oath.
يمنٌ Blessing, success, luck.
يمنة Right side or hand.
اليمنُ Yemen (Arabia Felix).
يُمنى ج يمنيات Right hand.
يمين Right side, right hand.
يمينٌ ج أيمنٌ وأيمانٌ Oath.
أيمُ وأيم الله By God.
التيمن The South.
ميمنةٌ ج ميامن Right Side. Right wing of an army.
ميمونٌ ج ميامين Fortunate.
ميمونُ الطائر Auspicious.

ينبوعٌ Fountain.
يانسونٌ (أنيسونٌ) Anise.
ينَع يينع. وأينع To ripen (fruit).
يانع ويَنيعٌ ج ينْع Ripe (fruit).
يهوديٌّ ج يهود. (See هود) Jew
يومٌ ج أيّام Day. Time; season
يوماً فيوماً Day by day.
من يومه The same day.
يوماً ما Once, some day.
ذات يوم On a certain day, once.
اليومُ To-day.
يوميٌّ Daily.
يومياً Day by day, daily.
يومئذ On that day.
يُونس (يونانٌ) Jonah.
اليُونانُ The Greek nation.
بلادُ اليُونان Greece.
يونانيٌّ ج يُونانيُّون Greek. Grecian.
اليُونانيَّة The Greek language.

SUPPLEMENT

ARABIC-ENGLISH

It was impossible, for technical reasons, to follow the conventional arrangement according to roots in this Arabic-English supplement. The words are, therefore, arranged strictly alphabetically.

metabolism *n.* إِبْدَالُ ٱلْمَوَادِّ فِى ٱلْجِسْمِ

Soviet Union *n.* إِتِّحَادُ ٱلسُّوفْيِتِ

authorize *v.* أَجَازَ

authorization *n.* إِجَازَةٌ

patent *n.* إِجَازَةُ ٱلْحَصْرِ

living wage *n.* أَجْرٌ كَافٍ

minimum wage *n.* اَلْأَجْرُ ٱلْأَصْغَرُ

red tape *n.* إِجْرَاءَاتٌ عَقِيمَةٌ

enemy alien *n.* أَجْنَبِىٌّ عَدَائِىّ

inferiority complex *n.* إِحْسَاسُ ٱلْإِنْحِطَاطِ

statistician *n.* إِحْصَائِىٌّ

statistics *n.* إِحْصَائِيَّةٌ

jurisdiction *n.* إِخْتِصَاصٌ

specialist *n.* إِخْتِصَاصِىٌّ

nutritionist *n.* إِخْتِصَاصِىٌّ بِٱلْغِذَاءِ

chiropodist *n.* إِخْتِصَاصِىٌّ لِمُعَالَجَةِ ٱلْأَقْدَامِ

fingerprint *v.* أَخَذَ طَابِعَ ٱلْأَصَابِعِ

camouflage *v.* أَخْفَى

defrost *v.* أَذَابَ ٱلْجَلِيدَ فِى خِزَانَةِ ٱلثَّلْجِ

broadcast *v.* أَذَاعَ

telecast *v.* أَذَاعَ بِٱلتَّلْفَزَةِ

broadcast *n.* إِذَاعَةٌ

newscast *n.* إِذَاعَةُ ٱلْأَخْبَارِ

telecast *n.* إِذَاعَةٌ تَلْفَزِيَّةٌ

radio broadcast *n.* إِذَاعَةٌ لَاسِلْكِيَّةٌ

mixup *n.* إِرْتِبَاكٌ

traffic jam *n.* إِرْتِبَاكُ ٱلْحَرَكَةِ

terrorism *n.* إِرْهَابٌ

terrorist *n.* إِرْهَابِىٌّ

أَرْهَبَ	terrorize *v.*
أَسْبِيرِينٌ	aspirin *n.*
إِسْتِبْدَادٌ	dictatorship *n.*
إِسْتَرَقَ إِلَى	infiltrate *v.*
إِسْتِعْرَاضٌ	revue *n.*
إِسْتِفْتَاءُ ٱلشَّعْبِ	plebiscite *n.*
إِسْتِقْلَالٌ	autonomy *n.*
إِسْتِكْشَافٌ	reconnaissance *n.* (mil.)
إِسْتِهْلَاكٌ	amortization *n.*
إِسْتَهْلَكَ	amortize *v.*
أُسْطُوَانَةٌ	record *n.* (phonograph)
إِسْعَافٌ	first aid *n.*
إِسْمٌ مُسْتَعَارٌ	pseudonym *n.*
أَسِيرٌ	internee *n.*
إِشَارَةٌ	tip-off *n.*
إِشَارَةُ ٱلْخَطَرِ	alert *n.*
إِشْتِرَاكِيٌّ	socialist *n.*, socialist(ic) *a.*
إِشْتِرَاكِيَّةٌ	socialism *n.*
أَشِعَّةُ رُنْتْجِن أَوْ إِكْس	x-ray *n.*
أَصْلَحَ	ameliorate *v.*
إِضْرَابٌ	walkout *n.*
إِطْفَائِيَّةٌ	fire department *n.*
إِعَادَةُ إِذَاعَةٍ	rebroadcast *n.*
إِعَادَةُ ٱلتَّنْظِيمِ	reorganization *n.*
إِعَانَةٌ	subsidy *n.*
إِعْتِدَاءٌ	aggression *n.*
إِعْلَانٌ	advertisement *n.*
إِعْلَانُ ٱلطَّلَبِ	want ad *n.*
إِعْلَانٌ مُبَوَّبٌ	classified ad *n.*
إِفْتِتَاحِيَّةٌ	editorial *n.*

إِقْتِدَارٌ	efficiency *n.*
إِقْطَاعِيَّةٌ	feudalism *n.*
إِكْثَارٌ	boost *n.*
إِلْتِهَابُ ٱلْمَفَاصِلِ	arthritis *n.*
أَلْإِلْتِهَابُ ٱلسَّحَائِيُّ	meningitis *n.*
إِلْحَاقٌ	annexation *n.*
أَلْحَقَ	annex *v.*
أَلْفُ مِلْيُونٍ	billion *n.*
آلَةٌ ٱسْتِكْتَابِيَّةٌ	dictaphone *n.*
آلَةُ ٱلْبَيْعِ	vending machine *n.*
آلَةُ ٱلتَّسْخِينِ	heater *n.*
آلَةُ ٱلتَّصْفِيحِ	rolling mill *n.*
آلَةُ ٱلتَّصْوِيرِ	camera *n.*
آلَةُ ٱلتَّفْرِيخِ	incubator *n.*
آلَةٌ حَاسِبَةٌ	calculating machine *n.*
آلَةٌ لِحَرْقِ ٱلْفَضَلَاتِ	incinerator *n.*
آلَةُ ٱلْخِيَاطَةِ	sewing machine *n.*
آلَةُ ٱلْغَسْلِ	washing machine *n.*
آلَةُ ٱلْكِتَابَةِ	typewriter *n.*
آلَةُ لَعْبِ ٱلْقِمَارِ	slot machine *n.*
آلَةٌ مُسَخِّنَةٌ	radiator *n.*
إِلْهَابٌ	ignition *n.*
إِمْكَانِيَّةٌ	potential *n.*
أَلْأَمْنُ ٱلْمُشْتَرَكُ	collective security *n.*
أَمِينٌ	trustee *n.*
إِنْتِظَارُ ٱلْحَيَاةِ	life expectancy *n.*
إِنْتِقَادٌ	book review *n.*
إِنْهِيَالُ ٱلْأَرْضِ	landslide *n.*
أُورِيُومِيسِين	aureomycin *n.*
إِنْسُولِينٌ	insulin *n.*

بَابٌ دَوَّارٌ turnstile *n.*

أَلْبَحْرِيَّةُ ٱلتِّجَارِيَّةُ merchant marine *n.*

بَدَلَ pinch-hit *n.*

بِدُونَ ٱسْمٍ anonymous *a.*

بِدُونَ تَطَوُّرٍ كَافٍ underdeveloped *a.*

بَرَّادَةٌ air conditioner *n.*

بَرْقِيَّةٌ cablegram *n.*

أَلْبَرِيدُ ٱلْجَوِّيُّ air mail *n.*

بُرُوتِئِين protein *n.*

بَسْتِيلِيَّةٌ لِلسُّعْلَةِ coughdrop *n.*

بِطِّيخٌ أَصْفَرُ honeydew melon *n.*

بَقَايَا leftover *n.*

بَقَايَا عَمَلٍ backlog *n.*

بِلَادٌ مُتَوَقِّفَةٌ satellite country *n.*

بُلُوتُونِيُوم plutonium *n.*

بَنْزِينٌ gasoline *n.*

بِنِيسِلِّينٌ penicillin *n.*

بِيجَامَا pajamas *n. pl.*

تَاجِرُ ٱلْجُمْلَةِ wholesaler *n.*

تَأْلِيفُ فَحَّاشٍ pornography *n.*

تَأْمِينٌ ٱجْتِمَاعِيٌّ social security *n.*

تَأْمِينٌ ضِدَّ ٱلأَمْرَاضِ health insurance *n.*

تَأْمِينٌ عَلَى ٱلْحَيَاةِ life insurance *n.*

تَأْمِينٌ عَلَى ٱلمَسْؤُولِيَّةِ liability insurence *n.*

تَبَادُلُ ٱلْخَوَاطِرِ telepathy *n.*

تَجْرِيب trial balloon *n.*

تَحَالُف coalition *n.*

تَحْتَ ٱلْمِقْيَاسِ substandard *a.*

تَحْكِيمٌ	arbitration *n.*
تَحْلِيلٌ	analysis *n.*
تَحْلِيلٌ نَفْسِيٌّ	psychoanalysis *n.*
تَخْدِيرٌ	anesthesia *n.*
تَخْزِينٌ	storage *n.*
تَدْبِيرٌ نَجْمِيٌّ	installment plan *n.*
تَدَرُّنٌ	tuberculosis *n.*
تَدْمِيجٌ	shorthand *n.*
تَذْكِرَةُ ٱلْأَصْلِ	certificate of origin *n.*
تَذْكِرَةُ إِثْبَاتِ ٱلشَّخْصِيَّةِ	identification *n.*
تَرَامٌ	trolley car *n.*
تَرْتِيبٌ	layout *n.*
تَرْوِيسَةٌ	headline *n.*
تَسْجِيلٌ	registration *n.*
تَسْخِينٌ	heating *n.*
أَلتَّسْيِيرُ ٱلنَّفَّاثِيُّ	jet propulsion *n.*
تَسْوِيَةٌ بِمِقْيَاسٍ أَحَدٍ	standardization *n.*
تَشْخِيصُ مَرَضٍ	diagnosis *n.*
تَشْرِيحٌ	autopsy *n.*
تَشَنُّجِيٌّ	spastic *a.*
تَصَوَّرَ	visualize *v.*
تَصْوِيرٌ وَقْتِيٌّ	time exposure *n.*
تَضَخُّمٌ نَقْدِيٌّ	inflation *n.*
تَطَوَّرَ	develop *v.*
تَعَطُّلٌ	unemployment *n.*
تَعْقِيمٌ	sterilization *n.*
تَفَرُّجٌ	sightseeing *n.*
تَكْيِيفُ ٱلْهَوَاءِ	air-conditioning *n.*

تَلْخِيصٌ	synopsis *n.*
تَلْفَزَ	televise *v.*
تَلْفَزَةٌ	television *n.*
تَلْقِيحٌ	vaccination *n.*
تِلْمِيذَةٌ	coed *n.*
تِلِيفُونٌ	phone *n.*
تَمْوِيجٌ	permanent wave *n.*
تَنْزِيلُ ٱلْأَثْمَانِ بِٱلتَّزَاحُمِ	price-cutting *n.*
تَنْزِيلُ ٱلثَّمَنِ	markdown *n.*
تَنْزِيلٌ نَقْدِيٌّ	devaluation *n.*
تَنْظِيفُ ٱلْأَظْفَارِ	manicure *n.*
تَنْظِيفُ أَظْفَارِ ٱلْأَرْجُلِ	pedicure *n.*
تَنْوِيمٌ	hypnosis *n.*
تَنْوِيمٌ	narcosis *n.*
تَوَاتُرٌ عَالٍ	high frequency *n.*
تَوَاتُرٌ لَاسِلْكِيٌّ	radio frequency *n.*
تَوْزِيعٌ مُسْتَعْجِلٌ	special delivery *n.*
تَوْصِيلٌ مُتَكَاثِرٌ	hookup *n.*
تَيَّارٌ	current *n.*
تَيَّارٌ مُتَبَادَلٌ	alternate current *n.*
ثَمَنُ ٱلتَّذْكِرَةِ	carfare *n.*
ثَوْرَوِيٌّ	subversive *a.*
ثِيَابٌ لِطِفْلٍ وَلِيدٍ	layette *n.*
جَانِبِيٌّ	collateral *n.*
جَذْبٌ جِنْسِيٌّ	sex appeal *n.*
جَذْمُ ٱلزَّائِدَةِ ٱلدُّودِيَّةِ	appendectomy *n.*
جَذْمُ ٱللَّوْزَتَيْنِ	tonsilectomy *n.*
جُرْثُومَةٌ	bacillus *n.*

جَرِيدَةٌ نَاطِقَةٌ newsreel *n.*

جِسْرٌ مُعَلَّقٌ suspension bridge *n.*

جَمْعِيَّةٌ تَعَاوُنِيَّةٌ co-operative *n.*

جُنْدِيُّ ٱلْمِظَلَّةِ parachutist *n.*

جَهَّزَ بِصَنَائِعَ industrialize *v.*

جَوْلَةٌ hike *n.*

جَوْلَةٌ وَعَوْدَةٌ roundtrip *n.*

جَوِّيٌّ atmospheric *a.*

حَاجِبُ ٱلْهَوَاءِ airtight *a.*

حَارِسُ ٱلْمُقَاوَمَةِ ٱلْجَوِّيَّةِ air warden *n.*

حَاطِمَةُ ٱلْجَلِيدِ ice breaker *n.*

حَافِزٌ initiative *n.*

حَافِلَةٌ bus *n.*

حَاكٍ phonograph *n.*

حَاكٍ loudspeaker *n.*

حَامِضٌ بُورِقِيٌّ boric acid *n.*

حَامِلَةُ ٱلطَّائِرَاتِ aircraft carrier *n.*

حِجَابٌ حَرِيرِيٌّ silkscreen *n.*

حُجْرَةٌ مُظْلِمَةٌ لِتَوْصِيحِ تَصَاوِيرَ darkroom *n.*

حَرَارِيَّةٌ calorie *n.*

حَرَّاقَةٌ torpedo *n.*

أَلْحَرْبُ ٱلْبَرِيدَةُ cold war *n.*

حَرْبُ ٱلطَّبَقَاتِ class struggle *n.*

حَرَكَةٌ سِيَاسِيَّةٌ سِرِّيَّةٌ . underground *n.* (polit.)

أَلْحُرُوفُ ٱلْمَجْمُوعَةُ typesetting *n.*

حِزَامُ ٱلْأَمْنِ safety belt *n.*

حِسَابٌ bank account *n.*

حِسَابُ ٱلتَّفَاضُلِ differential calculus *n.*

حِسِّيَّات	emotions *n.*
حَصْرُ ٱلتَّموين	rationing *n.*
حِصَّة فى ٱلرِّبْح	dividend *n.* (profit share)
حِفْظ	upkeep *n.*
حُقْنَة	injection *n.*
حَقِيبَة	suitcase *n.*
أَلْحُكْمُ ٱلْمُطْلَق	totalitarianism *n.*
حَلُّ ٱلْجَيْش	demobilization *n.*
حَلَّ ٱلْجَيْش	demobilize *v.*
أَلْحَمَوَان	in-laws *n.*
حَوَالَة سَفَرِيَّة	travelers' check *n.*
خَالِص مِنَ ٱلْكُمْرُك	duty-free *a.*
خَانَ	doublecross *v.*
خَدَّرَ	anesthesize *v.*
خِدْمَة اجْتِمَاعِيَّة	social service *n.*, social work *n.*
أَلْخِدْمَةُ ٱلسِّرِّيَّة	secret service *n.*
خِزَانَةُ ٱلثَّلْج	icebox *n.*
خِزَانَةُ ٱلثَّلْج	refrigerator *n.*
خِزَانَةُ ٱلْمَلَفَّات	filing cabinet *n.*
خَصَّصَ	earmark *v.*
خَطِر	touch-and-go *a.* [risky]
خَيَالِىّ	utopian *a.*
دَافِعُ الضَّرَائِب	taxpayer *n.*
دَائِرَة قَصِيرَة	short circuit *n.*
دَائِرَةُ ٱلْمَعَارِف	encyclopedia *n.*
دَبَّابَة	tank *n.* (mil.)
دَبُّوس إِنكليزِى	safety pin *n.*
دَرَّاجَة	bicycle *n.*
أَلدَّرَجَةُ ٱلثَّالِثَةُ فى سَفِينَة	tourist class *n.*
دَرَجَةُ ٱلْعَقْل	I.Q. *n.*

دَعَاوَةٌ — propaganda *n.*

دُكَّانُ جَرَائِدَ — newsstand *n.*

دُكَّانُ ٱلْعِطَارَةِ — drugstore *n.*

دَلِيلٌ — directory *n.*

دَوْرَةُ ٱلْبَرْدِ — cold wave *n.*

دَوْرَةُ ٱلْحَرَارَةِ — heatwave *n.*

أَلدُّوَلُ ٱلْمُوَقِّعَةُ — signatory powers *n. pl.*

دَوْلَةٌ مُتَوَسِّطَةٌ وَمُتَحَايِدَةٌ — buffer state *n.*

دُونَ ٱلْأَحْمَرِ — infrared *a.*

ذَرِّيٌّ — atomic *a.*

ذَرِيرَةٌ طَلْقِيَّةٌ — talcum powder *n.*

ذُو رَادِيُوم فَاعِلٍ — radioactive *a.*

ذُو ٱللَاسَامِيَّةِ — antisemite *n.*, anti-semitic *a.*

رَابِحٌ — profiteer *n.*

رَأْسُ ٱلْجِسْرِ — bridgehead *n.*

رَأْسْمَالِيٌّ — capitalist *n.*

رَأْسْمَالِيَّةٌ — capitalism *n.*

رَامِي ٱللَّهِيبِ — flame thrower *n.*

رَئِيس بِٱلْإِسْمِ — figurehead *n.*

رَبْطَةُ ٱلسَّاقِ — suspender *n.*

رَثٌّ — hack *a.*

رَثْيَةٌ — rheumatism *n.*

رَدَّ — refund *v.*

رَدُّ ٱلْفِعْلِ ٱلْمُسَلْسَلِ — chain reaction *n.*

رَدُّ ٱلنُّقُودِ — refund *n.*

رِسَالَةٌ لَاسِلْكِيَّةٌ — radiogram *n.*

رَسْمٌ قَلْبِيٌّ — cardiogram *n.*

blueprint *n.*	رَسْمٌ هَنْدَسِيٌّ
hush money *n.*	رِشْوَةٌ
tugboat *n.*	رَقَّاص
lay-off *n.*	رَفْتٌ
detective story *n.*	رِوَايَةٌ بُولِيسِيَّةٌ
kindergarten *n.*	رَوْضَةُ ٱلْأَطْفَالِ
nursery school *n.*	رَوْضَةُ ٱلْأَطْفَالِ
sport *n.*	رِيَاضَةٌ
tail wind *n.*	رِيحٌ وَرَائِيَّةٌ
appendix *n.*	زَائِدَةٌ دُودِيَّةٌ
ringleader *n.*	زَعِيمٌ
hypertrophy *n.*	زِيَادَةٌ مُفْرِطَةٌ
lubricating oil *n.*	زَيْتُ تَشْحِيمٍ
make-up *n.*	زِينَةُ ٱلْوَجْهِ
wristwatch *n.*	سَاعَةُ يَدٍ
chauffeur *n.*	سَائِقٌ
motorist *n.*	سَائِقُ سَيَّارَةٍ
track meet *n.*	سِبَاقٌ
blackboard *n.*	سَبُّورَةٌ
iron curtain *n.*	أَلسِّتَارُ ٱلْحَدِيدِيُّ
pullover *n.*	سُتْرَةٌ صُوفِيَّةٌ
physiognomy *n.*	سَحْنَةٌ
traffic light *n.*	سِرَاجُ ٱلْحَرَكَةِ
top-secret *a.*	سِرِّيٌّ جِدًّا
rate of exchange *n.*	سِعْرُ ٱلصَّرْفِ
bank rate *n.*	سِعْرُ ٱلْفَائِدَةِ
cutthroat *n.*	سَفَّاحٌ
space travel *n.*	سَفَرٌ فِى ٱلْفَضَاءِ
space ship *n.*	سَفِينَةٌ فَضَائِيَّةٌ
saccharine *n.*	سَكَارِينٌ

standardize *v.*	سَوَّى بِمِقْيَاسٍ أَحَدٍ
automobile *n.*	سَيَّارَةٌ
taxicab *n.*	سَيَّارَةُ ٱلْأُجْرَةِ
armored car *n.*	سَيَّارَةٌ مُصَفَّحَةٌ
motor truck *n.*	سَيَّارَةُ ٱلنَّقْلِ
network *n.*	شَبَكَةٌ
radio network *n.*	شَبَكَةٌ لَاسِلْكِيَّةٌ
diagnose *v.*	شَخَّصَ مَرَضًا
military police *n.*	أَلشُّرْطَةُ ٱلْعَسْكَرِيَّةُ
patrolman *n.*	شُرْطِيٌّ
insurance company *n.*	شِرْكَةُ ٱلتَّأْمِينِ
holding company *n.*	شِرْكَةُ ٱلشِّرْكَاتِ
subsidiary *n.* (fin.)	شِرْكَةٌ مُسَاعِدَةٌ
Inc. *a.*	شِرْكَةٌ مُسَجَّلَةٌ
subway *n.*	سِكَّةُ تَحْتَ ٱلْأَرْضِ
elevated railway *n.*	سِكَّةُ ٱلْحَدِيدِ ٱلْمُرْتَفِعَةُ
barbed wire *n.*	سِلْكٌ شَائِكٌ
escalator *n.*	سُلَّمٌ مُتَحَرِّكٌ
fire escape *n.*	سُلَّمُ ٱلنَّجَاةِ
fertilizer *n.*	سَمَادٌ
audition *n.*	سَمَاعٌ
telephone receiver *n.*	سَمَّاعَةٌ
poison ivy *n.*	أَلسُّمَّاقُ ٱلسَّامُّ
broker *n.*	سِمْسَارٌ
stockbroker *n.*	سِمْسَارُ ٱلْأَسْهُمِ
brokerage *n.*	سَمْسَرَةٌ
IOU *n.*	سَنَدٌ
stock market *n.*	سُوقُ ٱلْأَسْهُمِ
labor market *n.*	سُوقُ ٱلْعَمَلِ

شريط غرائي	Scotch tape *n.*
شريط ناطق	soundtrack *n.*
شريك الدين	correligionist *n.*
شريك المدعى عليه	codefendant *n.*
شغل جانبي	side line *n.*
شق	fission *n.*
شق الذرة	atomic fission *n.*
شقة	compartment *n.*
شقلبة طائرة	tail spin *n.*
الشلل الطفلي	polio(myelitis) *n.* infantile paralysis *n.*
شمعة الشرارة	spark plug *n.*
شهد قانونيا	notarize *v.*
شيوعي	communist *n.*
شيوعية	communism *n.*
صاحب دار الزينة	beautician *n.*
صاروخ	rocket *n.*
صباغ	pigment *n.*
صبياني	juvenile *a.*
صعد	take off *v.* (av.)
صعود	take-off *n.* (av.)
صف الدم	blood group *n.*
صناعي	industrial *a.*
صندوق سينماء أو مرسح	box office *n.*
صندوق القمامة	garbage can *n.*
صندوق مسجل	cash register *n.*
صندوق للمكاتيب	mailbox *n.*
صورة حالية	snapshot *n.*
صورة متحركة	motion picture *n.*
صورة هزلية	cartoon *n.*
ضابط الصف	petty officer *n.*
ضرب طفلا	spank *v.*
ضغط عال	high pressure *n.* high tension *n.*

battle fatigue *n.*	ضَنَى الحَرْبِ
rear light *n.*	ضَوْءٌ خَلْفِي
neon light *n.*	ضَوْءٌ نيوني
fingerprint *n.*	طَابِعُ الأَصَابِعِ
freshman *n.*	طَالِبُ السَّنَةِ الاولى
horoscope *n.*	طَالِعٌ فِي التَّنْجِيمِ
airplane *n.* aircraft *n.*	طَائِرَةٌ
dive bomber *n.*	طَائِرَةُ الانْقِضَاضِ
hydroplane *n.*	طَائِرَةٌ بَحْرِيَّةٌ
glider *n.*	طَائِرَةٌ شِرَاعِيَّةٌ
helicopter *n.*	طَائِرَةٌ عَمُودِيَّةٌ
fighter bomber *n.*	طَائِرَةُ القِتَالِ القَذَّافَةُ
pursuit plane *n.*	طَائِرَةُ المُطَارَدَةِ
jet plane *n.*	طَائِرَةٌ نَفَّاثَةٌ
pediatrics *n.*	أَلطِّبُّ الطِّفْلِي
socialized medicine *n.*	أَلطِّبُّ المُشْتَرَكُ
psychiatry *n.*	أَلطِّبُّ النَّفْسَانِي
topsoil *n.*	طَبَقَةُ التُّرْبَةِ الفَوْقَانِيَّةُ
ground floor *n.*	الطَّبَقَةُ السُّفْلَى
pediatrician *n.*	طَبِيبُ أَمْرَاضِ الأَطْفَالِ
diagnostician *n.*	طَبِيبٌ تَشْخِيصِي
obstetrician *n.*	طَنِيبٌ مُوَلِّدٌ
highway *n.*	طَرِيقٌ عَام
therapy *n.*	طَرِيقَةُ الشِّفَاءِ
side dish *n.*	طَعَامٌ جَانِبِي
sibling *n.*	طِفْلٌ
aviator *n.*	طَيَّارٌ
aeronautics *n.*	طَيَرَانٌ
insulator *n.*	عَازِلٌ

عَاهِرَةٌ	streetwalker *n.*
عَجَلَةٌ نَارِيَّةٌ	motorbike *n.*
عَدَسَةٌ	lens *n.*
عَرَبَةُ ٱلأَكْلِ	dining car *n.*
عُرْيَانِيَّةٌ	nudism *n.*
عُزْلَةٌ سِيَاسِيَّةٌ	isolationism *n.*
عَسَاكِرُ ٱلْهُجُومِ	shock troops *n. pl.*
عُصْبَةُ ٱلأُمَمِ	League of Nations *n.*
عَطَّارٌ	druggist *n.*
عَفَّارَةٌ	atomizer *n.*
عَقْدٌ فَرْعِيٌّ	subcontract *n.*
أَلْعَقْلُ ٱلْبَاطِنُ	subconscions *n.*
عِلَاجٌ كَهْرَبَائِيٌّ	diathermy *n.*
عَلَّاقٌ	hanger *n.*
عَلَامَةٌ تِجَارِيَّةٌ	trade mark *n.*
عِلْمُ ٱلإِجْتِمَاعِ	sociology *n.*
عِلْمُ ٱلأَحْيَاءِ	biology *n.*
عِلْمُ ٱلْجَرَاثِيمِ	bacteriology *n.*
عِلْمُ ٱلذَّرَّاتِ	nuclear physics *n.*
عِلْمُ ٱلصِّحَّةِ	hygiene *n.*
عِلْمُ ٱلطَّبِيعَةِ	physics *n.*
عِلْمُ ٱلْكَهَارِبِ	electronics *n.*
عِلْمُ وَظَائِفِ ٱلأَعْضَاءِ	physiology *n.*
أَلْعَمَلُ بِٱلْقِطْعِ	piecework *n.*
عَمَلِيَّةٌ قَيْصَرِيَّةٌ	caesarian section *n.*
عَمُودٌ كَهْرَبَائِيٌّ	electrode *n.*
عَنْتَرِيٌّ	bra(ssiere) *n.*
غَارَةٌ جَوِّيَّةٌ	air raid *n.*
غَازَلَ	flirt *v.*
غُدَّةٌ دَرَقِيَّةٌ	thyroid gland *n.*
غُدَّةٌ صَمَّاءُ	endocrine gland *n.*
غُرْفَةُ ٱلإِنْتِظَارِ	waiting room *n.*

shipping room *n.*	غرفة الشحن
checkroom *n.*	غرفة لحفظ الثياب
hangover *n.*	غشيان بعد الشرب
boner *n.*	غلطة كبيرة
submarine *n.*	غواصة
fascist *n.*	فاشي
fascism *n.*	فاشية
retroactive *a.*	فاعل إلى الماضي
paralysis *n.*	فالج
topnotch *a.*	فائق
can opener *n.*	فتاحة.
turn on the radio	فتح
checkup *n.* (med.)	فحص
blood test *n.*	فحص الدم
small change *n.*	فراطة
firing squad *n.*	فرقة الإعدام
standing room *n.*	فسحة الواقفين
washout *n.* (sl.) [failure]	فشل
fluorescent *a.*	فلوري
jackpot *n.*	ألفوز الأكبر في المقامرة
receiver *n.*	قابل
motorboat *n.*	قارب ناري
boycott *v.*	قاطع
supreme commander *n.*	ألقائد العام
airbase *n.*	قاعدة جوية
catalogue *n.*	قائمة
black list *n.*	قائمة سوداء
menu *n.*	قائمة الطعام
electrocute *v.*	قتل بالكهرباء
electrocution *n.*	قتل بالكهرباء

قَدَّاحٌ	lighter *n.*
قَدَّمَ إِعَانَةً	subsidize *v.*
قَرَأَ مَكْتُوبًا شِفْرِيًّا	decode *v.*
قَطَعَ	turn off the radio
قَلَّبَ	revolutionize *v.*
قَلْبِيٌّ	cardiac *a.*
قَلَمُ ٱلْحِبْرِ	fountain pen *n.*
قَلَمُ ٱلْحِبْرِ ٱلْجَافِّ	ball point pen *n.*
قَمَرَةُ ٱلدَّرَجَةِ ٱلْأُولَى	stateroom *n.*
قُنْبُلَةٌ دَمْعِيَّةٌ	tear bomb *n.*
قُنْبُلَةٌ ذَرِّيَّةٌ	atom bomb *n.*
قُنْبُلَةٌ مُضَادَّةٌ لِلْغَوَّاصَاتِ	depth charge *n.*
قُوَّةُ حِصَانٍ	horsepower *n.*
قُوَّةُ عِرَاكٍ	task force *n.*
قُوَّةُ ٱلنَّارِ	fire power *n.*
كَاذِبٌ	phony *a.*, *n.*
كَاسِبٌ	wage earner *n.*
كَاسِرُ ٱلْإِضْرَابِ	strikebreaker *n.*
كَافِرٌ	atheist *n.*
كِتَابُ ٱلْمَرْجِعِ	reference book *n.*
كِتَابَةٌ بِٱلْآلَةِ	typewriting *n.*
كِتَابَةٌ عَلَى ٱلسَّمَاءِ	skywriting *n.*
كَرَاهَةُ ٱلْأَجَانِبِ	xenophobia *n.*
كُرْسِيٌّ دَائِرٌ	swivel chair *n.*
كَشْفِيٌّ	boyscout *n.*
كَشْكُولٌ	scrapbook *n.*
كَعْكَةُ طَاجِنٍ	pancake *n.*
كُفْرَانٌ	atheism *n.*
كَفَلَ	sponsor *v.*
كَفِيلٌ	sponsor *n.*

كَلَامُ ذِي لِسَانَيْنِ	double talk *n.*
كَهْرَب	electron *n.*
كَهْرَبَائِيّ	electrician *n.*
كَهْرَبَة	electrification *n.*
كَهَارِبِيّ	electronic *a.*
كُوخ	shack *n.*
كِيمِيَاءُ أَحْيَائِيَّة	biochemistry *n.*
كِينَا	quinine *n.*
لَاسَامِيَّة	antisemitism *n.*
لَاسِلْكِيّ	radio *n.*, wireless *a.*
لَاقِطَةُ الْأَلْغَام	mine sweeper *n.*
لَجْنَةٌ تَحْكِيمِيَّة	arbitration board *n.*
لُصُوصِيَّة	stickup *n.*
لَعْبُ كُرَةِ الْقَدَم	soccer *n.*
لِفَافَةُ الْكِتَاب	book jacket *n.*
لُغْزُ قِطَعٍ كَثِيرَة	jig saw puzzle *n.*

لَقَّحَ	vaccinate *v.*
لُقْمَةٌ ذَاتَ كُرَى	ball bearing *n.*
لَوْلَب	spring *n.* (techn.)
مَائِيّ	hydraulic *a.*
مُبَارَاةُ نِصْفِ نِهَائِيّ	semifinal *n.*
مُبْدِلُ الأُسْطُوَانَات	record changer *n.*
مَتْحَف	museum *n.*
مُتَحَرِّك بِذَاتِه	automatic *a.*
مُتَطَرِّف	extremist *n.*
مُتَفَرِّق	sporadic *a.*
مَثَّلَ	assimilate *v.*
مِجْرَاف بُخَارِيّ	steam shovel *n.*
مُجَرَّدٌ عَنِ الْمَاء	dehydrated *a.*
مَجَلَّةٌ نِصْفِ شَهْرِيَّة	semimonthly *n.*
مِجْهَر	microscope *n.*
مُحَارَبَةٌ ذَرِّيَّة	atomic warfare *n.*

مُحَاصَرَةٌ	blockade *n.*
مُحْتَرِفٌ	professional *a.*
مُحْتَرَفٌ	studio *n.*
مِحْرَاثٌ آلِيٌّ	motor plough *n.*
مُحَرِّرٌ	editor *n.*
مُحَرِّضٌ لِلْحَرْبِ	warmonger *n.*
مُحَرَّمٌ على ٱلعَساكِرِ	off limits *n.*
مَحَطَّةٌ لاسِلْكِيَّةٌ	radio station *n.*
مِحَفَّةٌ	stretcher *n.*
مُحَكِّمٌ	arbitrator *n.*
مَحَلُّ إِحْرَاقِ ٱلجُثَثِ	crematory *n.*
مَحَلُّ ٱلبَنْزِينِ	gas station *n.*
مُحَلَّفٌ	juror *n.*
مُخْبِرُ جَرِيدَةٍ	reporter *n.*
مُخْبِرٌ شُرْطِيٌّ	plainclothes man *n.*
مُخَدِّرٌ	anesthetic *n.*
مَخْرَجُ عِنْدَ ٱلضَّرُورَةِ	emergency exit *n.*
مَخْزَنُ ٱلدَمِ	blood bank *n.*
مَدْخَلٌ	intake *n.*
مَدْخَلٌ لِلسَّيَّارَاتِ	driveway *n.*
مُدَرَّبٌ	trainee *n.*
مَدْرَسَةٌ أَوَّلِيَّةٌ	elementary school *n.*
مَدْرَسَةٌ تِجارِيَّةٌ	commercial college *n.*
مَدْرَسَةُ ٱلصَّنَائِعِ	vocational school *n.*
مُدْرِكُ طَبَقَتِهِ	class-conscious *a.*
مِدْفَعٌ مُضَادٌّ لِلدَّبَّابَاتِ	tank destroyer *n.*
مُدَمِّجٌ	stenographer *n.*
مُدِيرُ ٱلجَوْقِ	band leader *n.*

مُرَاقِبٌ	spotter *n.*
مُرَتِّبٌ	moderator *n.*
مِرْحَاضٌ	water closet *n.*
مُرْسِلَةٌ	radio transmitter *n.*
مَرَضُ ٱلْبَوْلِ ٱلسُّكَّرِيِّ	diabetes *n.*
مَرَضٌ سِرِّيٌّ	venereal disease *n.*
مِرْفَعَةٌ	derrick *n.*
مَرْكَزُ ٱلتِّلِيفُونِ	switchboard *n.*
مِرْوَحَةٌ	propeller *n.*
مِرْوَدٌ	lipstick *n.*
مَرِيضٌ نَفْسِيٌّ	psychopath *n.*
مُزَخْرِفٌ	interior decorator *n.*
مَزْلَقَانِ ذَوَا عَجَلَاتٍ	roller skate *n.*
مُسْتَخْدَمَةُ ٱلْإِسْتِقْبَالِ	receptionist *n.*
مُسْتَرَاحٌ	rest room *n.*
مُسْتَقْبِلٌ	receiver *n.* (radio)
مُسْتَقْبِلُ أَمْوَالِ ٱلْإِفْلَاسِ؛	(in bankruptcy)
مُسْتَقِلٌّ	autonomous *a.*
مُسْتَوَى ٱلْحَيَاةِ	standard of living *n.*
مُسَدَّسٌ	revolver *n.*
مُشَهٍّ	appetizer *n.*
مَشَى عَلَى غَفْلَةٍ	jaywalk *v.*
مِصْبَاحُ ضَوْءٍ فَوْقَ ٱلْبَنَفْسَجِيِّ	sunlamp *n.*
مَصَحٌّ	sanitarium *n.*
مِصْعَدَةٌ	elevator *n.*
مِصْفَاةُ ٱلْقَهْوَةِ	percolator *n.*
مَصْلَحَةُ ٱلتَّرْبِيَةِ	board of education *n.*

board of health *n.* مَصْلَحَةُ ٱلصِّحَّةِ
microphone *n.* مِصْوَاتٌ
contraceptive *n.* مُضَادَّاتٌ لِلْحَبَلِ
insecticide *n.* مُضَادَّاتٌ حَشَرِيَّةٌ
airfield *n.* مَطَارٌ
fire extinguisher *n.* مِطْفَاةٌ
detergent *n.* مُطَهِّرٌ
spectroscope *n.* مِطْيَافٌ
parachute *n.* مِظَلَّةٌ وَاقِيَةٌ
tax-exempt *a.* مُعَافًى مِنَ ٱلْمُكُوسِ
collective agreement *n.* مُعَاهَدَةٌ جَمَاعِيَّةٌ
nonaggression pact *n.* مُعَاهَدَةُ عَدَمِ ٱلإِعْتِدَاءِ
overpass *n.* مَعْبَرٌ
aggressor *n.* مُعْتَدٍ

commissar *n.* مُعْتَمَدٌ شُيُوعِيٌّ
toothpaste *n.* مَعْجُونُ ٱلأَسْنَانِ
coefficient *n.* مُعَدَّلٌ
concentration camp *n.* مُعَسْكَرُ ٱلاعْتِقَالِ
ceiling price *n.* مُعْظَمُ ٱلثَّمَنِ
disinfectant *n.* مُعَقِّمٌ
aseptic *a.* مُعَقِّمٌ
visual aid *n.* مِعْوَانٌ نَظَرِيٌّ
flirt *n.* مُغَازَلَةٌ
electromagnet *n.* مَغْنَطِيسٌ كَهْرَبَائِيٌّ
vacationist *n.* مُفَرِّصٌ
commentator *n.* مُفَسِّرُ ٱلأَخْبَارِ
heckler *n.* مُقَاطِعُ ٱلْكَلَامِ
subcontractor *n.* مُقَاوِلٌ فَرْعِيٌّ

مقاومة antagonism *n.*

مقرر الميزانية budget *n.* (pol.)

مقمر كهربائي toaster *n.*

مقنبلة bomber *n.*

مكب spool *n.*

مكبر amplifier *n.*

مكتب التخديم employment agency *n.*

مكتبة إعارية lending library *n.*, rental library *n.*

مكتر ثان subtenant *n.*

مكتوب بآلة الكتابة typescript *n.*

ملتجئ refugee *n.*

ملجأ عسكري bunker *n.*

مماثلة analogy *n.*

ممثل سينمائي screen actor *n.*

ممحاة eraser *n.*

ممكن potential *a.*

مناورة maneuver *n.*

منح نفقة لتلميذ scholarship *n.* (grant)

منزل apartment house *n.*, tenement house *n.*

منضح shower bath *n.*

منطاد balloon *n.*

منطقي dialectic *a.*

منظر الغواصة periscope *n.*

منفذ executive *n.*

منفضة vacuum cleaner *n.*

مهواة ventilator *n.*

مواقيت time table *n.*

موج قصير short wave *n.*

موقف parking lot *n.*

موكب سيارات motorcade *n.*

مُوَلِّدٌ	generator *n.*
مُؤَلِّفٌ	author *n.*
مِيعَادٌ آخِرٌ	deadline *n.*
مِيكَانِي	mechanized *a.*
مِينَا جَوِّيَّةٌ	airport *n.*
نَاطِحَةُ ٱلسَّحَابِ	skyscraper *n.*
نَائِبٌ عَام	public prosecutor *n.*
نِبَاتِي	vegetarian *n.*
نَزْعُ ٱلسِّلَاحِ	disarmament *n.*
نَزْلَةٌ صَدْرِيَّةٌ	bronchitis *n.*
نَزْلَةٌ وَافِدَةٌ	grippe *n.*
نُزُولٌ مَجْبُورٌ	forced landing *n.*
نُزُولِيٌّ	bearish *a.*
نَزِيفٌ	hemorrhage *n.*
نَسَّافَةٌ	torpedoboat *n.*
نِسْبَةُ ٱلْمَوْتِ	death rate *n.*
نِسْبِيَّةٌ	relativity *n.*
نُسْخَةٌ فُوتُوغْرَافِيَّةٌ	photostat *n.*
نَسَقُ ٱلْأَفْكَارِ	ideology *n.*
نَسَقُ مُوَظَّفِيٌّ	bureaucracy *n.*
نَشْرٌ بِتَسَلْسُلٍ	serialization *n.*
نَشَرَ بِتَسَلْسُلٍ	serialize *v.*
نُصْبَةٌ	signpost *n.*
نِصْفُ شَهْرِيٍّ	semimonthly *a.*
نَظَرِيَّةُ ٱلْكَمِّ	quantum theory *n.*
نِفْطٌ	kerosene *n.*
نِقَابَةٌ	syndicate *n.*
نِقَابَةٌ	union *n.* (labor)
نِقَابَةُ ٱلْعُمَّالِ	trade union *n.*
نَقَّادٌ	reviewer *n.*
نَقْلُ ٱلدَّمِ	blood transfusion *n.*

نَكَّتَ	wisecrack *v.*
نُكْتَةٌ	wisecrack *n.*
نَهْبٌ	holdup *n.*
نُورٌ كَاشِفٌ	searchlight *n.*
نُورٌ كَشَّافٌ	floodlight *n.*
هُجُومٌ بِالْغَازِ	gas attack *n.*
هَنْدَسَةٌ	technology *n.*
هَوَائِي	pneumatic *a.*
هَوَائِيٌّ	aerial *n.*
هُورْمُونٌ	hormone *n.*
هِيدْرُوجِينٌ	hydrogen *n.*
هَيْئَةُ أَرْكَانِ ٱلْحَرْبِ	general staff *n.*
وَرَقَةُ سُؤَالَاتٍ	questionnaire *n.*
وَزْنٌ ثَقِيلٌ	heavyweight *n.*
وَغْدٌ	hoodlum *n.*
وَكْرٌ	hangar *n.*
وَكَالَةُ ٱلْإِشْهَارِ	advertising agency *n.*
يُودٌ	iodine *n.*

ENGLISH-ARABIC

ABBREVIATIONS. إِخْتِصَارَاتٌ

---

a. = adjective.	صفة	*ppr. = present participle.*	اسم فاعل
ad. = adverb.	حال او ظرف	*p. pron. = personal pronoun.*	ضمير
con. = conjunction.	حرف عطف	*int. = interrogation.*	اسم استفهام
n. = noun.	اسم	*rel. = relative.*	اسم موصول
pl. = plural.	جمع	*dem. = demonstrative.*	اسم إشارة
pp. = past participle.	اسم مفعول	*pp. = preposition.*	حرف جر

ENGLISH-ARABIC DICTIONARY

قاموس انكليزي وعربي

A

A *or* an. حَرْفُ نَكِرَة

Abaft *ad.* عِنْدَ مُؤَخَّرِ ٱلْمَرْكَبِ

Abandon *v. t.* تَرَكَ . هَجَرَ ـُ

Abase *v. t.* أَذَلَّ . وَضَعَ ـَ . حَطَّ ـُ

Abasement *n.* ذِلٌّ . ضِعَةٌ .

Abash *v. t.* خَجَّلَ . أَخْجَلَ

Abate *v. t.* or *i.* نَقَّصَ . نَقَصَ

Abatement *n.* تَقْلِيلٌ . تَخْفِيضٌ

Abbess *n.* رَئِيسَةُ دَيْرٍ

Abbey *n.* دَيْرٌ

Abbot *n.* رَئِيسُ دَيْرٍ

Abbreviate *v. t.* قَصَّرَ . إِخْتَصَرَ

Abbreviation *n.* تَقْصِيرٌ . إِخْتِصَارٌ

Abdicate *v. t.* or *i.* خَلَعَ نَفْسَهُ مِنْ

Abdication *n.* تَنَازُلٌ عَنْ

Abdomen *n.* بَطْنٌ

Abdominal *a.* بَطْنِيٌّ

Abduct *v. t.* خَطَفَ ـ إِخْتَلَسَ

Abduction *n.* خَطْفٌ . إِخْتِلَاسٌ

Abet *v. t.* حَرَّضَ . عَاوَنَ . عَاضَدَ

Abhor *v. t.* مَقَتَ . كَرِهَ

Abhorrence *n.* مَقْتٌ . كَرَاهَةٌ

Abide *v. i.* or *t.* أَقَامَ بِ . إِنْتَظَرَ

Abiding *a.* ثَابِتٌ . مُسْتَمِرٌّ

Ability *n.* قُدْرَةٌ . طَاقَةٌ . إِسْتِطَاعَةٌ

Abject *a.* ذَلِيلٌ . دَنِيٌّ . حَقِيرٌ

Abjure *v. t.* رَفَضَ . إِرْتَدَّ عَنْ

Able *a.* قَادِرٌ . مُسْتَطِيعٌ

Able-bodied *a.* صَحِيحُ ٱلْجِسْمِ

Ablution *n.* غَسْلٌ . وُضُوءٌ

Ably *ad.* بِقُدْرَة . بِمَهَارَة

Abnegation *n.* إِنْكَارُ ٱلنَّفْس

Abnormal *a.* غَيْرُ قِيَاسِيٍّ . شَاذٌّ

Aboard *ad.* فِي ٱلسَّفِينَة

Abode *n.* مُقَامٌ . مَنْزِلٌ . مَسْكِنٌ

Abolish *v. t.* نَسَخَ . ـَ أَلْغَى . أَبْطَلَ

Abolition *n.* نَسْخٌ . إِلْغَاء

Abominable *a.* كَرِيهٌ . قَبِيحٌ

Abominate *v. t.* كَرِهَ ـَ إِسْتَقْبَحَ

Abomination *n.* قَبِيحَةٌ . رِجْسٌ

Aborigines *n. pl.* (سُكَّانٌ) أَصْلِيُّون

Abortion *n.* سِقْطٌ . إِسْقَاطُ ٱلْجَنِين

Abortive *a.* مُخَيِّبٌ . غَيْرُ مُنْتِجٍ

Abound *v. i.* كَثُرَ . ـُ وَفَرَ يَفِرُ

About *pr.* حَوْلَ نَحْوَ

Above *pr.* فَوْقَ . أَكْثَرُ مِنْ

Abrasion *n.* كَشْطٌ . إِحْتِكَاكٌ

Abridge *v. t.* قَصَّرَ . أَوْجَزَ . إِخْتَصَرَ

Abridgement *n.* إِيجَازٌ . إِخْتِصَارٌ

Abroad *ad.* خَارِجًا . فِي ٱلْخَارِجِ

Abrogate *v. t.* أَلْغَى . أَبْطَلَ . نَسَخَ

Abrupt *a.* فُجَائِيٌّ . مَقْطُوعٌ

Abruptness *n.* مُفَاجَأَةٌ . إِنْقِطَاعٌ

Abcess *n.* خُرَّاجٌ . خُرَّاجَة

Abscond *v. i.* تَوَارَى . إِخْتَفَى . إِنْسَلَّ

Absence *n.* غَيْبَةٌ . غِيَابٌ

Absent *a.* **Absentee** *n.* غَائِبٌ

Absolute *a.* غَيْرُ مُقَيَّدٍ . مُطْلَقٌ

Absolutely *ad.* مُطْلَقًا . قَطْعًا

Absolution *n.* حَلٌّ . غُفْرَانٌ

Absolve *v. t.* حَلَّ ـُ . غَفَرَ ـِ

Absorb *v. t.* إِمْتَصَّ . إِسْتَغْرَقَ

Absorption *n.* إِمْتِصَاصٌ

Abstain *v. i.* إِمْتَنَعَ عَنْ

Abstenious *a.* قَلِيلُ ٱلْأَكْلِ . عَفِيفٌ

Abstinence *n.* إِمْتِنَاعٌ . عِفَّةٌ

Abstinent *a.* زَاهِدٌ عَفِيفٌ
Abstract *v. t.* جَرَّدَ . إِخْتَلَس
Abstract *a.* مُجَرَّدٌ . تَجْرِيدِيٌّ
Abstraction *n.* تَجْرِيدٌ . (غَيْبَة)
Abstractly *ad.* مُجَرَّدًا
Abstruse *a.* عَوِيصٌ مُشْكِلٌ
Absurd *a.* باطِلٌ . مُخَالِفٌ ٱلْعَقْلَ
Absurdity *n.* بُطْلٌ . بُطْلَانٌ
Abundance *n.* كَثْرَةٌ . وَفْرٌ
Abundant *a.* كَثِيرٌ . وافِرٌ
Abuse *v. t.* شَتَمَ ـ أَسَاءَ ٱسْتِعْمَالَهُ
Abuse *n.* شَتِيمَةٌ . سُوءُ ٱلاسْتِعْمَالِ
Abusive *a.* شَاتِمٌ مُهِينٌ
Abyss *n.* هاوِيَةٌ . وَهْدَةٌ
Acacia *n.* شَجَرُ ٱلسنْطِ
Academy *n.* مَدْرَسةُ ٱلْعُلُومِ أَوْمَجمَعُهَا
Accede *v. t.* قَبِلَ . رَضِيَ بِهِ ـ
Accelerate *v. t.* اسْرَعَ . عَجَّلَ

Accent *n.* شِدَّةٌ فِي ٱللَّفظِ . نَبْرَةٌ
Accentuate *v. t.* شَدَّدَ . أَظْهَرَ أَهَمِّيَّتَهُ
Accept *v. t.* قَبِلَ ـ رَضِيَ
Acceptable *a.* مَقْبُولٌ . مَرْضِيٌّ
Acceptance *n.* قَبُول
Acceptation *n.* قُبُولٌ . مَعْنًى
Accepted *a.* مَقْبُولٌ
Access *n.* دُخُولٌ . وُصُولٌ
Accessible *a.* سَهْلُ ٱلْوصُولِ . اليفٌ
Accession *n.* { زِيَادَةٌ . وُصُولٌ / جُلُوسٌ (ملك) }
Accident *n.* عَرَضٌ . آفَة
Accidental *a.* عَرَضِيٌّ . إِتِّفَاقِيٌّ
Acclamation *n.* تصفِيقٌ . إِستِحسَانٌ
Acclimate / Acclimatize *v. t.* عَوَّدَ عَلَى ٱلْمَنَاخِ
Acclimation *n.* تَعَوُّدُ ٱلْمَنَاخِ
Acclivity *n.* مَطْلَعٌ . مَصْعَدٌ
Accommodate *v. t.* أَمَدَّ . وَفَّقَ

Accommodating *a.* مُوَفِّقٌ.مُلَاطِفٌ
Accommodation *n.* مُوَافَقَةٌ
Accompaniment *n.* مُرَافَقَةٌ
Accompany *v. t.* رَافَقَ
Accomplice *n.* شَرِيكٌ فِي ذَنْبٍ
Accomplish *v. t.* أَكْمَلَ . أَنْجَزَ
Accomplishment *n.* إِنْجَازٌ . إِتْمَامٌ
Accord *n.* إِتِّفَاقٌ . إِتِّحَادٌ
Accordance *n.* إِتِّفَاقٌ
According to. عَلَى مُوجِبِ . بِحَسَبِ
Accordingly *ad.* لِذَلِكَ
Accost *v. t.* خَاطَبَ كَلَّمَهُ أَوَّلاً
Account *v. t.* حَسَبَ ـُ . عَدَّ
Account *n.* حِسَابٌ . قِصَّةٌ . خَبَرٌ
Accountability *n.* مَسْؤُولِيَّةٌ
Accountable *a.* مَسْؤُولٌ
Accountant *n.* كَاتِبُ ٱلْحِسَابَاتِ
Accrue *v. i.* زَادَ . نَشَا ـَ . أُضِيفَ

Accumulate *v. t.* or *i.* جَمَعَ ـَ . إِزْدَادَ
Accumulation *n.* إِزْدِيَادٌ . تَجَمُّعٌ
Accumulative *a.* جَامِعٌ . مُزْدَادٌ
Accuracy *n.* ضَبْطٌ . إِتْقَانٌ
Accurate *a.* مَضْبُوطٌ . مُتْقَنٌ
Accurately *ad.* بِضَبْطٍ . بِإِتْقَانٍ
Accursed *a.* مَلْعُونٌ
Accusation *n.* إِشْتِكَاءٌ . شِكَايَةٌ
Accuse *v. t.* شَكَا . إِتَّهَمَ . سَعَى بِهِ
Accuser *n.* شَاكٍ . مُتَّهِمٌ
Accustom *v. t.* عَوَّدَ
Acerbity *n.* حَرَافَةٌ . فَظَاظَةٌ
Ache *n.* وَجَعٌ . أَلَمٌ
Ache *v. i.* تَوَجَّعَ . تَأَلَّمَ
Achieve *v. t.* عَمِلَ . تَمَّمَ . فَازَ
Achievement *n.* عَمَلٌ . إِنْجَازُ أَمْرٍ
Acid *n.* حَامِضٌ
Acidity *n.* حُمُوضَةٌ

Acknowledge *v. t.* إعترف . أقرّ

Acme *n.* رأسٌ . قمّة

Acknowledgement *n.* إعترافٌ

Acorn *n.* بلّوطٌ

Acoustics *n.* علمُ السّمعيّات

Acquaint *v. t.* أعلمَ . عرّفَ

Acquaintance *n.* معرفةٌ. أحدُ المعارفِ

Acquiesce *v. t.* قبلَ . رضيَ ب

Acquire *v. t.* حصّلَ . إقتنى

Acquisition *n.* تحصيلٌ . قنيةٌ

Acquit *v. t.* برّأ . أطلقَ

Acquittal *n.* تبرئةٌ . إطلاقٌ

Acre *n.* فدّانٌ (إنكليزيٌّ)

Acreage *n.* عددُ الفدادينِ في ارضٍ

Acrid *a.* قارصٌ . حرّيفٌ

Acrimony *n.* حرافةٌ . حدّةٌ

Across *pr.* عرضاً . عبرَ

Act *n.* فعلٌ . عملٌ

Act *v. t.* or *i.* فعلَ . عملَ ـَ . تصرّفَ

Action *n.* فعلٌ . معركةٌ . دعوى

Active *a.* فعّالٌ ـَ نشيطٌ

Actively *ad.* بنشاطٍ . بهمّةٍ

Activity *n.* نشاطٌ . همّةٌ

Actor *n.* فاعلٌ . مشخّصٌ في ملعبٍ

Actual *a.* فعليٌّ . حقيقيٌّ

Actually *ad.* فعلاً . حقّاً

Actuate *v. t.* حمله على . ساقَ إلى

Acumen *n.* ذكاءٌ . حذاقةٌ

Acuminate *a.* محدّدُ الرّأسِ. مسنّنٌ

Acute *a.* حادٌّ . ذكيٌّ . حاذقٌ

Acuteness *n.* حدّةٌ . حذاقةٌ

Adage *n.* مثلٌ

Adamant *n.* حجرٌ صلبٌ . ماسٌ

Adapt *v. t.* ناسبَ . وافقَ

Adapted *a.* جديرٌ به . مناسبٌ

Adaptable *a.* قابلُ المناسبةِ

Adaptation *n.* مُنَاسَبَةٌ . مُوَافَقَةٌ

Add *v. t.* جَمَعَ ـَ أَضَافَ إِلَى

Adder *n.* أَفْعَى ج أَفَاعٍ

Addict *v. t.* اولِعَ ب . عَكَفَ عَلَى

Addicted *pp,* مُوْلَعٌ . مُنْعَكِفٌ

Addition *n.* جَمْعٌ . إِضَافَةٌ

Additional *a.* مُضَافٌ . زَائِدٌ

Addle *v. t. & a.* أَفْسَدَ . قَذَرَ

Address *v. t.* خَاطَبَ . عَنْوَنَ

Address *n.* خِطَابٌ . عَنْوَانٌ . حِذَاقَةٌ

Adduce *v. t.* أَوْرَدَ . جَآءَ بِ

Adept *n.* مَاهِرٌ . لَبِيبٌ

Adequate *a.* كَافٍ . مُسَاوٍ

Adhere *v. t.* لَصِقَ . لَزِقَ ـَ

Adherence *n.* لَصْقٌ . لُزُوقٌ

Adherent *a. n.* حَلِيفٌ . مُلْتَصِقٌ بِ

Adhesion *n.* لَصَقٌ . إِلْتِصَاقٌ

Adhesive *a.* لَزِجٌ . دَابِقٌ

Adieu *ad.* أَستَوْدِعُكُم ٱللهَ

Adjacent *a.* مُجَاوِرٌ . مُتَاخِمٌ

Adjective *n.* نَعْتٌ . صِفَةٌ

Adjoin *v. t.* or *i.* إِتَّصَلَ بِ . جَاوَرَ

Adjoining *a.* مُتَّصِلٌ بِ

Adjourn *v. t.* أَجَّلَ . اخَّرَ

Adjournment *n.* تَأْجِيلٌ . تَأْخِيرٌ

Adjudicate *v. t.* قَضَى ـِ حَكَمَ

Adjunct *n.* or *a.* مُضَافٌ . مُلْحَقٌ

Adjure *v. t.* إِستَحْلَفَ

Adjust *v. t.* نَاسَبَ . ضَبَطَ

Adjustment *n.* ضَبْطٌ . تَعْدِيلٌ

Adjutant *n.* مُعَاوِنٌ عَسْكَرِيٌّ

Administer *v. t.* أَدَارَ . أَجْرَى

Administration *n.* إِدَارَةٌ . إِجْرَآءٌ

Administrator *n.* مُدِيرٌ . وَكِيلٌ

Admirable *a.* عَجِيبٌ . بَاهِرٌ

Admiral *n.* أَمِيرُ ٱلْبَحْرِ

Admiralty *n.* إِمَارَةُ ٱلْبَحْرِيَّةِ
Admiration *n.* تَعَجُّبٌ . إِسْتِحْسَانٌ
Admire *v. t.* تَعَجَّبَ مِنْ . إِسْتَحْسَنَ
Admissible *a.* مُسَلَّمٌ بِهِ . جَائِزٌ
Admission *n.* تَسْلِيمٌ بِ . دُخُولٌ
Admit *v. t.* سَلَّمَ بِهِ . أَدْخَلَ
Admittance *n.* دُخُولٌ . تَسْلِيمٌ
Admix *v. t.* مَزَجَ ـُ . خَلَطَ ـِ
Admixture *n.* مَزِيجٌ
Admonish *v. t.* نَبَّهَ . أَنْذَرَ
Admonition *n.* إِنْذَارٌ . نَصِيحَةٌ
Admonitive *a.* }
Admonitory *a.* } مُنْذِرٌ
Ado *n.* تَعَبٌ . ضَجِيجٌ
Adolescence *n.* شُبُوبِيَّةٌ . مُرَاهَقَةٌ
Adopt *v. t.* تَبَنَّى . إِتَّخَذَ
Adoption *n.* تَبَنٍّ . إِتِّخَاذٌ
Adorable *a.* مُسْتَحِقٌّ ٱلْعِبَادَةِ
Adoration *n.* عِبَادَةٌ . مَحَبَّةٌ فَائِقَةٌ
Adore *v. t.* عَبَدَ ـُ أَحَبَّ

Adorn *v. t.* زَيَّنَ . زَخْرَفَ
Adornment *n.* تَزْيِينٌ . زِينَةٌ
Adrift *a.* or *ad.* عَائِمٌ . سَائِبٌ
Adroit *a.* مَاهِرٌ . أَرِيبٌ . حَاذِقٌ
Adroitness *n.* مَهَارَةٌ . حَذَاقَةٌ
Adulation *n.* تَمَلُّقٌ . إِطْرَاءٌ
Adulatory *a.* مُتَمَلِّقٌ . مُطْرٍ
Adult *n.* بَالِغُ ٱلسِّنِّ
Adulterate *v. t.* أَفْسَدَ . غَشَّ
Adulterer *n.* }
Adulterous *a.* } زَانٍ
Adultery *n.* زِنًى
Advance *v. i.* or *t.* تَقَدَّمَ . قَدَّمَ . رَقَّى
Advance *n.* تَقَدُّمٌ . تَرَقٍّ
Advance guard *n.* طَلِيعَةُ ٱلْجَيْشِ
Advanced *a.* مُقَدَّمٌ . مُرَقًّى . مُتَقَدِّمٌ
Advancement *n.* تَقْدِيمٌ . تَرْقِيَةٌ
Advantage *n.* فَائِدَةٌ . مَصْلَحَةٌ
Advantageous *a.* مُفِيدٌ . نَافِعٌ

Advent *n.* مَجِيءٌ . ظُهُورٌ

Adventitious *a.* عَرَضِيٌّ

Adventure *n.* حَادِثَةٌ غَرِيبَةٌ
مَشْرُوعٌ

Adventurous / Adventuresome } *a.* مُخَاطِرٌ بِنَفْسِهِ

Adverb *n.* ظَرْفٌ أَوحَالٌ

Adverbial *a.* ظَرْفِيٌّ أَوحَالِيٌّ

Adversary *n.* خَصْمٌ . مُقَاوِمٌ

Adverse *a.* مُضَادٌّ . مُعَاكِسٌ

Adversity *n.* مُصِيبَةٌ . بَلِيَّةٌ

Advert *v. i.* إِلْتَفَتَ إِلَى . أَشَارَ

Advertise *v. t.* أَعْلَنَ . اخْبَرَ

Advertisement *n.* إِعْلاَن . إِخْبَارٌ

Advice *n.* نَصِيحَةٌ . مَشْوَرَةٌ

Advisable *a.* مُوَافِقٌ . مُسْتَحْسَنٌ

Advise *v. t.* نَصَحَ . أَخْبَرَ

Advisory *n.* شُورِيٌّ

Advocacy *a.* مُحَامَاةٌ . شَفَاعَةٌ

Advocate *n.* مُحَامٍ (أَفُوكَاتُو)

Advocated *v. t.* حَامَى عَنْ . عَضَدَ

Advocation *n.* مُحَامَاةٌ . إِحْتِجَاجٌ

Adz *or* Adge *n.* قَدُومٌ

Aerial *a.* هَوَائِيٌّ . عَالٍ

Aerolite *n.* حَجَرٌ جَوِّيٌّ . نَيْزَكٌ

Aeronaut *n.* مُسَافِرٌ فِي ٱلْهَوَاءِ

Aesthetics *n. pl.* عِلْمُ ٱلْجَمَالِ

Afar *ad.* عَلَى بُعْدٍ

Affability *n.* انْسٌ وَبَشَاشَةٌ

Affable *a.* انِيسٌ . لَيِّنُ ٱلْجَانِبِ

Affably *ad.* بِبَشَاشَةٍ . بِلُطْفٍ

Affair *n.* أَمْرٌ . شَأْنٌ . قَضِيَّةٌ

Affect *v. t.* أَثَّرَ فِي . هَيَّجَ . تَصَنَّعَ

Affectation *n.* تَصَنُّعٌ

Affected *a.* مُتَأَثِّرٌ . مُصَابٌ . مُتَصَنِّعٌ

Affecting *a.* مُؤَثِّرٌ

Affection *n.* مَحَبَّةٌ . مَوَدَّةٌ

Affectionate *a.* مُحِبٌّ . وَدُودٌ

Affective *a.* مُهَيِّجُ الْعَوَاطِفِ

Affiance *v. t.* خَطَبَ ـُ (اَلْمَرْأَةَ)

Affidavit *n.* إِقْرَارٌ بِالْيَمِينِ

Affiliate *v. t.* تَبَنَّى . أَشْرَكَ

Affiliation *n.* تَبَنٍّ . إِشْرَاكٌ

Affinity *n.* قَرَابَةٌ . مُجَانَسَةٌ

Affirm *v. t.* حَقَّقَ . أَكَّدَ

Affirmable *a.* مُمْكِنٌ تَأْكِيدُهُ

Affirmation *n.* تَأْكِيدٌ . إِيجَابٌ

Affirmative *a.* or *n.* إِيجَابِيٌّ . مُوجَبٌ

Affirmatory *a.* مُثَبِّتٌ

Affix *v* أَلْصَقَ بِ وَصَلَ

Affix *n* مُضَافٌ

Afflict *v. t.* كَدَّرَ . ضَايَقَ

Afflicting
Afflictive مُكَدِّرٌ . مُغِمٌّ

Affliction *n.* ضِيقَةٌ . بَلِيَّةٌ

Affluence *n.* غِنًى . وَفْرَةٌ

Affluent *a.* غَنِيٌّ . وَافِرٌ

Afford *v. t.* أَنْتَجَ . قَدَّمَ . قَدَرَ عَلَى

Affray *n.* مُشَاجَرَةٌ . شَغَبٌ

Affright *v. t.* أَفْزَعَ . خَوَّفَ

Affront *v. t.* أَهَانَ . عَيَّرَ

Affront *n.* إِهَانَةٌ . تَعْيِيرٌ

Affusion *n.* سَكْبٌ . رَشٌّ

Afloat *ad.* عَائِمٌ

Afoot *ad.* مَاشٍ . جَارٍ

Aforesaid *a.* اَلْمَارُّ ذِكْرُهُ

Afraid *a.* خَائِفٌ . مُرْتَعِبٌ

Afresh *ad.* حَدِيثًا . أَيْضًا

Aft *a.* or *ad.* عِنْدَ الْمُؤخِرِ

After *ad.* or *pr.* بَعْدُ . خَلْفُ . بِحَسَبِ

Afternoon *n.* بَعْدَ الظُّهْرِ

After-thought *n.* تَأَمُّلٌ . مُعَادٌ

Afterwards *ad.* بَعْدَ ذَلِكَ

Again *ad.* أَيْضًا . مَرَّةً أُخْرَى

Against *pr.* ضِدٌّ . تُجَاهَ

Age *n.* عُمْرٌ . عَصْرٌ

Aged *a.* طَاعِنٌ فِي ٱلسِّنِّ

Agency *n.* فَاعِلِيَّةٌ . وَكَالَةٌ

Agent *n.* فَاعِلٌ . وَكِيلٌ

Agglomerate *v. t.* كَتَّلَ

Agglomeration *n.* تَكْتِيلٌ . تَرَاكُمٌ

Agglutinate *v. t.* غَرَّى . أَلْصَقَ

Agglutination *n.* تَغْرِيَةٌ . إِلْزَاقٌ

Aggrandize *v. t.* عَظَّمَ . كَبَّرَ

Aggrandizement *n.* تَعْظِيمٌ

Aggravate *v. t.* زَادَ . بَالَغَ فِي

Aggravation *n.* زِيَادَةٌ . تَثْقِيلٌ

Aggregate *v. t.* جَمَعَ ـَ . بَلَغَ ـُ

Aggregate *n.* or *a.* ٱلْكُلُّ . مَجْمُوعٌ

Aggregation *n.* جَمْعٌ

Aggress *v. t.* تَعَدَّى عَلَى

Aggression *n.* تَعَدٍّ

Aggressive *a.*
Aggressor *n.* مُتَعَدٍّ

Aggrieve *v. t.* أَحْزَنَ . كَدَّرَ

Aghast *ad.* مُنْذَهِلٌ . مَرْعُوبٌ

Agile *a.* حَرِكٌ . خَفِيفٌ

Agility *n.* خِفَّةٌ . سُرْعَةٌ

Agitate *v. t.* حَرَّكَ . هَيَّجَ . أَقْلَقَ

Agitation *n.* تَحْرِيكٌ . إِنْزِعَاجٌ

Agitator *n.* مُهَيِّجٌ . مُحَرِّكٌ

Ago *ad.* سَابِقًا . مِنْ مُدَّةٍ

Agonize *v. i.* تَعَذَّبَ

Agony *n.* أَلَمٌ شَدِيدٌ . نَزْعٌ

Agrarian *a.* مُخْتَصٌّ بِٱلْحُقُولِ

Agrarian *n.* مَنْ يَطْلُبُ قِسْمَةَ ٱلْأَرَاضِي بِٱلتَّسَاوِي

Agree *v. i.* إِتَّفَقَ عَلَى . سَلَّمَ بِ

Agreable *a.* مُرْضٍ . سَارٌّ

Agreement *n.* إِتِّفَاقٌ . عَهْدٌ

Agricultural *a.* زِرَاعِيٌّ . فَلاحِيٌّ

Agriculture *n.* اَلْفِلَاحَةُ . اَلزِّرَاعَةُ

Agriculturist *n.* فَلَّاحٌ . زَارِعٌ

Aground *ad.* عَلَى ٱلْأَرْضِ (مَرْكَبٌ)

Ague *n.* بُرَدَاءُ . بَرْدِيَّةٌ

Ah ! / Aha ! *ex.* آه . آهاً

Ahead *ad.* امَامَ . إِلَى قُدَّامٍ

Aid *v. t.* سَاعَدَ . أَعَانَ

Aid *n.* مُسَاعَدَةٌ . عَوْنٌ . مَدَدٌ

Ail *v. i.* إِعْتَلَّ . تَشَكَّى مِنْ مَرَضٍ

Ail *n.* / Ailment *n.* عِلَّةٌ . مَرَضٌ

Aim *v. t.* or *i.* قَصَدَ . إِغْتَرَضَ . صَوَّبَ

Aim *n.* قَصْدٌ . غَرَضٌ

Aimless *a.* بِلَا قَصْدٍ أَوْ غَرَضٍ

Air *n.* هَوَاءٌ . نَغْمَةٌ . هَيْئَةٌ

Air *v. t.* عَرَّضَ لِلْهَوَاءِ . هَوَّى

Airing *n.* تَنَزُّهٌ

Airless *a.* بِلَا هَوَاءٍ

Airy *a.* مَكْشُوفٌ لِلْهَوَاءِ . مَرِحٌ

Akin *a.* ذُو قَرَابَةٍ . نَسِيبٌ

Alacrity *n.* إِسْتِعْدَادٌ لِلْعَمَلِ . نَشَاطٌ

Alarm *v. t.* خَوَّفَ . أَرْعَبَ

Alarm *n.* إِنْذَارٌ بِٱلْخَطَرِ . خَوْفٌ

Alarm-clock *n.* سَاعَةٌ مُنَبِّهَةٌ

Alarming *a.* مُخِيفٌ . مُفْزِعٌ

Alas ! *ex.* وَا أَسَفَاهُ

Albeit *ad.* مَعَ أَنَّ وَلَوْ أَنَّ

Albumen *n.* زُلَالٌ

Alchemy *n.* الكِيمْيَاءُ ٱلْقَدِيمَةُ

Alcohol *n.* (ٱلْكُحُولُ)

Alcoholic *a.* (كُحُولِيٌّ)

Alderman *n.* شَيْخُ بَلَدٍ

Ale *n.* جِعَةٌ

Alert *a.* مُنْتَبِهٌ . مُتَيَقِّظٌ . خَفِيفٌ

Alertness *n.* خِفَّةٌ . يَقْظَةٌ . نَشَاطٌ

Algebra *n.* عِلْمُ ٱلْجَبْرِ

Algebraist *n.* مَاهِرٌ فِي عِلْمِ ٱلْجَبْرِ

Algerine *a.* جَزَائِرِيٌّ

Alien *a.* or *ad.* أَجْنَبِيٌّ

Alienate *v. t.* نَقَلَ . أَبْعَدَ

Alienation *n.* بَيْعٌ . نَقْلٌ . هِجْرَانٌ

Alight *v. i.* تَرَجَّلَ . وَقَعَ عَلَى

Alignment *n.* تَرْتِيبٌ عَلَى خَطٍّ

Alike *a.* شَبِيهٌ . نَظِيرٌ

Aliment *n.* غِذَاءٌ ج أَغْذِيَةٌ

Alimental, alimentary *a.* مُغَذٍّ

Alive *a.* حَيٌّ

Alkali *n.* أَلْقِلْيُ . الْقِلَى

Alkaline *n.* قَلَوِيٌّ

Alkoran *n.* الْقُرْآنُ

All *a.* or *n.* كُلٌّ . الْكُلُّ

Allay *v. t.* أَخْمَدَ . خَفَّفَ . خفض

Allegation *n.* تَأْكِيدٌ . حجَّةٌ . إِدِّعَاءٌ

Allege *v. t.* صَرَّحَ . إِدَّعَى

Allegiance *n.* طَاعَةٌ . امانة

Allegory *n.* مَجَازٌ . رَمْزٌ

Alleviate *v. t.* خَفَّفَ . لَطَّفَ

Alleviation *n.* تَسْكِينٌ . تَلْطِيفٌ

Alley *n.* زُقَاقٌ ج أَزِقَّةٌ

Alliance *n.* مُعَاهَدَةٌ . مُحَالَفَةٌ . مُصَاهَرَةٌ

Allied *pp.* مُتَعَاهِدٌ . مُنْتَسِبٌ . مُصَاهِرٌ

Alligator *n.* ضَرْبٌ مِنَ التِّمْسَاحِ

Allot *v. t.* خَصَّصَ . أَعْطَى نَصِيباً

Allotment *n.* نَصِيبٌ . تَقْسِيمٌ

Allow *v. t.* سَمَحَ . أَذِنَ . أَجَازَ

Allowable *a.* جَائِزٌ . مُبَاحٌ

Allowance *n.* إِذْنٌ . رَاتِبٌ

Alloy *v. t.* or *n.* مَزِيجُ الْجَيِّدِ مَعَ الرَّدِي

Allude *v. t.* اشَارَ أَوْ لَمَّحَ إِلَى

Allure *v. t.* إِسْتَمَالَ . إِجْتَذَبَ . اغوى

Allurement *n.* جَذْبٌ . إِسْتِمَالَةٌ . إِغْوَاءٌ

Alluring *a.* مُسْتَمِيلٌ . مُغْوٍ

Allusion *n.* إشَارَةٌ . تَلْمِيحٌ

Alluvium *n.* غَرْبَل . رُسُوبُ آلْمَاء

Ally *n.* or *v. t.* مُحالِفٌ . مُعاهِدٌ . حَالف

Almanac *n.* رُزْنَامَةٌ . تَقْوِيمُ آلسنةِ

Almighty *a.* or *n.* قَادِر على كلِّ شيْء

Almond *n.* لوزٌ

Almoner *n.* وَكِيلٌ أو مُوَزِّع صدَقات

Almost *ad.* تَقْرِيبًا

Alms *n.* صدَقَةٌ . إحْسان

Aloft *ad.* في آلْعَالي . فوْق

Alone *a.* علَى آنْفِرَاد . وَحدَهُ

Along *ad.* or *pr.* إِلَى قُدَّامٍ . بِجَانِبٍ

Aloof *ad.* بمَعزِل عنْ . على بعْد

Aloud *ad.* بصوْت وَاضح او عال

Alphabet *n.* حرُوف آلهجاء

Alphabetic *a.* نسبة لحرُوف آلْهِجاء

Alpine *a.* مختص بجبل عال

Already *ad.* قد

Also *ad.* ايضا . كَذَلِك

Altar *n.* مذبحٌ

Alter *v. t.* غيَّرَ . بدَّلَ . حوَّل

Alterable *a.* قَابِلُ آلتَّغْيِير

Alteration *n.* تغْيِير . تحْوِيل

Altercation *n.* مُخاصَمَة . مشاجَرَةٌ

Alternate *a.* متبادِلٌ . متعَاقِبٌ

Alternate *v. i.* بَادَلَ . نَاوبَ

Alternation *n.* تبادُلٌ . تَنَاوُب

Alternative *n.* احَد امْرَيْن

Although *con.* مع انَّ . وَلَوْ ان

Altitude *n.* عُلُوٌّ . إرْتِفَاعٌ

Altogether *ad.* جُمْلَةً . آلْكل معاً

Alum *n.* شبٌّ ابْيَضُ

Always *ad.* دائمًا . علَى آلدَّوَام

Amalgamate *v. t.* خلَط مَعْدَنًا بالزئبق مزَجَ

Amalgamation *n.* مزْجُ آلْمَعَادِنِ بالزئبق

Amanuensis *n.* كَاتِبُ ما يُمْلَى عليهِ
Amass *v. t.* جَمَعَ . كَوَّمَ
Amateur *n.* مغرومٌ بالفنون هاوٍ
Amatory *a.* حُبِّيٌّ . عِشْقِيٌّ
Amaze *v.t.* أَدْهَشَ . أَذْهَلَ
Amazement *n.* دَهْشَةٌ . إِنْذِهَالٌ
Amazing *a.* مُدْهِشٌ . عَجِيبٌ
Amazon *n.* إِمْرَأَةٌ حَرْبِيَّةٌ . سَلِيطَةٌ
Ambassador *n.* سَفِيرٌ ج سُفَرَاء
Amber *n.* كَهْرَبَاء
Ambergris *n.* عَنْبَرٌ
Ambiguity *n.* اِلْتِبَاسٌ . إِبْهَامٌ
Ambiguous *a.* مُلْتَبِسٌ . مُبْهَمٌ
Ambition *n.* طَلَبُ ٱلرِّفْعَةِ . حُبُّ ٱلرِّآسَةِ
Ambitious *a.* طَالِبُ ٱلرِّفْعَةِ . مُحِبُّ ٱلرِّآسَةِ
Amble *v. i.* خَبَّ ـُ . رَهَا ـُ
Ambler *n.* خَابٌّ . رَهْوَانٌ
Ambrosia *n.* عَنْبَرِيَّةٌ . طَعَامُ ٱلآلِهَةِ
Ambulance *n.* مَحْمِلُ ٱلْمَرْضَى
Ambuscade *n.* مَكْمَنٌ
Ambush *n.* كَمِينٌ
Ameliorate *v. t.* حَسَّنَ . أَصْلَحَ
Amelioration *n.* تَحْسِينٌ
Amenable *a.* مَسْئُولٌ . مُطَالَبٌ
Amend *v. t.* اَصْلَحَ . عَدَّلَ . حَسَّنَ
Amendment *n.* إِصْلَاحٌ . تَحْسِينٌ
Amends *n.* تَعْوِيضٌ
Amenity *n.* لُطْفٌ . أُنْسٌ
Amerce *v. t.* غَرَّمَ
Amethyst *n.* جَمَشْتٌ . بَنَفْشٌ
Amiable *a.* أَنِيسٌ . مَحْبُوبٌ
Amiably *ad.* بِلُطْفٍ . بِرِقَّةٍ . بِوُدٍّ
Amiable *a.* سَلْمِيٌّ . وِدَادِيٌّ
Amid *pr.* بَيْنَ . فِيمَا بَيْنَ

Amiss *a.* or *ad.* غَيْرُ مُوَافِقٍ . بِخَطَآءٍ

Amity *n.* مَحَبَّةٌ . صُحْبَةٌ

Ammonia *n.* نُشَادِرٌ

Ammunition *n.* مُؤُنَةُ ٱلْحَرْبِ

Amnesty *n.* أَمَانٌ . عَفْوٌ

Among / **Amongst** } *pr.* بَيْنَ . فِيمَا بَيْنَ

Amorous *a.* عَاشِقٌ . غَرَامِيٌّ

Amount *v. i.* or *n.* بَلَغَ . مَبْلَغٌ

Amphibious *a.* (حَيَوَانٌ) مَائِيٌّ بَرِّيٌّ

Amphitheatre *n.* مَلْعَبٌ مُدَوَّرُ ٱلْبِنَاءِ

Ample *a.* فَسِيحٌ . وَاسِعٌ . كَافٍ

Amplification *n.* تَوْسِيعٌ . إِسْهَابٌ

Amplify *v. t.* وَسَّعَ . أَسْهَبَ

Amplitude *n.* إِتِّسَاعٌ . كِبَرٌ

Amply *ad.* كِفَايَةً . بِسِعَةٍ

Amputate *v. t.* بَتَرَ . قَطَعَ

Amputation *n.* بَتْرٌ . قَطْعٌ

Amulet *n.* عُوذَةٌ . تَمِيمَةٌ

Amuse *v. t.* سَلَّى . أَلْهَى

Amusement *n.* تَسْلِيَةٌ

Amusing *a.* مُسَلٍّ . مُضْحِكٌ

Anachronism *n.* خَطَأٌ تَارِيخِيٌّ

Anæsthetic *n.* مُخَدِّرٌ

Analogous *a.* مُمَاثِلٌ . تَمْثِيلِيٌّ

Analogy *n.* تَمْثِيلٌ . مُمَاثَلَةٌ

Analysis *n.* تَحْلِيلٌ . تَفْصِيلٌ

Analytic *a.* تَحْلِيلِيٌّ . مُفَصَّلٌ

Analyze *v. t.* حَلَّلَ . فَصَّلَ

Anarchic *a.* بِلَا حُكُومَةٍ أَوْ تَرْتِيبٍ

Anarchy *n.* عَدَمُ ٱلْحُكْمِ . فَوْضَى

Anathema *n.* حَرْمٌ

Anathematize *v. t.* حَرَمَ

Anatomical *a.* تَشْرِيحِيٌّ

Anatomist *n.* عَالِمٌ فِي ٱلتَّشْرِيحِ

Anatomy *n.* عِلْمُ ٱلتَّشْرِيحِ

Ancestor *n.* سَلَفٌ . جَدٌّ

Ancestral *a.*	مُختَصٌّ بالأجْدَادِ
Ancestry *n.*	سلسِلَةُ ٱلأَجْدَادِ نَسَبٌ
Anchor *n.*	مِرْسَاةٌ ج مَرَاسٍ
Anchorage *n.*	مَرْسًى . مَرْفَأ
Anchorite *n.*	نَاسِكٌ . زَاهِدٌ
Ancient *a.*	قَدِيمٌ
Ancients *n. pl.*	ٱلقُدَمَاءُ
And *con.*	وَاوُ ٱلعَطْف
Anecdote *n.*	حِكَايَةٌ . قِصَّةٌ
Anemone *n.*	شَقِيقَةٌ . (نَبَاةٌ)
Anew *ad.*	جَدِيدًا . أَيْضاً
Angel *n.*	مَلَاكٌ
Angelic *a.*	مَلَكِيٌّ
Anger *n.*	غَضَبٌ . غَيظٌ
Angle *n.*	زَاوِيَةٌ ج زَوَايَا
Angle *v.i.*	صَادَ (ٱلسَّمَكَ) بِالصِّنَّارَةِ
Angler *n.*	صَيَّادٌ بِٱلصِّنَّارَةِ
Anglican *a.*	تَابِعُ ٱلْكَنِيسَةِ ٱلإِنْكِلِيزِيَّةِ
Anglicism *n.*	لَهْجَةٌ إِنْكِلِيزِيَّةٌ
Anglicize *v. t.*	حَوَّلَ إِلَى ٱلانْكِلِيزِيِّ
Angling *n.*	صَيْدٌ بِٱلصِّنَّارَةِ
Angrily *ad.*	بِغَيظٍ . بِغَضَبٍ
Angry *a.*	غَضْبَانُ . مُغْتَاظٌ
Anguish *v.*	عَذَابٌ . أَلَمٌ شَدِيدٌ
Angular *a.*	ذُو زَوَايَا
Animadversion *v.*	مَلَامَةٌ . تَنْكِيتٌ
Animadvert *v. i.*	إِلْتَفَتَ إِلَى. نَكَّتَ
Animal *n.*	حَيَوَانٌ
Animalcule *n.*	حُوَيْوِينَةٌ
Animate *v. t.*	أَحْيَا . انْعَشَ . نَشَّطَ
Animating *a.*	مُحْيٍ . مُنَشِّطٌ
Animation *n.*	نَشَاطٌ . حَيَاةٌ . رُوحٌ
Animosity *n.*	بُغْضٌ . حِقْدٌ
Ankle *n.*	رُسْغُ ٱلْقَدَمِ
Anklet *n.*	خَلْخَالٌ
Annalist *n.*	مُؤَرِّخٌ

Annals *n.* أَخْبَارٌ سَنَوِيَّةٌ مُتَتَابِعَةٌ
Annex *v. t.* أَوْصَلَ اضَافَ
Annexation *n.* إِيصَالٌ . إِضَافَةٌ
Annihilate *v. t.* أَعْدَمَ . ابَادَ
Annihilation *n.* إِعْدَامٌ . إِبَادَةٌ
Anniversary *n.* or *a.* عِيدٌ سَنَوِيٌّ
Annotate *v. t.* شَرَحَ . حَشَّى
Annotation *n.* شَرْحٌ . حَاشِيَةٌ
Annotator *n.* شَارِحٌ . مُحَشٍّ
Announce *v. t.* أَعْلَنَ . أَخْبَرَ . أَنْبَأَ
Announcement *n.* إِعْلَانٌ إِنْبَاءٌ
Annoy *v. t.* كَدَّرَ . أَزْعَجَ
Annoyance *n.* إِزْعَاجٌ . أَمْرٌ مُكَدِّرٌ
Annual *a.* or *n.* سَنَوِيٌّ . نَبَاتٌ سَنَوِيٌّ
Annually *ad.* سَنَوِيًّا
Annuity *n.* مَعَاشٌ سَنَوِيٌّ
Annul *v. t.* أَلْغَى . أَبْطَلَ
Annular *a.* حَلَقِيٌّ . مُسْتَدِيرٌ
Annulment *n.* إِلْغَاءٌ إِبْطَالٌ
Annulet *v. t.* زَرَدَةٌ . حَلَقَةٌ
Annunciate *v. t.* أَعْلَنَ . أَتَى بِأَخْبَارٍ
Annunciation *n.* إِعْلَانٌ . خَبَرٌ . بِشَارَةٌ
Anoint *v. t.* مَسَحَ
Anointing *n.* مَسْحٌ
Anomalous *a.* غَيْرُ قِيَاسِيٍّ . شَاذٌّ
Anomaly *n.* شُذُوذٌ . عَدَمُ نِظَامٍ
Anon *ad.* عَنْ قَرِيبٍ . حَالاً
Anonymous *a.* بِلَا اسْمٍ
Another *a.* آخَرُ غَيْرُ
Answer *n.* or *v. t.* جَوَابٌ . اجَابَ
Answerable *a.* مَسْئُولٌ . مُوَافِقٌ
Ant *n.* نَمْلَةٌ
Antagonism *n.* مُضَادَّةٌ . مُقَاوَمَةٌ
Antagonist *n.* مُقَاوِمٌ . خَصْمٌ
Antagonistic *a.* مُضَادٌّ . مُقَاوِمٌ
Antagonize *v. t.* ضَادَّ . قَاوَمَ

Antractic a. مُخْتَصٌّ بِٱلْقُطْبِ ٱلْجَنُوبِيِّ

Antecedence n. أَسْبَقِيَّةٌ . سَبْقٌ

Antecedent a. سَابِقٌ

Antechamber n. غُرْفَةٌ مُقَدَّمَةٌ

Antedata v. t. أَرَّخَ قَبْلُ (التَّارِيخِ الحَقِيقِيّ)

Antediluvian a. or n. قَبْلَ ٱلطُّوفَانِ

Antelope n. رِئْمٌ ج آرَام

Antepenult a. مَقْطَعُ ٱلْكَلِمَةِ قَبْلَ ٱلأَخِيرِ

Anterior a. سَالِفٌ . مُتَقَدِّمٌ

Anthem n. نَشِيدٌ

Anteroom n. غُرْفَةٌ . قُدَّام غُرْفَةٍ

Anther n. طَرَفُ سِدَاةِ النَّبَاتِ

Anthracite n. فَحْمٌ حَجَرِيٌّ صَلِبٌ

Anthropology n. عِلْمٌ يَبْحَثُ عَنِ ٱلإِنْسَانِ

Antichrist n. ضِدِّ ٱلْمَسِيحِ

Anticipate v. t. سَبَقَ — رَأَى مِنْ قَبْلُ

Anticipation n. سَبْقٌ . حِسٌّ . سَابِقٌ

Antidote n. تِرْيَاقٌ

Antimony n. إِثْمِدٌ . انتيمُن

Antipathy n. نُفُورٌ . كَرَاهَةٌ

Antipodes n. السَّاكِنُونَ أَقْطَارَ ٱلأَرْضِ ٱلْمُتَقَابِلَةِ

Antiquarian a. مُخْتَصٌّ بِٱلزَّمَانِ ٱلْقَدِيمِ

Antiquarian n.
Antiquary n. } عَالِمٌ بِٱلآثَارِ ٱلْقَدِيمَةِ

Antiquated a. or pp. قَدِيمٌ . عَتِيقٌ

Antique a. or n. أَثَرٌ قَدِيمٌ . قَدِيمٌ

Antiquity n. ٱلزَّمَانُ ٱلْقَدِيمُ . أَثَرٌ قَدِيمٌ

Antiseptic a. or n. مُضَادٌّ ٱلْفَسَادِ وَٱلْعُفُونَةِ

Antithesis n. تَبَايُنٌ فِي ٱلْكَلَامِ

Antitype n. ٱلْمَرْمُوزُ إِلَيْهِ

Antler *n.* قَرْنُ الْوَعْلِ

Anus *n.* إِسْتٌ

Anvil *n.* سِنْدَانٌ . زُبْرَةٌ

Anxiety *n.* هَمٌّ . قَلَقٌ

Anxious *a.* مُهْتَمٌّ . مشغولُ الْبَالِ

Any *a.* احَدٌ . ايّاً كَان

Apace *ad.* سَرِيعاً

Apart *ad.* عَلَى جانِبٍ . على حِدَةٍ

Apartment *n.* غُرْفَةٌ . مُخدَعٌ

Apathetic *a.* غَيْرُ حاسٍّ أَوْ مُبَالٍ

Apathy *n.* عَدَمُ الاِكْتِرَاثِ أَوِ الْمُبَالَاةِ

Ape *n.* or *v. t.* قِرْدٌ . قَلَّدَ

Aperient *a.* مُسْهِلٌ . خفيفٌ . مُلَيِّنٌ

Aperture *n.* نَافِذَةٌ . ثَقْبٌ

Apex *n.* قِمَّةٌ . رأسٌ

Apiary *n.* مَنْحِلة

Apiece *ad.* نصيبُ كلٍّ . لِكلٍّ وَاحِدٍ

Apish *a.* قِرْدِيٌّ . نَظِيرُ الْقِرْدِ

Apocalypse *n.* الرُّؤْيَا . سِفْرُ الرُّؤْيَا

Apocrypha *n.* الكُتُبُ غيرُ القَانونيةِ

Apocryphal *a.* غيرُ ثابتٍ . بَاطِلٌ

Apologetic *a.* إِعْتِذارِيٌّ . إِحتِجاجِيٌّ

Apologist *n.* مُحتَجٌّ . مُحامٍ

Apologize *v. i.* إِعْتَذَرَ . دَافَعَ عنْ

Apology *n.* اعْتِذارٌ . مُحاماةٌ

Apoplexy *n.* دَاءُ السَّكْتَةِ

Apostasy *n.* إِرْتِدادٌ . جُحُودُ الدِّينِ

Apostate *n.* مُرْتَدٌّ . جاحِدٌ

Apostatize *v. t.* إِرْتَدَّ . جَحَدَ الإِيمَانَ

Apostle *n.* رَسُولٌ ج رُسُلٌ

Apostleship *n.* رَسُولِيَّةٌ . رِسَالَةٌ

Apostolic *a.* رَسُولِيٌّ

Apostrophe *n.* حَذْفُ حَرْفٍ وعلامتهُ

Apothecary *n.* اجْزَائِيٌّ (صَيْدَلانِيٌّ)

Appall *v. t.* أَرْعَبَ . راعَ

Appalling *a.* مُرْعِبٌ . رَائِعٌ
Apparatus *n.* ادَوَاتٌ
Apparel *n.* لِبَاسٌ . كِسَاءٌ
Apparent *a.* ظَاهِرٌ . وَاضِحٌ
Apparently *ad.* بِحَسَبِ الظاهِرِ
Apparition *n.* ظُهُورٌ . طَيْفٌ
Appeal *v. t.* رَفَعَ الدَّعْوَى
Appeal *n.* إِسْتِئْنَافٌ . رَفْعُ الدَّعْوى
Appear *v. t.* ظَهَرَ ـَ . بانَ ـَ
Appearance *n.* ظُهُورٌ
Appease *v. t.* سَكَّنَ (غَيْظَهُ) . هَدَّأَ
Appellant *n.* رَافِعُ الدَّعْوَى
Appellation *n.* لَقَبٌ . تَسْمِيَةٌ
Appellative *a.* or *n.* عَامٌّ . إِسْمٌ عَامٌّ
Append *v. t.* عَلَّقَ اوْ الْحَقَ بِ
Appendage *n.* مُلْحَقٌ . ذَيْلٌ
Appendix *n.* مُلْحَقٌ . ذَيْلُ كِتَابٍ
Appertain *v. i.* إِخْتَصَّ بِ

Appetite *n.* (قَابِلِيَّةٌ) شَهْوَةُ الْأَكْلِ
Appetizing *a.* مُهَيِّجٌ لِشَهْوَةِ الْأَكْلِ
Applaud *v. t.* مَدَحَ . صَفَّقَ مَدْحاً
Applause *n.* مَدْحٌ . تَصْفِيقٌ . اسْتِحْسَانٌ
Apple *n.* تُفَّاحَةٌ
Appliance *n.* وَضْعٌ . تَخْصِيصٌ . وَاسِطَةٌ
Applicable *a.* مُطَابِقٌ . مُوَافِقٌ
Applicant *n.* طَالِبٌ ج طَلَبَةٌ
Application *n.* مُوَاظَبَةٌ . طَلَبٌ . وَضْعٌ
Apply *v. t.* or *i.* أَطْلَقَ على . إِسْتَعْمَلَ لِ
Apply to-for *v. t.* طَلَبَ مِنْ
Appoint *v. t.* عَيَّنَ . اقَامَ عَلَى
Appointee *n.* مُعَيَّنٌ لِوَظِيفَةٍ
Appointment *n.* تَعْيِينٌ . رَاتِبٌ
Apportion *v. t.* قَسَّمَ . أَحَصَّ
Apportionment *n.* تَقْسِيمٌ . إِحْصَاصٌ
Apposite *a.* مُوَافِقٌ . لَائِقٌ
Apposition *n.* بَدَلٌ (فِي النَّحْوِ)

Appraisal / Appraisment *n.* تَثْمِينٌ .(تَقْدِيرٌ)

Appraise *v. t.* ثَمَّنَ (قَدَّرَ)

Appreciable *a.* قَابِلُ ٱلتَّثْمِينِ وَٱلتَّقْدِيرِ

Appreciate *v. t.* ثَمَّنَ . إِعْتَبَرَ

Appreciation *n.* تَثْمِينٌ . إِعْتِبَار

Apprehend *v. t.* فَهِمَ . أَدْرَكَ . قَبَضَ

Apprehension *n.* إِدْرَاكٌ . خَوْفٌ

Apprehensive *a.* مُدْرِكٌ . خَائِفٌ

Apprentice *n.* تِلْمِيذُ صِنَاعَة

Apprise *v. t.* أَخْبَرَ . اعْلَمَ

Approach *v. t.* دَنَا . قَرُبَ . مِنْ

Approachable *a.* سَهْلُ ٱلإِقْتِرَابِ إِلَيْهِ

Approbation *n.* إِسْتِحْسَانٌ . رِضَى

Appropriate *v. t.* خَصَّصَ . أَفْرَزَ

Appropriate *n.* مُنَاسِبٌ . لَائِقٌ

Appropriate *a.* تَخْصِيصٌ

Approval *n.* إِسْتِحْسَانٌ . قُبُولٌ

Approve *v. t.* إِسْتَحْسَنَ . رَضِيَ بِهِ

Approximate *v. t.* or *a.* إِقْتَرَبَ إِلَى . تَقْرِيبِيٌّ

Approximately *ad.* تَقْرِيباً

Approximation *n.* تَقْرِيبٌ . إِقْتِرَابٌ

Appurtenance *n.* مُلْحَقٌ . مُخْتَصٌّ

Apricot *n.* مِشْمِشَةٌ

April *n.* نِيسَانُ

Apron *n.* (مِرْيُولٌ) وَزْرَةٌ

Apt *a.* مُسْتَعِدٌّ . خَلِيقٌ بِ

Aptitudes / Aptness *n.* مَيْلٌ طَبِيعِيٌّ . اهْلِيَّةٌ

Aptly *ad.* كَمَا يَجِبُ . بِلِيَاقَةٍ

Aquarium *n.* حَوْضُ ٱلسَّمَكِ وَٱلنَّبَاتِ

Aquatic *a.* عَائِشٌ فِي ٱلْمَاءِ

Aqueduct *n.* قَنَاةُ مَاءٍ

Aqueous *a.* مَائِيٌّ

Arabian *a.* عَرَبِيٌّ

Arabic *n.* أَلْعَرَبِيَّةُ

Arable *a.* صَالِحٌ لِلْحَرْثِ او ٱلزَّرْعِ

Arbiter / Arbitrator *n.* فَيْصَلٌ . حَكَمٌ

Arbitrary *n.* غَيْرُ مُقَيَّدٍ . مُسْتَبِدٌّ

Arbitrate *v. t.* or *i.* تَوَسَّطَ بِحُكْمٍ بَيْنَ

Arbitration *n.* حُكْمُ ٱلْفَيَاصِلِ

Arbour *n.* عَرِيشٌ ج عَرَائِشُ

Arboreous *a.* شَجَرِيٌّ

Arc *d.* قَوْسٌ ج قِسِيٌّ

Arcade *n.* رِوَاقٌ ج أَرْوِقَةٌ

Arch *n.* or *v. t.* قَنْطَرَةٌ . قَنطَرَ

Archæology *n.* عِلْمُ ٱلْآثَارِ ٱلْقَدِيمَةِ

Archaïc *a.* قَدِيمٌ

Archangel *n.* رَئِيسُ مَلَائِكَةٍ

Archbishop *n.* رَئِيسُ أَسَاقِفَةٍ

Archbishop-ric *n.* مَقَامُ رَئِيسِ ٱلْأَسَاقِفَةِ

Archduchess *n.* أَمِيرَةٌ فِي دَوْلَةِ ٱلنَّمْسَا

Archduke *n.* أَمِيرٌ فِي دَوْلَةِ ٱلنَّمْسَا

Arched *a.* مُقَوَّسٌ . مُقَبَّوٌّ

Archer *n.* رَامِي ٱلسِّهَامِ . رَامٍ

Archery *n.* صِنَاعَةُ ٱلرَّمْيِ بِٱلْقَوْسِ

Archetype *n.* أُنْمُوذَجٌ أَصْلِيٌّ

Archipelago *n.* مَجْمُوعُ جَزَائِرَ . أَرْخَبِيلٌ

Architect *n.* مُهَنْدِسٌ بَنَّاءٌ

Architectural *a.* مُتَعَلِّقٌ بِعِلْمِ ٱلْبِنَاءِ

Architecture *n.* عِلْمُ ٱلْبِنَاءِ وَهَنْدَسَتُهُ

Archives *n. pl.* سِجِلَّاتٌ وَخَزَائِنُهَا

Archway *n.* مَمْشًى تَحْتَ قَنَاطِرَ

Arctic *a.* مُخْتَصٌّ بِٱلْقُطْبِ ٱلشِّمَالِيِّ

Ardent *a.* حَارٌّ . غَيُورٌ

Ardour *n.* حَرَارَةٌ . حَمِيَّةٌ . حَمَاسَةٌ

Arquous *a.* صَعْبٌ . شَاقٌّ

Area *n.* سَاحَةُ أَرْضٍ . إِتِّسَاعُهَا

Arena *n.* مَيْدَانٌ ج مَيَادِينُ

Arenaceous *a.* رَمْلِيٌّ

Argillaceous *a.* صَلْصَالِيٌّ

Argue *v. i.* or *t.* نَاظَرَ . إِحْتَجَّ . جَادَلَ

Argument *n.* دَلِيلٌ . حُجَّةٌ

Argumentation *n.* إِقَامَةُ ٱلدَّلِيلِ

Argumentation *n.* إِحتِجَاجِيٌّ

Arid *a.* قَاحِلٌ . جَافٌّ

Aridity *n.* قُحُولَةٌ . يُبُوسَةٌ

Aries *n.* بُرْجُ ٱلْحَمَلِ

Aright *ad.* مُسْتَقِيمًا

Arise *v. i.* قَامَ ـُ . طَلَعَ . ظَهَرَ ـَ

Aristocracy *n.* الأَشْرَافُ . حُكُومَتُهُمْ

Aristocrat *n.* أَحَدُ ٱلْأَشْرَافِ

Aristocratic *a.* مُخْتَصٌّ بِٱلْاشْرَافِ

Arithmetic *n.* عِلْمُ الْحِسَابِ

Arithmetical *a.* حِسَابِيٌّ

Arithmetician *n.* عَالِمٌ بِٱلْحِسَابِ

Ark *n.* فُلْكٌ . تَابُوت

Arm *n.* ذِرَاعٌ . سَاعِدٌ . فَرْعٌ مِنَ ٱلْعَسْكَرِ

Arm *v. t.* سَلَّحَ

Armada *n.* مَجْمُوعُ بَوَارِجَ . اسْطُولٌ

Armament *n.* جِهَازٌ لِلْحَرْبِ

Arm-chair *n.* كُرْسِيٌّ ذُو يَدَيْنِ

Armful *n.* مِلْءُ قَبْضَةِ الذِّرَاعِ

Armhole *n.* ثَقْبُ ثَوب لِلذِّرَاعِ

Armistice *n.* هُدْنَةٌ

Armlet *n.* سِوَارٌ

Armour *n.* عُدَّةُ حَرْب . سِلَاحٌ

Armoured *a.* مُصَفَّحٌ بِٱلْحَدِيدِ . مُلَبَّسٌ بِصَفَائِحِ حَدِيدٍ

Armourer *n.* صَانِعُ أَسْلِحَةٍ أَوْ بَائِعُهَا.

Armoury *n.* مَخْزَنُ اسلِحَةٍ

Armpit *n.* إِبْطٌ ج آبَاطٌ

Arms *n. pl.* عُدَّةُ حَرْب . اسلِحة

Army *n.* جَيْشٌ ج جُيُوشٌ

Aroma *n.* رَائِحَةٌ عِطْرِيَّةٌ

Aromatic *a.* عَطِرٌ . طَيِّبٌ

Around *pr.* or *ad.* حَوْلَ

Arouse *v. t.* أَيْقَظ . نَبَّهَ . حَرَّضَ

Arraign *v. t.* دَعَيَ لِلْمُحَاكَمَةِ

Arraignment *n.* مُحَاكَمَةٌ

Arrrange *v. t.* رَتَّبَ . دَبَّرَ

Arrangement *n.* تَرْتِيبٌ . تَدْبِيرٌ

Arrant *a.* شَهِيرٌ بِٱلشَّرِّ

Array *n.* مُصَافٌّ . لِبَاسٌ

Array *v. t.* صَفَّ . لَبَّسَ . زَيَّنَ

Arrears *n. pl.* بَقَايَا دَيْنٍ مُسْتَحِقٍّ

Arrest *v. t.* اَلْقَى ٱلْقَبْضَ عَلَى . وَقَفَ

Arrest *n.* إِلْقَاءُ ٱلْقَبْضِ . تَوْقِيفٌ

Arrival *n.* مَجِيءٌ . وُصُولٌ

Arrive *v. i.* أَتَى . وَصَلَ . بَلَغَ

Arrogance *n.* غَطْرَسَةٌ . تَكَبُّرٌ

Arrogant *a.* مُتَجَبِّرٌ . مُتَكَبِّرٌ

Arrogate *v. t.* إِدَّعَى . نَسَبَ لِنَفْسِهِ

Arrow *n.* سَهْمٌ ج سِهَامٌ

Arsenal *n.* مَخْزَنُ مُؤْنَةٍ حَرْبِيَّةٍ

Arsenic *n.* زِرْنِيخٌ . سَمُّ ٱلْفَارِ

Arson *n.* حَرَقَ بَيْتٍ عَنْ ضَغِينَةٍ

Art *n.* فَنٌّ . صِنَاعَةٌ . مَكْرٌ

Arterial *a.* شَرْيَانِيٌّ

Artery *n.* شَرْيَانٌ ج شَرَايِينُ

Artful *a.* مَكَّارٌ . مَاهِرٌ

Artichoke *n.* (أَرْضِي شَوْكِي) خُرْشُوفٌ

Article *n.* بَنْدٌ . مَادَّةٌ . آل ٱلتَّعْرِيفِ

Articulate *a.* ذو مَفَاصِلَ اوْ مَقَاطِعَ

Articulate *v. t.* لَفَظَ وَاضِحًا

Articulation *n.* لَفْظٌ . مَفْصِلٌ . إِتِّصَالٌ

Artifice *n.* حِيلَةٌ تَدْبِيرٌ

Artificer *n.* صَاحِبُ حِرْفَةٍ . مُخْتَرِعٌ

Artificial *a.* مُصَنَّعٌ . غَيْرُ حَقِيقِيٍّ

Artillery *n.* مَدَافِعُ (طُوبْجِيَّةٌ)

Artisan *n.* صَاحِبُ صِنَاعَةٍ

Artist *n.* إِسْتَاذُ صِنَاعَةٍ . مُصَوِّرٌ

Artistic *a.* مُطَابِقٌ لِلصِّنَاعَةِ . نَفِيسٌ

Artless *a.* سَاذِجٌ سَلِيمُ ٱلنِّيَّةِ

As *ad.* كَمَا . مِثْلُ . لَمَّا . بَيْنَمَا

Ascend *v. t.* or *i.* صَعِدَ . طَلَعَ ـَ

Ascendant *a.* or *n.* فَائِقٌ . سَطْوَةٌ

Ascendency *n.* سَطْوَةٌ . سَلْطَةٌ

Ascension *n.* صُعُودٌ

Ascent *n.* طُلُوعٌ . مَرْقًى . إِرْتِقَاءٌ

Ascertain *v. t.* كَشَفَ ـَ حَقَّقَ

Ascetic *n.* نَاسِكٌ . زَاهِدٌ

Asceticism *n.* تَنَسُّكٌ . زُهْدٌ

Ascribe *v. t.* نَسَبَ ـِ إِلى

Ascription *n.* نَسْبَةٌ . تَخْصِيصٌ

Ash *n.* دَرْدَارٌ (شَجَرَة)

Ashamed *a.* خَجْلَانُ . مُسْتَحٍ

Ashen *a.* دَرْدَارِيٌّ . رَمَادِيٌّ

Ashes *n. pl.* رَمَادٌ

Ashore *ad.* عَلَى ٱلْبَرِّ اوْ إِلَيهِ

Ashy *a.* رَمَادِيٌّ . مُصْفَرٌّ

Asiatic *a.* نِسبَةٌ لآسيَّا

Aside *ad.* عَلَى جَانِبٍ . عَلَى إِنفِرَادٍ

Asinine *a.* حِمَارِيٌّ . بَلِيدٌ

Ask *v. t.* طَلَبَ ـُ سَأَلَ

Asleep *a.* نَائِمٌ . رَاقِدٌ

Asp *n.* صِلٌّ . افْعَى

Asparagus *n.* هَلْيُونٌ

Aspect *n.* مَنْظَرٌ . هَيْئَةٌ

Asperity *n.* خُشُونَة . غِلَاظَةٌ

Asperse *v. t.* قذفَ ـِ طَعَنَ في

Aspersion *n.* قَذْفٌ . طَعْنٌ . رَشٌّ

Asphyxia *n.* إِخْتِنَاقٌ

Aspirant *n.* طَالِبٌ . تَوَّاقٌ

Aspirate *n.* صَوْتٌ كَٱلْهَاءِ

Aspiration *n.* شَوْقٌ . مَطْ . بٌ . تَلَهُّفٌ

Aspire *v. i.* طَلَبَ بِشَوْقٍ . تَاقَ إِلى

Ass *n.* حِمَارٌ ج حَمِيرٌ

Assail *v. t.* هَجَمَ عَلَى . إِقْتَحَمَ

Assailant *n.* مُهَاجِمٌ . مقْتَحِمٌ

Assassin *n.* قاتلٌ سِرًّا

Assassinate *v. t.* قَتَلَ سِرًّا

Assassination *n.* قتلٌ سِرًّا

Assault *v. t.* or *n.* هَاجَمَ مُهَاجَمَةٌ

Assay *v. t.* or *i.* or *n.* جَرَّبَ إِمتِحَان

Assayer *n.* مُمْتَحِنُ ٱلْمَعَادِنِ

Assemblage *n.* إِجتِمَاعٌ . مَحْفَلٌ

Assemble *v. i.* or *t.* جَمَعَ . إِجتَمَعَ

Assembly *n.* مَجْمَعٌ . مَجْلِسٌ

Assent *v. i.* or *n.* سَلَّمَ . تسلِيمٌ

Assert *v. t* زَعَمَ . إِدَّعَى . تَأَكَّدَ

Assertion *n.* زَعْمٌ . إِدِّعَاءٌ . تَأْكِيدٌ

Assess *v. t.* قَدَّرَ . ثَمَّنَ

Assessment *n.* تثمِينٌ

Assessor *n.* مُثَمِّنٌ . مَنْ يَضَعُ الرَّسْمَ

Assets *n. pl.* مَوْجُودَاتٌ

Asseverate *v. t.* اكَّدَ صَرَّحَ

Assiduity *n.* مُوَاظَبَةٌ . مُثَابَرَةٌ

Assiduous *a.* مُوَاظِبٌ . مُثَابِرٌ

Assign *v. t.* خَصَّصَ . أَفْرَزَ

Assignation *n.* تعيِينٌ . مِيعَادُ لِقَاءٍ

Assignee *n.* مَنْ يُسلَّمُ لَهُ شَيءٌ

Assignment *n.* تعيِينٌ . تحْوِيلٌ

إِحالَةُ امُورِ مفْلِسٍ إِلى وُكلاء

Assimilate *v. t.* مَثَّلَ . شبَّهَ . أَدْغَمَ

Assist *v. t.* أَعَانَ . ساعَدَ . اغاث

Assistance *n.* مُسَاعَدَةٌ . عَوْنٌ

Assistant *n.* مُسَاعِدٌ . مُعِينٌ

Assizes *n.* محكَمَةٌ . مَجْلِسُ ٱلْحقُوقِ

Associate *v. t.* or *i.* اشرَكَ . إِشْتَرَكَ

Associate *n.* or *a.* شَرِيكٌ . رَفِيقٌ

Association *n.* مشَارَكَةٌ . جَمْعِيَّةٌ

Assort *v. t.* رَتَّبَ . جَنَّسَ

Assorted *a.* متَنَوِّعٌ . مُشَكَّلٌ

Assortment ترْتِيبٌ . بَضَائِعُ متَنَوِّعَةٌ

Assuage *v. t.* خَفَّفَ . اخمَدَ

Assume *v. t.* ادَّعَى . إِتَّخَذَ

Assuming *a.* مُدَّعٍ . مُتَكَبِّرٌ . مُعْجَبٌ

Assumption *n.* إِدِّعَاءٌ . إِتِّخَاذٌ

Assurance *n.* تأْكِيدٌ . يَقِينٌ

Assure *v. t.* أكَّدَ . حقق

Asteroid *n.* سَيَّارٌ صَغِيرٌ

Astern *ad.* عَلَى مُؤَخَّرِ ٱلسَّفِينَةِ أَوْ خَلْفَهَا

Asthma *n.* دَاءُ ٱلرَّبْوِ

Asmatic *a.* مُصَابٌ بِدَاءِ ٱلرَّبْوِ

Astonish *v. t.* أَدْهَشَ . حَيَّرَ

Astonishing *a.* مُدْهِشٌ . مُحَيِّرٌ

Astonishment *n.* دَهْشَةٌ . تَعَجُّبٌ

Astound *v. t.* أَدْهَشَ حَيَّرَ

Astray *ad.* تَائِهاً . شَارِداً

Astrine *ad.* مفرْشحاً

Astringent *a.* or *n.* قَابِضٌ ج قَوَابِضُ

Astrologer *n,* مُنَجِّمٌ

Astrology *n.* عِلْمُ ٱلتَّنْجِيمِ

Astronomer *n.* عَالِمٌ بِعِلْمِ ٱلْهَيْئَةِ

Astronomy *n.* عِلْمُ ٱلْهَيْئَةِ

Astute *a.* ذَكِيٌّ . حَاذِقٌ

Astuteness *n.* دَهَاءٌ فِرَاسَةٌ

Asunder *ad.* مَفْصُولاً عَنْ

Asylum *n.* مَلْجأٌ . بِيمَارِسْتَانٌ

At *pr.* عِنْدَ . في

Atheism *n.* إِنْكَارُ وُجُودِ ٱللهِ

Atheist *n.* مُنْكِرُ وُجُودِ ٱللهِ . مُلْحِدٌ

Athirst *a.* عَطْشَانُ . ظَمْآنُ

Athlete *n.* مُصَارِعٌ . مُتْقِنُ ٱلرِّيَاضَةِ

Athletic *a.* قَوِيُّ ٱلْجِسْمِ . ضَلِيعٌ

Athwart *ad.* عَرْضاً

Atlas *n.* (أَطْلَسٌ . مَجْمُوعُ خَارِطَاتٍ)

Atmosphere *n.* هَوَاءٌ . جَوٌّ

Atmospheric *a.* هَوَائِيٌّ . جَوِّيٌّ

Atom *n.* ذَرَّةٌ . جَوْهَرٌ ٱلْفَرْدِ

Atomic *a.* مختَصٌّ بِجَوْهَرِ ٱلْفَرْدِ

Atone v. t. or i. كَفَّرَ عَنْ

Atonement n. كَفَّارَةٌ

Atrocious a. فَظِيعٌ . فَاحِشٌ

Atrocity n. كَبِيرَةٌ . فَظَاعَةٌ

Attach v. t. وَصَلَ ـ . عَلَّقَ

Attachment n. ضَبْط . حَجْزُ (آلامْوَال) . وُدٌّ

Attack v. t. or n. هَاجَمَ . مُهَاجَمَةٌ

Attain v. t. حَصَّلَ . بَلَغَ ـُ

Attainment n. تَحْصِيلٌ . بُلُوغٌ

Attaint v. t. أَفْسَدَ . أَثْبَتَ خِيَانَتَهُ

Attempt v. t. or n. جَرَّبَ . حَاوَلَ تَجْرِبَةٌ

Attend v. t. or i. رَافَقَ . إِعْتَنَى . حَضَرَ

Attendance n. حُضُورٌ . مُلَازَمَةٌ

Attendant n. تَابِعٌ . خَادِمٌ . إِصْغَاءٌ

Attention n. إِنْتِبَاهٌ . مَعْرُوفٌ

Attentive a. مُصْغٍ . مُلَازِمٌ

Attenuate v. t. رَقَّقَ . خَفَّفَ

Attenuation n. تَرْقِيقٌ . تَخْفِيفٌ

Attest v. t. شَهِدَ . اثْبَتَ . أَكَّدَ

Attestation n. شَهَادَةٌ . إِثْبَاتٌ

Attire v. t. or n. أَلْبَسَ . لِبَاسٌ

Attitude n. حَالَةٌ . هَيْئَةٌ

Attorney n. وَكِيلُ دَعَاوٍ

Attract a. t. جَذَبَ ـ إِسْتَمَال

Attraction n. جَذْبٌ . جَاذِبِيَّةٌ

Attracting / Attractive a. جَاذِبٌ . مُسْتَمِيلٌ . سَارٌّ

Attractiveness n. صِفَةُ ٱلْجَذْبِ جَاذِبَة . حُسْنٌ

Attribute v. t. or n. نَسَبَ إِلَى . صِفَةٌ

Attribution n. نِسْبَةٌ . وَصْفٌ

Attrition n. فَرْكٌ . سَحْقٌ

Attuned pp. مُوَفَّقٌ . مَدْوَزَن

Auction n. مَزَادٌ . حَرَاجٌ

Auctioneer n. دَلَّالٌ

Audacious *a.* جَسُورٌ . وَقِحٌ

Audacity *n.* جَسَارَةٌ . وَقَاحَةٌ

Audible *a.* مَسْمُوعٌ

Audience *n.* ٱلسَّامِعُونَ ٱلْحَاضِرُونَ

Audit *v. t.* فَحَصَ حِسَابًا وَضَبَطَهُ

Auditor *n.* فَاحِصُ حِساب . سَامِعٌ

Auditory *a.* سَمْعِيٌّ

Auger *n.* مِثْقَبٌ

Aught *n.* شَيْءٌ ما

Augment *v. t.* or *i.* زَادَ . إِزْدَادَ

Augment / **Augmentation** *n.* زِيَادة

Augury *n.* فَأْلٌ. تطَيُّرٌ

August *a.* عظِيمٌ .سَامِي ٱلشأْنِ

August *n.* شَهْرُ آبِ

Aunt *n.* عَمَّةٌ أَوْ خَالَةٌ

Auricle *n.* صِيوَانَةُ ٱلاذُنِ أُذَينَةُ ٱلْقَلْبِ

Auriferous *a.* ذُو ذَهبٍ

Aurora *n.* شَفَقٌ

Auspicious *a.* ذُو حَظٍّ . سَعِيدٌ

Austere *a.* عَابِسٌ . صَارِمٌ

Austerity *n.* صَرَامَةٌ . عُبُوسٌ

Authentic *a.* حَقِيقِيٌّ

Authenticate *v. t.* حَقَّقَ . أَثْبَتَ

Authenticity *n.* حَقِيقَةٌ . حَقَّانِيَّةٌ

Author *n.* مُؤَلِّفٌ . مُصَنِّفٌ . مُسَبِّبٌ

Authoritative *a.* جَازِمٌ .ذُو سُلْطَةٍ

Authority *n.* سُلْطَةٌ . حقُّ ٱلتَّسَلُّطِ

Authorization *n.* تَفْوِيضٌ . إِجَازَةٌ

Authorize *v. t.* فَوَّضَ.أَجَازَ.رَخَّصَ

Authorship *n.* صِنَاعَةُ ٱلتَّأْلِيفِ

Autobiography *n.* تَرْجَمَةُ ٱلإِنْسَانِ لِحَيَاتِهِ

Autocracy *n.* سُلْطَةٌ مُطْلَقَةٌ

Autocrat *n.* حَاكِمٌ مُطْلَقٌ

Autograph *n.* خطُّ ٱلْمُؤَلِّفِ . إِمْضَاءٌ

Automatic *a.* مُتحَرِّكٌ مِنْ ذَاتِهِ

Autonomy *n.* حُكْمٌ ذاتِيٌّ إِستِقْلاَلِيٌّ

Autopsy *n.* تَشْرِيحُ جُثَّةٍ

Autumn *n.* أَلْخَرِيفُ

Autumnal *a.* خَرِيفِيٌّ

Auxiliary *a.* or *n.* مُسَاعِدٌ

Avail *v. i.* or *t.* or *n.* نَفَعَ. أَفَادَ. نفعٌ

Available *a.* مَوْجُودٌ. مُفِيدٌ

Avails *n. pl.* أَلْحَاصِلُ مِنْ بيْعٍ

Avalanche *n.* هَيَارُ آلثَّلْجِ مِنْ جَبَلٍ

Avarice *n.* بُخْلٌ . شِحٌّ

Avaricious *a.* بَخِيلٌ . شَحِيحٌ

Avenge *v. t.* إِنْتَقَمَ مِنْ . عَاقَبَ

Avenger *n.* مُنتَقِمٌ

Avenue *n.* شارِعٌ عَرِيضٌ . مَدْخلٌ

Aver *v. t.* اكَّدَ . جزَمَ

Average *n.* or *v. t.* مُعَدَّلٌ . عَدَّلَ

Averse *a.* غيْرُ رَاضٍ . مُنَافٍ . كَارِهٌ

Aversion *n.* نفورٌ . كَرَاهَةٌ

Avert *v. t.* حَوَّلَ عَنْ . منَعَ

Aviary *n.* قَفَصٌ . بَيْتُ آلطُّيُورِ

Avidity *n.* شَرَهٌ . حِرْصٌ

Avocation *n.* حِرْفَةٌ . مَشْغَلَةٌ

Avoid *v. t.* جَانَبَ . تحَوَّلَ عَنْ

Avoirdupois *n.* عِيَارٌ فيهِ آللِّيبْرَا ١٦ أُوقيَّةً إِنْكلِيزِيَّةً

Avouch *v. t.* اكَّدَ . صَرَّحَ بِ

Avow *v. t.* صَرَّحَ . أَقرَّ بِ

Avowal *n.* إِقْرَارٌ . إِشْهَارٌ

Await *v. t.* إِنْتَظَرَ . توَقَّعَ

Awake / **Awaken** } *v. t.* or *i.* ايقَظَ إِستَيْقَظَ

Awake *a.* يَقْظَانُ

Award *v. t.* or *n.* حَكَمَ قَضَى . حُكْمٌ

Aware *a.* عارِفٌ مُنتَبِهٌ

Away *ad.* عَلَى بُعْدٍ . غَائِباً

Awe *n.* or *v. t.* رَوْعَةٌ . خشية . ارْعب

Awe-struck *a.* مُرْتَعِدٌ . رَاهِبٌ

Awful *a.* مُخِيفٌ . هَائِلٌ

Awhile *ad.* إِلَى حِينٍ . مُدَّةً

Awkward *a.* أَخْرَقُ . مُتَلَبِّكٌ

Awkwardness *n.* خَرَقٌ . تَلَبُّكٌ

Awl *n.* مَخْرَزٌ ج مَخَارِزُ

Awning *n.* مَظَلَّةٌ ج مَظَالُّ

Awry *a.* or *ad.* مُنْحَرِفٌ مُعَوَّجٌ بِانْحِرَافٍ

Ax *or* **Axe** *n.* فَأْسٌ ج فُؤُوسٌ

Axillary *a.* ابطيٌّ

Axiom *n.* مبدأ . اوَّلِيَّةٌ

Axiomatic *a.* مَبْدَئِيٌّ . اوَّلِيٌّ

Axail *a.* مِحْوَرِيٌّ

Axis *n.* مِحْوَرٌ

Axle *n.* مِحْوَرُ دُولاب . قِطْبٌ

Ay *or* **Aye** *adv.* بَلَى . نعمْ . دَائِماً

Azure *a.* or *n.* اسمانجوني

B

Babble *v. i.* or *n.* بقّ . هذر . هذرٌ

Babbler *n.* بقباقٌ . مِهْذَارٌ

Babe *or* **Baby** } *n.* طِفْلٌ ج اطفالٌ

Baboon *n.* نوعٌ من القرودِ

Babyish *a.* سَرِيعُ التَّكدُّرِ كَالطِّفل

Bachelor *n.* عَزَبٌ ج عُزَّابٌ

Bachelorship *n.* عُزُوبَةٌ

Back *n.* or *ad.* ظَهْرٌ ج ظُهُورٌ
إِلَى الْوَرَاءِ

Back and forth *ad.* إِقْبَالاً وَإِدْبَارًا

To go back رَجَعَ ـِ

Backbite *v. t.* غَابَ . إِغْتَابَ

Backbiting *n.* غِيبَةٌ . إِغْتِيَابٌ

Backbone *n.* اَلسِّلْسِلَةُ الْفَقْرِيَّةُ

Backing *n.* عَوْنٌ . سَنَدٌ . بِطَانَةٌ

Backside *n.* ظَهْرٌ . قَفَاءٌ

Backslide *v. i.* مَالَ عَنْ . إِرْتَدَّ

Backward *ad.* or *a.* إِلَى الْخَلْفِ . مُتَأَخِّرٌ

Bacon *n.* لَحْمُ خِنْزِيرٍ مُجَفَّفٌ

Bad *a.* شِرِّيرٌ . رَدِيءٌ . مُضِرٌّ

Bade *v. t.* أَمَرَ (مَاضِي bid)

Badge *n.* عَلاَمَةٌ (نِيشَانٌ)

Baffle *v. t.* خَيَّبَ . غَلَبَ بِحِيلَةٍ

Bag *n.* كِيسٌ ج اكْيَاسٌ

Bag *v. t.* وَضَعَ فِي كِيسٍ

Baggage *n.* أَمْتِعَةُ السَّفَرِ

Bagging *n.* خَيْشٌ لِلأَكْيَاسِ

Bail *n.* or *v. t.* كَفِيلٌ كَفَالَةٌ
أَطْلَقَ بِكَفَالَةٍ

Bait *n.* or *v. t.* طُعْمٌ لِلسَّمَكِ . طَعَّمَ

Bake *v. t.* طَبَخَ بِفُرْنٍ . خَبَزَ

Baker *n.* فَرَّانٌ . خَبَّازٌ

Bakery *n.* مَخْبَزٌ . دُكَّانُ الْخُبْزِ

Balance *n.* or *v. t.* مِيزَانٌ . وَازَنَ

Balcony *n.* شُرْفَةٌ . كُشْك

Bald *a.* أَقْرَعُ

Baldness *n.* قَرَعٌ

Bale *n.* (طَرْدٌ) حِزْمَةٌ ج حِزَمٌ

Baleful *a.* مُضِرٌّ . مُحْزِنٌ . مُكَدِّرٌ

Balk *v. t.* خَيَّبَ أَعَاقَ

Ball *n.* كُرَةٌ . رَصَاصَةٌ (طَابَةٌ)

Ballad *n.* أُغْنِيَةٌ . اغَانٍ

Ballast *n.* or *v. t.* صَابُورَةٌ . صَبَّرَ

Balloon *n.* مَرْكَبَةٌ هَوَائِيَّةٌ (بالُون)

Ballot *n.* or *v. t.* وَرَقَةُ انْتِخَاب. إِنْتَخَبَ بِهَا

Balm *n.* رِيحَان. مَرْهَمٌ عِطْرٌ

Balmy *a. n.* عِطْرٌ. لَطِيفٌ. لَذِيذٌ

Balsam *n.* بَلْسَمٌ

Balustrade *n.* دَرَابْزُون

Bamboo *n.* خَيْزُرَانٌ

Ban *n.* نَهْيٌ عَامٌّ. لَعْن (حِرْمٌ)

Banana *n.* مَوْزٌ

Band *n.* or *v. t.* رِبَاطٌ. فِرْقَة. إِرْتَبَطَ عِصَابَةٌ. ضِمَادَةٌ

Bandage *n.* or *v. t.* لَفَّ ـُ. ضَمَدَ

Bandbox *n.* عُلْبَةٌ لِلْبَرَانِيطِ

Bandit *n.* قَاطِعُ الطَّرِيقِ

Bane *n.* سُمٌّ. أَذِيَّةٌ. شَرٌّ

Baneful *a.* سَامٌّ. مُضِرٌّ. مُهْلِك

Bang *v. t.* or *n.* ضَرَبَ ـِ. صَوْت بِشِدَّة. ضَرْبَةٌ

Banish *v. t.* نَفَى ـ طَرَدَ ـُ

Banishment *n.* نَفْيٌ

Bank *n.* شَطٌّ. سَدٌّ. مَقْعَدٌ. بَنْكٌ

Bank-bill / Bank-note *n.* إِيرَادُ بَنْكٍ. بَنْكنُوت

Banker *n.* صَاحِبُ بَنْكٍ صَرَّافٌ ج صَيَارِفَة

Banking *n.* (صَرَافَة)

Bankrupt *a.* or *n.* مُفَلَّسٌ

Bankruptcy *n.* إِفْلَاسٌ

Bank-stock *n.* أَسْهُمُ بَنْكٍ

Banner *n.* رَايَةٌ. بَيْرَق

Banquet *n.* وَلِيمَةٌ. مَأْدَبَة

Banter *v. i.* or *n.* مَزَحَ ـَ. سَخِرَ ـَ. مَزْحٌ

Baptism *n.* مَعْمُودِيَّة

Baptist *n.* مُعْتَقِدٌ بِالتَّغْطِيس فِي الْمَعْمُودِيَّةِ

Baptize *v. t.* عَمَّدَ

Bar *n.* or *v. t.* سَدٌّ. قَضِيبٌ. (دِقْوٌ)

Barb *n.* سِنَان . شَوْكَة

Barbarian *n.* بَرْبَرِيٌّ . مُتَوَحِّشٌ

Barbaric / Barbarous *a.* بِرْبَرِيٌّ . فَظِيع

Barbarism *n.* بَرْبَرِيَّة . تَوَحُّشٌ

Barbarity *n.* فَظَاظَة . قَسَاوَة

Barbed *n.* ذُو سِنَانٍ اوْ شَوْكٍ

Barber *n.* حَلَّاقٌ

Bard *n.* شَاعِرٌ . مُغَنٍّ . مُنْشِدٌ

Bare *a.* or *v. t.* عَارٍ . مُجَرَّدٌ . عَرَّى

Barefaced *a.* وَقِحٌ بِدُونِ حَيَاءٍ

Barefoot *a.* حَافٍ

Bareheaded *a.* مَكْشُوفُ ٱلرَّأْسِ

Barely *ad.* بِالْجَهْدِ . فَقَطْ

Bareness *n.* عُرِيَة

Bargain *n.* or *v. i.* مُسَاوَمَة . سَاوَمَ

Barge *n.* جَرْمٌ . سَفِينَةٌ لِلشَّحْنِ

Bark *n* or *v. t.* or *i.* قِشْرٌ . قَشَّرَ . قَلَّفَ . نَبَحَ

Bark / Barque *n.* سَفِينَةٌ بِثَلَاثَةِ صَوَارٍ

Barking *n.* نَبِيحٌ . عُوَاءٌ

Barley *n.* شَعِيرٌ

Barn *n.* هُرْيٌ . بِنَاءٌ لِلْمَوَاشِي

Barometer *n.* مِيزَانٌ لِلْهَوَاءِ

Baron *n.* (بَارُونٌ)

Baronage *n.* رُتْبَةٌ مِنَ ٱلْأَشْرَاف

Baronet *n.* رُتْبَةٌ دُونَ ٱلْبَارُون

Barrack *n.* قِشْلَاقٌ . ثُكْنَة

Barrel *n.* بِرْمِيلٌ

Barren *a.* عَاقِرٌ . عَقِيمٌ . مَحْلٌ

Barrenness *n.* عُقْرٌ . مَحْلٌ

Barricade *n.* or *v. t.* سَدٌّ . حَاجِزٌ . سَدَّ

Barrier *n.* سَدٌّ . حَاجِزٌ . حَدٌّ . مَانِعٌ

Barrister *n.* وَكِيلُ دَعَاوٍ

Barter *n.* or *v.t.* مُبَادَلَة . بَادَلَ ٱلْبَضَائِعَ

Basalt *n.* حَجَرٌ نَارِيٌّ أَسْوَدُ

Base *n.* or *a.* قَاعِدَة . دَنِيٌّ . خَسِيسٌ

Baseless *a.* بِلَا أَسَاس . بَاطِلٌ

Basement *n.* طَبَقَةُ ٱلْبَيْتِ ٱلسُّفْلِي

Baseness *n.* دَنَاءَة . لُؤْمٌ

Bashful *a.* مُسْتَحٍ . خَجِلٌ

Bashfulness *n.* حِشْمَةٌ . حَيَاءٌ

Basin *n.* طَسْت . حَوْضٌ

Basilisk *n.* حَيَّةٌ خُرَافِيَّةٌ اوْ تِنِّين

Basis *n.* أَسَاسٌ . أَصْلٌ

Bask *v. i.* تَشَمَّسَ

Basket *n.* سَلَّةٌ ج سِلَالٌ . قُفَّةٌ ج قُفَفٌ

Bastard *n.* نَغْلٌ إِبْنُ زِنَا

Baste *v. t.* شَلَّ ـُ شَرَّجَ

Bastinade / **Bastinado** } *v. t.* or *n.* ضَرَبَ بِعَصاً خَاصَّةً عَلَى أَسْفَلِ ٱلْقَدَمَيْنِ . ضَرْبٌ بِهِ

Bastion *n.* بُرْجٌ اوِ ٱلْبَارِز مِنْهُ

Bat *n.* وَطْوَاطٌ . خُفَّاشٌ

Batch *n.* كَمِّيَّةٌ مِقْدَارٌ

Bated *a.* خَفِيٌّ (صَوْت)

Bath *n.* حَمَّامٌ

Bathe *v.t.* or *i.* حَمَّمَ . غَسَلَ . إِستحَمَّ

Bathing *n.* إِستِحْمَامٌ . إِغْتِسَالٌ

Battalion *n.* تَابُورٌ ج تَوَابِيرُ . اورْطَة

Batter *v. t.* هَدَمَ ـِ . هَدَّ

Battering-ram *n.* مَنْجَنِيقٌ

Battery *n.* مَجْمُوعُ مَدَافِعَ . بَطَّارِيَّةٌ

Battle *n.* قِتَالٌ . معْرَكَةٌ . حَرْبٌ

Battle-axe *n.* بَلْطَةٌ

Battlement *n.* شرْفَة ج شُرَفٌ

Bauble *n.* لُعْبَةٌ . شَيْءٌ زهِيدٌ

Bawl *v. i.* صَرَخَ ـُ . صَيَّحَ

Bay *a.* أَحْمَرُ ٱللَّوْنِ

Bay *n.* خَلِيجٌ . شجَرُ ٱلْغَارِ

Bayonet *n.* حَرْبَةٌ

Bazaar *n.* سُوقٌ ج أَسْوَاقٌ

Be *v. i.* (was, been) كَانَ يَكُون

Beach *n.* شَطٌّ (رَمْلِيٌّ) شَاطِئٌ

Beacon *n.* مَنَارَةٌ ج مَنَائِرُ

Bead *n.* خَرَزَةٌ ج خَرَزٌ

Beak *n.* مِنْقَادٌ . مِنْقَارٌ

Beaker *n.* كَأْسٌ قَدَحٌ

Beam *v. t.* اشْرَقَ لَاحَ

Beam *n.* جِسْرُ خَشَبٍ . شُعَاعٌ

Bean *n.* حَبَّةٌ مِنَ ٱللُّوبِيَا اوْ ٱلْفُولِ

Bear *n.* دُبٌّ ج اَدْبَابٌ . شَرِسٌ

Bear *v. t. or i.* حَمَلَ ـِ وَٱحْتَمَلَ . اثْمَرَ

Bearable *a.* مَا يُحْتَمَلُ اوْ يُطَاقُ

Beard *n.* لِحْيَةٌ ج لِحًى

Bearded *a.* ذُو لِحْيَةٍ أَوْ شَوْكٍ

Beardless *a.* بِلَا لِحْيَةٍ . امْرَدُ

Bearer *n.* حَامِلٌ . نَاقِلٌ

Beast *n.* بَهِيمَةٌ ج بَهَائِمُ . وَحْشٌ

Beat *v. t.* ضَرَبَ ـِ غَلَبَ ـُ

Beating *n.* ضَرْبٌ بَالِغٌ

Beatitude *n.* غِبْطَةٌ . طُوبَى

Beau *n.* لَبِق . بَشُوشٌ لِلنِّسَاءِ

Beau-ideal *n.* خَيَالٌ . غَايَةُ ٱلْجَمَالِ

Beauteous *a.* حَسَنٌ . جَمِيلٌ

Beautiful *a.* حَسَنٌ . جَمِيلٌ

Beautify *v. t* حَسَّنَ . زَخْرَفَ

Beauty *n.* حُسْنٌ . جَمَالٌ

Beaver *n.* كَلْبُ ٱلْمَاءِ

Becalm *v. t.* هَدَّأَ . سَكَّنَ

Because *con.* لِأَنَّ . بِسَبَبِ ان

Beckon *v. t.* أَوْمَأَ . أَشَارَ

Become *v. i.* or *t.* صَارَ ـِ . لَاقَ

Becoming *a.* لَائِقٌ . مُوَافِقٌ

Bed *n.* فِرَاشٌ . مَجْرَى (نَهْرٍ)

Bedaub *v. t.* طَلَي . دَهَنَ ـُ

Bedding *n.* فِرَاشٌ وَمَفْرُوشَاتُهُ

Bedeck *v. t.* زَيَّنَ . زَخْرَفَ

Bedew *v. t.* نَدَّى

Bedim *v. t.* اظْلَمَ

Bedlam *n.* بيمارستان

Bed-quilt *n.* لحافٌ ج لُحُفٌ

Bedridden *n.* مُلازِمُ الفِراشِ

Bedroom *n.* غُرْفةُ النَّوْمِ

Bedstead *n.* تختٌ . سَرِيرٌ

Bee *n.* نحْلةٌ

Beef *n.* لَحْمُ بَقَرٍ

Beefsteak *n.* شريحةُ بَقَرٍ لِلشَّيِّ

Bee-hive *n.* خليَّة . كُوَّارةٌ

Beer *n.* جِعَةٌ (بيرا)

Beeswax *n.* شَمْعٌ عَسَلِيٌّ

Beet *n.* (شَمَنْدُوْرٌ) . (بَنْجَرٌ)

Beetle *n.* خنفساءُ

Beeves (*pl.* of *beef.*) بقرٌ

Befall *v. t.* اصَابَ . إعْترى

Befit *v. t.* ناسَبَ . لاَقَ ـ

Befool *v. t.* إفتتَنَ . خدَعَ

Before *ad.* or *pr.* قَبْلُ . قدَّامُ . امَامُ

Beforehand *ad.* قَبْلاً . مِنْ قَبْلُ

Befoul *v. t.* وَسَّخ . دَنسَ . لوَّثَ

Befriend *v. t.* وَالَى . اعَانَ

Beg *v. t.* or *i.* إلْتَمَسَ . تَسَوَّلَ

Beget *v. t.* وَلَدَ يَلِدُ . أَنْتجَ

Beggar *n.* or *v. t.* شحَّاذٌ . افقَرَ

Beggarly *a.* حقيرٌ . دَنِيءٌ

Beggary *n.* فقرٌ . مسْكَنَة

Begging *n.* تسوَّل . شِحاذَةٌ

Begin *v. t.* بدَأَ ـَ . إبْتَدَأَ ب

Beginning *n.* بدْءٌ . بدَاءة

Begird *v. t.* زَنَّرَ . نطَّق . طوَّق

Begrudge *v. t.* حَسَدَ ـُ عَلَى

Beguile *v. t.* غرَّ ـُ . خدَعَ

Begun(*pp.* of *Begin*) مَبْدُوءٌ

Behalf *n.* منفعةٌ . لِأَجْلِ . بالنِّيابَةِ عنْ

Behave *v. i.* تصرفَ . أحسَنَ سُلوكَهُ

Behaviour *n.* تصرُّفٌ . سيرة

Behead *v. t.* قَطَعَ رَأْسَهُ

Beheld *v. t.* (*Behold.* رَأَى (مَاضِي

Behind *pr.* or *ad.* وَرَآءَ . خَلْفُ

Behindhand *ad.* مُتَأَخِّراً

Behold *v.t.* or *ad.* رَأَى ـَ هُوَ ذَا

Beholden *a.* (to) شَاكِرٌ لِ

Beholder *n.* مُشَاهِدٌ . مُعَايِنٌ

Behoove *v. t.* لَزِمَ ـَ . وَجَبَ ـِ

Being *n.* كَوْنٌ . وُجُودٌ . كَائِنٌ

Belabour *v. t.* ضَرَبَ ـِ كَثِيرًا

Belate *v. t.* أَخَّرَ . أَبْطَأَ

Belch *v. t.* قَذَفَ ـِ تَجَشَّأَ

Beleaguer *v. t.* حَاصَرَ . أَحَاطَ بِ

Belfry *n.* قُبَّةُ ٱلْجَرَسِ

Belie *v. t.* كَذَّبَ

Belief *n.* تَصْدِيقٌ . إِعْتِقَادٌ

Believe *v. t.* صَدَّقَ . إِعْتَقَدَ . آمَنَ

Believer *n.* مُصَدِّقٌ . مُؤْمِنٌ

Bell *n.* جَرَسٌ ج أَجْرَاسٌ

Belle *n.* إِمْرَأَةٌ حَسَنَةٌ . حَسْنَاءُ

Belles-lettres *n.* آدَابُ ٱللُّغَةِ

Belligerent *a.* مُحَارِبٌ

Bellow *v. i.* or *n.* جَأَرَ . صَرَخَ . جَأْرٌ

Bellows *n.* مِنْفَخٌ . مِنْفَاخٌ

Belly *n.* بَطْنٌ . جَوْفٌ

Belly-band *n.* حِزَامُ ٱلْفَرَسِ

Belong *v. i.* إِخْتَصَّ بِ

Belonging *a.* مُخْتَصٌّ . ذَيْلٌ

Beloved *a.* مَحْبُوبٌ . حَبِيبٌ

Below *pr.* or *ad.* تَحْتَ . دُونَ

Belt *n.* زُنَّارٌ . حِزَامٌ . مِنْطَقَةٌ

Bemoan *v. t.* نَدَبَ ـُ . نَاحَ ـُ

Bench *n.* مَقْعَدٌ . دَكَّةُ ٱلْقُضَاةِ

Bend *v. t.* or *i.* حَنَا . ثَنَى . تَلَوَّى

Bend *n.* حَنْوٌ . ثَنْيٌ . عَطْفٌ

Beneath *pr.* or *ad.* تَحْتَ . أَسْفَلَ

Benediction *n.* بَرَكَةٌ إِنعَامٌ

Benefaction *n.* إِحْسَانٌ . خَيْرٌ

Benefactor *n.* مُحْسِنٌ . عَامِلُ خَيْرٍ

Beneficence *n.* إِحْسَان عَمَلُ ٱلْخَيْرِ

Beneficent *a.* مُحْسِنٌ . جَوَّاد

Beneficial *a.* مُفِيدٌ . نَافِعٌ

Beneficiary *n.* أَلْمُحْسَنُ إِلَيْهِ

Benefit *n.* نَفَعٌ فَائِدَةٌ

Benevolence *n.* إِحْسَانٌ جُودٌ

Benevolent *n.* مُحْسِنٌ . مُحِبٌّ ٱلْخَيْرِ

Benighted *a.* ذَاهِبٌ فِي الظَّلَامِ

Benign *a.* حَلِيمٌ . لَطِيفٌ

Benignity *n.* حِلْمٌ . لُطْفٌ

Bent *a.* or *n.* مَعْطُوفٌ . مَيْلٌ

Benumb *v. t.* خَدَّرَ

Bequeath *v. t.* وَصَّى بِ

Bequest *n.* وَصِيَّةٌ . أَلْمُوَصَّى بِهِ

Berate *v. t.* عَنَّفَ . وَبَّخَ

Bereave *v. t.* أَثْكَلَ . أَفْقَدَ

Bereavement *n.* فُقْدَانُ ٱلْحَبِيبِ

Bereft *(pp. of Bereave).* فَاقِدٌ

Berry *n.* تُوتَةٌ . حَبَّةُ تُوتٍ

Berth *n.* سَرِيرٌ فِي سَفِينَةٍ . مَنْصِبٌ

Beseech *v. t.* تَوَسَّلَ تَضَرَّعَ إِلَى

Beseem *v. t.* لَاقَ . وَافَقَ

Beseemly *a.* لَائِقٌ . مُوَافِقٌ

Beset *v. t.* أَحَاطَ . لَازَمَ

Besetting *a.* مُحِيطٌ . مُلَازِمٌ

Beside *pr.* بِجَانِبِ عِنْدَ

Besides *ad.* فَضْلاً عَنْ . عَدَا . غَيْرَ

Besiege *v. t.* حَاصَرَ

Besmear *v. t.* طَلَى ـ . لَوَّثَ

Besotted *a.* سِكِّيرٌ . أَبْلَهُ

Besought *(pret of Beseech).* تَوَسَّلَ

Bespangle *v. t.* زَيَّنَ . رَصَّعَ

Bespatter *v. t.* لَطَخَ

Besprinkle *v. t.* رَشَّ

Best *a.* أَلْأَحْسَنُ. الأَفْضَلُ

Bestial *a.* بَهِيمِيٌّ . قَذِرٌ

Bestir *v. t.* حرَّكَ

Bestow *v. t.* اعطى وَهبَ يهِبُ

Bestowal / Bestowment } *n.* إِعطَاءٌ . مَنْحٌ

Bestride *v. t.* فَرْشَحَ رَكِبَ

Bet *n.* or *v. t.* or *i.* مُرَاهَنَةٌ . رَاهَنَ

Betake *v. t.* لَجَا إِلى . عكف

Bethink *v. t.* فطِنَ ـُ . تَامَّلَ

Betide *v. t.* or *i.* حَدَثَ ـُ . صارَ ـِ

Betimes *ad.* في وَقْتٍ مُنَاسِبٍ . بَاكِراً

Betoken *v. t.* أَشارَ . دلَّ ـِ

Betray *v. t.* سَلَّمَ . خَانَ

Betrayal *n.* تسْلِيمٌ. خيَانَةٌ

Betroth *v. t.* خطَبَ ـُ (إِمْرَأَةً)

Betrothal *n.* خُطْبَةٌ

Better *a.* احْسنُ . افضلُ . خيْرٌ

Bettor *n.* مُرَاهِنٌ

Between / Betwixt } *pr.* بَيْنَ . مَا بَيْن

Beverage *n.* شرَابٌ . مَشْرُوبٌ

Bevy *n.* سِرْبٌ . جَمَاعَةٌ

Bewail *v. t.* نَاحَ . نَدَبَ ـُ

Beware *v. t.* حَذِرَ ـ . تَحَرَّزَ مِنْ

Bewilder *v. t.* حَيَّرَ

Bewitch *v. t.* إِفْتَتَنَ . سَحَرَ

Beyond *ad.* or *pr.* عبْرٌ . بَعدَ

Bias *n.* or *v. t.* مَيْلٌ. إِنْحِرَافٌ. امَالَ

Bib *n.* صدْرِيَّةُ اَلطِّفْلِ

Bibber *n.* شِرِّيبٌ

Bible *n.* الْـكِتَابُ ٱلْمُقَدَّسُ

Biblical *a.* مُخْتَصٌّ بِالْـكِتَابِ ٱلْمُقَدَّسِ

Bibliography *n.* تَارِيخُ اَلْـكُتُبِ أَوْ وَصْفُهَا

Bicephaleus *a.* ذو رَأْسَيْنِ

Bid *v. t.* or *n.* امَرَ ـُ . زَايَدَ . دَفعٌ

Bidden *(pp. Bid)* مَأْمُورٌ

Bidding *n.* أَمْرٌ . دَعْوَةٌ

Bid *v. t.* or *i.* إِنْتَظَرَ . أَقَامَ . سَكَنَ

Biennial *a.* حَادِثٌ مَرَّةً كُلَّ سَنَتَيْنِ

Bier *n.* نَعْشٌ ج نُعُوشٌ

Bifold *a.* مُزْدَوِجٌ . ذُو ثَنْيَتَيْنِ

Big *a.* كَبِيرٌ . ضَخْمٌ

Bigamy *n.* اَلتَّزَوُّجُ بِامْرَأَتَيْنِ مَعًا

Bight *n.* خَلِيجٌ صَغِيرٌ

Bigness *n.* كُبْرٌ . ضَخَامَة

Bigot *n.*
Bigoted *a.* } مُتَعَصِّبٌ بِالدِّينِ

Bigotry *n.* تَعَصُّبٌ بِالدِّينِ

Bile *n.* صَفْرَاءُ . مِرَّةٌ

Bilingual *n.* ذُو لُغَتَيْنِ

Bilious *a.* صَفْرَاوِيٌّ

Bill *n.* مِنْقَارٌ . قَائِمَةُ حِسَابٍ

Bill of exchange *n.* سُفْتَجَة

Billet *n.* رُقْعَةٌ . كُتَيْبَةٌ

Billion *n.* أَلْفُ مِلْيُونٍ أَو أَلْفُ أَلْفِ أَلْفٍ

Billow *n.* مَوْجَةٌ ج مَوْجَاتٌ

Billowy *a.* مُتَمَوِّجٌ

Bimonthly *a.* مَا يَظْهَرُ كُلَّ شَهْرَيْنِ

Bin *n.* صُنْدُوقٌ لِلْمُؤْنَةِ

Binary *a.* مُزْدَوِجٌ . ثُنَائِيٌّ

Bind *v. t.* رَبَطَ ـُ . أَوْثَقَ . جَلَّدَ

Binder *n.* مُجَلِّدُ كُتُبٍ

Bindery *n.* مَحَلُّ اَلتَّجْلِيدِ

Binding *n.* رَبْطٌ . تَجْلِيدٌ

Biographer *n.* كَاتِبُ تَرْجَمَةِ إِنْسَانٍ

Biography *n.* تَرْجَمَةُ إِنْسَانٍ

Biology *n.* عِلْمُ اَلْحَيَاةِ

Biped *n.* ذُو رِجْلَيْنِ أَوْ سَاقَيْنِ

Birch *n.* بَتُولَا (شَجَرٌ) قَضِيبٌ

Bird *n.* طَائِرٌ . عُصْفُورٌ

Bird-lime *n.* دَابُوق (دِبْقٌ)

Birth *n.* وِلَادَةٌ . مَوْلِدٌ

Birthday *n.* مِيلَادٌ . مَوْلِدٌ

Birthplace *n.* مَسْقَطُ ٱلرَّأْسِ . مَوْلِدٌ

Birthright *n.* بَكُورِيَّة

Biscuit *n.* (بَقْسَمَاط)

Bisect *v. t.* نَصَّفَ . شَطَرَ ـُ

Bisection *n.* شَطْرٌ . تَنْصِيفٌ

Bishop *n.* أُسْقُفٌ ج اسَاقِفَة

Bishopric *n.* أَبْرَشِيَّةُ اسْقُفٍ

Bisextile *n.* سَنَةٌ كَبِيسَة

Bison *n.* جَامُوسٌ أَمْرِيكَانِيٌّ

Bit *n.* شَكِيمَة . قِطْعَةٌ صَغِيرَة

Bitch *n.* كَلْبَةٌ

Bite *v. t.* or *n.* عَضَّ ـَ . عَضَّة

Bitter *a.* مُرٌّ . شَدِيدٌ . مُحْزِن

Bitterness *n.* مَرَارَةٌ . بُغْضَةٌ . حُزْن

Bitumeen *n.* حُمَرٌ وَحُمَّرٌ

Bituminous *a.* حُمَرِيٌّ

Bivalve *n.* or *a.* صَدَفٌ . صَدَفِيٌّ

المَبِيتُ فِي ٱلْعَرَاءِ بَاتَ بِدُونِ خِيَمٍ

Bivouac *n.* or *v. t.*

Blab *v. t.* or *i.* افْشَى ٱلسِّرَّ . هَذِرَ

Blackguard *n.* ثَالِبٌ . وَبَشٌ

Block *a.* or *n.* أَسْوَدُ . زِنْجِيٌّ

Blackberry *n.* تُوتٌ اسْوَدٌ

Blackboard *n.* لَوْحٌ أَسْوَدٌ

Blacken *v. t.* سَوَّدَ

Blacksmith *n.* حَدَّادٌ

Bladder *n.* مَثَانَة

Blade *n.* نَصْلٌ . وَرَقَةُ عِشْبٍ

Blamable / Blameworthy } *n.* مُسْتَحِقٌّ ٱللَّوْمِ

Blame *n.* or *v.t.* لَوْمٌ . لَامَ ـُ . عَاتَبَ

Blameless *a.* بِلَا لَوْمٍ . بَرِيءٌ

Blanch *v. t.* بَيَّضَ . قَصَّرَ

Bland *a.* لَطِيفٌ . أَنِيسٌ

Blandish *v. t.* لَاطَفَ . مَلِقَ ـَ

Blandishment *n.* مُلَاطَفَةٌ . مَلَقٌ

Blandness *n.* لُطْفٌ . مُؤَانَسَة

Blank *a.* or *n.* خَالٍ .وَرَقَةٌ بَيْضَاءُ

Blanket *n.* حِرَامٌ. دِثَارٌ

Blaspheme *v. t.* جَدَّفَ

Blasphemous *a.* تَجْدِيفِيٌّ . مُجَدِّفٌ

Blasphemy *n.* تَجْدِيفٌ

Blast *v. t.* لَفَحَ ـَ . فَجَّرَ (بِلُغْمٍ)

Blast *n.* هَبَّةُ رِيحٍ . لَفُوحٌ . (لُغْمٌ)

Blaze *v. i.* or *n.* إِلْتَهَبَ . أَذَاعَ . لَهِيبٌ

Bleach *v. t.* بَيَّضَ . قَصَرَ ـُ

Bleaching *n.* تَبْيِيضٌ . قِصَارَةٌ

Bleak *a.* بَارِدٌ . مُعَرَّضٌ لِلرِّيحِ ٱلْبَارِدَةِ

Blear *v t.* سَبَّبَ ٱلْعَمَشَ

Blear-eyed *a.* اعْمَشُ

Bleat *v. i.* or *n.* ثَغَا يثغو . ثُغَاءٌ

Bleed *v. i.* or *i.* فَصَدَ ـِ . نَزَفَ

Bleeding *n.* فَصَادٌ . نَزْفٌ

Blemish *v. t.* or *n.* أَعَابَ . عَيْبٌ

Blend *v. t.* or *i.* مَزَجَ ـُ إِمْتَزَجَ

Bless *v. t.* بَارَكَ . حَمَدَ ـ

Blessed *a.* مُبَارَكٌ . مَغْبُوطٌ . سعِيْدٌ

Blessedness *n.* غُبْطَةٌ . سَعَادَةٌ

Blessing *n.* بَرَكَةٌ . نِعْمَةٌ

Blight *v. t.* or *n.* لَفَحَ ـَ لَفُوحٌ . آفَةٌ

Blind *a.* or *n.* أَعْمَى . ضَرِيرٌ . غَبِيٌّ

Blind *v. t.* أَعْمَى . عَمَّى

Blindfold *v. t.* غَطَّى ٱلْعَيْنَيْنِ

Blindness *n.* عَمًى . غَبَاوَةٌ

Blindly *ad.* بِدُوْنِ فِكْرٍ . بِغَبَاوَةٍ

Blink *v. i.* غَمَزَ ـِ . جَهَرَ ـَ

Bliss, Blissfulness *n.* سَعَادَةٌ . غبْطَةٌ

Blissful *a.* سَعِيدٌ . مَغْبُوط

Blister *n.* or *v. t.* نَفْطَةٌ. حَرَّاقَةٌ . نَقَّطَ

Blithe, Blithsome *a.* فَرِحٌ. مُبْتَهِجٌ. مَسْرُوْرٌ

Bloat *v. t.* or *i.* وَرَّمَ . نَفَخَ . إِنْتَفَخَ

Block *n.* or *v. t.* قِطْعَةُ خَشَبٍ . سَدَّ

Blockade *v. t.* or *n.* حَاصَرَ . احَاطَ . حِصَارٌ

Blockhead *n.* بَلِيدٌ . أَبْلَهُ

Block-house *n.* بُرْجٌ مِنْ أَخْشَابٍ ضَخْمَةٍ

Blood *n.* دَمٌ

Blood-hound *n* كَلْبُ صَيْدٍ كَبِيرٌ

Bloodless *a.* بِلَا دَمٍ

Bloodshed *n.* سَفْكُ ٱلدَّمِ . قَتْلٌ

Blood-thirsty *a.* سَفَّاكُ ٱلدَّمِ

Blood-vessel *n.* وِعَاءٌ دَمَوِيٌّ . عِرْقٌ

Bloody *n.* دَمَوِيٌّ . مُلَطَّخٌ بِالدَّمِ

Bloom *n.* or *v. i.* زَهْرَةٌ . جَمَالٌ . أَزْهَرَ

Blooming *a.* مُزْهِرٌ . نَضِيرٌ . جَمِيلٌ

Blossom *n.* or *v. i.* زَهْرَةٌ . ازْهَرَ

Blot *n.* or *v. t.* لَطْخَةٌ . عَارٌ . لَطَخَ . مَحَا ـُ

Blotch *n.* لَمْعَةٌ . بَثْرَةٌ

Blotting-paper *n.* وَرَقٌ نَشَّاشٌ

Blow *n.* or *v. t.* or *i.* ضَرْبَةٌ . هَبَّ ـُ

Blower *n.* نَافِخٌ . مِنْفَخٌ

Blubber *n.* شَحْمُ الحُوتِ

Blue *a.* ازْرَقُ

Blueness *n.* زُرْقَةٌ

Bluff *n.* or *a.* جُرْفٌ شَاهِقٌ . فَظٌّ

Bluish *a.* ضَارِبٌ إِلَى ٱلزُّرْقَةِ

Blunder *n.* or *v. i.* خَطَأ . غَلِطَ ـَ

Blundering *a.* كَثِيرُ ٱلْخَطَإِ

Blunt *a.* or *v. t.* كَلِيلٌ . شَرِسٌ فَلَّ حَدَّ السِّكِّينِ

Bluntness *n.* كَلَالٌ . خُشُونَةٌ

Blur *n.* or *v. t.* لَطْخَةٌ . لَاثَ ـُ

Blurred *pp.* غَيْرُ وَاضِحٍ

Blush *v.i.* or *n.* خَجِلَ ـَ . إِحْمِرَارٌ

Bluster *v. t.* or *n.* هَاجَ . تَصَلَّفَ . تَصَلُّفٌ

Boa *n.* ضَرْبٌ مِنَ ٱلْحَيَّاتِ ٱلضَّخْمَةِ

Boar *n.* خِنْزِيرٌ

Board *n.* لَوْحُ خَشَبٍ . قُوتٌ . مَجْلِسٌ

Board *v. t.* or *i.* غَطَّى بِأَلْوَاحٍ . صَعَدَ إِلَى مَرْكَبٍ . أَكَلَ قُوتَ ـُ

Boarder *n.* نَزِيلٌ بِٱلْأُجْرَةِ

Boarding *n.* تَسْمِيرُ الْوَاحٍ . طعامٌ
Boast *v. i.* or *n.* إِفتخرَ . إِفْتِخَارٌ
Boastful *a.* مُفْتَخِرٌ . مُتَعَظِّمٌ
Boasting *n.* إِفْتِخَارٌ . تعظمٌ
Boat *n.* قَارِبٌ . زَوْرَقٌ . سفينةٌ
Boating *n.* اَلتَّنَزُّهُ بِالْقَارِب
Boatman *n.* بَحْرِيٌّ
Boatswain *n.* مُدِيرُ قَارِب
Bob *v. i.* إِهتزَّ . إِرتَجَّ
Bode *v. t.* or *i.* انبَا بِهِ . شَوَّمَ
Bodiless *a.* بِلاَ جِسْمٍ اوْ جسدٍ
Bodily *a.* or *ad.* جَسَدِيٌّ . كُلِّيًّا
Body *n.* جِسْمٌ . جَسَدٌ . بَدَنٌ
Bog *n.* مُسْتَنْقَعٌ
Boggy *a.* مُسْتَنْقَعِيٌّ
Bogus *a.* مُزَوَّرٌ . كَاذِبٌ
Boil *n.* or *v. i.* or *v. t.* دُمَّلٌ . غَلَى ـِ . سَلَقَ ـُ
Boiler *n.* مِرْجَلٌ (دَسْتٌ)

Boisterous *a.* هائِجٌ . صَيَّاحٌ
Bold *a.* جَسُورٌ . شُجَاعٌ
Boldness *n.* جسارَةٌ شَجَاعة
Bolster *n.* or *v. t.* وِسَادَةٌ . سندَ
Bolt *n.* or *v. t.* مِزْلاَجٌ (دُقرَة . دَقر)
Bomb *n.* (قُنبرَةٌ) قُنبلَة
Bombard *v. t.* رَمَى بِالْقَنَابِلِ
Bombardment *n.* اطْلاَقُ الْقَنَابِلِ
Bombast *n.* التفخر فِي الكَلاَمِ
Bond *n.* قيد . رِباط . عَهد
Bondage *n.* عبُودِية
Bondman / **Bondservant** } *n.* عَبْدٌ . رَقِيقٌ
Bondsman *n.* كَافِلٌ . ضامِنٌ
Bone *n.* عَظْمٌ ج عِظَام
Bone-setter *n.* مُجبِّرُ الْعِظَام
Bonfire *n.* نارٌ تُشْعَلُ لِلْفرح
Bonnet *n.* قُبَّعَةٌ . بُرْنَيْطَةٌ
Bonny *a.* جمِيلٌ . بَدِيعٌ . فرِحٌ

Bonus *n.* نافِلَةٌ . جزءٌ فَوْقَ ٱلْمفرُوض

Bony *a.* كَثيرُ العِظَامِ . ضَلِيعٌ

Booby *n.* أَبْلَهُ . غَبِيٌّ

Book *n.* كِتَابٌ . سِفْرٌ

Book-binder *n.* مُجَلِّد كُتبٍ

Book-case *n.* خِزَانَةُ كُتُبٍ

Book-keeping *n.* مَسْكُ ٱلدَّفَاتِرِ

Book-store *n.* مَخْزَنُ كُتُبٍ

Book-worm *n.* مُغْرَمٌ بِالْكُتُبِ

Boom *v. i.* or *n.* عَجَّ . هَدَرَ . زَئِيرٌ

Booming *n.* مُنْقَضٌّ بِشِدَّةٍ . عَاجٌّ

Boon *n.* or *a.* هِبَةٌ . بَشُوشٌ

Boor *n.*
Boorish *a.* } غَلِيظٌ . جافٍ . غَيْرُ مُهَذَّبٍ

Boot *n.* or *v. t.* حِذَاءٌ (جَزْمَةٌ) . نَفَعَ ـَ

Booth *n.* خَيْمَةٌ . مَظَلَّةٌ

Bootless *n.* غَيْرُ نَافِعٍ . عَبَثٌ

Booty *n.* غَنِيمَةٌ

Borax *n.* بَوْرَقٌ

Border *n.* حَافَّةٌ . حَدٌّ . تَخْمٌ

Bore *v. t.* قَدَحَ ـَ . أَتْعَبَ . اضجَرَ

Bore *n.* (قَدْحٌ) ثَقْبٌ . مُضْجِرٌ

Boreal *n.* شِمَالِيٌّ

Born *p.p.* of *bear.* مَوْلُودٌ

Borne *p.p.* of *bear.* مَحْمُولٌ

Borrow *v. t.* إِسْتَعَارَ . إِسْتَقْرَضَ

Bosom *n.* حُضْنٌ . صَدْرٌ

Botanist *a.* عَالِمٌ بِالنَّبَاتِ

Botanize *v. t.* جَمَعَ ٱلنَّبَاتَ

Botany *n.* عِلْمُ ٱلنَّبَاتِ

Botch *n.* or *v. t.* رَقْعٌ رَدِيءٌ . رَقَعَ رَدِيئاً

Both *a.* كِلاَ وَكِلْتَا

Bother *n.* or *v. t.* إِنْزِعَاجٌ . ازعَجَ

Bottle *n.* زُجَاجَةٌ . قَارُورَةٌ

Bots *n. pl.* دُودُ إِمْعَاءِ ٱلْخَيْلِ

Bottom *n.* قَعْرٌ . قَاعٌ . اسفَل

Bottomless *a.* بِلاَ قَعْرٍ

Bough *n.* غُصْنٌ

Bought *p.p.* of *buy.* مُبْتَاعٌ

Bounce *v. i.* or *n.* وَثَبَ . وَثْبَةٌ

Bound *p.p.* of *bind.* مُقَيَّدٌ . مُلْتَزِمٌ

Bound *v. t.* or *i.* حَدَّدَ . قَفَزَ

Bound / **Boundary** } *n.* حَدٌّ . تَخْمٌ

Bounteous / **Bountiful** } *a.* كَرِيمٌ . جَوَّادٌ

Bounty *n.* كَرَمٌ . سَخَاءٌ

Bouquet *n.* بَاقَةُ زُهُورٍ

Bout *n.* دَوْرٌ

Bovine *a.* بَقَرِيٌّ

Bow *v. t.* or *i.* حَنَا ـُ إِنْحَنَى

Bow *n.* إِنْحِنَاءٌ . قَوْسٌ

Bowlder *n.* صَخْرَةٌ كَبِيرَةٌ كُرَوِيَّةٌ

Bowman *n.* رَامٍ بِالْقَوْسِ

Bowels *n. pl.* امْعَاءٌ . احْشَاءٌ

Bower *n.* مَظَلَّةٌ . عَرِيشٌ

Bowl *n.* كَأْسٌ . طَاسٌ

Bowsprit *n.* خَشَبَةُ مُقَدَّمِ السَّفِينَةِ

Bowstring *n.* وَتَرُ الْقَوْسِ

Box *n.* or *v. t.* صُنْدُوقٌ . لَكَمَ

Boxer *n.* مُقَاتِلٌ بِقَبْضَةِ الْيَدِ

Boy *n.* صَبِيٌّ . غُلَامٌ

Boyhood *n.* صَبْوَةٌ

Boyish *a.* وَلَدِيٌّ . طَفِيفٌ

Brace *n.* or *v. t.* مَشَدٌّ . شَدَّ ـُ

Bracelet *n.* سُوَارٌ ج اسَاوِرُ

Bracket *n.* رَفٌّ صَغِيرٌ بَارِزٌ مِنَ الْحَائِطِ

Brackets *n. pl.* هِلَالَانِ كَذَا ( )

Brackish *a.* مَالِحٌ . مَائِلٌ لِلْمُلُوحَةِ

Brad *n.* مِسْمَارٌ صَغِيرٌ بِلَا رَأْسٍ

Brag *v. i.* تَصَلَّفَ . فَاخَرَ

Braggadocio / **Braggart** } *n.* مُتَصَلِّفٌ . نَفَّاخٌ

Braid *v. t.* or *n.* ضَفَرَ ـِ . ضَفِيرَةٌ

Brain *n.* دِمَاغٌ ج ادْمِغَةٌ

Brake *n.* آلَةٌ لِتَوْقِيفِ دُولَابٍ. (فَرْمَلَةٌ)

Bramble *n.* عَوْسَجٌ . عُلَّيْقٌ

Bran *n.* نُخَالَةٌ

Branch *n.* or *v. i.* غُصْنٌ . تَفَرَّعَ

Brand *v. t.* وَسَمَ ـِ . عَابَ ـ

Brand *n.* وَسْمٌ أَوْسِمَةٌ . عَيْبٌ

Brandish *v. t.* هَزَّ . حَرَّكَ

Brandy *n.* كُونْيَاكٌ

Brasier *n.* كَانُونٌ . نُحَاسٌ

Brass *n.* نُحَاسٌ أَصْفَرُ

Brassy *n.* نُحَاسِيٌّ

Bravado *n.* تَصَلُّفٌ . تَعَظُّمٌ

Brave *a.* or *n.* شُجَاعٌ . بَاسِلٌ

Brave *v. t.* إِقْتَحَم . بَارَز

Bravery *n.* شَجَاعَةٌ . بَسَالَةٌ

Bravo *n.* or *int.* جَسُورٌ . أَحْسَنْتَ

Brawl *n.* or *v. i.* مُشَاجَرَةٌ . تَشَاجَرَ

Brawny *a.* قَوِيٌّ . ضَلِيعٌ

Bray *v. t.* or *i.* سَحَقَ ـ . شَهَقَ ـُ

Bray / **Braying** *n.* شَهِيقٌ . نَهِيقٌ

Brazen *a.* نُحَاسِيٌّ

Brazen / **Brazen-faced** *a.* جَسُورٌ . وَقِحٌ

Breach *n.* خَرْقٌ . نَكْثٌ

Bread *n.* خُبْزٌ . عَيْشٌ

Breadstuff *n.* دَقِيقٌ . حُبُوبٌ

Breadth *n.* عَرْضٌ

Break *v. t.* or *i.* كَسَرَ ـِ . إِنكَسَرَ

Break *n.* كَسْرٌ . فَتْحَةٌ

Breakage *n.* كَسْرٌ

Breaker *n.* كَاسِرٌ . صَخْرَةٌ بَحْرِيَّةٌ

Breakfast *n.* or *v. i.* فُطُورٌ . فَطَرَ ـُ (تَرَوَّقَ)

Breakwater *n.* سَدٌّ لِمَنْعِ الْأَمْوَاجِ

Breast *n.* or *v. t.* صَدْرٌ . صَادَرَ

Breastplate *n.* دُرْعٌ ج دُرُوعٌ

Breastwork *n.* مَتْرَاسٌ

Breath *n.* نَفَسٌ . نَسْمَةٌ

Breathe *v. i.* تَنَفَّسَ

Breathing *n.* تَنَفُّسٌ

Breathless *n.* مَقْطُوعُ ٱلنَّفَس

Breeches *n. pl.* سَرَاوِيلُ.(سِرْوَالٌ)

Breed *v. t.* or *i.* وَلَّدَ . رَبَّى . وَلَدَ

Breed *n.* ذُرِّيَّةٌ. نَسْلٌ . جِنْسٌ

Breeding *n.* تَوْلِيدٌ . تَرْبِيَةٌ. سجايا

Breeze *n.* نَسِيمٌ

Brethren *n. pl.* of *brother.* إِخْوَةٌ

Brevity *n.* إِخْتِصارٌ . إِيجَازٌ

Brew *v. t.* خَمَّرَ(جعة (بِيرا)

Brewery *n.* مَصْنَعُ ٱلْجِعَةِ

Bribe *n.* or *v. t.* بَرْطِيلٌ . بَرْطَل

Bribery *n.* بَرْطَلة . رَشْوَةٌ

Brick *n.* آجُرٌّ . قِرْمِيدٌ

Brick-bat *n.* قِطْعَةُ قِرْمِيدٍ

Brick-kiln *n.* أَتُونُ ٱلآجُرِّ

Bridal *a.* or *n.* عُرْسِيٌّ . عُرْسٌ

Bride *n.* عَرُوسٌ

Bridegroom *n.* عَرِيسٌ

Bridemaid / Bride's maid } *n.* شَبِينَةُ ٱلْعَرُوسِ

Bridge *n.* or *v. t.* جِسْرٌ. قَنْطَرَةٌ . نَصَبَ جِسْرًا

Bridle *n.* or *v. t.* لِجَامٌ . أَلْجَمَ

Brief *a.* or *n.* قَصِيرٌ. عَرْضحَالٌ مُخْتَصَرٌ

Brier *n.* عُلَّيقٌ . عَوْسَجٌ

Brig *n.* سَفِينَةٌ ذَاتُ صَارِيَيْنِ

Brigade *n.* لِوَاءٌ مِنَ ٱلْجُنْدِ

Brigadier *n.* قَائِدٌ فَوْقَ امِيرِ الآيِ .لِوَاءٌ

Brigand *n.* لِصٌّ . قَاطِعُ طُرُقٍ

Brigandage *n.* قَطْعُ ٱلطُّرُقِ

Bright *a.* لَامِعٌ . بَرَّاقٌ . ذَكِيٌّ

Brighten *v. t.* or *i.* أَنَارَ . لَمَعَ

Brightness *n.* لَمَعَانٌ . رَوْنَقٌ

Bright's disease *n.* مَرَضٌ فِي ٱلْكُلْيَتَيْنِ

Brilliancy *n.* رَوْنَقٌ . بَهَاءٌ

Brilliant *a.* بَهِيٌّ . لَامِعٌ

Brim *n.* شَفَةٌ . حَرْفٌ . حَافَّةٌ

Brimful / Brimming } *a.* مَمْلُوءٌ إِلَى شَفَتِهِ

Brimstone *n.* كِبْرِيتٌ

Brine *n.* مَاءٌ كَثِيرُ ٱلْمُلُوحة

Bring *v. t.* أَتَى بِهِ . احضَر

Brink *n.* حَافَةٌ

Brisk *a.* نَشِيطٌ . سَرِيعٌ. خَفِيفٌ

Briskness *n.* نَشَاطٌ . خِفَّةٌ

Bristle *n.* or *v. i.* هُلْبَةٌ . تَنَفَّشَ

Bristly *a.* اهْلَبُ اوْ هُلْبِيٌّ

Brittle *a.* قَصِمٌ . قَصِفٌ

Brittleness *n.* سُرْعَةُ ٱلْإِنْكِسَارِ

Broad *a.* عَرِيضٌ . مُتَّسِعٌ

Broadcloth *n.* جُوخٌ

Broaden *v. t.* or *i.* أَوْسَعَ . عَرَّضَ . إِتَّسَعَ

Broadside *n.* إِطْلَاقُ مَدَافِعِ جَانِبِ ٱلْبَارِجَةِ

Brocade *n.* دِيبَاجٌ . سُنْدُسٌ

Brochure *n.* كُرَّاسَةٌ

Brouge *n.* لَفْظٌ فَاسِدٌ

Broil *v.t.* or *n.* شَوَى . إِنْشَوَى . خِصَامٌ

Broken *pp.* (break مَكْسُورٌ (مِنْ

Broker *n.* سِمْسَارٌ ج سَمَاسِرَةٌ

Brokerage *n.* سَمْسَرَةٌ

Bronchitis *n.* إِلْتِهَابُ شُعَبِ ٱلرِّئَةِ

Bronze *n.* خَلِيطٌ مِنْ نُحَاسٍ وَقَصْدِيرٍ

Brooch *n.* دَبُّوسٌ لِلصَّدْرِ

Brood *n.* فرخ ج فِرَاخٌ . نسلٌ

Brood *v. t.* حَضَنَ ٱلْفِرَاخَ

Brood *v. i.* ثَابَرَ عَلَى ٱلْهَمِّ

Brook *n.* or *v. t.* سَاقِيَةٌ . إِحتَمَلَ

Brooklet *n.* سَاقِيَةٌ صَغِيرَةٌ

Broom *n.* مِكْنَسَةٌ ج مَكَانِسُ

Broomstick *n.* قَضِيبُ مِكْنَسَةٍ

Broth *n.* مَرَقٌ

Brothel *n.* بَيْتُ ٱلْعَوَاهِرِ

Brother *n.* أَخٌ . إِخْوَةٌ

Brotherhood *n.* اخوِيَّةٌ ج إِخَاءٌ

Brought *pp.* of *bring.* مُحْضَرٌ . مُؤْتًى بِهِ

Brow *n.* جَبْهَةٌ . جَبِينٌ . حَافَةٌ

Brown *a.* or *v. t.* أَسْمَرُ . جَعَلَهُ اسْمَرَ

Brownish *a.* مَائِلٌ إِلَى ٱلسُّمْرَةِ

Browse *v. t.* or *i.* رعَى . إِرْتَعَى

Bruin *n.* لَقَبٌ لِلدُّبِّ

Bruise *v. t.* رَضَّ ـُ رضرض

Brunt *n.* شِدَّةٌ . صَدْمَةٌ

Brush *n.* فُرْشَةٌ . اغصانٌ مقطوعة

Brush *v. i.* or *t.* مَسَحَ (بِالفُرْشَةِ)

Brusque *a.* خَشِنُ ٱلْمُعَامَلَةِ . عنيفٌ

Brutal / Brutish } *a.* وحشيٌّ . فظٌّ

Brutality *n.* وحشيَّةٌ . فَظَاظَة

Brutalize *v. t.* وَحَّشَ

Brute *n.* وَحْشٌ . جافٍ . قاس

Bubble *n.* فُقَّاعَةٌ . مشروعٌ بَاطِلٌ

Buck *n.* ذَكَرُ ٱلْغَنَمِ وَٱلْوَعِلِ

Bucket *n.* دَلْوٌ . سَطل

Buckle *n.* or *v.t.* إِبْزِيمٌ . شَدَّ (بِهِ)

Buckler *n.* تُرْسٌ ج اتْرَاسٌ

Bud *n.* or *v. i.* بُرْعُمٌ . أَخْرَجَ البَرَاعِمَ

Budge *v. i.* تحَرَّكَ . إِنطَلَقَ

Budget *n.* قَائِمَة مَالِيَّة . مِيزَانِيَّة

Buffalo *n.* جامُوسٌ ج جَوَامِيسُ

Buffet *v. t.* لكَمَ ـُ . لَطَمَ ـِ . قَاوَمَ

Buffoon *n.* مَازِحٌ . مَاجِنٌ

Bug *n.* بقّة . فسفسٌ ج فسَافِس

Bugbear *n.* هائلٌ . وَهْمِيٌّ

Bugle *n.* نَفِير

Build *v. t.* بنى ـ عَمَّرَ

Building *n.* بِنَاءٌ . عِمَار

Built *pp.* of *build.* مبنيٌّ

Bulb *n.* بَصَلَة نَبَاتٍ

Bulbous *a.* ذُو بَصَلٍ

Bulge *v. i.* تَقَبَّبَ . بَرَزَ

Bulk *n.* حجم . مِقْدَارٌ

Bulky *n.* جسيمٌ . ضخمٌ . كبيرٌ

Bull *n.* ثورٌ ج ثيران

Bull-dog *n.* كَلْبٌ كَبِيرٌ ضَارٌّ

Bullet *n.* كُلَّةُ بُنْدُقِيَّةٍ . رَصَاصَةٌ

Bulletin *n.* تَقْرِيرٌ رَسْمِيٌّ

Bull-frog *n.* ضِفْدَعٌ كَبِيرٌ

Bullion *n.* سَبَائِكُ ذَهَبٍ أَوْ فِضَةٍ

Bullock *n.* ثَوْرٌ صَغِيرٌ أَوْ خَصِيٌّ

Bully *n.* مُتَوَعِّدٌ . مُتَصَلِّفٌ

Bullrush *n.* حَلْفَاءٌ . بَرْدِيٌّ

Bulwark *n.* حِصْنٌ . مِتْرَاس

Bumble-bee *n.* نَحْلَةٌ كَبِيرَةٌ

Bump *n.* صَدْمَةٌ . لَطْمَةٌ . وَرَمٌ

Bump *v. t.* or *i.* صَدَمَ بِصَوْتٍ قَوِيٍّ

Bumper *n.* كَأْسٌ مَمْلُوءَةٌ

Bun *n.* نَوْعٌ مِنَ ٱلْكَعْكِ

Bunch *n.* or *v. t.* عُنْقُودٌ . عِذْقٌ . جَمَعَ

Bundle *n.* رَبْطَةٌ . رِزْمَةٌ . حُزْمَة

Bung *n.* سِدَادُ بَرْمِيلٍ

Bungle *v. i.* خَبَّصَ

Bunion *n.* ثُؤْلُولٌ فِي ٱلرِّجْل

Bunting *n.* نَسِيجُ صُوفٍ لِلرَّايَاتِ

Buoy *n.* عَوَّامَةٌ لِدَلَالَةِ ٱلْمَرَاكِبِ

Buoyant *n.* عَائِمٌ . خَفِيفٌ . مَسْرُورٌ

Bur or burr *n.* غُلَافُ نَبَاتٍ ذُوْشَوْكٍ

Burden *n.* or *v. t.* حِمْلٌ . ضَايَق

Burdensome *a.* ثَقِيلٌ . مُتْعِبٌ

Bureau *n.* خِزَانَةٌ . مَكْتَبٌ

Burglar *n.* سَارِقُ بَيْتٍ بِٱللَّيْل

Burglary *n.* سِرْقَةُ بَيْتٍ بِٱللَّيْلِ

Burial *n.* دَفْنٌ . جَنَازَةٌ

Burlesque *a* or *n.* مُضْحِكٌ . أُضْحُوكَةٌ

Burly *a.* جَسِيمٌ . ضَخْمٌ

Burn *v. t.* or *n.* حَرَقَ ـِ . إِحْتَرَقَ . كَيٌّ

Burnish *v. t.* صَقَلَ ـُ

Burrow *n.* or *v. i.* وِجَارٌ . إِحْتَفَرَ

Burst *v. t.* or *i.* فَجَرَ . إِنْفَجَرَ . إِنْفَلَق

Bury *v. t.* دَفَنَ ـِ . قَبَرَ ـُ

Bush *n.*	شُجَيْرَةٌ . دَغَلٌ
Bushel *n.*	مِكْيَالٌ انكِلِيزِيٌّ
Bushy *a.*	كَثٌّ
Busily *ad.*	بِجِدٍّ أَوْ بِاجْتِهَادٍ
Business *n.*	شُغْلٌ . مَصْلَحَةٌ . حِرْفَةٌ
Bust *n.*	تِمْثَالُ الرَّاسِ إِلَى الصدْرِ
Bustle *n.* or *v. i.*	جَلَبَةٌ . عَجَلَةٌ . — ضَجَّ
Busy *a.*	مَشْغُولٌ . مُهْتَمٌّ
Busybody *n.*	فُضُولِيٌّ
But *conj.* or *pr.*	لَكِنَّ . غَيْرَ ان . إِلاَّ
Butcher *n.*	لَحَّامٌ . قَصَّابٌ . جَزَّارٌ
Butchery *n.*	ذَبْحٌ . قَتْلٌ عَظِيمٌ
Butler *n.*	سَاقِي الْخَمْرِ
Butt *n.*	هَدَفٌ . بَرْمِيلٌ كَبِيرٌ
Butter *n.*	زُبْدَةٌ . سَمْنٌ
Buttery *n.*	بَيْتُ الْمُونَةِ
Butterfly *n.*	فَرَاشَةٌ ج فَرَاشٌ
Buttock *n.*	عَجُزٌ ج أَعْجَازٌ
Button *n.*	زِرٌّ ج ازْرَارٌ
Buttonhole *n.*	عُرْوَةٌ لِلزِّرِّ
Buttress *n.*	دِعَامَةٌ
Buxom *a.*	جَسِيمٌ . طَرِبٌ
Buy *v. t.*	إِبْتَاعَ . إِشْتَرَى
Buzz *v. i.* or *n.*	دَوَى . دَوِيٌّ
Buzzard *n.*	ضَرْبٌ مِنَ الْبَازِ
By *pr.*	عِنْدَ . قُرْبَ . بِ
By-and-by *ad.*	بَعْدَ حِينٍ
By-path / **By-way** *n.*	مَسْلَكٌ صَغِيرٌ
By-word *n.*	عِبْرَةٌ . مَثَلٌ

C

Cab *n.* نَوْعٌ مِنَ ٱلْمَرْكَباتِ

Cabal *n.* عُصبةٌ سِرِّيَّةٌ

Cabbage *n.* كُرُنبٌ . ملْفوفٌ

Cabin *n.* كُوخٌ . حُجْرَةٌ في سفِينَةٍ

Cabinet *n.* خِزَانَةٌ . وِزَارةٌ

Cabinet-maker *n.* نَجَّارٌ

Cable *n.* جُمَّلٌ (حبْلُ المِرْساة أوْ سلسِلتها) . حبْلٌ غلِيظٌ

Cackle *v. i.* or *n.* قاق ـُ . قوْق

Cadaverous *a.* شَبِيه بِالجُثَةِ . مُصْفَرٌّ

Cadence *n.* هُبُوط ٱلصَّوت . لَحْنٌ

Cadet *n.* تِلْمِيذ مَدْرَسَةٍ حرْبِيَّةٍ

Café *n.* قَهْوَةٌ

Cage *n.* قفَصٌ

Cajole *v. t.* دَاهَنَ . تَمَلَّقَ

Cake *n.* قُرصٌ . كَعْكَةٌ

Calamitous *a.* مُسِيءٌ . نَكْبِيٌّ

Calamity *n.* مُصِيبَةٌ . بَلِيَّةٌ

Calcareous *a.* كِلسِيٌّ

Calcedony *n.* عقِيقٌ أَبْيَضُ

Calcine *v. t.* كَلَّسَ بِٱلنَّارِ

Calculate *v. t.* حسَبَ ـُ . احْصى

Caldron *n.* قِدْرٌ . خلْقِينٌ

Calendar *n.* تَقْوِيمُ ٱلسَّنَةِ (رُزنامةٌ)

Calf (*pl.* calves) *n.* عِجْل ج عُجُولٌ

Calf of the leg *n.* بطْن السَّاقِ

Calibre *n.* قُطْرٌ . إِتِّسَاعٌ . عيارٌ

Calico *n.* شيتٌ . خامٌ

Call *v. t.* or *i.* دعَا . سمَّى . نادَى

Call *n.* دَعْوَةٌ . طَلَبٌ . مُنَادَاةٌ
Calling *n.* حِرْفَةٌ . مَصْلَحَةٌ . مُنَادَاةٌ
Callous *a.* مُتَصَلِّبٌ . مُكْتَنِبٌ
Calm *a.* or *v. t.* هَادِئٌ . هَدَّأَ . اسْكَنَ
Calm / **Calmness** } *n.* هُدُوءٌ . سُكُونٌ
Caloric *n.* أَلْحَرَارَةُ
Calorific *n.* مُوَلِّدٌ لِلْحَرَارَةِ
Calumniate *v. t.* وَشَى بِ . نَمَّ ـُ ـِ
Calumny *n.* نَمِيمَةٌ . إِفْتِرَاءٌ
Calve *v. t.* وَلَدَتْ (أَلْبَقَرَةُ)
Calyx *n.* كَأْسُ ٱلزَّهْرَةِ
Came (Come ماضي) *v. i.* جَاءَ . أَتَى
Camel *n.* جَمَلٌ . بَعِيرٌ . نَاقَةٌ
Camelopard *n.* زَرَافَةٌ
Cameo *n.* حَجَرٌ كَرِيمٌ نَافِرُ ٱلنَّقْشِ
Camera *n.* آلَةٌ لِلتَّصْوِيرِ ٱلشَّمْسِي
Camomile / **Chamomile** } *n.* بَابُونَجٌ
Camp *n.* مَحَلَّةٌ . مُعَسْكَرٌ

Campaign *n.* غَزْوَةٌ . حَرْبٌ
Camphor *n.* كَافُورٌ
Can *v. i.* or *n.* قَدَرَ ـُ . كُوزٌ
Canal *n.* قَنَاةٌ . تُرْعَةٌ
Canary *n.* عُصْفُورٌ مُغَرِّدٌ
Cancel *v. t.* مَحَا . أَلْغَى . أَبْطَلَ
Cancellation *n.* مَحْوٌ
Cancer *n.* سَرَطَانٌ
Cancerous *a.* سَرَطَانِيٌّ
Candid *a.* مُخْلِصٌ . سَلِيمُ ٱلنِّيَّةِ
Candidate *n.* طَالِبُ ٱلإِنْتِخَابِ
Candidly *ad.* بِإِخْلَاصٍ . مُخْلِصًا
Candy *n.* قَنْدٌ . نَوْعٌ مِن الحَلْوَى
Candle *n.* شَمْعَةٌ . قِنْدِيلٌ
Candlestick *n.* شَمْعَدَانٌ . مَغَارَةٌ
Candour *n.* إِخْلَاصٌ . سَلَامَةُ ٱلنِّيَّةِ
Cane *n.* قَصَبَةٌ . عَصًا
Canine *a.* كَلْبِيٌّ
Canine-tooth *n.* نَابٌ

Canker *n.* or *v i.* قُرْحٌ اكَّالٌ .فسدَ — ُ
Canker-worm *n.* دُودُالنَّبَاتَات
Cannibal *n.* آكل لُحُوم البَشَر
Cannibalism *n.* أَكْلُ لُحُومِ ٱلْبَشَر
Cannon *n.* مَدْفَعٌ ج مَدَافِعُ
Cannonade *n.* ضَرْبٌ بِالْمَدَافِعِ
Cannoneer / **Cannonier** } *n.* أَلرَّامِي بِالْمَدَافِع
Canoe *n.* قَارِبٌ هِنْدِيٌّ
Canon *n.* قَانُونٌ
Canonical *a.* قَانُونِيٌّ
Canonize *v. t.* صَرَّحَ بِقِدَاسةِ مَيْت
Canopy *n.* مِظَلَّة
Cant *n.* or *v. i.* تظاهُرٌ بكَلَامِ ٱلتقْوَى.تظاهَرَ
Canter *v. i.* or *n.* خَبَّ . خَبَبٌ
Canto *n.* قصيدَةٌ
Canton *n.* مُقَاطعَةٌ . إِقليمٌ
Cantonment *n.* مَحلَّة
Canvas *n.* جنفيصٌ .خَيْشٌ
Canvass *v. t.* بحثَ عَنْ — طَلَبَ
Cap *n.* or *v. t.* (طرْبوشٌ) . غطَّى
Capability *n.* مقْدَرَةٌ . طَاقَةٌ
Capable *a.* قادِرٌ. اهْلٌ
Capacious *a.* متسعٌ فسيحٌ
Capacity *n.* سعَة . قُدْرَة
Cap-a-pie *ad.* مِنَ ٱلرَّأْسِ إِلَى ٱلقدَم
Cape *n.* رَاسٌ (أَرْض) بُرْنسٌ
Capillary *a.* or *n.* شعْرِيٌّ
Capital *n.* or *a.* رَاسُ مَال . قصَبَة مَمْلكَةٍ . رَئِيسِيٌّ . نَفِيسٌ
Capitalist *n.* ذُو مَال مُثْر
Capitol *n.* سَرَايَ ٱلحُكُومة ٱلأميركيَّةِ
Capitulate *v. i.* سَلَّمَ تحْتَ شُرُوطٍ
Caprice *n.* تقَلُّبُ ٱلخَاطِرِ
Capricious *a.* مُتقلِّبٌ
Capsize *v. t.* or *i.* قلَّبَ . إِنقَلَب
Captain *n.* قبْطَان . يُوز بَاشِي

Capricorn *n.* بُرْجُ الجَدْي
Captious *a.* كَثِيرُ الانْتِقاد
Captivate *v. t.* أَسَرَ ـــِ ُ إِفْتَتَن
Captive *n.* or *a.* أَسِيرٌ . مسْبِيٌّ
Captivity *n.* أَسْرٌ . سَبْيٌ
Captor *n.* آسِرٌ . سالِبٌ
Capture *n.* or *v. t.* قَبْضٌ . قَبَض عَلى
Car *n.* عَجلَة . مرْكَبَة
Carat *n.* قِيرَاط (في وزن الذهب)
Caravan *n.* قَافِلَةٌ ج قَوَافِلُ
Caraway *n.* كَرَوْيَاءُ (كَرَاوِيَا)
Carbine *n.* (قرَابِينَة) بُنْدُقِيَّةٌ قَصِيرَةٌ
Carbon *n.* فحمٌ (كَرْبُونٌ)
Carbonaceous *a.* فَحْمِيٌّ
Carbonize *v. t.* صَيَّرَهُ فَحْماً
Carbuncle *n.* دُمَّلٌ كَبِيرٌ
Carcass *n.* جُثَّةٌ جِيفَةٌ
Card *n.* وَرَقَةُ زِيَارَةٍ . مُشْطٌ للصُّوف
Card *v. t.* مَشَّط . حلَجَ
Cardiac *a.* مُخْتَصٌّ بِالقَلْب
Cardinal *n.* or *a.* كَرْدِنَالٌ . أَوَّلِيٌّ
Care *n.* or *v. i.* إِعْتِنَاءٌ . همٌّ . إِعْتَنَى
Careen *v.i.* or *t.* مَالَتْ السَّفِينَةُ . أَمَالَهَا
Career *n.* مَجْرًى . مَسِيرٌ
Careful *a.* حذِرٌ . كَثِيرُ الاعْتِنَاء
Carefulness *n.* إِعْتِنَاءٌ . مُبَالَاة
Careless *a.* غيْرُ مُبالٍ . غافِلٌ
Carelessness *n.* إِهْمَالٌ . غَفْلَةٌ
Caress *v. t* or *n.* لاطَف . دَلَّلَ . مُلاطَفَةٌ
Cargo *n.* شَحْنٌ . وَسْقُ سَفِينَةٍ
Caricature *n.* صُورَةٌ هَزْلِيَّةٌ
Carious *a.* نَخِرٌ
Carmine *n.* لونٌ دُودِيٌّ
Carnage *n.* مَلْحَمَةٌ . مَقْتَلَةٌ عَظِيمَةٌ
Carnal *a.* جسدَانِيٌّ . شَهْوَانِيٌّ
Carnally *ad.* بِشَهْوَةٍ جَسَدِيَّةٍ

Carnival *n.* مَرْفَعٌ ج مَرَافِعُ

Carnivorous *a.* آكِلُ لُحُومٍ . ضارٍ

Carob *n.* خَرُّوبٌ

Carol *n.* or *v. i.* اغْنِيَّةٌ . غَنَّى

Carousal *n.* وَلِيمَةٌ لِلشُّرْبِ وَٱلْفَرَحِ

Carouse *v. i.* شَرِبَ وَفَرِحَ . قَصَفَ

Carp *v. i.* لامَ ـُ . عذَلَ ـُ

Carpenter *n.* نَجَّارٌ

Carpet *n.* سُجَّادَةٌ . بِسَاطٌ

Carriage *n.* مَرْكَبَةٌ . (عَرَبِيَّةٌ)

Carrion *n.* جِيفَةٌ . لَحْمٌ نَتِنٌ

Carrot *n.* جَزَرَةٌ ج جَزَرٌ

Carry *v. t.* حَمَلَ ـِ . نَقَلَ ـُ

Cart *n.* عَجَلَةُ ٱلنَّقْلِ

Cartage *n.* نَقْلٌ . اجْرَةُ النقلِ

Carter *n.* سَائِقُ عَجَلَةِ النَّقْلِ

Cartilage *n.* غُضْرُوفٌ ج غَضَارِيفُ

Cartilaginous *a.* غُضْرُوفِيٌّ

Cartridge *n.* (فَشَكَةٌ ج فَشَكٌ)

Carve *v. t.* نَقَشَ ـُ . قَطَعَ (لَحْمًا)

Cascade *n.* شَلَّالٌ

Case *n.* صُنْدُوقٌ . حَالٌ . قَضِيَّةٌ

Casement *n.* صُنْدُوقُ شُبَّاكٍ

Cash *n.* or *v. t.* نُقُودٌ . قَبَضَ ـِ نَقْدًا

Cash-book *n.* دَفْتَرُ ٱلنُّقُودِ

Cashier *n.* or *v. t.* أَمِينُ ٱلصُّنْدُوقِ . عَزَلَ

Cashmere *n.* كَشْمِيرٌ

Casing *n.* غِطَاءٌ . بِرْوَازٌ

Cask *n.* بَرْمِيلٌ

Casket *n.* عِلْبَةٌ لِلْحُلِيِّ أَوْ لِكُلِّ شَيْءٍ ثَمِينٍ

Casque *n.* خُوذَةٌ ج خُوَذٌ

Cast *v. t.* رَمَى . صَبَّ . سَبَكَ

Cast *n.* رَمْيَةٌ . هَيْئَةٌ . سَبِيكَةٌ

Castaway *n.* مَرْفُوضٌ . مَرْذُولٌ

Caste *n.* طَائِفَةٌ . فِئَةٌ

Castigate *v. t.* أدب. ضَرَبَ بِٱلسَّوْطِ

Casting *n.* رَمْيٌ . سبيكة

Cast-iron *n.* حَدِيدٌ صَبٍّ

Castor-oil *n.* زَيْتُ خَرْوَع

Castle *n.* حِصْنٌ . قَلْعَةٌ . صَرْحٌ

Castrate *v. t.* خَصَى —

Casual *a.* عَرَضِيٌّ . إِتِّفَاقِيٌّ

Casually *ad.* عَرَضاً . إِتِّفَاقاً

Casualty *n.* حَادِثَةٌ عَرَضِيَّةٌ

Cat *n.* قِطٌّ . هِرٌّ

Catacomb *n.* مَغَارَةٌ لِلدَّفْنِ تَحْتَ الْارْضِ

Catalogue *n.* قَائِمَةٌ . جَدْوَلٌ

Cataract *n.* شَلَّالٌ . مَاءٌ أَزْرَقُ فِي الْعَيْنَيْنِ

Catarrh *n.* زُكَامٌ

Catastrophe *n.* مُصِيبَةٌ . نَكْبَةٌ

Catch *v. t.* أَدْرَكَ . قَبَضَ . تَنَاوَلَ

Catching *a.* مُعْدٍ

Catechetical *a.* بِالسُّؤَالِ وَالْجَوَابِ

Catechise *v. t.* عَلَّمَ بِالسُّؤَالِ

Catechism *n.* اصُولُ الْإِيمَانِ

Categorical *a.* صَرِيحٌ . قَاطِعٌ

Category *n.* صَفٌّ . طَبَقَةٌ

Cater *v. t.* زَوَّدَ . قَدَّمَ طَعَاماً

Caterpillar *n.* دُودَةٌ . فَرَاشَةٌ

Catgut *n.* وَتَرٌ مِنْ مِعًى

Cathartic *n.* or *a.* مُسْهِلٌ

Cathedral *n.* كَنِيسَةُ اسْقُفٍ

Catholic *a.* جَامِعٌ . كَاثُولِيكِيٌّ

Catholocism *n.* النِّظَامُ الْكَاثُولِيكِيُّ

Cattle *n. pl.* مَاشِيَةٌ ج مَوَاشٍ

Caudal *a.* ذَنَبِيٌّ

Caught *pp.* of *catch.* مَقْبُوضٌ

Caul *n.* ثَرْبٌ

Cauliflower *n.* قَرْنَبِيط أَو قنبيط

Causal *a.* سَبَبِيٌّ

Causalty *n.* سَبَبِيَّةٌ

Causation *n.* تَسْبِيبٌ

Causative *a.* مُسَبِّبٌ
Cause *n.* سَبَبٌ . عِلّة
Caustic *a.* or *n.* حَارِقٌ . كَاوٍ
Cauterize *v. t.* كَوَى ـِ . وَسَمَ ـِ
Cautery *n.* كَيٌّ
Caution *n.* or *v. t.* حَذَرٌ . حذرَ
Cautious *a.* حَذِرٌ . مُحْتَرِسٌ
Cavalcade *n.* مَوْكِبُ فُرْسانٍ
Cavalier *n.* فارِسٌ . خَيَّالٌ
Cavalry *n.* فُرْسَانٌ . خَيَّالَةٌ
Cave / **Cavern** } *n.* مَغَارَةٌ ج مغائِرُ
Cavil *v. i.* or *n.* ماحك. مُماحَكة
Cavity *n.* وَقْبَةٌ . تجْوِيفٌ
Cease *v. i.* كَفَّ عَنْ . إنقطعَ
Cedar *n.* ارْز
Cede *v. t.* تَرَكَ ـُ . تخَلَّى عَن
Ceil *v. t.* سَقَفَ ـُ طَيَّن . بطَّن
Ceiling *n.* سَقْفٌ (طَوَان)
Celebrate *v. t.* عظمَ . إحْتَفَل
Celebrated *a.* مَشْهُورٌ
Celebrity *n.* شُهْرَةٌ . صِيتٌ
Celerity *n.* سُرْعة . عَجَلَةٌ
Celery *n.* كَرَفْسٌ
Celestial *a.* سَمَاوِيٌّ
Celibacy *n.* عزُوبة . عزبة
Cell *n.* صوْمَعَة . خَلِيَّة . حُوَيْصَلَةٌ
Cellar *n.* قَبْوٌ . بَيْتٌ تَحْتَانِيٌّ
Cellular *n.* حُوَيْصَلِيٌّ . ذُو تجَاوِيفٌ
Cement *n.* or *v. t.* مِلاطٌ . مَلط
Cemetry مَقْبَرَة
Censer *n.* مَبْخَرَةٌ . مِجْمَرَةٌ
Censor *n.* مُرَاقِبٌ . مُؤَدِّبٌ . منتَقِدٌ
Censorious *a.* قاسٍ . كَثِيرُ ٱلْمَلاَمَة
Censurable *a.* قَابِلُ ٱلْمَلاَمَةِ
Censure *v. t.* or *n.* لاَم . مَلاَمَةٌ
Census *n.* تَعْدَادُ ٱلنُّفُوسِ
Cent *n.* جُزْءٌ مِنَ ٱلْمِئَة مِنَ ٱلرِّيَال
Centaur *n.* فَرَس خُرَافِيٌّ لَهُ رَأْسُ إِنْسانٍ

Centennial *a.*	مَرَّةً كُلَّ مِئَةِ سَنَةٍ
Centenarian *n.*	ذُو مِئَةِ سَنَةٍ
Centigrade *a.*	قِيَاسُ مِئَةِ دَرَجَة
Centipede *n.*	ذُو مِئَةِ رِجْلٍ . أُمُّ أَرْبَعٍ وَارْبَعِين
Central *a.*	مَرْكَزِيٌّ
Centrality *n.*	مَرْكَزِيَّة
Centre *n.*	مَرْكَزٌ . وَسْط
Centrifugal *a.*	مَائِلٌ عَنِ ٱلْمَرْكَز
Centripetal *n.*	مَائِلٌ إِلَى ٱلْمَرْكَزِ
Centurion *n.*	قَائِدُ مِئَةٍ
Century *n.*	مِئَةُ سَنَةٍ . قَرْن
Cereals *n. pl.*	حُبُوبٌ تُؤْكَلُ
Cerebrum *n*	الدِّمَاغ
Cerebral *a.*	دِمَاغِيٌّ
Ceremonial *a.*	إِحْتِفَالِيٌّ . طَقْسِي
Ceremonial / Ceremony } *n.*	إِحْتِفَالٌ . طَقْسٌ
Certain *a.*	أَكِيدٌ . مُحَقَّقٌ
Certainly *n.*	مُحَقَّقًا
Certainty *n.*	يَقِينٌ . قَطْع
Certificate *n.*	شَهَادَةٌ . وَثِيقَة
Certify *v. t.*	حَقَّقَ . شَهِدَ بِ
Certitude *n.*	يَقِينٌ . عَدَمُ ٱلشَّكِّ
Cerulean *a.*	سَمَاوِيُّ ٱللَّوْنِ
Cessation *n.*	إِنْقِطَاعٌ . تَوَقُّف
Cession *n.*	تَسْلِيمٌ . تَخْلِيَة
Cess-pool *n.*	مَحَلُّ ٱلأَقْذَارِ . بَالُوعَة
Chafe *v.i.*or *t.*	دَعَكَ . ضَجِرَ
Chaff *n.* or *e. i.*	عُصَافَةٌ . مَازَح
Chaffer *v. i.*	سَاوَمَ
Chagrin *n.* or *v.t.* }	خَجَلٌ . ضَجَر . أَزْعَجَ
Chain *n.* or *v. i.*	سِلْسِلَةٌ . رَبَطَ بِهَا
Chair *n.*	كُرْسِيٌّ ج كَرَاسِيٌّ
Chairman *n.*	صَاحِبُ ٱلْكُرْسِيِّ
Chaise *n.*	مَرْكَبَةٌ بِعَجَلَتَيْن
Chalcedony *n.*	عَقِيق ابْيَضُ

Chalice *n.* كَأْسُ ٱلْعَشَآءِ ٱلرَّبَّانِي

Chalk *n.* طَبَاشِيرُ

Challenge *v. t.* or *n.* إِسْتَدْعَى لِلْمُبَارَزَةِ . تَحَدٍّ

Chamber *n.* غُرْفَةٌ . حُجْرَةٌ

Chamberlain *n.* حَاجِب

Chameleon *n.* حِرْبَآءٌ

Champ *v.t.*or *i.* صَكَّمَ عَلَى . عَضَّ

Champagne *n.* شَمْبَانِيَا

Champion *n.* مُبَارِزٌ . مُحَامٍ . بَطَلٌ

Chance *n.* صُدْفَةٌ . عَرَضٌ . إِتِّفَاقٌ

Chance *v. i.* إِتَّفَقَ . حَدَثَ

Chancellor *n.* وَزِيرٌ . رَئِيسُ قُضَاةٍ

Chandler *n.* بَائِعُ شَمْعٍ

Change *n.* or *v. t.* تَغْيِيرٌ . غَيَّرَ

Changeable *a.* قَابِلُ ٱلتَّغْيِيرِ . مُتَقَلِّبٌ

Channel *n.* مَجْرًى . مَضِيقٌ . تَلْم

Channelled *a.* مُتَلَّمٌ

Chant *v. t.* or *i.* or *n.* أَنْشَدَ . غَنَّى . نَشِيد

Chaos *n.* هَيُولِيٌّ . عَدَمُ ٱنْتِظَام

Chaotic *a.* غَيْرُ مُنْتَظِمٍ . مُشَوَّش

Chapel *n.* مَعْبَدٌ . كَنِيسَةٌ

Chaplain *n.* قِسِّيسٌ فِي ٱلْجَيْش

Chaplet *n.* إِكْلِيلُ زَهْرٍ اوْ أَوْرَاقٍ

Chapter *n.* بَابٌ . فَصْلٌ

Char *v. t.* صَبَّرَ فَحْمًا . حَرَق

Character *n.* سَجِيَّةٌ . خُلْقٌ . صِفَةٌ

Characteristic *a.*or *n* خَاصٌّ . مَزِيَّةٌ

Characterize *v. t.* وَصَفَ . مَيَّزَ

Charcoal *n.* فَحْمٌ (مِنْ خَطَبٍ)

Charge *v. t.* or *n.* هَاجَمَ . شَكَا . أَوْصَى . دَكٌّ . مُهَاجَمَةٌ . شَكْوَى

Charge *n.* قَيْدٌ فِي حِسَابٍ

Charger *n.* صِحْفَةٌ . جَوَادٌ

Chariot *n.* مَرْكَبَةٌ

Charitable *a.* مُحْسِنٌ . مُتَصَدِّق

Charity *n.* صَدَاقَةٌ . إِحْسَان

Charlatan *n.*	دَجَّالٌ
Charm *n.*	طَلْسَمٌ . حُسْنٌ . لُطْفٌ
Charm *v.t.*	سَحَرَ ـَ . فَتَنَ ـِ . ابْهج
Charming *a.*	سَارٌّ جِدًّا . مُبْهِجٌ
Chart *n.*	خَرِيطَةٌ
Charter *n.* or *v. t.*	صَكٌّ . إِمْتِيَازٌ . إِسْتَأْجَرَ
Chary *a.*	حَذِرٌ . مُتَيَقِّظٌ
Chase *v. t.*	طَارَدَ . إِصْطَادَ
Chase *n.*	مُطَارَدَةٌ . صَيْدٌ
Chasm *n.*	شَقٌّ عَمِيقٌ فِي الْأَرْضِ
Chaste *a.*	عَفِيفٌ
Chasten *v. t.*	أَدَّبَ
Chastise *v. t.*	قَاصَّ . ادب
Chastisement *n.*	قِصَاصٌ . تَأْدِيبٌ
Chastity *n.*	عِفَّةٌ
Chat *v. i.*	حَادَثَ . كَالَمَ
Chatter *v. i.*	هَذَرَ . بَقَّ ـُ
Chatterer *n.*	بَقْبَاقٌ
Cheap *a.*	رَخِيص
Cheapen *v. t.*	رَخَّصَ
Cheapness	رُخْصٌ
Cheat *v. t.*	غَشَّ ـُ . غَبَنَ ـِ
Cheat *n.*	مُحْتَالٌ . خِدَاعٌ
Check *v. t.*	رَدَعَ . اوْقَفَ . عَاقَ
Check *n.*	رَدْعٌ . تَوْقِيفٌ . تَحْوِيلٌ
Checker *v. t.*	نَوَّعَ
Checkers *n. pl.*	لِعْبُ الدَّامَا
Cheek *n.*	خَدٌّ . خُدُوْدٌ . وَجْنَة
Cheer *v. t.* or *n.*	فَرَّجَ . شَرَحَ . إِنْشِرَاحٌ
Cheerful / **Cheery** } *n.*	مَسْرُوْرٌ . بَشَّاش
Cheese *n.*	جبْن
Chemical *a.*	كِيمِيٌّ اوْ كِيمَاوِيٌّ
Chemicals *n. pl.*	مَوَادُّ كِيمِيَّةٌ
Chemise *n.*	قَمِيصُ آمْرَأَةٍ
Chemist *n.*	عَالِمٌ بِالْكِيمِيَا
Chemistry *n.*	أَلْكِيمِيَا

Cheque *n.*	تَحْوِيلٌ (مَالِيٌّ)
Cherish *v. t.*	رَبَّى. أَعَزَّ. لَاطَفَ
Cherry *n.* or *a.*	كَرَزٌ. كَرَزِيُّ ٱللَّوْنِ.
Cherub *n.*	كَرُوبٌ أَوْ كَرُوبِيمُ
Chess *n.*	شَطَرَنْجٌ
Chest *n.*	صُنْدُوقٌ. صَدْرٌ
Chestnut *n.*	كَسْتَنَا. أَبُو فَرْوَة
Chevalier *n.*	فَارِسٌ (شَفَلِيرٌ)
Chew *v. t.*	مَضَغَ ـُ
Chick / **Chicken** } *n.*	فَرْخ ج فُرُوخ وَفِرَاخ
Chicken-pox *n.*	جَدَرِيُّ ٱلْمَاء
Chick-peas *n. pl.*	حِمَّصٌ
Chide *v. t.*	عَاتَبَ زَجَرَ ـُ
Chief *a.*	رَئِيسِيٌّ. أَوَّلِيٌّ. اهَمٌّ
Chief / **Chieftain** } *n.*	رَئِيسٌ. قَائِدٌ
Chiefly *ad.*	خُصُوصاً. بِالْأَخَصِّ
Child *pl.* **Children** *n.*	وَلَدٌ ج اوْلَادٌ
Childhood *n.*	زَمَانُ ٱلصِّبَا. صَبْوَة
Childish *a.*	وَلَدِيٌّ. بَاطِلٌ
Chill *a.* or *n.*	بَارِدٌ. قَشْعَرِيرَةٌ
Chilly *v. t.*	بَرَّدَ
Chilly *a.*	بَارِدٌ
Chime *n.*	الْحَانُ اجْرَاسٍ مُوَقَّعَةٍ
Chimera *n.*	تَصَوُّرٌ وَهْمِيٌّ
Chimerical *a.*	وَهْمِيٌّ. بَاطِلٌ
Chimney *n.*	مَدْخَنَةٌ. دَاخِنَةٌ
Chin *n.*	ذَقْنٌ ج ذُقُونٌ
China *n.*	خَزَفٌ صِينِيٌّ. بِلَادُ ٱلصِّينِ.
Chinese *a.*	صِينِيٌّ
Chine *n.*	فَقَارَةٌ
Chink *n.*	شَقّ ضَيِّقٌ
Chink *v. i.* or *t.*	إِنْشَقَّ. طَنَّ. أَطَنَّ.
Chintz *n.*	شِيتٌ مُخْتَلِفُ ٱلْأَلْوَانِ
Chip *n.*	قِطْعَةُ خَشَبٍ صَغِيرَةٌ
Chirography *n.*	خُطّ. صِنَاعَةُ ٱلْكِتَابَةِ.
Chirp *v. i.*	غَرَّدَ. صَوَّتَ

Chisel *n.* or *v. t.* إِزْمِيلٌ ج ازَاميلُ. نَحَتَ بِهِ
Chivalrous *a.* شَرِيفٌ . ذُو شَهَامَةٍ
Chivalry *n.* فُرُوسِيَّةٌ . بَسَالَةٌ
Chloroform *n.* بَنْجٌ (كُلُورُفُورم)
Chocolate *n.* (شُوكَلَاتَا)
Choice *n.* or *a.* إِخْتِيَارٌ . نَفِيسٌ. فَاخِرٌ
Choir *n.* زُمْرَةُ مُرَنِّمِين
Choke *v. t.* or *i.* خَنَقَ. سَدَّ. إِخْتَنَقَ
Choler *n.* صَفْرَآءُ . غَضَبٌ
Cholera *n.* أَلْهَوَآءُ ٱلْأَصْفَرُ
Choleric *a.* سَرِيعُ ٱلْغَضَبِ. غَضُوبٌ
Choose *v. i.* إِخْتَارَ . إِنْتَخَبَ
Chop *v. t.* or *n.* قَطَعَ . قِطْعَةُ لَحْمٍ
Chord *n.* وَتْرٌ وَوَتَرٌ ج أَوْتَارٌ
Chorister *n.* مُغَنٍّ . مُرَنِّمٌ
Chorus *n.* قَرَارٌ فِي ٱلتَّرْنِيمِ / زُمْرَةُ مُرَنِّمِينَ
Christ *n.* أَلْمَسِيحُ
Christen *v. t.* عَمَّدَ . سَمَّى
Christendom *n.* أَلْعَالَمُ ٱلْمَسِيحِيُّ
Christening *n.* مَعْمُودِيَّةٌ مَعَ تَسْمِيَةٍ
Christian *a.* or *n.* مَسِيحِيٌّ
Christianity *n.* أَلدِّيَانَةُ ٱلْمَسِيحِيَّةُ
Christianize *v. t.* نَصَّرَ
Christmas *n.* عِيدُ ٱلْمِيلَادِ
Chromatic *a.* مُخْتَصٌّ بِٱلْأَلْوَانِ
Chronic *n.* مُزْمِنٌ
Chronicle *n.* سِفْرُ ٱلْأَخْبَارِ. تَأْرِيخٌ
Chronological *a.* تَارِيخِيٌّ
Chronologer / **Chronologist** *n.* عَالِمٌ بِٱلتَّارِيخِ
Chronology *n.* حِسَابُ ٱلتَّوَارِيخِ
Chronometer *n.* سَاعَةٌ تَضْبُطُ نَفْسَهَا
Chrysalis *n.* شَرْنَقَةٌ ج شَرَانِقُ
Chubby *a.* ضَخْمُ ٱلْجِسْمِ وَقَصِيرُهُ
Chuckle *v. i.* ضَحِكَ سِرًّا
Chum *n.* زَمِيلٌ . رَفِيقٌ

Church *n.* كنيسة

Churchyard *n.* مَقبَرَة

Churl *n.* خَشِنٌ . فَظٌّ

Churn *v. t.* or *n.* مَخَضَ ـُ مِمْخَضٌ

Cicatrice / Cicatrix } *n.* نَدْبَة

Cider *n.* عصيرُ التفَّاحِ

Cigar *n.* سيكارَة

Ciliary *a.* هُدْبيٌّ . شَعْرِيٌّ

Cimeter / Cimerer } *n.* سيفٌ مقوَّسٌ

Cincture *n.* زُنَّارٌ . مِنْطَقَة

Cinders *n. pl.* بقايا الوَقيدِ المَحرُوقِ

Cinnamon *n.* قِرْفَة

Cipher *n.* صِفْرٌ

Ciphering *v.* حِسَابُ الأرْقامِ

Circle *n.* or *v. i.* دَائِرَة . دَارَ ـُ

Circuit *n.* دَوَرَانٌ . إقْليمٌ

Circuitous *a.* دَوْرِيٌّ . غيرُ مُستقيمٍ

Circular *a.* مُدَوَّرٌ . نشْرَة

Circulate *v. i.* or *t.* دَارَ . نَشَرَ ـُ

Circulation *n.* دَوَرَانٌ . نَشْرٌ

Circulatory *a.* دَائِرٌ

Circumambulate *v. t.* طافَ ـُ حَوْلَ

Circumcise *v. t.* خَتَنَ ـِ . طَهَّرَ

Circumcision *n.* خِتان

Circumference *n.* مُحيط

Circumflex *n.* (ˆ) عَلامَة مَدّ حَرْف

Circumjacent *a.* مُحيطٌ (بِهِ)

Circumlocution *n.* إسهَابٌ

Circumnavigate *v. t.* طافَ بحْراً

Circumnavigation *n.* أَطْوَافُ بحْراً

Circumscribe *v. t.* أَحَاطَ بِهِ . حَصَرَ ـُ

Circumscription *n.* إحَاطَة . حَصْرٌ

Circumspect *a.* حَذِرٌ . مُحترِسٌ

Circumspection *n.* حذرٌ . إحترَاسٌ

Circumspectly *ad.* بحذرٍ . إحترَاساً

Circumstance *n.* حَالَة . ظَرْفٌ

Circumstantial *a.* مُفَصَّلٌ. عَرَضِيٌّ

Circumvent *v. t.* غَلَبَهُ بِالْحِيلَةِ

Circus *n.* مَلْعَبٌ مُسْتَدِيرٌ لِلْخَيْلِ

Cistern *n.* صِهْرِيجٌ. حَوْضٌ

Citadel *n.* بُرْجٌ. قَلْعَةٌ

Citation *n.* إِقْتِبَاس. إِسْتِدْعَاءٌ

Cite *v. t.* اِقْتَبَسَ. إِسْتَشْهَدَ. إِسْتَدْعَى

Citizen *n.* مَدَنِيٌّ تابِع لِدَوْلَةٍ

Citizenship *n.* حقوقُ الْمَدَنِيَّةِ

Citron *n.* لَيْمُونٌ حَامِضٌ. اتْرُجٌّ

Citric *n.* لَيْمُونِيٌّ. اتْرُجِيٌّ

City *n.* مَدِينَةٌ. بَلْدَةٌ

Civil *a.* مَدَنِيٌّ. سِيَاسِيٌّ. انِيسٌ

Civilian *n.* مَدَنِيٌّ. عَالِمٌ بِالشَّرِيعة الْمَدَنِيَةِ

Civilry *n.* انسٌ. لطفٌ

Civilization *n.* تَمَدُّنٌ. تهذِيب

Civilize *v. t.* مدن. هَذَّبَ

Clack *v. i.* or *n.* طقطق. قَعْقَعَ. طقطقة

Clad *pp.* of clothe لابسٌ. مَكْسُوٌّ

Claim *v. t.* or *n.* إِدَّعَى بِهِ. إِدِّعَاءٌ

Claimant *n.* طالبٌ. مُدَّعٍ

Clam *n.* بَطْلِينُوس

Clamber *v. i.* تسَلَّق

Clammy *a.* دَبِقٌ. لزِجٌ

Clamour *n.* صِيَاحٌ. ضَجَّةٌ

Clamorous *a.* صياح. صَخاب

Clamp *v. t.* or *n.* شَدَّ بِكلاب. كُلَّابٌ

Clan *n.* عَشِيرَةٌ. قَبِيلَةٌ

Clandestine *a.* خفِيٌّ. مَسْتُورٌ

Clang *v. t.* or *n.* طَنَّ. رَنَّ

Clangour *n.* طنينٌ

Clank *n.* or *v.* t. قعقعة. قعقع

Clap *v. t.* or *n.* صَفَّقَ. تصفيقٌ

Claper *n.* مِدَقُّ الْجَرَس او الْبَاب

Claret *n.* نوْعُ خَمْرٍ فرنساوِيةٍ

Clarify *v. t.* صَفَّى . رَوَّقَ

Clarion *n.* بُوقٌ ج أَبْوَاقٌ

Clash *v. i.* or *t.* إِصْطَدَمَ . ضَادَّ

Clashing *n.* or *a.* تَصَادُمٌ . تَعَارُضٌ

Clasp *n.* or *v. t.* إِبْزِيمٌ . عَانَقَ . قَبَضَ

Class *n.* صَفٌّ . فَصِيلَةٌ . رُتْبَةٌ

Classic *a.* or *n.* مُؤَلَّفٌ شَهِيرٌ

Classification *n.* صَفٌّ . تَرْتِيبٌ

Classify *v. t.* صَفَّ . رَتَّبَ

Clatter *n.* or *v. i.* طَقْطَقَ . طَقْطَقَةٌ

Clause *n.* جُزْءُ جُمْلَةٍ . عِبَارَةٌ

Clavicle *n.* تَرْقُوَةٌ ج تَرَاقٍ

Claw *n.* or *v. t.* مِخْلَبٌ . خَلَبَ

Clay *n.* طِينٌ . صَلْصَالٌ

Clayey *a.* طِينِيٌّ . صَلْصَالِيٌّ

Clean *a.* or *ad.* نَظِيفٌ . نَقِيٌّ . تَمَامًا

Clean *v. t.* نَظَّفَ . نَقَّى

Cleanliness *n.* نَظَافَةٌ . نَقَاوَةٌ

Cleanse *v. t.* طَهَّرَ . نَقَّى

Clear *a.* صَافٍ . رَائِقٌ

Clear *v. t.* or *i.* صَفَّى . بَرَّأَ . إِنْجَلَى

Clearance *n.* تَصْفِيَةٌ . إِجَازَةٌ

Clearly *ad.* وَاضِحًا . جَلِيًّا

Clearness *n.* وُضُوحٌ . بَيَانٌ . بَهَاءٌ

Cleavage *n.* شَقٌّ . شَقٌّ إِلَى طَبَقَاتٍ

Cleave *v. t.* or *i.* شَقَّ ـُ . إِلْتَصَقَ

Cleft *n.* or *pp.* شَقٌّ . مَشْقُوقٌ

Clemency *n.* رَأْفَةٌ . حِلْمٌ

Clement *a.* رَؤُوفٌ . حَلِيمٌ

Clergy *n.* إِكْلِيرُوسٌ

Clergyman *n.* قَسٌّ أَوْ قِسِّيسٌ

Clerical *a.* إِكْلِيرِيٌّ

Clerk *n.* كَاتِبٌ ج كُتَّاب

Clerkship *n.* مَقَامُ ٱلْكَاتِبِ

Clever *a.* ذَكِيٌّ . حَاذِقٌ . ارِيبٌ

Cleverness *n.* ذَكَاءٌ . حَذَاقَةٌ

Clew *n.* دَلِيلٌ . إِشَارَةٌ

Click *v. i.* or *a.* تَكْتَكَ . تَكْتَكَةٌ

Client *n.* زَبُونُ ٱلْمُحَامِي . تَابِعٌ

Cliff *n.* صَخْرَةٌ شَاهِقَةٌ

Climate / **Clime** } *n.* مَنَاخٌ . إِقْلِيمٌ

Climatic *a.* إِقْلِيمِيٌّ

Climax *n.* نِهَايَةٌ . تَدَرُّجٌ

Climb *v. t.* or *i.* تَسَلَّقَ . صَعِدَ ـَ

Clinch *v. t.* ضَبَطَ ـِ شَدَّ ـُ . أَثْبَتَ

Clincher *n.* كُلَّابٌ . بُرْهَانٌ قَاطِعٌ

Cling *v. i.* إِلْتَصَقَ بِ . تَعَلَّقَ عَلَى

Clinic / **Clinical** } *n.* (كلينيك) . سَرِيرِيٌّ

Clink *v. i.* or *t.* طَنَّ ـِ رَنَّ ـِ

Clip *v. t.* قَرَمَ ـُ قَصَّرَ . قَلَّمَ

Clipper *n.* سَفِينَةٌ سَرِيعَةُ ٱلسَّيْرِ

Clique *n.* عُصْبَةٌ

Cloak *n.* or *v.t.* رِدَاءٌ . سَتَرَ ـُ

Clock *n.* سَاعَةٌ كَبِيرَةٌ

Clock-maker *n.* سَاعَاتِيٌّ

Clockwork *n.* آلَاتُ سَاعَةٍ

Clod *n.* or *v. i.* مَدَرٌ . تَكَتَّلَ

Clog *v. t.* or *n.* عَاقَ . ثَقَّلَ . عَائِقٌ

Cloister *n.* دَيْرٌ

Close *v. t.* or *n.* غَلَقَ . أَنْجَزَ . خِتَامٌ

Close *a.* ضَيِّقٌ . مَحْصُورٌ . قَرِيبٌ

Closely *ad.* مُلَاصِقًا . عَنْ قُرْبٍ

Closet *n.* مُخْدَعٌ . حُجْرَةٌ صَغِيرَةٌ

Closing *n.* or *a.* نِهَايَةٌ . خِتَامٌ . آخِرٌ

Closure *n.* إِنْجَازٌ . خَتْمٌ . حَوْشٌ

Clot *n.* or *v. i.* خِثْرَةٌ . خَثَرَ ـَ

Cloth *n.* نَسِيجٌ . قُمَاشٌ . جُوخ

Clothe *v. t.* كَسَا ـُ أَلْبَسَ

Clothes / **Clothing** } *n.* لِبَاسٌ . ثِيَابٌ . كُسْوَةٌ

Clothes-line *n.* حَبْلُ ٱلْغَسِيلِ

Clothier *n.* صَانِعُ ثِيَابٍ وَبَائِعُهَا

Cloud *n.* غَيْمٌ . سَحَابٌ

Cloud *v. t.* or *i.* اظلمَ . سَوَّدَ . تغيَّمَ

Cloudiness *n.* تغيُّمٌ

Cloudy *a.* مُغيِّمٌ . مُظْلِمٌ

Cloves *n. pl.* كَبْشُ القرنفل

Cloven *pp.* of cleave. مَشْقُوق

Cloven-footed *a.* مَشْقوق الظِّلْفِ

Clover *n.* نَفَلَةٌ . بَرْسِيمٌ

Clown *n* فَظٌّ . مُهَرِّجٌ

Clay *v. t.* ملأ . أشْبَعَ

Club *n.* عصاً . نبُّوتٌ . مُنتدَى

Club-footed أَخْنَفُ

Clue *see* clew دَليلٌ . إشَارَة

Clump *n.* دَغْلٌ (مِنْ شَجَرٍ)

Clumsy *a.* أَخْرَقُ

Clung *pp.* of cling. تَعَلَّقَ علَى وَبِ

Cluster *n.* or *v. i.* عنقودٌ . تجمَّعَ

Clutch *v. t.* or *n.* قبضَ بِ . قبْضٌ

Coach *n.* عَجلَةٌ . عَرَبَةٌ . مَرْكَبة

Coachman *n.* سَائِقُ مَرْكَبَةٍ

Coadjutor *n.* مُعَاوِنٌ . مُسَاعِدٌ

Coagulate *v. t.* or *i.* خثَّرَ . خَثُرَ

Coagulation *n.* رَوْبٌ . تَجَمُّدٌ . خَثْرٌ

Coal *n.* فَحْمٌ . فحمٌ حَجَرِيٌّ

Coal *v.* إتحدَ . إتَّصَلَ

Coaling *n.* تقْدِيمُ فحْمٍ

Coalition *n.* إعتصابٌ . إتحاد

Coal-mine *n.* معْدِنُ فَحْمٍ حَجَرِيٍّ

Coarse *a.* خَشِنٌ . ثَخِين . غَلِيظ

Coarseness *n.* خُشُونَةٌ . فَظَاظَة

Coast *n.* شَاطِئُ ٱلْبَحْرِ

Coaster *n.* مُسَافِرٌ قُرْب ٱلشَّاطِئِ

Coat *n.* رِدَاءٌ . جُبَّةٌ

Coating *n* تغطيَةٌ . غطاءٌ

Coax *v. t.* تملَّقَ

Cobble *v. t* رَقَعَ (أحذِيَةً)

Cobble-stone *n.* حَصَاةٌ مُسْتَدِيرَة

Cobbler *n.* مُرَقِّعُ احذِيَةٍ

Cobweb *n.* نَسِيجُ ٱلعَنكَبُوتِ

Cock *n.* دِيكٌ . حَنَفِيَّةٌ

Cockade *n.* عُقْدَةُ شَرِيطٍ لِلرَّأْسِ

Cockatrice *n.* افعُوَانٌ

Cockle *n.* نَوْعٌ مِنَ ٱلصَّدَفِ

Cockroach *n.* صُرْصُورٌ

Cockscomb *n.* عُرْفُ ٱلدِّيكِ

Cockswain *n.* رَئِيسُ قَارِبٍ

Cocoanut *n.* جَوْزُ هِندٍ . نَارجِيلٌ

Cocoon *n.* شَرْنَقَةٌ

Cod, Codfish } *n.* نَوْعٌ مِنَ ٱلسَّمَكِ

Coddle *v. t.* دَلَّلَ

Code *n.* دُستُورُ شَرَائِعَ . مَجَلَّةٌ

Codicil *n.* ذَيْلُ وَصِيَّةٍ

Codify *v. t.* جَمَعَ . لَخَّصَ ٱلشَّرَائِعَ

Co-efficient *n.* or *a.* مُعَيِّنٌ . مُسَاعِدٌ

Co-equal *a.* كُفْوءٌ . مَثِيلٌ . عَدِيلٌ

Coerce *v. t.* غَصَبَ . أَجْبَرَ

Coercion *n.* غَصْبٌ . إِجْبَارٌ

Coercive *a.* غَاصِبٌ . مُجْبِرٌ

Coeval *a.* or *n.* مُعَاصِرٌ . مُتَسَاوٍ

Co-existent *a.* مَوْجُودٌ فِي زَمَانٍ وَاحِدٍ

Co-existence *n.* أَلتَّعَادُلُ فِي ٱلْوُجُودِ

Co-extensive *a.* مُعَادِلٌ فِي ٱلامْتِدَادِ

Coffee *n.* بُنٌّ . قَهْوَةٌ

Coffer *n.* صُنْدُوقٌ لِلْمَالِ

Coffin *n.* تَابُوتٌ . نَعْشٌ

Cog *n.* سِنُّ دُولَابٍ

Cogency *n.* قُوَّةٌ . شِدَّةٌ

Cogent *a.* قَوِيٌّ . مُقْنِعٌ

Cogitate *v. i.* تَأَمَّلَ . فَكَّرَ

Cogitation *n.* تَأَمُّلٌ . تَفْكِيرٌ

Cognate *n.* نَسِيبٌ . مُجَانِسٌ

Cognition *n.* عِلْمٌ . إِدْرَاكٌ

Cognizable *a.* قَابِلُ ٱلمَعْرِفَةِ

Cognomen *n.* إِسْمُ ٱلعائِلَةِ

Cogwheel *n.* دُولَابٌ ذُوْ اسْنَانٍ

Cohabit *v. i.* سَاكَنَ

Co-heir *n.* قسيمُ ٱلمِيرَاثِ

Cohere *v. i.* إِلْتَصَقَ . إِتَّحَدَ

Coherence / **Cohesion** *n.* إِلْتِصَاقٌ . إِلْتِحَامٌ

Coherent *a.* مُلْتَصِقٌ . مُنْتَظِمٌ

Cohesive *a.* لَزِجٌ مُلْتَصِقٌ

Cohort *n.* كَتِيبَةٌ

Coil *v. t.* or *n.* لَفَّ . طَوَى ـ لَفَّةٌ

Coin *n.* or *v. t.* قِطْعَةُ نُقُودٍ . سَكَّ ـُ

Coinage *n.* سَكُّ ٱلنُّقُودِ. أَلمَسكُوكَاتُ

Coincide *v. i.* إِتَّفَقَ

Coincidence *n.* إِتِّفَاقٌ . مُطَابَقَةٌ

Coincident *n.* مُتَّفِقٌ . مُطَابِقٌ

Coke *n.* نَوْعُ فَحْمٍ حَجَرِيٍّ

Cold *a.* or *n.* بَارِدٌ . بَرْدٌ . زُكَامٌ

Coldly *ad.* بَارِداً. بِعَدَمِ اكْتِرَاثٍ

Coldness *n.* بُرُودَةٌ . بَرْدٌ

Colic *n.* مَغْصٌ . (قُولَنْجٌ)

Collaborator *n.* شَرِيكٌ فِي عَمَلٍ

Collapse *v. i.* or *n.* هَبَطَ ـُ . تَهَوُّرٌ

Collar *n.*or *v.t.* طَوْقٌ . قَبَّةٌ . طَوَّقَ

Collate *v. i.* قَابَلَ . جَمَعَ . رَتَّبَ

Collateral *a.* مُجَانِبٌ مُرَافِقٌ

Collation *n.* مُقَابَلَةٌ . لُمْجَةٌ

Colleague *n.* شَرِيكٌ . رَصِيفٌ

Collect *v. t.* or *i.* جَمَعَ . إِجْتَمَعَ

Collected *pp.* or *a.* مَجْمُوعٌ.رَزِينٌ

Collection *n.* جَمْعٌ . مَجْمُوعٌ

Collectively *ad.* جُمْلَةً . بِالإِجْمَالِ

Collector *n.* جَامِعٌ. جَابٍ

College *n.* مَدْرَسَةٌ عَالِيَةٌ أَوْ كُلِّيَّةٌ

Collegiate *a.* مُخْتَصٌّ بِمَدْرَسَةٍ كُلِّيَّةٍ

Collide *v. i.* تَصَادَمَ

Collier *n.* فَحَّامٌ. سَفِينَةٌ لِحَمْلِ ٱلْفَحْمِ

Colliery *n.* مَعْدِنُ ٱلْفَحْمِ

Collision *n.* تَصَادُمٌ

Collocate *v. t.* رَتَّبَ . نَظَّمَ

Colloquial *n.* عَامِيٌّ . تحَاوُرِيٌّ

Colloquy *n.* مُحَاوَرَةٌ

Collude *v. i.* تَآمَرَ

Collusion *n.* مُؤَامَرَةٌ لِلْخِدَاعِ

Collusive *a.* خِدَاعِيٌّ

Colon *n.* علَامَةُ وَقْفٍ (:)

Colonel *n.* أَمِيرُ آلَايٍ

Colonial *a.* مُخْتَصٌّ بِمُسْتَعْمَرَةٍ

Colonist *n.* مُسْتَعْمِرٌ . مُهَاجِرٌ

Colonization *n.* إِنْشَاءُ مُسْتَعْمَرَاتٍ

Colonize *v. t.* أَنْشَا مُسْتَعْمَرَةً

Colonade *n.* صَفٌّ أَعْمِدَةٍ

Colony *n.* مُسْتَعْمَرَةٌ . مُهَاجِرُونَ

Colossal *a.* جَسِيمُ ٱلْقَدِّ

Colossus *n.* تِمْثَالٌ عَظِيمُ ٱلْقَدِّ

Colour *n.* or *v. t.* or *i.* لَوْنٌ . لَوَّنَ . إِحْمَرَّ

Colouring *n.* تَلْوِينٌ . تَلَوُّنٌ . صِبْغٌ

Colours *n. pl.* رَايَةٌ . عَلَمٌ

Colporteur *n.* بَيَّاعٌ يَدُورُ بِكُتُبٍ

Colt *n.* فِلْوٌ . مُهْرٌ

Column *n.* عَمُودٌ ج اعْمِدَةٌ

Columnar *a.* عَمُودِيٌّ

Comb *n.* مُشْطٌ ج أَمْشَاطٌ

Combat *n.* or *v. t* قِتَالٌ . قَاتَلَ

Combatant *n.* مُقَاتِلٌ

Combative *a.* مَائِلٌ إِلَى ٱلْقِتَالِ . خَصُومٌ

Combination *n.* إِتِّحَادٌ . إِتِّفَاقٌ

Combine *v. i.* or *t.* إِجْتَمَعَ . جَمَعَ

Combustible *a.* قَابِلُ ٱلإِشْتِعَالِ

Combustion *n.* إِشْتِعَالٌ . إِحْتِرَاقٌ

Come *v. i.* (came, come) جَآءَ . اتى

Comedian *n.* كَاتِبُ رِوَايَاتٍ هَزْلِيَّةٍ . مُشَخِّصُهَا

Comedy *n.* رِوَايَةٌ هَزْلِيَّةٌ

Comely *a.* حَسَنُ ٱلصُّورَةِ

Comet *n.* نَجْمٌ ذُو ذَنَبٍ

Comfort *n.* or *v. t.* تَعْزِيَةٌ . عَزَّى

Comfortable *a.* مُرِيحٌ . مُسْتَرِيحٌ

Comforter *n.* مُعَزٍّ . أَلرُّوحُ ٱلْقُدُسُ

Comic / **Comical** } *a.* مُضْحِكٌ . هَزْلِيٌّ

Coming *a.* or *n.* آتٍ إِتْيَانٌ . مَجِيءٌ

Comma *n.* (,) عَلَامَةُ وَقْفٍ قَصِيرٍ

Command *v. t.* or *n.* أَمَرَ . أَمْرٌ

Commandant / **Commander** } *n.* أَمِيرٌ . قَائِدٌ

Commanding *ppr.* آمِرٌ . مُشْرِفٌ عَلَى

Commandment *n.* أَمْرٌ . وَصِيَّةٌ

Commemorable *a.* مُسْتَحِقُّ ٱلذِّكْرِ

Commemorate *v. t.* إِحْتَفَلَ . عَيَّدَ

Commemorative *a.* تَذْكَارِيٌّ

Commence *v. t.* or *i.* بَدَأَ . إِبْتَدَأَ

Commencement *n.* بَدَاءٌ

Commend *v. t.* مَدَحَ ـ إِسْتَوْدَعَ

Commendable *a.* مُسْتَحِقُّ ٱلْمَدْحِ

Commendation *n.* مَدْحٌ . تَوْصِيَةٌ

Commensurable / **Commensurate** } *a.* مُتَسَاوٍ

Comment *v. i.* or *n.* شَرَحَ . تَفْسِيرٌ

Commentary *n.* تَفْسِيرٌ . شَرْحٌ

Commentator *n.* مُفَسِّرٌ . شَارِحٌ

Commerce *n.* تِجَارَةٌ . مَتْجَرٌ

Commercial *a.* تِجَارِيٌّ . مَتْجَرِيٌّ

Commingle *v. t.* or *i.* مَزَجَ ـ إِمْتَزَجَ

Commiserate *v. t.* أَشْفَقَ عَلَى

Commiseration *n.* شَفَقَةٌ

Commissary *n* } مُفَوَّضٌ . مَأْمُورُ ٱلْمَأْكُولَاتِ فِي جَيْشٍ

Commission *n.* وَكَالَةٌ . لَجْنَةٌ

Commission *v. t.* فَوَّضَ إِلَى

Commissioner *n.* وَكِيلٌ مُفَوَّضٌ

Commit *v. t.* سَلَّمَ . إِرْتَكَبَ

Commitment *n.* إِبْدَاعٌ . سِجْنٌ

Committal *n.* تَسْلِيمٌ . إِرْتِكَابٌ

Committee *n.* لَجْنَةٌ . وُكَلاءُ

Commodious *a.* مُرِيحٌ . رَحْبٌ

Commodity *n.* سِلْعَةٌ . بِضَاعَةٌ

Commodor *n.* رَئِيسُ أُسْطُولٍ

Common *a.* عَامٌّ . إِعْتِيَادِيٌّ

Commoner *n.* احَدُ ٱلْعَامَّةِ

Commonly *a.* غَالِبًا . إِعْتِيَادِيًّا

Common-wealth *n.* حُكُومَةٌ جَمْهُورِيَّةٌ

Commotion *n.* ضَجَّةٌ . إِضْطِرَابٌ

Commune *v. i.* إِشْتَرَكَ . كَالَمَ

Communicant *n.* مُشْتَرِكٌ

Communicate *v. t.* ابْلَغَ . أَخْبَرَ

Communication *n.* تَبْلِيغٌ . مُرَاسَلَةٌ

Communicative *a.* مُبَلِّغٌ

Communion *n.* مُخَالَطَةٌ . إِشْتِرَاكٌ

Community *n.* جَمَاعَةٌ . إِشْتِرَاكٌ

Commutable *a.* قَابِلُ ٱلاسْتِبْدَالِ

Commutation *n.* تَبَادُلٌ . إِسْتِبْدَالٌ

Commute *v. t.* إِسْتَبْدَلَ . غَيَّرَ

Compact *a.* or *n.* مُتَلَبِّدٌ . مُعَاهَدَةٌ

Compactness *n.* تَلَبُّدٌ . مَتَانَةٌ

Compánion *n.* رَفِيقٌ . عَشِيرٌ

Companionable *a.* أَنِيسٌ

Companionship *n.* مُعَاشَرَةٌ . صُحْبَةٌ

Company *n.* جَمَاعَةٌ . شِرْكَةٌ

Comparable *a.* قَابِلُ ٱلْمُقَابَلَةِ

Comparative *a.* or *n.* نِسْبِيٌّ . أَفْعَلُ التَّفْضِيلِ

Compare *v. t.* or *i.* قَابَلَ . شَابَهَ

Comparison *n.* مُقَابَلَةٌ . مُشَابَهَةٌ

Compartment *n.* قِسْمٌ . بَيْتٌ

Compass *v.t.* أَحَاطَ بِ . أَنْجَزَ . نَالَ

Campass *n.* مُحِيطٌ . حُكٌ

Compasses *n. pl.* بِرْكَارٌ أَوْ بِيكَارٌ

Compassion شَفَقَةٌ . رَأْفَةٌ

Compassionate *a.* شَفُوقٌ . رَؤُوفٌ

Compatibility *n.* مُوَافَقَةٌ . مُلاَءَمَة

Compatible *a.* مُوَافِقٌ . مُلاَئِم

Compeer *n.* قَرِينٌ . شَرِيك

Compel *v.* أَجْبَرَ أَلْزَمَ . غَصَبَ

Compend / Compendium *n.* مُخْتَصَرٌ

Compensate *v. t.* عَوَّضَ . كَافَأَ

Compensation *n.* مُكَافَأَةٌ . تَعْوِيضٌ

Compete *v. i.* سابَقَ . بَارَى . نَاظَرَ

Competence / Competency *n.* كِفَايَةٌ . جدَارة

Competent *a.* جَدِيرٌ . قَادِرٌ عَلَى

Competition *n.* مُسَابَقَةٌ . مُبَارَاة

Competitor *n.* مُسَابِقٌ . مُبَارٍ

Competitive *a.* سِبَاقِيٌّ

Compilation *n.* مَجْمُوعَة . تَأْلِيف

Compile *v. t.* جَمَعَ ـَ . أَلَّفَ

Complacence *n.* سُرُورٌ بِ . رِضىً بِ

Complacent *a.* رَاضٍ بِ . مَسْرُورٌ بِ

Complain *v. i.* شَكَا ـُ تَظَلَّمَ مِنْ

Complainant / Complainer *n.* مشْتَكٍ

Complaint *n.* شَكَايَةٌ . عِلَّةٌ

Complaisance *n.* مُلاَطَفَةٌ . مُرَاعَاةٌ

Complaisant *a.* مُلاَطِفٌ . مُرَاعِي ٱلْخَاطِرِ

Complement *n.* تَتِمَّةٌ . تَكْمِلَةٌ

Complemental *a.* مُتَمِّمٌ . تَكْمِيلِيٌّ

Complete *v. t.* or *a.* تَمَّمَ . أَكْمَلَ . كَامِلٌ

Completely *ad.* تَمَاماً

Completement / Completion *n.* إِتمَامٌ . تَكْمِيلٌ

Complex *a.* مُرَكَّبٌ . مُشْتَبِكٌ

Complexion *n.* لَوْنُ ٱلْوَجْهِ

Complexity *n.* إِشْتِبَاكٌ . تَعَقُّد

Compliance *n.* إِذْعَانٌ . إِجَابَةٌ

Compliant *a.* مُذْعِنٌ . مُنْقَادٌ

Complicate *v.t.* or *a.* عَرْقَلَ . مُعَقَّدٌ

Complicated *a.* مُعَرْقَلٌ . مُعَقَّدٌ

Complication *n.* عَرْقَلَةٌ . تَشْوِيشٌ
Complicity *n.* إِشْتِرَاكٌ فِي ذَنْبٍ
Compliment *n.* قَولُ مَدْحٍ . تَحِيَّةٌ
Complimentary *a.* مَادِحٌ
Comply *v. i.* أَذْعَنَ . اجَابَ . إِنْقَادَ
Component *a.* or *n.* تَرْكِيبِيٌّ . جُزْءٌ
Comport *v. i.* وافَقَ . لاَءَمَ
Compose *v. t.* رَكَّبَ . الَّفَ . هَدَّأَ
Composed *a.* مُرَكَّبٌ . مُؤَلَّفٌ رَزِينٌ
Composer *n.* مُؤَلِّفٌ . جَامِعٌ
Composite *a.* مُرَكَّبٌ مِنْ أَجزاء
Composition *n.* تَرْكِيبٌ . تَأْلِيفٌ
Compositor *n.* صَفَّافُ احْرُفٍ لِلطبع
Compost *n.* سَمَادٌ
Composure *n.* رَزَانَةٌ . هُدُوءٌ
Compound *a.* or *n.* مُرَكَّبٌ . مَزِيجٌ
Compound *v. t.* رَكَّبَ . مزج ـُ
Component *a.* or *n.* مُرَكَّبٌ . جُزْءٌ جَوْهَرِيٌّ

Comprehend *v. t.* ادْرَكَ . فَهِمَ ـَ
Comprehensible *a.* مُمْكِنٌ إِدْرَاكُهُ
Comprehension *n.* إِدْرَاكٌ . شُمُولٌ
Comprehensive *a.* شَامِلٌ . جَامِعٌ
Compress *v. t.* كَبَسَ ـَ ضَغَطَ ـَ
Compression *n.* كَبْسٌ
Comprise *v. t.* تَضَمَّنَ . إِشْتَمَلَ عَلَى
Compromise *v.t.* or *n.* إِتَّفَقَ . إِتِّفَاقٌ
Compulsion *n.* غَصْبٌ . إِكْرَاهٌ
Compulsive / Compulsory *a.* غَاصِبٌ . مُجْبِرٌ
Compunction *n.* تَوْبِيخُ ٱلضَّمِيرِ
Computable *a.* قَابِلُ ٱلإِحْصَاءِ
Compute *v. t.* احْصَى . حَسَبَ ـَ
Comrade *n.* رَفِيقٌ . صَاحِبٌ
Con *v. t.* تَأَمَّلَ . دَرَسَ ـُ
Concatenation *n.* تَسَلْسُلٌ . سِلْسِلَةٌ
Concave *a.* مُقَعَّرٌ . مُجَوَّفٌ
Concavity *n.* تَجْوِيفٌ . قَعْرَةٌ

Conceal *v. t.* اخفى . سَتَرَ ـِ . كَتَمَ ـُ

Concealment *n.* إِخفَاءٌ . كِتمَانٌ

Concede *v. t.* مَنَحَ — سَلَّمَ بِهِ

Conceit *n.* تَخَيُّلٌ . رَأْيٌ . عُجْبٌ

Conceited *a.* مُعْجَبٌ بنفسِهِ

Conceivable *a.* مُمْكِنٌ تَصَوُّرُهُ

Conceive *v. t.* تَصَوَّرَ فِي ٱلذِّهْنِ

Concentrate *v. t.* جَمَعَ فِي مَرْكَزٍ

Concentration *n.* جَمْعٌ . تَجَمُّعٌ

Concentric *a.* ذُو مَرْكَزٍ وَاحِدٍ

Conception *n.* تَصَوُّرٌ . فِكْرٌ . حَبَلٌ

Concern *v. t.* or *n.* هَمَّ ـُ . هَمٌّ . قَضِيَّةٌ

Concerning *pr.* بِخُصُوصِ . مِنْ جِهَةِ

Concert *v. t.* or *i.* دَبَّرَ . إِتَّفَقَ

Concert *n.* إِتِّفَاقٌ . مَحْفَلٌ مُوسِيقِيٌّ

Concession *n.* تَسْلِيمٌ بِ . هِبَةٌ . رُخْصَةٌ

Conciliate *v. t.* سَالَمَ . وَفَّقَ بَيْنَ

Conciliation *n.* مُسَالَمَةٌ

Conciliatory *a.* مُسْتَعْطِفٌ . مُسَالِمٌ

Concise *a.* مُخْتَصَرٌ . وَجِيزٌ

Conciseness *n.* إِخْتِصَارٌ . إِيجَازٌ

Conclave *n.* مَجْمَعٌ سِرِّيٌّ

Conclude *v. t.* or *i.* انهى . إِسْتَنْتَجَ

Concluding *a.* خَاتِمٌ . أَخِيرٌ

Conclusion *n.* خَاتِمَةٌ . نَتِيجَةٌ

Conclusive *a.* قَاطِعٌ . جَازِمٌ

Concoct *v.* دَبَّرَ . رَكَّبَ طَبِيخًا

Concoction *n.* هَضْمٌ . تَدْبِيرٌ

Concomitant *a.* مُرَافِقٌ . مُلَازِمٌ

Concord *n.* إِتِّفَاقٌ . وِفَاقٌ

Concordance *n.* فِهْرِسٌ

Concordat *n.* صَكٌّ . إِتِّفَاقٌ

Concourse *n.* إِجْتِمَاعٌ

Concrete *a.* or *n.* مُتَجَمِّدٌ . مُرَكَّبٌ

Concretion *n.* كُتْلَةٌ مُتَجَمِّدَةٌ

Concubine *n.* سُرِّيَّةٌ ج سَرَارِيُّ

Concupiscence *n.* شَهْوَة . هَوًى

Concur *v. i.* إِتَّفَقَ

Concurrence *n.* إِتِّفَاقٌ

Concurrent *a.* مُرَافِقٌ . مجَارٍ

Concussion *n.* هَزٌّ . صَدْمَةٌ

Condemn *v. t.* حَكَمَ عَلَى . دَانَ ـِ

Condemnation *n.* حُكْمٌ . دَيْنُونَةٌ

Condemnatory *a.* دائِنٌ . حَاكِمٌ بَدَيْنُونَةٍ

Condensation *n.* تَكْثِيفٌ

Condense *v. t.* كَثَّفَ . اوْجَزَ . قَطَّرَ

Condescend *v. i.* تَنَازَلَ . تَسَاهَلَ

Condescension *n.* تَنَازُلٌ

Condign *a.* مُسْتَحِقٌّ . مُوَافِق

Condiment *n.* تابِلٌ ج تَوَابِلُ

Condition *n.* or *v. t.* حالَةٌ . شَرْط . إِشْتَرَطَ

Conditional *a.* شرْطِيٌّ

Conditioned *a.* مشْرُوطٌ او مُشْتَرَط

Condole *v. i.* or *t.* حَزِنَ مَعَ غَيْرِهِ

Condolence *n.* الأَسَفُ مَعَ الْغَيْرِ

Condone *v. t.* غَفَرَ ـِ . سَامَحَ

Condor *n.* حَدَأَةٌ أَمِيرِكِيَّةٌ كَبِيرَة

Conduce *v. i.* أفضى أَوْ آلَ إِلَى

Couducible / Conducive *a.* مُفْضٍ أَوْ آيِلٌ إِلَى

Conduct *v. t.* قَادَ ـِ . أَدَارَ

Conduct *n.* تَصَرُّفٌ . قِيَادَة

Conductor *n.* قائِدٌ . مُوْصِلٌ كَهْرَبَائِيٌّ

Conduit *n.* قَنَاةٌ ج قُنِيٌّ وَقَنَوَات

Cone *n.* مَخْرُوطٌ

Confection / Confectionery *n.* حَلْوَى أَوْ حَلْوَاء

Confectioner *n.* حَلْوَانِيٌّ

Confederacy *n.* عُصْبَة . مُعَاهدة

Confederate *v. i.* or *a.* إِعْتَصَبَ . متعَاهِد

Confederation *n.* تعَاهُدٌ . تحَالفٌ

Confer *v.i.* or *t.* تَشَاوَرَ . مَنَحَ ـ

Conference *n.* مشاوَرَة . مُؤْتَمر

Confess *v. t.* أَقَرَّ . إِعْتَرَفَ

Confessedly *ad.* بِإِقْرَارِ الْعُمُومِ

Confession *n.* إِعْتِرَافٌ . إِقْرَارٌ

Confessional *n.* كُرْسِيُّ الإِعْتِرَاف

Confessor *n.* مُعَرِّفٌ . مُعْتَرِفٌ

Confidant *n.* صَفِيٌّ . خِلٌّ امِينٌ

Confide *v. i.* or *t.* امِنَ ـَ أَرْكَنَ إِلَى

Confidence *n.* ثِقَةٌ . إِرْكَان

Confident *a.* مُتَأَكِّدٌ . وَاثِق

Confidential *a.* سِرِّيٌّ . امِين

Configuration *n.* صُورَةٌ . هَيْئَةٌ

Confine *v. t.* حَجَزَ ـُ . حَصَرَ ـِ

Confinement *n.* حَصْرٌ . حَبْسٌ

Confirm *v. t.* اثْبَتَ . شَدَّدَ

Confirmation *n.* إِثْبَاتٌ . تَأْيِيد

Confirmative / Confirmatory *a.* مُثَبِّت . مُؤَيِّد

Confiscate *v. t.* ضبَطَ مُلْكاً (الحكومة)

Confiscation *n.* ضَبْطُ الْملك

Conflagration *n.* إِحْتِرَاقٌ . حَرِيق

Conflict *n.* or *v.t.* قِتَالٌ . خِصَامٌ . نَازَع

Conflicting *a.* مُتَنَاقِضٌ . مُتَخَالِفٌ

Confluent *a.* جَارٍ مَعَ غَيْرِه

Conform *v. t.* or *i.* شَاكَلَ . إِمْتَثَلَ

Conformable *a.* مُطَابِقٌ . مُوَافِقٌ

Conformation *n.* تَرْكِيبٌ . جِبْلَة

Conformity *n.* مُوَافَقَة . مُطَابَقَة

Confound *v. t.* خلَطَ . حَيَّرَ

Confounded *a.* مُخْتَلِطٌ . مُتَحَيِّرٌ

Confront *v. t.* وَاجَهَ . قَابَلَ

Confuse *v. t.* خلطَ ـِ . بَلْبَلَ . أَخْجَلَ

Confusion *n.* بِلْبَالٌ . تَشْوِيشٌ

Confutation *n.* دَحْضٌ . إِبطَالٌ

Confute *v. t.* ادْحَض . أَبْطَلَ

Congeal *v. t.* or *t.* جَمَّدَ . جَمُدَ ـ

Congelation *n.* جَمْدٌ أَوْ جمُود

Congenial *n.* مِنْ خُلقٍ وَاحِدٍ . مُوَافِق

Congeniality *n.* مُوَافَقَةُ ٱلْخُلْق

Congenital *a.* خِلْقِيٌّ . مِنَ الْخِلْقَةِ

Congested *a.* مُحْتَقِنٌ

Congestion *n.* إِحْتِقَانٌ

Conglomerate *v. t.* or *a.* كَتَّلَ . مُكَتَّلٌ

Conglomeration *n.* تَكَتُّلٌ

Congratulate *v. t.* هَنَّأَ

Congratulation *n.* تَهْنِئَةٌ

Congratulatory *a.* مُهَنِّي

Congregate *v. t.* or *i.* حَشَدَ ـُ . إِحْتَشَدَ

Congregation *n.* جَمَاعَةٌ . مَحْفَلٌ

Congregational *a.* جُمْهُورِيٌّ (فِي الدِّينِ)

Congress *n.* مُؤْتَمَرٌ . مَجْمَعٌ

Congruity *n.* مُنَاسَبَةٌ . مُطَابَقَةٌ

Congruous *a.* مُنَاسِبٌ . مُوَافِقٌ

Conical *a.* مَخْرُوطِيُّ ٱلشَّكْلِ

Conicsections *n.* عِلْمُ قَطْعِ ٱلْمَخْرُوطِ

Coniferous *a.* ذُو ثَمَرٍ كَالصَّنَوْبَرِ

Conjectural *a.* حَدْسِيٌّ . تَخْمِينِيٌّ

Conjecture *n.* حَدْسٌ . تَخْمِينٌ

Conjoin *v. t.* وَصَلَ ـِ . قَرَنَ ـِ

Conjointly *ad.* مَعاً

Conjugal *a.* زَوَاجِيٌّ . بَعْلِيٌّ

Conjugate *v. t.* صَرَّفَ (ٱلْفِعْلَ)

Conjugation *n.* تَصْرِيفُ ٱلْفِعْلِ

Conjunction *n.* وَصْلٌ . حَرْفُ عَطْفٍ

Conjunctive *a.* عَاطِفٌ . مُوْصِلٌ

Conjuncture *n.* إِتِّحَادٌ . وَقْتٌ مُهِمٌّ

Conjure *v. t.* or *i.* رَقَّى ـِ . إِسْتَحْلَفَ

Conjurer *n.* رَاقٍ . مُشَعْوِذٌ

Connect *v. t.* وصَلَ ـِ . قَرَنَ ـِ

Connection, Connexion *n.* وَصْلٌ . إِتِّصَالٌ

Connective *n.* or *a.* مُوْصِلٌ . رَابِط

Connivance *n.* إِغْضَاءٌ عَنْ زَلَّةٍ

Connive *v. t.* تَغَاضَى عَنْ

Connubial *a.* زِيجِيٌّ اوْ زَوْجِيٌّ

Conoid / Conoidal } a. شَبِيهٌ بِالْمَخْرُوط

Conquer v. t. غَلَبَ ـِ . ظَفِرَ بِـ ـَ

Conqueror n. غَالِبٌ . ظَافِرٌ . فَاتِح

Conquest n. غَلَبَةٌ . ظَفَرٌ . فَتْحٌ . فُتُوح

Consanguinity n. قَرَابَة . نَسَبٌ

Conscience n. اَلضَّمِيرُ . ذِمَّة

Conscientious a. صَاحِبُ ذِمَةٍ . أَمِين

Conscientiousness n. ذِمَّةٌ . امَانَة

Conscious a. عَارِفٌ . يقظَان

Consciously ad. عَنْ عِلْمٍ . عَمْداً

Consciousness n. إِدْرَاك . يقْظَة

Conscript a. جُنْدِيٌّ مَاخُوذ بالْقُرْعةِ

Conscription n. } قُرْعَةُ اَلْعَسْكَرِ / إِكْتِتَابٌ

Consecrate v. t. قَدَّسَ . كَرَّسَ

Consecration n. تقْدِيسٌ . تَكْرِيسٌ

Consecutive a. مُتَتَابِعٌ . مُتَوَالٍ

Consent n. or v. i. رِضي . رَضِيَ ب

Consentient a. مُتفق اَلرَّأْي

Consequence n. نَتِيجَةٌ . اهَمِّيَّةٌ

Consequent a. or n. تَابِعٌ . تَال

Consequential a. نَاتِجٌ . مُهِمٌّ . مُعْجِبٌ

Consequently ad. مِن ثَمَّ . إِذاً

Conservation n. حِفْظٌ . وِقَايَةٌ

Conservatism n. } اَلْمُحَافظَةُ عَلَى / اَلنِّظَامُ اَلحَالِيِّ

Conservative a. or n. مُحَافِظٌ

Conservatory a. or n. } حَافِظ . كِنٌّ لِلنبَاتِ

Conserve v. t. حَفِظَ ـَ . صَانَ ـُ

Consider v. t. or i. إِعْتَبَرَ . تَبَصَّرَ

Considerable a. } مُسْتَحِقٌّ اَلإِعْتِبَارِ . وَافِرٌ

Considerate a. مُتبَصِّرٌ . حَازِمٌ

Consideration n. تَفَكُّرٌ . إِعْتِبَارٌ

Considering ppr. نظراً إِلَى . مُتَأَمِّلٌ

Consign v. t. سَلَّمَ إِلَى . اوْدَعَ

Consignee n. اَلْمُتَسَلِّمُ . اَلْمُرْسَلُ إِلَيْهِ

Consignment *n.* تسليمٌ . إرْسَاليَّة

Consist *v. i.* تَكَوَّنَ (مِنْ)

Consistence / Consistency *n.* قوامٌ . مُوَافَقَةٌ

Consistent *a.* جَامِدٌ . مُوَافِقٌ

Consistently *ad.* مُطَابَقَةً لِ

Consolable *a.* قَابِلُ ٱلتَّعْزِيَةِ

Consolation *n.* تعْزِيَةٌ . سَلْوى

Consolatory *a.* مُعَزٍّ . مُسَلٍّ

Console *v. t.* عزى . سَلّى

Consolidate *v. t.* or *i.* ثَبَّتَ . مَكَّن . تجمد

Consolidation *n.* تَثْبِيتٌ . تَجَمُّدٌ

Consonant *a.* or *n.* مُوَافِقٌ . أَلحرْف ٱلصَّحِيحُ

Consort *n.* زَوْجٌ اوْ زَوْجَةٌ . قَرِينٌ

Consort *v. i.* تشَارَكَ . تَرَافَق

Conspicuous *a.* بيّنٌ . جليٌّ . ظاهِرٌ

Conspiracy *n.* فتْنَة . مُؤَامَرَة

Conspirator *n.* مُتَآمِرٌ

Conspire *v. i.* فتنَ ـَ . تآمرَ

Constable *n.* مَأْمورٌ لحفظِ ٱلسلاَم

Constant *a.* ثَابتٌ . دائِمٌ . امينٌ

Constancy *n.* ثَبَات . عَزْمٌ . امانةٌ

Constantly *ad.* على ٱلدَّوَام

Constellation *n.* جماعةُ نجومٍ . برجٌ

Consternation *n.* دهْشَةَ . رُعْبٌ

Constipate *v. t.* قَبَضَ ٱلامعآء

Constipation *n.* قَبْضُ ٱلامْعَآءِ

Constituency *n.* جَمَاعَةُ ٱلْمُنْتَخِبِين

Constituent *a.* or *n.* مكوّن . مُوَكِّلٌ . جوْهريٌّ

Constitute *v. t.* قامَ . نصَب . رَكب

Constitution *n.* بُنْيَةٌ . نظامٌ

Constitutional *a.* نُظَامِيٌّ . مِزَاجِيٌّ

Constitutive *a.* مقِيمٌ . مُكَوّن

Constrain *v. t.* اجْبرَ . الزَمَ

Constraint *n.* إِلْزَامٌ . حَصْر

Constrict *v. t.* شدَّ ـُ . ضغط ـ

Constriction *n.* شَدٌّ. ضغطٌ. إِنقباضٌ

Constringent *a.* قَابِضٌ. مُقلِّصٌ

Construct *v. t.* بنى ـ أنشأ . دَبَّرَ

Construction *n.* بِنَاءٌ . تركيبٌ

Constructor *n.* بَانٍ . بَنَّاءٌ

Constructive *a.* بَانٍ . إِستِدلاليٌّ

Construe *v. i.* فسَّرَ معنى . أَعرَبَ

Consul *n.* قنصلٌ ج قناصِلُ

Consular *a.* قُنصليٌّ

Consulship *n.* مقامُ القُنصلِ

Consulate *n.* مكتبُ القُنصلِ

Consult *v. t.* or *i.* شاوَرَ . تشاوَرَ

Consultation *n.* مُشاوَرَةٌ . مفاوَضَةٌ

Consume *v. t.* or *i.* أتلفَ . أباد . فَنِيَ ـ

Consumer *n.* آكلٌ . مُستعمِلٌ . نافِذٌ

Consummate *a.* تامٌّ . مُكمَّلٌ

Consummate *v. t.* كمَّلَ . تمَّمَ

Consummation *n.* إتمامٌ . إنجازٌ

Consumption *n.* إتلافٌ . داءُ السُّلِّ

Consumptive *a.* مُصابٌ بالسُّلِّ

Contact *n.* مُمَاسَّة . مُلامَسَة

Contagion *n.* عَدْوَى مِنَ المُماسةِ

Contagious *a.* مُعْدٍ بمُمَاسَّةٍ

Contain *v. t.* وَسِعَ ـ . إحتَوَى

Contaminate *v. t.* أفسَدَ . دَنَّسَ

Contamination *n.* إفسَاد . تنجيسٌ

Contemn *v. t.* أهَانَ . كرِهَ ـ

Contemplate *v. t.* or *i.* تأمَّلَ . قَصَدَ ـ

Contemplation *n.* تأمُّلٌ

Contemplative *a.* مُتَفَكِّرٌ

Contemporaneous *a.* مُعاصِرٌ

Contempt *n.* إهَانَةٌ . إحتِقارٌ

Contemptible *a.* مُحتَقَرٌ . دَنِيءٌ

Contemptuous *a.* مُحتقِرٌ . مُهِينٌ

Contend *v. t.* نَازَعَ . حَاجَّ . قَاوَمَ

Content *v. t.* أرضَى . أقنَعَ

Content *n.* المضْمُوْنُ . فَحْوَى

Content / Contented *n.* رَاضٍ. مُكْتَفٍ. قَانِعٌ

Contention *n.* مُنَازَعَةٌ . مشاجَرَةٌ

Contentious *a.* مشَاجِرٌ . خصومٌ

Contentment *n.* قناعَةٌ . رِضَى

Contest *n.* مُجَاهَدَةٌ . مقاوَمَةٌ

Contest *v. t.* نازَعَ . قَاوَمَ . نَاظَرَ

Contstant *n.* مقاوِمٌ . مُناظِرٌ

Conterminous *a.* مُتَاخِمٌ . مُجَاوِرٌ

Context *n.* قَرِيْنَةٌ. سِيَاقُ ٱلْكَلامِ

Contiguity *n.* مُمَاسَّةٌ . قربٌ

Contiguous *a.* مُمَاسٌّ . مُتَّصِلٌ ب

Continence / Continency *n.* عِفَّةٌ . إِمْسَاكٌ

Continent *a.* or *n.* عفيفٌ . قَارَّةٌ

Continental *a.* مُخْتَصٌّ بِقَارَّةٍ

Contingence / Contingency *n.* حَادِثَةٌ عَرَضِيَّةٌ

Contingent *a.* or *n.* عَرَضِيٌّ. مشْرُوْطٌ. عَارِضٌ

Contingently *ad.* عَرَضاً . إِتِّفَاقاً

Continual *a.* دَائِمٌ . مُسْتَمِرٌّ

Continuance *n.* دَوَامٌ . بقَاءٌ

Continuation *n.* تَتَابُعٌ . تَوَالٍ

Continue *v. i.* or *t.* دَامَ ـُ . دَاوَمَ

Continuity *a.* مُوَاصلةٌ . إِتِّصَالٌ

Continuous *a.* مُتَّصِلٌ . دائِمٌ

Contortion *n.* إِعْوِجَاجٌ . تفتُّلٌ

Contort *v. t.* فَتَلَ ـ . لوَى ـ

Contour *a.* صُوْرَةُ حُدُوْدِ ٱلشَّيْءِ

Contraband *a.* مَمْنُوْعٌ شَرْعاً

Contract *n.* عقدٌ. شَرْطٌ . إِتِّفاقٌ

Contract *v. t.* or *i.* قلَّصَ . شارَطَ . تقبَّضَ

Contracted *a.* متقَلِّصٌ مُنقبِضٌ ضَيِّقٌ

Contractible *a.* قَابِلُ ٱلتَّقَلُّصِ

Contraction *n.* تقَلُّصٌ . إِنْقِبَاضٌ

Contractor *n.* مُشَارِطٌ . مُعَاقِدٌ. مقاوِلٌ

Contradict *v. t.* نَاقَضَ . ضَادَّ . نَافَى

Contradiction *n.* مُناقَضَةٌ . تَناقُضٌ

Contradictory *a.* مُتَنَاقِضٌ

Contrariety *n.* مُعَاكسة . مغايرَةٌ

Contraries *n. pl.* اضْدَادٌ

Contrary *n.* مُضَادٌّ . ضِدٌّ . مُخالفٌ

Contrast *n.* or *v. t.* or *i.* تبَايُنٌ . قابَلَ . مَيَّزَ بَيْنَ

Contravene *v. t.* خَالفَ . عَارَضَ

Contravention *n.* مُخالفَةٌ . مُعَارَضة

Contribute *v. t.* وَهَبَ ـ . أَعْطَى

Contribution *n.* هبَة . إِعْطَآء

Contributive *a.* آئِلٌ إِلى . مُفيدٌ

Contributor *n.* مُعْطٍ

Contrite *a.* مُنْكَسِرُ ٱلْقَلْبِ . مُتَخَشِّعٌ

Contrition *n.* إِنْكِسَارُ ٱلْقَلْبِ . تَخَشُّعٌ

Contrivance *n.* حِيلَة . تدْبيرٌ

Contrive *v. t.* دَبَّرَ . إِبْتَدَعَ

Control *n.* or *v. t.* سُلْطَةٌ . ادَارَ . سَادَ

Controllable *a.* مُمكِنٌ إِدَارَتُهُ

Controller *n.* مُدِيرٌ . مُرَاقِبٌ

Controversial *a.* جَدَلِيٌّ

Controversy *n.* جدَالٌ . مُناظَرَة

Controvert *v. t.* خاصَمَ . جادَلَ

Controvertible *n.* ممكِنٌ مُقَاوَمَتهُ

Contumacious *a.* عَنِيدٌ . مَارِدٌ

Contumacy *n.* عِنادٌ

Contumelious *a.* مهِين . عَاتٍ . شَاتِمٌ

Contumely *n.* شتِيمَةٌ . إِهَانَة

Contusion *n.* رَضٌّ . رَضَّة

Conundrum *n.* ضَرْبٌ مِنَ ٱللُّغْزِ

Convalescense *n.* نَقَهٌ . تعَافٍ

Convalescent *a.* نَاقهٌ . مُتَعَافٍ

Convene *v. t.* or *i.* جَمَعَ ـ . إِلْتَأَمَ

Convenience *n.* مُوَافقَةٌ . رَاحة

Convenient *a.* مُوَافِق . مُلاَئِمٌ . مُرِيح

Conveniently *ad.* بِسهُولَةٍ . بِرَاحةٍ

Convent *n.* دَيْرٌ ج أَدْيِرَة

Conventicle *n.* إِجتِمَاعٌ دِينِيٌّ

Convention *n.* مَجْمَعٌ . مُؤْتَمَرٌ . مُعَاهَدَة

Conventional *a.* إِصْطِلَاحِيٌّ . إِعْتِيَادِيٌّ

Converge *v. i.* إِتَّجَهَ إِلَى مَرْكَزٍ

Convergence *n.* إِتِّجَاهٌ إِلَى مَرْكَزٍ

Convergent / **Converging** *a.* مُتَقَارِبٌ . مُتَّجِهٌ إِلَى مَرْكَزٍ

Conversant *a.* عَارِفٌ . خَبِيرٌ

Conversation *n.* مُفَاوَضَةٌ . حَدِيث

Conversational *a.* مُخْتَصٌّ بِٱلْحَدِيثِ

Converse *v. i.* تَفَاوَضَ . تَحَادَث

Converse *n.* or *a.* عَكْسٌ . مَعْكُوسٌ

Conversly *ad.* بِٱلْعَكْسِ

Conversion *n.* تَحْوِيلٌ . تَوْبَة

Convert *v. t.* حَوَّلَ . بَدَّلَ . هَدَى

Convert *n.* مُهْتَدٍ إِلَى دِينٍ

Convertible *a.* قَابِلُ ٱلتَّبْدِيل

Convex *a.* مُحَدَّبٌ

Convexity *n.* تَحَدُّبٌ

Convey *v. t.* نَقَلَ . حَمَلَ ـِ

Conveyance *n.* نَقْلٌ . مَرْكَبَةٌ

Convict *v.* t. or *n.* أَثْبَتَ ذَنْبَهُ . مُذْنِبٌ

Conviction *n.* إِثْبَاتَ ٱلذَّنبِ . يَقِين

Convince *v. t.* اَقْنَعَ

Convivial *a.* مُبْهِجٌ . قَصُوفِيٌّ

Conviviality *n.* إِنْشِرَاحٌ . قُصُوفٌ

Convocation *n.* جَمْعٌ . مَجْمَعٌ

Convoke *v. t.* إِستَدْعَى . جَمَعَ ـَ

Convolute / **Convoluted** *a.* مُلْتَفٌّ

Convolution *n.* لَفٌّ . إِلْتِفَافٌ

Convoy *v. t.* or *n.* خَفَرَ ـُ . خَفَرٌ

Convulse *v. t.* شَنَّجَ . رَجَّ ـُ

Convulsive *a.* مُشَنَّجٌ

Cony *n.* وَبْرٌ ج وُبُورٌ

Coo *v. i.* هَدَرَ . سَجَعَ ـُ

Cook *v. t.* or *n.* طَبَخَ ـَ . طَبَّاخٌ (عَشِّيٌّ)

Cookery *n.* صِنَاعَةُ ٱلطَّبْخ

Cool *a.* بَارِدٌ . مُعْتَدِلُ ٱلْبُرُودَةِ

Cool *v. t.* or *i.* بَرَّدَ . هَدَّأَ . بَرَدَ ـُ

Cooler *n.* بَرَّادَةٌ . مُبَرِّدٌ

Coolly *ad.* بِهُدُوءٍ . بِضَبْطِ ٱلنفسِ

Coolness *n.* بُرُودَةٌ . رِبَاطَةُ جَأْشٍ

Coop *n.* or *v. t.* قَفَصٌ . حَبَسَ في قَفَصٍ

Cooper *n.* صَانِعُ بَرَامِيلَ

Co-operate *v. i.* تَعَاوَنَ . تَشَارَكَ

Co-operative *a.* مُشْتَرِكٌ في عَمَلٍ

Co-ordinate *a.* مُتَسَاوِي ٱلرُّتْبَةِ

Co-partner *n.* شَرِيك ج شُرَكَاءُ

Co-partnership *n.* شِرْكَة

Cope *v.i.* بَارَى . سَابَقَ . نَاظَرَ

Copious *a.* وَافِرٌ . غَزِيرٌ

Copper *n.* نُحَاسٌ احْمَرُ

Copperas *n.* زَاجٌ

Copper-smith *n.* نَحَّاسٌ

Copse *n.* غَابَةُ اشْجَارٍ صغِيرَةٍ . دَغَلٌ

Copt *n.* / Coptic *a.* قُبْطِي

Copula *n.* رَابِط . صلة

Copulate *v. t.* or *i.* جَامَعَ

Coping *n.* إِفْرِيز . سَقِيفَةُ حائطٍ

Copy *n.* or *v. t.* نُسْخَةٌ . نَسَخَ ـَ

Copyer / Copyist *n.* نَاسِخ

Copyright *n.* حقُّ طبْعِ كِتَاب

Coquet *v. i.* غَنِجَ ـَ

Coquetry *n.* غُنْجٌ ـ غُنَاجٌ

Coquette *n.* غَنِيجَةٌ . (غَنوجة)

Coquettish *a.* غَانِجٌ . غَنِجٌ

Coral *n.* or *a.* مَرْجَانٌ . مَرْجَانِيٌّ

Cord *n.* or *v. t.* مَرَسٌ . شدَّ بمَرَسٍ

Cordage *n.* حِبَالُ ٱلسَّفِينَةِ

Cordate *a.* قَلْبِيُّ ٱلشَّكْلِ

Cordial *v.* or *n.* قَلْبِيٌّ . مُخْلِصٌ . / شَرَابٌ مُنْعِشٌ

Cordiality *n.* وُدٌّ . إِخْلَاصٌ

Cordon *n.* نطَاقٌ مِنَ الْجُنْد

Core *n.* قَلْبٌ . لُبٌّ

Coriander *n.* كُزْبَرَةٌ

Cork *n.* or *v. t.* (فَلّينٌ) .سَدَّادةٌ. سَدَّ بِهَا

Corky *a.* (فَلّينِيٌّ)

Cork-screw *n.* بِيرَمٌ . (بَرِّيمَةٌ)

Corn *n.* حبٌّ . ذُرَةٌ . مِسْمَارٌ

Cornea *n.* قَرْنية ٱلْعَيْنِ

Cornelian *n.* عقيقٌ

Corner *n.* زَاوِيَةٌ . قُرْنَةٌ

Corner-stone *n.* حجَرُ ٱلزَّاوِيَةِ

Cornet *n.* صُورٌ . نَفِيرٌ

Cornice *n.* إِفْرِيزٌ . طُنُفٌ

Corolla *n.* تُوَيْجُ زَهْرَةٍ

Corollary *n.* تابِعَةٌ . نتِيجةٌ

Coronation *n.* تَتْوِيجٌ

Coroner *n.* مَأْمُورٌ يفحُصُ سَبَبَ مَوْتٍ فُجائِيٍّ

Coronet *n.* تاجُ ٱلاشْرَاف.إِكْلِيل

Corporal *a.* or *n.* جَسَدِيٌّ . (أُونْبَاشِي)

Corporation *n.* شِرْكَةٌ

Corporeal *a.* ذو جَسَدٍ . جَسَدَانِيٌّ

Corps *n.* فَيْلَقُ عسْكَرٍ . جَمَاعَةٌ

Corpse *n.* جُثَّةُ ٱلْمَيْتِ

Corpulence, Corpulency *n.* سَمَانَةٌ . جَسَامَةٌ

Corpulent *a.* سمينٌ . جَسِيمٌ

Corpuscle *n.* ذرَّةٌ . جُسَيْمٌ

Correct *v. t.* اصْلَحَ . نقَّحَ . ادَّبَ

Correct *a.* صَحِيحٌ . مَضْبُوط

Correction *n.* إِصْلاَحٌ.تنْقِيحٌ تَأْدِيبٌ

Corrective *a.* مُصْلِحٌ . تَأْدِيبِيٌّ

Correctly *ad.* بِضَبْطٍ . تَمَاماً

Correctness *n.* ضَبْط . مُطَابَقَةٌ لِلْحقِّ

Correlate *v.t.* or *i.* نَاسَبَ . تَنَاسَبَ

Correlation *n.* نِسْبَةٌ . مُنَاسَبَة

Correlation *n.* نِسْبَةٌ مُتَبَادلَة

Correlative *a.* or *n.* } نِسْبِيٌّ مُتَبَادَلٌ . ذُوْ نِسْبَةٍ مُتَبَادَلَةٍ

Correspond *v. i.* طَابَقَ . رَاسَلَ

Correspondence *n.* مُرَاسَلَةٌ . مُنَاسَبَةٌ

Correspondent *n.* or *a.* مُرَاسِلٌ . مُنَاسِبٌ

Corridor *n.* رِوَاق . أَرْوِقَة

Corroborate *v. t.* شَدَّدَ . اثْبَتَ . أَيَّدَ

Corroboration *n.* إِثْبَاتٌ . تَأْيِيْدٌ

Corrode *v. i.* or *t.* صَدِئَ . قرض ـ

Corrodent / Corrosive } *a.* آكِلٌ . قَارِضٌ

Corrosion *n.* صَدَأٌ . قَرْضٌ

Corrugation *n.* تَجَعُّدٌ

Corrupt *v. t.* or *a.* } افْسَدَ . نَجَّس . فَاسِدٌ

Corruptible *a.* فَاسِدٌ . فَانٍ

Corruption *n.* فَسَادٌ . نَجَاسَةٌ

Corruptive *a.* مُفْسِدٌ . مُنَجِّسٌ

Corruptness *n.* فَسَادٌ

Corsair *n.* قُرْصَانُ ٱلْبَحْرِ

Corselet *n.* زَرْدِيَّةٌ . دِرْعٌ

Corset *n.* مَشَدٌّ لِلنِّسَاءِ

Cortege *n.* مَوْكِبٌ

Coruscate *v. i.* بَرَقَ . لَمَعَ ـ

Corvée *n.* سُخْرَةٌ

Corvette *n.* بَارِجَةٌ صَغِيرَةٌ

Cosmetic *a.* or *n.* } مُحَسِّنٌ لِلَوْنِ ٱلْوَجْهِ

Cosmogony *n.* عِلْمُ تَكْوِينِ ٱلْكَوْنِ

Cosmography *n.* عِلْمُ وَصْفِ ٱلْكَوْنِ

Cosmology *n.* عِلْمٌ يَبْحَثُ عَنِ ٱلْكَوْنِ

Cosmopolitan *n.* رَجُلٌ وَطَنُهُ ٱلْعَالَمِ

Cost *n.* or *v. t.* or *i.* قِيمَةٌ . سِعْرٌ . كَلَّفَ

Costal *a.* ضِلْعِيٌّ

Costive *a.* قَابِضُ ٱلامْعَاءِ

Costiveness *n.* قَبْضُ ٱلامْعَاءِ

Costliness *n.* غَلاَءٌ

Costly *a.* غَالٍ

Costume *n.* زِيٌّ ج أَزْيَاءٌ

Cot *n.* كُوخ . فِرَاشٌ صَغِيرٌ

Cote *n.* حَظِيرَةٌ . صِيرَةٌ

Coterie *n.* جَمَاعَةُ اصْحَابٍ

Cotemporaneous *a.*
Cotemporary *n.* } مُعَاصِرٌ

Cottage *n.* كُوخ . بَيْتٌ صَغِيرٌ

Cottager *n.* سَاكِنُ كُوخٍ

Cotton *n.* or *a.* قُطْنٌ . قُطْنِيٌّ

Cotton-gin *n.* مَحْلَجُ ٱلْقُطْنِ

Cotyledon *n.* فِلْقَةُ بِزْرَةٍ

Couch *v. i.* or *t.* { إِضْطَجَعَ . كَمَنَ . أَضْجَعَ

Couch *n.* فِرَاشٌ

Cough *v. i.* or *n.* سَعَلَ ـُ سُعَالٌ

Council *n.* مَجْلِسُ ٱلشُّوْرَى

Councillor *n.* عَضْوُ مَجْلِسٍ . مُشِيرٌ

Counsel *n.* or *v. t.* نَصِيحَةٌ . نَصَحَ

Counsellor *n.* نَاصِحٌ . مُشِيرٌ . فَقِيهٌ

Count *v. t.* or *n.* عَدَّ . احْصَى . امِيرٌ

Countenance *n.* مُحَيَّا . طَلْعَةٌ

Countenance *v. t.* عَضَدَ ـُ

Counter *n.* or *ad.* } مَائِدَةٌ مَخْزَنٍ . ضِدٌّ

Counteract *v. t.* ضَادَّ . خَيَّبَ

Counteraction *n.* مُضَادَّةٌ . إِبْطَالٌ

Counterbalance *n.* or *v. t.* } مُوَازَنَة . وَازَنَ . عَادَلَ

Counterfeit *a.* or *n.* or *v. t.* } مُزَوَّرٌ . زَوَّرَ

Countermand *n.* or *v. t.* } أَمْرٌ يُبْطِلُ امْرًا . أَلْغَى

Countermarch *v. i.* or *n.* } قَهْقَرَ . قَهْقَرَى

Counterpane *n.* لِحَافُ فِرَاشٍ

Counterpart *n.* قِسْمٌ مُقَابِلَ قِسْمٍ

Counterplot *n.* حِيلَةٌ ضِدَّ حِيلَةٍ

Counterpoise *n.* or *v. t.* } ثِقْلٌ . مُوَازِنٌ . وَازَنَ

Countersign *n.* كَلِمَةُ سِرِّ ٱللَّيْلِ

Countersign *v. t.* { امْضَى إِثْبَاتًا لِإِمْضَاءٍ

Countess *n.* امِيرَةٌ

Counting-house *n.* مَكْتَبُ ٱلتَّاجِرِ

Countless *a.* مَا لا يُحْصَى

Country *n.* بِلَاد . بَرِّيَّة

Countryman *n.* إِبْنُ بِلَادٍ . فلاحٌ

County *n.* لِوَاءٌ مِنْ بِلادٍ

Couple *n.* or *v. t.* زَوْجٌ . إِثْنَانِ . وَصَلَ

Couplet *n.* بَيْتَا شِعْرٍ

Coupling *n.* رَابِطٌ . مُوْصِلٌ . وَصْلٌ

Courage *n.* شَجَاعَة . بَسَالَةٌ

Courageous *a.* شُجَاعٌ . بَاسِلٌ

Courier *n.* رَسُوْلٌ . بَرِيْدٌ

Course *n.* سَيْرٌ . طَرِيقٌ . نَاحِيَةٌ

Courser *n.* فَرَسٌ سَرِيعٌ

Court *n.* or *v. t.* دَارٌ . مَحْكَمَةٌ . تَملق

Courteous *a.* انِيْسٌ . ادِيْبٌ

Courtesan *n.* زَانِيَةٌ . فاجِرَةٌ

Courtesy *n.* انسٌ . ادَبٌ . إِنْسَانِيَةٌ

Courtier *n.* مُلازِمُ بِلَاطِ الْمَلِك

Courtliness *n.* ادَبٌ . لُطْفٌ مَعَ شَرَفٍ

Courtly *a.* ادِيْبٌ . شَرِيْفٌ

Court-martial *n.* محكمة عسكرِيَّة

Court-plaster *n.* لُزُوْقٌ مِنْ حَرِيْرٍ

Courtship *n.* تَمَلُّقٌ

Courtyard *n.* حَوْشٌ . دَارٌ

Cousin *n.* إِبْنُ عَمٍّ اوْ عَمَّةٍ اوْ خَالٍ أَوْ خَالَةٍ اوْ إِبْنَتُهُمْ

Cove *n.* خَلِيْجٌ صَغِيْرٌ . خَوْرٌ

Covenant *n.* or *v. t.* عَهْدٌ . عَاهَدَ

Cover *v. t.* or *n.* سَتَرَ . غَطَّى . غِطَاءٌ

Covering *n.* غِطَاءٌ . سِتْرٌ

Coverlet *n.* لِحَافٌ . دِثَارٌ

Covert *n.* or *a.* مَأْوًى . مَسْتُوْرٌ . سِرِّيٌّ

Covertly *ad.* سِرًّا . خُفْيَةً

Covet *v. t.* إِشْتَهَى . طَمِعَ فِي ـ

Covetous *a.* مُشْتَهٍ . طَمَّاعٌ

Covetousness *n.* شَهْوَةٌ . طَمَعٌ

Covey *n.* سِرْبٌ مِنْ (طُيُوْرٍ)

Cow *n.* بَقَرَةٌ

Coward *n.* جَبَانٌ ج جُبَنَاء

Cowardice *n.* جَبَانَة . جُبْن

Cowardly *a.* or *ad.* جَبَانٌ . بِجَبَانَةٍ

Cower *v. i.* خَرَّ أَوْ تَرَدَّدَ مِنَ ٱلْخَوْفِ

Cowherd *n.* رَاعِي بَقَرٍ

Cowhide *n.* جِلْدُ بَقَرٍ أَوْ سَوطٌ مِنْهُ

Cowl *n.* قَلَنسُوَةٌ ج قَلَانِسُ

Coxcomb *n.* مُعْجَبٌ . مُتَحَذْلِقٌ . بِٱلتَّعَانِي

Cowpox *n.* جُدَرِيُّ ٱلْبَقَرِ

Coy *a.* مُتَصَاوِنٌ . مُعْتَزِلٌ عَنِ ٱلْمُعَاشَرَةِ

Cozen *v. t.* خَدَعَ ـَ . غَشَّ

Cozy *a.* مُسْتَرِيحٌ

Crab *n.* سَرَطَانٌ

Crabbed *a.* خَشِنُ ٱلْجَانِبِ . فَظٌّ

Crack *n.* or *v. t.* or *i.* شَقٌّ . شَقَّ . تَشَقَّقَ (طَقَّ)

Cracker *n.* كَعْكٌ يَابِسٌ . بَقْسُمَاط

Crackle *v. i.* (قَرْقَعَ . طَقْطَقَ)

Cradle *n.* or *v. t.* سَرِيرٌ . وَضَعَ فِي سَرِيرٍ

Craft *n.* حِرْفَة سَفِينَةٌ صَغِيرَة

Craft, Craftiness *n.* دَهَاءٌ . مَكْرٌ

Craftsman *n.* صَانِعٌ . مُحْتَرِفٌ

Crafty *a.* دَاهٍ . مُحْتَالٌ

Crag *n.* صَخْرٌ شاهِقٌ . غَلِيظ

Cragged, Craggy *a.* صَخْرِيٌّ . غَلِيظ

Cram *v. t.* or *i.* حَشَا ـُ أَفْعَمَ

Cramp *n.* or *v. t.* كُزَازٌ . كُلَّابٌ ضَيَّقَ عَلَى . اعَاقَ

Crane *n.* كُرْكِيٌّ . آلَة لِرَفْعِ ٱلْأَثْقَالِ

Cranial *a.* قِحْفِيٌّ

Cranium *n.* جُمْجُمَة . قِحْفٌ

Crank *n.* يَدُ دُولَابٍ أَوْ آلَةُ ٱلتَّدْوِيرِ

Crape *n.* (كُرَيْشَة) . نَسِيجٌ

Crash *v.i.* or *n.* صَوَّتَ صَوْتُ كَسْرٍ

Crass *a.* خَشِنٌ . غَلِيظ

Crate *n.* قَفَصٌ لِنَقْلِ صُحُون فَخَارِيةٍ

Crater *n.* فُوهَةُ بُرْكَان

Craunch *v. t.* مَضغ ـ . سَحَق بِالاسْنَان

Cravat *n.* رَبْطَةُ رَقَبَةٍ

Crave *v. t.* إِشْتَهَى . إِشْتَاق . طَلَب

Craven *a.* or *n.* جَبَانٌ . نَذْلٌ

Craving *n.* تَلَهُّفٌ . إِشْتِهَاءٌ

Crawl *v. i.* دَبَّ ـِ . زَحَفَ ـَ

Crayon *n.* or *v. t.* قَلَمُ رَصَاصٍ . رَسَمَ به

Craze *v. t.* جَنَّنَ

Craziness *n.* جُنُونٌ . إِخْتِلَالُ ٱلْعَقْلِ

Crazy *a.* مَجْنُونٌ . مُخْتَلُّ ٱلْعَقْلِ

Creak *v. i.* صَرَف ـِ صَرِيفًا

Cream *n.* زُبْدَةُ ٱللَّبَنِ . قِشْدَة

Crease *v. t.* or *n.* غَضَّنَ . غَضْنٌ

Create *v. t.* خَلَقَ ـُ . بَرَأَ ـ ابدَع

Creation *n.* خَلْقٌ خَلِيقَةٌ . بَرِيَّةٌ

Creative *a.* خَالِقٌ . مُبْدِعٌ

Creator *n.* خَالِق . أَلْبَارِئُ

Creature *n.* خَلِيقَة . مَخْلُوقٌ . برِية

Credence *n.* ثِقَةٌ . تَصْدِيقٌ

Credentials *pl.* شَهَادَاتٌ رَسْمِيَّةٌ

Credibility *n.* إِسْتِحْقَاقُ ٱلتَّصْدِيقِ

Credible *a.* مُسْتَحَقٌّ ٱلتَّصْدِيقِ

Credit *n.* or *v. t.* ثِقَةٌ . امَّنَ

Creditable *a.* مَوْثُوق بِهِ . مُعْتَبَرٌ

Creditor *n.* دَائِنٌ . صَاحِبُ دَيْنٍ

Credulity *n.* سُهُولَةُ ٱلتَّصْدِيقِ

Credulous *a.* سَهْلُ ٱلتَّصْدِيقِ

Creed *n.* مَذْهَبٌ . قَانُون ٱلإِيمَانِ

Creek *n.* جُون . نَهْرٌ صَغِيرٌ

Creep *v. i.* دبَّ ـِ . زَحَفَ ـَ

Creeper *n.* نَبْتٌ مُتَعَرِّشٌ او مُتَسَلِّق

Cremation *n.* حَرْق . حَرْقُ ٱلْجُثَّةِ

Crescent *n.* هِلَالٌ

Cress *n.* رَشَادٌ . قُرَّةُ ٱلْعَيْنِ

Crest *n.* قُنْبُرَة . قِمَّة

Crest-fallen *a.* مُنْحَط . ذَلِيلٌ

Cretacious *a.* طَبَاشِيرِيٌّ

Crevice *n.* شَقٌّ ج شقوق

Crew *n.* مَلاَّحُو ٱلسَّفِينَةِ . جَمَاعَةٌ

Crib *n.* مِذْوَدٌ. مَهْدٌ

Cricket *n.* صُرْصُرٌ

Crier *n.* مُنَادٍ . مُؤَذِّنٌ

Crime *n.* جَرِيمَةٌ . جِنَايَةٌ. جُنَاحٌ

Criminal *n.* or *a.* مُذْنِبٌ . جِنَائِيٌّ

Criminality *n.* جِنَائِيَّةٌ .ذَنْبِيَّةٌ

Criminate *v. t.* إِسْتَذْنَبَ . جَنَّحَ

Crimination *n.* إِسْتِذْنَابٌ . تَجْنِيحٌ

Crimp *v. t.* or *a.* جَعَّدَ . قَصِمٌ

Crimson *n.* or *a.* قِرْمِزٌ . قِرْمِزِيٌّ

Cringe *v. i.* تَذَلَّلَ لِ

Cringer / Cringeling } *n.* مُتَذَلِّلٌ

Cripple *n.* or *v. t.* كَسِيحٌ . صَيَّرَ كَسِيحاً

Crisis *n.* بُحْرَانٌ . نُقْطَةُ ٱلْخَطَرِ وَٱلتَّغَيُّرِ . أَزْمَةٌ

Crisp *a.* قَصِمٌ . مُجَعَّدٌ

Criterion *n.* دَلِيلٌ . مِقْيَاسٌ

Critic *n.* مُنْتَقِدٌ . مُنَكِّتٌ

Critical *a.* إِنْتِقَادِيٌّ .مُدَقِّقٌ . مُخْطِرٌ

Criticise *v. t.* إِنْتَقَدَ . نَكَّتَ

Criticism / Critique } *n.* إِنْتِقَادٌ. تَنْكِيتٌ

Croak *v. i.* or *n.* نَعَقَ ـَ . نَعِيقٌ

Croaker *n.* نَاعِقٌ . مُتَذَمِّرٌ

Crockery *n.* خَزَفٌ . فَخَّارٌ

Crocodile *n.* تِمْسَاحٌ

Crocus *n.* زَعْفَرَانٌ

Crony *n.* خِلٌّ . نَدِيمٌ

Crook *v. t.* or *n.* عَقَفَ ـِ . عَصَا ٱلرَّاعِي

Crooked *a.* أَعْقَفُ . مُلْتَوٍ

Crookedness *n.* إِعْوِجَاجٌ . إِنْعِقَافٌ

Crop *n.* غَلَّةٌ . حَوْصَلَةٌ

Crosier *n.* عُكَّازُ ٱلأُسْقُفِ

Cross *n.* or *a.* صَلِيبٌ. نَكِدٌ

Cross *v. t.* or *i.* عَبَرَ ـُ عَارَضَ

Cross-bow *n.* قَوْسُ ٱلسِّهَامِ

Cross-eyed *a.* أَحْوَلُ

Crossing *n.* مَعبَرٌ . عُبُورٌ

Crossgrained *a.* شَابِكٌ . نَكِدٌ

Crosslegged *a.* مُتَرَبِّعٌ

Cross-purpose *n.* قَصْدٌ مُتَضَادٌّ

Cross-question *v. t.* إِسْتَنطَقَ . حقَّقَ

Cross-road *n.* مُصلَّبُ ٱلطُّرُقِ

Crosswise *ad.* عَرْضاً

Crotch *n.* مَفْرَقُ أَغْصَانٍ

Crotchet *n.* وَهْمٌ . تَصَوُّرٌ بَاطِلٌ

Crouch *v. i.* رَبَضَ . جَثَا ـُ

Croup *n.* دَآءُ ٱلذَّبْحَةِ

Crow *n.* or *v. i.* غُرَابٌ . صَاحَ (ٱلدِّيكُ)

Crow-bar *n.* مُخْلٌ ج أَمْخَالٌ

Crowd *n.* or *v. t.* زَحْمَةٌ . زَاحَمَ

Crown *n.* or *v. t.* تَاجٌ . تَوَّجَ

Crown-prince *n.* وَلِيُّ ٱلْعَهْدِ

Crucial *a.* صَلِيبِيٌّ . شَدِيدٌ . حَتْمِيٌّ

Crucible *n.* بُوْتَقَةٌ

Crucifix *n.* صَلِيبٌ عَلَيْهِ صُوْرَةُ ٱلمَسِيحِ

Crucifixion *n.* صَلْبٌ

Cruciform *a.* صَلِيبِيُّ ٱلشَّكْلِ

Crucify *v. t.* صَلَبَ ـِ

Crude *a.* نِيٌّ . غَيْرُ مُتْقَنٍ

Crudity, Crudeness *n.* عَدَمُ إِتْقَانٍ . فَجَاجَة

Cruel *a.* قَاسٍ . صَارِمٌ

Cruelty *n.* قَسَاوَةٌ . صَرَامَةٌ

Cruet *n.* قَارُوْرَةٌ

Cruise *n.* or *v. i.* طَافَ ـُ . طَوَافٌ بَحْراً

Cruiser *n.* بَارِجَةٌ طَوَّافَةٌ أَوْ سَرِيعَة

Crum, Crumb *n.* كِسْرَةٌ صَغِيرَةٌ

Crumble *v. t.* or *i.* فَتَّتَ . تَفَتَّتَ

Crumple *v. t.* or *i.* غَضَّنَ تَغَضَّنَ

Crupper *n.* (قُوشٌ) . (اصاَلٌ)

Crusade *n.* حَرْبُ ٱلصَّلِيبِيَّةِ . جِهَادٌ

Crusader *n.* مُحَارِبٌ صَلِيبِيٌّ

Crush *v. t.* سَحَقَ . حَطَّمَ . اذَلَّ

Crust *n.* or *v. t.* قِشْرٌ . لَبَّسَ بِقِشْرٍ

Crustacious *a.* ذُو قِشْرٍ أَوْصَدَفَةٍ

Crusty *a.* فَظٌّ . شَرِسٌ . قِشْرِيٌّ

Crutch *n.* عُكَّازٌ

Cry *v. i.* or *n.* صَرَخَ ـُ . بَكَى ـِ . صُرَاخ

Crying *a.* صَارِخٌ . مَشْهُورٌ . عَظِيمٌ

Crypt *n.* مُخْدَعٌ تَحْتَ ٱلأَرْضِ

Crystal *n.* بَلُّوْرٌ وَبِلَّوْرٌ

Crystalline *a.* بَلُّوْرِيٌّ . شَفَّافٌ

Crystallize *v. i.* or *t.* تَبَلْوَرَ . بِلْوَرَ

Cub *n.* جَرْوٌ . شِبْلٌ

Cube *n.* or *v. t.* كَعْبٌ . مُكَعَّبٌ . كَعَّبَ

Cubic / Cubiform } *a.* مُكَعَّبُ ٱلشَّكْلِ

Cubit *n.* ذِرَاعٌ ج أَذْرُعٌ

Cucumber *n.* خِيَارٌ . قِثَّآءٌ

Cud *n.* جِرَّةٌ

Cuddle *v. i.* or *t.* إِسْتَكَنَّ عِنْدَ . حَضَنَ

Cudgel *n.* نَبُّوتٌ . هِرَاوَةٌ

Cue *n.* ذَيْلٌ . إِشَارَةٌ . تَلْمِيحٌ

Cuff *n.* or *v. t.* كُمُّ ٱلْقَمِيصِ . لَطَمَ ـِ

Cuirass *n.* دِرْعٌ ج ادْرَاعٌ وَدُرُوْعٌ

Cuirassier *n.* لَابِسُ دِرْعٍ . مُدَرَّعٌ

Culinary *a.* طَبْخِيٌّ

Cull *v. t.* نَخَبَ ـُ . إِنْتَخَبَ

Cullender *n.* مِصْفَاةٌ

Culminate *v. i.* بَلَغَ اعْلاهُ

Culmination *n.* غَايَةُ ٱلْبُلُوْغِ

Culpable *a.* مَلُوْمٌ . مُخْطِئٌ

Culpability *n.* ذَنْبٌ . إِسْتِحْقَاقُ ٱللَّوْمِ

Culprit *n.* مُذْنِبٌ

Cultivable *a.* قَابِلُ ٱلْحِرَاثَةِ

Cultivate *v. t.* حَرَثَ ـُ . هَذَّبَ

Cultivation / Culture } *n.* حِرَاثَةٌ . تَهْذِيبٌ

Cumber *v. t.* ثَقَّلَ . أعاقَ . لَبَّكَ

Cumbersome / Cumbrous } *a.* ثَقِيلٌ . مُلَبِّكٌ

Cumulate *v. t.* رَكَمَ ـُ كَوَّمَ

Cumulative *a.* مُتَجَمِّعٌ . مُتَزَايِدٌ

Cuneiform / Cuniform } *a.* إِسْفِينِيُّ ٱلشَّكْلِ

Cunning *a.* or *n.* دَاهٍ. دَاهِيَة. دَهَاءٌ

Cup *n.* or *v. t.* كَاسٌ. فِنْجَان. حَجَمَ ـُ

Cupbearer *n.* سَاقٍ . سَاقِي مَلِكٍ

Cupboard *n.* (خِزَانَةٌ) (دُولاَبٌ)

Cupidity *n.* طَمَعٌ . جَشَعٌ

Cupola *n.* قُبَّةٌ

Cur *n.* كَلْبٌ . شَاكِسٌ . فَظٌّ

Curable *a.* قَابِلُ ٱلشِّفَاءِ

Curacy *n.* مَقَامُ قَسِّيسٍ أَوْ خُورِيّ

Curate *n.* قَسِّيسٌ . خُورِيٌّ

Curative *a.* شَافٍ

Curator *n.* وَكِيلٌ . حافِظ

Curb *n.* or *v. t.* شَكِيمَة . صَدٌّ . كَبَحَ ـَ

Curd *n.* رَوْبٌ . خَثْرَة . لَبَنٌ رَائِبٌ

Curdle *v. i.* or *t.* خَثَرَ . خَثَّرَ

Cure *v. t.* or *n.* شَفَى . شِفَاءٌ

Curiosity *n.* إِسْتِطْلاَعٌ . نَادِرَة

Curious *a.* مُسْتَطْلِعٌ . نَادِرٌ

Curl *n.* or *v. t.* or *i.* جُعْدَة . جَعَّدَ . تَجَعَّدَ

Curly *a.* مُتَجَعِّدٌ . جُعْدِيٌّ

Currants *n. pl.* عِنَبُ ٱلثعلَبِ. كِشْمِشٌ

Currency *n.* مُعَامَلَة. نُقُودٌ . جرَيَانٌ

Current *a.* or *n.* جَارٍ . مَجْرًى

Currier *n.* مُصْلِحُ جُلُودٍ مَدْبُوغَةٍ

Curry *v. t.* اصْلَحَ (جُلُوداً) حَسَّ (فَرَساً)

Curse *v. t.* or *n.* لَعِنَ . لَعْنَة

Cursed *a.* مَلْعُونٌ . مَكْرُوهٌ

Cursorily *ad.* بِسُرْعَةٍ . بِلاَ دِقَّةٍ

Cursory *a.* سَرِيعٌ . غَيْرُ مُدَقَّق

Curt *a.* قَصِيرٌ . فَظٌّ

Curtail *v. t.* قَصَّرَ . اوْجَزَ

Curtain *n.* or *v. t.* سِتَارٌ نَصَبَ سِتَاراً

Curvature / Curve } *n.* إِنْحِنَاءٌ . قَوْسٌ

Curve *v. t.* or *i.* قَوَّسَ . إِنْحَنَى

Cushion *n.* وِسَادَةٌ . مِخَدَّةٌ

Custodian *n.* وَكِيلٌ . مُحَافِظ

Custody *n.* وِكَالَةٌ . مُحَافَظَة . حَبْسٌ

Custom *n.* عَادَة . دَأْبٌ

Customary *a.* إِعْتِيَادِيٌّ . مَأْلُوفٌ

Cutomer *n.* زُبُون ج زُبَنَاءُ

Custom-house *n.* (جُمْرُكٌ) دِيوَان الرُّسُومَاتِ

Customs *n.* رُسُومَاتٌ . (جمَارِك)

Cut *v. t.* or *n.* قَطَعَ . قَطْعٌ

Cutaneous *a.* جِلْدِيٌّ

Cuticle *n.* بَشَرَةُ الْجِلْدِ

Cutlass *n.* سَيْفٌ عَرِيضٌ قَصِيرٌ

Cutlery *n.* ادَوَاتُ الْقَطْعِ كَالسَّكَاكِينِ

Cutlet *n.* قِطعة لَحمٍ لِلشَّيّ (كستلاتا)

Cutter *n.* سَفِينَةٌ صَغِيرة

Cutting *a.* or *n.* قَاطِعٌ . مُؤْلِمٌ . قِطعَة

Cwt *n.* عَلَامَةُ مِئَةِ لِيبْرَا انكليزيَّة

Cyclamen *n.* بَخُورُ مَرْيَمُ (نبات)

Cycle *n.* دَائِرَة . دَوْرٌ

Cyclone *n.* زَوْبَعَة عَظِيمة

Cyclopean *a.* كَبِير جِدًّا

Cyclopedia *n.* دَائِرَةُ الْمَعَارِفِ

Cylinder *n.* اسْطُوَانَةٌ ج اسَاطِينُ

Cylindrical *a.* اسْطُوَانِيٌّ

Cymbal *n.* صَنْجٌ ج صُنُوجٌ

Cynic *n.* / Cynical *a.* } شَرِسٌ . فَظٌّ

Cypress *n.* سَرْوٌ . سَرْوَة

Cyprian / Cypriote } *a.* or *n.* قُبْرُسِيٌّ

Cyst *n.* كِيسٌ غِشَائِيٌّ

Czar *n.* قَيْصَرُ رُوسيًّا

Czarina *n.* إِمْرَاةُ الْقَيْصَرِ

Czarowitz *n.* وَلِيُّ عَهْدِ رُوسيًّا

D

Dab *v. t.* مَلَثَ ـُ لطخَ ـ

Dabble *v. i.* لَعِبَ فِي وبرٍ . لَطخَ

Dad, Daddy *n.* أَبٌ (بِلُغَةِ ٱلاوْلاَدِ)

Daft *a.* بَلِيدٌ . مَجْنُونٌ

Dagger *n.* خَنْجَرٌ ج خَنَاجِرُ

Dahlia *n.* دَالِيَا (نَبَاتٌ)

Daily *a.* or *ad.* يَوْمِيٌّ . يَوْمِيًّا

Daintly *ad.* بِتَأَنُّقٍ

Daisy *n.* أُقحُوَانٌ

Dainty *a.* نَفِيسٌ . أَنِيقٌ

Dairy *n.* مَلْبَنٌ . مَجْبَنَةٌ

Dale *n.* وَادٍ ج اوْدِيَةٌ

Dalliance *n.* مُدَاعَبَةٌ . مُلاَعَبَةٌ

Dally *v. i.* دَاعَبَ . غَازَلَ . لاَعَبَ

Dam *v. t.* سَدَّ ـُ . حَجَرَ

Dam *n.* سَدٌّ . امٌّ بَهِيمَةٍ

Damage *n.* or *v. t.* ضَرَرٌ . أَضرَّ

Damask *n.* نَسِيجٌ نَفِيسٌ مُنَقَّشٌ

Dame *n.* سَيِّدَةٌ

Damn *v. t.* دَانَ ـِ . لعَنَ ـَ

Damnable *a.* مَلْعُونٌ . مَكْرُوهٌ

Damnation *n.* دَيْنُونَةٌ . هَلاَكٌ

Damp *a.* or *n.* رَطِبٌ . رُطُوبَةٌ .

Dampen *v. t.* رَطَّبَ . بَلَّ ـُ

Damper *n.* صِمَامُ مَدْخَنَةٍ

Dampness *n.* رُطُوبَةٌ

Damsel *n.* فَتَاةٌ . بِنْتٌ

Dance *v. i.* or *n.* رَقَصَ ـُ . رَقصٌ

Dandelion *n.* نَابُ الْاسدِ (نَبَاتٌ)
Daddle *v. t.* رَقَّصَ (طِفْلاً) . دَلَّلَ
Dandruff *n.* هِبْرِيَةُ ٱلرَّأْسِ . أَلْقِشْرَةُ
Dandy *n.* أَنِيقٌ . مُتَأَنِّقٌ
Danger *n.* خَطَرٌ
Dangerous *a.* خَطِرٌ . مُخْطِرٌ
Dangle *v. i.* تَدَلَّى
Dank *a.* مُبْتَلٌّ . رَطْبٌ
Dapple / **Dappled** *a.* أَرْقَطُ
Dard *v. i.* or *t.* تجَاسَرَ . إِقْتَحَمَ
Daring *a.* مِتَجَاسِرٌ . جَسُورٌ
Dark *a.* or *n.* مُظْلِمٌ . أَغْبَشُ . ظَلَامٌ
Darken *v. t.* or *i.* أَظْلَمَ . عَتَّمَ
Darkly *ad.* مُظْلِماً
Darkness *n.* ظَلَامٌ . قِتَامٌ
Darling *a.* or *n.* عزِيزٌ . حَبِيبٌ
Darn *v. t.* رَتَقَ ـُ . رفَا ـَ
Darnel *n.* زوَانٌ
Dart *n.* or *v. t.* or *i.* سَهْمٌ . رَمَى . إِنْقَضَّ
Dash *v. t.* صَدَمَ ـِ . إِقْتَحَمَ . كَسَّرَ
Dash *n.* عَلَامَةُ فَصْلٍ كَذَا (—)
Dastard *n.* خسِيسٌ . لَئِيمٌ
Dastardly *a.* جَبَانٌ . لَئِيمٌ
Data *n. pl.* مَوَادٌّ . مَوْضُوعٌ
Date *n.* or *v. t.* تَارِيخٌ . تَمْرَةٌ . أَرَّخَ
Daub *v. t.* طَيَّنَ . دَهَنَ
Daughter *n.* بِنْتٌ أَوْ ابْنَةٌ
Daughter-in-law *n.* كَنَّةٌ
Daunt *v. t.* افْزَعَ . ارْهَبَ
Dauntless *a.* جَسُورٌ . جَرِيءٌ
Dauphin *n.* وَلِيُّ عَهْدِ فَرَنْسَا
Dawn *n.* or *v. i.* فَجْرٌ . أَفْجَرَ
Day *n.* يَوْمٌ . نَهَارٌ
Day-break / **Day-spring** *n.* فَجْرٌ . فَلَقٌ
Daylight *n.* ضَوْءُ ٱلنَّهَارِ
Daze / **Dazzel** *v. t.* جَهَرَ ـَ . أَسْدَرَ

Deacon *n.* شَمَّاسٌ ج شَمَامِسَةٌ

Dead *a.* or *n.* مَيْتٌ ج أَمْوَاتٌ

Deaden *v. t.* أَضْعَفَ . أَخْمَدَ

Dead-letter *n.* مُهْمَلٌ

Deadlock *n.* وَرْطَةٌ . مُعْضِلَة

Deadly *a.* مُهْلِكٌ . مُمِيتٌ

Deaf *a.* اصَمُّ . اطرَشُ

Deafen *v. t.* أَصَمَّ

Deaf-mute *n.* أَطرَشُ . اخرَسُ

Deafness *n.* صمَمٌ . طرَشٌ

Deal *v. t.* or *i.* وَزَّعَ. تَاجَرَ . عَامل

Dealer *n.* تَاجِرٌ . بَيَاعٌ

Dean *n.* ثَانِي ٱلْاسْقُفِ. رَئِيسُ عُمْدَةِ مَدْرَسَةٍ أَوْ كَاتِبُهَا

Dear *a.* عزِيزٌ . غَال

Dearth *n.* مَجَاعَةٌ . قَحْطٌ

Death *n.* مَوْتٌ

Deathless *a.* خَالِدٌ

Debar *v. t.* مَنَعَ ـ . صدَّ عَنْ

Debase *v. t.* أَذلَّ . افْسَدَ

Debasement *n.* إِذْلَالٌ . دَنَاءَةٌ

Debasing *a.* مُفْسِدٌ . مُذِلٌّ

Debate *v.t.*or*n.* نَاظَرَ بَاحَثَ. مُنَاقَشَةٌ

Debauch *n.* or *v. t.* خَلَاعَة. أَفْسَدَ

Debauchery *n.* خَلَاعَةٌ . فِسْقٌ

Debilitate *v. t.* أَضْعَفَ . اوْهَنَ

Debility *n.* ضَعْفٌ. وَهْنٌ . وَنَاءٌ

Debt *n.* دَيْنٌ ج دُيُونٌ

Debtor *n.* مَدْيُون

Decade *n.* مُدَّةُ عَشْرِ سِنِينَ

Decadence *n.* إِنحطاطٌ

Decalogue *n.* أَلْوَصَايَا ٱلْعَشْرُ

Decamp *v. i.* بَرِحَ ٱلْمَحَلَةَ . إِنسلَّ

Decanter *n.* قَنِّينة

Decapitate *v. t.* قَطَعَ ٱلرَّأْسَ

Decay *v. i.* or *n.* } إِنْحطَّ . فَنِيَ ـ فَنَاءٌ

Decease *v. i.* or *n.* مَاتَ . مَوْتٌ . وَفَاة
Deceased *a.* مَيْتٌ . مَرْحُومٌ
Deceit *n.* غِشٌّ . مَكْرٌ . خَدِيعَة
Deceitful *a.* غَاشٌّ . خَدَّاعٌ
Deceive *v. t.* غَشَّ ـُ . خَدَعَ . خَادع
December *n.* شَهْرُ كَانُونَ الاوَّلِ
Decency *n.* لِيَاقة . حِشْمَة
Decennial *a.* حَادِثٌ كُلَّ عَشْرِ سِنِين مَرَّة
Decent *a.* لاَئِقٌ. مُوَافِقٌ
Deception *n.* خَدِيعَة . غرُورٌ . غش
Deceptive *a.* غرَّارٌ . غَاشٌّ
Decide *v. t.* عَزَمَ ـِ . حتمَ ـ . أنهى
Decided *a.* مَحتُومٌ . عَزُومٌ . واضِحٌ
Decimal *a.* عَشْرِيٌّ
Decimate *v. t.* قَتلَ عُشْرًا
Decipher *v. t.* فَسَّرَ . حلَّ
Decision *n.* حَتْمٌ . حُكمٌ . فَتوى
Decisive *a.* قاطِع . جازمٌ . حَتْمِيٌّ
Deck *v.t.* or *n.* زيَّنَ . ظَهْرُ السَّفِينَة
Declaim *v. i.* خَطَبَ ـُ . اكْثَرَ الكَلاَم
Declamation *n.* خطابٌ . خُطْبَة
Declamatory *a.* خِطابِيٌّ كَثِيرُ الْكَلاَمِ
Declaration *n.* قَرارٌ . تصْرِيحٌ
Declare *v. t.* اقرَّ . صَرَّحَ بِ . شهرَ
Declension *n.* تصْرِيفُ الاسْمَاءِ إِنحِرَافٌ
Declination *n.* إِنحِرَافٌ . رَفْضٌ
Decline *v. t.* or *i.* صَرَّفَ . إِنْحَرَفَ . إِنحَطَ
Declivity *n.* احْدُورٌ . متَحَدِّرٌ
Decoct *v. t.* غَلَى ـَ
Decoction *n.* مَغْلِيٌّ
Decompose *v.t.* or *i.* حَلَّ . فَسَدَ ـُ
Decomposition *n.* إِنحِلاَلٌ . فَسَادٌ
Decorate *v. t.* زَيَّنَ . زَخْرَفَ
Decoration *n.* زِينَة . نِيشَانٌ

Decorative *a.* مُزَيَّنٌ. مُزَخْرَفٌ

Decorous *a.* اديبٌ . لائقٌ

Decorum *n.* أَدَبٌ. لياقةُ التَّصَرُّفِ

Decoy *v. t* or *n.* أَغْوَى . حيلةٌ

Decrease *v. t.* or *i.* or *n.* قَلَّلَ . نَقَصَ ـُ نَقْصٌ

Decree *v. t.* or *n.* أَصْدَرَ أَمْرًا . أَمْرٌ

Decreed *a.* or *pp.* مَحْتُومٌ . مُقَدَّرٌ

Decrepitude *n.* هَرَمٌ . عَجْزٌ

Dedicate *v. t.* قَدَّسَ . كَرَّسَ (دَشَّنَ)

Dedication *n.* تَقْدِيسٌ. تَكْرِيسٌ

Deduce *v. t.* إِسْتَدَلَّ . إِسْتَنْتَجَ

Deducible *a.* مُمْكِنٌ إِسْتِنْتَاجُهُ

Deduct *v. t.* طَرَحَ ـَ أَسْقَطَ

Deduction *n.* إِسْقَاطٌ . إِسْتِنْتَاجٌ

Deed *n.* عَمَلٌ . فِعْلٌ

Deem *v. t.* or *i.* ظَنَّ ـُ إِرْتَأَى

Deep *a.* or *n.* عَمِيقٌ . أَلْبَحْرُ

Deepen *v. t.* or *i.* عَمَّقَ . زَادَ عُمْقًا

Deer *n.* ايّلٌ إِيَّلٌ ج ايائِلُ

Deface *v. t.* شَوَّهَ . مَحَا ـُ

Defacement *n.* تَشْوِيهٌ

Defalcation *n.* إِخْتِلَاسٌ

Defamation *n.* هَتْكَةٌ . وِشَايَةٌ

Defame *v. t.* وَشَى يَشِي بِهِ . هَتَكَ

Default *v. t.* or *n.* إِخْتَلَسَ مالاً قَصَّرَ عَنْ

Default *n.* إِخْتِلَاسٌ. ذَنْبٌ. تَقْصِيرٌ

Defeat *v. t.* or *n.* غَلَبَ ـِ هَزَمَ ـِ هَزِيمَةٌ

Defect *n.* نَقْصٌ . خَلَلٌ . عَيْبٌ

Defection *n.* تَرْكٌ . خِيَانَةٌ

Defective *a.* نَاقِصٌ . كَثِيرُ ٱلْخَلَلِ

Defence / Defense *n.* حِمَايَةٌ . مُدَافَعَةٌ

Defenceless *a.* خَالٍ مِنَ ٱلْحِمَايَةِ

Defend *v. t.* حَمَى . دَفَعَ عَنْ

Defendant *n.* مُدَافِعٌ مُدَّعًى عَلَيْهِ

Defender *n.* مُحَامٍ . مُدَافِعٌ

Defensive *a.* دِفَاعِيٌّ

Defer *v. t.* أَمْهَلَ . أَخَّرَ . أَجَّلَ

Deference *n.* إِحْتِرَامٌ . إِعْتِبَارٌ

Deferential *a.* إِحْتِرَامِيٌّ

Defiance *n.* تَحَدٍّ . تَعْيِيرٌ

Deficiency *n.* نَقْصٌ . قُصُورٌ

Deficient *a.* نَاقِصٌ . قَاصِرٌ

Deficit *n.* نَقْصٌ فِي ٱلْمَالِ

Defile *v. t.* or *i.* دَنَّسَ . مَشَى صَفًّا

Defile *n.* مَضْيَقٌ

Defilement *n.* نَجَاسَةٌ . تَدْنِيسٌ

Definable *a.* قَابِلُ ٱلتَّحْدِيدِ

Define *v. t.* حَدَّدَ . عَرَّفَ . بَيَّنَ

Definite *a.* مَحْدُودٌ . وَاضِحٌ

Definition *n.* حَدٌّ . تَعْرِيفٌ

Definitive *a.* مُحَدِّدٌ . قَاطِعٌ . جَازِمٌ

Deflect *v. t.* or *i.* حَرَّفَ . إِنْحَرَفَ

Deflection *n.* تَحْرِيفٌ . إِنْحِرَافٌ

Deform *v. t.* شَوَّهَ . بَشَّعَ

Deformed *a.* مُشَوَّهٌ . مَعْيُوبُ ٱلْخِلْقَةِ

Deformity *n.* عَيْبُ ٱلْخِلْقَةِ

Defraud *v. t.* غَبَنَ ـ . خَدَعَ ـ

Defry *v. t.* قَامَ بِٱلنَّفَقَةِ

Defunct *a.* مُتَوَفًّى . مَيْتٌ

Defy *v. t.* تَحَدَّى . بَارَزَ . عَيَّرَ

Degenerate *a.* or *v. i* مُنْحَطٌّ . إِنْحَطَ . فَسَدَ

Degeneracy, Degeneration *n.* فَسَادٌ . إِنْحِطَاطٌ

Degradation *n.* ذُلٌّ . هَوَانٌ

Degrade *v. t.* اذَلَّ . حَطَّ الشَّانَ ـُ

Degraded *a.* مُذَلٌّ . مُحْتَقَرٌ

Degrading *a.* مُذِلٌّ . شَائِنٌ

Degree *n.* رُتْبَةٌ . دَرَجَةٌ

Deify *v. t.* أَلَّهَ

Deign *v. i.* تَنَازَلَ . تَكَرَّمَ

Deism *n.* إِعْتِقَادٌ بِٱللهِ دُونَ ٱلْوَحْيِ

Deist *n.* مُعْتَقِدٌ بِٱللهِ دُونَ ٱلْوَحْيِ

Deity *n.* الوهيَّةٌ . إِلٰهٌ

Deject *v. t.* اَغَمَّ . بَرَّدَ هِمَّتَهُ

Dejected *a.* كَئِيبٌ . مَغْمُومٌ

Dejection *n.* غَمٌّ . كَآبَةٌ

Delay *v.t.* or *n.* أَخَّرَ . أَعَاقَ . تَأَخُّرٌ

Delectable *a.* مُبْهِجٌ . سَارٌّ جِدًّا

Delegate *v. t.* or *n.* فَوَّضَ . نَائِبٌ . رَسُولٌ

Delegation *n.* تَفْوِيضٌ . جَمَاعَةُ نُوَّابٍ

Deleterious *a.* ضَارٌّ . مُؤْذٍ . مُهْلِكٌ

Deliberate *v. i.* or *t.* تَأَمَّلَ . تَبَصَّرَ

Deliberate *a.* مُتَمَهِّلٌ . مَقْصُودٌ . مُتَأَمِّلٌ

Deliberately *ad.* مُتَمَهِّلاً . عَمْداً

Deliberation *n.* تَأَمُّلٌ . تَبَصُّرٌ . تَمَهُّلٌ

Delicacy *n.* رِقَّةٌ . حِشْمَةٌ . لَذَّةٌ

Delicate *a.* بَضٌّ . لَطِيفٌ . لَذِيذٌ

Delicious *a.* شَهِيٌّ . لَذِيذٌ

Delight *n.* or *v. i.* بَهْجَةٌ . إِبْتَهَجَ

Delighted *a.* مُبْتَهِجٌ . مَسْرُورٌ جِدًّا

Delightful *a.* مُبْهِجٌ . سَارٌّ

Delineate *v. t.* رَسَمَ ـُ صَوَّرَ . وَصَفَ ـِ

Delineation *n.* رَسْمٌ . وَصْفٌ

Delinquency *n.* قُصُورٌ . خَطَأٌ

Delinquent *a.* مُقَصِّرٌ . مُذْنِبٌ

Delirious *a.* هَاذٍ

Delirium *n.* هَذَيَانٌ (بُحْرَانٌ)

Deliver *v. t.* نَجَّى . اطْلَقَ . سَلَّمَ

Deliverance *n.* نَجَاةٌ . إِطْلَاقٌ . تَخْلِيصٌ

Delivery *n.* نَجَاةٌ . تَسْلِيمٌ . وِلَادَةٌ

Dell *n.* وَادٍ صَغِيرٌ

Delta *n.* قِطْعَةُ ارْضٍ مُثَلَّثَةٌ

Delude *v. t.* خَدَعَ ـَ أَغْوَى . اضَلَّ

Deluge *n.* or *v. t.* طُوفَانٌ . غَمَرَ ـَ

Delusion *n.* وَهْمٌ . ضَلَالٌ . غُرُورٌ

Delusive *a.* خَادِعٌ . مُضِلٌّ

Demagogue *n.* زَعِيمُ ٱلْعَوَامِّ . مُهَيِّجُهُمْ

Demand *v.t.* or *n.* طَلَبَ ـُ . طَلَبٌ

Demarcation / Demarkation *n.* تَخْطِيطُ ٱلْحُدُود

Demean *v. t.* سَلَكَ ـُ. تَصَرَّفَ. دَنَّا

Demeanor *n.* سُلُوْك . تَصَرُّفٌ

Demented *a.* مُخْتَلُّ ٱلعَقْلِ

Demerit *n.* نَقْصٌ ادبِيٌّ . قُصُوْر

Demigod *n.* نِصفُ إِلهٍ . بَطَلٌ

Demise *n.* وَفَاة . مَوْتٌ

Democracy *n.* حُكمٌ جُمْهُوْرِيٌّ

Democrat *n.* أَحَدُ حِزْبِ ٱلْجُمْهُورِيّين

Democratic / **Democratical** } *a.* جُمْهُوْرِيٌّ

Demolish *v. t.* هَدَمَ ـِ . هَدَّ ـُ

Demolition *n.* هَدْمٌ . هَدٌّ

Demon *n.* جِنِّيٌّ . رُوْحٌ نجِسٌ

Demoniac *n.* مَنْ بِهِ رُوْحٌ نجِسٌ . مَجْنُوْنٌ

Demonstrate *v. t.* بَرْهَنَ . أَثْبت

Demonstration *n.* إِثْبَاتٌ . دَلاَلَةٌ

Demonstrative *a.* دَالٌّ مُظهِرُ عَوَاطفِهِ

Demoralization *n.* فَسادُ ٱلآدَابِ

Demoralize *v. t.* افسَدَ ٱلآدَابَ او ٱلنخْوَةَ

Demur *v. i.* تَرَدَّدَ فِيْ . تَأَخرَ

Den *n.* عرِينٌ . عِرِّيسٌ

Denial *n.* إِنْـكَارٌ . رَفضٌ

Denizen *n.* سَاكِنٌ

Denominate *v. t.* لَقَّبَ . سَمَّى

Denomination *n.* تسمِيَة . طَائِفَةٌ

Denominator *n.* مَخْرَجُ ٱلـكُسُوْرِ

Denote *v. t.* أَشَارَ إِلَى . دَلَّ على

Denounce *v. t.* شَهَّرَ . إِشْتَـكى على

Dense *a.* كَـثِيفٌ . مُلْتَفٌّ . مُتَلَبِّدٌ

Density *n.* كَـثَافَة

Dent *n.* or *v. t.* نَقيْرَةٌ . نَقرَ قَلِيلاً

Dental *a.* سِنِّيٌّ اوْ ضِرْسِيٌّ

Dentate *n.* ذُوْ اسْنَانٍ

Dentiform *a.* شَبِيهٌ بالسِّنِّ

Dentist *n.* طبِيبُ ٱلأَسْنَانِ

Dentistry *n.* طِبُّ ٱلاسْنَانِ

Dentition *n.* زَمَنُ ٱلتَّسْنِينِ . بُرُوزُ ٱلأَسْنَانِ

Denude *v. t.* عرَّى . جَرَّدَ

Denunciation *n.* تَعْدِيلٌ . تَهْدِيدٌ

Deny *v. t.* أَنْكَرَ . رَفَضَ طَلَبًا

Deodorize *v. t.* أَزالَ ٱلرَّائِحَةَ

Depart *v. i.* ذَهَبَ ـَ رَحَلَ

Department *n.* دائِرَةُ اعمَالٍ . قِسْمٌ

Departure *n.* ذهَابٌ . رَحِيلٌ

Depend *v. i.* إِسْتَنَدَ إِلَى . وَثِقَ ب . تَدَلَّى

Dependence *n.* إِتِّكَالٌ . إِسْتِنَادٌ . تَعَلُّقٌ

Dependent *a.* مُسْتَنِدٌ . تَابِعٌ اوْ خاضِعٌ لِ

Depict *v. t.* صَوَّرَ . وَصَفَ ـِ

Deplorable *a.* مُحْزِنٌ . مَا يُرْثَى لَهُ

Deplore *v. t.* اسِفَ ـَ عَلَى . حَزِنَ على

Depopulate *v. t.* قَرَضَ ٱلسُّكَّانَ

Depopulation *n.* إِنْقِرَاضُ ٱلسُّكَّانِ

Deport *v. t.* تَصَرَّفَ . نَقَلَ . نَفَى

Deportation *n.* إِجْلَاءُ ٱلسُّكَّانِ

Deportment *n.* تَصَرُّفٌ . سُلُوكٌ

Depose *v. t.* or *i.* عَزَلَ ـِ شَهِدَ ـَ

Deposit *v. t.* or *n.* أَوْدَعَ . وَضَعَ ـَ وَدِيعَةٌ

Deposition *n.* عَزْلٌ . شَهَادَةٌ

Depository *n.* مَخْزَنٌ . مُسْتَوْدَعٌ

Depot *n.* مَخْزَنٌ . مَحَطَّةٌ

Deprave *v. t.* أَفْسَدَ

Depraved *a.* فَاسِدٌ . شِرِّيرٌ

Depravity *n.* فَسَادٌ . شَرٌّ

Deprecate *v. t.* تَوَسَّلَ . أَسِفَ عَلَى

Depreciate *v. t.* or *i.* وَكَّسَ . وَكَسَ

Deprecia-tion *n.* إِسْتِخْفَافٌ . هُبُوطُ ٱلْقِيمَةِ

Depredation *n.* سَلْبٌ . نَهْبٌ

Depress *v. t.* خَفَّضَ . أَذَلَّ . أَغَمَّ

Depressing *a.* مُكَدِّرٌ . مُغِمٌّ

Depression *n.* تَخَفُّضٌ . كَآبَةٌ . كَسَادٌ

Deprivation *n.* نَزْعٌ . فُقْدَانٌ . حِرْمَانٌ

Deprive *v. t.* أَخَذَ مِنْ . نَزَعَ ـِ

Depth *n.* عُمْقٌ

Deputation *n.* تَوْكِيلٌ . وَفْدٌ

Depute *v. t.* وَكَّلَ . أَوْفَدَ

Deputy *n.* نائِبٌ . وَكِيلٌ . وَافِدٌ

Derange *v. t.* قَلَبَ ـِ . شَوَّشَ

Deranged *a.* مَقلوبٌ . مُشَوَّشٌ . مُخْتَلٌّ

Derangement *n.* تَشْوِيشٌ . إِخْتِلَالٌ

Deride *v. t.* إِزْدَرَى بِ . هَزَأَ بِ ـَ

Derisive / Derisory *a.* إِسْتِهْزَائِيٌّ . إِزْدِرَائِيٌّ

Derision *n.* إِزْدِرَاءٌ . هُزْءٌ

Derivation *n.* إِشْتِقَاقٌ

Derivative *a.* or *n.* مُشْتَقٌّ

Derive *v. t.* إِشْتَقَّ . إِسْتَخْرَجَ مِنْ

Derogate *v. t.* or *i.* نَقَصَ . إِسْتَخَفَّ بِ

Derogative / Derogatory *a.* مُسْتَخِفٌّ . مُسْتَحْقِرٌ

Dervish *n.* دَرْوِيشٌ

Descend *v. i.* نَزَلَ ـِ . إِنْحَدَرَ

Descendant *n.* سَلِيلٌ . أَحَدُ الذُّرِّيَّةِ

Descent *n.* نُزُولٌ . أُحْدُورٌ

Describe *v. t.* وصَفَ ـِ أَوْضَحَ

Description *n.* وصْفٌ

Descriptive *a.* وَصْفِيٌّ . وَاصِفٌ

Descry *v. t.* رَأَى . اوْ مِنْ بعيدٍ

Desecrate *v. t.* نَجَّسَ . دَنَّسَ

Desert *v. t.* or *i.* تَرَكَ ـُ . هَجَرَ ـُ

Desert *n.* قَفْرٌ . صَحْرَآءُ . إِسْتِحْقَاقٌ

Deserter *n.* هارِبٌ . آبِقٌ

Deserve *v. t.* إِسْتَحَقَّ . إِسْتَوْجَبَ

Desiccate *v. t.* نَشَّفَ . جَفَّفَ

Desideratum *n.* مَطْلوبٌ . بُغْيَةٌ

قَصَدَ ـُ . نَوَى ـِ . قَصْدٌ

Design *v. t.* or *n.* رَسَمَ ـُ رَسْمٌ

Designate *v. t.* دلَّ . عَيَّنَ . أَشَارَ إِلَى

Designation *n.* تَعيِينٌ . دَلاَلَةٌ

Designedly *ad.* قَصْدًا . عَمْدًا

Designer *n.* مُسْتَنْبِطٌ. رَاسِمٌ. مُصَوِّرٌ

Designing *a.* رَاسِمٌ . مُحْتَالٌ . دَاهٍ

Desirable *a.* مَرْغُوبٌ . مُبْتَغًى

Desire *n.* or *v. t.* رِغْبَة.بُغْيَةٌ.إِبْتَغَى

Desirous *a.* رَاغِبٌ . مُبْتَغٍ

Desist *v. i.* كَفَّ عَنْ ـُ . عَدَلَ عَنْ

Desistance *n.* تَرْكٌ . كَفٌّ عَنْ

Desk *n.* مائِدَةٌ لِلْكِتَابَةِ

Desolate *v. t.* or *a.* دَمَّرَ . خَرَّبَ . مُقْفِرٌ

Desolation *n.* دَمَارٌ.وَحْشَةٌ . خَرَابٌ

Despair *v. i.* or *n.* يَئِسَ ـ . يَاسٌ. قُنُوطٌ

Despairing *a.* يَآئِسٌ . بِلاَ رَجَاءٍ

Despatch *see* Dispatch.

Desperado *n.* / **Desperate** *a.* } يَآئِسٌ. فَاتِكٌ . هَائِجٌ

Desperation *n.* يَأْسٌ . قنوطٌ

Despicable *a.* خَسِيسٌ.مُحْتَقَرٌ. مُهَانٌ

Despise *v. t.* إِحْتَقَرَ . اهَانَ

Despite *n.* ضَغِينَةٌ . حِقْدٌ

Despite of. رَغْماً عَنْ

Despoil *v. t.* نَهَبَ . سَلَبَ

Despond *v. i.* يَئِسَ ـَ . قَنِطَ

Despondency *n.* يَأْسٌ . قُنُوطٌ

Despondent / **Desponding** } *a.* خَائِبُ ٱلأَمَلِ. قَانِطٌ

Despot *n.* / **Despotic** *a.* } حَاكِمٌ مُطْلَقٌ.ظَالِمٌ

Despotism *n.* سُلْطَةٌ مُطْلَقَةٌ . ظُلْمٌ

Dessert *n.* فَاكِهَةٌ أَوْحَلْوَى بَعْدَ ٱلطَّعَامِ

Destination *a.* مَكَانٌ مَقْصُودٌ

Destinate / **Destine** } *v. t.* قَدَّرَ. عَيَّنَ. خَصَّصَ

Destiny *n.* قَدْرٌ . قِسْمَةٌ . نَصِيبٌ

Destitute *a.* مُحْتَاجٌ. خَالٍ مِنْ . فَقِيرٌ

Destitution *n.* فَاقَةٌ . عوزٌ

Destroy *v. t.* اهْلَكَ . أَبَاد . ازَالَ

Destruction *n.* إِبَادَةٌ. هلاَكٌ

Destructive *a.* مُهْلِكٌ . مُمِيتٌ

Desultory *a.* غَيْرُ مُنْتَظِمٍ . مُنْقَطِعٌ

Detach *v. t.* فَصَلَ ـُ فَكَّ ـُ

Detachment *n.* سَرِيَّةٌ مِنَ ٱلْجُنْدِ

Detail *n.* or *v. t.* تَفْصِيلٌ . اسْهَابٌ . اسْهَبَ

Detain *v. t.* حَجَزَ ـُ . صَدَّ ـُ . مَنَعَ ـَ

Detect *v. t.* كَشَفَ ـِ . وَجَدَ ـِ

Detection *n.* كَشْفٌ . إِظْهَارٌ

Detention *n.* حَجْزٌ . تَوْقِيفٌ . تَأْخِيرٌ

Deter *v.t.* أَعَاقَ . صَدَّ . مَنَعَ ـَ

Deteriorate *v.i.* إِنْحَطَّ . فَسَدَ ـُ

Deterioration *n.* إِنْحِطَاطٌ . فَسَادٌ

Determinable *a.* قَابِلُ ٱلتَّحْدِيدِ أَوِ ٱلتَّعْرِيفِ

Determinate *a.* مَحْدُودٌ . جَازِمٌ

Determination *n.* تَحْدِيدٌ . عَزْمٌ . حُكْمٌ

Determine *v. t.* حَكَمَ فِي . عَزَمَ عَلَى حَقَّقَ

Determined *a.* عَزُومٌ . مَحْكُومٌ بِهِ

Detest *v. t.* كَرِهَ ـَ . مَقَتَ ـُ

Detestable *a.* مَكْرُوهٌ . مَمْقُوتٌ

Detestation *n.* كُرْهٌ . مَقْتٌ

Dethrone *v. t.* خَلَعَ عَنِ ٱلْمُلْكِ

Dethronement *n.* خَلْعٌ

Detonation *n.* صَوْتُ ٱنْفِجَارٍ

Detour *n.* دَوْرَةٌ

Detract *v. t.* قَلَّلَ . ذَمَّ ـَ

Detraction *n.* ذَمٌّ . نَمِيمَةٌ

Detriment *n.* ضَرَرٌ . خَسَارَةٌ

Detrimental *a.* مُضِرٌّ

Deuteronomy *n.* سِفْرُ ٱلتَّثْنِيَةِ

Devastate *v. t.* خَرَّبَ . دَمَّرَ

Devastation *n.* تَخْرِيبٌ . دَمَارٌ

Develop *v.i.* or *t.* نَشَأَ ـَ . إِنْتَشَرَ ـُ نَشَرَ

Development *n.* نُشُوءٌ . نَشْرٌ

Deviate *v. i.* حَادَ ـِ . مَالَ ـِ

Deviation *n.* إِنْحِرَافٌ . حَيَدَانٌ

Device *n.* حِيلَةٌ . تَدْبِيرٌ . عَلَامَةٌ

Devil *n.* شَيْطَانٌ

Devilish *a.* شَيْطَانِيٌّ . خبيثٌ

Deviltry *n.* شَيْطَنَةٌ. تَصَرُّفٌ شَيْطَانِيٌّ

Devious *a.* زَائِغٌ . مُنْحَرِفٌ مُعْوَجٌّ

Devise *v. t.* دَبَّرَ . إِختَرَعَ . وَصَّى بَعْدَ ٱلْمَوْتِ

Devoid *a.* خَالٍ . مُجَرَّدٌ . فارِغٌ

Devolve *v. t.* or *i.* كَلَّفَ . سَلَّمَ . إِنْتقَلَ

Devote *v. t.* أَفْرَزَ . خَصَّصَ

Devoted *a.* مفْرَزٌ

Devotedness *n.* غيرَةٌ . وُلوعٌ

Devotee *n.* زَاهِدٌ . مُتعبِّدٌ

Devotion *n.* غيْرَةٌ . عِبَادة

Devour *v. t.* إِبْتَلَعَ . إِفْتَرَس

Devout *a.* دَيِّن . تَقِيٌّ

Dew *n.* نَدًى . طَلٌّ

Dexterity *n.* خفَّةٌ . مَهَارَةٌ

Dexterous *a.* خَفِيفٌ . مَاهِرٌ

Diabolic / Diabolical *a.* شَيْطَانِيٌّ خَبِيثٌ

Diadem *n.* تَاجٌ . عِصَابَة

Diagnosis *n.* تَشْخِيصٌ

Diagonal *n.* خَطٌّ بَيْنَ زَاوِيَتَينِ مُتَقَابِلَتَينِ

Diagram *n.* رَسْمٌ . شَكْلٌ هَنْدَسِيٌّ

Dial *n.* مِينَا سَاعَةٍ . شَمْسِيَّةٌ

Dialect *n.* لُغَةٌ . لَهْجَةٌ

Dialectic / Dialectical *a.* نُطْقِيٌّ . لَهْجِيٌّ

Dialogue *n.* مُحَاوَرَةٌ . مُكَالَمَةٌ

Diameter *n.* قُطْرُ دَائِرَةٍ

Diametrical *a.* قُطْرِيٌّ أَبْعَدُ مَا يُمْكِنُ

Diamond *n.* مَاسٌ

Diaphragm *n.* حِجَابٌ . اَلْحِجَابُ اَلْحَاجِزُ (فِي الطِّبِّ)

Diarrhœa *n.* إِسْهَالٌ

Diary *n.* يَوْمِيَّةٌ

Dice *n. pl.* of *Die* زَهْرُ النَّرْدِ

Dicephalous *a.* ذُو رَأْسَيْنِ

Dictate *v.* or *n.* أملى على . أمر ـُ . أمرٌ
Dictation *n.* إملاء . أمرٌ
Dictator *n.* مطلق السلطة
Dictatorial *a.* مستبدّ
Diction *n.* أسلوب الكلام
Dictionary *n.* قاموس ج قواميس
Dictum *n.* قول جازم
Didactic / Didactical *a.* تعليميّ . موافق للتعليم
Die *v. i.* مات ـُ . توفّي
Diet *n.* or *v. i.* طعام . إحتمى بالطعام
Differ *v. i.* إختلف . تباين
Difference *n.* إختلاف . فرق
Different *a.* مختلف
Difficult *a.* صعب . عسر . شاقّ
Difficulty *n.* صعوبة . عاقة . إرتباك
Diffident *a.* غير واثق بنفسه
Diffuse *v. t.* or *a.* نشر ـُ . منتشر . مسهب
Diffusion *n.* نشر . إمتداد
Diffusive *a.* ممتدّ . منتشر . مسهب
Dig *v. t.* or *i.* (dug) حفر ـِ . نقب ـُ
Digest *v. t.* or *n.* هضم ـِ . مجموع شرائع
Digestible *a.* سهل الهضم
Digestion *n.* هضم
Digestive *a.* هاضم
Dignified *a.* ذو وقار
Dignify *v.t.* كرّم . شرّف . وقّر
Dignitary *n.* صاحب رتبة عالية
Dignity *n.* وقار . كرامة . جاه
Digress *v. i.* حاد ـِ . إستطرد
Digression *n.* حيدان . إستطراد
Digressive *a.* مستطرد . معتسف
Dike *n.* سدّ . خندق
Dilapidated *a.* خرب . متساقط
Dilate *v. t.* or *i.* وسّع . مدّ ـُ . إتّسع
Dilatory *a.* بطيء . متكاسل . متراخٍ
Dilemma *n.* مشكل . ورطة

Diligence *n.* جِدٌّ . مُثَابَرَةٌ . مُوَاظَبَةٌ

Diligent *a.* مُجْتَهِدٌ . مُثَابِرٌ

Dilute *v. t.* خَفَّفَ سَائِلاً . أَضَافَ مَاءً

Dilution *n.* تَخْفِيفٌ

Dim *a.* or *v. t.* مُظْلِمٌ . مُكَدَّرٌ . كَدَّرَ

Dimension *n.* قِيَاسٌ . إِمْتِدَادٌ . قَدْرٌ

Diminish *v. t.* or *i.* قَلَّلَ . نَقَصَ . قَلَّ . نَقَصَ

Diminution *n.* تَقْلِيلٌ . نَقْصٌ

Diminutive *n.* or *a.* إِسْمُ التَّصْغِيرِ . صَغِيرٌ جِدًّا

Dimly *ad.* مُكَدَّرًا

Dimple *n.* نُونَة . (غَمَّازَة)

Dimpled *a.* ذُو نُونَاتٍ

Din *n.* or *v. t.* صَخَبٌ . قَعْقَعَة . قَعْقَعَ

Dine *v. i.* تَغَدَّى . تَعَشَّى

Dinginess *n.* غُبْسَة

Dingy *a.* مُكْمَدُّ اللَّوْنِ

Dinner *n.* غَدَاءٌ . فُطُورٌ

Diocese *n.* ابرَشِيَّة

Dip *v. t.* or *n.* غَمَسَ ـِ حُدُورٌ

Diphthong *n.* إِجْتِمَاعُ حَرْفَيْ عِلَّةٍ بِصَوْتٍ وَاحِدٍ

Diploma *n.* شَهَادَةٌ مَدْرَسِيَّةٌ

Diplomacy *n.* سِيَاسَةُ الدُّوَلِ

Diplomatic *a.* مختَصٌّ بِالسِّيَاسَةِ

Diplomatist *n.* خَبِيرٌ بِالسِّيَاسَةِ الدَّوْلِيَةِ

Dipper *n.* غَاطِسٌ . مِغْرَفَة

Dire *a.* هَائِلٌ . مُرْعِبٌ

Direct *v. t.* or *a.* أَرْشَدَ . أَدَارَ . أَمَرَ ـُ . مُسْتَقِيمٌ

Direction *n.* جِهَةٌ . إِرْشَادٌ . أَمْرٌ

Directly *ad.* رَأْسًا . بِإِسْتِقَامَةٍ . حَالاً

Directness *n.* إِسْتِقَامَةٌ . خُلُوصٌ

Director *n.* مُدِيرٌ . مُدَبِّرٌ . نَاظِرٌ

Directory *n.* جَمَاعَةُ مُدِيرِينَ . كِتَابُ مُرْشِدٌ . دَلِيلٌ

Direful *a.* هَائِلٌ . رَائِعٌ

Dirge *n.* تَرْنِيمَةُ جَنَازَةٍ

Dirk *n.* خَنْجَرٌ ج خَنَاجِرُ

Dirt *n.* وَسَخٌ . قَذَرٌ

Dirtly *a.* وَسِخٌ . قَذِرٌ

Disability *n.* عَجزٌ . عَدَمُ اقْتِدَار

Disable *v. t.* اعْجَزَ . أَوْهَنَ

Disabuse *v. t.* بَيَّنَ غَلَطَهُ . أَصْلَحَ فِكْرَهُ

Disadvantage *n.* خِسَارَةٌ . عَاقَةٌ

Disadvantageous *a.* غَيْرُ نَافِعٍ

Disaffected *a.* فَاتِرُ الْمَحَبَّةِ . سَاخِطٌ

Disagree *v. i.* تَخَالَفَ

Disagreeable *a.* غَيرُ مُرْضٍ . غَيْرُ مَقْبُولٍ

Disagreement *n.* إِختِلَافٌ . إِنْشِقَاقٌ

Disallow *v. t.* أَنكَرَ عَلَى . رَفَضَ

Disappear *v. i.* غَابَ ـِ تَوَارَى

Disappearance *n.* مُوَارَاةٌ . إِخْتِفَاءٌ

Disappoint *v. t.* خَيَّبَ . خَذَلَ ـُ

Disappointment *n.* خَيبَةٌ . خِذْلَانٌ

Disapprobation / **Disapproval** *n.* إِنكَارٌ عَلَى . عَدَمُ رِضًى

Disapprove *v. t.* أَنكَرَ عَلَى . عَابَ ـَ

Disarm *v. t.* جَرَّدَ مِنَ السِّلَاحِ . نَزَعَ الْقُوَّةَ

Disarrange *v. t.* أَخَلَّ بِالتَّرْتِيبِ . قَلَبَ ـِ

Disaster *n.* مُصِيبَةٌ . نَازِلَةٌ . نَكْبَةٌ

Disastrous *a.* مَشْؤُومٌ . جَالِبُ مُصِيبَةٍ

Disavow *v. t.* أَنكَرَ . رَفَضَ ـِ

Disavowal *n.* إِنكَارٌ . رَفْضٌ

Disband *v. t.* فَضَّ . فَرَّقَ

Disbelief *n.* عَدَمُ تَصدِيقٍ

Disbelieve *v. t.* أَنكَرَ . كَفَرَ

Disburden *v. t.* نَزَعَ حِمْلَهُ

Disburse *v. t.* انفق . صرّف

Disbursement *n.* إِنْفَاقٌ . صَرفٌ

Disc *n. see* **Disk.**

Discard *v. t.* رفضَ ـِ . أبعدَ . طَرَحَ ـَ

Discern *v. t.* رَأَى ـَ . مَيَّزَ

Discernible *a.* مُمْكِنٌ مُشَاهَدَته

Discerning *a.* مُمَيِّزٌ . بصيرٌ

Discernment *n.* تَمْيِيز. إِدْرَاك. فطنَة

Discharge *v. t.* or *n.* أَطلقَ.طَرَدَ.صَرَفَ أَجْرَى . تَخْلِيَة

Disciple *n.* تِلْمِيذٌ ج تلاَمِيذ وَتَلاَمِذَة

Disciplinary *a.* تَأْدِيبِيٌّ

Disicpline. *v. t.* or *n.* أَدَّبَ . هَذَّبَ . تَأْدِيبٌ

Disclaim *v. t.* انكَرَ . رَفَضَ ـُ

Disclose *v. t.* أَظْهَرَ . بَيَّنَ . أَعْلَنَ

Disclosure *n.* إِظْهَارٌ. إِعْلاَنٌ. إِبَاحة

Discolour *v. t.* غَيَّرَ لَوْنَهُ . لَطَّخ

Discomfit *v. t.* هَزَمَ ـِ . كَسَرَ ـِ

Discomfiture *n.* هَزِيمَة . خَيْبَة

Discomfort *n.* كَدَرٌ. عَدَمُ رَاحَةٍ

Discommode *v. t.* أَقْلَقَ . ثَقلَ عَلَى

Discompose *v. t.* شَوَّشَ . بَلْبَلَ

Disconcert *v. t.* اقْلَقَ . حَيَّرَ

Disconnect *v. t.* فصلَ ـِ . قَطَعَ ـَ

Disconsolate *a.* كَئِيبٌ . حَزِينٌ

Discontented *a.* غيْرُ رَاضٍ.ضَجِرَ

Discontent / **Discontentment** } *n.* عدَمُ رِضًى ضَجَرٌ

Discontinue *v. t.* or *i.* ابْطَلَ . إِنْقَطَعَ

Discontinuous *a.* مُنْقَطِعٌ

Discord *n.* خِصَامٌ . عَدَمُ إِتِّفاقٍ

Discordant *a.* غيْرُ مُتَّفِق . مغَايِرٌ

Discount *v. t.* or *n.* خَفَضَ الثَّمَنَ. إِسقَاطٌ (خَصْمٌ)

Discountenance *v. t.* عَارَضَ.قاوَمَ

Discourage *v. t.* بَرَّدَ هِمَّتَهُ فَشَّلَ . ضَعَّفُ

Discouragement *n.* الْعَزْم

Discouraging *a.* مُضْعِفُ الْعَزْمِ وَالرَّجَاءِ

Discourse *n.* or *v.i.* خِطَابٌ . خَاطَبَ

Discourtesy *n.* سُوءُ الادَب . فَظَاظَةٌ

Discover *v. t.* كَشَفَ ـ وَجَدَ ـ إِكْتَشَفَ

Discovery *n.* إِكْتِشَافٌ . إِخْتِرَاعٌ

Discredit *v. t.* or *n.* لَمْ يُصدِّقْ . شَيْنٌ

Discreditable *a.* شَائِنٌ. مُخِلٌّ بِالشَّرَفِ

Discreet *a.* عَاقِلٌ . حازِمٌ

Discreetness, Discretion *n.* تَعقُّلٌ. بَصِيرَةٌ. تَمِيزٌ

Discretionary *a.* مَتْرُوكٌ لِحُكْمِهِ

Discrepance, Discrepancy *n.* إِخْتِلَافٌ . مُغَايَرَةٌ

Discriminate *v. t.* مَيَّزَ بَيْنَ

Discuss *v. t.* بَحَثَ ـَ فِي اوْ بَاحث

Discussion *n.* مُبَاحثَة

Disdain *v. t.* or *n.* إِزدَرَى بِـ . إِحْتِقَارٌ

Disdainful *a.* مُسْتَحْقِرٌ . متَعَجْرِفٌ

Disease *n.* مَرَضٌ . دَآءٌ . عِلَّة

Diseased *a.* مَرِيضٌ . سَقِيمٌ

Disembark *v. t.* or *i.* نَزَّلَ أَوْ نَزَلَ مِنْ سَفِينَةٍ

Disembarrass *v. t.* أَزَالَ آرْتِبَاكًا

Disenchant *v.t.* حَرَّرَ مِنْ سِحْرٍ اوْ رُقْيَةٍ

Disencumber *v. t.* حَرَّرَ مِنْ أَثْقَال

Disengage *v. t.* فكَّ مِنْ عَهْدٍ . أَطْلَقَ

Disentangle *v. t.* فَكَّ ـُ . حَلَّ ـُ

Disfavour *n.* عَدَمُ قُبُولٍ . نُفُورٌ

Disfiguration *n.* تَشْوِيهٌ

Disfigure *v. t.* شَوَّهَ . أَخَلَّ بِالْهَيْئَةِ

Disfranchise *v. t.* نزَعَ الْحُقوقَ السِّيَاسِيَّةَ

Disgorge *v. t.* اخْرَجَ . قَذَفَ . إِسْتَفْرَغَ

Disgrace *v. t.* or *n.* فضَحَ ـَ. شَانَ. عَيَّبَ . عَارٌ

Disgraceful *a.* شَائِنٌ . مُعِيبٌ

Disguise *v.t.* or *n.* سَتَّرَ . اخْفَى . تَسَتُّرٌ. تَنَكُّرٌ

Disgust *n.* or *v. t.* كُرْهٌ . قَزَّزَ

Disgusting *a.* مُقَزِّزٌ . كَرِيهٌ

Dish *n.* صَحْنٌ . قَصْعَةٌ . طَبَقٌ

Dishearten *v. t.* أَضْعَفَ الْعَزْمَ اوِ الْهِمَّةَ

Dishonest *a.* غَيْرُ أَمِينٍ . غَابِنٌ

Dishonesty *n.* غَبْنٌ . عَدَمُ أَمَانَةٍ
Dishonour *n.* or *v. t.* هَوَانٌ . عَارٌ . أَهَانَ
Dishonorable *a.* شَائِنٌ . مُعِيبٌ
Disinclination *n.* مَيْلٌ عَنْ . نُفُورٌ
Disincline *v. t.* أَمَالَ عَنْ . نَفَّرَ
Disinfect *v.t.* طَهَّرَ مِنْ أَسْبَابِ ٱلْعَدْوى
Disingenuous *a.* غَيْرُ مُخْلِصٍ
Disinherit *v. t.* حَرَمَ مِنَ ٱلْإِرْثِ
Disintegrate *v.t.* حَلَّ . فَرَّقَ أَجْزَآءَهُ
Disinterested *a.* صَافِي ٱلنِّيَّةِ
Disjoin *v. t.* فَصَلَ ـِ
Disjoint *v. t.* خَلَعَ ـَ
Disk or Disc *n.* قُرْصٌ ج اقْرَاصٌ
Dislike *v. t.* or *n.* كَرِهَ ـَ . سَئِمَ ـَ
Dislocate *v. t.* خَلَعَ ـَ ازَاحَ
Dislocation *n.* خَلْعٌ . إِزَاحَةٌ
Dislodge *v. t.* أَخْرَجَ مِنْ مَكَانِهِ
Disloyal *a.* خَائِنٌ . غَيْرُ امِينٍ

Disloyalty *n.* خِيَانَةٌ عَدَمُ امانَةٍ
Dismal *a.* مُظْلِمٌ . مُغِمٌّ
Dismantle *v. t.* عَرَّى . نَزَعَ أَدَوَاتِ ٱلتَّحْصِينِ
Dismast *v. t.* نَزَعَ سَوَارِيَ سَفِينَةٍ
Dismay *n.* or *v. t.* رَوْعٌ . رَوَّعَ
Dismember *v. t.* فَصَلَ ـِ ٱلْاجْزَآءَ
Dismiss *v. t.* صَرَفَ ـِ . طَرَدَ ـُ
Dismissal / **Dismission** *n.* فَصْلٌ . عَزْلٌ
Dismount *v. i.* or *t.* نَزَلَ عَنْ دَابَّةٍ . نَزَّلَ
Disobedience *n.* عَدَمُ طَاعَةٍ . عِصْيَانٌ
Disobey *v.t.* عَصَى ـِ . خَالَفَ أَمْراً
Disoblige *v. t.* خَالَفَ خَاطِرَهُ اوْ كَدَّرَهُ
Disorder *n.* or *v. t.* تَشْوِيشٌ . شَوَّشَ
Disorderly *a.* مُشَوَّشٌ . غَيْرُ مُنْتَظِمٍ
Disorganize *v. t.* أَخَلَّ بِنِظَامٍ او تَرْتِيبٍ
Disown *v. t.* رفَضَ ـُ . أَنْكَرَ
Disparage *v. t.* عَبَ . إِحْتَقَرَ

Dispassionate رَزِينٌ.هَادِئُ ٱلطَّبْعِ .

Dispatch *v.t.* ارْسَلَ . أَنْجَزَ

Dispatch *n.* سِرْعَةٌ . رِسَالَةٌ

Dispel *v. t.* بَدَّدَ . ازَالَ

Dispensary *n.* صَيْدَلِيَّةٌ. مَجَّانِيَّةٌ

Dispensation *n.* نِظَامٌ . تَحْلِيلٌ إِجَازَةٌ

Dispense *v.t.* اعفَى مِنْ.وَزَّعَ. اجْرَى

Disperse *v. t.* بَدَّدَ . شَتَّتَ

Dispersion *n.* تَشْتِيتٌ . تَشَتُّتٌ

Dispirited *a.* فَشِلٌ. مُنْكَسِرُ ٱلْعَزْمِ

Displace *v. t.* أَزَاحَ مِنْ مَكَانِهِ

Displacement *n.* إِزَاحةٌ مِنْ مَكَانِهِ

Display *v.t.* or *n.* اظْهَرَ. مَنْظَرٌ بَاطِلٌ

Displease *v. t.* كَدَّرَ. غَمَّ ـُ . احْزَنَ

Displeasure *n.* كَدَرٌ. غَمٌّ . (زَعَلٌ)

Disposal *n.* تَصَرُّفٌ. تَرْتِيبٌ. تَدْبِيرٌ

Dispose *v. t.* رَتَّبَ. تَصَرَّفَ فِي. امَالَ

Disposition *n.* تَرْتِيبٌ. خُلْقٌ . مَيْلٌ

Dispossess *v. t.* حَرَمَهُ مُلْكَهُ . سَلَبَ ـُ

Disproportion *n.* عَدَمُ تَنَاسُبٍ اوْ تَعَادُلٍ

Disproof *n.* إِدْحَاضٌ . رَدٌّ

Disprove *v. t.* أَدْحَضَ . رَدَّ

Disputable *a.* قَابِلُ ٱلرَّدِّ .فِيهِ خِلَافٌ

Disputant *n.* مُنَاظِرٌ . مُجَادِلٌ

Disputation *n.* مُجَادَلَةٌ . مُنَاظَرَةٌ

Dispute *v. t.* or *i.* جَادَلَ . نَازَعَ

Disqualify *v.t.* ازَالَ اهْلِيَّتَهُ.اعْجَزَ

Disquiet *v. t.* أَزْعَجَ . أَخَلَّ بِالرَّاحَةِ

Disregard *v. t.* or *n.* إِسْتَخَفَّ بِهِ.إِهْمَالٌ

Disrelish *n.* or *v. t.* كُرْهٌ . تَقَزَّزَ

Disreputable *a.* شَائِنٌ.مُضِرٌّ بِالصِّيتِ

Disrepute *n.* صِيتٌ رَدِيٌّ اوْ مُعِيبٌ

Disrespect *n.* جَفَاءٌ . عَدَمُ ٱحْتِرَامٍ

Disrespectful *a.* جَافٍ . مُهِينٌ

Disrobe *v. t.* خَلَعَ ـَ ٱلثِّيَابَ

Dissatisfaction *n.* عَدَمُ ٱلرِّضى

Dissatisfactory *a.* غَيْرُ رَاضٍ

Dissatisfied *a.* غَيْرُ رَاضٍ أَوْ مُكْتَفٍ

Dissatisfy *v. t.* أَضْجَرَ . لَمْ يُرْضِ

Dissect *v. t.* شَرَّحَ

Dissemble *v. t.* or *i.* تَظَاهَرَ . تَسَتَّرَ . رَاءَى

Disseminate *v. t.* بَثَّ ـُ . نَثَرَ ـُ

Dissension *n.* إِنْشِقَاقٌ . نِزَاعٌ

Dissent *v. i.* or *n.* خَالَفَ الرَّأْيَ . خِلَافٌ

Dissenter *n.* مُخَالِفٌ خَاصَّةً فِي الدِّينِ

Dissertation *n.* خِطَابٌ . مَقَالَةٌ

Dissever *v. t.* فَصَلَ ـِ . قَطَعَ ـَ

Dissimilar *a.* مُخْتَلِفٌ . غَيْرُ مُشَابِهٍ

Dissimilarity / **Dissimiltude** } *n.* إِخْتِلَافٌ

Dissimulation *n.* تَظَاهُرٌ . رِيَاءٌ

Dissipate *v. t.* بَذَّرَ . أَسْرَفَ . شَتَّتَ

Dissipated *a.* مُتَشَتِّتٌ . خَلِيعٌ

Dissipation *n.* خَلَاعَةٌ . لَهْوٌ . إِسْرَافٌ

Dissoluble *a.* قَابِلُ ٱلذَّوَبَانِ

Dissolute *a.* خَلِيعٌ . فَاجِرٌ

Dissolution *n.* إِنْحِلَالٌ . فَنَاءٌ . مَوْتٌ

Dissolve *v. t.* or *i.* ذَوَّبَ . حَلَّ ـُ . ذَابَ ـُ

Dissolvent *n.* مُحَلِّلٌ . مُذِيبٌ

Dissuade *v. t.* ثَنَى عَنْ

Dissuasion *n.* إِقْنَاعٌ بِالْعُدُولِ عَنْ

Dissuasive *a.* مُمِيلٌ عَنْ . ثَانٍ عَنْ

Dissyllable *n.* لَفْظَةٌ ذَاتُ مَقْطَعَيْنِ

Distaff *n.* عِرْنَاسٌ ج عَرَانِيسُ

Distance *n.* or *v. t.* بُعْدٌ . مَسَافَةٌ . سَبَقَ ـِ

Distant *a.* بَعِيدٌ

Distaste *n.* عَيْفٌ . كَرَاهَةٌ

Distasteful *a.* كَرِيهٌ . غَيْرُ لَذِيذٍ

Distemper *n.* مَرَضٌ . سُوءُ الْخُلْقِ

Distend *v.t.* or *i.* وَسَّعَ . مَدَّدَ . إِنْتَفَخَ

Distill *v. t.* or *i.* قَطَّرَ . تَقَطَّرَ

Distillery *n.* مَعْمَلُ المسكرات

Distinct *a.* وَاضِحٌ . بَيِّنٌ . مُمْتَازٌ

Distinction *n.* تَمْيِيزٌ . سُمُوٌّ . رِفْعَةٌ

Distinctive *a.* مُمَيِّزٌ . فَاصِلٌ

Distinctly *ad.* وَاضِحاً . بَيِّناً

Distinctness *n.* وُضُوحٌ . صَرَاحة

Distinguish *v. t.* مَيَّزَ . فَصَلَ بَيْنَ

Distinguished *a.* مُمْتَاز . شَهِيرٌ

Distort *v. t.* لَوَى . عَوَّجَ . حَرَّفَ

Distract *v. t.* شَوَّشَ . حَيَّرَ . أَلْهَى

Distraction *n.* تَشْوِيشٌ . لَهْوٌ

Distress *n.* or *v.t.* ضِيقٌ . أَلَمٌ شَدِيدٌ . ضَايَق

Distressing / Distressful *a.* مُؤْلِمٌ . شَاقٌّ . مُكَدِّرٌ

Distribute *v. t.* وَزَّعَ . قَسَّمَ

Distribution *n.* تَوْزِيعٌ . تَقْسِيمٌ

District *n.* اقْلِيمٌ . كُورَةٌ . مَرْكَزٌ

Distrust *n.* or *v. t.* عَدَمُ ثِقَةٍ . إِرْتَاب

Distrustful *a.* غَيْرُ وَاثِقٍ . مُرْتَابٌ

Disturb *v. t.* أَقْلَقَ . شَوَّشَ . ازْعَجَ

Disturbance *n.* تَشْوِيشٌ . إِضْطِرَابٌ

Disunion *n.* إِنْشِقَاقٌ . إِنْفِصَالٌ

Disunite *v. t.* فَصَلَ ـِ . فَرَّقَ

Disuse *v. t.* or *n.* أَهْمَلَ . إِهْمَالٌ

Ditch *n.* خَنْدَقٌ . حُفْرَةٌ

Ditto *n.* مِثْلُهُ . ذَاتُ ٱلشَّيْءِ

Diurnal *a.* يَوْمِيٌّ . نَهَارِيٌّ

Divan *n.* دِيوَانٌ . مَقْعَدٌ

Dive *v. i.* or *n.* غَطَسَ ـِ . غَاصَ ـُ غَطْسَةٌ

Diverge *v. i.* إِفْتَرَقَ . إِنْحَرَفَ

Divergence *n.* تَشَعُّبٌ . إِفْتِرَاقٌ

Divergent / Diverging *a.* مُفْتَرِقٌ . مُنْفَصِلٌ

Divers / Diverse *a.* مُخْتَلِفٌ . مُتَنَوِّعٌ

Diversify *v. t.* نَوَّعَ . جَعَلَهُ أَشْكَالاً

Diversion *n.* تَحْوِيلٌ . لَهْوٌ . تَسْلِيَةٌ

Diversity *n.* تَنَوُّعٌ . تَعَدُّدُ ٱلاشْكَال

Divert *v. t.* أَلْهَى عَنْ . سَلَّى

Diverting *a.* مُلْهٍ . مُسَلٍّ . مُحَوِّلٌ

Divest *v. t.* عَرَّى . نَزَعَ ـَ

Divide *v. t.* قَسَمَ ـِ . جَزَّأَ . فَصَلَ ـِ

Dividend *n.* حِصَّةٌ . أَلْعَدَدُ ٱلْمَقْسُومُ

Divider *n.* قَاسِمٌ . قَسَّامٌ

Divine *a.* or *v. t.* إِلٰهِيٌّ . تَكَهَّنَ

Divinity *n.* أُلُوهِيَّةٌ . لَاهُوتٌ

Divisible *a.* قَابِلُ ٱلْقِسْمَةِ

Division *n.* قِسْمَةٌ . تَقْسِيمٌ . فِرْقَة

Divisor *n.* مَقْسُومٌ عَلَيْهِ

Divorce *v. t.* or *n.* طَلَّقَ . طَلَاقٌ

Divulge *v. t.* اذاعَ . بَاحَ ب

Dizziness *n.* دُوَارٌ . رَنْحٌ

Dizzy *a.* مُصَابٌ بِٱلدُّوَار . مُتَرَنِّحٌ

Do *v. t.* (did, done). عَمِلَ ـَ . فَعَلَ ـَ

Docile *a.* سَهْلُ ٱلتَّعْلِيمِ . مُطِيعٌ

Docility *n.* إِنْقِيَادٌ

Dock *n.* or *v.t.* مَرْبَطُ ٱلسُّفُنِ . قَصَّرَ

Dockyard *n.* تَرْسَخَانَةٌ

Doctor *n.* طَبِيبٌ (دَكْتُورٌ)

Doctorate *n.* رُتْبَةُ ٱلدَّكْتُورِ

Doctrine *n.* تَعْلِيمٌ دِينِيٌّ . عَقِيدَةٌ

Document *n.* رَقِيمٌ . صَكٌّ

Doged *v. t.* or *i.* جَانَبَ . تَنَحَّى عَنْ

Doe *n.* ظَبْيَةٌ . انثى ٱلإِيِّلِ اوِ ٱلْوَعْلِ

Doff *v. t.* نَزَعَ ـَ كُسْوَةً

Dog *n.* كَلْبٌ ج كِلَابٌ

Dog-days *n. pl.* ايامُ ٱلشِّعْرَى

Dogged *a.* عَنِيدٌ . عَازِمٌ . فَظ

Dogma *n.* عَقِيدَةٌ . مَذْهَبٌ

Dogmatic / **Dogmatical** } *a.* جَازِمُ ٱلرَّأْيِ . تَجَبُّرٌ

Dogmatism *n.* جَزْمُ ٱلرَّأْيِ . تَجَبُّرٌ

Dogmatize *v. t.* جَزَمَ فِي ٱلرَّأْيِ

Dog-star *n.* ٱلشِّعْرَى (نَجْمَةٌ)

Dole *n.* or *v. t.* نَصِيبٌ . هِبَةٌ حَقِيرَةٌ
اعطى صَدَقَةً زَهِيدَةً

Doleful *a.* مُغِمٌّ . مُحْزِنٌ

Doll *n.* اَلْعُوْبَة . لُعْبَةٌ

Dollar *n.* رِيَالٌ ج رِيَالَاتٌ

Dolorous *a.* مُؤْلِمٌ . مُحْزِنٌ

Dolphin *n.* دُلْفِينٌ ج دَلَافِينُ

Dolt *n.* بَلِيدٌ . أَبْلَهُ

Domain *n.* مُلْكٌ . رِزقٌ . مَمْلَكَةٌ

Dome *n.* قُبَّةٌ

Domestic *a.* بَيْتِيٌّ . عَائِلِيٌّ . دَاجِنٌ

Domesticate *v. t.* دَجَّنَ . أنَّسَ

Domicile *n.* or *v. t.* مَسْكَنٌ . مَقَامٌ . اسْكَنَ

Dominant *a.* مُتَسَلِّطٌ . سَائِدٌ . شَائِعٌ

Domination *n.* تَسَلُّطٌ . سِيَادَةٌ

Domineer *v. i.* تَسَلُّطٌ . بِغَطْرَسَةٍ وَتَعَجْرُفٍ

Dominion *n.* مَمْلَكَةٌ . تَسَلُّطٌ

Don *v. t.* لَبِسَ ـَ

Donate *v. t.* مَنَحَ ـَ وَهَبَ . يَهِبُ

Donation *n.* هِبَةٌ . هَدِيَّةٌ

Donkey *n.* حِمَارٌ ج حَمِيرٌ

Donor *n.* وَاهِبٌ . مُعْطٍ

Doom *n.* قَضَاءٌ . نَصِيبٌ . هَلَاكٌ

Doomsday *n.* يَوْمُ ٱلدَّيْنُونَةِ

Door *n.* بَابٌ . مَدْخَلٌ

Dormant *n.* نَائِمٌ . غَيْرُ عَامِلٍ

Dormitory *n.* غُرْفَةُ ٱلنَّوْمِ . مَنَامٌ

Dorsal *a.* ظَهْرِيٌّ

Dose *n.* or *v. t.* جَرْعَةٌ . سَقَى جُرْعَةً

Dot *n.* or *v. t.* نُقْطَةٌ . نَقَطَ

Dotage *n.* خَرَفٌ . ضَعْفُ الْعَقْلِ كِبَرًا

Dotard *n.* خَرِفٌ

Dote *v. i.* خَرِفَ ـَ وَلِعَ

Double *a.* or *v. t.* مُزْدَوِجٌ . ضَاعَفَ

Double-dealing *n.* خِدَاعٌ . مُخَاتَلَةٌ

Doubt *n.* or *v. t.* شَكٌّ . رَيْبٌ . شَكَّ ـُ

Doubtful *a.* مَشْكُوكٌ فِيهِ . مُرْتَابٌ

Doubtless *ad.* بِلَا شَكٍّ أَوْ رَيْبٍ

Dough *n.* عَجِينٌ

Dove *n.* حَمَامَةٌ ج حَمَامٌ

Dove-cote *n.* بُرْجُ حَمَامٍ

Dower / Dowry *n.* صَدَاقٌ . مَهْرٌ

Down *pr.* or *n.* إِلَى تَحْتٍ . زَغَبٌ

Downfall *n.* هُبُوطٌ . خَرَابٌ

Downcast / Downhearted *a.* مَكْسُورُ ٱلْخَاطِرِ مَغْمُومٌ

Downright *a.* وَاضِحٌ . صَافٍ . مُسْتَقِيمٌ

Downward / Downwards *ad.* إِلَى تَحْت او اسفل

Doxology *n.* تَسْبِحَةٌ

Doze *v. i.* نَعَسَ ـَ نَامَ خَفِيفاً

Dozy *a.* نَاعِسٌ . نَعْسَانٌ

Dozen *n.* إِثْنَا عَشَرَ (دَزِّينَة)

Drachm *n.* دِرْهَمٌ

Draft *n.* سَحْبٌ . سفتجة . حوالة

Drag *v. t.* or *i.* سَحَبَ ـ جَرَّ ـَ . تَأَخَّرَ

Dragoman *n.* تُرْجُمَانٌ

Dragon *n.* تِنِّينٌ

Dragoon *n.* جُنْدِيٌّ مِنَ ٱلْفُرْسَانِ

Drain *n.* or *v. t.* قَنَاةٌ . فَرَّغَ بِقَنَاةٍ

Drainage *n.* صَرْفٌ . قَنَوَاتُ مَاءٍ

Drake *n.* ذَكَرُ ٱلْبَطِّ

Dram *n.* دِرْهَمٌ . جُرْعَةٌ مُسْكِرَةٌ

Drama *n.* رِوَايَةٌ تَشْخِيصِيَّةٌ

Dramatic *a.* مُخْتَصٌّ بِرِوَايَةٍ تَشْخِيصِيَّةٍ

Dramatist *n.* مُؤَلِّفُ رِوَايَاتٍ

Dramatize *v. t.* كَتَبَ رِوَايَاتٍ تَشْخِيصِيَّةً

Drape *v. t.* غَطَّى بِسُتْرٍ او سُجُوفٍ

Draper *n.* تَاجِرٌ بِالنسج ٱلصُّوفِيَّةِ

Drapery *n.* أَصْوَافٌ سُجُوفٌ

Draught *n.* مَجْرَى هَوَاءٍ . جَرْعَة

Draughts *n.* لَعْبُ ٱلدَّامَا

Draughtsman *n.* رَسَّام

Draw *v. t.* سَحَبَ ـ جَرَّ ـُ جذب

Drawback *n.* عَاقَة . مَانِعٌ

Drawer *n.* سَاحِبٌ . (جَرَّارٌ) . (دَرْجٌ)

Drawers *n. pl.* سِرْوَالٌ تَحْتِيٌّ

Drawing *n.* رَسْمٌ . تَخْطِيطٌ . سَحْبٌ

Drawing-room *n.* غُرْفَةُ إِسْتِقْبَالٍ

Drawl *v. i.* or *n.* اطَالَ ٱلصَّوْتَ فِي ٱلنُّطْقِ

Dray *n.* مَرْكَبَةٌ لِنَقْلِ ٱلْبَضَائِعِ

Dread *n.* or *v. t.* خَوْفٌ . هَوْلٌ . خَافَ

Dreaded / **Dreadful** *a.* هَائِلٌ . مُخِيفٌ

Dream *n.* or *v. i.* حُلْمٌ . حَلَمَ ـُ

Dreamless *a.* خَالٍ مِنَ ٱلْأَحْلَامِ

Dreamy *a.* كَثِيرُ ٱلاحْلَامِ

Dreariness *n.* وَحْشَةٌ . كَآبَة

Dreary *a.* مُغِمٌّ . مُسْتَوْحِشٌ

Dredge *v. t.* or *n.* جَرَفَ ـُ . مِجْرَفَةٌ بَحْرِيَّةٌ

Dregs *n. pl.* ثُفْلٌ . دُرْدِيٌّ

Drench *v. t.* بَلَّلَ

Dress *n.* or *v. t.* لِبَاسٌ . أَلْبَسَ . كَسَا

Dressmaker *n.* خَيَّاطَةٌ

Dribble *v. i.* قَطَرَ ـِ

Driblet *n.* كَمِّيَّةٌ قَلِيلَةٌ . جُزْءٌ صَغِيرٌ

Drift *v. i.* or *n.* تَكَوَّمَ إِنْسَاقَ . كَوْمَةُ ثَلْجٍ

Drill *n.* تَمْرِينُ ٱلْجُنُودِ . مِثْقَبٌ

Drill *v. t.* ثَقَبَ . مَرَّنَ ٱلْجُنودَ

Drink (drank, drunk) *v. t.* شَرِبَ ـَ

Drip *v. i.* قَطَرَ ـُ

Drive *v. t.* or *i.* سَاقَ ـُ . حَرَّضَ . أَلْزَمَ

Drizzle *v. i.* or *n.* أَرَذَّ . نَضَّ . رَذَاذٌ

Droll *a.* مُضْحِكٌ

Drollery *n.* مَزْحٌ . دُعَابَةٌ

Dromedary *n.* بَعِيرٌ مُسْرِعٌ . هَجِينٌ

Drone *n.* ذَكَرُ ٱلنَّحْلِ . كَسْلَانٌ

Droop *v. i.* ذَبُلَ ـُ . ضَنِيَ ـَ

Drop *n.* or *v. t.* قَطْرَةٌ . قَطَرَ . أَسْقَطَ

Dropsy *n.* إِسْتِسْقَاءٌ

Dropsical *a.* مُسْتَسْقٍ

Dross *n.* رَغْوَةُ مَعْدَنٍ (زَغَلٌ)

Drought *n.* قَيْظٌ . قَحْطٌ

Drove *n.* قَطِيعٌ ج قُطْعَانٌ

Drown *v. t.* or *i.* غَرَّقَ . غَرِقَ ـَ

Drowsiness *n.* نعَاسٌ

Drowsy *a.* نَعْسَانُ

Drudge *n.* or *v. i.* كَثِيرُ ٱلْكَدِّ . كَدَّ .جَدَّ

Drudgery *n.* عَنَآءٌ . شُغْلٌ مُمِلٌّ

Drug *n.* or *v. t.* عَقَّارٌ . عَالَجَ بِٱلْعَقَاقِيرِ

Drugget *n.* لِبْدٌ ج لُبُودٌ

Druggist *n.* صَيْدَلاَنِيٌّ . اجْزَائِيٌّ

Drum *n.* or *v. i.* طَبْلٌ . طَبَّلَ

Drummer *n.* طَبَّال

Drunk / **Drunken** } *a.* سَكْرَانُ ج سكَارى

Drunkard *n.* سِكِّيرٌ

Drunkenness *n.* سُكْرٌ

Dry *a.* or *v. t.* يَابِسٌ . يَبَّسَ

Dry-goods *n. pl.* منْسُوجاتٌ

Dryly *ad.* بِتَهَكُّمٍ

Dryness *n.* يُبُوسَةٌ

Dual *a.* مثَنًّى

Dub *v. t.* سَمَّى . لَقَّبَ

Dubious *a.* مَشْكُوكٌ فِيهِ . مُشْتَبَهٌ

Ducal *a.* أَمِيرِيٌّ . دُوقِيٌّ

Ducat *n.* دِينَارٌ اورُبِّيٌّ

Duchess *n.* أَمِيرَةٌ إِمْرَأَةُ دُوقٍ

Duchy / **Dukedom** } *n.* إِيَالَةُ دُوقٍ

Duck *n.* or *v. t.* بَطٌّ . غَطَّسَ

Duckling *n.* فَرْخُ ٱلْبَطِّ

Duct *n.* انْبُوبَةٌ . قَنَاةٌ

Ductile *a.* مُتَمَغِّطٌ . مَرِنٌ

Ductility *n.* لينَة . إِمْتِغَاطِيَّةٌ

Due *n.* or *a.* حَقٌّ . مُسْتَحِقٌّ . مَطْلُوبٌ

Duel *n.* مُبَارَزَةُ ٱثْنَيْنِ

Duelist / **Dueller** } *n.* مُبَارِزٌ

Dug *pp.* or *n.* مَحْفُورٌ . ضَرْعٌ ج ضُرُوعٌ

Duke *n.* اميرٌ (دُوقٌ)

Dull *a.* or *v. t.* كَالٌّ . بَلِيدٌ . اكَلَّ

Dullness *n.* كَلاَلَةٌ . بَلاَدَةٌ . بَلاَهة

Duly *ad.* كَمَا يَجِبُ . فِي حِينِهِ

Dumb *a.* أَخْرَسُ . أَبْكَمُ

Dumbness *n.* خَرَسٌ . بَكَمٌ

Dumpish *a.* كَئِيبٌ . مَغْمُومٌ . بَلِيدٌ

Dun *a.* or *v. t.* كُمَيْتُ ٱللَّوْنِ . طَلَبَ بِلَجَاجَةٍ

Dunce *n.* غَبِيٌّ . أَبْلَهُ

Dung *n.* or *v. t.* زِبْلٌ . سَمَادٌ . دمَالٌ . سَمَّدَ

Dungeon *n.* حَبْسٌ . غَائِرٌ

Duodecimal *a.* or *n.* إِثْنَاعَشَرِيٌّ . جُزْءٌ مِنْ ١٢

Duodenum *n.* أَلْمَعَى ٱلاِثْنَا عَشَرِيُّ

Dupe *n.* or *v. t.* غَرِيرٌ . غَرَّ ـُ

Duplicate *n.* or *v. t.* نُسْخَةٌ ثَانِيَةٌ . ثَنَّى

Duplicity *n.* مُخَادَعَةٌ . مُخَاتَلَةٌ

Durability / **Durableness** *n.* صِفَةُ ٱلْبَقَاءِ

Durable *a.* مُسْتَمِرٌّ . بَاقٍ

Duration *n.* بَقَاءٌ . دَوَامٌ . مُدَّةٌ

During *pr.* اثْنَاءَ . مُدَّةَ . خِلاَلَ

Dusk *n.* غَسَقٌ . غَبَشٌ

Dusky *a.* غَاسِقٌ . مَائِلٌ إِلَى ٱلسَّوَادِ

Dust *n.* or *v. t.* غُبَارٌ . مَسَحَ مِنَ ٱلْغُبَارِ

Duster *n.* مَاسِحُ ٱلْغُبَارِ . مِمْسَحَةٌ

Dustpan *n.* مَجْرُودُ ٱلْغُبَارِ

Dusty *a.* مُغَبَّرٌ . مُتَعَفِّرٌ

Duteous / **Dutiful** *a.* مُتَمِّمٌ وَاجِبَاتِهِ . مُطِيعٌ

Duty *n.* فَرْضٌ . وَاجِبٌ . رَسْمُ جُمْرُكٍ

Dwarf *n.* or *a.* / **Dwarfish** *a.* قَزَمٌ . قَصِيرُ ٱلْقَدِّ

Dwarf *v. t.* صَيَّرَهُ قَزَمًا . مَنَعَ نُمُوَّهُ

Dwell *v. i.* سَكَنَ ـُ . قَطَنَ ـُ

Dwelling *n.* مَسْكَنٌ . بَيْتٌ

Dwindle *v. i.* صَغُرَ . إِنْحَطَّ . قَلَّ

Dye *v. t.* or *n.* صَبَغَ ـُ . صَبْغَةٌ . صِبَاغٌ

Dyeing *n.* صَبْغٌ صِبَاغَةٌ

Dyer *n.* صَبَّاغٌ

Dying *pp.* of *die.* مَائِتٌ . فَانٍ

Dynasty *n.* دَوْلَةُ مُلوكٍ

Dysentery *n.* سَحْجٌ . دُوسَنْطَارْيَا

Dyspepsia *n.* سُوءُ ٱلْهَضْمِ . تُخْمَةٌ

Dyspeptic *a.* or *n.* متَعَلِّقٌ بِالتُّخْمَةِ . مُصَابٌ بِهَا

E

Each *a.* كُلٌّ . كَلُّ وَاحِدٍ

Eager *a.* رَاغِبٌ . تَائِق . مُلْهِفٌ لِ

Eagerness *n.* رَغْبَةٌ . شَوْقٌ

Eagle *n.* نَسْرٌ ج نُسُورٌ

Eaglet *n.* فَرْخُ نَسْرٍ

Ear *n.* أُذُنٌ ج آذَانٌ

Ear of corn *n.* سُنْبُلَةٌ

Earl *n.* رِتْبَةٌ بَيْنَ امَرَاءِ ٱلانكليز

Early *a.* or *ad.* مُبَكِّرٌ . بَاكِراً

Earn *v. t.* إِسْتَحَقَّ اجْرَةً . كَسَبَ ـِ

Earnest *a.* or *n.* جَادٌّ . عَرْبُونٌ

Earnestness *n.* غَيْرَةٌ . جِدٌّ . إِهْتِمَامٌ

Earnings *n.* أَجْرٌ . كَسْبٌ

Ear-ring *n.* قُرْطٌ ج أَقْرَاطٌ

Earth *n.* الأَرْضُ . تُرَابٌ

Earthen *a.* تُرَابِيٌّ . مِنْ طِينٍ

Earthen-ware *n.* أَوَانٍ خَزَفِيَّةٌ

Earthquake *n.* زَلْزَلَةٌ ج زَلَازِلُ

Ease *n.* or *v. t.* رَاحَةٌ سُهُولَةٌ . ارَاحَ

Easiness *n.* سُهُولَةٌ . رَاحَةٌ

East *n.* الشَّرْقُ . ٱلْمَشْرِقُ

Easter *n.* عِيدُ ٱلْفِصْحِ

Easterly } *a.* شَرْقِيٌّ
Eastern }

Eastward *ad.* نَحْوَ ٱلشَّرْقِ . شَرْقاً

Easy *a.* سَهْلٌ . هَيِّنٌ

Eat *v.t.* or *i.* أَكَلَ ـُ

Eatable *n.* or *a.* مَأْكُولٌ . مَا يُؤْكَلُ

Eaves *n. pl.* أَطْنَافُ ٱلسَّقْفِ

Ebb *v. i.* or *n.* جَزْرٌ . جَزَرَ ـِ

Ebony *n.* أَبَنُوسٌ

Ebullition *n.* غَلَيَانٌ . فَوَرَانٌ

Eccentric *n.* or *a.* مُنْحَرِفٌ . غَرِيبٌ

Ecclesiastic *n.* } أَكْلِيرِكِيٌّ كَنَائِسِيٌّ
Ecclesiastical *a.* }

Eaves *n.* or *v. i.* or *t.* صَدًى . أَصْدَى

Eclipse *n.* كُسُوفٌ . خُسُوفٌ

Ecliptic *n.* مَدَارُ ٱلشَّمْسِ

Economic } *a.* إِقْتِصَادِيٌّ
Economical }

Economize *v. t.* or *i.* إِقْتَصَدَ

Economy *n.* إِقْتِصَادٌ

Ecstasy *n.* شَغَفٌ . ذُهُول

Ecstatic *n.* شَغَفِيٌّ . مُفْتِنٌ

Eddy *n.* دَرْدُورٌ

Eden *n.* عَدْنٌ

Edge *n.* حَدٌّ . حَافَّةٌ

Edgewise *ad.* جَانِبِيّاً

Edible *see* eatable.

Edict *n.* أَمْرٌ سُلْطَانِيٌّ . فَرَمَانٌ

Edifice *n.* بِنَاءٌ . عِمَارَةٌ

Edify *v. t.* بَنَى . أَفَادَ . هَذَّبَ

Edit *v.t.* هَذَّبَ لِلطَّبْعِ . نَقَّحَ

Edition *n.* طَبْعٌ . طَبْعَةٌ

Editor *n.* مُهَذِّبٌ . رَئِيسُ تَحْرِيرِ جَرِيدَةٍ

Educate *v. t.* عَلَّمَ . رَبَّى . دَرَّبَ

Education *n.* تَعْلِيمٌ . تَرْبِيَةٌ . تَهْذِيبٌ

Educe *v. t.* إِسْتَخْرَجَ . انْتَجَ

Eel *n.* سَمَكٌ كَالْحَيَّةِ . حَنْكَلِيسٌ

Efface *v. t.* مَحَا ـُ . طَلَسَ ـِ

Effect *n.* or *v. t.* نَتِيجَة . تَأْثِيرٌ . سَبَّبَ

Effective } *a.* فَعَّالٌ . مُنْتِجٌ . عَامِلٌ
Effectual }

Effects *n. pl.* أَمْتِعَةٌ . أَثَاثٌ

Effeminacy *n.* خُنَاثَةٌ . تَخَنُّثٌ

Effeminate *a.* or *v. t.* خَنِثٌ . خَنَّثَ

Effervesce *v. t.* فَارَ . ازْبَدَ

Effervescence *n.* فَوَرَانٌ

Effervescent *a.* فَوَّارٌ . مُزْبِدٌ

Effete *a.* غَيْرُ مُنْتِجٍ . مَنْهُوك

Efficacious *a.* فَعَّالٌ . عَامِلٌ

Efficacy, Efficiency *n.* قُوَّة فَعَّالة . فَاعِلِيَّة

Efficient *a.* فَعَّالٌ . مُنْتِجٌ

Effigy *n.* تِمْثَالٌ . صُورَة

Efflorescence *n.* إِزْهَارٌ

Effort *n.* إِجْتِهَادٌ . سَعْيٌ

Effrontery *n.* وَقَاحَةٌ . عَجْرَفَةٌ

Effulgence *n.* بَهَاءٌ . رَوْنَقٌ

Effulgent *a.* بَهِيٌّ . لَامِعٌ

Effusion *n.* سَفْكٌ . إِهْرَاقٌ

Egg *n.* بَيْضَة ج بُيُوضٌ وَبَيْضَات

Egg-plant *n.* بَاذِنْجَانٌ

Egoism, Egotism *n.* عُجْبٌ . تَعْظِيمُ ٱلذَّات

Egotist *n.*, Egotistic *a.* مُعْجَبٌ بِنَفْسِهِ

Egregious *a.* فَائِقٌ (فِي ٱلسُّوءِ)

Egress *n.* خُرُوجٌ . مَخْرَجٌ

Egyptian *a.* مِصْرِيٌّ

Eight *n.* ثَمَانِيَة . ثَمَانٍ

Eighth *a.* أَلثَّامِنُ

Eighteen *n.* ثَمَانِيَةَ عَشَرَ وَثَمَانِي عَشْرَةَ

Eighty *n.* ثَمَانُونَ

Either *a.* or *pron.* إِمَّا . كُلٌّ مِنِ ٱثْنَيْنِ

Ejaculate *v. t.* نَطَقَ بِصُرَاخٍ او دُعَاءٍ

Eject *v. t.* قَذَفَ . أَخْرَجَ . طَرَدَ ـُ

Ejection *n.* قَذْفٌ . إِخْرَاجٌ

Elaborate *v. t.* or *a.* تَمَّمَ . أَتْقَنَ . مُتْقَنٌ

Elapse *v. i.* مَضَى ـِ . إِنْقَضَى

Elastic *a.* مَرِنٌ . لَدْنٌ

Elasticity *n.* مُرُونَة . لُدُونَة

Elated *pp.* مُفْتَخِرٌ . مُبْتَهِجٌ

Elation *n.* تَشَامُخٌ . إِبْتِهَاجٌ

Elbow *n.* or *v. t.* مِرْفَقٌ دَفَعَ بِهِ

Elder *a.* or *n.* اكْبَرُ عُمْراً . شَيْخٌ

Elder *n.* (plant). بَلَسَانٌ

Elderly *a.* مُتَقَدِّمٌ فِي ٱلسِّنِّ

Eldest *a.* الأَكْبَرُ فِي ٱلْعُمْرِ

Elect *v. t.* or *a.* or *n.* إِنْتَخَبَ . مُخْتَارٌ

Election *n.* إِنْتِخَابٌ

Electric / Electrical } *a.* كَهْرَبَائِيٌّ

Electricity *n.* كَهْرَبَائِيَّةٌ

Electrify *v. t.* كَهْرَبَ

Elegance *n.* ظَرَافَةٌ . لَبَاقَةٌ

Elegant *a.* ظَرِيفٌ . كَيِّسٌ . مَلِيحٌ

Elegy *n.* مَرْثَاةٌ ج مَرَاثٍ

Element *n.* عُنْصُرٌ . مَبْدَأٌ

Elemental / Elementary } *a.* عُنْصُرِيٌّ . اوَّلِيٌّ

Elephant *n.* فِيلٌ ج افْيَال

Elevate *v. t.* رَفَعَ . رَقَّى . على

Elevation *n.* رَفْعٌ . إِرْتِفَاعٌ

Elevator *n.* رَافِعٌ . مُعَلٍّ

Eleven *n.* احَدَ عَشَرَ

Eleventh *a.* أَلْحَادِي عَشَرَ

Elicit *v. t.* إِسْتَخْرَجَ . إِسْتَبَانَ

Elide *v. t.* حَذَفَ

Eligible *a.* جَدِيرٌ بِٱلإِنْتِخَاب

Eliminate *v. t.* اخْرَجَ . حَذَفَ

Elimination *n.* إِخْرَاجٌ

Elision *n.* حَذْفٌ

Elk *n.* نَوْعٌ مِنَ ٱلإِيَّلِ

Ellipse *n.* إِهْلِيلَجٌ

Elliptical *a.* إِهْلِيلَجِيُّ ٱلشَّكْلِ

Elm *n.* دَرْدَارٌ (نَوْعٌ مِنَ ٱلشَّجَرِ)

Elocution *n.* نُطْقٌ . فَصَاحَةٌ

Elocutionist *n.* إِسْتَاذُ ٱلْخِطَابَةِ

Elongate *v. t.* أَطَالَ طَوَّلَ

Elope *v. i.* هَرَبَ سِرًّا

Eloquence *n.* فَصَاحَةٌ. بلاغَةٌ

Eloquent *a.* فَصِيحٌ. بَلِيغٌ

Else *pron.* or *a.* غَيْرُ. وَإِلا

Elsewhere *ad.* بِغَيْرِ مَكَانٍ

Elucidate *v. t.* اوْضَحَ. شَرَحَ ـَ

Elude *v. t.* تَمَلَّصَ مِنْ. تَجَنَّبَ

Emaciate *v. i.* or *t.* هَزَلَ ـُ

Emaciation *n.* هُزَالٌ

Emancipate *v. t.* حَرَّرَ. اعْتَقَ

Emancipation *n.* تَحْرِيرٌ

Emanate *v. i.* نَشَأَ ـَ. صَدَرَ ـُ

Emasculate *v. t.* اضْعَفَ. خَصَى

Embalm *v. t.* حَنَطَ

Embankment *n.* سَدٌّ. حَاجِزٌ

Embargo *n.* حَجْزُ آلسُّفُنِ عَنِ آلسفرِ

Embark *v. t.* رَكِبَ سَفِينَةً. بَاشَرَ

Embarkation *n.* نُزُولٌ في سَفِينَةٍ

Embarrass *v. t.* لَبَّكَ. رَبَكَ ـُ

Embarrassment *n.* إِرْتِبَاكٌ. لَبْكَةٌ

Embassy *n.* سَفَارَةٌ

Embellish *v. t.* زَيَّنَ. زَخْرَفَ

Embellishment *n.* زِينَةٌ. زَخْرَفَةٌ

Embezzle *v.* إِخْتَلَسَ

Embezzlement *n.* إِخْتِلَاسٌ

Emblem *n.* رَمْزٌ. كِنَايَةٌ

Emblematic / Emblematical } *a.* رَمْزِيٌّ

Embody *v. t.* جَسَّمَ. ضَمَّنَ

Embolden *v. t.* شَجَّعَ. جَرَّأَ

Embrace *v. t.* or *n.* عَانَقَ. تَضَمَّنَ. مُعَانَقَةٌ

Embroider *v. t.* طَرَّزَ

Embroidery *n.* تَطْرِيزٌ

Embroil *v. t.* شَوَّشَ. هَيَّجَ. افْتَنَ

Embryo *n.* جَنِينٌ ج اجِنَّةٌ. جُرْثُومَةٌ

Embryology *n.* عِلْمٌ يَبْحَثُ عَنِ آلاجِنَّةِ

Emerald *n.* زُمُرُّدٌ

Emerge *v. i.* خَرَجَ ـُ . ظَهَرَ ـَ

Emergency *n.* حَادِثَةٌ غَيْرُ مُنْتَظَرَةٍ . ضَرُورَةٌ

Emetic *a.* or *n.* مُقَيِّئٌ

Emigrant *n.* مُهَاجِرٌ

Emigrate *v. i.* هَاجَرَ ٱلْوَطَنَ

Emigration *n.* مُهَاجَرَةٌ

Eminence *n.* إِرْتِفَاعٌ . سُمُوٌّ

Eminent *a.* سَامٍ . شَهِيرٌ

Emissary *n.* رَسُولٌ . جَاسُوسٌ

Emission *n.* إِصْدَارٌ . نَشْرٌ

Emit *v. t.* اصْدَرَ . نَشَرَ ـُ

Emollient *a.* مُلَيِّنٌ

Emotion *n.* انْفِعَالٌ نَفْسَانِيٌّ

Emotional *a.* انْفِعَالِيٌّ . سَرِيعُ ٱلانْفِعَالِ

Empale *v. t.* خَوْزَقَ

Emperor *v. t.* سُلْطَانٌ (امْبَرَاطُورٌ)

Emphasis *n.* تَأْكِيدٌ . تَشْدِيدُ ٱلصَّوْتِ

Emphasize *v. t.* أَكَّدَ . شَدَّدَ ٱللَّفْظَ

Emphatic *a.* مُؤَكَّدٌ . مُشَدَّدٌ

Empire *n.* مَمْلَكَةٌ . سَلْطَنَةٌ

Employ *v. t.* إِسْتَخْدَمَ . شَغَّلَ

Employé *n.* مُسْتَخْدَمٌ . اجِيرٌ

Employer *n.* مُسْتَخْدِمٌ . مُشَغِّلٌ

Employment *n.* شُغْلٌ . مَصْلَحَةٌ

Empower *v. t.* قَدَّرَ . مَكَّنَ . فَوَّضَ

Empress *n.* سُلْطَانَةٌ (أَمْبَرَاطُورَةٌ)

Emptiness *n.* فَرَاغٌ . خُلُوٌّ

Empty *a.* خَالٍ . فَارِغٌ . بَاطِلٌ

Empty *v. t.* افْرَغَ

Emulate *v. t.* نَافَسَ . بَارَى

Enable *v. t.* قَدَّرَ . مَكَّنَ

Enact *v. t.* سَنَّ . رَسَمَ ـُ

Enactment *n.* سُنَّةٌ . شَرِيعَةٌ

Enamel *n.* or *v. t.* مِينَاءٌ . غَشَّى بِٱلْمِينَاءِ

Enamour *v. t.* عَشِقَ . افْتَتَنَ

Encamp *v. t.* or *i.* نَزَلَ ـِ . عَسْكَرَ
Encampment *n.* مَحلة . معسكرٌ
Enchain *v. t.* غَلَّ . سَلْسَلَ . أَوْثَقَ
Enchant *v. t.* سَحَرَ ـَ . فَتَنَ ـِ . رَقَى
Enchantment *n.* سحرٌ . رُقْيَةٌ
Encircle *v. t.* أَحَاطَ . أَحْدَقَ ب
Enclosure *n.* حَوْشٌ . سِيَاجٌ
Encompass *v. t.* احَاطَ . أَحْدَقَ بِ
Encounter *n.* or *v. t.* مُصَادَفَةٌ . معركةٌ . صَادَفَ . بَارَزَ
Encourage *v. t.* شَجَّعَ ، حَرَّضَ عَلَى
Encouragement *n.* تَشْجِيعٌ
Encouraging *a.* مشجّعٌ . مُقوّي ٱلْأَمَلِ
Encroach *v. t.* تعدى على
Encroachment *n.* تعدٍّ عَلَى
Encumber *v. t.* ثَقَّلَ . أَعَاقَ . عَرْقَلَ
Encumbrance *n.* ثِقْلٌ . إِعَاقَةٌ
Encyclopedia *n.* دَائِرَةُ ٱلْمَعَارِفِ

End *n.* or *v. t.* نِهَايَةٌ . غَايَة . أَنْهى
Endanger *v. t.* أَوْقَعَ فِي ٱلْخَطرِ
Endear *v. t.* حَبَّبَ . صَيَّرَ عَزِيزاً
Endeavour *v. t.* or *n.* إِجْتَهَدَ . سَعَى ـَ
Ending *n.* إِنْتِهَاءٌ . خِتَامٌ
Endless *a.* غَيْرُ مُتَنَاهٍ . بِلاَ نِهَايَةٍ
Endow *v. t.* وَقَفَ لَهُ رِزْقًا . امْهَرَ
Endowment *n.* وَقْفٌ . مَهْرٌ
Endurable *a.* مُمْكِنٌ إِحتِمَالُهُ . محتمِلٌ
Endurance *n.* إِحْتِمَالٌ . بَقَاءٌ
Endure *v. t.* or *i.* بَقِيَ ـَ . إِحْتَمَلَ
Enemy *n.* عَدُوٌّ ج أَعْدَاءٌ
Energetic / Energetical } *a.* نَشِيطٌ . هُمَامٌ
Energize *v. t.* قَوَّى . شَدَّدَ
Energy *n.* هِمَّةٌ . جِدٌّ . نَشَاطٌ
Enervate / Enfeeble } *v. t.* اضْعَفَ . أَوْهَنَ
Enforce *v. t.* أَجْرَى . أَنفَذَ
Enforcement *n.* إِجْرَآءٌ . إِنْفَاذٌ

Enfranchise *v. t.* مَنَحَ حُقُوقَ ٱلْامَّةِ
Engage *v. t.* عَاهَدَ . إِسْتَخْدَمَ . بَارَزَ
Engaged *a.* مَشْغُولٌ.مُقَيَّدٌ . مَخْطُوبٌ
Engagement *n.* وَعْدٌ . خِطْبَةٌ قِتَالٌ
Engaging *a.* فَاتِنٌ.مُسْتَمِيلُ ٱلْعَوَاطِفِ
Engender *v. t.* وَلَّدَ . أَوْجَدَ . سَبَّبَ
Engine *n.* آلَةٌ بُخَارِيَّةٌ
Engineer *n.* مُهَنْدِسٌ
English *a.* or *n.* إِنْكِلِيزِيٌّ.ٱلْإِنْكِلِيزُ
Engrave *v. t.* حَفَرَ ـِ. نَقَشَ ـُ
Engraver *n.* حَفَّارٌ. نَقَّاشٌ
Engraving *n.* نَقْشٌ . صُورَةٌ مَحْفُورَةٌ
Engross *v. t.* شَغَلَ.نَسَخَ بِخَطٍّ وَاضِحٍ
Engulf *v. t.* إِبْتَلَعَ
Enhance *v. t.* رَقَّى . عَظَّمَ
Enigma *n.* لُغْزٌ . احْجِيَّةٌ
Enigmatic / Enigmatical *a.* لُغْزِيٌّ . غَامِضٌ
Enjoin *v. t.* أَمَرَ ـُ

Enjoy *v. t.* إِلْتَذَّ . تَمَتَّعَ بِ
Enjoyable *a.* لَذِيذٌ . مُفْرِحٌ
Enjoyment *n.* لَذَّةٌ . حظ . تَمَتُّعٌ
Enlarge *v. t.* or *i.* وَسَّعَ . إِتَّسَعَ
Enlargement *n.* تَوْسِيعٌ . تَوَسُّعٌ
Enlighten *v. t.* عَلَّمَ . أَنَارَ
Enlist *v. t.* or *i.* ضَمَّ. دَوَّنَ ٱسْمًا
Enlistment *n.* تَقْيِيدٌ . تَدْوِينٌ
Enliven *v. i.* انعَشَ . أَبْهَجَ
Enmity *n.* عَدَاوَةٌ
Ennoble *v. t.* شَرَّفَ . رَقَّى
Enormity *n.* جَسَامَةٌ . فَظَاعَةٌ
Enormous *a.* عَظِيمٌ جِدًّا. مُفْرِطٌ
Enough *n.* or *ad.* كاف
Enrage *v. t.* أَغَاظَ . أَغْضَبَ
Enrich *v. t.* أَغْنَى . أَخْصَبَ
Enrol *v. t.* سجَّلَ . دَوَّنَ
Ensign *n.* عَلَمٌ . ضَابِطٌ

Enslave *v. t.* إستعبد . إسترق

Ensnare *v. t.* أخذ بحيلة . شبك

Ensue *v. i.* تلا ـ تبع ـ

Entail *v. t.* أوقف . جر

Entangle *v. t.* عرقل . شبك ـ

Enter *v. t.* or *i.* أدخل أو دخل ـ

Enterprise *n.* مسعى . مشروع

Eeterprising *a.* ذو إقدام . همام

Entertain *v. t.* ضاف . سلى

Entertaining *a.* مسل . سار

Entertainment *a.* تسلية . ضيافة

Enthrone *v. t.* أجلس على العرش

Enthusiasm *n.* حماسة . نشاط

Enhusiast *n.*
Enthusiastic *a.* } حمس . نشيط

Entice *v. t.* أغوى . راود . تملق

Entire *a.* كامل . كل . صحيح

Entirely *ad.* تماماً . بكليته

Entitle *v. t.* لقب . أعطى حقا في

Entomb *v. t.* قبر ـ . دفن ـ

Entrails *n. pl.* أحشاء . أمعاء

Entrance *n.* مدخل . دخول

Entrance *v. t.* سحر ـ . أبهج

Entrap *v. t.* شبك ـ . أخذ بحيلة

Entreat *v. t.* توسل . تضرع

Entreaty *n.* توسل . إلتماس

Entry *n.* دخول . مدخل . تقييد

Entwine *v. t.* فتل ـ . حبك ـ

Enumerate *v. t.* عد ـ . أحصى

Enunciate *v. t.* أعلن . نطق ـ

Envelop *v. t.* غلف . لف ـ

Envelope *n.* غلاف . ظرف

Envenom *v. t.* صم ـ . أحقد

Enviable *a.* مهيج الحسد . مشتهى

Envious *a.* حاسد . حسود

Environ *v. t.* أحاط . أحدق به

Environment *n.* إحاطة

Environs *n. pl.* سَوَادٌ . ضَوَاحٍ

Envoy *n.* رَسُوْلٌ . مُعْتَمَدٌ . سَفِيرٌ

Envy *n.* or *v. t.* حَسَدٌ . حَسَدَ

Ephemeral *a.* فَانٍ . قَلِيلُ ٱلْبَقَاءِ

Epic *a.* or *n.* قِصَّةٌ شِعْرِيَّةٌ

Epicure *n.* / Epicurean *a.* } مُتَنَعِّمٌ . شَهْوَانِيٌّ

Epidemic *n.* or *a.* وَبَاءٌ . وَبَائِيٌّ

Epidermis *n.* بَشَرَةٌ

Epiglottis *n.* لِسَانُ ٱلْمِزْمَارِ

Epigram *n.* شِعْرٌ . قَصِيرٌ . فَكِهٌ

Epilepsy *n.* دَاءُ ٱلصَّرْعِ

Epileptic *a.* صَرِيعٌ . مُصَابٌ بِٱلصَّرْعِ

Episcopal *a.* / Episcopalian *n.* } أُسْقُفِيٌّ

Episode *n.* حَادِثَةٌ . إِسْتِطْرَادِيَّةٌ

Epistle *n.* رِسَالَةٌ

Epitaph *n.* كِتَابَةٌ عَلَى قَبْرٍ

Epithet *n.* صِفَةٌ . لَقَبٌ

Epitome *n.* مُخْتَصَرٌ . خُلَاصَةٌ

Epitomize *v. t.* لَخَّصَ . أَوْجَزَ . إِخْتَصَرَ

Epoch *n.* عَصْرٌ . زَمَنٌ

Equable *a.* مُتَسَاوٍ

Equal *a.* or *n.* or *v. t.* مُسَاوٍ . قَرِينٌ . سَاوَى

Equality *n.* مُسَاوَاةٌ . مُعَادَلَةٌ

Equalize *v. t.* سَاوَى . عَدَّلَ

Equanimity *n.* هُدُوءُ ٱلْعَقْلِ

Equation *n.* تَسْوِيَةٌ . مُعَادَلَةٌ جَبْرِيَّةٌ

Equator *n.* خَطُّ ٱلْإِسْتِوَاءِ

Equatorial *a.* مَنْسُوبٌ لِخَطِّ ٱلْإِسْتِوَاءِ

Equestrian *a.* or *n.* مُتَعَلِّقٌ بِرُكُوبِ ٱلْخَيْلِ . خَيَّالٌ . فَارِسٌ .

Equiangular *a.* مُتَسَاوِي ٱلزَّوَايَا

Equidistant *a.* مُتَسَاوِيَ ٱلْبُعْدِ

Equilateral *a.* مُتَسَاوِيَ ٱلْأَضْلَاعِ

Equilibrium *n.* تَوَازُنٌ

Equinoctial *a.* إِعْتِدَالِيٌّ

Equinox *n.* إِعْتِدَالُ ٱللَّيْلِ وَٱلنَّهَارِ

Equip *v. t.* جَوَّزَ . أهبَ

Epuipage *n.* مُهِمَّاتٌ . اتبَاعٌ

Equipment *n.* تَجْهِيزٌ . جهازٌ

Equitable *a.* عَادِلٌ . مُنْصِفٌ

Equity *n.* عَدْلٌ . إِنْصَافٌ

Equivalent *n.* مُسَاوٍ . مُعَادِلٌ

Equivocal *a.* ذُو مَعْنَيَيْنِ . مُشْتَبِهٌ

Equivocate *v. t.* لَبَّسَ فِي ٱلْكَلَامِ

Era *n.* عَصْرٌ . مُدَّةٌ

Eradicate *v. t.* إِسْتَأْصَلَ

Erase *v. t.* مَحَا ـُ . سَحَقَ ـَ

Erasure *n.* مَحْوٌ

Ere *ad.* قَبْلَ أَنْ . قَبْلُ

Erect *a.* or *v. t.* مُنْتَصِبٌ . نَصَبَ ـُ . اقام

Erection *n.* إِقَامَةٌ . نَصْبٌ

Erelong *ad.* بَعْدَ قَلِيلٍ

Erosion *n.* قَضْمٌ . قَرْضٌ

Erosive *a.* آكِلٌ . قَاضِمٌ

Err *v. i.* غَلِطَ ـَ . ضَلَّ ـِ . خَطِئَ

Errand *n.* عَرَضٌ

Erratic *a.* ضَالٌ . زَائِغٌ . غَيْرُ مَضْبُوطٍ

Erratum / Errata *pl. n.* } *n.* غَلَطٌ . خَطَأٌ

Erroneous *a.* مَغْلُوطٌ

Error *n.* غَلَطٌ . خَطَأٌ

Erudition *n.* عِلْمٌ غَزِيرٌ

Eruption *n.* إِنْفِجَارٌ . بَثَرٌ

Erysipelas *n.* مَرَضُ ٱلْحُمْرَةِ

Escape *n.* or *v. i.* نَجَاةٌ . نَجَا ـُ

Eschew *v. t.* رَفَضَ ـِ ـُ . تَنَحَّى عَنْ

Escort *v. t.* or *n.* خَفَرَ ـِ ـُ . خَفَرٌ

Esophagus *n.* أَلْمَرِيءُ

Especial *a.* خَاصٌّ . خُصُوصِيٌّ

Especially *ad.* خَاصَّةً

Espouse *v. t.* خَطَبَ ـُ (إِمْرَأَةً)

Espy *v. t.* إِسْتَطْلَعَ . إِسْتَكْشَفَ

Esquire *n.* سَيِّدٌ

Essay *v. t.* جَرَّبَ

Essay *n.* تجربة . مَقَالَة

Essence *n.* مَاهِيَّة . عِطْر

Essential *a.* جَوْهَرِيّ . ضَرُورِيّ

Essentially *ad.* حَقِيقَةً

Establish *v. t.* اقَامَ . ثَبَّتَ

Establishment *n.* إِقَامَة . بِنَاء

Estate *n.* حَال . مُلْك

Real-estate *n.* أَلْأَمْلَاكُ غَيْرُ ٱلْمَنْقُولَة

Esteem *n.* or *v. t.* إِعْتِبَار . إِعْتَبَرَ

Estimable *a.* مُسْتَحِقُّ ٱلْمَدْحِ

Estimate *v. t.* حَسَبَ . ثَمَّنَ

Estimation *n.* تَثْمِين . إِعْتِبَار

Estrange *v. t.* نَفَّرَ

Estuary *n.* مَصَبُّ نَهرٍ

Eternal *a.* سَرْمَدِيّ . أَبَدِيّ

Eternity *n.* أَلْأَبَد . أَلْأَزَل

Ether *n.* إِثِير

Ethical *a.* ادَبِيّ

Ethics *n. pl.* عِلْمُ ٱلْآدَابِ

Ethnology *n.* أَلْبَحْثُ عَنْ أَجْنَاسِ ٱلْبَشَرِ

Etiquette *n.* آدَابُ ٱلْإِكْرَامِ

Etymology *n.* إِشْتِقَاقُ ٱلْكَلَامِ

Eulogy *n.* تَقْرِيظ . تَابِين

Eunuch *n.* خَصِيّ

European *n.* اورُبِيّ

Evacuate *v. t.* أَخْلَى . تَرَكَ

Evacuation *n.* إِخْلَاء . تَرْك

Evade *v. t.* إِجْتَنَبَ . مَلَصَ مِنْ

Evanescent *a.* فَانٍ . زَائِل

Evangelical *a.* إِنْجِيلِيّ

Evangelist *n.* مُبَشِّر إِنْجِيلِيّ

Evaporate *v. i.* تَحَوَّلَ بُخَاراً

Evasion *n.* إِجْتِنَاب . مُوَارَبَة

Evasive *a.* مُجْتَنِب . مُحَاوِل . مُوَارِب

Eve / Evening } *n.* مساء . عَشِيَّة

Even *a.* سَهْلٌ . مُسْتَوٍ

Even *ad.* حَتَّى . كَذَلِكَ . ايضاً

Event *n.* حَادِثَةٌ . نَتِيجَةٌ

Eventful *a.* كَثِيرُ ٱلْحَوَادِثِ

Eventually *a.* فِي ٱلنِّهَايَةِ . أَخِيراً

Ever *ad.* دَائِماً . كُلَّ حِينٍ

Evergreen *n.* نَبَات دَائِمُ ٱلْإِخْضِرارِ

Everlasting *a.* أَبَدِيٌّ . بَاقٍ

Evermore *ad.* دَائماً . أَبداً

Every *a.* كُلّ

Everywhere *ad.* فِي كُلِّ مَكَانٍ

Evict *v. t.* أَخْرَجَ . طَرَدَ ـُ

Evidence *n.* بُرْهَانٌ . دَلِيلٌ . شَهَادَةٌ

Evident *a.* وَاضِحٌ . ظَاهِرٌ . جَلِيٌّ

Evil *n.* or *a.* شَرٌّ . شِرِّيرٌ

Evince *v. t.* اظْهَرَ . بَيَّنَ

Evoke *v. t.* إِسْتَدْعَى

Evolution *n.* نَشْرٌ . نُشُوءٌ

Evolve *v. t.* نَشَرَ ـُ اخْرَجَ

Ewe *n.* شَاةٌ . نَعْجَةٌ

Exact *a.* or *v. t.* مَضْبُوطٌ . أَلْزَمَ

Exaction *n.* بَلْصٌ . ظُلْمٌ فِي ٱلْأَخْذ

Exactly *ad.* تَمَاماً . بِضَبْطٍ

Exactness *n.* ضَبْطٌ . إِتْقَانٌ

Exaggerate *v. t.* بَالَغَ . غَالَى فِي

Exaggeration *n.* مُبَالَغَةٌ . مُغَالَاةٌ

Exalt *v. t.* رَقَّى . عَظَّمَ . فَخَّمَ

Exaltation *n.* تَرْقِيَةٌ . سُمُوٌّ . رِفْعَةٌ

Exalted *a.* مُرْتَفِعٌ . سَامٍ

Examination *n.* فَحْصٌ . إِمْتِحَانٌ

Examine *v. t.* فَحَصَ . إِمْتَحَنَ

Example *n.* مِثَالٌ . نَمُوذَجٌ . قِدْوَة

Exasperate *v. i.* أَغَاظَ . أَسْخَطَ

Exasperation *n.* إِغَاظَةٌ . حَنَقٌ

Excavate *v. t.* حَفَرَ ـِ . نَبَشَ ـُ

Excavation *n.* حَفْرٌ . حُفْرَةٌ

Exceed *v.t.* or *i.* زَادَ ـِ . فَاقَ ـُ . جَاوَزَ

Exceeding *a.* فَائِقٌ . عَظِيمٌ جِدًّا

Exceedingly *ad.* جِدًّا . لِلْغَايَةِ

Excel *v. t.* or *i.* فَاقَ ـُ . سَبَقَ ـُ

Excellence / Excellency *n.* فَضْلٌ . جُودَةٌ . سُمُوٌّ

Excellent *a.* فَاضِلٌ . فَاخِرٌ . نَفِيسٌ

Except *v. t.* إِسْتَثْنَى مِنْ

Except / Excepting *pr.* إِلَّا . غَيْرُ . مَا عَدَا

Exception *n.* إِسْتِثْنَاءٌ . شُذُوذٌ

Exceptional *a.* شَاذٌّ . إِسْتِثْنَائِيٌّ

Excess *n.* زِيَادَةٌ . مُجَاوَزَةُ ٱلْحَدِّ

Excessive *a.* زَائِدٌ جِدًّا . مُفْرِطٌ

Exchange *v. t.* or *n.* بَادَلَ . مُبَادَلَةٌ

Excision *n.* قَطْعٌ . بَتْرٌ

Excitable *a.* سَرِيعُ ٱلْهَيَجَانِ

Excite *v. t.* هَيَّجَ . أَثَارَ . حَرَّكَ

Excited *a.* مُتَهَيِّجٌ . ثَائِرٌ

Exciting *a.* مُهَيِّجٌ . مُحَرِّكٌ

Excitement *n.* هَيَجَانٌ . ثَوَرَانٌ

Exclaim *v. i.* صَاحَ ـِ . صَرَخَ ـُ

Exclamation *n.* صُرَاخٌ . صَيْحَةٌ

Exclude *v. t.* اخْرَجَ . إِسْتَثْنَى

Exclusion *n.* إِخْرَاجٌ . نَفْيٌ . مَنْعٌ

Exclusive *a.* نَافٍ . مَانِعٌ . خَاصٌّ

Excommunicate *v. t.* حَرَمَ ـِ

Excommunication *n.* حِرْمٌ

Excrement *n.* بَرَازٌ . رَوْثٌ

Excrescence *n.* نُتُوءٌ غَيْرُ طَبِيعِيٍّ

Excretion *n.* إِفْرَازُ ٱلْفُضُولِ

Excruciating *a.* أَلِيمٌ جِدًّا . مُعَذِّبٌ

Exculpate *v. t.* بَرَّأَ . زَكَّى

Excursion *n.* سَفْرَةٌ قَصِيرَةٌ

Excusable *a.* مَعْذُورٌ

Excuse *v. t.* عَذَرَ ـِ . سَامَحَ

Excuse *n.* عُذْرٌ

Execrate *v. t.* لَعَنَ ـَ . كَرِهَ ـَ

Execute *v. t.* انجَزَ . أعدَمَ (الحَيَاة)

Executioner *n.* مُعدِمُ الحَيَاةِ . جَلَّادٌ

Executive *a.* or *n.* مُجرٍ . مُنفِذ . رَئِيسٌ

Executor *a.* وَكِيلُ تَرِكَةٍ . وَصِيٌّ

Exemplary *a.* مُستَحِقٌّ الاِقتِدَاءِ بِهِ

Exemplify *v. t.* مَثَّلَ . نَسَخَ ـَ

Exempt *v. t.* أعفَى مِنْ

Exemption *n.* إعفَاءٌ . تَحرِيرٌ مِنْ

Exercise *n.* مُمَارَسَةٌ . رِيَاضَةٌ

Exert *v. t.* بَذَلَ الجُهدَ ـُ . سَعَى ـَ

Exertion *n.* إجتِهَادٌ . سَعيٌ . جِدٌّ

Exhale *v. i.* or *t.* زَفَرَ ـِ

Exhaust *v. t.* فَرَّغَ . أفنَى

Exhaustion *n.* نَفَادٌ . كَلَالٌ

Exhaustive *a.* مُدَقِّقُ البَحثِ . كَامِلٌ

Exhibit *v. t.* أظهَرَ . عَرَضَ ـِ

Exhibiton *n.* إظهَارٌ . مَعرَضٌ

Exhilarate *v. t.* ابهَجَ . أنعَش

Exhort *v.* وَعَظَ . انذَرَ . حَثَّ ـُ

Exhortation *n.* وَعظ . إنذَارٌ

Exhume *v. t.* نَبَشَ ـَ المَدفُونَ

Exigence / **Exigency** *n.* إحتِيَاجٌ . إضطِرَارٌ

Exile *n.* or *v. t.* مَنفَى . نَفَى ـِ

Exist *v. i.* كَانَ ـُ . وُجِدَ

Existence *n.* وُجُودٌ

Existent *a.* / **Existing** *ppr.* or *a.* مَوجُودٌ . كَائِنٌ

Exodus *n.* خُرُوجٌ . سِفرُ الخُرُوجِ

Exonerate *v. t.* بَرَّأ

Exorbitant *a.* مُفرِطٌ . بَاهِظٌ

Exotic *a.* or *n.* أجنَبِيٌّ . (نَبَات)

Expand *v. t.* or *i.* مَدَّ ـُ . إمتَدَّ

Expanse *n.* إنبِسَاطٌ . فُسحَةٌ

Expantiate *v. i.* اطنَبَ . تَوَسَّعَ فِي

Expatriate *v. t.* أجلَى عَنِ الوَطَنِ

Expect *v. t.* إنتَظَرَ . تَوَقَّع

Expectancy / **Expectation** *n.* إنتِظَارٌ . تَوَقُّعٌ

Expectorate *v. t.* بَصَقَ ـُ . نَفَثَ ـُ

Expectoration *n.* بصْق . نَفْث

Expedience / Expediency } *n.* مُوَافَقَةٌ . مُنَاسَبَةٌ

Expedient *a.* مُوَافِقٌ . نَافِعٌ

Expedient *n.* وَسِيلَةٌ . وَاسِطَةٌ

Expedite *v. t.* عَجَّلَ . بَعَثَ ـَ

Expedition *n.* سُرْعَةٌ . إِرْسَالِيَّةٌ

Expel *v. t.* طَرَدَ ـُ . أَخْرَجَ

Expend *v. t.* صَرَفَ ـِ . أَنْفَقَ

Expenditure *n.* صَرْفٌ . نَفَقَةٌ

Expense *n.* نَفَقَةٌ . مَصْرُوفٌ

Expensive *a.* غَالٍ . (مُكَلِّفٌ)

Experience *n.* or *v. t.* إِخْتِبَارٌ . إِخْتَبَرَ

Experienced *a.* خَبِيرٌ . مُخْتَبِرٌ

Experiment *n.* إِمْتِحَانٌ . تَجْرِبَةٌ

Expert *n.* مَاهِرٌ . بَارِعٌ . خَبِيرٌ

Expiate *v. t.* كَفَّرَ عَنْ

Expiration *n.* إِنْقِضَاءٌ . نِهَايَةٌ

Expire *v. i.* مَاتَ . إِنْقَضَى . زَفَرَ ـِ

Explain *v. t.* فَسَّرَ . أَوْضَحَ

Explanation *n.* تَفْسِيرٌ . إِيضَاحٌ

Explanatory *a.* مُفَسِّرٌ . تَفْسِيرِيٌّ

Explicit *a.* صَرِيحٌ . وَاضِحٌ

Explode *v. i.* إِنْفَجَرَ

Exploration *n.* إِكْتِشَافٌ . رَوْدٌ

Explore *v. t.* زَادَ ـُ . إِكْتَشَفَ

Explosion *n.* إِنْفِجَارٌ

Explosive *a.* or *n.* مُسَبِّبُ ٱلْإِنْفِجَارِ

Export *v. t.* أَصْدَرَ بَضَائِعَ

Exports *n. pl.* بَضَائِعُ صَادِرَةٌ

Expose *v. t.* كَشَفَ ـِ . عَرَضَ ـِ

Exposition *n.* عَرْضٌ . تَفْسِيرٌ

Expostulate *v. i.* نَصَحَ ـَ عَاقَبَ

Exposure *n.* كَشْفٌ . عَرْضٌ

Expound *v. t.* فَسَّرَ . شَرَحَ ـَ

Express *a.* or *n.* صَرِيحٌ . خَاصٌ

Express *n.* رَسُولٌ خَاصٌّ . مَرْكَبَةٌ خَاصَّةٌ

Express *v. t.* عَصَرَ ـ أَظْهَرَ

Expressed *a.* مَقُولٌ . مَنْطُوق بِهِ

Expression *n.* عِبَارَةٌ . أُسْلُوبُ ٱلنُّطْقِ

Expressive *a.* بَلِيغٌ . مُفِيدُ ٱلْمَعْنَى

Expressly *ad.* خَاصَّةً . صَرِيحاً

Expulsion *n.* طَرْدٌ . إِخْرَاجٌ

Expunge *v. t.* مَحَا ـُ أَزَالَ

Expurgate *v. t.* طَهَّرَ . نَقَّحَ

Exquisite *a.* نَفِيسٌ . فَاخِرٌ

Extant *a.* بَاقٍ فِي ٱلْوُجُودِ

Extemporaneous } *a.* مُرْتَجَلٌ
Extemporary }

Extempore *ad.* إِرْتِجَالاً

Extemporize *v. t.* إِبْتَدَهَ . إِرْتَجَلَ

Extend *v. t.* or *i.* مَدَّ . إِمْتَدَّ

Extension *n.* مَدٌ . إِمْتِدَادٌ . إِتِّسَاعٌ

Extensive *a.* مُمْتَدٌّ . مُتَّسِعٌ

Extent *n.* إِمْتِدَادٌ . سِعَةٌ

Extenuate *v. t.* خَفَّفَ . خَفَّضَ

Exterior *a.* or *n.* خَارِجِيٌّ . ٱلْخَارِجُ

Exterminate *v. t.* إِستَأْصَلَ . أَبَادَ

External *a.* خَارِجِيٌّ . عَرَضِيٌّ

Extinct *a.* مُنْقَرِضٌ . مَعْدُومٌ

Extinction *n.* إِنْقِرَاضٌ

Extinguish *v. t.* أَطْفَأَ . أَزَالَ

Extirpate *v. t.* إِسْتَأْصَلَ . أَبَادَ

Extol *v. t.* مَجَّدَ . فَخَّمَ

Extort *v. t.* بَلَصَ

Extortion *n.* بَلْصٌ

Extortionate *a.* } بَلَّاصٌ
Extortioner *n.* }

Extra *n.* or. *a.* زِيَادَةٌ . زَائِدٌ

Extract *n.* جُمْلَةٌ مُقْتَبَسَةٌ . خُلَاصَةٌ

Extract *v. t.* إِسْتَخْرَجَ . إِقْتَبَسَ

Extraction *n.* إِسْتِخْرَجٌ . نَسَبٌ

Extraordinary *a.* فَوْقَ ٱلْعَادَةِ . غَرِيبٌ

Extravagance *n.* إِسْرَافٌ . إِفْرَاطٌ

Extravagant *a.* مُسْرِفٌ . مفْرِط . مبَالِغٌ

Extreme *a.* اقْصَى . اشَد

Extremely *ad.* لِلْغَايَةِ . جِدًّا

Extreme / Extremity *n.* طَرَفٌ . حَاجَةٌ شَدِيدَةٌ

Extricate *v. t.* نَشَلَ ـَ . أنْقَذَ . فكّ

Exuberance *n.* وَفْرَةٌ . غَزَارَةٌ . خِصْبٌ

Exude *v. t.* or *i.* رَشَحَ . أفْرَزَ

Exult *v. i.* إِبْتَهَجَ . تَهَلَّلَ

Eye *n.* or *v. t.* عَيْنٌ ج أَعْيُنٌ . رَاقَبَ

Eyeball *n.* مقْلَةٌ . مقَلٌ

Eye-brow *n.* حَاجِبٌ ج حَوَاجِبُ

Eye-glass *n.* مَنْظَرٌ

Eye-lashes *n. pl.* هدْبٌ ج أَهْدَابٌ

Eyelid *n.* جَفْنٌ ج أَجْفَانٌ

Eye-sight *n.* بَصَرٌ . عيَان

Eye-tooth *n.* Tusk. نَابٌ ج أنْيَابٌ

F

Fable *n.* خُرَافَةٌ . خُزَعْبَلَةٌ

Fabric *n.* بِنْيَةٌ . نَسِيجٌ

Fabricate *v. t.* صَنَعَ . إِخْتَلَقَ

Fabulous *a.* خُرَافِيٌّ . خُزَعْبَلِيٌّ

Face *n.* or *v. t.* وَجْهٌ . سطْحٌ . وَاجَهَ

Facetious *a.* مَازِحٌ . هَازِلٌ

Facilitate *v. t.* سَهَّلَ . يَسَّرَ

Facility *n.* سُهُولَةٌ . يُسْرٌ

Fac-simile *n.* نُسْخَةٌ طِبْقُ ٱلْأَصْلِ

Fact *n.* حَقِيقَةٌ . أَمْرٌ . وَاقِعٌ

Faction *n.* عُصْبَةٌ . حِزْبٌ

Factious *a.* تَحَزُّبِيٌّ . مُتَحَزِّبٌ

Factitious *a.* مُصَنَّعٌ

Factor *n.* عَامِلٌ . أَصْلُ ٱلْحَاصِلِ . ضِلْعٌ

Factory *n.* مَعْمَلٌ

Faculty *n.* قُوَّةٌ . طَاقَةٌ . (عُمْدَةٌ)

Fade *v. i.* ذَبُلَ ـُ . جَرِدَ ـَ . بَاخَ ـُ

Fagot *n.* حُزْمَةُ قُضْبَانٍ

Fail *v. t.* or *i.* خَابَ ـِ افْلَسَ

Failure *n.* خَيْبَةٌ . إِفْلَاسٌ

Fain *a.* or *ad.* مَسْرُورٌ . بِرِضًى

Faint *a.* or *v. i.* مُعْيٍ . أُعْيِيَ . غُشِيَ عَلَيْهِ

Faint-hearted *a.* جَبَانٌ . خَائِفٌ

Faintly *ad.* بِضُعْفٍ . قَلِيلاً

Faintness *n.* إِعْيَاءٌ . إِغْمَاءٌ

Fair *a.* or *n.* حَسَنٌ . صَافٍ . سُوقٌ

Fairly *ad.* بِإِسْتِقَامَةٍ . بِعَدْلٍ

Fairness *n.* عَدَالَةٌ . حُسْنٌ . بَيَاضٌ

Fairy *n.* or *a.* جِنِّيَّةٌ . جِنِّيٌّ

Faith *n.* إِيمَانٌ . إِعْتِقَادٌ . مَذْهَبٌ

Faithful *a.* أَمِينٌ . صَادِقٌ

Faithfulness *n.* أَمَانَةٌ

Faithless *a.* غَيْرُ مُؤْمِنٍ . خَائِنٌ

Falcon *n.* بَازٌ . صَقْرٌ

Falconer *n.* مُرَبِّي اوْ مُطَبِّعُ ٱلْبُزَاةِ

Fall *v. i.* or *n.* سَقَطَ ـُ وَقَعَ ـَ . سُقُوطٌ

Fallacious *a.* خَادِعٌ . سَفْسَطِيٌّ

Fallacy *n.* خَطَأٌ . إِسْتِدْلَالٌ . فَاسِدٌ

Fallible *a.* قَابِلُ ٱلْخَطَا اوْ ٱلزَّلَلِ

Fallow *a.* or *n.* أَرْضٌ غَيْرُ مَزْرُوعَةٍ

False *a.* كَاذِبٌ . مُزَوَّرٌ . بَاطِلٌ

Falsehood *n.* كِذْبٌ . زُورٌ

Falsify *v. t.* or *i.* زَوَّرَ . كَذَّبَ

Falter *v. i.* تَرَدَّدَ . قَصَّرَ . لَعْثَمَ

Fame *n.* صيتٌ عظيمٌ . شُهْرَةٌ

Famed *a.* مشهورٌ . شهيرٌ

Familiar *a.* or *n.* مألوفٌ . معروفٌ

Familiarity *n.* أُلفَة . صَدَاقةٌ . معرِفة

Familiarize *v. t.* ألّف . عوّدَ . سهّل

Family *n.* عائلة . آلٌ . نسبٌ

Famine *n.* مجاعَةٌ . قحطٌ . غَلاءٌ

Famish *v. i.* or *t.* مات جُوعاً . جوّع

Famous *a.* شهيرٌ . كثير الذِّكرِ

Fan *n.* or *v. t.* مِرْوَحةٌ . هوّى . روّح

Fanatic *n.* / Fanatical *a.* } متعصبٌ في الدِّين

Fancied *a.* موْهومٌ . متصوَّرٌ

Fanciful *a.* وَهْميٌّ . تصوُّريٌّ

Fancy *n.* or *v. t.* or *i.* وَهْمٌ . تصوّر

Fang *n.* نابٌ . مخلبٌ

Fantasm *n.* وَهْمٌ . خيالٌ

Fantastic / Fantastical } *a.* وَهْميٌّ . خياليٌّ

Fantasy *n.* وهمٌ . تصوُّرٌ . باطِلٌ

Far *a.* or *ad.* بعيدٌ . بعيداً

Farce *n.* روايةٌ سخريّةٌ . بطْلٌ

Farewell *n.* الوداعُ

Farm *n.* or *v. t.* مزرَعةٌ . فلَحَ . اقطعَ

Farmer *n.* فلاّحٌ . ملْتزِمٌ

Farming *n.* فِلاحَةٌ

Farrier *n.* بيطارٌ ج بياطِرَة

Farther *a.* أبعدُ . أيضاً

Farthing *n.* فَلْسٌ ج فُلوسٌ

Fascinate *v. t.* فتنَ . خلَبَ

Fascination *n.* إفْتِتَانٌ

Fashion *n.* or *v. t.* زيٌّ . عادةٌ . جَبَلَ

Fashionable *a.* بحسَبِ الزّيِّ او العادَةِ

Fast *a.* سَرِيعٌ . ثابتٌ . ماكِنٌ

Fast *n.* or *v. i.* صَوْمٌ . صامَ

Fasten *v. t.* مكّنَ . ثبّتَ . شدَّ

Fastidious *a.* صعبُ الإرْضاء

Fat *n.* or *a.* دُهْنٌ . سَمِينٌ

Fatal *a.* مُمِيتٌ . مُهْلِكٌ

Fatalism *n.* اَلْإِعْتِقَادُ بِالْقَدَرِ

Fatalist *n.* مُعْتَقِدٌ بِالْقَدَرِ

Fatally *ad.* مُمِيتاً

Fatality / **Fate** *n.* قَدَرٌ . قَضَاءٌ

Fated *a.* مُقَدَّرٌ . مَقْضِيٌّ بِهِ

Fates *n. pl.* تَقَادِيرُ

Father *n.* أَبٌ ج آبَاءٌ . وَالِدٌ

Father-in-law *n.* حَمٌ أَوْ حَمُو

Fatherland *n.* وَطَنٌ ج أَوْطَانٌ

Fatherless *a.* بِلاَ أَبٍ . يَتِيمٌ

Fatherly *a.* أَبَوِيٌّ

Fathom *n.* or *v. t.* قَامَةٌ . سَبَرَ ـُ

Fathomless *a.* عَمِيقٌ لاَ يُسْبَرُ غَوْرُهُ

Fatigue *n.* or *v. t.* وَنًى . تَعَبٌ . اتْعَبَ

Fatling *n.* مُسَمَّنٌ . مَعْلُوفٌ

Fatness *n.* سَمَانَةٌ . دَسَمٌ

Fatten *v. t.* سَمَّنَ . دَسَّمَ

Fatty *a.* دَسِمٌ . دَهِنٌ

Faucet *n.* انْبُوبَةٌ . حَنَفِيَّةٌ

Fault *n.* عَيْبٌ . ذَنْبٌ . غَلَطٌ

Faultless *a.* بِلاَ عَيْبٍ . كَامِلٌ

Faulty *a.* عَائِبٌ . مَغْلُوطٌ . نَاقِصٌ

Favour *v. t.* أَحْسَنَ إِلَى . اعَانَ

Favour *n.* مَعْرُوفٌ . نِعْمَةٌ . رِضًى

Favourable *a.* مُوَافِقٌ . لَطِيفٌ

Favourite *n.* or *a.* خَلِيلٌ . عَزِيزٌ . حَبِيبٌ

Favouritism *n.* مُحَابَاةٌ

Fawn *v. t.* تَذَلَّلَ لَهُ . دَاهَنَ

Fawn *n.* or *a.* وَلَدُ الْإِيِلِ . مِنْ لَوْنِهِ

Fealty *n.* أَمَانَةٌ . طَاعَةٌ

Fear *n.* or *v. t.* خَوْفٌ . خَافَ ـَ

Fearful *a.* خَائِفٌ . مُخِيفٌ . رَائِعٌ

Fearfulness *n.* خَوْفٌ . حَالَتُهُ

Fearless *a.* بِلاَ خَوْفٍ . جَسُورٌ

Feasible *n.* مُمْكِنٌ فِعْلُهُ

Feast *n.* or *v. t.* or *i.* عِيدٌ . وَلِيمَةٌ . أَوْلَمَ

Feat *n.* عَمَلٌ . عَجِيبٌ

Feather *n.* رِيشَةٌ ج رِيشٌ

Feature *n.* هَيْئَةٌ . طَلْعَةٌ . صِفَةٌ

February *n.* شَهْرُ شُبَاطٍ (فبراير)

Fecund *a.* مُخْصِبٌ . مُثْمِرٌ (لِلْحَيَوَانِ)

Fee *n.* or *v. t.* أُجْرَةٌ . هِبَةٌ . آجَرَ

Feeble *a.* ضَعِيفٌ . عَاجِزٌ

Feebleness *n.* ضَعْفٌ . وَهْنٌ

Feed *a.* or *v. t.* عَلَفٌ . أَطْعَمَ

Feel *v. t.* or *i.* لَمَسَ ـِ . حَسَّ ـُ

Feeling *n.* حَسٌّ . شُعُورٌ . إِنْفِعَالٌ

Feign *v. t.* تَظَاهَرَ . تَرَآءَى

Feint *n.* حِيلَةٌ . تَظَاهُرٌ

Felicitate *v. t.* هَنَّأَ

Felicity *n.* سَعَادَةٌ . غِبْطَةٌ

Fell *v. t.* رَمَى . أَلْقَى

Fellow *n.* رَفِيقٌ . قَرِينٌ

Fellowship *n.* أُلْفَةٌ . صُحْبَةٌ . شَرِكَةٌ

Felon
Felonious *a.* } مُجْرِمٌ بِذَنْبٍ عَظِيمٍ

Felony *n.* جَرِيمَةٌ عَظِيمَةٌ . جِنَايَةٌ

Felt *n.* لِبْدٌ ج لُبُودٌ . وَأَلْبَادٌ

Female *n.* or *a.* أُنْثَى ج اِنَاثٌ

Feminine *a.* مُؤَنَّثٌ . أُنْثَوِيٌّ

Fen *n.* مُسْتَنْقَعٌ

Fence *n.* or *v. t.* سِيَاجٌ . سَيَّجَ

Ferment
Fermentation } *a.* إِخْتِمَارٌ . هَيَجَانٌ

Ferment *v. i.* or *t.* خَمَرَ ـُ . إِخْتَمَرَ

Fern *n.* خِنْشَارٌ (نَبَاتٌ)

Ferocious *a.* ضَارٍ . مُفْتَرِسٌ

Ferocity *n.* تَوَحُّشٌ . قَسَاوَةٌ

Ferry *n.* or *v. t.* مَعْبَرٌ . عَبَّرَ

Fertile *a.* مُخْصِبٌ . مُثْمِرٌ

Fertility *n.* خِصْبٌ

Fertilize *v. t.* خَصَّبَ . لَقَّحَ

Fervency *n.* حَرَارَةٌ . حَمَاسَةٌ

Fervent / **Fervid** } *a.* حَارٌّ . غَيُورٌ . حَادٌّ

Fervour *n.* حَرَارَةٌ . حَمَاسَةٌ . حَمِيَّةٌ

Festal *a.* مُفْرِحٌ . عِيدِيٌّ

Fester *v. i.* or *n.* تَقَيَّحَ . قَيْحٌ

Festival *n.* عِيدٌ . فَرَحٌ

Festivity *n.* فَرَحٌ . بَسْطٌ . عِيدٌ

Fetch *v. t.* جَاءَ بِهِ . أَحْضَرَ

Fetid *a.* مُنْتِنٌ . مُخِمٌ

Fetter *n.* or *v. t.* قَيْدٌ . قَيَّدَ

Fetus *n.* جَنِينٌ ج أَجِنَّة

Feud *n.* نِزَاعٌ . شِقَاقٌ

Fever *n.* حُمَّى

Feverish *a.* مَحْمُومٌ

Few *a.* قَلِيلٌ . يَسِيرٌ

Fib *n.* or *v. i.* كِذْبَة . كَذَبَ

Fibre / **Fibril** } *n.* لِيفَةٌ . لِيفٌ . لُوَيْفَةٌ

Fickle *a.* مُتَقَلِّبٌ . مُتَرَدِّدٌ

Fickleness *n.* تَقَلُّبٌ . طَيْشٌ

Fiction *n.* خِرَافَةٌ . كِذْبٌ

Fictitious *a.* كَاذِبٌ . وَهْمِيٌّ

Fiddle *n.* كَمَنْجَة

Fidelity *n.* أَمَانَةٌ . صِدْقٌ

Fidget *v. t.* قَلِقَ ـ ضَجِرَ ـ

Fidgety *a.* قَلِقٌ . مُضْطَرِبٌ . ضَجِرٌ

Field *n.* حَقْلٌ . سَاحَة

Field-piece *n.* مَدْفَعٌ . صَغِيرٌ

Fiend *n.* عَدُوٌّ . خَبِيثٌ . شَيْطَان

Fierce *a.* عَنِيفٌ . حَادٌّ . شَرِسٌ

Fiery *a.* نَارِيٌّ . حَادُّ ٱلطَّبْعِ

Fife *n.* مِزْمَارٌ

Fifteen *a.* خَمْسَةَ عَشَرَ . خَمْسَ عَشْرَةَ

Fifteenth *a.* أَلْخَامِسَ عَشَرَ

Fifth *a.* or *n.* خَامِسٌ . خُمْسٌ

Fiftieth / **Fifty** } *a.* أَلْخَمْسُونَ . خَمْسُونَ

Fig *n.* تِينَةٌ

Fight *n.* or *v. t.* قِتَالٌ . قَاتَلَ

Figurative *a.* مَجَازِيٌّ . إِسْتِعَارِيٌّ

Figure *n.* or *v.t.* or *i.* صُورَةٌ . صَوَّرَ . حَسَبَ . ظَهَرَ

Filbert *n.* بُنْدُقَةٌ

Filch *v. t.* سَرَقَ ـِ . أَسَلَّ

File *n.* or *v. t.* مِبْرَدٌ . صَفٌّ . بَرَدَ ـُ

Filial *a.* بَنَوِيٌّ . وَلَدِيٌّ

Fill *v. t.* مَلأَ . أَفْعَمَ

Filly *n.* فَلُوٌّ . مُهْرَةٌ

Film *n.* غِشَاوَةٌ

Filter *n.* or *v. t.* مِصفَاةٌ . صَفَّى

Filth / **Filthness** } *n.* وَسَخٌ . قَذَرٌ

Filthy *a.* وَسِخٌ . قَذِرٌ

Filtrate *v. t.* صَفَّى

Fin *n.* زِعْنِفَةُ (ٱلسَّمَكِ)

Final *a.* نِهَائِيٌّ . أَخِيرٌ

Finally *ad.* أَخِيراً

Finance *n.* مَالِيَّةٌ

Financial *a.* مَالِيٌّ

Financier *n.* مَاهِرٌ بِٱلْأُمُورِ ٱلْمَالِيَّةِ

Find *v. t.* (*pp.* Found) وَجَدَ ـِ

Fine *a.* دَقِيقٌ . نَاعِمٌ

Fine *n.* or *v. t.* غَرَامَةٌ . غَرَّمَ

Fineness *n.* دِقَّةٌ . رِقَّةٌ

Finery *n.* زِينَةٌ . حِلْيَةٌ

Finesse *n.* دَهَاءٌ . حِيلَةٌ

Finger *n.* or *v.t.* إِصْبَعٌ . مَسَّ . جَسَّ ـُ

Finish *v. t.* أَنْهَى . أَنْجَزَ . أَكْمَلَ

Finite *a.* مَحْدُودٌ . مُتَنَاهٍ

Fir *n.* شَرْبِينٌ . (شَجَرٌ)

Fire *n.* نَارٌ . حَرَارَةُ ٱلْخُلْقِ

Fire *v. t.* اوْقَدَ . أَطْلَقَ (ٱلْأَسْلِحَةَ)

Fire-arms *n. pl.* أَسْلِحَةٌ . نَارِيَةٌ

Fire-engine *n.* آلَةٌ لِإِطْفَاءِ ٱلنَّارِ

Firefly *n.* حُبَاحِبُ

Fire-place *n.* مَوْقِدٌ

Fireside *n.* مَوْقِدُ ٱلْعَائِلَةِ . ٱلْبَيْتُ

Fireworks *n. pl.* أَلْعَابٌ . نارِيَةٌ

Firm *a.* or *n.* ثابتٌ. رَاسِخ شِرْكَةٌ (تجار)

Firmament *n.* جَلَدٌ . جوٌّ

Firman *n.* فرمان

Firmly *ad.* بثَبَاتٍ . بعزمٍ

Firmness *n.* ثَبَات . عزْمٌ . متانَةٌ

First *a.* or *ad.* ٱلاوَّل. أَوَّلاً. إِبْتِدَآءً

First-born *n.* بِكْرٌ ج أَبْكَارٌ

First-rate *a.* عَال . فَائِقٌ

Fiscal *a.* مُختَصٌّ بٱلمَالِيَّةِ

Fish *n.* or *v. t.* or *i.* سَمَكٌ. صادَ ـِ

Fisherman *n.* صَيَّادُ سَمَكٍ

Fishery *a.* صيْدُ ٱلسَّمَكِ او محلهُ

Fish-hook *n.* صِنَّارَةُ ٱلصَّيْدِ

Fishing *n.* صَيْدُ ٱلسَّمك

Fissure *n.* شِقٌّ . فَلْقٌ

Fist *n.* قَبْضَةُ ٱليَدِ

Fit *n.* نَوْبة. صرْعٌ . دَوْرٌ

Fit *a.* or *v. t.* مُنَاسِبٌ. نَاسَبَ

Fitful *a.* مُتَغَيِّرٌ. غيرُ مضبُوْطٍ

Fitness *n.* لياقَة . مُنَاسبَةٌ

Five *n.* or *a.* خَمْسَةٌ

Fivefold *a.* or *ad.* خَمْسَةُ أَضْعَافٍ

Fix *v. t.* or *i.* ثَبَّتَ . مَكَّنَ . أَرْسخَ ـَ

Fizz *v. i.* / Fizzle *v. i.* صفرَ ـِ (نَارٌ)

Flabby / Flaccid *a.* رَخْوٌ. مُرْتَخٍ

Flag *n.* حلفَآءُ . رَايةٌ . بَلَاطَةٌ

Flag *v. t.* ضَعُفَ ـُ. إِسْتَرْخَى

Flagitious *a.* خَبِيث .فَاجِرٌ

Flagon *n.* إِبْرِيقٌ لِلْمُسْكِرَاتِ

Flagrant *a.* مفْرِطٌ . قَبِيحٌ

Flag-ship *n.* بَارِجَةُ أَمِيْرِ البَحْرِ

Flag-staff *n.* سَارِيَةُ ٱلرَّايَةِ

Flag-stone *n.* بَلَاطَةٌ

Flake *n.* صَفِيحَةٌ رَقِيقَةٌ

Flame *n.* or *v. i.* لَهِيبٌ. إِلْتَهَبَ

Flaming *a.* مُلْتَهِبٌ . بَرَّاقٌ . مُحْتَدٌّ

Flank *n.* or *v.* خَاصِرَةٌ أَتَى ٱلْجَانِبَ

Flannel *n.* نَسِيجٌ صُوفِيٌّ (فَلَانِلَّا)

Flap *n.* or *v. t.* or *i.* ذَيْلٌ (ثَوْبٍ) خَفَقَ ـِ

Flare *v. i.* خَفَقَ (ٱللَّهِيبُ) تَأَلَّقَ

Flash *n.* or *v. i.* وَمِيضٌ . أَوْمَضَ . بَرَقَ ـُ

Flask *n.* قِنِّينَةٌ . قَارُورَةٌ

Flat *a.* or *n.* مُسَطَّحٌ . طَبَقَةٌ . سَهْلٌ

Flatten *v. t.* or *i.* سَطَّحَ . تَسَطَّحَ

Flatter *v. t.* مَلِقَ ـَ . دَاهَنَ

Flatterer / **Flattering** مُتَمَلِّقٌ . مُدَاهِنٌ

Flattery *n.* مَلَقٌ . مُدَاهَنَةٌ

Flavour *n.* or *v. t.* طَعْمٌ . رَائِحَةٌ . تَبَّلَ

Flaw *n.* عَيْبٌ . خَلَلٌ . شَقٌّ

Flax *n.* كَتَّانٌ (نَبَاتٌ) قُنَّبٌ

Flay *v. t.* سَلَخَ ـُ . كَشَطَ ـِ

Flea *n.* بُرْغُوثٌ ج بَرَاغِيثُ

Flee(**Fled**) *v. i.* هَرَبَ ـُ . فَرَّ ـِ

Fleece *n.* or *v. t.* جَزَّةٌ . جَزَّ . سَلَبَ

Fleet *a.* or *n.* سَرِيعٌ . اسْطُولٌ

Fleeting *a.* وَقْتِيٌّ . فَانٍ

Flesh *n.* لَحْمٌ . جَسَدٌ . أَلْبَشَرُ

Fleshly *a.* حَيَوَانِيٌّ . شَهْوَانِيٌّ

Fleshy *a.* سَمِينٌ . لَحْمِيٌّ

Flew *pret. of fly* طَارَ

Flexibility *n.* لِينٌ . مُرُونَةٌ

Flexible *a.* لَيِّنٌ . مَرِنٌ . مُنْقَادٌ

Flicker *v. i.* خَفَقَ ـِ لَأْلَأَ

Flight *n.* طَيَرَانٌ . هَرَبٌ . فِرَارٌ

Flighty *a.* طَائِشٌ . مُتَخَيِّلٌ

Flimsy *a.* سَخِيفٌ . ضَعِيفٌ . بَاطِلٌ

Fling *v. t.* or *n.* رَمَى ـِ . طَرَحَ ـَ . رَمْيٌ

Flint *n.* صَوَّانٌ

Flippant *a.* خَفِيفُ ٱلْكَلَامِ . بِقْبَاقٌ

Flirt *v. t., i.* or *n.* غَازَلَ . غَنِجَ . غُنْجَةٌ

Flirtation *n.* غُنْجٌ . مُغَازَلَةٌ

Flit *v. i.* / **Flitter** *v. i.* هَفَتَ ـِ .حَامَ ـُ

Float *v. t.* or *i.* عَامَ ـَ. سَبَّحَ

Flock *n.* or *v.i.* قَطِيعٌ .سِرْبٌ تَجَمَّعَ

Flog *v. t.* جَلَدَ ـِ . سَاطَ ـُ

Flogging *n.* جَلْدٌ . سَوْطٌ

Flop *v. t.* صَفَقَ . تَقَلَّبَ

Flood *n.* or *v. t.* طُوفَانٌ . غَمَرَ ـُ

Floor *n.* or *v. t.* أَرْضُ ٱلْبَيْتِ.طَبَقَةٌ . بَلَّطَ

Flora *n.* نَبَاتُ إِقْلِيمٍ . شَرْحُهُ

Floral *a.* زَهْرِيٌّ

Florid *a.* أَحْمَرُ . زَاهِرٌ .مُزَوَّقٌ

Florist *n.* مُرَبِّي ٱلزُّهُورِ

Flotilla *n.* أُسْطُولٌ صَغِيرٌ

Flounce / **Flounder** *v. i.* تَمَرَّغَ . تَقَلَّبَ

Flour *n.* طَحِينٌ . دَقِيقٌ

Flourish *v.t.* or *i.* هَزَّ ـِ . أَزْهَرَ . أَفْلَحَ

Flow *v. i.* جَرَى ـِ سَالَ ـِ .نَبَعَ ـِ ـُ

Flower *n.* زَهْرَةٌ . زُبْدَةٌ

Flowery *a.* زَهْرِيٌّ . أَزْهَرَ . زَاهِرٌ

Flown *see* **Fly.** طَارَ . طَيَّرَ

Fluctuatte *v.i.* تَقَلَّبَ . تَرَدَّدَ

Fluency *n.* طَلاَقَةُ ٱللِّسَانِ

Fluent *a.* ذَلِقٌ . طَلِقُ ٱللِّسَانِ

Fluid *n.* سَائِلٌ . مَائِعٌ

Fluidity *n.* سَيَلاَنٌ . مَيْعٌ

Flush *n.* or *v. i.* إِحْمِرَارٌ . إِحْمَرَّ

Flute *n.* نَايٌ

Flutter *v. i.* or *n.* خَفَقَ ـِ . خَفَقَانٌ

Fly *v. i.* or *t.* طَارَ . طَيَّرَ

Fly *n.* ذُبَابَةٌ ج ذِبَّانٌ وَذُبَابٌ

Fly-leaf *n.* وَرَقَةٌ بَيْضَاءُ فِي كِتَابٍ

Foal *n.* or *v. i.* فَلْوٌ. وَلَدَتْ (فَرَسٌ

Foam *n.* or *v. i.* رَغْوَةٌ . زَبَدٌ ازْبَدَ

Foamy / **Foaming** *a.* مُزْبِدٌ

Focus *n.* نُقْطَةُ ٱلإِحْتِرَاقِ

Fodder *n.* or *v. t.* عَلَفٌ . عَلَفَ ـِ

Foe *n.* عَدُوٌّ . خَصْمٌ

Fog *n.* ضَبَابٌ

Foil *v. t.* or *n.* خَيَّبَ . صَفِيحَةٌ . رَقِيقَةٌ

Fold *n.* ضِعْفٌ . ثِنْيٌ . حَظِيرَةٌ

Fold *v. t.* ثَنَى ـِ . زَرَبَ ـُ

Foliage *n.* أَوْرَاقُ ٱلنَّبَاتِ

Folk *n.* أَهْلٌ . قَوْمٌ . اناسٌ

Follow *v. t.* or *i.* تَبِعَ ـَ . نَتَجَ مِنْ

Follower *n.* تَابِعٌ . تِلْمِيذٌ

Following *n.* قَوْمٌ . اتْبَاعٌ

Folly *n.* جَهَالَةٌ . حَمَاقَةٌ . سَفَهٌ

Foment *v. t.* اثَارَ . هَيَّجَ

Fond *a.* مُوْلَعٌ . مُحِبٌّ

Fondle *v. t.* دَالَّ . لَاطَفَ

Fondness *n.* غَرَامٌ . وِدَادٌ

Font *n.* طَقْمُ احْرُف . نَبْعٌ

Food *n.* طَعَامٌ . قُوْتٌ

Fool *n.* / Foolish *a.* } جَاهِلٌ . غَبِيٌّ . سَفِيهٌ

Foolishness *n.* جَهْلٌ . حَمَاقَةٌ

Foolhardy *a* مُتَهَوِّرٌ . مُخَاطِرٌ بِنَفْسِهِ جَهْلاً

Foot *n.* قَدَمٌ رِجْلٌ . وَزْنُ شِعْرٍ

Footman *n.* خَادِمٌ . تَابِعٌ

Foot-path *n.* مَمْشًى . مَسْلَكٌ (لِلرَّاجِلِ)

Footstep *n.* خَطْوَةٌ . أَثَرُ ٱلْقَدَمِ

Footstool *n.* كُرْسِيٌّ لِلرِّجْلَيْنِ

For *pr.* or *conj.* لِأَجْلِ . لِ . لِأَنْ

Forage *n.* عَلَفٌ . عُلُوفَةٌ

Forasmuch *conj.* حَيْثُ . بِمَا أَنْ

Foray *n.* غَزْوَةٌ . غَارَةٌ

Forbear *v. t.* or *i.* إِمْتَنَعَ . كَفَّ ـُ

Forbearance *n.* إِحْتِمَالٌ . إِمْتِنَاعٌ

Forbid *v. t.* نَهَى ـَ . مَنَعَ ـَ

Force *n.* or *v. t.* قُوَّةٌ . فَاعِلِيَّةٌ . أَلْزَمَ

Forceps *n. pl.* مِلْقَطٌ . جِرَاحِيٌّ

Forcible *a.* قَوِيٌّ . فَعَّالٌ

Ford *n.* or *v. t.* مَخَاضَةٌ . خَاضَ ـَ

Fore-arm *n.* سَاعِدٌ

Forebode *v.t.* تَشَاءَمَ . أَنْبَأَ بِشَرٍّ

Forecast *n.* or *v.t.* تَدْبِيرٌ سَابِقٌ . دَبَّرَ

Forecastle *n.* أَعْلَى مقدمِ ٱلسَّفِينَةِ

Forefather *n.* جَدٌّ . سَلَفٌ

Forefinger *n.* سَبَّابَةٌ

Forefoot *n.* قَائِمَةٌ . مُقَدَّمَةٌ لِلْبَهِيْمَةِ

Forego *v. t.* تَنَازَلَ عَنْ . تَرَكَ ـُ

Foregoing *a.* مُتَقَدِّمٌ . سَالِفٌ

Foregone *a.* مَعْزُومٌ عَلَيْهِ . مَحْتُومٌ

Forehead *n.* جَبْهَةٌ

Foreign / Foreigner *n.* أَجْنَبِيٌّ . غَرِيبٌ

Forejudge *v. t.* سَبَقَ فَقَضَى

Foreknow *v. t.* سَبَقَ فَعَرَفَ

Foreknowledge *n.* عِلْمٌ سَابِقٌ

Forelock *n.* نَاصِيَةٌ ج نَوَاصٍ

Foreman *n.* نَاظِرٌ . رَئِيسُ شُغْلٍ

Foremast *n.* سَارِيَةُ ٱلْمُقَدَّمِ

Foremost *a.* الاوَّلُ . أَلْمُتَقَدِّمُ

Forenoon *n.* مَا قَبْلَ ٱلظُّهْرِ

Foreordain *v. t.* سَبَقَ فَعَيَّنَ

Foresee *v. t.* سَبَقَ فَنَظَرَ أَو عَرَفَ

Foresight *v.* سَبَقُ ٱلنَّظَرِ . عِنَايَةٌ

Forest *n.* غَابَةٌ . عَرِينٌ

Forestall *n. n.* سَبَقَ إِلَى

Foretell *v. t.* سَبَقَ فَاخْبَرَ . أَنْبَأَ

Forethought *n.* فِكْرٌ سَابِقٌ . تَبَصُّرٌ

Forever *ad.* إِلَى ٱلْابَدِ

Forewarn *v.t.* سَبَقَ فَحَذَّرَ . انْذَرَ

Forfeit *v.t.* or *n.* غَرَّمَ فِي جِنَايَةٍ . غَرَامَةٌ

Forge *n.* or *v. t.* كُورٌ . زَوَّرَ

Forger *n.* حَدَّادٌ . مُزَوِّرٌ

Forgery *n.* تَزْوِيرٌ . زَيْفٌ

Forget *v. t.* (Forgot) نَسِيَ ـَ

Forgetful *a.* نَاسٍ . غَافِلٌ

Forgetfulness *n.* نِسْيَانٌ . غَفَلٌ

Forgive *v. t.* غفرَ لهُ

Forgiveness *n.* غُفْرَانٌ . مَغْفِرَةٌ

Fork *n.* or *v. t.* شَوْكَةٌ . تَشَعَّبَ

Forked *a.* مُتَشَعِّبٌ . مُتفرِّعٌ

Forlorn *a.* مُهْمَلٌ . بائِسٌ

Form *n.* رَسْمٌ . شَكْلٌ . هيئةٌ

Form *v. t.* كوَّنَ . صوَّرَ . عَمِلَ

Formal *a.* رَسْمِيٌّ . خَارِجِيٌّ

Formality *n.* عَادَةٌ رَسْمِيَّةٌ . تَكْلِيفٌ

Formally *ad.* رَسْماً . بِالظَّاهِرِ فقط

Formation *n.* تَكوِينٌ . تَرْكِيبٌ

Former *a.* سَابِقٌ . اوَّلُ ٱثْنَيْنِ

Formerly *ad.* سَابِقاً . قَبْلاً

Formidable *a.* عَظِيمٌ . مُخِيفٌ

Formulate *v. t.* صَرَّحَ بِهِ رَسْمِيًّا

Formication *n.* زِنًى . عِهَارَةٌ

Forsake *v. t.* تَرَكَ . هَجَرَ

Forsaken *a.* مَتْرُوكٌ

Fort *n.* حِصْنٌ . قَلْعَةٌ

Forth *ad.* خَارِجاً . فَصاعِداً

Forthcoming *a.* آتٍ . قَرِيبُ ٱلْحُضُورِ

Forthwith *ad.* حَالاً . عَلَى ٱلْفَوْرِ

Fortieth *a.* الأَرْبَعُونَ

Fortification *n.* حِصْنٌ . تَحْصِينٌ

Fortify *v. t.* حَصَّنَ . قَوَّى

Fortitude *n.* تَجَلُّدٌ . عَزْمٌ . ثَبَاتٌ

Fortnight *n.* اسْبُوعَانِ

Fortress *n.* حِصْنٌ . قَلْعَةٌ

Fortuitous *a.* عَرَضِيٌّ . إِتِّفَاقِيٌّ

Fortunate *a.* سَعِيدٌ . حَظِيظٌ

Fortune *n.* حَظٌّ . نَصِيبٌ

Forty *a.* أَرْبَعُونَ

Forward *a.* or *ad.* مُقَدَّمٌ . إِلَى قُدَّامٍ

Forward *v. t.* أَرْسَلَ . عَجَّلَ

Fossil *n.* or *a.* مُتَحَجِّرٌ

Foster *v. t.* رَبَّى . عَالَ . اعَانَ

Foul *a.* قَذِرٌ . نَجِسٌ . قَبِيحٌ

Foul *v. t.* وَسَّخَ . نَجَّسَ . لَوَّثَ

Found *v. t.* اسَّسَ . انشأَ . سَبَكَ

Foundation *n.* اسَاسٌ . اصْلٌ

Founder *n.* مُؤَسِّسٌ . سَبَّاكٌ

Foundling *n.* وَلَد . لَقِيطٌ

Foundry / **Foundery** *n.* مَعْمَلُ ٱلسَّبْكِ

Fount / **Fountain** *n.* نَبْعٌ . يَنْبُوعٌ

Four *a.* ارْبَعَة او ارْبَعُ

Fourfold *a.* ارْبَعَةُ اضْعَافٍ

Fourfooted *a.* ذَوَاتُ ٱلْارْبَع

Fourscore *a.* ثَمَانُونَ

Fourteen *a.* ارْبَعَةَ عَشَرَ . ارْبَعَ عَشَرَة

Fourteenth *a.* الرَّابِعُ عَشَرَ

Fowl *n.* طَيْرٌ . دُجَاجَة

Fowler *n.* صَيَّادٌ

Fowling-piece *n.* بَارُودَة . بُنْدُقِيَّةٌ

Fox *n.* ثَعْلَبٌ . مَكَّار

Fraction *n.* كَسْرٌ . جُزْءٌ

Fracture *n.* or *v. t.* كَسْرٌ . كَسَرَ

Fragile *a.* قَصِمٌ . سَهْلُ ٱلْانْكِسَارِ

Fragment *n.* قِطْعَةٌ . كِسْرَةٌ

Fragmentary *a* مُؤَلَّفٌ مِنْ كِسَرٍ

Fragrance *n.* رَائِحَة . ذَكِيَّةٌ

Fragrant *a.* عَطِرٌ . ذَكِيُّ ٱلرَّائِحَةِ

Frail *a.* نَحِيفٌ . ضَعِيفٌ . وَاهٍ

Frailty *n.* ضَعفٌ . وَهْنٌ . عجز

Frame *n.* بِنْيَةٌ . قَالِبٌ . بِرْوَازٌ

Franchise *n.* إِمْتِيَازٌ سِيَاسِيٌّ

Frank *a.* or *n.* مُخْلِصٌ . سَلِيمُ ٱلنِّيَّةِ . إِفْرَنْجِيٌّ

Frankincense *n.* بَخُورٌ . لُبَانٌ

Frankness *n.* إِخْلَاصٌ . صَفْوُ ٱلنِّيَّةِ

Frantic *a.* مَجْنُون . هَائِجٌ غَيْظًا

Fraternal *a.* أَخَوِيٌّ

Fraternity *n.* إِخَاء وَإِخَاوَة . شَرِكَةٌ

Fraternize *v. t.* آخَى . تَآخَى

Fratricide *n.* قَاتِلُ ٱلْأَخِ . قتل ٱلْاخِ
Fraud *n.* خِدَاعٌ . غُبْنٌ . مَكر
Freak *n.* غَرَابَةُ خلقٍ أو فِعْلٍ
Freckle *n.* or *v. t.* كَلَفٌ . كَلِفَ ـَ
Freckled / Freckly *a.* أَكلفُ
Free *v. t.* حَرَّرَ . أَعتق
Free *a.* حرٌّ . بَرِيءٌ . مَجَّانيٌّ
Freedom *n.* حرِّيةٌ . بَرَاءَةٌ . خلُوصٌ
Freely *ad.* مجَّاناً . طَوْعاً . بِسَخَاءٍ
Freeman *n.* حرٌّ
Freemason *n.* فرْمَاسون
Freeness *n.* حرِّيةٌ . سَخَاءٌ
Free-thinker *n.* مُنْكِرُ الْوَحيِ
Freewill *n.* إِرَادَةٌ حرَّةٌ
Freeze *v. t.* or *i.* قَرَّسَ . قرس ـ
Freight *n.* شَحْنٌ . اجرتهُ
French *n.* or *a.* فَرَنساويٌّ
Frenzy *n.* جنُونٌ . غيظ

Frequent *a.* كَثِيرُ ٱلْوُقُوعِ . مُتَوَاتِرٌ
Frequent *v. t.* تَرَدَّدَ إِلى . لازَمَ
Frequently *ad.* تكرَاراً . كثيراً مَا
Fresco *n.* or *v. t.* تَصوِيرٌ علَى جَصٍّ
Fresh *a.* جَدِيدٌ . رَطْبٌ
Freshen *v.t.* or *i.* حَلَّى . رَطَّبَ . أَنْعَشَ . إِشتد
Freshet *n.* سَيْلٌ . طُغيَانٌ
Freshman *n.* مبتَدِئٌ (في مَدْرَسَةٍ)
Freshness *n.* نضَارَةٌ . عذُوبَةٌ
Fret *v.t.* or *i.* كَدَّرَ . تَكَدَّرَ . ضَجِرَ
Fretful *a.* نَكِدٌ . شَاكٍ
Fretfulness *n.* نَكَدٌ . ضَجَرٌ
Friar *n.* رَاهِبٌ ج رُهْبَانٌ
Friction *n.* فرْكٌ . حَكٌّ . دَلْكٌ
Friday *n.* يوم ٱلْجُمْعَةِ
Friend *n.* صَاحِبٌ . صدِيقٌ . خِلٌّ
Friendless *a.* بِلاَ صَدِيقٍ . مهمَل
Friendly *a.* وَدُودٌ . مُسَالِمٌ

Friendship *n.* صَدَاقَةٌ . أُلْفَةٌ

Frigate *n.* بَارِجَةٌ حَرْبِيَّةٌ

Fright *n.* خَوف . فَزَع . رُعْبٌ

Frighten *v. t.* خَوَّفَ . افزعَ

Frightful *a.* مُرعِبٌ . مُخِيف . هَائِلٌ

Frigid *a.* بَارِدٌ . قَارِس

Frill, Fringe } *n.* هُدْبٌ . حَاشِيَةٌ

Frisk *v. t.* قَفَزَ فَرَحاً . مَرِحَ ـ

Frisk, Erisky } *a.* مَرِحٌ . خَفِيفٌ

Frivolity *n.* طَيْشٌ . بُطْلٌ

Frivolous *a.* عَبَثٌ . بَاطِلٌ

Frock *n.* قُفْطَانٌ . (فسطَانٌ)

Frog *n.* ضِفْدَعٌ ج ضَفَادِعُ

Frolic *n.* or *v. i.* لِعْبٌ . مَرِحَ ـ

From *pr.* مِنْ . عَنْ . من عِنْد

Front *n.* مُقَدَّمٌ . صَدْرٌ

Frontier *n.* حَدٌّ . تَخْمٌ

Frost *n.* صَقِيعٌ . جَلِيدٌ

Froth *n.* رَغْوَةٌ . زَبَدٌ

Froward *a.* مُتَمَرِّدٌ . عَاتٍ

Frown *n.* or *v. t.* عُبُوسَةٌ . عَبَسَ ـِ

Froze *see* Freeze. فَرَّسَ

Fructify *v. t.* جَعَلَهُ مُثْمِراً . لَقَّحَ

Frugal *a.* مُقْتَصِدٌ

Frugality *n.* إِقْتِصَادٌ

Fruit *n.* ثَمَرٌ . فَاكِهَةٌ . حَاصِل

Fruitful *a.* مُثْمِرٌ . مُخْصِبٌ . مُنْتِجٌ

Fruitlessly *ad.* عَبَثاً . بَاطِلاً

Frustrate *v. t.* خَيَّبَ . أَبطَلَ

Fry *v. t.* or *i.* قَلَى ـ . إِنْقَلَى

Frying-pan *n.* مِقْلاة

Fuel *n.* وَقِيدٌ . وُقُود

Fugitive *n.* or *a.* هَارِبٌ . زَائِلٌ

Fulcrum *n.* مُسْنَدٌ . دَارِكٌ

Fulfil *v. t.* اكْمَلَ . اتَمَّ

Fulfilment *n.* إِتْمَامٌ . وَفَاء

Full *a.* or *v.t.* مَلْآنٌ. وَافِرٌ. تَامٌّ. قَصَرَ

Fuller *n.* قَصَّارٌ

Fully *ad.* تَمَاماً

Fume *n.* or *v. i.* بُخَارٌ . إِغْتَاظ . دَخَّنَ

Fumigate *v. t.* بَخَّرَ . دَخَّنَ

Fumigation *n.* تَبْخِيرٌ . تَدْخِينٌ

Fun *n.* مُزَاحٌ . هَزْلٌ

Function *n.* وَظِيفَةٌ . شُغْلٌ

Fund *n.* مَالٌ . رَأْسُ مَالٍ

Fundamental *a.* أَسَاسِيٌّ . جَوْهَرِيٌّ

Funeral *n.* جَنَازَةٌ

Fungus *n.* فُطْرٌ (نَبَاتٌ)

Funnel *n.* قُمْعٌ . مِدْخَنَةٌ

Funny *a.* مُضْحِكٌ

Fur *n.* فَرْوٌ . بَيَاضُ ٱللِّسَانِ

Furious *a.* هَائِجٌ غَضَباً . مُزْبِدٌ

Furl *v. t.* طَوَى ـِ لَفَّ ـُ

Furlong *n.* فَرْسَخٌ ج فَرَاسِخُ

Furlough *n.* رُخْصَةٌ لِلْغِيَابِ (إِجَازَةٌ)

Furnace *n.* كُورٌ . اتُونٌ

Furnish *v. t.* جَهَّزَ . اَهَّبَ

Furniture *n.* أَثَاثٌ . أَمْتِعَةٌ

Furrier *n.* فَرَّاءٌ . تَاجِرُ ٱلْفَرْوِ

Furrow *n.* or *v. t.* ثَلْمٌ . خَدَّةٌ . خَدَّ ـُ

Further *a.* or *ad.* ابْعَدُ . ثُمَّ . ايضاً

Further *v. t.* سَاعَدَ . ايَّدَ

Furthermore *ad.* ثُمَّ . ايضاً

Furthermost, Furthest } *a.* ٱلأَبْعَدُ . ٱلأَقْصَى

Furtive *a.* سِرِّيٌّ . خَفِيٌّ

Fury *n.* غَيْظٌ مُزْبِدٌ . جُنُونٌ

Fuse *v. t.* or *i.* أَذَابَ . ذَابَ ـُ

Fuse *n.* فَتِيلَةُ ٱللَّغَمِ

Fuss *n.* ضَجِيجٌ . شَغَبٌ

Futile *a.* بَاطِلٌ . عَبَثٌ

Futility *n.* عَبَثٌ . عَدَمُ ٱلْفَائِدَةِ

Future *n.* or *a.* مُسْتَقْبَلٌ . آتٍ

Futurity *n.* ٱلزَّمَانُ ٱلْمُقْبِلُ

G

Gabble *v. i.* or *n.* ثَرْثَرَ . ثَرْثَرَة

Gable *n.* (جملون)

Gag *v. t.* or *n.* سَدَّ الفم

Gage *n.* or *v. t.* رَهْنٌ . عِيَار . عَايَرَ

Gaily / Gayly *ad.* سُرُوراً . بَهْجَةً

Gain *n.* or *v. t.* or *i.* كَسْبٌ . رَبِحَ

Gainful *a.* مُكْسِبٌ . مُرْبِحٌ

Gainings *n. pl.* أَرْبَاح

Gainsay *v. t.* نَاقَضَ . قَاوَمَ

Gait *n.* أَلْمَشْيُ أو نوعه

Gaiter *n.* جُرْمُوقٌ

Galaxy *n.* أَلْمَجَرَّةُ . مَوْكِبٌ

Gale *n.* ريحٌ شَدِيدَةٌ . عَاصِفَةٌ

Gall *n.* صفرَاء . مَرَارَةٌ . عفصٌ

Gallant *a.* شُجَاع . لَطِيف . عَاشِق

Gallantry *n.* بَسَالَة . شهَامَةٌ

Gallery *n.* رِوَاقٌ . دِهْلِيزٌ

Galley *n.* نَوْع مِنَ السُّفُن

Gallic *a.* غَالِيٌّ ، فَرَنْسَاوِيٌّ

Gallon *n.* مِكْيَالٌ للسَّائِلَاتِ

Gallop *n.* or *v. i.* رَكْضٌ (اَلْفَرَسِ)

Gallows *n. pl.* مِشْنَقَةٌ

Galvanic *a.* كَهْرَبَائِيٌّ . كَلْفَانِيٌّ

Galvanize *v.t.* كَهْرَبَ . لبسَ بالمعدن

Gamble *v. t.* or *i.* قَامَرَ

Gambler *n.* مُقَامِرٌ

Gambling *n.* مُقَامَرَةٌ

Gambol *n.* or *v. i.* قَمْصٌ . قَمَصَ

Game *n.* لِعْبَة . قَنَص . صَيداً
Gamester *n.* لاَعِبٌ . مُقَامِر
Gander *n.* ذَكَرُ ٱلْوَزّ
Gang *n.* زُمْرَةٌ . جَمَاعَةٌ
Gangrene *n.* or *v. i.* غَنْغَرِينٌ تَغَنْغَرَ
Gangway *n.* مَعْبَرٌ . مَمَرٌّ
Gaol *n.* سِجْنٌ . حَبْس
Gap *n.* شَقٌّ . فَتحة
Gape *v. t.* فَغَرَ
Garb *n.* لِبَاسٌ . هَيْئَةٌ
Garden *n.* بُسْتَانٌ . جُنَيْنَة
Gardener *n.* بُستَانِيٌّ
Gargle *v. t.* or *n.* غَرْغَر . غَرْغَرَة
Garland *n.* إِكْلِيلُ زَهرٍ
Garlic *n.* ثُومٌ
Garment *n.* ثَوْبٌ . كِساءٌ
Garner *n.* or *v. t.* شُونَةٌ خَزَنَ
Garnish *v. t.* زَيَن . زَخْرَف

Garrison *a.* or *v. t.* حَرَسُ حِصْنٍ . جَهَّزَ بِحَرَسٍ
Garrulity *n.* ثَرْثَرَة . بَقَاق
Garrulous *a.* ثَرْثَار . بِقْبَاق
Garter *n.* رُبَاط ٱلساق . (وِسَامٌ إِنْكِلِيزِيٌّ)
Gas *n.* غَاز
Gaseous *a.* غَازِيٌّ
Gash *n.* جُرْحٌ
Gas-light *n.* نُورُ غَاز
Gasometer *n.* مِقيَاسُ غَاز . مَخزنه
Gasp *v. i.* or *n.* إِلتهث . لَهْثَة
Gastric *a.* مَعِدِيٌّ
Gate *n.* بَابٌ . مَدخَلٌ
Gateway *n.* مَدْخَل في حَائِط
Gather *v. t.* or *i.* جَمَعَ . إِجتَمع
Gaudy *a.* مزخرَف بلا ذَوق
Gauge *v. t.* or *n.* قَاس . مِقيَاسٌ
Gaunt *a.* هَزِيل . ضامِر . اعجَف
Gauntlet *n.* كَفٌّ مِن حَدِيدٍ

Gawky a. or n.	غَشِيم . غَلِيظ ٱلتَّصرُّفِ
Gauze n.	نَسِيج رَقِيق
Gay a.	مُبتَهِج . مَرِح . فَاخِر
Gayety n.	بَهجَة . بَسْط . سُرُورٌ
Gaze n. or v.t.	نَظرَةٌ ثَابِتَةٌ . تَفَرَّسَ
Gazelle n.	غَزَال ج غِزْلاَن
Gazette n.	جَرِيدَةٌ ج جَرَائِد
Gazetteer n.	كِتَابُ وَصْفِ ٱلْبُلْدَان
Gear n.	عُدَّةٌ . جِهَازٌ . أَدَوَاتٌ
Gear v. t.	لَبَّسَ بِعُدَّةٍ
Gelatine n.	هُلاَم
Gelding n.	حِصَان مَخْصِيٌّ
Gem n.	جَوْهَرَةٌ . فَصٌّ
Gender n.	جِنْس ج أَجْنَاس
Genealogical a.	نَسَبِيٌّ
Genealogy n.	سِلْسِلَةُ ٱلنَسَب
General a. or n.	عَامٌّ . شَائِع . قَائِد
Generality n.	عُمُومِيَّة . اغلَبِيَة
Generalize v. t.	عَمَّمَ
Generally ad.	غَالِباً . عُمُوماً
Generate v. t.	وَلَدَ . سَبَّبَ . أَحدَثَ
Generation n.	حَبَلٌ . تَنَاسُل
Generative a.	مُوَلِّد . مُنْتِج
Generic / Generical a.	جِنسِيٌّ . شَامِلٌ
Generosity n.	سَخَاءٌ . كَرَمٌ
Generous a.	كَرِيمٌ . سَخِيٌّ
Genesis n.	تَوْلِيد . سِفرُ ٱلتَكْوِين
Genial a.	مُبْهِجْ . بَشُوشٌ
Genii n. pl.	جَانٌّ
Genitive n.	ٱلْمُضَافُ إِلَيْهِ
Genius n.	حِذْقٌ . قَرِيحَةٌ . صَاحِبُهَا
Genteel a.	مُهَذب . لَطِيفٌ
Gentile n. or a.	اممي . وَثَنِيٌّ
Gentility n.	رِقَّةٌ . تَهْذِيبٌ . ادَبٌ
Gentle a.	لَطِيفٌ . دَمِث . انيس
Gentleman n.	مُهَذَّبٌ . (خَوَاجَا) سَيِّد

Gentleness *n.* رِقة . دَماثة . لُطْف

Gently *ad.* بلطافة . برقة

Gentry *n.* أَلخاصة . ألنجباء . ألاعيان

Genuine *a.* حَقِيقيّ . صَحيح . خالص

Genuineness *n.* حَقِيقة . حَقِيقيّة

Genus (*pl.* Genera) *n.* جنس . نوْع

Geographic
Geographical } *a.* جغرافيّ

Geography *n.* جِغرافيا . رَسمُ الارضِ

Geologic
Geological } *a.* جيولوجيّ

Geologist *n.* عالِمٌ بالجيولوجيا

Geology *n.* عِلمُ طبقاتِ الأرضِ

Geometric
Geometrical } *a.* هندسيّ

Geometrician *n.* ماهر بعِلمِ الهندسةِ

Geometry *n.* عِلمُ الهندسةِ

Germ *n.* جُرثومة . اصلٌ

German
Germanic } *a.* أَلمانيّ . جرمانيّ

Germinate *v. i.* نبتَ ـُ . افرخَ

Gestation *n.* حَملٌ . مدةُ الحمل

Gesticulate *v. i.* اومَأ في الخِطابِ

Gesticulation
Gesture } *n.* إيماء . حركة جسديّة

Get (Got) *v. t.* حصَلَ . إقتنى

Ghastliness *n.* إصفِرارُ الوجهِ

Ghastly *a.* فظيعُ المنظرِ

Ghost *n.* رُوحٌ . طيفٌ . خيالٌ

Ghostly *a.* خياليّ . رُوحانيّ

Ghoul *n.* غولٌ ج غيلانٌ

Giant *n.* or *a.* جبّار . عظيمٌ جدًّا

Gibberish *n.* تمتمة

Gibbet *n.* or *v. t.* مِشنقة . شنَقَ

Gibe *v. i.* or *n.* إزدرى . هزَأ . هزء

Gibralter *n.* جبَلُ طارق

Giddiness *n.* دُوارٌ . طيشٌ

Giddy *a.* مُصاب بالدُّوارِ . طائشٌ

Gift *n.* عطيّة . هِبة

Gifted *a.* حاذِق . ذو مواهِبَ

Gig *n.* مَرْكَبَةٌ ذَات دُولاَبَيْنِ

Gigantic *a.* كَبِيرٌ جِدا . ضَخْمٌ

Gild *v. t.* مَوَّهَ . ذَهَّبَ

Gilt *n.* مِكْيَال صَغِيرٌ لِلسَّوَائِلِ

Gilt *a.* مُذَهَّب . مُمَوَّه

Gimlet *n.* بَيْرَم صَغِير . بَرِّيمَة

Gin *n.* نَوْع مِنَ ٱلْعَرَقِ . فَخّ

Ginger *n.* زَنْجَبِيل

Gipsy / Gypsy *n.* نُورِي . غَجَرِي

Giraffe *n.* زَرَافَة

Gird *v. t.* نَطَّق . زَنَّرَ ـَ . رَبَطَ ـ

Girder *n.* جِسْرٌ كَبِيرٌ

Girdle *n.* مِنطَقَة . زُنَّار . حِزَام

Girl *n.* صَبِيَّة . إِبْنَةٌ . فَتَاة

Girth *n.* حِزَام

Gist *n.* خُلاَصَة . زُبْدَة . جل

Give *v. t.* أَعْطَى . وَهَب ـ

Giving *n.* إِعْطَاء . إِهْدَاء

Gizzard *n.* قَانِصَةٌ ج قَوَانِصُ

Glacier *n.* جُرْفُ جَلِيدٍ

Glad *a.* مَسْرُورٌ . فَرْحَان . مَبسُوطٌ

Gladden *v. t.* فَرَّحَ . أَسَرَّ . ابْهَجَ

Glade *n.* مَعْبَرٌ او فسحةٌ فِي غَابَةٍ

Gladiator *n.* مُصَارِع

Gladness *n.* سُرُوْر . فَرَحٌ . بسط

Glance *n.* or *v. i.* لَمْحَةٌ . لَمَحَ ـ . إِنْعَكَس

Gland *n.* غُدَّة ج غدد

Glandular / Glandulous *a.* غُدِي ذُو غُدَدٍ

Glare *n.* or *v.i.* لَمَعَانٌ . مُبْهِرٌ . تَوَهَّج

Glaring *a.* لاَمِعٌ . مُبْهِرٌ . فَاحِشٌ

Glass *n.* زُجَاج . مِرْآةٌ . نَظَّارَةٌ

Glassy *a.* زُجَاجِيٌّ

Glaze *v. t.* جَهَّزَ بِزُجَاج

Gleam *n.* or *v. i.* وَمِيضٌ . بَرْقٌ . وَمَضَ ـ

Glean *v. t.* إِلْتَقَط . جمعَ ٱلْفَضَلاَتِ

Glee *n.* سُرُورٌ . إِبْتِهَاج

Gleeful *a.* مَسْرُورٌ . فَرِحٌ . مُبْتَهِجٌ

Glen *n.* وَادٍ ضَيِّقٌ مُنفَرِدٌ

Glibness *n.* نُعُومَةٌ . طَلَاقَةُ ٱللِّسَانِ

Glide *v. i.* تَزَلَّقَ تَزَلَّجَ

Glimmer *v. i.* تَلَأْلَأَ . خَفِيفاً

Glimmering *n.* تَلَأْلُؤٌ

Glimpse *n.* لَمْحَةٌ . نَظْرَةٌ قَصِيرَةٌ

Glisten / Glitter *v. i.* or *n.* تَلَأْلَأَ . لَمَعَانٌ

Gloat *v. i.* تَفَرَّسَ بِعَيْنِ ٱلشَّرِّ

Globe *n.* كُرَةُ ٱلْأَرْضِ

Globular / Globulous *a.* كُرَوِيٌّ

Globule *a.* كُرَيَّةٌ

Glomerate *v. t.* كَتَّلَ

Gloom *n.* قَتَامٌ . غَمٌّ

Gloomy *a.* مُغِمٌّ . مُكَدِّرٌ

Glorify *v. t.* مَجَّدَ . عَظَّمَ . اجَلَّ

Glorious *a.* مَجِيدٌ . جَلِيلٌ

Glory *n.* مَجْدٌ . جَلَالَةٌ . شُهْرَةٌ

Gloss / Glossiness *n.* لَمَعَانٌ . تَأْوِيلٌ

Glossary *n.* فِهْرِسُ كَلِمَاتٍ مَشْرُوحَةٍ

Glossy *a.* مَصْقُولٌ . لَامِعٌ

Glottis *n.* مِزْمَارُ ٱلْحَنْجَرَةِ

Glove *n.* كَفٌّ ج كُفُوفٌ

Glow *n.* or *v.i.* تَوَهَّجَ . تَوَقَّدَ . إِحْتَدَمَ

Glowing *a.* مُتَوَهِّجٌ . مُتَأَجِّجٌ . لَامِعٌ

Glow-worm *n.* يَرَاعَةٌ (حَشَرَةٌ)

Glue *n.* or *v. t.* غِرَاءٌ . غَرَّى

Glum *a.* مَغْمُومٌ . عَبُوسٌ

Glut *v. t.* أَشْبَعَ

Glutinous *a.* دَبِقٌ . لَزِجٌ

Glutton *n.* / Gluttonous *a.* أَكُولٌ . نَهِمٌ . شَرِهٌ

Gluttony *n.* شَرَهٌ . نَهَمٌ

Gnarled / Gnarly *a.* مُعَقَّدٌ . مُلْتَفٌّ

Gnash *v. t.* صَرَّ اسْنَانَهُ

Gnat *n.* بَعُوضَةٌ . نَامُوسَةٌ

Gnaw *v. t.* قَرَضَ ـِ . قَضَمَ ـَ

Go (went, gone) *v. i.* ذَهَبَ ـَ . مضَى ـ

Goad *n.* or *v. t.* منخَسٌ . نخَس ـ

Goal *n.* أمد . غَايَة . غَرَضٌ

Goat *n.* ماعِزٌ . عَنْزٌ . تَيْس

Goat-herd *n.* مَعازٌ

Gobble *v. t.* or *i.* إِزدَرَدَ . لَهِمَ

Go-between *n.* وَسيطٌ

Goblet *n.* قَدَحٌ . كَأْسٌ

Goblin *n.* جِنّيٌّ . عِفْرِيتٌ

God *n.* إِلهٌ ج آلِهَةٌ . اللهُ

Goddess *n.* إِلاهةٌ

Godfather *n.* عرَّابٌ

Godless *a.* كَافِرٌ . شِرِّيرٌ . فَاجِرٌ

Godliness *n.* تقوَى

Godly *a.* تقيٌّ . صَالِحٌ

Godson *n.* فَلْيُونٌ

Gold *n.* ذَهَبٌ

Golddust *n.* دَقِيقُ ٱلذَّهَبِ . تِبْرٌ

Golden *a.* ذَهَبِيٌّ

Goldfinch *n.* حَسُّونٌ . (طَائِرٌ)

Goldsmith *n.* صائِغٌ ج صاغَةٌ

Gondola *n.* زَوْرَقٌ . قَارِبٌ

Gong *n.* نَاقُوسٌ

Good *a.* صَالِحٌ . جَيِّد . طَيِّبٌ

Good *n.* خير . نَفْعٌ . فَائِدَةٌ

Good-by / Good-bye *n.* or *int.* تَوْدِيعٌ
بِامَانِ ٱللهِ

Good-humour *n.* بَشَاشَةٌ

Goodly *a.* جَمِيلٌ . حسن

Good-natured *a.* حَسَنُ ٱلأَخْلَاق

Goodness *n.* صَلَاح . جُوْدَةٌ . فَضِيلَةٌ

Goods *n. pl.* بَضَائِعُ . سِلَعٌ . امْلَاكٌ

Good-will *n.* إِحسَانٌ . مَسَرَّةٌ . معرُوفٌ

Goose *n.* (*pl.* geese) وَزَّةٌ . غَبِيٌّ

Gore *v.* or *v.t.* دَمٌ . نَطَحَ ـَ . طَعَنَ ـ

Gorge *v. t.* إِلْتَهَم

Gorgeous *a.* فَاخِرٌ . زَاهٍ . بَهِيٌّ

Gorilla *n.* اكبرُ ٱلقُرُودِ . جُورِلاَّ

Gory *a.* دَمَوِيٌّ . مُضَرَّجٌ بِٱلدَّمِ

Gosling *n.* فَرْخُ ٱلوَزِّ

Gospel *n.* إِنْجِيلٌ . بِشَارَة

Gossip *n.* or *v. i.* فُضُولِيٌّ . مِهْذَارٌ . هَذَرَ

Gouge *n.* or *v. t.* إِزْمِيلٌ . نَقَرَ

Gourd *n.* قَرْعٌ . (نَبَاتٌ)

Gout *n.* نِقْرِسٌ . دَاءُ ٱلمُلُوكِ

Gouty *a.* مُصَابٌ بِٱلنِّقْرِسِ

Govern *v. t.* مَلَكَ . سَادَ . حَكَمَ

Governess *n.* مُعَلِّمَةُ عَائِلَةٍ

Government *n.* حُكُومَة . سِيَاسَه

Governor *n.* حَاكِمٌ . وَالٍ . مُدِيرٌ

Governorship *n.* مَنْصِبُ ٱلحَاكِمِ . وِلاَيَةٌ

Gown *n.* قُفْطَانٌ . جُبَّةُ ٱلعُلَمَاءِ

Grab *v.t.* or *n.* مَسَكَ . خَطَفَ . خَطْف

Grace *n.* نِعْمَة . عَفْو . حُسْن

Grace *v. t.* زَيَّنَ . ظَرَّفَ . اكْرَمَ

Graceful *a.* رَقِيقٌ . لَطِيفٌ . مُهَذَّبٌ

Graceless *a.* شِرِّيرٌ . خَبِيثٌ

Gracious *a.* مُنعِمٌ . جَوَّادٌ . رَحِيمٌ

Graciously *ad.* بِلَطَافَةٍ . تَكَرُّماً

Gradation *n.* تَدْرِيجٌ . تَدَرُّجٌ

Grade *n.* دَرَجَة . رِتْبَة

Gradual *a.* تَدْرِيجِيٌّ

Graduate *v. i.* نَالَ رِتْبَةً عِلْمِيَّةً

Graduation *n.* نَيْلُ رِتْبَةٍ . تَدْرِيجٌ

Graft *n.* or *v.t.* تَطْعِيمُ ٱلغُصْنِ . طَعَّمَ

Grain *n.* حَبَّةٌ . حُبُوبٌ . حِنطَةٌ

Gram *n.* وَزْنُ الجِرَامِ

Grammar *n.* عِلْمُ ٱلصَّرْفِ وَٱلنَّحوِ

Grammarian *n.* نَاحٍ ج نُحَاةٌ

Grammatical *a.* حَسَبَ ٱلنَّحوِ

Granary *n.* مَخْزَنُ ٱلحُبُوبِ . هُرْيٌ

Grand *a.* عَظِيمٌ . فَاخِرٌ . جَلِيلٌ

Grand-child *n.* حفيد . حفيدة

Granted *pp.* مسلّم به . لنفرض

Grandee *n.* احد الشرفاء او الأعيان

Grandeur *n.* عظمة . سموّ . فخامة

Grandfather, Grandsire *n.* جدّ ج جدود

Grandma, Grandmother *n.* جدّة

Grandson *n.* حفيد

Granite *n.* نوع من الحجر الصلب

Grant *n.* or *v.t.* هبة وهب ـ . أجاب

Granular, Granulate *a.* حبّيّ . محبّب

Granulate *v. t.* or *i.* حبّب . تحبّب

Granule *n.* حبيبة . دقيقة

Grape *n.* حبّة عنب

Grape-shot *n.* دكّة رصاصات

Grape-vine *n.* دالية . كرمة

Graphic, Graphical *a.* خطّيّ . بليغ الوصف

Grapple *v. t.* or *n.* قبض . صارع . قبض

Grasp *v.t.* or *n.* قبض . مسك . قبض

Grasping *a.* طمّاع

Grass *n.* حشيش . كلأ . عشب

Grasshopper *n.* جندب

Grassy *a.* عشب . معشب

Grate *v. t.* or *i.* حكّ . كدّر . صرف

Grate *n.* كانون . وجاق

Grateful *a.* شكور . مرض

Gratefulness *n.* إمتنان . شكر

Gratification *n.* إرضاء . جبر الخاطر

Gratify *v. t.* أرضى . طيّب الخاطر

Grating *n.* شعريّة

Gratis *ad.* مجّانًا

Gratitude *n.* شكر

Gratuitous *a.* مجّاني . بلا داع

Gratuity *n.* عطيّة . هديّة

Grave *n.* or *a.* قبر . مهمّ . رصين

Gravel *n.* or *v. t.* حصى او دقيقها . فرش به

Graven *a.* منحوت . منقوش

Graver *n.* نَقَّاش . حَفَّار

Gravestone *n.* رُجْمَةٌ ج رُجَم

Graveyard *n.* مَقْبَرَةٌ

Gravitate *v. i.* مَالَ إِلى . إِنْجَذَبَ

Gravity *n.* رَزَانَةٌ . عَظَمَةٌ . أَلْجَاذِبِيَّةُ

Gravy *n.* مَرَقٌ

Gray *a.* أَشْيَبُ . أَشْهَبُ

Grayish *a.* ضَارِب إِلَى ٱلشَّيْبِ

Grayness *n.* شَيْب . شُبْهَةٌ

Graze *v. t.* or *i.* رَعَى ـَ . مسَّ ـَ

Grazing *n.* مَرْعًى

Grease *n.* or *v. t.* دُهْن . دهنَ ـُ

Greasiness *n.* دُهْنِيَّةٌ

Greasy *a.* دَهِنٌ

Great *a.* عَظِيمٌ . كَبِيرٌ . سامٍ

Greatly *ad.* كَثِير جدًّا

Greatness *n.* عَظَمَةٌ . سُمُوٌّ . كِبْرٌ

Greaves *n. pl.* جُرْمُوق . دِرْع لِلْأَرْجُلِ

Grecian *a.* يُونَانِيٌّ . رُومِيٌّ

Greedily *ad.* شرِهًا . نَهِمًا . تَائِقًا

Greediness *n.* شَرَهٌ . شَهْوَةٌ . طَمَعٌ

Greedy *a.* شَرِهٌ . أَكُولٌ . طَامع

Greek *a.* or *n.* يُونَانِيٌّ

Green *a.* أَخْضَرُ . فَجٌّ . عَدِيمُ ٱلْخِبْرَةِ

Greenhouse *n.* كِنَانٌ لِتَرْبِيَةِ ٱلنَّبَاتِ

Greens *n. pl.* خُضَر . بُقُولٌ

Greet *v. t.* حَيَّا . سلَّم على

Greeting *n.* تَحِيَّةٌ . سَلَامٌ

Greyhound *n.* كَلْب سَلُوقِيٌّ

Griddle / Gridion *n.* مِقْلَاةٌ . سَفُّودٌ . (مُصَبَّع)

Grief *n.* حُزْن . كَآبَةٌ

Gregarious *a.* عَائِشٌ سِرْبًا (حيوان)

Grievance *n.* شَكْوَى . ضِيق . اذِيَّةٌ

Grieve *v. i.* or *t.* حَزِنَ ـَ . أَحْزَنَ

Grievous *a.* مُحْزِنٌ . شَاقَ . شَدِيدٌ

Grill *v. t.* شَوَى ـ

Grim *a.* عَبُوس . هائِل . شَرِس

Grimace *n.* إعوِجاجُ الوَجْهِ لِقصدٍ

Grime *v. t.* or *n.* قَذَرَ . لوَّث . وَسَخ

Grin *n.* or *v. t.* كَشْرَة . كَشَرَ ـِ

Grind *v. t.* سَنَّ . طَحَنَ . جَرَشَ ـِ

Grind *v.t.* (the teeth) قَرَعَ اسْنَانَهُ

Grinder *n.* سَنَّانٌ . مِطْحَنَةٌ . ضِرْسٌ

Grindstone *n.* جَلْخ . مِسَنٌّ

Grip / Gripe *n.* or *v. t.* قَبْضٌ . قَبَضَ ـِ . مَغْص

Grist *n.* طَحْنَة

Gristel *n.* غضرُوف ج غَضَارِيف

Gristmill *n.* طَاحُونٌ ج طَوَاحِين

Grit *n.* رَمل . جَرِيشُ الطَّحِين

Grizzled / Grizzly *a.* اشْيَبُ . أَرْبَد

Groan *v. t.* or *n.* ان . تأوَّهَ . انِين

Groaning *n.* انِين . تأوُّه

Grocer *n.* بدَّال (بقَّال) . عطار

Grocery *n.* دُكان المأكُولاتِ

Grog *n.* شَرَابٌ مُسكِر

Groin *n.* ارْبِيَّة

Groom *n.* or *v. t.* سائِسٌ . سَاسَ ـُ (الخَيل)

Groove *n.* خُدَّة . خطٌّ محفُور . ثلم

Grope *v. i.* تَلَمَّسَ . تجَسَّسَ

Gross *a.* غَلِيظ . ضَخم . فَظٌّ

Gross *n.* جُمْلَة . ١٢ دستة (دزّينة)

Grossness *n.* غَلاظَة . خُشُونَة

Grotto *n.* كَهْفٌ ج كُهُوف

Grotesque *a.* غَريب . مضحِك

Ground *n.* ارْض . اساس . دليل

Ground *v. t.* or *i.* اسَّسَ . شَطَّطَتْ (سفِينَة)

Groundless *a.* بَاطِلٌ . لا اصلَ له

Groundwork *n.* اساس . أصل

Group *n.* or *v. t.* جَمَاعَة . زُمْرَة . جَمَّعَ

Grove *n.* غابَة . حَرَجَة

Grovel *v. t.* تذَلَّلَ . دبَّ ـِ

Grow *v. t.* or *i.* ربى . نما . زادَ ـِ

Growl *v. t.* or *i.* هَمْهَمَ . تقمقم

Growth *n.* نُمُوٌّ . زِيَادَةٌ . تقدُّم

Grub *n.* شحمَةُ ٱلْأَرْض . دودَة ٱلخنفساء

Grudge *n.* or *v. t.* ضَغِينَةٌ . حَسَدَ ـُ

Gruel *n.* ثَرِيدٌ لِلْمَرِيض

Gruff *a.* عبُوس . شَرِسٌ

Grumble *v. i.* تذمَّرَ . تَقمقم

Grunt *v. i.* or *n.* قَبَعَ ـَ . قَبِيعَة

Guarantee *v. t.* or *n.* كَفَلَ ـِ . كَفَالَة . كَفِيلٌ

Guard *n.* or *v. t.* حِرَاسَةٌ . حُرَّاسٌ حَرَسَ ـِ ـُ

Guardian *n.* حَارِسٌ . وَصِيٌّ . وَلِيٌّ

Guardianship *n.* وِصَايَة . حِرَاسَةٌ

Guess *v. t.* or *n.* خَمَّنَ . تَخْمِينٌ

Guest *n.* ضَيف ج ضُيُوف

Guidance *n.* إِرْشَاد . هِدَايَة . دِلاَلَة

Guide *v. t.* ارشد . دَلَّ ـُ . هدَى ـِ

Guide *n.* مرشِدٌ . دَلِيلٌ

Guile *n.* مكرٌ . خدَاعٌ . غِشٌّ

Guileless *a.* مُخْلِصٌ . بَرِيءٌ

Guillotine *n.* آلَةٌ لِلْإِعْدَام بِقَطْعِ ٱلرَّأس

Guilt / Guiltiness *n.* ذَنْبٌ

Guiltless *a.* بريءٌ لا ذَنبَ فِيهِ

Guilty *a.* مُذْنِبٌ . مُستَحِقٌّ ٱلقِصَاصِ

Guinea *n.* ٢١ شِلِنًا . جنيهٌ

Guise *n.* اسْلُوبٌ . هَيئَةٌ . زِيٌّ

Guitar *n.* قِيثَارٌ . ج قيَاثِير

Gulf *n.* خَلِيجٌ . جُوْن

Gull *v. t.* or *n.* خدَعَ . طَائِرٌ بحرِيٌّ

Gullet *n.* أَلْمَرِيء . أَلْبُلْعُوْم

Gully *n.* مَجْرًى عَمِيقٌ ضَيِّقٌ

Gulp *v. t.* or *n.* لَهِمَ . جرَعَ . جرْعة

Gum *n.* لِثَةٌ . صَمْغٌ

Gun *n.* بُارُودَةٌ . بُنْدُقِيَّة . مَدْفع

Gunner *n.* طوبجيٌّ

Gunpowder *n.* بارُودٌ

Gunsmith *n.*	صَانِعُ ٱلْأَسْلِحَةِ
Gurgle *v. i.*	تَغَرْغَرَ
Gush *v. i.*	دَفَقَ ـُ
Gust *n.*	نَفْخَة رِيحٍ قَوِيَّة
Gust *n.*	مِعىً ج أَمعاء
Gutter *n.*	قَنَاة . بَالُوعَة
Guttural *a.* or *n.*	حَلْقِيٌّ . حَرْفُ ٱلْحَلْق
Guy *n.*	حَبْلٌ لِلإِسْنَادِ
Gymnasium *n.*	مَدْرَسَةُ ٱلرِّيَاضَةِ
Gymnastic *a.*	رِيَاضِيٌّ . جَسَدِيٌّ

H

Ha ! *ex.*	عَجَبًا . ها
Habiliment *n.*	ثَوْبٌ
Habit *n.*	عَادَة . دَأْبٌ . ثَوْبٌ
Habitable *a.*	قَابِلُ ٱلسُّكْنَى
Habitation *n.*	مَسْكَنٌ
Habitual *a.*	عَادِيٌّ . إِعْتِيَادِيٌّ
Habituate *v.t.*	عَوَّدَ . أَلَّفَ
Habitude *n.*	عَادَةٌ
Hack *v. t.* or *n.*	قَطَعَ . فَرَّضَ . كَدِيشٌ
Hackneyed *a.*	كَثِيرُ ٱلإِسْتِعْمَالِ
Hackney-coach *n.*	مَرْكَبَةٌ لِلْكِرَاءِ
Haddock *n.*	نَوْعٌ مِنَ ٱلسَّمَكِ
Haft *n.*	مَقْبَضٌ وَمِقْبَضٌ . نِصَابٌ
Hag *n.*	عَجُوزٌ . قَبِيحَةٌ
Haggard *a.*	خَاسِفُ ٱلْوَجْهِ
Haggle *v. t.* or *i.*	دَقَّقَ فِي ٱلْمُسَاوَمَة . قَطَّعَ
Hail *n.* or *v. t.*	بَرَدَ . نَادَى . حيا
Hailstones *n. pl.*	بَرَدَ

Hair *n.* شَعْرٌ . شَعْرَة

Hairless *a.* أَجْرَدُ

Hairy *a.* أَشْعَرُ

Hale *a.* مُتَعَافٍ . صَحِيحُ ٱلْجِسْمِ

Half *n.* (*pl.* Halves) نِصْف

Hall *n.* دِهْلِيز . قَاعَة . مُنْتَدَى

Halloo *n.* or *v. i.* صَيْحَة . صَاحَ ـِ

Hallow *v. t.* قَدَّس

Hallucination *n.* وَهْم . تَوَهُّم

Halo *n.* هَالَة . دائِرَة مُنيرَة

Halt *n.* or *a.* وُقُوفٌ . أَعْرَجُ

Halt *v. t.*, or *i.* وَقَّفَ . وَقَفَ ـِ . عَرَجَ ـُ

Halter *n.* or *v.t.* رَسَنٌ . شِنَاقٌ . رسَنَ

Halve *v. t.* نَصَفَ ـُ . شَطَرَ ـُ

Ham *n.* فَخْذُ خِنْزِيرٍ مُمَلَّحٌ

Hamlet *n.* مَزْرَعَة

Hammer *n.* مِطْرَقَة . شَاكُوش

Hammer *v. t.* طَرَقَ ـُ . دَقَّ ـُ

Hammock *n.* سَرِيرٌ مُعَلَّق

Hamper *n.* or *v. t.* قُفَّة . عَاقَ . قَيَّدَ

Hamstring *n.* or *v. t.* عُرْقُوب . عَرْقَبَ

Hand *n.* or *v.t.* يَدٌ . كَفٌّ . نَاوَلَ

Handbook *n.* كِتَابٌ مُخْتَصَرٌ لِلدَّلاَلَة

Handcraft, Handicraft *n.* حِرْفَة . صَنْعَةُ ٱلْيَدِ

Handcuff *n.* غُلٌّ . قَيْدٌ لِلْيَدِ

Handful *n.* قَبْضَة . شِرْذِمَة

Handily *ad.* بِمَهَارَةٍ . بِسُهُولَةٍ

Handiwork *n.* شُغْلُ ٱلْيَدِ

Handkerchief *n.* (مَحْرَمَة) . مِنْدِيلٌ

Handle *n.* or *v. t.* مِقْبَضٌ . مَسَّ ـَ

Handmaid *n.* جَارِيَة . أَمَة

Hand-mill *n.* جَارُوشٌ ج جَوَارِيشُ

Handsome *a.* جَمِيلٌ . حَسَن

Handy *a.* مَاهِر . قَرِيبٌ

Hang *v. t.* or *i.* عَلَّقَ . شَنَقَ . تَعَلَّقَ

Hangings *n. pl.* سَتَائِرُ . مُعَلَّقَات

Hangman *n.* جَلّاد

Hanker *v. i.* تاقَ ـُ إِلى

Hap-hazard *n.* عَرَض . صدفة

Hapless *a.* نحس . مَنكود الحظّ

Happen *v. i.* حَدَثَ ـُ صارَ ـِ

Happiness *n.* سعادة . غبطة

Happy *a.* سعيد . مغبوط . فرِح

Harangue *n.* or *v. t.* خِطاب . خاطب

Harass *v. t.* أزعج . اضجر . أتعب

Harassing *a.* مزعج . متعب

Harbinger *n.* سابق . مُبشّر

Harbour *n.* or *v. t.* ميناء . مرفأ . آوى

Hard *a.* قاسٍ . صلب . صعب

Harden *v. t.* or *i.* صلّب . قسّى . تصلّب

Hard-hearted *a.* قاسي القلب

Hardihood *n.* جراءة . إقدام

Hardly *ad.* بصعوبة . بالجهد

Hardness *n.* صلابة . قساوة

Hardship *n.* مشقّة . صعوبة

Hardware *n.* بضائع معدنيّة

Hardy *a.* شديد . باسل . ضليع

Hare *n.* أرنب

Hare-brained *a.* طائش

Harelip *n.* شفة شرماء

Harem *n.* حريم

Hark *v. i.* أصغى إلى

Harlot *n.* زانية . عاهرة

Harm *n.* or *v. t.* أذية . ضرر . آذى

Harmful *a.* مؤذٍ . مضرّ

Harmless *a.* غير مضرّ . سليم

Harmonious *a.* متوافق . متناسب

Harmonize *v. t.* وفّق . ساوى

Harmony *n.* إتّفاق . موازنة

Harness *n.* عدّة الفرس او العسكريّ

Harness *v. t.* ألبسه العدّة . كدن ـُ

Harp *n.* or *v. i.* عود . ضرب عليه

Harper *n.* ضارِبٌ بِالْعُودِ

Harpoon *n.* خُطَّافُ ٱلصَّيْدِ

Harrow *n.* or *v. t.* مِسْلَفَة . كَدَرَ . سَلَفَ

Harry *v. t.* نَهَبَ . سَلَبَ . ازْعَجَ

Harsh *a.* صَارِمٌ . فَظ . خَشِن

Harshness *n.* جَفَاءٌ . خُشُونَةٌ

Hart *n.* إِيَّلٌ . وَعْلٌ ج وُعُول

Harvest *n.* or *v. t.* حِصَادٌ . حَصَدَ ـُ

Hash *n.* or *v. t.* (لَحْم مَفْرُومٌ) . قَطَعَ

Haste / Hasten *v. i.* or *t.* أَسْرَعَ . عَجَّلَ

Haste *n.* عَجَلَةٌ . مُبَادَرَة

Hasty *a.* عَجُولٌ . مُسْرِعٌ . حَادٌّ

Hat *n.* بُرْنَيْطَةٌ . قَلَنْسُوَة

Hatch *v.t.* or *i.* فَقَسَ ـ . إِنْفَقَسَ

Hatchet *n.* فَأْسٌ

Hatchway *n.* مَدْخَل فِي ٱلسَّفِينَة

Hate *n.* or *v. t.* بُغْضٌ . أَبْغَضَ . مَقَتَ

Hateful *a.* مَمْقُوتٌ . مَكْرُوه

Hatred *n.* بُغْضٌ . مَقْتٌ

Hatter *n.* صَانِعُ ٱلْبَرَانِيطِ اوْ بَائِعُهَا

Haughty *a.* مُتَكَبِّرٌ . متعَجْرِف

Haul *v. t.* جَذَبَ . سَحَبَ

Haunch *n.* وَرْكٌ

Haunt *n.* or *v. t.* مَزَارٌ . تَرَدَّدَ إِلَى

Haunted *a.* مَأْوَى ٱلْجَانّ أَو ٱلطيفِ

Have *v. t.* مَلَكَ ـِ . لَهُ

Haven *n.* مِينَاءٌ . مَرْسى

Havoc *n.* خَرَاب . مَقْتَلَةٌ

Hawk *n.* بَازٍ ج بُوَازٍ . صَقْرٌ ج صُقُورٌ

Hawser *n.* حَبْلٌ ضَخْمٌ

Hawthorn *n.* زُعْرُورٌ (نَبَاتٌ)

Hay *n.* قَشٌّ . تِبْنٌ . كَلَأٌ

Hazard *n.* or *v.t.* خَطَرٌ . خَاطَرَ بِ

Hazardous *a.* مُخْطِرٌ . خَطِرٌ

Haze *n.* ضَبَابَةٌ . إِغْبِرَارٌ

Hazel *n.* or *a.* شَجَرُ ٱلْبُنْدُقِ . بُنْدُقِيٌّ

Haziness *n.* إِغْبِرَارٌ

Hazy *a.* ضَبَابِيٌّ . مُغْبَرٌّ

He *pron.* هُوَ

Head *n.* or *v. t.* رَأْسٌ . قَادَ . تَرَأَّسَ

Headache *n.* وَجَعُ ٱلرَّأْسِ . صُدَاعٌ

Head-dress *n.* كِسَاءُ ٱلرَّاسِ

Heading *n.* أَوَّلُ ٱلشَّيْءِ . عُنْوَانٌ

Headland *n.* رَاسٌ (فِي ٱلْبَحْرِ)

Headlong *a.* or *ad.* اَلرَّأْسُ إِلَى أَسْفَلَ

Head-quarters *n.* مَرْكَزُ ٱلْقَائِدِ أَوِ ٱلْحُكُومَةِ

Headship *n.* رِئَاسَةٌ

Headstrong *a.* عَنِيدٌ . صَلْبُ ٱلرَّأْسِ

Heal *v.t.* or *i.* شَفَى ـِ . تَعَافَى . إِنْدَمَلَ

Health *n.* صِحَّةٌ . عَافِيَةٌ

Healthful *a.* مُتَعَافٍ . مُفِيدٌ لِلصِّحَّةِ

Healthfulness / Healthiness *n.* صِحَّةٌ . عَافِيَةٌ

Healthy *a.* صَحِيحٌ . نَافِعٌ لِلصِّحَّةِ

Heap *n.* or *v. t.* كَوْمَةٌ . عُرْمَةٌ . كَوَّمَ

Hear *v. t.* سَمِعَ ـَ . اصْغَى . أَطَاعَ

Hearing *n.* سَمْعٌ . مَسْمَعٌ

Hearken *v. t.* أَصْغَى . إِسْتَمَعَ

Hearsay *n.* قَوْلٌ . قَالٌ وَقِيلٌ

Hearse *n.* مَرْكَبَةٌ لِحَمْلِ ٱلْمَوْتَى

Heart *n.* قَلْبٌ . لُبٌّ

Heart-felt *a.* قَلْبِيٌّ . مُخْلِصٌ

Hearth *n.* مَوْقَدَةٌ

Heartily *a.* قَلْبِيًّا . بِنَشَاطٍ

Heartiness *n.* خُلُوصٌ . هِمَّةٌ

Heartless *a.* قَاسٍ . بِلَا رَأْفَةٍ

Hearty *a.* قَلْبِيٌّ . مُخْلِصٌ . مُتَعَافٍ

Heat *n.* or *v. t.* حَرَارَةٌ . سَخَّنَ

Heathen *n.* / Heathenish *a.* وَثَنِيٌّ

Heathenism *n.* الدِّيَانَةُ ٱلْوَثَنِيَّةُ

Heave *v. t.* رَفَعَ ـَ . رَمَى ـِ

Heaven *n.* اَلسَّمَاءُ

Heavenly *a.* سَمَاوِيٌّ

Heaviness *n.* ثقل . غمّ

Heavy *a.* ثقيل . شديد . بطيء

Hebraic *a.* / Hebrew *n.* عبراني

Hedge *n.* or *v. t.* سياج . سيّج

Hedgehog *n.* قنفذ ج قنافذ

Heed *v. t.* بالى . أصغى إلى

Heed *n.* إكتراث . إعتناء

Heedful *a.* مبال . منتبه

Heedless *a.* غافل . غير مبال

Heedlessness *n.* عدم المبالاة

Heel *n.* عقب ج اعقاب

Hegira *n.* هجرة

Heifer *n.* عجلة

Height *n.* علوّ

Heighten *v. t.* زاد . على

Heinous *a.* فظيع

Heir *n.* وارث ج ورثة

Heir-apparent *n.* وليّ عهد

Hell *n.* جهنّم . جحيم

Hellenic *a.* يوناني

Helm *n.* دفة . قيادة

Helmet *n.* خوذة ج خوذ

Helmsman *n.* مدير الدفّة

Help *v. t.* or *n.* ساعد . مساعدة

Helpful *a.* مساعد . معاون

Helpless *a.* عاجز . لا معين له

Helpmate *n.* معين . رفيق

Hem *n.* or *v.t.* كفّة . حاشية . كفّ

Hemisphere *n.* نصف كرة

Hemlock *n.* شوكران

Hemorrhage *n.* نزف الدم

Hemp *n.* قنّب

Hen *n.* دجاجة

Henbane *n.* بنج (نبات)

Hence *ad.* من هنا . لهذا . إذاً

Henceforth / Henceforward *ad.* من الآن فصاعداً

Hencoop *n.* قَفَص . قُنٌّ

Heptagon *n.* مُسَبَّع

Her *pro.* لَهَا . هَا (ضمير)

Herald *n.* or *v. t.* مُنَادٍ . مُخْبِرٌ . اخْبَرَ

Herb *n.* عُشْبٌ . بَقْلٌ . نَبْت

Herbaceous *a.* عُشْبِيٌّ

Herbage *n.* كَلأٌ . خُضْرَةٌ

Herbarium *n.* مَنْبَت

Harbivorous *a.* آكِلُ ٱلنَّبَاتِ

Herculean *a.* عَظِيمٌ جِدًّا . صَعْبٌ

Herd *n.* or *v. i.* قَطِيعٌ . إِجْتَمَعَ

Herdsman *n.* رَاعٍ ج رُعَاة

Here *ad.* هُنَا . هَا هُنَا

Hereabouts *ad.* فِي هٰذِهِ ٱلنَّوَاحِي

Hereafter *ad.* فِيمَا بَعْدُ . بَعْدَ هٰذَا

Hereby *ad.* بِهٰذَا . مِنْ هٰذَا

Hereditary *a.* إِرْثِيٌّ . مَوْرُوث

Herein *ad.* فِي هٰذَا . مِنْ هٰذَا . لِهٰذَا

Heresy *n.* (هَرْطَقَةٌ) بِدْعَة

Heretic *n.* / Heretical *a.* (هَرْطُوقِي) . خَارِجِي

Heretofore *ad.* فِيمَا مَضَى . سَابِقًا

Hereupon *ad.* عِنْدَ ذَلِكَ . مِنْ ثَمَّ

Herewith *ad.* بِهٰذَا . مِنْ هٰذَا

Heritage *n.* مِيرَاث

Hermetically *ad.* بِضَبْطٍ (مَسْدُودٌ)

Hermit *n.* نَاسِكٌ . زَاهِدٌ

Hermitage *n.* مَنْسَكٌ

Hernia *n.* فِتْق

Hero *n.* (*pl.* Heroes). صِنْدِيدٌ . بَطَلٌ

Heroic *a.* صِنْدِيدِيٌّ . مَجِيدٌ

Heroine *n.* صِنْدِيدَة . بَطَلَةٌ

Heroism *n.* بَسَالَةٌ . إِقْدَامٌ

Herring *n.* نَوْعٌ مِنَ السَّمَكِ

Herself *pro.* نَفْسُهَا . ذَاتُهَا

Hesitancy / Hesitation *n.* تَرَدُّدٌ . إِرْتِيَاب

Hesitate *v. i.* تَرَدَّدَ . إِرْتَابَ

Heterogeneous *a.* مُخْتَلِفُ ٱلْجِنْسِ

Hew *v. t.* نَحَتَ ـ . قَطَّعَ

Hexagon *n.* مُسَدَّسٌ
Hexangular *a.* مُسَدَّسُ ٱلزَّوَايَا
Hibernal *a.* شَتَوِيٌّ
Hibernate *v. i.* شَتَّى (لِلْبَهَائِمِ)
Hibernian *n.* إِرْلَانْدِيٌّ
Hiccough *n.* or *v. i.* فُوَاق . فَاقَ ـَ
Hidden *a.* مُخْفِيٌّ . مَسْتُور
Hide *v. t.* or *i.* أَخْفَى . إِخْتَفَى
Hideous *a.* قَبِيحٌ . كَرِيهُ ٱلْمَنْظَرِ
Hierarchy *n.* رِئَاسَة دِينِيَّة
Hieroglyphics *n. pl.* خَط بِصُوَر
High *a.* عَالٍ . سَامٍ
Highland *n.* نَجْد . ارْض جَبَلِيَّة
Highly *ad.* كَثِيراً . جِدًّا
Highness *n.* سُمُوٌّ . رِفْعَة
High-priest *n.* رَئِيسُ ٱلْكَهَنَةِ
Hight *see* Height *n.* عُلُوٌّ
High-water *n.* أَعْلَى ٱلْمَدّ
Highway *n.* سِكَّة سُلْطَانِيَّة
Highwayman *n.* قَاطِعُ ٱلطُّرُقِ
Hilarity *n.* طَرَب فَرَحٌ
Hill *n.* تَلٌّ . أَكَمَةٌ
Hillock *n.* قَلِيل . كَثِيب
Hilly *a.* كَثِيرُ ٱلتِّلَالِ
Hilt *n.* مِقْبَضٌ . نِصَابٌ
Himself *pro.* نَفْسُهُ . ذَاتُهُ
Hind *a.* or *n.* مُؤَخَّرُ ٱلشَّيْء . إِيلَةٌ
Hinder *v. t.* عَاقَ . صَدَّ ـُ مَنَعَ ـَ
Hinderance / Hindrance *n.* عَائِقٌ . مَانِعٌ
Hindermost / Hindmost *a.* أَلاخِيرُ
Hindoo *n.* هِنْدِيٌّ
Hinge *n.* or *v. i.* مَفَصَّلَةٌ . دَار عَلَى
Hint *v. t.* or *i.* or *n.* اوْمَأَ . لَمَّحَ . إِيمَاءٌ . تَلْمِيح
Hip *n.* وِرْك
Hippodrome *n.* مِيدَانٌ لِلْخَيْلِ
Hippopotamus *n.* فَرَسُ ٱلْمَاءِ
Hire *n.* or *v. t.* اجرٌ . كِرَاءٌ . إِسْتَأْجَرَ
Hireling *n.* or *a.* اجِيرٌ

His *pro.* لهُ

Hiss *v. t.* or *i.* or *n.* صفر ـِ . فحّ ـُ . فحيح

Historian *n.* مؤرّخ

Historical *a.* تاريخيّ

History *n.* تأريخ

Hit *v. t.* or *n.* اصابَ . إصابة

Hitch *v. t.* or *n.* علَّقَ . ربَطَ . عرقلة

Hither *ad.* إلى هنا

Hitherto *ad.* إلى الآن

Hive *n.* قفير

Hoar / Hoary *a.* أشيبُ . أبيضُ

Hoard *v. t.* or *n.* ذخَرَ ـَ . ذخيرة

Hoarfrost *n.* ملّاح . صقيع

Hoariness *n.* شيب

Hoarse *a.* ابحّ . مبحوح

Hoarseness *n.* بحّة

Hoax *n.* or *v. t.* غشّ . ألعوبة . غشَّ . مكرَ

Hobble *v. i.* or *t.* عرِجَ . شكّلَ

Hobby / Hobbyhorse *n.* ما يُولَعُ بهِ

Hobgoblin *n.* غول

Hock *n.* or *v. t.* عرقوب . عرقبَ

Hod *n.* نقيرج نقران

Hoe *n.* or *v. t.* مجرفة . مِعزقة . عزَق ـِ

Hog *n.* خنزير ج خنازير

Hogshead *n.* برميل كبير

Hog-sty *n.* زريبة الخنازير

Hoist *v. t.* رفعَ ـَ

Hold *n.* ضبط . داخل سفينةٍ

Holde *v. t.* ضبطَ . حجزَ ـُ . وسعَ ـَ

Hole *n.* ثقب . خرق . وجار

Holiday *n.* يوم بطالةٍ

Holiness *n.* قداسة

Hollow *a.* فارغ . مجوّف . باطل

Hollow *v. t.* جوّفَ

Hollow *n.* إنخفاض . غوط . جوف

Hollow-hearted *a.* خائن . مراء

Hollyhock *n.* الخطميّ

Holy *a.* مُقَدَّسٌ . قُدُّوسٌ

Homage *n.* إِكْرَام . عِبَادَة . إِحْتِرَامٌ

Home *n.* بَيْتٌ . وَطَنٌ

Homely *a.* عَدِيمُ ٱلْحُسْنِ . بَيْتِيٌّ

Homeopathy *n.* اَلْعِلَاجُ بِالْمِثْلِ

Homesick *a.* مُشْتَاقٌ لِلْوَطَنِ او لِلْبَيْتِ

Homestead *n.* دَارُ عَائِلَةٍ

Homeward *ad.* نَحْوَ ٱلْبَيْتِ او ٱلْوَطَنِ

Homicide *n.* قَاتِل . قَتْلٌ

Homogeneous *a.* مُتَجَانِسٌ

Hone *n.* or *v. t.* مِسَنٌّ رَفِيعٌ . سَنَّ ـُ

Honest *a.* مُسْتَقِيمٌ . أَمِينٌ . مُخْلِصٌ

Honesty *n.* أَمَانَةٌ . إِسْتِقَامَةٌ

Honey *n.* عَسَلٌ

Honeycomb *n.* شَهْدُ ٱلْعَسَلِ

Honeymoon *n.* شَهْرُ ٱلزَّوَاجِ

Honour *n.* or *v. t.* إِكْرَامٌ . أَكْرَمَ

Honorable *a.* مُكْرَمٌ . شَرِيفٌ

Honorary *a.* إِكْرَامِيٌّ

Hood *n.* قَلَنْسُوَةٌ . قُبَّعَةٌ

Hoodwink *v. t.* خَدَعَ . خَتَلَ ـِ

Hoof *n.* حَافِرٌ . ظِلْفٌ ج ظُلُوفٌ

Hook *n.* شِصٌّ . كَلَّابٌ . خُطَّافٌ

Hoop *n.* or *v.t.* إِطَارٌ . طَوْق . شَدَّ بِإِطَارٍ

Hooping-cough *n.* مَرَضُ ٱلشَّهْقَةِ

Hoot *n. v. i.* صَيْحَةٌ . نَعْقٌ . نَعَقَ ـ

Hop *v. i.* قَفَزَ عَلَى رِجْلٍ وَاحِدَةٍ

Hop *n.* قَفْزَةٌ . حَشِيشَةُ ٱلدِّينَارِ

Hope *n.* or *v. i.* رَجَاءٌ . رَجَا ـُ

Hopeful *a.* كَثِيرُ الرَّجَاءِ . مَرْجُوٌّ

Hopeless *a.* بِلَا رَجَاءٍ . بَائِسٌ

Horde *n.* قَوْمٌ . قَبِيلَةٌ

Horizon *n.* افق

Horizontal *a.* افقيٌّ

Horn *n.* قَرْنٌ . بُوْن . نَاقُوْرٌ

Horned *a.* ذو قُرُون

Hornet *n.* زُنبُورٌ

Horrible *a.* هَائِلٌ . فَظِيعٌ

Horrid *a.* فَظِيعٌ . قَبِيحٌ

Horrify *v. t.* أَرْعَبَ . أَفْظَعَ

Horror *n.* هَولٌ . رُعْبٌ

Horse *n.* فَرَسٌ . حِصَانٌ ج احْصِنَةٌ

Horseback *n.* ظَهْرُ ٱلْفَرَسِ

Horseman *n.* خيَّالٌ . فَارِسٌ

Horsemanship *n.* فَنُّ رُكُوبِ ٱلْخَيلِ

Horseshoe *n.* نَعْلُ ٱلْفَرَسِ

Horsewhip *n.* سَوْطٌ . كُرْبَاجٌ

Hospitable *a.* مِضْيَافٌ . كَرِيم

Hospital *n.* مُسْتَشْفَى

Hospitality *n.* تَضْيِيفٌ . ضِيَافَةٌ

Host / Hostess *n.* مُضِيفٌ مُضَيِّفٌ . مُضَيِّفَةٌ

Hostage *n.* رَهْنٌ . رَهِينٌ

Hostile *a.* عِدَائِيٌّ . مُضَادٌّ

Hostility *n.* عَدَاوَةٌ . خِصَامٌ

Hostler *n.* سَائِسُ الخَيلِ

Hot *a.* حَارٌّ . سُخْن . حَامٍ

Hotel *n.* فندُقٌ . لوكَنْدَة

Hotly *ad.* بِحَمِيةٍ . بشِدَّةٍ

Hound *n.* كَلْبُ ٱلصَّيْدِ

Hour *n.* سَاعَةٌ . زَمَان

Hour-glass *n.* سَاعَةٌ . رَمْليَّةٌ

Hourly *a.* or *ad.* كلَّ سَاعَةٍ

House *n.* بَيْتٌ . دَوْلَةٌ . شِرْكَة

House-breaker *n.* لِصٌّ ج لُصُوص

Household *n.* أَهْلُ ٱلبَيْتِ

Housekeeper *n.* مُدَبِّرُ ٱلْمَنْزِلِ

Houseless *a.* بِلا مَسْكَنٍ

Hovel *n.* كُوخٌ . خُصٌّ

Hover *v. i.* حَامَ ـُ . تَرَدَّدَ بِقُرْبٍ

How *ad.* كَيْفَ

However *ad.* كَيْفَمَا . إِلَّا انَّ

Howl *v. i.* or *n.* عَوَى ـِ . عُوَاءٌ

Hub *n.* بَطِّيخَة ٱلدُّولَاب

Hubbub *n.* ضَوْضَاء . ضَجِيجٌ

Huddle *v. t.* اسْرَعَ . خَلَطَ ـ إِزْدَحَمَ

Hue *n.* لَوْنٌ

Hug *v. t.* or *n.* عَانَقَ . عِنَاقٌ

Huge *a.* كَبِير جِدًّا . جَسِيمٌ

Hull *n.* قِشْرُ ٱلْجَوْزَةِ . بَدَنُ ٱلسَّفِينَةِ

Hull *v. t.* قَشَّرَ

Hum *v. i.* or *n.* دَنْدَنَ . دَنْدَنَة . دَوِيٌّ

Human *a.* بَشَرِيٌّ . إِنْسَانِي

Humane *a.* ذُو إِنْسَانِيَّةٍ . لَطِيف

Humanity *n.* إِنْسَانِيَّةٌ . لُطْفٌ

Humble *a.* وَدِيعٌ . مُتَوَاضِعٌ

Humble *v. t.* ذَلَّلَ . وَضَعَ ـ حَطَّ

Humbug *n.* or *v. t.* شَعْبَذَةٌ . غَشَّ ـ

Humid *a.* رَطْب . مُنَدًّى

Humidity *n.* رُطُوبَة . نَدًى

Humiliate *v. t.* ذَلَّلَ . حَطَّ شَأْنَهُ

Humiliation *n.* ذُلٌّ . إِنْحِطَاطٌ

Humility *n.* تَوَاضُعٌ . خُشُوعٌ

Humour *v. t.* لَاطَفَ . دَارَى

Humour *n.* طَبْعٌ . سَجِيَّةٌ . فُكَاهَة

Humorist *n.* / Humorous *a.* مَازِح . مُضْحِكٌ

Hump *n.* حَدَبَةٌ . سِنَامٌ

Humpback / Hunchback *n.* أَحْدَب . حَدْبَاء

Hundred *n.* مِئَة ومِائَةٌ

Hundredth *a.* أَلْمِئَةُ

Hunger *n.* or *v. i.* جُوعٌ . جَاعَ

Hungry *a.* جَائِعٌ . جُوعَان

Hunt *v. t.* or *n.* إِصْطَادَ . صَيْدٌ . قَنْصٌ

Hunter / Huntsman *n.* قَانِصٌ . صَيَّادٌ

Hurl *v. t.* or *n.* أَلْقَى . رَمَى ـ رَمْيَةً

Hurrah ! *ex.* هُتَافُ ٱلْفَرَحِ

Hurricane *n.* زَوْبَعَةٌ

Hurry *v. t.* or *i.* عَجَّلَ . إِسْتَعْجَلَ

Hurt *n.* or *v. t.* ضَرَر . أَضَرَّ . آذَى

Hurtful *a.*	مُؤْذٍ . مُضِر
Husband *n.* or *v. t.*	زَوْج . بَعلٌ . إِقْتَصد
Husbandman *n.*	فلاحٌ . كرَّامٌ
Husbandry *n.*	فَلَاحَةٌ
Hush *v. t.* or *i.*	اسْكَتَ . سَكَتَ ـُ
Husk *n.* or *v. t.*	قِشْرَةٌ . قشرَ
Husky *a.*	أَبَحُّ
Hustle *v. t.*	زَحَمَ ـَ . دَفع ـَ عَجَّلَ
Hut *n.*	كُوْخ
Huzza *n.*	هِتَافُ ٱلْإِستِحْسَان
Hybrid *n.*	مَوْلُودٌ مِنْ نَوْعَين
Hydraulics *n. sing.*	عِلْمُ ٱلسَّوَائِلِ
Hydrogen *n.*	هِدرُوجِينٌ
Hydrophobia *n.*	دَآءُ ٱلْكَلْب
Hygiene / Hygienics *n.*	عِلْمُ حِفْظُ ٱلصِّحَّةِ
Hyena *n.*	ضَبْع ج ضِبَاع
Hymn *n.*	تَرْنِيمَةٌ
Hymnal *n.*	كِتَابُ تَرْنِيمَاتٍ
Hyperbola *n.*	قَوْسُ قَطْعِ ٱلْمَخْرُوطِ
Hyperbole *n.*	مُبَالَغَةٌ
Hyphen *n.*	عَلَامَةُ وَصْلٍ (ـَ)
Hypochondria *n.*	سَوْدَآء
Hypocrisy *n.*	رِيَاءٌ . نِفَاقٌ
Hypocrite *n.*	مُرَآءٍ . مُنَافِقٌ
Hypothenuse *n.*	وَتَرُ زَاوِيَةٍ قَائِمَةٍ
Hypothssis *n.*	حَدْسٌ . فَرْضٌ
Hyssop *n.*	زوفَا
Hysterical *a.*	(هِستِيرِي)
Hysteria / Hysterics *n.*	(هِستِيرِيَا)

I

I *pro.* انا

Ice *n.* جَلِيدٌ

Iceberg *n.* جَبَلُ جَلِيدٍ عَائِمٌ

Ice-cream *n.* (بُوزٌ جِلاَتِه . دَنْدُرْمَه)

Icicle *n.* جَلِيدٌ مَخْرُوطِيُّ ٱلشَّكْلِ

Icy *a.* جَلِيدِيٌّ . قَارِسٌ

Idea *n.* صُورَةٌ عَقْلِيَّةٌ . فِكْرٌ

Ideal *a.* تَصَوُّرِيٌّ . كَامِلٌ

Idealize *v. t.* تَصَوَّرَ

Identic, Identical *a.* عَيْنُهُ . ذَاتُهُ

Identify *v. t.* حَقَّقَ أَنَّهُ هُوَ

Idiocy *n.* بَلَاهَةٌ . عَتَه

Idiom *n.* إِصْطِلَاحٌ

Idiomatic, Idiomatical *a.* إِصْطِلَاحِيٌّ

Idio *n.*, Idiotic *a.* أَبْلَهُ . مَعْتُوهٌ

Idle *a.*, Idler *n.* بَطَّال . كَسْلَانُ

Idleness *n.* كَسَلٌ . بَطَالَةٌ

Idol *n.* صَنَمٌ . وَثَنٌ

Idolater *n.* وَثَنِيٌّ . عَابِد اصْنَامٍ

Idolatrous *a.* مُخْتَصٌّ بِعِبَادَةِ ٱلاوْثَانِ

Idolize *v. t.* أَفْرَطَ فِي ٱلْحُبِّ . وَلِعَ بِ

Idolatry *n.* عِبَادَةُ ٱلْاوْثَانِ

If *conj.* لَوْ . إِنْ . إِذَا

Igneous *a.* نَارِيٌّ

Ignite *v. t.* أَوْقَدَ . أَشْعَلَ

Ignoble *a.* دَنِيءٌ . خَسِيسٌ

Ignominious *a.* مُوجِبُ ٱلْعَارِ . مُخْزٍ

Ignominy *n.* عَارٌ . فَضِيحَةٌ . إِبَّةٌ

Ignoramus *n.* / Ignorant *a.*	جَاهِلٌ . غَبِي
Ignorance *n.*	جَهَالَة . غَبَاوَة
Ignore *v. t.*	تَجَاهَلَ . أَهمَلَ
Ill *a.* or *a.*	مَرِيضٌ . سُوءٌ
Ill-bred *a.*	غَيْرُ مُهَذَّبٍ . فَظ
Illegal *a.*	غَيْرُ شَرْعِيٍّ
Illegible *a.*	مُمْتَنِعٌ قِرَاءَتُهُ
Illegitimate *a.*	غَيْرُ شَرْعِيٍّ . نَغْل
Ill-fated *a.*	نَحْس . مَشْؤُومٌ
Ill-favoured *a.*	اشْوَهُ . سَيِّئُ ٱلْمَنْظَرِ
Illiberal *a.*	بَخِيلٌ . خَسِيسٌ
Illicit *a.*	مُحَرَّمٌ . مَمْنُوعٌ
Illimitable *a.*	غَيْرُ مَحْدُودٍ
Illiterate *a.*	أُمِّيٌّ
Ill-nature *n.*	سُوءُ ٱلطَّبْعِ
Illness *n.*	مَرَضٌ . عِلَّة
Illogical *a.*	غَيْرُ مَنْطِقِيٍّ
Ill-omened *a.*	مَشْؤُومٌ
Ill-starred *a.*	مَشْؤُومٌ
Ill-timed *a.*	فِي غَيْرِ وَقْتِهِ
Illumine / Illuminate *v. t.*	أَنَارَ . اضَاءَ
Illumination *n.*	إِنَارَةٌ
Illusion *n.*	وَهْمٌ
Illusive / Illusory *a.*	غَرَّارٌ . غَيْرُ حَقِيقِيٍّ
Illustrate *v. t.*	بَيَّنَ . شَرَحَ
Illustration *n.*	إِيضَاحٌ . تَصْوِيرٌ
Illustrious *a.*	شَهِيرٌ . جَلِيلٌ
Ill-will *n.*	ضَغِينَة . سُوءُ نِيَّةٍ
Image *n.*	تِمْثَالٌ . صُورَةٌ
Imagery *n.*	ٱلتَّصَوُّرُ فِي ٱلْكَلَامِ
Imaginable *a.*	قَابِلُ ٱلتَّصَوُّرِ
Imaginary *a.*	تَصَوُّرِيٌّ . وَهْمِيٌّ
Imagination *n.*	التَّصَوُّرُ . ٱلْمُخَيِّلَة
Imaginative *a.*	كَثِيرُ ٱلتَّصَوُّرِ
Imagine *v. t.*	تَصَوَّرَ . تَخَيَّلَ
Imbecile *a.*	سخيف . عاجز

Imbecility *n.* سخافة . عجز

Imbedded *pp.* مغروز . مدفون

Imbibe *v. t.* شرب ـــ . تشرّب

Imbrue *v. t.* بلّل . نقع . لطّخ

Imbue *v. t.* صبغ ـــ . أثّر

Imitate *v. t.* تمثّل به . حاكى

Imitation *n.* إقتداء . تزوير

Immaculate *a.* بلا دنس . نقيّ

Immalleable *a.* لا يُمطل بالطَّرق

Immaterial *a.* غيرُ ماديّ . غيرُ مُهمّ

Immature *a.* فِج . غيرُ بالغ

Immeasurable / Immensurable } *a.* لا يُقاس

Immediate *a.* غيرُ متأخّر . قريب

Immediately *ad.* حالاً . على الفور

Immemorial *a.* قديم جدًّا

Immense *a.* عظيم جدًّا

Immensity *n.* كُبْرٌ لا يُقاس

Immerse *v. t.* غطّس ـــ . غمس ـــ

Immersion *n.* غطس . غمس

Immigrant *a.* مُهاجر إلى

Immigrate *v. i.* هاجر إلى

Imminent *a.* قريب . مُوشك

Immoderate *a.* مُفرط . متجاوز الحدّ

Immodest *a.* عديم الحشمة او الحياء

Immolate *v. t.* ذبح ـــ

Immoral *a.* فاسد . فاجر

Immorality *n.* فساد الآداب

Immortal *a.* خالد

Immortality *n.* خلود

Immortalize *v. t.* خلّد

Immovable *a.* in *pl. n.* ثابت . راسخ . عقار

Immunity *n.* براءة . إمتياز

Immure *v. t.* حبس ـــ

Immutability *n.* عدم التغيّر

Immutable *a.* عديم التغيّر

Imp *n.* عفريت صغير

Impact *n.* صَدْمٌ . دَفْعٌ

Impair *v. t.* أَفْسَدَ . أَخَلَّ بِهِ . أَضَرَّ

Impale *v. t.* خَوْزَقَ

Impalpable *a.* مَا لَا يُدْرَكُ بِٱللمس

Impart *v. t.* مَنَحَ . ـــ . أَخْبَرَ بِهِ

Impartial *a.* عَدِيمُ ٱلْمُحَابَاةِ . عَادِلٌ

Impartiality *n.* عَدَمُ ٱلْمُحَابَاةِ

Impassable *a.* مَا لَا يُعْبَرُ

Impassioned *a.* ثَائِرٌ . مُهَيَّجٌ . مُتَهَيِّجٌ

Impatience *n.* عَدَمُ ٱلصبر

Impatient *a.* عَدِيمُ ٱلصَّبْرِ . جَزِعٌ

Impeach *v. t.* أَقَامَ دَعْوَى عَلَيْهِ

Impede *v. t.* عَاقَ

Impediment *n.* عَائِقٌ

Impel *v. t.* دَفَعَ — حَرَّضَ

Impending *a.* مُوشِكٌ . مُتَوَعِّدٌ

Impenetrable *a.* غَيْرُ قَابِلِ ٱلإِخْتِرَاقِ

Impenitence *n.* عَدَمُ ٱلتَّوْبَةِ

Impenitent *a.* عَدِيمُ ٱلتَّوْبَةِ

Imperative *a.* or *n.* ضَرُورِيٌّ . أَمْرٌ

Imperceivable / Imperceptible } *a.* لَا يُشْعَرُ بِهِ

Imperfect *a.* نَاقِصٌ . غَيْرُ كَامِلٍ

Imperfection *n.* نقص

Imperial *a.* سُلْطَانِيٌّ

Imperil *v. t.* اوقع فِي خَطَرٍ

Imperious *a.* مُتَجَبِّرٌ . ضَرُورِيٌّ

Imperishable *a.* عَدِيمُ ٱلزَّوَالِ

Impermeable *a.* مَا لَا يَتَخَلَّلُهُ سَائِلٌ

Impersonal *a.* غَيْرُ شَخْصِيٍّ

Impersonate *v. t.* شَخَّصَ

Impertinence *n.* وَقَاحَةٌ

Impertinent *a.* وَقِحٌ . فُضُولِيٌّ

Imperturbable *a.* رَكِينٌ لَا يُقْلَقُ

Impervious *a.* مَا لَا يُخْرَقُ وَيُتَخَلَّلُ

Impetuosity *n.* إِقْتِحَامٌ . حِدَّةٌ

Impetuous *a.* مُقْتَحِمٌ . مُحْتَدٌّ

Impetus *n.* قُوَّةٌ دَافِعَةٌ

Impiety *n.* عَدَمُ ٱلتَّقوَى

Impious *a.* شرِّيرٌ . أَثِيمٌ

Implacable *a.* حَنِقٌ لَا يُرْضَى

Implant *v. t.* غَرَسَ فِي . أَدْخَلَ

Implement *n.* آلَةٌ . أَدَاةٌ

Implicate *v. t.* أَوْقَعَ فِي . عَرَّضَ

Implication *n.* تَضَمُّنُ مَعْنًى

Implicit *a.* مُتَضَمَّنٌ . مَوْثُوقٌ بِهِ

Implicitly *ad.* بِثِقَةٍ تَامَّةٍ . مَعْنَوِيًّا

Implore *v. t.* تَوَسَّلَ . إِسْتَغَاثَ

Imply *v. t.* تَضَمَّنَ . دَلَّ عَلَى

Impolite *a.* قَلِيلُ ٱلْأَدَبِ . فَظٌّ

Impoliteness *n.* قِلَّةُ ٱلادَبِ

Impolitic *a.* بِغَيْرِ حِكْمَةٍ . غَيْرُ مُنَاسِبٍ

Imponderable *a.* عَدِيمُ ٱلثِّقَلِ

Import *v. t.* جَلَبَ بِـ . ادْخَلَ إِلَى

Import *n.* وَارِدٌ . مَعْنًى . اهمِّيَةٌ

Importance *n.* أَهَمِّيَّةٌ . عَظَمَةٌ

Important *a.* مُهِمٌّ . خَطِيرٌ

Importation *n.* جَلْبٌ مِنْ خَارِجٍ

Importunate *a.* لَجُوجٌ . مُلِحٌّ

Importune *v. t.* لَجَّ بِـ . أَلَحَّ عَلَى

Importunity *n.* لَجَاجَةٌ . إِلْحَاحٌ

Impose *v. t.* وَضَعَ عَلَى . غَشَّ

Imposing *a.* عَظِيمٌ . مُؤَثِّرٌ

Imposition *n.* تَكْلِيفٌ . مَكْرٌ

Impossibility *n.* عَدَمُ ٱلإِمْكَانِ

Impossible *a.* غَيْرُ مُمْكِنٍ . مُسْتَحِيلٌ

Impost *n.* ضَرِيبَةٌ . مَكْسٌ

Impostor *n.* خَدَّاعٌ . دَجَّالٌ

Imposture *n.* خُدْعَةٌ

Impotence *n.* عَجْزٌ . وَهَنٌ

Impotent *a.* عَاجِزٌ . وَاهِنٌ

Impoverish *v. t.* أَفْقَرَ . أَعْوَزَ

Impracticable *a.* مُمْتَنِعٌ عَمَلُهُ

Imprecate *v. t.* دَعَا عَلَى

Impregnable *a.* مَنِيعٌ

Impregnate *v. t.* لَقَّحَ . أَشْرَبَ

Impregnation *n.* تَلْقِيحٌ . إِشْرَابٌ

Impress *v. t.* أَثَّرَ . سَخَّرَ . خَتَمَ

Impress *n.* رَسْمٌ . أَثَرٌ . صُورَةٌ

Imprsesion *n.* ظَنٌّ . عَلَامَةٌ . طَبْعَةٌ

Impressive *a.* مُؤَثِّرٌ

Imprint *v. t.* or *n.* طَبَعَ . وَسَمَ . وَسْم

Imprison *v. t.* حَبَسَ . سَجَنَ

Imprisonment *n.* حَبْسٌ . سِجْنٌ

Improbable *a.* غَيْرُ مُحْتَمَلٍ

Improper *a.* غَيْرُ لَائِقٍ

Impropriety *n.* عَدَمُ لِيَاقَةٍ

Improve *v. t.* or *i.* حَسَّنَ . تَقَدَّمَ

Improvement *n.* تَحَسُّنٌ . تَقَدُّمٌ

Improvident *a.* عَدِيمُ الْعِنَايَةِ . مُتَغَفِّلٌ

Improvise *v. i.* إِرْتَجَلَ . إِبْتَدَهَ

Imprudence *n.* قِلَّةُ الْحَزْمِ أَوِ الْبَصِيرَةِ

Imprudent *a.* غَيْرُ بَصِيرٍ أَو حَازِمٍ

Impudence *n.* وَقَاحَة . سَفَهٌ

Impudent *a.* وَقِحٌ . سَفِيهٌ

Impugn *v. t.* نَاقَضَ . عَارَضَ

Impulse / Impulsion *n.* قُوَّةٌ دَافِعَةٌ

Impulsive *a.* مُنْدَفِعٌ . دَافِعٌ

Impunity *n.* عَدَمُ عِقَابٍ . أَمْنٌ

Impure *a.* فَاسِدٌ . نَجِسٌ

Impurity *n.* فَسَادٌ . قَذَرٌ

Imputation *n.* إِتِّهَامٌ . ذَمٌّ

Impute *v. t.* نَسَبَ إِلَى . حَسِبَ لَهُ

In *pr.* فِي . بِ . دَاخِلِ

Inability *n.* عَجْزٌ . عَدَمُ قُدْرَةٍ

Inaccessible *a.* مَنِيعٌ

Inaccuracy *n.* عَدَمُ ضَبْطٍ أَو صِحَّةٍ

Inaccurate *a.* غَيْرُ مَضْبُوطٍ أَو صَحِيحٍ

Inaction / Inactivity *n.* عَدَمُ حَرَكَةٍ . بَطَالَةٌ

Inactive *a.* سَاكِنٌ . مُتَكَاسِلٌ

Inadequate *a.* غَيْرُ كَافٍ . نَاقِصٌ

Inadmissible *a.* مُمْتَنِعٌ قَبُولُهُ

Inadvertence / Inadvertency } *n.* غَفْلَةٌ . سَهْوٌ

Inalienable *a.* لَا يُبَاعُ وَلَا يُوهَبُ

Inane *a.* فَارِغٌ . غَيْرُ مُفِيدٍ . خَاوٍ

Inanimate *a.* عَدِيمُ ٱلْحَيَاةِ

Inapplicable *a.* غَيْرُ مُطَابِقٍ

Inappreciable *a.* مَالَا يُحْسَبُ . زَهِيدٌ

Inappropriate *a.* غَيْرُ مُنَاسِبٍ

Inapt *a.* غَيْرُ جَدِيرٍ . غَيْرُ مُنَاسِبٍ

Inaptitude *a.* عَدَمُ جَدَارَةٍ أَوْ مُنَاسَبَةٍ

Inarticulate *a.* غَيْرُ مَلْفُوظٍ

Inasmuch *ad.* بِمَا أَنَّ

Inattention *n.* عَدَمُ مُبَالَاةٍ . غَفْلَةٌ

Inattentive *a.* غَيْرُ مُبَالٍ . مُتَغَافِلٌ

Inaudible *a.* غَيْرُ مَسْمُوعٍ

Inaugural *a.* إِفْتِتَاحِيٌّ . إِحْتِفَالِيٌّ

Inaugurate *v. t.* إِفْتَتَحَ . رَسَمَ . قَلَّدَ

Inauguration *n.* إِفْتِتَاحٌ . تَقْلِيدٌ

Inauspicious *a.* مَشْؤُومٌ

Inborn / Inbred } *a.* غَرِيزِيٌّ . طَبِيعِيٌّ

Incalculable *a.* مَا لَا يُحْصَى

Incandescent *a.* وَهَّاجٌ

Incantation *a.* رُقْيَةٌ

Incapability *n.* عَجْزٌ . قُصُورٌ

Incapable *a.* عَاجِزٌ . غَيْرُ قَادِرٍ

Incapacitate *v. t.* اعْجَزَ

Incapacity *n.* عَجْزٌ

Incarcerate *v. t.* حَبَسَ

Incarceration *n.* حَبْسٌ

Incarnate *a.* مُتَجَسِّدٌ

Incarnation *n.* تَجَسُّدٌ

Incase *v. t.* وَضَعَ فِي صُنْدُوقٍ

Incautious *a.* غَافِلٌ . غَيْرُ مُتَحَذِّرٍ

Incendiary *a.* or *n.* حَارِقُ بُيُوتٍ عَمْدًا

Incense *n.* / Incense *v. t.* } بَخُورٌ . بَخَّرَ . اغَاظَ

Incentive *n.* بَاعِث . حَثّ

Inception *n.* بَدَاءَةٌ . شُرُوعٌ

Incertitude *n.* عَدَمُ يَقِين . شك

Incessant *a.* غَيْرُ مُنْقَطِعٍ

Incest *n.* أَلزِّنَا بَيْنَ اقْرِبَاء

Inch *n.* عُقْدَة

Incidence *n.* وُقُوعٌ . حُدُوثٌ

Incident *n.* وَاقِعٌ . حَادِثَةٌ

Incidental *a.* عَرَضِي . إِتِّفَاقِيٌّ

Incipient *a.* إِبْتِدَائِيٌّ

Incision *n.* شَقٌّ . تَشْرِيط

Incisive *a.* قَاطِعٌ . صَارِمٌ . حَادٌّ

Incisor *n.* قَاطِعٌ . ثَنِيَّةٌ . (سِن)

Incite *v. t.* حَمَلَ عَلَى. أَغْوَى. هَيَّجَ

Incivility *n.* غَلَاظَةٌ . عَدَمُ انسٍ

Inclement *a.* صَارِمٌ . قَارِسٌ

Inclinable *a.* مَائِلٌ إِلَى

Inclination *n.* مَيْل

Incline *v. t.* or *i.* أَمَالَ . مَالَ ـِ

Inclose *v. t.* أَحَاطَ . سَيَّجَ . ضَمَّنَ

Inclosure *n.* حَائِطٌ . حَظِيرَةٌ . ضِمْنٌ

Include *v. t.* حَوَى ـِ . شَمِلَ ـَ

Including *pp.*
Inclusive *a.* } شَامِلٌ . حَاوٍ

Incognito *n.* or *ad.* تَنَكُّرٌ

Incoherence *n.* عَدَمُ ارْتِبَاطٍ . هَذْيٌ

Incoherent *a.* هَذَآء . بِلَا مُطَابَقَةٍ

Incombustible *a.* مَالَا يُحْرَقُ

Income *n.* إِيرَادٌ . دَخْلٌ

Incommode *v. t.* ثَقَّلَ عَلَى . اتعَبَ

Incommodious *a.* مُتعِبٌ

Incommunicative *a.* كَتُومٌ

Incomparable *a.* فَرِيدٌ

Incompatible *a.* مُغَايِرٌ . مُتَنَافٍ

Incompetence *n.* قُصُورٌ . عَجْزٌ

Incompetent *a.* قَاصِرٌ . عَاجِزٌ

Incomplete *a.* نَاقِصٌ

Incompleteness *n.* نَقْصٌ

Incomprehensible *a.* مُمْتَنِعٌ إِدْرَاكُهُ

Inconceivable *a.* مَا لَا يُتَصَوَّرُ

Inconclusive *a.* غَيْرُ مُقْنِعٍ

Incongruent / Incongruous *a.* غَيْرُ مُتَنَاسِبٍ

Incongruity *n.* عَدَمُ تَنَاسُبٍ

Inconsiderable *a.* زَهِيدٌ

Inconsiderate *a.* غَيْرُ مُبَالٍ

Inconsistency *n.* تَنَاقُضٌ

Inconsistent *a.* مُخَالِفٌ . مُنَاقِضٌ

Inconsolable *a.* لَا يَتَعَزَّى

Inconspiciuous *a.* غَيْرُ بَيِّنٍ أَوْ وَاضِحٍ

Inconstancy *n.* تَقَلُّبٌ

Inconstant *a.* مُتَقَلِّبٌ . مُتَغَيِّرٌ

Incontestable *a.* مَا لَا يُنْكَرُ

Incontinence / Incontinency *n.* عَدَمُ الْعِفَّةِ وَالضَّبْطِ

Incontinent *a.* غَيْرُ عَفِيفٍ . فَاسِقٌ

Incontrovertible *a.* مَا لَا يُرَدُّ

Inconvenience *n.* عَائِقٌ

Inconvenient *a.* غَيْرُ مُوَافِقٍ

Incorporate *v. t.* ضَمَّ إِلَى . أَدْخَلَ / أَقَامَ شَرْعاً

Incorporeal *a.* غَيْرُ مَادِّيٍّ . بِلَا جِسْمٍ

Incorrect *a.* غَيْرُ مُصِيبٍ . خَطَأٌ

Incorrectness *n.* خَطَأٌ . عَدَمُ ضَبْطٍ

Incorrigible *a.* مَا لَا يُصْلَحُ

Incorrupt *a.* غير فاسدٍ . طَاهِرٌ

Incorruptible *a.* عَدِيمُ الْفَسَادِ

Increase *v. t.* or *i.* زَادَ ـــِ نَمَا ـــُ

Increment / Increase *n.* زِيَادَةٌ . نُمُوٌّ

Incredible *a.* مُمْتَنِعٌ تَصْدِيقُهُ

Incredulity *n.* عَدَمُ تَصْدِيقٍ

Incredulous *a.* غَيْرُ مُصَدِّقٍ

Incriminate *v. t.* إِسْتَذْنَبَ . إِتَّهَمَ

Incrust *v. t.* لَبَّسَ بِقِشْرَةٍ

Incubation *n.* حضَانة . رَخْمٌ

Incubus *a.* كَابُوسٌ ج كَوَابِيس

Inculcate *v. t.* اوصى . أَلَحَّ . عَلَّمَ
Incumbent *a.* or *n.* وَاجِبٌ عَلَى . مُتَوَظِّفٌ
Incumbrance *n.* عَائِقٌ . ثِقْلٌ
Incur *v.t.* تَعَرَّضَ لَهُ . جَلَبَ عَلَى نَفْسِهِ
Incurable *a.* عَدِيمُ ٱلشِّفَاءِ
Incursion *n.* غَزْوَةٌ . غَارَةٌ
Indebted *n.* مَدْيُونٌ
Indecency *n.* رَذِيلَةٌ . قَبَاحَةٌ
Indecent *a.* رَذِيلٌ . قَبِيحٌ
Indecipherable *a.* مَا لَا يُقْرَأُ أَوْ يُحَلُّ
Indecision *n.* تَرَدُّدٌ . عَدَمُ ثَبَاتٍ
Indecisive *a.* غَيْرُ جَازِمٍ
Indeclinable *a.* غَيْرُ مُتَصَرِّفٍ . مَبْنِيٌّ
Indecorous *a.* مُخَالِفُ ٱلْأَدَبِ
Indecorum *n.* مُخَالَفَةُ ٱلْأَدَبِ
Indeed *ad.* حَقًّا . صَحِيحٌ
Indefatigable *a.* جَادٌّ لَا يَكِلُّ
Indefensible *a.* مَا لَا يُحَامَى عَنْهُ
Indefinite *a.* غَيْرُ مَحْدُودٍ . مُبْهَمٌ
Indefiniteness *n.* عَدَمُ تَحْدِيدٍ
Indelible *a.* ثَابِتٌ لَا يُمْحَى
Indelicacy *n.* قِلَّةُ ٱلْأَدَبِ
Indelicate *a.* قَلِيلُ ٱلْأَدَبِ
Indemnification / **Indemnity** } *n.* تَعْوِيضٌ غَرَامَةٌ
Indemnify *v. t.* عَوَّضَ عَنْ
Indent *v. t.* فَرَضَ — . قَيَّدَ لِخِدْمَةٍ
Indentation *n.* فَرْضٌ . أَثَرٌ
Independence / **Independency** } *n.* اسْتِقْلَالٌ
Independent *a.* مُسْتَقِلٌّ
Indescribable *a.* مَا لَا يُوصَفُ
Indestructible *a.* مَا لَا يَفْنَى
Indeterminable *a.* مَا لَا يُحَدَّدُ
Indeterminate *a.* غَيْرُ مُحَدَّدٍ
Index *n.* دَلِيلٌ . فِهْرِسٌ . سَبَّابَةٌ
Indian *n.* هِنْدِيٌّ
Indiaman *n.* سَفِينَةٌ تُسَافِرُ إِلَى ٱلْهِنْدِ

India-rubber n. (مُغَّيطٌ) . (لَسْتِك)

Indicate v. t. اشَارَ إِلَى . دَلَّ

Indication n. إِشَارَةٌ . دَلاَلَةٌ

Indicative a. } Indicator n. } مُشِيرٌ . دَالٌّ

Indict v. t. أَقَامَ دَعْوَى عَلَيْهِ

Indictment n. إِقَامَةُ ٱلدَّعْوَى

Indifference n. عَدَمُ ٱكْتِرَاثٍ

Indifferent a. غَيْرُ مُكْتَرِثٍ . سَوَاءٌ

Indigence n. فَقْرٌ . فَاقَةٌ

Indigenous a. وَطَنِيٌّ . بَلَدِيٌّ

Indigent a. فَقِيرٌ . مُعْوِزٌ

Indigestible a. مَالاَ يُهْضَمُ

Indigestion n. تُخْمَةٌ . سُوءُ هَضْمٍ

Indignant a. مُغْتَاظٌ

Indignation n. غَيْظٌ . غَضَبٌ .

Indignity n. إِهَانَةٌ . إِحْتِقَارٌ

Indigo n. نِيلٌ (الصباغ المعروف)

Indirect a. غَيْرُ مُسْتَقِيمٍ . مُنْحَرِفٌ

Indirectness n. إِنْحِرَافٌ

Indiscernible a. مَالاَ يُرَى أَوْ يُمَيَّزُ

Indiscoverable a. مَالاَ يُكْشَفُ

Indiscreet a. غَيْرُ حَازِمٍ اوْ بَصِيرٍ

Indiscretion n. حَمَاقَةٌ . رُعُونَةٌ

Indiscriminate a. غَيْرُ مُمَيَّزٍ . بِلاَ فَرْقٍ

Indiscrimination n. عَدَمُ تَمْيِيزٍ

Indispensable a. ضَرُورِيٌّ

Indisposed a. مُنْحَرِفُ ٱلصِّحَّةِ نَافِرٌ مِنْ

Indisposition n. إِنْحِرَافُ ٱلصِّحَّةِ

Indisputable a. مَالاَ يُنْكَرُ . مُسَلَّمٌ

Indissoluble } Indissolvable } a. مَالاَ يَنْحَلُّ

Indistinct n. غَيْرُ وَاضِحٍ . مُبْهَمٌ

Indistinctness n. عدمُ وُضُوحٍ

Indistinguishable a. مَالاَ يُمَيَّزُ

Indite v. t. أَلَّفَ . كَتَبَ . أَملَى ب

Individual n. شَخْصٌ . فَرْدٌ

Individualism } Individuality } n. ذَاتِيَّةٌ . فَرْدِيَّةٌ

Individualize *v. t.* ميز على حدة

Individually *ad.* إفرادًا . شخصيًّا

Indivisible *n.* مالا ينقسم

Indocile *a.* غير طائعٍ . عاص

Indolence *n.* كسل . توانٍ

Indolent *a.* كسلان

Indomitable *a.* مالا يقهر او يذلَّل

Indorse *v. t.* صادق على

Indorsement *n.* مصادقة على

Indubitable *a.* لا ريب فيه

Induce *v. t.* اغرى . امال . رغب

Inducement *n.* داعٍ . موجب

Induction *n.* إدخال . إستدلال

Inductive *a.* إستدلالي

Indue *v. t.* منح — . البس . قلد

Indulge *v. t.* or *i.* ارضى . اولع ب

Indulgence *n.* تلذذ . عفو

Indulgent *a.* مدلِّل . مسامح

Industrial *a.* صناعي

Industrious *a.* جادّ . مثابر

Industry *n.* جد . مثابرة . صناعة

Inebriate *v. t.* or *n.* أسكر . سكير

Inebriation, Inebriety *n.* سكر

Inedited *a.* غير مطبوعٍ

Indeffable *a.* مالا يعبر عنه

Ineffaceable *a.* مالا يمحى

Ineffective, Ineffectual, Inefficacious *a.* غير فعالٍ . عبث

Inefficacy, Inefficiency *n.* عدم فاعلية

Inefficient *a.* غير فعالٍ . عاجز

Inelegant *a.* غير ظريفٍ

Inelegant *a.* لا يجوز إنتخابه

Inequality *n.* عدم مساواةٍ

Inert *a.* غير متحركٍ . بليد

Inestimable *a.* فائق التثمين

Inevitable *a.* مالا مفرّ منه

Inexact *a.* غيرُ مَضبُوطٍ

Inexactness *n.* عدمُ ضَبطٍ . غَلَطٌ

Inexcusable *a.* بِلا عُذْرٍ

Inexhaustible *a.* مَالا يفْرَغ

Inexorable *a.* غيرُ مُتغيّرٍ . ثَابِتُ ٱلْعَزْمِ

Inexpedience / Inexpediency — عدمُ مُنَاسَبَةٍ

Inexpedient *a.* غيرُ مُنَاسِبٍ

Inexpensive *a.* رَخِيصٌ

Inexperience *n.* عَدَمُ ٱلإِختِبَارِ

Inexpiable *a.* مَالَا يُعفَى أَو يُكَفَّرُ عَنهُ

Inexplicable *a.* مَالَا تفْسِيرَ لَهُ

Inexpressible *a.* مَالَا يُعَبَّرُ عَنهُ

Inexpressive *a.* غيرُ مُعبِّرٍ عَن

Inextinguishable *a.* مَالَا يَنْطَفِئُ

Inextricable *a.* مَالَا يُحَلُّ . مُعَقَّدٌ

Infallibility *n.* عِصْمَةٌ

Infallible *a.* مَعْصُومٌ

Infamous *n.* كَرِيهُ ٱلصّيتِ

Infamy *n.* فَضِيحَةٌ . عَارٌ . قَبِيحَةٌ

Infancy *n.* طُفُولِيَّةٌ

Infant *n.* طِفلٌ . رَضِيعٌ

Infanticide *n.* قَتْلُ ٱلأَطْفَالِ

Infantile / Infantine — *a.* طِفْليٌّ

Infantry *n.* جُنُودٌ مُشَاةٌ

Infatuate *v. t.* فَتَنَ بِـ . شَغَفَ حُبًّا

Infatuation *n.* إِفْتِتَانٌ . كَلَفٌ . وُلُوعٌ

Infect *v. t.* اعدى . افْسَدَ

Infection *n.* عَدْوَى . إِفْسَادٌ

Infectious *a.* مُعْدٍ . مُفْسِدٌ

Infelicitous *a.* نَحْسٌ . فِي غَيْرِ مَحَلِّهِ

Infelicity *n.* نَحْسٌ . بَلِيَّةٌ

Infer *v. t.* إِستَنْتَجَ . إِستَدَلَّ

Inferable / Inferential — *a.* نَاتِجٌ عَنْ . مُسْتَدَلٌّ

Inference *n.* نَتِيجة . إِستِدْلَالٌ

Inferior *a.* دَنِيٌّ . دُونٌ

Inferiority *n.* دُونِيَّةٌ . اسفَلِيَّةٌ

Infernal *a.* جهنّميّ. جحيميّ

Infertility *n.* عدمُ خِصْب

Infest *v. t.* كدّر. أكثر في

Infidel *n.* كافرٌ ج كفّارٌ وكفرة

Infidelity *n.* كُفْرٌ. خيانة

Infinite *a.* غيرُ محدودٍ

Infinitely *ad.* بلا نهايةٍ. جدًّا

Infiniteness / Infinity } *n.* عدمُ حدٍّ أو نهايةٍ

Infinitesimal *a.* دقيقٌ جدًّا

Infinitive *a.* صيغة المصدر

Infirm *a.* عاجزٌ. ضعيفٌ

Infirmary *n.* مُستشفى

Infirmity *n.* ضعفٌ. عجز

Inflame *v. t.* اضرمَ. هيّج

Inflammable *a.* قابلُ الالتهابِ

Inflammation *n.* إلتهابٌ

Inflammatory *a.* ملهبٌ. مهيّج

Inflate *v. t.* نفخ —. ملأ هواءً

Inflect *v. t.* حنى —. صرّف

Inflection / Inflexion } *n.* حِنايةٌ. تصريفٌ

Inflexibility *n.* صلابةٌ. إصرارٌ

Inflexible *a.* لا يُحنى. مُصرٌّ

Inflict *v. t.* أبلى بهِ. حمّل بهِ

Infliction *n.* بليّةٌ. عقابٌ

Influence *n.* تأثيرٌ. نفوذٌ. قوّةٌ

Influence *v. t.* أثّر في. أمالَ

Influential *a.* ذو سطوةٍ او نفوذٍ

Influenza *n.* زكامٌ وافدي

Influx *n.* ورودٌ بوفرةٍ

Infold *v. t.* لفّ —. عانقَ

Inform *v. t.* اخبرَ. أعلمَ

Informal *a.* غيرُ رسميٍّ

Informality *n.* مخالفةُ الرسومِ

Information *n.* خبرٌ. إنباءٌ

Infraction / Infringement } *n.* نكثٌ. تعدٍّ

Infrequent *a.* نادرٌ

Infringe *v. t.* خَالَفَ . تَعَدَّى عَلَى

Infuriate *v. t.* أَغَاظَ . هَيَّجَ غَضَباً

Infuse *v. t.* ادْخَلَ . نَقَعَ

Infusion *n.* إِدْخَال . نَقِيعٌ

Ingathering *n.* حصَادٌ . جَمْعٌ

Ingenious *a.* حَاذِقٌ . لَبِيبٌ

Ingenuity *n.* حذَاقَةٌ . مَهارَةٌ

Ingenuous *a.* صَفِيٌّ . مُخْلِصٌ . نَبِيل

Inglorious *a.* عَدِيمُ ٱلْمَجْدِ . مُخْزٍ

Ingot *n.* سَبِيكَةٌ ج سَبَائِك

Ingratiate *v. t.* إِستَعْطَفَ

Ingratitude *n.* كُنُودٌ . عَدَمُ ٱلشُّكْرِ

Ingredient *a.* عُنْصُرُ مَزِيج

Ingress *n.* دُخُول . مَدْخَلٌ

Ingulf *v. t.* إِبْتَلَعَ

Inhabit *v. t.* or *i.* سَكَنَ ـُ . قَطَنَ ـُ

Inhabitable *a.* قَابِلُ ٱلسَّكَن

Inhabitant *n.* سَاكِن . قَاطِنٌ

Inhale *v. t.* إِستَنْشَقَ

Inhere *v. i.* إِخْتَصَّ بِهِ . طُبِعَ عَلَيْهِ

Inherent *a.* مُلَازِمٌ . حَالٌ فِي

Inherit *v. t.* وَارِثَ ـُ

Inheritance *n.* مِيرَاثٌ ج مَوَارِيث

Inheritor *n.* وَارِثٌ ج وَرَثَةٌ

Inhibit *v. t.* نَهَى ـَ . مَنَعَ ـَ عَارَضَ

Inhospitable *a.* غَيْرُ مِضْيَافٍ

Inhospitality *n.* عَدَمُ إِكْرَامِ ٱلضَّيفِ

Inhuman *a.* عَدِيمُ ٱلإِنْسَانِيَّةِ

Inhumanity *n.* عَدَمُ ٱلإِنْسَانِيَّةِ

Inimical *a.* عُدْوَانِيٌّ . مُقَاوِمٌ

Inimitable *a.* لَا يُحَاكَى . لَا مَثِيلَ لَهُ

Iniquitous *a.* اثِيمٌ . شِرِّيرٌ جِدًّا

Iniquity *n.* إِثْمٌ . شَرٌّ

Initial *a.* or *n.* إِبْتِدَائِيٌّ . اوَّلُ ٱسْمٍ

Initiate *v. t.* أَدخَلَ فِي . بَدَّأَ . عَلَّمَ

Initiative / Initiatory } *a.* إِبْتِدَائِي . إِنْشَائِيٌّ

Inject *v. t.* حَقَنَ ـُ . أَدخَلَ فِي

Injection *n.* حُقْنَة

Injudicious *a.* غيرُ مُوَافِقٍ او بَصِير

Injunction *n.* أَمْرٌ . حُكْمٌ

Injure *v. t.* أَضَرَّ . آذَى

Injurious *a.* مُضِرٌّ . مُؤْذٍ

Injury *n.* ضَرَرٌ . أَذِيَّةٌ

Injustice *n.* ظُلْمٌ . جَوْرٌ . بَغْيٌ

Ink *n.* حِبْرٌ . مِدَاد

Inkhorn / **Inkstand** *n.* دَوَاةٌ . مِحْبَرَةٌ

Inkling *n.* تَلْمِيحٌ . إِشَارَةٌ

Inland *n.* دَاخِلَ ٱلْبَرِّ

Inlay *v. t.* (*pp.* inlaid) رَصَّعَ

Inlet *n.* مَدْخَلٌ . خَلِيجٌ . جُونٌ

Inmate *n.* سَاكِنٌ مَعَ غَيْرِهِ

Inmost / **Innermost** *a.* الاكثرُ دَاخِلِيَّةً

Inn *n.* فُنْدُقٌ . خَانٌ

Innate *a.* غَرِيزِيٌّ . بَدِيهِيٌّ

Inner *a.* دَاخِلِيٌّ

Inkeeper *n.* صَاحِبُ ٱلْفُنْدُقِ . خَانَاتِيٌّ

Innocence *n.* بَرَاءَة . طَهَارَةٌ

Innocent *a.* بَرِيءٌ . سَلِيمُ ٱلْقَلْبِ

Innocuous *a.* غيرُ مُضِرٍّ . سَلِيمٌ

Innovation *n.* بِدْعَةٌ . إِحْدَاثٌ

Innovator *n.* مُبْدِعٌ . مُحْدِثٌ

Innoxious *a.* غيرُ مُضِرٍّ . سَلِيمٌ

Innuendo *n.* تَلْمِيحٌ خَفِيٌّ . دَسِيسَةٌ

Innumerable *a.* فَائِقُ ٱلإِحْصَاءِ

Innutricious / **Innutritive** *a.* غيرُ مُغَذٍّ

Inoculate *v. t.* طَعَّمَ . لَقَّحَ

Inoculation *n.* تَطْعِيمٌ . تَلْقِيح

Inodorous *a.* عَدِيمُ ٱلرَّائِحَةِ

Inoffensive *a.* غيرُ مُسِيءٍ . بَسِيط

Inoperative *a.* غيرُ عَامِلٍ

Inopportune *a.* فِي غَيْرِ أَوَانِهِ

Inordinate *a.* مُفْرِطٌ . زَائِدٌ
Inorganic *a.* غَيْرُ آلِيّ . غَيْرُ عُضْوِيٍّ
Inquest *n.* فَحْصٌ . تَفْتِيشٌ
Inquire *v. t.* إِسْتَخْبَرَ . سَأَلَ
Inquirer *n.* مُسْتَخْبِرٌ . طَالِبٌ
Inquiry *n.* سُؤَالٌ . فَحْصٌ . بَحْثٌ
Inquisition *n.* تَفْتِيشٌ . دِيوَانُهُ
Inquisitive *a.* كَثِيرُ ٱلسُّؤَالِ
Inquisitor *n.* مُفَتِّشٌ . فَاحِصٌ
Inroad *n.* غَزْوَةٌ . هَجْمَةٌ
Insalubrious *a.* وَخِيمٌ . وَبِيلٌ
Insalubrity *n.* وَبَالٌ . وَخَامَةٌ
Insane *a.* مَجْنُونٌ . مُخْتَلُّ ٱلْعَقْلِ
Insanity *n.* جُنُونٌ . إِخْتِلَالُ ٱلْعَقْلِ
Insatiable, Insatiate *a.* لَا يَشْبَعُ
Inscribe *v. t.* كَتَبَ . حَفَرَ
Inscription *n.* كِتَابَةٌ
Inscrutable *a.* مَا لَا يُكْشَفُ لَا يُفْهَمُ

Insect *n.* دُوَيْبَةٌ . حَشَرَةٌ
Insectivorous *a.* آكِلُ ٱلْحَشَرَاتِ
Insecure *a.* غَيْرُ مُطْمَئِنٍّ . خَطِرٌ
Insecurity *n.* عَدَمُ ٱلْأَمْنِ
Insensate *a.* عَدِيمُ ٱلْحِسِّ . بَلِيدٌ
Insensibility *n.* عَدَمُ ٱلْحِسِّ
Insensible *a.* عَدِيمُ ٱلْحِسِّ
Inseparable *a.* مَا لَا يُفْصَلُ أَوْ يَنْفَكُ
Insert *v. t.* أَدْخَلَ . أَدْرَجَ
Insertion *n.* إِدْخَالٌ . إِدْرَاجٌ
Inside *ad.* or *a.* or *n.* دَاخِلًا . دَاخِلٌ
Insidious *a.* غَدَّار . مُخَاتِلٌ
Insight *n.* بَصِيرَةٌ . فِطْنَةٌ
Insignia *n.* عَلَامَاتٌ
Insignificant *a.* زَهِيدٌ . طَفِيفٌ
Insincere *a.* غَيْرُ مُخْلِصٍ
Insincerity *n.* عَدَمُ إِخْلَاصٍ
Insinuate *v. t.* لَمَّحَ . دَسَّ

Insinuation *n.* تَلْمِيحٌ . دَسِيسَةٌ

Insipid *a.* تَفِهٌ . بَارِدٌ . نَاشِفٌ

Insipidity *n.* تَفَاهَةٌ . بَلَادَةٌ

Insist *v. i.* أَصَرَّ . أَلَحَّ

Insistence *n.* إِصْرَارٌ . إِلْحَاحٌ

Insolence *n.* وَقَاحَةٌ . عُتُوٌّ

Insolent *n.* وَقِحٌ . عَاتٍ

Insolubility *n.* عَدَمُ الذَّوَبَانِ

Insoluble *a.* مَا لَا يَذُوبُ . لَا يُحَلُّ

Insolvable *a.* مَا لَا يُحَلُّ . لَا يُفَسَّرُ

Insolvency *n.* إِفْلَاس

Insolvent *a.* مُفْلِسٌ

Insomuch *ad.* حَتَّى أَنْ

Inspect *v. t.* فَحَصَ ـ . فَتَّشَ

Inspection *n.* فَحْصٌ . تَفْتِيشٌ

Inspector *n.* نَاظِرٌ . مُفَتِّشٌ

Inspiration *n.* شَهِيقٌ . وَحْيٌ

Inspire *v. t.* شَهَقَ ـ أَلْهَمَ

Inspiring *a.* مُشَجِّعٌ . مُفَرِّحٌ . مُنَشِّطٌ

Instability *n.* عَدَمُ ثَبَاتٍ . تَقَلُّبٌ

Instable *a.* غَيْرُ ثَابِتٍ . مُتَغَيِّرٌ

Install *v. t.* قَلَّدَ مَنْصِبًا . أَقَامَ

Installment *n.* قِسْطٌ . تَقْلِيدٌ

Instance *n.* مِثَالٌ . حَادِثَةٌ

Instant *a.* or *n.* حَالِي . مُهِمٌّ . لَحْظَةٌ

Instantaneous *a.* حَالِي . فُجَائِي

Instantly *ad.* حَالًا عَلَى ٱلْفَوْرِ

Instead *ad.* عِوَضًا عَنْ

Instep *n.* ظَهْرُ ٱلْقَدَمِ

Instigate *v. t.* حَمَلَ عَلَى . أَغْرَى

Instigation *n.* إِغْرَاءٌ . تَهْيِيجٌ

Instigator *n.* مُغْرٍ . مُهَيِّجٌ

Instill *v. t.* أَدْخَلَ . تَدْرِيجًا . لَقَّنَ

Instinct *n.* سَلِيقَةٌ . فِطْرَةٌ . غَرِيزَةٌ

Instinctive *a.* غَرِيزِيٌّ

Institute *v. t.* أَقَامَ . أَنْشَأَ

Institution *n.* إقامة. منصب. دارٌ للتعليم وما أشبه
Instruct *v. t.* علّم. أوصى
Instruction *n.* تعليم. أمر
Instructive *a.* مفيدٌ. مثقّف
Instructor *n.* معلّم. مدرّس
Instrument *n.* آلة. واسطة
Instrumental *a.* آليّ. مفضٍ إلى
Instrumentality *n.* واسطة
Insubordination *n.* عصيان
Insufferable *a.* مالا يطاق
Insufficiency *n.* نقص
Insufficient *a.* غير كاف. ناقص
Insular *a.* مختصّ بجزيرة. محاطٌ بماء
Insulate *v. t.* أفرد. قطع عن
Insulator *n.* قاطع مجرى الكهربائيّة
Insult *n.* or *v. t.* إهانة. أهان
Insulting *a.* مهين. شاتم
Insuperable *a.* مالا يغلب
Insupportable *a.* مالا يحتمل
Insurance *n.* تأمين. ضمان
Insure *v. t.* أمّن. ضمن
Insurgent *a.* ثائرٌ. ماردٌ. عاصٍ
Insurmountable *a.* مالا يقوى عليه
Insurrection *n.* ثورة. فتنة
Insusceptible *a.* غير متأثر
Intangible *a.* مالا يحسّ به
Intact *a.* كاملٌ. سالمٌ. غير ممسوس
Integer *n.* عددٌ صحيحٌ او تامٌّ
Integral *n.* or *a.* صحيح. كامل
Integrate *v. t.* تمّم. شمل. جدّد
Integrity *n.* إستقامة. كمال
Intellect *n.* عقل. ذهن
Intellectual *a.* عقليّ. ذكيّ
Intelligence *n.* فهم. ذكاء
Intelligent *a.* ذكيّ. عاقل

Intelligible *a.*	مَفْهُومٌ . معقول
Intemperance *n.*	افْرَاطٌ . سُكر
Intemperate *a.*	مُفْرِط . سِكّيرٌ
Intend *v. t.* or *i.*	قَصَدَ ـِ . نَوَى ـ
Intense *a.*	شَدِيدٌ جدًّا
Intensely *ad.*	جدًّا . بِشِدةٍ
Intensify *v. t.*	شَدَّدَ . قَوَّى
Intensive *a.*	مشَدِّدٌ . مقوّ
Intent *n.* or *a.*	قَصْدٌ . مُنْصَبٌّ على
Intention *n.*	قَصْدٌ . نِيَّةٌ
Intentional *a.*	مَقْصود . عَمْدِيٌّ
Intentionally *ad.*	عمْدًا
Inter *v. t.*	دَفَنَ ـ . قَبَرَ ـُ
Intercede *v. i.*	شَفَعَ . تَوَسَّطَ
Intercept *v. t.*	عَارَضَ . وَقَّفَ
Interception *n.*	مُعَارَضَةٌ . تَوْقِيفٌ
Intercession *n.*	شفَاعَةٌ
Intercessor *n.*	شَفِيعٌ . وَسِيطٌ
Interchange *v.t.* or *n.*	بادَلَ . تبَادُلٌ
Intercourse *n.*	مُبَاشرَةٌ . مُخَالَطَةٌ
Interdict *v.t.* or *n.*	مَنَعَ . نَهْيٌ
Interest *n.*	فَائدَةٌ . رَغبَةٌ . نَفْعٌ
Interest *v. t.*	إِسْتَعْمَالَ . رَغبَ
Interested *a.*	مَائِل . مُهْتَمٌّ
Interesting *a.*	مُلِذٌّ . مُفِيدٌ
Interfere *v. i.*	تَدَاخَلَ فِي . عَارَضَ
Interference *n.*	مُدَاخَلَةٌ . مُعَارَضَةٌ
Interim *n.*	اثْنَاء . خِلاَلَ
Interior *a.* or *n.*	دَاخِلِيٌّ . أَلدَّاخِلُ
Interjection *n.*	حَرْفُ نِدَاء
Interlace *v. t.*	شَبَكَ ـِ
Interleave *v. t.*	أَدْخَلَ أَوْراقًا بَيْنَ غَيْرِهَا
Interline *v. t.*	خَطَّ بَيْنَ خُطُوطٍ
Interloper *n.*	فُضُولِيٌّ . طُفَيْلِيٌّ
Intermarriage *n.*	تَزَاوُجٌ
Intermeddle *v. i.*	تَدَاخَلَ

Intermediate *a.* مُتَوَسِّط

Intermediation *n.* وَسَاطَةٌ . تَوَسُّط

Interment *n.* دَفْنٌ . جِنَازَة

Interminable *a.* لَانِهَايَةَ لَهُ

Intermingle *v.t.* or *i.* خَالَطَ . تَخَالَطَ

Intermission *n.* فَتْرَةٌ . تَوَقُّف

Intermit *v. t.* or *i.* وَقَّفَ . تَوَقَّفَ

Intermittent *a.* مُتَقَطِّعٌ . مُتَنَاوِبٌ

Intermix *v. t.* or *i.* مَازَجَ . تَخَالَطَ

Internal *a.* دَاخِلِيٌّ . بَاطِنِيٌّ

International *a.* مُشْتَرِكٌ بَيْنَ الْامَمِ

Internecine *a.* مُتَبَادِلُ الْقَتْلِ . مُهْلِكٌ

Interpalate *v. t.* أَفْسَدَ كِتَابًا اوْ ادْخَلَ فِيهِ

Interpose *v. i.* ادْخَلَ أَوْ دَخَلَ بَيْنَ

Interposition *n.* مُدَاخَلَةٌ · تَوَسُّطٌ

Interpret *v. t.* تَرْجَمَ . فَسَّرَ

Interpretation *n.* تَرْجَمَةٌ . تَفْسِيرٌ

Interpreter *n.* مُتَرْجِمٌ · مُفَسِّرٌ

Interregnum *n.* فَتْرَةٌ فِي السَّلْطَنَةِ

Interrogate *v.t.* سَأَلَ ـَ . (إِسْتَنْطَقَ)

Interrogation *n.* سُؤَالٌ . (إِسْتِنْطَاقٌ)

Interrogative *a.* إِسْتِفْهَامِي

Interrupt *v. t.* قَطَعَ ـَ . تَعَرَّضَ لِ

Interruption *n.* قَطْعٌ . إِنْقِطَاعٌ . مَانِعٌ

Intersect *v. t.* قَاطَعَ . تَقَاطَعَ

Intersection *n.* تَقَاطُعٌ

Intersperse *v. t.* بَذَرَ بَيْنَ

Interstice *n.* فَسْحَةٌ ضَيِّقَةٌ

Intertwine / **Intertwist** *v.t.* شَبَكَ ـِ . حَبَكَ ـُ

Interval *n.* خِلَالُ . فَتْرَةٌ

Intervene *v. i.* تَخَلَّلَ . تَوَسَّطَ

Intervention *n.* مُدَاخَلَةٌ . تَوَسُّطٌ

Interview *n.* مُقَابَلَةٌ . مُحَادَثَةٌ

Interweave *v. t.* حَاكَ . نَسَجَ مَعًا

Intestate *a.* بِدُونِ وَصِيَّةٍ

Intestine *a.* دَاخِلِي . وَطَنِيٌّ

Intestines *n. pl.* أَمْعَاء

Inthrall *v. t.* إِستَعْبَدَ

Intimacy *n.* مَوَدَّة . خَاصة

Intimate *v. t.* اشَارَ . لَمَّحَ

Intimate *a.* or *n.* خَاصٌّ . خَلِيلٌ

Intimation *n.* تَلْمِيحٌ . إِعْلَانٌ

Intimidate *v. t.* أَخَافَ . هَدَّدَ

Intimidation *n.* تَهْدِيدٌ

Into *prep.* فِي . إِلَى دَاخِلِ

Intolerable *a.* مَالَا يُطَاقُ

Intolerance *n.* تَعَصُّبٌ

Intolerant *a.* مُتَعَصِّبٌ

Intone *v. t.* نَغَّمَ . لَحَّنَ فِي ٱلْقِرَاءَةِ

Intoxicate *v. t.* أَسْكَرَ

Intoxication *n.* سُكْرٌ

Intractable *a.* مَالَا يُذَلَّلُ . عَنِيدٌ

Intransitive *a.* لَازِمٌ (فِعْلٌ)

Intrench *v. t.* خَنْدَقَ . حَصَّنَ

Intrenchment *n.* تَحْصِينٌ . مِتْرَاسٌ

Intrepid *a.* جَسُورٌ . شُجَاعٌ

Intrepidity *n.* جَسَارَة . جَرَاءَةٌ

Intricacy *n.* تَعْقِيدٌ

Intricate *a.* مُعَقَّدٌ . مُشْكِلٌ

Intrigue *n.* or *v. i.* دَسِيسَةٌ . إِحْتَالَ

Intriguer *n.* مُحْتَالٌ . صَاحِبُ دَسَائِسَ

Intrinsic *a.* حَقِيقِيٌّ . جَوْهَرِيٌّ

Introduce *v. t.* دَخَلَ . عَرَّفَ . أَنْشَأَ

Introduction *n.* إِدْخَالٌ مُقَدِّمَةٌ

Introductory *a.* إِفْتِتَاحِي . دِيبَاجِيٌّ

Introspection *n.* نَظَرٌ إِلَى دَاخِلِ

Intrude *v. i.* تَطَفَّلَ . تَعَدَّى

Intrusion *n.* تَطَفُّلٌ

Intrusive *a.* مُتَطَفِّلٌ

Intrust *v. t.* امَّنَ أَوْدَعَ

Intuition *n.* بَدَاهَةٌ . فِطْرَةٌ

Intuitive *a.* بَدِيهِيٌّ

Inundate *v. t.* غَمَرَ ـُ . اغْرَقَ

Inundation *n.* طُفُوحٌ . فَيَضَانٌ

Inure *v. t.* عَوَّدَ

Inutility *n.* عَدَمُ فَائِدَةٍ

Invade *v. t.* هَجَمَ عَلَى . إِفْتَتَحَ

Invader *n.* مُهَاجِمٌ . فَاتِحٌ . غَازٍ

Invalid *a.* or *n.* مَرِيضٌ . بَاطِلٌ

Invalidate *v. t.* أَبْطَلَ . أَوْهَنَ

Invalidity *n.* بُطْلَانٌ . فَسَادٌ

Invaluable *a.* فَائِقُ ٱلثَّمَنِ . سَامٍ

Invariable *a.* غَيْرُ مُتَغَيِّرٍ . ثَابِتٌ

Invasion *n.* مُهَاجَمَةٌ . فُتُوحٌ . غَزْوٌ

Invective *n.* شَتِيمَةٌ . سَبٌّ

Inveigh *v. t.* طَعَنَ ـَ . سَعَى بِهِ

Inveigle *v. t.* اغْوَى . أَضَلَّ . وَرَّطَ

Invent *v. t.* إِخْتَرَعَ . إِخْتَلَقَ

Invention *n.* إِخْتِرَاعٌ . إِخْتِلَاقٌ

Inventive *a.* }
Inventor *n.* } مُخْتَرِعٌ . مُبْدِعٌ

Inventory *n.* قَائِمَةٌ . تَقْيِيدٌ

Inversion *n.* عَكْسٌ . قَلْبٌ

Invert *v. t.* عَكَسَ ـِ . قَلَبَ ـِ

Invertebrate *a.* عَدِيمُ ٱلْفَقَرَاتِ

Inverse *a.* مُنْعَكِسٌ . مَقْلُوبٌ

Inverted *a.* مَقْلُوبٌ . مَعْكُوسٌ

Invest *v. t.* قَلَّدَ . وَقَفَ لِلْفَائِدَةِ

Investigate *v. t.* فَحَصَ . إِسْتَقْصَى

Investigation *n.* فَحْصٌ . إِسْتِقْصَاءٌ

Investiture *n.* تَقْلِيدٌ . إِقَامَةٌ

Investment *n.* إِلْبَاسٌ . وَضْعُ مَالٍ

Inveterate *a.* مُتَأَصِّلٌ . مُتَعَوِّدٌ

Invidious *a.* مُهَيِّجُ ٱلْحَسَدِ أَوِ ٱلْبُغْضِ

Invigorate *v. t.* قَوَّى . شَدَّدَ . نَشَّطَ

Invincible *a.* مَنِيعٌ . لَا يُغْلَبُ

Inviolable *a.* مُحَرَّمٌ . مَا لَا يُنْقَضُ

Inviolate *a.* مَصُونٌ . مَحْفُوظٌ

Invisible *a.* غَيْرُ مَنْظُورٍ

Invitation *n.* دعوة . إستدعاء

Invite *v. t.* دعا . إستدعى

Invocation *n.* دعاء . صلاة

Invoice *n.* قائمة بضائع

Invoke *v. t.* دعا . إستغاث

Involuntary *a.* غير إختياري

Involution *n.* ترقية العدد (في الحساب)

Involve *v. t.* لفّ . تضمّن . عرقل

Invulnerable *a.* مصون . ما لا يجرح

Inward *a.* داخلي . باطني

Inwrought *a.* مرصّع . موشّى

Iodine *n.* يود (دوا)

Irascible *a.* نزق . سريع الغضب

Ire *n.* غضب . غيظ

Iridescent *a.* ملوّن كقوس قزح

Iris *n.* قوس قزح . قزحية العين

Irksome *a.* ممل . مضجر . متعب

Iron *n.* or *a.* حديد . حديدي

Ironical *a.* تهكمي . إستهزائي

Irony *n.* تهكم . إستهزاء

Irradiate *v. t.* أضاء . أشعّ . انار

Irrational *a.* غير معقول

Irreclaimable *a.* ما لا يستردّ

Irreconcilable *a.* ما لا يصالح

Irrecoverable *a.* ما لا يردّ . ما لا يعاد

Irredeemable *a.* ما لا يفدى او يفك

Irrefutable *a.* ما لا يدحض

Irregular *a.* غير قياسي . شاذّ

Irregularity *n.* عدم انتظام . شذوذ

Irrelevant *a.* غير مطابق

Irreligion *n.* كفر . زندقة

Irreligious *a.* قليل الدين

Irremediable *a.* ما لا يشفى او يصلح

Irremovable *a.* ما لا ينقل او ينزع

Irreparable *a.* ما لا يعوّض

Irrepressible *a.* ما لا يردع او يضبط

Irreproachable *a.* مَا لَا يُلَامُ

Irresistible *a.* مَالَا يُقَاوَمُ اوْ يُدْفَعُ

Irresolute *a.* مُتَرَدِّدٌ . مُتَقَلْقِلٌ

Irresoluteness / Irresolution } *n.* تَرَدُّدٌ . تَقَلُّبٌ

Irrespective *a.* بِلَا ٱلْتِفَاتٍ إِلَى

Irresponsible *a.* غَيْرُ مَسْؤُولٍ

Irretrievable *a.* مَالَا يُعَوَّضُ

Irreverence *n.* عَدَمُ ٱحْتِرَامٍ

Irrevocable *a.* مَا لَا يُلْغَى اوْ يُرَدُّ

Irrigate *v. t.* سَقَى ـِ أَرْوَى

Irrigation *n.* سَقْيٌ . رَيٌّ

Irritabiliy *n.* سُرْعَةُ ٱلتَّهَيُّجِ

Irritable *a.* نَكِدٌ . نَزِقٌ

Irritant *a.* or *n.* مُهَيِّجٌ

Irritate *v. t.* هَيَّجَ . أَثَارَ . أَغَاظَ

Irritation *n.* تَهْيِيجٌ . إِلْتِهَابٌ

Irruption *n.* هُجُومٌ . غَارَةٌ . إِنْفِجَارٌ

Is (see *to be*) كَائِنٌ . يَكُونُ

Islam / Islamism } *n.* اَلْإِسْلَامُ

Island / Isle } *n.* جَزِيرَةٌ ج جَزَائِر

Islet *n.* جَزِيرَةٌ صَغِيرَةٌ

Isolate *v. t.* افْرَدَ

Isosceles *n.* مُتَسَاوِي ٱلضِّلْعَيْنِ

Israelite *n.* إِسْرَائِيلِيٌّ

Issue *v. t.* or *i.* أَصْدَرَ . صَدَرَ ـُ

Issue *n.* نَتِيجَةٌ . نَسْلٌ . صُدُورٌ

Isthmus *n.* بَرْزَخٌ

It *pro.* هُوَ . هِيَ

Italian *n.* or *a.* إِيطَالِيٌّ

Italics *n. pl.* حُرُوفُ ٱلطَّبْعِ ٱلْمَائِلَةُ

Itch *n.* or *v. t.* جَرَبٌ . حِكَّةٌ . حَكَّ

Item *n.* أَيْضًا . نُفْذَةٌ

Iterate *v. t.* كَرَّرَ

Itinerant *a.* دَائِرٌ . جَائِلٌ

Itinerate *v. i.* دَارَ . جَالَ ـُ

Itinerary *n.*	سِيَاحَةٌ أَوْ كِتَابُهَا
Itself *pro.*	ذَاتُه . نَفْسُه
Ivory *n.* or *a.*	عَاجٌ . عَاجِيٌّ
Ivy *n.*	لَبْلَابٌ أَوْ عَاشِقُ ٱلشَّجَرِ (نَبَاتٌ)

J

Jabber *v. i.*	بَقَّ ـُ . تَمْتَمَ
Jack *n.*	آلَةٌ لِقَلْعِ ٱلْأَحْذِيَةِ اوْ لِرَفْعِ ٱلْأَثْقَالِ
Jackal *n.*	إِبْنُ آوَى ج بَنَاتُ آوَى
Jackass *n.*	حِمَارٌ ج حَمِيرٌ
Jackdaw *n.*	نَوْعٌ مِنَ ٱلزَّاغِ
Jacket *n.*	جُبَّةٌ قَصِيرَةٌ
Jack-knife *n.*	سِكِّينُ ٱلْجَيْبِ
Jade *n.*	كَدِيشٌ . جَارِيَةٌ
Jaded *a.*	مُعْيٍ . تَعِبٌ
Jagged *a.*	مَحْزُوزٌ . مُشَقُوقٌ
Jail *n.*	حَبْسٌ . سِجْنٌ
Jailer *n.*	سَجَّانٌ
Jam *n.* or *v. t.*	مُرَبًّى . زَحْمَةٌ . زَحَمَ ـَ
Janitor *n.*	حَاجِبٌ . بَوَّابٌ
Janizary *n.*	إِنْكِشَارِيٌّ . يَسْقَجِيٌّ
January *n.*	كَانُونُ ٱلثَّانِي . يَنَايِرُ
Jar *v. t.* or *i.*	هَزَّ ـُ . إِهْتَزَّ
Jar *n.*	جَرَّةٌ . حَزَّةٌ . خِصَامٌ
Jargon *n.*	رَطَانَةٌ
Jasmine / Jessamine *n.*	يَاسْمِينٌ . فُلٌّ
Jasper *n.*	يَشْبٌ
Jaundice *n.*	يَرْقَانٌ
Jaunty *n.*	مَرِحٌ . خَفِيفٌ

Javelin *n.*	مِزْرَاقٌ ج مَزَارِيقُ
Jaw *n.*	فَكٌّ ج فُكُوكٌ
Jealous *a.*	غَيُورٌ . مِغْيَارٌ
Jealousy *n.*	غَيْرَةٌ
Jeer *v. i.* or *n.*	هَزَأَ ـَ . هَزْءٌ
Jelly *n.*	هُلَامٌ
Jeopard / Jeopardize } *v. t.*	أَلْقَى فِي خَطَرٍ
Jeopardy *n.*	خَطَرٌ
Jerboa *n.* (حَيَوَان)	يَرْبُوعٌ ج يَرَابِيعُ
Jerk *v. t.*	رَمَى . شَدَّ بَغْتَةً
Jest *v. i.* or *n.*	مَزَحَ ـَ مَزْحٌ
Jester *n.*	مَازِحٌ . مَاجِنٌ
Jesting *n.*	مَزْحٌ
Jesuit *n.* / Jesuitical *a.* }	يَسُوعِيٌّ
Jesuitism *n.*	مَبَادِئُ يَسُوعِيَّةٌ
Jet *n.*	غَايَةُ ٱلسَّوَادِ . فَوَّارَةٌ
Jetty *n.*	لِسَانٌ صِنَاعِيٌ فِي ٱلْبَحْرِ
Jew *n.* / Jewish *a.* }	يَهُودِيٌّ
Jewel *n.*	جَوْهَرَةٌ . دُرَّةٌ
Jeweller *n.*	صَائِغٌ . جَوْهَرِي
Jewelry *n.*	مَصَاغٌ . حُلْيٌ
Jib *n.*	شِرَاعُ مُقَدَّمِ ٱلسَّفِينَةِ
Jibe *v. i.* or *n.*	هَزَأَ ـَ . هَزْءٌ
Jilt *v. t.*	رَفَضَتْ عَاشِقَهَا
Jingle *v. t.*	طَنَّ ـِ . رَنَّ ـِ
Job *n.* (أَيُّوبُ ٱلنَّبِيِّ)	شُغْلَةٌ . مُقَاوَلَةٌ .
Jockey *n.*	تَاجِرٌ بِٱلْخَيْلِ . مَكَّارٌ
Jocose / Jocular } *a.*	مَازِحٌ . دَاعِبٌ
Jog / Joggle } *v. t.*	هَزَّ ـِ . وَكَزَ يَكِزُ
Jog on *v. t.* or *i.*	مَشَى عَلَى مَهْلٍ
Join *v. t.* or *i.*	وَصَلَ ـِ . إِتَّصَلَ
Joiner *n.*	نَجَّارٌ
Joint *n.* or *a.*	مَفْصَلٌ . عُقْدَةٌ . مُشْتَرَكٌ
Jointed *a.*	ذُو مَفَاصِلَ اوْ عُقَدٍ
Jointly *ad.*	مَعاً . بِٱشْتِرَاكٍ
Joist *n.*	جِسْرٌ . خَشَبَةٌ مُعْتَرِضَةٌ

Joke *n.* or *v. t.* مَزْحٌ. هَزَلَ ـِ
Jolly *a.* مَرِحٌ . فَرِحٌ . بَهِيجٌ
Jolt *v. t.* or *i.* رَجَّ ـُ . (خَضَّ ـُ) إِرْتَجَّ
Jostle *v. t.* صَدَمَ . رَجَّ ـُ
Jot *n.* or *v. t.* جزْءٌ دَقِيقٌ . دَوَّنَ
Journal *n.* (يَوْمِيَّةٌ . جَرِيدَةٌ)
Journalism *n.* كِتَابَةُ جَرِيدَةٍ . تَحْرِيرٌ
Journalist *n.* كَاتِبُ جَرِيدَةٍ . مُحَرِّرٌ
Journey *n.* or *v. i.* سَفَرٌ . سَافَرَ
Jovial *a.* مَرِحٌ . فَرِحٌ
Jowl *n.* خَدٌّ . فَكٌّ
Joy *n.* فَرَحٌ . سُرُورٌ . بَهْجَةٌ
Joyful, Joyous *a.* فَرِحٌ . مُبْتَهِجٌ مَسْرُورٌ
Joyless *a.* عَدِيمُ ٱلْفَرَحِ . كَئِيبٌ
Jubilant *a.* كَثِيرُ ٱلِٱبْتِهَاجِ . مُتَهَلِّلٌ
Jubilee *n.* يُوبِيلٌ
Judaism *n.* دِيَانَةُ ٱلْيَهُودِ
Judge *n.* قَاضٍ . دَيَّانٌ
Judge *v. t.* قَضَى ـِ . حَكَمَ ـُ
Judgment *n.* قَضَاءٌ . حُكْمٌ . تَمْيِيزٌ
Judicatory *a.* مُخْتَصٌّ بِمَحْكَمَةٍ . حُكْمِيٌّ
Judicial *a.* قَضَائِيٌّ . قِصَاصِيٌّ
Judiciary *a.* or *n.* قَضَائِيٌّ . دَائِرَةُ ٱلْقُضَاةِ
Judicious *a.* حَكِيمٌ . حَازِمٌ
Jug *n.* إِبْرِيقٌ . كُوزٌ
Juggle *v. i.* شَعْوَذَ . غَبَنَ ـِ
Juggler *n.* مُشَعْوِذٌ . مَكَّارٌ
Jugglery, Juggling *n.* شَعْوَذَةٌ
Jugular *a.* or *n.* عُنُقِيٌّ . حَبْلُ ٱلْوَرِيدِ
Juice *n.* عَصِيرٌ . عُصَارَةٌ
Juicy *n.* غَضٌّ . ذُو عُصَارَةٍ
July *n.* تَمُّوزُ . يُولْيُو
Jumble *v. t.* or *n.* خَلَطَ . خِلْطٌ
Jump *v. i.* or *n.* قَفَزَ . قَفْزَةٌ
Junction *n.* وَصْلٌ . مُلْتَقًى

Juncture *n.* آن . وَقْتٌ مُهِمٌّ
June *n.* حَزِيرَان . يُونيُو
Jungle *n.* غَابَةٌ . اجَمٌ
Junior *n.* اصغَرُ عُمْراً
Juniper *n.* عَرْعَرٌ (نَبَاتٌ)
Junk *n.* سَفِينَةٌ صِينِيَّةٌ . مَوَاد عتِيقَة
Juno *n.* الإِلَاهَةُ رُومَانِيَّةٌ . إِحدَى ٱلسَّيَّارَاتِ ٱلصغِيرَةِ
Jupiter *n.* الْمُشْتَرِي (سَيَّارٌ)
Jurisdiction *n.* حُكْمٌ أَوْ دَائِرَتُه
Jurisprudence *n.* علمُ ٱلْفِقْهِ
Juror / **Juryman** *n.* عضوُ مَحْكَمَةِ ٱلتَّحقِيقِ
Jury *n.* مَحْكَمَةٌ تَحْقِيقِيَّةٌ
Just *a.* or *ad.* عَادِلٌ . بَارٌّ . تَمَاماً
Justice *n.* عَدْلٌ . إِستِقَامَةٌ . قَاضٍ
Justifiable *a.* يَتَبَرَّرُ . جَائِزٌ
Justification *n.* تَبْرِيرٌ . تَبْرِئَةٌ
Justify *v. t.* بَرَّرَ . بَرَّأَ
Justly *ad.* بِعَدْل . بِٱستِحْقَاقٍ
Jut *v. i.* بَرَزَ ـُ . نَتَأَ ـَ
Juvenile *a.* or *n.* وَلَدِيٌّ . وَلَدٌ
Juxtaposition *n.* مُقَارَبَةٌ

K

Keel *n.* قاعِدَةُ ٱلسفِينَةِ
Keen *a.* حَادٌّ . ذَكِيٌّ
Keep *v. t.* حفظَ ـَ . ضَبطَ ـُ
Keeper *n.* حَافِظٌ . حَارِسٌ

Keepsake *n.* شَيْءٌ لِلتَّذْكَارِ

Keg *n.* بَرْمِيلٌ صَغِيرٌ

Ken *v. t.* or *n.* عَلِمَ ـَ . عِلْمٌ

Kennel *n.* زَرِيبَةُ ٱلْكِلَابِ

Kerchief *n.* مِنْدِيلٌ

Kernel *n.* حَبَّةٌ . نَوَاةٌ . لُبٌّ

Kerosene *n.* زَيْتٌ مَعْدَنِيٌّ

Kettle *n.* قِدْرٌ . غَلَّايَةٌ

Key *n.* مُفْتَاحٌ . تَفْسِيرٌ

Key-stone *n.* أَعْلَى حَجَرِ ٱلْقَنْطَرَةِ

Kick *v. t.* or *i.* or *n.* لَبَطَ ـُ . رَفَسَ ـِ

Kid *n.* جَدْيٌ ج جِدَاءٌ

Kidnap *v. t.* إِخْتَلَسَ بَشَرًا

Kidney *n.* كُلْيَةٌ ج كُلًى

Kill *v. t.* قَتَلَ ـُ . اخْمَدَ

Kiln *n.* أَتُّونٌ

Kilo / Kilogramme } *n.* أَلْفُ جِرَامٍ

Kilometre *n.* أَلْفُ مِتْرٍ

Kin *n.* اقَارِبُ . أَنْسِبَاءُ

Kind *a.* or *n.* لُطِيفٌ . مُحْسِنٌ . نَوْعٌ

Kindle *v. t.* اضْرَمَ . اشْعَلَ

Kindliness *n.* لُطْفٌ . مَعْرُوفٌ

Kindly *ad.* or *a.* بِلُطْفٍ . لَطِيفٌ

Kindness *n.* لُطْفٌ . مَعْرُوفٌ

Kindred *n.* اقَارِبُ . أَنْسِبَاءُ

Kine *n. pl.* بَقَرٌ

King *n.* مَلِكٌ ج مُلُوكٌ

Kingdom *n.* مَمْلَكَةٌ

Kink *v. i.* or *n.* إِلْتَوَى . لَيَّةٌ

Kinsman *n.* نَسِيبٌ . قَرِيبٌ

Kiss *n.* or *v. t.* قُبْلَةٌ . قَبَّلَ

Kitchen *n.* مَطْبَخٌ

Kite *n.* حِدَأَةٌ . طَيَّارَةٌ

Kitten *n.* جَرْوُ ٱلْقِطِّ . قُطَيْطَةٌ

Knack *n.* خِفَّةٌ . بَرَاعَةٌ . مَلَكَةٌ

Knapsack *n.* مِزْوَدُ ٱلْجُنْدِيِّ

Knarled *a.* مُعَقَّدٌ

Knave *n.*
Knavish *a.* } خَبِيثٌ . مَكَّارٌ

Knavery
Knavishness } *n.* خَبَاثَةٌ . مَكْرٌ

Knead *v. t.* عَجَنَ ـِ

Knee *n.* رُكْبَةٌ ج رُكَبٌ

Kneel *v. i.* رَكَعَ ـَ . جَثَا ـُ

Knee-pan *n.* رَضْفَةُ ٱلرُّكْبَةِ

Knell *n.* دَقُّ ٱلْجَرَسِ لِمَيْتٍ

Knife *n.* سِكِّينٌ

Knight *n.* فَارِسٌ . لَقَبُ شَرَفٍ

Knighthood *n.* فُرُوسِيَّةٌ رُتْبَةُ شَرَفٍ

Knit *v. t.* or *i.* حَبَكَ ـُ . إِحْتَبَكَ

Knob *n.* عُجْرَةٌ

Knock *v. t.* or *n.* قَرَعَ ـَ . ضَرْبَةٌ

Knocker *n.* مِقْرَعَةٌ . مِطْرَقَةٌ

Knoll *n.* تَلَّةٌ . رَابِيَةٌ صَغِيرَةٌ

Knot *n.* or *v. t.* عُقْدَةٌ . عَقَّدَ

Knotted
Knotty } *a.* مُعَقَّدٌ . كَثِيرُ ٱلْعُقَدِ

Know *v. t.* عَلِمَ ـَ . عَرَفَ ـِ

Knowable *a.* مَا يُعْلَمُ أَوْ يُعْرَفُ

Knowingly *ad.* عَمْدًا

Knowledge *n.* عِلْمٌ . مَعْرِفَةٌ

Knuckle *n.* مَفْصَلُ ٱلْإِصْبَعِ

Koran *n.* أَلْقُرْآنُ

L

Label *n.* or *v. t.* وُرَيْقَةٌ لِعُنْوَانٍ . عَنْوَنَ

Laboratory *n.* مَعْمَلٌ لِفَنٍّ

Laborious *a.* شَاقٌّ . كَدُودٌ

Labour *n.* or *v. i.* كَدَّ . إِشْتَغَلَ

Labourer *n.* فَاعِلٌ . شَغَّالٌ

Labyrinth *n.* أَمْرٌ مُعَقَّدٌ . أَلْغَازٌ

Lace *n.* or *v. t.* (تَخْرِيمٌ). شَدَّ بِخَيْطٍ

Lacerate *v. t.* شَرَّطَ . مَزَّقَ

Laceration *a.* تَشْرِيطٌ . تَمْزِيقٌ

Lachrymal *a.* دَمْعِيٌّ

Lack *n.* or *v. t.* or *i.* عَوَزٌ . عَازَ . أَعْوَزَ

Laconic / **Laconical** *a.* مَا قَلَّ وَدَلَّ (مِنَ ٱلْكَلَامِ)

Lacteal / **Lactic** *a.* لَبَنِيٌّ

Lad *n.* صَبِيٌّ . وَلَدٌ . فَتًى

Ladder *n.* سُلَّمٌ ج سَلَالِمُ

Lade *v. t.* حَمَلَ . شَحَنَ ـَ

Lading *n.* حَمْلٌ . شَحْنٌ

Ladle *n.* مِغْرَفَةٌ

Lady *n.* سَيِّدَةٌ . خَاتُونٌ

Ladyship *n.* مَقَامُ ٱلسَّيِّدَةِ

Lag *v. i.* تَأَخَّرَ . أَبْطَأَ

Laggard *n.* مُتَأَخِّرٌ . مُتَكَاسِلٌ

Lagoon *n.* بُحَيْرَةٌ قَلِيلَةُ ٱلْمَاءِ

Laid, lain, *see* Lay. مَوْضُوعٌ

Lair *n.* عَرِينٌ . وِجَارٌ ج أَوْجِرَةٌ

Laity *n.* أَلْعَوَامُّ . غَيْرُ ٱلْإِكْلِيرُسِ

Lake *n.* بُحَيْرَةٌ

Lamb *n.* خَرُوفٌ . حَمَلٌ

Lambkin *n.* خَرُوفٌ صَغِيرٌ

Lame *a.* or *v. t.* أَعْرَجُ . عَرَّجَ

Lameness *n.* عَرَجٌ

Lament *n.* or *v. t.* نَاحَ ـُ . رَثَى ـِ

Lamentable *a.* مُحْزِنٌ . مَا يُرْثَى لَهُ

Lamentation *n.* نَوْحٌ . مَرْثَاةٌ

Lamp *n.* مِصْبَاحٌ . سِرَاجٌ . قِنْدِيلٌ

Lampoon *v. t.* or *n.* هَجَا . هَجْوٌ

Lance *n.* or *v. t.* رُمْحٌ . رَمَحَ . طَعَنَ ـُ

Lanceolate *a.* رُمْحِيُّ ٱلشَّكْلِ

Lancet *n.* مِشْرَطٌ . مِبْضَعٌ

Land *n.* ارضٌ . بَرٌّ . بِلَادٌ

Land *v. t.* or *i.* انزَلَ او نزَلَ من سفينة

Landlocked *a.* مُحاط بالبَرّ

Landlord *n.* ربّ ارضٍ او منزلٍ

Landmark *n.* علامة حدّ . تخم

Landscape *n.* منظر من الارضِ

Lane *n.* زقاق . مضيق

Language *n.* لغة . كلام . لسان

Languid *a.* متوانٍ . متراخٍ

Languish *v. i.* خارَ . إنضنى . إرتخى

Languor *n.* رخاوة . ضعف

Lank *a.* رخو . نحيف

Lantern *n.* (فنار . فانوس)

Lap *n.* ذيل . حضن . حجر

Lap *v. t.* or *i.* ولغَ . طوى . إنثنى

Lapse *v. i.* مضى وقته . سقطَ

Larceny *n.* سرقة

Lard *n.* دهن الخنزير

Larder *n.* بيت المؤونة

Large *a.* كبير . فسيح

Largely *ad.* بوفرة . كثيراً

Lark *n.* قبّرة او قنبرة (طائر)

Larynx *n.* حنجرة ج حناجر

Lascivious *a.* شهوانيّ . فاسق

Lash *n.* or *v.t.* سوط . ساطَ . شدّ

Lass *n.* فتاة . صبيّة

Lassitude *n.* إسترخاء . عياء

Last *n.* or *a.* قالب الحذاء . الأخير

Last *v. i.* بقي . دامَ . إستمرّ

Lastly *ad.* أخيراً

Latch *n.* or *v. t.* سقّاطة . اوصد (الباب)

Latchet *n.* شراك . سير

Late *a.* متأخّر

Lately *ad.* حديثاً

Lateness *n.* تأخّر . فوات الوقت

Latent *a.* مستتر . كامن

Lateral *a.* جنبيّ . جانبي

Lather *n.* مَخْرَطَةٌ

Lather *n.* رَغْوَةُ ٱلصابُون

Latin *a.* or *n.* لاتينيٌّ . أَللغةُ ٱللاتينيَّةُ

Latitude *n.* عَرْضٌ

Latter *a.* أَلاخِيرُ . أَلثَّاني

Latterly *ad.* حَدِيثًا

Lattice *n.* شُبَّاكٌ

Laud *v. t.* مَدَحَ ـَ . حَمَدَ ـَ

Laudable *a.* مَمْدُوحٌ . جَدِيرٌ بِالْمَدْحِ

Laudanum *a.* صِبْغَةُ أَفْيُون

Laudatory *a.* مَدْحِيٌّ . مادِحٌ

Laugh *n.* or *v. i.* ضَحْكَةٌ . ضَحِكَ ـَ

Laughable *a.* مُضْحِكٌ

Laughing } Laughter } *n.* ضِحْكٌ

Laughing-stock *n.* اُضْحُوكَةٌ

Launch *v. t.* أَنْزَلَ فِي ٱلْمَاءِ

Laundress *n.* غَسَّالَةٌ

Laundry *n.* مَغْسَلٌ

Laurel *n.* غارٌ (شَجَرٌ)

Lava *n.* مَوَادُّ تَقْذِفُ مِنْ جَبَلِ ٱلنَّار

Lavatory *n.* مِرْحَضَةٌ . مَغْسَلَةٌ . حَمَّامٌ

Lave *v. t.* غَسَلَ ـِ

Laver *n.* مِرْحَضَةٌ . جُرْنٌ لِلْغَسْلِ

Lavish *a.* or *v. t.* مُسْرِفٌ . أَسْرَفَ . بَذَّرَ

Law *n.* شَرِيعَةٌ . نَامُوسٌ . سُنَّةٌ

Lawful *a.* شَرْعِيٌّ . جائِزٌ . مُبَاحٌ

Lawfulness *n.* جَوَازٌ

Lawless *a.* مُخَالِفُ ٱلشَّرِيعَةِ . عَاصٍ

Lawn *n.* سُهْلَةٌ خَضْرَاءُ . (شَاشٌ)

Lawsuit *n.* دَعْوَى ج دَعَاوٍ

Lawyer *n.* فَقِيهٌ . مُحَامٍ (أَفُوكَاتُو)

Lax *a.* مُتَرَاخٍ . مُتَسَاهِلٌ

Laxative *a.* مُسَهِّلٌ

Laxity *n.* تَرَاخٍ . فَسَادٌ

Lay *n.* or *a.* نَشِيدٌ . عَامِّيٌّ

Lay *v. t.* وَضَعَ ـَ . نَظَمَ . بَسَطَ ـُ

Layer *n.* طَبَقَةٌ
Laziness *n.* كَسَل . تَوانٍ
Lazy *a.* كَسْلَانٌ
Lead *n.* رَصَاصٌ
Lead *v. t.* قَادَ ـُ . هدى ـ
Leader *n.* قَائِدٌ . مرْشِدٌ
Leadership *n.* قِيَادَةٌ . رِيَاسَةٌ
Leaf *n.* وَرَقَةٌ . مِصْرَاعٌ
Leaflet *n.* وُرَيقَةٌ
Leafy *a.* مُوْرِقٌ . ذو وَرَق
League *n.* مُحَالَفَةٌ . عصْبَةٌ . فرْسَخٌ
Leak *n.* or *v. i.* فُجْرَة . وَكَفَ ـ
Leakage *n.* وَكْفٌ . تَلَفٌ منه
Leaky *a.* واكفٌ . غيرُ مضبوطٍ
Lean *a.* or *v. i.* نَحِيفٌ . هزيل . مَالَ ـ
Leanness *n.* هزَالٌ . نَحَافَة
Leap *n.* or *v. t.* قَفزَة . قفزَ ـ . وثَبَ
Leap-year *n.* سنة كَبِيسَةٌ

Learn *v. t.* تَعَلَّمَ . عَلِمَ ـَ
Learned *a.* عَالِمٌ . مَاهِرٌ
Learner *n.* مُتَعَلِّمٌ . تلميذ
Learning *n.* عِلْمٌ . معرِفَة
Lease *n.* or *v. t.* إِيجَارٌ . آجر
Least *a.* الأَصْغَرُ . الأَقَلّ . الأدنى
Leather *n.* جِلْدٌ مَدْبُوغ
Leathern / Leathery *a.* مِنْ جِلْدٍ . جِلْدي
Leave *n.* or *v. t.* إِذْنٌ . تَرَكَ ـ
Leaven *n.* or *v. t.* خَمِيرَة . خَمَرَ ـ
Lecture *n.* خِطَابٌ
Lecturer *n.* خَطِيبٌ . مُدَرِّسٌ
Led *pp.* of Lead. مَقُودٌ
Ledge *n.* طَبَقَة . صُخُورٌ بَارِزَة
Ledger *n.* دَفْتَرٌ مُختَصرِ الحِسَابَات
Leech *n.* عَلَقَة
Lee *n.* or *a.* أَلجَانبُ الْمَخفور مِن الرِّيحِ
Leeward *a.* or *ad.* مع الرِّيح

Leeway *n.* حركة جنبية مع الريح

Left *a.* or *n.* يسار . شمال

Left-handed *a.* أعسر

Leg *n.* رجل . ساق . قائمة

Legacy *n.* وصية . وقف

Legal *a.* شرعي . قانوني . جائز

Legality *n.* شرعية . جواز

Legalize *v. t.* جعله شرعيا

Legate *n.* نائب . قاصد

Legatee *n.* الموصى له . وارث

Legation *n.* سفارة

Legend *n.* خرافة . عنوان

Legendary *a.* خرافي

Legerdemain *n.* شعوذة . شعبذة

Legging *n.* جورب للرجل

Legible *a.* ما يقرأ . واضح

Legion *n.* كتيبة . جوق

Legislate *v. i.* سن شرائع

Legislation *n.* سن الشرائع

Legislative *a.* مختص بسن الشرائع

Legislator *n.* مشترع

Legislature *n.* مجلس المشترعين

Legitimacy *n.* شرعية

Legitimate *a.* شرعي . نظامي

Leisure *n.* عطلة . فراغ

Leisurely *ad.* بطيئا . رويدا

Lemon *n.* ليمون

Lemonade *n.* شراب الليمون

Lend *v. t.* أقرض . أعار

Length *n.* طول

Lengthen *v.t.* or *i.* أطال . طال

Lengthwise *ad.* طولا

Lengthy *a.* طويل

Lenient *a.* لطيف . حليم

Lenity *n.* لطف . مساهلة

Lens *n.* بلورة محدبة او مقعرة

Lent *n.* or *pp.* اَلصَّوْمُ اَلْكَبِيرُ . مُقْرَضٌ

Lentil *n.* عَدَسَةٌ

Leopard *n.* نِمْرٌ . نَمِرٌ

Leper *n.* / Leprous *a.* } *a.* مَجْذُومٌ

Leprosy *n.* جُذَامٌ

Less *a.* اقَلُّ

Lesion *n.* أَذِيَّةٌ . ضَرَرٌ . هَتْكٌ

Lessen *v. i.* or *t.* قَلَّ ـِ . نَقَصَ ـُ . قَلَّلَ

Lesson *n.* مَآلَةٌ . تَعْلِيمٌ . عِبْرَةٌ

Lest *conj.* لِئَلاَّ

Let *v. t.* سَمَحَ ـَ . رَخَّصَ . آجر

Lethargy *n.* سُبَاتٌ . تغافُلٌ

Letter *n.* حَرْفٌ . كِتَابٌ . تَحْرِيرٌ

Letters *pl.* آدَابٌ . تَهْذِيبٌ

Lettuce *n.* خَسٌّ

Levant *n.* شَرْقِيُّ بَحْرَ الرُّوم

Level *a.* or *v.t.* مُسْتَوٍ . سَهْلٌ . سوَّى

Level *n.* سَطْحٌ مُسْتَوٍ مِيزَانٌ (مَنْسُوبٌ)

Levelling *n.* تَسْوِيَةٌ . تسطِيحٌ

Lever *n.* مُخْلٌ . عَتَلَة

Levity *n.* خِفَّةٌ . طَيْشٌ

Levy *v. t.* ضَرَبَ عَلَى . جَبَى ـِ

Lewd *a.* شَهْوَانِيٌّ . مُفْسِدٌ . فَاسِقٌ

Lewdness *n.* فِسْقٌ . فُجُورٌ

Lexicographer *n.* مؤَلِّفُ قَامُوسٍ

Lexicon *n.* قَامُوسٌ

Liable *a.* مُعَرَّضٌ لِ . مسؤُولٌ

Liability *n.* تَعَرُّضٌ لِ . مسؤُولِيَةٌ

Liar *n.* كَذَّابٌ

Libel *n.* هَجْرٌ . طَعْنٌ (قَذْفٌ)

Libeler *n.* هَاجٍ . طَعَّانٌ (قَاذِفٌ)

Libelous *a.* هَجَائِيٌ . طَاعِنٌ

Liberal *a.* سَخِيٌّ . كَرِيمٌ

Liberality *n.* سَخَاءٌ . كَرَمٌ

Liberalize *v. t.* حرَّرَ مِنَ اَلتَّعَصُّبِ

Liberate *v. t.* حرَّرَ . اعتَقَ . أَطْلَقَ

Liberation *n.* تَحْرِيرٌ . إِطْلَاقٌ

Liberator *n.* مُحَرِّرٌ . مُعْتِق

Libertine *n.* خَلِيعٌ . فَاسِقٌ . فَاجِرٌ

Liberty *n.* حُرِّيَّة . إِسْتِقْلَال

Librarian *n.* مُدِيرُ مَكْتَبَةٍ

Library *n.* مَكْتَبَةٌ

Lice *n. pl.* قَمْلٌ

License *n.* إِجَازَةٌ . غُلُوٌّ . خَلَاعَةٌ

Licensed *a.* / Licentiate *n.* } ذُو ٱمْتِيَازٍ أَوْ رُخْصَةٍ

Licentious *a.* شَهْوَانِيٌّ . خَلِيعٌ

Licentiousness *n.* خَلَاعَةٌ . دَعَارَةٌ

Lick *v. t.* لَحَسَ ـَ . لَعِقَ ـَ

Licorice / Liquorice } *n.* سُوسٌ (نَبَاتٌ)

Lid *n.* غِطَاءٌ ج اغْطِيَة

Lie *n.* كِذْبٌ

Lie *v. i.* كَذَبَ . إِضْطَجَعَ . إِتَّجَهَ . مَكَثَ

Lieutenant *n.* نَائِبٌ . (مُلَازِمٌ)

Life *n.* حَيَاة . عُمْرٌ . نَشَاطٌ

Life-boat *n.* قَارِبٌ لَا يَغْرَقُ

Lifelike *a.* مِثْلُهُ . طِبْقُ ٱلْاصْلِ

Lifelong *a.* مَا يَدُومُ مَدَى ٱلْحَيَاةِ

Lift *v. t.* or *n.* رَفَعَ ـَ . عَلَّى . رَفْعٌ

Ligament *n.* رُبَاطٌ . عَصَبٌ

Ligature *n.* عِصَابَةٌ

Light *n.* or *a.* نُورٌ . ضَوْءٌ . خَفِيفٌ

Light / Lighten } *v. t.* أَنَارَ . أَضَاءَ

Lighten *v. i.* or *t.* بَرَقَ ـُ خَفَّفَ

Lighter *n.* جَرْمٌ . مَاعُونٌ

Light-headed *a.* طَائِشٌ . فِرْفَارٌ

Light-house *n.* مَنَارَةٌ

Lightly *ad.* بِخِفَّةٍ

Lightness *n.* خِفَّةٌ . فَرْفَرَةٌ

Lightning *n.* بَرْقٌ

Lightsome *a.* نَيِّرٌ . فَرِحٌ . مُفْرِحٌ

Like *ad.* عَلَى مِثَالِ

Like *a.* or *n.* مِثْلٌ . شَبِيه . نَظِيرٌ

Like *v. t.* احَبَّ . إِسْتَحْسَن

Likely *a.* or *ad.* مُحْتَمَلٌ . مُمْكِنٌ

Liken *v. t.* شَبَّهَ . مَثَّل

Likeness *n.* شِبْهٌ . صُورَةٌ

Likewise *ad.* ايْضاً . كَذَلِكَ

Liking *n.* إِسْتِحْسَانٌ . مَيْلٌ إِلَى

Lily *n.* زَنْبَقٌ . سُوسَن

Limb *n.* غُصْنٌ . عُضْوٌ

Line *n.* كِلْسٌ . (جِيرٌ)

Lime-kiln *n.* أَتُّون كِلْسٍ

Lime-stone *n.* حَجَرُ ٱلْكِلْسِ

Limit *n.* or *v. t.* حَدٌّ . تَخْمٌ . حَدَّدَ

Limitable *a.* قَابِلُ ٱلتَحْدِيدِ

Limitation *n.* تَحْدِيدٌ . حَصْرٌ

Limitless *a.* لاَحَدٍّ . غَيْرُ مَحْدُودٍ

Limp *v. i.* or *a.* عَرَجَ . رَخْوٌ

Limpid *a.* صَافٍ . رَائِقٌ

Line *n.* خَطٌّ . سَطْرٌ . صَفٌّ . مَرَس

Line *v. t.* بَطَّنَ . خَطَّطَ . سَطَّر

Lineage *n.* نَسَبٌ . ذُرِّيَّةٌ

Lineal *a.* نَسَبِيٌّ

Lineament *n.* رَسْمٌ . هَيْئَةٌ

Linear *a.* خَطِّي . مُسْتَقِيمٌ

Linen *n.* كَتَّانٌ . ثِيَابٌ مِنْ كَتَّانٍ

Linger *v. i.* ابْطَا . تَرَدَّد

Lingering *a.* إِبْطَاءٌ . تَأَخرٌ

Lingual *a.* لِسَانِيٌّ

Linguist *n.* عَالِمٌ بِاللُّغَاتِ

Linguistic / Linguistical } *a.* مُخْتَصٌّ بِعِلْمِ ٱللُّغَاتِ

Lining *n.* بِطَانَةٌ . تَبْطِينٌ

Liniment *n.* مَرْهَمٌ . دِهْنٌ

Link *n.* or *v. t.* حَلْقَةٌ . زَرَدَةٌ . سَلْسَلَ

Linseed *n.* بِزْرُ كَتَّان

Lint *n.* كَتِيتٌ . مُشَاقَةٌ

Lintel *n.* عَتَبَةٌ ج . عَتَبٌ

Lion *n.* أَسدٌ ج اسُودٌ

Lioness *n.* لَبْوَةٌ

Lip *n.* شِفَةٌ

Liquify *v. t.* ذَوَّبَ . اماعَ

Liquid *n.* مَائِعٌ . سَائِلٌ

Liquidate *v. t.* صَفَّى ٱلحِساب . اوْفَى ـِ

Liquidation *n.* تَصْفِيَةُ ٱلحِسَابِ إِيفَاءٌ

Liquor *n.* سَائِلٌ . شَرابٌ . مُسْكِرٌ

Liquorice *n.* نَبَاتُ ٱلسُّوسِ اوربه

Lisp *v. i.* or *n.* لَثِغَ ـَ . لُثْغَةٌ

List *n.* قَائِمَةٌ . جَدْوَلٌ . مَيْلٌ

Listen *v. i.* اصغَى إِلَى . إِستَمَعَ

Listless *a* غَافِلٌ . غَيرُ مُبَالٍ

Literal *a.* حرْفِيٌّ

Literary *a.* آدَابِيٌّ . عِلْمِيٌّ

Literature *n.* آدَابُ ٱللُّغَةِ . كُتُبٌ

Lithe / Lithesome } *a.* مَرِنٌ . لَيِّنٌ

Lithograph *v. t.* or *n.* طَبَعَ عَلَى حجرٍ

Lithographer *n.* طَابِعٌ عَلَى حجر

Lithography *n.* صِنَاعَةُ ٱلطَّبْعِ ٱلحَجَرِيِّ

Litigant *n.* خَصِيمٌ . مُدَّعٍ

Litigate *v. i.* خَاصَمَ . اقَام دَعْوَى

Litigation *n.* مُخَاصَمَةٌ . إِجْرَاءُ ٱلدَّعَاوِي

Litter *n.* مَحْمَلٌ . نُشَارَةٌ . أَجْرِيَةٌ

Little *a.* or *ad.* صَغِيرٌ . قَلِيلٌ . قَلِيلاً

Liturgy *n.* خِدْمَةُ ٱلْعِبَادَةِ

Live *v. i.* عَاشَ ـِ . أَقَامَ ـِ . تَصَرَّفَ

Live *a.* حَيٌّ . نَشِيطٌ

Livelihood *n.* مَعَاش . مَعِيشَة

Liveliness *n.* خِفَّةٌ . نَشَاط

Lively *a.* خَفِيفٌ . نَشِيط . بَشَّاشٌ

Liver *n.* كَبِدٌ ج اكْبَادٌ

Livery *n.* زِيّ رَسْمِيّ لِلْخَدم

Live-stock *n.* خَيْلٌ . موَاشٍ

Livid *a.* ازْرَق مُسْوَدٌّ

Living *a.* or *n.* حَيٌّ . مَعِيشَةَ

Lizard *n.* حرْذَوْن . ضَب

Lo ! *ex.* هوَ ذَا . إِذَا بِ . هَا

Load *n.* or *v. t.* حِمْلٌ . حَمَّلَ . شَحَنَ ـ

Loadstone *n.* حَجَرٌ مَغْنَطِيس

Loaf *n.* رغيفٌ . قَالِبُ (سُكر)

Loafer *n.* بَطَّال . كَسْلاَن

Loam *n.* تربةٌ مُخصبَة

Loan *v.* or *n.* اقْرَضَ . اعَار . قِرْضٌ

Loath *a.* غيرُ رَاضٍ . نَافِر

Loathe *v. t.* كَرِهَ ـ . سئِم

Loathsome *a.* مَكْرُوهٌ

Loathsomeness *n.* كَرَاهة

Lobe *n.* فَصٌّ ج فُصُوصٌ

Lobster *n.* سرطَانٌ بَحْرِيٌّ

Local *a.* مَحلِّيٌّ

Locality *n.* مَحَلٌّ . موقِعٌ

Locate *v. t.* وضَعَ ـ . انزَلَ

Location *n.* وضعٌ . موضِع

Lock *n.* or *v. t.* قفلٌ . اقفَلَ

Locket *n.* حميلَةٌ

Locksmith *n.* قَفَّالٌ . (قَرَدَحجي)

Locomotion *n.* سيْرٌ . إِنْتِقَالٌ

Locomotive *n.* آلةُ ٱلْبُخَارِ لِلسَّيْرِ

Locust *n.* جَرادةٌ

Lodge *n.* or *v. i.* مَأْوى . آوى . بَاتَ ـ

Lodger *n.* نَزِيلٌ . بَائتٌ

Lodging *n.* مَبيتٌ . منزِلٌ

Loftiness *n.* عُلُو . تَشَامُخٌ

Lofty *a.* عَالٍ . رَفِيعٌ . متَشَامِخٌ

Log *n.* خَشَبَةٌ ضَخْمَة

Logarithms *n. pl.* علمُ ٱلأنسَابِ

Log-book *n.* كِتَابُ سيرِ سفينةٍ

Logic *n.* علمُ ٱلْمَنْطِقِ

Logical *a.* منْطِقِي . قِيَاسيٌّ

Logician *n.* عَالِمٌ بِٱلْمَنْطِقِ

Loin *n.* صُلبٌ ج اصْلاَبٌ

Loiter *v. t.* تاخَّرَ . أبطَأَ

Lone *a.* مُنْفَرِدٌ . مُتَوَحِّدٌ

Loneliness *n.* وَحْدَةٌ

Lonely / **Lonesome** *a.* مُسْتَوْحِشٌ

Long *a.* or *v. i.* طَوِيلٌ . تَاقَ . إِشْتَاقَ

Longevity *n.* طُولُ ٱلعمرِ

Longing *n.* إِشْتِيَاقٌ . شَوْق

Longitude *n.* طُولٌ

Long-suffering *n.* or *a.* طولُ ٱلْأَنَاةِ . طَوِيلُهَا

Look *v. i.* نَظَرَـُ . فَتَشَ . ظَهَرَـ

Looking-glass *n.* مِرْآةٌ

Loom *n.* or *v. i.* نَوْلٌ . ظَهَرَـ

Loop *n.* عُرْوة

Loop-hole *n.* فَرَاغُ ٱلْعُرْوَةِ . مَهْرَب

Loose / **Loosen** *v.t.* حَلَّـُ . فَكَّـُ . أَطْلَقَ

Loose *n.* مَحْلُول . رَخْو . مُسْتَرْسِلٌ

Looseness *n.* رَخَاوَةٌ . إِنْحِلَالٌ

Lop *v. t.* قَضَبَـ . إِسْتَمَالَ

Loquacious *a.* كَثِيرُ ٱلْكَلَامِ

Lord *n.* رَبٌّ . سَيِّدٌ . شَرِيفٌ

Lordly *a.* شَرِيفٌ . مُتَعَظِّمٌ . سَامٍ

Lordship *n.* رَبُوبِيَّةٌ . سِيَادَةٌ

Lose *v. t.* ضَيعَ . خَسِرَـ . فَقَدَـ

Loss *n.* خِسَارَةٌ . فَقْدٌ . تَلَفٌ

Lot *n.* نَصِيبٌ . حِصَّةٌ . قُرْعَة

Lotion *n.* غَسُلٌ . غَسْلَةٌ

Lottery *n.* قُرْعَةٌ . قِمَارٌ

Lotus *n.* جَنْدَقُوقٌ

Loud *a.* عَالٍ . مُجْهِرٌ . جَهُورٌ

Loudness *n.* عُلُوٌّ (ٱلصَّوْتِ) . جَهَارَةٌ

Lounge *v. i.* تَقَاعَدَ . تَكَاسَلَ

Louse *n.* (*pl.* **Lice**). قَمْلَةٌ ج قَمْلٌ

Lovable / **Lovely** *a.* مَحْبُوبٌ . جَدِيرٌ بِالْمَحَبَّةِ

Love *n.* or *v. t.* مَحَبَّةٌ . أَحَبَّ

Loveliness *n.* حُسْنٌ . جَمَالٌ

Lover *n.* / **Loving** *a.* مُحِبٌّ . عَاشِقٌ

Low *a.* مُنْخَفِضٌ . دَنِيٌّ . رَخِيصٌ

Lower *v. t.* خَفَّضَ . أَنْزَلَ

Lowering *a.* مُظْلِمٌ . عَابِسٌ

Lowland *n.* أَرْضٌ مُنْخَفِضَةٌ

Lowliness *n.* مَسْكَنَةٌ . ضعة

Lowly *a.* مُتَوَاضِعٌ . وَدِيعٌ

Low-spirited *a.* كَئِيبٌ

Loyal *a.* أَمِين . مُخْلِص ٱلطَّاعة

Loyalty *n.* أَمَانَةٌ . طَاعَة

Lubricate *v. t.* دهَنَ. زَيَّتَ . ملَّس

Lucid *a.* وَاضِحٌ . صَاف

Lucidness / **Lucidity** *n.* وُضُوحٌ . صفَاءٌ

Luck *n.* حَظٌّ . نَصِيبٌ

Luckily *ad.* بِحُسْنِ ٱلْحَظِّ . بِسعْدٍ

Luckless *a.* مَنْكُودُ ٱلْحَظِّ

Lucky *a.* حَظِيظ . سعِيدٌ

Lucrative *a.* مُكسِبٌ . مفِيد

Lucre *n.* رِبْحٌ . مَكْسَبٌ

Ludicrous *a.* مُضْحِك

Luggage *n.* أَمْتِعة

Lukewarm *a.* فَاتِرٌ

Lull *v.t.* or *i.* or *n.* هدَّأَ . هَدَا . هدوٌّ

Lumbre *n.* سَقْطُ ٱلْمَتَاعِ . اخْشَاب

Luminary *n.* جِرْمٌ مُضِيءٌ

Luminous *a.* مُضِيءٌ نَيِّرٌ

Lump *n.* كُتْلَةٌ . جُمْلة

Lunacy *n.* جُنُونٌ

Lunar / **Lunary** *a.* قَمَرِيٌّ

Lunatic *n.* or *a.* مَجْنُونٌ . جُنُونِيٌّ

Lunatic-asylum *n.* بِيمَارِسْتَانُ

Lunch *n* or *v. i.* غدَاءٌ . تغَدَّى

Lung *n.* رِئَةٌ

Lurch *v. i.* or *n.* إِنْدَفَعَ جَانِبًا

Lure *v. t.* اغْوَى . غرَّ ـُ

Lurid *a.* مُصْفَرٌّ . مغِمٌّ . مُكَدِّر

Lurk *v. i.* كمَنَ ـُ . إِخْتَبأَ

Luscious *a.* حلوٌ . لَذِيذ

Lust *n.* or *v. i.* شَهْوَةٌ . إِشْتَهى

Lustful *a.* شَهْوَانِيٌّ

Lustily *a.* بِبَأسٍ بِشِدَّةٍ

Lustre *n.* بَهَاءٌ . رَوْنَقٌ . شهرةٌ

Lustrous *a.* لاَمِعٌ . بهِيٌّ

Lusty *a.* ضَلِيعٌ . نَشِيطٌ

Lute *n.* عودٌ

Luxuriance *n.* رَتْعٌ .خصْبٌ . تَرفٌ

Luxuriant *a.* خَصِبٌ . تَارِفٌ

Luxuriate *v. i.* رُتِعَ . تَنَعَّمَ

Luxurious *a.* مُتَنَعِّمٌ . مُتَرَفِّهٌ

Luxury *n.* تَرَفٌ . تنعُّمٌ . رفَاهة

Lyceum *n.* جَمْعِيةٌ عِلْمِيَّةٌ

Lying *n.* or *a.* كِذْبٌ . كَاذِبٌ

Lync *v. t.* قَاصَّ اوْ قَتَلَ بِلاَ حُكمٍ شَرعِيٍّ

Lynx *n.* نَوْعٌ منَ ٱلْفَهْدِ

Lyre *n.* قِيثَارٌ

Lyric / **Lyrical** *a.* غنَائِيٌّ . قِيثَارِيٌّ

M

Macadamize *v. t.* رَصَفَ بِٱلْحَصى

Mace *n.* عصاً . صَوْلَجَانٌ

Macerate *v. t.* نقَعَ . انْحَفَ

Machination *n.* مؤَامَرَةٌ. مَكْرٌ

Machine *n.* آلَةٌ

Machinery *n.* آلاَتٌ اوْ اجزَآؤُهَا

Machinist *n.* صَانِعُ ٱلآلاتِ

Mackerel *n.* سمكٌ بَحرِيٌّ منقَّطٌ

Mackintosh *n.* مُشَمَّعٌ

Mad *a.* مَجْنُونٌ . أحمق

Madam *n.* سيِّدَة

Madden *v. t.* أَغْضَبَ . جَنَّنَ

Madhouse *n.* بِيمَارِسْتَان

Madly *ad.* بِجُنُون . بِحَمَاقَةٍ

Madman *n.* مَجْنُونٌ

Madness *n.* جُنُونٌ . حَمَاقَةٌ

Magazine *n.* مَخْزَن (جرِيدَة)

Maggot *n.* دُودَةٌ

Magic *n.* سِحْرٌ . رُقْيَةٌ

Magic, Magical *a.* سِحْرِيٌّ

Magician *n.* سَاحِرٌ . رَاقٍ

Magisterial *a.* سُلْطَانِيٌّ . مُتَجَبِّرٌ

Magistracy *n.* مَأْمُورِيَّةُ حَاكِمٍ

Magistrate *n.* حَاكِمٌ . مَأْمُور

Magnanimity *n.* شَرَفُ ٱلنَّفْس

Magnanimous *a.* شَرِيفُ ٱلنَّفْسِ

Magnate *n.* عَظِيم . كَبِيرٌ . وجِيهٌ

Magnet *n.* مَغْنَطِيسٌ

Magnetic, Magnetical *a.* مَغْنَطِيسِيٌّ

Magnetism *n.* مَغْنَطِيسِيَّةٌ

Magnetize *v. t.* مَغْنَطَ

Magnificence *n.* جَلَالٌ . بَهَاءٌ

Magnificent *a.* بَهِيٌّ . فَاخِرٌ . جَلِيلٌ

Magnify *v. t.* كَبَّرَ . عَظَّمَ . بَجَّلَ

Magnitude *n.* كِبَرٌ . قَدْر . أَهَمِّيَةٌ

Magpie *n.* نَوْعٌ مِنَ ٱلْعَقْعَقِ (طَائِر)

Maid, Maiden *n.* فَتَاة . عَذْرَاءُ . جَارِيَة

Maiden-hair *n.* كُزْبَرَةُ ٱلْبِئْرِ (نبات)

Mail *n.* بَرِيدٌ . دِرْعٌ

Mail *v. t.* أَرْسَلَ بِٱلْبَرِيد . دَرَّعَ

Maim *v. t.* جَدَعَ . بَتَرَ

Main *a.* or *n.* رَئِيسِيٌّ . اهَمُّ . قُوَّةٌ

Mainland *n.* ٱلْيَابِسَةُ . (غَيْرُ جَزِيرَةٍ)

Mainly *ad.* غَالِبًا . فِي ٱلْأَكْثَرِ

Mainmast *n.* الصَّارِي ٱلاكْبَر

Mainsail *n.* الشِّرَاعُ الأَكْبَرُ

Maintain *v. t.* حَفِظَ . قَامَ بِ . أكدَ

Maintenance *n.* إِعَالَةٌ . حِفْظٌ. قِيَامٌ

Maize *n.* ذُرَةٌ صَفْرَآء

Majestic *a.* جَلِيلٌ . رَفِيعٌ . عَظِيمٌ

Majesty *n.* جَلَالَةٌ . عَظَمَة

Major *a.* or *n.* أَكْبَرُ. كُبْرَى . (بِكْبَاشِي)

Major-general *n.* قَائِدُ لِوَآء

Majority *n.* أَلأَكْثَرِيَّةُ . سِنُّ ٱلْبُلُوغِ

Make *v. t.* عَمِلَ ـَ . صَنَعَ ـَ . اوْجَبَ

Maker *n.* عَامِلٌ . صَانِعٌ . خَالِقٌ

Maladministration *n.* سُوءُ إِدَارَةٍ

Malady *n.* مَرَضٌ . عِلَّةٌ . دَآء

Malaria *n.* فَسَادُ ٱلْهَوَآءِ. مَلَارِيَا

Malcontent *a.* غَيْرُ رَاضٍ

Male *n.* ذَكَرٌ ج ذُكُورٌ

Malediction *n.* لَعْنَةٌ . شَتِيمَةٌ

Malefactor *n.* مُذْنِب . مُجْرِمٌ

Malevolent *a.* سَيِّءُ ٱلنِّيةِ . ضَاغِنٍ

Malformation *n.* سُوءُ ٱلْخِلْقَةِ . تَشَوُّهٌ

Malice *n.* ضَغِينَةٌ . حِقْدٌ

Malicious *a.* ضَاغِنٌ . حَقُودٌ

Malign *v. t.* هَتَكَ . نَمَّ ـُ . إِفْتَرَى

Malignancy, Malignity } *n.* ضَغِينَةٌ . خَبَاثَةٌ

Malignant *a.* ضَاغِنٌ. حَقُودٌ. خَبِيثٌ

Malleable *a.* قَابِلُ ٱلْمَطْلِ بِٱلتطْرِيق

Mallet *n.* مِطْرَقَةٌ

Malpractice *n.* سُوءُ ٱلْعَمَلِ

Maltreat *v. t.* عَامَلَ بِٱلسُّوءِ

Maltreatment *n.* مُعَامَلَةٌ . سَيِّئَةٌ

Mameluke *n.* مَمْلُوكٌ ج مَمَالِيكُ

Mamma *n.* أُمٌّ

Mammali *n.*, Mammalia *n. pl.* } ذَوَاتُ ٱلثَّدْيِ

Man *n.* (*pl.* Men) الإِنْسَانُ . رَجُلٌ

Manacle *v.t.* or *n.* غَلَّ ـّ . غُلٌّ ج اغْلَالٌ

Manage *v. t.* ادار . ساس . دبّر

Manageable *a.* سهل التدبير والضبط

Management *n.* تدبير . إدارة

Manager *n.* مدير . مدبّر

Mandate *n.* أمر رسمي

Mandrake *n.* لفّاح (نبات)

Mane *n.* عرف الفرس

Maneuvre / Manœuvre *n.* حركات العسكر حيلة

Manful *a.* رجلي . شهم

Mange *n.* جرب الحيوانات

Manger *n.* مذود . معلف

Mangle *v. t.* مزّق . فرّض

Mangy *a.* أجرب

Manhood *n.* رجولة . مروءة

Mania *n.* جنون . ولع . (هوس)

Maniac *n.* / Maniacal *a.* مجنون

Manifest *a.* or *v. t.* ظاهر . بيّن . أظهر

Manifestation *n.* إظهار . بيان

Manifesto *n.* إعلان . منشور

Manifold *a.* متنوّع . شتّى

Mankind *n.* نوع الإنسان . البشر

Manfully *ad.* بمروءة . بشهامة . بشجاعة

Manliness *n.* رجولية . شهامة

Manly *a.* شهم . ذو مروءة

Manna *n.* منّ

Manner *n.* كيفية . اسلوب . دأب

Manners *n. pl.* آداب

Man-of-war *n.* بارجة حربية

Manœuvre *see* Maneuvre.

Manor *n.* عقار . إقطاعة

Mansion *n.* دار . قصر

Manslaughter *n.* القتل خطأ

Mantel *n.* رف فوق الموقد

Mantle *n.* رداء . جبة

Manual *a.* or *n.* شغل اليد . كتاب مختصر

Manufactory *n.* معمل

Manufacture *n.* or *v. t.* عمَلٌ . إِصْطِنَاعٌ
Manufacturer *n.* صَانِعٌ . صَاحِبُ مَعْمَلٍ
Manure *n.* زِبْلٌ . سَمَادٌ . سَرْقِينٌ
Manuscript *n.* كِتَابُ خَطٍّ
Many *a.* كَثِيرٌ . عَدِيدٌ
Map *n.* (خَارِطَةٌ) . رسمُ بِلَادٍ
Mar *v. t.* أَضَرَّ . أَفْسَدَ . شَوَّه
Marauder *n.* / **Marauding** *a.* نَهَّابٌ . مغيرٌ لِلسَّلْبِ
Marble *n.* رُخَامٌ . مَرْمَرٌ
March *n.* or *v. i.* اذَارُ . مَسِيرٌ . سَارَ ـ
Mare *n.* أُنثَى ٱلْفَرَسِ
Margin *n.* حَاشِيَةٌ . حرفٌ . شَفِيرٌ
Marine *a.* / **Mariner** *n.* بَحْرِيٌّ
Marital *a.* زَوْجِيٌّ
Maritime *a.* بَحَرِيٌّ . مُجَاوِرُ ٱلْبَحْرِ
Mark *n.* عَلَامَةٌ . أَثَرٌ . هدفٌ
Mark *v. t.* عَلَّمَ عَلَى . لَاحَظَ
Market *n.* سُوقٌ ج اسْوَاقٌ

Marketable *a.* رَائِجٌ
Marksman *n.* رَامٍ . مَاهِرٌ بِٱلرَّمْيِ
Marmalade *n.* نوعٌ مِنَ ٱلْمُرَبَّى
Marriage *n.* عُرسٌ . زَوَاجٌ
Marriageable *a.* خليقٌ بِٱلزَّواج
Marrow *n.* مُخٌّ . لُبٌّ
Marry *v. t.* or *i.* زَوَّجَ . تَزَوَّج
Mars *n.* أَلْمَرِّيخ (سَيَّارٌ) . إِلٰهُ ٱلْحَرْبِ
Marsh *n.* مُسْتَنْقَعٌ . سَبْخَةٌ
Marshal *n.* or *v. t.* اكْبَرُ ٱلقوَّاد . صفَّ
Marshy *a.* مُسْتَنْقَعِيٌّ . سَبِخٌ
Martial *a.* حرْبِيٌّ . عَسْكَرِيٌّ
Martyr *n.* شَهِيدٌ ج شهدَاء
Martyrdom *n.* إِستِشْهَاد
Marvel *v. i.* or *n.* تَعجب . عَجِيبَةٌ
Marvelous *a.* عَجِيبٌ . غَرِيبٌ
Masculine *a.* مُذَكَّرٌ
Mash *v. t.* دقَّ ـُ . خَبِصَ ـِ

Mask *n.* or *v. t.* وَجْهٌ عَارِيَةٌ . تَنَكَّرَ . سَتَرَ

Mason *n.* بَنَّاءٌ . مِعْمَارٌ

Masonic *a.* مَاسُونِيٌّ

Masonry *n.* صِنَاعَةُ الْبِنَاءِ . مَاسُونِيَّةٌ

Masquerade *v. i.* or *n.* تَنَكُّرٌ لِلسُّخْرِيَةِ

Mass *n.* كَوْمٌ . مِقْدَارٌ . قُدَّاسٌ

Massacre *n.* or *v. t.* ذَبْحٌ . مَقْتَلَةٌ . قَتَلَ ـُ

Massive *a.* جَسِيمٌ . غَلِيظٌ

Mast *n.* صَارٍ . دَقَلٌ

Master *n.* or *v. t.* سَيِّدٌ . مُعَلِّمٌ . رَئِيسٌ . غَلَبَ

Master-piece *n.* شُغْلٌ سَامٍ فِي بَابِهِ

Mastery *n.* ظَفَرٌ . تَسَلُّطٌ

Mastic *n.* عِلْكٌ . (مَصْطِكَى)

Masticate *v. t.* مَضَغَ ـُ . عَلَكَ ـُ

Mastication *n.* مَضْغٌ . عَلْكٌ

Mastiff *n.* كَلْبٌ . كَبِيرٌ . قَوِيٌّ

Mat *n.* or *v. i.* حَصِيرَةٌ . تَلَبَّدَ

Match *n.* عُودٌ كِبْرِيتِيٌّ . قِرْنٌ . سِبَاقٌ

Match *v. t.* وَفَّقَ . أَزْوَجَ

Matchless *a.* لاَ نَظِيرَ لَهُ

Mate *n.* رَفِيقٌ . قَرِينٌ . ثَانِي قُبْطَانٍ

Material *n.* or *a.* مَادَّةٌ . مَادِّيٌّ

Materialism *n.* مَذْهَبُ الْمَادِّيِّينَ

Materialist *n.* دَهْرِيٌّ

Materially *ad.* مَادِّيًّا

Maternal *a.* أُمِّيٌّ

Maternity *n.* أُمِّيَّةٌ . وَظِيفَةُ الْأُمِّ

Mathematical *a.* رِيَاضِيٌّ

Mathematician *n.* عَالِمٌ بِالرِّيَاضِيَّاتِ

Mathematics *n. pl.* أَلْعُلُومُ الرِّيَاضِيَّةُ

Matricide *n.* قَتْلُ الْأُمِّ

Matriculate *v. t.* تَسَجَّلَ فِي مَدْرَسَةٍ عَالِيَةٍ

Matrimonial *a.* مُتَعَلِّقٌ بِالزِّيجَةِ

Matrimony *n.* أَلزِّيجَةُ

Matron *n.* شَيْخَةٌ . رَئِيسَةٌ . قَهْرَمَانَةٌ

Matted *a.* مُتَلَبِّدٌ

Matter *v. i.* هَمَّ . اغث

Matter *n.* مَادَّةٌ . هُيُولَى . أمرٌ

Mattock *n.* مِعْوَلٌ ج مَعَاوِلُ

Mattress *n.* فِرَاشٌ

Mature *a.* or *v. i.* نَاضِجٌ . بَالِغٌ . نَضَجَ

Matureness / Maturity } *n.* نَضْجٌ . بُلُوغٌ

Maul *v. t.* ضرَبَ شَدِيداً بعَصاً . جرَح

Mausoleum *n.* مقَامٌ . مزَخْرَفٌ لِمَيْتٍ

Maxim *n.* قَاعِدَةٌ . حِكْمَةٌ ج حِكَمٌ

Maximum *n.* غَايَةٌ . اعْلَى دَرَجَةٍ

May *n.* or *v. i.* أَيَّارُ . (مايو) . أَمْكَنَ

Mayor *n.* حَاكِمُ مَدِينَةٍ . رَئِيسُ بَلَدِيَّةٍ

Maze *n.* إِرْتِبَاكٌ . ورْطَةٌ

Mazy *a.* مُرْتَبِكٌ . مبهمٌ

Me *pron.* ضَمِيرُ ٱلْمُتَكَلِّمِ . بي . ي

Meadow *n.* مَرْجٌ . رَوْضَةٌ

Meagre *a.* هَزِيلٌ . زَهِيدٌ . سَخِيفٌ

Meal *n.* طَحِينٌ . أَكْلَةٌ وَاحِدَةٌ

Mealy *a.* نَاعِمٌ كَالطَّحِينِ

Mean *a.* حقيرٌ . دَنِيٌّ . وَسَطٌ

Mean *v. t.* عَنَى ـِ . قَصَدَ ـِ . نَوَى ـ

Meander *v. t.* إِنْعَرَجَ . جرَى عِوَجاً

Meaning *n.* معنىً . مُرَادٌ . مَرَامٌ

Meanly *ad.* بِدَنَاءَةٍ . خِسَّةٌ

Meanness *n.* خَسِيسَةٌ . دَنَاءَةٌ

Means *n. pl.* وَاسِطَةٌ . ثروَةٌ

Meantime / Meanwhile } *ad.* في أَثْنَاءِ ذلِكَ

Measles *n. pl.* حَصْبَةٌ (مَرَضٌ)

Measurable *a.* قَابِلُ ٱلْقِيَاسِ أَوِ ٱلْكَيْلِ

Measure *v. t.* قَاسَ . كَالَ ـِ . مَسَحَ ـَ

Measure *n.* قِيَاسٌ . كَيْلٌ . وَسِيلَةٌ

Measurement *n.* قِيَاسٌ . مِسَاحَةٌ

Meat *n.* لَحْمٌ . طَعَامٌ

Mechanic *n.* فَاعِلٌ يَعْمَلُ بالآلاتِ

Mechanical *a.* آلِيٌّ . صِنَاعِيٌّ

Mechanics *n. pl.* عِلْمُ ٱلْحِيَلِ

Mechanism *n.* تَرْكِيبُ آلاَتٍ

Medal *n.* نيشَانٌ . سِكَّةٌ تذْكَارِيَّةٌ

Medallion *n.* سكةٌ كَبِيرَةٌ . وِسَامٌ

Meddle *v. i.* تَطَفَّلَ . تَحَرَّشَ

Meddler *n.*
Meddlesome *a.* } مُتَحَرِّشٌ . مُتَطَفِّلٌ

Mediaeval *a.* مِنَ ٱلْقُرُونِ ٱلْمتوَسّطَةِ

Mediate *v. t.* تَوَسَّطَ . تَشَفَّعَ في

Mediation *n.* شَفَاعَةٌ . تَوَسُّطٌ

Mediator *a.* وسيطٌ . شَفِيعٌ

Medical *a.* طُبّيٌّ

Medicate *v. t.* خَلَطَ بِعَقَاقِيرِ . عَالَجَ

Medicinal *a.* عِلاجيٌّ . دَوَائِيٌّ

Medicine *n.* دَوَآءٌ . عِلاَجٌ

Mediocre *a.* وسَطٌ اوْ اقلُّ مِنْهُ

Mediocrity *n.* إِعْتِدَالٌ . قِلَّةٌ

Meditate *v. t.* or *i.* تَأَملَ . تفَكَّرَ . نوَى

Meditation *n.* تَأَمُّلٌ . تَفَكُّرٌ

Mediterranean *n.* ٱلْبَحْرُ ٱلْمتوَسّطُ

Medium *n.* وَاسِطَةٌ . وَسَطٌ . وسيطٌ

Medley *n.* خَلِيطٌ . عَدَمُ نِظَامٍ

Meek *a.* وَدِيعٌ . حَلِيمٌ . لَطِيفٌ . طَائِعٌ

Meekness *n.* وَدَاعَةٌ . حِلْمٌ

Meet *v. t.* or *i.* لَقِيَ . إِلْتقَى . إِجْتَمَعَ

Meet *a.* لاَئِقٌ . مُوَافِقٌ

Meeting *n.* إِجْتِمَاعٌ . مَجْمَعٌ . لِقَآءٌ

Melancholy *n.* غَمٌّ . سَوْدَآءُ

Meliorate *v.t.* حَسَّنَ . اصْلَحَ

Melioration *n.* تَحْسِينٌ

Mellow *a.* نَاضِجٌ . لَيِّنٌ . رُخْوٌ

Mellow *v. t.* or *i.* نَضَّجَ . نَضِجَ

Melodious *a.* مُطْرِبٌ . رخِيمٌ

Melody *n.* حسْنُ ٱلأَلْحَانِ . إِيقَاعُهَا

Melon *n.* جبْسٌ . بَطِّيخٌ

Melt *v. t.* or *i.* أَذَابَ . ذَابَ

Member *n.* عُضْوٌ . جزْءٌ

Membership *n.* عضْوِيَّةٌ

Membrane *n.* غشاء . نسيج
Membranaceous, Membranous *a.* غشائي
Memento *a.* تذكرة
Memoir *n.* ترجمة . تقرير
Memorable *a.* مستحق الذكر
Memorialize *v. t.* قدم عرض حال إلى
Memorandum *n.* تذكرة . مفكرة
Memorial *n.* or *a.* تذكرة . تقرير للتذكار
Memorize *v. t.* حفظ . غيب
Memory *n.* ذكر . الذاكرة . الحافظة
Menace *v. t.* or *n.* هدد . توعد . وعيد
Menagerie *n.* معرض الحيوانات
Mend *v. t.* or *i.* أصلح . رقع . تحسن
Mendacious *a.* كاذب
Mendacity *n.* كذب
Mendicancy, Mendicity *n.* تسول . شحاذة
Mendicant *n.* شحاذ . متسول
Menial *a.* or *n.* دني . ذليل . اجير

Menses *n. pl.*, Menstruation *n.* حيض , طمث
Menstrual *a.* حيضي . شهري
Menstruate *v. i.* حاضت . طمثت
Mensuration *n.* قياس . مساحة
Mental *a.* عقلي . ذهني
Mention *n.* or *v. t.* ذكر . ذكر
Mercantile *a.* تجاري
Mercenary *a.* or *n.* مستأجر . طماع
Merchandise *n.* بضائع . تجارة
Merchant *a.* تاجر
Merchantman *n.* سفينة تجارية
Merciful *a.* رحيم . رؤوف
Merciless *a.* عديم الرحمة . صارم
Mercurial *a.* زئبقي . حاد الطبع
Mercury *n.* زئبق . عطارد (سيار)
Mercy *n.* رحمة . رأفة
Mere *a.* مجرد . خالص
Merely *ad.* فقط . لا غير

Merge *v. t.* or *i.* غَطَسَ. إِخْتَفَى فِي

Meridian *n.* نِصْفُ ٱلنهَارِ وَخَطُّهُ

Merit *n.* or *v. t.* فَضْلٌ. إِسْتِحْقَاقٌ. إِسْتَحَقَّ

Merited *a.* مُسْتَحِق . مُسْتَوْجِبٌ

Meritorious *a.* مُسْتَحِقٌّ ٱلثَّنَاءِ أَوِ ٱلثَّوابِ

Merriment *n.* فَرَحٌ. طَرَبٌ. إِنْبِسَاطٌ

Merry *a.* فَرِحٌ . طَرِبٌ

Mesmerism *n.* تَنْوِيمٌ إِصْطِنَاعِيٌّ

Mess *n.* طَبْخَةٌ . حِصَّةٌ . خِلْطٌ

Message *n.* رِسَالَةٌ . بَلَاغٌ

Messenger *n.* رَسُولٌ . سَاعٍ

Messiah *n.* أَلْمَسِيحُ

Metal *a.* مَعْدِنٌ

Metallic *n.* مَعْدِنِيٌّ

Metallurgy *n.* عِلْمُ ٱلْمَعَادِنِ

Metaphor *n.* إِسْتِعَارَةٌ . مَجَازٌ

Metaphorical / Metaphoric *a.* إِسْتِعَارِيٌّ مَجَازِيٌّ

Metaphysical *a.* مُخْتَصٌّ بِعِلْمِ ٱلْمَعْقُولَاتِ

Metaphysician *n.* عَالِمٌ بِٱلْمَعْقُولَاتِ

Metaphysics *n.* عِلْمُ مَاوَرَاءَ ٱلطَّبِيعَةِ

Mete *v. t.* قَاسَ . كَالَ بِـ

Meteor *n.* شِهَابٌ

Meteorite / Meteorolite *n.* حَجَرٌ مِنَ ٱلْجَوِّ نَيْزَكٌ

Meteorology *n.* علمُ ٱلظَّوَاهِرِ ٱلْجَوِّيَّةِ

Meter *n.* مِقْيَاسُ ٱلْمَاءِ وَٱلْغَازِ

Metre *n.* مِتْرٌ. وَزْنُ ٱلشِّعْرِ

Method *n.* طَرِيقَةٌ. اسْلُوبٌ. نِظَامٌ

Methodic / Methodical *a.* بِتَرْتِيبٍ . بِنِظَامٍ

Metrical *a.* مَوْزُونٌ . نَظْمِيٌّ

Metropolis *n.* عَاصِمَةُ بِلَادٍ

Metropolitan *n.* مطرَانٌ مُخْتَصٌّ بِقَصَبَةٍ

Mettle *n.* مُرُوءَةٌ . نَخْوَةٌ . نَشَاطٌ

Mew *v. i.* مَاءَ كَالْقِطِّ . نَوَّى

Miasma *n.* أَبْخِرَةٌ سَامَّةٌ

Mice *n.* (*pl.* of Mouse). فِيرَانٌ

Microscope *n.* مِجْهَرٌ . (مِكْرُسْكُوبٌ)

Midday *n.* نِصفُ ٱلنَّهارِ . مُنْتَصَفُهُ

Middle *a.* or *n.* مُنْتَصَفٌ أَوْسَط . وسَطٌ

Middling *a.* متوَسِّط . بَيْنَ بَيْنَ

Midnight *n.* مُنْتَصَفُ ٱللَّيْل

Midriff *n.* الحِجَابُ ٱلحَاجِز

Midshipman *n.* ضابِطٌ صَغيرٌ في بارِجةٍ

Midst *n.* وَسْطٌ

Midway *n.* مُنْتَصَفُ ٱلمَسافة

Midwife *n.* قابِلَةٌ ج قَوَابِل . (دايَةٌ)

Midwifery *n.* قُبَالَة

Mien *n.* هَيْئَةٌ . طَلْعَةٌ

Might *n.* قُوَّةٌ . بَأْسٌ . شِدَّةٌ

Mightily *ad.* بِشِدَّةٍ . جِدًّا

Mighty *a.* قَوِيٌّ . قَدِيرٌ . عزِيزٌ

Migrate *v. i.* هَاجَر . إِنْتَقَلَ

Migration *n.* مُهَاجَرَةٌ . إِنْتِقَالٌ

Migratory *a.* راحِلٌ . مُتَنَقِّلٌ

Mild *a.* لَطِيفٌ . حَلِيمٌ . مُعْتَدِلٌ

Mildew *n.* عُفُونَةٌ

Mildness *n.* لُطْفٌ . حِلْمٌ . رِقَّةٌ

Mile *n.* مِيلٌ ج أَمْيَالٌ

Militant *a.* مُحارِبٌ . مُجَاهِدٌ

Military *a.* حَرْبِيٌّ . عَسْكَرِيٌّ

Militia *n.* جُنْدُ ٱلرَّدِيفِ

Milk *n.* or *v. t.* حَلِيبٌ . لَبَنٌ . حَلَبَ

Milkyway *n.* المَجَرَّةُ

Mill *n.* or *v. t.* مِطْحَنَةٌ . مَعْمَلٌ . طَحَنَ

Millennium *n.* أَلْفُ سَنَةٍ

Miller *n.* طَحَّانٌ

Millet *n.* ذُرَةٌ

Milliner *n.* خَيَّاطَةُ لِبَاسِ ٱلنِّسَاءِ

Millinery *n.* مَلْبُوسَاتُ ٱلنِّسَاءِ

Million *n.* أَلْفُ أَلْفٍ . مَلْيُونٌ

Millionaire *n.* وافِرُ ٱلغِنَى

Millstone *n.* حَجَرُ طَاحُونٍ . رحى

Milt *n.* طِحال

Mimic *n.* or *v. t.* مُقَلِّدٌ . قَلَّدَ هزْلاً

Minaret *n.* مأذَنَة ج مآذن

Mince *v. t.* or *i.* قرَّطَ . (فَرَمَ) تَخَطر

Mind *n.* عَقْل . ذهْن . نِيَّة

Mind *v. t.* بالَى بِهِ . إِكْتَرَثَ . إِعْتَنَى

Minded *a.* مُتَفَكِّرٌ . مَائِل إِلَى

Mindful *a.* مُبَالٍ . مُكْتَرِثٌ . مُعْتَنٍ

Mine *pron.* or *n.* لِي . مَعْدِن . لُغْمٌ

Miner *n.* صَانِعٌ فِي مَنَاجِمَ

Mineral *n.* or *a.* جَمَاد . جَمَادِيٌّ

Mineralogist *n.* عَالِمٌ بِالْجَمَادَاتِ

Mineralogy *n.* عِلْمُ ٱلْجَمَادِ وَٱلْمَعَادِنِ

Mingle *v. t.* or *i.* خَلَطَ ـِ مَزَجَ ـُ . إِمْتَزَجَ

Miniature *n.* صُورَةٌ . صَغِيرَةٌ

Minimum *n.* ٱلْأَقَلّ . أَقَلُّ مِقْدَار

Mining *n.* مُعَالَجَةُ ٱلْمَعَادِنِ او ٱللغوم

Minister *v.t.* خَدَمَ ـِ ـُ . امَدَّ . قَدَّمَ ل

Minister *n.* خَادِمُ قَسِّيسٌ . سَفِيرٌ . وَزِيرٌ

Ministerial *a.* قُسُوسِيٌّ . وَزِيرِيٌّ

Ministration *n.* خِدْمَةٌ

Ministry *n.* خِدْمَة . وِزَارَة

Minor *a.* اصْغَرُ عُمْراً . قَاصِرٌ . اصغَرُ

Minority *n.* ٱلْعَدَدُ ٱلْاقَلُّ . سِنُّ ٱلْقُصُورِ

Minstrel *n.* مُغَنٍّ . عَوَّاد

Mint *n.* مَضْرِبُ نُقُودٍ . نَعْنَعٌ

Minuend *n.* الْمَطْرُوحُ مِنْهُ

Minus *a.* عَلَامَةُ ٱلطَّرْح (—). إِلَّا

Minute *n.* دَقِيقَةٌ . تَذْكِرَةٌ

Minute *a.* دَقِيقٌ . مُدَقِّقٌ

Minutely *ad.* بِدِقَّةٍ . بِضَبْطٍ

Minuteness *n.* دِقَّةٌ . صِغَرٌ

Miracle *n.* آيَةٌ . مُعْجِزَةٌ . عَجِيبَةٌ

Miraculous *a.* عَجِيبٌ . خَارِقُ ٱلْعَادَةِ

Mirage *n.* سَرَابٌ . لَعْلَعٌ

Mire *n.* وَحْلٌ . حَمَاةٌ

Mirror *n.* مِرْآة ج مَرَايَا

Mirth *n.* فَرَحٌ . سُرُورٌ . طَرَبٌ

Mirthful *a.* طَرِبٌ . فَرِحٌ

Miry *a.* ذُو وَحَلٍ

Misanthrope *n.* / Misanthropic *a.* مبغِضُ ٱلْبَشَرِ

Misanthropy *n.* بُغْضُ ٱلْبَشَرِ . وَحْشَةٌ

Misapplication *n.* سُوءُ ٱلاِسْتِعْمَالَ

Misapply *v. t.* أَسَاءَ ٱلاِسْتِعْمَالَ

Misapprehend *v. t.* أَسَاءَ ٱلْفَهْمَ

Misapprehension *n.* سُوءُ ٱلْفَهْمِ

Misbehave *v. i.* أَسَاءَ ٱلتصرُّفَ

Misbehaviour *n.* سُوءُ ٱلتَّصرُّفِ

Misbelief *n.* إِعْتِقَادٌ . فَاسِدٌ

Misbelieve *v. t.* أَسَاءَ ٱلاِعْتِقَادَ

Miscalculate *v. t.* أَسَاءَ ٱلْحِسَابَ

Miscarriage *n.* خَيْبَةٌ . إِسْقَاطُ ٱلْجَنِينِ

Miscarry *v. i.* خَابَ ـِ . اسْقَطَتْ

Miscellaneous *a.* مُتَنوِّعٌ . شَتَّى

Miscellany *n.* مَجْمُوعُ أَشْيَآءَ . شَتَّى

Mischance *n.* مُصِيبَةٌ

Mischief *n.* ضَرَرٌ . سُوءٌ . شَرٌّ

Mischievous *a.* مُضِرٌّ . مُسِيءٌ مُكَدِّرٌ

Misconceive *v. t.* أَسَاءَ ٱلْفَهْمَ . غَلِطَ ـَ

Misconception *n.* سُوءُ ٱلْمَفْهُومِيَةِ . غَلَطٌ

Misconduct *n.* سُوءُ ٱلتَّصَرُّفِ

Misconstrue *v.t.* اسَاءَ ٱلتَّاوِيلَ . حَرَّفَ

Miscount *v. t.* غلطَ فِي ٱلْعَدِّ

Miscreant *n.* كَافِرٌ . شِرِّيرٌ . فَاجِرٌ

Misdate *v. t.* أَرَّخَ غَلَطًا

Misdeed *n.* فِعْلٌ شِرِّيرٌ . سَيِّئَةٌ

Misdemeanor *n.* سُوءُ ٱلسِّيرَةِ . ذَنْبٌ

Misdirect *v. t.* أَرْشَدَ او عَنْوَنَ خَطَأً

Misdoing *n.* إِسَاءَةٌ . خَطِيئَةٌ

Miser *n.* / Miserly *a.* بَخِيلٌ . شَحِيحٌ

Miserable *a.* تَعِيسٌ شَقِيٌّ . مِسْكِينٌ

Misery *n.* مَسْكَنَةٌ . شَقَآءٌ . تَعَاسَةٌ

Misfortune *n.* مُصِيبَةٌ . بَلِيَّةٌ . نَكْبَةٌ

Misgiving *n.* ريبة . قلق النفس

Misgovern *v. t.* أساء السياسة

Misgovernment *n.* سوء الإدارة

Misguide *v. t.* أساء الإرشاد. أضل

Mishap *n.* مصيبة . نازلة

Misinform *v.t.* أخبر بغير الواقع

Misinterpret *v. t.* أساء التفسير

Misjudge *v. t.* اخطأ في الحكم

Mislay *v. t.* وضع في غير محله

Mislead *v. t.* أضل . اغوى

Mismanagement *n.* سوء التدبير

Misname *v. t.* اخطأ في التسمية

Misnomer *n.* إسم في غير محله

Misplace *v. t.* وضع في غير محله

Misprint *n.* غلط في الطبع

Mispronounce *v. t.* غلط في اللفظ

Mispronunciation *n.* خطأ في اللفظ

Misquote *v. t.* اخطأ في الإقتباس

Misrepresent *v. t.* حرف كلامه. موه

Misrule *n.* سوء السياسة والحكم

Miss *n.* فتاة . إخطاء

Miss *v. t.* اخطأ لم يصب . اعوزه

Misshaped / Misshapen *a.* مشوه. قبيح الخلقة

Missile *n.* مرماة

Missing *a.* مفقود. ضائع

Mission *n.* إرسالية . جماعة مرسلة

Missionary *n.* مرسل . مبشر

Missive *n.* رسالة

Misspell *v. t.* أخطأ في التهجئة

Misspend *v. t.* صرف باطلا

Misstatement *n.* تحريف. تمويه

Mist *n.* or *v. i.* ضباب رذاذ . ارذ

Mistake *n.* or *v. t.* خطأ . سهو . اخطأ

Mistaken *a.* مخطئ

Mister *n.* سيد . افندي . خواجا

Mistranslate *v. t.* اخطأ في الترجمة

Mistress *n.* سَيِّدَةٌ. مُعَلِّمَةٌ. سرِّيةٌ

Mistrust *n.* or *v. t.* عدم ثِقَةٍ. شَكَّ في

Mistrustful *a.* عَدِيمُ ٱلثِّقَة

Misty *a.* ذُو ضَبَاب. ضَبَابِيٌّ

Misunderstand *v. t.* اساءَ ٱلْفَهْمَ

Misunderstanding *n.* سُوءُ فَهْمٍ. خِلَافٌ

Misuse *v. t.* or *n.* أَسَاءَ ٱلْاسْتِعْمَالَ

Mite *n.* شَيْءٌ يَسِيرٌ. فِلْسٌ. سُوَيْسَةٌ

Mitre *n.* تَاجُ اسْقُفٍ أَوْ قَلَنْسُوَتُهُ

Mitigate *v. t.* خَفَّضَ. خَفَّفَ. لَيَّنَ

Mitten *n.* كَفٌّ بِلاَ اصَابِعٍ

Mix *v. t.* or *i.* مَزَجَ. إِمْتَزَجَ

Mixture *n.* مَزِيجٌ

Moan *v. i.* or *n.* أَنَّ ـِ. أَنِينٌ

Moat *n.* خَنْدَقُ تَحْصِينٍ

Mob *n.* or *v. t.* الاوْبَاشُ. قَامَ ٱلاوْبَاشُ عَلَيْهِ

Mobile *a.* سَهْلُ الحَرَكَةِ اوْ ٱلتَّغيُّر

Mobility *n.* سُهُولَةُ ٱلْحَرَكَةِ. خِفَّةٌ

Mobilize *v. t.* عَبَّأَ (جَيْشًا) لِلْحَرْبِ

Mock *v. t.* or *a.* هَزَأَ ـَ. سَخِرَ ـَ. مُصَنَّعٌ

Mockery *n.* هُزْءٌ. سُخْرَةٌ

Mode *n.* كَيْفِيَّةٌ. أُسْلُوبٌ. عَادَةٌ

Model *n.* or *v. t.* نُمُوذَجٌ. مِثَالٌ. عَمِلَ عَلَى ٱلرَّسْمِ

Moderate *a.* or *v. t.* مُعْتَدِلٌ. خَفَّفَ. خَفَّضَ

Moderation *n.* إِعْتِدَالٌ. ضَبْطُ ٱلنَّفْسِ

Modern *a.* حَدِيثٌ. مُتَأَخِّرٌ

Modest *a.* مُحْتَشِمٌ. حَيِيٌّ. مُعْتَدِلٌ

Modesty *n.* حِشْمَةٌ. حَيَاءٌ

Modification *n.* تَغْيِيرٌ. نَوْعٌ

Modify *v. t.* غَيَّرَ صِفَاتِهِ. نَوَّعَ

Modulate *v. t.* اوْقَعَ عَلَى وَزْنٍ

Mohammedan *n.* or *a.* مُسْلِمٌ. إِسْلَامِيٌّ

Moiety *n.* نِصْفٌ

Moist *a.* رَطْبٌ. مُنَدًّى

Moisten *v. t.* رَطَّبَ. نَدَّى. ثَرَّى

Moisture *n.* رُطُوبَةٌ. نَدًى

Molasses *n. pl.* دِبْسُ سُكَّرٍ

Mold / Mould *n.* or *v. i.* or *t.* عَفَنٌ . قَالِبٌ . تَعَفَّنَ . صَبَّ فِي قَالِبٍ

Moldy / Mouldy *a.* مُتَعَفِّنٌ

Molder / Moulder *v.i.* إِنْحَلَّ . بَلِيَ

Mole *n.* خَالٌ . خُلْدٌ . سَدٌّ فِي ٱلْبَحْرِ

Molecule *a.* ذَرَّةٌ

Molest *v. t.* كَدَّرَ . ازْعَجَ

Mollify *v. t.* لَيَّنَ . طَيَّبَ الخَاطِرَ

Molten *a.* ذَائِبٌ . مَسْبُوكٌ

Moment *n.* دَقِيقَةٌ . أَهَمِّيَّةٌ

Momentary *a.* لِلَحْظَةٍ . وَقْتِيٌّ

Momentous *n.* مُهِمٌّ جِدًّا . خَطِيرٌ

Momentum *n.* قُوَّةُ ٱلاِنْدِفَاعِ

Monarch *n.* مَلِكٌ . سُلْطَانٌ

Monarchical *a.* مَلَكِيٌّ

Monarchy *n.* مَمْلَكَةٌ . مَلَكِيَّةٌ

Monastery *n.* دَيْرٌ ج أَدْيِرَةٌ

Monastic *a.* رَهْبَانِيٌّ . نُسْكِيٌّ

Monday *n.* يَوْمُ ٱلاِثْنَيْنِ

Money *n.* دَرَاهِمُ . نُقُودٌ

Moneyed *a.* ذُو مَالٍ . غَنِيٌّ

Mongrel *a.* or *n.* نَغْلٌ . خِلَاسِيٌّ

Monition *n.* إِنْذَارٌ . إِنْبَاءٌ . تَنْبِيهٌ

Monitor *n.* مُنْذِرٌ . عَرِيفٌ

Monk *n.* رَاهِبٌ . نَاسِكٌ

Monkey *n.* قِرْدٌ . (سَعْدَانٌ)

Monogamy *n.* زَوَاجٌ بِٱمْرَأَةٍ وَاحِدَةٍ

Monogram *n.* طُغْرَاءُ

Monomaniac *a.* مَجْنُونٌ فِي أَمْرٍ وَاحِدٍ

Monopolize *v. t.* إِحْتَكَرَ . خَصَّصَ لِنَفْسِهِ

Monopoly *n.* إِحْتِكَارٌ . إِمْتِيَازٌ فِي أَمْرٍ

Monosyllable *n.* لَفْظَةٌ مِنْ مَقْطَعٍ وَاحِدٍ

Monotheism *n.* التَّوْحِيدُ

Monotonous *a.* مُمِلٌّ . بَارِدٌ

Monotony *n.* عَدَمُ تَغَيُّرٍ او تَنَوُّعٍ

Monster *n.* وحشٌ غريبُ الخلقة

Month *n.* شهرٌ ج اشهرٌ وشهور

Monthly *a.* شهريٌّ

Monument *a.* بناءٌ للتذكار. ضريحٌ

Monumental *a.* تذكاريٌّ

Mood *n.* حالةٌ. منوالٌ. صيغة فعلٍ

Moody *a.* مهمومٌ. مغمومٌ. نكدٌ

Moon *n.* قمرٌ ج اقمارٌ

Moonshine *n.* ضوء القمر. تظاهرٌ

Moor *v.t.* or *n.* ربطَ سفينةً. مغربيٌّ

Moorings *n. pl.* رُبطُ السفينة

Mop *n.* or *v. t.* ممسحةٌ. مسحَ بها

Mope *v. i.* ملَّ. ضجرَ

Moral *a.* أدبيٌّ. فاضلٌ. مستقيمٌ

Moral *n.* مغزى مثلٍ او مقصدهُ

Morality *n.* إستقامةُ السيرة. فضيلةٌ

Moralize *v. t.* فسَّرَ بمعنىً أدبيٍّ

Morally *ad.* أدبيًّا

Morals *n. pl.* الآدابُ. صفاتٌ ادبية

Morass *n.* مستنقعٌ. سبخةٌ

Morbid *a.* سقيمٌ. وبيلٌ. مغتمٌّ

More *a.* or *ad.* اكثرُ. ازيدُ

Moreover *ad.* ايضاً. ثمَّ

Morn / Morning } *n.* صباحٌ. صبحٌ

Morose *a.* عبوسٌ. نكدٌ

Moroseness *n.* عبوسةٌ. شراسةٌ

Morrow *n.* غدٌ. بكرةٌ

Morsel *n.* لقمةٌ. قطعةٌ. صغيرةٌ

Mortal *a.* مائتٌ. فانٍ. قاتلٌ

Mortals *n. pl.* بشرٌ

Mortality *n.* موتٌ. هلاكٌ

Mortally *ad.* للموتِ. مميتاً

Mortar *n.* طينٌ. هاوونٌ. مدفع قصير

Mortgage *n.* or *v.t.* رهنٌ. رهنَ

Mortification *n.* فسادٌ. قهرٌ. خجلٌ

Mortify *v. i.* or *t.* فسدَ. أذلَّ. قمعَ

Mosaic *n.* or *a.* فُسَيْفَسَاءُ . فُسَيْفَسِيٌّ

Moslem *n.* مُسْلِمٌ

Mosque *n.* جَامِعٌ . مَسْجِدٌ

Mosquito *n.* نَامُوسَةٌ . بَعُوضَةٌ

Moss *n.* طَحْلَبٌ . اشْنَةٌ

Most *a.* أَكْثَرُ . أَلاكْثَرُ

Mote *n.* قَذًى . هَبْوَةٌ

Moth *n.* فَرَاشَةٌ . عُثَّةٌ

Mother *n.* أُمٌّ . وَالِدَةٌ

Mother-in-law *n.* حَمَاةٌ

Motion *n.* or *v. i.* حَرَكَةٌ . أَشَارَ إِلَى

Motive *n.* بَاعِثٌ . دَاعٍ . مُوجِبٌ

Motley *a.* مُلَوَّنٌ . مُتَنَوِّعٌ

Motor *n.* مُحَرِّكٌ

Mottled *a.* كَثِيرُ ٱلْبُقَعِ ٱلْمُلَوَّنَةِ

Motto *n.* عِبَارَةٌ عُنْوَانِيَّةٌ . شِعَارٌ

Mould *etc.* *see* Mold *etc.*

Mound *n.* اكَمَةٌ . تَلٌّ . مِتْرَاسٌ

Mount *n.* or *v. t.* جَبَلٌ . صَعِدَ . رَكِبَ

Mountain *n.* or *a.* جَبَلٌ . جَبَلِيٌّ

Mountaineer *n.* سَاكِنُ الجَبَلِ

Mountainous *a.* كَثِيرُ ٱلجِبَالِ

Mountebank *a.* مُشَعْبِذٌ . دَجَّالٌ

Mourn *v. i.* or *t.* نَاحَ . ـُ . حَزِنَ

Mourner *n.* نَائِحٌ . نَادِبٌ . حَزِينٌ

Mournful *a.* مَحْزُونٌ . مُكْرِبٌ

Mourning *n.* نَوْحٌ . حُزْنٌ . حِدَادٌ

Mouse *n.* (*pl.* Mice). فَارَةٌ ج فِيرَانٌ

Moustache *n.* شَارِبٌ ج شَوَارِبُ

Mouth *n.* فَمٌ . فُوهٌ . مَدْخَلٌ

Mouthful *n.* لُقْمَةٌ ج لُقَمٌ . اكْلَةٌ

Mouthpiece *n.* فَمُ ٱلْمِزْمَارِ وَمَا اشْبَهَ
نَائِبٌ فِي ٱلْكَلَامِ

Movable *a.* مِمَّا يُحَرَّكُ اوْ يُنْقَلُ

Movables *n. pl.* بَضَائِعُ . اثَاثٌ

Move *v. t.* or *i.* نَقَلَ . حَرَّكَ . تَحَرَّكَ

Movement *n.* حَرَكَةٌ . تَحْرِيكٌ

Mow *v. t.* or *n.* حَشَّ ـِ . كُدْسٌ

Much *a.* or *ad.* كَثِيرٌ . وَافِرٌ . كَثِيرًا

Mucilage *n.* لُعَابٌ . صَمْغٌ ذَائِبٌ

Mucous *a.* مُخَاطِيٌّ

Mucus *n.* مُخَاطٌ

Mud *n.* وَحْلٌ . طِينٌ . حَمْأَةٌ

Muddle *v. t.* or *n.* عَكَّرَ . شَوَّشَ . إِرْتِبَاكٌ

Muddy *a.* ذُو وَحَلٍ

Muff *n.* فَرْوَةٌ لِلْيَدَيْنِ

Muffle *v. t.* سَتَرَ ـُ . لَفَّ ـُ . خَمَرَ

Mug *n.* كُوزٌ . قَدَحٌ . إِبْرِيقٌ

Mulatto *n.* خِلَاسِيٌّ

Mulberry *n.* تُوتٌ . تُوتَةٌ

Mule *n.* بَغْلٌ ج بِغَالٌ

Muleteer *n.* بَغَّالٌ . مُكَارٍ

Mulish *a.* عَنِيدٌ كَالْبَغْلِ

Multiform *a.* مُتَعَدِّدُ ٱلْهَيْئَةِ

Multiple *n.* عَدَدٌ يُقْسَمُ عَلَى غَيْرِهِ بِلَا بَاقٍ

Multiplicand *n.* أَلْمَضْرُوبُ (عَدَدٌ)

Multiplication *n.* أَلضَّرْبُ . تَكْثِيرٌ

Multiplicity *n.* تَضَاعُفٌ . تَعَدُّدٌ

Multiplier *n.* أَلْمَضْرُوبُ فِيهِ

Multiply *v. t.* كَثَّرَ . ضَرَبَ إِزْدَادَ

Multitude *n.* جُمْهُورٌ . فَوْجٌ

Mumble *v. t.* هَمَسَ ـِ دَنْدَنَ

Mummery *n.* سُخْرَةٌ . مُجُونٌ

Mummy *n.* جُثَّةٌ مُحَنَّطَةٌ

Mumps *n. pl.* إِلْتِهَابُ ٱلْغُدَّةِ ٱلنَّكْفِيَّةِ

Munch *v. t.* or *i.* مَضَغَ ـُ لَاكَ ـُ

Municipal *a.* بَلَدِيٌّ

Municipality *n.* بَلَدِيَّةٌ . إِدَارَةُ مَدِينَةٍ

Mundane *a.* عَالَمِيٌّ . دُنْيَوِيٌّ

Munificence *n.* سَخَاءٌ . كَرَمٌ

Munificent *a.* جَوَّادٌ . كَرِيمٌ جِدًّا

Munitions *n. pl.* ذَخَائِرُ حَرْبِيَّةٌ

Mural *a.* حَائِطِيٌّ . سُورِيٌّ جِدَارِيٌّ

Murder *n.* or *v. t.* قَتْلٌ . قَتَلَ ـَ

Murderer *n.* قَاتِل

Murderous *a.* مُهْلِكٌ . قَاصِدُ ٱلْقَتْلِ

Murky *a.* مُظْلِمٌ . كَدِرٌ (هَوَآء)

Murmur *v. i.* or *n.* تَذَمَّرَ . دَنْدَنَ

Murrain *n.* وَبَا ٱلْمَوَاشِي

Muscle *n.* عَضَلَةٌ . صَدَفٌ

Muscular *a.* عَضَلِيٌّ

Muse *n.* or *v. t.* إِلَاهَةُ ٱلشّعْرِ . تَأَمل

Museum *n.* مَعْرِضُ ٱلتُّحَفِ . مَتْحَفٌ

Mushroom *n.* فَطَرٌ

Music *n.* صِنَاعَةُ ٱلالحَانِ . موسِيقِى

Musical *a.* مُوسِيقِيٌّ . مُطْرِبٌ

Musician *n.* عَالِمٌ بِالْمُوسِيقَى

Musk *n.* مِسْكٌ

Musket *n.* بُنْدُقِيَّةٌ . بَارُودَةٌ

Muskmelon *n.* شَمَّامٌ . بَطِّيخٌ اصفرُ

Muslin *n.* نَسِيجٌ رَقِيقٌ . شَاشٌ

Mussulman *n.* مُسْلِمٌ

Must *v. i.* (*aux.*) يَجِبُ . يَنْبَغِي

Mustard *n.* خَرْدَلٌ

Muster *v. t.* or *i.* حَشَدَ ـُ . جَمَعَ ـَ . إِجْتَمَعَ

Muster *n.* حَشْدُ ٱلْعَسَاكِرِ . دَفْتَرُهُمْ

Musty *a.* عَفِنٌ . فَاسِدٌ

Mutability *n.* عَدَمُ ثَبَاتٍ او بَقَآءٍ

Mutable *a.* مُتَغَيِّرٌ . مُتَقَلِّبٌ

Mute *a.* or *n.* صَامِتٌ . أَخْرَسُ

Mutilate *v. t.* جَدَعَ ـَ . جَذَمَ ـُ

Mutineer *n.* / Mutinous *a.* } عَاصٍ . ثَائِرٌ . مُتَمَرِّدٌ

Mutiny *n.* عِصْيَانٌ . ثَوْرَةٌ . فِتْنَةٌ

Mutter *v. t.* هَمَسَ ـِ . دَمْدَمَ

Muttering *n.* هَمْسٌ . دَمْدَمَةٌ

Mutton *n.* لَحْمُ ضَأْنٍ

Mutual *a.* مُشْتَرَكٌ . مُتَبَادِلٌ

Mutually *ad.* إِشْتِرَاكًا . تَبَادُلاً

Muzzle *v. t.* or *n.* كَمَّ ـُ . كِمَامٌ . فَمٌ

Myriad *n.* رَبْوَةٌ . عَدَدٌ عظِيمٌ

Myrrh *n.* مُرٌّ

Myrtle *n.* آسٌ

Myself *pron.* نفسِي . ذَاتِي

Mysterious *a.* غرِيبٌ . سِرّيٌّ

Mystery *n.* سِرٌّ . لُغْزٌ

Mystic *a.* or *n.* / Mystical *a.* غَامِضٌ . خَفِيٌّ . صُوفِيٌّ

Mystify *v. t.* حَيَّرَ وَخَاتَلَ

Myth *n.* خُرَافَةٌ . حِكَايَةٌ

Mythology *n.* عِلْمُ ٱلْخُرَافَاتِ . مَجْمُوعُهَا

N

Nag *n.* or *v. t.* حِصَانٌ صَغِيرٌ . نَكَدَ

Nail *n.* or *v. t.* مِسْمَارٌ . ظُفْرٌ . سَمَّرَ

Naive *a.* مُخْلِصٌ . صَافِي ٱلْقَلْبِ

Naked *a.* عُرْيَانٌ . مَكْشُوفٌ

Nakedness *n.* عُرْيٌ . عَوْرَةٌ

Name *n.* or *v. t.* إِسْمٌ . سَمَّى . ذَكَرَ

Nameless *a.* بِلاَ ٱسْمٍ . مَجْهُولٌ

Namely *ad.* أَيْ . يَعْنِي

Namesake *n.* سَمِيٌّ

Nap *n.* نَوْمَةٌ قَصِيرَةٌ . زَغَبٌ

Nape *n.* قَفَا ٱلْعُنُقِ

Napkin *n.* فُوطَةٌ . مِنْشَفَةٌ

Narcotic *a.* مُخَدِّرٌ . مُنَوِّمٌ

Narrate *v. t.* حَدَّثَ . قَصَّ . رَوَى

Narration / Narrative *n.* حَدِيثٌ . قِصَّةٌ . رِوَايَةٌ

Narrator *n.* مُحَدِّثٌ . رَاوٍ

Narrow *a.* ضَيِّقٌ . مَحْصُورٌ

Narrow *v. t.* or *i.* ضَيَّقَ . تَضَيَّقَ

Nasal *a.* انفيٌّ . اغنُّ

Nasty *a.* وَسِخٌ . قذِرٌ . قبيحٌ

Natal *a.* وَطَنِيٌّ . موْلِدي

Nation *n.* أمه . شَعْبٌ

National *a.* امميٌّ . وطَنيٌّ

Nationality *n.* وَطنيّةٌ . جِنْسيّةٌ

Native *a.* وَطَنيٌّ . أهْليٌّ

Nativity *a.* موْلِدٌ . ولادَةٌ

Natural *a.* طَبيعيٌّ . فِطْرِيٌّ . خَلقيٌّ

Naturalist *n.* عالِمٌ بالطبيعيّاتِ

Naturalize *v.t.* ضمّ إلى تبعيةِ دولةٍ

Naturalness *n.* طَبيعيّةٌ . عَدَمُ تصنّعٍ

Nature *n.* الطَّبيعةُ . خَليقةٌ . ماهيّةٌ

Naught *n.* لا شيءٌ . بطْلٌ . عدمٌ

Naughtiness *n.* تمرُّدٌ . رَدَاءةٌ . شرٌّ

Naughty *a.* متمرّدٌ . فاسدٌ . شرّيرٌ

Nausea *n.* غَثَيانٌ

Nauseate *v. t.* سبَّبَ ٱلغَثَيانَ

Nauseous *a.* مُسَبّبُ ٱلغَثَيانِ . كَرِيهٌ

Nautical *a.* منوطٌ بٱلسفرِ بحْراً . نوْتيٌّ

Naval *a.* منوطٌ بالسفُنِ اوٱلبوَارِجِ

Nave *n.* صحْنُ ٱلكنيسةِ

Navel *n.* سُرَّةٌ

Navigable *a.* صالحٌ لِسَيْرِ ٱلسفُنِ

Navigate *v. t.* سافرَ في سفينةٍ . سيّرَها

Navigation *n.* السيْرُ في ٱلسفُنِ . علْمهُ

Navigator *n.* قائدُ سفينةٍ . مُدِيرُها

Navy *n.* أسْطولٌ . مجموعُ بوارجَ

Nay *ad.* لا . كلا

Nazarite *n.* نذيرٌ

Near *a.* or *v.t.* قريبٌ . قرُبَ ـُ . دنا ـُ

Near / Nearly } *ad.* قريباً . تقريباً

Nearness *n.* قرْبٌ

Neat *a.* نظيفٌ . مرتّبٌ . بقَريٌّ

Neatness *n.* نظافةٌ . إتقانٌ

Nebula *n.* سَديمٌ

Nebular / Nebulous a. سَدِيمِيٌّ

Necessary a. لاَزِمٌ. ضَرُورِيٌّ. وَاجِبٌ

Necessitate v. t. أَلْزَمَ. احْوَجَ

Necessitous a. مُحْتَاجٌ. مُفْتَقِرٌ

Necessity n. حَاجَةٌ. عوزٌ. ضَرُورَةٌ

Neck n. عُنُقٌ. رَقَبَةٌ.

Necklace n. قِلاَدَةٌ. عِقْدٌ

Necromancy n. سِحْرٌ. خُرافة

Necropolis n. مَقْبَرَةٌ. مَدْفَنٌ

Nectar n. شَرَابُ ٱلآلِهَةِ. شَرابٌ نَفِيسٌ

Need n. or v. t. or i. حَاجةٌ. فَاقَةٌ. إِحتَاجَ

Needful a. ضَرُورِيٌّ. لاَزِمٌ

Needle n. إِبْرَةٌ. مِسَلَّةٌ

Needless a. لا حَاجَةَ إِلَيْهِ

Needs ad. لا بُدَّ من

Needy a. مُحْتَاجٌ. فَقِيرٌ

Nefarious a. شَنِيعٌ. غَايَةٌ فِي ٱلشرِّ

Negation n. نَفْيٌ. إِنكَارٌ. سَلْبٌ

Negative a. or v. t. نافٍ. سَلْبِيٌّ. أَدْحَضَ. رَفَضَ

Neglect v. t. or n. اهْمَلَ. تَغَافَلَ. إِهمَالٌ

Neglectful / Negligent a. مُهْمِلٌ. مُتَغَافِلٌ

Negligence n. إِهْمَالٌ. تَغَافلٌ

Negotiate v. t. تَاجَرَ. فَاوَضَ. قاولَ

Negotiation n. تَدْبِيرُ امْرٍ. مُفَاوضَةٌ

Negotiator n. مُدَبِّرُ امْرٍ اوْ مُعَاهَدَةٍ

Negro n. زِنْجِيٌّ. عَبْدٌ. أَسْوَدُ

Neigh v. t. صَهَلَ ـِ. حَمْحَمَ

Neighbour n. جَارٌ. قَرِيبٌ

Neighbouring a. مُجَاوِرٌ

Neighbourhood n. جِوَارٌ

Neither pro. لاَ. لاَ احَدَ (إِثْنَيْنِ)

Nephew n. إِبْنُ اخٍ اوْ اخْتٍ

Nerve n. or v.t. عَصَبٌ. قُوَّةٌ. قوَّى

Nervous a. عَصَبِيٌّ. سَرِيعُ ٱلتَّأْثرِ

Nest n. عُشٌّ. وَكْرٌ

Nestle v. t. إِسْتَكَنَّ. (فَرْخٌ). آوَى

Net *n.* or *a.* شَبَكَةٌ . شَرَكٌ . صَاف

Net *v. t.* حَبَكَ ـُ . رَبِحَ ـَ رِبْحاً خَالِصاً

Nether *a.* أَسْفَلُ . جَحِيمِيٌّ

Netting *n.* شَبَكَةٌ . شَبَكٌ

Nettle *n.* or *v. t.* قُرَّاصٌ . قَرَصَ ـُ . نَكَى

Neuralgia *n.* وَجَعُ الْعَصَبِ

Neuter *n.* لاَمُذَكَّرٌ وَلاَمُؤَنَّثٌ . لاَزِمٌ

Neuter / Neutral *a.* or *n.* مُحَايِدٌ

Neutrality *n.* حِيَادٌ . مُحَايَدَةٌ

Neutralize *v. t.* أَبْطَلَ فِعْلَهُ

Never *ad.* أَبَدًا . قَطُّ (مَعْ نَفْيٍ)

Nevertheless *ad.* مَعْ ذَلِكَ

New *a.* جَدِيدٌ . حَدِيث

Newness *n.* جِدَّةٌ

News *n.* أَخْبَارٌ . حَوَادِثُ

Newspaper *n.* جَرِيدَةٌ

Next *a.* or *ad.* أَلتَّالِي . الثَّانِي . قَادِمٌ . بَعْدُ

Nib *n.* رَأْسٌ . طَرَفٌ

Nibble *v. t.* قَرَضَ ـَ . قَضِمَ ـَ

Nice *a.* لَذِيذٌ . حَسَنٌ . مُدَقِّقٌ

Nicety *a.* دِقَّةٌ . رِقَّةٌ . تَأَنُّقٌ

Niche *n.* مِشْكَاةٌ

Nickel *n.* مَعْدِنٌ أَبْيَض

Nickname *n.* or *v. t.* لَقَّبَ . لَقَبٌ

Niece *n.* بِنْتُ أَخٍ أَو اخْتٍ

Niggard / Niggardly *n.* بَخِيلٌ . شَحِيحٌ

Nigh *a.* or *ad.* قَرِيبٌ . قَرِيبًا

Nighness *n.* قُرْبٌ

Night *n.* لَيْلٌ ج لَيَالٍ

Night-fall *n.* عَشِيَّةٌ . غَسَقٌ

Nightingale *n.* بُلْبُلٌ ج بَلاَبِل

Nightly *a.* or *ad.* لَيْلِيٌّ . كُلَّ لَيْلَةٍ

Nightmare *n.* كَابُوسٌ . ضَاغُوطٌ

Nilometer *n.* مِقْيَاسٌ لِمَاءِ النِّيلِ

Nimble *a.* خَفِيفٌ . حَرِكٌ . نَشِيطٌ

Nimbleness *n.* خِفَّةٌ . نَشَاطٌ

Nine *a.* تِسْعٌ . تِسعةٌ

Ninefold *a.* تِسعةُ أَضعَاف

Nineteen *a.* تِسْعةَ عشَرَ . تِسعَ عَشَرةَ

Nineteenth *a.* أَلتاسِعُ عشَرَ

Ninetieth / Ninety } *a.* تِسعونَ

Ninth *a.* أَلتَّاسِعُ . تُسْعٌ

Nip *v. t.* or *n.* قَرَصَ ـُ قَرسَ ـِ . قَرْص

Nippers *n. pl.* ملقَطٌ صَغِيرٌ

Nipple *n.* حَلَمَةٌ . بز

Nitre *n.* مِلْحُ بَارُودٍ

No *a.* or *ad.* لاَ . لَيْس . كَلاَّ

Nobility *n.* شَرَف . كَرَامَةٌ . الأَشْرافُ

Noble *a.* شَرِيفٌ . جَلِيلٌ . كَرِيمٌ

Nobleman *n.* شَرِيفُ ٱلأَصْلِ

Nobody *n.* لاَ أَحَدٌ . لَيْسَ أَحَدٌ

Nocturnal *a.* لَيليٌّ

Nod *n.* or *v. t.* حَنْيَةُ ٱلرَّاس . حنَاهُ

Node *n.* عُقْدَةٌ ج عُقَدٌ

Nodose / Nodular } *a.* ذُو عُقَدٍ

Noise *n.* صَوْتٌ . ضَجَّةٌ . جَلَبَةٌ

Noiseless *n.* بِلاَ صَوْتٍ

Noisome *a.* مُؤْذٍ . كَرِيهٌ . مُهْلِكٌ

Noisy *a.* صَيَّاحٌ . صَوَّاتٌ

Nomad *n.* / Nomadic *a.* } بَدَوِيٌّ

Nomenclature *n.* تَسمِيَةٌ عِلْمِيَّةٌ

Nominal *a.* إِسْمِيٌّ . بِٱلاْسْمِ فَقَطْ

Nominate *v. t.* سَمَّى . عَيَّنَ

Nominative *a.* فَاعِلٌ . مُبْتَدأ

Nominee *n.* مُسَمًّى . مُعَيَّنٌ

Non-conductor *n.* غَيْرُ مُوصِلٍ لِلْكَهْرَبَائِيَّةِ

None *a.* لاَ أَحدٌ . لَيس أَحَدٌ

Non-existence *n.* عَدَمُ وُجُودٍ

Non-resident *n.* غَيْرُ ساكِنٍ مَحَلَّ مُعينٍ

Nonsense *n.* هَذَيَانٌ . هَذْرٌ

Nonsensical *a.* بِلاَ مَعْنًى . هَذِرِيٌّ

Nook *n.* زَاوِيَةٌ

Noon / Noonday } *n.* أَلظُّهْر. مُنْتَصَفُ ٱلنَّهَارِ

Noose *n.* أُنْشُوطَةٌ. رِبْقَةٌ

Nor *conj.* وَلاَ

Normal *a.* قَانُونِيٌّ. طَبِيعِيٌّ

North *n.* ٱلشَّمَالُ

North / Northern } *a.* شَمَالِيٌّ

Northward *ad.* شَمَالاً

Nose *n.* أَنْفٌ. مَنْخَرٌ

Nostril *n.* مِنْخَرٌ

Not *ad.* لاَ. مَا. لَيْس. لَمْ. لَنْ

Notable *a.* شَهِيرٌ. وَجِيهٌ. عَجِيبٌ

Notary *n.* مُسَجِّلُ ٱلصُّكُوكِ

Notation *n.* تَرْتِيبُ ٱلأَرْقَامِ

Notch *n.* or *v.t.* حَزَّةٌ. فَرْضٌ. فَرَّضَ

Note *n.* or *v. t.* عَلاَمَةٌ. رُقْعَةٌ. كَتَبَ

Note-book *n.* دَفْتَرُ تَذْكِرَةٍ

Noted *a.* مُقَيَّدٌ. مَشْهُورٌ. شَائِعٌ

Noteworthy *a.* مُسْتَحِقٌّ ٱلذِّكْرِ

Nothing *n.* لاَ شَيْءَ

Nothingness *n.* عَدَمٌ

Notice *n.* إِعْلاَنٌ. إِلْتِفَاتٌ. تَنْبِيهٌ

Notice *v. t.* لاَحَظَ. إِلْتَفَتَ إِلى

Noticeable *a.* مِمَّا يُلاَحَظُ. مِمَّا يُذْكَرُ

Notification *n.* تَنْبِيهٌ إِعْلاَنٌ إِخْطَارٌ

Notify *v. t.* أَخْبَرَ. أَعْلَنَ. أَعْلَمَ

Notion *n.* فِكْرٌ. تَصَوُّرٌ. رَأْيٌ

Notional *a.* وَهْمِيٌّ. خَيَالِيٌّ

Notoriety *n.* شُهْرَةٌ. صِيتٌ رَدِيٌّ

Notorious *a.* مَشْهُورٌ. سَيِّئُ ٱلصِّيتِ

Notwithstanding *conj.* مَعْ أَنْ وَلَوْ

Nought *n.* see Naught.

Noun *n.* إِسْمٌ ج أَسْمَاءٌ

Nourish *v. t.* قَاتَ ـُ. رَبَّى. غَذَّى

Nourishment *n.* قُوتٌ. غِذَاءٌ

Novel *a.* or *n.* جَدِيدٌ. غَرِيبٌ. رِوَايَةٌ

Novelist *n.* مُؤَلِّفُ ٱلرِّوَايَاتِ

Novelty *n.* جِدَّةٌ . نَادِرَةٌ

November *n.* تِشْرِينُ ٱلثَّانِي (نُوفَمبِرْ)

Novice *n.* مُبْتَدِئٌ . تِلْمِيذٌ جَدِيدٌ

Novitiate *n.* مُدَّةُ ٱلتَّلْمَذَةِ ٱلإِبْتِدَائِيَّةِ

Now *ad.* أَلآنَ . حَالاً

Nowadays *ad.* فِي هٰذِهِ ٱلأَيَّامِ

Noway, Nowise *n.* كَلَّا . لَا . ٱلْبَتَّةَ

Nowhere *ad.* غَيْرُ مَوْجُودٍ أَصْلاً

Noxious *a.* مُضِرٌّ . سَامٌّ . مُهْلِكٌ

Nozzle *n.* أَنْفٌ . خُرْطُومٌ . طَرَفٌ

Nucleus *n.* (نَوَاةٌ) . مَرْكَزُ ٱلْجَوْهَرِ

Nudge *v. t.* وَكَزَ بِٱلْمِرْفَقِ

Nudity *n.* عَرَاءٌ . عُرْيٌ

Nugget *n.* كُتْلَةٌ مِنْ تِبْرٍ . شَذْرَةٌ

Nuisance *n.* مَكْرَهَةٌ . مُكَدِّرٌ

Null *a.* بَاطِلٌ . سَاقِطٌ . غَيْرُ عَامِلٍ

Nullify *v. t.* أَبْطَلَ . أَلْغَى

Nullity *n.* بُطْلَانٌ . سُقُوطٌ

Numb *a.* or *v. t.* خَدِرٌ . خَدَّرَ

Number *n.* or *v. t.* عَدَدٌ . عِدَّةٌ . عَدَّ

Numberless *a.* لَا يُعَدُّ أَوْ يُحْصَى

Numbers *n.* سِفْرُ ٱلْعَدَدِ (فِي ٱلتَّوْرَاةِ)

Numbness *a.* خَدَرٌ

Numeral *n.* or *a.* عَدَدٌ . رَقْمٌ . عَدَدِيٌّ

Numerate *v. t.* عَدَّ . قَرَأَ ٱلأَرْقَامَ

Numerator *n.* صُورَةُ ٱلْكَسْرِ

Numeric, Numerical *a.* عَدَدِيٌّ

Numerous *a.* كَثِيرٌ . عَدِيدٌ

Numismatics *n.* عِلْمُ ٱلنُّقُودِ

Numskull *n.* بَلِيدٌ . أَبْلَهُ

Nun *n.* رَاهِبَةٌ

Nuncio *n.* قَاصِدُ ٱلْبَابَا (نَائِبُهُ)

Nunnery *n.* دَيْرُ ٱلرَّاهِبَاتِ

Nuptial *a.* زَوَاجِيٌّ . عُرْسِيٌّ

Nuptials *n.* عُرْسٌ

Nurse *n.* مُرْضِعٌ (ة) مُمَرِّضَةٌ . مُرَبِّيَةٌ

Nurse *v. t.* أرضع . مرّض . ربّى

Nursery *n.* حُجرة الأولاد . (مشتل)

Nursling *n.* رضيع

Nurture *n.* or *v. t.* تربية . ربّى

Nut *n.* جوزة . بندقة

Nutmeg *n.* جوز الطيب

Nutriment *n.* غذاء . قوت

Nutrition *n.* غذاء . قوت . تغذية

Nutritious, Nutritive *a.* مغذٍ

Nymph *n.* الاهة الماء والجبال

O

Oak *n.* سنديان . بلوط

Oaken *a.* من سنديان

Oar *n.* مجذاف ج مجاذيف

Oarsman *n.* جذّاف

Oasis *n.* واحة ج واحات

Oats *n. pl.* (شوفان)

Oath *n.* قسم . حلف . يمين

Oatmeal *n.* دقيق شوفان

Obduracy *n.* عناد . صلابة القلب

Obdurate *a.* عنيد . متصلب القلب

Obedience *n.* طاعة . إذعان

Obedient *a.* مطيع . خاضع

Obeisance *n.* سجود . خرور

Obelisk *n.* عمود . مربّع . مسلّة

Obese *a.* سمين . شحيم

Obey *v. t.* أطاع . خضع ل

Obituary *n.* ترجمة مختصرة لميت

Object n. شيءٌ . غايةٌ . مرامٌ . مَفعولٌ بهِ

Object v. t. إعترَضَ . قاوَمَ

Objection n. إعتِراضٌ . مانِعٌ

Objectionable a. غيرُ مقبولٍ

Objective a. خارِجٌ عَنِ ٱلعقلِ

Objector n. مُعترِضٌ . مقاوِمٌ

Oblation n. تَقدِمةٌ . قُرْبانٌ

Obligation n. فَرْضٌ . وُجوبٌ . إمتِنانٌ

Obligatory a. مَفرُوضٌ . واجِبٌ

Oblige v. t. أَوْجَبَ . عَمِلَ مَعرُوفاً

Obliged a. ممنونٌ . مُلتزِمٌ . شاكِرٌ

Obliging a. ذُو معرُوفٍ . لَطيفٌ

Oblique a. مُنحرِفٌ . مائِلٌ

Obliquity n. إنحِرافٌ . إنحِناءٌ

Obliterate v. t. محا ـُ . دَرَسَ ـِ

Oblivion n. نسيانٌ . عفوٌ

Oblivious a. ناسٍ . غافِلٌ

Oblong a. مُستطِيل

Obloquy n. طَعْنٌ . لُؤْمٌ . ذَمٌّ

Obnoxious a. مَكروهٌ . مُعرَّضٌ ل

Obscene a. قَبيحٌ . فَاحِشٌ . مُفسِدٌ

Obscenity n. قَباحَةٌ . كَلامٌ قَبيحٌ

Obscure v. t. or a. أَظْلَمَ . أَبهَمَ . مُلتَبِسٌ

Obscureness, Obscurity n. ظُلْمَةٌ . غمُوضٌ . إلتِباسٌ

Obsequies n. pl. جِنازةٌ

Obsequious a. خاضِعٌ . ذَليلٌ

Observable a. مما يُلاحَظُ أو يُراعَى

Observance n. مُراعاةٌ . حِفظٌ . إجراءٌ

Observant a. مُلاحِظٌ . مُنتَبِهٌ

Observation n. مُلاحَظَةٌ . مُراقَبةٌ . رَصدٌ

Observatory n. مرْصِدٌ فلكِيٌّ

Observe v. t. لاَحَظَ . رَاعَى . رَصَدَ ـُ

Obsolete a. غيرُ مُستعمَلٍ . مُهمَلٌ

Obstacle n. مانِعٌ . عائِقٌ

Obstetrics n. عِلمُ ٱلوِلادَةِ أو ٱلتَّوليدِ

Obstinacy *n.* عنَادٌ . إِصْرَارٌ . مُكَابَرَةٌ

Obstinate *a.* عنِيدٌ . مُصِرٌّ . مُكَابِرٌ

Obstruct *v. t.* مَانَعَ . صَدَّ ـُ . عَاقَ

Obstruction *n.* مَانِعٌ . سَدٌّ . عَارِضٌ

Obtain *v. t.* حَصَّلَ . نَالَ ـَ . أَدْرَكَ

Obtainable *a.* مُمْكِنٌ تَحْصِيلُهُ . يُنَالُ

Obtrude *v. t.* أَلَحَّ . تَدَاخَلَ . تعرَّضَ

Obtrusive *a.* فُضُولِيٌّ . مُتَدَاخِلٌ

Obtuse *a.* كَلِيل . بَلِيدٌ . مُنْفَرِجٌ

Obtuseness *n.* كَلّ . بَلَادَةٌ

Obverse *n.* وجْهُ ٱلسِّكَّةِ أَو ٱلنقُودِ

Obviate *v. t.* أَزَالَ . رَدَّ ـُ . نَجَا مِن

Obvious *a.* ظَاهِرٌ . وَاضِحٌ

Occasion *n.* فُرْصَةٌ . سَبَبٌ . حَاجَةٌ . مَرَّةٌ

Occasional *a.* إِتِّفَاقِيٌّ . حَادِثٌ أَحْيَانًا

Occident *n.* ٱلْغَرْبُ . الاقْطَارُ ٱلْغَرْبِيَّةُ

Occidental *a.* غَرْبِيٌّ . مغرِبِيٌّ

Occult *n.* سِرِّيٌّ . مَكْتُومٌ

Occupancy *n.* تَمَلُّكٌ . إِقَامَةٌ فِي

Occupant, Occupier *n.* سَاكِنٌ . مُتَمَتِّعٌ

Occupation *v.* حِرْفَةٌ . إِحْتِلَالٌ . تَمَتُّعٌ

Occupy *v. t.* حَلَّ فِي شَغَلَ . إِسْتَوْلَى

Occur *v. i.* حَدَثَ . خَطَرَ بِٱلْبَالِ

Occurrence *n.* حَادِثَةٌ . حُدُوثٌ

Ocean *n.* أَلْبَحْرُ ٱلْمُحِيطُ . أُوقِيَانُوسٌ

Oceanic *a.* بَحْرِيٌّ

Oceanica *n.* جَزَائِرُ ٱلْبَحْرِ ٱلْمُحِيطِ

Octagon *n.* شَكْلٌ مُثَمَّنٌ

Octagonal *a.* ذُو ثَمَانِي زَوَايَا

Octangular *a.* مُثَمَّنُ ٱلزَّوَايَا

October *n.* تِشْرِينُ ٱلأَوَّل (أُكتوبر)

Octogenarian *n.* إِبْنُ ثَمَانِينَ سَنَةً

Ocular *a.* بَصَرِيٌّ . عِيَانِيٌّ

Oculist *n.* طَبِيبُ ٱلْعُيُونِ

Odd *a.* فَرْدٌ . غَرِيبٌ . زَائِدٌ

Oddity, Oddness *n.* غَرَابَةٌ . شُذُوذٌ

Ode *n.*	قصيدةٌ . نشيدٌ
Odious *a.*	ممقوتٌ . كَرِيهٌ . قبيحٌ
Odium *n.*	مقتٌ . كُرهٌ . كَرَاهِيَةٌ
Odorous *a.*	ذَكِيُّ ٱلرَّائِحَةِ
Odour *n.*	رَائِحَةٌ
Of *prep.*	مِنْ . عَنْ . علامة ٱلإِضَافَةِ
Off *ad.*	بَعِيدًا . على بُعْدٍ
Offal *n.*	سَقَطُ الذبيحِ . زُبَالَةٌ
Offence / **Offense** } *n.*	إِغَاظَةٌ . غَيْظٌ . تَعَدٍّ
Offend *v. t.*	اغَاظَ . كَدَّرَ . اخطأَ
Offender *n.*	مذنبٌ . مُكَدِّرٌ . خَاطِئٌ
Offensive *a.*	مُغِيظٌ . كَرِيهٌ . مُعْتَدٍ
Offer *v. t.* or *i.*	قَدَّمَ . أَهْدَى . عَرَضَ ـِ
Offer *n.*	إِهْدَاءٌ . عَرْضٌ . تَقْدِمَةٌ
Offering *n.*	ذَبِيحَةٌ . تَقْدِمَةٌ
Office *n.*	مَنْصَبٌ . خِدْمَةٌ . مكتبٌ
Officer *n.*	مَأْمُورٌ . ضَابِطٌ
Official *a.* or *n.*	رَسْمِيٌّ . مَأْمُورٌ
Officiate *v. i.*	قَامَ بِخِدْمَةٍ أَوْ وَظِيفَةٍ
Officious *a.*	مُتَكَلِّفٌ . فُضُولِيٌّ
Officiousness *n.*	فُضُولٌ . تعرُّضٌ
Offscouring *n.*	سُقَاطَةٌ . نُفَايَةٌ . نَجَاسَةٌ
Offset *v. t.* or *n.*	وَازَنَ . بَادَلَ . بَدَلٌ
Offshoot *n.*	فَرْعٌ . عُسْلُجٌ
Offspring *n.*	ذُرِّيَّةٌ . نَسْلٌ
Oft / **Often** } *ad.*	كَثِيرًا مَا . مِرَارًا
Ogle *v. t.*	غَمَزَ ـِ عِشْقًا
Oh *inter.*	آه . اوَّاه
Oh that !	يَا لَيْتَ
Oil *n.* or *v. t.*	زَيْتٌ . دهنٌ . زَيَّتَ
Oil-cloth *n.*	مُشَمَّعٌ
Oily *a.*	دهنٌ . زَيْتِيٌّ
Ointment *n.*	دِهْنٌ . مَرْهَمٌ
Old *a.*	طَاعِنٌ فِي ٱلسِّنِّ . شَيْخٌ . عَتِيقٌ
Olden *a.*	قَدِيمٌ
Oleander *n.*	دِفْلَى . دِفْلٌ

Olive *n.* زَيْتُونَةٌ

Omelet *n.* عُجَّةٌ

Omen *n.* فَأْلٌ . طِيرة . عَلَامَةٌ

Ominous *a.* مُنْذِرٌ بالسُّوءِ

Omission *n.* إِهْمَالٌ . تَرْكٌ . إِسْقَاطٌ

Omit *v. t.* تَرَكَ ـُ . أَهْمَلَ . أَسْقَطَ

Omnibus *n.* عَجَلَةٌ كَبِيرَةٌ

Omnipotence *n.* أَلْقُدْرَةُ عَلَى كُلِّ شَيْءٍ

Omnipotent *a.* أَلْقَادِرُ عَلَى كُلِّ شَيْءٍ

Omnipresence *n.* أَلْحُضُورُ فِي كُلِّ مَكَانٍ

Omnipresent *a.* أَلْحَاضِرُ فِي كُلِّ مَكَانٍ

Omniscience *n.* أَلْعِلْمُ بِكُلِّ شَيْءٍ

Omniscient *a.* أَلْعَالِمُ بِكُلِّ شَيْءٍ

Omnivorous *a.* آكِلٌ مِنْ كُلِّ شَيْءٍ

On *pr.* or *ad.* عَلَى . عِنْدَ . إِلَى قُدَّامٍ

Once *ad.* مَرَّةً . قَبْلاً . وَقْتًا مَّا

One *a.* or *n.* وَاحِدٌ (ة) . أَحَدٌ . ذَات

One-eyed *a.* أَعْوَرُ

Oneness *n.* وَحْدَانِيَّةٌ

Onerous *a.* ثَقِيلٌ . شَاقٌّ

Onion *n.* بَصَلَةٌ

Only *a.* وَحِيدٌ . وَحْدَهُ . لَا غَيْرُ

Onset / Onslaught } *n.* هُجُومٌ . حَمْلَةٌ . بَطْشٌ

Onward / Onwards } *ad.* إِلَى قُدَّامٍ . تَقَدُّمًا

Onyx *n.* جَزْعٌ (حَجَرٌ كَرِيمٌ)

Ooze *v. i.* رَشَحَ ـَ . نَضَّ ـِ

Opaque *a.* مُظْلِمٌ . غَيْرُ شَفَّافٍ

Open *v. t.* or *i.* or *a.* فَتَحَ ـَ . إِنْفَتَحَ . مَفْتُوحٌ

Opening *n.* فَتْحَةٌ . شَقٌّ . بَابٌ

Openly *ad.* عَلَانِيَةً . جِهَارًا

Openness *n.* خُلُوصٌ . مُجَاهَرَةٌ

Opera *n.* رِوَايَةٌ مُوسِيقِيَّةٌ

Operate *v. i.* or *t.* جَرَى ـِ . أَثَّرَ . عَمِلَ ـَ

Operation *n.* عَمَلٌ إِجْرَاءٌ . عَمَلِيَّةٌ

Operative *a.* عَامِلٌ . مُؤَثِّرٌ . عَمَلِيٌّ

Operator *n.* عَامِلٌ . جَرَّاحٌ

Ophthalmic *a.* عينيٌّ

Ophthalmia *n.* إِلْتِهَابُ ٱلْعَيْنِ . رَمَدٌ

Opiate *n.* دَوَاءٌ أَفْيُونِيٌّ . مُنَوِّمٌ

Opinion *n.* رَأْيٌ . ظَنٌّ . إِعْتِقَادٌ

Opinionated / **Opinionative** *a.* عَنِيدُ ٱلرَّأْيِ

Opium *n.* أَفْيُونٌ

Opponent *n.* خَصْمٌ . مُقَاوِمٌ

Opportune *a.* فِي مَحَلِّهِ أَوْ حِينِهِ

Opportunity *n.* فُرْصَةٌ

Oppose *v. t.* ضَادَّ . عَارَضَ . مَانَعَ

Opposite *a.* مُقَابِلٌ . حِذَاءَ . مُضَادٌّ

Opposition *n.* مُضَادَّةٌ . مُعَارَضَةٌ

Oppress *v. t.* ظَلَمَ ـ . بَغَى ـ . ضَايَقَ

Oppression *n.* ظُلْمٌ . جَوْرٌ

Oppressive *a.* / **Oppressor** *n.* ظَالِمٌ . مُضَايِقٌ . بَاغٍ

Opprobrious *a.* مُعِيبٌ . مُحَقِّرٌ . مُخْزٍ

Opprobrium *n.* عَارٌ . عَيْبٌ . خِزْيٌ

Optic / **Optical** *a.* بَصَرِيٌّ . مُخْتَصٌّ بِعِلْمِ ٱلنُّورِ

Optician *n.* صَانِعُ آلَاتٍ بَصَرِيَّةٍ

Optics *n.* عِلْمُ ٱلنُّورِ وَٱلْإِبْصَارِ

Optimism *n.* اَلتَّفَاؤُلُ بِٱلْخَيْرِ

Option *n.* خِيَارٌ

Optional *a.* إِخْتِيَارِيٌّ

Opulence *n.* ثَرْوَةٌ . يُسْرٌ

Opulent *a.* غَنِيٌّ . مُوسِرٌ

Or *conj.* أَوْ . أَمْ

Oracle *n.* وَحْيٌ . رَأْيٌ حَكِيمٌ

Oracular *a.* مُتَكَلِّمٌ بِسُلْطَةٍ

Oral *a.* شِفَاهِيٌّ . لَفْظِيٌّ

Orange *n.* بُرْتُقَالٌ

Orang-outang *n.* قِرْدٌ يُشْبِهُ ٱلْإِنْسَانَ

Oration *n.* خُطْبَةٌ

Orator *n.* خَطِيبٌ

Oratorical *n.* خِطَابِيٌّ . بَلِيغٌ

Oratory *n.* عِلْمُ ٱلْخِطَابَةِ . مُصَلًّى

Orb *n.* كُرَةٌ

Orbit *n.* مَدَارُ كَوْكَبٍ. تَجْوِيفُ ٱلْعَيْنِ

Orchard *n.* بُسْتَانٌ . حَدِيقَةٌ

Orchestra *n.* جَمَاعَةُ عَازِفِينَ مَوْقِفُهُمْ

Ordain *v. t.* أَقَامَ . أَمَرَ . رَسَمَ

Ordeal *n.* إِمْتِحَانٌ شَدِيدٌ . مِحْنَةٌ

Order *v. t.* أَمَرَ . رَتَّبَ . دَبَّرَ

Order *n.* أَمْرٌ . تَرْتِيبٌ . رُتْبَةٌ

Orderly *a.* (مُرَاسَلَةٌ) . مُرَتَّبٌ . مُنْتَظِمٌ

Ordinance *n.* سُنَّةٌ . فَرْضٌ . حُكْمٌ

Ordinarily *ad.* إِعْتِيَادِيًّا . غَالِبًا

Ordinary *a.* إِعْتِيَادِيٌّ . مَأْلُوفٌ

Ordination *n.* إِقَامَةٌ . تَعْيِينٌ . رَسْمٌ

Ordnance *n.* مَدَافِعُ وَمُتَعَلِّقَاتُهَا

Ore *n.* خَلِيطٌ يُسْتَخْرَجُ ٱلْمَعْدِنُ مِنْهُ

Organ *n.* (ارْغُن) عُضْوٌ . وَاسِطَةٌ

Organic *a.* عُضْوِيٌّ . آلِيٌّ . أَسَاسِيٌّ

Organism *n.* بِنَاءٌ . آلِيٌّ

Organist *n.* عَازِفٌ عَلَى ٱلارْغُنِ

Organization *n.* نِظَامٌ . تَرْتِيبٌ

Organize *v. t.* نَظَّمَ . رَتَّبَ . جَهَّزَ

Orgies *n. pl.* بَطَرٌ مُفْرِطٌ . سُكْرٌ

Orient *n.* ٱلشَّرْقُ ٱلأَقْطَارُ ٱلشَّرْقِيَّةُ

Oriental *a.* or *n.* شَرْقِيٌّ . شَرْقِيُّ ٱلْوَطَنِ

Orientalism *n.* إِصْطِلَاحٌ شَرْقِيٌّ

Orientalist *n.* عَالِمٌ بِلُغَاتِ ٱلشَّرْقِ

Orifice *n.* مَنْفَذٌ . فَتْحَةٌ

Origin *n.* أَصْلٌ . مَبْدَأٌ . مَصْدَرٌ

Original *a.* أَصْلِيٌّ . أَوَّلِيٌّ . غَرِيبٌ

Original *n.* أَصْلٌ . صُورَةٌ أَصْلِيَّةٌ

Originality *n.* أَصْلِيَّةٌ . إِبْدَاعٌ . ذَكَاءٌ

Originate *v. t.* or *i.* أَبْدَعَ . أَوْجَدَ . نَشَأَ

Originator *n.* مُبْدِعٌ . مُخْتَرِعٌ . مُبْتَكِرٌ

Orion *n.* أَلْجَبَّارُ . أَلْجَوْزَاءُ

Ornament *n.* زِينَةٌ . زَخْرَفَةٌ

Ornament *v. t.* زَيَّنَ . زَخْرَفَ

Ornamental *a.* زِينيٌّ . مزيَّن

Ornate *a.* مُزَخْرَفٌ . مزوَّقٌ

Ornithology *n.* عِلْمٌ يبْحَثُ فِيهِ عَنِ ٱلطُّيورِ

Orphan *n.* يَتِيمٌ ج أَيْتَامٌ . يتَامَى

Orphanage *n.* دَارُ ٱلْيتَامَى

Orthodox *a.* قَوِيمُ ٱلْمَذْهَبِ (ارثوذكس)

Orthodoxy *n.* صِحَّةُ ٱلْمَذْهَبِ

Orthography *n.* عِلْمُ ٱلتَّهجِئَة

Oscillate *v. i.* ذَبْذَبَ . إِرْتَجَجَ . خطَرَ

Oscillation *n.* ذَبْذَبةٌ . إِرْتِجَاجٌ

Osseous *a.* عَظْمِيٌّ

Ossify *v. t.* or *i.* حَوَّلَهُ أَوْ تَحَوَّلَ عَظْماً

Ostensible *a.* ظَاهِرٌ . مُدَّعًى

Ostentation *n.* تَفَاخُرٌ . مُبَاهَاةٌ

Ostentatious *a.* مُتَفَاخِرٌ . مُتَبَاهٍ

Osteology *n.* عِلْمُ ٱلْعِظَامِ

Ostracise *v. t.* نَفَى ـِ . طَرَدَ ـُ

Ostrich *n.* نَعَامَةٌ

Other *a.* آخَرُ . ذَاكَ

Otherwise *ad.* وَإِلَّا . خِلَافاً لِذَلِكَ

Ottar *n.* عِطْرٌ

Otter *n.* كَلْبُ ٱلْمَاءِ

Ottoman *n.* عُثْمَانِيٌّ

Ought *v. i.* وَجَبَ ـِ . لَزِمَ ـَ

Ounce *n.* اوْقِيَّةٌ أَنْكِلِيزِيَّةٌ أَوْ طِبِّيَّةٌ

Our, Ours *pro.* لَنَا . نَا

Ourselves *pro. pl.* نَحْنُ . انْفُسُنَا

Oust *v. t.* طَرَدَ ـُ أَخْرَجَ

Out *ad.* خَارِجاً

Outbid *v. t.* زَايَدَ

Outbreak, Outburst *n.* ثَوْرَةٌ . إِنْفِجَارٌ

Outcast *n.* مَطْرُودٌ . مَنْفِيٌّ

Outcry *n.* صِيَاحٌ . صرَاخ

Outdo *v. t.* فَاقَ . سَبَقَ ـُ

Outdoor *a.*, Outdoors *adv.* خَارِجَ ٱلْبَيْتِ

Outer *a.* خَارِجِيٌّ

Outermost *a.* أَلأَبْعَدُ عَنِ ٱلْمَرْكَزِ

Outfit *n.* جَهَازٌ. لَوَازِمُ

Outgrow *v. t.* سَبَقَ نُمُوًّا. زَادَ عَلَى

Outhouse *n.* بَيْتٌ خَارِجُ ٱلدَّارِ

Outlandish *a.* غَرِيبٌ. بَرْبَرِيٌّ

Outlaw *n.* فَاقِدُ ٱلْحُقُوقِ ٱلشَّرْعِيَّةِ

Outlay *n.* نَفَقَةٌ. مَصْرُوفٌ

Outlet *n.* مَخْرَجٌ. مَنْفَذٌ. مَصَبٌّ

Outline *n.* or *v. t.* رَسْمٌ مُخْتَصَرٌ. رَسَمَ ـُ

Outlive *v. t.* عَاشَ بَعْدَهُ

Outlook *n.* مَنْظَرٌ. مُرَاقَبَةٌ

Outlying *a.* بَعِيدٌ عَنِ ٱلْمَرْكَزِ. خَارِجِيٌّ

Outmost *a.* أَلأَبْعَدُ عَنِ ٱلْمَرْكَزِ

Outpost *n.* مَرْكَزُ حَرَسٍ خَارِجِيٌّ

Outrage *v. t.* فَضَحَ ـَ. أَسَاءَ إِلَى

Outrage *n.* فَظِيعَةٌ. إِهَانَةٌ. بَغْيٌ

Outrageous *a.* فَظِيعٌ. مُفْرِطُ ٱلْبَغْيِ

Outrider *n.* فَارِسٌ. تَابِعٌ

Outright *ad.* حَالاً. تَمَامًا

Outrun *v. t.* سَبَقَ رَكْضًا

Outset *n.* بَدَاءَةٌ. مَطْلَعٌ

Outside *n.* أَلْخَارِجُ ظَاهِرُهُ

Outskirt *n.* ظَاهِرُ بَلَدٍ. ضَاحِيَةٌ

Outspread *v. t.* بَسَطَ ـُ. مَدَّ ـُ

Outstanding *a.* بَارِزٌ. غَيْرُ مَدْفُوعٍ

Outstrip *v. t.* سَبَقَ ـِ

Outward *a.* or *ad.* خَارِجِيٌّ. ظَاهِرٌ. إِلَى خَارِجٍ

Outweigh *v. t.* رَجَحَ ـَ. زَادَ وَزْنًا

Outwit *v. t.* فَاقَ حِيلَةً

Outwork *n.* اِسْتِحْكَامٌ. خَارِجِيٌّ

Oval, Ovate *a.* بَيْضِيُّ ٱلشَّكْلِ. إِهْلِيلَجِيٌّ

Ovary *n.* مَبِيضٌ فِي ٱلنَّبَاتِ وَٱلْحَيَوَانِ

Ovation *n.* مَوْكِبٌ. إِكْرَامِيٌّ

Oven *n.* فُرْنٌ. تَنُّورٌ

Over *pr.* or *ad.* فَوْقُ. عَلَى. زِيَادَةً

Overbalance *v. t.* رَجَحَ ـُ. فَاقَ وَزْنًا

Overbearing *a.* مُتَجَبِّرٌ . غَطْرِيسٌ
Overboard *ad.* مِنَ ٱلسَّفِينَةِ . فِي ٱلْبَحْرِ
Overcautious *a.* زَائِدُ ٱلْحَذَرِ
Overcharge *v. t.* أَفْرَطَ فِي ٱلثَّمَنِ أَوِ ٱلْحِمْلِ
Overcoat *n.* جُبَّةٌ فَوْقَانِيَّةٌ
Overcome *v. t.* غَلَبَ ـِ . قَهَرَ ـَ
Overdo *v. t.* أَفْرَطَ فِي ٱلْعَمَلِ
Overdose *n.* جَرْعَةٌ مُفْرِطَةٌ
Over-due *a.* فَائِتُ ٱلِٱسْتِحْقَاقِ (دين)
Overestimate *v. t.* أَفْرَطَ فِي ٱلتَّقْدِيرِ
Overflow *v.t.* or *n.* فَاضَ ـِ . فَيَضَانٌ
Over-grown *a.* كَثِيرُ ٱلنَّبَاتِ . مُفْرِطُ ٱلنُّمُوِّ
Overhang *v. t.* أَشْرَفَ عَلَى . بَرَزَ ـُ
Overhead *ad.* فَوْقَ ٱلرَّأْسِ
Overhear *v. t.* سَمِعَ ٱتِّفَاقًا
Overland *a.* بِٱلْبَرِّ (سَفَرٌ)
Overlay *v. t.* غَشَّى بِ
Overload *v. t.* ثَقَّلَ ٱلْحِمْلَ
Overlook *v. t.* أَشْرَفَ عَلَى . أَهْمَلَ . عَفَا ـُ
Overmatch *n.* أَقْدَرُ مِنْ
Overmuch *a.* زَائِدٌ . مُفْرِطٌ
Overnight *ad.* مُدَّةَ ٱللَّيْلِ ٱلْمَاضِي
Overpay *v. t.* أَوْفَى فَوْقَ ٱلْحَقِّ
Overplus *n.* فَضْلَةٌ . بَقِيَّةٌ . زِيَادَةٌ
Overpower *v.t.* قَوِيَ عَلَى . قَهَرَ ـَ
Overrate *v. t.* أَفْرَطَ فِي ٱلتَّثْمِينِ
Overreach *v. t.* غَبَنَ ـِ . جَاوَزَ
Overrule *v. t.* أَبْطَلَ تَأْثِيرَهُ أَوْ حَوَّلَهُ
Overruling *a.* مُتَسَلِّطٌ . ضَابِطٌ
Overrun *v. t.* أَفْرَطَ . غَطَّى . غَزَا ـُ
Oversee *v. t.* نَاظَرَ
Overseer *n.* نَاظِرٌ . وَكِيلٌ
Overshoe *n.* جُرْمُوقٌ (كَالُوش)
Oversight *n.* إِهْمَالٌ . سَهْوٌ . مُنَاظَرَةٌ
Oversleep *v. t.* تَأَخَّرَ فِي ٱلنَّوْمِ
Overspread *v. t.* إِنْتَشَرَ عَلَى . غَطَّى

Overstep *v. t.* جَاوَزَ . تجَاوَزَ

Overt *a.* ظَاهِرٌ . شَائِعٌ

Overtake *v. t.* لَحِقَ ـَ . أَدْرَكَ . أَلَمَّ ب

Overtask / Overtax } *v. t.* كَلَّفَ فَوْقَ ٱلطَّاقَةِ

Overtax *v. t.* أَفْرَطَ فِي ٱلضَّرِيبَةِ

Overthrow *v. t.* قَلَبَ ـِ . هَزَمَ . هَدَمَ ـِ

Overtly *ad.* ظَاهِرًا . جِهَارًا

Overtop *v. t.* عَلَا ـُ . فَاقَ ـُ

Overture *n.* عَرْضٌ . مُفَاوَضَةٌ . فَاتِحَةٌ

Overturn *v. t.* قَلَبَ . نَكَّسَ

Overweening *a.* مُعْجَبٌ بِنَفْسِهِ . مزهٍ

Overwhelm *v. t.* غَمَرَ ـُ . قَهَرَ ـَ

Overwork *v. t.* شَغَّلَ فَوْقَ ٱلطَّاقَةِ

Oviparous *a.* بَائِضٌ . بَيُوضٌ

Ovum *n.* بَيْضَةٌ . بِزْرَةٌ . جُرْثُومَةٌ

Owe *v. t.* كَانَ مَدْيُونًا . عَلَيْهِ دَيْنٌ

Owing *a.* مَدْيُونٌ . مَطْلُوبٌ . نَاشِئٌ عَنْ

Owl *n.* بُومَةٌ ج بُومٌ

Own *a.* or *v. t.* خَاصَّتُهُ . مَلَكَ ـِ . أَقَرَّ بِ

Owner *n.* صَاحِبٌ . مَالِكٌ . رَبٌّ

Ownership *n.* مِلْكٌ

Ox (*pl.* Oxen). ثَوْرٌ

Oxalis *n.* حُمَّاضٌ (نَبَاتٌ)

Oyster *n.* نَوْعٌ مِنَ ٱلصَّدَفِ . مَحَارَةٌ

P

Pace *n.* or *v. t.* خُطْوَةٌ . خَطَا . مَشَى ـِ

Pacer *n.* رَهْوَان (فَرَسٌ)

Pacific *a.* or *n.* مُسَالِمٌ سِلْمِيٌّ . البَحْرُ المحيط

Pacify *v. t.* سَالَمَ . هَدَّأَ

Pack *v. t.* رَزَمَ ـُ . حَزَمَ ـِ . كَبَسَ ـِ

Pack, **Package** *n.* رِزْمَةٌ . حُزْمَةٌ . فَرْدَةٌ

Packet *n.* حُزْمَةٌ . سَفِينَةٌ سَرِيعَةٌ

Pack-horse *n.* فَرَسٌ لِلحَمْلِ . كَدِيشٌ

Pack-saddle *n.* جُلٌّ (جِلَالٌ)

Pad *n.* or *v. t.* وِسَادَةٌ . حَشَا . بَطَّنَ

Paddle *v. i.* or *n.* جَذَفَ . مِجْذَافٌ

Padlock *n.* قُفْلٌ ج أَقْفَالٌ

Pagan *n.* وَثَنِيٌّ

Paganism *n.* عِبَادَةُ ٱلأَوْثَانِ

Page *n.* صَفْحَةٌ . غُلَامٌ

Page *v. t.* رَقَمَ ٱلأَعْدَادَ عَلَى ٱلصَّفَحَاتِ

Pageant, **Pageantry** *n.* مَوْكِبٌ . إِحْتِفَالٌ . بَهَاءٌ

Pail *n.* دَلْوٌ . سَطْلٌ

Pain *n.* or *v. t.* وَجَعٌ . أَلَمٌ . أَوْجَعَ

Painful *a.* مُوجِعٌ . مُؤْلِمٌ . مُكَدِّرٌ

Painless *a.* بِلَا أَلَمٍ

Pains *n.* إِعْتِنَاءٌ . إِهْتِمَامٌ . دِقَّةٌ

Paint *n.* or *v. t.* دِهَانٌ . دَهَنَ ـُ . صَوَّرَ

Painter *n.* دَهَّانٌ . مُصَوِّرٌ

Painting *n.* دَهْنٌ . تَصْوِيرٌ . صُورَةٌ

Pair *n.* or *v. t.* or *i.* زَوْجٌ . زَاوَجَ . تَزَاوَجَ

Palace *n.* قَصْرٌ . بَلَاطُ ٱلمَلِكِ

Palanquin *n.* تَخْتَرَوَانٌ

Palatable *a.* مَقْبُولٌ لِلذَّوْقِ . لَذِيذٌ

Palate *n.* حَنَكٌ . سَقْفُ ٱلحَلْقِ

Palatial *a.* جَلِيلٌ . عَظِيمٌ . قَصْرِيٌّ

Pale *a.* or *v. i.* مُصْفَرٌّ . بَاهِتٌ . إِصْفَرَّ

Paleness *n.* إِصْفِرَارٌ . بَهْتُ ٱللَّوْنِ

Paleography *n.* خَطُّ ٱلقُدَمَاءِ وَعِلْمُهُ

Paleontology *n.* عِلْمُ ٱلمُتَحَجِّرَاتِ ٱلآلِيَّةِ

Palisade *n.* سِيَاجٌ مِنْ أَوْتَادٍ لِلدِّفَاعِ

Pall *n.* غِطَاءُ ٱلنَّعْشِ . رِدَاءٌ

Pallet *n.* فِرَاشٌ حَقِيرٌ . لَوْحُ مُصَوِّرٍ

Palliate *v. t.* سَتَرَ أَوْ خَفَّفَ بِعُذْرٍ

Palliative *n.* مُسَكِّنُ وَجَعٍ

Pallid *a.* مُصْفَرٌّ

Palm *n.* نَخْل. رَاحَةُ ٱلْيَدِ

Palm-Sunday *n.* أَحَد ٱلشَّعَانِين

Palpable *a.* مَا يُلْمَسُ . وَاضِحٌ

Palpitate *v. i.* خَفَقَ ـُ

Palpitation *n.* خَفَقَانٌ

Palsied *a.* مَفْلُوجٌ

Palsy *n.* فَالِجٌ

Paltry *n.* حَقِيرٌ . خَسِيسٌ

Pamper *v. t.* أَشْبَعَ . فَتَقَ

Pamphlet *n.* كُرَّاسَةٌ . رِسَالَة

Pan *n.* طَاجَنٌ . لَكَنٌ

Panacea *n.* عِلَاجٌ لِكُلِّ دَاءٍ

Pancreas *n.* بَنْكَرْيَاسٌ

Pandemonium *n.* مَجْمَعُ ٱلشَّيَاطِين

Pander *v. i.* صَدَمَ شَهَوَاتِ غَيْرِهِ

Pane *n.* لَوْحُ . زُجَاجٍ

Panegyric *n.* مَدِيحٌ . تَبْجِيل

Panel *n.* لَوْحٌ . (حَشْوَةُ بَابٍ)

Pang *n.* أَلَمٌ وَقْتِيٌّ شَدِيدٌ . مَخَاضٌ

Panic *n.* رَوْعٌ فُجَائِيٌّ بَاطِلٌ

Pannier *n.* قُفَّةٌ . زِبِّيل أو زِنْبِيل

Panoply *n.* درعٌ كَامِلَةٌ

Panorama *n.* مَنْظَرٌ . شَامِلٌ

Pant *v. i.* نَهَجَ ـَ لَهِثَ ـَ

Pantalets / Pantaloons *n.* سِروَالٌ ج سَرَاوِيلُ

Pantheism *n.* مَذْهَبُ أُلُوهِيَّةِ ٱلْكَوْنِ

Pantheist *n.* مُعْتَقِدٌ بِأُلُوهِيَّةِ ٱلْكَوْنِ

Panther *n.* نَمِرٌ ج نُمُرٌ وَنُمُورَةٌ

Pantomime *n.* تَشْخِيصٌ بِٱلْإِشَارَات

Pantry *n.* بَيْتُ ٱلْمُونَةِ

Papa *n.* أَبٌ . بَابَا

Papacy *n.* ٱلْبَابَوِيَّة (مَذْهَبٌ)

Papal *a.* بَابَوِيٌّ

Paper *n.* or *a.* وَرَق . جَرِيدَة . مِن وَرَقٍ

Papist *n.* بَابَوِيٌّ تَابِع ٱلْبَابَا

Papyrus *n.* قَصَبُ آلبَرْدِيّ . قِرْطَاسَةٌ
Par *n.* مُسَاوَاة . مُعَادَلَةُ آلقِيمَةِ
Parable *n.* مَثَلٌ ج أَمْثَالٌ
Parabola *n.* قَطْعُ مَخْرُوطِيٌّ . شَلْجَمِيٌّ
Parade *n.* or *v. t.* مَوْكِبٌ . إِحْتَفَلَ
Paradise *n.* فِرْدَوْس . جَنَّةٌ
Paradox *n.* تَنَاقُضٌ بِآلظَّاهِرِ فَقَطْ
Paragraph *n.* فَقْرَةٌ . فَصْلٌ . جُمْلَةٌ
Parallel *n.* or *a.* مُوَازَاةٌ . مُشَابَهَةٌ . مُوَازٍ
Parallelogram *n.* مُرَبَّعٌ مُسْتَطِيلٌ
Paralysis *n.* فَالِجٌ . شَلَلٌ
Paralytic *a.* مَفْلُوجٌ . أَشَلُّ
Paralyze *v. t.* أَشَلَّ
Paramount *a.* رَئِيسِيٌّ . أَلأَعْظَمُ . فَائِقٌ
Paramour *n.* عَاشِقٌ أَو عَاشِقَةٌ
Parapet *n.* مِتْرَاسٌ . سُورٌ
Paraphrase *n.* or *v.t.* تَأْوِيل . فَسَّرَ
Parasite *n.* نَبَات أَو حَيَوَان طُفَيْلِيٌّ

Parasol *n.* شَمْسِيَّةٌ صَغِيرَةٌ
Parcel *n.* or *v. t.* حُزْمَةٌ . رَبْطَةٌ . قَسَمَ ـِ
Parch *v. t.* or *i.* جَفَّفَ . لَفَحَ ـَ . تَجَفَّفَ
Parchment *n.* رِقٌّ مِنْ جِلْدٍ
Pardon *n.* or *v. t.* عَفْوٌ . غُفْرَانٌ . عَفَا ـُ
Pardonable *n.* مِمَّا يُغْفَرُ لَهُ . يُصْفَحُ عَنْهُ
Pare *v. t.* قَشَرَ ـِ . جَلَفَ ـُ . نَقَصَ
Parent *n.* وَالِدٌ (ة) . مَنْشَأٌ
Parentage *n.* أَصْلٌ . نَسَبٌ
Parental *a.* وَالِدِيٌّ
Parenthesis *n.* هِلاَلاَنِ وَجُمْلَةٌ بَيْنَهُمَا
Parenthetical *a.* مُعْتَرِضٌ
Paring *n.* قِشْرَةٌ . قُصَاصَةٌ
Parish *n.* ابْرَشِيَّةٌ
Parity *n.* مُسَاوَاةٌ . مُعَادَلَةٌ . مُشَابَهَةٌ
Park *n.* مُنْتَزَهٌ . غَابَةٌ
Parley *n.* or *v. i.* مُفَاوَضَةٌ . إِئْتَمَرَ
Parliament *n.* مَجْلِسُ آلنُّوَّابِ

Parliamentary *a.* مَنُوطٌ بِٱلْبَارْلَمَنْتِ

Parlour *n.* غُرْفَةُ ٱلْإِسْتِقْبَالِ

Parole *n.* كَلَامُ شَرَفٍ . عَهْدٌ

Paroxysm *n.* نَوْبَةُ مَرَضٍ . دَوْرٌ

Parricide *n.* قَتْلُ ٱلْوَالِدَيْنِ أَوْ أَقَارِبِهِمَا

Parrot *n.* بَبْغَاءُ

Parry *v. t.* دَفَعَ ـَ . جَانَبَ . إِجْتَنَبَ

Parse *v. t.* أَعْرَبَ

Parsimonious *n.* قَتُورٌ . شَحِيحٌ

Parsimony *n.* قَتْرٌ . إِقْتِصَادٌ زَائِدٌ

Parsley *n.* بَقْدُونِسٌ

Parsnip *n.* جَزَرٌ أَبْيَضُ

Parson *n.* قِسِّيسٌ . خُورِيٌّ

Parsonage *n.* بَيْتُ ٱلْقِسِّيسِ

Part *n.* قِسْمٌ . حِصَّةٌ . جَانِبٌ

Part *v. t.* or *i.* فَصَلَ ـِ . قَاسَمَ . إِفْتَرَقَ

Partake *v. t.* إِشْتَرَكَ . تَنَاوَلَ

Partial *a.* جُزْئِيٌّ . مُحَابٍ

Partially *ad.* جُزْئِيًّا . بِمُحَابَاةٍ

Participant *n.* مُشْتَرِكٌ . مُتَنَاوِلٌ

Participate *v. t.* إِشْتَرَكَ . أَخَذَ حِصَّةً

Participation *n.* إِشْتِرَاكٌ . إِتِّخَاذٌ

Participle *n.* إِسْمُ فَاعِلٍ أَوْ مَفْعُولٍ

Particle *n.* ذَرَّةٌ . دَقِيقَةٌ . حَرْفٌ

Particular *a.* خَاصٌّ . مُدَقِّقٌ

Particular *n.* مَادَّةٌ . خَاصَّةٌ . تَفَاصِيلُ

Particularity *n.* خَاصِّيَّةٌ . دِقَّةٌ . تَفْصِيلٌ

Particularize *v. t.* خَصَّصَ . فَصَّلَ . دَقَّقَ

Parting *n.* إِفْتِرَاقٌ . وَدَاعٌ

Partisan *n.* حَلِيفٌ . مُتَحَزِّبٌ

Partition *n.* تَقْسِيمٌ . قِسْمَةٌ . حَاجِزٌ

Partly *ad.* بَعْضًا . جُزْئِيًّا

Partner *n.* شَرِيكٌ . رَفِيقٌ

Partnership *n.* شِرْكَةٌ

Partridge *n.* حَجَلٌ

Party *n.* حِزْبٌ . جَمَاعَةٌ . فَرِيقٌ

Paschal *a.* خاصٌّ بعيدِ ٱلفِصْحِ

Pashalic *n.* ولايةُ باشا

Pass *n.* ممرٌّ . تذكرة . حال

Pass *v. t.* or *i.* إجتاز . عبَرَ . عبّرَ . مرَّ ب

Passable *a.* ممَّا يُمرُّ عليهِ . جائزٌ

Passage *n.* ممرٌّ . مرورٌ . جملة

Passenger *n.* مسافرٌ . راكبٌ

Passing *a.* مارٌّ . وقتيٌّ . زائل

Passion *n.* انفعالٌ شديدٌ . هوًى

Passionate *a.* سريع ٱلغضب . محتدٌّ

Passive *a.* قابِل تأثيرٍ . ساكنٌ . ٱلمجهول

Passover *n.* عيد ٱلفِصْح

Passport *n.* تذكرة ٱلمرور

Past *pr.* or *a.* or *n.* وراءَ . عبرٌ . ماضٍ

Paste *n.* or *v. t.* عصيدةٌ . لازقةٌ . ألزقَ

Pasteboard *n.* ورقٌ سميك . كرتون

Pastime *n.* لعبٌ . لهوٌ

Pastor *n.* راعٍ . قسّيسٌ

Pastoral *a.* رعويٌّ . قسّيسيٌّ

Pastry *n.* كعك . فطائرُ

Pasturage / Pasture *n.* مرعًى . مرتعٌ

Pat *v. t.* or *n.* لطمَ خفيفاً ولطفاً

Pat *a.* في محلّهِ . غايةِ ٱلموافقة

Patch *n.* or *v. t.* رقعةٌ . رقَّعَ . رفأَ

Pate *n.* رأس . هامة

Patent *n.* or *v. t.* امتيازٌ . أعطى امتيازاً

Patent *a.* واضحٌ . جليٌّ . جهاريٌّ

Paternal *a.* أبويٌّ . إرثيٌّ

Paternity *n.* أبوّةٌ

Path *n.* سبيل . صراطٌ . سلوك

Pathetic *a.* مؤثّرٌ في ٱلعواطف

Pathless *a.* ما لا يُسلَك . لا طريقَ فيهِ

Pathology *n.* عِلمُ ٱلأمراض

Pathos *n.* ما يُهيّجُ ٱلعواطف

Pathway *n.* مسلك . طريقٌ . ممرٌّ

Patience *n.* صبرٌ . أناة

Patient *a.* or *n.* صَبُورٌ . مَرِيضٌ

Patois *n.* لغوٌ . لَهْجَةٌ غَيْرُ فَصِيحَةٍ

Patriarch *n.* رَئِيسُ ٱلآبَاءِ . بطرك

Patriarchate *a.* بطرَكِيَّة

Patrician *n.* or *a.* نَجِيبٌ . شَرِيفٌ

Patrimony *n.* مِيرَاثٌ

Patriot *n.* }
Patriotic *a.* } مُحِبُّ ٱلْوَطَنِ

Patriotism *n.* مَحَبَّةُ ٱلْوَطَنِ

Patrol *n.* or *v. i.* عسسٌ . دوْرِيَّة . عسَّ ـُ

Patron *n.* وَلِيٌّ . مُحَامٍ . نَصِيرٌ

Patronage *n.* مُوَالَاةٌ . مُحَامَاةٌ

Patronize *v. t.* وَالَى . عَضَدَ ـُ . أَيَّدَ

Pattern *n.* or *v. t.* انْمُوذَجٌ . مِثَالٌ . تَمَثَّلَ بِ

Paucity *n.* قِلَّةٌ

Paunch *n.* بَطْنٌ . جَوْفٌ

Pauper *n.* فَقِيرٌ . عَائِشٌ مِنْ صَدَقَاتٍ

Pauperism *n.* فَقْرٌ . مَسْكَنَةٌ

Pauperize *v. t.* افْقَرَ

Pause *n.* or *v.i.* وَقْفٌ . فِتْرَةٌ . وَقَفَ

Pave *v. t.* بَلَطَ . رَصَفَ ـُ . سَهَّلَ

Pavement *n.* بَلَاطٌ . رَصْفٌ . تَبْلِيطٌ

Pavillion *n.* خَيْمَةٌ . مِظَلَّةٌ

Paw *n.* or *v. i.* كَفُّ ٱلْحَيَوَانِ . بَحَثَ بِهِ

Pawn *n.* or *v. t.* رَهِينَةٌ . رَهَنَ ـَ

Pawnbroker *n.* مُرْتَهِنٌ . مُسْتَرْهِنٌ

Pay *n.* or *v. i.* أُجْرَةٌ . أَوْفَى . ادَّى

Payable *a.* مُسْتَحِقٌّ . مَا يُوْفَى

Paymaster *n.* مُؤَدِّي ٱلاجْرَةِ

Payment *n.* إِيفَاءٌ . دَفْعٌ . قِسْطٌ

Pea *n.* جِلْبَانٌ . بِسِلَّةٌ

Peace *n.* سَلَامٌ . صُلْحٌ . رَاحَةٌ

Peaceable *a.* مُسَالِمٌ . مُطْمَئِنٌّ

Peaceful *a.* سَلْمِيٌّ . سَاكِنٌ

Peacemaker *n.* مُصَالِحٌ . صَانِعُ سَلَامٍ

Peach *n.* (دُرَّاق . خَوْخ) . دُرَاقِنٌ

Peacock *n.* طَاوُوسٌ ج طَوَاوِيسُ

Peak *n.* قِمَّة . رَأْسُ جَبَلٍ
Peal *n.* or *v. i.* صَوْت قَوِيّ . صَوَّت
Pear *n.* إِنْجَاص . إِجَّاص . كُمَّثْرى
Pearl *n.* لُؤْلُؤَة . دُرَّة
Peasant *n.* فلاح
Peasantry *n.* أَلْفَلاَّحُون
Pebble *n.* حَصَاة ج حَصَيَات وَحَصًى
Peck *n.* مِكْيَال يَسَعُ نَحْوَ مُدٍّ
Pectoral *a.* صَدْرِيّ
Peculation *n.* سَرِقَة . إِخْتِلاَس
Peculiar *a.* خَاصّ . نَادِر
Peculiarity *n.* خَاصِّيَّة . غَرَابَة
Pecuniary *a.* مَالِي . منوط بِالدَّرَاهِمِ
Pedagogue *n.* مُعَلِّمُ أَوْلاَدٍ
Pedant *n.* / **Pedantic** *a.* } مُتَظَاهِر بِالعِلْم
Peddle *v. t.* دَارَ يَبيع
Peddler *n.* عِنْقَاش . بَيَّاع
Pedestal *n.* قَاعِدَةُ عَمُودٍ
Pedestrian *n.* مَاشٍ
Pedigree *n.* نَسَب
Peel *v. t.* or *n.* قَشَرَ . جَرَّدَ . قِشْرَة
Peep *v. i.* or *n.* لاَصَ ـُ . سَارَق نَظْرَة
Peer *n.* نَظِير . شَرِيف . قَرِين
Peerage *n.* رُتْبَةُ الشُّرَفَاءِ . جَمَاعَتُهُمْ
Peerless *a.* فَائِق . لاَ نَظِيرَ لَهُ
Peevish *a.* نَكِد
Peg *n.* or *v. t.* وَتَد . مُسْمَار خَشَبِيّ . سَمَّرَ بِهِ
Pelican *n.* بَجَع (طَائِر)
Pelf *n.* ربح . مَال (خَاصَّة) حَرَام
Pellet *n.* كُرَيَّة . حَبَّة
Pell-mell *ad.* شَذَرَ مَذَرَ
Pelt *v. t.* رَمَى ـ . رَجَمَ ـ
Peltry *n.* جُنُود
Pen *n.* or *v. t.* قَلَم . زَرِيبَة . كَتَبَ ـُ
Penal *a.* قِصَاصِيّ . جَزَائِيّ . عِقَابِيّ
Penalty *n.* قِصَاص . عِقَاب

Penance *n.* كفّارة. عقوبة. تكفيرية

Pencil *n.* or *v. t.* قلم . رسم به

Pendant *n.* شيء معلّق . قرط

Pendent *a.* معلّق . متدلّ

Pending *a.* معلّق . غير مقضيّ

Pendulum *n.* رقّاص ساعة

Penetrate *v. t.* خرق ـِ . تخلّل . أدرك

Penetration *n.* دخول. فطنة. ذكاء

Penetrating *a.* نافذ. حادّ . ذكيّ

Peninsula *n.* شبه جزيرة

Peninsular *a.* على صورة شبه جزيرة

Penitence *n.* توبة . إنسحاق القلب

Penitent *a.* تائب. نادم

Pentientiary *n.* سجن

Penknife *n.* سكّين صغير . (مطوى)

Penman *n.* عالم بالخطّ . كاتب

Penmanship *n.* صناعة الخطّ

Pennant / Pennon *n.* راية . بيرق صغير

Penniless *a.* فقير . مفلس

Penny *n.* (*pl.* pence) نقود أنكليزية = ٢٠ بارة

Pension *n.* راتب . معاش تقاعد

Pensioner *n.* صاحب راتب التقاعد

Pensive *n.* متفكّر . مشغول البال

Pent-up *a.* محصور . محجوز

Pentagon *n.* / Pentagonal *n.* مخمّس الزوايا

Pentateuch *n.* اسفار موسى الخمسة

Pentecost *n.* يوم الخمسين. العنصرة

Penult *n.* مقطع الكلمة قبل الاخير

Penurious *n.* بخيل

Penury *a.* فقر . فاقة . عوز

People *n.* or *v. t.* شعب. أهل. أناس. عمّر

Pepper *n.* or *v. t.* فلفل . فلفل

Peppermint *n.* ضرب من النعنع

Peradventure *ad.* لعلّ . عسى

Perambulate *v. t.* دار ـُ . طاف ـُ

Perceivable *a.* ما يرى . ما يدرك

Perceive *v. t.* رَأَى ـَ شعرَ ـُ . أَدْرَكَ

Percent *ad.* بِالْمِئَةِ

Percentage *n.* نِسبةٌ في الْمِئَةِ

Perceptible *a.* *see* Perceivable.

Perception *n.* شعورٌ . إِدْرَاكٌ

Perch *v. t.* جثَمَ ـُ

Perchance *ad.* لَعَلَّ . رُبَّمَا

Percipient *a.* مدْرِكٌ . شَاعِرٌ

Percolate *v. i.* or *t.* رَشَحَ ـَ . صفى

Percolation *n.* رَشْحٌ . تَصْفِيَةٌ

Percussion *n.* طَرْقٌ . صدْمٌ . قَرْعٌ

Perdition *n.* تَلَفٌ . هلاكٌ

Peremptory *a.* جازِمٌ . قَطْعِيٌّ

Perennial *a.* مستَمِرٌّ طُولَ السَّنَةِ

Perfect *a.* تَامٌّ . كَامِلٌ

Perfect *v. t.* كَمَّلَ . أَنْجزَ . أَنفذَ

Perfection *n.* كَمَالٌ . سَلامَةٌ

Perfidious *n.* غَدَّارٌ . خوَّانٌ

Perfidy *n.* غدْرٌ . خيانَةٌ . خِداعٌ

Perforate *v. t.* ثَقَبَ ـُ . خرَق ـُ

Perforation *n.* ثَقْبٌ . خرْقٌ

Perforce *ad.* رغماً . جبْرًا

Perform *v. t.* عمِلَ ـَ . أَنْجزَ . أَجرَى

Performance *n.* عمَل ـ إِنْجازٌ

Performer *n.* عامِلٌ . مُشَخِّصٌ

Perfume *n.* or *v. t.* عِطْرٌ . عطرَ

Perfumery *n.* عِطْرٌ

Perhaps *ad.* رُبَّمَا . عسَى . لَعَلَّ

Pericardium *n.* شغَافٌ . غِلافُ الْقَلْبِ

Peril *n.* or *v. t.* خطَرٌ . خاطَرَ بِ

Perilous *a.* خطِرٌ . مُخْطِرٌ

Period *n.* مدة . عصْرٌ . دَوْرٌ

Periodic / Periodical *a.* دَوْرِيٌّ

Periodical *n.* نَشْرَةٌ . جرِيدَةٌ

Periosteum *n.* سمْحَاقٌ . غشَاءُ الْعَظْمِ

Perish *v. i.* هلَكَ ـِ . بادَ ـ فني ـَ

Perishable *a.* سرِيعُ الزَّوَالِ أَوْ الْفسادِ

Perjure v. t. حَنَثَ ـ فِي. حَلَفَ ـِ زُوراً

Perjury n. حِنْثٌ . يَمِين زُورٍ

Permanence / Permanency n. دَوَامٌ . بَقَاءٌ

Permanent a. بَاقٍ . ثَابِتٌ . مُسْتَمِرٌّ

Permeable a. مَا يَتَخَلَّلُ. مَا يَنفُذُ فِيهِ

Permeate v. t. تَخَلَّلَ . نَفَذَ ـ فِي

Permissible a. مُبَاحٌ . جَائِزٌ

Permission n. إِذْنٌ . رُخْصَةٌ

Permit v. t. أَذِنَ ـ . سَمَحَ ـ

Pernicious a. مُؤْذٍ . مُهْلِكٌ . مُفْسِدٌ

Perpendicular a. عَمُودِيٌّ . قَائِمٌ

Perpetrate v. t. فَعَلَ ـَ . ارْتَكَبَ

Perpetrator n. فَاعِلٌ . مُرْتَكِبٌ

Perpetual a. دَائِمٌ . مُسْتَمِرٌّ . مُؤَبَّدٌ

Perpetuate v. t. أَدَامَ . خَلَّدَ

Perpetuity n. دَوَامٌ . بَقَاءٌ

Perplex v. t. بَهَتَ ـ . حَيَّرَ. شَوَّشَ

Perplexing a. مُحَيِّرٌ.مُشَوِّشٌ.مُشْكِلٌ

Perplexity n. حَيْرَةٌ . إِرْتِبَاكٌ

Perquisite n. رَاتِبٌ إِضَافِيٌّ.عَرَضِيٌّ

Persecute v.t. إِضْطَهَدَ.عَنَّتَ.ظَلَمَ ـِ

Persecution n. إِضْطِهَادٌ . تَعَدٍّ

Persecutor n. مُضْطَهِدٌ

Perseverance n. مُوَاظَبَةٌ . مُدَاوَمَةٌ

Persevere v.t. وَاظَبَ. دَاوَمَ. لاَزَمَ

Persian a. عَجَمِيٌّ . فَارِسِيٌّ

Persist v. i. أَصَرَّ عَلَى. ثَابَرَ عَلَى

Persistence / Persistency n. إِصْرَارٌ .مُثَابَرَةٌ

Persistent / Persisting a. مُصِرٌّ . مُثَابِرٌ

Person n. شَخْصٌ . أَلذَاتُ . أُقْنُومٌ

Personal a. شَخْصِيٌّ . ذَاتِيٌّ

Personate / Personify v. t. شَخَّصَ . مَثَّلَ

Personification n. تَشْخِيصٌ

Perspicacity n. ذَكَاءٌ . بَصِيرَةٌ

Perspicuous n. جَلِيٌّ . وَاضِحٌ

Perspiration n. عَرَقٌ . رَشِيحٌ

Perspire *v. i.* عَرِقَ . رَشَحَ ـَ

Persuade *v. t.* أَقنعَ . حَمَلَ على

Persuasion *n.* إِرْضَاءٌ . إِقْنَاع . إِعتِقَادٌ

Persuasive *a.* مُرْضٍ . مستميل

Pert *a.* وَقِحٌ . سلِيط

Pertain *v. i.* إِختصَّ ب

Pertinacious *a.* مُصِرٌّ . عنيد

Pertinacity *n.* إِصْرَارٌ . عنادٌ

Pertinence / **Pertinency** *n.* مُوَافقَةٌ . ملاءمة

Pertinent *a.* سدِيدٌ . مناسبٌ

Perturbation *n.* قلَقٌ . إِقلاقٌ

Perusal *n.* قِرَاءَة . مطَالعة

Peruse *v. t.* قرَأَ ـَ . طَالعَ

Pervade *v. t.* شمِلَ ـُ . عمَّ ـُ . تخلَّل

Pervasion *n.* تخلّلٌ . شمُولٌ

Perverse *a.* متمرّدٌ . شَكِسٌ

Perversion *n.* إِضلالٌ . إِفسادٌ . تحْرِيفٌ

Perversity *n.* عِنادٌ . شكَاسَةٌ

Pervert *v. t.* أَضَلَ . حَرَّفَ . افسدَ

Pest *a.* وَبَاءٌ . ضرَرٌ شدِيدٌ

Pester *v. t.* اقلَقَ . أَضْجَرَ . ازعجَ

Pesthouse *n.* مستشفًى لِأَمْرَاضٍ معْدِيَةٍ

Pestiferous / **Pestilential** *a.* وَبَائِيٌّ مُضِرٌ . مفْسِدٌ

Pestilence *n.* وَبَاءٌ

Pestilent *a.* مُضِرٌّ . مُفْسِدٌ

Pestle *n.* مِدَقَّةٌ . مِطْرَقَة

Pet *n.* or *v. t.* عَزِيزٌ . مدلَّلٌ . دَلل

Petal *n.* وَرَقَةُ زَهرَةٍ

Petiole *n.* سَاقُ وَرَقَةٍ

Petition *n.* طَلَبٌ . دُعَاءٌ . عرِيضة

Petition *v. t.* طَلَبَ ـُ . قَدمَ عَرِيضةً

Petrifaction *n.* تحجرٌ . مُحَجَّرَة

Petrify *v. t.* or *i.* حَجَّرَ . تحَجَّرَ

Petroleum *n.* زَيتٌ . معْدَنيٌّ . بترُولٌ

Petticoat *n.* فُسْتَانٌ تحتيٌّ . تنورَة

Pettish *a.* نَكِدٌ . شَكِسٌ

Petty *a.* صَغِيرٌ . طَفِيفٌ . دَنِيءٌ

Petulance *n.* نَكَدٌ . شَرَاسَة

Petulant *a.* نَكِدٌ . شَرِسٌ . مُتَذَمِّرٌ

Pew *n.* مَقْعَدٌ فِي كَنِيسَةٍ

Pewter *n.* مُرَكَّبُ ٱلْقَصْدِيرِ وَٱلرَّصَاصِ

Phalanx *n.* كَتِيبَة . كَثِيفَةٌ مُرَبَّعَة

Phantasm *n.* تَصَوُّرٌ . خَيَال

Phantom *n.* طَيْفٌ . خَيَالٌ

Pharaoh *n.* فِرْعَوْن

Pharissee *n.* فَرِّيسِيٌّ

Pharisaic *a.* مِثْلَ ٱلْفَرِّيسِيِّ . مُرَاءٍ

Pharisaism *n.* رِيَاءٌ . مَذْهَبُ ٱلْفَرِّيسِيِّ

Pharmaceutic / Pharmaceutical *a.* صَيْدَلِيٌّ أَجْزَائِيٌّ

Pharmacist *n.* صَيْدَلِيٌّ

Pharmacopœia *n.* ٱلْأَقْرَابَاذِين

Pharmacy *n.* أَجْزَائِية . صَيْدَلِيَّة .

Pharos *n.* مَنَارَةٌ

Pharynx *n.* بُلْعُومٌ

Phase *n.* مَنْظَرٌ . صُورَةٌ . حَالٌ

Phenomenon *n.* ظَاهِرَةٌ . حَادِثَةٌ

Phial *n.* قَارُورَةٌ . (قِنِّينَةٌ)

Philanthropist *n.* مُحِبُّ ٱلْبَشَرِ

Philanthropy *n.* مَحَبَّةُ ٱلْبَشَرِ

Philippic *n.* خُطْبَةُ طَعْنٍ

Philology *n.* عِلْمُ ٱللُّغَة

Philosopher *n.* فَيْلَسُوفٌ

Philosophic / Philosophical *a.* فَلْسَفِيٌّ

Philsophy *n.* فَلْسَفَة

Phlegm *n.* بَلْغَمٌ

Phlegmatic *a.* بَلْغَمِيٌّ . بَارِدٌ

Phonetic *a.* صَوْتِيٌّ

Phosphorescent *a.* مُضِيءٌ بِضَوْءٍ خَفِيفٍ

Phosphorus *n.* فُصْفُور

Photograph *n.* صُورَةٌ شَمْسِيَّة

Photography *n.* ٱلتَّصْوِيرُ ٱلشَّمْسِيُّ

Phrase *n.* عِبَارَةٌ . جُمْلَة

Phraseology *n.* صُورَةُ ٱلْكَلَام

Phthisis *n.* دَاءُ آلسِلِّ

Physic *n.* أَلطِّبُّ. دَوَاءٌ

Physical *n.* طَبِيعِيٌّ

Physician *n.* طَبِيبٌ

Physics *n.* عِلْمُ آلطَّبِيعِيَّاتِ

Physiognomy *n.* هَيْئَةُ آلوَجْهِ

Physiology *n.* عِلْمُ آلفِسيُولوجِيَا

Piazza *n.* رِوَاقٌ . سَاحَةٌ

Pick *v. t.* اِلْتَقَطَ — . إِنتَخَبَ

Pick / Pick-axe } *n.* مِعْوَلٌ

Picket *n.* وَتَدٌ . طَلِيعَةُ حَرَسٍ

Pickle *v. t.* or *n.* كَبَسَ فِي خَلٍّ . كَبِيس

Picnic *n.* تَنَزُّهٌ

Pickpocket *n.* لِصٌّ. نَشَّالٌ

Pictorial *a.* تَصَوُّرِيٌّ. صُورِيٌّ

Picture *n.* صُورَةٌ

Picturesque *a.* جَمِيلُ آلمَنظَرِ

Pie *n.* نَوْعٌ مِنَ آلحَلْوَى مَحْشُوٌّ

Piece *n.* قِطْعَةٌ . جُزْءٌ

Piecemeal *ad.* قِطْعَةً فَقِطْعَةً

Pier *n.* دِعَامَة رَصِيفٌ مُمْتَدٌّ فِي آلبَحرِ

Pierce *v. t.* خَرَقَ —ُ . ثَقَبَ —ُ . طَعَنَ

Piercing *a.* خَارِقٌ . حَادٌّ

Piety *n.* تَقْوَى . تَدَيُّنٌ

Pig *n.* خِنوصٌ. خِنْزِيرٌ صَغِيرٌ

Pigeon *n.* حَمَامَةٌ . يَمَامَةٌ

Pigmy *n.* قَزَمُ آلجِنْسِ

Pike *n.* رُمْحٌ . حَرْبَةٌ

Pile *n.* or *v. t.* كَوْمَةٌ . وَتَدٌ. كَوَّمَ

Piles *n. pl.* بَوَاسِيرُ

Pilfer *v. t.* سَرَقَ أَشْيَاءَ طَفِيفَةً

Pilgrim *n.* حَاجٌّ . زَائِرٌ

Pilgrimage *n.* حَجٌّ

Pill *n.* حَبَّةٌ (لِلْعِلَاجِ)

Pillage *n.* or *v. t.* نَهْبٌ سَلْبٌ نَهَبَ

Pillar *n.* عَمُودٌ. اسطُوَانَةٌ

Pillow *n.* مخدة . وسادة

Pilot *n.* or *v.t.* دليل لسفينة . هدى

Pimple *n.* بثرة صغيرة

Pin *n.* or *v. t.* دبوس . ضبط به

Pinch *v. t.* or *n.* قبض ـَ قرص ـَ ضيق على

Pincers / Pinchers } *n.* ملقط . كماشة

Pincushion *n.* وسادة للدبابيس

Pine *n.* or *v. t.* صنوبر . نحل ـَ . تاق ـُ

Pink *n.* or *a.* قرنفل وردي اللون

Pinnacle *n.* قمة . شرفة

Pint *n.* مكيال يسع نحو ٢٠٠ درهم

Pioneer *n.* ممهد الطريق . متقدم

Pious *a.* تقي . متدين

Pipe *n.* قسطل . مزمار . قصبة

Piper *n.* زمار

Pique *n.* or *v.t.* غيظ . ضجر . هاج

Pirates *n.* لصوص البحر . قرصان

Pistachio *n.* فستق

Pistil *n.* مدقة الزهر

Pistol *n.* فرد . طبنجة

Pit *n.* حفرة . هاوية . نقرة

Pitch *n.* قير . درجة الصوت

Pitch *v. t.* طلى بالقير ـِ . رمى . وقع

Pitch *v. i.* or *t.* حط ـُ . نزل . ضرب

Pitcher *n.* إبريق . كوز

Pitfall *n.* حفرة صيد . اغوية

Pith *n.* أب . زبدة . خلاصة

Pithy *a.* سديد

Pitiable *a.* ما يرثى له

Pitiful *a.* شفوق . زهيد . حقير

Pitiless *a.* بلا شفقة . صارم

Pittance *n.* مبلغ زهيد . صدقة زهيدة

Pity *n.* or *v. t.* شفقة . أشفق على

Pivot *n.* محور . مدار

Placard *n.* إعلان

Placate *v. t.* طيب النفس . سكن غيظه

Place *n.* or *v. t.* مكَان . مَوْضِعٌ . وَضَعَ ـَ
Placid *a.* هَادِئٌ . سَاكِنٌ
Plagiarize *v. i.* تَنَحَّلَ . إِنتَحَلَ
Plague *n.* طاعون . وَبَاءٌ . بَلِيَة
Plague *v. t.* أَزْعَجَ . عَنى . كَدَّر
Plain *n.* سَهْلٌ . مِهَادٌ
Plain *a.* سَهْلٌ . وَاضِحٌ . بسيطٌ
Plainly *ad.* جليا . بإِخْلاَصٍ بِبَسَاطةٍ
Plainness *n.* وُضُوحٌ . بَسَاطة . بيَان
Plaint *n.* شَكْوَى . حَنينٌ
Plaintiff *n.* مدَّعٍ شَرْعِيٌّ
Plaintive *a.* محزِنٌ . حَزِينٌ
Plait *v. t.* or *n.* ضفرَ ـِ . ثَنى — . ضَفِيرَة
Plan *n.* تَدْبيرٌ . قَصْدٌ . رَسْمٌ
Plan *v. t.* دَبَّرَ . رَسَمَ — هَنَأَ
Plane *a.* or *n.* مسطَّحٌ . سَطْحٌ . (فَارَة) نجارٍ
Planet *n.* سيارٌ (نجمة)
Planetary *a.* سيَّارِيٌّ

Plank *n.* لَوحٌ سَميكٌ
Plant *n.* or *v. t.* نبتٌ . غرَسَ ـِ
Plantation *n.* منبت . مزرَعَةٌ
Plaster *n.* or *v. t.* طينٌ . لَزْقَة . طَينَ
Plastering *n.* تَكْلِيسٌ . وَرَقَةٌ
Plate *n.* صَحنٌ . آنيَة فِضِيَّةٌ أَوْ ذَهَبيةٌ
Plate *v. t.* لَبس بمَعْدنٍ
Plateau *n.* سَهْلٌ مُرْتَفِعٌ . هضبةٌ
Platform *n.* مِنْبَرٌ . سَطْحٌ مُرْتَفِعٌ
Platter *n.* قَصعَةٌ ج قِصَاعٌ
Plaudit *n.* إِستِحْسَان . مَدْحٌ
Plausible *a.* مُرْضٍ . مِمَّا يصدَّقُ
Play *v. t.* لَعِبَ ـَ . شَخَّصَ . عَزَفَ ـِ
Play *n.* لعبٌ . تسلية
Playful *a.* لعُوبٌ . دَعِبٌ
Playfellow / **Playmate** *n.* رَفيقٌ فِي اللِّعْب
Plaything *n.* لعبة . ألعُوبة
Plea *n.* حُجَّة . إِعتذَارٌ . دُعاء

Plead *v. i.* إِحتَجَّ . إِبتَهَلَ . رَافع

Pleasant / **Pleasing** *a.* سَارٌّ . طَيِّبٌ . انِيسٌ

Pleasantry *n.* مَزْحٌ . هَزْل

Please *v. t.* سَرَّـُ . أَرْضَى . أَعْجَبَ

Pleasure *n.* سُرُورٌ . لَذَّةٌ . إِنْشِرَاحٌ

Plebeian *a.* or *n.* عَامِيٌّ . أَحدُ ٱلْعَوَامِّ

Pledge *v. t.* رَهَنَ . تعهَّدَ . عَرْبَنَ

Pledge *n.* رَهْنٌ . عَهْدٌ . ضَمَانٌ

Plenary *a.* تَامٌّ . كَامِلٌ . عَام

Plenipotentiary *n.* سَفِيرٌ . مُطْلَقٌ

Plenteous / **Plentiful** *a.* وَافِرٌ . غَزِيرٌ . كَثِيرٌ

Plenty *n.* وَفْرٌ . كَثْرَة . غزَارَة

Pleurisy *n.* دَآءُ ذَاتِ ٱلْجَنْبِ

Pliable / **Pliant** *a.* لَيِّنٌ . مُذْعِنٌ

Plight *n.* or *v. t.* عَهْد . حَالٌ . عَهَدَ

Plod *v. t.* سَعَى بِمَشَقَّةٍ . كَدَّ

Plot *n.* مَكِيدَةٌ . مؤَامَرَة . بقعة

Plot *v. t.* or *i.* رَسَمَ . دَبَّرَ . إِحْتَالَ

Plow / **Plough** *n.* or *v. t.* مِحْرَاثٌ . حَرَثَ

Plowshare / **Ploughshare** *n.* سِكَّةُ مِحْرَاثٍ

Pluck *v. t.* or *n.* قَلَعَ . قَطَفَ . شَجَاعَةٌ

Plug *n.* or *v. t.* سِدَادٌ . سَدَّ

Plum *n.* خَوْخٌ . خَوْخَةٌ (بَرْقوق)

Plumage *n.* رِيشٌ

Plume *n.* رِيشَةٌ . وِسَامُ شَرَفٍ

Plummet *n.* مِقْيَاسٌ لِلعُمْقِ . شَاقُول

Plump *a.* or *ad.* سَمِينٌ . مُشْحِمٌ . فَجْأَة

Plunder *v. t.* or *n.* نَهَبَ . سَلَبَ . غَنِيمَةٌ

Plunge *v. t.* or *i.* غَمَسَ . غَطَسَ . خَاضَ

Plural *a.* or *n.* أَكْثَرُ مِنْ وَاحِدٍ . أَلْجَمْعُ

Plurality *n.* أَكْثَرِيَّةٌ . تَعَدُّدٌ

Plus *n.* عَلَامَةُ ٱلْجَمْعِ (+)

Ply *v. t.* or *n.* أَلَحَّ . شغَلَ . جدَّ . ثَنْيَة

Pneumatics *n. sing.* عِلْمُ ٱلْهَوَآءِ

Pneumonia *n.* دَآءُ ذَات ٱلرِّئَةِ

Poach *v. t.* سَرَقَ صَيْدًا . نَهَبَ

Pocket *n.* or *v. t.* جَيْبٌ . وَضَعَ فِيهِ

Pod *n.* قُرْنَةُ نَبَاتٍ

Poem *n.* قَصِيدَةٌ

Poesy *n.* شِعْرٌ . عِلْمُ ٱلنظْمِ

Poet *n.* شَاعِرٌ

Poetic / Poetical *a.* شعرِيٌّ . نَظْمِيٌّ

Poetry *n.* شِعْرٌ . ديوانُ شعرٍ

Poignant *a.* شَدِيد . حَادٌّ . شَاقٌّ

Point *n.* رَأْسٌ . نُقْطَةٌ . مُرَادٌ

Point *v. t.* or *i.* أَشَارَ . سَنَّ . نَقَّطَ . وَجَّهَ

Pointer *n.* دَلِيلٌ . كَلْبُ صَيْدٍ

Pointless *n.* كَلِيلٌ . بِلاَ مَعْنًى

Poise *n.* ثِقْلٌ . مُوَازَنَةٌ

Poison *n.* or *v. t.* سَمٌّ . سَمَّ

Poisonous *a.* سَامٌّ

Poke *n.* or *v. t.* دَفْعٌ . دَفَعَ . وَكَزَ

Poker *n.* مِحْرَاكٌ

Polar *n.* قُطْبِيٌّ

Polarity *n.* أَلاِتِّجَاه نَحْوَ ٱلقُطْبِ

Polarize *v. t.* أَعطَاهُ خَاصِيَةَ ٱلاِتِّجَاه للقُطْبِ

Pole *n.* قُطْبٌ . قَضِيبٌ طَوِيل

Pole-star *n.* نَجْمُ ٱلقُطْبِ

Police *n.* ضَابِطَة مَدِينَةٍ . بُولِيسٌ

Policy *n.* سِيَاسَةٌ . تَدْبِيرٌ

Polish *n.* or *v. t.* صَقْلٌ . صَقَلَ ـُ

Polite *a.* أَدِيبٌ . أَنِيسٌ

Politeness *n.* أَدَبٌ . أُنسٌ

Politic *a.* بَصِيرٌ . فَطِنٌ

Political *a.* سِيَاسِيٌّ

Politics *n. sing.* امُور ٱلسِّيَاسَةِ

Polity *n.* نِظَامُ دوْلَةٍ أَو سِيَاسَةٍ

Poll *n.* or *v. t.* رَاسٌ . إِنْتِخَابٌ . قَيَّدَ ٱلأَسْمَاء

Pollen *n.* هَبَاءُ أَسْدِيَة ٱلنَّبَات

Poll-tax *n.* ضَرِيبَة على ٱلشَّخصِ

Pollute *v. t.* أَفسَدَ . نَجَّسَ . وسَّخَ

Pollution *n.* نَجَاسَةٌ . رَجَاسَة

Poltroon *n.* جَبانٌ . خسيسٌ

Polygamy *n.* تَعَدُّدُ ٱلزَّوْجَاتِ . ضرٌّ

Polygon *n.* كَثِيرُ ٱلاضلاع

Polysyllable *n.* لَفْظَةٌ معدَّدَةُ ٱلْمَقَاطِعِ

Polytheism *n.* أَلْقَوْل بِكَثْرَةِ ٱلآلِهةِ

Pomade *n.* دهان ٱلشعْرِ

Pomegranate *n.* رُمَّانَة

Pommel *v. t.* or *n.* ضَرَبَ — ِ .قَرَبُوسٌ

Pomp *n.* مُبَاهَاةٌ . مَوْكِبٌ

Pompous *a.* مبَاهٍ . فَخورٌ . متاَنِّه

Pond *n.* بِرْكَةٌ ج. برك

Ponder *v. i.* تَأَملَ . تَفَكر

Ponderous *a.* ثَقِيلٌ . مُهِمٌّ

Poniard *n.* or *v.t.* خَنجَرٌ . طعن به

Pontiff *n.* حَبْرٌ . رئِيسُ ٱلْكَهَنَةِ

Pontifical *a.* حَبْرِيٌّ . بَابَوِيٌّ

Pony *n.* فَرَسٌ صَغِيرٌ

Poodle *n.* كُلَيْبٌ

Pool *n.* بِرْكَةٌ . غَدِيرٌ

Poor *a.* فَقِيرٌ . مِسْكِين . حَقِيرٌ

Poorly *ad.* بِحَالَةٍ سَيِّئَةٍ

Pop *n.* or *v.i.* صوْت انفِجَار. إِنفَجَر

Pope *n.* بَابَا

Popery *n.* مَذْهَبُ ٱلْبَابَا

Popish *a.* بَابَوِيٌّ

Poplar *n.* شَجَرُ ٱلْحَوْرِ

Poppy *n.* خَشْخَاشٌ

Populace *n.* أَلْعَامَّةُ . رعاعُ ٱلنَّاسِ

Popular *a.* مقبول عِنْدَ ٱلْجُمهورِ

Popularity *n.* قُبُولٌ عِنْدَ ٱلنَّاسِ

Popularize *v. t.* جَعَلَ مَقْبُولاً عِنْدَ ٱلنَّاسِ

Populate *v. t.* أَعْمر

Population *n.* أَهْلٌ . سُكَّانٌ

Populous *a.* كَثِير ٱلسُّكَّانِ

Porcelain *n.* خَزَفٌ صِينِيٌّ

Porch *n.* رِوَاقٌ . إِيوانٌ

Porcupine *n.* قُنْفُذ ج قنافذ

Pore *n.* مَسَمٌّ ج مسامّ

Pork *n.* لَحمُ خِنزِير

Porous *a.* ذو مسامّ

Porridge *n.* ثَرِيد . عَصِيدَة

Port *n.* ميناء . يسارُ سفينةٍ . مرفأ

Portable *a.* خفيفٌ . يُمْكِنُ نقلُهُ

Portage *n.* نَقلٌ . اجرتُهُ

Portal *n.* بابٌ . مدخلٌ

Porte *n.* البابُ العالي

Portend *v. t.* دلَّ على . أنبأَ بهِ

Portent *n.* علامةُ سوء . شؤمٌ

Portentous *a.* مُنذِرٌ بسُوء

Porter *n.* حمّالٌ . بوّابٌ (عتّالٌ . شيّال)

Port-hole *n.* كوة مدفع في سفينة

Portico *n.* رواقٌ

Portion *n.* or *v. t.* جزء . حصة . قسم

Portly *a.* جسيمٌ . مهيب الهيئة

Portmanteau *n.* صندوقُ سفرٍ صغيرٌ

Portrait *n.* صورة شخص

Portray *v. t.* صوَّر . وصف —

Position *n.* مقامٌ . مركز . حال

Positive *a.* أكيدٌ . متيقّنٌ . جازم

Possess *v. t.* ملَكَ — حازَ — . إقتنى

Possession *n.* ملكٌ . تملّكٌ

Possessive *a.* ملكيٌّ . المضافُ إليهِ

Possessor *n.* مالك . صاحبٌ . ربٌّ

Possibility *n.* إمكانٌ

Possible *a.* مُمْكِنٌ . مُحتملٌ

Post *v. t.* (accounts) شطَّب حساباً

Post *n.* عمودٌ . بريدٌ . منصبٌ

Postage *n.* اجرة البريد

Postal *a.* مختصٌّ بالبريد

Posterior *a.* خلفيٌّ . بعد . تال

Posterity *n.* ذرّيّة . أهل المستقبل

Post-haste *ad.* بغاية السرعة

Postman *n.* سَاعِي ٱلْبَرِيدِ (بُوسْطَجِيٌّ)

Post-master *n.* مُدِيرُ ٱلْبَرِيدِ

Post-office *n.* مَرْكَزُ إِدَارَةِ ٱلْبَرِيدِ

Postpone *v. t.* أَخَّرَ . أَجَّلَ

Postscript *n.* ذَيْلٌ . مُلْحَق

Postulate *n.* فَرْضٌ . قَضِيَّةٌ أَوَّلِيَّةٌ

Posture *n.* وَضْعٌ . هَيْئَة . حَالَة

Posy *n.* زَهْرَةٌ . بَاقَة

Pot *n.* قِدْرٌ . مِرْجَلٌ

Potash *n.* قِلْيٌ . قلى

Potable *a.* صَالِحٌ لِلشُّرْبِ

Potato *n.* بَطَاطِسٌ

Potency *n.* عِزَّة . قُوَّةٌ . صَوْلَة

Potent *a.* قَوِيٌّ . مُقْتَدِرٌ . عَزِيز

Potentate *n.* مُسَلَّط . مَلِك

Potential *a.* مُمْكِنٌ وُجُودُه

Potion *n.* جَرْعَةٌ . شَرْبَة

Pottage *n.* طَبِيخٌ مِنْ لَحْمٍ وَخُضَرٍ

Potter *n.* خَزَّافٌ . فَخَارِيٌّ

Pottery *n.* خَزَفٌ . فَخَارٌ

Pouch *n.* كِيسٌ . جِرَابٌ . حَوْصَلَة

Poultice *n.* or *v. t.* لَزُوقٌ . عَالَجَ بِهِ

Poultry *n.* دَجَاجٌ

Pounce *v. i.* إِنْقَضَّ عَلَى

Pound *n.* رَطْلٌ أَنْكِلِيزِيٌّ . لِيرَةٌ أَنْكِلِيزِيَّة

Pound *v. t.* مَسْحُوقٌ — . دَقّ

Pour *v.t.* or *i.* صَبَّ . سَكَبَ . تَدَفَّق

Poverty *n.* فَقْرٌ . فَاقَة

Powder *n.* مَسْحُوقٌ . سَفُوفٌ . بَارُودٌ

Power *n.* قُوَّةٌ . قُدْرَة . سُلْطَانٌ

Powerful *a.* قَوِيٌّ . مُقْتَدِرٌ . قَدِيرٌ

Powerless *a.* عَاجِزٌ

Pox *n.* أَلدَّاءُ الزُّهْرِيُّ

Small-pox *n.* أَلْجُدَرِيُّ

Practicability *n.* إِمْكَانُ ٱلْعَمَلِ

Practicable *a.* مُمْكِنٌ عَمَلُهُ

Practical *a.* مُوافِقٌ لِلْحالِ أَوْ لِلْعَمَلِ

Practice *n.* or *v. t.* مُمارسَةٌ . عادَة . مارَسَ

Practitioner *n.* طبيبٌ . عامِل

Prairie *n.* فَلاةٌ ذاتُ كَلاءٍ

Praise *n.* or *v. t.* مَدْحٌ . حمد . مدح . سَبَّحَ

Praiseworthy *a.* خَلِيقٌ بِالْمَدْحِ

Prance *v. i.* شَبَّ — ُ (حصان)

Prate *v. i.* هَذَرَ —

Pratique *n.* براءة الصِّحَّةِ . براتيكه

Prattle *n.* or *v. i.* ثَرْثَرَةُ الوَلَد . ثَرْثَرَ

Pray *v. t.* or *i.* تَوَسَّلَ . تَضَرَّعَ . صَلَّى

Prayer *n.* تَوَسُّلٌ . طَلَبٌ . صَلاةٌ

Preach *v. i.* or *t.* كَرَزَ — . بَشَّرَ . وَعَظَ —

Preacher *n.* وَاعِظ . مُبَشِّرٌ

Preamble *n.* دِيباجَة . مُقَدَّمَة

Precarious *a.* غَيْرُ ثابِتٍ أَوْ مَوْثُوقٍ بِهِ

Precaution *n.* حَذَرٌ . إِحْتِياط

Precautional / Precautionary *a.* حَذَرِيٌّ إِحْتِياطِيٌّ

Precede *v. t.* سَبَقَ — ُ . تَقَدَّمَ

Precedence / Precedency *n.* تَقَدُّمٌ . أَفْضَلِيَّة

Precedent *a.* or *n.* مُقَدَّمٌ . سابِقَةٌ

Precept *n.* مَبْدَأٌ . سُنَّةٌ . أَمْرٌ

Preceptor *n.* مُعَلِّمٌ . مُهَذِّبٌ

Precious *a.* ثَمِينٌ . عَزِيز . نَفِيسٌ

Precipice *n.* جُرْفٌ شاهِق . وهدة

Precipitance / Precipitancy *n.* عَجَلَة . تَهَوُّرٌ

Precipitant *a.* مُتَهَوِّرٌ . عَجُول

Precipitate *v. t.* رَسَّبَ . اِعْجَلَ

Precipitate *a.* or *n.* مُتَهَوِّرٌ . رُسُوب

Precipitation *n.* تَهَوُّرٌ . تَرْسِيب

Precipitous *a.* شامِخ . عَجُول

Precise *a.* مُدَقِّق . مَضْبُوطٌ . مُتَأَنِّقٌ

Preciseness / Precision *n.* ضَبْط . إِتْقَان

Preclude *v. t.* مَنَعَ . أَغْلَق . سَدَّ عَلَى

Precocious *a.* بالِغٌ قَبْلَ أَوانِه . مبتسر

Precociousness / Precocity *n.* بُلوغٌ قَبْلَ الوَقْتِ

Preconceive *v. t.* سبق فتصوّر

Preconcerted *a.* مُتّفَقٌ عليه سابقًا

Precursor *n.* سابقٌ . علامةٌ . بشيرٌ

Predaceous *a.* عائشٌ بالصيد . مفترسٌ

Predatory *n.* ناهبٌ خاطفٌ . مفترسٌ

Predecessor *n.* سابقٌ . سالفٌ

Predestinate / Predestine *v. t.* سبق فقضى قدّر

Predetermine *v. t.* سبق فحتم

Predicament *n.* حالٌ . ورطةٌ

Predicate *n.* or *v. t.* خبرٌ . مُسنَدٌ . اسنَد

Predict *v. t.* أنبأ به

Prediction *n.* نبوءةٌ . إنباءٌ

Predispose *v. t.* سبق فأمال أو هيأ

Predisposition *n.* ميلٌ سابق

Predominant *n.* غالبٌ . مستعلٍ

Predominate *v. i.* فاق . غلب —

Preeminence *n.* أسبقيةٌ

Preeminent *a.* فائقٌ . سابقٌ

Preemption *n.* حقّ الشُّفعة

Preengagement *n.* تعهدٌ سابقٌ

Preexistence *n.* سبقُ الوجود

Preexistent / Preexisting *a.* كائنٌ سابقًا

Preface *n.* or *v. t.* مقدّمةٌ . صدّر . فتح

Prefatory *a.* إفتتاحيٌّ . ديباجيٌّ

Prefer *v. t.* آثر . فضّل . عرض —

Preferable *a.* أفضل . أولى

Preference *n.* تفضيلٌ . إيثارٌ

Preferment *n.* ترقيةٌ . تقديمٌ

Prefigure *v. t.* رمز إلى . سبق فمثّل

Prefix *v. t.* صدّر . أدخل على

Prefix *n.* إضافةٌ إبتدائيّةٌ

Pregnancy *n.* حبلٌ . حملٌ

Pregnant *a.* حبلى . متضمّنٌ كثيرًا

Prejudge *v. t.* حكم قبل الفحص

Prejudice *n.* ميلٌ أو حكمٌ سابقٌ . ضررٌ

Prejudicial *a.* مضرٌّ . مؤذٍ

Prelate *n.* أُسقفٌ

Preliminary *a.* إِفتِتَاحِيٌّ

Prelude *n.* فاتِحَة . مقدَّمَة

Premature *a.* قَبْلَ وقتِهِ . مُبْتَسَرٌ

Premeditate *v. t.* سَبَقَ فتأمل

Premeditated *a.* عَمْدِيٌّ . مقصودٌ

Premier *n.* أَوَّل . وزيرٌ أَوَّل

Premise *v. t.* or *i.* صَدَّر كَلامَهُ ب

Premises *n. pl.* مُقدَّمَات قِيَاس

Premium *n.* رِبًا . جزَ آءِ إِكْرَامِيٌّ

Preoccupy *v. t.* سبق فَمَلَكَ . شغَلَ البال

Preordain *v. t.* سَبَقَ فَعَيَّن أَوْ أَعَدَّ

Preparation *n.* إِسْتِعْدَادٌ . تَهْيِئَةٌ

Preparative / Preparatory } *a.* مُهَيِّئٌ إِسْتِعْدَادِيٌّ

Prepare *v. t.* هيأَ . أَعَدَّ

Prepay *v. t.* سلَّف الاجْرَة

Preponderate *v. i.* رجح ـِ . زاد على

Preposition *n.* حرْفُ جَرٍّ

Prepossessing *a.* مستَميل مستَعطِفٌ

Prepossession *n.* تَمَلُّك أَوْ رَأْيٌ سابِق

Preposterous *a.* مخالِفُ العَقْلِ . عبث

Prerequisite *a.* or *n.* لازِمٌ . لزُومٌ . سابِق

Prerogative *n.* إِمتِيَاز

Presage *n.* or *v. t.* إِنْذارٌ . أَنْذَر

Presbyter *n.* قسيسٌ

Presbytery *n.* مَشْيَخَة الكَنِيسَةِ

Prescribe *v. t.* أمر ـُ . فرض ـِ . وصف ـِ

Prescription *n.* وصفَة علاجٍ

Presence *n.* حضُور . وُجُودٌ . حَضْرَة

Present *a.* or *n.* حاضِرٌ . الحاضِرُ . هَدِيَة

Present *v. t.* أهدَى . أَظْهر . قَدَّم

Presentation *n.* إِهدَآء . تَقْدِيمٌ

Presentiment *n.* رَأْيٌ سابِقٌ . هاجِس

Presently *ad.* حالاً . عنْ قرِيبٍ

Preservation *n.* حِفظٌ . أَمْن

Preserve *v. t.* حَفِظَ ـَ . صَانَ

Preside *v. t.* رَأَسَ . أَدَارَ

Presidency *n.* رَآسَة

President *n.* رَئِيسٌ

Press *v. t.* ضَغَطَ ـَ كَبَسَ ـِ . حَثَّ ـُ

Press *n.* مِكْبَسٌ . مَطْبَعَة

Pressing *a.* مُهِمٌّ . ضَرُورِيٌّ

Pressure *n.* ضَغْط . حَصْرٌ . إِلْحَاحٌ

Prestige *n.* نُفُوذ . جَاه

Presumable *a.* مُوَافِق آلظَّنّ . مُحْتَمَل

Presume *v. t.* or *i.* ظَنَّ . خَمَّنَ . تَجَرَّأَ

Presumption *n.* ظَنٌّ . تَجَبُّرٌ . تَرْجِيحٌ

Presumptive *a.* مَظْنُونٌ . مُرَجَّحٌ

Presumptuous *a.* مُتَجَبِّرٌ . مُعْجَبٌ

Presuppose *v.t.* سَبَقَ فَظَنَّ أَوْ فَرَضَ

Pretend *v. t.* إِدَّعَى . تَظَاهَرَ

Pretence / Pretension *n.* إِدِّعَاء . حُجَّةٌ

Pretentious *a.* مُبَالِغ فِي آلادِّعَاء

Preternatural *a.* فَوْق آلطَّبِيعَةِ

Pretext *n.* حُجَّةٌ . إِدِّعَاء . عُذْرٌ

Pretty *a.* حَسَنٌ . جَمِيل . ظَرِيفٌ

Prevail *v. i.* غَلَبَ ـِ . فَاقَ ـُ . عَمَّ ـُ

Prevalence *n.* إِسْتِيلَاء . إِنتِشَارٌ

Prevalent / Prevailing *a.* مُنْتَشِرٌ . مُشْتَدٌّ

Prevaricate *v. i.* مَوَّهَ . وَارَبَ

Prevent *v. t.* مَنَعَ ـَ . صَدَّ ـُ

Preventable *a.* مِمَّا يُمْنَعُ

Preventative / Preventive *n.* or *a.* مَانِع

Previous *a.* سَابِق . سَالِف . مَاضٍ

Prey *n.* or *v. t.* فَرِيسَةٌ . غَنِيمَةٌ . إِفْتَرَسَ

Price *n.* ثَمَن . سِعْرٌ

Priceless *a.* مَا لَا يُثَمَّنُ . فَوْق كُلّ ثَمَن

Prick *v. t.* or *n.* نَخَسَ ـُ نَخَزَ ـَ . نَخْسَة

Prickle *n.* شُوَيْكَةٌ

Prickly *a.* كَثِيرُ الشَّوْك

Prickly-pear *n.* صَبِّيرٌ (تِينٌ بِشَوكه)

Pride *n.* كِبْرِيَاء . عِزَّةُ آلنَّفْسِ

Priest *n.* كَاهِنٌ . خُورِي

Priesthood *n.* كَهَنُوتٌ

Priestly *a.* كَهَنُوتِيٌّ

Prim *a.* مُتَأَنِّق

Primary *a.* أَوَّلِيٌّ . أَصْلِيٌّ

Prime *a.* or *n.* أَوَّل . أَلأَعْلَى درَجَةً

Primer *n.* كِتَابُ مَبَادِئَ

Primeval *a.* مِنَ ٱلعُصُورِ الاولَى

Primitive *a.* إِبْتِدَائِيٌّ . أَصْلِيٌّ

Primness *n.* تَأَنُّق

Prince *n.* أَمِير . إِبْنُ ملكٍ

Princess *n.* أَمِيرَة . إِبْنَةُ ملكٍ

Principal *a.* or *n.* أَعْظَمُ . أَوَّلٌ . رَئِيس

Principality *n.* سَلْطَنَة . إِمَارَة

Principle *n.* مَبْدَأٌ . قَاعِدَةٌ

Print *v. t.* or *n.* طَبَعَ . وَسَمَ . أَثَر

Printer *n.* طَبَّاعٌ . صَاحِبُ مَطْبَعَةٍ

Printing *n.* طَبْع

Prior *a.* or *n.* سَابِقٌ . رَئِيسُ دَيْر

Prioress *n.* رَئِيسَةُ دَيْر

Priority *n.* أَسْبَقِيَّةٌ . تَقَدُّم

Prism *n.* مَوْشُورٌ . مَنْشُور

Prismatic *n.* مَوْشُورِي

Prison *n.* سِجْنٌ . حَبْس

Prisoner *n.* مَحْبُوسٌ . أَسِير

Privacy *a.* إِنْفِرَادٌ . عُزْلَةٌ . سِرٌّ

Private *a.* سِرِّيٌّ . مُنْفَرِدٌ . خَاصٌّ

Privateer *n.* سَفِينَةٌ حَرْبِيَّةٌ خَاصَّةٌ

Privation *n.* حِرْمَانٌ . عَوَزٌ . عَدَم

Privilege *n.* إِمْتِيَازٌ . فَائِدَة . رخصة

Privily *ad.* سِرًّا . خِفْيَةً

Privy *a.* or *n.* عارف سِرًّا . خَاصٌّ . خَلَاءٌ

Prize *n.* or *v. t.* جَائِزَة . جُعَالَة . اعزّ

Probability *n.* تَرْجِيحٌ

Probable *a.* مُرَجَّحٌ

Probation *n.* إِمْتِحَانٌ

Probe *v. t.* or *n.* سبر ـُ . مِسبار
Probity *n.* إستقامة . امانة
Problem *n.* مسألة . قضية
Problematical *a.* غير ظاهر . مبهم
Proboscis *n.* خرطوم
Proceed *v. i.* تقدم . شرع في . صدر ـُ
Proceeding *n.* عمل . تصرف
Proceeds *n. pl.* حاصل . دخل
Process *n.* فعل . كيفية . طريقة
Procession *n.* موكب
Proclaim *v. t.* نادى ب . صرح
Proclamation *n.* مناداة . إعلان
Proclivity *n.* ميل . إنعطاف
Procrastinate *v. t.* or *i.* أجل . تأخر
Procreate *v. t.* ولد ـِ . أنتج
Procumbent *a.* ملقى على وجهه
Procurable *a.* ما يحصل
Procure *v. t.* حصل . فاز ب

Prodigal *a.* مسرف . مبذر
Prodigality *n.* تبذير . إسراف
Prodigious *a.* عظيم . عجيب
Prodigy *a.* معجزة . آية
Produce *v. t.* or *n.* انتج . أورد . غلة
Product *n.* نتيجة . حاصل
Productive *a.* منتج . مثمر . مسبب
Profanation *n.* تدنيس مقدس
Profane *a.* or *v. t.* دنس . دنيوي . دنس
Profaneness, Profanity } *n.* دناسة . تجديف
Profess *v. t.* أقر . تظاهر . قال ب
Profession *n.* إقرار . عقيدة . حرفة
Professor *n.* مقر . استاذ
Professorship *n.* وظيفة استاذ
Proffer *v. t.* or *n.* قدم . أدى . تقديم
Proficiency *n.* تقدم في العلوم
Proficient *a.* ماهر . بارع
Profile *n.* رسم جانبي للوجه

Profit *n.* or *v. i.* رِبْح . رَبِحَ ـَ

Profitable *a.* مُكْسِبٌ . مُفِيدٌ

Profligacy *n.* خَلاَعَة . فُجُورٌ

Profligate *a.* خليع . فَاجِر

Profound *a.* عَمِيق . خارق . متعمّق

Profuse *a* وَافِرٌ . مفرِط . فَيَاض

Profusion *n.* وفرة . فَيْض . تبذِير

Progenitor *n.* جَد . سلف

Progeny *n.* ذرّيةٌ . نَسْلٌ

Prognosis *n.* إِنْذار بنتيجة مرضٍ

Prognosticate *v. t.* أَنْبَأَ أو أَنْبَأ بِهِ

Programme *n.* لَائِحَةٌ . تعريفٌ

Progress *n.* تَقَدُّمٌ . نَجَاح

Progress *v. i.* تقدَّمَ . نَجَح ـَ

Progressive *a.* مُتَقَدِّم . متتابِع

Prohibit *v. t.* منع ـَ . نَهى ـَ . حرَّم

Prohibition *n.* نَهْي . مَنْع

Prohibitive / **Prohibitory** *a.* مانِع . ناهٍ

Project *v. i.* or *t.* برز ـُ . قصد ـِ . أَلْقى

Project *n.* قَصْد . تدْبِير . مَشْرُوع

Projectile *n.* مِرْمَاة . قُنْبلة

Prolific *a.* مثمر . مُنْتِج كثِيراً

Prolix *a.* مُسْهِب . مُمِل

Prolixity *n.* إِسهَاب . إِطْنَاب

Prolong *v. t.* أَطَال . مَدّ ـُ

Prolongation *n.* إِطَالَة

Promenade *n.* تَنَزُّهٌ . منتَزَه

Prominence / **Prominency** *n.* عُلُوٌّ . بُرُوزٌ

Prominent *a.* بَارِز . ظَاهِر . شهِير

Promiscuous *a.* مختَلِطٌ . غير مرتب

Promise *n.* or *v. t.* موعد . وَعْد . يعِد

Promissory *a.* وعديٌّ . تعهديٌّ

Promontory *n.* رأس عَالٍ في البَحر

Promote *v. t.* سَاعَد . نجح . رقّي

Promotion *n.* تَرْقِيةٌ . تقديم

Prompt *a.* مُستعدٌ . سَرِيعُ الفِعْل

Promptitude / Promptness *n.* إستعداد . سُرْعة

Promulgate *v. t.* نَشَرَ . أذاعَ

Prone *a.* ملقىً على وجهه . مائِل . منعطِف

Prong *n.* شعبة

Pronoun *n.* ضمير

Pronounce *v. t.* لفظ — . صرَّح ب

Pronunciation *n.* لفظ . نطق

Proof *n.* برهان . بيِّنة . إمتحان

Proof *a.* ما لا يؤثِّر فيه

Proof-sheet *n.* مُسوَّدة

Prop *n.* or *v. t.* دعامة . سَنَد . دعَم —

Propagate *v. t.* ولد . نشر — اذاع

Propel *v. t.* دفع — . ساق —

Propensity *n.* ميل . صبو . إنعطاف

Proper *a.* لائِق . مُوافِق . خاص

Property *n.* مُلك . خاصة . صِفة

Prophecy *n.* نبوءة ونبوّة

Prophesy *v. i.* أنبأ . اخبر بالغيب

Prophet *n.* نبيّ ج أنبياء

Prophetic / Prophetical *a.* نبويّ

Propitiate *v. t.* إستعطف

Propitiation *n.* إستعطاف . كفَّارة

Propitious *a.* منعم . مُوافق . مفيد

Proportion *n.* نسبة . مناسبة . حِصة

Proportional / Proportionate *a.* نِسبيّ . متناسِب

Proposal *n.* عرْض . قصد . رأي

Propose *v. t.* عرض — . قدم

Proposition *n.* عرْض . قضية . مطلب

Propound *v. t.* عرض — . طرح — . قدم

Proprietor *n.* صاحِب . ربّ . مالك

Propriety *n.* لِياقة . مُوافقة

Propulsion *n.* دفع . سوق

Prorogue *v. t.* أجل . أخر

Prosaic / Prosaical *a.* نثريّ . مُمِلّ

Proscribe *v. t.* حرّم . طرد —

Prose *n.* نثر

Prosecute *v. t.* تتبع . ادعى على

Prosecutor *n.* مدعٍ . مواظب

Proselyte *n.* or *v. t.* دخيل . جلب إلى دين

Prosody *n.* علم العروض

Prospect *n.* منظر . أمل . منتظر

Prospective *a.* مستقبل . منتظر

Prosper *v. i.* نجح — أفلح

Prosperity *n.* نجاح . فلاح

Prosperous *a.* ناجح . مفلح

Prostitute *n.* عاهرة . فاجرة

Prostitute *v. t.* إستعمل لغاية رذيلة

Prostrate *a.* ساجد . متمدد

Prostrate *v. t.* ألقى . سجد — . خوّر

Prosy *a.* مملّ . مضجر

Protect *v. t.* حمى — . وقى — . صان —

Protection *n.* حماية . وقاية

Protective *a.* }
Protector *n.* } حامٍ . حافظ

Protectorate *n.* حماية

Protegé *n.* محميّ . مولّي

Protest *v.i.* or *t.* أكد . صرّح بعدم قبول

Protestation *n.* إقامة الحجة . تأكيد

Protocol *n.* لائحة (بروتوكول)

Protract *v. t.* أطال . أخّر

Protrude *v. t.* or *i.* أخرج . برز — . نتأ —

Protuberance *n.* نوء . بروز

Proud *a.* متكبّر . مشامخ . معجب

Prove *v. t.* or *i.* برهن . جرّب . تبيّن

Provender *n.* عليق . علف

Proverb *n.* مثل ج أمثال

Proverbial *a.* يضرب به المثل

Provide *v. t.* جهّز . قدم . أمد

Providence *n.* عناية . تدبير

Provident *a.* ذو عناية . مدبّر

Providential *a.* من عناية الله

Province *n.* إقليم . ولاية

Provincial *a.* إقليميّ . غير مهذب

Provison *n.* جِهَازٌ . مُؤْنَةٌ .شَرْطٌ

Provisional / Provisionary } *a.* وَقْتِيٌّ. شَرْطِيٌّ

Provocation *n.* إِغَاظَةٌ . تَهْيِيجٌ

Provocative *a.* مُهَيِّجٌ . مُحَرِّكٌ

Provoke *v. t.* أَغَاظَ . هَيَّجَ . أَثَارَ

Prow *n.* مُقَدَّمُ سَفِينَةٍ

Prowess *n.* بَسَالَةٌ .شَجَاعَةٌ . سَطْوَةٌ

Prowl *v. i.* جَالَ ـُ. جَالَ يَفْتَرِسُ

Proximate *a.* أَلأَقْرَبُ.سَابِقٌ أَوْتَالٍ

Proximity *n.* قُرْبٌ

Proxy *n.* وَكِيلٌ . وَكَالَةٌ

Prudence *n.* حَزْمٌ . بَصِيرَةٌ إِحْتِيَاطٌ

Prudent *a.* حَازِمٌ . فَطِنٌ . حَذِرٌ

Prudish *a.* مُتَصَنِّعٌ بِالْحِشْمَةِ

Prune *n.* or *v. t.* خَوْخَةٌ مُجَفَّفَةٌ .شَذَّبَ .قَضَّبَ

Pry *v. i.* تَجَسَّسَ . رَفَعَ بِمُخْلٍ

Psalm *n.* مَزْمُورٌ ج مَزَامِيرُ

Psalmist *n.* مُؤَلِّفُ ٱلْمَزَامِيرِ. مُرَنِّمٌ

Psalter *n.* كِتَابُ ٱلْمَزَامِيرِ

Psychic / Psychical } *a.* مَنُوطٌ بِالنَّفْسِ

Psychology *n.* أَلْفَلْسَفَةُ ٱلْعَقْلِيَّةُ

Puberty *n.* سِنُّ ٱلْبُلُوغِ

Public *a.* or *n.* عُمُومِيٌّ . شَائِعٌ .ٱلْجُمْهُورُ

Publican *n.* عَشَّارٌ . خَمَّارٌ

Publication *n.* إِذَاعَةٌ . نَشْرٌ

Publicity *n.* شُيُوعٌ . إِشْتِهَارٌ

Publish *v. t.* نَشَرَ ـُ . أَشَاعَ

Pucker *v.i.* or *n.* جَعَّدَ . جَعْدَةٌ . ثَنْيَةٌ

Puddle *n.* مَنْقَعُ وَحْلٍ

Puerile *a.* وَلَدِيٌّ. رَكِيكٌ.(صِبْيَانِيٌّ)

Puff *n.* or *v. i.* نَفْخَةٌ . نَفَخَ ـُ

Pugilist *n.* مُلاَكِمٌ

Pugnacious *a.* خَصُومٌ. مُحِبُّ ٱلْمُنَازَعَةِ

Pull *v. t.* شَدَّ ـُ. جَرَّ ـُ قَلَعَ ـَ

Pulley *n.* بَكَرَةٌ

Pulmonary / Pulmonic } *a.* رِئَوِيٌّ

Pulp *n.* لُبٌّ . شَحْمٌ

Pulpit *n.* مِنْبَرٌ

Pulsate *v. i.* نَبَضَ ـِ

Pulsation *n.* نَبْضَة . نبض

Pulse *n.* أَلنَّبْضُ . أَلْقَطَانِيُّ

Pulverize *v. t.* سحق ـَ . دق ـُ

Pump *n.* or *v.t.* طُلُمْبَةٌ . رَفَعَ مَآءً بِهَا

Pun *n.* تَوْرِيَةٌ (فِي آلبَيَانِ)

Punch *v. t.* ثَقَبَ ـُ . دَفَعَ ـَ

Punch *n.* نَوْعٌ مِنَ آلْمُسْكِرِ . مِثْقَب

Punctual *a.* مُرَاعِي آلْوَقْت . مُدَقِّق

Punctuality *n* أَلتَّدْقِيقُ فِي الْمِيعَادِ

Punctuate *v.t.* وَضَعَ عَلَامَاتِ آلْوَقْف

Puncture *n.* or *v.t.* ثَقْبَةٌ . ثَقَبَ ـُ

Pungent *a.* حِرِّيفٌ . حَادٌّ

Punish *v. t.* عَاقَبَ . قَاصَّ

Punishment *n.* عِقَاب . قِصَاصٌ

Punitive *a.* عِقَابِيٌّ . قِصَاصِيٌّ

Punster *n.* مَاهِرٌ بِآلتَّوْرِيَةِ

Puny *a.* هَزِيلٌ . ضَعِيف

Pup / Puppy *n.* جَرْوُ كَلْبٍ

Pupil *n.* تِلْمِيذٌ . بُؤْبُؤُ آلعَيْنِ

Puppet *n.* أُلْعُوبَةٌ

Pur or Purr *v. i.* or *n.* خَرْخَرَةُ آلْهِرِّ

Purchase *v. t.* إِبْتَاعَ . إِشْتَرَى

Purchaser *n.* مُشْتَرٍ

Pure *a.* صَافٍ . طَاهِر . صِرْفٌ

Purely *ad.* فَقَطْ

Purgative *a.* or *n.* مُطَهِّرٌ . مُسْهِل

Purgatory *n.* أَلْمَطْهَرُ

Purge *v. t.* طَهَّرَ . اسهل

Purification *n.* تَطْهِير . غَسْلٌ

Purify *v. t.* طَهَّرَ . نَقَّى . مَحَّصَ

Purity *n.* طَهَارَةٌ . نَقَاوَةٌ . عِفَّةٌ

Purloin *v. t.* إِخْتَلَسَ . سَرَقَ ـِ

Purple *n.* or *a.* أرْجوَان . ارجوَانِيٌّ

Purport *n.* or *v. t.* مَضْمُون . مَعْنًى . افَادَ

Purpose *n.* or *v. t.* قَصْد . نِيَّة . قَصَدَ ـِ

Purposely *ad.* عَمْدًا . قَصْدًا

Purse *n.* كِيسُ دَرَاهِمَ

Pursue *v. t.* تَبِعَ ـَ طَارَدَ . سَعَى فِي

Pursuit *n.* مُطَارَدَة . إِتِّبَاع . حِرْفَة

Pursuance *n.* إِتِّبَاع

Purvey *v. t.* قَدَّمَ مَؤُونَة . جَهَّزَ

Purveyor *n.* مُجَهِّزُ ٱلْمَؤُونَةِ

Pus *n.* صَدِيد . قَيْح . مِدَّة

Push *v. t.* or *n.* دَفَعَ ـَ . حَرَّضَ . نَشَاط

Pusillanimity *n.* جَبَانَة

Pusillanimous *a.* جَبَان صَغِيرُ ٱلنَّفْسِ

Puss / Pussy } *n.* هِرّ . قِطّ

Pustule *n.* بَثْرَة . دُمَّل

Put *v. t.* وَضَعَ . جَعَلَ ـَ . حَرَّضَ

Putrefaction *n.* فَسَاد . عُفُونَة

Putrefy *v. i.* فَسَدَ ـُ عَفِنَ

Putrid *a.* عَفِن . فَاسِد

Puzzle *n.* or *v. t.* إِرْتِبَاك . حَيْرَة . حَيَّرَ

Pygmy *n.* قَزَم جِنْسًا

Pyramid *n.* هَرَم ج اهْرَام

Pyre *n.* عُرْمَة وَقِيدٍ

Q

Quack *v. i.* or *n.* بَطْبَطَ . دَجَّال

Quackery *n.* تَدْجيل . مُخاتَلة

Quadrangle *n.* مُرَبَّع . دَارٌ مُرَبَّعة

Quadrant *n.* رُبْعُ دَائِرَةٍ

Quadratic *a.* مُرَبَّعيٌّ

Quadrilateral *a.* ذُو أَرْبَعِ أَضْلاَعٍ

Quadroon *n.* وَلَدُ أَبٍ ابْيَضَ وَأُمٍّ خلاسيةٍ

Quadruped *n.* ذُو أَرْبَعِ قَوَائِمَ

Quadruple *a.* أَرْبَعَةُ أَضْعَافٍ

Quaff *v. t.* شَرِبَ ـَ

Quagmire *n.* نَقْعٌ . حَمْأَةٌ

Quail *n.* or *v. i.* سَلْوَى (سِمَّان) . خَافَ

Quaint *a.* غَرِيبٌ . أَنِيقٌ

Quake *v. i.* إِرْتَعَدَ . رَعَشَ ـَ

Quakers *n. pl.* طَائفَة مِنَ ٱلْمَسِيحيِّين

Qualification *n.* أَهْلِيَّةٌ . قَيْدٌ

Qualify *v. t.* أَهَّلَ . نَعَتَ ـَ . قَيَّدَ

Quality *n.* صِفَةٌ . خَصْلَةٌ . نَبَالَةٌ

Qualm *n.* غَثَيَانٌ . قَلَقُ ٱلضَّمِيرِ

Quantity *n.* مِقْدَار . كَمِّيَّة

Quarantine *n.* حَجْرٌ صِحِّيٌّ

Quarrel *n.* or *v. i.* خِصَامٌ . خَاصَمَ

Quarrelsome *a.* خَصُومٌ . مُحِكٌّ

Quarry *n.* مَقْلَعٌ . صَيْدٌ

Quart *n.* مِكْيَال وَهُوَ رُبْعُ جَالُونٍ

Quarter *n.* رُبْعٌ . جِهَةٌ . مَحَلٌّ

Quarterly *a.* or *ad.* كُلَّ ثَلاَثَةِ أَشْهُرٍ

Quartermaster *n.* مَأْمُورُ ٱلْمُونَةِ

Quartett } n. أَرْبَعَةٌ يغنُّون مَعًا
Quartet

Quarto n. كِتَابٌ مُرَبَّعُ ٱلشَّكْلِ

Quartz n. ضَرْبٌ مِنَ ٱلْحَجَرِ ٱلصلْب

Quash v. t. سَحقَ . أَبْطَلَ

Quaver v. i. or n. رَجَّ (ٱلصَّوْتَ)

Quay n. إِسْكِلَةٌ . بنْطٌ . رَصِيف

Queen n. مَلِكَةٌ

Queer a. غَيْرُ مَأْلُوفٍ . غَرِيبٌ

Queerness n. غَرَابَةٌ

Quell v. t. أَخْمَدَ . سَكَّنَ

Quench v. t. أَطْفَأَ . أَرْوَى

Querulous a. مُتَذَمِّرٌ . مُتَشَكٍّ

Query n. or v. t. إِسْتِفْهَامٌ سَأَلَ . شَكَّ

Quest n. طَلَبٌ . تَفْتِيش

Question n. سُؤَالٌ . مَطْلَبٌ . قَضِيَّةٌ

Question v. t. سَأَلَ . إِرْتَابَ

Questionable a. فِيهِ نَظَرٌ أَوْ رَيْبٌ

Quibble n. or v. i. حِيلَةٌ . رَاوَغَ

Quibbler n. مُرَاوِغٌ فِي ٱلْكَلَامِ

Quick a. سَرِيعٌ . ذَكِيٌّ . حَيٌّ

Quicken v. t. أَسْرَعَ . أَحْيَا . حَرَّكَ

Quicklime n. كِلْسٌ غَيْرُ مصوَّل

Quickness n. سُرْعَةٌ . عَجَلَةٌ

Quicksand n. رَمْلٌ يُغْرَقُ فِيهِ

Quicksilver n. زِئْبَقٌ

Quiescence n. سُكُونٌ

Quiescent a. سَاكِنٌ

Quiet v. t. هَدَّأَ . سَكَّنَ . أَرَاحَ

Quiet n. or a. سكون رَاحةٌ سَاكِنٌ

Quietness } a. هُدُوءٌ . سُكُونٌ
Quietude

Quill n. رِيشَةٌ . قَلَمُ رِيشَةٍ

Quilt n. or v. t. لِحَاف . دِثَارٌ . خاطَ لِحَافًا

Quince n. سَفَرْجَلَةٌ ج سَفَارِجُ

Quinine n. كِينَا

Quinsy n. إِلْتِهَابُ ٱللَّوْزَتَيْنِ

Quintal n. مِئَةُ لِيبْرَا

Quire *n.* رِزْمَةُ وَرَق

Quit *v. t.* تَرَكَ . قَضَى ٱلْوَاجِبَ

Quit *a.* مُحَرَّرٌ مِنْ . بَرِيءٌ مِن

Quite *ad.* تَمَامًا بِٱلْكُلِّيَّةِ

Quittance *n.* تَبْرِئَةٌ مِنْ دَيْن . وَصْلٌ

Quiver *n.* or *v. i.* جَعْبَةٌ . إِهْتَزَّ . إِرْتَجَفَ

Quiz *v. t.* خَيَّرَ . سَخِرَ بِهِ

Quondam *a.* سَابِقٌ

Quorum *n.* عَدَدُ أَعْضَاءٍ كَافٍ لِلأَشْغَالِ

Quota *n.* حِصَّةٌ . نَصِيبٌ

Quotation *n.* إِقْتِبَاسٌ

Quote *v. t.* إِقْتَبَسَ . ذَكَرَ (شِعْرًا)

Quoth *v. t.* قَالَ

Quotient *n.* خَارِجُ ٱلْقِسْمَةِ

R

Rabbi *n.* مُعَلِّمٌ . حَاخَامٌ

Rabbinic / **Rabbinical** *a.* حَاخَامِي . تَلْمُودِي

Rabbit *n.* ارْنَبٌ ج أَرَانِب

Rabble *n.* رَعَاعٌ . أَوْبَاشٌ

Rabid *a.* هَائِجٌ . مَجْنُونٌ . كَلِب

Race *n.* سِبَاق . جِنْسٌ . أَصْلٌ

Race *v. i.* or *t.* سَابَقَ . جَعَلَ يُسَابِقُ

Raceme *n.* عُرْجُون

Rack *n.* آلَةُ تَعْذِيبٍ . عَذَاب . رَفٌّ

Racket *n.* ضَجَّةٌ . جَلَبَة

Radiance *n.* ضِيَاءٌ . بَهَاءٌ . لَمَعَانٌ

Radiant *a.* لَامِعٌ . نَيِّرٌ

Radiate *v. i.* or *t.* شَعَّ . أَشَعَّ

Radical *a.* or *n.* أَصْلِيٌّ . جَوْهَرِي . أَصْلٌ . جِذْر

Radicle *n.* جَذْرٌ

Radish *n.* فُجلةٌ

Radius *n.* نِصفُ قُطْرٍ . كُعْبرةٌ

Raft *n.* رَمَثٌ ج أَرْمَاثٌ

Rafter *n.* رافِدٌ ج روافد

Rag *n.* خِرْقَةٌ . رِثَّةٌ

Rage *n.* or *v.i.* غَيظٌ . غضبٌ . إِغتَاظ

Ragged *a.* رَثٌّ . بالٍ

Raging *a.* هائِجٌ . ثائِرٌ . حنِقٌ

Raid *n.* غَزْوَةٌ . غارةٌ

Rail *n.* قضيب حدِيدٍ

Rail *v. t.* or *i.* سَيَّجَ . عيَّرَ . إِفترى

Railing *n.* تعييرٌ . إِفتراءٌ . دَرَابْزونٌ

Raillery *n.* هزْلٌ . مزحٌ . مُدَاعَبَةٌ

Railroad } *n.* سِكَّةُ حَدِيدٍ
Railway }

Raiment *n.* لِباس . كِسوة

Rain *n.* or *v. i.* مطرٌ . امطَرَ

Rainbow *n.* قَوْسُ قُزَحَ

Rainy *a.* مُمْطِرٌ

Raise *v. t.* رَفعَ — . أَقَامَ . ربَّى

Raisin *n.* زَبيبةٌ ج زَبِيبٌ

Rake *n.* خليعٌ . مَجْرَفَةٌ كَالْمُشْطِ

Rally *v. t.* ضَمَّ الشَّارِدِينَ . دَاعَبَ

Ram *n.* كبْشٌ . منجنيقٌ . بُرْجُ الحَمَلِ

Ramble *v. i.* جَالَ . طَافَ —

Rambling *a.* جائِلٌ . غيرُ سَدِيدٍ

Ramify *v. t.* or *i.* فرَّعَ . تفرَّعَ . تشعَّبَ

Rampant *a.* مُفْرِطٌ . غيرُ مَحْصُورٍ

Rampart *n.* سُورٌ . مِتْراسٌ

Ramrod *n.* مدكُ البُنْدُقِيَّةِ

Rancid *a.* زَنِخٌ

Rancour *n.* حِقدٌ . غِلٌّ . ضغينةٌ

Rancorous *a.* مُغِلٌ . حقود

Random *a.* or *n.* عَاسِفٌ غيرُ مُتعمِّدٍ

Range *n.* مدًى . صفٌّ

Range *v. t.* or *i.* صفَّ — جَالَ . طَافَ —

Rank *a.* مُخْصِبٌ . زَنِخٌ . شَدِيدٌ

Rank *n.* or *v. i.* رُتْبَةٌ . صَفٌّ . لَهُ رُتْبَةٌ

Rankle *v. i.* إِشْتَدَّ . إِحْتَدَ

Ransack *v. t.* فَتَّشَ كَثِيراً . نَهَبَ ـُ

Ransom *n.* or *v. t.* فِدْيَةٌ . إِفْتَدَى . فَكَّ ـُ

Rant *v. i.* أَفْرَطَ بِالْكَلَامِ

Rap *n.* or *v. i.* لَكْمَةٌ . ضَرَبَ . دَقَّ ـُ

Rapacious *a.* طَمَّاعٌ . ضَارٍ . سَالِبٌ

Rapacity *n.* طَمَعٌ . إِخْتِطَافٌ

Rape *n.* إِغْتِصَابٌ . فَضْحٌ

Rapid *a.* سَرِيعٌ . مُسْرِعٌ

Rapidity / Rapidness } *n.* سُرْعَةٌ . عَجَلَةٌ

Rapids *n. pl.* سَيْلُ مَاءٍ سَرِيعٍ

Rapier *n.* سَيْفٌ خَفِيفٌ ضَيِّقُ ٱلنَّصْلِ

Rapine *n.* نَهْبٌ . إِخْتِطَافٌ

Rapture *n.* سُرُورٌ مُفْرِطٌ

Rapturous *a.* مُفْتَتِنٌ . سَالِبُ ٱلْعَقْلِ

Rare *a.* نَادِرٌ . نَفِيسٌ . لَطِيفٌ

Rarefy *v. t.* or *i.* رَقَّقَ . لَطَّفَ

Rarely *ad.* نَادِراً

Rareness / Rarity } *n.* قِلَّةُ ٱلْوُجُودِ . نُدْرَةٌ

Rascal *n.* خَبِيثٌ . مُحْتَالٌ

Rascality *n.* خُبْثٌ . غَبِينَةٌ

Rase *v. t.* خَرَّبَ . هَدَّمَ . مَحَا ـُ

Rash *a.* هَيِّرٌ . مِسْرَاعٌ . عَجُولٌ

Rashness *n.* تَهَوُّرٌ . عَدَمُ عِنَايَةٍ

Raspberry *n.* ثَمَرُ ٱلْعُلَّيْقِ

Rat *n.* جُرَذٌ ج جِرْذَانٌ

Ratan *n.* خَيْزُرَانٌ

Rate *n.* سِعْرٌ . كَمِّيَّةٌ . نِسْبَةٌ

Rather *ad.* بِٱلْحَرِيِّ . أَكْثَرُ

Ratify *v. t.* أَمْضَى . أَثْبَتَ . وَقَّعَ

Ratio *n.* نِسْبَةٌ . دَرَجَةٌ

Ration *n.* جِرَايَةُ ٱلْجُنْدِيِّ

Rational *a.* نَاطِقٌ . مُوَافِقٌ لِلْعَقْلِ

Rationalist *n.* قَائِلٌ بِكَفَاءَةِ ٱلْعَقْلِ دُونَ ٱلْوَحْيِ

Ratsbane *n.* سَمُّ ٱلْفَار

Rattle *v. i.* or *t.* or *n.* صَلَّ ـِ . صليل

Ravage *v. t.* نَهَبَ ـَ . خرَّبَ

Rave *v. i.* هذى ـِ . هذرَ ـُ

Ravel *v. t.* or *i.* فكَّكَ . حلَّ ـُ . إنفكَّ

Raven *n.* غُرابٌ ج غِرْبان

Ravenous *a.* أَنهمٌ . نَهِمٌ . كاسِرٌ

Ravine *n.* وادٍ عميقٌ ضيّق

Raving *a.* هاذٍ . هائجٌ

Ravish *v. t.* خطفَ ـَ . إغتصبَ . أفتنَ

Ravishment *n.* إغتصابٌ . وَلَه

Raw *a.* نِيٌّ . غيرُ خبير . مسحوجٌ

Rawhide *n.* سوْطٌ مِنْ جلدٍ غيرِ مدبوغٍ

Ray *n.* شُعاعٌ . نوْعٌ مِنَ ٱلسَّمك

Raze *v. t.* محا ـُ . هدَّ تماماً

Razor *n.* موسى ج مواسٍ

Reach *v. t.* or *i.* بلغَ ـُ . لَحِقَ . إمتدَّ

React *v. t.* or *i.* ردَّ ٱلفعل

Reaction *n.* ردُّ ٱلْفِعْل

Read *v. t.* or *i.* قرأ ـَ . تلا ـُ

Readable *a.* مُسْتَحِق ٱلقِراءَة . يُقْرأ

Readily *ad.* بسهولةٍ

Readiness *n.* تأهُّبٌ . مُبادرةٌ

Reading *n.* قِراءَة . مطالعة

Readmit *v. t.* عادَ فأدْخَلَ

Ready *a.* مُسْتعِدٌ . حاضرٌ . مهيَّأ

Reaffirm *v. t.* كرَّر . عاد فأكَّدَ

Real *a.* حقيقيٌّ . فعليٌّ . صحيحٌ

Real-estate *n.* ألأموالُ غيرُ ٱلمنقولة

Reality *n.* حقيقة . وُجودٌ

Realise *v. t.* انجز . أوْجدَ . تحقَّقَ

Realm *n.* مملكةٌ

Ream *n.* ماعونٌ (منَ ٱلورق)

Reanimate *v. t.* أحيا . أنعشَ

Reap *v. t.* or *i.* حصدَ ـُ . حصَّلَ . تمتَّعَ

Reaper *n.* حاصِد . آلةُ ٱلحصاد

Reappear *v. i.* عَادَ فَظَهَرَ

Reappoint *v. t.* عَيَّنَ ثَانِيَةً

Rear *n.* or *a.* or *v. t.* مُؤَخَّر . أَقَامَ . رَبَّى

Rear-guard *n.* سَاقَةُ ٱلْجَيْش

Reason *v. i.* or *t.* حَاجَّ . ٱسْتَدَلَّ . أَقْنَعَ

Reason *n.* سَبَب . بُرْهَان . عَقْل

Reasonable *a.* مَعْقُول . مُعْتَدِل . عَاقِل

Reasoning *n.* مُحَاجَّة . إِسْتِدْلَال

Reassure *v. t.* أَكَّدَ ثَانِيَةً . أَمَّنَ

Rebel *n.* or *v. i.* خَائِن . عَاص . عَصَى ـِ

Rebellion *n.* عِصْيَان

Rebellious *a.* عَاص

Rebound *v. i.* or *n.* إِرْتَدَّ . إِرْتِدَاد

Rebuff *n.* or *v. t.* رَدّ . رَفْض . رَفَضَ ـِ

Rebuke *v. t.* or *n.* وَبَّخَ . تَوْبِيخ زَجْر

Rebut *v. t.* رَدَّ دَلِيلًا . دَفَعَ ـَ

Recall *v. t.* إِسْتَرْجَعَ . ذَكَرَ ـُ . نَقَضَ ـُ

Recant *v.t.* or *i.* إِرْتَدَّ عَنْ . أَنْكَرَ

Recapitulate *v. t.* كَرَّرَ مُلَخَّصًا

Recede *v. i.* رَجَعَ ـِ . تَقَهْقَرَ

Receipt *n.* or *v.t.* وَصْل . أَعْطَى وَصْلًا

Receive *v. t.* قَبِلَ ـَ . قَبَضَ ـِ . نَالَ ـَ

Recent *a.* حَدِيث . جَدِيد

Receptacle *n.* وُعَاء . غِلَاف

Reception *n.* قُبُول . إِسْتِقْبَال . أَخْذ

Receptive *a.* قَابِل

Recess *n.* إِعْتِزَال . فَرَاغ . فَتْرَة

Recipe *n.* وَصْفَةُ دَوَاء

Recipient *n.* مُسْتَلِم . قَابِل . نَائِل

Reciprocal *a.* مُتَبَادِل . مُعَاوِض

Reciprocate *v. t.* or *i.* عَاوَضَ . تَبَادَلَ

Reciprocity *n.* تَبَادُلُ ٱلْفِعْلِ أَوْ ٱلْفَائِدَة

Recital *n.* قِرَاءَة . رِوَايَة . قِصَّة

Recitation *n.* تِلَاوَة عَنْ ظَهْرِ ٱلْقَلْبِ

Recite *v. t.* قَرَأَ ـَ . تَلَا ـُ

Reckless *a.* مُتَهَوِّر . غَيْرُ مُبَال

Reckon *v. t.* حسبَ ـُ . أَحْصى

Reckoning *n.* حساب. مُحاسبة

Reclaim *v. t.* إِسْترجع. أَصْلحَ

Recline *v. i.* إِتَّكأَ . إِسْتَند

Recluse *n.* or *a.* نَاسكٌ. مُعْتزلٌ

Recognisable *a.* مَا يعرفُ أو يُميَّز

Recognise *v. t.* عَرَفَ . قَبلَ صرِيحًا

Recoil *v. i.* or *n.* إِرْتدَّ . نكَصَ ـُ

Recollect *v. t.* ذكَرَ ـُ. جمعَ. ثانِيةً

Recollection *n.* ذكر وَذِكْرَى

Recommence *v. t.* بدأَ ثانيةً

Recommend *v. t.* وصَّى بهِ.مدَحَ

Recompense *v. t.* or *n.* جازَى. مُجازَاةٌ

Reconcile *v. t.* صالَحَ . وفَق بَيَّنَ

Recondite *a.* غَامض . عوِيص

Reconnaissance *n.* إِستطْلاع

Reconnoiter *v. t.* إِستطْلع . تجَسَّس

Reconquer *v. t.* فتَحَ ـَ . ثَانيةً

Reconsider *v. t.* اعاد آلنَّظَر فِي

Reconsideration *n.* مُرَاجَعَةٌ

Record *v. t.* or *n.* كَتَبَ . دوَّن . سِجلٌ

Recount *v. t.* قصَّ . رَوى بِتفْصِيل

Recourse *n.* إِلْتجا ءٌ . ملْجا

Recover *v. t.* or *i.* إِسْتَرد . تَعَافَى

Recoverable *a.* قابِلُ آلاسْتِرْدَاد

Recovery *n.* إِسْترْجاعٌ . شفا ءٌ

Recreant *a.* or *n.* خَائِن. جبَان. نَذْلٌ

Recreation *n.* تنزُّه . تَسْلِيَة

Recriminate *v. t.* or *i.* اتهمَ . تعايب

Recruit *v. t.* or *i.* أَمد . جدد. تعافى

Recruit *v. i.* or *n.* جنَّدَ . عسكرِي جَدِيد

Rectangle *n.* مُربَّعٌ مُستطِيل قَائمُ آلزَّوايا

Rectify *v. t.* قوَّم . أَصلحَ

Rectilinear *a.* مُسْتقِيمُ آلخُطُوط

Rectitude *n.* إِسْتقامةٌ

Rector *n.* مُديرٌ . قسِّيسُ أبْرشيَّة

Rectory *n.* كَنِيسَةُ أَبْرَشِيَّةٍ . بَيْتُ ٱلْقِسِّيسِ

Rectum *n.* ٱلْمُسْتَقِيمُ (مِنَ ٱلْأَمْعَاءِ)

Recumbent *a.* مُتَّكِئٌ

Recuperate *v. i.* تَعَافَى

Recuperative *a.* شَافٍ . مُعَافٍ

Recur *v. i.* عَادَ . تَكَرَّرَ . إِلْتَجَأَ

Recurrence *n.* عَوْدٌ . تَكْرَارٌ

Red *a.* أَحْمَرُ

Redden *v. t.* or *i.* حَمَّرَ . إِحْمَرَّ

Redeem *v. t.* فَدَى . فَكَّ

Redeemer *n.* فَادٍ . مُخَلِّصٌ

Redemption *n.* فِدْيَةٌ . فِدَاءٌ

Redness *n.* حُمْرَةٌ . إِحْمِرَارٌ

Redolent *a.* فَائِحٌ . عَبِقٌ

Redouble *v. t.* ضَاعَفَ . كَثَّرَ

Redoubt *n.* مِتْرَاسٌ . حِصْنٌ

Redress *v. t.* قَوَّمَ . عَدَلَ . أَنْصَفَ

Reduce *v. t.* قَلَّلَ . أَخْضَعَ . رَدَّ

Reduction *n.* رَدٌّ . تَحْوِيل (فِي ٱلْحِسَابِ)

Redundant *n.* زَائِد عَنِ ٱللُّزُومِ

Reduplicate *v. t.* ضَاعَفَ

Re-echo *v. t.* or *i.* رَدَّ ٱلصَّدَى

Reed *n.* قَصَبَةٌ . مِزْمَارٌ

Reef *n.* سِلْسِلَةُ صُخُورٍ فِي ٱلْمَاءِ

Reef *v. t.* طَوَى (ٱلْقُلُوعَ)

Reek *v. i.* فَاحَ بُخَارُهُ . بَخَرَ

Reel *n.* or *v. t.* or *i.* مِكَبٌّ . كَبَّ . تَرَنَّحَ

Re-elect *v. t.* إِنْتَخَبَ ثَانِيَةً

Re-embark *v. i.* or *t.* نَزَلَ ثَانِيَةً فِي سَفِينَةٍ

Re-enforce *v. t.* عَزَّزَ . أَمَدَّ

Re-engage *v. t.* جَدَّدَ ٱلْعَهْدَ أَوِ ٱلْقِتَالَ

Re-enter *v. t.* عَادَ فَدَخَلَ

Re-establish *v. t.* عَادَ فَأَقَامَ أَوْ أَثْبَتَ

Re-examine *v. t.* عَادَ فَفَحَصَ أَوِ ٱمْتَحَنَ

Refectory *n.* قَاعَةُ ٱلْأَكْلِ

Refer *v. t.* or *i.* وَجَّهَ أَوْ أَشَارَ إِلَى

Referee *n.* فيصل .حكم

Reference *n.* إشارة .شاهد .علاقة

Refine *v. t.* or *i.* محص .هذب .تنقى

Refinement *n.* ادب . تهذيب

Refinery *n.* معمل التمحيص أو التصفية

Refit *v. t.* عاد فجهز . أصلح

Reflect *v. i.* or *t.* تأمل . إنعكس

Reflective *a.* متأمل . عاكس

Reflector *n.* سطح عاكس . مرآة

Reflex *a.* مردود .منعكس

Reflexive *a.* مائل إلى الوراء أو الذات

Reform *v. t.* اصلح .قوم .جدد

Reform, Reformation } *n.* إصلاح . تجديد

Reformatory *a.* or *n.* مصلح (إصلاحية)

Reformer *n.* مصلح

Refract *v. t.* كسر شعاع النور

Refraction *n.* إنكسار النور

Refractory *a.* متمرد . شكس

Refrain *v. i.* إمتنع . امسك عن

Refrangible *n.* قابل الانكسار

Refresh *v. t.* أنعش . أراح

Refreshment *n.* إنعاش . طعام

Refrigerator *n.* آلة التبريد . مبرد

Refuge *n.* ملجأ . سبيل النجاة

Refugee *n.* ملتجئ .مهاجر .هارب

Refulgence, Refulgency } *n.* لمعان . بهاء

Refulgent *a.* بهي . نير

Refund *v. t.* أوفى . رد

Refusal *n.* رفض .حق الأخذ دون غيره

Refuse *n.* سقاطة . نفاية

Refuse *v. t.* أبى . رفض

Refute *v.t.* أدحض .نقض . رد

Regain *v. t.* إسترد . إستعاد

Regal *a.* ملكي

Regale *v. t.* أولم وليمة فاخرة

Regard *v. t.* or *n.* لاحظ . إعتبر .إعتبار

Regardless *a.* غير مكترث . غافل

Regency *n.* نيابةُ ملكٍ

Regenerate *v. t.* or *a.* جدد. متجدد

Regent *n.* نائبُ الملكِ

Regicide *n.* قاتل ملكٍ. قتلهُ

Regime *n.* شكل حكومةٍ

Regiment *n.* كتيبة. آلاي

Region *n.* قطر. جهة

Register *n.* or *v. t.* دفتر. سجل. سجل

Regress / Regression *n.* إرتداد. تقهقر

Regret *n.* or *v. t.* أسف تأسف على

Regular *a.* قياسي على ترتيب

Regularity *n.* ترتيب. إنتظام

Regulate *v. t.* رتب. نظم. دبر

Regulation *n.* قانون. نظام

Regulator *n.* مرتب. آلة ضبط

Rehearse *v. t.* قص. تلا مراجعة

Reign *n.* or *v. i.* ملك. ملك. إستولى

Reimburse *v. t.* أوفى كافاً

Rein *n.* or *v. t.* عنان. عنن. كبح

Reindeer *n.* نوع من الايل

Reins *n. pl.* كلى

Reinstall / Reinstate *v. t.* أعاد إلى منصبه

Reissue *v. t.* or *i.* or *n.* عاد فأصدر

Reiterate *v. t.* كرر

Reject *v. t.* نبذ. رفض

Rejoice *v. i.* or *t.* سر. فرح. فرح

Rejoicing *n.* فرح. سرور

Rejoin *v. t.* or *i.* لاقى بعد فراق. أجاب

Rejoinder *n.* مجاوبة. جواب

Rejuvenate *v. t.* جدد الشباب

Rekindle *v. t.* أشعل ثانية

Relapse *v.i.* or *n.* عاد إلى حالته. نكس نكس

Relate *v. t.* or *i.* قص. حدث. تعلق ب

Relation *n.* نسبة. رواية. نسيب

Relationship *n.* قرابة. نسب

Relative *n.* or *a.* نسيب. موصول. نسبي

Relax *v. t.* or *i.* أَرْخَى. خَفَّفَ. إِرْتَخَى

Relaxation *n.* إِرْخَاءٌ. إِرَاحة. فَرَحٌ

Relaxative / Relaxing *a.* مُرْخٍ. مُلَيِّن

Relay *n.* or *v. t.* بَدَلُ خيلٍ. عَادَ. فَوَضَعَ

Release *v. t.* or *n.* أَطْلَقَ. حرَّرَ. إِطْلَاقٌ

Relent *v. i.* رَقَّ لَهُ. سَامَحَ

Relentless *a.* بِلَا رَحْمَةٍ أَوْ عفوٍ

Relevant *a.* مُوَافِقٌ. في محلِّهِ

Reliable *a.* ما يُرْكَنُ إِلَيْهِ. مَوْثُوقٌ بِهِ

Reliance *n.* ثِقَةٌ. إِعْتِمَادٌ. إِتِّكَال

Relic *n.* بَقِيَّةٌ. أَثَرٌ. ذَخِيرَة

Relief *n.* إِسْعَافٌ، نَجْدَةٌ. إِرَاحة

Relieve *v. t.* أَرَاحَ. خَفَّفَ. أَمَدَّ

Religion *n.* دِيَانَةٌ. دِينٌ

Religious *a.* دَيِّن. دِينِيٌّ

Relinquish *v. t.* تَرَكَ. تَنَحَّى عَنْ

Relinquishment *n.* تَرْكٌ

Relish *n.* or *v. t.* لَذَّةُ طَعْمٍ. إِسْتَلَذَّ

Reluctance *n.* نُفُورٌ. مُضَادَّةٌ. كَرَاهَة

Reluctant *a.* نَافِرٌ. غَيْرُ رَاضٍ

Rely *v. i.* وَثِقَ بِ. إِتَّكَلَ عَلَى

Remain *v. i.* بَقِيَ. دَامَ. مَكَثَ

Remainder *n.* بَقِيَّةٌ. فَضْلَةٌ

Remains *n. pl.* بَقَايَا. جُثَّةٌ

Remand *v. t.* أَعَادَ. رَدَّ

Remark *v. t.* or *n.* لَاحَظَ. قَالَ. مُلَاحَظَةٌ

Remarkable *a.* مُسْتَحِقٌّ ٱلذِّكْرِ مَشْهُورٌ

Remediable *a.* قَابِلُ ٱلإِصْلَاحِ

Remedial *a.* عِلَاجِيٌّ. مُصْلِحٌ

Remedy *n.* or *v. t.* عِلَاجٌ. عَالَجَ

Remember *v. t.* تَذَكَّرَ. ذَكَرَ

Remembrance *n.* ذِكْرٌ. ذِكْرَى

Remind *v. t.* ذَكَّرَ. (فَكَّرَ)

Reminiscence *n.* ذِكْرٌ. تَذْكَارٌ

Remiss *a.* غَافِلٌ. مُتَوَانٍ

Remission *n.* غُفْرَانٌ. عَفْوٌ

Remit *v. t.* رَدَّ ـُ . أَرْسَلَ . عفا ـُ

Remittance *n.* ارْسالُ دَرَاهِم

Remittent *a.* مُتَقَطِّعٌ . مُتَرَدِّدٌ

Remnant *n.* فَضْلَةٌ

Remonstrance *n.* إِعْتِرَاضٌ

Remonstrate *v. i.* إِعْتَرَضَ عَلَى . وَبَّخَ

Remorse *n.* تَوْبِيخُ ٱلضَّمِيرِ

Remorseless *a.* بِلا رَحْمَةٍ . قاسٍ

Remote *a.* بعيدٌ

Remoteness *n.* بُعدٌ

Remount *v. t.* عادَ فَصَعِدَ أَوْ رَكِبَ

Removal *n.* نَقْلٌ . رَحِيلٌ . عَزْلٌ

Remove *v. t.* or *i.* نَقَلَ ـُ عَزَلَ ـِ إِرْتَحَلَ

Remunerate *v. t.* جازَى . كافَى

Remunerative *a.* مُكَافٍ . مُرَبِّحٌ

Renascence / **Renaissance** *n.* تَجْدِيدٌ . عَوْدَةٌ

Rend *v. t.* مَزَّقَ . شَقَّ ـُ

Render *v. t.* رَدَّ ـُ . أَعْطَى . صَيَّرَ

Renegade *n.* مُرْتَدٌّ . خائِنٌ

Renew *v. t.* جَدَّدَ

Renewable *a.* قَابِلُ ٱلتَّجْدِيدِ

Renewal *n.* تَجْدِيدٌ

Renounce *v. t.* رَفَضَ ـُ . نَبَذَ ـِ

Renovate *v. t.* جَدَّدَ

Renown *n.* صيتٌ شُهْرَةٌ ذِكْرٌ

Renowned *a.* شَهِيرٌ

Rent *v. t.* or *n.* آجَرَ . أُجْرَةٌ

Rent *n.* or *a.* شَقٌّ . فَتْقٌ . مَشْقُوقٌ

Renunciation *n.* رَفْضٌ . إِنْكارٌ

Reorganize *v. t.* رَتَّبَ أَوْ نَظَّمَ ثانِيَةً

Repair *v. t.* or *i.* أَصْلَحَ . رَمَّمَ . ذَهَبَ إِلَى

Reparation *n.* تَصْلِيحٌ . تَعْوِيضٌ

Repass *v. t.* or *i.* عادَ فَاجْتازَ أَوْ مَرَّ

Repast *n.* أَكْلَةٌ . طَعامٌ

Repay *v. t.* وفَى . يَفِي

Repel *v. t.* or *i.* نَسَخَ — . أَلْغَى نَسَخَ

Repeat *v. t.* كَرَّرَ . ثنى

Repel *v. t.* دَفع ـَ . دَافِعٌ

Repellent *a.* رَادّ . منفِّر

Repent *v. i.* تَابَ ـُ نَدِمَ ـَ

Repentance *n.* تَوْبة . نَدَامة

Repentant *a.* تائِبٌ . نَادِم

Repetition *n.* تكْرار

Repine *v. i.* تَشَكَّى . تَذَمَّر

Replace *v. t.* عوَّضَ . اعاد إِلى مكانِهِ

Replenish *v. t.* ملأَ أيضاً . سدَّ الْعوز

Replete *a.* محشوٌّ . مُمْتَلِئٌ . مفعم

Repletion *n.* فُعومة . إِمتلاءٌ

Reply *n.* or *v. t.* جوابٌ . جاوَبَ . أجابَ

Report *v. t.* قرَّر . أَخْبَرَ

Report *n.* تقرير . خَبر . صوْتٌ

Reporter *a.* مُقرِّرٌ . مخبرٌ

Repose *v. i.* or *n.* إِسْتَراحَ . راحةٌ

Repository *n.* مخزنٌ . مُسْتودعٌ

Repossess *v. t.* عاد فملك . إِسْترد

Reprehend *v. t.* وبَّخَ . لام ـُ

Reprehensible *a.* مُسْتحِقٌّ اللَّوْم

Represent *v. t.* مثَّل . صوَّر . ناب عنْ

Representation *n.* صُورَة . نِيَابة

Representative *n.* or *a.* نائبٌ . ممثّل

Repress *v. t.* منَعَ ـَ . قهرَ ـَ . قمعَ ـَ

Repressive *a.* قاهر . مانِع

Reprieve *v. t.* or *n.* أجَّلَ القصاصَ

Reprimand *v. t.* or *n.* وبَّخَ . توْبيخٌ

Reprint *v. t.* or *n.* طَبَعَ ثانيةً

Reprisal *n.* أخْذُ الثَّأْر . إِنْتقام

Reproach *v. t.* or *n.* عيَّر . عَار . تعْيير

Reprobate *n.* مرْفوضٌ . مرْذُول

Reproduce *v. t.* جدَّدَ . تَنَاسَلَ

Reproduction *n.* تجْديدَ . تَنَاسل

Reproductive *a.* مجدِّد . مُتَنَاسل

Reproof *n.* توْبيخ

Reprove *v. t.* وَبخ . عزل ـُ . لامَ ـ
Reptile *n.* زَحافةٌ
Republic *n.* جُمْهُورِيَّةٌ
Repulican *a.* جُمْهُورِي
Republicanism *n.* مَذْهبُ ٱلْجُمْهُورِيَةِ
Republish *v. t.* أَصْدَرَ ثانيةً
Repudiate *v. t.* رَفضَ ـِ . أَنْكرَ
Repugnance / Repugnancy } *n.* كَرَاهةٌ . نفُورٌ
Repugnant *a.* كَرِيهٌ . مُنَفِّرٌ
Repulse *n.* or *v. t.* رَدعٌ . رَدَّ ـُ
Repulsive *a.* رَادِع . قَبِيحٌ . كرِيهٌ
Reputable *a.* حَسَنُ ٱلصِيتِ . مُحْترَمٌ
Reputation / Repute } *n.* صِيتٌ . ذِكْرٌ . شُهرَةٌ
Reputed *a.* مَحْسوبٌ . مَظنونٌ
Request *n.* or *v. t.* طلبٌ . طلبَ ـُ . إِلْتمسَ
Requiem *n.* تَرْزِمةٌ اوْ قدَّاسٌ لِأَجْلِ ٱلمَوْتَى
Require *v. t.* إِحتاجَ . إِقتضى . أَلْزمَ
Requirement *n.* إِحْتِيَاجٌ . إِقْتِضاءٌ . إِلْزامٌ
Requisite *a.* مَطْلُوبٌ . لازِمٌ
Requisition *n.* إِقْتِضاءٌ . إِلْزامٌ
Requital *n.* مُكافاةٌ . جَزَاءٌ
Requite *v. t.* كَافأَ . جازَى . عَوَّضَ
Rescind *v. t.* نَسخَ ـَ . أَلْغى
Rescue *v. t.* or *n.* أَنْقذَ . خلَّصَ . نجَّى
Research *n.* تَفْتِيشٌ . بَحْثٌ
Resemblance *n.* مُشَابَهةٌ
Resemble *v. t.* شابَهَ . مَاثَلَ . أَشْبَهَ
Resent *v. t.* إِستاءَ . قاوَمَ
Resentful *a.* مغتاظٌ . حَقودٌ
Reservation *n.* إِبقاءٌ . تقييدٌ
Reserve *v. t.* حفِظَ . ابْقَى
Reserved *a.* محفُوظٌ . كَتومٌ . مُتَحَفِّظٌ
Reservoir *n.* حوْضٌ . صَهْرِيجٌ (خزان)
Reset *v. t.* وَضعَ ثَانيةً
Reside *v. i.* سكَنَ ـُ . اقامَ

Residence *n.* إقامَةٌ . سكنى

Resident *a.* ساكِن . مُتَوطِّن

Residual *a.* باقٍ . فاضِلٌ

Residue / Residuum *n.* بَقِيَّةٌ . فضلةٌ

Resign *v. t.* تخلَّى عن . سلم

Resignation *n.* تَسليمٌ

Resigned *a.* صبورٌ

Resin *n.* راتِينجٌ

Resist *v. t.* قاوم . ضادَّ . عارَض

Resistance *n.* مُقاوَمَةٌ

Resistless *a.* ما لا يُقاوَمُ

Resolute *a.* عَزُومٌ . ثابِتُ ٱلرَّأْيِ

Resolution *n.* عزمٌ . تقريرٌ . حلٌّ

Resolve *v. t.* or *n.* عزَمَ . حلَّ . عزْمٌ

Resolvent *n.* حَالٌّ . مُذيبٌ

Resonance *n.* رَدُّ ٱلصَّوْتِ . رنين

Resort *v.i.* or *n.* اِلْتَجأَ إلى . مُجْمَعٌ

Resound *v. t.* or *i.* أذاعَ ٱلصِّيتَ . رَنَّ

Resource *n.* ملْجأٌ . وَسِيلَةٌ

Respect *v. t.* or *n.* إحْترَمَ . إحْتِرَامٌ

Respectability *n.* إحْتِرَامٌ

Respecting *pr.* بخصُوصِ . مِنْ جهَةِ

Respective *a.* كُل عَلَى حِدَةٍ . نِسْبِيٌّ

Respectable *a.* مُحْترَمٌ . مُتَوَسِّطٌ

Respectful *a.* مُحْتَرِمٌ . مُحْتَشِمٌ

Respiration *n.* تنفُّسٌ . نفسٌ

Respiratory *a.* تنفسيٌّ

Respite *n.* or *v. t.* فِتْرَةٌ . أمهل

Resplendent *a.* بَهِي . لامِعٌ

Respond *v. i.* أجَابَ . وافَقَ

Response *n.* جوَابٌ

Responsibility *n.* مسئولِيَّةٌ

Responsible *a.* مسئُولٌ

Responsive *a.* مجيبٌ . مُرِيدُ ٱلجَوَابِ

Rest *v. t.* or *i.* رَاحَ . إسْتَرَاح

Rest *n.* سكونٌ . رَاحةٌ . بقية

Restaurant *n.* مَحَلُّ طَعَامٍ (مَطْعَمٌ)
Restitution *n.* رَدٌّ . تعويضٌ
Restive *a.* قَلِقٌ . جَمُوحٌ
Restless *a.* عَدِيمُ ٱلرَّاحةِ . جزِعٌ
Restoration *n.* رَدٌّ . إِصلاحٌ . شفاءٌ
Restorative *a.* شَافٍ . مقوٍّ
Restore *v. t.* رَدَّ . جدد
Restrain *v. t.* منع . حجز
Restraint *n.* حَجْرٌ . مَانِعٌ . ضبْطٌ
Restrict *v. t.* حصر . قَصَرَ على
Restriction *n.* حَصْرٌ . قَصْرٌ
Result *v. i.* or *n.* نَتَجَ مِنْ . نتيجةٌ
Resume *v. t.* إِستَرَدَّ . عَادَ إِلَى
Resumé *n.* خُلاصَةٌ . مُلَخصٌ
Resurrection *n.* قِيامَةٌ . بعثٌ
Resuscitate *v. t.* أَحيَا . انعش
Retail *v. t.* or *n.* بَاعَ بِٱلمُفرَّقِ
Retain *v. t.* امسك . ضبط
Retainer *n.* خَادِمٌ . تَابِعٌ
Retaliate *v. i.* أَخذ ٱلثأر . إِنْتَقمَ
Retard *v. t.* عَاقَ . أَخَّرَ
Retention *n.* إِمْساكٌ . حَجْزٌ
Retentive *a.* حافِظٌ . ضابِطٌ
Reticent *a.* كَتومٌ . كاظِمٌ
Retina *n.* شَبَكِيَّةُ ٱلعَيْنِ
Retinue *n.* حَشَمٌ . تَبَعٌ
Retire *v. i.* تقهقر . إِرتَدَّ
Retirement *n.* إِعتِزَالٌ . تَقَاعُدٌ
Retort *v. t.* or *i.* رَدَّ بِٱلمِثْلِ
Retort *n.* رَدٌّ . إِنبِيقٌ
Retrace *v. t.* رَجَعَ عَلَى ٱلأَثَرِ
Retract *v. t.* إِسْتَرَدَّ قَوْلاً
Retreat *n.* or *v. i.* إِرْتِدَادٌ . إِرْتَدَّ
Retrench *v. t.* نقَصَ . قلل ٱلمَصْرُوف
Retribution *n.* مُعَاقَبَةٌ . مُجَازَاةٌ
Retributive / Retributory } *a.* عقابي

Retrieve *v. t.* إِسْتَرَدَّ . أَصْلَحَ

Retroaction *n.* رَدُّ ٱلْفِعْلِ

Retrograde *a.* or *v. i.* مُرْتَدٌّ . تَقَهْقَرَ

Retrogression *n.* إِرْتِدَادٌ . إِنْحِطَاطٌ

Retrospect / Retrospection *n.* نَظَرٌ إِلَى ٱلْمَاضِي

Return *v. t.* or *i.* رَجَّعَ . رَجَعَ

Return *n.* رُجُوعٌ . تَعْوِيضٌ . رِبْحٌ

Reunion *n.* إِجْتِمَاعٌ بَعْدَ فِرَاقٍ

Reunite *v. t.* or *i.* ضَمَّ أَيْضاً . إِنْضَمَّ

Reveal *v. t.* أَعْلَنَ . كَشَفَ . أَظْهَرَ

Revel *n.* or *v. i.* بَطَرٌ . إِنْهَمَكَ بِاللَّذَّاتِ

Revelation *n.* إِعْلَانٌ . وَحْيٌ . تَنْزِيلٌ

Revelry *n.* بَطَرٌ . مَرَحٌ

Revenge *n.* or *v. t.* إِنْتِقَامٌ . إِنْتَقَمَ

Revengeful *v. i.* شَدِيدُ ٱلْاِنْتِقَامِ . ضَاغِنٌ

Revenue *n.* دَخْلٌ

Reverberate *v. i.* إِرْتَدَّ ٱلصَّوْتُ وَتَكَرَّرَ

Revere *v. t.* إِحْتَرَمَ . وَقَّرَ

Reverence *n.* إِحْتِرَامٌ

Reverend *a.* مُوَقَّرٌ . مُحْتَرَمٌ

Reverent / Reverential *a.* مُحْتَرِمٌ . إِحْتِرَامِيٌّ

Reverie / Revery *n.* شُرُودُ ٱلْأَفْكَارِ . تَأَمُّلٌ

Reversal *n.* قَلْبٌ . عَكْسٌ . نَقْضٌ

Reverse *v. t.* قَلَبَ . عَكَسَ . أَبْطَلَ

Reverse *n.* نَقِيضٌ . مُصِيبَةٌ . قَفاً

Revert *v. i.* عَادَ . رَجَعَ

Review *n.* or *v. t.* مُرَاجَعَةٌ . أَعَادَ ٱلنَّظَرَ

Revile *v. t.* شَتَمَ . سَبَّ

Revisal / Revision *n.* مُرَاجَعَةٌ . تَصْحِيحٌ

Revise *v. t.* رَاجَعَ . نَقَّحَ . صَحَّحَ

Revisit *v. t.* عَادَ فَزَارَ

Revival *n.* إِنْتِعَاشٌ . تَجْدِيدٌ

Revive *v. t.* or *i.* أَنْعَشَ . إِنْتَعَشَ

Revivify *v. t.* أَحْيَا . جَعَلَهُ يَنْتَعِشُ

Revocation *n.* فَسْخٌ . إِلْغَاءٌ

Revoke *v. t.* نَقَضَ . أَلْغَى . فَسَخَ

Revolt *v. i.* or *n.* عَصَى ـِ . عِصْيَانٌ

Revolution *n.* إِنقِلَابٌ . دَوَرَانٌ

Revolutionary *a.* آيِلٌ لِلفِتْنَةِ

Revolutionize *v. t.* غَيَّرَ كُلِّيًّا

Revolve *v. t.* or *i.* ادارَ . رَدَّدَ . دَارَ ـُ

Revulsion *n.* رَدٌّ . نفورٌ شَدِيدٌ

Reward *n.* or *v. t.* ثَوَابٌ . جَازَى

Rewrite *v. t.* عَادَ فَكَتَبَ

Rhetoric *n.* عِلْمُ ٱلْبَيَانِ

Rheumatism *n.* دَآءُ ٱلْمفَاصِلِ

Rhinoceros *n.* كَرْكَدَّنٌ

Rhubarb *n.* رَوَنْدٌ او رِوَنْدٌ

Rhyme *n.* سَجْعٌ . قَافِيَةٌ

Rhythm *n.* نَظْمُ ٱلشِّعْرِ

Rib *n.* ضِلْعٌ ج ضُلُوعٌ واضْلُعٌ

Ribalbry *n.* كَلَامٌ رَذِيلٌ أو فَاحِشٌ

Ribbed *a.* مُضَلَّعٌ . مُخَطَّطٌ

Ribbon *n.* شَرِيط ج شُرُط وشَرَائِطِ

Rice *n.* ارُزٌّ . رُزٌّ

Rich *a.* غَنِيٌّ . مُخْصِبٌ . دَسِمٌ

Riches *n. pl.* غِنًى . ثَرْوَة . مَالٌ

Richness *n.* خِصْبٌ . وُفُورٌ . دَسَمٌ

Rickets *n. pl.* دَآءُ ٱلْكُسَاحِ

Rickety *a.* كَسِيحٌ . رَكِيكٌ

Rid *v. t.* أَنْقَذَ . خَلصَ . نَجَّى

Riddle *n.* لغز . أُحْجِيَّةٌ

Ride *v. t.* or *n.* رَكِبَ ـَ . رِكْبَةٌ

Riding *n.* رُكُوبٌ

Ridge *n.* ظَهْرٌ . مُرْتَفِعٌ

Ridicule *n.* or *v. t.* هزْءٌ . سَخِرَ بِ

Ridiculous *a.* مُضْحِكٌ . سُخْرِيٌّ

Rifle *n.* or *v. i.* بُنْدُقِيَةٌ مُضَلَّعَةٌ . سَلَبَ ـ

Rift *n.* or *v. t.* شَقٌّ . فُرْجَةٌ . شَقَّ

Rig *v. t.* جَهَزَ ٱلسَّوَارِيَ . الْبَس

Rigging *n.* جِهَازُ سَفِينَةٍ

Right *a.* or *n.* مُصِيبٌ . مُستَقِيمٌ . حقٌّ . يمينٌ

Right *n.* صَوَابٌ . عَدْلٌ . إِمْتِيَازٌ

Righteous *n.* بَارٌّ . تَقِيٌّ . صَالِحٌ

Righteousness *n.* بِرٌّ

Rightful *a.* حَقٌّ . شَرْعِيٌّ . عَادِلٌ

Rigid *a.* مُتَوَتِّرٌ . مُتَصَلِّبٌ

Rigidity, Rigidness *n.* صَلَابَةٌ . عَدَمُ لُيُونَةٍ

Rigour *n.* عُنْفٌ . شِدَّة . صَرَامَةٌ

Rigorous *a.* شَدِيدٌ . عَنِيفٌ . صَارِمٌ

Rill *n.* سَاقِيَةٌ . جَدْوَلُ مَآءٍ

Rim *n.* حَافَّةٌ

Rind *n.* قِشْرٌ

Ring *n.* حَلَقَةٌ . خَاتِمٌ . رَنِين

Ring *v. t.* or *i.* دَقَّ ـُ . رَنَّ ـِ . طَنَّ ـِ

Ringleader *n.* رَئِيسُ ثَوْرَةٍ

Ringlet *n.* جُعَيْدَةُ شَعْرٍ

Ringworm *n.* أَلْقُوبَآءُ

Rinse *v. t.* شَطَفَ ـَ . مَضْمَضَ

Riot *n.* شَغْبٌ . فِتْنَةٌ . بَطَرٌ

Rioter *n.*, Riotous *a.* مُشَاغِبٌ . خَلِيعٌ . بَطِرٌ

Rip *v. t.* or *n.* فَتَقَ ـِ . مزق . فَتْقٌ

Ripe *a.* نَاضِجٌ . مُسْتَوٍ . كَامِلٌ

Ripen *v. t.* or *i.* أَنْضَجَ . نَضِجَ ـَ

Ripeness *n.* نَضْجٌ . كَمَالٌ . بُلُوغٌ

Ripple *n.* مَوْجَةٌ خَفِيفَةٌ

Rise *v. i.* إِرْتَفَعَ . قَامَ ـُ . أَشْرَقَ

Rising *n.* قِيَامٌ . طُلُوعٌ . إِرْتِفَاعٌ

Risk *n.* or *v. t.* خَطَرٌ . خَاطَرَ بِـ

Rite *n.* طَقْسٌ دِينِيٌّ . سُنَّةٌ

Ritual *a.* or *n.* طَقْسِيٌّ . كِتَابُ طُقُوسٍ

Rival *n.* or *v. t.* مُنَاظِرٌ . سَابَقَ

Rivalry *n.* مُسَابَقَةٌ . مُبَارَاةٌ

River *n.* نَهْرٌ ج أَنْهُرٌ وأَنْهَارٌ

Rivet *n.* or *v. t.* مِسْمَارٌ مُبَجَّنٌ . سَمَّرَ بِهِ

Rivulet *n.* نُهَيْرٌ . سَاقِيَةٌ

Road *n.* طَرِيقٌ . سِكَّةٌ . دَرْبٌ

Roadstead *n.* مَرْسًى . مَرْفَأٌ

Roam *v. i.* جَالَ ـُ . سَاحَ ـِ

Roan *a.* or *n.* فَرَسٌ كُمَيْتٌ مُبَقَّعٌ

Roar *v. i.* or *n.* زَمْجَرَ . زَأَرَ ـَ . زَئِيرٌ

Roast *v. t.* or *n.* شَوَى ـِ . مَشْوِي

Rob *v. t.* سَلَبَ ـُ . نَهَبَ ـَ

Robber *n.* لِصٌّ . سَرَّاقٌ

Robbery *n.* سَلْبٌ . سَرِقَةٌ

Robe *n.* or *v. t.* ثَوْبٌ . رِدَآءٌ . أَلْبَسَ

Robust *a.* ضَلِيعٌ . قَوِيُّ ٱلْجِسْمِ

Rock *n.* or *v. t.* صَخْرَةٌ . هَزَّ ـِ

Rocket *n.* سَهْمٌ نَارِيٌّ

Rocky *a.* صَخْرِيٌّ

Rod *n.* عَصًا

Roe *n.* أُنْثَى ٱلْأَيِّلِ

Rogue *n.* مَكَّارٌ . غَدَّارٌ . خَبِيثٌ

Roguery *n.* خُبْثٌ . مَكْرٌ . حِيَلٌ

Roil *v. t.* عَكَّرَ . كَدَّرَ . هَيَّجَ

Roll *v. t.* or *i.* دَحْرَجَ . تَدَحْرَجَ . طَوَى ـِ

Roll *n.* دَرْجٌ . قَائِمَةٌ . دَحْرَجَةٌ

Roller *n.* مِحْدَلَةٌ

Romance *n.* حِكَايَةٌ . خُرَافَةٌ

Romanism *n.* عَقَائِدُ كَنِيسَةٍ رُومِيَّةٍ

Romp *v. i.* or *n.* تَغَالَظَ فِي ٱللَّعِبِ . إِبْنَةٌ سَلِيطَةٌ

Roof *n.* سَقْفٌ . سَطْحٌ

Room *n.* مَكَانٌ . فَرَاغٌ . حُجْرَةٌ

Roomy *a.* فَسِيحٌ . رَحِيبٌ

Root *n.* or *v. i.* جِذْرٌ . أَصْلٌ . تَأَصَّلَ

Root *v. t.* نَبَشَ ـُ . إِسْتَأْصَلَ

Rope *n.* حَبْلٌ . مَرَسٌ

Rose *n.* وَرْدَةٌ

Rosette *n.* وَرْدَةٌ مِنْ شَرِيطٍ

Rosin *n.* رَاتِينَجٌ

Rosy *a.* وَرْدِيٌّ . مُحْمَرٌّ

Rot *v. i.* or *t.* or *n.* فَسَدَ ـُ . تَعَفُّنٌ

Rotary, Rotatory *a.* دَائِرٌ . دَوَّارٌ

Rotate *v. i.* or *t.* دَارَ ـُ . أَدَارَ

Rotation *n.* دَوَرَانٌ . تَنَاوُبٌ

Rotten *a.* فَاسِدٌ . عَفِنٌ

Rottenness *n.* فَسَادٌ . عُفُونَةٌ

Rotund *a.* كُرَوِيٌّ . مُسْتَدِيرٌ

Rotundity *a.* كُرَوِيَّةٌ

Rough *a.* خَشِنٌ . فَظٌّ . غَلِيظٌ

Roughness *n.* خُشُونَةٌ . غِلَاظَةٌ

Round *a.* or *n.* مُسْتَدِيرٌ . دَوْرٌ

Roundness *n.* إِسْتِدَارَةٌ . كُرَوِيَّةٌ

Rouse *v. t.* أَيْقَظَ . حَرَّكَ . حَرَّضَ

Rout *n.* or *v. t.* هَزِيمَةٌ . هَزَمَ ـِ

Route *n.* طَرِيقٌ

Routine *n.* أُسْلُوبٌ . عَادَةٌ

Rove *v. i.* جَالَ ـُ . سَاحَ ـِ

Row *n.* صَفٌّ . شَغَبٌ . خِصَامٌ

Row *v. t.* جَذَفَ ـِ . قَذَفَ ـِ

Royal *a.* مَلَكِيٌّ . مُلُوكِيٌّ

Royalist *n.* مَلَكِيُّ ٱلْحِزْبِ

Royalty *n.* مَلَكِيَّةٌ . مُلْكٌ . ضَرِيبَةٌ

Rub *v. t.* فَرَكَ ـُ . مَسَحَ ـَ . إِحْتَكَّ

Rub *n.* فَرْكٌ . حَكٌّ . صُعُوبَةٌ

Rubbish *n.* رَدْمٌ . نُفَايَةٌ . سَقَطٌ

Ruby *n.* or *a.* يَاقُوتَةٌ . يَاقُوتِيٌّ

Rudder *n.* دَفَّةُ ٱلسَّفِينَةِ

Ruddy *a.* أَحْمَرُ . أَشْقَرُ

Rude *a.* فَظٌّ

Rudeness *n.* غِلَاظَةٌ . فَظَاظَةٌ

Rudiment *n.* مَبْدَأٌ . أَصْلٌ

Rudimental / Rudimentary } *a.* إِبْتِدَائِيٌّ

Rue *v. t.* أَسِفَ ـَ . نَدِمَ ـَ

Rue *n.* (plant) سَذَابٌ

Ruff *n.* طَوْقٌ ذُو كَشْكَشٍ

Ruffian *n.* خَبِيثٌ . غَلِيظٌ . شَرِسٌ

Ruffle *v. t.* تَنَفَّشَ . أَضْجَرَ

Rug *n.* سَجَّادَةٌ . زُرْبِيَّةٌ

Rugged *a.* وَعْرٌ . خَشِنٌ

Ruin *v. t.* or *n.* خَرَبَ ـِ . خَرَابٌ

Ruinous *a.* خَرَابِيٌّ

Rule *n.* قَانُونٌ . قَاعِدَة . حُكْمٌ

Rule *v. t.* حَكَمَ ـُ . سَطَرَ

Ruler *n.* حَاكِمٌ . مُتَسَلِّطٌ . مِسْطَرَةٌ

Rumble *v. i.* خَرَّ ـُ . قَرْقَرَ

Ruminant *n.* حَيوانٌ مُجْتَرٌّ

Ruminate *n.* or *v. i.* إِجْتَرَّ . تَأَمَّلَ

Rummage *n.* or *v. t.* قَلَّبَ . فَتَّشَ

Rumour *n.* إِشَاعَةٌ . خَبَرٌ

Rump *n.* عَجُزٌ . إِلْيَةٌ

Rumple *v. t.* جَعَّدَ . غَضَّنَ

Run *v. i.* رَكَضَ ـُ . سَالَ ـِ جَرَى ـِ

Runaway *n.* هَارِبٌ . آبِق . شَارِدٌ

Rupture *n.* فَتْقٌ . شِقَاقٌ . إِنْفِجَارٌ

Rural *a.* رِيفِيٌّ . غَيْرُ مَدَنِيٍّ

Ruse *n.* حِيلَةٌ

Rush *n.* or *v. i.* إِقْتِحَامٌ . زَحْمَةٌ . إِقْتَحَمَ

Rush *n.* بَرْدِيٌّ (نَبَاتٌ)

Rust *n.* or *v. i.* صَدَأٌ . صَدِئَ ـَ

Rustic *a.* غَيْرُ مُهَذَّبٍ . خَشِنٌ

Rustle *v. i.* جَرَّ ـُ . خَشْخَشَ

Rusty *a.* صَدِئٌ

Ruthless *a.* قَاسٍ . بِلاَ رَأْفَةٍ

S

Sabbath *n.* سَبْتٌ . يَوْمُ ٱلأَحَدِ

Sabre *n.* سَيْفٌ ج سيوف

Sable *n.* or *a.* سَمُّورٌ (طَائِرٌ) . أَسْوَدُ

Saccharine *a.* سُكَّرِيٌّ

Sacerdotal *a.*	كَهْنُوتِيٌّ
Sack *n.* or *v. t.*	كِيسٌ . نَهَبَ ـُ
Sackcloth / Sacking } *n.*	خيشٌ . مِسْحٌ
Sacrament *n.*	سر دِينِيٌّ
Sacred *a.*	مقدسٌ . دِينِيٌّ . مُحَرَّمٌ
Sacredness *n.*	قُدْسٌ . حرْمِيَّةٌ
Sacrifice *n.* or *v. t.*	ذَبِيحَةٌ . ذَبَحَ ـَ . ضَحى
Sacrificial *a.*	ذَبِيحِيٌّ . قُرْبَانِيٌّ
Sacrilege *n.*	تَدْنِيسُ ٱلمقَدسِ
Sad *a.*	حَزِينٌ . كَئِيبٌ . مُحْزِنٌ
Sadden *v. t.*	أَحْزَنَ
Saddle *n.*	سَرْجٌ . بَرْذَعَه
Saddler *n.*	سَرَّاجٌ .(سُرُوجِيٌّ) بَرَاذِعِيٌّ
Sadducee *n.*	صَدُوقِيٌّ
Sadness *n.*	حزْنٌ . كآبَةٌ . غَمٌّ . لَهْفٌ
Safe *a.* or *n.*	سَالِمٌ . مَصُون . آمِنٌ
Safeguard *n.* or *v. t.*	حِمَايَةٌ . حَمى ـِ
Safety *n.*	أَمْنٌ . سَلَامَةٌ . نجَاةٌ
Safety-valve *n.*	صِمامُ آلَةٍ
Saffron *n.*	زَعفَرَان
Sag *v. i.*	حَطَّ ـُ مِنْ ثِقْلٍ
Sagacious *a.*	ذَكِيٌّ . فطِنٌ
Sagacity *n.*	ذَكَاءٌ . فِطْنَةٌ
Sage *a.* or *n.*	حَكِيمٌ . فَطِنٌ . قوَيْسَةٌ
Sail *n.* or *v. i.* or *t.*	قِلْعٌ . أَقْلَع . سَيَّرَ
Sailor *n.*	نوتِيٌّ . بَحْرِيٌّ . ملاحٌ
Saint *n.*	قَدِّيسٌ
Sake *n.*	قصدٌ . غَايَةٌ . شأنٌ
Salad *n.*	سَلَطَةٌ
Salary *n.*	راتِبٌ . معَاشٌ . مَاهِيَةٌ
Sale *n.*	بيْعٌ . رَوَاجٌ
Saleable *a.*	رَائِجٌ
Salient *a.*	بارِز . ظَاهِرٌ
Saline *a.*	مِلْحِيٌّ . مَالِحٌ
Saliva *n.*	لُعَابٌ . رِيق
Sallow *a.*	مُصْفَرّ

Sallowness *n.* إِصفِرَارٌ . صُفْرَةٌ

Sally *n.* or *v. i.* هُجومٌ . هَجَمَ عَلَى

Saloon *n.* غُرْفَةُ ٱستِقبَالٍ

Salt *n.* or *v. t.* مِلْحٌ . مَلَّحَ

Salt-cellar *n.* مَمْلَحَةٌ

Saltness *n.* مُلُوحَةٌ

Salt-petre *n.* مِلْحُ البارُودِ

Salubrious *a.* نَافِعٌ لِلصِّحَةِ

Salubrity *n.* مُلاَءَمَةٌ لِلصِّحَةِ

Salutary *a.* مُفِيدٌ . نَافِعٌ

Salutation *n.* تَحِيَّةٌ . سَلاَمٌ

Salute *v. t.* or *n.* سَلَّمَ عَلَى . تَسْلِيمٌ

Salvation *n.* خَلاَصٌ . نَجَاةٌ . إِنْقَاذٌ

Salve *n.* مَرْهَمٌ . دُهْنٌ

Salver *n.* طَبَقٌ ج أَطْبَاقٌ

Samaritan *n.* سامِرِيٌّ

Same *n.* ذَاتٌ . نفسٌ . هُوَ هُوَ

Sameness *n.* ذَاتِيَّةٌ . مُمَاثَلَةٌ

Sample *n.* عَيْنِيَّةٌ .(مَسْطَرَةٌ). نَمُوذَجٌ

Sanative / Sanatory } *a.* شَافٍ. مُفِيدٌ لِلصِّحَةِ

Sanctification *n.* تَقْدِيسٌ . تَطْهِيرٌ

Sanctify *v. t.* قَدَّسَ . طَهَّرَ

Sanctimonious *a.* مُتَظَاهِرٌ بِٱلتقوَى

Sanction *n.* or *v. t.* مُصَادَقَةٌ . أَثْبَتَ

Sanctity *n.* قَدَاسَةٌ . قُدْسٌ

Sanctuary *n.* مَقْدِسٌ . مَعْبَدٌ . مَلاَذٌ

Sand *n.* رَمْلٌ ج رِمَالٌ

Sandal *n.* حِذَاءٌ . نَعْلٌ

Sandal wood *n.* صَنْدَلٌ

Sandal-fly *n.* بَعوضَةٌ (سُكَيْت)

Sandstone *n.* حَجَرٌ رَمْلِيٌّ

Sandwich *n.* لَحْمٌ بَيْنَ قِطْعَتَي خُبْزٍ

Sandy *a.* رَمْلِي

Sane *a.* سَلِيمُ ٱلْعَقْلِ

Sanguinary *a.* دَمَوِيٌّ . سَفَّاكُ ٱلدمِ

Sanguine *a.* وَاثِقٌ . كَثِيرُ ٱلرَّجَاءِ

Sanitary *a.* صِحِّيٌّ . مفيد لِلصِّحةِ

Sanity *n.* سَلَامَةُ ٱلْعَقْلِ . صِحتهُ

Sap *n.* or *v. t.* عَصِيرُ ٱلنَّبَاتِ . هَدَمَ ٱلاساس

Sapient *a.* حَكِيمٌ . مُتَصَنِّعُ ٱلْحِكْمَةِ

Sapling *n.* شُجَيْرَةٌ

Sapphire *n.* يَاقُوتٌ ازرقُ

Saracen *n.* شَرْقِيٌّ . عَرَبِيٌّ

Sarcasm *n.* تَهَكُّمٌ . إِسْتِهْزَآءٌ

Sarcastic / Sarcastical *a.* تَهَكُّمِيٌّ

Sarcophagus *n.* نَاوُوسٌ (تابوت قديم)

Sardonic *a.* (ضَحْكٌ) . تَهَكُّمِيٌّ

Sash *n.* زُنَّارٌ . بِرْوَاز نافِذَةٍ

Satan *n.* إِبْلِيسٌ . ٱلشَّيْطَانُ

Satanic / Satanical *a.* إِبْلِيسِيٌّ . شَيْطَانِيٌّ

Satchel *n.* كِيسٌ صَغِيرٌ

Satellite *n.* تَابِعٌ . قَمَرٌ

Sate / Satiate *v. t.* شَبَّعَ . أَرْضَى . أَفْعَمَ

Satiety *n.* شَبَعٌ

Satin *n.* أَطْلَسُ حَرِيرٍ

Satire *n.* هِجَآءٌ

Satiric / Satirical *a.* هِجَآئِيٌّ

Satirize *v. t.* هَجَا ـُ

Satisfaction *n.* رِضًى . إِرْضَاءٌ

Satisfactory *a.* مُرْضٍ . كَافٍ

Satisfy *v. t.* أَرْضَى . أَقْنَعَ

Saturate *v. t.* أَشْرَبَ . أَشْبَعَ

Saturday *n.* يَوْمُ ٱلسَّبْتِ

Saturn *n.* زُحَلُ

Sauce *n.* مَرَقَةٌ

Saucer *n.* صَحْنٌ صَغِيرٌ . سُكُرُّجَةٌ

Saucy *a.* وَقِحٌ . سَلِيطٌ

Saunter *v. i.* مَشَى مُتَكَاسِلًا

Sausage *n.* مَقَانِقُ . سُجُقٌّ

Savage *n.* or *a.* هَمَجٌ . وَحْشِيٌّ . جَافٍ

Savageness *n.* تَوَحُّشٌ . قَسَاوَةٌ . هَمَجِيَّةٌ

Savant *n.* عَلَّامَةٌ

Save *v.t.* or *pr.* خلّص . إقتصد. إلا

Saving *a.* or *n.* مقتصد. إقتصادٌ. إستثناءٌ

Saviour *n.* مُخلّصٌ. فادٍ

Savour *n.* or *v. i.* طعمٌ. إتّصفَ ب

Savoury *a.* لذيذٌ. طيّبٌ. زكيٌّ

Saw *n.* or *v. t.* منشارٌ. نشرَ ـُ

Sawyer *n.* نشّارٌ

Say *v. t.* قالَ ـُ أخبرَ

Saying *n.* قولٌ . مثَلٌ

Scab *n.* جلبةٌ

Scabbard *n.* غمدٌ . قرابٌ

Scaffold *n.* صقالة

Scaffolding *n.* صقالات

Scald *v. t.* سلقَ ـُ. سمطَ ـِ

Scale *n.* كفّة ميزانٍ . حرشفٌ

Scale *v. t.* قشّرَ . تسوّر . تسلق

Scalp *n.* or *v. t.* فروةُ الرأسِ . نزعها

Scalpel *n.* مِشرط ج مشارطُ

Scaly *a.* ذو حراشف . حرشفيٌّ

Scamp *n.* خبيثٌ . شرّيرٌ

Scamper *v. i.* ركضَ ـُ. فرَّ ـِ

Scan *v. t.* تفرّسَ . وزنَ الشعرَ

Scandal *n.* عارٌ. إفتراءٌ. فضيحةٌ

Scandalize *v. t.* فضحَ . إفترى . اخجل

Scandalous *a.* معيبٌ. فاضحٌ. افترائيٌّ

Scant, Scanty *a.* ناقصٌ. قليلٌ

Scantiness, Scantness *n.* نقصٌ . قلةٌ

Scape-goat *n.* حاملُ ذنوبِ غيرهِ

Scar *n.* ندبةٌ. أثرُ جرحٍ

Scarce *a.* نادرٌ. قليلُ الوجودِ

Scarcely *ad.* بالجهدِ . نادراً

Scarcity *n.* قلةُ الوجودِ . ندرةٌ

Scare *v. t.* خوّفَ . أفزعَ . أرهبَ

Scarecrow *n.* شبحٌ للتخويفِ

Scarf *n.* وشاحٌ . حمالةٌ

Scarify *v. t.* شرطَ ـِ. حجمَ ـُ

Scarlatina / Scarlet-fever } n. اَلْحُمَّى اَلْقِرْمِزِيَّة

Scarlet a. or n. قِرْمِزِيٌّ . قِرْمِز

Scath / Scathe } v. t. آذَى . أَهْلَكَ

Scathless a. غَيْرُ مُؤْذًى . سالِمٌ

Scatter v. t. فَرَّقَ . بَدَّدَ

Scavenger n. زَبَّالٌ

Scene n. مَنْظَرٌ . فَصْل رِوَايَةٍ

Scenery n. مَنْظَرٌ

Scent n. or v. t. رَائِحَة . إِشْتَمَّ . عَطَّرَ

Sceptre n. صَوْلَجَانٌ . مُلْكٌ

Sceptic n. / Sceptical a. } مُرْتَابٌ

Scepticism n. إِرْتِيَابٌ . شَكٌّ

Schedule n. قَائِمَةٌ . جَدْوَلٌ

Scheme n. تَدْبِيرٌ . مَقْصَد . اسلُوبٌ

Scheme v. t. دَبَّرَ . إِخْتَرَعَ . رَسَمَ ـ

Schism n. شِقَاقٌ . إِخْتِلَافٌ

Schismatic n. or a. رَافِضِيٌّ خَارِجِيٌّ

Scholar n. تِلْمِيذٌ . طَالِبٌ . عَالِمٌ

Scholarly a. عَالِمٌ . عِلْمِيٌّ

Scholarship n. عِلْمٌ مَالٌ وَقْفٌ لِتِلْمِيذٍ

Scholastic a. مَدْرَسِيٌّ

School n. مَدْرَسَةٌ . مَذْهَبٌ

Schooling n. تَدْرِيسٌ . تَعْلِيمٌ

School-master n. مُعَلِّمُ مَدْرَسَةٍ

Schooner n. سَفِينَةٌ ذَاتُ سَارِيَتَيْنِ

Science n. عِلْمٌ . فَنٌّ

Scientific / Scientifical } a. عِلْمِيٌّ

Scintillate v. i. تَلَأْلَأَ . بَرَقَ ـُ

Scissors n. pl. مِقَصٌّ . مِقْرَاضٌ

Scoff n. or v. i. هُزْءٌ . هَزَأَ ـَ

Scold v. t. or i. وَبَّخَ . عَنَّفَ . زَجَرَ ـُ

Scolding n. تَعْنِيفٌ . زَجْرٌ

Scoop n. or v. t. مِغْرَفَةٌ . غَرَفَ ـِ . حَفَرَ ـِ

Scope n. مَدًى . مَجَالٌ . غَايَةٌ

Scorch v. t. حَرَقَ ـِ . كَوَى ـ شَوَّطَ

Score n. عِشْرُونَ . حِسَابٌ . شَأْنٌ

Score *v. t.* خَطَّطَ . قَيَّدَ في حِسَابٍ

Scorn *n.* or *v.t.* إِحْتِقَارٌ. إِزْدَرَى بِ

Scorner
Scornful } مُزْدَرٍ . مُحْتَقِرٌ

Scorpion *n.* عَقْرَبٌ

Scoundrel *n.* خَبِيثٌ . شِرِّيرٌ . قَبِيحٌ

Scour *v. t.* جَلَى ـِ . طَافَ عَاجِلاً

Scourge *n.* or *v. t.* سَوْطٌ . بَلِيَّةٌ . جَلَدَ ـُ

Scot-free *a.* مَعْفِيٌّ مِنْ . سَالِمٌ

Scout *n.* or *v. t.* جَاسُوسٌ . إِسْتَخَفَّ بِ

Scowl *n.* or *v. i.* عُبُوسَةٌ . عَبَّسَ . كَلَحَ ـَ

Scragged
Scraggy خَشِنٌ . نَحِيفٌ

Scramble *n.* or *v. i.* مُنَاوَشَةٌ . تَسَلَّقَ

Scrap *n.* قِطْعَةٌ صَغِيرَةٌ . حِتَّةٌ

Scrape *v. t.* حَتَّ ـُ . كَشَطَ ـِ . حَكَّ ـُ

Scraper *n.* مِكْشَطٌ . مِحَتٌّ

Scratch *v. t.* or *i.* خَدَشَ ـِ . حَكَّ ـُ

Scratch *n.* خَمْشٌ . خَدْشَة

Scrawl *n.* خط رَدِيءٌ

Scream
Screech } *v. i.* or *n.* صَاحَ ـِ . صَيْحَةٌ

Screen *n.* or *v. t.* سِتْرٌ . سَتَرَ ـُ

Screw *n.* or *v. t.* (برمه) . شَدَّ بها

Scribble *v.i.* or *t.* أَسَاءَ خَطًّا وَمَعْنًى

Scribbler *n.* مُؤَلِّفٌ رَكِيكٌ

Scribe *n.* كَاتِبٌ

Scrimp *v. t.* ضَيَّقَ . قَصَّرَ

Script *n.* أَحْرُفُ طَبْعٍ شَبِيهَةٌ بِالْخَطِّ

Scriptural *a.* مُطَابِقٌ لِلْكِتَابِ ٱلْمُقَدَّسِ

Scripture *n.* اَلْكِتَابُ ٱلْمُقَدَّسُ

Scrofula *n.* دَاءُ ٱلْخَنَازِيرِ

Scrofulous *a.* مُصَابٌ بِدَاءِ ٱلْخَنَازِيرِ

Scroll *n.* دَرْجٌ

Scrub *n.* or *v. t.* خَسِيسٌ . جَلَى ـِ . مَسَّحَ

Scruple *n.* or *v. i.* شَكٌّ . إِرْتِيَابٌ . تَرَدَّدَ

Scrupulous *a.* مُتَرَدِّدٌ . مُحْتَرِسٌ

Scrutinize *v. t.* دَقَّقَ ٱلنَّظَرَ . تَفَحَّصَ

Scrutiny *n.* فَحْصٌ مُدَقِّقٌ . إِنْعَامُ نَظَرٍ

Scuffle *n.* or *v. t.* مُصَارَعَةٌ . نَاوَشَ

Sculptor *n.* نَحَاتٌ . نَقَاشٌ

Sculpture *n.* صِنَاعَةُ ٱلنحتِ

Scum *n.* or *v. t.* رَغْوَةٌ . زَبَدٌ . نَزَعَهَا

Scurf *n.* هِبْرِيَةٌ . قِشْرَةُ ٱلرَّأْسِ

Scurrilous *a.* قَبِيحٌ . رَذِيلٌ . سَفِيهٌ

Scurvy *n.* or *a.* دَاءُ ٱلإِسْكُرْبُوطِ . خَسِيسٌ

Scuttle *n.* or *v.t.* سطْلُ فَحْمٍ . ثَقَبَ سَفِينَةً لِتَغْرَقَ

Scythe *n.* مِحْصَدٌ . مِنْجَلٌ

Sea *a.* بَحْرٌ

Seaboard / Seacoast } *n.* شَطُّ ٱلْبَحْرِ . رِيفٌ

Seafarer / Seafaring } *n.* مَلَّاحٌ . بَحْرِيٌّ

n. or *v.* خَتْمٌ . خَاتِمٌ خَتَمَ . عِجلُ ٱلْبَحْرِ

Seam *n.* دَرْزٌ . نَدْبَةٌ . طَبقَة

Seaman *n.* بَحْرِيٌّ

Seamanship *n.* مِلَاحه

Seamstress *a.* خَيَاطَةٌ

Seaport *n.* مِينَاءُ . فُرْضَةٌ

Sear *v. t.* كَوَى ـِ . جَفَّفَ . صَلَّبَ

Search *v. t.* or *n.* فَتَّشَ . تَفَحَّصَ . تَفْتِيشٌ

Searching *a.* مُسْتَقْصٍ . مُدَقِّقٌ . نَافِذٌ

Seasick *a.* مُصَابٌ بِدُوَارِ ٱلْبَحْرِ

Seaside *n.* سَاحِلُ ٱلْبَحْرِ . رِيفُهُ

Season *n.* فَصْلٌ . وَقْتٌ . مُدَّةٌ

Seasonable *a.* فِي وَقْتِهِ . فِي مَحَلِّهِ

Seasoning *n.* تَابِلٌ . تَتْبِيلٌ . تَجْفِيفٌ

Seat *n.* or *v. t.* مَقْعَدٌ . مَجْلِسٌ . أَجْلَسَ

Seaward *ad.* إِلَى جِهَةِ ٱلْبَحْرِ

Secede *v.i.* إِنْفَصَلَ . إِعْتَزَلَ . خَرَجَ ـُ

Secession *n.* إِنْفِصَالٌ . خُرُوجٌ

Seclude *v. t.* حَجَبَ ـُ . جَعَلَ بِعُزْلَةٍ

Seclusion *n.* عُزْلَةٌ . خُلُوٌّ

Second *n.* ثَانِيَةٌ ج ثَوَانٍ

Second *a.* or *n.* or *v. t.* ٱلثَّانِي . أَيَّدَ

Secondary *a.* ثَانَوِيٌّ . غَيْرُ مُهِمٍّ

Second-hand *a.* مُسْتَعْمَلٌ

Second-rate *a.* مِنَ ٱلدَّرَجَةِ ٱلثَّانِيَةِ

Secrecy *n.* سر . كتمان

Secret *a.* or *n.* سرّيّ . مكتوم . سرّ

Secretary *n.* كاتب . ناظر دائرة

Secrete *v. t.* اخفى . خبأ . افرز

Secretion *n.* إخفاء . إفراز

Sect *n.* طائفة . شيعة . مذهب

Sectarian *a.* }
Sectary *n.* } طائفي . تحزبي

Section *n.* قطعة . قسم . فصل

Secular *a.* غير ديني . عالمي

Secularize *v. t.* حوّل إلى غاية عالمية

Secure *a.* or *v. t.* مطمئنّ . حصل . أحرز

Security *n.* أمن طمأنينة . ضمان

Sedate *a.* رزين . هادي

Sedative *a.* or *n.* مسكّن

Sedentary *a.* قاعد . ملازم الجلوس

Sediment *n.* راسب . ثقل

Sedition *n.* فتنة . ثورة . شغب

Seditious *a.* مشاغب . مهيّج .. مثير

Seduce *v. t.* أغوى . أضلّ

Seductive *a.* مغو مفتتن . مضل

Sedulous *a.* كدود . مجتهد

See *v. t.* or *n.* رأى ـَ . نظر ـُ . ابرشية

Seed *n.* بزر . زرع . نسل

Seedling *n.* نبات من بزرة

Seed-time *n.* أبان الزرع

Seedy *a.* كثير البزر . بال

Seek *v. t.* طلب ـُ . فتّش . جدّ ـِ

Seeing *con.* بما أن

Seem *v. i.* ظهر ـَ . بان ـِ

Seemingly *ad.* بحسب الظاهر

Seemly *a.* لائق . حسن

Seer *n.* رائي . نبي

Seethe *v. t.* طبخ ـُ . غلى

Segment *n.* قطعة

Segregate *v. t.* فصل ـِ . أفرز

Seize *v.t.* قبض ـِ . خطف ـَ . إعترى

Seizure *n.* قَبْضٌ . ضَبْطٌ

Seldom *ad.* نَادِراً . قَلَمَا

Select *v. t.* or *a.* إِخْتَارَ . إِصْطَفَى . صَفِيٌّ

Self *n.* ذَاتٌ . نَفْسٌ

Self-conceit *n.* عُجْبٌ

Self-denial *n.* إِنْكَارُ ٱلذَّاتِ

Self-evident *a.* غَنِيٌّ عَنِ ٱلْبَيَانِ

Selfish *a.* مُحِبٌّ ٱلذَّات

Selfishness *n.* مَحَبَّة ٱلذاتِ

Self-respect *n.* إِحْتِرَامُ ٱلذاتِ

Self-same *a.* ذَاتٌ . بِعَيْنِهِ

Self-will *n.* عِنَادٌ

Sell *v. t.* بَاعَ ـِ

Semblance *n.* شِبْهٌ . شَكْل . صُورَةٌ

Semi *n.* نُصْفٌ (فِي ٱلتَّرْكِيبِ)

Semi-annual *a.* كُلَّ نُصْفِ سَنَةٍ

Semi-circle *n.* نصفُ دَائِرَةٍ

Semicolon *n.* (;) عَلاَمَة وَقْفٍ كَذَا

Seminary *n.* مَدْرَسَةٌ

Semitic *a.* سَامِيٌّ

Senate *n.* مَشْيَخَةٌ . مَجْلِسُ اعيَان

Senator *n.* عُضْوُ مَجْلِسِ ٱلأَعْيَانِ

Send *v. t.* أَرْسلَ . بَعَثَ ـَ

Senility *n.* شَيْخُوخَةٌ . كِبَرٌ

Senior *n.* or *a.* أَكْبَرُ عُمْراً . أَلْمتَقَدِّمُ

Seniority *n.* أَسْبَقِيَّةٌ سِنًّا أَوْ مَنْصِباً

Sensation *n.* حِسٌّ . شُعُورٌ . تَأْثِيرٌ

Sensational *a.* مُهَيِّجٌ ٱلْعَوَاطِفِ

Sense *n.* حِسٌّ . حَاسَّةٌ . مَعْنًى

Senseless *a.* بِلاَحِسٍّ أَوْمَعْنًى . مَغْشِيٌّ عَلَيْهِ

Sensibility *n.* حَاسِّيَّةٌ . رِقَّةُ ٱلنفْسِ

Sensible *a.* حَسَّاسٌ . عَاقِلٌ . مَحْسُوسٌ

Sensitive *a.* دَقِيقُ ٱلْحِسِّ وَٱلاَنْفِعَالِ

Sensual *a.*, Sensualist *n.* حَيَوَانِيٌّ . شَهْوَانِيٌّ

Sensualism, Sensuality *n.* شَهْوَانِيَّةٌ

Sentence *n.* جملَةٌ . قَضَاءٌ . حُكْمٌ

Sentient *n.* حَسَّاسٌ. مُدْرِكٌ بِٱلْحَسِّ

Sentiment *n.* حِس . عَاطِفَةٌ . مَعْنًى

Sentinel / Sentry } *n.* حَارِسٌ. خَفَرٌ

Separable *a.* قَابِلُ ٱلْفَصْلِ

Separate *v. t.* or *a.* فَصَلَ ـِ مُنْفَصِلٌ

Separation *n.* فَصْلٌ إِنْفِصَالٌ. مُفَارَقَة

Separatist *n.* مُعْتَزِلٌ . مُنْشَقٌّ

September *n.* شَهْرُ أَيْلُولَ. (سبتمبر)

Septennial *a.* كُلَّ سَبْعِ سِنِين

Septentrional *a.* شِمَالِيٌّ

Septuagenarian *n.* إِبْنُ ٧٠ سَنَةً

Septuagint *n.* أَلتَّرْجَمَةُ السَّبْعِينِيَّةُ

Sepulchre *n.* قَبْرٌ. ضَرِيحٌ

Sepulture *n.* دَفْنٌ

Sequel *n.* تَابِعٌ. تَالٍ . نَتِيجَةٌ

Sequence *n.* تَتَابُعٌ. تَال

Sequester / Sequestrate } *v. t.* ضَبَطَ ـُ حَجَزَ ـُ

Serdphic *a.* مَلَائِكِيٌّ . بَهِيٌّ

Serenade *n.* or *v. t.* عَزْفُ ٱلْمُوسِيقَى بِٱللَّيْلِ

Serene *a.* هَادِئٌ . صَافٍ . رَصِينٌ

Serenity *n.* صَفَاءٌ . هُدُوءٌ

Serf *n.* عَبْدٌ

Sergeant *n.* جَاوِيشٌ. شَاوِيشٌ

Serial *a.* or *n.* مُتَتَابِعٌ. رِوَايَةٌ تُطْبَعُ أَجْزَاءً مُتَتَابِعَةً

Series *n.* نَسَقٌ. سِلْسِلَةٌ

Serious *a.* رَزِينٌ. جَادٌّ . عَظِيمٌ

Sermon *n.* مَوْعِظَةٌ

Serpent *n.* حَيَّةٌ . ثُعْبَانٌ

Serpentine *a.* مُلْتَفٌّ كَٱلْحَيَّةِ

Servant *n.* خَادِمٌ. أَجِيرٌ

Serve *v. t.* خَدَمَ ـُ. عَبَدَ ـُ. صَلَحَ لِ

Service *n.* خِدْمَةٌ. عِبَادَةٌ . مَعْرُوفٌ

Serviceable *a.* مُفِيدٌ . صَالِحٌ لِ

Servile *a.* ذَلِيلٌ . خَاضِعٌ

Servility *n.* تَذَلُّلٌ . عُبُودِيَّة

Servitor *n.* خَادِمٌ . تَابِعٌ

Servitude *n.* عُبُودِيَّةٌ . رِقٌّ

Sesame *n.* سِمْسِمٌ

Session *n.* جَلْسَةٌ

Sesspool *n.* بَالُوعَةُ أَوْسَاخٍ

Set *v.t.* or *i.* وَضَعَ ـَ . جَبَرَ ـُ . غَابَ ـِ

Set *n.* طَقْمٌ . قَوْمٌ . حِزْبٌ

Settle *v. i.* سَكَنَ ـُ . أَثْقَلَ . هَدَأَ

Settle *v. t.* أَسْكَنَ . دَبَّرَ . أَنْجَزَ

Settlement *n.* مَسْكَنٌ . تَسْوِيَةٌ

Settlings *n. pl.* دُرْدِيٌّ . رُسُوبٌ

Seven *a.* سَبْعٌ أَوْ سَبْعَة

Seventh *a.* سَابِعٌ

Seventeen *a.* سَبْعَةَ عَشَرَ

Seventieth / Seventy *a.* سَبْعُونَ

Sever *v. t.* فَصَلَ ـِ . قَطَعَ ـَ

Several *a.* بَعْضٌ . بِضْعَةٌ . فَرْدٌ

Severally *ad.* أَفْرَادًا . عَلَى حِدَةٍ

Severance *n.* فَصْلٌ . قَطْعٌ

Severe *a.* قَاسٍ . صَارِمٌ . شَدِيدٌ

Severity *n.* صَرَامَةٌ . شِدَّةٌ . عُنْفٌ

Sew *v. t.* خَاطَ ـِ . خَيَّطَ

Sewer *n.* خَيَّاطٌ . بَالُوعَةٌ . سَرَبٌ

Sex *n.* جِنْسٌ

Sextant *n.* آلَةٌ لِقِيَاسِ ٱلزَّوَايَا

Sexton *n.* قَنْدَلَفْتٌ . حَفَّارُ ٱلْقُبُورِ

Sexual *a.* جِنْسِيٌّ . مُمَيِّزُ ٱلْجِنْسِ

Shabby *a.* رَثِيثٌ . خَسِيسٌ

Shackle *v. t.* قَيَّدَ . عَاقَ

Shackles *n. pl.* قُيُودٌ . أَغْلَالٌ

Shade *n.* or *v. t.* ظِلٌّ . خَيَالٌ . ظَلَّلَ

Shadow *n.* ظِلٌّ . رَمْزٌ

Shadowy *a.* مُظَلَّلٌ . وَهْمِيٌّ . مُبْهَمٌ

Shady *a.* مُظَلِّلٌ . كَثِيرُ ٱلظِّلِّ

Shaft *n.* سَهْمٌ . بِئْرٌ . عَرِيشٌ

Shagged / Shaggy *a.* أَشْعَرُ . كَثٌّ

Shake *v. t.* or *i.* or *n.* هَزَّ . اهتز . هزة

Shall *aux. v.* فِعلٌ إِضافي يدلُّ عَلَى ٱلإِستِقبَالِ

Shallow *a.* قَلِيلُ ٱلغَوْرِ . ضعيفٌ

Sham *n.* or *a.* or *v. i.* تصنُّعٌ . غِشٌّ

Shambles *n. pl.* مسلَخٌ . مجزَرٌ

Shame *n.* خزيٌ . عارٌ . خَجلٌ

Shamefaced *a.* مستَحٍ . خَجِلٌ

Shameful *a.* مُخزٍ . مُعيبٌ . قبيحٌ

Shameless *a.* بِلاَ حيَاءٍ

Shank *n.* ساقٌ . يَدُ آلَةٍ

Shanty *n.* كوخ

Shape *v.t.* or *n.* كَوَّنَ . صُورَةٌ . هيئَةٌ

Shapeless *a.* بِلاَ شَكلٍ أَوْ تَرتِيبٍ

Shapely *a.* جَمِيلُ ٱلشَّكلِ

Share *v. t.* or *i.* قَاسَمَ . شارَكَ

Share *n.* حصَّة . سهمٌ . سِكَة

Share-holder *n.* صَاحِبُ سهمٍ

Shark *a.* كَلبُ ٱلبَحرِ

Sharp *a.* حَادٌّ . حرِّيفٌ . خَارِقٌ . ذَكِي

Sharpen *v. t.* سنَّ . انهَضَ

Sharpness *n.* حِدَّةٌ . حِذقٌ . شِدَّةٌ

Shatter *v. t.* كَسَّرَ . قَصفَ . ابَادَ

Shave *v. t.* حَلَقَ ـِ . غَبَنَ ـِ

Shaving *n.* نُجَارَة . شَرِيحَة رَقِيقَةٌ

Shawl *n.* شَالٌ

She *pron.* هِيَ

Sheaf *n.* حزمَةُ قمحٍ

Shear *v. t.* جَزَّ ـُ

Shears *n. pl.* مجز . مِقَصٌّ

Sheath *n.* غِلاَفٌ . غِمدٌ

Sheathe *v. t.* غَلفَ ـِ . غَمَدَ ـُ

Shed *v.t.* سَفَكَ ـُ . ذَرَفَ ـِ . خَلَعَ ـَ

Sheep *n.* غَنَمٌ . ضَأن . شَاة

Sheep-fold *n.* حظِيرَةٌ . صِيرَة

Sheepish *a.* مستَحٍ . خَجِلٌ

Sheer *a.* مَحْضٌ . خَالِصٌ

Sheet *n.* مُلَاءَة . شَرْشَفٌ . طَلْحِيَّةٌ

Shelf *n.* رَفٌّ ج رُفُوفٌ

Shell *n.* قِشْرَةٌ . صَدَفَةٌ . قُنْبُلَةٌ

Shell *v. t.* قَشَرَ ـُ . رَمَى بِٱلْقَنَابِلِ

Shell-fish *n.* صَدَفٌ

Shelter *n.* or *v. t.* مَأْوًى . آوى . حَمَى ـِ

Shepherd *n.* رَاعٍ ج رُعَاةٌ

Sherbet *n.* شَرَابٌ

Sheriff *n.* مَأْمُورٌ يُجْرِي ٱلْأَحْكَامَ

Shield *n.* or *v. t.* تُرْسٌ . حَمَى ـِ . صَانَ

Shift *v. t.* or *n.* نَقَلَ . غَيَّرَ . حِيلَةٌ

Shiftless *a.* عَدِيمُ ٱلتَّدْبِيرِ . قَاصِرٌ

Shilling *n.* ١/٢٠ مِنَ ٱللِّيرَا ٱلْإِنكليزيَّةِ

Shin *n.* مُقَدَّمُ ٱلسَّاقِ

Shine *v. i.* أَضَاءَ . أَشْرَقَ

Shingle *n.* or *v. t.* لَوْحٌ رَقِيقٌ . غَطَّى بِهِ

Shining, Shiny } *a.* مُضِيءٌ لَامِعٌ

Ship *n.* or *v. t.* سَفِينَةٌ . أَنْزَلَ فِيهَا

Shipment *n.* إِرْسَالِيَّةُ بِضَاعَةٍ

Shipping *n.* مُجْتَمَعُ سُفُنٍ

Shipwreck *n.* ٱنْكِسَارُ سَفِينَةٍ

Shire *n.* مُقَاطَعَةٌ . لِوَاءٌ

Shirk *v. t.* تَجَنَّبَ (ٱلْوَاجِبَ)

Shirt *n.* or *v. t.* قَمِيصٌ ج قُمْصَانٌ . أَلْبَسَهُ

Shiver *v. i.* or *t.* اقْشَعَرَّ . حَطَّمَ

Shoal *n.* سِرْبٌ (سَمَكٍ) . ضَحْلٌ

Shock *n.* or *v. t.* صَدْمَةٌ . رَجَّةٌ . ارْعَبَ

Shocking *a.* هَائِلٌ . مُكَدِّرٌ

Shoe *n.* or *v. t.* حِذَاءٌ . نَعْلٌ . نَعَلَ ـَ

Shoemaker *n.* سَكَّافٌ . إِسْكَافٌ

Shoot *v. t.* or *i.* أَطْلَقَ . رَمَى ـِ . فَرَّخَ

Shoot *n.* فَرْخٌ . عُسْلُجٌ

Shop *n.* دُكَّانٌ . حَانُوتٌ

Shop-keeper *n.* صَاحِبُ دُكَّانٍ

Shopping *n.* شِرَاءٌ . مِسْوَاقٌ

Shore *n.* شط . شاطِئٌ

Short *a.* قَصيرٌ . نَاقِصٌ

Shorten *v. t.* or *i.* قَصَّرَ . تَقَصَّرَ

Short-lived *a.* قصيرُ ٱلْعُمْرِ

Shortness *n.* قِصَرٌ . إِيجَازٌ

Short-sighted *a.* قَصيرُ ٱلْبَصَرِ

Shot *n.* رَمْيَةٌ . خرْدُقٌ . رَامٍ

Should *pret.* of shall

Shoulder *n.* كَتِفٌ . مَنْكِبٌ

Shout *v. t.* or *n.* زَعَقَ ـَ . صَاحَ . هُتَافٌ

Shove *v. t.* or *n.* دَفَعَ ـَ دَفْعَةٌ

Shovel *n.* or *v. t.* مِجْرَفَةٌ . جَرَفَ ـُ

Show *v. t.* أَظْهَرَ . بَيَّنَ . هَدَى ـِ

Show *n.* مَعْرَضٌ . مَنْظَرٌ . تَظَاهُرٌ

Shower *n.* مَطْرَةٌ

Showy *a.* زَاهٍ . مزَخْرَفٌ

Shred *n.* or *v. t.* شِقَّةٌ . قِطْعَةٌ رَقيقَةٌ . قَطَعَ

Shrew *n.* سَلِيطَةٌ . صَخَّابَةٌ

Shrewd *a.* حَاذِقٌ . دَاهٍ

Shriek *v. i.* or *n.* صَرَخَ ـُ . صُرَاخٌ

Shrill *a.* حَادُّ ٱلصَّوْتِ

Shrine *n.* مَقَامٌ مُقَدَّسٌ . مَعْبَدٌ

Shrink *v. i.* تَقَلَّصَ . نَقَصَ . ٱشْمَأَزَّ

Shrivel *v. t.* or *i.* غَضَّنَ . تَغَضَّنَ

Shroud *n.* or *v.t.* كَفَنٌ . سِتْرٌ . سَتَرَ

Shrub *n.* نَجْمٌ ٱلأَشْجَارِ . شُجَيْرَةٌ

Shrubbery *n.* مُجْتَمَعُ أَنْجُمٍ

Shrubby *a.* نَجْمِيٌّ . كَثِيرُ ٱلأَنْجُمِ

Shrug *v. t.* or *n.* هَزَّ (ٱلأَكْتَافَ)

Shudder *n.* or *v. i.* ٱرْتِعَاشٌ . ٱرْتَجَفَ

Shuffle *v. t.* خَلَطَ . ٱحْتَالَ

Shun *v. t.* أَعْرَضَ عَنْ . ٱجْتَنَبَ

Shut *v. t.* or *i.* أَغْلَقَ . انْغَلَقَ

Shutter *n.* دَرْفَةٌ

Shuttle *n.* مَكُّوكٌ

Shy *a.* or *v.i.* مُسْتَحٍ . وَجِلٌ . أَجْفَلَ

Shyness *n.* حَيَاءٌ . وَجَلٌ

Sibyl *n.* كاهِنَةٌ . وثَنيّـةٌ . عرَّافَةٌ

Sick *a.* مَريضٌ. عَليل

Sicken *v. t.* or *i.* قزَّزَ . مَرِضَ

Sickish *a.* مقزِّز

Sickle *n.* مِنْجَل

Sickly *a.* وَخيمٌ . سَقيمٌ. ضَعيفٌ

Sickness *n.* مَرَضٌ. عِلَّةٌ

Side *n.* جَانبٌ . نَاحِيَةٌ . حزْبٌ

Sideboard *n.* خزَانَةُ السُّفْرَةِ

Sidelong *a.* جَانِبيٌّ . منْحَرِفٌ

Sidereal *a.* كَوْكَبيٌّ . نجْميٌّ

Side-saddle *n.* سَرْجٌ لِلنِّسَاءِ

Sidewise *ad.* بِالعَرْضِ . جَانباً

Siege *n.* مُحَاصَرَةٌ . حِصَارٌ

Siesta *n.* قَيْلُولَةٌ

Sieve *n.* مُنْخُلٌ . غرْبَالٌ

Sift *v. t.* غَرْبَلَ . تفَحَّصَ

Sigh *v. i.* or *n.* تَنَهَّدَ. زَفَرَ . زفِيرٌ

Sight *n.* نَظَرٌ . بَصَرٌ . مَنْظَرٌ

Sightless *a.* أَعْمَى

Sightly *a.* ظَاهِرٌ. شَهِيٌّ لِلنظَرِ

Sign *n.* عَلاَمَةٌ . إِشَارَةٌ . آيَة

Sign *v. t.* or *i.* أَمْضَى . أَشَارَ إِلَى

Signal *n.* or *a.* إِشَارَةٌ . ممتَازٌ

Signalize *v. t.* مَيَّزَ . شَهَرَ

Signature *n.* إِمْضَا

Signet *n.* خَتْمٌ . خَاتِمٌ

Significance } *n.* معْنًى . اَهَمِّيَّةٌ
Significance }

Significant *a.* دَال . مُهِمٌّ

Signification *n.* مَعْنًى . فَحْوَى

Signify *v. t.* افَادَ . عَنَى بِـ

Silence *n.* سُكُوتٌ . هُدُوءٌ. سُكُونٌ

Silence *v. t.* أَسْكَتَ . أَفْحَمَ

Silent *a.* سَاكِتٌ. سَاكِنٌ

Silk *n.* حَرِيرٌ. سُنْدُسٌ

Silk } *a.* حَريريٌّ
Silken }

Silk-worm *n.* دُودُ ٱلْقَزِّ

Silky *a.* نَاعِمٌ . أَمْلَسُ

Sill *n.* اُسْكُفَّةٌ (اسفلُ ٱلبَابِ أَوْ ٱلشُّبَّاكِ)

Silliness *n.* غَبَاوَةٌ . رُعُونَةٌ

Silly *a.* أَرْعَنُ . غَبِيٌّ

Silver *n.* or *a.* فِضَّةٌ . فِضِّيٌّ

Silversmith *n.* صَائِغٌ ج صَاغَةٌ

Silvery *a.* فِضِّيٌّ . كَالفِضَّةِ

Similar *a.* شَبِيهٌ . مِثْلٌ . مشَاكِلٌ

Similarity, Similitude *n.* مُشَابَهَةٌ

Simile *n.* تَشْبِيهٌ

Simmer *v. t.* غَلَى بِخِفَّةٍ

Simony *n.* شِرَآءُ رُتَبِ ٱلْكَنِيسَةِ

Simoom *n.* سَمُومٌ (رِيحٌ)

Simper *v. i.* تَبَسَّمَ كَالأَبْلَهِ

Simple *a.* بَسِيطٌ . هَيِّنٌ . وَاضِحٌ

Simpleton *n.* غَبِيٌّ . أَبْلَهُ

Simplicity *n.* بَسَاطَة . سَذَاجَة

Simplify *v. t.* جَعَلَهُ بَسِيطًا . سَهَّلَ

Simply *ad.* بِبَسَاطَةٍ . فَقَطْ

Simulate *v. t.* تَشَبَّهَ . تَظَاهَرَ بِ

Simultaneous *a.* فِي وَقْتٍ وَاحِدٍ

Sin *n.* or *v. i.* خَطِيئَةٌ . أَخْطَأَ

Since *ad.* or *pr.* or *con.* بَعْدُ . مُنْذُ . لِأَنَّ

Sincere *a.* مُخْلِصٌ . نَصُوحٌ

Sincerity *n.* إِخْلَاصٌ . صَفَآءُ ٱلنِّيَّةِ

Sine *n.* جَيْبٌ فِي (ٱلْهَنْدَسَةِ)

Sinew *n.* وَتَرٌ . أَصْلُ قُوَّةٍ

Sinewy *a.* قَوِيٌّ . ضَلِيعٌ . عَضِلٌ

Sinful *a.* خَاطِئٌ . أَثِيمٌ

Sinfulness *n.* خَطِيَّةٌ . حَالَةُ ٱلإِثْمِ

Sing *v. t.* رَنَّمَ . غَنَّى . رَتَّلَ

Singe *v. t.* مَسَّتْهُ ٱلنَّارُ قَلِيلاً

Singing *n.* غِنَآءٌ . تَرْنِيمٌ

Single *a.* فَرْدٌ . وَاحِدٌ . عَازِبٌ

Singleness *n.* وَحْدَةٌ . بَسَاطَةٌ

Singular *n.* مفرد . غريب . عجيب

Singularity *n.* وحدة . غرابة

Sinister *a.* يسار . مشوم

Sink *v. i.* or *t.* غرق ـ . انحط . أغرق

Sink *n.* مصب . بالوعة

Sinking-fund *n.* مال لاستهلاك دين

Sinless *a.* بلا خطية . بار

Sinner *n.* خاطئ

Sinuosity *n.* تعرج

Sinuous *a.* متعرج

Sip *n.* or *v. t.* مصة . تمصص

Sir *n.* سيد

Sire *n.* أب . مولى (للملوك)

Siren *n.* or *a.* جنية البحر . فتان

Sirocco *n.* ريح شرقية . سموم

Sirup *n.* عصير محلى . شراب

Sister *n.* اخت . شقيقة

Sister-in law *n.* سلفة . اخت الزوج أو الزوجة

Sister-hood *n.* جمعية نساء أو راهبات

Sit *v. t.* جلس ـ . استقر . حضن ـ

Site *n.* موقع . موضع

Sitting *n.* جلوس . جلسة

Situate / Situated *a.* واقع

Situation *n.* موقع . منصب . حال

Six *a.* ستة أو ست

Sixpence *n.* نصف شلين

Sixteen *a.* ستة عشر

Sixteenth *a.* السادس عشر

Sixth *a.* سادس

Sixty *a.* ستون

Size *n.* حجم . قدر . قد

Skate *n.* نعل للسير على الجليد

Skein *n.* شلة خيطان . خصلة

Skeleton *n.* هيكل حيوان

Skeptic *etc.* *see* Sceptic *etc.* مرتاب

Sketch *n.* or *v. t.* رسم . رسم ـ

Skiff *n.* قَارِبٌ . زَوْرَقٌ

Skilfulness, Skill *n.* مَهَارَةٌ

Skilful, Skilled *a.* مَاهِرٌ . خَبِيرٌ

Skim *v. t.* or *i.* نَزَعَ ـَ ٱلرَّغْوَةَ . سَفَّ ـَ

Skin *n.* or *v. t.* جِلْدٌ . قِشْرٌ . سَلَخَ ـُ

Skinny *a.* هَزِيلٌ . جِلْدِيٌّ

Skip *v. i.* or *t.* قَفَزَ ـِ . فَاتَ . تَرَكَ

Skipper *n.* رُبَّان سَفِينَةٍ صَغِيرَةٍ

Skirmish *n.* قِتَالٌ خَفِيفٌ

Skirt *n.* هُدْبٌ . تَخْمٌ

Skittish *a.* جَفُولٌ

Skulk *v. i.* ٱخْتَبَأَ دَهَاءً

Skull *n.* جُمْجُمَةٌ

Sky *n.* جَوٌّ . جَلَدٌ . سَمَاءٌ

Sky-lark *n.* قُنْبُرَةٌ ج قَنَابِرُ

Sky-light *n.* كُوَّةٌ فِي ٱلسَّقْفِ

Slab *n.* لَوْحُ حَجَرٍ أَوْ خَشَبٍ

Slack *a.* مُسْتَرْخٍ . مُتَغَافِلٌ

Slack, Slacken *v. t.* or *i.* أَرْخَى . خَفَّ ـِ

Slackness *n.* رَخَاءٌ . تَوَانٍ

Slain *pp.* of slay مَذْبُوحٌ

Slake *v. t.* رَوِيَ ـَ . صَوَّلَ

Slam *v. t.* أَغْلَقَ بِعُنْفٍ

Slander *v. t.* or *n.* نَمَّ ـِ . نَمِيمَةٌ

Slanderer *n.*, Slanderous *a.* نَمَّامٌ . مُفْتَرٍ

Slang *a.* كَلَامٌ عَامِّيٌّ

Slant *v. i.* or *t.* مَالَ ـُ . أَمَالَ

Slanting *a.* مَائِلٌ . غَيْرُ عَمُودِيٍّ

Slap *v. t.* or *n.* لَطَمَ ـِ . لَطْمَةٌ

Slash *v. t.* or *n.* شَقَّ ـُ . جَرَحَ ـَ

Slate *n.* or *v. t.* لَوْحُ حَجَرٍ . غَطَّى بِهِ

Slate-pencil *n.* قَلَمُ حَجَرٍ

Slaughter *n.* or *v. t.* ذَبْحٌ . ذَبَحَ ـَ

Slave *n.* عَبْدٌ . رَقِيقٌ . مَمْلُوكٌ

Slaver *n.* سَفِينَةٌ لِجَلْبِ ٱلْعَبِيدِ

Slavery *n.* عُبُودِيَّةٌ . رِقٌّ

Slavish *a.* عَبْدِيٌّ . ذَلِيلٌ

Slay *v. t.* (*pp.* Slain) قَتَلَ ـُ . ذَبَحَ

Sled / Sledge } *n.* مَرْكَبَةٌ لِلثَّلْجِ

Sledge *n.* مِهَدَّةٌ

Sleek *a.* أَمْلَسُ . لَيِّنٌ

Sleep *n.* or *v. i.* نَوْمٌ . رُقَادٌ . نَامَ ـَ

Sleepiness *n.* نُعَاسٌ

Sleepless *a.* بِلاَ نَوْمٍ

Sleepy *a.* نَعْسَانُ

Sleet *n.* ثَلْجٌ وَمَطَرٌ مَعًا

Sleeve *n.* كُمٌّ ج أَكْمَامٌ

Sleigh *n.* مَرْكَبَةٌ لِلثَّلْجِ

Sleight *n.* خِفَّةُ يَدٍ . حِيلَةٌ

Slender *a.* أَهْيَفُ . دَقِيقٌ . ضَعِيفٌ

Slenderness *n.* رِقَّةٌ . ضُعْفٌ

Slice *n.* or *v. t.* شَرِيحَةُ لَحْمٍ . شَرَّحَ

Slide *v. i.* or *t.* زَلَجَ ـِ . زَلِقَ ـَ . أَزْلَقَ

Slight *a.* or *n.* زَهِيدٌ . اسْتِخْفَافٌ

Slight *v. t.* أَهَانَ . اسْتَخَفَّ بِهِ

Slily *ad.* بِحِيلَةٍ . إِخْتِلاَسًا . خَفِيَّةً

Slim *a.* رَقِيقٌ . أَهْيَفُ

Slime *n.* رَدْغَةٌ . وَحْلٌ خَفِيفٌ

Sling *n.* or *v. t.* مِقْلاَعٌ . قَذَفَ بِهِ ـِ

Slink *v. i.* انْسَلَّ

Slip *v. i.* or *n.* زَلِقَ . زَلْقَةٌ ـَ . زَلَّةٌ

Slipper *n.* أَشْقَنٌ . بَابُوجٌ

Slippery *a.* زَلِقٌ . زَلِجٌ . مُتَقَلِّبٌ

Slit *n.* or *v. t.* شَرْمٌ . شَرَمَ ـِ

Sliver *n.* or *v. t.* شَظِيَّةٌ . شَقَّةٌ . شَظَّيَا

Sloop *n.* سَفِينَةٌ لَهَا سَارِيَةٌ وَاحِدَةٌ

Slope *n.* انْحُدُورٌ . حَدُورٌ

Sloppy *a.* قَذِرٌ . وَحِلٌ

Sloth *n.* (حيوان) كَسَلٌ . كَسْلاَنٌ

Slothful *a.* كَسْلاَنٌ . بَطِيءٌ

Slough *n.* مَحَلٌّ كَثِيرُ الْوَحْلِ

Sloven *a.* غَيْرُ مُهَنْدَمٍ

Slovenly *ad.* بِلاَ إِتْقَان

Slow *a.* بَطِيءٌ

Slowness *n.* بُطْوءٌ . تَأَخُّرٌ

Slug *n.* كَسْلاَنٌ . بَزَّاقَة . عُرْيَانَة

Sluggard *n.* } كَسْلاَنٌ . بَلِيدٌ
Sluggish *a.* }

Sluice *n.* مَنْفَذ ماء في سَدٍّ

Slumber *v. i.* or *n.* نعس ـَ . نام ـَ . نَوْمٌ

Slur *v. t.* or *n.* آسْتَخَفَّ . لَوَّثَ

Sut *n.* بَذَّة

Sly *a.* مُحْتَالٌ . داهٍ

Slyly *ad.* حِيلَةً . خُفْيَةً

Slyness *n.* دَهاءٌ . دَسٌّ . آسْتِخْفاءٌ

Smack *n.* سَفِينَة صَغِيرَة . قُبْلَة قَوِيَّة

Small *a.* صَغِيرٌ . دَقِيقٌ

Small-pox *n.* جُدَرِيٌّ

Smart *a.* نَشِيط . نَبِيهٌ . حاذِق

Smart *v. i.* or *n.* تَأَلَّمَ شَدِيدًا . أَلَمٌ

Smartness *n.* حَذَاقَة . حِدَّة

Smash *v. t.* or *n.* كَسَّرَ . حَطَّمَ

Smattering *n.* رُكَاكَة عِلْمٍ

Smear *v. t.* لطخ ـَ . وَسَّخ

Smell *n.* رَائِحَةٌ . شَمٌّ . حاسَّةٌ

Smell *v. t.* or *i.* شَمَّ ـُ . فاحَ ـُ

Smelt *v. t.* أَذَاب . أَمَاعَ

Smile *v. i.* or *n.* تَبَسَّمَ . تَبَسُّمٌ

Smirch *v. t.* وَسَّخَ . سَوَّدَ

Smite *v. t.* ضَرَبَ ـُ . قَتَلَ ـِ . لَفَحَ ـُ

Smith *n.* حَدَّادٌ . نَحَّاسٌ . صَائِغ

Smoke *n.* or *v. t.* دُخَان . دَخَنَ

Smoker *n.* شَارِبُ تُتُنٍ أَوْ دُخَانٍ

Smoky *a.* مُدَخِّنٌ . مُتَدَخِّنٌ

Smooth *a.* or *v. t.* مَلِسٌ . مُسْتَوٍ . مَلَّسَ

Smoothness *n.* مَلاَسَةٌ . آسْتِوَاءٌ

Smother *v. t.* خَنَقَ ـُ . أَطْفَأَ

Smoulder *v. i.* آحْتَرَقَ بِدُونِ لَهِيب

Smuggle *v. t.* هَرَّبَ . أَدْخَلَ خُلْسَةً

Smutty *a.* كَتِنٌ . وَسِخٌ

Snag *n.* خَشَبَةٌ تُصَادِمُهَا سَفِينَةٌ . مَانِعٌ

Snail *n.* بَزَّاقَةٌ . حَلَزُونَةٌ

Snake *n.* حَيَّةٌ . أَفْعَى

Snap *v. t.* or *i.* قَصَفَ ـِ آنْقَسَمَ بِصَوْتٍ

Snappish *a.* نَكِدٌ . حَادُّ ٱلْكَلَامِ

Snare *n.* شَرَكٌ . مَكِيدَةٌ

Snarl *v. i.* هَرَّ ـِ . هَمْهَمَ

Snatch *v. t.* خَطِفَ ـَ

Sneak *v. i.* آنسَلَ . آنْدَسَّ

Sneak *n.* / Sneaking *n.* } ذَلِيلٌ . دَسِيسٌ

Sneer *v. i.* or *n.* هَزَّأَ . آسْتَخَفَّ . هَزْءٌ

Sneeze *v. i.* عَطَسَ ـُ

Sniff *v. t.* اشْتَمَّ . آسْتَنْشَقَ

Snip *v. t.* قَطَعَ ـَ . قَرَضَ ـ

Snipe *n.* نَوْعٌ مِنَ ٱلْقَطَا

Snob *n.* Snobbish *a.* مُتَظَرِّفٌ . مُتَظَاهِرٌ بِالشَرَفِ

Snooze *v. i.* نَام نَوْمًا خَفِيفًا

Snore *v. i.* شَخَرَ ـُ خَرْخَرَ

Snort *v. i.* نَخَرَ ـِ

Snout *n.* خُرْطُومٌ . ج خَرَاطِيمُ

Snow *n.* or *v. i.* ثَلْجٌ . ثَلَجَ ـُ

Snow-drift *n.* كَوْمَةُ ثَلْجٍ

Snowy *a.* مُثْلِجٌ . أَبْيَضُ

Snub *v. t.* عامَلَ بِفَظَاظَةٍ . خَجَلَ

Snuff *n.* or *v. i.* سَعُوطٌ . نَزَعَ ٱلذُبَالَةَ

Snuff-box *n.* عِلْبَةُ ٱلسَعُوطِ

Snuffers *n. pl.* مِقْرَاضُ ٱلْفَتِيلَةِ

Snuffle *v. i.* نَخَرَ ـِ

Snug *a.* مُتَلَبِّدٌ . يُنَاسِبُ مَحَلَّهُ

Snuggle *v. i.* آسْتَكَنَّ

So *ad.* كَذَا . هٰكَذَا . كَذٰلِكَ

Soak *v. t.* or *i.* نَقَعَ ـَ . تَشَرَّبَ

Soap *n.* or *v. t.* صَابُونٌ . عَامَلَ بِهِ

Soapsuds *n.* رَغْوَةُ ٱلصَابُونِ

Soar *v. i.* آسْتَعْلَى (طَيْرٌ)

Sob *v. i.* or *n.* بَكَى مَعَ تَنَهُّدٍ

Sober / Soberminded *a.* رَزِينٌ. صاحٍ

Soberness / Sobriety *n.* رَزَانَةٌ. تَعَفُّفٌ

Sociability *n.* انْسٌ. عِشْرَة

Sociable *a.* انِيسٌ. أَلِيفٌ

Social *a.* أَلِيفٌ. جَمْهُورِي

Socialism *n.* مَذْهَبُ ٱلإِشْتِرَاكِيِّينَ

Society *n.* ٱلْهَيْئَةُ ٱلإِجْتِمَاعِيَّة

Sock *n.* جَوْرَبٌ

Socket *n.* نُقْرَةٌ. تَجْوِيفٌ

Sod *n.* مَدَرٌ فِيهِ جُذُورُ كَلَاء

Soda *n.* ٱلْقِلَى. نَطْرُونٌ

Sodden *a.* مَسْلُوقٌ. مَنْقُوعٌ

Sofa *n.* مَقْعَدٌ. دِيوَانٌ

Soft *a.* نَاعِمٌ. لَيِّنٌ. طِفْلٌ

Soften *v. t.* or *i.* لَيَّنَ. لاَنَ ـِ

Softness *n.* لِينٌ. نعومة

Soil *v. t.* or *n.* لَطَخَ ـَ وَسَّخَ. تُرْبَة

Sojourn *v.i.* or *n.* تَغَرَّبَ. غُرْبَةٌ

Sojourner *n.* مُتَغَرِّبٌ

Solace *v. t.* or *n.* سَلَّى عَزَّى. سَلْوَى

Solar *a.* شَمْسِيٌّ

Solder *n.* or *v. t.* لِحَامٌ. لَحَمَ ـُ

Soldier *n.* عَسْكَرِيٌّ. جُنْدِيٌّ

Soldiery *n.* عَسَاكِرُ

Sole *n.* نَعْلٌ. أَسْفَلُ ٱلْقَدَمِ

Sole *v. t.* or *a.* خَصَفَ ٱلنَّعْلَ. وَحِيدٌ

Solely *ad.* فَقَطْ

Solemn *n.* مُوَقَّرٌ. خَطِيرٌ

Solemnity *n.* ٱحْتِفَالٌ. وَقَارٌ

Solemnize *v. t.* ٱحْتَفَلَ. مَارَسَ سِرًّا

Solicit *v. t.* تَوَسَّلَ. طَلَبَ ـُ

Solicitation *n.* تَوَسُّلٌ. ٱلْتِمَاسٌ

Solicitor *n.* وَكِيلُ دَعَاوٍ

Solicitous *a.* مُهْتَمٌّ. رَاغِبٌ فِي

Solicitude *n.* هَمٌّ. رَغْبَةٌ

Solid *a.* جَامِدٌ . مَتِينٌ . مُجَسَّمٌ
Solidify *v. t.* or *i.* جَمَدَ . تَجَمَّدَ
Solidity *n.* جُمُودٌ . مَتَانَةٌ
Soliloquize *v. t.* كَلَّمَ نَفْسَهُ
Soliloquy *n.* مُخَاطَبَةُ ٱلذَّاتِ
Solitariness *n.* تَوَحُّدٌ . ٱنْفِرَادٌ
Solitary *a.* مُنْفَرِدٌ . مُعْتَزِلٌ
Solitude *n.* وَحْدَةٌ . عُزْلَةٌ
Solo *n.* غِنَاءُ شَخْصٍ وَحْدَهُ
Solstice *n.* نُقْطَةُ ٱنْقِلَابِ ٱلشَّمْسِ
Soluble *a.* قَابِلُ ٱلذَّوَبَانِ أَوِ ٱلْحَلِّ
Solution *n.* حَلٌّ . مَحْلُولٌ
Solvable *a.* قَابِلُ ٱلْحَلِّ أَوِ ٱلْوَفَاءِ
Solve *v. t.* حَلَّ . أَوْضَحَ
Solvency *n.* قُدْرَةٌ عَلَى ٱلْوَفَاءِ
Solvent *a.* قَادِرٌ عَلَى ٱلْوَفَاءِ
Solvent *n.* سَائِلٌ مُحَلِّلٌ أَوْ مُذَوِّبٌ
Sombre *a.* مُظْلِمٌ . مُغِمٌّ
Some *a.* بَعْضٌ
Somebody *n.* وَاحِدٌ . أَحَدٌ مَّا
Somehow *ad.* كَيْفَمَا كَانَ
Somersault / Somerest *n.* وَثْبَةٌ ٱنْقِلَابٍ
Something *n.* شَيْءٌ مَا
Sometime *ad.* وَقْتًا مَّا
Sometimes *ad.* أَحْيَانًا
Somewhat *ad.* or *n.* نَوْعًا . شَيْءٌ مَا
Somewhere *ad.* فِي مَكَانٍ مَّا
Somnambulism *n.* مَشْيٌ فِي ٱلنَّوْمِ
Somnambulist *n.* مَاشٍ فِي ٱلنَّوْمِ
Somnolence *n.* نُعَاسٌ
Son *n.* ٱبْنٌ ج أَبْنَاءٌ وَبَنُونَ
Son-in-law *n.* زَوْجُ ٱبْنَةٍ . صِهْرٌ
Song *n.* أُغْنِيَّةٌ . نَشِيدٌ
Songster *n.* مُغَنٍّ . مُغَرِّدٌ
Sonnet *n.* قَصِيدَةٌ قَصِيرَةٌ
Sonorous *a.* صَائِتٌ . رَنَّانٌ

Sonship *n.* بُنُوَّةٌ

Soon *ad.* عَنْ قَرِيبٍ . سَرِيعاً

Soot *n.* كَتَنٌ . سُخَامٌ

Soothe *v. t.* خَفَّفَ . لاَطَفَ . سكَّنَ

Soothsayer *n.* عَرَّافٌ . مُنَجِّمٌ

Sooty *a.* كَتَنِيٌّ . سُخَامِيٌّ

Sophism, Sophistry *n.* سَفْسَطَةٌ

Sophist *n.*, Sophistical *a.* سَفْسَطِيٌّ

Soporific *n.* or *a.* مُنَوِّمٌ

Sorcerer, Sorceress *n.* سَاحِرٌ . سَاحِرَةٌ

Sorcery *n.* سِحْرٌ

Sordid *a.* خَسِيسٌ . طَمَّاعٌ

Sore *a.* or *n.* مُؤْلِمٌ . شَدِيدٌ . قَرْحَةٌ

Sorely *ad.* جِدّاً

Sorrel *a.* or *n.* أَشْقَرُ . حَمَاضٌ

Sorrow *n.* or *v. i.* حُزْنٌ . حَزِنَ

Sorrowful *a.* حَزِينٌ . كَئِيبٌ

Sorry *a.* مُكَدَّرٌ . آسِفٌ . مُتَحَسِّرٌ

Sort *n.* نَوْعٌ . صِنْفٌ . شَكْلٌ

Sort *v. t.* رَتَّبَهُ عَلَى اشْكَالِهِ

Sot *n.*, Sottish *a.* سِكِّيرٌ . أَبْلَهُ

Sought *pp.* (Seek) مَطْلُوبٌ

Soul *n.* نَفْسٌ . رُوحٌ . حَيَاةٌ

Soulless *a.* بِلاَ نَفْسٍ . خَسِيسٌ

Sound *a.* or *n.* صَحِيحٌ . صَوْتٌ . مَضِيقٌ

Sound *v.t.* or *i.* سَبَرَ . صَاتَ

Soundings *n. pl.* قِيَاسُ عُمْقِ ٱلْبَحْرِ

Soundly *ad.* جَيِّداً بِصَوَابٍ

Soundness *n.* صِحَّةٌ . مَتَانَةٌ

Soup *n.* شَوْرَبَةٌ

Sour *a.* حَامِضٌ . شَكِسٌ

Source *n.* أَصْلٌ . مَصْدَرٌ . يَنْبُوعٌ

Sourness *n.* حُمُوضَةٌ . شَكَاسَةٌ

Souse *v. t.* غَطَّسَ . غَمَسَ

South *n.* or *a.* جَنُوبٌ . جَنُوبِيٌّ

South-east *n.* اَلْجَنُوبُ ٱلشَّرْقِيُّ

Southerly } a. جَنُوبِيٌّ
Southern }

Southward ad. جَنُوبًا . إِلَى ٱلْجَنُوب

South-west n. ٱلْجَنُوبُ ٱلْغَرْبِيُّ

Souvenir n. تَذْكَارٌ . تَذْكِرَةٌ

Souvereign n. or a. مَلِكٌ . سُلْطَانِيٌّ

Souvereignty n. مُلْكٌ . سَلْطَنَةٌ

Sow n. or v. t. خِنْزِيرَةٌ . زَرَعَ ـ أَذَاعَ

Space n. خَلَاءٌ . مَسَافَةٌ . مُدَّةٌ

Spacious a. فَسِيحٌ . رَحِيبٌ

Spade n. مِجْرَفَةٌ . مَرٌّ . لَوْحٌ

Span n. or v. t. شِبْرٌ . قَاسَ بِهِ

Spaniard n. } إِسْبَنْيُولِيٌّ
Spanish a. }

Spaniel n. نَوْعٌ مِنَ ٱلْكَلْبِ

Spank v. t. لَطَمَ عَلَى ٱلْعَجْزِ

Spar n. سَارِيَةٌ . حَجَرٌ مُتَبَلْوِرٌ

Spare a. يَسِيرٌ . نَحِيفٌ . فَارِغٌ

Spare v. t. عَفَا عَنْ . ٱسْتَحْيَا . ٱقْتَصَدَ

Spark n. شَرَارَةٌ . جُزْءٌ يَسِيرٌ

Sparkle v. i. أَخْرَجَ شَرَرًا . تَلَأْلَأَ

Sparrow n. عُصْفُورٌ دُورِيٌّ

Sparse a. مُتَشَتِّتٌ مُتَفَرِّق

Spasm n. تَشَنُّجٌ

Spasmodic a. تَشَنُّجِيٌّ . مُتَقَطِّعٌ

Spatter v. t. لَطَخَ ـَ

Spawn n. or v. i. بَيْضُ ٱلسَّمَكِ . بَاضَ ـِ

Speak v. i. تَكَلَّمَ . نَطَقَ ـِ

Speaker v. مُتَكَلِّمٌ . رَئِيسُ مَجْلِسٍ

Spear n. رُمْحٌ . حَرْبَةٌ

Special v. خَاصٌّ . خُصُوصِيٌّ

Speciality n. خُصُوصِيَّةٌ

Specie n. نُقُودٌ . مَسْكُوكَات

Species n. نَوْعٌ ج أَنْوَاعٌ

Specific a. نَوْعِيٌّ . خُصُوصِيٌّ . جَازِمٌ

Specification n. تَخْصِيصٌ . تَعْرِيفٌ

Specify v. t. خَصَّصَ . صَرَّحَ . عَرَّفَ

Specimen n. مِثَالٌ . مَسْطَرَةٌ . عَيِّنَةٌ

Specious *a.* حَسَنٌ أَوْحَقٌّ بالظاهِرِ

Speck *n.* نُقْطَةٌ . لَطْخَة

Speckled *n.* مُرَقَّطٌ . أرْقَط

Spectacle *n.* مَنْظَرٌ . مَشْهَد

Spectacles *n. pl.* مِنْظَرٌ (عُوَيْنَاتٌ)

Spectator *n.* شَاهِدٌ . مُتَفَرِّجٌ

Spectre *n.* خَيَالٌ . طَيْفٌ

Speculate *v. i.* تَأَمَّلَ . تَفَلْسَفَ

آبْتَاعَ بِانْتِظَارِ زِيَادَةِ آلثَّمَنِ . ضَارَبَ

Speculative *a.* نَظَرِيٌّ . فَلْسَفِيٌّ

Speculum *n.* مِرْآةٌ . مِنْظَارٌ

Speech *n.* كَلَامٌ . خِطَابٌ . لغَةٌ

Speechless *a.* صَامِتٌ . أَخْرَسُ

Speed *n.* سُرْعَةٌ . فَلَاحٌ . تَوفِيقٌ

Speedy *a.* سَرِيعٌ

Spell *n.* دَوْرٌ . بُرْهَةٌ

Spell *v. t.* هَجَى . تَهَجَى

Speller *n.* مُتَهَجٍّ . كِتَابٌ تَهْجِيَةٍ

Spend *v. t.* صَرَفَ . أَنْفَقَ . أَفْرَغَ

Spendthrift *n.* مُسْرِفٌ . مُبَذِّرٌ

Spew *v. t.* or *i.* آسْتَفْرَغَ . قَاءَ

Sphere *n.* كُرَةٌ . دَائِرَةٌ . مَقَامٌ

Spheric } *a.* كُرِوِيٌّ
Spherical }

Spheroid *n.* شِبْهُ كُرَةٍ

Sphinx *n.* ابُو آلْهَوْلِ

Spice *n.* طِيبٌ تَابِل

Spicy *a.* تَابِلِيٌّ . حَرِّيفٌ . مُطَيَّبٌ

Spider *n.* عَنْكَبُوتٌ . رُتَيْلاَء

Spike *n.* or *v. t.* سُنْبلَةٌ . مِسْمَارٌ كَبِيرٌ . سَمَّرَ بِهِ

Spikenard *n.* نَارَدِينٌ

Spill *v. t.* or *i.* أَرَاقَ . كَبَّ ـُ . آنْكَبَّ

Spin *v. t.* or *i.* غَزَلَ ـِ . بَرَمَ ـُ

Spinach } *n.* إِسْبَانَخٌ
Spinage }

Spinal *a.* فَقَرِيٌّ

Spindle *n.* or *v. i.* مَغْزَلٌ . طَالَ . آسْتَدَقَ

Spine *n.* آلْعَمُودُ آلْفَقَرِيُّ . شَوْكَةٌ

Spinster *n.* امرأةٌ. غيرُ متزوّجة

Spiral *a.* لَوْلَبِيٌّ

Spire *n.* بُرجٌ بِهيئةِ مسلّةٍ

Spirit *n.* رُوحٌ. نشاطٌ. طبعٌ

Spirited *a.* نشيطٌ

Spiritless *a.* خائرٌ. متراخٍ

Spiritual *a.* رُوحيٌّ. دينيٌّ

Spirituality *a.* رُوحانيّة

Spirituous *a.* رُوحِيٌّ. مُسْكِرٌ

Spit *n.* or *v. t.* سَفُودٌ. بُصاق بصَق ـــ

Spite *n.* or *v.t.* ضَغينةٌ. غِل. ضغِن ـــ حقد

Spiteful *a* ضَغِنٌ. مُغِلٌّ. حقودٌ

Spittle *n.* بُصاقٌ. لعابٌ. تفْلٌ

Spittoon *n.* مَبْصَقَة

Splash *v. t.* لَطَمَ السائلَ فرشّه

Spleen *n.* طِحالٌ. حِقْد

Splendid *a.* فاخرٌ. باهِرٌ. بَهِي

Splendour *n.* بهاءٌ. رونق. جلال

Splice *v. t.* or *n.* أوصلَ الطرَفين

Splint / Splinter } *n.* شَظيّةٌ. جَبِرَةٌ

Split *v. t.* شقّ ـــ. فَلَقَ ـــ

Spoil *v. t.* or *i.* نَهَبَ ـــ أَفْسَدَ. فسد ـــ

Spoil *n.* نَهْبٌ. غنيمة

Spokesman *n.* نائبٌ فِي التكلم

Spoliation *n.* نَهْبٌ. تشليح

Sponge *n.* or *v. t.* إسْفَنجةٌ. سفَنْجٌ. مَسَحَ بها

Spongy *a.* إسْفَنجِيٌّ

Sponsor *n.* كفيل. إشبين

Spontaniety *n.* فِعلٌ مِنْ تِلْقاءِ النفس

Spontaneous *a.* مِنَ النفسِ رأسًا

Spool *n.* مِسْلَكَةٌ (بَكَرَةٌ)

Spoon *n.* مِلْعقةٌ ج ملاعقُ

Spoonful *n.* مِلْءُ مِلعقة

Sporadic *a.* متوحّد. متفرّق

Spore *n.* بُزَيْرةٌ دقيقةٌ جدًّا

Sport *n.* لعبٌ. طَرَبٌ. صَيْدٌ

Sportsman *n.* صَيَّادٌ

Spot *n.* مَوْضِعٌ. بقعةٌ. لَطْخَةٌ

Spotless *a.* طاهرٌ. بِلاَعَيْبٍ

Spotted *a.* مَلَطَّخٌ. أَرْقَطُ

Spouse *n.* زوجٌ. زَوْجَةٌ

Spout *n.* or *v. i.* صُنْبُورٌ. تَفَجَّرَ

Sprain *n.* or *v. t.* وَثْيٌ. وَثِيَ

Sprawl *v. i.* اَسْتَلْقَى

Spray *n.* رِشَاشُ اَلْمَاءِ

Spread *v. t.* or *i.* نَشَرَ. اَنْتَشَرَ

Spree *n.* سَكْرَةٌ

Sprig *n.* شعبَةٌ. عُسْلُجٌ

Sprightful / Sprightly *a.* نشيطُ الجسدِ والعقلِ

Spring *v. i.* وثبَ. صَدَرَ. اَنْفَجَرَ

Spring *n.* وثْبَةٌ. نَبْعٌ. رَبِيعٌ. زَنْبُرُكٌ

Sprinkle *v.t.* or *i.* رشَّ. نَضَحَ

Sprite *n.* خَيَالٌ. طَيْفٌ

Sprout *v. i.* or *n.* نَبَتَ. فَرَّخَ. فرخ

Spry *a.* خَفِيفُ اَلْحَرَكَةِ. نشيطٌ

Spue *v. i.* اَسْتَفْرَغَ. تَقَيَّأَ

Spur *n.* مِهْمَازٌ. ظَهْرٌ بَارِزٌ

Spur *v. t.* حَثَّ. أَنْهَضَ. نَخَسَ

Spurious *a.* كَاذِبٌ. مزوَّرٌ

Spurn *v. t.* رَفَضَ. أَنِفَ مِنْ

Spurt *v. t.* or *i.* فجرَ. اَنْفَجَرَ

Spy *n.* or *v. t.* جاسُوسٌ. نَظَرَ

Spyglass *n.* نظَّارَةٌ صغيرَةٌ

Squabble *v. i.* شَاجَرَ. نَازَعَ

Squad *n.* شرْذِمَةٌ

Squadron *n.* كُرْدُوسَة. جَمَاعَةُ سفنٍ

Squalid *a.* قَذِرٌ. وَسِخٌ

Squall *n.* or *v. t.* هَبَّةٌ قَوِيَّةٌ. صَرَخَ

Squalor *n.* قَذَرٌ. وَسَخٌ

Squander *v. t.* بَذَّرَ. أَسْرَفَ

Square *a.* or *n.* مُرَبَّعٌ. عَادِلٌ. سَاحَةٌ

Square *v. t.* رَبَّعَ. كَعَّبَ. سَدَّد

Squash *n.* كُوسَى . لَقْطِينٌ

Squat *v. t.* قَعَدَ ٱلقُرْفُصَى

Squeak *n.* or *v. i.* صَرِيرٌ . صَرَّ ـَ

Squeal *v. i.* صَاحَ كَٱلخِنْزِيرِ

Squeeze *v. t.* ضَغَطَ ـَ . عَصَرَ ـِ

Squint *v. i.* or *n.* حَوِلَ ـَ . حَوَلٌ

Squint-eyed *a.* أَحْوَلُ

Squirrel *n.* سِنْجَابٌ

Stab *v. t.* or *n.* طَعَنَ ـَ . طَعْنَةٌ

Stability *n.* ثَبَاتٌ . رُسُوخٌ

Stable *n.* or *a.* إِصْطَبْلٌ . أَخُورٌ . ثَابِتٌ

Stack *n.* or *v. t.* كَوْمَةٌ . كَوَّمَ

Staff *n.* عُكَّازٌ . رُكْنٌ ج أَرْكَانٌ

Stag *n.* ذَكَرُ ٱلْإِيلِ

Stage *n.* دَكَّةٌ . دَرَجَةٌ . مَرْحَلَةٌ

Stagger *v. i.* or *t.* تَرَنَّحَ . تَمَايَلَ . أَرَابَ

Stagnant *a.* سَاكِنٌ . فَاسِدٌ . كَاسِدٌ

Stagnate *v.i.* سَكَنَ ـُ . فَسَدَ ـُ . كَسَدَ

Staid *a.* رَزِينٌ . رَصِينٌ

Stain *v. t.* or *n.* صَبَغَ ـُ . لَطَخَ ـُ . لَطْخَةٌ

Stainless *a.* بِلَا عَيْبٍ . نَقِيٌّ

Stairs / Stair-case } *n.* مِعْرَجٌ . سُلَّمٌ

Stake *n.* وَتَدٌ . رَهْنٌ . إِسْتِشْهَادٌ

Stake *v. t.* خَاطَرَ بِ . رَاهَنَ

Stale *a.* تَافِهٌ . عَتِيقٌ

Stalk *n.* سَاقُ نَبَاتٍ . رُجَيْلَةٌ

Stall *n.* مَعْلَفٌ . دُكَّانٌ

Stallion *n.* فَحْلٌ ج فُحُولٌ

Stalwart *a.* قَوِيٌّ . شُجَاعٌ

Stamen *n.* سَدَاةٌ ج أَسْدِيَةٌ

Stammer *v. i.* تَمْتَمَ . لَجْلَجَ

Stamp *v. t.* خَبَطَ ـِ . طَبَعَ ـَ . رَسَمَ ـِ

Stamp *n.* طَبْعٌ . رَسْمٌ . دَمْغَةٌ

Stampede *n.* هَزِيمَةٌ

Stanch *a.* or *v. t.* ثَابِتٌ . وَقَّفَ نَزَفًا

Stand *v. i.* وَقَفَ ـِ . ثَبَتَ ـُ . بَقِيَ

Stand *n.* مَوْقِفٌ. قَاعِدَةٌ. ثُبُوتٌ

Standard *n.* عَلَمٌ. مِقْيَاسٌ. قَاعِدَة

Standing *a.* قَائِمٌ. ثَابِت. دَائِمٌ

Stanza *n.* دوْرُ شِعْرٍ

Stable *n.* or *a.* زَرِيبَةٌ. حَاصِلٌ. رَئِيسِيٌّ

Star *n.* نَجمَة. كَوْكَبٌ

Starboard *n.* يمين ٱلسَّفِينَةِ

Starch *n.* or *v. t.* نَشَا. نَشّى

Stare *v. i.* تَفَرَّس. حَمْلَقَ

Stark *a.* مَحْضٌ. كُلِّيٌّ. جَامِدٌ

Starlight *n.* نورُ ٱلنجُومِ

Starry *a.* ذُو نجُومٍ أو كَثِيرهَا

Start *v. i.* or *t.* بَدا. أَجْفَل. حرَّك

Startle *v. t.* جَفَلَ. أَرْعَش

Starvation *n.* أَلْمَوْت جُوعاً

Starve *v. i.* or *t.* مات أوأَماتَ جُوعاً

State *n.* حالٌ. وِلاَيَةٌ. حُكومَةٌ

State *v. t.* قالَ ُ. قصَّ ـ. قرَّر

Stateliness *n.* ابَّهَةٌ. جلاَلَة

Stately *a.* جليلٌ. عَظِيمٌ. مُوَقرٌ

Statement *n.* قَوْلٌ. تَقْرِيرٌ

Statesman *n.* عالِمٌ بِٱلسِّيَاسَةِ

Statesmanship *n.* عِلمُ ٱلسِّيَاسَةِ

Station *n.* مَنْصِبٌ. رُتْبَةٌ. مَحَطَّةٌ

Station *v. t.* وَضَعَ ـَ. نَصبَ ـِ

Stationary *a.* وَاقِفٌ. ثَابِتٌ

Stationery *n.* أَدوَاتُ ٱلْكِتَابَةِ

Statistics *n.* عِلْمُ ٱلإِحْصَاءِ أوٱلتَّعدَاد

Statuary *n.* مجتَمَعُ تمَاثِيلَ

Statue *n.* تِمْثَالٌ

Stature *n.* قَدٌّ. قَامَةٌ

Statute *n.* سنة. نِظَامٌ

Stave *v. t.* كَسر. أَخَّرَ

Stave *n.* لَوْحٌ. ضَيِّقٌ لِبَرْمِيلٍ

Stay *v. i.* or *t.* استَمَرَّ. وَقفَ. دَعَمَ

Stead *n.* عوضٌ . بَدَل

Steadfast *a.* ثَابِتٌ . رَاسِخٌ

Steadfastness / Steadiness } *n.* حزمٌ . ثَبَات

Steady *a.* ثَابِتٌ . غَيْرُ مُتَقَلِّب

Steak *n.* شَرِيحَةُ لَحْمٍ

Steel *v. t.* or *i.* سَرَقَ ـِ . اَنْسَلَّ

Stealth *n.* اَنْسِلَالٌ . اَخْتِلَاسٌ

Stealthy *a.* مُنْسَلٌّ . مُخْتَلِسٌ

Steam *n.* or *v. i.* بُخَارٌ . بَخَرَ

Steam-boat / Steamer } *n.* بَاخِرَةٌ . وَابُورٌ

Steam-engine *n.* آلَةٌ بُخَارِيَّةٌ

Steed *n.* جَوَادٌ ج جِيَادٌ

Steel *n.* or *v. t.* فُولَاذٌ . قَسَّى

Steelyard *n.* قَبَّانٌ

Steep *a.* or *v. t* مُنْحَدِرٌ جِدًّا . نَقَعَ ـَ

Steeple *n.* مَنَارَةُ كَنِيسَةٍ

Steepness *n.* شِدَّةُ تَحَدُّرٍ

Steer *v. t.* أَدَارَ سَفِينَةً

Stellar *a.* نَجْمِي

Stem *v. t.* وَقَفَ . دَفَعَ ـَ

Stem *n.* سَاقٌ . مُقَدَّمُ سَفِينَةٍ

Stench *n.* رَائِحَةٌ قَبِيحَةٌ

Step *n.* or *v. i.* خُطْوَةٌ . خَطَا ـُ

Step-child *n.* وَلَدُ ٱلزَّوْجِ أَوِ ٱلزَّوْجَةِ

Step-father *n.* زَوْجُ ٱلأُمِّ . رَابٌّ

Step-mother *n.* زَوْجَةُ ٱلأَبِ . رَابَّةٌ

Stepping-stone *n.* وَسِيلَةٌ . مِرْقَاةٌ

Sterile *a.* عَقِيمٌ . أَجْدَبُ

Sterility *n.* جَدْبٌ . عُقْمٌ

Sterling *n.* or *a.* دَرَاهِمُ إِنْكِلِيزِيَّةٌ . حَقِيقِيٌّ

Stern *n.* or *a.* مُؤَخَّرٌ . عَبُوسٌ

Sternness *n.* عُبُوسٌ

Stethoscope *a.* مُسْتَقْصِيَةٌ . صَدْرِيَّةٌ

Stew *v. t.* or *n.* سَلَقَ ـُ رُوَيْدًا . يَخْنَةٌ

Steward *n.* وَكِيلٌ . قَهْرَمَانٌ

Stewardship *n.* وَكَالَةٌ . قَهْرَمَةٌ

Stick *n.* or *v.t.* قَضِيبٌ . اِلْزَقَ . طَعَنَ

Stickiness *n.* لُزُوجَةٌ

Stickle *v. i.* نَازَعَ مُكَابَرَةً

Sticky *a.* لَزِجٌ . دَبِقٌ

Stiff *a.* جَامِدٌ . صُلْبٌ . مُتَيَبِّسٌ

Stiffen *v. t.* or *i.* جَمَّدَ . جَمَدَ

Stiffness *n.* جُمُودٌ . اِشْتِدَادٌ . صَلَابَةٌ

Stiff-necked *a.* صُلْبُ ٱلرَّقَبَةِ

Stifle *v.* أَطْفَأَ . سَكَّنَ . خَنَقَ

Stigma *n.* عَيْبٌ . سِمَةٌ

Stigmatize *v.* عَيَّبَ . وَسَمَ

Still *v. t.* or *a.* سَكَّنَ . سَاكِنٌ . سَاكِتٌ

Still *ad.* إِلَى ٱلْآنَ . مَعْ ذَلِكَ

Still-born *a.* (وَلَدٌ) سِقْطٌ

Stillness *n.* سُكُونٌ . هُدُوٌّ

Stimulant *a.* or *n.* / Stimulative *a.* } مُنَبِّهٌ . مُنَشِّطٌ

Stimulate *v. t.* نَبَّهَ . حَرَّضَ

Stimulation *n.* تَحْرِيضٌ . تَهْيِيجٌ

Stimulus *n.* مُنَبِّهٌ . مُحَرِّكٌ

Sting *n.* or *v. t.* لَسْعَةٌ . لَسَعَ

Stinginess *n.* بُخْلٌ . شُحٌّ

Stingy *a.* بَخِيلٌ . شَحِيحٌ

Stink *n.* or *v. i.* نَتَانَةٌ . نَتِنَ

Stint *v. t.* or *a.* حَدَّدَ . حَدٌّ . عَمَلٌ مَحْدُودٌ

Stipend *v.* رَاتِبٌ . مَعَاشٌ

Stipulate *v. i.* اِشْتَرَطَ

Stipulation *n.* شَرْطٌ . إِتِّفَاقٌ

Stir *v. i.* or *t.* تَحَرَّكَ . حَرَّكَ . هَزَّ

Stirrup *n.* رِكَابٌ ج رُكُبٌ

Stitch *v. t.* خَاطَ . دَرَزَ

Stock *n.* أَصْلٌ . مَالٌ . سِلَعٌ

Stock *v. t.* جَهَّزَ . ذَخَرَ

Stockade *n.* سِيَاجٌ لِلتَّحْصِينِ

Stock-holder *n.* صَاحِبُ أَسْهُمٍ

Stocking *n.* جَوْرَبٌ

Stocks *n. pl.* أَسْهُمٌ مَالِيَّةٌ . مِقْطَرَةٌ

Stocky *a.* ضَخْمٌ . قَوِيُّ ٱلْجِسْمِ

Stoic *a.* or *n.* غَيْرُ مُبَالٍ بِمَا يَحْدُثُ

Stoicism *n.* مَذْهَبُ غَيْرِ ٱلْمُكْتَرِثِينَ بِٱلدَّهْرِ

Stole, Stolen, *see* Steal. سَرَقَ

Stolid *a.* بَلِيدٌ . أَبْلَهُ

Stolidity *n.* بَلَادَةٌ . بَلَاهَةٌ

Stomach *n.* or *v. t.* مَعِدَةٌ . ٱحْتَمَلَ

Stone *n.* or *v. t.* حَجَرٌ . نَوَاةٌ . رَجَمَ . أَخْرَجَ ٱلْبِزْرَةَ أَوِ ٱلنَّوَاةَ

Stone-cutter *n.* نَحَّاتٌ

Stone-ware *n.* آنِيَةٌ . حَجَرِيَّة

Stony *a.* مُحْجِرٌ

Stool *n.* كُرْسِيٌّ لِلرِّجْلَيْنِ . إِسْكَمْلَةٌ

Stoop *v. i.* ٱنْحَنَى . خَضَعَ ـَ

Stop *v. t.* or *i.* وَقَّفَ . وَقَفَ ـِ

Stop *n.* وَقْفٌ . وُقُوفٌ . سَدٌّ

Stoppage *n.* وَقْفٌ . تَوْقِيفٌ

Stopper / Stopple } *n.* سِدَادٌ . صِمَامٌ

Storage *n.* خَزْنٌ . إِدِّخَارٌ

Store *n.* or *v. t.* كَمِّيَّةٌ . مُؤْنَةٌ . مَخْزَنٌ . ذَخَرَ

Storied *a.* مَقُولٌ فِي رِوَايَةٍ . ذُو طَبَقَاتٍ

Stork *n.* بَجَعٌ

Storm *n.* نَوْءٌ . عَاصِفٌ . هُجُومٌ

Storm *v. t.* or *i.* هَجَمَ عَلَى . عَصَفَ ـِ

Stormy *a.* عَاصِفٌ . كَثِيرُ ٱلْأَنْوَاءِ

Story *n.* قِصَّةٌ . طَبَقَةُ بَيْتٍ

Stout *a.* قَوِيٌّ . جَسُورٌ . سَمِينٌ

Stoutness *n.* قُوَّةٌ . شِدَّةٌ . سِمْنٌ

Stove *n.* وُجَاقٌ . مَوْقِدٌ

Stow *v. t.* خَزَنَ ـُ . عَبَّى

Straddle *v. i.* or *t.* فَجَّ ـُ . رَكِبَ ـَ

Straggle *v. i.* شَرَدَ ـُ . عَنْ . هَامَ ـِ

Straggler *n.* شَارِدٌ

Straight *a.* or *ad.* مُسْتَقِيمٌ . رَأْسًا

Straighten *v. t.* قَوَّمَ . سَوَّى

Straightforwad *a.* مُسْتَقِيمٌ . عَادِلٌ

Straightway *ad.* حالاً . على ٱلْفَوْرِ

Strain *v. t.* شَدَّ ـُ . وَثَى ـِ . صفى

Strain *n.* جَهْدٌ . اسلوبٌ

Strainer *n.* مِصْفَاةٌ

Strait *a.* or *n.* ضَيّقٌ. ضيقةٌ. مضيقٌ

Straiten *v. t.* ضَيَّقَ . شَدَّ

Strand *n.* شَطٌّ . طَاقُ حَبْلٍ

Strange *a.* غريبٌ . عَجيبٌ

Strangeness *n.* غَرَابَة

Stranger *n.* غريبٌ . أَجْنَبِيٌّ

Strangle *v. t.* خَنَقَ ـُ

Strangulation *n.* خَنْق . آخْتِنَاقٌ

Strap *n.* or *v. t.* سَيْرٌ . شَدَّ بِهِ

Strapping *a.* طَوِيلٌ . خَلِيعٌ

Strata *n. pl.* طَبَقَاتٌ . صفوفٌ

Stratagem *n.* حيلةٌ . مَكِيدَة

Strategy *n.* علمُ إدارةِ ٱلْحَرْبِ

Stratification *n.* نضدُ ٱلطَّبَقَاتِ

Stratum *n.* طَبَقَةٌ

Straw *n.* قَش . تِبْن

Strawberry *n.* ثمرٌ كالتوتِ. فَرَاوْلا

Stray *v. i.* ضَلَّ ـِ . شَرَدَ ـُ تاهَ ـِ

Streak *n.* خَطٌّ

Streaked / Streaky } *a.* مُخَطَّطٌ

Stream *n.* or *v. i.* مجرى . نَهْرٌ . سَالَ ـ

Streamlet *n.* نُهَيْرٌ . ساقيةٌ

Street *n.* طَرِيقٌ . زُقَاقٌ . شَارِعٌ

Strength *n.* قوةٌ . مَتَانَة

Strengthen *v. t.* قَوَّى . شَدَّدَ

Strenuous *a.* عزومٌ . مُجِدٌّ

Stress *n.* ضَغْطٌ . شِدَّةٌ

Stretch *v. t.* or *i.* مدَّ ـُ . وَسَّعَ . إمتَدَ

Stretch *n.* آمْتِدَادٌ . آتّساعٌ

Strew *v. t.* بَذر . فَرَّقَ . نَشَرَ

Stricken *a.* مُصَابٌ . مُتَضَايِقٌ

Strict *a.* مدقِّقٌ . مشدِّدٌ . صَارِمٌ

Strictly *ad.* بضبطٍ بصرامةٍ بالتمامِ

Strictness *n.* تدقيقٌ . تشديد

Stricture *n.* تنكيت . تضيق

Stride *n.* or *v. i.* خطوةٌ طويلة

Strife *n.* نزاعٌ . مناظرةٌ

Strike *v. t.* ضربَ ـ . أثَّرَ . اصابَ

Striking *a.* مؤثّرٌ . غريبٌ

String *n.* خيط . وترٌ . سلسلة

String *v. t.* جهز بوترٍ . صفَّ

Stringent *a.* مشدّدٌ . خطيرٌ . مهمٌّ

Stringy *a.* ليفي . خيطيٌّ

Strip *v. t.* عرّى . قشرَ . نزعَ ـ

Strip *n.* قطعة . ضيقةٌ . سيرٌ

Stripe *n.* قلمٌ . خطٌّ . ضربةُ سوطٍ

Striped *a.* مخطط

Stripling *n.* ولدٌ . غلامٌ

Strive *v. i.* جدَّ ـ . كدَّ ـُ . إجتهد

Stroke *n.* ضربةٌ . مصيبة . إصابة

Stroke *v. t.* دلكَ ـُ . لاطفَ

Stroll *v. i.* جالَ ـُ . عارَ ـِ

Strong *a.* قويٌّ . متينٌ . شديدٌ

Stronghold *n.* حصنٌ . معقل

Structure *n.* هيئةٌ . بنيـة . بناءٌ

Struggle *v. i.* جدَّ . عاركَ

Struggle *n.* عراكٌ

Strumpet *n.* عاهرةٌ . فاجرةٌ

Strut *v. i.* تبخترَ . تخطرَ

Stubble *n.* هشيمٌ

Stubborn *a.* عنيد . ماردٌ

Stucco *n.* or *v. i.* جصٌّ . طلى بهِ

Stud *n.* طوَلة خيلٍ . ررٌّ

Studded *a.* مرصَّعٌ

Student *n.* تلميذٌ . طالبُ علمٍ

Studied *a.* مدروسٌ . مهيأ . مدبَّرٌ

Studious *a.* مجدٌّ في الدرسِ

Study *n.* or *v. t.* درسٌ . درسَ ـُ

Stuff *n.* مادةٌ . متَاعٌ . قُمَاشٌ

Stuff *v. t.* حَشَا . أفْعَمَ

Stuffing *n.* حَشْوٌ

Stultify *v. t.* جهَّلَ . حمَّقَ

Stumble *v. i.* عَثَرَ ـُ . زَلَّ ـَ . كَبَا ـُ

Stumbling-block *n.* حَجَرُ عثْرَةٍ

Stump *n.* قَرْمِيةٌ ج قرَامِيٌّ

Stun *v. t.* دَوَّخَ . حَيَّرَ . بَهَّتَ

Stunt *v. t.* وَقَّفَ عَنِ ٱلنمُوِّ

Stupefy *v. t.* أَدْخَلَ . بَهَّتَ . خدر

Stupendous *a.* عَظِيمٌ جدًّا . عَجيبٌ

Stupid *a.* بَليد . أَبْلَهُ . أَخْرَقُ

Stupidity *n.* خُرْقٌ . بَلَاهَةٌ

Stupor *n.* سُبَاتٌ . خَدَرٌ

Sturdy *a.* قَوِيٌّ . عَزومٌ

Stutter *v. i.* تَمْتَمَ . لَجْلَجَ

Sty *n.* زَرِيبةُ ٱلْخَنَازِيرِ . شَحَّاذُ ٱلْعَيْنِ

Style *n.* اُسْلُوبٌ . عِبَارَةٌ . زِيٌّ

Stylish *a.* بحَسَبِ ٱلزِّيِّ . انيقٌ

Suasive *a.* مُقْنِعٌ

Suavity *n.* لَطَافَةٌ . أَدَبٌ . عُذوبَةٌ

Subdivide *v. t.* جزَّا ايضاً

Subdivision *n.* تَجزِئَةُ ٱلْمُجَزَّإِ

Subdue *v. t.* أَخْضَعَ . غَلَبَ ـِ

Subject *n.* تابِعٌ . مَوضوعٌ . فَاعِلٌ

Subject *v. t.* or *a.* خَضَعَ . خَاضِعٌ . تَحْتَ

Subjection *n.* إِخْضَاعٌ . خضوع

Subjective *a.* باطِنِيٌّ . ذِهْنِيٌّ

Subjoin *v. t.* لَحْقَ بِهِ . ذَيَّلَ

Subjugate *v. t.* أَخْضَعَ . قَهرَ ـَ

Subjunctive *a.* مُلْحق . مَوْصُوْلٌ بِهِ

Sublime *a.* سَامٍ . جَليلٌ . رَفيعٌ

Sublimity *n.* سُمُوٌ . جلاَلَةٌ . رِفْعَةٌ

Submerge *v. t.* أَغْرَقَ . غَطَّسَ

Submersion *n.* تغْطِيسٌ

Submission *n.* خُضُوعٌ . تسْلِيمٌ

Submissive *a.* خاضِعٌ. طائِعٌ

Submit *v. i.* or *t.* خَضَعَ ـَ . سَلَّمَ

Subordinate *a.* تابِعٌ. دونٌ. ثانوي

Subordination *n.* خُضوعٌ. تَبَعِيَّةٌ

Suborn *v. t.* حَمَلَ عَلَى حَلْفِ زورٍ

Subscribe *v.t.* or *i.* أَمْضَى. رَضِيَ بِهِ. اشْتَرَكَ في

Subscriber *n.* مشْتَرِكٌ

Subscription *n.* قيمَةُ اشْتِراكٍ

Subsequent *a.* تالٍ. تابِعٌ

Subsequently *ad.* بَعْدُ. مِنْ بَعْدُ

Subserve *v. t.* خَدَمَ ـُ . أَفادَ

Subservient *a.* مُفيدٌ لَهُ. خاضِعٌ

Subside *v. i.* خَمَدَ ـُ . سَكَنَ ـُ

Subsidence *n.* سُكونٌ. هُبوطٌ

Subsidiary *a.* مُعاوِنٌ. إِضافِيٌّ

Subsidize *v. t.* أَعانَ بِدَراهِمَ لِخِدْمَةٍ

Subsidy *n.* إِعانَةٌ مالِيَّةٌ

Subsist *v. i.* اقْتاتَ. بَقِيَ ـَ وُجِدَ

Subsistence *n.* مَعيشَةٌ. وُجودٌ

Substance *n.* مادَّةٌ. جَوْهَرٌ. خُلاصَةٌ

Substantial *a.* حَقيقِيٌّ. جَوْهَرِيٌّ

Substantiate *v. t.* أَثْبَتَ. حَقَّقَ

Substantive *n.* or *a.* اسْمٌ. حَقيقِيٌّ

Substitute *n.* or *v. t.* عِوَضٌ. ابْدَلَ

Substitution *n.* إِبْدالٌ

Substruction / **Substructure** *n.* بِناءٌ تَحْتِيٌّ. أَساسٌ

Subtend *v. t.* قاطَعَ مِنْ أَسْفَلَ أَوْ مُقابِلاً

Subterfuge *n.* مُوارَبَةٌ. حيلَةٌ

Subterranean / **Subterraneous** *a.* تَحْتَ الأَرْضِ

Subtle *a.* داهٍ. مُحْتالٌ. مَكّارٌ

Subtilty / **Subtlety** *n.* حيلَةٌ. دَهاءٌ

Subtract *v. t.* طَرَحَ ـَ . أَسْقَطَ مِنْ

Subtraction *n.* طَرْحٌ

Subtrahend *n.* المَطْروح

Suburban *a.* مِنْ سَوادِ مَدينَةٍ

Suburbs *n. pl.* سَوادُ مَدينَةٍ

Subversion *n.* قلبٌ . هدْمٌ . تحرِيفٌ

Subversive *a.* مُخرّبٌ . مُحرِّفٌ

Subvert *v. t.* قَلَبَ ـِ . خرَّبَ . حرَّفَ

Succeed *v. t.* or *i.* تَبِعَ ـَ حَلَّ مَحَلَّهُ . نَجح

Success *n.* نجاحٌ . فوْزٌ

Successful *a.* ناجحٌ . ظَافرٌ

Succession *n.* تَتَابُعٌ . خِلَافَةٌ

Successive *a.* مُتتَابِعٌ . متعَاقِبٌ

Successor *n.* تَابِعٌ . خَلَفٌ . خَلِيفَةٌ

Succinct *a.* مُوجزٌ . مُلَخَّصٌ

Succour *n.* or *v. t.* إِغَاثَةٌ . أَغَاثَ . أَعَانَ

Succulent *a.* غَضٌ

Succumb *v. i.* خَضَعَ . مَاتَ

Such *a.* كَذَا . كَهَذَا . مِثْلُ هَذَا

Suck *v. t.* رَضَعَ ـَ امْتَصَّ

Sucker *n.* فرْخٌ . عُسْلجٌ . نَوْعٌ مِنَ السَّمَكِ

Suckle *v. t.* أَرْضَعَ

Suckling *n.* رَضِيعٌ ج رضعٌ

Suction *n.* مَصٌّ

Sudden *a.* فجَائِيٌّ . بَاغِتٌ

Suddenly *ad.* بَغْتَةً

Sue *v. t.* ادَّعَى عَلَيْهِ . حاكم . طَلَبَ

Suet *n.* شَحْمٌ

Suffer *v. t.* or *i.* احْتَمَلَ . قَاسَى . رَخَّصَ

Sufferable *a.* مَا يُحْتَمل

Sufferance *n.* رُخْصَةٌ . احتمَالٌ

Sufferer *n.* مُصابٌ . مُكَابِدٌ . مُتَألِّمٌ

Suffering *n.* الَمٌ . ضِيقٌ . عذَابٌ

Suffice *v. i.* or *t.* كَفَىِ ـِ . أَغْنَى

Sufficiency *n.* كِفَايَةٌ . مُكْنَةٌ

Sufficient *a.* كَافٍ . مغْنٍ

Suffix *n.* مُضَافٌ إِلى آخِرِهِ

Suffocate *v. t.* خَنَقَ . فطَّس

Suffocation *n.* خنْقٌ . اخْتِنَاق

Suffrage *n.* حقُّ صوتُ الإِنْتِخابِ

Suffuse *v. t.*	نَشَرَ ـُ . أَفْشَى
Sugar *n.*	سُكَّرٌ
Sugar-basin / **Sugar bowl** } *n.*	سُكَّرِيَّةٌ
Sugar-cane *n.*	قَصَبُ ٱلسُّكَّرِ
Sugar-loaf *n.*	رَأْسُ سُكَّرٍ
Sugar-plum *n.*	مُلَبَّسٌ
Suggest *v. t*	أَوْعَزَ . قَدَّمَ رَأْياً
Suggestion *n.*	تَقْدِيمُ رَأْيٍ . تَلْمِيحٌ
Suggestive *a.*	مُلَمِّحٌ . مُشِيرٌ إِلى
Suicidal *n.*	آيِلٌ لِقَتْلِ ٱلنَفْسِ
Suicide *n*	قَتْلُ ٱلنَّفْسِ . ٱنْتِحَارٌ
Suit *n.* or *v. t.*	حُلَّةُ ثِيَابٍ . دَعْوَى . نَاسَبَ
Suitable *a.*	مُوَافِقٌ . مُنَاسِبٌ
Suitableness *n.*	مُنَاسَبَةٌ
Suite *n.*	حَشَمٌ . طَقْمٌ
Suitor *n.*	طَالِبٌ . مُحِبٌّ . صَاحِبُ دَعْوَى
Sulky / **Sullen** } *a.*	عَبُوسٌ . حَرِيدٌ
Sully *v. t.*	لَطَخَ . ثَلَمَ ٱلصِّيتَ
Sulphur *n.*	كِبْرِيتٌ
Sulphureous / **Sulphurous** } *a.*	كِبْرِيتِيٌّ
Sultriness *n.* / **Sultry** *a.* }	عَكٌّ
Sum *n.*	مَجْمُوعٌ . حَاصِلٌ
Sumach *n.*	سُمَّاقٌ (شَجَرَةٌ)
Summarily *ad.*	مُلَخَّصاً . حَالاً
Summary *n.* or *a.*	مُلَخَّصٌ
Summer *n.*	صَيْفٌ . قَيْظٌ
Summit *n.*	قِمَّةٌ . رَأْسٌ
Summon *v. t.*	ٱسْتَدْعَى . ٱسْتَحْضَرَ
Summons *n. sing.*	ٱسْتِحْضَارٌ
Sumptuous *a.*	فَاخِرٌ . بَهِيٌّ . ثَمِينٌ
Sun *n.* or *v. t.*	شَمْسٌ . شَمَّسَ
Sun-beam *n.*	شُعَاعُ ٱلشَّمْسِ
Sunday *n.*	يَوْمُ ٱلأَحَدِ
Sunder *v. t.*	فَصَلَ ـِ
Sun-dial *n.*	سَاعَةٌ شَمْسِيَّةٌ
Sundries *n. pl.*	أَشْيَاءُ شَتَّى

Sundry *a.* شتّى

Sunken *a.* غارقٌ . تحتَ الماء

Sunlight *n.* نورُ الشمسِ

Sunlit *a.* منوَّرٌ مِنَ الشمسِ

Sunny *a.* شمسٌ . مُعرَّضٌ للشمسِ

Sunrise *n.* شروقُ الشمسِ

Sunset *n.* غروبُ الشمس

Sunshine *n.* ضوءُ الشمسِ

Sun-stroke *n.* رعنٌ

Sup *v. i.* تعشّى

Superabundance *n.* وَفرةٌ . فرْطٌ

Superabundant *a.* مُفرِطٌ . وَافِرٍ

Superannuated *a.* عاجزٌ مِنَ الكِبَرِ

Superb *a.* فاخرٌ . نفيسٌ . بهيٌّ

Supercilious *a.* متغطرسٌ . مُتجبّرٌ

Supereminent *a.* فائقٌ جدًّا

Supererogatory *a.* نافِليٌّ

Superficial *a.* سطحي . ظاهِري

Superfine *a.* نفيسٌ جدًّا . سَامٍ

Superfluity *n.* زِيادَةٌ . فضْل

Superfluous *a.* زائِد . فوْقَ اللازمِ

Superintend *v. t.* ناظرَ . توَكَّل على

Superintendence *n.* مُناظرَةٌ

Superintendent *n.* ناظِرٌ . وَكيلٌ

Superior *a.* or *n.* فائِقٌ . أعظَمَ . رئيس

Superiority *n.* سبْقٌ . أفضَليّةٌ

Superlative *a.* الأَفضَلُ . أَفْعَلُ التفضيلِ

Supernatural *a.* فوْقَ الطبيعةِ

Superscribe *v. t.* عنوَنَ

Superscription *n.* عنوانٌ

Supersede *v. t.* عزَلَ ـــِ . الغى

Supernal *n.* عَلوِي . سَماوي

Superstition *n.* وَهمٌ . خُرافةٌ

Superstitious *n.* متوَهِّمٌ . خُرافيٌّ

Superstructure *n.* بِناءٌ فوْقَ غيْرِهِ

Supervene *v. i.* حدَثَ عرَضًا

Supervise *v. t.* ناظَرَ . راقَبَ

Supervisor *n.* ناظِرٌ . مُناظِرٌ

Supine *a.* مُتَكاسِلٌ . غَيْرُ مُكْتَرِثٍ

Supineness *n.* تَوانٍ . تَهامُلٌ

Supper *n.* عَشاءٌ

Supplant *v. t.* اسْتَبْدَلَ حيلةً

Supple *a.* مَرِنٌ . لَيِّنٌ . مُنْقادٌ

Supplement *n.* مُلْحَقٌ . إضافةٌ

Supplemental / Supplementary *a.* إضافي

Suppleness *n.* مُرُونَةٌ . ليونةٌ

Suppliant / Supplicant *a.* مُتَوَسِّلٌ . مُتَضَرِّعٌ

Supplicate *v. t.* تَوَسَّل . تَضَرَّعَ إلى

Supplication *n.* تَوَسُّلٌ . اِلْتِماسٌ

Supplies *n. pl.* / Supply *n.* مُؤْنَةٌ . ذَخيرةٌ . كَفاءة

Supply *v. t.* جهز . قَدَّمَ . أَوْرَدَ

Support *v. t.* عَضَدَ . عالَ . امدَّ

Support *n.* سَنَدٌ . عولٌ . عَضَدٌ

Supportable *a.* يحتمل . يُطاق

Supposable *a.* مظنونٌ . مُحْتَمل

Suppose *v. t.* ظَنَّ ـ فَرَضَ ـ

Supposition *n.* ظنٌّ . فَرْضٌ

Suppositious *a.* غَيْرُ حَقيقيّ . مَظْنُونٌ

Suppress *v. t.* منعَ . أَبْطَلَ . أَخْمَدَ

Suppression *n.* إبْطالٌ . إخْمادٌ

Suppurate *v. i.* قاحَ ـُ تَقَيَّحَ

Suppremacy *n.* سُلْطَةٌ . رِياسةٌ تَفَوُّقٌ

Suppreme *a.* مُطْلَقُ التَّسلُّطِ . الأعْظَمُ

Sure *a.* اكيدٌ . يَقينٌ . مُحَقَّقٌ

Surety *n.* أَمْنٌ . كَفالةٌ . يَقينٌ

Surf *n.* أَمْواجٌ عَلَى الشَّطِّ

Surface *n.* سَطْحٌ . وَجْهٌ

Surfeit *n.* or *v. t.* كِظةٌ . كَظَّ ـُ

Surge *n.* or *v. i.* مَوْجٌ عَظيمٌ . تَمَوَّجَ

Surgeon *n.* جَرَّاحٌ

Surgery *n.* عِلْمُ الجِراحةِ

Surgical *a.* جراحي

Surly *a.* شَكِسٌ . فَظٌّ
Surmise *n.* or *v. t.* حَدْسٌ . خَمَّنَ
Surmount *v. t.* عَلاَ عَلَيْهِ . غَلَبَ
Surname *n.* اسْمُ الْعَائِلَةِ . لَقَبٌ
Surpass *v. t.* سَبَقَ . فَاقَ
Surpassing *a.* فَائِقٌ . جَيِّدٌ جِدًّا
Surplus *n.* فَضْلَةٌ . بَقِيَّةٌ
Surprise *n.* or *v. t.* تَعَجُّبٌ . جَا . ادْهَشَ
Surrender *v. t.* or *n.* سَلَّمَ . تَسْلِيمٌ
Surreptitions *a.* مَا يُفْعَلُ خُلْسَةً أَو غَدْرًا
Surround *v. t.* احَاطَ بِهِ . أَحْدَقَ
Survey *v. t.* عَايَنَ . فَحَصَ . مَسَحَ
Survey / Surveying *n.* مَسْحٌ . مِسَاحَةٌ
Surveyor *n.* مَسَّاحٌ
Survival *n.* بَقَاءٌ بَعْدَ آخَرَ
Survive *v. t.* عَاشَ بَعْدَهُ
Susceptibility *n.* حِسٌّ . تَأَثُّرٌ
Susceptible *a.* مُحِسٌّ . مُتَأَثِّرٌ . قَابِلٌ

Suspect *v. t.* اتَّهَمَ . اشْتَبَهَ
Suspend *v. t.* وَقَفَ . أَجَّلَ . عَلَقَ
Suspense *n.* تَرَدُّدٌ . حِيرَةٌ
Suspension *n.* تَوْقِيفٌ . تَعْطِيلٌ
Suspension *n.* تُهْمَةٌ . شُبْهَةٌ
Suspicious *a.* ظَنَّانٌ . مُشْتَبِهٌ
Sustain *v. t.* احْتَمَلَ . سَنَدَ . عَضَدَ
Sustenance *n.* قُوتٌ . عَضَدٌ
Suture *n.* دَرْزٌ
Suzerain *n.* مَوْلًى
Swab *n.* or *v. t.* مِمْسَحَةٌ . مَسَحَ بِهَا
Swaddle *v. t.* or *n.* قَمَطَ . قِمَاطٌ
Swagger *v. i.* or *n.* تَغَطْرَسَ . غَطْرَسَةٌ
Swain *n.* فَلاَّحٌ . فَلاَّحٌ عَاشِقٌ
Swallow *v. t.* or *n.* ازْدَرَدَ . سُنُونُو
Swamp *n.* مُسْتَنْقَعٌ . سَبَخَةٌ . غَمْقَةٌ
Swan *n.* نَوْعٌ مِنَ الاوَزِّ
Sward *n.* جَزْمَةٌ . أَرْضٌ كَثِيرَةُ الْكَلاِ

Swarm *n.* or *v. i.* ثَوْل . اَزْدَحَمَ

Swarthy *a.* أَسمَرُ

Sway *v. t.* or *i.* مَلَكَ . أَمَالَ . تَمَايَلَ

Swear *v. i.* حَلَفَ ـِ . اَقْسَمَ . شَتَمَ ـُ

Swearing *n.* حلف . تَجْدِيفٌ

Sweat *n.* or *v. i.* عَرَقٌ . عَرِقَ ـَ

Sweep *v. t.* كَنَسَ . جَرَفَ ـُ

Sweepings *n. pl.* كُنَاسَةٌ . زُبَالَةٌ

Sweet *a.* or *n.* حلوٌ . عذبٌ . حلْوَى

Sweeten *v.t.* or *i.* حَلَى . حَلاَ ـُ

Sweetheart *n.* عَاشِقٌ (ة) مَعْشوق (ة)

Sweetmeat *n.* حَلْوَى ج حَلاَوَى

Sweetness *n.* حَلاَوَةٌ . عذُوبَة

Swell *v. i.* or *n.* اَنْتَفَخَ . وَرمَ ـَ . عُبَابٌ

Swelling *n.* وَرَمٌ

Swelter *v. i.* تضَايَق مِنَ ٱلْحَرِّ

Swerve *v.* مَالَ ـِ انْحَرَفَ

Swift *a.* سَرِيعٌ

Swiftness *n.* سُرْعَةٌ

Swim *v. i.* سَبَحَ ـَ

Swimming *n.* سِبَاحَةٌ

Swimmingly *ad.* جَيِّدًا . بتَوْفِيقٍ

Swindle *v. t.* or *n.* غَبَنَ ـِ غَدَرَ ـُ

Swine *n.* خِنزِيرٌ ج خَنَازِيرُ

Swing *v. t.* or *i.* ارْجَحَ . اَرْتَجَحَ . تَمَايَلَ

Swing *n.* أَرْجُوحَةٌ . مَرْجُوحَةٌ

Switch *n.* قَضِيبٌ لَيِّنٌ

Swoon *v. i.* or *n.* غُشِيَ عَلَيْهِ . غَشْيَةٌ

Swoop *v. i.* اَنْقَضَّ عَلَى

Sword *n.* سَيْفٌ . ج سُيُوفٌ . حُسَامٌ

Sycamore *n.* جُمَّيْزٌ . جُمَّيْزَةٌ

Sycophant *n.* مُدَاهِنٌ

Syllable *n.* مَقْطَعُ كَلِمَةٍ

Syllabus *n.* خُلَاصَةٌ . مُخْتَصَرٌ

Syllogism *n.* قِيَاسٌ مَنْطِقِيٌّ

Sylvant *a.* غَابِيٌّ

Symbol *n.* رَمْزٌ . مِثَالٌ . عَلَامَةٌ
Symbolic / **Symbolical** *a.* رَمْزِي . اسْتِعَارِيٌّ
Symmetrical *a.* مُتَنَاسِبُ الأَجْزَاءِ
Symmetry *n.* تَنَاسُبُ الأَجْزَاءِ
Sympathetic مُشْتَرِكٌ فِي شُعُورِ غَيْرِهِ
Sympathize *v. i.* اشْتَرَكَ فِي شُعُورِهِ
Sympathy *n.* إِشْتِرَاكٌ فِي شُعُورِهِ
Symptom *n.* عَلَامَةٌ . عَرَضُ مَرَضٍ
Synagogue *n.* مَجْمَعُ الْيَهُودِ
Synchronism *n.* اتِّفَاقٌ فِي الْوَقْتِ
Syndicate *n.* وِكَالَةٌ أَوْ شَرِكَةٌ لإِجْرَاءِ أَشْغَالٍ
Synonym / **Synonyme** *a.* كَلِمَةٌ مُتَرَادِفَةٌ
Synonymous *a.* مُتَرَادِفٌ
Synopsis *n.* مُلَخَّصٌ . خُلَاصَةٌ
Synoptic / **Synoptical** *a.* مُلَخَّصِيٌّ . شَامِلٌ
Syntax *n.* عِلْمُ النَّحْوِ
Synthesis *n.* تَرْكِيبٌ . تَأْلِيفُ الأَفْكَارِ
Syriac *a.* سِرْيَانِيٌّ
Syringe *n.* or *v. i.* مِحْقَنَةٌ . عَالَجَ بِهَا
Syrup *n.* عَصِيرٌ . مُحَلًّى . شَرَابٌ
System *n.* تَرْتِيبٌ . نِظَامٌ . مَذْهَبٌ
Systematic / **Systematical** *a.* نِظَامِيٌّ . تَرْتِيبِيٌّ
Systematize *v. t.* نَظَّمَ . رَتَّبَ

T

Tabernacle *n.* خَيْمٌ . مَظَلٌّ
Table *n.* مَائِدَةٌ . سُفْرَةٌ . جَدْوَلٌ
Tableau *n.* صُورَةٌ . تَشْخِيصٌ
Table-land *n.* نَجْدٌ . هَضْبَةٌ . صَعِيدٌ
Tablet *n.* لَوْحٌ لِلْكِتَابَةِ
Tabular *a.* مُسَطَّحٌ . جَدْوَلِيٌّ

Tacit *a.* ساكِتٌ . مُضمَنٌ . مفهُومٌ

Taciturn *a.* سَكُوتٌ . كَتومٌ

Taciturnity *n.* سُكُوت

Tack *n.* مِسْمَارٌ صغِيرٌ. مَجرَى ٱلسَّفِينَة

Tack *v. t.* سَمَّرَ خَفِيفاً. غَيَّرَ مَجْرَى السَّفِينَةِ

Tackle *n.* or *v. t.* جِهازٌ. آلاتٌ. قَبَضَ . شَدَّ

Tackling *n.* جِهازُ ٱلسَّوَارِي وَٱلْقُلُوعِ

Tact *n.* مَهارَةٌ . لَبَاقَةٌ . فِراسَةٌ

Tactical *a.* مُختَصٌّ بِتَنْظِيمِ ٱلْجُيُوشِ

Tactics *n. sing.* عِلْمُ تَنْظِيمِ ٱلْجُيُوشِ

Tadpole *n.* وَلَدُ ٱلضِفْدَعِ

Tail n. ذَنَبٌ . ذَيلٌ . مُؤَخر

Tailor *n.* خَيَاطٌ

Taint *v. t.* or *n.* شَابَ ـُ لَطْخَةٌ

Take *v. t.* اخَذَ ـُ تَنَاوَلَ

Taking *a.* or *n.* جَاذِبٌ . أَخْذٌ

Tale *n.* قِصةٌ . حكايَة . رِوَايَةٌ

Tale-bearer *n.* نَمَّامٌ . وَاش

Talent *n.* وَزْنَةٌ . مَوْهَبَةٌ

Talented *a.* ذَكِيٌّ . لَوْذَعِيٌّ

Talisman *n.* طِلَسْمٌ ج طَلاَسِمٌ

Talk *n.* or *v. i.* كَلاَمٌ . تَكَلَّمَ

Talkative *a.* كَثِيرُ ٱلكَلاَمِ

Tall *a.* طَوِيلُ ٱلْقَامَةِ . عال

Talness *n.* طُولٌ . عُلوٌّ

Tallow *n.* شَحْمٌ

Tally *v. i.* طَابَقَ . اتَّفَقَ

Tallon *n.* مِخْلَبٌ . ظِفْرٌ

Tamable *a.* مَا يُؤَانَسُ . يُطَبَّعُ . يُذَلَّلُ

Tame *a.* or *v. t.* دَاجِنٌ . ذَلُولٌ . ذَلَّلَ

Tamely *ad.* تَذَلُّلاً

Tamper *v. i.* تَدَاخَلَ فِي . لعِبَ فِي

Tan *n.* or *v. t.* دِبْغَةٌ . دَبَغَ ـُ

Tangent *n.* خَط مُمَاسٌّ لقوس

Tangible *a.* مَا يُمَسُّ أو يُلْمَسُ . مَحسُوسٌ

Tangle *v. t.* or *n.* شَبَّكَ . عُقْدَةٌ

Tank *n.* حَوْضٌ . بِرْكَةٌ

Tanner *n.* دَبَّاغٌ

Tannery *n.* مَدْبَغَةٌ . دَبَّاغَةٌ

Tantalize *v. t.* عَذَّبَ بِرَجَاءِ ٱلْمُسْتَحِيلِ

Tantamount *a.* مُسَاوٍ

Tap *n.* دَقَّ ـُ خَفِيفًا . بَزَلَ ـُ

Tape *n.* شَرِيطٌ

Taper *n.* or *v. i.* شَمْعَةٌ . اِسْتَدَقَّ

Tap-root *n.* اَلْجِذْرُ ٱلْأَصْلِيُّ ٱلْمُسْتَقِيمُ

Tapestry *n.* أَنْسِجَةٌ مُوَشَّاةٌ لِلتَّعْلِيقِ

Tapeworm *n.* الدودةُ ٱلْعَرِيضَةُ

Tar *n.* or *v. t.* قَطْرَانٌ طَلَى بِهِ . نُوتِيٌّ

Tardiness *n.* تَأَخُّرٌ . بُطُوءٌ

Tardy *a.* مُتَأَخِّرٌ . بَطِيءٌ

Tare *n.* زُوَانٌ

Target *n.* هَدَفٌ . تُرْسٌ صَغِيرٌ

Tariff *n.* تَعْرِيفٌ . جَدْوَلُ جَمَارِكَ

Tarnish *v. t.* كَدَّرَ ٱللَّوْنَ . لَطَّخَ

Tarry *v. i.* مَكَثَ ـُ . أَبْطَأَ

Tart *a.* or *n.* حَامِضٌ . حَادٌّ . فَطِيرَةٌ

Tartar *n.* طَرْطِيرٌ . تَتَرِيٌّ

Tartness *n.* حُمُوضَةٌ . حِدَّةٌ

Task *n.* شُغْلٌ مَفْرُوضٌ . عَمَلٌ شَاقٌّ

Tassel *n.* شَرَّابَةٌ . زِرٌّ

Taste *v. t.* or *n.* ذَاقَ ـُ . ذَوْقٌ . مَشْرَبٌ

Tasteful / Tasty } *a.* بِحَسَبِ ٱلذَّوْقِ . أَنِيقٌ

Tasteless *a.* بِلَا طَعْمٍ . تَافِهٌ

Tatter *v. t.* or *n.* مَزَّقَ . خِرْقَةٌ . رِثَّةٌ

Tattle *v. i.* هَذَرَ ـِ . فَضَحَ ٱلسِّرَّ

Taunt *v. t.* عَيَّرَ . عَنَّفَ

Tavern *n.* فُنْدُقٌ . حَانَةٌ

Tawdry *a.* مُتَظَرِّفٌ بِلَا ذَوْقٍ

Tawny *a.* أَسْمَرُ

Tax *n.* ضَرِيبَةٌ . رَسْمٌ

Taxable *a.* تَحْتَ ضَرِيبَةٍ أَوْ رَسْمٍ

Taxation *n.* اَلضَّرَائِبُ بِجُمْلَتِهَا

Tea *n.* شَايٌ

Teach *v. t.* عَلَّمَ . دَرَّسَ

Teachable *a.* قَابِلُ ٱلتَّعْلِيمِ . طَوْعٌ

Teacher *n.* مُعَلِّمٌ . مُدَرِّسٌ

Team *n.* ثَوْرَا ٱلْحِرَاثَةِ . قِطَارُ دَوَابَّ

Tea-pot *n.* إِبْرِيقُ شَايٍ

Tear *n.* دَمْعَةٌ . شَرْمٌ . مَزْقَةٌ

Tear *v. t.* مَزَّقَ . شَقَّ ـُ

Tearful *a.* دَمِيعٌ

Tease *v. t.* نَكَّدَ . أَضْجَرَ

Teat *n.* حَلَمَةُ حَيَوَانٍ . بِزٌّ

Technical *a.* صِنَاعِيٌّ . ٱصْطِلَاحِيٌّ

Technology *n.* ٱلْبَحْثُ عَنِ ٱلصِّنَاعَاتِ وَحُدُودِهَا

Tedious *a.* مُتْعِبٌ . مُمِلٌّ . مُطَوَّلٌ

Tediousness } *n.* مَلَلٌ . ضَجَرٌ
Tedium }

Teem *v. i.* غَصَّ ـُ . أَنْتَجَ كَثِيرًا

Teens *n. pl.* ٱلْعُمْرُ بَيْنَ ١٣ و ١٩ سنة

Teeth *n. pl. of* Tooth أَسْنَانٌ

Teetotalism *n.* ٱلْامْتِنَاعُ عَنِ ٱلْمُسْكِرَاتِ

Telegram *n.* رِسَالَةٌ بَرْقِيَّةٌ

Telegraph *n.* سِلْكٌ بَرْقِيٌّ

Telephone *n.* آلَةٌ لِلتَّكَلُّمِ عَلَى بُعْدٍ

Telescope *n.* نَظَّارَةٌ . مِنْظَرٌ

Tell *v. t.* or *i.* خَبَّرَ . حَدَّثَ . قَالَ

Tell-tale *n.* وَاشٍ

Temerity *n.* تَهَوُّرٌ . ٱعْتِسَافٌ

Temper *n.* طَبْعٌ . خُلْقٌ

Temper *v. t.* مَزَجَ ـُ لَطَّفَ . عَدَّلَ

Temperament *n.* مِزَاجٌ

Temperance *n.* ٱعْتِدَالٌ . عِفَّةٌ

Temperate *a.* مُعْتَدِلٌ . عَفِيفٌ

Temperature *n.* دَرَجَةُ ٱلْحَرَارَةِ

Tempest *n.* عَاصِفَةٌ . نَوْءٌ

Tempestuous *a.* عَاصِفٌ . زَوْبَعِيٌّ

Temple *n.* هَيْكَلٌ . صُدْغٌ

Temporal *a.* زَمَنِيٌّ . صدغيٌّ
Temporarily *ad.* وَقْتِيًّا
Temporary *a.* وَقْتِيٌّ . إلى حين
Temporise *v. i.* دارَ مع الأحوال
Tempt *v. t.* جرَّبَ . أغوى
Temptation *n.* تجربة
Tempter *n.* مُجرِّب
Ten *a.* عشرة . عشر
Tenable *a.* قابِل التمسُّك به أو الإثبات
Tenacity *n.* تمسُّك . تشبُّث
Tenant *n.* مُستأجِر
Tenantry *n.* مُستأجِرو املاك
Tend *v. t.* or *i.* آلَ . مالَ إلى . إعتنى بِ
Tendency *n.* مَيْل . انعطاف
Tender *a.* غضٌّ . طريٌّ . حنون
Tender *n.* or *v. t.* عَرْضُ سعرٍ . عرَضَ
Tenderness *n.* حنوٌّ . رِقة
Tendon *n.* وَتَر

Tendril *n.* عُسلُج لَوْلَبِيٌّ للتَّعاليق
Tenement *n.* مَسْكن مُستأجَر
Tenet *n.* عقيدة . مذهب
Tenfold *n.* عشرة أضعاف
Tennis *n.* نوعٌ مِنْ لعبِ الكرة
Tenor *n.* فحوى . سياق
Tense *a.* or *n.* مشدود . زمان الفعل
Tension *n.* شدٌّ . اشتداد
Tent *n.* خيمة . صيوان . فسطاط
Tentacle *n.* قرن الحشرات
Tentative *a.* تجريبيٌّ
Tenth *a.* عاشر
Tenuity *n.* رِقّة . لطافة
Tenure *n.* استئجار
Tepid *a.* فاتر
Terebinth *n.* شجر البُطْم
Term *n.* عبارة . مدّة . شرط . حدّ
Term *v. t.* سمّى . دعا

Terminal *a.* فِي ٱلطَّرَفِ . آخِرٌ

Terminate *v. t.* أَنْهَى . إِنْتَهَى

Termination *n.* إِنْهَآءٌ . نِهَايَةٌ

Terminus *n.* تَخْمٌ . طَرَفٌ . حدّ

Terrace *n.* سَطْحُ بَيْتٍ . دَكَّةٌ

Terra-Cotta *n.* فَخَّارٌ

Terrestrial *a.* ارضِيٌّ

Terrible *a.* مُخِيفٌ . هَائِلٌ

Terrier *n.* ضَرْبٌ مِنْ كِلَابِ ٱلصَّيْدِ

Terrific *a.* مُسَبِّبُ خَوفٍ شَدِيدٍ

Terrify *v. t.* خَوَّفَ . فَزَّعَ

Territory *n.* إِقْلِيمٌ . ارضٌ مَمْلَكَةٍ

Terror *n.* هَوْلٌ . فَزَعٌ

Terse *a.* أَنِيقُ ٱلْعِبَارَة . مُوْجَزُهَا

Terseness *n.* إِيجَازٌ

Test *n.* or *v. t.* آمْتِحَانٌ . جَرَّبَ

Testament *n.* عَهْدٌ . وَصِيَّةٌ

Testamentary *a.* مَنُوطٌ بِوَصِيَّةٍ

Testator *n.* مُوصٍ

Testicle *n.* خِصْيَةٌ ج خِصًى

Testify *v. t.* شَهِدَ ـَ

Testimonial *a.* }
Testimony *n.* } شَهَادَةٌ

Testiness *n.* حِدَّةٌ . شَكَاسَةٌ

Tetanus *n.* دَآءُ ٱلْكُزَازِ

Tether *v. t.* شَكَلَ ـُ . شَكَّلَ

Teutonic *a.* جَرْمَانِيٌّ

Text *n.* مَتْنٌ . موضُوعٌ

Text-book *n.* كِتَابُ دَرْسٍ

Textile *a.* مَنْسُوجٌ . نَسِيجِيٌّ

Texture *n.* نَسِيجٌ

Than *conj.* مِنْ (بعدَ أفعلَ ٱلتَّفْضِيلِ)

Thank *v. t.* شَكَرَ ـُ . اثْنَى عَلَى

Thankful *a.* شَاكِرٌ . شَكُورٌ

Thankfulness *n.* شُكْرَانٌ . شُكْرٌ

Thankless *a.* عَدِيمُ ٱلشُّكْرِ

Thanks *n.* ([illegible])

Thanksgiving *n.* شُكْرٌ . حَمْدٌ

That *pron.* or *conj.* ذَلِكَ . أَنْ

Thatch *n.* or *v. t.* غمَآءٌ . غَمَى ـُ

Thaw *v. i.* or *t.* ذَابَ ـُ . أَذَابَ

The *def. article.* آلْ آلتَّعْرِيفِ

Theatre *n.* مَسْرَحٌ . مَلْعَبٌ

Theatric / **Theatrical** *a.* مَسْرَحِيٌّ

Thee *p. pron.* لِكَ (ضَمِيرُ آلْمُخَاطَبِ)

Theft *n.* سَرِقَةٌ

Theirs *a. pron.* الذِي لَهُمْ

Theism *n.* ٱلْإِعْتِقَادُ بِوُجُودِ آللهِ

Theist *n.* مُعْتَقِدٌ بِآللهِ

Them *p. pron.* هُمْ . هُنَّ (مَنْصُوبٌ او مَجْرُورٌ)

Theme *n.* مَوْضُوعٌ . جُمْلَةٌ . مَقَالَةٌ

Themselves *pron. pl.* هُمْ أَنْفُسُهُمْ

Then *ad.* عِنْدَ ذَلِكَ . حِينَئِذٍ . إِذًا

Thence *ad.* مِنْ هُنَاكَ

Thenceforth / **Thenceforward** *ad.* مِنْ ذَلِكَ آلْوَقْتِ

Theodolite *n.* آلَةٌ لِلْمِسَاحَةِ

Theologian *n.* عَالِمٌ بِاللَّاهُوتِ

Theologic / **Theological** *a.* لَاهُوتِيٌّ

Theology *n.* عِلْمُ آللاهُوتِ

Theorem *n.* قَضِيَةٌ هِنْدَسِيَّةٌ

Theoretic / **Theorotical** *a.* نَظَرِيٌّ . تَصَوُّرِيٌّ

Theorise *v. i.* نَظَرَ فِي . إِرْتَأَى

Theory *n.* نَظَرِيَّةٌ . رَأْيٌ

Therapeutic *a.* عِلَاجِيٌّ . شِفَائِيٌّ

There *ad.* هُنَاكَ . حَرْفُ ٱلِإبْتِدَاءِ

Thereabout *ad.* تَقْرِيباً

Thereafter *ad.* بَعْدَ ذَلِكَ . ثُمَّ

Thereby *ad.* بِذَلِكَ . لِذَلِكَ

Therefore *ad.* لِذَلِكَ . لِأَجْلِ ذَلِكَ

Therein *ad.* فِي ذَلِكَ . هُنَاكَ

Thereof *ad.* مِنْ ذَلِكَ . مِنْهُ

Thereupon *ad.* حِينَئِذٍ . عِنْدَ ذَلِكَ

Therewith *ad.* لِذَلِكَ . بِهِ

Thermal *a.* مَنُوطٌ بالحَرِّ
Thermometer *n.* ميزان الحَرَارَة
Thesaurus *n.* خَزْنَةٌ . قَامُوسٌ جَامِعٌ
These *pron. pl. of* this هؤُلاءِ
Thesis *n.* مَوْضُوعٌ . مَبْحَثٌ . مقالة
They *pl. pron.* هُمْ هُنَّ (مرفوعٌ)
Thick *a.* سميكٌ . كثيفٌ . ثَخِينٌ
Thicken *v. t.* or *i.* سمك . كَثُفَ
Thicket *n.* أَجَمَةٌ . دَغَل
Thickness *n.* سَمْك . كَثَافَة
Thick-set *a.* ضَخْمٌ
Thief *n.* سَارِقٌ . لِصٌّ
Thieve *v. i.* لصَّ
Thievish *a.* مُتَلَصِّصٌ
Thigh *n.* فَخِذٌ ج أَفْخَاذ
Thimble *n.* قِمْعٌ . كِشْتُبَان
Thin *a.* رقيق . نَحِيفٌ
Thine *a. pron.* لَكَ . الذي لَكَ

Thing *n.* شيءٌ . أمرٌ
Think *v. i.* or *t.* افْتَكَرَ . ظَنَّ
Third *a.* or *n.* ثَالِثٌ . ثُلْثٌ
Thirst *n.* or *v. i.* عَطَشٌ . عَطِشَ
Thirsty *a.* عَطْشَانُ م عَطْشَى
Thirteen *a.* ثَلَثَةَ عَشَرَ
Thirteenth *a.* الثالِثُ عَشَرَ
Thirtieth *a.* الثَلاثُونَ
Thirty *a.* ثَلاثُونَ
This *pron.* هَذَا . هَذِهِ
Thistle *n.* شَوْكٌ . حَسَك
Thither *ad.* إِلَى هُنَاكَ
Thong *n.* سَيْرٌ . شِرَاكٌ
Thorax *n.* الصَّدْرُ
Thorn *n.* شَوْكٌ . اشْوَاك
Thorny *a.* كَثِيرُ الشَوْكِ . عسِرٌ
Thorough *a.* كَامِلٌ . شَامِل
Thoroughfare *n.* سِكَّة . شارِعٌ

Those *pl. of* that اولئِكَ

Thou *pron.* أَنْتَ

Though *conj.* مَعْ ان . وَلَوْ . وَانْ

Thought *n.* فِكْرٌ . رَأْيٌ

Thoughtful *a.* مُتَفَكِّرٌ . رَزِينٌ . مُهْتَمٌ

Thoughtless *a.* طائِشٌ . غافِلٌ

Thousand *a.* or *n.* الْفٌ

Thousandth *n.* أَلالْفُ

Thraldom / **Thralldom** *n.* عُبُودِيَّةٌ . رِقٌّ

Thrash *v. t.* دَرَسَ ٱلْحُبُوبَ . ضَرَبَ

Thread *n.* or *v. t.* خَيْطٌ . أَدْخَلَهُ فِي إِبْرَةٍ

Threadbare *a.* بالٍ

Threat *n.* تَهْدِيدٌ . وعيد

Threaten *v. t.* or *i.* هددَ . اوعَدَ . هَمَّ بِ

Threatening *a.* مُهَدِّدٌ . مُوشِكٌ

Three *a.* ثلثة . ثلاثة . ثلاث

Threefold *a.* ثلاثة أضعافٍ

Threescore *a.* سِتون

Thresh *v. t.* دَرَسَ ُ ٱلْحُبُوبَ

Threshold *n.* أُسْكُفَّةٌ . مَدْخَلٌ

Thrice *ad.* ثَلاثَ مَرَّاتٍ

Thrift *n.* نجاحٌ . اقْتِصادٌ

Thriftless *a.* عَدِيمُ ٱلتَّدْبِيرِ وَٱلنَّجاح

Thrifty *a.* ناجِحٌ . مقتصدٌ

Thrill *v. t.* or *n.* حَرَّكَ . هاجَ . اهْتِزازٌ

Thrilling *a.* مُهَيِّجٌ . مؤثِّرٌ جِدًّا

Thrive *v. i.* نَجَحَ ِ . أَفْلَحَ

Throat *n.* حُلْقُومٌ . بُلْعُومٌ حَلْقٌ

Throb *v. i.* خَفَقَ ُ . اخْتَلَجَ

Throe *n.* أَلَمٌ شَدِيدٌ . مخاضٌ

Throne *n.* عَرْشٌ

Throng *n.* or *v. t.* or *i.* زَحْمَةٌ . تقاطَرَ

Throttle *v. t.* خَنَقَ ُ

Through *pr.* مِنَ ٱلأَوَّلِ إِلَى ٱلآخِرِ . بِوَاسِطَةِ

Throughout *pr.* or *ad.* فِي كُلِّهِ

Throw *v. t.* or *n.* رَمَى ِ . رَمْيَةٌ

Thrust *v. t.* or *n.* دَفَعَ . طَعَنَ ـُ دَفْعَةٌ
Thumb *n.* or *v. t.* إِبْهَامٌ ج أَبَاهِمُ . وَسَّخَ بِهَا
Thump *n.* or *v. t.* ضَرَبَ . وَكَزَ . ضَرْبَةٌ
Thunder *n.* or *v. i.* رَعْدٌ . رَعَدَ ـَ
Thunder-bolt *n.* صَاعِقَةٌ
Thunder-struck *a.* صَعِقٌ . مَدْهُوشٌ
Thursday *n.* يَوْمُ ٱلْخَمِيسِ
Thus *ad.* هٰكَذَا . كَذَا
Thwart *v. t.* عَارَضَ . عَطَّلَ
Thy *poss. pron.* ـكَ
Thyme *n.* سَعْتَرٌ
Thyself *pron.* أَنْتَ نَفْسُكَ
Tick *n.* or *v. i.* قُرَّاضَةٌ . تَكْتَكَ
Ticket *n.* تَذْكِرَةٌ إِجَازَةٍ
Tickle *v. t.* دَغْدَغَ
Tide *n.* مَدُّ ٱلْبَحْرِ وَجَزْرُهُ
Tidings *n. pl.* أَخْبَارٌ
Tidy *a.* نَظِيفٌ . مُرَتَّبٌ

Tie *v. t.* رَبَطَ ـُ . عَقَدَ ـِ . قَيَّدَ
Tier *n.* طَبَقَةٌ . صَفٌّ
Tiger *mas.* / **Tigress** *fem.* } *n.* نَمِرٌ . نَمِرَةٌ ج نُمُورٌ
Tight *a.* شَدِيدٌ . مَشْدُودٌ
Tighten *v. t.* شَدَّ ـُ أَحْكَمَ . مَكَّنَ
Tile *n.* or *v. t.* قَرْمِيدَةٌ . غَطَّى بِهَا
Till *ad.* or *n.* حَتَّى . إِلَى . صَنْدُوق دَرَاهِمَ
Till *v. t.* حَرَثَ ـُ . فَلَحَ ـَ
Tillage *n.* حِرَاثَةٌ . فِلَاحَةٌ
Tilt *v. t.* أَمَالَ . طَعَنَ ـَ
Timber *n.* خَشَبٌ
Time *n.* زَمَانٌ . وَقْتٌ مَرَّةٌ
Timely *ad.* فِي وَقْتِهِ . فِي مَحَلِّهِ
Time-piece *n.* سَاعَةٌ
Timid / **Timorous** } *a.* خَائِفٌ . جَبَانٌ
Timidity *n.* جَبَانَةٌ . حَيَاءٌ
Tin *n.* قَصْدِيرٌ . تَنَكٌ . صَفِيحٌ
Tincture *n.* صِبْغَةٌ . لَوْنٌ

Tinder *n.* صُوفَانٌ

Tinge *v. t.* لَوَّنَ خَفِيفًا

Tingle *v. i.* تَأَلَّمَ شَدِيدًا

Tinker *n.* or *v. t.* سَنْكَرِيٌّ . اصْلَحَ أَوْعِيَةً

Tinkle *v. i.* طَنَّ ـِ

Tinkling *n.* طَنِينٌ

Tinman, Tinner *n.* تَنْكَارِيٌّ

Tinsel *n.* or *a.* بَهْرَجٌ . لَامِعٌ

Tint *n.* لَوْنٌ خَفِيفٌ

Tiny *a.* صَغِيرٌ جِدًّا . زَهِيدٌ

Tip *n.* or *v. t.* طَرَفٌ . رَاسٌ . أَمَالَ

Tippler *n.* سِكِّيرٌ

Tipsy *a.* سَكْرَانُ

Tiptoe *n.* أَطْرَافُ أَصَابِعِ ٱلْقَدَمِ

Tiptop *n.* اعلاهُ . سَامٍ غَايَةً فِي ٱلْجُودَةِ

Tirade *n.* شَتْمٌ

Tire *v. t.* or *n.* اتْعَبَ . طَبَانٌ

Tired *a.* مُتْعَبٌ

Tiresome *a.* مُتْعِبٌ . مُمِلٌّ

Tissue *n.* نَسِيجٌ

Tithe *v. t.* or *n.* عَشَّرَ . عُشْرٌ

Title *n.* لَقَبٌ . عِنْوَانٌ . حَقٌّ

Titular *a.* بِٱلِاسْمِ فَقَطْ . اسْمِيٌّ

To *pr.* إِلَى . نَحْوَ . لِ

Toad *n.* نَوْعٌ مِنَ ٱلضِّفْدَعِ

Toadstool *n.* فُطْرٌ

Toast *v. t.* or *n.* حَمَّصَ . خُبْزٌ مُحَمَّصٌ

Tobacco *n.* تَبْغٌ . تُتُنٌ . دُخَانٌ

To-day *n.* اليَوْمُ

Toddle *v. i.* دَبَّ ـِ

Toddy *n.* شَرَابٌ مُسْكِرٌ

Toe *n.* اصْبَعُ ٱلْقَدَمِ

Together *ad.* مَعًا

Toil *v. i.* or *n.* تَعِبَ ـَ . تَعَبٌ . كَدٌّ

Toilet *n.* زِينَةٌ . لِبَاسٌ . مَائِدَةٌ لِلُّبْسِ

Toilsome *a.* مُتْعِبٌ . شَاقٌّ

Token *n.* تَذْكِرَةٌ . عَلاَمَةٌ

Tolerable *a.* مُحْتَمَلٌ . مُعْتَدِلٌ

Tolerance / Toleration *n.* اِحْتِمَالٌ . تَسَامُحٌ

Tolerate *v. t.* أَبَاحَ . اِحْتَمَلَ

Toll *n.* or *v. t.* رَسْمٌ . دقّ

Tomahawk *n.* فَاسٌ حَرْبِيَّةٌ لِلْهُنُودِ

Tomato *n.* (بَنَدُورَةٌ . طَمَاطِمُ)

Tomb *n.* قَبْرٌ . ضَرِيحٌ

Tombstone *n.* حَجَرُ قَبْرٍ

Tome *n.* كِتَابٌ . مُجَلَّدٌ

To-morrow *n.* اَلْغَدُ

Ton *n.* وَزْنٌ = ٢٠٠٠ لِيبْرَا

Tone *n.* صَوْتٌ . نَغَمَةٌ

Tongs *n. pl.* مِلْقَطٌ

Tongue *n.* لِسَانٌ . لُغَةٌ

Tongue-tied *a.* مَعْقُود اللِّسَانِ

Tonic *a.* or *n.* مقوٍّ

To-night *n.* هَذِهِ اللَّيْلَةَ

Tonnage *n.* وَزْنُ مَا تَسَعهُ سَفِينَةٌ

Tonsil *n.* لَوْزَةُ الْحَلْقِ

Tonsure *n.* حَلْقُ قِمَّةِ الرَّأْسِ

Too *ad.* بِزِيَادَةٍ . أَيْضًا

Tool *n.* آلَةٌ . أَدَاةٌ

Tooth *n.* سِنٌّ . نَابٌ . ضِرْسٌ

Toothache *n.* وَجَعُ الأَسْنَانِ

Toothless *a.* بِلا أَسْنَانٍ

Tooth-pick *n.* سِوَاكٌ

Toothsome *a.* لَذِيذٌ

Top *n.* قِمَّةٌ . سَطْحٌ . دُوَّامَةٌ . (نَحْلَةٌ)

Toper *n.* سِكِّيرٌ

Tophet *n.* الْجَحِيمُ

Topic *n.* مَوْضُوعٌ . مَبْحَثٌ

Topical *a.* مَحَلِّيٌّ . مَوْضُوعِيٌّ

Topmost *a.* اَلأَعْلَى

Topography *n.* تَخْطِيطٌ . وَصْفٌ

Topple *v. i.* اهتَزَّ . انْقَلَبَ

Torch *n.*	مِشْعَلٌ
Torment *n.* or *v. t.*	عَذَابٌ . عَذَّبَ
Tormenter / Tormentor } *n.*	مُعَذِّبٌ
Tornado *n.*	زَوْبَعَةٌ
Torpedo *n.*	لَغْمٌ بَحْرِيٌّ . قَنْرَةٌ (سَمَكَةٌ)
Torpid *a.*	ثَقِيلُ ٱلْحَرَكَةِ
Torpidity / Torpor } *n.*	سُبَاتٌ . ثِقَلٌ
Torrent *n.*	سَيْلٌ
Torrid *a.*	حَارٌّ جِدًّا
Tortoise *n.*	سُلَحْفَاةٌ ج سَلَاحِفُ
Tortuous *a.*	مُعْوَجٌّ
Torture *n.*	عَذَابٌ . تَعْذِيبٌ
Toss *v. t.* or *i.*	طَرَحَ ـ . اِنْقَلَبَ
Total *a.* or *n.*	كُلِّيٌّ . جُمْلَةٌ . مَجْمُوعٌ
Totality *n.*	كُلِّيَّةٌ . جُمْلَةٌ
Totally *ad.*	بِأَسْرِهِ . جُمْلَةً
Totter *v. i.*	اِهْتَزَّ . هَمَّ بِٱلسُّقُوطِ
Touch *v. i.*	مَسَّ ـ . لَمَسَ ـ
Touching *a.*	لَامِسٌ . مُؤَثِّرٌ
Touchy *a.*	سَرِيعُ ٱلْغَيْظِ
Tough *a.*	صُلْبٌ . قَاسٍ
Toughen *v. t.*	صَلَّبَ . قَسَّى
Tour *n.*	سِيَاحَةٌ . سَفْرَةٌ
Tourist *n.*	سَائِحٌ . مُسَافِرٌ
Tournament *n.*	تَطَاعُنٌ لَعِبِيٌّ
Tow *n.* or *v. t.*	مُشَاقَةُ ٱلْكَتَّانِ . جَرَّ
Toward / Towards } *prep.*	إِلَى . نَحْوَ
Towel *n.*	مِنْشَفَةٌ
Tower *n.* or *v. t.*	بُرْجٌ . اِرْتَفَعَ
Towering *a.*	عَالٍ . مُرْتَفِعٌ
Tow-line *n.* (لِسَفِينَةٍ)	حَبْلُ ٱلْجَرِّ
Town *n.*	بَلْدَةٌ . مَدِينَةٌ
Township *n.*	بَلْدَةٌ مَعْ ضَوَاحِيهَا
Toxicology *n.*	عِلْمُ ٱلسُّمُومِ
Toy *n.* or *v. t.*	لُعْبَةٌ . لَاعَبَ . عَبِثَ
Trace *v. t.*	رَسَمَ ـُ . اِسْتَقْصَى

Trace *n.* أَثَرٌ . عَلَامَةٌ . رَسمٌ

Traces *n. pl.* سُيُورُ ٱلْخَيلِ

Traceable *a.* مَا يُسْتَدَلُّ عَلَيْهِ

Track *v. t.* تَأَثَّرَ . ٱقْتَفَى

Track *n.* مَسْلَكٌ . أثرٌ . اثرُ قَدَمٍ

Trackless *a.* لَا مَسْلَكَ فِيهِ وَلَا أَثَرَ

Tract *n.* إِقْلِيمٌ . مَقَالَةٌ

Tractable *a.* طَوْعٌ . طَائِعٌ

Tractability *n.* طَوْعِيَّةٌ . ٱنْقِيَادٌ

Traction *n.* جَذْبٌ . مَدٌّ . جَرٌّ

Trade *n.* or *v. i.* تِجَارَةٌ . حِرْفَةٌ تَاجَرَ

Trade-mark *n.* عَلَامَةُ بِضَائِعَ

Trader / **Tradesman** *n.* تَاجِرٌ ج تُجَّارٌ

Tradition *n.* تَقْلِيدٌ . حَدِيثٌ

Traditional / **Traditionary** *n.* تَقْلِيدِيٌّ

Traduce *v. t.* نَمَّ بِـ عَابَ بِـ

Traffic *n.* تِجَارَةٌ . مُعَامَلَةٌ

Tragedy *n.* رِوَايَةٌ او حَادِثَةٌ هَائِلَةٌ

Tragic / **Tragical** *a.* هَائِلٌ . فَظِيعٌ

Trail *v. t.* or *i.* جَرَّ ـُ انْسَحَبَ

Train *v. t.* هَذَّبَ . ادَّبَ

Trait *n.* صِفَةٌ . عَلَامَةٌ خُلُقٍ

Traitor *n.* / **Traitorous** *a.* خَائِنٌ

Trammel *v. t.* or *n.* عَاقَ . أَوْثَقَ . عَائِقٌ

Trample *v. t.* دَاسَ ـُ . ٱزْدَرَى بِـ

Trance *n.* غَيْبَةٌ

Tranquil *a.* هَادِئٌ مُسْتَرِيحٌ

Tranquilize / **Tranquillize** *v. t.* هَدَّأَ . أَمَّنَ

Tranquillity *n.* هُدُوءٌ

Transact *v. t.* قَضَى ـِ . أَجْرَى

Transaction *n.* عَمَلٌ . أَمْرٌ

Transcend *v. t.* فَاقَ ـُ . جَاوَزَ

Transcendent *a.* فَائِقٌ

Transcribe *v. t.* نَسَخَ ـَ . نَقَلَ ـُ

Transcript *n.* نُسْخَةٌ

Transcription *n.* نَسْخٌ

Transfer *v. t.* or *n.* نَقَلَ ـُ . نَقْلٌ

Transferable *a.* قَابِلُ ٱلنَّقْلِ أَوِ ٱلتَّحْوِيلِ

Transference *n.* نَقْلٌ. تَحْوِيلٌ

Transfigure *v. t.* جَلَّى. غَيَّرَ ٱلشَّكْلَ

Transfix *v. t.* خَرَقَ ـِ . أَنْفَذَ فِي

Transform *v. t.* غَيَّرَ . حَوَّلَ

Transformation *n.* تَغْيِيرٌ

Transgress *v. t.* خَالَفَ . تَعَدَّى

Transgression *n.* تَعَدٍّ . خَطِيَّةٌ

Transgressor *n.* خَاطِئٌ . مُخَالِفٌ

Tranship *v. t.* نَقَلَ مِنْ سَفِينَةٍ إِلَى أُخْرَى

Transient *a.* وَقْتِيٌّ . زَائِلٌ

Transit *n.* عُبُورٌ إِجْتِيَازٌ

Transition *n.* عُبُورٌ . ٱنْتِقَالٌ

Transitive *a.* مُتَعَدٍّ (فعل)

Transitory *a.* وَقْتِي . زَائِلٌ

Translatable *a.* قَابِلُ ٱلتَّرْجَمَةِ

Translate *v.* تَرْجَمَ . نَقَلَ ـُ

Translation *n.* تَرْجَمَةٌ . نَقْلٌ

Translator *n.* مُتَرْجِمٌ

Translucent *a.* شَفَّافٌ بَعْضَ ٱلشُّفُوفِ

Transmarine *a.* مَا وَرَاءَ ٱلْبَحْرِ

Transmigrate *v. t.* هَاجَرَ . ٱنْتَقَلَ

Transmigration *n.* مُهَاجَرَةٌ. تَنَاسُخٌ

Transmission *n.* إِرْسَالٌ . إِنْفَاذٌ

Transmit *v. t.* أَرْسَلَ. أَنْفَذَ إِلَى

Transmutation *n.* تَحْوِيلٌ. تَحَوُّلٌ

Transparency *n.* شُفُوفٌ

Transparent *a.* شَفَّافٌ. وَاضِحٌ

Transpire *v. i.* حَدَثَ ـُ . ذَاعَ ـِ

Transplant *v. t.* نَقَلَ ـُ غَرْساً

Transport *n.* نَقْلٌ. سَفِينَةُ نَقْلٍ. طَرَبٌ

Transport *v. t.* نَقَلَ ـُ أَبْهَجَ

Transportation *n.* نَقْلٌ . نَفْيٌ

Transpose *v. t.* بَدَّلَ . عَكَسَ ـِ

Transposition *n.* تَبْدِيلُ ٱلْمَكَانِ

Transverse *a.* مُعَارِضٌ

Trap *n.* or *v. t.* مَصِيدَةٌ . صادَ بها

Trapdoor *n.* بَابٌ مَخْفِيٌّ

Trapezium *n.* مُرَبَّعٌ مُنْحَرِفٌ

Trappings *n. pl.* عُدَّة زِينَةٍ لِلْخَيْلِ خَاصَّةً

Trash *n.* نُفَايَةٌ . سَقَط

Trashy *a.* بَاطِلٌ . خَسِيسٌ

Travail *v.i.* or *n.* تَعِبَ ـَ . تَمَخَّضَ مَخَاض

Travel *v. i.* سَافَرَ . سَاحَ ـ

Traveller *n.* مُسَافِرٌ . سَائِحٌ

Traverse *v. t.* قَطَعَ ـَ . عَارَض

Tray *n.* طَبقٌ . صِينِيَّةٌ

Treacherous *a.* خَائِنٌ . غَادِرٌ

Treachery *n.* خِيَانَةٌ ، غَدْرٌ

Treacle *n.* دُبْسٌ

Tread *v. i.* (trod) دَاسَ ـ

Treason *n.* خِيَانَةٌ

Treasonable *a.* ذُو خِيَانَةٍ

Treasure *n.* or *v. t.* كَنْزٌ . ذَخَرَ ـَ

Treasurer *n.* أَمِينُ الصُّنْدُوق . خَازِنٌ

Treasury *n.* خِزَانَةٌ . بَيْتُ الْمَال

Treat *v. t.* or *i.* عَامَلَ . بَحَثَ ـَ . عَالَج

Treatise *n.* مَقَالَةٌ . رِسَالَة

Treatment *n.* مُعَامَلَةٌ . مُعَالَجَة

Treaty *n.* مُعَاهَدَةٌ

Treble *a.* or *v. t.* or *i.* مُثَلَّثٌ . ثَلَثَ . تَثَلَّث

Tree *n.* شَجَرَةٌ

Trellis *n.* عَرِيشٌ . شُبَّاكٌ

Tremble *v. i.* إِرْتَجَفَ . إِرْتَعَد

Tremendous *a.* عَظِيمٌ . هَائِلٌ

Tremor *n.* قُشَعْرِيرَةٌ . رَجْفَةٌ

Tremulous *a.* مُرْتَجِفٌ . مُرْتَعِشٌ

Trench *n.* خَنْدَقٌ ج خَنَادِقُ

Trepidation *n.* إِرْتِجَافٌ . فَزَعٌ

Trespass *v. i.* or *n.* تَعَدَّى . أَخْطَأَ . تَعَدٍّ

Tress *n.* خُصْلَةٌ . ضَفِيرَةٌ

Triad *n.* إِتِّحَادُ ثَلَاثَةٍ فِي وَاحِدٍ

Trial *n.* تَجْرِبَةٌ . مُحَاكَمَةٌ . بَلِيَّةٌ

Triangle *n.* مُثَلَّثٌ

Triangular *a.* مُثَلَّثُ ٱلشَّكْلِ

Tribe *n.* قَبِيلَةٌ . سِبْطٌ . جِنْسٌ

Tribulation *n.* ضِيقٌ . شِدَّةٌ

Tribunal *n.* مَحْكَمَةٌ . مَجْلِسٌ . دِيوَانٌ

Tribune *n.* حَاكِمٌ رُومَانِيٌّ . مِنْبَرٌ

Tributary *a.* تَحْتَ ٱلْجِزْيَةِ . فَرْعُ نَهْرٍ

Tribute *n.* جِزْيَةٌ . خَرَاجٌ

Trice *n.* لَحْظَةٌ . لَمْحَةٌ

Trick *n.* حِيلَةٌ . مَكِيدَةٌ

Trickery *n.* إِحْتِيَالٌ . خِدَاعٌ

Trickish *a.* مُحْتَالٌ . غَشَّاشٌ

Trickle *v. i.* نَضَّ ـِ . نَزَّ ـِ

Tri-coloured *a.* ذُو ثَلَاثَةِ أَلْوَانٍ

Trident *n.* صَوْلَجَانٌ ذُو ثَلَاثِ شَوْكَاتٍ

Tridnnial *a.* كُلَّ ثَلَاثِ سِنِينَ

Trifle *n.* or *v. t.* شَيْءٌ زَهِيدٌ . عَبِثَ ـَ

Trifling *n.* زَهِيدٌ مَا لَا يُعْتَبَرُ . عَبَثٌ

Triform *a.* مُثَلَّثُ ٱلشَّكْلِ

Trigger *n.* زِنَادُ ٱلْبُنْدُقِيَّةِ

Trigonometry *n.* عِلْمُ ٱلْمُثَلَّثَاتِ

Trilateral *a.* ذُو ثَلَاثَةِ جَوَانِبَ

Triliteral *a.* ذُو ثَلَاثَةِ أَحْرُفٍ

Trill *n.* or *v. t.* تَطْرِيبٌ . طَرَّبَ

Trim *a.* or *v. t.* أَنِيقٌ . قَصَّ ـُ . زَيَّنَ

Trimming *n.* زِينَةٌ (خَرْجٌ)

Trinity *n.* ثَالُوثٌ

Trinket *n.* حِلْيَةٌ . شَيْءٌ زَهِيدٌ

Trio *n.* ثَلَاثَةٌ مُتَّحِدُونَ

Trip *v. i.* مَشَى بِخِفَّةٍ . عَثَرَ ـُ . كَبَا ـُ

Trip *n.* عَثْرَةٌ . سَفْرَةٌ

Triple *a.* مُثَلَّثٌ . ثُلَاثِيٌّ

Triplet *n.* ثَلَاثَةُ أَبْيَاتِ شِعْرٍ عَلَى قَافِيَةٍ وَاحِدَةٍ

Tripod *n.* ذُو ثَلَاثِ قَوَائِمَ

Trisyllabic *a.* / **Trisyllable** *n.* } ذَاتُ ثَلٰثَةِ مَقَاطِعَ

Trite *a.* كَثِيرُ ٱلْاِسْتِعْمَالِ. مُبْتَذَلٌ

Triumph *n.* or *v. i.* نُصْرَةٌ. إِنْتَصَرَ

Triumphal / **Triumphant** } *a.* مَنْصُورٌ. نَصْرِيٌّ

Triumvirate *n.* حُكْمُ ثَلٰثَةٍ

Triune *n.* مُثَلَّثُ ٱلْأَقَانِيمِ. ثَالُوثِيٌّ

Trivial *a.* زَهِيدٌ. حَقِيرٌ

Trodden *pp. of* **tread.** مَدُوسٌ

Troop *n.* جَمَاعَةٌ. كَتِيبَةٌ

Trooper *n.* جُنْدِيٌّ. فَارِسٌ

Trophy *n.* عَلَامَةُ نُصْرَةٍ

Tropic *n.* مِنْطَقَةٌ حَارَّةٌ

Tropical *a.* مُخْتَصٌّ بِٱلْمِنْطَقَةِ ٱلْحَارَّةِ

Trot *v. i.* or *n.* خَبَّ ـُ. خَبَبٌ

Trouble *v. t.* or *n.* كَدَّرَ. أَزْعَجَ. ضِيقٌ

Troublesome *a.* مُكَدِّرٌ. شَاقٌ

Troublous *a.* مُضْطَرِبٌ. شَاقٌ

Trough *n.* حَوْضٌ

Trousers / **Trowsers** } *n.* سَرَاوِيلُ

Trousseau *n.* جَهَازُ عَرُوسٍ

Trowel *n.* مِلْعَقَةُ ٱلْبَنَّاءِ

Truant *a.* or *n.* كَسْلَانٌ. مُهْمِلُ ٱلْوَاجِبَاتِ

Truce *n.* هُدْنَةٌ

Trudge *v. i.* مَشَى ـِ. تَعِبَ فِي ٱلْمَشْيِ

True *a.* حَقِيقِيٌّ. أَكِيدٌ. امِينٌ. صَحِيحٌ

Truly *ad.* حَقًّا

Trump / **Trumpet** } *n.* بُوقٌ

Trumpery *n.* خِدَاعٌ. عَبْثٌ

Trumpeter *n.* بَوَّاقٌ

Truncate / **Truncated** } *a.* أَقْطَعُ. مَجْزُومٌ

Trunk *n.* صُنْدُوقٌ. سَاقٌ. خُرْطُومٌ

Trust *n.* ثِقَةٌ. وَدِيعَةٌ. إِئْتِمَانٌ

Trust *v. i.* or *t.* وَثِقَ ـِ. صَدَّقَ

Trustee *n.* وَكِيلٌ. أَمِينٌ

Trustful *a.* وَاثِقٌ

Trustiness *n.* أَمَانَةٌ

Trusty / **Trustworthy** *a.* أَمِينٌ. مَوْثُوقٌ بِهِ

Truth *n.* حَقٌّ. صِدْقٌ. صَوَابٌ

Truthful *a.* صَادِقٌ

Try *v. t.* or *i.* جَرَّبَ ـ حَاوَلَ

Trying *a.* مُجَرِّبٌ. شَاقٌّ. مُكَدِّر

Tub *n.* مِرْجَل

Tube *n.* انْبُوبَة

Tubercle *n.* عُجْرَةٌ . دَرَنَة

Tubercular / **Tuberculous** *a.* دَرَنِي

Tuck *n.* or *v. t.* ثِنْيَةٌ. طَيَّةٌ. طَوَى ـِ

Tuesday *n.* يَوْمُ ٱلثَّلَاثَاء

Tuft *n.* خُصْلَةٌ . قُنْبُرَةٌ

Tug *v. t.* or *i.* شَدَّ ـُ . جَذَبَ ـِ

Tug-boat *n.* وَابُورٌ جَرَّارٌ

Tuition *n.* اجرَةُ تَعْلِيمٍ

Tulip *n.* ضَرْبٌ مِنَ الزَنْبَقِ

Tumble *v. i.* سقطَ ـُ هَبَطَ ـ تقَلَّبَ

Tumbler *n.* قدحٌ ج اقْدَاحٌ

Tumid *a.* مُنْتَفِخٌ . وَارِمٌ

Tumour *n.* وَرَمٌ . خُرَاجٌ

Tumult *n.* شَغَبٌ . ضَجَّةٌ. جَلَبَة

Tumultuary / **Tumultuous** *a.* شَاغِبٌ

Tune *n.* or *v. t.* نَغْمَةٌ. لَحْنٌ. أَوْقَعَ

Tunnel *n.* or *v. t.* سِرْدَابٌ . سَرَبٌ حفرهُ

Turban *n.* عِمَامَةٌ. لفة

Turbid *a.* عكِرٌ . كَدِرٌ

Turbulence / **Turbulency** *n.* تَشْوِيشٌ. شَغَبٌ

Turbulent *a.* مُشَاغِبٌ . مُهَيِّجٌ

Turf *n.* ارْضٌ كَثِيرَةُ ٱلْكَلَإِ

Turgid *a.* وَارِمٌ . مُنْتَفِخٌ

Turkey *n.* تُرْكِيَّا. دِيكٌ رُومِيٌّ

Turquoise *n.* فَيْرُوزٌ

Turmoil *n.* إِضْطِرَابٌ. شَغَبٌ

Turn *v. t.* or *i.* خَرَطَ ـِ . أَدَار . دَارَ ـ

Turn *n.* دَوْرَةٌ . بَرْمَة

Turner *n.* خَرَّاطٌ

Turnip *n.* لِفْتٌ
Turnkey *n.* بَوَّابُ سِجْنٍ
Turpentine *n.* رَاتِينَجُ ٱلصَّنَوْبَرِ
Turpitude *n.* قَبَاحَةٌ
Turret *n.* بُرْجٌ
Turreted *a.* ذُو أَبْرَاجٍ
Turtle *n.* سُلَحْفَاةٌ
Turtledove *n.* حَمَامَةٌ . يَمَامَةٌ
Tusk *n.* نَابٌ ج أَنْيَابٌ
Tussle *n.* مُصَارَعَةٌ
Tutelage *n.* حِمَايَةٌ . وِكَالَةٌ
Tutelar / Tutelary *a.* حَافِظٌ . مُحَامٍ
Tutor *n.* مُعَلِّمٌ . مُهَذِّبٌ
Twain *n.* إِثْنَانِ م إِثْنَتَانِ
Twang *v. i.* or *n.* رَنَّ ـِ . رَنِينٌ
Tweezers *n. pl.* مِلْقَطٌ صَغِيرٌ
Twelfth *a.* أَلثَّانِي عَشَرَ
Twelve *a.* إِثْنَا عَشَرَ وَٱثْنَتَا عَشَرَةَ
Twentieth *a.* ٱلْعِشْرُونَ
Twenty *a.* عِشْرُونَ
Twice *ad.* مَرَّتَيْنِ
Twig *n.* عُسْلُوجٌ ج عَسَالِيجُ
Twilight *n.* شَفَقٌ
Twin *n.* تَوْأَمٌ
Twine *n.* or *v. i.* خَيْطُ دَوْبَارَةٍ . فَتَلَ ـِ
Twinge *v. i.* or *n.* تَأَلَّمَ . أَلَمٌ
Twinkle *v. i.* تَلَأْلَأَ . لَمَعَ ـَ
Twinkle / Twinkling *n.* لَأْلَأَةٌ . لَمَعَانٌ
Twirl *v. t.* or *i.* بَرَمَ ـَ دَوَّرَ . دَارَ
Twist *v. t.* فَتَلَ ـِ . جَدَلَ ـُ ـِ . حَرَّفَ
Twitch *v. t.* or *n.* شَدَّ بِهِ بَغْتَةً
Twitter *v. i.* غَرَّدَ
Two *a.* إِثْنَانِ م إِثْنَتَانِ
Two-edged *a.* ذُو حَدَّيْنِ
Twofold *a.* مُثَنًّى . مُضَاعَفٌ
Tympanum *n.* طَبْلَةُ ٱلْأُذُنِ

Type *n.* رَمْزٌ . صُورَةٌ . حَرْفُ طَبْعٍ

Typhoid *a.* or *n.* اَلْحُمَّى ٱلتِّيفُودِيَّةُ

Typhus *a.* or *n.* أَلْحُمَّى ٱلتِّيفُوسِيةُ

Typical *a.* رَمْزِيٌّ . مِثَالِيٌّ

Typify *v. t.* رَمَزَ ـِ اشارَ إِلى

Typographical *a.* مَنُوطٌ بِالطَّبْعِ

Typography *n.* صِنَاعَةُ ٱلطَّبْعِ

Tyrannical / **Tyrannic** *a.* ظَالِمٌ . طَاغٍ

Tyrannize *v. t.* ظَلَمَ ـِ

Tyranny *n.* ظُلْمٌ . بَغْيٌ

Tyrant *n.* ظَالِمٌ . طَاغٍ . بَاغٍ

U

Ubiquity *n.* حُضُورٌ في كُلِّ مَكَانٍ

Udder *n.* ضَرْعٌ ج ضُرُوعٌ

Ugliness *n.* بَشَاعَةٌ . قَبَاحَةُ ٱلْمَنْظَرِ

Ugly *a.* قَبِيحُ ٱلْمَنْظَرِ

Ulcer *n.* قُرْحَةٌ

Ulcerate *v. i.* تَقَرَّحَ

Ulceration *n.* تَقَرُّحٌ

Ulna *n.* زَنْدٌ

Ulterior *a.* أَبْعَدُ . وَرَآءُ

Ultimate *a.* الأَبْعَدُ . نِهَائِيٌّ

Ultimatum *n.* قَرَارٌ نِهَائِيٌّ

Ultra *a.* مُفْرِطٌ . مُتَجَاوِزُ ٱلْحَدِّ

Umbel *n.* صِيوَانُ أَزْهَارٍ

Umbelliferous *a.* صِيوَانِيٌّ

Umbrage *n.* غَيْظٌ . حِقْدٌ

Umbrageous *a.* ظَلِيلٌ

Umbrella *n.* شَمْسِيَّةٌ

Umpire *n.* فَيْصَلٌ . حَكَمٌ

Un حَرْفُ نَفْيٍ فِي ٱلتَّرْكِيبِ
Unable *a.* غَيْرُ قَادِرٍ
Unabridged *a.* غَيْرُ مُخْتَصَرٍ . مُطَوَّلٌ
Unacceptable *a.* غَيْرُ مَقْبُولٍ
Unaccommodating *a.* غَيْرُ مُسَاهِلٍ
Unaccompanied *a.* غَيْرُ مُرَافَقٍ
Unaccountable *a.* غَيْرُ مَسْؤُولٍ . غَيْرُ مَفْهُومٍ
Unaccustomed *a.* غَيْرُ مُعْتَادٍ
Unacknowledged *a.* غَيْرُ مُسَلَّمٍ بِهِ
Unacquainted *a.* غَيْرُ عَارِفٍ بِهِ
Unadvisable *a.* غَيْرُ مُوَافِقٍ
Unaffected *a.* غَيْرُ مُؤَثَّرٍ
Unaided *a.* غَيْرُ مُسَاعَدٍ . وَحْدَهُ
Unalterable *a.* مَا لَا يَتَغَيَّرُ . ثَابِتٌ
Unamiable *a.* غَيْرُ لَطِيفٍ . شَرِسٌ
Unanimity *n.* إِجْمَاعُ ٱلرَّأْيِ
Unanimous *a.* مُجْمِعُ ٱلرَّأْيِ
Unanswerable *a.* مَا لَا يُرَدُّ عَلَيْهِ
Unappreciated *a.* غَيْرُ مُعْتَبَرٍ
Unapproachable *a.* مَا لَا يُدْنَى مِنْهُ
Unappropriated *a.* غَيْرُ مُخَصَّصٍ
Unarmed *a.* غَيْرُ مُتَسَلِّحٍ
Unasked *a.* غَيْرُ مَطْلُوبٍ
Unaspiring *a.* غَيْرُ طَالِبِ ٱلرِّفْعَةِ
Unassailable *a.* لَا يُهَاجَمُ . مَنِيعٌ
Unassisted *a.* غَيْرُ مُسَاعِدٍ . وَحْدَهُ
Unassuming *a.* غَيْرُ مُعْجَبٍ . مُتَوَاضِعٌ
Unattainable *a.* لَا يُحَصَّلُ
Unattended *a.* غَيْرُ مُرَافَقٍ . وَحْدَهُ
Unauthorised *a.* غَيْرُ مُبَاحٍ
Unavailing *a.* غَيْرُ مُفِيدٍ . عَبَثٌ
Unavoidable *a.* مَا لَا بُدَّ مِنْهُ
Unaware *a.* غَيْرُ عَارِفٍ
Unawares *ad.* عَلَى غَفْلَةٍ
Unbar *v. t.* رَفَعَ ٱلْمِغْلَاقَ . فَتَحَ

Unbecoming *a.* غيرُ لائقٍ

Unbelief *n.* عدمُ إيمانٍ أوْ تصديق

Unbeliever *n.* / **Unbelieving** *a.* غيرُ مؤمنٍ

Unbending *a.* متصلّبٌ

Unbiassed *a.* غيرُ متحاملٍ أوْ متحزّب

Unbind *a.* حلَّ . فكَّ

Unblemished *a.* بلا عيبٍ

Unblushing *a.* بلا حياءٍ . وقحٌ

Unbolt *v. t.* فتحَ المغلاقَ

Unborn *a.* غيرُ مولودٍ

Unbosom *v. t.* صرّحَ بهِ . أقرَّ

Unbounded *a.* غيرُ محدودٍ

Unbridle *v. i.* فكَّ اللّجامَ . أطلقَ

Unbroken *a.* غيرُ منقطعٍ

Unbuckle *v. t.* فكَّ الإبزيمَ

Unburden *v. t.* نزعَ حملاً . أراحَ

Unburied *a.* غيرُ مدفونٍ

Unbutton *v. t.* فكَّ الأزرارَ

Uncanonical *a.* غيرُ قانونيٍّ

Unceasing *a.* غيرُ منقطعٍ . دائمٌ

Unceremonious *a.* عديمُ التّكليفِ

Uncertain *a.* غيرُ مؤكّدٍ. مشكوكٌ فيهِ

Uncertainty *n.* عدمُ يقينٍ . شكٌّ

Unchain *v. t.* فكَّ القيدَ أوِ الزّنجيرَ

Unchangeable / **Unchanging** *a.* غيرُ متغيّرٍ

Uncharitable *a.* عديمُ المحبّةِ

Unchaste *a.* غيرُ عفيفٍ . نجسٌ

Unchristian *a.* مخالفُ المسيحيّةِ

Uncivil *a.* غيرُ أنيسٍ . فظٌّ

Uncivilized *a.* غيرُ متمدّنٍ

Uncle *n.* عمٌّ . خالٌ

Unclean *a.* غيرُ طاهرٍ . نجسٌ

Uncleanness *n.* نجاسةٌ

Unclose *v. t.* فتحَ . كشفَ

Uncoil *v. t.* فكَّ الملتفَّ. أرخى

Uncomely *a.* غيرُ كيّسٍ أوْ ظريفٍ

Uncomfortable *a.* غَيْرُ مُسْتَرِيحٍ شَاقٌّ

Uncommon *a.* غَيْرُ مَعْهُودٍ . نَادِرٌ

Uncomplaining *a.* غَيْرُ شَاكٍ

Uncompromising *a.* غَيْرُ مُتَرَاضٍ . عَنِيدٌ

Unconcern *n.* عَدَمُ اكْتِرَاثٍ

Unconditional *a.* بِلَا شَرْطٍ . مُطْلَقٌ

Uncongenial *a.* غَيْرُ مُؤَانِسٍ

Unconqurable *a.* لَا يُغْلَبُ

Unconscious *a.* غَيْرُ شَاعِرٍ اوْ عَالِمٍ

Unconsciousness *n.* غَيْبَةٌ

Unconstitutional *a.* مُخَالِفُ النِّظَامِ

Uncontrollable / Uncontrolled *a.* لَا يُضْبَطُ

Unconverted *a.* غَيْرُ تَائِبٍ أَوْ مُتَغَيِّرٍ

Uncork *v. t.* أَخْرَجَ السِّدَادَ

Uncorrupt / Uncorrupted *a.* غَيْرُ فَاسِدٍ غَيْرُ مُرْضٍ

Uncounted *a.* غَيْرُ مَعْدُودٍ

Uncourteous *a.* عَدِيمُ الْأُنْسِ . فَظٌّ

Uncouth *a.* غَيْرُ مَأْلُوفٍ . أَخْرَقُ

Uncover *v. t.* كَشَفَ ـِ . فَتَحَ ـَ

Unction *n.* مَسْحَةٌ

Unctuous *a.* دِهْنٌ . ذُو زَيْتٍ

Uncultivated *a.* غَيْرُ مَحْرُوثٍ . غَيْرُ مُهَذَّبٍ

Uncut *a.* غَيْرُ مَقْصُوصٍ أَوْ مَقْطُوعٍ

Undaunted *a.* جَسُورٌ . غَيْرُ خَائِفٍ

Undeceive *v. t.* أَزَالَ الْغُرُورَ وَالْغَلَطَ

Undecided *a.* مُتَرَدِّدٌ

Undefiled *a.* غَيْرُ مُدَنَّسٍ . طَاهِرٌ

Undefined *a.* غَيْرُ مَحْدُودٍ

Undeniable *a.* لَا يُنْكَرُ

Under *prep.* تَحْتَ

Underbid *v. i.* عَرَضَ أَقَلَّ

Underbrush *n.* أُنْجُمٌ تَحْتَ شَجَرٍ

Undercurrent *n.* مَجْرًى تَحْتَ الْمَاءِ

Undergo *v. i.* إِحْتَمَلَ . قَاسَى

Undergraduate *n.* تِلْمِيذُ مَدْرَسَةٍ

Underground *v.* تَحْتَ الْأَرْضِ

Undergrowth n. شُجَيْرَاتٌ تَحْتَ شَجَرٍ

Underhand / Underhanded a. مَسْتُورٌ . غَادِرٌ

Underlie v. t. وُجِدَ تَحْتَ

Underline v. t. خَطَّ تَحْتَ ٱلسَّطْرِ

Underling n. شَخْصٌ دُونٌ . أَجِيرٌ

Undermine v. t. حَفَرَ تَحْتَ . نَقَضَ ـُ

Underneath ad. تَحْتَ

Underpinning n. حِجَارَةُ ٱلأَسَاسِ

Underrate v. t. إِسْتَصْغَرَ . إِسْتَخَفَّ

Underscore v. t. رَسَمَ تَحْتَهُ . خَطًّا

Undersell v. t. بَاعَ بِأَقَلِّ ثَمَنٍ

Understand v. t. فَهِمَ ـَ . أَدْرَكَ

Understanding n. ذِهْنٌ . إِدْرَاكٌ

Undertake v. t. تَعَاطَى . إِلْتَزَمَ

Undertaker n. مُدَبِّرُ ٱلدَّفْنِ

Undertaking n. مَسْعًى . مَشْرُوعٌ

Undertone n. صَوْتٌ مُنْخَفِضٌ

Undervalue v. t. بَخَسَ ـَ . إِسْتَخَفَّ بِهِ

Undeserved a. غَيْرُ مُسْتَحَقٍّ

Undeserving a. غَيْرُ مُسْتَحِقٍّ

Undesigned a. غَيْرُ مَقْصُودٍ . إِتِّفَاقِيٌّ

Undesirable a. غَيْرُ شَهِيٍّ أَوْ مَرْغُوبٍ فِيهِ

Undeviating a. غَيْرُ مُنْحَرِفٍ . مُسْتَقِيمٌ

Undignified a. غَيْرُ لَائِقٍ ٱلشَّأْنِ

Undisguisied a. غَيْرُ مُسْتَتِرٍ . ظَاهِرٌ

Undismayed a. غَيْرُ خَائِفٍ

Undivided a. غَيْرُ مُنْقَسِمٍ . مُتَّحِدٌ

Undo v. t. حَلَّ ـُ . أَبْطَلَ . عَكَسَ ـِ

Undone a. مُعَطَّلٌ . هَالِكٌ

Undoubted a. لَا رَيْبَ فِيهِ . مُقَرَّرٌ

Undress v. t. نَزَعَ ٱلثِّيَابَ . خَلَعَ ـَ

Undue a. مُفْرِطٌ . زَائِدٌ

Undulated a. مُتَمَوِّجٌ . غَيْرُ مُسْتَوٍ

Undulation n. تَمَوُّجٌ

Unduly ad. بِزِيَادَةٍ . فِي غَيْرِ مَحَلِّهِ

Undutiful a. غَيْرُ مُطِيعٍ

Undying *a.* غَيْرُ مَائِتٍ . خَالِدٌ

Unearth *v. t.* نَبَشَ ـُ . كَشَفَ ـِ

Unearthly *n.* غَيْرُ طَبِيعِيٍّ

Uneasiness *n.* إِضْطِرَابٌ . هَمٌّ . قَلَق

Uneasy *a.* غَيْرُ مُسْتَرِيحٍ . مُهْتَمٌّ

Uneducated *a.* غَيْرُ مُهَذَّبٍ . أُمِّيٌّ

Unembarrassed *a.* غَيْرُ مُرْتَبِكٍ

Unending *a.* غَيْرُ مُتَنَاهٍ

Unengaged *a.* غَيْرُ مَرْبُوطٍ . مُتَفَرِّغٌ

Unenlightened *a.* جَاهِلٌ

Unenviable *a.* غَيْرُ شَهِيٍّ . مَكْرُوهٌ

Unequal *a.* غَيْرُ مُتَسَاوٍ . عَاجِزٌ

Unequalled *a.* فَرِيدٌ . فَائِقٌ

Unequivocal *a.* غَيْرُ مُبْهَمٍ . صَرِيحٌ

Unerring *a.* غَيْرُ مُخْطِئٍ . مُصِيبٌ

Uneven *a.* غَيْرُ مُسْتَوٍ

Unevenness *n.* عَدَمُ ٱسْتِوَاءٍ

Unexpected *a.* غَيْرُ مُنْتَظَرٍ

Unexpressed *a.* غَيْرُ مَنْطُوقٍ بِهِ

Unfaded / Unfading *a.* غَيْرُ ذَابِلٍ

Unfailing *a.* غَيْرُ مُنْقَضٍ . بَاقٍ

Unfair *a.* غَيْرُ عَادِلٍ

Unfairness *n.* عَدَمُ إِنْصَافٍ

Unfaithful *n.* غَيْرُ أَمِينٍ

Unfaithfulness *n.* عَدَمُ امَانَةٍ

Unfashionable *a.* خِلَافُ ٱلزِّيِّ

Unfasten *v. t.* فَكَّ ـُ . حَلَّ ـُ

Unfathomable *a.* مَا لَا يُسْبَرُ

Unfavourable *a.* مُخَالِفُ ٱلْمَطْلُوبِ

Unfeeling *a.* غَيْرُ مُتَأَثِّرٍ . بِلَا رَحْمَةٍ

Unfeigned *a.* بِلَا رِيَاءٍ . مُخْلِصٌ

Unfelt *a.* غَيْرُ مَشْعُورٍ بِهِ

Unfilial *a.* غَيْرُ لَائِقٍ بِٱلْبَنِينَ

Unfinished *a.* غَيْرُ مُتَمَّمٍ أَوْ مُنْجَزٍ

Unfit *a.* غَيْرُ لَائِقٍ . غَيْرُ أَهْلٍ

Unfold *v. t.* نَشَرَ ـُ كَشَفَ ـِ فَسَّرَ

Unforeseen *a.* غيرُ منتظَرٍ

Unforetold *a.* غيرُ مُخبَرٍ بهِ

Unforgiven *a.* غيرُ مغفورٍ

Unfortunate *a.* نحِسٌ . مَنكودُ ٱلحظِّ

Unfounded *a.* بلا أساسٍ

Unfrequent *a.* نادِرٌ

Unfrequented *a.* غيرُ مُترَدَّدٍ إليهِ

Unfriendly *a.* غيرُ وَدُودٍ . خَصيمٌ

Unfruitful *a.* غيرُ مُثمرٍ

Unfurl *v. t.* نَشَرَ ـُ

Ungainly *a.* أخرَق

Ungenerous *a.* غيرُ كريمٍ . شَحيحٌ

Ungentlemanly *a.* غيرُ أديبٍ

Ungodliness *n.* عَدَمُ تقوًى . شَرٌّ

Ungodly *a.* عَديمُ ٱلتقوى . شِرّيرٌ

Ungovernable *a.* ما لا يُضبَطُ

Ungraceful *a.* غيرُ ظريفٍ . أخرَق

Ungracious *a.* غيرُ لطيفٍ . سَيّئٌ

Ungrammatical *a.* مُخالِفٌ لِعِلمِ ٱلنَّحوِ

Ungrateful *a.* غيرُ شكورٍ . كنودٌ

Ungratefulness *n.* عَدَمُ الشكرِ

Ungrounded *a.* ما لا أصلَ لهُ

Unguarded *a.* غيرُ مَصُونٍ . مُتغافِلٌ

Unguent *n.* دُهنٌ . مَرهَمٌ

Unhallowed *a.* غيرُ مُقَدَّسٍ . مُحرَّمٌ

Unhappiness *n.* غَمٌّ . كَدَرٌ

Unhappy *a.* مَغمُومٌ . تَعيسٌ

Unharness *v. i.* نزَعَ عُدَّةَ ٱلخَيلِ

Unhealthful / Unhealthy } *a.* غيرُ موافِقِ ٱلصِّحةِ . وَخيمٌ

Unheard *a.* غيرُ مَسمُوعٍ

Unheeded *a.* غيرُ مُكتَرَثٍ لهُ

Unhesitating *a.* غيرُ مُتردّدٍ

Unhinge *v. t.* خَلَعَ ـُ

Unhitch *v. t.* فكَّ ـُ حَلَّ ـُ

Unholy *a.* غيرُ مقدَّسٍ . دَنِسٌ

Unhonoured *a.* غَيْرُ مُكَرَّمٍ

Unhook *v. t.* فَكَّ ـُ

Unhorse *v. t.* رَمَى عَنْ ٱلْفَرَسِ

Unhurt *a.* غَيْرُ مُؤْذًى. سَلِيمٌ

Unicorn *n.* وَحِيدُ ٱلْقَرْنِ

Uniform *a.*, عَلَى نَسَقٍ وَاحِدٍ

Uniform *n.* بِذْلَةٌ رَسْمِيَّةٌ

Uniformity *n.* وَحْدَةُ ٱلشَّكْلِ أَوِ ٱلنِّظَامِ

Unimpeachable *a.* مَا لَا يُعَابُ

Unimportant *a.* غَيْرُ مُهِمٍّ

Unimproving *a.* غَيْرُ مُتَقَدِّمٍ

Uninhabitable *a.* مَالَا يُسْكَنُ

Unintelligible *a.* مَالَا يُفْهَمُ

Unintended, Unintentional *a.* غَيْرُ مَقْصُودٍ

Uninteresting *a.* غَيْرُ لَذِيذٍ. مُمِلٌّ

Uninterrupted *a.* غَيْرُ مُنْقَطِعٍ

Uninvited *a.* غَيْرُ مَدْعُوٍّ. طُفَيْلِي

Union *n.* إِتِّحَادٌ . ضَمٌّ صِلَة

Unionist *n.* مُرِيدُ ٱلِٱتِّحَادِ

Unique *a.* فَرِيدٌ . وَحِيدٌ

Unison *n.* إِتِّفَاقُ ٱلأَصْوَاتِ

Unit *n.* فَرْدٌ . وَاحِدٌ

Unitarian *n.* مُوَحِّدٌ. مُنْكِرُ ٱلثَّالُوثِ

Unite *v.t.* or *i.* ضَمَّ ـُ. وَصَلَ. إِتَّحَدَ

United *a.* مُتَّحِدٌ . مُتَّصِلٌ

Unity *n.* وَحْدَانِيَّةٌ . وَحْدَةٌ

Univalve *n.*, Univalvular *a.* ذُو مِصْرَاعٍ وَاحِدٍ

Universal *a.* عَامٌّ. شَامِلٌ

Universalist *n.* ٱلْقَائِلُ بِخَلَاصِ ٱلْجَمِيعِ

Universality *n.* عُمُومِيَّةٌ . كُلِّيَّةٌ

Universe *n.* ٱلْكَوْنُ

University *n.* مَدْرَسَةٌ جَامِعَةٌ

Unjust *a.* غَيْرُ عَادِلٍ . ظَالِمٌ

Unjustifiable *a.* مَالَا يُبَرَّرُ أَوْ يُعْذَرُ

Unkind *a.* عَدِيمُ ٱلْمَعْرُوفِ . مُسِيءٌ

Unkindness *n.* إِسَاءَةٌ

Unknowingly *ad.* سَهْواً . غفْلَةً

Unknown *a.* غَيْرُ معْرُوفٍ . مَجْهُولٌ

Unlace *v. t.* حَلَّ ٱلشَّرِيطَ

Unlade *v. i.* فَرَّغَ مَرْكَباً

Unlawful *a.* غَيْرُ شَرْعِيٍّ أَوْ جَائِزٍ

Unlearn *v. t.* تعَلَّم خِلاَفَهُ . نَسِيَ

Unlearned *a.* أُمِّيٌّ . مَنْسِيٌّ

Unleavened *a.* غَيْرُ مُخْتَمِرٍ . فَطِيرٌ

Unless *cong.* مَالَمْ اَوْ اَمْ . إِنْ لَمْ

Unlettered *a.* أُمِّيٌّ

Unlike *a.* غَيْرُ مُشَابِهٍ . مُخَالِفٌ

Unlikely *ad.* بَعِيدُ ٱلوُقُوعِ

Unlikeness *n.* عَدَمُ مُشَابَهَةٍ

Unlimited *a.* غَيْرُ مَحْدُودٍ

Unload *v. t.* حَطَّ ٱلحِمْلَ . فَرَّغَهُ

Unlock *v. t.* فَتَحَ قُفْلاً

Unloveliness *n.* عَدَمُ جَمَالٍ أَوْ لُطْفٍ

Unlovely *a.* غَيْرُ جَمِيلٍ . غَيْرُ مَحْبُوبٍ

Unlucky *a.* نَحِسٌ . مَشْؤُومٌ

Unman *v. t.* اوهَنَ . خَوَّفَ

Unmanageable *a.* مَالاَ يُضْبَطُ

Unmanly *a.* قَلِيلُ ٱلْمُرُوَّةِ . خَنِثٌ

Unmannered / Unmannerly *a.* قَلِيلُ ٱلأَدَبِ

Unmarried *a.* عَازِبٌ

Unmask *v. t.* كَشَفَ ٱلسِّتَارَ

Unmeaning *a.* بِلا مَعْنىً

Unmerciful *a.* بِلا شَفَقَةٍ

Unmerited *a.* غَيْرُ مُسْتَوْجِبٍ

Unmindful *a.* مُتَغَافِلٌ

Unmingled *a.* غَيْرُ مَمْزُوجٍ . صِرْفٌ

Unmitigated *a.* غَيْرُ مُلَطَّفٍ . مَحْضٌ

Unmotherly *a.* مُخَالِفٌ لِصِفَةِ ٱلأُمِّ

Unmurmuring *a.* غَيْرُ مُتَذَمِّرٍ

Unmusical *a.* غَيْرُ مُطْرِبٍ

Unnatural *a.* غَيْرُ طَبِيعِيٍّ

Unnecessary *a.* غَيْرُ لاَزِمٍ

Unneighbourly *a.* مُخَالِفُ حَقِّ ٱلْقَرِيب

Unnerve *v. t.* أَوْهَنَ

Unnumbered *a.* غَيْرُ مَعْدُودٍ

Unobjectionable *a.* ما لا يُعْتَرَضُ عَلَيْهِ

Unobservable *a.* مَا لَا يُلاحَظُ

Unobserving *a.* غَيْرُ مُلاحِظٍ أو منْتَبِهٍ

Unobtrusive *a.* غَيْرُ فَضُولِيٍّ

Unoccupied *a.* غَيْرُ مَشْغُولٍ . فَارِغٌ

Unoffending *a.* غَيْرُ مُكَدِّرٍ

Unofficial *a.* غَيْرُ رَسْمِيٍّ

Unostentatious *a.* غَيْرُ مُتَفَاخِرٍ

Unpack *v. i.* فكّ ٱلْمَحْزُومَ أَوِ ٱلْمُعَبَّى

Unpaid *a.* غَيْرُ مَدْفُوعٍ

Unpalatable *a.* غَيْرُ لَذِيذٍ

Unparalleled *a.* لَا مَثِيلَ لَهُ

Unpardonable *a.* لَا يُغْفَرُ

Unparliamentary *a.* مُخَالِفُ قانونِ مَجْلِسٍ

Unphilosophical *a.* مُخَالِفُ ٱلْفَلْسفَةِ

Unpitied *a.* غَيْرُ مَشْفُوقٍ عَلَيْهِ

Unpitying *a.* غَيْرُ شفوقٍ

Unpleasant *a.* غَيْرُ مُرْضٍ كَرِيهٌ

Unpleasantness *a.* كَدَرٌ

Unpoetical *a.* عَدِيمُ رُوحِ ٱلشِّعْرِ

Unpolished *a.* غَيْرُ مَصْقُولٍ أَو مُهَذَّب

Unpolite *a.* غَيْرُ أَدِيبٍ

Unpolluted *a.* غَيْرُ مُفْسَدٍ . طَاهِرٌ

Unpopular *a.* غَيْرُ مَقْبُولٍ عِنْدَ ٱلناسِ

Unprecedented *a.* لَا سَابِقَ لَهُ

Unprejudiced *a.* خَالٍ مِنَ ٱلْغَرَضِ

Unpremeditated *a.* غَيْرُ مَقْصُودٍ

Unprepared *a.* غَيْرُ مُسْتَعِدٍّ

Unpretending *a.* متوَاضِعٌ . بَسِيطٌ

Unprincipled *a.* غَيْرُ مُرَاعِي ٱلْحَقِّ

Unprinted *a.* غَيْرُ مَطْبُوعٍ

Unproductive *a.* غَيْرُ مثمِرٍ . عقيم

Unprofitable *a.* غَيْر مُرْبِحٍ أو مفيدٍ

Unpromising *a.* مَا لا أمَلَ فِيهِ

Unpropitious *a.* غَيْرُ مُوَافِقٍ

Unprotected *a.* غَيْرُ مَصُونٍ

Unpublished *a.* غَيْرُ مَنْشُورٍ أوْ مُذَاعٍ

Unqualified *a.* غَيْرُ أَهْلٍ لَه

Unquenchable *a.* مَا لاَ يُطْفَا

Unquestionable *a.* مَا لاَ رَيْبَ فِيهِ

Unravel *v. t.* حَلَّ ـُ. فَكَّ ـُ

Unreal *a.* غَيْرُ حَقِيقِيٍّ . وَهْمِيٌّ

Unreasonable *a.* لاَ يُوَافِقُ الْعَقْلَ. غَيْرُ عَادِلٍ

Unredemeed *a.* غَيْرُ مَفْدِيٍّ أو مُوفًى

Unregenerate *a.* غَيْرُ مُتَجَدِّدِ الْقَلْبِ

Unregistered *a.* غَيْرُ مُسَجَّلٍ

Unrelenting *a.* غَيْرُ مسَامِحٍ . مصِرٌّ

Unremitting *a.* مُسْتَمِرٌّ

Unrepenting *a.* غَيْرُ تائِبٍ

Unrequited *a.* غَيْرُ مُكَافَاٍ

Unreserved *a.* غَيْرُ كَتُومٍ . مُخْلِصٌ

Unresisting *a.* غَيْر مقَاوِمٍ

Unrestrained *a.* غَيْرُ مَحْصُورٍ

Unrewarded *a.* غيْرُ مُجَازَى

Unrighteous *a.* غيْرُ بَارٍّ . أَثِيمٌ

Unrighteousness *n.* إِثْمٌ

Unripe *a.* غيْرُ نَاضِجٍ . فِجٌّ

Unrivalled *a.* لا مَثِيلَ لَهُ

Unrobe *v. t.* خَلَعَ الثِّيَاب

Unroll *v. t.* فَتَحَ دَرْجًا . نَشَرَهُ

Unroof *v. t.* رَفَعَ السَّطْحَ عن

Unruffled *a.* غيْرُ مُهَيَّجٍ . هَادِئٌ

Unruly *a.* ما لاَ يُضْبَطُ . عنيد

Unsaddle *v. t.* رَفَعَ السَّرْجَ عَنْهُ

Unsafe *a.* غيْرُ امِينٍ . مُخْطِرٌ

Unsaid *a.* غيْرُ مَقولٍ

Unsaleable *a.* مَا لاَ يُبَاعُ . كَاسِدٌ

Unsanctified *a.* غيْرُ مُقَدَّسٍ أو مُطَهَّرٍ

Unsatisfactory / Unsatisfying } *a.* غَيْرُ مُرضٍ

Unsavoury *a.* غَيْرُ مَقْبُولٍ لِلذَّوْقِ

Unsay *v. t.* أَبْطَلَ ٱلْقَوْلَ

Unscrew *v. t.* فَكَّ ٱللَّوْلَبَ

Unscriptural *a.* ضِدُّ ٱلْكِتَابِ ٱلْمُقَدَّسِ

Unseal *v. t.* فَكَّ ٱلْخَتْمَ

Unsearchable *a.* مَا لَا يُفْحَصُ أَوْ يُسْتَقْصَى

Unseasonable *a.* فِي غَيْرِ آنِهِ

Unseemly *a.* غَيْرُ لَائِقٍ

Unseen *a.* غَيْرُ مَنْظُورٍ

Unselfish *a.* غَيْرُ مُحِبِّ ٱلذَّاتِ

Unserviceable *a.* غَيْرُ نَافِعٍ

Unsettle *v. t.* أَزْعَجَ . شَوَّشَ

Unshaken *a.* غَيْرُ مُزَعْزَعٍ

Unsheathe *v. t.* إِسْتَلَّ مِنْ غِمْدِهِ

Unshod *a.* حَافٍ

Unshrinking *a.* غَيْرُ مُرْتَدٍّ . جَسُورٌ

Unsightliness *n.* قَبَاحَةُ ٱلْمَنْظَرِ . بَشَاعَةٌ

Unsightly *a.* قَبِيحُ ٱلْمَنْظَرِ . بَشِعٌ

Unskillfull / Unskilful *n.* غَيْرُ مَاهِرٍ

Unsociable *a.* غَيْرُ أَلِيفٍ

Unsocial *a.* غَيْرُ أَلِيفٍ . آبِدٌ

Unsold *a.* مَا لَمْ يُبَعْ

Unsolicited *a.* غَيْرُ مَطْلُوبٍ

Unsophisticated *a.* بَسِيطٌ . سَاذِجٌ

Unsought *a.* غَيْرُ مَطْلُوبٍ

Unsound *a.* غَيْرُ صَحِيحٍ أَوْ سَالِمٍ

Unsoundness *n.* إِخْتِلَالٌ . إِعْتِلَالٌ

Unsparing *a.* غَيْرُ مُقْتَصِدٍ . قَاسٍ

Unspeakable *a.* مَا لَا يُنْطَقُ بِهِ

Unspent *a.* غَيْرُ مَصْرُوفٍ . بَاقٍ

Unspotted *a.* غَيْرُ مُلَطَّخٍ . طَاهِرٌ

Unstable *a.* غَيْرُ ثَابِتٍ . مُتَرَدِّدٌ

Unstained *a.* غَيْرُ مُلَوَّثٍ . بِلَا عَيْبٍ

Unsteady *a.* غَيْرُ ثَابِتٍ . مُتَقَلِّبٌ

Unstinted *a.* غَيْرُ مَحْدُودٍ

Unstrung *a.* مَحْلُولٌ : مَرْخِيٌّ

Unsubstantial *a.* غَيْرُ حَقِيقِيّ أَوْ مَتِينٍ
Unsuccessful *a.* غَيْرُ نَاجِحٍ
Unsuitable } *a.* غَيْرُ مُلَائِمٍ
Unsuited }
Unsullied *a.* غَيْرُ مَعِيبٍ
Unsupported *a.* غَيْرُ مُسْنَدٍ
Unsurpassed *a.* مَالَمْ يَفُقْهُ شَيْءٌ
Unsusceptible *a.* غَيْرُ حَاسٍّ
Unsuspicious *a.* غَيْرُ ظَنَّانٍ . وَاثِقٌ
Unsystematic *a.* غَيْرُ مُنْتَظِمٍ
Unstained *a* غَيْرُ فَاسِدٍ
Untasted *a.* غَيْرُ مَذُوقٍ
Untaught *a.* غَيْرُ مُعَلَّمٍ . أُمِّيٌّ
Untenable *a.* مَالَا يُؤَيَّد . بَاطِلٌ
Unthankful *a.* غَيْرُ شَكُورٍ
Unthankfulness *a.* عَدَمُ شُكْرٍ
Unthinking } *a.* غَيْرُ مُنْتَبِهٍ . غَافِلٌ
Unthoughtful }
Unthrifty *a.* غَيْرُ مُقْتَصِدٍ
Untidy *a.* غَيْرُ نَظِيفٍ أَوْ مُرَتَّبٍ

Untie *v. t.* حَلَّ عُقْدَةً
Until *prep.* حَتَّى . إِلَى . أَنْ . إِلَى
Untimely *a.* فِي غَيْرِ وَقْتِهِ
Untiring *a.* مَالَا يَتْعَبُ أَو يَكِلُّ
Unto *prep.* حَتَّى . إِلَى
Untold *a.* غَيْرُ مَذْكُورٍ . غَيْرُ مُحْصًى
Untoward *a.* مَشْؤُومٌ . شَاقٌّ
Untractable *a.* مَالَا يُضْبَطُ . عَنِيدٌ
Untried *a.* غَيْرُ مُخْتَبَرٍ
Untrodden *a.* غَيْرُ مَسْلُوكٍ
Untrue *a.* كَاذِبٌ غَيْرُ أَمِينٍ
Untruth *n.* كِذْبٌ
Untruthful *a.* كَاذِبٌ
Untwist *v. t.* حَلَّ الْمَفْتُولَ
Unused *a.* غَيْرُ مُسْتَعْمَلٍ
Unusual *a.* نَادِرٌ . شَاذٌ
Unutterable *a.* مَالَا يُنْطَقُ بِهِ
Unveil *v. t.* كَشَفَ الْبُرْقُعَ . بَيَّنَ

Unvarnished *a.* غَيْرُ مَدْهُونٍ. بسيطٌ
Unvaried / Unvarying *a.* غَيْرُ مُتَغَيِّرٍ
Unwarlike *a.* غَيْرُ جدِيرٍ بِالْحَرْبِ
Unwarrantable / Unwarranted *a.* غَيْرُ جائِزٍ
Unwary *a.* غَيْرُ مُتحذِّرٍ . غافِلٌ
Unwearied *a.* غَيْرُ مُتْعَبٍ
Unwelcome *a.* غَيْرُ مُرَحَّبٍ بِهِ
Unwell *a.* مَرِيضٌ
Unwept *a.* غَيْرُ مأسُوفٍ عليهِ
Unwholesome *a.* ضارٌّ بِالصِّحَّةِ
Unwieldy *a.* ضَخْمٌ . ثقِيلٌ
Unwilling *a.* غَيْرُ راضٍ
Unwind *v. t.* حَلَّ الْمَلْفُوفَ
Unwise *a.* غَيْرُ حَكِيمٍ
Unwittingly *ad.* بِلا مَعْرِفَةٍ أَوْ قصد
Unwomanly *a.* غَيْرُ لائقٍ بِالْمَرْأَةِ
Unwonted *a.* غَيْرُ مُعْتادٍ . نادِرٌ
Unworn *a.* غَيْرُ مَلْبُوسٍ
Unworthily *ad.* بِلا استِحْقَاقٍ
Unworthiness *n.* عَدَمُ استِحْقَاقٍ
Unworthy *a.* غَيْرُ لائقٍ أَوْ مُسْتَحِقٍّ
Unwritten *a.* غَيْرُ مَكْتُوبٍ . شَفَهِيٌّ
Unyielding *a.* غَيْرُ مُذْعِنٍ . ثابِتٌ
Unyoke *v. t.* رَفَعَ النِّيرَ
Up *ad.* إِلَى فَوْقٍ . فَوْق
Upbraid *v. t.* وَبَّخَ . لامَ ـُ
Upheaval *n.* إِرْتِفَاعٌ . إِنْدِفَاعٌ
Upheave *v. t.* رَفَعَ ـَ
Uphill *a.* عَسِرٌ . شاق
Uphold *v. t.* سَنَدَ . ايَّدَ . عَضَدَ ـُ
Upholder *n.* مُؤَيِّدٌ . عاضِدٌ . ظَهِيرٌ
Upholsterer *n.* مُنَجِّدٌ
Upholstery *n.* مَفْرُوشَاتٌ
Upland *n.* نَجْدٌ . صَعِيدٌ
Uplift *v. t.* رَفَعَ . رَقَّى
Upon *prep.* عَلَى . عِنْدَ . حِينَ

Upper *a.* أَعْلَى . عَلَوِيٌّ . فَوْقَانِيٌّ

Upperhand *n.* أَسْبَقِيَّةٌ . غَلَبَةٌ

Uppermost *a.* الأَعْلَى

Upright *a.* مُسْتَقِيمٌ . قَائِمٌ

Uprightness *n.* إِسْتِقَامَةٌ

Uproar *n.* شَغَبٌ . ضَجَّةٌ . ضَوْضَاءٌ

Uproot *v. t.* قَلَعَ . إِسْتَأْصَلَ

Upset *v. t.* قَلَبَ . نَكَسَ

Upshot *n.* نَتِيجَةٌ . عَاقِبَةٌ

Upside-down *a.* مَقْلُوبٌ

Upstart *n.* or *a.* حَدِيثُ النِّعْمَةِ

Upward / **Upwards** *ad.* إِلَى فَوْق

Urban *a.* مَدَنِيٌّ

Urbane *a.* مُهَذَّبٌ . لَطِيفٌ . أَنِيسٌ

Urbanity *n.* أَدَبٌ . أُنْسٌ

Urchin *n.* وَلَدٌ خَبِيثٌ . قُنْفُذٌ

Urge *v. t.* حَرَّضَ . حَثَّ

Urgency *n.* لَجَاجَةٌ . ضَرُورَةٌ

Urgent *a.* مُلِحٌّ . ضَرُورِيٌّ

Urinary *a.* بَوْلِيٌّ

Urine *n.* بَوْلٌ

Urn *n.* جَرَّةٌ . قَارُورَةٌ

Us *pron.* ضَمِيرٌ مُتَّصِلٌ (نا)

Usage *n.* اسْتِعْمَالٌ . عَادَةٌ

Use *n.* or *v. t.* إِسْتِعْمَالٌ . إِسْتَعْمَلَ

Useful *a.* مُفِيدٌ . نَافِعٌ

Usefulness *n.* مَنْفَعَةٌ . فَائِدَةٌ

Useless *a.* بِلَا فَائِدَةٍ

Usher *n.* or *v. t.* عَرِيفٌ . أَدْخَلَ

Usual *a.* إِعْتِيَادِيٌّ . دَارِجٌ . جَارٍ

Usurer *n.* مُرَابٍ

Usurp *v. t.* إِغْتَصَبَ

Usurpation *n.* إِغْتِصَابٌ

Usurper *n.* مُغْتَصِبٌ

Usury *n.* رِبًا

Utensil *n.* آلَةٌ . وِعَاءٌ

Utility *n.* فَائِدَةٌ . نَفْعٌ

Utmost *a.* اَلْأَقْصَى

Utter *v. t.* نَطَقَ بِ . فَاهَ بِهِ

Utterance *n.* نُطْقٌ

Utterly *ad.* تَمَامًا بِالْكُلِّيَّةِ

Uttermost *a.* اَلْأَقْصَى . اَلْأَبْعَدُ

Uxorious *a.* مُفْرِطُ الْحُبِّ لِزَوْجَتِهِ

V

Vacancy *n.* فَرَاغ . مَنْصِبٌ خَالٍ

Vacant *a.* فَارِغ . خَالٍ

Vacate *a.* اَخْلَى . تَرَكَ

Vacation *n.* فَرَاغٌ . بِطَالَةٌ . فُرْصَة

Vaccinate *v. t.* طَعَّمَ

Vaccination *n.* تَطْعِيمٌ

Vaccine *n.* مَادَّة لِلتَّطْعِيمِ

Vacillate *v. i.* تَرَدَّدَ

Vacillation *n.* تَرَدُّدٌ

Vacuity / Vacuum *n.* فَرَاغٌ . خَلَاءٌ

Vagabond *n.* طَوَّافٌ. بَطَّالٌ .(مُتَشَرِّدٌ)

Vagabondage *n.* بِطَالَةٌ

Vagary *n.* تَصَوُّرٌ بَاطِلٌ . وَهْمٌ

Vagrancy *n.* جَوَلَانٌ لِلتَّسَوُّلِ

Vagrant *n.* تَائِهٌ. بَطَّالٌ . (مُعْتَرٌّ)

Vague *a.* مُبْهَمٌ . غَيْرُ وَاضِحٍ

Vail *n.* بُرْقُعٌ . قِنَاعٌ

Vain *a.* بَاطِلٌ . مُعْجِبٌ

Vainglorious *a.* مُتَصَلِّفٌ

Vale *n.* وَادٍ . وَهْدٌ

Valedictory *n.* خِطَابٌ وِدَاعِيٌّ

Valet *n.* خَادِمٌ شَخْصِيٌّ

Valiant *a.* بَاسِلٌ . شُجَاعٌ

Valid *a.* ثَابِتٌ . شَرْعِيٌّ . حَقِيقِيٌّ

Validity *n.* ثُبُوتٌ . شَرْعِيَّةٌ

Valise *n.* صَنْدُوقُ سَفَرٍ صَغِيرٌ

Valley *n.* وَادٍ ج أَوْدِيَةٌ

Valorous *a.* بَاسِلٌ . شُجَاعٌ

Valour *n.* شَجَاعَةٌ . بَسَالَةٌ إِقْدَامٌ

Valuable *a.* ثَمِينٌ

Valuation *n.* تَثْمِينٌ . تَقْدِيرٌ

Value *n.* ثَمَنٌ . قِيمَةٌ أَهَمِّيَّةٌ

Value *v. t.* ثَمَّنَ . إِعْتَبَرَ

Valve *n.* صِمَامٌ

Vampire *n.* وَطْوَاطٌ كَبِيرٌ

Van *n.* طَلِيعَةُ ٱلْجَيْشِ . عَرَبَةٌ

Vandal *n.* بَرْبَرِيٌّ مُخَرِّبٌ

Vandalism *n.* تَخْرِيبٌ بَرْبَرِيٌّ

Vane *n.* دَوَّارَةٌ تَدُلُّ عَلَى جِهَةِ ٱلرِّيحِ

Vanguard *n.* طَلِيعَةُ جَيْشٍ

Vanish *v. i.* إِخْتَفَى . زَالَ ـ

Vanity *n.* عُجْبٌ . تَكَبُّرٌ بُطْلٌ

Vanquish *v. t.* قَهَرَ ـ غَلَبَ ـ

Vantage-ground *n.* مَقَامٌ أَفْضَلُ

Vapid *a.* تَافِهٌ نَاشِفٌ بِلَا طَعْمٍ

Vapour *n.* بُخَارٌ

Vapour-bath *n.* حَمَّامٌ بُخَارِيٌّ

Vaporize *v. t.* حَوَّلَ إِلَى بُخَارٍ

Variable *a.* مُتَغَيِّرٌ . مُتَقَلِّبٌ

Variableness *n.* تَغَيُّرٌ . تَقَلُّبٌ

Variance *n.* إِخْتِلَافٌ . خِلَافٌ

Variation *n.* تَغَيُّرٌ . إِخْتِلَافٌ . فَرْقٌ

Variegate *v. t.* لَوَّنَ . رَقَشَ ـ

Variety *n.* نَوْعٌ . شَكْلٌ . تَنَوُّعٌ

Varioloid *n.* جُدَرِيٌّ خَفِيفٌ

Various *n.* مُتَنَوِّعٌ . شَتَّى .

Varlet *a.* دَنِيٌّ . خَبِيثٌ

Varnish *n.* نَوْعٌ مِنَ ٱلصِّبْغِ (فرنيش)

Vary *v. t.* or *i.* غيّر . نوّع . تغيّر

Vase *n.* إناء . ظرف

Vassal *n.* تابع . مزارع تابع

Vassalage *n.* خضوع . عبوديّة

Vast *a.* عظيم . فسيح . عديد

Vastness *n.* عظمة . إتّساع

Vat *n.* حوض ج أحواض

Vault *n.* قبو . قبّة . خشخاشة

Vault *v. t.* or *i.* عقد ـِ . قفز ـِ

Vaulted *n.* مقبّب . مقبوّ

Vaunt *v. i.* إفتخر . تصلّب

Veal *n.* لحم عجل

Veer *v. t.* or *i.* أدار . دار ـُ

Vegetable *n.* نبات . خضرة . بقل

Vegetate *v. t.* نبت ـُ . نما كالبقول

Vegetation *n.* عشب . نبات

Vehemence *n.* شدّة . عنف

Vehement *a.* عنيف . مشدّد

Vehicle *n.* مركبة . عربة

Veil *n.* برقع . نقاب . قناع

Veil *v. t.* تنقّبت . حجب ـُ

Vein *n.* عرق . وريد

Veined / Veiny *a.* ذو عروق او أوردة

Vellum *n.* رقّ للكتابة

Velocity *n.* سرعة السّير

Velvet *n.* مخمل . قطيفة

Velvety *a.* مخمليّ . املس

Venality *n.* إرتشاء . الميل إليه

Vend *v. t.* باع ـِ

Vender / Vendor *n.* بائع

Veneer *v. t.* لبّس . غشى

Venerable *a.* محترم . وقور

Venerate *v. t.* إحترم . وقّر

Veneration *n.* إحترام . توقير

Venereal *a.* زهريّ

Vengeance *n.* نقمة . ثأر

Vengeful *n.* مُنْتَقِمٌ . حَقُودٌ

Venial *n.* مِمَّا يُغْفَرُ أو يُعْذَرُ . زَهِيدٌ

Venison *n.* لَحْمُ ٱلصَّيْدِ

Venom *n.* سُمٌّ . حِقْدٌ

Venomous *a.* سَامٌّ . حَقُودٌ

Venous *a.* وَرِيدِيٌّ (لِلدَّمِ)

Vent *n.* مَنْفَذٌ . إِظْهَارٌ . نُطْقٌ

Vent *v. t.* نَفَثَ ـُ . أَظْهَرَ (حِقْداً)

Ventilate *v. t.* هَوَّى عَرَضَ لِلْهَوَاءِ

Ventilation *n.* تَهْوِيَةٌ

Ventilator *n.* مَنْفَذٌ لِلْهَوَاءِ

Ventriloquism *n.* اَلتَّكَلُّمُ مِنَ ٱلْجَوْفِ

Ventriloquist *n.* مُتَكَلِّمٌ مِنَ ٱلْجَوْفِ

Venture *n.* or *v. t.* مُخَاطَرَةٌ . تَجَرَّأَ

Venturesome / Venturous } *a.* مُخَاطِرٌ . جَسُورٌ

Venus *a.* اَلزُّهَرَةُ . إِلَاهَةُ ٱلْعِشْقِ

Veracious *a.* صَادِقٌ

Veracity *n.* صِدْقٌ

Veranda *n.* رِوَاقٌ ج أَرْوِقَةٌ

Verb *n.* فِعْلٌ ج أَفْعَالٌ

Verbal *a.* فِعْلِيٌّ . لَفْظِيٌّ

Verbally *ad.* شِفَاهاً . لَفْظاً

Verbatim *ad.* حَرْفِيّاً

Verbosity *n.* كَثْرَةُ ٱلْكَلَامِ

Verdant *a.* أَخْضَرُ . غَبِيٌّ . نَضِرٌ

Verdict *n.* حُكْمٌ . قَضَاءٌ . فَتْوَى

Verdigris *n.* زِنْجَارٌ

Verdure *n.* خُضْرَةٌ

Verge *n.* حَافَّةٌ . حَرْفٌ . حَدٌّ

Verge *v. i.* إِقْتَرَبَ . مَالَ ـِ

Verification *n.* تَحْقِيقٌ . إِثْبَاتٌ

Verify *v. t.* حَقَّقَ

Verily *ad.* حَقّاً

Verisimilitude *n.* مُشَابَهَةٌ إِمْكَانِيَّةٌ

Veritable *a.* حَقِيقِيٌّ . وَاقِعٌ

Verity *n.* حَقٌّ . حَقِيقَةٌ . صِدْقٌ

Vermillion *n.* زُنْجُفْرٌ . حُمْرَةٌ

Vermin *n.* حَشَرَاتٌ خَبِيثَةٌ

Vernacular *a.* وَطَنِيٌّ (لُغَةٌ)

Vernal *a.* رَبِيعِيٌّ

Versatile *a.* مُتَقَلِّبٌ . مَاهِرٌ

Versatility *n.* مَهَارَةٌ

Verse *n.* بَيْتُ شِعْرٍ . دَوْرٌ

Versed *a.* حَاذِقٌ . خَبِيرٌ . عَالِمٌ

Versification *n.* نَظْمٌ

Versify *v. i.* or *t.* نَظَمَ ـِ . شَعَرَ ـُ

Version *n.* تَرْجَمَةٌ

Vertebra *n.* فِقْرَةٌ ج فَقَارٌ

Vertebral *a.* فِقْرِيٌّ

Vertebrate *a.* ذُو فِقْرَاتٍ أَوْ فِقَارٍ

Vertex *n.* قِمَّةٌ . رَأْسٌ

Vertical *a.* عَمُودِيٌّ

Vertigo *n.* دُوَارٌ

Very *a.* or *ad.* حَقِيقِيٌّ . ذَاتٌ . جِدًّا

Vespers *n. pl.* صَلَاةُ ٱلْمَسَاءِ

Vessel *n.* مَرْكَبٌ . سَفِينَةٌ . وِعَاءٌ

Vest *n.* صُدْرِيَّةٌ . صُدْرَةٌ

Vestal *a.* or *n.* عَفِيفٌ . عَذْرَاءُ

Vested *a.* ثَابِتٌ . مُعَيَّنٌ . مُقَلَّدٌ

Vestibule *n.* دِهْلِيزٌ

Vestige *n.* أَثَرٌ . رَسْمٌ

Vestment *n.* لِبَاسٌ . حُلَّةٌ

Vesture *n.* ثَوْبٌ . لِبَاسٌ

Veteran *a.* مُجَرَّبٌ . مُتَمَرِّنٌ

Veterinary *a.* مَنُوطٌ بِطِبِّ ٱلْحَيَوَانَاتِ

Veto *n.* or *v. t.* نَهْيٌ . مَنْعٌ . رَفْضٌ . رَفَضَ

Vex *v. t.* أَضْجَرَ . كَدَّرَ . أَغَاظَ

Vexation *n.* كَدَرٌ . مُضَايَقَةٌ

Vexatious *n.* مُضَايِقٌ . مُكَدِّرٌ

Viaduct *n.* سِكَّةٌ مُرْتَفِعَةٌ . جِسْرٌ

Vial *n.* قَارُورَةٌ جَامٌ

Viands *n. pl.* أَطْعِمَةٌ

Vibrate v. t. or i. رَجَّ ـ . إِرْتَجَّ . إِهْتَزَّ

Vibration n. إِهْتِزَازٌ

Vicar n. نَائِبٌ . خُورِيٌّ . قِسِّيسٌ

Vicarious n. نَائِبٌ . مُوَكَّلٌ

Vice n. رَذِيلَةٌ . شَرٌّ . مِلْزَمَةٌ . عِوَضٌ

Vice-admiral n. نَائِبُ . رَئِيسِ أُسْطُولٍ

Vicegerent n. نَائِبٌ

Viceroy n. نَائِبُ مَلِكٍ

Vicinage
Vicinity } n. جُوَارٌ

Vicious a. فَاسِدٌ . شِرِّيرٌ . خَلِيعٌ

Vicissitude n. تقلبٌ

Victim n. قَتِيلٌ . ذَبِيحٌ

Victor n.
Victorious a. } قَاهِرٌ . غَالِبٌ . مَنْصُورٌ

Victory n. نَصْرٌ . غَلَبَةٌ . فَوز

Victual v. t. زَوَّدَ . مَوَّنَ

Victuals n. pl. طَعَامٌ . مَأْكُولَاتٌ

Vie v. i. بَارَى . سَابَقَ . نَافَسَ

View v. t. نَظَرَ ـُ . رَأَى ـَ . تَطَلَّعَ

View n. مَنْظَرٌ . رَأْيٌ

Vigil n. سَهَرٌ . صَلَاةٌ سَهَرِيَةٌ

Vigilance n. مُرَاقَبَةٌ . سَهَرٌ

Vigilant a. سَاهِرٌ . حَذِرٌ . مُنْتَبِهٌ

Vigorous a. قَوِيٌّ . نَشِيطٌ . شَدِيدٌ

Vigour n. شِدَّةٌ . قُوَّةٌ . نَشَاطٌ

Vile a. رَذِيلٌ . نَجِسٌ . قَبِيحٌ

Vileness n. قَبَاحَةٌ . خَسَاسَةٌ

Vilify v. t. عَابَ ـِ . شَتَمَ ـِ

Villa n. دَارُ سَكَنٍ خَارِجَ ٱلْمَدِينَةِ

Village n. قَرْيَةٌ . ضَيْعَةٌ

Villager n. قَرَوِيٌّ

Villain n.
Villainous a. } خَبِيثٌ . شِرِّيرٌ

Villainy
Villany } n. خُبْثٌ . شَرٌّ

Vindicate v. t. بَرَّأَ . بَرَّرَ . ثَبَّتَ

Vindication n. تَبْرِئَةٌ . إِثْبَاتٌ

Vindictive a. ضَغِنٌ . طَالِبُ ٱلْاِنْتِقَامِ

Vine n. كَرْمَةٌ . زَرَجُونٌ . دَالِيَةٌ

Vinegar *n.* خَل

Vineyard *n.* كَرْمٌ

Vintage *n.* قِطَافٌ. حاصِلُ ٱلْكَرْمِ

Viol, Viola *n.* كَمَنْجَةٌ كبيرة

Violate *v. i.* خَالَفَ . نكَثَ ـُ اغتَصَبَ

Violation *n.* مُخَالَفَةٌ . نَكْثٌ

Violence *n.* عُنفٌ . قوَّةٌ . غصْبٌ

Violent *a.* عَنِيفٌ . شَدِيدٌ . طَحُومٌ

Violet *n.* or *a.* بَنَفْسَجة . بَنفسَجِيٌّ

Violin *n.* كَمَنْجَةٌ

Viper *n.* أَفعَى . صِل

Virago *n.* سَلِيطَةٌ

Virgin *n.* عَذْرَاء

Virginity *n.* عُذْرَةٌ

Virile *a.* رَجلِيٌّ . مَرْئِيٌّ

Virility *n.* رُجُولِيةٌ

Virtual *a.* حَقِيقِي . بِٱلْحَقِيقَة

Virtue *n.* فَضِيلة . جُودَة . قوَّة

Virtuous *a.* عفيفٌ . نَقِيٌّ . صَالِحٌ

Virulence *n.* شِدَّة . عنفٌ . سَلاَقَةٌ

Virulent *a.* شَدِيدٌ . عَنِيفٌ . سَامٌّ

Virus *n.* سَمٌّ . صَدِيدٌ

Visage *n.* مُحَيًّا . وَجهٌ . طَلْعَةٌ

Viscera *n. pl.* أَحْشَاءٌ

Viscid, Viscous *a.* لَزِجٌ . دَبِقٌ

Viscount *n.* أَمِيرٌ . رُتبَةٌ أَمِيرِيَّةٌ

Visibility *n.* امكانِيَّة نَظَرِهِ . ظُهُورٌ

Visible *v. t.* ما ينظَرُ . ظَاهِرٌ

Vision *n.* نَظَرٌ . رُؤْيَةٌ . رُؤْيَا

Visionary *a.* خَيَالِيٌّ . وَهْمِيٌّ

Visit *n.* or *v. t.* زِيَارَةٌ . زَارَ ـُ . إِفتَقَدَ

Visitation *n.* إِفتِقَادٌ . مُصِيبَةٌ

Visitor *n.* زَائِرٌ . ضَيفٌ . مُفَتِّشٌ

Vista *n.* مَنظَرٌ (إِلى بَعِيدٍ)

Visual *a.* مَرْئِيٌّ . نَظَرِيٌّ . بَصَرِيٌّ

Vital *a.* حَيَوِيٌّ . ضَرُورِيٌّ

Vitality *n.* حَيَوِيَّةٌ رُوحُ ٱلْحَيَاةِ

Vitals *n. pl.* أَلأَحْشَاءُ ٱلرَّئِيسِيَّةُ

Vitiate *v. t.* أَفْسَدَ . أَبْطَلَ

Vitreous *a.* زُجَاجِيٌّ

Vitriol *n.* زَاجٌ . شَبٌّ

Vituperate *v. t.* شَتَمَ ـُـ . طَعَنَ ـَـ

Vivacious *a.* خَفِيفٌ . مَرِحٌ . ذَكِيٌّ

Vivacity *n.* خِفَّةٌ . مَرَحٌ . نَشَاطٌ

Vivid *a.* بَرَّاقٌ . مُؤَثِّرٌ

Vividness *n.* وُضُوحٌ . لَمَعَانٌ

Vivify *v. t.* أَحْيَا . أَنْعَشَ

Vivisection *n.* تَشْرِيحُ ٱلْجِسْمِ ٱلْحَيِّ

Vixen *n.* سَلِيطَةٌ . وَقِحَةٌ

Viz *ad.* أَيْ . يَعْنِي

Vizier *n.* وَزِيرٌ

Vocabulary *n.* قَامُوسٌ مُوجَزٌ

Vocal *a.* صَوْتِيٌّ . مَلْفُوظٌ

Vocalize *v. t.* لَفَظَ ـِـ . حَرَّكَ (الحروف)

Vocation *n.* حِرْفَةٌ . وَظِيفَةٌ . دَعْوَةٌ

Vociferate *v. t.* صَاحَ ـِـ . صَرَخَ ـُـ

Vociferous *a.* صَائِحٌ . هَاتِفٌ

Voice *n.* صَوْتٌ . صِيغَةُ ٱلْمَعْلُومِ أَوِ ٱلْمَجْهُولِ

Void *a.* or *n.* فَارِغٌ . خَالٍ . بَاطِلٌ . خَلَاءٌ

Volatile *a.* طَيَّارٌ . مُتَقَلِّبٌ

Volcanic *a.* بُرْكَانِيٌّ

Volcano *a.* بُرْكَانٌ . جَبَلُ نَارٍ

Volition *n.* إِرَادَةٌ . إِخْتِيَارٌ

Volley *n.* إِطْلَاقُ أَسْلِحَةٍ كَثِيرَةٍ مَعًا

Volublity *n.* كَثْرَةُ ٱلْكَلَامِ

Voluble *a.* كَثِيرُ ٱلْكَلَامِ

Volume *n.* مُجَلَّدٌ . جِرْمٌ . سِعَةٌ

Voluminous *a.* كَثِيرٌ . مُطَوَّلٌ

Voluntary *a.* إِخْتِيَارِيٌّ . طَوْعِيٌّ

Volunteer *n.* مُتَطَوِّعٌ . مُتَبَرِّعٌ

Voluptuary *n.* } شَهْوَانِيٌّ . مُتَنَعِّمٌ
Voluptuous *a.* }

Vomit *v. t.* or *n.* إِسْتَفْرَغَ . قَيْءٌ

Voracious *a.* نَهِمٌ . أَهْيَمُ . شَرِهٌ

Voracity *n.* نَهْمَةٌ . شَرَهٌ

Vortex *n.* دُرْدُورٌ

Votary *n.* مُتَعَبِّدٌ . نَذِيرٌ

Vote *n.* or *v. i.* صَوْتٌ فِي ٱلْاَنْتِخَابِ

Voter *n.* مَنْ لَهُ حَقٌّ فِي ٱلانْتِخَابِ

Votive *a.* نَذْرِيٌّ

Vouch *v. t.* or *i.* أَثْبَتَ . شَهِدَ ـ

Voucher *n.* شَاهِدٌ . بَيِّنَةٌ

Vouchsafe *v. t.* مَنَحَ . أَنْعَمَ عَلَى . وَهَبَ

Vow *n.* or *v. t.* نَذْرٌ . نَذَرَ ـ

Vowel *n.* حَرْفُ عِلَّةٍ

Voyage *n.* or *v. i.* سَفَرٌ . سَافَرَ

Voyager *n.* مُسَافِرٌ

Vulgar *a.* دَارِجٌ . دَنِيٌّ . خَسِيسٌ

Vulgarism *n.* إِصْطِلَاحٌ . دَارِجٌ

Vulgarity *n.* دَنَاءَةٌ . قِلَّةُ أَدَبٍ

Vulnerable *a.* قَابِلُ ٱلْجَرْحِ اوْ ٱلطَّعْنِ

Vulture *n.* نَسْرٌ . شُوحَةٌ

Vying *See* Vie مُنَافِسٌ

Vulgate *n.* تَرْجَمَةُ ٱلْكِتَابِ ٱلْمُقَدَّسِ ٱللَّاتِينِيَّةُ

W

Wabble *v. i.* تَرَنَّحَ . تَمَايَلَ

Wad *n.* or *v. t.* حَشْوَةٌ . حَشَا ـ

Wadded *a.* مَحْشُوٌّ

Waddle *v. i.* تَمَايَلَ فِي ٱلْمَشْيِ

Wade *v. i.* خَاضَ ـ

Wafer *n.* بُرْشَانَةٌ

Waft *v. t.* حَمَلَ ـِ (اَلرِّيحَ)

Wage *n.* or *v. t.* مَازِحٌ . هَزَّ ـ بِصَبْصَ

Wage *v. t.* رَاهَنَ. إِسْتَأْجَرَ. حَارَبَ

Wager *n.* or *v. t.* رَهْنٌ . رَاهَنَ

Wages *n. pl.* أَجْرٌ . كِرَاءٌ

Waggish *a.* مَازِحٌ . مَاجِنٌ

Waggon *n.* مَرْكَبَةٌ . عَرَبَةٌ

Waif *n.* لَقِيطٌ

Wail *v. i.* or *n.* وَلْوَلَ. عَوَّلَ. عَوِيلٌ

Waist *n.* خَصْرٌ . حَقْوٌ

Waistcoat *n.* صِدْرَةٌ . صَدْرِيَّةٌ

Wait *v. i.* إِنْتَظَرَ . إِسْتَأْنَى. تَرَبَّصَ

Waiter *n.* خَادِمٌ . طَبَقٌ

Waiting-maid *n.* خَادِمَةٌ . جَارِيَةٌ

Waive *v. t.* تَرَكَ ـُ. خَلَى. تَنَحَّى عَنْ

Wake *v. i.* إِسْتَيْقَظَ. إِنْتَبَهَ

Wake *n.* حِرَاسة مَيْتٍ . أَثَرُ سفينةٍ

Wakeful *a.* يَقِظٌ . سَاهِرٌ

Waken *v. i.* or *t.* تَيَقَّظَ . أَيْقَظَ. نَبَّهَ

Walk *v. t.* or *n.* مَشَى ـِ مَشْيٌ . مَمْشًى

Wall *n.* or *v. t.* حَائِطٌ . سُورٌ. حَوَّطَ

Wallet *n.* جِرَابٌ . كِيسٌ. قَلْعٌ

Wallow *v. i.* تَمَرَّغَ

Walnut *n.* جَوْزَةٌ . شَجَرُ ٱلْجَوْزِ

Waltz *n.* نَوْعٌ مِنَ ٱلرَّقْص

Wan *n.* أَصْفَرُ مُصْفَرٌّ

Wand *n.* قَضِيبٌ صَوْلَجَان

Wander *v. i.* تَاهَ ـِ ضَلَّ ـِ حَادَ ـِ

Wanderer *n.* تَائِهٌ . ضَالّ . جَائِلٌ

Wane *v. i.* تَنَاقَصَ . إِنْحَطَّ

Want *v. t.* or *i.* إِحْتَاجَ . ارَادَ نَقَصَ ـُ

Want *n.* حَاجَةٌ . فَاقَةٌ . نَقْصٌ

Wanting *a.* نَاقِصٌ مَفْقُودٌ

Wanton *a.* فَاجِرٌ. بَطِرٌ . لَاهٍ

War *n.* or *v. i.* حَرْبٌ . حَارَبَ

Warble *v. i.* غَرَّدَ

Warbler / Warbling } n. مُغَرِّدٌ

Ward n. حِرَاسَةٌ . قاصِرٌ لهُ وَصِيٌّ

Warden n. حَافِظٌ . وَكِيلٌ

Wardrobe n. خِزانَةُ ثِيَابٍ . لِبَاسٌ

Wares n. pl. سِلَعٌ . بَضَائِعُ

Warehouse n. مَخْزَنٌ

Warfare n. مُحارَبَةٌ . مُجاهَدَةٌ

Warily ad. بِحَذَرٍ . مُتَحَذِّراً

Wariness n. حَذَرٌ . إِحْتِيَاطٌ

Warlike a. حَرْبِيٌّ . مُحِبُّ ٱلْحَرْبِ

Warm a. or v. t. دَافِئٌ . حَارٌّ . سَخَّنَ

Warmly ad. بِحَمَاسَةٍ . بِغَيْرَةٍ

Warmth n. دِفْءٌ . حَرَارَةٌ

Warn v. t. حَذَّرَ . أَنْذَرَ

Warning n. إِنْذَارٌ . إِخْطَارٌ

Warp n. or v. t. سَدَاةٌ . حَرَّفَ

Warrant n. تَفْوِيضٌ . إِجَازَةٌ . أَمْرٌ

Warrant v. t. كَفَلَ . ضَمِنَ . بَرَّرَ

Warrantable a. جَائِزٌ

Warrior n. مُحارِبٌ . جُنْدِيٌّ

Wart n. ثُؤْلُولٌ ج ثَآلِيل

Wary a. مُتَحَذِّرٌ . مُحْتَرِسٌ . بَصِيرٌ

Was see Be. كَانَ يَكُونُ

Wash v. t. or i. غَسَلَ ـِ . إِغْتَسَلَ

Wash n. غَسْلٌ . غَسْلَةٌ

Washer-woman n. غَسَّالَةٌ

Washing n. غَسْلٌ . غَسَالَةٌ . غَسِيلٌ

Wasp n. زُنْبُورٌ ج زَنَابِيرُ

Waspish a. نَكِدٌ . سَرِيعُ ٱلْغَيْظِ

Waste v. t. or i. أَسْرَفَ . بَذَّرَ . ضَنِيَ ـَ

Waste n. إِسْرَافٌ . خَرَابٌ . صَحْرَاءُ

Wasteful a. مُسْرِفٌ . مُبَذِّرٌ

Watch n. خَفِيرٌ . هَزِيعٌ . ساعةٌ

Watch v. t. or i. حَرَسَ ـِ . رَاقَبَ . سَهِرَ ـَ

Watchful v. مُرَاقِبٌ . حَذِرٌ . مُنْتَبِهٌ

Watch-maker n. سَاعَاتِيٌّ

Watchman *n.* حَارِسٌ . رَقِيبٌ

Watch-tower *n.* بُرْجُ ٱلرَّقِيبِ

Watchword *n.* شِعَارٌ

Water *n.* or *v. i.* مَآءٌ . سقَى ـِ

Water-course *n.* مَجْرَى مَآءٍ

Water-cress *n.* قُرَّةُ ٱلْعَيْنِ (نبات)

Waterfall *n.* شَلَّالٌ

Water-melon *n.* بَطِّيخٌ أَحْمَرُ

Waterproof *n.* مُشَمَّعٌ

Water-spout *n.* عَمُودُ مَاءٍ

Watery *a.* مَائِيٌّ . خَفِيفٌ . تَافِهٌ

Wave *n.* or *v.t.* or *i.* مَوْجٌ . هَزَّ . هَاجَ ـَ

Waver *v. i.* تَرَدَّدَ . إِرْتَابَ . تَمَايَلَ

Wavy *a.* مُتَمَوِّجٌ

Wax *n.* or *v.t.* or *i.* شَمْعٌ . شَمَّعَ . زَادَ ـِ

Waxen *a.* شَمْعِيٌّ

Waxwork *n.* صُوَرٌ أو شُخُوصٌ شَمْعِيَّةٌ

Way *n.* طَرِيقٌ . مِنْوَالٌ . وَسِيلَةٌ

Wayfarer / Wayfaring *n.* مُسَافِرٌ . إِبْنُ ٱلسَّبِيلِ

Waylay *v. t.* اكْمَنَ لَهُ

Wayward *a.* جَامِحٌ غَيْرُ مُطِيعٍ

We *pron. pl.* نَحْنُ

Weak *a.* ضَعِيفٌ . وَاهِنٌ . وَمُرْتَخٍ

Weaken *v. t.* أَضْعَفَ . أَوْهَنَ

Weakness *n.* ضُعْفٌ . وَهْنٌ . سُقْمٌ

Weal *n.* خَيْرٌ . سَعَادَةٌ

Wealth *n.* ثَرْوَةٌ . غِنًى . وَفْرَةٌ

Wealthy *a.* غَنِيٌّ . ذُو ثَرْوَةٍ

Wean *v. t.* فَطَمَ ـِ

Weapon *n.* سِلَاحٌ

Wear *v. t.* لَبِسَ ـَ . أَبْلَى

Weariness *n.* تَعَبٌ . ضَنْكٌ . إِعْيَآءٌ

Wearisome *a.* مُتْعِبٌ . مُمِلٌّ

Weary *a.* or *v. t.* تَعِبٌ . أَتْعَبَ . ازعج

Weasel *n.* إِبْنُ عِرْسٍ نِمْسٌ

Weather *n.* حَالَةُ ٱلْجَوِّ . طَقْسٌ

Weather-cock *n.* دَوَّارَةُ ٱلرِّيحِ

Weave *v. t.* حَاكَ . نَسَجَ ـُ

Weaver *n.* حَائِكٌ . نَسَّاجٌ

Web *n.* نَسِيجٌ

Wed *v. t.* or *i.* تَزَوَّجَ

Wedding *n.* عُرْسٌ

Wedge *n.* سَفِينٌ

Wedlock *n.* زِيجَةٌ . زَوَاجٌ

Wednesday *n.* يَوْمُ ٱلْأَرْبِعَاءِ

Weld *n.* or *v. t.* عشْبٌ بَرّي . قَلَعَهُ

Week *n.* أُسْبُوعٌ

Weekday *a.* غَيْرُ يوْمِ ٱلاحَد

Weekly *a.* or *ad.* اسْبُوعِيٌّ . أسْبوعِيًّا

Weep *v. i.* بَكَى

Weevil *n.* سُوسٌ

Weigh *v. t.* وَزَنَ ـِ . تأمَّلَ . ثَقُلَ ـُ

Weight *n.* وَزْنٌ . ثِقْلٌ . أَهَمِّيَّةٌ

Weighty *a.* ثَقِيلٌ . مُهِمٌّ

Weir *n.* سَدُّ نَهْرٍ

Weird *a.* غَيْرُ طَبِيعِيٍّ . غَرِيبٌ

Welcome *n.* or *a.* تَأْهِيلٌ . مُرَحَّبٌ بِهِ

Weld *v. t.* لَحَمَ ـُ

Welfare / Well-being } *n.* خَيْرٌ . حظ . سَلَامَةٌ

Well *a.* or *ad.* مُعَافًى . جَيِّدٌ . حَسَنًا

Well *n.* or *v. i.* بِئْرٌ . نَبَعَ ـَ

Well-bred *a.* مُهَذَّبٌ . حسن ٱلتَّرْبِيَةِ

Well-nigh *ad.* تَقْرِيبًا

Well-spring *n.* نَبْعٌ

Welter *v. i.* تَمَرَّغَ . تَقَلَّبَ

Wen *n.* سِلْعَةٌ . غُدَّةٌ

Wench *n.* جَارِيَةٌ

Went *See* Go. ذَهَبَ ـَ

Were *See* Be. كَانُوا

West *n.* مَغْرِبٌ . غَرْبٌ

Western *a.* غَرْبِيٌّ

Westward *ad.* غَرْبًا . نَحْوَ ٱلْغَرْبِ

Wet *a.* مَبْلُول . رَطْبٌ . مَاطِرٌ

Wether *n.* كَبْش خصيٌّ

Whale *n.* حوتٌ

Wharf *n.* إِسْكِلَة . (رَصِيفٌ)

What *pron.* مَا . مَاذَا

Whatever / Whatsoever } *pron.* مَهْمَا . كُلَّمَا

Wheat *n.* قَمْحٌ . بِرٌّ . حِنْطَةٌ

Wheedle *v. t.* دَاهَنَ . دَارى . تَملَّق

Wheel *n.* دُولاَبٌ (عَجَلَةٌ)

Wheel-barrow *n.* عَجلَةُ ٱلْيَدِ

Whelp *n.* شِبْلٌ . جرْوٌ

When *ad.* متى . لما . عِندِ ما

Whence *ad.* مِنْ أَيْنَ . مِنْ حيْثُ

Whenever / Whensoever } *ad.* كُلَّمَا . مَتَى ما

Where *ad.* أَينَ . إِلَى أَيْنَ . حَيثُ

Whereabouts *ad.* or *n.* أَيْنَ . مَكَانٌ

Whereas *conj.* بِمَا أَنْ . عَلَى أَنَّ

Whereat *ad.* عِنْدَ ذلك

Whereby *ad.* أَلَّذِي بِهِ . مِنْ حَيْثُ

Wherefore *ad.* لِذَلِكَ . مِنْ ثَمَّ . لِمَاذَا

Wherein *ad.* حَيْثُ أينَ

Whereof *ad.* أَلَّذِي مِنْهُ

Whereon / Whereupon } *ad.* إِذْذاك . عِنْدَذَلِكَ

Wheresoever / Wherever } *ad.* حَيْثُمَا . أَيْنَمَا

Whereto / Whereunto } *ad.* إِلَى حَيْث

Wherewith / Wherewithal } *ad.* ما بِهِ . بِمَا

Whet *v. t.* سَنَّ ـُ . هَيَّجَ . شَوَّق

Whether *pron.* or *conj.* أَيُّهُمَا . إِنْ كَان

Whetstone *n.* مِسَنٌّ . مِشْحَذٌ . صُلَّبٌ

Whey *n.* مصلٌ

Which *pron.* مَا . مَنْ . أَلَّذي

Which-ever / Which-so-ever } *pron.* اَيُّمَا . هذَا أَوْ ذَاكَ

Whiff *n.* نَفْحَةٌ . نفسٌ

Whig *n.* مِن حِزْبِ ٱلأَحْرَارِ ٱلإِنْكِلِيز

While *n.* مدَّة . وقْتٌ . حينٌ

While / Whilst } *ad.* بينْما . حينما . لَمَّا . إِذْ

Whim *n.* وَهْمٌ . تَصَوُّرٌ باطِلٌ

Whimper *v. i.* بَكَى خَفِيفاً كَالْوَلَدِ

Whimsical *a.* وَهْمِيٌّ . غَرِيبٌ

Whine *v. i.* or *n.* هَرَّ ـِ . هَرِيرٌ

Whip *n.* or *v. t.* سَوْطٌ . سَاطَ ـُ

Whir *v. i.* دَارَ بِصَوْتٍ . خَرَّ

Whirl *v. t.* or *i.* دَوَّرَ ـُ دَارَ

Whirlpool *n.* دُرْدُورٌ

Whirlwind *n.* زَوْبَعَةٌ

Whisker *n.* لِحْيَةُ ٱلْعَارِضِ

Whisk *v. t.* حرَّكَ . جَرَّفَ بِسُرْعَةٍ

Whisky *n.* نَوْعٌ مِنَ ٱلْعَرَقِ . وِسْكِي

Whisper *n.* or *v. i.* وَسْوَسَةٌ . سَارَّ

Whistle *v. i.* or *n.* صَفَرَ ـِ . صَافُورَةٌ

Whit *n.* نُقْطَةٌ . ذَرَّةٌ . بَتَّةٌ

White *a.* or *n.* أَبْيَضُ . بَيَاضٌ

Whiten *v. t.* or *i.* بَيَّضَ . إِبْيَضَّ

Whiteness *n.* بَيَاضٌ

Whitewash *n.* بَيَاضُ ٱلْجِيرِ

Whither *ad.* إِلَى أَيْنَ

Whithersoever *ad.* أَيْنَمَا . حَيْثُمَا

Whitish *a.* ضَارِبٌ إِلَى ٱلْبَيَاضِ

Whittle *v. t.* قَشَرَ بِسِكِّينٍ . بَرَى ـِ

Whiz *n.* or *v. i.* صَفِيرُ ٱلسَّهْمِ . صَفَرَ ـِ

Who *rel.* or *int. pron.* ٱلَّذِي . أَيُّ . مَنْ

Whoever *rel. pron.* مَنْ . كُلُّ مَنْ

Whole *a.* كُلٌّ . صَحِيحٌ . كَامِلٌ

Wholesale *n.* or *a.* بَيْعٌ بِالْجُمْلَةِ

Wholesome *a.* سَلِيمٌ . مُوَافِقُ ٱلصِّحَّةِ

Wholly *ad.* جُمْلَةً . كَافَّةً . تَمَاماً

Whom *pron. See* Who. ٱلَّذِي

Whoop *n.* or *v. i.* صِيَاحٌ . صَاحَ ـِ . زَعَقَ

Whooping-cough *n.* دَاءُ ٱلشَّهْقَةِ

Whore *n.* زَانِيَةٌ . عَاهِرَةٌ . فَاجِرَةٌ

Whoredom *n.* عَهْرٌ . فُجُورٌ

Whose *poss. pron. See* Who
Whosoever *rel. pron. See* Whoever.
Why *ad.* لماذا . لِمَ
Wick *n.* فَتيلَة . شعيلَة
Wicked *a.* شِرّيرٌ . أثيمٌ . طالِحٌ
Wickedness *n.* شَرٌّ . إِثمٌ
Wicket *n.* بَابٌ صَغيرٌ
Wide *a.* وَاسِعٌ . فَسيحٌ . عَريضٌ
Widely *ad.* جِدًّا . شَائِعًا . إِتّساعًا
Widen *v. t.* or *i.* وَسَّعَ . إِتسَعَ
Widow *n.* أَرْمَلَةٌ ج أَرامِلُ
Widower *n.* ارْمَلُ
Widowhood *n.* تَرَمُّلٌ
Width *n.* عَرضٌ . إِتسَاعٌ
Wield *v. t.* إِستَعمَلَ . أَدارَ . دَبَّرَ
Wife *n.* زَوجَةٌ . قرينَةٌ . إِمرَأَةٌ
Wig *n.* شعرٌ مُستَعارٌ
Wigwam *n.* كُوخُ الهُنودِ
Wild *a.* برّيٌّ . وَحشيٌّ . فالِتٌ
Wilderness *n.* برّيَّةٌ . بادِيَةٌ
Wildly *ad.* بجنون . طَيْشًا
Wile *n.* حيلَةٌ . مَكيدَةٌ . خدْعَةٌ
Wilful *a.* عنيدٌ
Wilfulness *n.* عِنادٌ
Will *v. i.* سَوف
Will *v. t.* or *n.* أَرادَ . أَوصى . إِرادَةٌ . وَصيَّةٌ
Willing *a.* رَاض . مُريدٌ
Willingness *n.* رِضًى . قُبُولٌ
Willow *n.* صَفْصافٌ
Wilt *v. i.* ذَمُلَ ـ
Wily *a.* بَكّارٌ . مُختَالٌ . خَدّاعٌ
Win *v. t.* رَبِحَ ـ . فَازَ ـُ . أَرضى
Wince *v. i.* جفَلَ عَنْ
Wind *n.* ريحٌ
Wind *v. t.* or *i.* فَتلَ ـِ . دَارَ ـ
Winding-sheet *n.* كَفَنٌ ج أكفانٌ
Windlass *n.* آلَةٌ لِرَفعِ الأَثقالِ

Windmill *n.* طَاحُون تُدِيرهُ ٱلرِّيحُ

Window *n.* طَاقَةٌ . كُوَّةٌ . شُبَّاكٌ

Windpipe *n.* قَصبَة ٱلرِّئَةِ

Windward *ad.* إِلَى جِهَةِ ٱلرِّيحِ

Windy *a.* كَثِيرُ ٱلرِّيحِ . بَاطِلٌ

Wine *n.* خَمرٌ . نَبِيذٌ

Wine-bibber *n.* شِرِّيبُ خَمْرٍ

Wine-glass *n.* قَدَحٌ . كَاسٌ

Wing *n.* جَنَاحٌ . كَنَفٌ

Wink *v. i.* طَرَفَ ـِ . تَغَاضَى عَنْ

Winner *n.* فَائِزٌ . غَالِبٌ

Winning *a.* مُرْضٍ . مُسْتَمِيلُ ٱلْقَلْبِ

Winnow *v. t.* ذَرَّى

Winter *n.* فَصلُ ٱلشِّتَاءِ

Wintery / Wintry *a.* شَتَوِيٌّ . شَاتٍ . بَارِدٌ

Wipe *v. t.* مَسَحَ ـَ نَظَفَ . مَحَا ـ

Wire *n.* or *v. t.* شَرِيطٌ . سِلْكٌ . رَاسلَ بِهِ

Wiry *a.* شَرِيطِيٌّ . ضَلِيعٌ . قَوِيٌّ

Wisdom *n.* حِكْمَةٌ . فِطْنَةٌ

Wise *a.* حَكِيمٌ . عَاقِلٌ

Wish *v. t.* or *n.* ارَادَ تَمَنَّى . إِرَادَةٌ . بُغْيَةٌ

Wistful *a.* تَائِقٌ . رَاغِبٌ

Wit *n.* ذَكَاءٌ . حَذْقٌ . بَصِيرَةٌ

Witch *n.* سَاحِرَةٌ

Witchcraft *n.* سِحْرٌ . كَهَانَةٌ

Wichery *n.* سِحرٌ . فُتُونٌ

With *prep.* مَعْ . بِ . عِنْدَ . مِنْ

Withal *ad.* أَيضاً . مَعْ كُلِّهِ

Withdraw *v. t.* or *i.* إِسْتَرَدَّ . إِرْتَدَّ

Withdrawal *n.* إِسْتِرْجَاعٌ . إِرْتِدَادٌ

Wither *v. t.* or *i.* أَذْبَلَ . ذَبَلَ ـُ

Withers *n. pl.* حَارِكٌ (عَظْمٌ بِأَعْلَى ٱلظَّهْرِ)

Withhold *v. t.* أَمسكَ عَنْ

Within *prep.* دَاخِل . فِي . ضِمْنَ

Without *prep.* خَارِجٌ . بِدُونِ . مَالَمْ

Withstand *v. t.* قَاوَمَ . ثَبتَ ضِدَّ

Witless *a.* غَبِيٌّ . أَخْرَقُ

Witness *n.* or *v. i.* شَاهِدٌ . شَهَادَةٌ . شَاهَدَ

Witticism *n.* مُلْحَةٌ

Wittingly *ad.* قَصْداً . بِعِلْمٍ

Witty *a.* ذَكِيٌّ . ظَرِيفٌ

Wives *n. pl. See* Wife زَوْجَاتٌ

Wizard *n.* سَاحِرٌ

Woe *n.* وَيْلٌ . بَلِيَّةٌ . حُزْنٌ

Woe-begone *a.* حَزِينٌ . مَغْمُومٌ

Woeful / Woful } *a.* حَزِينٌ . مُحْزِن

Wolf *n.* ذِئْبٌ ج ذِئَابٌ

Woman *n.* (*pl.* Women). مَرْأَةٌ . إِمرَأَةٌ

Womanhood *n.* حَالةُ ٱلمَرْأَةِ . النِّسَاءُ

Woman-kind *n.* جِنْسُ ٱلنِّسَاءِ

Womb *n.* رَحِمٌ ج أَرْحَامٌ

Wonder *n.* تَعَجُّبٌ . غَرِيبَةٌ . مُعْجِزَةٌ

Wonderful / Wondrous } *a.* عَجِيبٌ . مُدْهِشٌ

Wont *a.* or *n.* مُعْتَادٌ . عَادَةٌ

Wonted *a.* مُعْتَادٌ

Woo *v. t.* تَوَدَّدَ إِلَى . إِسْتَعْطَفَ

Wood *n.* خَشَبٌ . حَطَبٌ . غَابَةٌ

Woodcock *n.* دُجَاجُ ٱلأَرْضِ

Woodcut *n.* نَقْشٌ عَلَى خَشَبٍ

Wooded *a.* ذُو أَشْجَار

Wooden *a.* خَشَبِيٌّ . مِنْ خَشَبٍ

Woodman *n.* حَطَّابٌ

Woody *a.* خَشَبِيٌّ . كَثِيرُ ٱلأَشْجَارِ

Woof *n.* لُحْمَةٌ

Wool *n.* صُوف

Woollen *a.* صُوفِي . من صُوف

Woolly *a.* صُوفِيٌّ . ذُو صُوفٍ

Word *n.* كَلِمَةٌ . وَعْدٌ . أَمْرٌ

Wording *n.* عِبَارَةٌ . تَرْكِيبُ عِبَارَةٍ

Wordy *a.* كَثِيرُ ٱلْكَلَامِ

Work *n.* or *v. i.* شُغْلٌ . عَمَلٌ . إِشْتَغَلَ

Worker / Workman } *a.* صَانِعٌ . فَاعِلٌ

Workmanship *n.* صَنْعَةٌ . عَمَلٌ

Workshop *n.* مَعْمَلٌ . دُكَّانُ شُغْلٍ

World *n.* عَالَمٌ . دُنْيَا

Worldliness *n.* مَحَبَّةُ ٱلدُّنْيَا

Worldly *n.* مُحِبُّ ٱلدُّنْيَا . دُنْيَوِيٌّ

Worm *n.* دُودَةٌ ج دُودٌ . دِيدَان

Worm-eaten *a.* مُسَوَّسٌ

Wormy *a.* مُدَوِّدٌ . كَثِيرُ ٱلدُّودِ

Worn *pp.* مَلْبُوسٌ . تَعِبٌ . مَنْهُوكٌ

Worry *v. t.* or *i.* كَدَّرَ . أَهَمَّ . إِهْتَمَّ

Worse *a.* or *ad.* أَرْدَأُ . شَرٌّ

Worship *n.* or *v. t.* عِبَادَةٌ . عَبَدَ ـُ

Worshipper *n.* عَابِدٌ . سَاجِدٌ

Worst *a.* or *v. t.* اَلْأَرْدَأُ . غَلَبَ ـِ

Worsted *n.* or *a.* غَزْلٌ صُوفِيٌّ

Worth *n.* or *a.* قِيمَةٌ . مُعَادِلٌ . مُسْتَحِقٌ

Worthily *ad.* بِٱسْتِحْقَاقٍ . بِلِيَاقَةٍ

Worthless *a.* بِلَا قِيمَةٍ . غَيْرُ نَافِعٍ

Worthy *a.* مُسْتَحِقٌّ . أَهْلٌ . فَاضِلٌ

Would (*See* Will.) سَوْفَ . يَالَيْتَ

Wound *n.* or *v. t.* جُرْحٌ . جَرَحَ ـَ

Wound *pp. of* Wind. مَفْتُولٌ . مَلْفُوفٌ

Wove / Woven } *See* Weave. مَنْسُوجٌ

Wrangle *v. i.* نَازَعَ . شَاجَرَ

Wrap *v. t.* لَفَّ ـُ

Wrapper / Wrapping } *n.* لِفَافَةٌ . غِلَافٌ

Wrath *n.* غَيْظٌ . سُخْطٌ . غَضَبٌ

Wrathful *a.* غَضُوبٌ . سَاخِطٌ . مُغْتَاظٌ

Wreak *v.* أَنْزَلَ عَلَى . أَحَلَّ بِهِ

Wreathe *n.* إِكْلِيلُ أَزْهَارٍ . ضَفِيرَةٌ

Wreathe *v. t.* ضَفَرَ ـِ . لَفَّ ـُ

Wreck *v. t.* or *n.* كَسَّرَ . خَرَّبَ . كَسْرٌ

Wren *n.* ضَرْبٌ مِنَ ٱلْعَصَافِيرِ

Wrench *v. t.* لَوَّى . إِغْتَصَبَ

Wrest *v. t.* إِغْتَصَبَ . خَطِفَ ـَ . حَرَّفَ

Wrestle *v. i.* صَارَعَ

Wrestling *n.* مُصَارَعَةٌ

Wretch *n.* شَقِيٌّ . خَبِيثٌ . حَقِيرٌ

Wretched *a.* شَقِيٌّ . تَعِسٌ . بَائِسٌ

Wriggle *v. i.* تَلَوَّى

Wright *n.* صَانِعٌ

Wring *v. t.* عَصَرَ ـِ . إِغْتَصَبَ

Wrinkle *n.* or *v. t.* جَعْدَةٌ . تَجَعَّدَ

Wrist *n.* مِعْصَمٌ . رُسْغٌ

Write *n.* كَتَبَ ـُ . حَرَّرَ . أَلَّفَ

Writer *n.* كَاتِبٌ . مُؤَلِّفٌ

Writhe *v. t.* تَلَوَّى

Writing *n.* كِتَابٌ . كِتَابَةٌ

Written *a.* مَكْتُوبٌ . خَطِّيٌّ

Wrong *n.* ظُلْمٌ . ضَرَرٌ . خَطَأٌ

Wrong *n.* غَيْرُ صَحِيحٍ . مُخْطِئٌ

Wrong *v. t.* ظَلَمَ ـِ . أَضَرَّ . أَسَاءَ إِلَى

Wrongful *a.* مُضِرٌّ . ظَالِمٌ . غَيْرُ عَادِلٍ

Wroth *a.* مُغْتَاظٌ . غَضْبَان

Wrought *a.* مَصْنُوعٌ

Wrung *See* Wring. مَعْصُورٌ

Wry *a.* أَزْوَرُ . مُعَوَّجٌ

Y

Yacht *n.* سَفِينَةٌ صَغِيرَةٌ لِلتَّنَزُّهِ . يَخْتٌ

Yard *n.* ذِرَاعٌ إِنْكِلِيزِيٌّ

Yarn *n.* غَزْلٌ . قِصَّةٌ . طَوِيلَةٌ

Yawl *n.* زَوْرَقٌ

Yawn *v. i.* or *n.* تَثَاءَبَ . تَثَاؤُبٌ

Ye *p. pron.* أَنْتُمْ . أَنْتُنَّ

Yea *ad.* نَعَمْ

Year *n.* سَنَةٌ . عَامٌ

Yearling *n.* حَوْلِيٌّ . إِبْنُ سَنَةٍ

Yearly *a.* سَنَوِيٌّ

Yearn *v. i.* إِشْتَاقَ إِلَى . حَنَّ ـِ

Yearning *n.* حَنِينٌ . شَوْقٌ

Yeast *n.* خَمِيرٌ

Yell *v. i.* or *n.* صَاحَ ـِ . صَيْحَةٌ

Yellow *a.* أَصْفَرُ

Yellowish *a.* ضَارِبٌ إِلَى ٱلصُّفْرَةِ

Yelp *v. i.* هَرَّ ـِ . نَبَحَ ـَ

Yeoman *n.* فَلَّاحٌ . صَاحِبُ مُلْكٍ

Yes *ad.* نَعَمْ . بَلَى

Yesterday *ad.* أَلْبَارِحَةَ . أَمْسِ

Yet *conj.* مَعَ ذَلِكَ . بَعْدُ

Yield *v. t.* or *i.* أَنْتَجَ . سَلَّمَ . أَذْعَنَ

Yielding *a.* or *p. pr.* مُذْعِنٌ . لَيِّنٌ . مُنْتِجٌ

Yoke *n.* or *v. t.* نِيرٌ . وَضَعَ ٱلنِّيرَ

Yoke-fellow *n.* أَلِيفٌ . شَرِيكٌ

Yolk / Yelk *n.* مُحُّ ٱلْبَيْضِ (الصفار)

Yon *a.* / Yonder *ad.* هُنَاكَ . ذَلِكَ

Yore *ad.* قَدِيماً

You *p. pron.* أَنْتَ أَنْتُمْ أَنْتُنَّ

Young *a.* or *n.* صَغِيرُ ٱلْعُمْرِ . طِفْلٌ

Younger *a.* أَصْغَرُ عُمْراً

Youngest *n.* الأَصْغَرُ عُمْراً

Youngster *n.* صَبِيٌّ . فَتًى

Your *poss. pron.* كَ . كُمْ . كُنَّ . كُمَا

Yours *pross. pron.* لَكَ . لَكُمْ . لَكُنَّ

Yourself *p. pron.* أَنْتَ نَفْسُكَ

Youth *n.* حَدَاثَةٌ صَبْوَةٌ

Youthful *a.* حَدِيثُ ٱلسِّنِّ . شَابٌّ

Z

Zeal *n.*	غيرة . مُرُوءَةٌ. إِقْدَامٌ
Zealot *n.* / **Zealous** *a.*	غيورٌ
Zebra *n.*	فَرَسٌ وَحشِيٌّ مُخَطَّطٌ
Zenith *n.*	سَمتُ ٱلرَّأْسِ
Zephyr *n.*	نَسِيمٌ
Zero *n.*	صِفْرٌ
Zest *n.*	شَهِيَّة . لَذَّةٌ
Zigzag *a.* or *n.*	مُتَعَرِّجٌ . تَعرِيجٌ
Zinc *n.*	تُوتِيَا
Zion *n.*	صِهيَوْن
Zodiac *n.*	مِنْطَقَةُ ٱلْبُرُوجِ
Zone *n.*	مِنطَقَةٌ
Zoological *a.*	منوطٌ بِعِلمِ ٱلْحَيَوَانِ
Zoologist *n.*	عالِمٌ بِٱلْحَيَوَانِ
Zoology *n.*	عِلْمُ ٱلْحَيَوَانِ

SUPPLEMENT

ENGLISH-ARABIC

advertisement *n.* إِعْلَانٌ

advertising agency *n.* وَكَالَةُ ٱلإِشْهَارِ

aerial *n.* هَوَائِيٌّ

aeronautics *n.* طَيَرَانٌ

aggression *n.* إِعْتِدَاءٌ

aggressor *n.* مُعْتَدٍ

airbase *n.* قَائِدَةٌ جَوِّيَةٌ

air conditioner *n.* بَرَّادَةٌ

air-conditioning *n.* تَكْيِيفُ ٱلْهَوَاءِ

aircraft *n.* طَائِرَةٌ

,, carrier *n.* حَامِلَةُ ٱلطَّائِرَاتِ

airfield *n.* مَطَارٌ

air mail *n.* أَلْبَرِيدُ ٱلْجَوِّيُّ

airplane *n.* طَائِرَةٌ

airport *n.* مِينَا جَوِّيَةٌ

air raid *n.* غَارَةٌ جَوِّيَهْ

airtight *a.* حَاجِبُ ٱلْهَوَاءِ

air warden *n.* حَارِسُ ٱلْمُقَاوَمَةِ ٱلْجَوِّيَةِ

alert *n.* إِشَارَةُ ٱلْخَطَرِ

alternate current *n.* تَيَّارٌ مُتَبَادَلٌ

ameliorate *v.* أَصْلَحَ

amortization *n.* إِسْتِهْلَاكٌ

amortize *v.* إِسْتَهْلَكَ

amplifier *n.* مُكَبِّرٌ

analogy *n.* مُمَاثَلَةٌ

analysis *n.* تَحْلِيلٌ

anesthesia *n.* تَخْدِيرٌ

anesthesize *v.* خَدَّرَ

anesthetic *n.* مُخَدِّرٌ

annex *v.* أَلْحَقَ

annexation *n.* إِلْحاقٌ

anonymous *a.* بِدُونَ اسْمٍ

antagonism *n.* مُقاوَمَةٌ

antisemite *n.*, antisemitic *a.* ذُو اللاسامِيَّةِ

antisemitism *n.* لاسامِيَّةٌ

apartment house *n.* مَنْزِلٌ

appendectomy *n.* جَذْمُ الزائِدَةِ الدُودِيَّةِ

appendix *n.* زائِدَةٌ دُودِيَّةٌ

appetizer *n.* مُشَهٍّ

arbitration *n.* تَحْكِيمٌ

arbitration board *n.* لَجْنَةٌ تَحْكِيمِيَّةٌ

arbitrator *n.* مُحَكِّمٌ

armored car *n.* سَيّارَةٌ مُصَفَّحَةٌ

arthritis *n.* إِلْتِهابُ المَفاصِلِ

aseptic *a.* مُعَقِّمٌ

aspirin *n.* أَسْبِيرِينٌ

assimilate *v.* مَثَّلَ

assimilation *n.* تَمَثُّلٌ

atheism *n.* كَفْرانٌ

atheist *n.* كافِرٌ

atmospheric *a.* جَوِّيٌّ

atom bomb *n.* قُنْبُلَةٌ ذَرِّيَّةٌ

atomic *a.* ذَرِّيٌّ

atomic fission *n.* شَقُّ الذَرَّةِ

atomic warfare *n.* مُحارَبَةٌ ذَرِّيَّةٌ

atomizer *n.* عَفّارَةٌ

audition *n.* سَماعٌ

aureomycin *n.* أُورْيُومِيسِينٌ

author *n.* مُؤَلِّفٌ

authorization *n.* إِجَازَةٌ

authorize *v.* أَجَازَ

automatic *a.* مُتَحَرِّكٌ بِذَاتِهِ

automobile *n.* سَيَّارَةٌ

autonomous *a.* مُسْتَقِلٌّ

autonomy *n.* إِسْتِقْلَالٌ

autopsy *n.* تَشْرِيحٌ

aviator *n.* طَيَّارٌ

bacillus *n.* جُرْثُومَةٌ

backlog *n.* بَقَايَا عَمَلٍ

bacteriology *n.* عِلْمُ ٱلْجَرَاثِيمِ

ball bearing *n.* لُقْمَةٌ ذَاتَ كُرًى

balloon *n.* مُنْطَادٌ

ball point pen *n.* قَلَمُ ٱلْحِبْرِ ٱلْجَافِّ

band leader *n.* مُدِيرُ ٱلْجَوْقِ

bank account *n.* حِسَابٌ

bank rate *n.* سِعْرُ ٱلْفَائِدَةِ

barbed wire *n.* سِلْكٌ شَائِكٌ

battle fatigue *n.* ضَنَى ٱلْحَرْبِ

beachhead *n.* قَائِدَةٌ حَرْبِيَّةٌ

bearish *a.* نُزُولِيٌّ

beautician *n.* صَاحِبُ دَارِ ٱلزِّينَةِ

bicycle *n.* دَرَّاجَةٌ

bifocals *n. pl.* نَظَّارَاتٌ ذَوَاتُ نُقْطَتَيِ اجْتِمَاعِ ٱلنُّورِ

big shot *n.* رَجُلٌ مُهِمٌّ

billion *n.* أَلْفُ مِلْيُونٍ

bimonthly *a.* مَا يَظْهَرُ كُلَّ شَهْرَيْنِ

biochemical *a.* مُخْتَصٌّ بِالْكِيمِيَاءِ الاحْيَائِيَّةِ

biochemistry *n.* كِيمِيَاءُ أَحْيَائِيَّةٌ

biology *n.* عِلْمُ الأَحْيَاءِ

bipartisan *a.* لِكِلَي ٱلحِزْبَيْنِ

bisexual *a.* لِكِلَي ٱلجِنْسَيْنِ

blackboard *n.* سَبُّورَةٌ

black list *n.* قَائِمَةٌ سَوْدَاءُ

blacklist *v.* قَاطَعَ

blockade *n.* مُحَاصَرَةٌ

blood bank *n.* مَخْزَنُ ٱلدَّمِ

blood group *n.* صَفُّ ٱلدَّمِ

blood test *n.* فَحْصُ ٱلدَّمِ

blood transfusion *n.* نَقْلُ ٱلدَّمِ

blueprint *n.* رَسْمٌ هَنْدَسِيٌّ

board of education *n.* مَصْلَحَةُ ٱلتَّرْبِيَةِ

board of health *n.* مَصْلَحَةُ ٱلصِّحَّةِ

bomber *n.* مُقَنْبِلَةٌ

bomb sight *n.* آلَةٌ تَصْوِيبِيَّةٌ لِلْقَذْفِ بِالْقَنَابِلِ

boner *n.* غَلْطَةٌ كَبِيرَةٌ

book jacket *n.* لِفَافَةُ ٱلْكِتَابِ

book review *n.* إِنْتِقَادٌ

boost *n.* إِكْثَارٌ

boric acid *n.* حَامِضٌ بُورِقِيٌّ

box office *n.* صُنْدُوقُ سِينَمَاءَ أَوْ مَرْسَحٍ

boycott *v.* قَاطَعَ

boyscout *n.* كَشْفِيٌّ

brass hat *n.* ضَابِطٌ عَالٍ

bra(ssiere) *n.* عَنْتَرِي

bridgehead *n.* رَأْسُ ٱلْجِسْرِ

broadcast *n.* إِذَاعَةٌ

broadcast *v.* أَذَاعَ

broker *n.* سِمْسَارٌ

brokerage *n.* سَمْسَرَةٌ

bronchitis *n.* نَزْلَةٌ صَدْرِيَّةٌ

budget *n.* (pol.) مُقَرَّرُ ٱلْمِيزَانِيَّةِ

buffer state *n.* دَوْلَةٌ مُتَوَسِّطَةٌ وَمُتَحَايِدَةٌ

bulldozer *n.* آلَةٌ لِبِنَاءِ ٱلطُّرُقِ

bungalow *n.* دَارٌ خَارِجَ ٱلْمَدِينَةِ

bunker *n.* مَلْجَأٌ عَسْكَرِيٌّ

bureaucracy *n.* نَسَقٌ مُوَظَّفِيٌّ

bus *n.* حَافِلَةٌ

cablegram *n.* بَرْقِيَّةٌ

caesarian section *n.* عَمَلِيَّةٌ قَيْصَرِيَّةٌ

calculating machine *n.* آلَةٌ حَاسِبَةٌ

calorie *n.* حَرَارِيَّةٌ

camera *n.* آلَةُ ٱلتَّصْوِيرِ

camouflage *v.* أَخْفَى

can opener *n.* فَتَّاحَةٌ

canopy *n.* مَظَلَّةٌ

capitalism *n.* رَأْسَمَالِيَّةٌ

capitalist *n.* رَأْسَمَالِيٌّ

cardiac *a.* قَلْبِيٌّ

cardiogram *n.* رَسْمٌ قَلْبِيٌّ

carfare *n.* ثَمَنُ ٱلتَّذْكَرَةِ

cartoon *n.* صُورَةٌ هَزْلِيَّةٌ

cash register *n.* صُنْدُوقٌ مُسَجِّلٌ

catalogue *n.* قَائِمَةٌ

ceiling price *n.* مُعْظَمُ ٱلثَّمَنِ

certificate of origin *n.* تَذْكَرَةُ ٱلْأَصْلِ

chain reaction *n.* رَدُّ ٱلْفِعْلِ ٱلْمُسَلْسَلُ

chauffeur *n.* سَائِق

checkroom *n.* غُرْفَةٌ لِحفْظِ ٱلثِيَابِ

checkup *n.* (med.) فَحْص

chiropodist *n.* إِخْتِصَاصِيٌّ لِمعَالَجةِ ٱلأَقْدَامِ

class-conscious *a.* مُدْرِكٌ طَبَقَتِه

classified ad *n.* إِعْلاَنٌ مبوَّب

class struggle *n.* حَرْبُ ٱلطَبَقَاتِ

coalition *n.* تَحَالُف

codefendant *n.* شَرِيكُ ٱلمُدَّعَى عَلَيْهِ

coed *n.* تِلْمِيذَةٌ

coefficient *n.* مُعَدَّل

cold war *n.* أَلْحَرْبُ ٱلبَرِيدَةُ

cold wave *n.* دَوْرَةُ ٱلبَرْدِ

collateral *n.* جَانِبيٌّ

collective agreement *n.* مُعَاهَدَةٌ جَمَاعِيَّةٌ

collective security *n.* الأَمَنُ ٱلمُشْتَرَك

commander-in-chief *n.* قَائِدٌ عام

commentator *n.* مُفَسِّرُ ٱلأَخْبَارِ

commercial college *n.* مَدْرَسَةٌ تِجَارِيَّةٌ

commissar *n.* مُعْتَمَدٌ شُيُوعِي

communism *n.* شُيُوعِيَّةٌ

communist *n.* شُيُوعِي

compartment *n.* شَقَّةٌ

concentration camp *n.* مُعَسْكَرُ ٱلاعْتِقَالِ،

contraceptive *n.* مُضَادَّاتٌ لِلْحَبَلِ

co-operative *n.* جَمْعِيَّةٌ تَعَاوُنِيَّةٌ

correligionist *n.* شَرِيكُ ٱلدِينِ

coughdrop *n.* بَسْتِيلِيَّةٌ لِلسُّعْلَةِ

crematory *n.* مَحَلُّ إِحْرَاقِ ٱلْجُثَثِ

current *n.* تَيَّارٌ

cutthroat *n.* سَفَّاحٌ

cyclotron *n.* سِيكْلُو تْرُون

darkroom *n.* حُجْرَةٌ مَظْلَمَةٌ لِتَوْضِيحِ تَصَاوِيرَ

deadline *n.* مِيعَادٌ آخِرٌ

death rate *n.* نِسْبَةُ ٱلْمَوْتِ

decode *v.* قَرَأَ مَكْتُوبًا شِفْرِيًّا

deep freeze *n.* بَرَّادَةٌ شَدِيدَةٌ

defrost *v.* أَذَابَ ٱلْجَلِيدَ فِى خِزَانَةِ ٱلثَّلْجِ

dehydrated *a.* مُجَرَّدٌ عَنِ ٱلْمَاءِ

demobilization *n.* حَلُّ ٱلْجَيْشِ .

demobilize *v.* حَلَّ ٱلْجَيْشَ

democracy *n.* دِيمُوقْرَاطِيَّةٌ

democrat *n.* دِيمُوقْرَاطِيٌّ

democratic *a.* دِيمُوقْرَاطِيٌّ

depth charge *n.* قُنْبُلَةٌ مُضَادَّةٌ لِلْغَوَّاصَاتِ

derrick *n.* مِرْفَعَةٌ

detective story *n.* رِوَايَةٌ بُولِيسِيَّةٌ

detergent *n.* مُطَهِّرٌ

devaluation *n.* تَنْزِيلٌ نَقْدِيٌّ

develop *v.* تَطَوَّرَ

diabetes *n.* مَرَضُ ٱلْبَوْلِ ٱلسُّكَّرِيِّ

diagnose *v.* شَخَّصَ مَرَضًا

diagnosis *n.* تَشْخِيصُ مَرَضٍ

diagnostician *n.* طَبِيبٌ تَشْخِيصِيٌّ

dialectic *a.* مَنْطِقِيٌّ

diathermy *n.* عِلَاجٌ كَهْرَبَائِيٌّ

dictaphone *n.* آلَةٌ اسْتِكْتَابِيَّةٌ

dictatorship *n.* إِسْتِبْدَادٌ

differential calculus *n.* حِسَابُ ٱلتَّفَاضُلِ

dining car *n.* عَرَبَةُ ٱلْأَكْلِ

directory *n.* دَلِيلٌ

disarmament *n.* نَزْعُ ٱلسِّلَاحِ

disinfectant *n.* مُعَقِّمٌ

dive bomber *n.* طَائِرَةُ ٱلِانْقِضَاضِ

dividend *n.* (profit share) حِصَّةٌ فِي ٱلرِّبْحِ

doublecross *v.* خَانَ

double talk *n.* كَلَامُ ذِي لِسَانَيْنِ

doughboy *n.* عَسْكَرِيٌّ أَمِيرِكِيٌّ

driveway *n.* مَدْخَلٌ لِلسَّيَّارَاتِ

druggist *n.* عَطَّارٌ

drugstore *n.* دُكَّانُ ٱلْعِطَارَةِ

duty-free *a.* خَالِصٌ مِنَ ٱلْكُمْرُوكِ

earmark *v.* خَصَّصَ

earphone *n.* سَمَّاعَةٌ

editor *n.* مُحَرِّرٌ

editorial *n.* إِفْتِتَاحِيَّةٌ

efficiency *n.* إِقْتِدَارٌ

electrician *n.* كَهْرَبَائِيٌّ

electrification *n.* كَهْرَبَةٌ

electrocute *v.* قَتَلَ بِٱلْكَهْرَبَاءِ

electrocution *n.* قَتْلٌ بِٱلْكَهْرَبَاءِ

electrode *n.* عَمُودٌ كَهْرَبَائِيٌّ

electromagnet *n.* مَغْنَطِيس كَهْرَبائِي

electron *n.* كَهْرَب

electronic *a.* كَهارِبي

electronics *n.* عِلْمُ ٱلْكَهارِب

elementary school *n.* مَدْرَسَةٌ أَوَّلِيَّة

elevated railway *n.* سِكَّةُ ٱلْحَدِيد ٱلْمُرْتَفِعَة

elevator *n.* مِصْعَدَة

emergency exit *n.* مَخْرَج عِنْدَ ٱلضَّرُورَة

emotions *n.* حِسِّيات

employment agency *n.* مَكْتَب ٱلتَّخْدِيم

encyclopedia *n.* دائِرَةُ ٱلْمَعارِف

endocrine gland *n.* غُدَّةٌ صَمَّاء

enemy alien *n.* أَجْنَبِي عَدائِي

eraser *n.* مِمْحاة

escalator *n.* سُلَّم مُتَحَرِّك

executive *n.* مُنَفِّذ

extremist *n.* مُتَطَرِّف

fascism *n.* فاشِيَّة

fascist *n.* فاشِي

fertilizer *n.* سَماد

feudalism *n.* إِقْطاعِيَّة

fighter bomber *n.* طائِرَةُ ٱلْقِتال ٱلْقَذَّافَة

figurehead *n.* رَئِيس بِالِاسْم

filing cabinet *n.* خِزانَةُ ٱلْمَلَفَّات

fingerprint *n.* طابِعُ ٱلْأَصابِع

fingerprint *v.* أَخَذَ طابِعَ ٱلْأَصابِع

fire department *n.* إِطْفائِيَّة

fire escape *n.* سُلَّمُ ٱلنَّجاة

fire extinguisher *n.* مِطْفَأَةٌ

fire power *n.* قُوَّةُ ٱلنَّارِ

firing squad *n.* فِرْقَةُ ٱلإِعْدَامِ

first aid *n.* إِسْعَافٌ

fission *n.* شِقٌّ

fissionable *a.* مَايَقْدِرْ أَنْ يَشَقّْ

flame thrower *n.* رَامِي ٱللَّهِيبِ

flirt *n.* مُغَازَلَةٌ

flirt *v.* غَازَلَ

floodlight *n.* نُورٌ كَشَّافٌ

fluorescent *a.* فُلُورِيٌّ

forced landing *n.* نُزُولٌ مَجْبُورٌ

fountain pen *n.* قَلَمُ ٱلْحِبْرِ

frankfurter *n.* مَقَانِقٌ صَغِيرٌ

freshman *n.* طَالِبُ السَّنَةِ ٱلأُولَى

garbage can *n.* صُنْدُوقُ ٱلْقُمَامَةِ

gas attack *n.* هُجُومٌ بِٱلْغَازِ

gasoline *n.* بَنْزِينٌ

gas station *n.* مَحَلُّ ٱلْبَنْزِينِ

general delivery *n.* يُطْلَبُ مِنَ ٱلْبُوسْطَةِ

general staff *n.* هَيْئَةُ أَرْكَانِ ٱلْحَرْبِ

generator *n.* مُوَلِّدٌ

gentile *n.* غَيْرُ ٱلْيَهُودِيِّ

glamour girl *n.* جَارِيَةٌ جَاذِبَةٌ

glider *n.* طَائِرَةٌ شِرَاعِيَّةٌ

golf *n.* كُلْفٌ

grippe *n.* نَزْلَةٌ وَافِدَةٌ

ground floor *n.* اَلطَّبَقَةُ ٱلسُّفْلَى

hack *a.* رَثٌّ

handout *n.* هَدِيَّةٌ

hangar *n.* وَكْرٌ

hanger *n.* عَلَّاقٌ

hangover *n.* غَشَيَانٌ بَعْدَ الشُّرْبِ

hay fever *n.* نَزْلَةٌ يُسَبِّبُهَا نَوْعُ عُشْبٍ

headline *n.* تَرْوِيسَةٌ

health insurance *n.* تَأْمِينٌ ضِدَّ الأَمْرَاضِ

heater *n.* آلَةُ التَّسْخِينِ

heating *n.* تَسْخِينٌ

heatwave *n.* دَوْرَةُ الْحَرَارَةِ

heavyweight *n.* وَزْنٌ ثَقِيلٌ

heckler *n.* مُقَاطِعُ الْكَلَامِ

helicopter *n.* طَائِرَةٌ عَمُودِيَّةٌ

hemorrhage *n.* نَزِيفٌ

highball *n.* وِيسْكِي

high frequency *n.* تَوَاتُرٌ عَالٍ

highlight *n.* أَلنُّقْطَةُ الْهُمّى

high pressure *n.*
high tension *n.* ضَغْطٌ عَالٍ

highway *n.* طَرِيقٌ عَامٌّ

hike *n.* جَوْلَةٌ

holding company *n.* شِرْكَةُ الشِّرْكَاتِ

holdup *n.* نَهْبٌ

honeydew melon *n.* بِطِّيخٌ أَصْفَرُ

hoodlum *n.* وَغْدٌ

hookup *n.* تَوْصِيلٌ مُتَكَاثِرٌ

hormone *n.* هُورْمُونٌ

horoscope *n.* طَالِعٌ فِي التَّنْجِيمِ

horsepower *n.* قُوَّةُ حِصَانٍ

hot dog *n.* مَقَانِقُ مَقْلِيٌّ

housewarming *n.* عِيدُ ٱلإِنْتِقَالِ إِلَى بَيْتٍ جَدِيدٍ

hush money *n.* رِشْوَةٌ

hydrant *n.* حَنَفِيَّةٌ فِى شَارِعٍ لِلْإِطْفَائِيَّةِ

hydraulic *a.* مَائِىٌّ

hydroelectric *a.* عَنِ ٱلْكَهْرَبَاءِ ٱلْمَائِيَّةِ

hydrogen *n.* هِيدرُوجِين

hydroplane *n.* طَائِرَةٌ بَحْرِيَّةٌ

hygiene *n.* عِلْمُ ٱلصِّحَّةِ

hypertrophy *n.* زِيَادَةٌ مُفْرِطَةٌ

hypnosis *n.* تَنْوِيمٌ

hypodermic *a.* تَحْتَ ٱلْأَدِيمِ

hysteria *n.* هِسْتِيرِيَا

icebox *n.* خِزَانَةُ ٱلثَّلْجِ

ice breaker *n.* حَاطِمَةُ ٱلْجَلِيدِ

identification *n.* تَذْكِرَةُ إِثْبَاتِ ٱلشَّخْصِيَّةِ

ideology *n.* نَسَقُ ٱلْأَفْكَارِ

ignition *n.* إِلْهَابٌ

incinerator *n.* آلَةٌ لِحَرْقِ ٱلفَضَلَاتِ

Inc. *a.* شِرْكَةٌ مُسَجَّلَةٌ

incubator *n.* آلَةُ ٱلتَّفْرِيخِ

industrial *a.* صِنَاعِىٌّ

industrialize *v.* جَهَّزَ بِصَنَائِعَ

infantile paralysis *n.* ٱلشَّلَلُ ٱلطِّفْلِىُّ

إِحْسَاس

inferiority complex *n.* اَلْإِنْحِطَاط

infiltrate *v.* إِسْتَرَقَ إِلَى

inflation *n.* تَضَخُّم نَقْدِي

infrared *a.* دُونَ ٱلْأَحْمَرِ

initiative *n.* حَافِزٌ

injection *n.* حُقْنَةٌ

in-laws *n.* أَلْحَمَوَان

insecticide *n.* مُضَادَّاتٌ حَشَرِيَّةٌ

installment plan *n.* تَدْبِيرٌ نَجْمِي

insulator *n.* عَازِلٌ

insulin *n.* إِنْسُولِين

شَرْكَةُ

insurance company *n.* اَلتَّأْمِين

intake *n.* مَدْخَلٌ

interior decorator *n.* مُزَخْرِفٌ

internee *n.* أَسِيرٌ

iodine *n.* يُودٌ

IOU *n.* سَنَدٌ

I.Q. *n.* دَرَجَةُ ٱلْعَقْلِ

iron curtain *n.* أَلسِّتَارُ ٱلْحَدِيدِيُّ

isolationism *n.* عُزْلَةٌ سِيَاسِيَّةٌ

isolationist *n.* تَابِعُ ٱلْعُزْلَةِ ٱلسِّيَاسِيَّةِ

jackpot *n.* أَلْفَوْزُ ٱلْأَكْبَرُ فِي ٱلْمُقَامَرَةِ

jalopy *n.* سَيَّارَةٌ رَثَّةٌ

jaywalk *v.* مَشَى عَلَى غَفْلَةٍ

jazz *n.* جَزٌّ

jeep *n.* سَيَّارَةٌ «جِيب»

jet plane *n.* طَائِرَةٌ نَفَّاثَةٌ

jet propulsion *n.* أَلتَّسْيِيرُ ٱلنَّفَّاثِيُّ

jig saw puzzle *n.* لُغْزُ قِطَعٍ كَثِيرَةٍ

jurisdiction *n.* إِخْتِصَاصٌ

juror *n.* مُحَلَّفٌ

juvenile *a.* صِبْيَانِيٌّ

kerosene *n.* نِفْطٌ

kindergarten *n.* رَوْضَةُ ٱلْأَطْفَالِ

know-how *n.* مَعْرِفَةٌ وَٱخْتِبَارٌ

labor market *n.* سُوقُ ٱلْعَمَلِ

landslide *n.* إِنْهِيَالُ ٱلْأَرْضِ

layer cake *n.* نَوْعُ كَعْكٍ

layette *n.* ثِيَابٌ لِطِفْلٍ وَلِيدٍ

lay-off *n.* رَفْتٌ

layout *n.* تَرْتِيبٌ

League of Nations *n.* عُصْبَةُ ٱلْأُمَمِ

leftover *n.* بَقَايَا

lending library *n.* مَكْتَبَةٌ إِعَارِيَّةٌ

lens *n.* عَدَسَةٌ

liability insurence *n.* تَأْمِينٌ عَلَى ٱلْمَسْؤُولِيَّةِ

life expectancy *n.* إِنْتِظَارُ ٱلْحَيَاةِ

life insurance *n.* تَأْمِينٌ عَلَى ٱلْحَيَاةِ

lighter *n.* قَدَّاحٌ

lipstick *n.* مِرْوَدٌ

living wage *n.* أَجْرٌ كَافٍ

loudspeaker *n.* حَاكٍ

lubricating oil *n.* زَيْتُ تَشْحِيمٍ

mailbox *n.* صُنْدُوقٌ لِلْمَكَاتِيبِ

make-up *n.* زِينَةُ ٱلْوَجْهِ

maneuver *n.* مُنَاوَرَةٌ

manicure *n.* تَنْظِيفُ ٱلْأَظْفَارِ

markdown *n.*	تنزيل الثمن
mechanized *n.*	ميكاني
meningitis *n.*	الالتهاب السحائي
menu *n.*	قائمة الطعام
merchant marine *n.*	البحرية التجارية
metabolism *n.*	إبدال المواد في الجسم
microfilm *n.*	ميكروفلم
microphone *n.*	مصوات
microscope *n.*	مجهر
military police *n.*	الشرطة العسكرية
mine sweeper *n.*	لاقطة الألفام
minimum wage *n.*	الأجر الأصغر
mixup *n.*	إرتباك
moderator *n.*	مرتب
motion picture *n.*	صورة متحركة
motorbike *n.*	عجلة نارية
motorboat *n.*	قارب نارى
motorcade *n.*	موكب سيارات
motorist *n.*	سائق سيارة
motor plough *n.*	محراث آلي
motor truck *n.*	سيارة النقل
museum *n.*	متحف
narcosis *n.*	تنويم
Nazi *n.*	نازى
neon light *n.*	ضوء نيوني
network *n.*	شبكة
neuralgia *n.*	نيورالجية
newscast *n.*	إذاعة الأخبار
newsreel *n.*	جريدة ناطقة

newsstand *n.* دُكّانُ جَرائِدَ

nonaggression pact *n.* مُعاهَدَةُ عَدَمِ ٱلإِعْتِداءِ

notarize *v.* شَهِدَ قانُونِيًّا

nuclear physics *n.* عِلْمُ ٱلذَّرّاتِ

nudism *n.* عُرْيانِيَّةٌ

nursery school *n.* رَوْضَةُ ٱلأَطْفالِ

nutritionist *n.* إِخْتِصاصِيٌّ بِٱلغِذاءِ

nylon *n.* نَيْلُونٌ

obstetrician *n.* طَنِيبٌ مُوَلِّدٌ

off limits *n.* مُحَرَّمٌ عَلى ٱلعَساكِرِ

overpass *n.* مَعْبَرٌ

pajamas *n. pl.* بِيجاما

pancake *n.* كَعْكَةُ طاجِنٍ

panel discussion *n.* مُباحَثَةٌ عُمُومِيَّةٌ

parachute *n.* مِظَلَّةٌ واقِيَةٌ

parachutist *n.* جُنْدِيُّ ٱلمِظَلَّةِ

paralysis *n.* فالِجٌ

paranoia *n.* جُنُونٌ

paratrooper *n.* جُنْدِيُّ ٱلمِظَلَّةِ

parking lot *n.* مَوْقِفٌ

patent *n.* إِجازَةُ ٱلحَصْرِ

patrolman *n.* شُرْطِيٌّ

pediatrician *n.* طَبِيبُ أَمْراضِ ٱلأَطْفالِ

pediatrics *n.* أَلطِّبُّ ٱلطِّفْلِيُّ

pedicure *n.* تَنْظِيفُ أَظْفارِ ٱلأَرْجُلِ

penicillin *n.* بِنِيسِلِّينٌ

percolator *n.* مِصْفاةُ ٱلقَهْوَةِ

periscope *n.* مِنْظَرُ ٱلغَوّاصَةِ

permanent wave *n.* تَموِيج

petty officer *n.* ضَابِطُ ٱلصَّفِّ

phone *n.* تَلِيفُونٌ

phonograph *n.* حَاكٍ

phony *a.*, *n.* كَاذِبٌ

photostat *n.* نُسْخَةٌ فُوتُوغْرَافِيَّةٌ

physics *n.* عِلْمُ ٱلطَّبِيعَةِ

physiognomy *n.* سَحْنَةٌ

physiology *n.* عِلْمُ وَظَائِفِ ٱلأَعْضَاءِ

picket *n.* صَفُّ مُضْرِبِينَ

picnic *n.* أَكْلٌ فِي ٱلعَرَاءِ

piecework *n.* أَلعَمَلُ بِٱلقِطَعِ

pigment *n.* صِبَاغٌ

pinch-hit *n.* بَدَلَ

pinup (girl) *n.* تَصْوِيرَةُ جَارِيَةٍ ٱلمُعَلَّقَةُ بِٱلجِدَارِ

plainclothes man *n.* مُخْبِرٌ شُرْطِيٌّ

plebiscite *n.* إِسْتِفْتَاءُ ٱلشَّعْبِ

plutonium *n.* بْلُوتُونِيُومُ

pneumatic *a.* هَوَائِيٌّ

poison ivy *n.* أَلسُّمَّاقُ ٱلسَّامُّ

polio(myelitis) *n.* أَلشَّلَلُ ٱلطِّفْلِيُّ

pornography *n.* تَأْلِيفٌ فَحَّاشٌ

potential *a.* مُمْكِنٌ

potential *n.* إِمْكَانِيَّةٌ

pressure cooker *n.* طَنْجَرَةٌ ذَاتُ بُخَارٍ مَضْغُوطٍ

price-cutting *n.* تَنْزِيلُ ٱلأَثْمَانِ بِٱلتَّزَاحُمِ

professional *a.* مُحْتَرِف

profiteer *n.* رَابِح

propaganda *n.* دَعَاوَة

propeller *n.* مِرْوَحَة

protein *n.* بُرُوتِين

pseudonym *n.* إِسْم مُسْتَعَار

psychiatry *n.* اَلطِّبُّ النَّفْسَانِي

psychoanalysis *n.* تَحْلِيل نَفْسِيّ

psychopath *n.* مَرِيض نَفْسِيّ

public prosecutor *n.* نَائِب عَامّ

pullover *n.* سُتْرَة صُوفِيَّة

pulp magazine *n.* مَجَلَّة رَائِجَة

pursuit plane *n.* طَائِرَةُ الْمُطَارَدَة

quantum theory *n.* نَظَرِيَّةُ الْكَمّ

questionnaire *n.* وَرَقَةُ سُؤَالَات

quinine *n.* كِينَا

racket *n.* شِرْكَةُ مُذْنِبِين

racketeer *n.* جَانٍ

radar *n.* رَادَار

radiator *n.* آلَة مُسَخِّنَة

radio *n.* لَاسِلْكِيّ

turn on the radio فَتَحَ

turn off the radio قَطَعَ

radio *v.* أَذَاعَ

radioactive *a.* ذُو رَادِيُوم فَاعِل

radio broadcast *n.* إِذَاعَة لَاسِلْكِيَّة

radio frequency *n.* تَوَاتُر لَاسِلْكِيّ

radiogram *n.* رِسَالَة لَاسِلْكِيَّة

radio network *n.* شَبَكَة لَاسِلْكِيَّة

radio station *n.* مَحَطَّة لَاسِلْكِيَّة

radio transmitter *n.* مُرْسِلَة

radium *n.* رَادِيوم

rate of exchange *n.* سِعْرُ الصَّرْف

rationalize *v.* وَجَدَ سَبَبًا فِى الذِّهْنِ

rationing *n.* حَصْرُ التَّمْوِين

rear light *n.* ضَوْءٌ خَلْفِى

rebroadcast *n.* إِعَادَةُ إِذَاعَة

receiver *n.* قَابِل

(in bankruptcy) مُسْتَقْبِلُ أَمْوَالِ الإِفْلَاسِ;

(tel.) سَمَّاعَة;

(radio) مُسْتَقْبِل

receptionist *n.* مُسْتَخْدَمَةُ الإِسْتِقْبَالِ

reconnaissance *n.* (mil.) إِسْتِكْشَاف

record *n.* (phonograph) أُسْطُوَانَة

record changer *n.* مُبَدِّلُ الأُسْطُوَانَات

red tape *n.* إِجْرَاءَاتٌ عَقِيمَة

reference book *n.* كِتَابُ الْمَرْجِع

refrigerator *n.* خِزَانَةُ الثَّلْج

refugee *n.* مُلْتَجِئٌ

refund *n.* رَدُّ النُّقُودِ

refund *v.* رَدَّ

registration *n.* تَسْجِيل

relativity *n.* نِسْبِيَّة

rental library *n.* مَكْتَبَةٌ إِعَارِيَّة

reorganization *n.* إِعَادَةُ التَّنْظِيم

reporter *n.* مُخْبِرُ جَرِيدَة

rest room *n.* مُسْتَرَاح

retroactive *a.* فَاعِلٌ إِلَى الْمَاضِى

reviewer *n.* نَقَّاد

revolutionize *v.* قَلَّبَ

revolver *n.* مُسَدَّس

revue *n.* إِسْتِعْرَاض

rheumatism *n.* رَثْيَة

ringleader *n.* زَعِيم

rocket *n.* صَارُوخ

roller skate *n.* مَزْلَقَان ذَوَا عَجَلاتٍ

rolling mill *n.* آلَةُ ٱلتَّصْفِيح

roundtrip *n.* جَوْلَةٌ وَعَوْدَة

saccharine *n.* سَكَارِين

safety belt *n.* حِزَامُ ٱلأَمْنِ

safety pin *n.* دَبُّوس إِنْكِلِيزِي

sanitarium *n.* مَصَحّ

satellite country *n.* بِلَادٌ مُتَوَقِّفَة

saxophone *n.* سَكْسُوفُن

scholarship *n.* (grant) مِنَحُ نَفَقَة لِتِلْمِيذٍ

Scotch tape *n.* شَرِيطٌ غِرَائِي

scrapbook *n.* كَشْكُول

screen actor *n.* مُمَثِّل سِينَمائِي

searchlight *n.* نُورٌ كَاشِف

secret service *n.* أَلْخِدْمَةُ ٱلسِّرِّيَّةُ

semifinal *n.* مُبَارَاة نِصْف نِهَائِيّ

semimonthly *a.* نِصْف شَهْرِيّ

semimonthly *n.* مَجَلَّةٌ نِصْف شَهْرِيَّة

serialization *n.* نَشْرٌ بِتَسَلْسُلٍ

serialize *v.* نَشَرَ بِتَسَلْسُلٍ

serviceman *n.* عَسْكَرِي

sewing machine *n.* آلَةُ ٱلخِيَاطَة

sex appeal *n.* جَذْب جِنْسِي

shack *n.* كُوخ

shipping room *n.* غُرْفَةُ ٱلشَّحْن

shock troops *n. pl.* عساكرُ الهجُوم

short-change *v.* (cheat) غبن

short circuit *n.* دَائرَة قصيرَة

shorthand *n.* تدْميج

short wave *n.* موْج قصِير

shower bath *n.* منْضح

sibling *n.* طفْل

side dish *n.* طعَام جانِبي

side line *n.* شغْل جانِبي

sightseeing *n.* تفرّج

signatory powers *n. pl.* الدُّوَل الموَقّعة

signpost *n.* نصْبة

silkscreen *n.* حجاب حرِيري

skyscraper *n.* ناطحَةُ السَّحاب

skywriting *n.* كِتَابَة على السماء

slacks *n. pl.* جِنْس بنْطلُون

slick magazine *n.* مجلّة ظرِيفة

slot machine *n.* آلةُ لعْبِ القِمارِ

small change *n.* فُرَاطة

snapshot *n.* صُورَة حاليّة

soccer *n.* لَعْب كُرَة القدَم

socialism *n.* إشْترَاكيّة

socialist *n*, socialist(ic) *a.* إشْترَاكِي

socialized medicine *n.* الطّبّ المشْترَك

sociology *n.* عِلم الإجْتماعِ

social security *n.* تأمِين اجْتماعِي

social service *n.*, social work *n.* خدْمَة اجْتماعيّة

soda fountain (counter) *n.* مائدَة الأشْرِبة

sophisticated *a.* أَدِيبٌ

soundtrack *n.* شَرِيطٌ نَاطِقٌ

Soviet Union *n.* إِتِّحَادُ ٱلسُّوفْيَت

space ship *n.* سَفِينَةٌ فَضَائِيَّةٌ

space travel *n.* سَفَرٌ فِى ٱلْفَضَاءِ

spank *v.* ضَرَبَ طِفْلاً

spark plug *n.* شَمْعَةُ ٱلشَّرَارَةِ

spastic *a.* تَشَنُّجِىٌّ

special delivery *n.* تَوْزِيعٌ مُسْتَعْجِلٌ

specialist *n.* إِخْتِصَاصِىٌّ

spectroscope *n.* مِطْيَافٌ

sponsor *n.* كَفِيلٌ

sponsor *v.* كَفَلَ

spool *n.* مِكَبٌّ

sporadic *a.* مُتَفَرِّقٌ

sport *n.* رِيَاضَةٌ

spotter *n.* مُرَاقِبٌ

spring *n.* (techn.) لَوْلَبٌ

standardization *n.* تَسْوِيَةٌ بِمِقْيَاسٍ أَحَدٍ

standardize *v.* سَوَّى بِمِقْيَاسٍ أَحَدٍ

standard of living *n.* مُسْتَوَى ٱلْحَيَاةِ

standing room *n.* فُسْحَةُ ٱلْوَاقِفِينَ

stateroom *n.* قَمَرَةُ ٱلدَّرَجَةِ ٱلأُولَى

statistician *n.* إِحْصَائِىٌّ

statistics *n.* إِحْصَائِيَّةٌ

steam shovel *n.* مِجْرَافٌ بُخَارِىٌّ

stenographer *n.* مُدَمِّجٌ

stenography *n.* تَدْمِيجٌ

sterilization *n.* تَعْقِيمٌ

stickup *n.* لُصوصِيَّة

stockbroker *n.* سِمْسارُ ٱلأَسْهُم

stock market *n.* سوقُ ٱلأَسْهُم

storage *n.* تخزِين

streetwalker *n.* عاهِرَة

stretcher *n.* مِحَفَّة

strikebreaker *n.* كاسِرُ ٱلاِضْراب

studio *n.* مُحْتَرَف

stuffed shirt *n.* (fig.) رَجُل مُتَكَبِّر

subconscions *n.* أَلْعَقْلُ ٱلباطِن

subcontract *n.* عَقْد فَرْعِيّ

subcontractor *n.* مُقاوِل فَرْعِيّ

submarine *n.* غَوَّاصَة

subsidiary *n.* (fin.) شَرِكَة مُساعِدَة

subsidize *v.* قَدَّمَ إِعانَةً

subsidy *n.* إِعانَة

substandard *a.* تَحْتَ ٱلمِقْياس

subtenant *n.* مُكْتَرٍ ثانٍ

subversive *a.* ثَوْرَوِيّ

subway *n.* سِكَّة تَحْتَ ٱلأَرْض

suitcase *n.* حَقيبَة

sunlamp *n.* مِصْباح ضَوْء فَوْقَ ٱلبَنَفْسَجِيّ

supreme commander *n.* أَلقائِدُ ٱلعامّ

suspender *n.* رَبْطَةُ ٱلسَّاق

suspension bridge *n.* جِسْر مُعَلَّق

switchboard *n.* مَرْكَزُ ٱلتِّلِيفون

swivel chair *n.* كُرْسِيّ دائِر

syndicate *n.* نِقابَة

synopsis *n.*	تَلْخِيص
tabloid *n.*	جَرِيدَةٌ صَغِيرَةُ ٱلْحَجْمِ
tail spin *n.*	شَقْلَبَةُ طَائِرَةٍ
tail wind *n.*	رِيحٌ وَرَائِيَّةٌ
take-off *n.* (av.)	صُعُودٌ
take off *v.* (av.)	صَعِدَ
talcum powder *n.*	ذَرِيرَةٌ طَلْقِيَّةٌ
tank *n.* (mil.)	دَبَّابَةٌ
tank destroyer *n.*	مِدْفَعٌ مُضَادٌّ لِلدَّبَّابَاتِ
task force *n.*	قُوَّةُ عِرَاكٍ
tax-exempt *a.*	مُعَافًى مِنَ ٱلْمُكُوسِ
taxicab *n.*	سَيَّارَةُ ٱلْأُجْرَةِ
taxpayer *n.*	دَافِعُ ٱلضَّرَائِبِ
tear bomb *n.*	قُنْبُلَةٌ دُمْعِيَّةٌ
technology *n.*	هَنْدَسَةٌ
telecast *n.*	إِذَاعَةٌ تَلْفَزِيَّةٌ
telecast *v.*	أَذَاعَ بِٱلتَّلْفَزَةِ
telepathy *n.*	تَبَادُلُ ٱلْخَوَاطِرِ
telephone receiver *n.*	سَمَّاعَةٌ
televise *v.*	تَلْفَزَ
television *n.*	تَلْفَزَةٌ
tenement house *n.*	مَنْزِلٌ
terrorism *n.*	إِرْهَابٌ
terrorist *n.*	إِرْهَابِيٌّ
terrorize *v.*	أَرْهَبَ
therapy *n.*	طَرِيقَةُ ٱلشِّفَاءِ
thyroid gland *n.*	غُدَّةٌ دَرَقِيَّةٌ
tideland *n.*	أَلْبَرُّ ٱلَّذِي يَغْطُوهُ مَدُّ ٱلْبَحْرِ
time exposure *n.*	تَصْوِيرٌ وَقْتِيٌّ

time table *n.* مَوَاقِيت

tip-off *n.* إِشَارَة

toaster *n.* مُقَمِّرٌ كَهْرَبَائِي

tonsilectomy *n.* جَذْمُ ٱللَّوْزَتَيْنِ

toothpaste *n.* مَعْجُونُ ٱلأَسْنَانِ

topnotch *a.* فَائِق

top-secret *a.* سِرِّي جِدًّا

topsoil *n.* طَبَقَةُ ٱلتُّرْبَةِ ٱلفَوْقَانِيَّة

torpedo *n.* حَرَّاقَة

torpedoboat *n.* نَسَّافَة

totalitarianism *n.* أَلْحُكْمُ المُطْلَق

touch-and-go *a.* [risky] خَطِر

tourist class *n.* أَلدَّرَجَةُ ٱلثَّالِثَةُ فِي سَفِينَة

track meet *n.* سِبَاق

trade mark *n.* عَلَامَةٌ تِجَارِيَّة

trade union *n.* نِقَابَةُ ٱلعُمَّال

traffic jam *n.* إِرْتِبَاكُ ٱلحَرَكَة

traffic light *n.* سِرَاجُ ٱلحَرَكَةِ

trainee *n.* مُدَرَّب

travelers' check *n.* حَوَالَةٌ سَفَرِيَّه

trial balloon *n.* تَجْرِيب

trolley car *n.* تَرَام

trouble-shooter *n.* مُسَهِّلُ ٱلمَصَاعِبِ

trustee *n.* أَمِين

tuberculosis *n.* تَدَرُّن

tugboat *n.* رَقَّاص

turnstile *n.* بَابٌ دَوَّار

tycoon *n.* ذُو نُفُوذٍ كَثِير

typescript *n.* مَكْتُوبٌ بِآلَةِ ٱلكِتَابَة

typesetting *n.* أَلْحُرُوفُ المَجْمُوعَة

typewriter *n.* آلَةُ ٱلْكِتَابَةِ

typewriting *n.* كِتَابَةٌ بِٱلآلَةِ

underdeveloped *a.* بِدُونِ تَطَوُّرٍ كَافٍ

underdog *n.* مُضْطَرٌّ

underground *n.* (polit.) حَرَكَةٌ سِيَاسِيَّةٌ سِرِّيَّةٌ

underprivileged *a.* مِسْكِينٌ

unemployment *n.* تَعَطُّلٌ

union *n.* (labor) نِقَابَةٌ

unionize *v.* نَظَّمَ نِقَابَةً

upkeep *n.* حِفْظٌ

utopian *a.* خَيَالِيٌّ

vacationist *n.* مُفَرِّصٌ

vaccinate *v.* لَقَّحَ

vaccination *n.* تَلْقِيحٌ

vacuum cleaner *n.* مِنْفَضَةٌ

vegetarian *n.* نَبَاتِيٌّ

vending machine *n.* آلَةُ ٱلْبَيْعِ

venereal disease *n.* مَرَضٌ سِرِّيٌّ

ventilator *n.* مِهْوَاةٌ

visual aid *n.* مِعْوَانٌ نَظَرِيٌّ

visualize *v.* تَصَوَّرَ

vocational school *n.* مَدْرَسَةُ ٱلصَّنَائِعِ

wage earner *n.* كَاسِبٌ

waiting room *n.* غُرْفَةُ ٱلإِنْتِظَارِ

walkout *n.* إِضْرَابٌ

walkover *n.* نَصْرٌ سَهْلٌ

want ad *n.* إِعْلَانُ ٱلطَّلَبِ

warmonger *n.* مُحَرِّضٌ لِلْحَرْبِ

washed-up *a.* مُضْنًى

washing machine *n.* آلَةُ ٱلْغَسْلِ

washout *n.* (sl.) [failure] فَشَلٌ

water closet *n.* مِرْحَاضٌ

white-collar worker *n.* عَامِلٌ بِعَقْلِهِ

wholesaler *n.* تَاجِرُ ٱلْجُمْلَةِ

wireless *a.* لَاسِلْكِيٌّ

wisecrack *n.* نُكْتَةٌ

wisecrack *v.* نَكَّتَ

wristwatch *n.* سَاعَةُ يَدٍ

xenophobia *n.* كَرَاهَةُ ٱلْأَجَانِبِ

x-ray *n.* أَشِعَّةُ رُنْتْجِن أَوْ إِكْس

xylophone *n.* آلَةٌ مُوسِيقِيَّةٌ

Yugoslavia *n.* يُوغُوسْلَافِيَا

Other Standard Dictionaries from Hippocrene . . .

ALBANIAN-ENGLISH STANDARD DICTIONARY
510pp • 5 ¼ x 7 ½ • 20,000 entries
0-87052-077-6 • $14.95pb • (293)

ARABIC-ENGLISH/ENGLISH-ARABIC STANDARD DICTIONARY
900pp • 5 ½ x 8 ½
0-7818-0383-7 • $24.95 • (195)

CAMBODIAN-ENGLISH/ENGLISH-CAMBODIAN STANDARD DICTIONARY
355pp • 5 ½ x 8 ¼ • 15,000 entries
0-87052-0099-4 • $8.95pb • (411)

DUTCH-ENGLISH/ENGLISH-DUTCH STANDARD DICTIONARY
578pp • 5 ½ x 8 ¼ • 35,000 entries
0-7818-0541-4 • $16.95pb • (629)

GREEK-ENGLISH/ENGLISH-GREEK STANDARD DICTIONARY
686pp • 5 ½ x 8 ½ • 30,000 entries
0-7818-0600-3 • $16.95pb • (695)

HINDI-ENGLISH/ENGLISH-HINDI STANDARD DICTIONARY
800pp • 6 x 9 • 30,000 entries
0-7818-0470-1 • $27.50pb • (559)
0-7818-0387-X • $37.50hc • (280)

HUNGARIAN-ENGLISH STANDARD DICTIONARY
650pp • 4 ½ x 8 ½ • 40,000 entires
0-7818-0390-X • $40.00pb • (43)

ENGLISH-HUNGARIAN STANDARD DICTIONARY
541pp • 4 ½ x 8 ½ • 40,000 entries
0-7818-0391-8 • $40.00pb • (48)

MALAY-ENGLISH/ENGLISH-MALAY STANDARD DICTIONARY
631pp • 7 ¼ x 5 • 21,000 entries
0-7818-0103-6 • $16.95pb • (428)

PERSIAN-ENGLISH STANDARD DICTIONARY
700pp • 5 ½ x 8 ½ • 22,500 entries
0-7818-0055-2 • $19.95 • (350)

ENGLISH-PERSIAN STANDARD DICTIONARY
700pp • 5 ½ x 8 ½ • 40,000 entries
0-7818-0056-2 • $19.95pb • (365)

POLISH-ENGLISH/ENGLISH-POLISH STANDARD DICTIONARY, Revised Edition with Business Terms
780pp • 5 ½ x 8 ½ • 32,000 entries
0-7818-0282-2 • $19.95pb • (298)

PULAAR-ENGLISH/ENGLISH-PULAAR STANDARD DICTIONARY
275pp • 5 ½ x 8 ¼ • 30,000 entries
0-7818-0479-5 • $19.95pb • (600)

ROMANIAN-ENGLISH/ENGLISH-ROMANIAN STANDARD DICTIONARY
800pp • 4 ⅜ x 7 • 18,000 entries
0-7818-0444-2 • $17.95pb • (99)

RUSSIAN-ENGLISH/ENGLISH-RUSSIAN STANDARD DICTIONARY, Revised Edition with Business Terms
418pp • 5 ½ x 8 ½ • 32,000 entries
0-7818-0280-6 • $18.95pb • (322)

Related Titles from Hippocrene . . .

ARABIC-ENGLISH DICTIONARY
450pp • 5 ½ x 8 ¼ • 15,000 entries
0-7818-0153-2 • $14.95pb • (487)

ARABIC HANDY DICTIONARY
120pp • 5 x 7 ¾
0-87052-960-9 • $8.95pb • (463)

ARABIC-ENGLISH LEARNER'S DICTIONARY
467pp • 18,000 entries
0-87052-914-5 • $18.95pb • (flex plastic)

ENGLISH-ARABIC LEARNER'S DICTIONARY
1242pp • 20,000 entries
0-87052-155-9 • $24.95pb • (flex plastic)

MODERN MILITARY DICTIONARY: ENGLISH-ARABIC/ARABIC-ENGLISH
250pp • 5 ½ x 8 ½
0-7818-0243-1 • $14.95pb • (214)

SAUDI ARABIC BASIC COURSE: URBAN HAJAZI DIALECT
288pp • 6 ½ x 8 ½ • 50 lessons
0-7818-0257-1 • $14.95pb • (171)

ENGLISH-HEBREW/HEBREW-ENGLISH CONVERSATIONAL DICTIONARY
Romanized, Revised Edition
160pp • 5 ½ x 8 ½ • 7000 entries
0-7818-0137-0 • $8.95pb • (257)

ROMANIZED ENGLISH-HEBREW/HEBREW-ENGLISH COMPACT DICTIONARY
157pp • 3 ⅛ x 4 ⅝ • 7000 entries
0-7818-0568-6 • $7.95pb • (687)

ENGLISH-HEBREW/HEBREW-ENGLISH DICTIONARY
604pp • 4 ¾ x 6 ½ • 50,000 entries
0-07818-0431-0 • $16.95pb • (484)

KURDISH-ENGLISH/ENGLISH-KURDISH DICTIONARY
400pp • 4 x 6 • 8000 entries
0-7818-0246-6 • $11.95pb • (218)

PERSIAN-ENGLISH STANDARD DICTIONARY
700pp • 5 ½ x 8 ½ • 22,500 entries
0-7818-055-2 • $19.95pb • (350)

ENGLISH-PERSIAN STANDARD DICTIONARY
700pp • 5 ½ x 8 ½ • 40,000 entries
0-7818-0056-0 • $19.95pb • (365)

ENGLISH-TURKISH/TURKISH-ENGLISH CONCISE DICTIONARY
288pp • 3 ⅝ x 5 ⅜
0-7818-0161-3 • $8.95pb • (338)

ENGLISH-TURKISH/TURKISH-ENGLISH POCKET DICTIONARY
523pp • 4 ¾ x 6 ¼ • 35,000 entries
0-87052-812-2 • $14.95pb • (148)

TURKISH HANDY DICTIONARY
120pp • 5 x 7 ¾
0-87052-982-X • $8.95pb • (375)

ENGLISH-TURKISH/TURKISH-ENGLISH STANDARD DICTIONARY
887pp • 5 ½ x 8 ½ • 70,000 entries
0-7818-0381-0 • $29.50pb • (469)

TURKISH-ENGLISH COMPREHENSIVE DICTIONARY
650pp • 6 ¼ x 9 ¾
0-7818-0468-X • $60.00hc • (578)

ENGLISH-TURKISH COMPREHENSIVE DICTIONARY
1293pp • 6 ¼ x 9 ¾
0-7818-0469-8 • $90.00hc • (548)

PRACTICAL ENGLISH-TURKISH HANDBOOK
416pp • 4 ¼ x 6 ½
0-7818-0476-0 • $14.95pb • (558)

Tutorial

ARABIC GRAMAR OF THE WRITTEN LANGUAGE
560pp • 5 ½ x 8 ½
0-87052-101-2 • $19.95pb • (397)

ARABIC FOR BEGINNERS
186pp • 5 ¼ x 8 ¼
0-7818-0114-1 • $9.95pb • (18)

LET US CONVERSE IN ARABIC
156pp • 5 ½ x 8 ½
0-7818-0562-7 • $11.95 • (702)

MASTERING ARABIC
320pp • 5 ¼ x 8 ¼
0-87052-922-6 • $14.95pb • (501)

MALTESE-ENGLISH/ENGLISH-MALTESE DICTIONARY AND PHRASEBOOK
175pp • 3 ¾ x 7 • 1500 entries
0-7818-0565-1 • $11.95pb • (697)

BEGINNER'S PERSIAN
150pp • 5 ½ x 8
0-7818-0567-8 • $14.95pb

THE MODERN PUSHTU INSTRUCTOR
Script and romanized form
343pp • 4 x 8
0-7818-0204-0 • $22.95 • (174)

Cookbooks

THE ART OF PERSIAN COOKING
Forough Hekmat
This collection features such traditional Persian dishes as *Abgushte Adas* (Lentil Soup), *Mosamme Khoresh* (Eggplant Stew), *Lamb Kebab*, *Cucumber Borani* (Special Cucumber Salad), *Sugar Halva* and *Gol Moraba* (Flower Preserves).
190pp • 5 ½ x 8 ½
0-7818-0241-5 • $9.95pb • (125)

THE ART OF TURKISH COOKING
308pp • 5 ½ x 8 ½
0-7818-0201-6 • $12.95pb • (162)

ADDITIONAL TITLES OF INTEREST FROM HIPPOCRENE . . .

Dictionaries

ENGLISH BENGALI DICTIONARY
1354pp • 5 ½ x 8 ½ • 38,000 entries
0-7818-037-X • $28.95hc • (166)

BENGALI-ENGLISH DICTIONARY
1074pp • 5 ½ x 8 ½ • 38,000 entries
0-7818-0372-1 • $28.95hc • (177)

HINDI-ENGLISH/ENGLISH-HINDI STANDARD DICTIONARY
800pp • 6 x 9 • 30,000 entries
0-7818-0470-1 • $27.50pb • (559)
0-7818-0387-X • $37.50hc • (280)

HINDI-ENGLISH/ENGLISH-HINDI PRACTICAL DICTIONARY
745pp • 4 ⅜ x 7 • 25,000 entries
0-7818-0084-6 • $19.95pb • (442)

ENGLISH-HINDI PRACTICAL DICTIONARY
399pp • 4 ⅜ x 7 • 15,000 entries
0-87052-978-1 • $11.95pb • (362)

LEARNER'S HINDI-ENGLISH DICTIONARY
758pp • 5 ½ x 8 ¾ • 10,000 entries
0-7818-0187-7 • $22.50 • (102)

NEPALI-ENGLISH/ENGLISH-NEPALI CONCISE DICTIONARY
286pp • 4 x 6 • 6,000 entries
0-87052-106-3 • $8.95pb • (398)

A SHORTER ENGLISH-NEPALI DICTIONARY
154pp • 4 ¾ x 7 • 2500 entries
0-87052-894-7 • $11.95 • (277)

ENGLISH-PUNJABI DICTIONARY ROMANIZED
498pp • 5 ½ x 8 ½
0-7818-0105-2 • $14.95 • (144)

CONCISE SANSKRIT-ENGLISH DICTIONARY
366pp • 5 x 7 • 18,000 entries
0-7818-0203-2 • $14.95pb • (605)

SINHALESE-ENGLISH DICTIONARY
276pp • 5 ¾ x 8 ¾ • 20,000 entries
0-87052-0219-9 • $24.95 • (319)

URDU-ENGLISH GEM POCKET DICTIONARY
480pp • 4 x 5 • 16,000 entries
0-87052-911-0 • $7.95 • (289)

ENGLISH-URDU DICTIONARY
764pp • 6 x 9
0-7818-0221-0 • $24.95 • (364)

Tutorial

LEARN BENGALI
160pp • 5 x 7
0-7818-0224-5 • $7.95pb • (190)

TEACH YOURSELF HINDI
207pp • 4 ¾ x 7
0-87052-831-9 • $8.95pb • (170)

LEARN KANNADA
160pp • 5 x 7
0-7818-0177-X • $7.95pb • (122)

INTENSIVE COURSE IN KASHMIRI
300pp • 5 x 8
0-7818-0176-1 • $18.95 - (129)

LEARN MALAYALAM
164pp • 4 ¾ x 7
0-7818-0058-7 • $7.95pb • (229)

TEACH YOURSELF MARATHI
143pp • 4 ½ x 7
0-87052-620-0 • $7.95pb • (236)

LEARN ORIYA
160pp • 5 x 7
0-7818-0182-6 • $7.95pb • (137)

INTENSIVE COURSE IN SINDHI
282pp • 6 x 9
0-7818-0389-6 • $29.95 • (455)

LEARN TAMIL
160pp • 5 x 7
0-7818-0062-5 • $7.95pb • (256)

LEARN TELUGU
160pp • 5 x 7
0-7818-0206-7 • $7.95pb (320)

Proverbs
A CLASSIFIED COLLECTION OF TAMIL PROVERBS
499pp • 3644 entries • 0-7818-0592-9 • $19.95pb • (699)

Cookbooks

ART OF SOUTH INDIAN COOKING
Alamelu Vairavan and Patricia Marquardt
192pp • 5 ½ x 8 ½
0-7818-0525-2 • $22.50hc • (635)

BEST OF GOAN COOKING
Gilda Mendonsa
106pp • 12pp color illus • 7 x 9 ¼
0-7818-0584-8 • $8.95pb